McGraw-Hill's
10 ACT Practice Tests

ABOUT THE AUTHOR

Steve Dulan has been involved with the ACT since 1982, when he received a score of 32 on his own test as a high school junior at Iron Mountain High School. That score qualified him for the State of Michigan Competitive Scholarship in 1983. In 1989, after serving as a U.S. Army infantry Sergeant, and during his time as an undergraduate at Michigan State University, Steve became an ACT instructor. He has been helping students to prepare for success on the ACT and other standardized exams ever since. Steve attended The Thomas M. Cooley Law School on a full Honors Scholarship after achieving a 99th percentile score on his Law School Admission Test (LSAT). In fact, Steve scored in the 99th percentile on every standardized test he has ever taken. While attending law school, Steve continued to teach standardized test prep classes (including ACT, SAT, PSAT, GRE, GMAT, and LSAT) an average of thirty hours each week, and tutored some of his fellow law students in a variety of subjects and in essay exam writing techniques. Steve has also served as an instructor at the college and law school levels.

Thousands of students have benefited from Steve's instruction, coaching, and admissions consulting and have gone on to the colleges of their choice. His students have gained admission to some of the most prestigious institutions in the world and received many scholarships of their own. A few of them even beat his ACT score! Since 1997, Steve has served as the President of Advantage Education (www.AdvantagEd.com), a company dedicated to providing effective and affordable test prep education in a variety of settings, including classes and seminars at high schools and colleges around the country, summer College Prep Camps at The University of Michigan, and one-on-one via the Internet worldwide.

McGraw-Hill's
10 ACT Practice Tests

SECOND EDITION

Steven W. Dulan
and the faculty of
Advantage Education

New York   Chicago   San Francisco   Lisbon   London   Madrid   Mexico City
Milan   New Delhi   San Juan   Seoul   Singapore   Sydney   Toronto

The McGraw-Hill Companies

Library of Congress Cataloging-in-Publication Data

Dulan, Steven W.
    McGraw-Hill's 10 ACT practice tests / Steven W. Dulan and the faculty of Advantage Education. – 2nd ed.
        p. cm.
    ISBN-13: 978-0-07-159146-1
    ISBN-10: 0-07-159146-X
    1. ACT Assessment–Study guides. 2. Achievement tests–Study guides. I. Advantage Education (Firm)
II. McGraw-Hill Companies. III. Title. IV. Title: McGraw-Hill's 10 American College Testing practice tests.
V. Title: McGraw-Hill's ten ACT practice tests. VI. Title: McGraw-Hill's ten American College Testing
practice tests. VII. Title: 10 ACT practice tests.
    LB2353.48.D85 2008
    378.1'662–dc22   2008016002

4 5 6 7 8 9 0 QPD/QPD 0 1 3 2 1 0 9

ISBN-13: 978-0-07-159146-1
ISBN-10: 0-07-159146-X

This book is printed on acid-free paper.

McGraw-Hill books are available at special quantity discounts for use as premiums and sales promotions, or for
use in corporate training programs. For more information, please write to the Director of Special Sales,
McGraw-Hill Professional, Two Penn Plaza, New York, NY 10121-2298. Or contact your local bookstore.

This publication is designed to provide accurate and authoritative information in regard to the subject matter
covered. It is sold with the understanding that neither the author nor the publisher is engaged in rendering legal,
accounting, or other professional services. If legal advice or other expert assistance is required, the services of a
competent professional person should be sought.

> *–From a Declaration of Principles jointly adopted*
> *by a Committee of the American Bar*
> *Association and a Committee of Publishers.*

**ACT is a registered trademark of ACT, Inc., which was not involved in the production of, and does not
endorse, this product.**

CONTENTS

ACKNOWLEDGMENTS

The author would like to acknowledge the contribution of the faculty and staff of Advantage Education. You are not only the smartest, but also the best. Special thanks to Lisa DiLiberti, Amy Dulan, Matt Mathison, Kathy Matteo, Blair Morley, Ryan Particka, Andrew Sanford, Kim So, and Amanda Thompson. All of you put in extra effort to make this book a success.

INTRODUCTION: USING THIS BOOK

This book contains ten simulated ACT practice tests. You can use these tests as "dress rehearsals" to get you ready for the whole experience of taking an ACT exam.

If you have enough time between now and your ACT (at least three weeks but preferably twelve to eighteen weeks), you should work through this entire book. If you have only a few days, try to complete as many practice tests as time allows. Even just a few hours of study and practice can have a beneficial impact on your ACT score.

Use this book as a companion to McGraw-Hill's ACT prep book.

HOW TO USE THE PRACTICE TESTS

Each practice test in this book is a full-length simulated ACT. Written by ACT experts, these tests are designed to be as close as you can get to the actual exam. The tests contain some variations in style and mix of question type. This approach is intentional so that you can get a taste of all of the various formats and styles that can appear on an ACT exam. If you work through all of the material provided, you can rest assured that there won't be any surprises on test day. However, you should keep your score results in perspective. Generally, students tend to score slightly higher on each successive practice test. But the truth is that ACT exams are sensitive to factors such as fatigue and stress. The time of the day that you take the exams, your surroundings, and other things going on in your life can have an impact on your scores. Don't get worried if you see some variations due to an off day or because the practice test exposed a weakness in your knowledge base or skill set. Just use the information that you gather as a tool to help you improve.

There is an explanation for each of the practice questions in this book. You will probably not need to read absolutely all of them. Sometimes you can tell right away why you got a particular question wrong. We have seen countless students smack themselves on the forehead and say "stupid mistake." We try to refer to these errors as "concentration errors." Everyone makes them from time to time, and you should not worry when they occur. There is a good chance that your focus will be a little better on the real test as long as you train yourself properly with the aid of this book. You should distinguish between those concentration errors and any understanding issues or holes in your knowledge base. If you have the time, it is worth reading the explanations for any of the questions that were at all challenging for you. Sometimes, students get questions correct but for the wrong reason, or because they guessed correctly. While you are practicing, you should mark any questions that you want to revisit and be sure to read the explanations for those questions.

A NOTE ON SCORING THE PRACTICE TESTS

The tests in this book are simulations created by experts to replicate the question types, difficulty level, and content areas that you will find on your real ACT. The Scoring Worksheets provided for each test are guides to computing approximate scores. Actual ACT exams are scored from tables that are unique to each test. The actual scaled scores depend on a number of factors, which include the number of students who take the test, the difficulty level of the items, (questions and answer choices), and the performance of all of the students who take the test. This means that "your mileage may vary." Do not get too hung up on your test scores; the idea is to learn something from each practice experience and to get used to the "look and feel" of the ACT.

Each Scoring Worksheet has formulas for you to work out an approximate scaled score for each section, as well as an overall Composite Score. Each computation includes a "correction factor," which is an average correction derived from analysis of recent ACT exams. The correction factor is most valid for students whose scores are in the middle 50% of all scores. The correction factor starts to lose a bit of its effectiveness at the top and bottom of the scoring scale. This is not a major flaw in the practice tests; your actual ACT score report will include a "band" around each score. ACT, Inc., says right on the student's score report that they do this to highlight the fact that all test scores are just estimates.

UNDERSTANDING THE ACT

WHAT IS THE ACT?

The authors of the ACT insist that the ACT is an achievement test, meaning that it is designed to measure your readiness for college instruction. There is ongoing debate about how well the ACT accomplishes that mission. What is not debated is that the ACT is not a direct measure of intelligence. It is not an IQ test. The ACT is certainly not a measure of your worth as a human being. It is not even a perfect measure of how well you will do in college. Theoretically, each of us has a specific potential to learn and acquire skills. The ACT doesn't measure your natural, inborn ability. If it did, we wouldn't be as successful as we are at raising students' scores on ACT exams.

The ACT actually measures a certain knowledge base and skill set. It is "trainable," meaning that you can do better on your ACT if you work on gaining the knowledge and acquiring the skills that are tested.

The ACT is broken up into four multiple-choice tests and one optional essay. The multiple-choice tests are called English, Mathematics, Reading, and Science Reasoning, respectively. They are always given in the same order. In fact, there is a lot of predictability when it comes to the ACT. The current exam still has very much in common with ACT exams from past years. This means that we basically know what is going to be on your ACT in terms of question types and content. The ACT Structure chart on the next page provides more information on the format of the ACT.

ACT offers a thirty-minute Writing Test as an optional component to the ACT. Many colleges and universities require applicants to take the Writing Test. Be sure to check with your schools of choice prior to registering for the test.

WHO WRITES THE ACT?

There is a company called ACT, Inc. that decides exactly what is going to be on your ACT exam. This group of experts consults with classroom teachers at the high school and college level. They look at high school and college curricula and they employ educators and specialized psychologists called "psychometricians" (measurers of the mind), who know a lot about the human brain and how it operates under various conditions. We picture them as "evil genius" researchers gleefully rubbing their hands together and trying to think up ways to keep you out of college. Don't fear, however; we are the "good geniuses" trying to get you into the college of your choice. We'll lay out the details of how you will be tested so that you can get yourself ready for the "contest" on test day.

REGISTERING FOR THE ACT

You must register for the ACT in advance. You can't just show up on test day with a number 2 pencil and dive right in. The best source of information for all things ACT is, not surprisingly, the ACT Web site: **www.act.org**. There is also a very good chance that a guidance counselor and/or pre-college counselor at

ACT Structure

English	
75 Questions 45 Minutes	

Content/Skills	Number of Questions
Usage/Mechanics	**40**
Punctuation	10
Grammar/Usage	12
Sentence Structure	18
Rhetorical Skills	**35**
Strategy	12
Organization	11
Style	12

Mathematics	
60 Questions 60 Minutes	

Content	Number of Questions
Pre-Algebra and Elementary Algebra	24
Intermediate Algebra and Coordinate Geometry	18
Plane Geometry	14
Trigonometry	4

Reading	
40 Questions 35 Minutes	

Passage Type	Number of Questions
Prose Fiction	10
Social Science	10
Humanities	10
Natural Science	10

Science Reasoning	
40 Questions 35 Minutes	

Format	Number of Questions
Data Representation - 3 passages	15
Research Summaries - 3 passages	18
Conflicting Viewpoints - 1 passage	7
Content Areas: Biology, Physical Sciences, Chemistry, Physics	

The ACT includes an optional 30-minute Writing Test, which comes after the Science Reasoning Test.

your school has an *ACT Registration Book*, which includes all of the information that you need for your test registration.

WHY DO ACT EXAMS EXIST?

Back in the mid-twentieth century, some people noticed that there was a disturbing trend in college admissions. Most of the people who were entering college came from a fairly small group of people who went to a limited number of high schools. Many had parents who had attended the same colleges. There wasn't much opportunity for students from new families to "break into" the higher education system. Standardized entrance exams were an attempt to democratize the situation and create a meritocracy where admissions decisions were based on achievement and not just social status. The ACT was not the first standardized college entrance exam. It came a little later as an attempt at improving on the older SAT.

Colleges use the ACT for admissions decisions and, sometimes, for advanced placement. It is also used to make scholarship decisions. Since there are variations among high schools around the country, the admissions departments at colleges use the ACT, in part, to help provide a standard for comparison. There are studies that reveal a fair amount of "grade inflation" at some schools. So, colleges cannot simply rely upon grade point averages when evaluating academic performance.

ACT SCORES

Each of the multiple-choice sections of the ACT is called a Test. Each test is given a score on a scale of 1 to 36. These four "scaled scores" are then averaged and rounded according to normal rounding rules to yield a Composite Score. It is this Composite Score that is most often meant when someone refers to your ACT score.

Your actual score report will also refer to "subscores," which are reported for your English, Mathematics, and Reading tests. These are based on your performance on a subset of the questions on each of these tests. Our experience has been that there is nothing to be gained from discussing them in detail with students. Reports indicate that many college admissions professionals don't have the faintest idea how to utilize them when making admissions decisions.

One important thing that can be said about scores is that you don't have to be perfect to get a good score on the ACT. The truth is that you can miss a fair number of questions and still get a score that places you in the top 1% of all test takers. In fact, this test is so hard and the time limit is so unrealistic for most test takers that you can get a score that is at the national average (about a 21) even if you get almost half of the questions wrong. Use the scoring guidelines provided in this book to estimate your ACT score at each stage of your preparation.

WRITING TEST SCORING GUIDELINES

The ACT Writing Test is scored on a 2-point through 12-point scale. Two professional, trained readers will evaluate your answer, and each of them will assign a point value of 1 (worst) through 6 (best); the two scores are then totaled. If the two readers assign scores that differ by more than 1 point, then a 3rd reader will be called in to read your essay and make the final decision regarding your score.

The scores are *holistic* scores, which means that your essay is judged as a whole without assigning point values to the specific characteristics that the graders are looking for. Use the following guidelines when scoring your essays based on the sample prompts included in this book.

Score of 6: The essay takes a clear position and discusses other perspectives, including perspectives that may differ from the author's. The essay is logical and complete. There are good transitions and very little or no irrelevant information. The introduction and conclusion are solid and consistent with each other and with the argument. The essay predicts and deals with counter arguments. While there may be a few errors, they are minor and infrequent. Grammar, spelling, and punctuation are nearly perfect. Vocabulary is effective and appropriate.

Score of 5: The essay takes a clear position on the topic and might give an overall context. The essay deals with some of the complex issues surrounding the topic and at least raises some counter arguments. There are specific examples given. Organization is clear and concise even if it is not creative. Transition signals are used. The author uses language competently and there is some variation in word choice. Any errors present are relatively minor and not distracting.

Score of 4: The essay demonstrates an understanding of the issue and the purpose of the essay is clear. The author states a position on the main issue and at least raises some potential counter arguments. There is adequate development of ideas and some specific reasons and/or examples are given. There is some logical sequence. Most transitions are simple. There is some variety in sentence length and word choice. There are some distracting errors but the essay is still understandable.

Score of 3: The essay reveals that the author has some understanding of the task. There is a clear position but no real overall context is provided. There may be some mention of counter arguments but they are cursory or not clearly stated. The essay may be repetitious or redundant. The essay stays within the general subject but may stray from the specific issue. The organization is simple and predictable. Transitions, if any, are simple and predictable. Introduction and conclusion are present but not well developed. Word choice is generally appropriate and sentences lack variety in length or structure. There are distracting errors that impact understandability.

Score of 2: The essay shows that the author misunderstood the assignment. There is no position taken on the main issue or there are no reasons given. There may be a general example or two but no specific examples offered. There are problems with the relevance of some of the statements made. Transition words may be incorrect or misleading. There are several distracting errors that affect the understandability of the essay.

Score of 1: The author demonstrates almost no grasp of the assignment. The essay fails to take a position or fails to support a position taken. May be excessively redundant. There is little or no structure or coherence. There are several errors that nearly prevent understanding the author's point, if any.

Score of 0: The answer document is blank, the essay is on a topic of the author's own choosing, the essay is either completely or nearly illegible, or the essay is not written in English.

■■■ **ANSWER SHEET**

ACT PRACTICE TEST 1
Answer Sheet

ENGLISH

1 Ⓐ Ⓑ Ⓒ Ⓓ	21 Ⓐ Ⓑ Ⓒ Ⓓ	41 Ⓐ Ⓑ Ⓒ Ⓓ	61 Ⓐ Ⓑ Ⓒ Ⓓ
2 Ⓕ Ⓖ Ⓗ Ⓙ	22 Ⓕ Ⓖ Ⓗ Ⓙ	42 Ⓕ Ⓖ Ⓗ Ⓙ	62 Ⓕ Ⓖ Ⓗ Ⓙ
3 Ⓐ Ⓑ Ⓒ Ⓓ	23 Ⓐ Ⓑ Ⓒ Ⓓ	43 Ⓐ Ⓑ Ⓒ Ⓓ	63 Ⓐ Ⓑ Ⓒ Ⓓ
4 Ⓕ Ⓖ Ⓗ Ⓙ	24 Ⓕ Ⓖ Ⓗ Ⓙ	44 Ⓕ Ⓖ Ⓗ Ⓙ	64 Ⓕ Ⓖ Ⓗ Ⓙ
5 Ⓐ Ⓑ Ⓒ Ⓓ	25 Ⓐ Ⓑ Ⓒ Ⓓ	45 Ⓐ Ⓑ Ⓒ Ⓓ	65 Ⓐ Ⓑ Ⓒ Ⓓ
6 Ⓕ Ⓖ Ⓗ Ⓙ	26 Ⓕ Ⓖ Ⓗ Ⓙ	46 Ⓕ Ⓖ Ⓗ Ⓙ	66 Ⓕ Ⓖ Ⓗ Ⓙ
7 Ⓐ Ⓑ Ⓒ Ⓓ	27 Ⓐ Ⓑ Ⓒ Ⓓ	47 Ⓐ Ⓑ Ⓒ Ⓓ	67 Ⓐ Ⓑ Ⓒ Ⓓ
8 Ⓕ Ⓖ Ⓗ Ⓙ	28 Ⓕ Ⓖ Ⓗ Ⓙ	48 Ⓕ Ⓖ Ⓗ Ⓙ	68 Ⓕ Ⓖ Ⓗ Ⓙ
9 Ⓐ Ⓑ Ⓒ Ⓓ	29 Ⓐ Ⓑ Ⓒ Ⓓ	49 Ⓐ Ⓑ Ⓒ Ⓓ	69 Ⓐ Ⓑ Ⓒ Ⓓ
10 Ⓕ Ⓖ Ⓗ Ⓙ	30 Ⓕ Ⓖ Ⓗ Ⓙ	50 Ⓕ Ⓖ Ⓗ Ⓙ	70 Ⓕ Ⓖ Ⓗ Ⓙ
11 Ⓐ Ⓑ Ⓒ Ⓓ	31 Ⓐ Ⓑ Ⓒ Ⓓ	51 Ⓐ Ⓑ Ⓒ Ⓓ	71 Ⓐ Ⓑ Ⓒ Ⓓ
12 Ⓕ Ⓖ Ⓗ Ⓙ	32 Ⓕ Ⓖ Ⓗ Ⓙ	52 Ⓕ Ⓖ Ⓗ Ⓙ	72 Ⓕ Ⓖ Ⓗ Ⓙ
13 Ⓐ Ⓑ Ⓒ Ⓓ	33 Ⓐ Ⓑ Ⓒ Ⓓ	53 Ⓐ Ⓑ Ⓒ Ⓓ	73 Ⓐ Ⓑ Ⓒ Ⓓ
14 Ⓕ Ⓖ Ⓗ Ⓙ	34 Ⓕ Ⓖ Ⓗ Ⓙ	54 Ⓕ Ⓖ Ⓗ Ⓙ	74 Ⓕ Ⓖ Ⓗ Ⓙ
15 Ⓐ Ⓑ Ⓒ Ⓓ	35 Ⓐ Ⓑ Ⓒ Ⓓ	55 Ⓐ Ⓑ Ⓒ Ⓓ	75 Ⓐ Ⓑ Ⓒ Ⓓ
16 Ⓕ Ⓖ Ⓗ Ⓙ	36 Ⓕ Ⓖ Ⓗ Ⓙ	56 Ⓕ Ⓖ Ⓗ Ⓙ	
17 Ⓐ Ⓑ Ⓒ Ⓓ	37 Ⓐ Ⓑ Ⓒ Ⓓ	57 Ⓐ Ⓑ Ⓒ Ⓓ	
18 Ⓕ Ⓖ Ⓗ Ⓙ	38 Ⓕ Ⓖ Ⓗ Ⓙ	58 Ⓕ Ⓖ Ⓗ Ⓙ	
19 Ⓐ Ⓑ Ⓒ Ⓓ	39 Ⓐ Ⓑ Ⓒ Ⓓ	59 Ⓐ Ⓑ Ⓒ Ⓓ	
20 Ⓕ Ⓖ Ⓗ Ⓙ	40 Ⓕ Ⓖ Ⓗ Ⓙ	60 Ⓕ Ⓖ Ⓗ Ⓙ	

MATHEMATICS

1 Ⓐ Ⓑ Ⓒ Ⓓ Ⓔ	16 Ⓕ Ⓖ Ⓗ Ⓙ Ⓚ	31 Ⓐ Ⓑ Ⓒ Ⓓ Ⓔ	46 Ⓕ Ⓖ Ⓗ Ⓙ Ⓚ
2 Ⓕ Ⓖ Ⓗ Ⓙ Ⓚ	17 Ⓐ Ⓑ Ⓒ Ⓓ Ⓔ	32 Ⓕ Ⓖ Ⓗ Ⓙ Ⓚ	47 Ⓐ Ⓑ Ⓒ Ⓓ Ⓔ
3 Ⓐ Ⓑ Ⓒ Ⓓ Ⓔ	18 Ⓕ Ⓖ Ⓗ Ⓙ Ⓚ	33 Ⓐ Ⓑ Ⓒ Ⓓ Ⓔ	48 Ⓕ Ⓖ Ⓗ Ⓙ Ⓚ
4 Ⓕ Ⓖ Ⓗ Ⓙ Ⓚ	19 Ⓐ Ⓑ Ⓒ Ⓓ Ⓔ	34 Ⓕ Ⓖ Ⓗ Ⓙ Ⓚ	49 Ⓐ Ⓑ Ⓒ Ⓓ Ⓔ
5 Ⓐ Ⓑ Ⓒ Ⓓ Ⓔ	20 Ⓕ Ⓖ Ⓗ Ⓙ Ⓚ	35 Ⓐ Ⓑ Ⓒ Ⓓ Ⓔ	50 Ⓕ Ⓖ Ⓗ Ⓙ Ⓚ
6 Ⓕ Ⓖ Ⓗ Ⓙ Ⓚ	21 Ⓐ Ⓑ Ⓒ Ⓓ Ⓔ	36 Ⓕ Ⓖ Ⓗ Ⓙ Ⓚ	51 Ⓐ Ⓑ Ⓒ Ⓓ Ⓔ
7 Ⓐ Ⓑ Ⓒ Ⓓ Ⓔ	22 Ⓕ Ⓖ Ⓗ Ⓙ Ⓚ	37 Ⓐ Ⓑ Ⓒ Ⓓ Ⓔ	52 Ⓕ Ⓖ Ⓗ Ⓙ Ⓚ
8 Ⓕ Ⓖ Ⓗ Ⓙ Ⓚ	23 Ⓐ Ⓑ Ⓒ Ⓓ Ⓔ	38 Ⓕ Ⓖ Ⓗ Ⓙ Ⓚ	53 Ⓐ Ⓑ Ⓒ Ⓓ Ⓔ
9 Ⓐ Ⓑ Ⓒ Ⓓ Ⓔ	24 Ⓕ Ⓖ Ⓗ Ⓙ Ⓚ	39 Ⓐ Ⓑ Ⓒ Ⓓ Ⓔ	54 Ⓕ Ⓖ Ⓗ Ⓙ Ⓚ
10 Ⓕ Ⓖ Ⓗ Ⓙ Ⓚ	25 Ⓐ Ⓑ Ⓒ Ⓓ Ⓔ	40 Ⓕ Ⓖ Ⓗ Ⓙ Ⓚ	55 Ⓐ Ⓑ Ⓒ Ⓓ Ⓔ
11 Ⓐ Ⓑ Ⓒ Ⓓ Ⓔ	26 Ⓕ Ⓖ Ⓗ Ⓙ Ⓚ	41 Ⓐ Ⓑ Ⓒ Ⓓ Ⓔ	56 Ⓕ Ⓖ Ⓗ Ⓙ Ⓚ
12 Ⓕ Ⓖ Ⓗ Ⓙ Ⓚ	27 Ⓐ Ⓑ Ⓒ Ⓓ Ⓔ	42 Ⓕ Ⓖ Ⓗ Ⓙ Ⓚ	57 Ⓐ Ⓑ Ⓒ Ⓓ Ⓔ
13 Ⓐ Ⓑ Ⓒ Ⓓ Ⓔ	28 Ⓕ Ⓖ Ⓗ Ⓙ Ⓚ	43 Ⓐ Ⓑ Ⓒ Ⓓ Ⓔ	58 Ⓕ Ⓖ Ⓗ Ⓙ Ⓚ
14 Ⓕ Ⓖ Ⓗ Ⓙ Ⓚ	29 Ⓐ Ⓑ Ⓒ Ⓓ Ⓔ	44 Ⓕ Ⓖ Ⓗ Ⓙ Ⓚ	59 Ⓐ Ⓑ Ⓒ Ⓓ Ⓔ
15 Ⓐ Ⓑ Ⓒ Ⓓ Ⓔ	30 Ⓕ Ⓖ Ⓗ Ⓙ Ⓚ	45 Ⓐ Ⓑ Ⓒ Ⓓ Ⓔ	60 Ⓕ Ⓖ Ⓗ Ⓙ Ⓚ

READING

1 (A)(B)(C)(D)	11 (A)(B)(C)(D)	21 (A)(B)(C)(D)	31 (A)(B)(C)(D)
2 (F)(G)(H)(J)	12 (F)(G)(H)(J)	22 (F)(G)(H)(J)	32 (F)(G)(H)(J)
3 (A)(B)(C)(D)	13 (A)(B)(C)(D)	23 (A)(B)(C)(D)	33 (A)(B)(C)(D)
4 (F)(G)(H)(J)	14 (F)(G)(H)(J)	24 (F)(G)(H)(J)	34 (F)(G)(H)(J)
5 (A)(B)(C)(D)	15 (A)(B)(C)(D)	25 (A)(B)(C)(D)	35 (A)(B)(C)(D)
6 (F)(G)(H)(J)	16 (F)(G)(H)(J)	26 (F)(G)(H)(J)	36 (F)(G)(H)(J)
7 (A)(B)(C)(D)	17 (A)(B)(C)(D)	27 (A)(B)(C)(D)	37 (A)(B)(C)(D)
8 (F)(G)(H)(J)	18 (F)(G)(H)(J)	28 (F)(G)(H)(J)	38 (F)(G)(H)(J)
9 (A)(B)(C)(D)	19 (A)(B)(C)(D)	29 (A)(B)(C)(D)	39 (A)(B)(C)(D)
10 (F)(G)(H)(J)	20 (F)(G)(H)(J)	30 (F)(G)(H)(J)	40 (F)(G)(H)(J)

SCIENCE

1 (A)(B)(C)(D)	11 (A)(B)(C)(D)	21 (A)(B)(C)(D)	31 (A)(B)(C)(D)
2 (F)(G)(H)(J)	12 (F)(G)(H)(J)	22 (F)(G)(H)(J)	32 (F)(G)(H)(J)
3 (A)(B)(C)(D)	13 (A)(B)(C)(D)	23 (A)(B)(C)(D)	33 (A)(B)(C)(D)
4 (F)(G)(H)(J)	14 (F)(G)(H)(J)	24 (F)(G)(H)(J)	34 (F)(G)(H)(J)
5 (A)(B)(C)(D)	15 (A)(B)(C)(D)	25 (A)(B)(C)(D)	35 (A)(B)(C)(D)
6 (F)(G)(H)(J)	16 (F)(G)(H)(J)	26 (F)(G)(H)(J)	36 (F)(G)(H)(J)
7 (A)(B)(C)(D)	17 (A)(B)(C)(D)	27 (A)(B)(C)(D)	37 (A)(B)(C)(D)
8 (F)(G)(H)(J)	18 (F)(G)(H)(J)	28 (F)(G)(H)(J)	38 (F)(G)(H)(J)
9 (A)(B)(C)(D)	19 (A)(B)(C)(D)	29 (A)(B)(C)(D)	39 (A)(B)(C)(D)
10 (F)(G)(H)(J)	20 (F)(G)(H)(J)	30 (F)(G)(H)(J)	40 (F)(G)(H)(J)

RAW SCORES		**SCALE SCORES**		DATE TAKEN:
ENGLISH	_____	ENGLISH	_____	
MATHEMATICS	_____	MATHEMATICS	_____	ENGLISH/WRITING _____
READING	_____	READING	_____	
SCIENCE	_____	SCIENCE	_____	_____
				COMPOSITE SCORE

Refer to the Scoring Worksheet on page 66 for help in determining your Raw and Scale Scores.

You may wish to remove these sample answer document pages to respond to the practice ACT Writing Test.

Cut Here

Begin WRITING TEST here.

If you need more space, please continue on the next page.

Do not write in this shaded area.

WRITING TEST

If you need more space, please continue on the back of this page.

Do not write in this shaded area.

Cut Here

WRITING TEST

If you need more space, please continue on the next page.

PLEASE DO NOT WRITE IN THIS AREA.

WRITING TEST

_____

_____

_____

_____

_____

_____

_____

_____

_____

_____

_____

_____

_____

_____

_____

_____

_____

_____

_____

_____

_____

_____

_____

_____

_____

_____

_____

_____

STOP here with the Writing Test.

4

1 ■ ■ ■ ■ ■ ■ ■ ■ 1

ENGLISH TEST

45 Minutes—75 Questions

DIRECTIONS: In the passages that follow, some words and phrases are underlined and numbered. In the answer column, you will find alternatives for the words and phrases that are underlined. Choose the alternative that you think is best, and fill in the corresponding bubble on your answer sheet. If you think that the original version is best, choose "NO CHANGE," which will always be either answer choice A or F. You will also find questions about a particular section of the passage, or about the entire passage. These questions will be identified either by an underlined portion or by a number in a box. Look for the answer that clearly expresses the idea, is consistent with the style and tone of the passage, and makes the correct use of standard written English. Read the passage through once before answering the questions. For some questions, you should read beyond the indicated portion before you answer.

PASSAGE I

Hair-raising Problems

Why is it that we are so completely <u>obsessive</u> with the
                                        1
hair on our heads? Millions of dollars are spent each year

on cutting hair, lengthening hair, bleaching hair,

straightening hair, curling hair, highlighting hair, and even

growing hair; whatever you can do to hair, someone is

willing to <u>pay the money</u> to do it. Natural redheads long
            2

<u>for to be</u> brunettes and dishwater blondes dream of shiny
  3
golden tresses. Both men and women cringe at the sight of

each gray hair, <u>so</u> teenagers enjoy weekly experiments
                 4
with magenta dyes, spikes, and tangerine streaks.

All of these thoughts cross my mind as I examine the

<u>result of</u> my most recent hair adventure. As a mature
  5

1. **A.** NO CHANGE
   B. obsessed
   C. obsessing
   D. obsessioned

2. **F.** NO CHANGE
   G. pay
   H. paying money
   J. have paid

3. **A.** NO CHANGE
   B. to have
   C. to be
   D. becoming for

4. **F.** NO CHANGE
   G. however
   H. yet
   J. and

5. **A.** NO CHANGE
   B. result for
   C. result with
   D. result by

GO ON TO THE NEXT PAGE.

1 ■ ■ ■ ■ ■ ■ ■ ■ **1**

woman watching the gray hairs <u>mixing in rapidly</u> with my
                                        6

natural brunette tones, I decided over a year <u>ago, to</u>
                                                    7
approach my stylist with the idea of highlights. Having

seen many of my peers go this route, I figured that

highlighting <u>was for to be</u> the answer to my reluctance to
              8
look my age.

[1] The monthly highlighting went <u>well: excepting</u> for
                                          9
those times when my hair turned out a little too subdued,

making me look partially gray instead of brunette. [2] I

suffered through it remarkably well, saying to myself,

"She'll get it right the next time." [3] <u>For the most part,</u>
                                                10
I've enjoyed my year of highlights, so much so that I

bravely approached Donna, my stylist, two months ago

and proclaimed that I was done with wimpy highlighting

and ready to go blonde. [4] The result was not quite what

I expected, but I resolved to live with it! [11] [5] Donna was

surprised at my suggestion, but quickly began sharing my

unbridled enthusiasm as <u>she gathers</u> the appropriate
                                12
chemicals and concoctions that would soon transform me.

Three months later, I find myself seesawing between

tears <u>and</u> laughter as I attempt to cover up a patch of
      13
nearly bald scalp on the top of my head. For someone who

has long been fanatical about the appearance of her hair,

this absence of hair has proven to be quite a challenge to

my ego and self-confidence. I've always enjoyed styling

my hair, and suddenly, I have nothing to style.

6. **F.** NO CHANGE
   G. rapidly mixing
   H. mixed rapidly in
   J. rapidly mix in to

7. **A.** NO CHANGE
   B. ago to
   C. ago: to
   D. ago to,

8. **F.** NO CHANGE
   G. was being
   H. could of been
   J. was

9. **A.** NO CHANGE
   B. well, except
   C. well except
   D. well. Except

10. **F.** NO CHANGE
    G. Also
    H. Instead
    J. In light of this

11. For the sake of logic and coherence, Sentence 5 should
    be placed:
    A. where it is now.
    B. before Sentence 1.
    C. after Sentence 2.
    D. before Sentence 4.

12. **F.** NO CHANGE
    G. she was gathering
    H. she had been gathering
    J. she gathered

13. **A.** NO CHANGE
    B. along with
    C. or
    D. as well as

GO ON TO THE NEXT PAGE.

1 ■ ■ ■ ■ ■ ■ ■ ■ 1

Each time I begin to experience a new pang of disgust and despair over this new hair anomaly, I once again ask myself why we are so obsessed with the hair on our heads. The answer always comes to me in a flash, in a simple two-word phrase: pure vanity. Soon after this realization, I cease my crying. 14

14. The writer is considering deleting the preceding sentence. If the sentence was deleted, the essay would primarily lose:
   F. a summary of the essay.
   G. the narrator's ability to put her situation into perspective.
   H. a stylistic link to the essay's introduction.
   J. an understanding of the author's purpose in writing the essay.

Question 15 asks about the preceding passage as a whole.

15. Suppose the writer had chosen to write a how-to article for people wanting to change their hair color. Would this essay fulfill the writer's goal?
   A. Yes, because the author's approach to changing her own hair color would ease the anxiety of others wishing to do the same.
   B. Yes, because this essay emphasizes the universality of people changing their hairstyles and hair color.
   C. No, because this article only deals with the narrator's own experimentation with her hair and does not provide steps for others to do the same.
   D. No, because the essay discourages people from changing their hair color.

PASSAGE II

A Modern Blacksmith

You will probably never find his name in a history book, but to this day, Walker Lee continues to contribute to America heritage. Walker Lee is an old-fashioned, modern-
16

day blacksmith who still practices the fine art of
17
manipulating metal over a hot fire. In his words, "Blacksmithing is no dying art!"

16. F. NO CHANGE
    G. American heritage.
    H. Americas heritage.
    J. American's heritage.

17. A. NO CHANGE
    B. who still continues to practice
    C. who continues to still practice
    D. who practices still

GO ON TO THE NEXT PAGE.

1 ■ ■ ■ ■ ■ ■ ■ ■ 1

Walker Lee had began his career in hand-forged
                    18
ironwork at the age of 30. The idea of creating an object

out of iron, a most intractable material, appealed to him.
         19
He started on this new venture by collecting and reading

every book he could find that described the process of

blacksmithing: its history, its practical and decorative uses,

and the equipment needed to establish and outfit his own

smithy. During the course of his research, Lee discovered a

tool necessary for the success of any blacksmith: the anvil,

a heavy block of iron or steel upon which the blacksmith

hammered and shaped the malleable metal.

Lee bought his first anvil from 84-year-old Hurley

Alford Templeton of Philadelphia, lugging it home to
                                        20
Michigan in the back of a 4-H county bus. This anvil

weighed 100 pounds, about the minimum size Walker Lee

needed to get started in his craft.
         21

Lee's first anvil cost him $100, and four months later,

he paid $75 for an additional implement—a vice—from

Cornell University in New York. This important tool also

made its way back to Michigan in the back of Lee's 4-H bus.
     22

Lee had spent the summer carting 4-H groups out
                    23
from Michigan to the east coast for
         23

---

18. **F.** NO CHANGE
    G. had begun
    H. begun
    J. began

19. Which of the following alternatives to the underlined
portion would NOT be acceptable?
    A. one of the most intractable metals, iron,
    B. a most intractable material, that being iron
    C. iron (a most intractable material)
    D. a most intractable material, iron,

20. Which choice most emphasizes the difficulty in moving
the large anvil?
    F. NO CHANGE
    G. taking
    H. driving
    J. transporting

21. At this point, the writer wants to express how Lee first
began the craft of blacksmithing. Which choice would
most effectively accomplish this task?
    A. NO CHANGE
    B. continue
    C. keep going
    D. move on

22. **F.** NO CHANGE
    G. it's
    H. its'
    J. the

23. **A.** NO CHANGE
    B. Carting 4-H groups out from Michigan to the east
coast for various county fairs and expositions, Lee
had spent the summer.
    C. Lee had spent the summer, for various county
fairs and expositions, carting 4-H groups out from
Michigan to the east coast.
    D. OMIT the underlined portion.

GO ON TO THE NEXT PAGE.

1 ■ ■ ■ ■ ■ ■ ■ ■ ■ 1

various county fairs and expositions.
                                    23

Once Lee obtained his first portable forge, he was
                                    24
ready to build his blacksmith shop, commonly referred to
                                    24
as a "smithy." In the interest of economy, he constructed
    24
this shop out of inexpensive oak planks and tarpaper. It

was a crude little shack but stood for only nine years. Lee,
                          25
who by then was completely hooked on blacksmithing,

replaced his first shop with a finer one made of more

expensive wood; this shop also had glass windows, a

definite improvement over Lee's original "smithy."

[1] The very first object Lee forged was a

long, pointed Hudson Bay dagger.
    26
[2] Many people refer to this type of knife as a "dag."

[3] As he recalls that event he says, "From the minute

I first saw the thing take shape, I was hooked . . . still am.

There's an element of magic in it to me. You heat it up and

pound it with a hammer and it goes where you want it to

go." [4] Years later at a family event Lee, discovered
                 27
that his Italian ancestors were accomplished coppersmiths.

[5] During the gathering, Lee's great uncle Johnny

was proclaiming that Lee's propensity for blacksmithing
    28
was "in the blood" as he happily presented Lee with a new

125-pound anvil. [29]

---

24. Given that all of the choices are true, which one would most effectively introduce the subject of this paragraph?
F. NO CHANGE
G. Obtaining a portable forge for the shop proved to be Lee's biggest challenge.
H. Blacksmith shops can be difficult to construct, but the most challenging task is moving the necessary equipment into it.
J. A blacksmith's forge requires some type of blower in order to keep the fire hot enough to bend the steel.

25. A. NO CHANGE
B. that stood for
C. which standing for
D. and stands for

26. F. NO CHANGE
G. long pointed,
H. long, and pointed
J. long-pointed

27. A. NO CHANGE
B. later at a family, event Lee
C. later, at a family event, Lee,
D. later, at a family event, Lee

28. F. NO CHANGE
G. proclaimed
H. had been proclaiming
J. having proclaimed

29. Which of the following sentences in this paragraph is LEAST relevant to the main focus of the essay and, therefore, could be deleted?
A. Sentence 2
B. Sentence 3
C. Sentence 4
D. Sentence 5

GO ON TO THE NEXT PAGE.

1 ■ ■ ■ ■ ■ ■ ■ ■ 1

As an outside observer <u>watches</u> Walker Lee
₃₀
bending and shaping a hot metal rod into some

recognizable form, it is difficult to discern the origin of the

magic Lee spoke of; is it in the glowing, orange steel or in

Walker himself?

PASSAGE III

Scorpion Scare

   As my sister <u>begins</u> by telling me about the
₃₁
scorpion in her bed that stung her as she

<u>slumbered, I could</u> feel my eyes popping out of my head
₃₂
and my jaw dropping to the floor. She seemed so calm

telling me this story, and all I <u>could think</u> about was
₃₃

<u>how that she's</u> lucky to be alive. Diana's terrifying story
₃₄
continued, detailing how her husband threw back the bed

covers, began beating the dreaded thing with a broom, and

then quickly <u>flushed</u> it down the toilet. Only later did they
₃₅
learn that the corpse should have been kept for

identification purposes. Some Arizonan scorpions

<u>are deadlier than others</u>, and it is important to know which
₃₆
species is responsible for a given attack.

   My sister characteristically chose not to seek medical

treatment as her upper arm first swelled, then ached

with pain, and finally became numb and useless. [37]

As her condition worsened, she searched the Internet for

general information, discovering time and again that

species identification is important in administering proper

care to the sting victim.

---

30. F. NO CHANGE
   G. was watching
   H. had been watching
   J. watched

31. A. NO CHANGE
   B. begun
   C. had begun
   D. began

32. F. NO CHANGE
   G. slumbered I could
   H. slumbered I could,
   J. slumbered, I could,

33. A. NO CHANGE
   B. could have thought
   C. think
   D. had thought

34. F. NO CHANGE
   G. because she is
   H. how she is
   J. she is

35. A. NO CHANGE
   B. flush
   C. flushing
   D. flushes

36. F. NO CHANGE
   G. are more deadlier than others
   H. being more deadly than others
   J. more deadly than others

37. Assuming that all of the choices are true, which one
best links the preceding sentence with the rest of the
paragraph?
   A. You could say that Diana is afraid of hospitals,
doctors, and nurses.
   B. Most scorpion bites should be examined by a
medical professional.
   C. My sister's physician had treated many scorpion
bites.
   D. Symptoms of a scorpion sting can vary from one
person to another.

GO ON TO THE NEXT PAGE.

1 ■ ■ ■ ■ ■ ■ ■ ■ 1

Scorpions will sting anyone they accidentally encounter as they crawl inadvertently into human habitats. Most
38
problems occur at construction sites where the

scorpions natural homes have been upset and uprooted by
39

bulldozers and dump trucks. Of the ninety scorpion
40
species native to the United States, 30 percent live in
40
Arizona. Unfortunately, one of those species is the
40

Bark Scorpion, just about the only species whose venom is
41
considered truly dangerous and often fatal to humans.

My sister and her husband just moved into a new home a year ago, and dozens of homes are still being built all around them. This, indeed, is a perfect explanation for the presence of a scorpion in their bedclothes. Scorpions hide during the day and search for food and water at night. Arizonans will tell you that it's a good idea to refrain from going barefoot in the dark, both outside and inside.
42
Checking your shoes and clothes before putting them on wouldn't hurt, either, particularly if you know you're in an area where scorpions have been found. Wherever there is one scorpion, there are probably dozens more that can be easily detected with a black light at night when they're on the move.

[1] If a scorpion happens to sting you, please don't
43
follow my sister's example. [2] All medical facilities in Arizona have antivenin on hand. [3] Seek medical

38. F. NO CHANGE
G. inadvertently crawl
H. are crawling inadvertently
J. crawl

39. A. NO CHANGE
B. scorpion's naturally
C. scorpion natural
D. scorpions' natural

40. F. NO CHANGE
G. In Arizona, about 30 percent of the ninety scorpion species native to the United States live.
H. Arizona has about 30 percent of the ninety scorpion species, living in the United States.
J. Of the ninety species of scorpions, 30 percent native to the United States live in Arizona.

41. A. NO CHANGE
B. Bark Scorpion which is just about the only species
C. only one that is the Bark Scorpion species,
D. Bark Scorpion, yet just about the only species

42. If the author were to delete the phrase "both outside and inside," the essay would primarily lose a detail that:
F. adds essential information to the discussion of Arizona.
G. is not particularly necessary to the impact of the essay.
H. supports the reference to the scorpions' behavior.
J. adds an element of humor to the essay's theme.

43. A. NO CHANGE
B. happened to sting
C. happen to sting
D. stung

GO ON TO THE NEXT PAGE.

treatment immediately, especially if you've flushed the critter down the toilet and have no way of knowing the exact nature of the perpetrator! [4] This way, you will certainly save yourself from some amount of pain and discomfort, and you might even save your life. [44]

44. For the sake of coherence, Sentence 2 should be placed:
  F. Where it is now.
  G. Before sentence 1.
  H. After sentence 3.
  J. Omit it; it is not relevant to the paragraph.

Question 45 asks about the preceding passage as a whole.

---

45. Suppose the writer had intended to write a medical column that would offer professional advice on the treatment of scorpion stings. Would this essay successfully fulfill this goal?
  A. Yes, because this essay describes the steps that need to be taken if a person is stung by a scorpion.
  B. Yes, because it is clear in the essay that the writer possesses professional knowledge on the topic of scorpion stings.
  C. No, because the writer is describing only one personal incident about a scorpion sting and is offering personal, not professional, advice.
  D. No, because there are too many species of scorpions to allow a short essay to provide professional advice on the treatment of scorpion stings.

PASSAGE IV

Unfulfilled Promises

If you have ever entered a contest of any sort—you are well aware of the legal requirements, exclusions, and
    46

disclaimers that always accompany the contest's entry
                       47
form. Many laws today regulate a contest sponsor's responsibilities to the entrants, and courts are filled with lawsuits asserting with non-compliance on both sides.
            48
However, this was not always the case.

In 1896, a contest motivated a Norwegian immigrant, Helga Estby, to travel nearly 3,500 miles on foot from the
                                                49
state of Washington to New York City. Unfortunately, as is still sometimes true, Helga won the competition

46. **F.** NO CHANGE
  G. sort; you
  H. sort you
  J. sort, you

47. **A.** NO CHANGE
  B. always are accompanying
  C. accompany always
  D. are accompanying

48. **F.** NO CHANGE
  G. lawsuits asserting non-compliance
  H. lawsuits of non-compliance asserting
  J. non-compliance lawsuits asserting

49. **A.** NO CHANGE
  B. on foot, 3,500 miles
  C. 3,500 miles on feet
  D. 3,500 miles per foot

GO ON TO THE NEXT PAGE.

1 ■ ■ ■ ■ ■ ■ ■ ■ 1

only to find that the <u>promise $10,000</u> award was
₅₀
mysteriously absent.

[1] Helga <u>had been living</u> on her farm with her husband
₅₁
and nine children in Spokane, Washington, when she read
of a $10,000 prize being offered to a woman who was
willing to walk across the country. [2] Because the Estby
farm was facing foreclosure, Helga decided that walking
across the country in a bicycle skirt for that kind of money
was a small price to pay for a <u>greater rewarding</u>. [3] At the
₅₂

time, this style of skirt was considered to be inappropriate
because it revealed the female ankle. [4] The only
requirement, from all accounts, was that she wear a
modern, newfangled bicycle skirt as she traveled. [53]

So, in May of 1896, Helga and her 18-year-old
daughter, Clara, <u>had set off</u> on their long journey.
₅₄

<u>Helga carried a revolver and a spray gun containing red</u>
₅₅
<u>pepper for protection.</u> Presumably, Helga and Clara found
₅₅
food and shelter along the way, and they arrived in
New York City in December, seven months after their
departure. The contest sponsors, however, <u>were to be</u>
₅₆
<u>found nowhere</u>.
₅₆
This story of bravery and persistence
<u>had therefore been kept a secret</u> for nearly a century,
₅₇
primarily because Helga's seven-month absence from the
farm wreaked havoc on her family. Two of her children
died of diphtheria while she was gone. Even worse, her
husband had sequestered the surviving children in an

50. F. NO CHANGE
G. promise for the
H. promised
J. promising

51. A. NO CHANGE
B. been living
C. has been living
D. had lived

52. F. NO CHANGE
G. greatly rewarding
H. great reward
J. greatest reward

53. Which of the following sequences of sentences makes
this paragraph most logical?
A. NO CHANGE
B. 1, 3, 2, 4
C. 3, 2, 4, 1
D. 1, 4, 3, 2

54. F. NO CHANGE
G. have set off
H. set off
J. went to set off

55. A. NO CHANGE
B. For protection, Helga carried a revolver as well as
a red pepper-containing spray gun.
C. Helga, for protection, she carried a revolver and a
spray gun containing red pepper.
D. Carried by Helga for protection were a revolver
and a spray gun containing red pepper.

56. F. NO CHANGE
G. were nowhere when found
H. to be found nowhere
J. were nowhere to be found

57. A. NO CHANGE
B. had been kept a secret
C. had been actually kept a secret
D. had in fact been kept a secret

GO ON TO THE NEXT PAGE.

1 ■ ■ ■ ■ ■ ■ ■ ■ 1

unheated shed, thinking that this was the only way to keep them from being infected with the disease. Since the contest sponsor failed to award Helga the money, the Estbys ended up losing the farm; her expedition had been a disaster.

At the time, Helga's trip was considered an embarrassment by the Norwegian-American community and was kept utterly quiet. After Helga's death, her own children burned the hundreds of pages Helga had written through the years, leaving only a small scrapbook of
                              58
newspaper clippings and very few details of Helga's life or her ill-fated trip. Looking back 100 years, one can only marvel at the boldness and bravery that must have energized Helga Estby to make that journey on foot across the country in an effort to save her family farm. [60]
                                                    59

58. F. NO CHANGE
    G. years leaving only
    H. years; leaving only
    J. years leaving only,

59. Given that all of the choices are true, which one would best conclude the sentence while providing the reader with the most specific explanation for Helga's motivation to walk across the country?
    A. NO CHANGE
    B. to win $10,000.
    C. in an effort to save her children from diphtheria.
    D. to help her daughter Clara gain experience.

Question 60 asks about the preceding passage as a whole.

60. At this point, the writer is considering adding the following sentence:

    In 1984, Helga's great-great-grandson wrote a story about his ancestor for a history assignment.

    Should the writer make this addition here?
    F. Yes, because it links the ending of the essay to its introduction.
    G. Yes, because this information is highly relevant to the rest of the essay.
    H. No, because this story might not focus on Helga's farm.
    J. No, because this information introduces a new subtopic of the essay.

GO ON TO THE NEXT PAGE.

1 ■ ■ ■ ■ ■ ■ ■ ■ **1**

PASSAGE V

> The following paragraphs may or may not be in the most logical order. You may be asked questions about the logical order of the paragraphs, as well as where to place sentences logically within any given paragraph.

Jet Lag

[1]

Traveling across time zones <u>particularly</u> via airplane, can
₆₁
be very disconcerting to the human body, both physically
and mentally. When you "gain" or "lose" time going from
Point A to Point B, <u>a condition (*desynchronosis*)</u> likely
₆₂
affects you in some form. Jet lag is medically considered a
sleeping disorder, although it is normally a temporary

condition and <u>not as serious</u> as other sleeping dysfunctions.
₆₃

[2]

[64] The term "circadian" originates from the Latin *circa*,
meaning "about," and *diem* or "day." Circadian rhythms
refer to a variety of daily bodily functions such as
temperature changes, sleep patterns, and digestive
functions. Normally, the body operates on a
24-hour time period that coincides with the earth's
24-hour cycle of night and day. The human body generally
falls into a routine of sleeping and <u>waking; that is, regular</u>
₆₅
changes in body temperature, breathing, and digestion

take place. <u>In addition</u>, most
₆₆

<u>who's inner clocks</u> cause more sleepiness from 3:00 p.m.
₆₇
to 5:00 p.m. and again from 3:00 a.m. to 5:00 a.m. Body
temperature usually rises as the day goes on, quickly drops
around midnight, and then begins

61. A. NO CHANGE
  B. zones; particularly
  C. zones, particularly,
  D. zones, particularly

62. Given that all of the choices are true, which one would provide the most detailed and relevant information at this point in the essay?
  F. NO CHANGE
  G. a condition called *desynchronosis*, commonly known as jet lag,
  H. a condition known as *desynchronosis*
  J. a condition of jet lag

63. A. NO CHANGE
  B. not serious
  C. serious as not
  D. as serious as

64. Which of the following sentences would most effectively introduce the subject of this paragraph and act as a transition from the preceding paragraph?
  F. Many scientific words have Latin origins.
  G. Sleeping disorders can produce a great deal of stress and anxiety.
  H. Most travelers are unaware of the exact moment that they leave one time zone and enter another.
  J. Traveling across time zones over a short period of time disturbs the body's circadian rhythms.

65. A. NO CHANGE
  B. waking regular
  C. waking, during which regular
  D. waking. Regular

66. F. NO CHANGE
  G. Likewise
  H. Instead
  J. For example

67. A. NO CHANGE
  B. of our inner clocks
  C. whose inner clocks
  D. of us inner clock's

GO ON TO THE NEXT PAGE.

1

the cycle of rising again just before 6:00 a.m. Since these changes occur on a twenty-four-hour cycle, so abrupt time zone changes can understandably upset the body's

highly well-tuned in system of regulation.

[3]

Some symptoms of jet lag include excessive daytime sleepiness or some level of insomnia at night, changes in appetite and/or digestion, moodiness, and difficulty concentrating. Often, after traveling on a plane for long periods, people will also experience headaches, dry sinuses, earaches, and bloating. However, these symptoms are more likely being attributable to the conditions of the

airplane cabin, which has a very dry pressurized, atmosphere, and are not symptomatic of jet lag.

[4]

[1] There are steps that can be taken to alleviate the effects of jet lag, primarily as preventive measures. [2] First, it might be helpful to slightly alter your sleeping schedule for several days before your trip. [3] If you are going east, for example, go to bed one hour earlier and rise the next day an hour earlier so that you will be somewhat more acclimated to the new time zone. [4] Regulating your exposure to light can also be helpful, since light and darkness serve as triggers to the brain. [5] Before traveling west, expose yourself to evening light and avoid early morning light for several days as a way of simulating the new time zone you're headed toward. [6] Some say it takes about one day for every hour of time zone change to completely adjust to the new time zone. [7] Unfortunately

68. F. NO CHANGE
   G. However, these
   H. Because these
   J. These

69. A. NO CHANGE
   B. well-tuned
   C. highly tuned well
   D. high

70. F. NO CHANGE
   G. Often, after doing a lot of traveling on a plane for long periods
   H. After traveling for long periods on a plane sometimes
   J. Traveling for long periods on a plane

71. A. NO CHANGE
   B. are more likely to be attributable
   C. are attributable, more likely,
   D. are more likely attributable

72. F. NO CHANGE
   G. dry, pressurized
   H. dry, pressurized,
   J. dry pressurized

73. Which of the following alternatives to the underlined portion would NOT be acceptable?
   A. trip. When traveling east, for example,
   B. trip; if you are going east for example,
   C. trip. For example, if you are going east,
   D. trip, if you are going east for example,

GO ON TO THE NEXT PAGE.

1 ■ ■ ■ ■ ■ ■ ■ ■ 1

for many, that formula often coincides precisely with

the return trip. [8] Avoiding caffeine and alcohol

may also aid your body in adjusting to its new

environment. 74

74. For the sake of the logic and coherence of this paragraph, Sentence 8 should be placed:
   F. where it is now.
   G. after Sentence 4.
   H. before Sentence 6.
   J. before Sentence 7.

Question 75 asks about the preceding passage as a whole.

75. The writer wishes to add the following sentence in order to show that jet lag can sometimes be a more serious problem:

There are those, however, who routinely fly across continents either for pleasure or business, and jet lag can become a more serious issue for these people.

The new sentence would best support and be placed at the end of Paragraph:
   A. 1
   B. 2
   C. 3
   D. 4

END OF THE ENGLISH TEST.
STOP! IF YOU HAVE TIME LEFT OVER, CHECK YOUR WORK ON THIS SECTION ONLY.

2 △ △ △ △ △ △ △ △ **2**

MATHEMATICS TEST

60 Minutes—60 Questions

DIRECTIONS: Solve each of the problems in the time allowed, then fill in the corresponding bubble on your answer sheet. Do not spend too much time on any one problem; skip the more difficult problems and go back to them later. You may use a calculator on this test. For this test you should assume that figures are NOT necessarily drawn to scale, that all geometric figures lie in a plane, and that the word *line* is used to indicate a straight line.

DO YOUR FIGURING HERE.

1. Shannon walked $1\frac{2}{3}$ miles on Wednesday and $2\frac{3}{5}$ miles on Thursday. What was the total distance, in miles, Shannon walked during those 2 days?
   A. $3\frac{5}{8}$
   B. $3\frac{2}{5}$
   C. $4\frac{4}{15}$
   D. $4\frac{1}{3}$
   E. $5\frac{1}{3}$

2. $4x^3 \times 3xy^2 \times 2xy^2$ is equivalent to:
   F. $9x^3y^4$
   G. $9x^5y^4$
   H. $24x^3y^4$
   J. $24x^5y^4$
   K. $24x^5y^6$

3. Mr. Wilk is a high school math teacher whose salary is $33,660 for this school year, which has 180 days. In Mr. Wilk's school district, substitute teachers are paid $85 per day. If Mr. Wilk takes a day off without pay and a substitute teacher is paid to teach his classes, how much less does the school district pay in salary by paying a substitute teacher instead of Mr. Wilk for that day?
   A. $57
   B. $85
   C. $102
   D. $114
   E. $187

4. A student has earned the following scores on four 100-point tests this marking period: 63, 72, 88, and 91. What score must the student earn on the fifth and final 100-point test of the marking period to earn an average test grade of 80 for the five tests?
   F. 79
   G. 86
   H. 89
   J. 94
   K. The student cannot earn an average of 80.

GO ON TO THE NEXT PAGE.

2 △ △ △ △ △ △ △ △ 2

5. The oxygen saturation of a lake is found by dividing the amount of dissolved oxygen the lake water currently has per liter by the dissolved oxygen capacity per liter of the water, and then converting that number into a percent. If the lake currently has 6.4 milligrams of dissolved oxygen per liter of water and the dissolved oxygen capacity is 9.5 milligrams per liter, what is the oxygen saturation level of the lake, to the nearest percent?

A. 64%
B. 67%
C. 70%
D. 89%
E. 95%

6. A rectangular lot that measures 125 feet by 185 feet is completely fenced. What is the length, in feet, of the fence?

F. 310
G. 435
H. 620
J. 740
K. 1,240

7. The expression $a[(b - c) + d]$ is equivalent to:

A. $ab + ac + ad$
B. $ab - ac + d$
C. $ab - ac + ad$
D. $ab - c + d$
E. $a - c + d$

8. If $6x - 3 = -5x + 7$, then $x =$?

F. $\dfrac{4}{11}$

G. $\dfrac{10}{11}$

H. $\dfrac{11}{10}$

J. $\dfrac{1}{2}$

K. 10

9. What two numbers should be placed in the blanks below so that the difference between the consecutive numbers is the same?

13, __, __, 34

A. 19, 28
B. 20, 27
C. 21, 26
D. 23, 24
E. 24, 29

10. If x is a real number such that $x^3 = 729$, then $x^2 + \sqrt{x} =$?

F. 9
G. 27
H. 30
J. 84
K. 90

DO YOUR FIGURING HERE.

GO ON TO THE NEXT PAGE.

2 △ △ △ △ △ △ △ △ **2**

11. The formula for the volume, V, of a sphere with radius r is $V = \left(\dfrac{4}{3}\right)\pi r^3$. If the radius of a baseball is $1\dfrac{1}{3}$ inches, what is the volume to the nearest cubic inch?

   A. 6
   B. 8
   C. 10
   D. 14
   E. 15

12. If a gumball is randomly chosen from a bag that contains exactly 6 yellow gumballs, 5 green gumballs, and 4 red gumballs, what is the probability that the gumball chosen is NOT green?

   F. $\dfrac{2}{3}$

   G. $\dfrac{1}{3}$

   H. $\dfrac{2}{5}$

   J. $\dfrac{3}{5}$

   K. $\dfrac{4}{15}$

13. The number of students participating in fall sports at a certain high school can be shown with the following matrix:

Tennis	Soccer	Cross-Country	Football
25	30	50	80

The athletic director estimates the ratio of the number of sports awards that will be earned to the number of students participating with the following matrix:

Tennis	0.2
Soccer	0.5
Cross-Country	0.3
Football	0.4

Given these matrices, what is the athletic director's estimate for the number of sports awards that will be earned for these fall sports?

   A. 55
   B. 60
   C. 65
   D. 67
   E. 74

DO YOUR FIGURING HERE.

2 △ △ △ △ △ △ △ △ **2**

Use the following information to answer questions 14–15.

The following chart shows the current enrollment in all social studies classes—Geography, US History, World Cultures, and Government—at Iron Mountain High School.

Course title	Section	Period	Enrollment
Geography	A	1	23
	B	2	24
US History	A	2	25
	B	3	29
	C	4	24
World Cultures	A	3	27
Government	A	4	26
	B	6	27

14. What is the average number of students enrolled per section in US History?
    F. 25
    G. 26
    H. 27
    J. 29
    K. 34

15. The school wants to have all of the students enrolled in social studies classes read the same book at the same time so that the author of the book can speak to the students at an assembly. The school originally purchased two classroom sets of 30 books each, but now one set is missing 3 books and the other is missing 5. For which of the following class periods, if any, are there NOT enough books available for each student to have one book?
    A. Period 2 only
    B. Period 3 only
    C. Period 4 only
    D. Period 3 and 4 only
    E. There are enough books for each class period

DO YOUR FIGURING HERE.

GO ON TO THE NEXT PAGE.

16. What expression must the center cell of the table below contain so that the sums of each row and each column are equivalent?

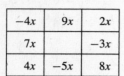

$-4x$	$9x$	$2x$
$7x$		$-3x$
$4x$	$-5x$	$8x$

    F. $5x$
    G. $3x$
    H. 0
    J. $-x$
    K. $-4x$

17. Point A is to be graphed in a quadrant, not on an axis, of the standard (x, y) coordinate plane below.
If the x-coordinate and the y-coordinate of point A are to have the same signs, then point A *must* be located in:

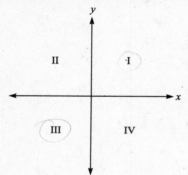

    A. Quadrant I only
    B. Quadrant II only
    C. Quadrant III only
    D. Quadrant I or II only
    E. Quadrant I or III only

18. Reggie knows how to make 5 different entrees, 4 different side dishes, and 6 different desserts. How many distinct complete meals, each consisting of an entrée, a side dish, and a dessert, can Reggie make?
    F. 16
    G. 26
    H. 72
    J. 120
    K. 144

19. At a bottling plant, 10,000 liters of carbonated water are needed to produce 3,000 bottles of soda. How many liters of carbonated water are needed to produce 750 bottles of soda?
    A. 225
    B. 1,500
    C. 2,500
    D. 4,000
    E. 5,000

DO YOUR FIGURING HERE.

GO ON TO THE NEXT PAGE.

2   △ △ △ △ **2**

20. If a rectangle measures 20 meters by 48 meters, what is the length, in meters, of the diagonal of the rectangle?

   F. 52
   G. 68
   H. 72
   J. 112
   K. 2,704

21. For all positive integers a, b, and c, which of the following expressions is equivalent to $\dfrac{a}{c}$?

   ✓ A. $\dfrac{a \times b}{c \times b}$

   B. $\dfrac{a \times a}{c \times c}$

   C. $\dfrac{a \times c}{c \times a}$

   D. $\dfrac{a - b}{c - b}$

   E. $\dfrac{a + b}{c + b}$

22. What is the slope-intercept form of $6x - 2y - 4 = 0$?

   F. $y = 6x - 2$
   G. $y = 3x + 2$
   H. $y = 3x - 2$
   J. $y = -3x + 2$
   K. $y = -6x - 4$

23. Which of the following is a solution to the equation $x^2 + 25x = 0$?

   A. 50
   B. 25
   C. 5
   D. −5
   E. −25

24. For the right triangle $\triangle ABC$ shown below, what is $\tan B$?

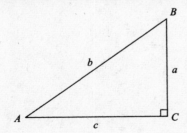

   F. $\dfrac{a}{b}$

   G. $\dfrac{a}{c}$

   H. $\dfrac{b}{a}$

   J. $\dfrac{c}{a}$

   K. $\dfrac{c}{b}$

DO YOUR FIGURING HERE.

GO ON TO THE NEXT PAGE.

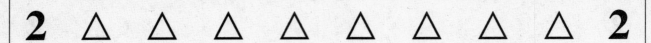

25. A chord 8 inches long is 3 inches from the center of a circle, as shown below. What is the radius of the circle, to the nearest tenth of an inch?

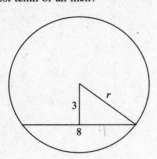

DO YOUR FIGURING HERE.

    A. 4.0
    B. 4.3
    C. 5.0
    D. 6.9
    E. 8.5

26. The length L, in meters, of a spring is given by the equation $L = \left(\dfrac{2}{3}\right)F + 0.05$, where F is the applied force in newtons. Approximately what force, in newtons, must be applied for the spring's length to be 0.23 meters?
    F. 0.12
    G. 0.18
    H. 0.20
    J. 0.24
    K. 0.27

27. After a snowstorm, city workers removed an estimated 12,000 cubic meters of snow from the downtown area. If this snow were spread in an even layer over an empty lot with dimensions 62 meters by 85 meters, about how many meters deep would the layer of snow be?
    A. Less than 1
    B. Between 1 and 2
    C. Between 2 and 3
    D. Between 3 and 4
    E. More than 4

GO ON TO THE NEXT PAGE.

2   **2**

28. The hypotenuse of the right triangle *LMN* shown below is 22 feet long. The cosine of angle *L* is $\frac{3}{4}$. How many feet long is the segment *LM*?

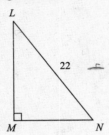

F. 18.4
G. 16.5
H. 11.0
J. 6.7
K. 4.7

29. The table below shows the number of pounds of apples grown last year in 4 cities. (Each whole apple on the graph represents 1,000 pounds of apples.) According to the graph, what fraction of the apples grown in all 4 cities were grown in Appleton?

City	Apples grown
Golden Hills	
Red Falls	
Appleton	
Shady Acres	

A. $\frac{5}{24}$

B. $\frac{1}{4}$

C. $\frac{1}{6}$

D. $\frac{5}{19}$

E. $\frac{3}{16}$

30. Points *B* and *C* lie on segment *AD* as shown below. The length of segment *AD* is 25 units; the segment *AC* is 19 units long; and the segment *BD* is 14 units long. How many units long, if it can be determined, is the segment *BC*?

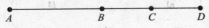

F. 5
G. 6
H. 8
J. 11
K. Cannot be determined from the given information.

DO YOUR FIGURING HERE.

GO ON TO THE NEXT PAGE.

2 △   △ △ △ △ △ **2**

31. What is the *x*-coordinate of the point in the standard (x, y) coordinate plane at which the two lines $y = -2x + 7$ and $y = 3x - 3$ intersect?

  A. 10
  B. 5
  C. 3
  D. 2
  E. 1

32. For all pairs of real numbers S and T where $S = 4T - 7$, $T = ?$

  F. $\dfrac{S}{4} - 7$

  G. $\dfrac{S}{4} + 7$

  H. $4S + 7$

  J. $\dfrac{S - 7}{4}$

  K. $\dfrac{S + 7}{4}$

33. Parallelogram *ABCD*, with dimensions in inches, is shown in the diagram below. What is the area of the parallelogram, in square inches?

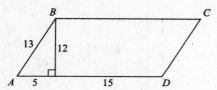

  A. 60
  B. 72
  C. 180
  D. 240
  E. 260

34. If $b = a + 3$, then $(a - b)^4 = ?$

  F. 81
  G. 27
  H. −3
  J. −27
  K. −81

GO ON TO THE NEXT PAGE.

2 △ △ △ △ △ △ △ △ **2**

DO YOUR FIGURING HERE.

35. A park has the shape and dimensions, in miles, given below. The park office is located halfway between point A and point D. Which of the following is the location of the park office from point A? (Note: The park's borders run east–west or north–south.)

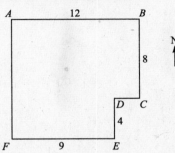

A. 3 miles east and $4\frac{1}{2}$ miles north

B. $4\frac{1}{2}$ miles east and 4 miles south

C. 4 miles east and $4\frac{1}{2}$ miles south

D. 6 miles east and 4 miles south

E. 6 miles east and $4\frac{1}{3}$ miles south

36. The larger of two numbers exceeds three times the smaller number by 4. The sum of twice the larger number and 4 times the smaller number is 58. If x is the smaller number, which equation below determines the correct value of x?

F. $3(2x+4)+4x=58$
G. $3(2x-4)+3x=58$
H. $2(3x+4)+2x=58$
J. $2(3x+4)+4x=58$
K. $2(2x-4)+4x=58$

37. Members of the fire department lean a 26-foot ladder against a building. The side of the building is perpendicular to the level ground so that the base of the ladder is 10 feet away from the base of the building. To the nearest foot, how far up the building does the ladder reach?

A. 12
B. 15
C. 20
D. 22
E. 24

GO ON TO THE NEXT PAGE.

2 △ △ △ △ △ △ △ △ **2**

38. A square is circumscribed about a circle of a 5-foot radius, as shown below. What is the area of the square, in square feet?

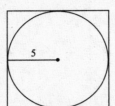

  F. 144
  G. 100
  H. 25π
  J. 50
  K. 25

39. The ratio of the side lengths for a triangle is exactly 7:11:13. In a second triangle similar to the first, the shortest side is 9 inches long. To the nearest tenth of an inch, what is the length of the longest side of the second triangle?
  A. 14.1
  B. 15
  C. 16.7
  D. 17.3
  E. Cannot be determined from the given information.

40. In the figure below, *ABCD* is a trapezoid. *E* lies on line *AD*, and angle measures are as marked. What is the measure of angle *CDB*?

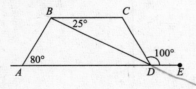

  F. 25°
  G. 30°
  H. 55°
  J. 80°
  K. 100°

DO YOUR FIGURING HERE.

GO ON TO THE NEXT PAGE.

2 △ △ △ △ △ △ △ △ **2**

41. In the figure shown below, each pair of intersecting line segments meets at a right angle, and all the lengths are given in inches. What is the perimeter, in inches, of the figure?

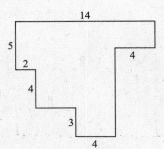

DO YOUR FIGURING HERE.

A. 30
B. 36
C. 42
D. 52
E. 62

42. Of the 517 graduating seniors at Brighton High School, approximately $\frac{4}{5}$ will be attending college, and approximately $\frac{1}{2}$ of those going to college will be attending a state college. Which of the following is the closest estimate of the number of graduating seniors who will be attending a state college?

F. 170
G. 200
H. 260
J. 300
K. 320

43. Let $x \boxast y = (x - 2y)^2$ for all integers x and y. Which of the following is the value of $5 \boxast (-3)$?

A. 121
B. 64
C. 41
D. 1
E. −31

44. If 125% of a number is 425, what is 65% of the number?

F. 221
G. 276
H. 284
J. 308
K. 340

45. What is the distance in the standard (x, y) coordinate plane between the points (2,3) and (5,5)?

A. 3
B. 5
C. $\sqrt{11}$
D. $\sqrt{13}$
E. $\sqrt{25}$

GO ON TO THE NEXT PAGE.

2 △ △ △ △ △ △ △ △ **2**

46. The ratio of the radii of two circles is 9:16. What is the ratio of their circumferences?

  F. 3:4
  G. 9:16
  H. 18:32
  J. 3:4π
  K. 9π:16

47. A circle in the standard (x, y) coordinate plane is tangent to the x-axis at 4 and tangent to the y-axis at 4. Which of the following is an equation of the circle?

  A. $x^2 + y^2 = 4$
  B. $x^2 + y^2 = 16$
  C. $(x - 4)^2 + (y - 4)^2 = 4$
  D. $(x - 4)^2 + (y - 4)^2 = 16$
  E. $(x + 4)^2 + (y + 4)^2 = 16$

48. Using the complex number i, where $i^2 = -1$, $\dfrac{2}{(1 - i)} \times \dfrac{(1 + i)}{(1 + i)} = ?$

  F. $1 + i$
  G. $i - 1$
  H. $1 - i$
  J. $2(1 + i)$
  K. $2(1 - i)$

49. Which of the following describes the total number of dots in the first n rows of the triangular arrangement below?

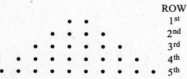

ROW
1st
2nd
3rd
4th
5th

  A. 30
  B. $2n$
  C. n^2
  D. $n(n + 1)$
  E. $2n + 2(n - 1)$

50. After polling a class of 24 students by a show of hands, you find that 9 students play soccer and 21 students play basketball. Given that information, what is the number of students in the class who must play both soccer and basketball?

  F. 0
  G. 1
  H. 3
  J. 6
  K. 9

GO ON TO THE NEXT PAGE.

2 △ △ △ △ △ △ △ △ 2

51. Which of the following is the set of all real numbers x such that $x + 2 > x + 5$?
    A. The set containing only zero
    B. The set containing all nonnegative real numbers
    C. The set containing all negative real numbers
    D. The set containing all real numbers
    E. The empty set

52. Pentagons have 5 diagonals, as illustrated below. How many diagonals does the heptagon (7 sides) below have?

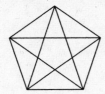 

Pentagon   Heptagon

    F. 7
    G. 12
    H. 14
    J. 21
    K. 28

53. John wants to draw a circle graph showing his friends' favorite ice cream flavors. When he polled his friends asking each their favorite flavor of ice cream, 35% of his friends said chocolate, 20% of his friends said vanilla, 15% of his friends said strawberry, 25% of his friends said mint chocolate chip, and 5% of his friends said flavors other than those previously listed. What will be the degree measure of the vanilla sector of the circle graph?
    A. 126°
    B. 108°
    C. 90°
    D. 72°
    E. 36°

DO YOUR FIGURING HERE.

GO ON TO THE NEXT PAGE.

2 △ △ △ △ △ △ △ △ **2**

54. If $\sin \theta = \dfrac{4}{5}$ and $\dfrac{\pi}{2} < \theta < \pi$, then $\tan \theta = ?$

F. $-\dfrac{5}{4}$

G. $-\dfrac{4}{3}$

H. $-\dfrac{3}{5}$

J. $\dfrac{4}{3}$

K. $\dfrac{3}{4}$

55. Which of the following systems of inequalities is represented by the shaded region of the graph below?

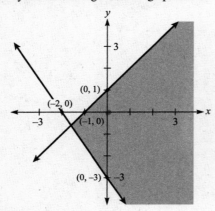

A. $y \le x + 1$ or $y \ge x - 3$

B. $y \le x + 1$ and $y \ge x - 3$

C. $y \le x + 1$ or $y \ge \left(-\dfrac{3}{2}\right)x - 3$

D. $y \le x + 1$ and $y \le \left(-\dfrac{3}{2}\right)x - 3$

E. $y \le x + 1$ and $y \ge \left(-\dfrac{3}{2}\right)x - 3$

56. If $f(x) = 2x^2 + 3$, then $f(x + h) = ?$

F. $2x^2 + h^2$

G. $2x^2 + h + 3$

H. $2x^2 + 2h^2 + 3$

J. $x^2 + 2xh + h^2 + 3$

K. $2x^2 + 4xh + 2h^2 + 3$

DO YOUR FIGURING HERE.

GO ON TO THE NEXT PAGE.

2 △ △ △ △ △ △ △ △ **2**

57. Which of the following is the graph, in the standard (x, y) coordinate plane, of $y = \dfrac{x^2 + 3x}{x}$?

A.

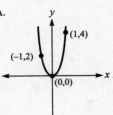

D.

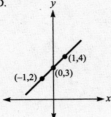

B.

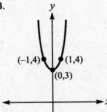

E.

C.

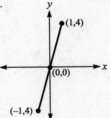

DO YOUR FIGURING HERE.

58. A triangle, $\triangle ABD$, is reflected across the y-axis to have the image $\triangle A'B'D'$ in the standard (x, y) coordinate plane: thus A reflects to A'. The coordinates of point A are (m, n). What are the coordinates of point A'?

F. $(-m, n)$
G. $(m, -n)$
H. $(-m, -n)$
J. (n, m)
K. Cannot be determined from the given information.

GO ON TO THE NEXT PAGE.

2 △ △ △ △ △ △ △ △ **2**

59. If $x = 3r - 4$ and $y = 3r + 2$, which of the following expresses y in terms of x?
A. $y = x + 2$
B. $y = x + 6$
C. $y = 9r + 14$
D. $y = 6r - 2$
E. $y = 3x + 14$

60. What is $\cos \dfrac{\pi}{12}$ given that $\dfrac{\pi}{12} = \dfrac{\pi}{3} - \dfrac{\pi}{4}$ and that $\cos(\alpha - \beta) = (\cos \alpha)(\cos \beta) + (\sin \alpha)(\sin \beta)$?

θ	$\sin \theta$	$\cos \theta$
$\dfrac{\pi}{6}$	$\dfrac{1}{2}$	$\dfrac{\sqrt{3}}{2}$
$\dfrac{\pi}{4}$	$\dfrac{\sqrt{2}}{2}$	$\dfrac{\sqrt{2}}{2}$
$\dfrac{\pi}{3}$	$\dfrac{\sqrt{3}}{2}$	$\dfrac{1}{2}$

F. $\dfrac{1}{4}$

G. $\dfrac{1}{2}$

H. $\dfrac{\sqrt{6} + \sqrt{2}}{4}$

J. $\dfrac{\sqrt{3} + \sqrt{2}}{2}$

K. $\dfrac{\sqrt{6} + 2}{4}$

DO YOUR FIGURING HERE.

END OF THE MATHEMATICS TEST.
STOP! IF YOU HAVE TIME LEFT OVER, CHECK YOUR WORK ON THIS SECTION ONLY.

3 ▬▬▬▬▬▬▬▬▬▬▬▬▬▬▬▬▬▬▬▬▬▬▬▬ **3**

READING TEST

35 Minutes—40 Questions

DIRECTIONS: This test includes four passages, each followed by ten questions. Read the passages and choose the best answer to each question. After you have selected your answer, fill in the corresponding bubble on your answer sheet. You should refer to the passages as often as necessary when answering the questions.

PASSAGE I

PROSE FICTION: *This passage is adapted from Joseph Conrad's* The Heart of Darkness © 1899.

The *Nellie*, a cruising ship, swung to her anchor without a flutter of the sails, and was at rest. The tide had come in, the wind was nearly calm, and being bound down the river, the only thing for the ship was
5 to come to and wait for the turn of the tide.
The Director of Companies was our captain and our host. We four affectionately watched his back as he stood in the bow looking toward the sea. On the whole river there was nothing that looked half so nautical.
10 He resembled a pilot, which to a seaman is trustworthiness personified. It was difficult to realize his work was not out there in the luminous estuary, but behind him, within the brooding gloom.
Between us there was, as I have already said
15 somewhere, the bond of the sea. Besides holding our hearts together through long periods of separation, it had the effect of making us tolerant of each other's stories—and even convictions. The Lawyer—the best of old fellows—had, because of his many years and
20 many virtues, the only cushion on deck, and was lying on the only rug. The Accountant had brought out already a box of dominoes, and was toying architecturally with the pieces. Marlow sat cross-legged, leaning against the mast. He had sunken cheeks, a
25 yellow complexion, a straight back, and, with his arms dropped, the palms of his hands outwards, resembled an idol. The Director, satisfied the anchor had good hold, made his way forward and sat down amongst us. We exchanged a few words lazily. Afterwards there
30 was silence on board the yacht. For some reason or another we did not begin that game of dominoes. We felt meditative, and fit for nothing but placid staring.
"And this also," said Marlow suddenly, "has been one of the dark places of the earth." He was the only
35 man of us who still "followed the sea." The worst that could be said of him was that he did not represent his class—always the same. In their unchanging surroundings, the foreign shores, the foreign faces glide past, veiled not by a sense of mystery but by a slightly
40 disdainful ignorance; for there is nothing mysterious

to a seaman unless it be the sea itself, which is the mistress of his existence and as inscrutable as destiny. For the rest, after his hours of work, a casual stroll or a casual spree on shore suffices to unfold for him the
45 secret of a whole continent, and generally he finds the secret not worth knowing. The stories of seamen have a direct simplicity, the whole meaning of which lies within the shell of a cracked nut. But Marlow was not typical, and to him the meaning of an episode was not
50 inside like a kernel but outside, enveloping the tale, which brought it out only as a glow brings out a haze, in the likeness of one of these misty halos that sometimes are made visible by the spectral illumination of moonshine.
55 His remark did not seem at all surprising. It was just like Marlow. It was accepted in silence. No one took the trouble to grunt even; and presently he said, very slow—"I was thinking of very old times, when the Romans first came here, nineteen hundred years
60 ago." And at last, in its curved and imperceptible fall, the sun sank low, and from glowing white changed to a dull red without rays and without heat, as if about to go out suddenly, stricken to death by the touch of that gloom brooding over a crowd of men.
65 Marlow broke off. Flames glided in the river, small green flames, red flames, white flames, pursuing, overtaking, joining, crossing each other—then separating slowly or hastily. The traffic of the great city went on in the deepening night upon the sleepless river. We
70 looked on, waiting patiently—there was nothing else to do; but it was only after a long silence, when he said, in a hesitating voice, "I suppose you fellows remember I did once turn fresh-water sailor for a bit," that we knew we were fated, before the ebb began to run, to
75 hear about one of Marlow's inconclusive experiences.

1. The narrator's point of view is that of:
A. an omniscient observer.
B. a member of the ship's crew.
C. another ship's captain.
D. a person watching from shore.

GO ON TO THE NEXT PAGE.

3   **3**

2. It can reasonably be inferred from the passage that the crew most likely did not play dominoes because:
   F. they were simply too tired.
   G. they did not get along well enough to play a game together.
   H. the Director would not have approved of game-playing.
   J. the sea was too rough.

3. Which of the following are explanations given by the narrator as to why the Lawyer used the ship's only cushion?
   I. He was very old.
   II. He would not allow anyone else to use it.
   III. He was greatly respected by the ship's crew.
   A. I and II only
   B. I only
   C. I and III only
   D. II only

4. As it is used in line 32 of the passage, the word *placid* most nearly means:
   F. calm.
   G. straightforward.
   H. nervous.
   J. playful.

5. According to the passage, how was Marlow unlike typical seamen?
   A. Marlow was content to stay in one place, while most men of the sea prefer to roam and explore.
   B. Marlow believed his home was the ship, while most sailors believed their home was the sea.
   C. Marlow found the sea inexplicable and full of secrets, while a typical sailor understands the mysteries of the water.
   D. Marlow wove complicated and ambiguous tales, while most seamen prefer to tell simple and clear tales.

6. It can be reasonably inferred from the passage that Marlow is about to tell a story:
   F. that explains why he is now a freshwater sailor.
   G. that is short and funny, like most of the stories he tells.
   H. that is not clear and self-contained but is instead rather nebulous.
   J. about a man that he saved from drowning in a river.

7. According to the passage, how did the men aboard the *Nellie* feel about the Director?
   A. They respected and trusted him.
   B. They felt that he was lazy.
   C. They despised and rejected him.
   D. They thought that he was gloomy.

8. The reaction of the narrator to Marlow's story can be most accurately described as:
   F. malicious annoyance.
   G. resigned tolerance.
   H. genuine interest.
   J. sincere appreciation.

9. According to the passage, which of the following was not an effect of the "bond of the sea" (line 15)?
   A. It allowed the men to look past each other's criminal backgrounds.
   B. The men did not mind listening to each other's meandering tales.
   C. It eased the loneliness of extended periods of time away from each other.
   D. The men were able to be more tolerant of each other's beliefs.

10. The main point of the second paragraph is:
   F. The ship's captain is better suited to be an aviator than a sailor.
   G. The captain is unaware of the great amount of hard work that lies ahead of him.
   H. An unqualified and inexperienced businessman is serving as the captain of the Nellie.
   J. The narrator and other crew members greatly respect their ship's captain.

GO ON TO THE NEXT PAGE.

3 ███████████████████████████████████████ **3**

PASSAGE II

SOCIAL SCIENCE: *This passage discusses some social and economic issues regarding liquid natural gas as an energy source.*

Although oil and gasoline remain important energy sources, it is natural gas that currently supplies around 25 percent of America's energy needs. A recent study shows that natural gas use was roughly 22 trillion
5 cubic feet (TCF) annually. Natural gas demand is increasing at phenomenal rates because of its ability to create cleaner fuel for electrical power. Experts predict that annual demand is likely to increase to almost 32 TCF in less than a decade. At a consumption rate
10 of 32 TCF per year, the United States would only have about a five-year supply of natural gas. Known natural gas reserves in North America are quickly becoming exhausted. In fact, in the past thirty years, known supplies have dwindled from almost 300 TCF to around
15 150 TCF.

It is no wonder that natural gas has become a controversial and critical topic of discussion among politicians, business leaders, and consumers. It is apparent that the United States will need to drastically increase
20 imports of natural gas to relieve shortages. One way that economists believe this can be done is by importing liquid natural gas. Experts predict that liquid natural gas imports will increase by almost 500 percent in a few short years. Currently, the country imports very little
25 liquid natural gas. The process of transporting liquid natural gas is complicated and expensive. This is the most obvious reason why America has been reluctant to choose liquid natural gas over other energy sources. Converting natural gas into liquid natural gas involves
30 cooling natural gas as it is collected to −260°F. This transforms the gas into a liquid, which is then injected into a specially designed vessel for transport. When the liquid natural gas reaches its destination, the liquid is reheated into its original gaseous state and allowed
35 to flow into a pipeline. Even though new technology has considerably decreased transportation costs for liquid natural gas, it is still often uneconomical. This is especially true for nations with other energy sources.

One of the largest misconceptions about liquid
40 natural gas is that it is an abundant source of natural gas. While liquid natural gas imports continue to increase, the public demand for natural gas increases at an even higher rate. Even though the United States has several facilities that can process liquid natural gas,
45 these facilities are consistently unable to obtain enough liquid natural gas to operate at their fullest capacity. Even when liquid natural gas is obtainable, there is a fear that low natural gas prices in the United States will make liquid natural gas uneconomical. Most business
50 leaders and politicians are reluctant to create new facilities to process liquid natural gas because these facilities are expensive and risky. This limits the capacity to process liquid natural gas even if it becomes more readily available.
55 The United States also faces competition from Asia in securing liquid natural gas. Competition for liquid natural gas will most likely become even more ferocious as other populous countries like Japan and

China become more desperate for fuel sources. Some
60 of the more daring politicians and business leaders believe that building new liquid natural gas facilities will help companies and consumers take advantage of future increased liquid natural gas imports. Currently, Canada is the largest liquid natural gas supplier for
65 the United States. However, liquid natural gas imports from Canada will decrease considerably in the next decade as Canadian consumption increases and supplies of natural gas dwindle. Therefore, consumers and business leaders should not rely on liquid natural gas
70 to solve America's energy needs and consumers should continue to expect high prices as demand grows and supplies decline.

11. According to the passage, current known North American supplies of natural gas are:
   A. sufficient to provide the United States with natural gas for the next thirty years.
   B. down approximately 50 percent from thirty years ago.
   C. decreasing at a rate of 25 percent per year.
   D. extremely difficult to access.

12. The author of the passage would most likely agree with which of the following statements?
   F. Liquid natural gas will never be a viable source of energy in the United States.
   G. America's energy needs will not be met by the use of liquid natural gas alone.
   H. The populations of Japan and China are growing too rapidly to be served by liquid natural gas.
   J. Until another reliable energy source is discovered, liquid natural gas is the best solution to the world's energy problems.

13. One of the main ideas of the passage is that:
   A. energy sources are dwindling around the world.
   B. natural gas supplies one-quarter of America's energy needs.
   C. liquid natural gas takes millions of years to form.
   D. the known supply of liquid natural gas is limited.

14. It can be inferred from the second paragraph (lines 16–38) that America's reluctance to choose liquid natural gas over other energy sources will:
   F. not prevent America from importing more liquid natural gas from other countries.
   G. induce Japan and China to build new liquid natural gas processing facilities.
   H. most likely continue until the cost and problems associated with liquid natural gas can be reduced.
   J. lead to a decrease in the current demand for liquid natural gas in other countries, such as Canada.

GO ON TO THE NEXT PAGE.

3 ████████████████████████████████████ **3**

15. According to the passage, which of the following countries supplies the most liquid natural gas to the United States?
  A. Japan.
  B. China.
  C. Canada.
  D. Asia.

16. According to the third paragraph (lines 39–54), misconceptions exist about liquid natural gas regarding:

    I. its abundance.
    II. the expense of converting it.
    III. public demand for it.

  F. I only
  G. II only
  H. II and III only
  J. I, II, and III

17. As it is used in line 6, the word *phenomenal* most nearly means:
  A. annual.
  B. efficient.
  C. extraordinary.
  D. inconsequential.

18. The passage states that all of the following are reasons for America's reluctance to choose liquid natural gas EXCEPT:
  F. the expense of transporting liquid natural gas.
  G. the increasing demand for liquid natural gas.
  H. the difficulty in processing liquid natural gas.
  J. the possibility of low natural gas prices.

19. The passage states that which of the following is true about natural gas?
  A. It currently supplies more than half of America's energy needs.
  B. The United States has an unlimited supply of natural gas.
  C. Canada is the world's largest exporter of natural gas.
  D. Annual demand for natural gas is increasing at a rapid rate.

20. As it is used in line 32, the word *vessel* most nearly means:
  F. process.
  G. source.
  H. facility.
  J. container.

PASSAGE III

HUMANITIES: *This passage is adapted from* The Nature of Goodness *by George Herbert Palmer ©1903.*

My reader may well feel that goodness is already the most familiar of all the thoughts we employ, and yet he may at the same time suspect that there is something about it perplexingly remote. Familiar it certainly is. It
5 attends all our wishes, acts, and projects as nothing else does, so that no estimate of its influence can be excessive. When we take a walk, read a book, pick out a dress, visit a friend, attend a concert, cast a vote, enter into business, we always do it in the hope of attaining
10 something good. Since they are so frequently encountering goodness, both laymen and scholars are apt to assume that it is altogether clear and requires no explanation. But the very reverse is the truth. Familiarity obscures. It breeds instincts and not understanding. So
15 woven has goodness become with the very web of life that it is hard to disentangle.

Consequently, we employ the word or some synonym of it during pretty much every waking hour of our lives. Wishing some test of this frequency I turned
20 to Shakespeare, and found that he uses the word "good" fifteen hundred times, and its derivatives "goodness," "better," and "best," about as many more. He could not make men and women talk right without incessant reference to this concept.

25 How then do we employ the word "good"? I do not ask how we ought to employ it, but how we actually do. For the present, we shall be engaged in a psychological inquiry, not an ethical one. We need to get at the plain facts of usage. I will therefore ask each reader
30 to look into his own mind, see on what occasions he uses the word, and decide what meaning he attaches to it. Taking up a few of the simplest possible examples, we will through them inquire when and why we call things good.

35 Here is a knife. When is it a good knife? Why, a knife is made for something, for cutting. Whenever the knife slides evenly through a piece of wood, and with a minimum of effort on the part of him who steers it, when there is no disposition of its edge to bend or
40 break, but only to do its appointed work effectively, then we know that a good knife is at work. Or, looking at the matter from another point of view, whenever the handle of the knife neatly fits the hand, following its lines and presenting no obstruction, we may say that
45 in these respects also the knife is a good knife. That is, the knife becomes good through adaptation to its work, an adaptation realized in its cutting of the wood and in its conformity to the hand. Its goodness always has reference to something outside itself, and is measured
50 by its performance of an external task.

Or take something not so palpable. What glorious weather! When we woke this morning, drew aside our curtains and looked out, we said "It is a good day!" And of what qualities of the day were we thinking? We
55 meant, I suppose, that the day was well fitted to its various purposes. Intending to go to our office, we saw there was nothing to hinder our doing so. We knew that the streets would be clear, people in an amiable mood,

business and social duties would move forward easily.
60 In fact, whatever our plans, in calling the day a good day we meant to speak of it as excellently adapted to something outside itself.

A usage more curious still occurs in the nursery. There when the question is asked, "Has the baby
65 been good?" one discovers by degrees that the anxious mother wishes to know if it has been crying or quiet. This elementary life has as yet not acquired positive standards of measurement. It must be reckoned in negative terms, a failure to disturb.

70 This signification of goodness is lucidly put in the remark of Shakespeare's Portia, "Nothing I see is good without respect." We must have some respect or end in mind in reference to which the goodness is compared. Good always means good "for." That little preposition
75 cannot be absent from our minds, though it need not audibly be uttered. The knife is good for cutting and the day for business. Omit the "for," and goodness ceases. To be bad or good implies external reference. To be good means to be an efficient means; and the end to
80 be furthered must be already in mind before the word good is spoken.

In short, whenever we inspect the usage of the word good, we always find behind it an implication of some end to be reached. Good is a relative term. The
85 good is the useful, and it must be useful for something. Silent or spoken, it is the mental reference to something else which puts all meaning into it. So Hamlet says, "There's nothing either good or bad, but thinking makes it so." No new quality is added to an object or
90 act when it becomes good.

21. One of the main arguments the author is trying to make in the passage is that:
   A. the word *good* always connotes the same idea no matter the context of the usage, whether people realize it or not.
   B. although the word *good* is used frequently, the exact definition and connotation of the word is difficult to identify precisely.
   C. things or people are either good or not good; goodness is not a quality that is debatable.
   D. a debate of ethics, not psychology, will most clearly identify the exact definition and connotation of the word *good.*

22. The main idea of the sixth paragraph (lines 63–69) is that:
   F. it is irrelevant for a mother to inquire if her baby has been well-behaved or not.
   G. a baby has not been alive long enough to be judged as either good or bad.
   H. since the baby is so young, it is not judged as good by what it does, but rather what it does not do.
   J. whether or not a baby has been crying is not a significant standard upon which to determine its goodness.

GO ON TO THE NEXT PAGE.

3 ███ **3**

23. According to the passage, why does the author concern himself with Shakespeare's usage of the word *good*?
   A. He was seeking confirmation for his belief that both the use of the word and the concept of *good* are strikingly common.
   B. He was looking for a definition of the concept of *good* and turned to Shakespeare for inspiration.
   C. He was trying to understand the lack of the concept of *good* and *goodness* in the works of Shakespeare.
   D. He was seeking support for his belief that Shakespeare was able to use the concept of *good* more effectively than any other author.

24. The author of the passage asserts that the weather and a knife are similar because:
   F. both are defined as good if and only if they can be helpful to many people for a variety of reasons.
   G. neither can be defined as good unless they remain consistent and unchanged in the wake of fluctuating circumstances.
   H. both are defined as good when their characteristics serve appropriate external circumstances.
   J. neither one can be good unless a universal definition of the concept is accepted.

25. As it is used in line 70, the word *lucidly* most nearly means:
   A. obscurely.
   B. inappropriately.
   C. enthusiastically.
   D. coherently.

26. The author argues that a knife may be described as good:
   F. only if it cuts wood.
   G. only if it is made for something other than cutting.
   H. only as it relates to something other than itself.
   J. only if it requires extra effort in its use.

27. As it is used in the passage, the word *palpable* most nearly means:
   A. apparent.
   B. powerful.
   C. drab.
   D. complicated.

28. The main argument that the author tries to make in the seventh paragraph (lines 70–81) is that:
   F. it is always clear what is meant when someone describes something as *good*.
   G. the concept of being *good* is entirely different than the concept of being *good for*.
   H. it is often easier to understand the concept of *good* without using the phrase *good for*.
   J. the word *good* is relative, finding meaning only when there is a specific end in mind.

29. It can be reasonably inferred from the passage that the author would agree that the word *good* actually means:
   A. measurable.
   B. significant.
   C. persistent.
   D. practical.

30. When, referring to the role of goodness in life, the author states, "no estimate of its influence can be excessive" (lines 6–7), he most likely means that:
   F. people must be careful not to allow the search for goodness to monopolize their lives.
   G. it is impossible to over-emphasize the power that the quest for goodness has on us.
   H. it is impossible to conceptualize and grasp the definition of the word good.
   J. people often inaccurately describe the role that goodness plays in their own lives.

3 ▮▮▮▮▮▮▮▮▮▮▮▮▮▮▮▮▮▮▮▮▮▮▮ **3**

PASSAGE IV
NATURAL SCIENCE: *The Armored Armadillo*

Meandering along the shoulder of the highway, the armadillo is surprisingly unaffected by its surroundings. This nomad of the desert appears to have no cares in the world, and really, why should he, when
[5] he carries on his back a natural suit of armor? He looks far more awkward than do most animals, yet this alien creature handles himself remarkably well. For such a small animal, the armadillo can withstand a surprising amount of aggression from most predators. Although
[10] his shell is far from impenetrable, the armadillo can rest assured that he is safer than many animals who wander the Texas roads.

The *Dasypus novemcinctus*, or nine-banded armadillo, is characterized by the bands that arch across
[15] its back. The bands are made of bony plates and are covered with leathery skin—these plates, in fact cover the animal's back, sides, tail, and the top of its head, creating a somewhat turtle-like shell. The interesting thing about the nine-banded armadillo is
[20] that the number of bands on its back may be anywhere between seven and eleven; nine is just the most common number. Contrary to popular belief, only one species of armadillo can roll itself into a ball; the three-banded armadillo does this as its primary defense
[25] against predators. Other armadillos often scurry under thorn bushes, rather like tanks strengthening their position.

Armadillos are, on average, two and a half feet long and they typically weigh between eight and
[30] sixteen pounds, although across different species those numbers can vary dramatically. Nine-banded females give birth once a year, generally to four identical young, which come from a single fertilized egg. The nine-banded armadillo is the only species of animal in which
[35] this remarkable trait occurs. The four-month-long gestation period is more than enough time for the offspring to develop, as they are born fully formed with their eyes open. After a few hours they begin to walk and are able to distance themselves from their mothers after only a
[40] few months. Few animals are able to outrun a startled armadillo, and if chased into its burrow, the animal is able to arch its armor against the burrow walls, making the armadillo nearly impossible to become dislodged; this is quite frustrating to dogs and other animals who
[45] would like to eat the armadillo. In addition to threats of being eaten by an opportunistic predator, the armadillo must also endure a more severe danger: automobiles. A significant number of armadillos die each year after being struck by cars.
[50] Armadillos can be found in the northern parts of South America and as far north as the State of Texas. Nine-banded armadillos prefer warm climates and like to build burrows in the wet soil near streambeds, which they often share with other species, such as rabbits and
[55] opossums. Armadillos are nocturnal, and they spend their evenings digging for grubs and other invertebrates which make up the majority of their diet.

Most Texans see the armadillo as a pest, since the creatures have a tendency to ruin corn by eating the
[60] parts of the plants that are low to the ground; they occasionally will eat other farm vegetables as well. Armadillos provide some benefits however, as they eat many annoying and harmful insects and are often used in medical research. Interestingly enough, they are the
[65] only mammal besides humans that can contract leprosy.

While armadillos are seen as strange and often troublesome animals, they are unique and valuable for research. This armored native of the south will most likely continue to fascinate and charm people for many
[70] years to come.

31. The author likens armadillos scurrying under thorn bushes to "tanks strengthening their position" in Paragraph 2 because:
   A. armadillos are well armored and thorn bushes give them even more protection.
   B. an armadillo's shell is as hard as steel.
   C. the scurrying of an armadillo sounds like a tank rolling over land.
   D. the armadillo resembles a tank in appearance.

32. The author calls the armadillo an "alien creature" in the first paragraph because:
   F. not much is known about armadillos.
   G. armadillos come from another planet.
   H. armadillos are very aggressive.
   J. an armadillo's unique appearance makes it stand out.

33. The passage indicates that, unlike some other desert animals, the armadillo:
   A. lacks a means of defending itself.
   B. can go without drinking water for long periods of time.
   C. reproduces many times each year.
   D. can withstand most predators' attacks.

34. As it is used in the passage (line 42), the phrase "arch its armor" most nearly means:
   F. to construct.
   G. to curve.
   H. to dig.
   J. to fight.

35. Based on information in the passage, the author feels that the nine-banded armadillo is especially unique because:
   A. it can curl into a ball.
   B. it is the rarest type of armadillo.
   C. it gives birth to four identical young.
   D. its diet consists entirely of grubs.

GO ON TO THE NEXT PAGE.

3 ████████████████████████████ **3**

36. The passage indicates that most Texans consider the armadillo to be both:
 F. rare and sacred.
 G. strange and interesting.
 H. annoying and helpful.
 J. valued and dangerous.

37. What does the passage state is one of armadillo's greatest threats?
 A. farmers.
 B. cars.
 C. opossums.
 D. dogs.

38. The passage states that, in the Southern United States, armadillos do damage to:
 F. crops.
 G. deserts.
 H. rivers.
 J. houses.

39. The passage indicates that, at birth, armadillos:
 A. are utterly helpless.
 B. are identical to adults.
 C. are able to see.
 D. are totally independent.

40. According to the passage, the scientific name *Dasypus novemcinctus* is unique to:
 F. the three-banded armadillo.
 G. the six-banded armadillo.
 H. all armadillos.
 J. the nine-banded armadillo.

END OF THE READING TEST.
STOP! IF YOU HAVE TIME LEFT OVER, CHECK YOUR WORK ON THIS SECTION ONLY.

4 ◯ ◯ ◯ ◯ ◯ ◯ ◯ ◯ ◯ **4**

SCIENCE REASONING TEST

35 Minutes—40 Questions

DIRECTIONS: This test includes seven passages, each followed by several questions. Read the passage and choose the best answer to each question. After you have selected your answer, fill in the corresponding bubble on your answer sheet. You should refer to the passages as often as necessary when answering the questions. You may NOT use a calculator on this test.

PASSAGE I

Some students performed three studies to measure the average speed on a flat surface of a remote-controlled car with different types of wheels. Each study was conducted indoors in a temperature-controlled room. A straight track was constructed and measured to be 75 feet long. The car's travel time was measured from start to finish with a stopwatch. The temperature in the room was kept constant at 20° F and the surface was returned to its original condition after each trial. No modifications were made to the car aside from changing the wheels, and the car's batteries were fully charged before each trial.

Study 1

The students fitted the car with hard rubber wheels, which had deep treads, and placed it on the surface. One student started the car as another student simultaneously started the stopwatch. The student stopped the stopwatch as the car crossed the 75-foot mark. The students calculated the results of three separate trials and averaged the results (see Table 1).

Table 1		
Trial	Time (s)	Speed (ft/s)
1	22.8	3.28
2	23.2	3.23
3	22.5	3.33
Average:	22.8	3.28

Study 2

The students repeated the procedure used in Study 1, except they fitted the car with soft rubber wheels, which were smooth and lacked treads. The results are shown in Table 2.

Table 2		
Trial	Time (s)	Speed (ft/s)
1	57	1.31
2	56.4	1.33
3	56.7	1.32
Average:	56.7	1.32

Study 3

The students repeated the procedure used in Study 1, except they fitted the car with hard rubber wheels, which had studs imbedded into them instead of treads. The results are shown in Table 3.

Table 3		
Trial	Time (s)	Speed (ft/s)
1	11.3	6.64
2	11.6	6.47
3	12.1	6.20
Average:	11.7	6.44

1. The fastest times resulted from using which wheels?
   A. The speeds remained constant.
   B. Hard rubber wheels with studs imbedded in them.
   C. Soft rubber wheels with no treads.
   D. Hard rubber wheels with deep treads.

GO ON TO THE NEXT PAGE.

2. According to Study 1, the average speed for all three trials was:
   F. greater than the speed measured in Trial 3.
   G. less than the speed measured in Trial 1.
   H. greater than the speed measured in Trial 2.
   J. equal to the speed measured in Trial 2.

3. Which of the following statements is best supported by the results of all three studies?
   A. The average speed of a car with deeply treaded hard rubber wheels is approximately $\frac{1}{2}$ the average speed of car with soft rubber wheels.
   B. The average speed of a car with studded, hard rubber wheels is approximately $\frac{1}{2}$ the average speed of car with deeply treaded hard rubber wheels.
   C. The average speed of a car with soft rubber wheels lacking treads is approximately twice the average speed of car with deeply treaded hard rubber wheels.
   D. The average speed of a car with studded, hard rubber wheels is approximately twice the average speed of car with deeply treaded hard rubber wheels.

4. Based on the passage, the higher average speeds were probably the result of:
   F. greater friction.
   G. temperature variations.
   H. too much sunlight.
   J. statistical error.

5. During which of the following was the travel time of the car the slowest?
   A. Study 2, Trial 1
   B. Study 2, Trial 2
   C. Study 3, Trial 1
   D. Study 1, Trial 2

4 ◯ ◯ ◯ ◯ ◯ ◯ ◯ ◯ 4

PASSAGE II

The ninth planet of our solar system, Pluto, was discovered in 1930. It is the smallest planet in the solar system, with a surface area more than 300 times smaller than Earth's. Recently, Pluto's categorization as a planet has been debated. Two scientists discuss whether Pluto is a planet or another celestial object.

Scientist 1

Pluto is most certainly a planet. Some astronomers have suggested that Pluto be stripped of its planetary status, arguing that it is more accurately categorized as an asteroid or comet. However, with a 1,413 mile diameter, Pluto is almost 1,000 times bigger than an average comet, and it does not have a tail of dust and gas as comets do. A planet can be described as a non-moon, sun-orbiting object that does not generate nuclear fusion and is large enough to be pulled into a spherical shape by its own gravity. Strictly by definition alone, Pluto is a planet. Pluto is clearly not a moon, as it does not orbit another planet. Although Pluto's orbital path is irregular as compared with the other planets of the solar system, it undisputedly orbits the sun. Pluto does not generate heat by nuclear fission, distinguishing it from a star. It is large enough to be pulled into a spherical shape by its own gravitational force, distinguishing it from either a comet or an asteroid.

Scientist 2

There are many facts about Pluto suggesting that it is actually not a planet but a member of the Kuiper Belt, a group of sizable comets that orbit the sun beyond Neptune. First, Pluto is composed of icy material, as are the comets in the Kuiper Belt, while the other planets of the solar system fall into one of two categories: rocky or gaseous. The four inner planets, Mercury, Venus, Earth, and Mars are rocky planets; Jupiter, Saturn, Uranus, and Neptune are gaseous. Pluto is neither rocky nor gaseous but has an icy composition. In addition, Pluto is much too small to be a planet. It is less than half the diameter of the next smallest planet, Mercury. The Earth's moon is even larger than Pluto. Finally, the eccentricity of Pluto's orbit indicates that it is not a planet. Pluto is generally considered the ninth planet, but for twenty years of its 249 year orbit, it is actually closer to the sun than is Neptune, making it the eighth planet during that period of time. This irregular orbit is shared by over seventy Kuiper Belt comets.

6. Which of the following phrases best describes the major point of difference between the two scientists' viewpoints?
   F. The actual location of Pluto in the solar system.
   G. The length of Pluto's orbit.
   H. The shape of Pluto.
   J. The classification of Pluto as a planet.

7. According to Scientist 2's viewpoint, compared to other planets of the solar system, Pluto's surface is:
   A. less icy.
   B. more icy.
   C. more gaseous.
   D. more rocky.

8. Scientist 1's viewpoint indicates that Pluto differs from asteroids and comets in all of the following ways EXCEPT:
   F. Pluto can generate heat through nuclear fission.
   G. Pluto is pulled into a spherical shape by its own gravitational force.
   H. Asteroids and comets have a tail of gas and dust particles.
   J. Asteroids and comets are much smaller than Pluto.

9. The polar ice caps on Pluto's surface melt one time during every 249-year orbit, exposing Pluto's truly rocky surface, which is similar to that of Mars. Based on the information provided, this finding, if true, would most likely weaken the position(s) of:
   A. Scientist 1 only.
   B. Scientist 2 only.
   C. both Scientist 1 and Scientist 2.
   D. neither Scientist 1 nor Scientist 2.

10. With which of the following statements would both scientists most likely agree?
    F. The size of Pluto indicates that it could actually be a satellite of another planet.
    G. Pluto should be classified as neither a planet nor a comet; a new category is indicated.
    H. The surface composition of Pluto is irrelevant and should not be considered in its classification.
    J. Pluto's erratic orbit differentiates it from all other planets in the solar system.

11. Scientist 1's viewpoint would be weakened by which of the following observations, if true?
    A. Scientists have recently discovered a Kuiper Belt comet with a radius of almost 1,500 miles.
    B. Pluto only has one moon, Charon, which is half the size of Pluto.
    C. Planets can be distinguished from comets by the lack of gas and dust particles in the wake of their orbits.
    D. Comets and asteroids are capable of generating nuclear fission.

12. Which of the following statements best describes how Scientist 2 likens Pluto to a Kuiper Belt comet?
    F. Neither Pluto nor Kuiper Belt comets have identifiable atmospheres.
    G. Neither Pluto nor Kuiper Belt comets are trailed by a cloud of gases and dust.
    H. Both Pluto and Kuiper Belt comets have similar eccentric orbital patterns.
    J. Both Pluto and Kuiper Belt comets are roughly half the size of the next smallest planet, Mercury.

GO ON TO THE NEXT PAGE.

4 ○ ○ ○ ○ ○ ○ ○ ○ ○ **4**

PASSAGE III

A *solute* is any substance that is dissolved in another substance, which is called the *solvent*.

A student tested the *solubility* (a measure of how much solute will dissolve into the solvent) of six different substances. The solubility of a substance at a given temperature is defined as the concentration of the dissolved solute that is in equilibrium with the solvent.

Table 1 represents the concentration of dissolved substances in 100 grams of water at various temperatures. The concentrations are expressed in grams of solute per 100 grams of water.

Table 1						
Concentration of solute (g/100 g H_2O)						
Temp (°C)	KCl	NaNO$_3$	HCl	NH$_4$Cl	NaCl	NH$_3$
0	28	72	83	29	37	90
20	33	86	72	37	37	55
40	39	105	63	46	38	36
60	45	125	55	55	38	23
80	51	145	48	66	39	14
100	57	165	43	77	40	8

13. According to Table 1, the concentrations of which of the following substances varies the least with temperature?
A. HCl
B. NH$_3$
C. NaCl
D. KCl

14. The graph below best represents the relationship between concentration and temperature for which of the following substances?

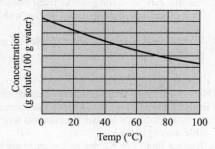

F. HCl
G. NaNO$_3$
H. NaCl
J. KCl

15. The data shown in Table 1 support the conclusion that, for a given substance, as the temperature of the water increases, the amount of solute that can be dissolved:
A. increases only.
B. decreases only.
C. varies, but there is a trend depending on the substance.
D. varies, but with no particular trend.

16. According to Table 1, HCl would most likely have which of the following concentrations at 70°C?
F. 25.5 g/100g H$_2$O
G. 37.0 g/100g H$_2$O
H. 48.5 g/100g H$_2$O
J. 51.5 g/100g H$_2$O

17. A scientist wants to dissolve at least 50 grams of NH$_4$Cl in 100 g of water in order for the solution to be the proper concentration for use in an experiment. A reasonable minimum temperature for the solution would be:
A. 25°C
B. 30°C
C. 35°C
D. 50°C

GO ON TO THE NEXT PAGE.

4 ○ ○ ○ ○ ○ ○ ○ ○ ○ **4**

PASSAGE IV

Salt pans are unusual geologic formations found in deserts. They are formed in *endorheic basins*, which are lowland areas where water collects but has no outflow. Any rain that falls or any water that is collected in an *endorheic basin* remains there permanently, except for what is lost through evaporation. This type of closed system often leads to a high concentration of salt and other minerals.

Study 1

Four different salt pans around the world were studied. The volumes of mineral deposits were estimated from the surface areas of the salt pans and the average thickness of the deposits. The ages of the salt pans were also estimated based on the mineral volume. The estimates are shown in Table 1.

Table 1		
Salt pan	Estimated mineral volume (km^3)	Estimated age (million years)
A	2,000,000	4.5
B	4,500,000	5.7
C	5,700,000	10.8
D	12,150,000	21.0

Study 2

The same four salt pans were excavated for fossils. Fossil remnants of extinct plant species were found within each of the salt pans. The ages of the fossils found were similar to the ages of the salt pans (See Table 2). Scientists hypothesize that flooding of each salt pan may have led to the extinction of the plant species.

Table 2		
Salt pan	Type of fossils found	Estimated age of fossils (million years)
A	Plant species *q*	4.4
B	Plant species *r*	5.5
C	Plant species *s*	10.2
D	Plant species *t*	19.9

18. Which of the following statements is best supported by information in the passage?
    F. Water that has collected in *endorheic basins* is at least 21.0 million years old.
    G. The age of fossilized plant species cannot be precisely estimated.
    H. More water has collected in and evaporated from older salt pans.
    J. Any *endorheic basin* that is less than 2.0 million years old contains no fossils.

19. Which one of the following graphs best represents the relationship between the mineral volume and the age of the salt pans, according to Study 1?

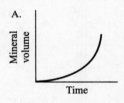
A.

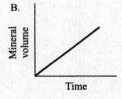
B.

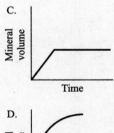
C.

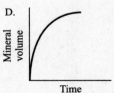
D.

GO ON TO THE NEXT PAGE.

20. Is the conclusion that Salt pan A contains more extinct plant fossils than does Salt pan D supported by information in the passage?

F. Yes, because Salt pan A is younger than Salt pan D.

G. Yes, because the passage suggests that it is easier for plants to grow in areas with a lower mineral volume.

H. No, because Salt pan D contains a different type of fossilized plant.

J. No, because the passage does not include data regarding the quantity of plant fossils found in the salt pans.

21. From the results of Table 1, you could conclude that a salt pan formed more than 21 million years ago would have a mineral value:

A. between 5,700,000 km^3 and 12,150,000 km^3.

B. equal to approximately $\frac{1}{2}$ the mineral volume of Salt pan B.

C. greater than 12,150,000 km^3.

D. less than 2,000,000 km^3.

22. A fossilized plant approximately 9.7 million years old was recently discovered in a salt pan in North America. It was most likely found in a salt pan similar to:

F. Salt pan A.

G. Salt pan B.

H. Salt pan C.

J. Salt pan D.

GO ON TO THE NEXT PAGE.

4 ◯ ◯ ◯ ◯ ◯ ◯ ◯ ◯ **4**

PASSAGE V

Petroleum, or crude oil, is refined by separating it into different by-products. This process is called *fractional distillation*, whereby the crude oil is heated and each different product is distilled, or drawn off, at different stages. Each product is distilled at certain temperature ranges and collected in separate receivers. Petroleum refining is carried out in a boiler and a fractionating tower. The crude oil is super-heated in the boiler to about 600°C, which vaporizes the crude oil. The vapors then rise in the tower to certain levels where they cool and condense, according to their chemical structure. When the vapor reaches a height in the tower where the temperature in the column is equal to the boiling point of the substance, the vapor turns into liquid (condenses), collects in troughs, and flows into various tanks for storage, as shown in Figure 1. Table 1 below summarizes the characteristics of the by-products obtained from the fractional distillation of petroleum.

Table 1	
Petroleum by-product	Condensation temperature (°C)
Petroleum gas	20–40
Gasoline	40–70
Kerosene	100–120
Gas oil	120–200
Lubricating oil stocks	200–300
Residue	600

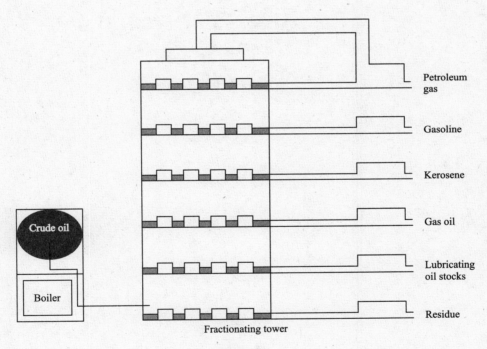

Fractionating tower

Figure 1

23. According to the passage, the temperature at which gasoline condenses is most likely:
    A. less than 0°C.
    B. less than 40°C.
    C. greater than 20°C.
    D. greater than 70°C.

24. According to the passage, which by-product formed in the fractionating tower condenses first?
    F. Petroleum gas
    G. Kerosene
    H. Gas oil
    J. Residue

GO ON TO THE NEXT PAGE.

4

25. According to Figure 1, fractional distillation uses which of the following as a raw material?
    A. Gasoline
    B. Residue
    C. Crude oil
    D. Gas oil

26. Given that naptha, another by-product of petroleum distillation, has a condensation point of approximately 90°C, between which two petroleum by-products would this substance be found in a fractionating tower?
    F. Gasoline and kerosene
    G. Lubricating oil stocks and gas oil
    H. Kerosene and gas oil
    J. Residue and lubricating oil stocks

27. According to the passage, at what temperature is most of the crude oil vaporized?
    A. 600°C
    B. 300°C
    C. 100°C
    D. 20°C

28. According to the passage, as the vapor rises in the fractionating tower:
    F. the condensation temperature increases only.
    G. the condensation temperature decreases only.
    H. the condensation temperature increases quickly, then slowly decreases.
    J. the condensation temperature remains stable at 600°C.

GO ON TO THE NEXT PAGE.

4 ◯ ◯ ◯ ◯ ◯ ◯ ◯ ◯ ◯ 4

PASSAGE VI

Scientists theorize that the release of X-rays by distant stars and the amount of distortion or "bending" the X-rays endure as they travel out of their solar system can help indicate the presence of planets orbiting these stars. The distortion of the X-rays would be caused by the gravitational pull exerted by the planets. Specifically, high 'bending' in these rays would indicate the presence of large planets, while a low level of bending would most likely signify the presence of smaller planets.

In addition to determining whether or not there are planets circling a distant star, the amount of X-ray distortion can determine the planets' orbital pattern. A circular orbit produces increasing or decreasing distortions of the same level. For instance, if a star's X-rays are bent 1 meter the first day, 2 meters the fourth day, 4 meters the seventh day, and so on, it indicates a circular orbit. See Figure 1. If however, the pattern of bending is random, as in a bending of 5 meters the first day, 3 meters the second day, 0 meters the third day, and 7 meters the fourth day, then the planet's orbit is elliptical. See Figure 2. Further, if the paths of the X-rays are not bent in any way, it is assumed that the star lacks any planets.

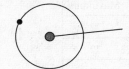

Figure 1   Circular orbit

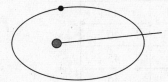

Figure 2   Elliptical orbit

Table 1 shows the amount of distortion of X-rays released by 4 different stars over a period of 10 days.

Table 1			
X-ray distortion (m)			
	Day 1	Day 4	Day 7	Day 10
Star 1	1.00	1.75	2.50	3.25
Star 2	0.00	0.00	0.00	0.00
Star 3	8.00	4.00	2.00	1.00
Star 4	0.20	0.10	0.11	0.11

Note: Assume that there are no other objects that could affect the X-rays.

29. According to Table 1, which star most likely has no planets?
A. Star 1
B. Star 2
C. Star 3
D. Star 4

30. Based on the information in the passage, how many of the stars listed in Table 1 have at least one planet with a circular orbit?
F. 0
G. 2
H. 3
J. 4

31. Which of the following statements is best supported by information in the passage?
A. Star 3 is likely orbited by at least one large planet.
B. Star 4 has a circular orbit.
C. Star 1 has an elliptical orbit.
D. Star 2 is likely orbited by several small planets.

32. If X-ray distortion were observed for an additional three days, one could predict that the path of the X-rays produced by Star 1 on day 13 would be distorted by:
F. 0.75 meters.
G. 1.00 meter.
H. 3.75 meters.
J. 4.00 meters.

33. According to information in the passage, which of the following assumptions could be true?
A. X-rays are affected by certain physical forces.
B. X-rays are simply bits of energy and are, therefore, unaffected by physical forces.
C. Planets with elliptical orbits are more common than are planets with circular orbits.
D. The presence of planets orbiting a star can only be detected using X-ray distortion.

34. Based on information in the passage, which of the following stars most likely has at least one planet with an elliptical orbit?
F. Star 2 only
G. Star 4 only
H. Stars 1 and 3 only
J. Stars 1, 3, and 4 only

GO ON TO THE NEXT PAGE.

4 ○ ○ ○ ○ ○ ○ ○ ○ ○ **4**

PASSAGE VII

Bacteria can be categorized by how they respond, as indicated by reproduction and growth, to certain temperatures. They are grouped into four categories—psychrophiles, psychrotrophs, mesophiles, and thermophiles—based on their growth response to certain temperatures. Minimal growth temperature is the lowest point at which the bacteria will reproduce. Optimum growth point is the temperature at which the bacteria reproduce most efficiently. Maximum growth point is the very highest temperature to which the bacteria will respond, beyond which the bacteria will not reproduce at all. Table 1 lists the types of bacteria as well as the growth points for each.

Table 2 represents a list of common bacteria and their growth points.

Table 1			
Growth points or ranges (°C)			
Classifications	Minimum	Optimum	Maximum
Psychrophile	below 0	10–15	below 20
Psychrotroph	0–5	15	30
Mesophile	5–25	18–45	30–50
Thermophile	25–45	50–60	60–90

Table 2			
Cardinal growth points (°C)			
Bacteria name	Minimum	Optimum	Maximum
Anoxybacillus flavithermus	30	60	72
Bacillus flavothermus	30	60	72
Clostridium perfringens	15	45	50
Escherichia coli	10	37	45
Listeria monocytogenes	1	34	45
Micrococcus cryophilus	0	15	30
Staphylococcus aureus	10	37	45
Streptococcus pyogenes	20	37	40
Streptococcus pneumoniae	25	37	42

35. The category of bacteria appearing the most frequently in Table 2 is:
  A. psychrophile.
  B. psychrotroph.
  C. mesophile.
  D. thermophile.

36. The type of bacteria found in Table 2 that does not fit exactly into any of the categories listed in Table 1 is:
  F. Clostridium perfringens.
  G. Listeria monocytogenes.
  H. Micrococcus cryophilus.
  J. Streptococcus pneumoniae.

37. Average human body temperature is 40°C. According to Table 2, which of the following bacteria would grow most successfully in the human body?
  A. Anoxybacillus flavithermus.
  B. Clostridium perfringens.
  C. Escherichia coli.
  D. Listeria monocytogenes.

38. A new bacteria was discovered by scientists. It reproduces best at 55°C and does not show any new growth if exposed to temperatures above 65°C. This bacteria can most likely be categorized as a:
  F. psychrophile.
  G. psychrotroph.
  H. mesotroph.
  J. thermophile.

GO ON TO THE NEXT PAGE.

4 ◯ ◯ ◯ ◯ ◯ ◯ ◯ ◯ ◯ **4**

39. Based on the information in Table 2, which bacteria has the smallest growth range?
   A. *Listeria monocytogenes*.
   B. *Micrococcus cryophilus*.
   C. *Streptococcus pneumoniae*.
   D. *Streptococcus pyogenes*.

40. According to information provided in the passage, *Listeria monocytogenes* stop reproducing at what temperature?
   F. >1°C, but <10°C
   G. >10°C, but <34°C
   H. >34°C, but <45°C
   J. >45°C

END OF THE SCIENCE REASONING TEST.
STOP! IF YOU HAVE TIME LEFT OVER, CHECK YOUR WORK ON THIS SECTION ONLY.

WRITING TEST PROMPT

DIRECTIONS: This test is designed to assess your writing skills. You have 30 minutes to plan and write an essay based on the stimulus provided. Be sure to take a position on the issue and support your position using logical reasoning and relevant examples. Organize your ideas in a focused and logical way, and use the English language to clearly and effectively express your position.

   When you have finished writing, refer to the Scoring Rubrics discussed in the Introduction (page 4) to estimate your score.

Foreign-language instruction is declining in public high schools in the United States. Some people think this reflects the rise of English as the accepted language of commerce around the world, and that knowledge of foreign languages is of lessening importance. Other people see the reduction in language study as a sign of the United States' failure to integrate with the rest of the world and a threat to the nation's vitality in an increasingly cross-cultural marketplace.

In your opinion, should greater support be given to foreign language programs in high schools in the United States?

In your essay, take a position on this question. You may write about one of the points of view mentioned above, or you may give another point of view on this issue. Use specific examples and reasons for your position.

■ **ANSWER KEY**

English Test

1. B	21. A	41. B	61. D
2. G	22. F	42. H	62. G
3. C	23. D	43. A	63. A
4. J	24. F	44. J	64. J
5. A	25. B	45. C	65. C
6. G	26. F	46. J	66. J
7. B	27. D	47. A	67. B
8. J	28. G	48. G	68. J
9. B	29. A	49. A	69. B
10. F	30. F	50. H	70. F
11. D	31. D	51. A	71. D
12. J	32. F	52. H	72. G
13. A	33. A	53. D	73. D
14. G	34. H	54. H	74. H
15. C	35. A	55. A	75. A
16. G	36. F	56. J	
17. A	37. A	57. B	
18. J	38. J	58. F	
19. B	39. D	59. A	
20. F	40. F	60. J	

Mathematics Test

1. C	21. A	41. D
2. J	22. H	42. G
3. C	23. E	43. A
4. G	24. J	44. F
5. B	25. C	45. D
6. H	26. K	46. G
7. C	27. C	47. D
8. G	28. G	48. F
9. B	29. A	49. D
10. J	30. H	50. J
11. C	31. D	51. E
12. F	32. K	52. H
13. D	33. D	53. D
14. G	34. F	54. G
15. B	35. B	55. E
16. G	36. J	56. K
17. E	37. E	57. D
18. J	38. G	58. F
19. C	39. C	59. B
20. F	40. H	60. H

Reading Test

1. B	21. B
2. F	22. H
3. C	23. A
4. F	24. H
5. D	25. D
6. H	26. H
7. A	27. A
8. G	28. J
9. A	29. D
10. J	30. G
11. B	31. A
12. G	32. J
13. D	33. D
14. F	34. G
15. C	35. C
16. F	36. H
17. C	37. B
18. G	38. F
19. D	39. C
20. J	40. J

Science Reasoning Test

1. B	21. C
2. H	22. H
3. D	23. C
4. F	24. J
5. A	25. C
6. J	26. F
7. B	27. A
8. F	28. G
9. B	29. B
10. J	30. G
11. A	31. A
12. H	32. J
13. C	33. A
14. F	34. G
15. C	35. C
16. J	36. G
17. D	37. C
18. H	38. J
19. B	39. C
20. J	40. J

▆▆▆ SCORING GUIDE

Your final reported score is your COMPOSITE SCORE. Your COMPOSITE SCORE is the average of all of your SCALE SCORES.

Your SCALE SCORES for the four multiple-choice sections are derived from the Scoring Table on the next page. Use your RAW SCORE, or the number of questions that you answered correctly for each section, to determine your SCALE SCORE. If you got a RAW SCORE of 60 on the English test, for example, you correctly answered 60 out of 75 questions.

Step 1 Determine your RAW SCORE for each of the four multiple-choice sections:

English _____

Mathematics _____

Reading _____

Science Reasoning _____3____

The following Raw Score Table shows the total possible points for each section.

RAW SCORE TABLE	
KNOWLEDGE AND SKILL AREAS	**RAW SCORES**
ENGLISH	75
MATHEMATICS	60
READING	40
SCIENCE REASONING	40
WRITING	12

Multiple-Choice Scoring Worksheet

Step 2 Determine your SCALE SCORE for each of the four multiple-choice sections using the following Scoring Worksheet. Each SCALE SCORE should be rounded to the nearest number according to normal rules. For example, $31.2 \approx 31$ and $31.5 \approx 32$. If you answered 61 questions correctly on the English section, for example, your SCALE SCORE would be 29.

English _____ $\times$ 36 = _____ $\div$ 75 = _____
RAW SCORE $-\ 2$ (*correction factor)

_____
SCALE SCORE

Mathematics _____ $\times$ 36 = _____ $\div$ 60 = _____
RAW SCORE $+\ 1$ (*correction factor)

_____
SCALE SCORE

Reading _____ $\times$ 36 = _____ $\div$ 40 = _____
RAW SCORE $+\ 2$ (*correction factor)

_____
SCALE SCORE

Science Reasoning _____ $\times$ 36 = _____ $\div$ 40 = _____
RAW SCORE $+\ 1.5$ (*correction factor)

_____
SCALE SCORE

   *The correction factor is an approximation based on the average from several recent ACT tests. It is most valid for scores in the middle 50% (approximately 16–24 scale composite score) of the scoring range.
   The scores are all approximate. Actual ACT scoring scales vary from one administration to the next based upon several factors.

   If you take the optional Writing Test, you will need to combine your English and Writing scores to obtain your final COMPOSITE SCORE. Once you have determined a score for your essay out of 12 possible points, you will need to determine your ENGLISH/WRITING SCALE SCORE, using both your ENGLISH SCALE SCORE and your WRITING TEST SCORE. The combination of the two scores will give you an ENGLISH/WRITING SCALE SCORE, from 1 to 36, that will be used to determine your COMPOSITE SCORE mentioned earlier.
   Using the English/Writing Scoring Table, find your ENGLISH SCALE SCORE on the left or right hand side of the table and your WRITING TEST SCORE on the top of the table. Follow your ENGLISH SCALE SCORE over and your WRITING TEST SCORE down until the two columns meet at a number. This number is your ENGLISH/WRITING SCALE SCORE and will be used to determine your COMPOSITE SCORE.

Step 3   Determine your ENGLISH/WRITING SCALE SCORE using the English/Writing Scoring Table on the following page:

English   _____

Writing   _____

English/Writing   _____

ENGLISH/WRITING SCORING TABLE

ENGLISH SCALE SCORE	WRITING TEST SCORE											ENGLISH SCALE SCORE
	2	3	4	5	6	7	8	9	10	11	12	
36	26	27	28	29	30	31	32	33	34	32	36	36
35	26	27	28	29	30	31	31	32	33	34	35	35
34	25	26	27	28	29	30	31	32	33	34	35	34
33	24	25	26	27	28	29	30	31	32	33	34	33
32	24	25	25	26	27	28	29	30	31	32	33	32
31	23	24	25	26	27	28	29	30	30	31	32	31
30	22	23	24	25	26	27	28	29	30	31	32	30
29	21	22	23	24	25	26	27	28	29	30	31	29
28	21	22	23	24	24	25	26	27	28	29	30	28
27	20	21	22	23	24	25	26	27	28	28	29	27
26	19	20	21	22	23	24	25	26	27	28	29	26
25	18	19	20	21	22	23	24	25	26	27	28	25
24	18	19	20	21	22	23	23	24	25	26	27	24
23	17	18	19	20	21	22	23	24	25	26	27	23
22	16	17	18	19	20	21	22	23	24	25	26	22
21	16	17	17	18	19	20	21	22	23	24	25	21
20	15	16	17	18	19	20	21	21	22	23	24	20
19	14	15	16	17	18	19	20	21	22	23	24	19
18	13	14	15	16	17	18	19	20	21	22	23	18
17	13	14	15	16	16	17	18	19	20	21	22	17
16	12	13	14	15	16	17	18	19	20	20	21	16
15	11	12	13	14	15	16	17	18	19	20	21	15
14	10	11	12	13	14	15	16	17	18	19	20	14
13	10	11	12	13	14	14	15	16	17	18	19	13
12	9	10	11	12	13	14	15	16	17	18	19	12
11	8	9	10	11	12	13	14	15	16	17	18	11
10	8	9	9	10	11	12	13	14	15	16	17	10
9	7	8	9	10	11	12	13	13	14	15	16	9
8	6	7	8	9	10	11	12	13	14	15	16	8
7	5	6	7	8	9	10	11	12	13	14	15	7
6	5	6	7	7	8	9	10	11	12	13	14	6
5	4	5	6	7	8	9	10	11	12	12	13	5
4	3	4	5	6	7	8	9	10	11	12	13	4
3	2	3	4	5	6	7	8	9	10	11	12	3
2	2	3	4	5	6	6	7	8	9	10	11	2
1	1	2	3	4	5	6	7	8	9	10	11	1

Step 4   Determine your COMPOSITE SCORE by finding the sum of all your SCALE SCORES for each of the four sections: English only (if you do not choose to take the optional Writing Test) *or* English/Writing (if you choose to take the optional Writing Test), Math, Reading, and Science Reasoning, and divide by 4 to find the average. Round your COMPOSITE SCORE according to normal rules. For example, $31.2 \approx 31$ and $31.5 \approx 32$.

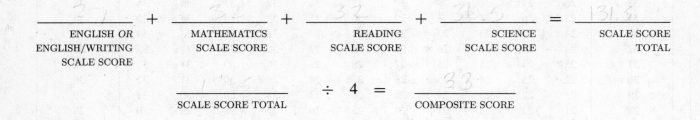

_____ +	_____ +	_____ +	_____ =	_____
ENGLISH *OR* ENGLISH/WRITING SCALE SCORE	MATHEMATICS SCALE SCORE	READING SCALE SCORE	SCIENCE SCALE SCORE	SCALE SCORE TOTAL

_____ ÷ 4 = _____

SCALE SCORE TOTAL   COMPOSITE SCORE

ANSWERS AND EXPLANATIONS

English Test Explanations

PASSAGE I

1. **The best answer is B.** In this sentence, the word "obsessed" is most appropriate to describe the action taking place. The word "obsessive" can be used as an adjective. The participle "obsessing" is not appropriate, and "obsessioned" is not a word, so answer choices C and D can be eliminated.

2. **The best answer is G.** Answer choice G is the most clear and concise, because it simply uses the verb "pay." As it is written, the sentence is wordy and redundant. Answer choice H, "paying money," sounds awkward and is grammatically incorrect in conjunction with the phrase that precedes it, "is willing to." Answer choice J is written in the past tense while the rest of the sentence is written in the present tense and, therefore, must be eliminated.

3. **The best answer is C.** Answer choice C is grammatically correct and makes sense idiomatically. Answer choices A and B indicate that natural redheads actually want to possess brunettes, which does not make sense. Answer choice D does not make sense and is not correct for standard written English.

4. **The best answer is J.** The first part of the sentence and the second part of the sentence are independent clauses that refer to different hairstyles. Answer choice J, "and," makes most sense here. Answer choice G, "however," requires punctuation to fit in the sentence (normally between commas). Answer choice F implies that teenagers enjoy experimenting with their hair as a result of men and women cringing at the sight of gray hair. Answer choices G and H imply that the two phrases negate each other.

5. **The best answer is A.** The correct preposition to use here is "of." The phrase "result of" is idiomatic.

6. **The best answer is G.** This answer choice correctly precedes the verb "mixing" with its modifier "rapidly."

7. **The best answer is B.** The sentence does not have a natural pause at this point in the sentence, so a comma is inappropriate. In addition, you can eliminate answer choices A and D. A colon should be used after a complete statement to introduce directly related information, such as a list or an example, so answer choice C should be eliminated.

8. **The best answer is J.** The word "was" makes the most sense in the sentence, because it clearly and simply indicates the past tense. The phrase "could of become" can never be correct. "Could of been" is not appropriate in standard written English. Some people incorrectly use "could of" when they should use "could've," which is the contraction of "could have."

9. **The best answer is B.** The sentence is composed of a main clause ("The monthly highlighting went well") followed by a subordinator ("except for"), then an extended noun phrase ("those times when my hair turned out a little too subdued, making me look partially gray instead of brunette."). Especially as it is preceded by a subordinator, such a lengthy component of the sentence calls to be offset by a comma.

10. **The best answer is F.** The sentence as it is written makes the most sense in context. It sufficiently indicates that, despite some setbacks, the author's experience with highlights has been mostly positive. Answer choice G implies that the author was making some sort of list regarding her and her feelings towards her highlights. Answer choice H indicates some sort of contrast that is simply not present in the paragraph. Answer choice J suggests that the hairdresser's mistakes pleased the author.

11. **The best answer is D.** Sentence 5 follows from the information in Sentence 3. Likewise, Sentence 4 relies on Sentence 5, and also creates a good transition into the next paragraph.

12. **The best answer is J.** To maintain parallel tense in the sentence, since Donna "was" surprised at the author's request, the simple past tense of the verb "gather" also needs to be used. The sentence is written in the present tense; therefore answer choice F can be eliminated. Answer choices G and H are not in the parallel tense.

13. **The best answer is A.** The coordinating conjunction "and" is the most concise choice; it joins two functionally parallel elements within the

sentence—here, two nouns: "tears" and "laughter." The phrases "along with" and "as well as" serve a similar function to the coordinating conjunction "and," but they are awkward and neither clear nor concise. Answer choice C is incorrect because "or" does not make sense in this context with "seesawing."

14. **The best answer is G.** Since the preceding sentence does not summarize the essay or relate to the introduction, answer choices F and H can be eliminated. This sentence is specifically about the narrator ceasing her crying, which is not the purpose of the essay. Eliminate answer choice J. The realization of her vanity puts her situation in perspective; therefore, answer choice G is the best answer.

15. **The best answer is C.** The passage simply discusses the narrator's experiences in dyeing her own hair. It is unlikely that the author's decision to change her hair color would ease the apprehension of others who were considering dyeing their hair. The fact that dyeing her hair gave her a bald spot would probably deepen the fears of those who were feeling anxious about dyeing their hair. Eliminate answer choice A. Answer choice B can also be eliminated; the passage only discusses the author and other "mature" women dyeing their hair. Answer choice D is incorrect because the passage as a whole is neutral and does not attempt to influence people regarding changing hair color.

PASSAGE II

16. **The best answer is G.** Answer choice G is a common phrase, and sounds the best in the context of this sentence. It is appropriate to use "American" as an adjective to describe the noun "heritage." The other answer choices are grammatically incorrect. Also, answer choice J suggests that the "heritage" belongs to only one "American," which does not fit the context of the paragraph.

17. **The best answer is A.** To state that Walker Lee "still practices" is clear and concise. Answer choices B and C are wordy and redundant in saying that Lee "still continues to practice" and "continues to still practice." Answer choice D is awkward.

18. **The best answer is J.** This passage is written in the past tense. "Began" is the simple past form of the verb "begin," therefore answer choice J is correct. Answer choice F is written in the past perfect tense, and therefore does not maintain the

parallel between verbs. Answer choices G and H use "begun," the past participle of "begin," and can therefore be eliminated.

19. **The best answer is B.** The phrase "that being iron" does not make sense. The rest of the answer choices correctly use parentheses or commas in setting off their respective appositive phrases.

20. **The best answer is F.** The word "lugging" is the most descriptive word. It signifies carrying or pulling something heavy. None of the other answer choices addresses the effort it took to move the anvil from Pennsylvania to Michigan.

21. **The best answer is A.** The phrase "get started" in answer choice A clearly indicates that Lee was just beginning his career in blacksmithing. The other answer choices suggest that his career had already started.

22. **The best answer is F.** In the context of the sentence, "its" is in the possessive form; therefore, no apostrophe is necessary. "It's" means "it is." "Its'" (note the apostrophe *at the end*) does not exist in English beacuse "it" is a singular pronoun.

23. **The best answer is D.** Omitting the underlined portion of the sentence is the best choice in this instance. In any form, the information provided in this sentence is distractive—not related to the main topic of the essay—and is therefore unnecessary.

24. **The best answer is F.** Answer choice F provides a logical and relevant introduction to the topic of the paragraph. Answer choice H is incorrect because the paragraphs preceding and following this sentence have nothing to do with moving equipment. Answer choices G and J can be eliminated because neither has anything to do with the construction of Lee's first blacksmith shop, the subject of the paragraph.

25. **The best answer is B.** This answer choice is correct because it is the only one that is grammatically proper and makes sense. Answer choice A does not make sense because "but" is used to introduce a contradictory element; a "crude" structure standing "only nine years" appears to be instead a correlational relationship. Answer choice C is ungrammatical and D violates tense agreement with "was."

26. **The best answer is F.** If two adjectives modify a noun in the same way, they must either be separated by a comma or joined with the word "and" with no comma.

27. **The best answer is D.** The phrase "at a family event" is a descriptive phrase that must be set off by commas. Answer choice C is incorrect because subject and verb must not be separated by a comma. Similarly, in B, a comma makes an incorrect division of a compound.

28. **The best answer is G.** The act of proclaiming took place during the event, so it is a completed action and should be in the past tense.

29. **The best answer is A.** The information given in Sentence 2 merely describes the knife from the preceding sentence, and has nothing to do with the creation of Lee's first object.

30. **The best answer is F.** No specific person or point in time is mentioned, and the remainder of the sentence is written in the present tense. Thus, the present tense of the verb "watch" must be used.

PASSAGE III

31. **The best answer is D.** Using the past tense verb "began" makes the most sense because the narrator is recalling what *happened* when she *heard* the story.

32. **The best answer is F.** Answer choice F correctly places a comma following the clause that begins with the subordinator "As," which describes what happened that caused the narrator's eyes to pop out of her head and her jaw to drop. Answer choice G creates a run-on sentence. Answer choices H and J incorrectly place commas following the word "could," which creates awkward and ungrammatical sentences.

33. **The best answer is A.** An easy way to figure out the answer to this question is to look at the preceding sentence. In that sentence, the narrator says, "I could." To maintain verb parallelism in the paragraph, the phrase "I could" should be repeated.

34. **The best answer is H.** In this sentence, the word "that" is unnecessary, because the normal clause-introducing function of the word "that" is satisfied by "how." Answer choice G is wrong because "because" does not make sense after "about." Answer choice J lacks a clause-introducer.

35. **The best answer is A.** This question tests your ability to maintain parallel structure in a sentence. Each verb in the sequence of events is written in the past tense. Since the sister's husband "*threw* back the bedcovers" and "*began* beating the dreaded

thing with a broom," he would have to have "*flushed*" it down the toilet.

36. **The best answer is F.** This part of the sentence requires a verb, so you can eliminate answer choice J. The adjective "deadly" is used to describe the scorpions. If the word "deadlier" is used, the word "more" cannot precede it; therefore, answer choice G can be eliminated. The comma before "and" indicates the phrase preceding it must be an independent clause, meaning one that contains a verb phrase that could stand alone in a sentence. The gerund ("-ing") form violates this test.

37. **The best answer is A.** This answer choice gives a logical explanation for why Diana would not seek professional help as the condition of her arm continued to worsen. The remaining choices are not supported by the context.

38. **The best answer is J.** This question tests your ability to express yourself clearly and simply. Because the sentence states that scorpions will sting anyone they *accidentally* encounter, using the word "inadvertently" would be redundant and unnecessary. The word "crawl" is the clearest and most concise choice.

39. **The best answer is D.** This question tests your ability to accurately create the possessive form of words. In this case, the narrator is talking about the homes of many scorpions instead of the home of one specific scorpion. The plural possessive form of scorpion, "scorpions'," must be used. To make a plural word possessive, you must place an apostrophe after the pluralizing "s."

40. **The best answer is F.** Answer choice G is awkward because its components are not written in logical order. Answer choice H places an unnecessary comma after the word "species." Answer choice J is ambiguous as to whether the "ninety species" in question constitute all the world's scorpions or just those native to the United States.

41. **The best answer is B.** In this part of the sentence, the word "which" introduces a clause descriptive of the noun that precedes it, "the Bark Scorpion."

42. **The best answer is H.** This question tests your ability to discern which details are important to the subject of an essay. In this case, the author previously mentioned that scorpions can be found in the home, and it is obvious that they still live outside. The underlined portion reinforces the notion that scorpions can be found both inside the home and outside the home.

43. The best answer is A. This sentence follows a standard verb pattern for hypothetical situations. "If" begins a clause in simple present tense, which precedes a clause in the imperative (command) form. For example, "If you *swim* today, *apply* sunscreen."

44. The best answer is J. This question requires you to put things in logical order, and to decide whether the underlined portion is relevant to the paragraph. In this case, it is best to omit the underlined portion because it does not add any necessary information to the paragraph; it is an irrelevant detail. The rest of the sentences are already in the most logical order.

45. The best answer is C. Answer choices A and B can be eliminated immediately because the simple answer to the question is no. This essay does not provide professional advice on the treatment of scorpion stings. The essay is merely a recollection of a time when the narrator's sister was stung by a scorpion and the narrator is offering advice based solely on personal experience and opinion.

PASSAGE IV

46. The best answer is J. Answer choice F is incorrect because dashes should only be used to place special emphasis on a certain word or phrase in a sentence, which is unnecessary here. Answer choice G is incorrect because the preceding phrase is not an independent clause, thus must not be separated by a semicolon. Answer choice H is incorrect because it creates a run-on sentence. Answer choice J correctly identifies the fact that the word "if" begins a clause that must be separated from the rest of the sentence by a comma wherever the clause ends. In this case, the second clause clearly begins with repetition of the subject "you."

47. The best answer is A. This is the most clear and concise answer choice. The others are awkward. Answer choice C is incorrect because "always" modifies "accompany" and must, in this case, precede it. Answer choice D does not include the word "always," which causes the sentence to lose a key detail.

48. The best answer is G. "Non-compliance" describes the wrong each side feels the other committed, thus the lawsuits assert "non-compliance on both sides." This eliminates all answer choices except answer choice G.

49. The best answer is A. Answer choice B uses an unnecessary comma. Answer choices C and D can be eliminated because they are incorrect as idiomatic phrases.

50. The best answer is H. In this case, the word "promised" is used as an adjective. Thus, answer choices F and G can be eliminated. Answer choice J is an adjective, but the definitions of "promised" and "promising" differ. The reward was assured, or promised, to Helga. It was not likely to develop nor did it show potential, both aspects of the definition of "promising," thus answer choice J can be eliminated.

51. The best answer is A. Answer choice B creates an incomplete sentence, so it can be eliminated. Since the action was continuously occurring in the past, you would say that she "had been living."

52. The best answer is H. Answer choice J can be eliminated because the underlined portion is preceded by the article "a." The article "the" must precede the word "greatest." Since "reward" serves correctly as a noun in this sentence, answer choices F and G can be eliminated. A "great reward," answer choice H, is the best and most reasonable choice.

53. The best answer is D. Sentence 1 explains how Helga became interested in the contest, so it must be first. This eliminates answer choice C. It makes sense that the requirements would be listed next and that the comments about the bicycle skirt would follow. The last sentence, Sentence 4, explains why Helga decided to make the journey despite the embarrassment of wearing a bicycle skirt.

54. The best answer is H. The actions of Helga and her daughter should be written in the simple past tense in order to maintain verb parallelism throughout the paragraph. Answer choice J is in the past tense, but it is wordy. "Have," in any form, is not necessary to this phrase.

55. The best answer is A. This answer choice is the clearest and most concise. The other choices are wordy and awkward.

56. The best answer is J. "Nowhere to be found" is a common idiomatic phrase, making it the most clear and concise choice. The other answer choices are awkward.

57. The best answer is B. Answer choice A indicates that the following sentence is a result of what comes before. In this case, the phrases are not causally connected, so answer choice A is incorrect. Answer choice C is awkward and answer choice D is wordy. The phrase "in fact" is not necessary to this passage. Answer choice B is the clearest and most concise choice.

58. The best answer is F. The words "leaving only" begin a descriptive clause, which must be set off by a comma. Answer choice G creates a run-on sentence. Semicolons must be used to separate two independent clauses; therefore, answer choice H is incorrect. Answer choice J uses a comma incorrectly, separating "only" from the phrase it modifies.

59. The best answer is A. Answer choice A gives a specific reason as to what Helga intended to use the $10,000 prize for. The passage clearly states that without this prize money, the Estby farm would face foreclosure. Answer choice B simply restates the fact that Helen wanted the $10,000 she would win if she completed the cross-country walk, but does not explain what she would use the money for. Answer choice C is incorrect because no logical connection between the prize money and the children's diphtheria is made in the passage. Answer choice D is outside the scope of the passage as well; there is no mention of Clara gaining experience anywhere in the passage.

60. The best answer is J. Answer choices F and G are incorrect because the writer should not make this addition to the passage; it is irrelevant. Answer choice H identifies an unimportant detail of the great-great-grandson's story as the reason the sentence does not belong.

PASSAGE V

61. The best answer is D. Appositives, like "particularly via airplane," must be separated from the sentence by commas. They are easily identified because they can be omitted from the sentence without rendering the sentence ungrammatical.

62. The best answer is G. Because the author wishes to add more detail, the best answer choice will be the one that includes the most descriptive language. Answer G is the best alternative because it includes the explanatory detail "also known as jet lag" and correctly sets it apart with commas.

63. The best answer is A. The sentence identifies jet lag as a "sleeping disorder," but the word "although" indicates that what follows are mitigating factors. First, jet lag is a "temporary condition" and second, jet lag is "not as serious" as other sleeping disorders. Answer choice B appears to define correctly the lack of seriousness, but is missing the critical first "as" to make a comparison.

64. The best answer is J. Before a term is defined, its relevance to the passage must be stated. Furthermore, among the other answer choices, circadian rhythms are not specifically mentioned.

65. The best answer is C. While the sentence as it is written may be grammatical, its use of punctuation is excessive. Answer choice C provides a fluid, concise transition to the details of the human "sleeping and waking" cycle.

66. The best answer is J. This sentence elaborates on the statement from the previous sentence by citing an example. It does not provide supplementary (Answer choice F: "In addition"), parallel (G: "Likewise"), or opposing (H: "Instead") evidence.

67. The best answer is B. It is appropriate to use the plural possessive pronoun "our" when referring to the inner clocks of human beings.

68. The best answer is J. The sentence introduces a factor adversely affecting circadian rhythms, which does not require additional transition words. Answer choices F and H create incomplete sentences.

69. The best answer is B. "Well-tuned" stands by itself as a satisfactory idiomatic expression meaning "optimized." Introducing "high" or "highly" makes the sentence unnecessarily wordy.

70. The best answer is F. Answer choices G and H may be eliminated for their wordiness. Answer choice J may be eliminated because it makes too strong an assertion about the link between long air travel and headaches. Answer choice F correctly uses "Often" to define the frequency of passengers' headaches.

71. The best answer is D. As it is written in the passage, this verb phrase is wordy, as it is written in passive voice ("being"). This same principle eliminates answer choice B. Answer choice C may be eliminated for its unnecessary use of commas.

72. The best answer is G. When adjectives modify a noun in a similar way, they are separated from each other with commas or "and," just as in a list. Therefore, there must be a comma between "dry" and "pressurized." It is not necessary to include a comma after "pressurized," because it is followed directly by the noun that is being modified (atmosphere).

73. The best answer is D. Using a comma to join independent clauses creates a comma splice. The other choices present several acceptable ways to separate independent clauses.

74. **The best answer is H.** This answer choice mentions the body's "new environment." Logical places for the sentence, thus, would be after the technique cited for acclimating to eastbound travel (before Sentence 4) and after the technique cited for acclimating to westbound travel (after Sentence 5).

Choice H corresponds to the latter location, "before Sentence 6."

75. **The best answer is A.** This sentence would provide a reason why understanding ways to correct jet lag—which is the focus of the essay—is important. It follows that the sentence would be placed after the assertion that jet lag is considered a minor sleep disorder.

Mathematics Test Explanations

1. **The correct answer is C.** To find the total distance in miles that Shannon walked, add $1\frac{2}{3}$ and $2\frac{3}{5}$. To add mixed numbers, find the least common denominator. The least common denominator of 3 and 5 is 3×5, or 15. To convert $\frac{2}{3}$, multiply by $\frac{5}{5}$ (*hint:* $\frac{5}{5} = 1$, and multiplication by 1 does not change the value of a number). The result is $\frac{10}{15}$. To convert $\frac{3}{5}$, multiply by $\frac{3}{3}$. The result is $\frac{9}{15}$. To add $1\frac{10}{15}$ and $2\frac{9}{15}$, first add 1 and 2 and then $\frac{10}{15}$ and $\frac{9}{15}$. The result is $3\frac{19}{15}$, which reduces to $4\frac{4}{15}$.

   Answer choice A is the most popular incorrect answer and comes from adding the whole numbers and then adding the numerators and the denominators separately.

2. **The correct answer is J.** To find an equivalent expression, multiply the constants ($4 \times 3 \times 2 = 24$), combine the x terms ($x^3 \times x \times x$) $\rightarrow x^{3+1+1} \rightarrow x^5$, and combine the y terms ($y^2 \times y^2 \rightarrow y^{2+2} \rightarrow y^4$). The result is $24x^5y^4$.

   The most common incorrect answers are F and H, which come from multiplying the exponents of the x and y terms instead of adding them. If you chose G, you probably added the constants instead of multiplying them.

3. **The correct answer is C.** To find Mr. Wilk's pay per day, divide his annual salary, $33,660, by the total number of days he works, 180. His pay per day is $\frac{33,660}{180}$, or $187. When Mr. Wilk takes a day off without pay and the school pays a substitute $85, the school district saves the difference in these amounts, $187 - 85$, or $102.

   Answer choice E, the most common incorrect answer, is simply Mr. Wilk's pay per day and not the difference between his pay and a substitute's pay.

4. **The correct answer is G.** To find the score on the fifth 100-point test that will yield an average score of 80, first calculate the total of the four scores already obtained: $63 + 72 + 88 + 91 = 314$. To obtain an average of 80 on 5 tests, the total score of all 5 tests must be 80×5, or 400. The score needed on the last test is equivalent to $400 - 314$, or 86.

Answer choice A is the average of the 4 scores, rounded to the nearest whole point.

5. **The correct answer is B.** To find the oxygen saturation level, divide the current number of milligrams per liter by the capacity milligrams per liter: $\frac{6.4}{9.5}$. Convert the result (0.6737) into a percent by multiplying by 100: 67.37% is approximately equal to 67%.

6. **The correct answer is H.** To find the length of fence needed to surround a rectangular lot 125 feet by 185 feet, calculate the perimeter. The formula for perimeter of a rectangle is 2 times the sum of the length and width, or $P = 2(l + w)$. Calculate the perimeter as follows: $2(125 + 185) = 2(310)$, or 620.

7. **The correct answer is C.** To find an equivalent expression, simply distribute the a, as follows: $ab - ac + ad$. Remember to keep track of the negative sign.

8. **The correct answer is G.** To solve for x in the equation $6x - 3 = -5x + 7$, add $5x$ and 3 to both sides of the equation, which results in the equation $11x = 10$. Divide both sides by 11, which results in $x = \frac{10}{11}$.

9. **The correct answer is B.** These four numbers will form an arithmetic sequence, a sequence in which each pair of successive terms differs by the same number. To find the difference, define d as that difference, 13 as the first term, and 34 as the fourth term. By definition, the second term is $13 + d$. The fourth term, 34, can also be written as $(13 + d + d) + d$. Using that expression, obtain the equation $34 = 13 + d + d + d$, or $34 = 13 + 3d$. After subtracting 13 from both sides, divide by 3, which results in $7 = d$. The difference is 7. Thus the second term is $13 + 7$, or 20, and the third term is $20 + 7$, or 27.

10. **The correct answer is J.** To calculate the value of $x^2 + \sqrt{x}$, first solve $x^3 = 729$ for x. The solution is the cube root of 729, which is 9. Substitute 9 into the original expression, arriving at $9^2 + \sqrt{9}$. This expression simplifies to $81 + 3$, or 84.

11. **The correct answer is C.** To find the volume, substitute $\frac{4}{3}$ for r in the equation $V = \left(\frac{4}{3}\right)\pi r^3$ as follows:

$$\left(\frac{4}{3}\right)\pi\left(\frac{4}{3}\right)^3$$

$$= \left(\frac{4}{3}\right)\pi\left(\frac{64}{27}\right)$$

$$= \left(\frac{256}{81}\right)\pi$$

Recall that π = approx. 3.14, so $\left(\frac{256}{81}\right)(3.14)$ is about 9.92, or 10 when rounded to the nearest cubic inch.

12. **The correct answer is F.** The probability that the gumball chosen will NOT be green when there are 6 yellow gumballs, 5 green gumballs, and 4 red gumballs is the number of favorable outcomes (the number of times a yellow or red gumball can be chosen) divided by the number of total outcomes (the total number of gumballs). The number of favorable outcomes is 10 because there are 6 yellow gumballs and 4 red gumballs. The total number of outcomes is $6+5+4$, or 15. Thus the probability of the gumball NOT being green is $\frac{10}{15}$, which can be reduced to $\frac{2}{3}$.

Answer choice G is incorrect because it is the probability that a chosen gumball *will* be green.

13. **The correct answer is D.** To find the number of sports awards earned, multiply the number of participants in each sport by the ratio for that sport, and then add these 4 products. This is a matrix multiplication, as shown below:

$$[25\ 30\ 50\ 80]\begin{bmatrix} 0.2 \\ 0.5 \\ 0.3 \\ 0.4 \end{bmatrix}$$

$$= 25(0.2) + 30(0.5) + 50(0.3) + 80(0.4)$$

$$= 5 + 15 + 15 + 32 = 67$$

14. **The correct answer is G.** To find the average number of students per section enrolled in US History, find the total number of students in all sections and divide by the number of sections. Add $25+29+24$ to get 78, then divide by 3. This results in an average of 26 students enrolled per section in US History.

If you selected answer choice F, you found the median, or middle number (which is not always the average), of 24, 25, and 29.

15. **The correct answer is B.** The total number of books available is $(30-3) + (30-5)$, or $27+25$, which is 52. To find the class periods for which there are not enough books, find the total number

of books needed for each period, as given in the table below.

PERIOD	1	2	3	4	5
BOOKS NEEDED	23	49	56	50	27

The only entry in the table with more than 52 is 56 for period 3.

If you selected answer choice E, you probably used 60 as the number of available books and did not take into account the 8 missing books.

16. **The correct answer is G.** Because the sum of each row is equivalent, the sum of row 1 is the same as the sum of row 2.

Row 1: $(-4x) + 9x + 2x = 7x$
Row 2: $7x + ? + (-3x) = 4x + ?$

The question mark must represent $3x$, because $7x = 4x + 3x$. You could also perform these calculations using the sum values in column 1 and column 2.

If you selected answer choice K, you may have thought that each sum must be 0 and found that $-4x$ would make the sums of row 2 and column 2 equal 0.

17. **The correct answer is E.** The x-coordinate is positive if A is to the right of the y-axis. The y-coordinate is positive if y is above the x-axis. The table below shows the sign of x and the sign of y in the four quadrants.

QUADRANT	SIGN OF x	SIGN OF y
I	+	+
II	−	+
III	−	−
IV	+	−

Thus the signs are the same in Quadrants I and III only.

18. **The correct answer is J.** To find the number of distinct complete meals that Reggie can make from 5 different entrees, 4 different sides, and 6 different desserts, multiply the quantities in the 3 different groups together. Thus, there are $(5)(4)(6)$, or 120 distinct meals that Reggie can make. The figure below shows that for each meal, there are 4 sides, and for each side there are 6 desserts.

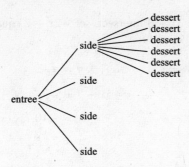

19. The correct answer is C. To find the number of liters of carbonated water needed to produce 750 bottles of soda, set up a proportion with ratios of liters of carbonated water to bottles of soda, as follows:

$$\frac{10,000}{3,000} = \frac{x(\text{liters carbonated water})}{750}.$$

Cross-multiply and solve for x.

$$3,000x = 7,500,000$$

$$x = 2,500$$

20. The correct answer is F. To find the length of the diagonal, apply the Pythagorean Theorem; the sides of the rectangle are the legs of a right triangle and the diagonal of the rectangle is the hypotenuse of the right triangle. Thus $c^2 = 20^2 + 48^2$, and $c = 52$.

21. The correct answer is A. To find an equivalent expression for $\frac{a}{c}$, either multiply or divide both the numerator and denominator by the same value. Because the question asks for all positive integers a, b, and c, and you are looking for an expression that is equivalent to $\frac{a}{c}$, multiply $\frac{a}{c}$ by $\frac{b}{b}$ to get $\frac{(a \times b)}{(c \times b)}$, answer choice A.

22. The correct answer is H. The slope-intercept form of the equation of a line states that $y = mx + b$. To find the slope-intercept form of the equation $6x - 2y - 4 = 0$, you must isolate y on the left side of the equation, as follows:

$$6x - 2y - 4 = 0$$

$$-2y - 4 = -6x$$

$$-2y = -6x + 4$$

$$y = 3x - 2$$

If you selected answer choice J, you probably forgot to switch the signs when dividing by -2.

It is crucial to multiply all terms on both sides of the equation to arrive at a correct answer.

23. The correct answer is E. To solve the quadratic equation $x^2 + 25x = 0$ for x, factor out an x on the left side of the equation: $x(x + 25)$. Now, apply the zero product rule: $x = 0$ or $x + 25 = 0$. If $x + 25 = 0$, then $x = -25$, which is answer choice E.

24. The correct answer is J. To find $\tan B$ in $\triangle ABC$, take the ratio of the length of the opposite side to the length of the adjacent side: AC to $BC = c$ to a, or $\frac{c}{a}$.

Answer choice F is $\cos B$; answer choice G is $\cot B$; answer choice H is $\sec B$; answer choice K is $\sin B$.

25. The correct answer is C. To find the radius, use the right triangle shown in the diagram. Half of the length of the chord is 4 inches, which is the length of one leg. The other leg is 3 inches long, and the hypotenuse is r inches long. (Note: this is a right triangle because the distance between a point and a line is measured perpendicular to the line.) Use the Pythagorean Theorem, as follows: $r^2 = 3^2 + 4^2 \rightarrow r^2 = 9 + 16 \rightarrow r^2 = 25 \rightarrow r = 5$ inches.

If you selected answer choice E, you probably used 8 and 3 for the leg lengths and got $r^2 = 73$, which makes r equivalent to about 8.5 inches.

26. The correct answer is K. To find the force F (in newtons) corresponding to the spring length, L, of 0.23 meters when the relationship is given by the equation $L = \left(\frac{2}{3}\right)F + 0.05$, first substitute 0.23 for L to get $0.23 = \left(\frac{2}{3}\right)F + 0.05$. Next, subtract 0.05 from both sides to get $0.18 = \left(\frac{2}{3}\right)F$. Finally, multiply by $\left(\frac{3}{2}\right)$, since dividing by a fraction is equal to multiplying by its reciprocal, to arrive at $0.27 = F$.

27. The correct answer is C. To find the uniform depth, use the formula for volume, V, of a rectangular prism with the height h, length l, and width w, $V = (l)(w)(h)$. Substitute the given values for the variables and solve for h: $12,000 = (62)(85)(h)$, or $12,000 = 5,270h$. Thus $h = \frac{12,000}{5,270}$, or about 2.277, which is between 2 and 3.

28. The correct answer is G. To find the length of the segment LM in $\triangle LMN$, where the length of the hypotenuse is 22 and the cosine of angle L is

$\frac{3}{4}$, use the definition of cosine, which is the ratio of the length of the adjacent side to the length of the hypotenuse. In $\triangle LMN$, the cosine of angle L is the ratio of the length of segment LM to the length of the hypotenuse. Substitute the length of the hypotenuse and solve for LM, as follows:

$$\frac{3}{4} = \frac{LM}{22}$$

$$4 \times LM = 22 \times 3$$

$$LM = \frac{66}{4}, \text{ or } 16.5, \text{ answer choice G.}$$

29. **The correct answer is A.** To find the fraction of apples grown in Appleton, divide the number of apples grown in Appleton by the total number of apples grown. The table below shows the conversion of apple symbols to numbers for the 4 cities, as well as the total number of apples grown.

CITY	NUMBER OF APPLES GROWN
Golden Hills	4,500
Red Falls	3,000
Appleton	2,500
Shady Acres	2,000
All Cities	12,000

The fraction of apples grown in Appleton is $\frac{2,500}{12,000}$, or $\frac{5}{24}$.

If you selected answer choice D, the most common incorrect answer, you probably used the number grown in Appleton divided by the total number of apples from the other 3 towns only.

30. **The correct Answer is H.** You are given that the length of AC is 19 units and the length of BD is 14 units. In addition, points are along segment AD as shown in the problem. Segment BC is the intersection of segment AC and segment BD. Therefore, the sum of the lengths AC and BD is the same as the sum of the lengths AD and BC. Substitute the actual lengths in $AC + BD = AD + BC$ as follows: $19 + 14 = 25 + BC \rightarrow 33 = 25 + BC \rightarrow 8 = BC$.

31. **The correct answer is D.** To find the x-coordinate where the lines with equations $y = -2x + 7$ and

$y = 3x - 3$ intersect, set $-2x + 7$ equal to $3x - 3$ and solve for x:

$$-2x + 7 = 3x - 3$$

$$-5x + 7 = -3$$

$$-5x = -10$$

$$x = 2$$

32. **The correct answer is K.** To solve the equation $S = 4T - 7$ for T, add 7 to both sides to get $S + 7 = 4T$, and divide by 4 on both sides to get $\frac{(S + 7)}{4}$.

33. **The correct answer is D.** The area for a parallelogram with base b and corresponding height h is $(b)(h)$. For parallelogram $ABCD$, segment AD is the base, with length $5 + 15$, or 20 inches, and the corresponding height is 12 inches. Therefore, the area is $(20)(12)$, or 240 square inches.

The most common incorrect answer is E, which is the result of multiplying the two side lengths: $(5 + 15)(13) = 20(13)$, or 260.

34. **The correct answer is F.** To find $(a - b)^4$ given $b = a + 3$, substitute $a + 3$ for b, as follows:

$$(a - (a + 3))^4$$

$$= (a - a - 3)^4$$

$$= (-3)^4, \text{ or } 81.$$

If you get stuck on this one, you can try choosing a specific value for a, such as 2. Then $b = 5$ and $(a - b)^4 = (2 - 5)^4 = 81$.

If you selected answer choice K, you might have gotten -3 for $(a - b)$, but solved $-(3^4)$ instead of $(-3)^4$, thus arriving at an answer of -81. Remember that when you have an even numbered exponent, you can eliminate negative answer choices.

35. **The correct answer is B.** To find the location of the park office located halfway between points A and D, it makes sense to give coordinates to the points in relation to an origin (see diagram below). In this case it makes sense to choose point F as the origin because it is in the bottom left of the figure. The first coordinate is the number of miles east of the origin, and the second coordinate is the number of miles north of the origin.

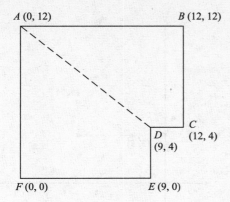

The park office is at the midpoint of the segment *AD*, and so the midpoint formula applies. For points with coordinates (x_1, y_1) and (x_2, y_2), the midpoint has coordinates $\left[\dfrac{(x_1 + x_2)}{2}, \dfrac{(y_1 + y_2)}{2}\right]$. For *A* (0,12) and *D* (9,4), the midpoint is $\left(\dfrac{[0+9]}{2}, \dfrac{[12+4]}{2}\right)$, or $\left(\dfrac{9}{2}, 8\right)$. However, the problem asks you to relate the location of the office to its distance and direction from point *A*. To do so, subtract the coordinates of point *A* from the coordinates of the midpoint: $\left(\dfrac{9}{2} - 0, 8 - 12\right)$, or $\left(\dfrac{9}{2}, -4\right)$. Thus, the location of the office relative to point *A* is $4\dfrac{1}{2}$ miles east and 4 miles south.

36. The correct answer is J. A simple way to solve this problem is to let the larger number be *y*. Therefore, you know that $y = 3x + 4$, and that $2y + 4x = 58$. Substitute $3x + 4$ for *y* in the last equation to arrive at $2(3x + 4) + 4x = 58$. This equation allows you to solve for *x*.

37. The correct answer is E. To find out how far a 26-foot ladder reaches up a building when the base of the ladder is 10 feet away from the building, it is useful to draw a picture, as shown below:

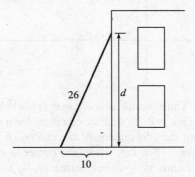

As you can see, the ladder forms the hypotenuse of a right triangle with a length of 26, and the base of the ladder is 10 feet away from the building. Using the Pythagorean Theorem, $26^2 = 10^2 + d^2$, where *d* is the distance up the building. Simplifying, you get $676 = 100 + d^2 \rightarrow 576 = d^2 \rightarrow 24 = d$.

38. The correct answer is G. Recall that the area of a square with side *s* is s^2. Finding the diameter of the circle, as shown below, it is clear that the side of the square is equal to the diameter of the circle, or $2(5) = 10$. Thus the area of the square is 10^2, or 100 square feet.

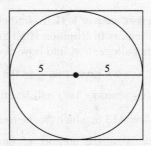

39. The correct answer is C. To find the length of the longest side of the second triangle, use ratios of corresponding sides of each triangle. For example, $\dfrac{9}{7} = \dfrac{x}{13}$, where *x* is the longest side of the second triangle. Cross-multiply to arrive at $117 = 7x$. Divide by 7 to get $x =$ about 16.7.

If you selected answer choice B, the most common incorrect answer, you might have noticed that the difference in lengths of the smallest sides was 2 and then simply added 2 to the longest side of the first triangle to get 15 for the longest side of the second triangle.

40. The correct answer is H. To find the measure of angle *CDB* in the figure, it is helpful to recognize that the sides *BC* and *AD* are parallel (definition of trapezoid) and are connected by the transversal *BD*. Angles *CBD* and *ADB* are alternate interior angles, and thus are equal and both measure 25°. Because *A*, *D*, and *E* all lie along the same line, angle $ADE = 180°$. Because angle *ADE* is made up of angles *ADB*, *CDB*, and *CDE*, the measures of these three angles add up to 180° : $25° + CDB + 100° = 180°$, thus the measure of angle *CDB* is 55°.

41. The correct answer is D. This figure has 10 sides, but the lengths are given for only 7 sides. Those lengths add up to 36 inches. The perimeter is greater than this because of the missing 3 sides so you can eliminate answer choices A and B. To solve this problem, use the information given to find the missing sides; based on the figure, you can see that the sum of right-facing sides equals the sum of left-facing sides, and the sum of top-facing sides equals the sum of bottom-facing sides. It is easy to see that the bottom-facing sides will equal the top-facing side, which has a length of 14. Since we have the values for all of the left-facing sides ($5 + 4 + 3 = 12$), the right-facing sides also have the sum of 12. Thus the perimeter is $14 + 14 + 12 + 12$, or 52.

42. The correct answer is G. To find out how many of the 517 seniors in Brighton High School are going to a state college, first find how many are going to college. You are given that $\frac{4}{5}$ of the total number of graduating seniors (517) will be attending college: $\frac{4}{5}$ of $517 = 413.6$, which can be rounded up to 414. Now, calculate the number of those 414 seniors who are going to a state college: $\left(\frac{1}{2}\right)(414)$, or about 207 seniors are going to a state college. This is closest to 200, answer choice G.

43. The correct answer is A. You are given that $x \boxdot y = (x - 2y)^2$ and are asked to solve $5 \boxdot (-3)$. To do this, simply replace x with 5, and y with -3, as follows:

$$x \boxdot y = (x - 2y)^2$$
$$5 \boxdot (-3) = (5 - 2(-3))^2$$
$$5 \boxdot (-3) = (5 - (-6))^2$$
$$5 \boxdot (-3) = (5 + 6)^2$$
$$5 \boxdot (-3) = (11)^2$$
$$5 \boxdot (-3) = 121$$

44. The correct answer is F. Because 125% of "the number" is 425, then "the number" is $425 \div 1.25$, which equals 340. Calculate 65% of 340: $340 \times 0.65 = 221$.

45. The correct answer is D. To find the distance between 2 points in the standard (x, y) coordinate plane, use the distance formula, which states that $d = \sqrt{[(x_2 - x_1)^2 + (y_2 - y_1)^2]}$. Therefore, the distance is $\sqrt{[(5 - 2)^2 + (5 - 3)^2]}$, or $(3^2 + 2^2)$, which equals $\sqrt{13}$.

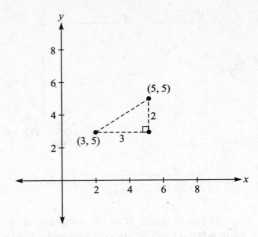

Another way to look at this problem would be to draw a picture as shown above. Then you can use the Pythagorean Theorem to find the hypotenuse of the triangle that is formed from the given points.

46. The correct answer is G. To find the ratio of the circumference of 2 circles for which the ratio of their radii is 9:16, recognize that both circumference and radius are 1-dimensional attributes of a circle. Because of that, the ratios should be the same, 9:16. Another way is to use the ratio of the radii and let $9x$ and $16x$ be the radii of the two circles. Their circumferences would be $2\pi(9x)$ and $2\pi(16x)$, respectively. When you put them in a ratio you see that the ratio $2\pi(9x) : 2\pi(16x)$ simplifies to 9:16.

47. The correct answer is D. The best approach to this question is to draw a diagram as shown below:

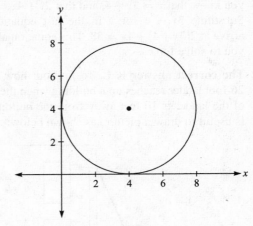

The equation of a circle is $(x - h)^2 + (y - k)^2 = r^2$. One way to find an equation for a circle is by using the coordinates of the center, (h, k), and the radius, r. For this circle, the center is at (4, 4) and the radius is 4. Given center (4, 4) and radius 4, the circle has equation $(x - 4)^2 + (y - 4)^2 = 4^2$, or $(x - 4)^2 + (y - 4)^2 = 16$.

If you selected answer choice B, a common incorrect answer, you centered the circle at $(0, 0)$.

48. **The correct answer is F.** To find an equivalent expression for $\dfrac{2}{(1-i)} \times \dfrac{(1+i)}{(1+i)}$, simply perform the calculations, as follows:

$$\frac{2(1+i)}{(1-i)(1+i)} = \frac{2(1+i)}{(1-i^2)}$$

$$\frac{2(1+i)}{(1-i^2)} = \frac{2(1+i)}{2}$$

$$\frac{2(1+i)}{2} = 1+i$$

49. **The correct answer is D.** One approach to solving this problem is to make a table like the one below, showing the number of rows and the cumulative number of dots.

Row	1	2	3	4	5
Number of dots per row	2	4	6	8	10
Cumulative number of dots	2	2 + 4 = 6	6 + 6 = 12	8 + 12 = 20	10 + 20 = 30

The total number of dots in rows 1 and 2 is $2(2+1)$; the total number of dots in row 3 is $3(3+1)$, and so on. You should be able to see that for the nth row, the total is the product of n and $n + 1$, or $n(n + 1)$.

50. **The correct answer is J.** You are given that the total number of students is 24. If 21 students play basketball, and 9 students play soccer, there must be some overlap between basketball players and soccer players. The total number of students who play basketball and/or soccer is $21 + 9$, or 30; therefore, $30 - 24$, or 6 students must play both sports.

51. **The correct answer is E.** To find the real numbers x such that $x + 2 > x + 5$, subtract x and 2 from both sides. The result is $0 > 3$, and because that inequality is never true, there is no solution for x. The solution set is the empty set.

52. **The correct answer is H.** As shown below, there are 4 diagonals coming from each vertex point.

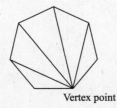

Vertex point

Because there are 7 vertex points, you might be tempted to conclude that there are 7×4, or 28 diagonals. But this method counts each diagonal exactly twice. Therefore, there are $\dfrac{28}{2}$, or 14 diagonals.

53. **The correct answer is D.** You are given that 20% of John's friends selected vanilla ice cream as their favorite flavor. This means that 20% of the 360° in the circle will represent vanilla; 20% of 360 is equivalent to $(0.20)(360°)$, or 72°. If you chose one of the other answers, you may have found the degree measure of any of the other flavors.

54. **The correct answer is G.** One way to find $\tan \theta$ given that $\sin \theta = \dfrac{4}{5}$ and $\dfrac{\pi}{2} < \theta < \pi$, is to first find $\cos \theta$, then find $\dfrac{\sin \theta}{\cos \theta}$, which is equivalent to $\tan \theta$. To find $\cos \theta$, use the identity $\sin^2 \theta + \cos^2 \theta = 1$ and the fact that $\cos \theta < 1$ in Quadrant II $\left(\dfrac{\pi}{2} < \theta < \pi \text{ would place the angle in Quadrant II} \right)$. Use substitution to get $\left(\dfrac{4}{5} \right)^2 + \cos^2 \theta = 1$, or $\dfrac{16}{25} + \cos^2 \theta = 1$. After subtracting $\dfrac{16}{25}$, you get $\cos^2 \theta = \dfrac{9}{25}$. After taking the square root of both sides, you get $\cos \theta = \pm \dfrac{3}{5}$. Because $\cos \theta < 1$ is in Quadrant II, $\cos \theta = -\dfrac{3}{5}$. Substitute this value into $\dfrac{\sin \theta}{\cos \theta}$ to get $\dfrac{(4/5)}{(-3/5)}$, which equals $-\dfrac{4}{3}$.

Another way you could solve this problem would be to construct an angle in Quadrant II with $\sin \theta = \dfrac{4}{5}$, as shown below.

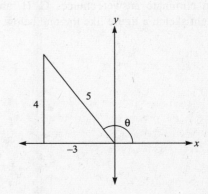

By virtue of the Pythagorean Theorem, the missing side of the right triangle is 3 units long, and is negative because it is along the negative side of the x-axis. From this triangle, knowing that tangent $= \dfrac{\text{opposite}}{\text{adjacent}}$, you can get $\tan \theta = -\dfrac{4}{3}$.

55. The correct answer is E. To find the system of inequalities represented by the shaded region of the graph, first find the equations of the line through $(-1, 0)$ and $(0, 1)$ and the line through $(-2, 0)$ and $(0, -3)$. These are $y = x + 1$ (the y-intercept is 1) and $y = \left(-\dfrac{3}{2}\right)x - 3$ (the y-intercept is -3), respectively. Pay attention to the coordinating conjunctions, *and/or*.

56. The correct answer is K. To find $f(x + h)$ when $f(x) = 2x^2 + 3$, substitute $(x + h)$ for x in $f(x) = 2x^2 + 3$, as follows:

$$f(x + h) = 2(x + h)^2 + 3$$

$$2(x + h)^2 = 2(x^2 + 2xh + h^2) + 3$$

$$2(x^2 + 2xh + h^2) = 2x^2 + 4xh + 2h^2 + 3$$

57. The correct answer is D. The equation $y = \dfrac{x^2 + 3x}{x}$ can be simplified to $y = \dfrac{x(x + 3)}{x}$. Therefore, the graph of this seemingly complicated equation actually looks like a line, not a parabola, so eliminate answer choices A and B. This is equivalent to $y = x + 3$ except when $x = 0$. When $x = 0$, the original equation is undefined. So the correct graph is $y = x + 3$, with a point removed where $x = 0$.

58. The correct answer is F. To find the coordinates of vertex A after it is reflected across the y-axis, remember that a reflection across the y-axis does not change the sign of the y-coordinate but does change the sign of the x-coordinate. Therefore, you can eliminate answer choices G, H, and J. You might sketch a figure like the one below.

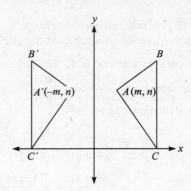

The reflection of $A\,(m, n)$ across the x-axis is $A'\,(-m, n)$. The most popular incorrect answer is J, which gives the reflection of A over the line $y = x$.

59. The correct answer is B. To obtain an expression for y in terms of x when $x = 3r - 4$ and $y = 3r + 2$, first solve $x = 3r - 4$ for r as follows:

$$x = 3r - 4$$

$$x + 4 = 3r$$

$$\frac{x + 4}{3} = r$$

Substitute that expression for r into $y = 3r + 2$, and solve for y:

$y = 3\left[\dfrac{x + 4}{3}\right] + 2$, which simplifies to $y = (x + 4) + 2$, or $y = x + 6$.

60. The correct answer is H. To find $\cos \dfrac{\pi}{12}$ using $\cos(\alpha - \beta) = (\cos \alpha)(\cos \beta) + (\sin \alpha)(\sin \beta)$ given that $\dfrac{\pi}{12} = \dfrac{\pi}{3} - \dfrac{\pi}{4}$, you can first substitute $\dfrac{\pi}{3}$ for α and $\dfrac{\pi}{4}$ for β and get $\cos\left(\dfrac{\pi}{3} - \dfrac{\pi}{4}\right) = \left(\cos \dfrac{\pi}{3}\right)\left(\cos \dfrac{\pi}{4}\right) + \left(\sin \dfrac{\pi}{3}\right)\left(\sin \dfrac{\pi}{4}\right)$. Using the table of values to substitute into that equation, you get $\cos \dfrac{\pi}{12} = \left(\dfrac{1}{2}\right)\left(\dfrac{\sqrt{2}}{2}\right) + \left(\dfrac{\sqrt{3}}{2}\right)\left(\dfrac{\sqrt{2}}{2}\right)$, or $\dfrac{(\sqrt{6} + \sqrt{2})}{4}$.

Reading Test Explanations

PASSAGE I

1. **The best answer is B.** The passage takes place on a ship, the *Nellie*, and the narrator is one of the crew members. He uses words like "we" and "us" when referring to the crew, implying his membership to this group. The other answer choices are not supported by the passage.

2. **The best answer is F.** Although the passage states, "for some reason or another we did not begin that game of dominoes," it is reasonable to assume that it was because they were too tired from the use of the words "lazily" and "meditative." The other answer choices are not supported by the passage.

3. **The best answer is C.** The passage states that "the Lawyer ... had, because of his many years and many virtues, the only cushion on deck," indicating that since he was the eldest crew member and had the other crew members' respect, he was afforded the comfort of the cushion. The other answer choices are not supported by the passage.

4. **The best answer is F.** The definition of "placid" is "not easily excited or upset; calm." Since the men on the ship were feeling "meditative" and seemed not to have an abundance of energy, it makes sense that they simply wanted to sit calmly. The other answer choices are not supported by the context of the passage.

5. **The best answer is D.** In the fifth paragraph the narrator is describing how Marlow is unlike most sailors: "The stories of seamen have a direct simplicity, the whole meaning of which lies within the shell of a cracked nut. But Marlow was not typical ... and to him the meaning of an episode was not inside like a kernel but outside ..." This is to say that typical sailors tell simple, uncomplicated tales, while Marlow tends to tell stories that are layered and complex. This best supports answer choice D.

6. **The best answer is H.** According to the passage, "Marlow was not typical, and to him the meaning of an episode was not inside like a kernel but outside ..." This suggests that Marlow's story will be unlike the usual straightforward tales told by seamen and will instead be vague and nebulous.

7. **The best answer is A.** The passage states that, "The Director of Companies was our captain and our host. We four affectionately watched his back as he stood in the bow looking toward the sea. On the whole river there was nothing that looked half so nautical. He resembled a pilot, which to a seaman is trustworthiness personified." This best supports answer choice A.

8. **The best answer is G.** There are clues in the passage to indicate that the narrator, as well as the other crew members, were not thrilled when Marlow began to speak. Marlow's very first comment was "accepted in silence" and "no one took the trouble to grunt even." In the next paragraph the narrator begins to realize that the crew was "fated, before the ebb began to run, to hear about one of Marlow's inconclusive experiences." Since resigned means "accepting that something can not be avoided" and tolerance means "patience," making G the best answer.

9. **The best answer is A.** In the third paragraph the passage states that the men's mutual interest in the sea created a bond between them capable of "holding (their) hearts together through long periods of separation," "making (them) tolerant of each other's yarns," and making them accepting of each other's "convictions." Answer choice A is not mentioned in the passage.

10. **The best answer is J.** The passage states that the crewmen watched him "affectionately," meaning "showing fondness or liking." The captain is also described as "trustworthiness personified," indicating that the other crew members have the utmost faith and trust in him. This best supports answer choice J.

PASSAGE II

11. **The best answer is B.** As stated in the passage, "in the past 30 years, known supplies have dwindled from almost 300 TCF to around 150 TCF," or known supplies have decreased by about 50 percent. Answer choice A is incorrect because the passage states that at predicted rates of consumption, the United States' natural gas supply would be exhausted in approximately five years. Answer choice C is incorrect because natural gas provides for roughly 25 percent of America's energy needs, which has nothing to do with the decrease in supply. Answer choice D is incorrect because the passage states that it is extremely difficult to obtain natural gas from other countries, not from within the US.

12. **The best answer is G.** At the end of the passage, the author states that "consumers and business leaders should not rely on liquid natural gas to solve America's energy needs." This can also be inferred from the point that natural gas is currently only supplying approximately 25 percent of the nation's energy needs, and even at this level there is much concern over whether supplies will run out. Answer choice H may appear to be correct, but the passage merely states that countries such as Japan and China will also be searching for fuel sources, including liquid natural gas, outside of their own countries in the future.

13. **The best answer is D.** This question can be difficult if you do not read the answer choices carefully. The third paragraph is devoted to a discussion on the limited availability of liquid natural gas, and the expense of processing the gas, which makes answer choice D the best selection. Answer choice A may appear to be correct; however, the passage focuses on the supply and use of liquid natural gas around the world. The passage does not discuss the supply and use of any other energy sources. Answer choice B was mentioned briefly in the passage, but is not a main idea. Answer choice C is beyond the scope of the passage.

14. **The best answer is F.** As stated in the second paragraph, it is predicted that "liquid natural gas imports will increase by almost 500 percent in a few short years." Although America may be reluctant to import liquid natural gas, it is necessary for the nation to do so in order to relieve and/or avoid shortages. Answer choice H may appear to be correct; however, the author states that even though transportation costs have been substantially decreased due to new technology, importing liquid natural gas "is still often uneconomical." Answer choices G and J are beyond the scope of the passage.

15. **The best answer is C.** According to the passage, "Currently, Canada is the largest liquid natural gas supplier for the United States." Japan and China, two countries in Asia, are providing competition in attaining liquid natural gas.

16. **The best answer is F.** The first sentence of the third passage states "One of the largest misconceptions about liquid natural gas is that it is an abundant source of natural gas." While the passage goes on to discuss the expense of creating new processing facilities and prices making liquid natural gas uneconomical, the only misconception mentioned is the fact that liquid natural gas is an abundant

source of natural gas. The other answer choices are not supported by the passage.

17. **The best answer is C.** The context surrounding the word *phenomenal* discusses the surprisingly large growth expected in natural gas demand and the huge impact that such growth will have on depletion of the resource. This context clearly indicates that the demand is increasing at "phenomenal," or extraordinary, rates. The other answer choices are not supported by the context of the passage.

18. **The best answer is G.** Answer choice G is the only reason that America is choosing liquid natural gas; consumers are demanding it so America must provide it. Answer choices F and H express current problems with choosing liquid natural gas; transportation and processing are both very costly relative to other fuel sources. Answer choice J is a potential problem. Liquid natural gas is inherently expensive due to its transportation and processing costs. If natural gas prices are low, the market for liquid natural gas will plummet, making liquid natural gas an uneconomical choice for consumers.

19. **The best answer is D.** As stated in the paragraph, "natural gas demand is increasing at phenomenal rates" and its consumption is expected to grow from 22 trillion cubic feet per year to 32 trillion cubic feet per year in less than a decade. Answer choice C may appear to be correct; however, the passage simply states that Canada is the largest liquid natural gas supplier for the United States alone. The passage does not compare Canada's liquid natural gas exports to those of any other country; therefore, we do not know whether or not Canada is the world's largest exporter. Likewise, the other answer choices are not supported by the passage.

20. **The best answer is J.** In the paragraph, the *vessel* in question is described as something that the liquid natural gas is injected into for transportation. It does not make sense that a liquid would be injected into a "process," "source," or "facility" for transportation. Answer choice J, "container," is the most logical choice.

PASSAGE III

21. **The best answer is B.** Throughout the passage, the author talks about the prevalence of the word "good," further discusses several different meanings and methods for interpreting the word, and suggests that there is no one specific denotation for the word "good." The other answer choices are not supported by the context of the passage.

22. The best answer is H. As stated by the author, babies are so young and powerless ("this elementary life has not yet acquired positive standards or measurement"), that they can only be judged in negative terms, "a failure to disturb." Answer choice G may appear to be correct; however, the "anxious mother" is still able to judge whether her baby has been good by what the baby did or did not do—in this case, cry.

23. The best answer is A. The author states that "we employ the word or some synonym of it during pretty much every waking hour of our lives. Wishing some test of this frequency, I turned to Shakespeare." In simpler terms, the author is asserting that we use the word "good" or some form of it constantly, and he believed that the works of Shakespeare would provide a good test of this notion. In other words, if Shakespeare used forms of the word "good" as often as the author predicted, the author's theory on use of the word would be proven true. This best supports answer choice A.

24. The best answer is H. The author writes "goodness always has reference to something outside itself, and is measured by its performance of an external task." The author goes on to write, "The knife is good for cutting and the day for business ... To be bad or good implies external reference." This best supports answer choice H.

25. The best answer is D. The author describes a quote by Shakespeare's Portia as being spoken "lucidly," and goes on to analyze and apply Portia's quotation. The author does so in a positive light, thus eliminating answer choices A and B. It does not make sense that Portia's quote was "enthusiastic," or excited. Answer choice D makes the most sense within the context of the passage; "coherently" means "logically and meaningfully."

26. The best answer is H. When discussing the knife, the author states, "Its goodness always has reference to something outside itself." Although the passage mentions cutting wood, the author never says that a knife is good *only* if it cuts wood. Answer choices G and J are not supported by the context of the passage.

27. The best answer is A. The author begins by discussing the goodness of a clear, tangible object—a knife. The author then moves on to discussing the goodness of the weather—something "not so *palpable*." Answer choice A, "apparent," makes the most sense. The goodness of an intangible thing, such as the weather, is not nearly as "evident or clear" as that of a tangible object.

The goodness of the weather is not less "complicated" than that of the knife; likewise, it does not make sense that the goodness of the weather would be less "powerful" or "drab" than that of the knife.

28. The best answer is J. The author states, "We must have some respect or end in mind in reference to which the goodness is compared." In other words, in order to understand what "good" means, you must know specifically what is being referred to as "good" before interpreting the definition of "good." Answer choice G may appear to be correct, but the passage states that "good always means good 'for;'" thereby asserting that the two are actually identical concepts.

29. The best answer is D. Throughout the passage the author refers to the actual application of the word "good," and that the word "must be useful for something." This best supports answer choice D.

30. The best answer is G. According to the author, goodness in life "attends all our wishes, acts, and projects as nothing else does, so that no estimate of its influence can be excessive." The author furthers this point by adding that every action we take is in hopes of achieving something good. In simpler terms, the author is saying that because our pursuit of goodness has such a huge impact on our lives, there is no way we could overestimate or over-emphasize the influence this has on us. Answer choice F is incorrect because it is the opposite of what the author is trying to say. Answer choices H and J are beyond the scope of the passage.

PASSAGE IV

31. The best answer is A. At this point in the passage, the defense mechanisms of armadillos are being discussed. If tanks were strengthening their positions, they would be improving their safety and increasing their level of protection from enemies. Therefore, if armadillos "often scurry under thorn bushes, rather like tanks strengthening their position," they are giving themselves better protection against their predators. This best supports answer choice A.

32. The best answer is J. The first paragraph states that armadillos look "far more awkward than most animals." The passage then goes on to describe the armadillo as an "alien creature," which suggests that the armadillo's awkward appearance is what makes it an alien creature. The other answer choices are not supported by the passage.

33. The best answer is D. According to the passage, the armadillo is "safer than most animals who wander the Texas roads" because its shell protects its from predators. Answer choices A through C are beyond the scope of the passage and, therefore, are incorrect.

34. The best answer is G. The author's statement that "if chased into its burrow, the animal is able to arch its armor against the burrow walls making the armadillo nearly impossible to became dislodged" suggests that the armadillo curves its back against the burrow walls, wedging itself into the burrow. The other answer choices are not supported by the passage.

35. The best answer is C. Information in the passage indicates that "The nine-banded armadillo is the only species of animal in which this remarkable trait occurs," which is speaking in reference to their ability to have four identical offspring emerging from the same egg. This best supports answer choice C.

36. The best answer is H. According to the passage, most Texans feel the armadillo is a "pest" when it destroys crops and other plants that are low to the ground; however, most Texans also see that armadillos provide "benefits" as well, such as its eating harmful insects and aiding in medical research. This best supports answer choice H.

37. The best answer is B. Although the passage mentions both opossums and farmers, neither are identified as predators of the armadillo. Both dogs and cars are acknowledged as predators of the armadillo; however, the passage explicitly states that "In addition to threats of being eaten by an opportunistic predator, the armadillo must also endure a more severe danger: automobiles." Therefore, automobiles are more dangerous to armadillos than are any other predator. This best supports answer choice B.

38. The best answer is F. The passage states that, "Texans see the armadillo as a pest, since the creatures have a tendency to ruin corn by eating the parts of the plants that are low to the ground." This suggests that armadillos are damaging crops. The other answer choices are not supported by the passage.

39. The best answer is C. According to the passage, armadillos "are born fully formed with their eyes open" so it makes sense that they would be able to see. The other answer choices contradict statements made elsewhere in the passage, or are unsupported by the passage.

40. The best answer is J. The only scientific name mentioned, *Dasypus novemcincts*, is directly defined as being the name for the nine-banded armadillo. The other choices are similar species of armadillo, but not mentioned in reference to that specific scientific name.

Science Reasoning Test Explanations

PASSAGE I

1. **The best answer is B.** Based on the data in all three tables, the highest average speed was recorded in Table 3, which shows the results of Study 3. Therefore, the highest average speeds resulted from using studded, hard rubber wheels, answer choice B.

2. **The best answer is H.** The average speed recorded in Table 1 is 3.28 feet per second. This speed is not greater than the speed recorded in Trial 2 (3.33 ft/s); likewise, it is not less than the speed recorded in Trial 1 (3.28 ft/s); eliminate answer choices F and G. The speed recorded in Trial 2 (3.23 ft/s) is less than the average speed recorded in Table 1 (3.28 ft/s), so answer choice H must be correct.

3. **The best answer is D.** To answer this question, you must remember that Table 1 is associated with deeply treaded hard rubber wheels, Table 2 is associated with soft rubber wheels lacking treads, and Table 3 is associated with studded, hard rubber wheels. When you compare the average recorded speed, you will see that the average speed of a car with studded, hard rubber wheels (6.44 ft/s) is approximately twice the average speed of a car with deeply treaded hard rubber wheels (3.28 ft/s) answer choice D.

4. **The best answer is F.** Since the passage indicates that all three of the studies were, "conducted indoors in a temperature controlled room," you can eliminate answer choices G and H. The studies also dealt with different types of wheels, and the traction they would provide, so the most likely reason for the highest average speeds is greater friction, answer choice F.

5. **The best answer is A.** During which of the following Trials did the car travel most slowly?

   A. Study 2, Trial 1 = 57 seconds
   B. Study 2, Trial 2 = 56.4 seconds
   C. Study 3, Trial 1 = 11.3 seconds
   D. Study 1, Trial 2 = 23.2 seconds

   Because it took the car in Study 2, Trial 1 longer to travel the constant distance of 75 feet, that car must have been traveling more slowly than the cars in each of the other answer choices.

PASSAGE II

6. **The best answer is J.** The two scientists are discussing how the planet Pluto should be classified: as a planet, or as some other celestial object. Scientist 1 believes it Pluto should retain its status as a planet, while Scientist 2 believes Pluto would be more accurately categorized as a Kuiper Belt comet. This best supports answer choice J.

7. **The best answer is B.** Scientist 2 explains that currently two categorizations of planets exist: rocky and gaseous. The scientist then goes on to say that Pluto does not fit into either of these categories because it is composed of an icy material. This best supports answer choice B.

8. **The best answer is F.** The questions asks for the identification of the characteristic that does *not* differentiate Pluto from asteroids and comets. Neither Pluto nor asteroids and comets can generate heat through nuclear fission, so this is not a differentiating characteristic, making this answer choice the best.

9. **The best answer is B.** Scientist 2 maintains that Pluto is not like the other planets due to its icy surface. If the ice melted and revealed that Pluto's surface was similar to Mars, Scientist 2's argument would be significantly weakened.

10. **The best answer is J.** Both scientists mention the irregularity of Pluto's orbit in their respective arguments. Scientist 1 states, "Pluto's orbital path is irregular as compared with the other planets of the solar system, and Scientist 2 also makes note of the "eccentricity of Pluto's orbit."

11. **The best answer is A.** One of the arguments that Scientist 1 makes for Pluto not being a comet is that Pluto is far too massive. If a comet were discovered with a diameter of 1,500 miles, it would be even larger than Pluto, which has a diameter of 1,413 miles. This would nullify the scientist's argument that Pluto cannot be a comet because comets are much smaller than Pluto.

12. **The best answer is H.** One reason that Scientist 2 offers to support the argument for Pluto to be a Kuiper Belt object is that both have strange, atypical orbital patterns.

PASSAGE III

13. **The best answer is C.** The question asks you to look at the overall trends of the data sets for each substance. A good way to measure the degree to which data varies would be to find the range, meaning subtract the lowest value from the highest value for each individual substance. In this problem it is clear that NaCl varies the least with temperature.

14. **The best answer is F.** In this question you are asked to look at the trends of the substances, especially at how their concentrations change with increasing temperature. In the data set, some substances become more soluble with increasing temperature, while some become less soluble. The graph represents the solubility curve for a substance that gets less soluble with increasing temperature. Looking at the possible answer choices, HCl is the only logical choice.

15. **The best answer is C.** It is clear from the table that each substance reacts differently in its solubility depending on the temperature. However, each substance does show a clear trend in whether it gets more or less soluble with increasing temperature.

16. **The best answer is J.** According to Table 1, HCl has a concentration of 55 g/100 g H_2O at 60°C, and a concentration of 48 g/100 g H_2O at 80°C. Therefore, at 70°C it would likely have a concentration of $55 + 48 \div 2 = 51.5$ g/100 g H_2O.

17. **The best answer is D.** By looking at the trend in concentration for NH_4Cl, 50g are dissolved between the 40°C and 60°C measurements. The logical answer choice would then be 50°C.

PASSAGE IV

18. **The best answer is H.** As shown in Table 1, the estimated mineral volume of the oldest salt pan (21 million years old) is 12,150,000 cubic kilometers; the estimated mineral volume of the youngest salt pan (4.5 million years old) is only 2,000,000 cubic kilometers. The deposits were formed as collected water evaporated, so the much larger volume of minerals in the oldest basin suggests that more water has collected and evaporated there.

19. **The best answer is B.** As Table 1 shows for Study 1, there is a direct, positive relationship between mineral volume and age of the salt pans. As the age increased, the mineral volume is also shown to increase in each of the four cases. This direct relationship is shown in the graph in answer choice B.

20. **The best answer is J.** There is no information contained within either Study 1 or Study 2, or in either of the tables that makes reference to the quantity of plant fossils. The only references to plant fossils are that they were found in each salt pan, that the ages were similar, and that the flooding was thought to cause plant extinction. Plant species is not shown by the data to influence quantity of fossils.

21. **The best answer is C.** Since there is a direct, positive relationship between salt pan age and mineral volume, if a salt pan were to have formed before the oldest salt pan in the study, then it would likely contain a greater volume of minerals than that pan is shown to contain. Since the oldest pan in the study contained 12,150,000 cubic kilometers of minerals, a pan older than that would have a higher mineral value.

22. **The best answer is H.** Since the ages of the fossils are stated in Study 2 to be similar to the ages of the salt pans, a fossil that is 9.7 million years old would be closest in age to Salt pan C (10.8 million years old) and, therefore, would most likely be found in a similar salt pan.

PASSAGE V

23. **The best answer is C.** As shown in Table 1, the temperature of gasoline is between 40 and 70°C, which makes it greater than 20°C. Despite this being the lowest temperature for petroleum gas, it is still correct as the choices of less than 40 and greater than 70°C exclude gasoline completely.

24. **The best answer is J.** Figure 1 shows a diagram of the fractioning tower, which places residue as the first substance to be condensed and drawn off. Additionally, the passage states that the vapor rises through the tower and cools, condensing at the appropriate points—this means that the substance with the hottest condensation temperature would be first.

25. **The best answer is C.** Within the passage is says that, "this process is called fractional distillation, whereby the crude oil is heated ..." Gasoline, residue, and gas oil are all products that result from the process of fractional distillation. The passage clearly discusses crude oil in the context of a raw material.

26. **The best answer is F.** A condensation point of 90°C would place naptha in Table 1 between gasoline (40–70°C) and kerosene (100–120°C), as it is above the upper end of gasoline and below the lower end of kerosene.

27. **The best answer is A.** Within the passage it is discussed that "the crude oil is super-heated in the boiler to about 600°C, which vaporizes the crude oil." Since this is the temperature at which crude oil vaporizes, answer choice A is correct.

28. **The best answer is G.** As the passage states, "the vapors rise in the tower to certain levels where

they cool and condense, according to their chemical structure." The condensation temperature would continuously decrease then as the vapor moves up the fractionating tower.

PASSAGE VI

29. **The best answer is B.** As stated in the passage, "if the paths of the X-rays are not bent in any way, it is assumed that the star lacks any planets." Since Table 1 shows there to be no X-ray distortion for Star 2 over a ten day period, it can be assumed then that Star 2 has no planets.

30. **The best answer is G.** Since the passage states that "a circular orbit produces increasing or decreasing distortions of the same level" and Table 1 shows that Star 1 has distortions increasing by 0.75, and Star 3 has distortions decreasing by half, both of those stars are likely to have planets with circular orbits.

31. **The best answer is A.** Since Table 1 shows that there is indeed a decrease in X-ray distortion for Star 3, and the note instructs that there are no other objects that could affect the X-rays, it is reasonable to believe that Star 3 is orbited by at least one planet. The passage further states that X-ray distortion is caused by the pull from planets. This best supports answer choice A.

32. **The best answer is J.** According to the table, every three days the X-ray distortion for Star 1 increases by 0.75 meters. Since 4.00 is an increase of 0.75 over the 3.25 meters measured on day 10, 4.00 is the likely predicted distortion on day 13.

33. **The best answer is A.** According to the passage, the X-rays are distorted by the force of gravity, which best support answer choice A.

34. **The best answer is G.** The passage indicates that when "the pattern of bending is random, as in a bending of 5 meters the first day, 3 meters the second day, 0 meters the third day, and 7 meters the fourth day, then the planet's orbit is elliptical." Table 1 shows the X-ray distortion for Star 4 to go from 0.20 meters to 0.10 meters to 0.11 meters and to stay at 0.11 meters; this bending pattern can be considered random when compared to the example

within the passage and thus indicates a planet with an elliptical orbit.

PASSAGE VII

35. **The best answer is C.** Five of the nine bacteria listed in Table 2 can be classified as mesophiles, given their stated minimum, optimum, and maximum growth points. No other type of bacteria appears as frequently within the table.

36. **The best answer is G.** *Listeria monocytogenes* is a bacteria with a minimum growth point of 1°C, which would make it appear to be a psychrophile; however its optimum growth point is 34°C, which is far above the maximum growth range for psychrophiles. For that reason it cannot be precisely classified.

37. **The best answer is C.** Since the question states that human body temperature is 40°C, a bacteria with an optimum growth point close to 40°C would grow most successfully in the human body. *Escherichia coli* has an optimum growth point of 37°C, which is two degrees closer to 40°C than that of *Clostridium perfringens* at 45°C.

38. **The best answer is J.** Thermophiles are shown by Table 2 to reproduce best, that is to have an optimum growth point, between 50° and 60°C. A bacteria that reproduces at 55°C would likely be classified there. Further, if the bacterium does not show any new growth above 65°C, that also fits within the range of maximum growth points for thermophiles of between 60° and 90°C.

39. **The best answer is C.** The growth range of *Streptococcus pneumoniae* is between 25°C at the minimum and 42°C at the maximum, for a total range of 17°C. *Listeria monocytogenes* has the greatest range of the bacteria choices at 44°C. *Micrococcus cryophilus* is next with 30°C of growth range, and *Streptococcus pyogenes* is next smallest with 20°C.

40. **The best answer is J.** Table 1 shows that maximum growth point of *Listeria monocytogenes* is 45°C, which means that 45°C is the temperature "beyond which the bacteria will not reproduce at all," as stated in the passage.

Writing Test Explanation

Because grading the essay is subjective, we've chosen not to include any "graded" essays here. Your best option is to have someone you trust, such as your personal tutor, read your essays and give you an honest critique. If you plan on grading your own essays, review the grading criteria and be as honest as possible regarding the structure, development, organization, technique, and appropriateness of your writing. Focus on your weak areas and continue to practice in order to improve your writing skills.

■■■ **ANSWER SHEET**

ACT PRACTICE TEST 2
Answer Sheet

ENGLISH

1 Ⓐ Ⓑ Ⓒ Ⓓ	21 Ⓐ Ⓑ Ⓒ Ⓓ	41 Ⓐ Ⓑ Ⓒ Ⓓ	61 Ⓐ Ⓑ Ⓒ Ⓓ
2 Ⓕ Ⓖ Ⓗ Ⓙ	22 Ⓕ Ⓖ Ⓗ Ⓙ	42 Ⓕ Ⓖ Ⓗ Ⓙ	62 Ⓕ Ⓖ Ⓗ Ⓙ
3 Ⓐ Ⓑ Ⓒ Ⓓ	23 Ⓐ Ⓑ Ⓒ Ⓓ	43 Ⓐ Ⓑ Ⓒ Ⓓ	63 Ⓐ Ⓑ Ⓒ Ⓓ
4 Ⓕ Ⓖ Ⓗ Ⓙ	24 Ⓕ Ⓖ Ⓗ Ⓙ	44 Ⓕ Ⓖ Ⓗ Ⓙ	64 Ⓕ Ⓖ Ⓗ Ⓙ
5 Ⓐ Ⓑ Ⓒ Ⓓ	25 Ⓐ Ⓑ Ⓒ Ⓓ	45 Ⓐ Ⓑ Ⓒ Ⓓ	65 Ⓐ Ⓑ Ⓒ Ⓓ
6 Ⓕ Ⓖ Ⓗ Ⓙ	26 Ⓕ Ⓖ Ⓗ Ⓙ	46 Ⓕ Ⓖ Ⓗ Ⓙ	66 Ⓕ Ⓖ Ⓗ Ⓙ
7 Ⓐ Ⓑ Ⓒ Ⓓ	27 Ⓐ Ⓑ Ⓒ Ⓓ	47 Ⓐ Ⓑ Ⓒ Ⓓ	67 Ⓐ Ⓑ Ⓒ Ⓓ
8 Ⓕ Ⓖ Ⓗ Ⓙ	28 Ⓕ Ⓖ Ⓗ Ⓙ	48 Ⓕ Ⓖ Ⓗ Ⓙ	68 Ⓕ Ⓖ Ⓗ Ⓙ
9 Ⓐ Ⓑ Ⓒ Ⓓ	29 Ⓐ Ⓑ Ⓒ Ⓓ	49 Ⓐ Ⓑ Ⓒ Ⓓ	69 Ⓐ Ⓑ Ⓒ Ⓓ
10 Ⓕ Ⓖ Ⓗ Ⓙ	30 Ⓕ Ⓖ Ⓗ Ⓙ	50 Ⓕ Ⓖ Ⓗ Ⓙ	70 Ⓕ Ⓖ Ⓗ Ⓙ
11 Ⓐ Ⓑ Ⓒ Ⓓ	31 Ⓐ Ⓑ Ⓒ Ⓓ	51 Ⓐ Ⓑ Ⓒ Ⓓ	71 Ⓐ Ⓑ Ⓒ Ⓓ
12 Ⓕ Ⓖ Ⓗ Ⓙ	32 Ⓕ Ⓖ Ⓗ Ⓙ	52 Ⓕ Ⓖ Ⓗ Ⓙ	72 Ⓕ Ⓖ Ⓗ Ⓙ
13 Ⓐ Ⓑ Ⓒ Ⓓ	33 Ⓐ Ⓑ Ⓒ Ⓓ	53 Ⓐ Ⓑ Ⓒ Ⓓ	73 Ⓐ Ⓑ Ⓒ Ⓓ
14 Ⓕ Ⓖ Ⓗ Ⓙ	34 Ⓕ Ⓖ Ⓗ Ⓙ	54 Ⓕ Ⓖ Ⓗ Ⓙ	74 Ⓕ Ⓖ Ⓗ Ⓙ
15 Ⓐ Ⓑ Ⓒ Ⓓ	35 Ⓐ Ⓑ Ⓒ Ⓓ	55 Ⓐ Ⓑ Ⓒ Ⓓ	75 Ⓐ Ⓑ Ⓒ Ⓓ
16 Ⓕ Ⓖ Ⓗ Ⓙ	36 Ⓕ Ⓖ Ⓗ Ⓙ	56 Ⓕ Ⓖ Ⓗ Ⓙ	
17 Ⓐ Ⓑ Ⓒ Ⓓ	37 Ⓐ Ⓑ Ⓒ Ⓓ	57 Ⓐ Ⓑ Ⓒ Ⓓ	
18 Ⓕ Ⓖ Ⓗ Ⓙ	38 Ⓕ Ⓖ Ⓗ Ⓙ	58 Ⓕ Ⓖ Ⓗ Ⓙ	
19 Ⓐ Ⓑ Ⓒ Ⓓ	39 Ⓐ Ⓑ Ⓒ Ⓓ	59 Ⓐ Ⓑ Ⓒ Ⓓ	
20 Ⓕ Ⓖ Ⓗ Ⓙ	40 Ⓕ Ⓖ Ⓗ Ⓙ	60 Ⓕ Ⓖ Ⓗ Ⓙ	

MATHEMATICS

1 Ⓐ Ⓑ Ⓒ Ⓓ Ⓔ	16 Ⓕ Ⓖ Ⓗ Ⓙ Ⓚ	31 Ⓐ Ⓑ Ⓒ Ⓓ Ⓔ	46 Ⓕ Ⓖ Ⓗ Ⓙ Ⓚ
2 Ⓕ Ⓖ Ⓗ Ⓙ Ⓚ	17 Ⓐ Ⓑ Ⓒ Ⓓ Ⓔ	32 Ⓕ Ⓖ Ⓗ Ⓙ Ⓚ	47 Ⓐ Ⓑ Ⓒ Ⓓ Ⓔ
3 Ⓐ Ⓑ Ⓒ Ⓓ Ⓔ	18 Ⓕ Ⓖ Ⓗ Ⓙ Ⓚ	33 Ⓐ Ⓑ Ⓒ Ⓓ Ⓔ	48 Ⓕ Ⓖ Ⓗ Ⓙ Ⓚ
4 Ⓕ Ⓖ Ⓗ Ⓙ Ⓚ	19 Ⓐ Ⓑ Ⓒ Ⓓ Ⓔ	34 Ⓕ Ⓖ Ⓗ Ⓙ Ⓚ	49 Ⓐ Ⓑ Ⓒ Ⓓ Ⓔ
5 Ⓐ Ⓑ Ⓒ Ⓓ Ⓔ	20 Ⓕ Ⓖ Ⓗ Ⓙ Ⓚ	35 Ⓐ Ⓑ Ⓒ Ⓓ Ⓔ	50 Ⓕ Ⓖ Ⓗ Ⓙ Ⓚ
6 Ⓕ Ⓖ Ⓗ Ⓙ Ⓚ	21 Ⓐ Ⓑ Ⓒ Ⓓ Ⓔ	36 Ⓕ Ⓖ Ⓗ Ⓙ Ⓚ	51 Ⓐ Ⓑ Ⓒ Ⓓ Ⓔ
7 Ⓐ Ⓑ Ⓒ Ⓓ Ⓔ	22 Ⓕ Ⓖ Ⓗ Ⓙ Ⓚ	37 Ⓐ Ⓑ Ⓒ Ⓓ Ⓔ	52 Ⓕ Ⓖ Ⓗ Ⓙ Ⓚ
8 Ⓕ Ⓖ Ⓗ Ⓙ Ⓚ	23 Ⓐ Ⓑ Ⓒ Ⓓ Ⓔ	38 Ⓕ Ⓖ Ⓗ Ⓙ Ⓚ	53 Ⓐ Ⓑ Ⓒ Ⓓ Ⓔ
9 Ⓕ Ⓖ Ⓗ Ⓙ Ⓚ	24 Ⓕ Ⓖ Ⓗ Ⓙ Ⓚ	39 Ⓐ Ⓑ Ⓒ Ⓓ Ⓔ	54 Ⓕ Ⓖ Ⓗ Ⓙ Ⓚ
10 Ⓕ Ⓖ Ⓗ Ⓙ Ⓚ	25 Ⓐ Ⓑ Ⓒ Ⓓ Ⓔ	40 Ⓕ Ⓖ Ⓗ Ⓙ Ⓚ	55 Ⓐ Ⓑ Ⓒ Ⓓ Ⓔ
11 Ⓐ Ⓑ Ⓒ Ⓓ Ⓔ	26 Ⓕ Ⓖ Ⓗ Ⓙ Ⓚ	41 Ⓐ Ⓑ Ⓒ Ⓓ Ⓔ	56 Ⓕ Ⓖ Ⓗ Ⓙ Ⓚ
12 Ⓕ Ⓖ Ⓗ Ⓙ Ⓚ	27 Ⓐ Ⓑ Ⓒ Ⓓ Ⓔ	42 Ⓕ Ⓖ Ⓗ Ⓙ Ⓚ	57 Ⓐ Ⓑ Ⓒ Ⓓ Ⓔ
13 Ⓐ Ⓑ Ⓒ Ⓓ Ⓔ	28 Ⓕ Ⓖ Ⓗ Ⓙ Ⓚ	43 Ⓐ Ⓑ Ⓒ Ⓓ Ⓔ	58 Ⓕ Ⓖ Ⓗ Ⓙ Ⓚ
14 Ⓕ Ⓖ Ⓗ Ⓙ Ⓚ	29 Ⓐ Ⓑ Ⓒ Ⓓ Ⓔ	44 Ⓕ Ⓖ Ⓗ Ⓙ Ⓚ	59 Ⓐ Ⓑ Ⓒ Ⓓ Ⓔ
15 Ⓐ Ⓑ Ⓒ Ⓓ Ⓔ	30 Ⓕ Ⓖ Ⓗ Ⓙ Ⓚ	45 Ⓐ Ⓑ Ⓒ Ⓓ Ⓔ	60 Ⓕ Ⓖ Ⓗ Ⓙ Ⓚ

READING

1 Ⓐ Ⓑ Ⓒ Ⓓ	11 Ⓐ Ⓑ Ⓒ Ⓓ	21 Ⓐ Ⓑ Ⓒ Ⓓ	31 Ⓐ Ⓑ Ⓒ Ⓓ
2 Ⓕ Ⓖ Ⓗ Ⓙ	12 Ⓕ Ⓖ Ⓗ Ⓙ	22 Ⓕ Ⓖ Ⓗ Ⓙ	32 Ⓕ Ⓖ Ⓗ Ⓙ
3 Ⓐ Ⓑ Ⓒ Ⓓ	13 Ⓐ Ⓑ Ⓒ Ⓓ	23 Ⓐ Ⓑ Ⓒ Ⓓ	33 Ⓐ Ⓑ Ⓒ Ⓓ
4 Ⓕ Ⓖ Ⓗ Ⓙ	14 Ⓕ Ⓖ Ⓗ Ⓙ	24 Ⓕ Ⓖ Ⓗ Ⓙ	34 Ⓕ Ⓖ Ⓗ Ⓙ
5 Ⓐ Ⓑ Ⓒ Ⓓ	15 Ⓐ Ⓑ Ⓒ Ⓓ	25 Ⓐ Ⓑ Ⓒ Ⓓ	35 Ⓐ Ⓑ Ⓒ Ⓓ
6 Ⓕ Ⓖ Ⓗ Ⓙ	16 Ⓕ Ⓖ Ⓗ Ⓙ	26 Ⓕ Ⓖ Ⓗ Ⓙ	36 Ⓕ Ⓖ Ⓗ Ⓙ
7 Ⓐ Ⓑ Ⓒ Ⓓ	17 Ⓐ Ⓑ Ⓒ Ⓓ	27 Ⓐ Ⓑ Ⓒ Ⓓ	37 Ⓐ Ⓑ Ⓒ Ⓓ
8 Ⓕ Ⓖ Ⓗ Ⓙ	18 Ⓕ Ⓖ Ⓗ Ⓙ	28 Ⓕ Ⓖ Ⓗ Ⓙ	38 Ⓕ Ⓖ Ⓗ Ⓙ
9 Ⓐ Ⓑ Ⓒ Ⓓ	19 Ⓐ Ⓑ Ⓒ Ⓓ	29 Ⓐ Ⓑ Ⓒ Ⓓ	39 Ⓐ Ⓑ Ⓒ Ⓓ
10 Ⓕ Ⓖ Ⓗ Ⓙ	20 Ⓕ Ⓖ Ⓗ Ⓙ	30 Ⓕ Ⓖ Ⓗ Ⓙ	40 Ⓕ Ⓖ Ⓗ Ⓙ

SCIENCE

1 Ⓐ Ⓑ Ⓒ Ⓓ	11 Ⓐ Ⓑ Ⓒ Ⓓ	21 Ⓐ Ⓑ Ⓒ Ⓓ	31 Ⓐ Ⓑ Ⓒ Ⓓ
2 Ⓕ Ⓖ Ⓗ Ⓙ	12 Ⓕ Ⓖ Ⓗ Ⓙ	22 Ⓕ Ⓖ Ⓗ Ⓙ	32 Ⓕ Ⓖ Ⓗ Ⓙ
3 Ⓐ Ⓑ Ⓒ Ⓓ	13 Ⓐ Ⓑ Ⓒ Ⓓ	23 Ⓐ Ⓑ Ⓒ Ⓓ	33 Ⓐ Ⓑ Ⓒ Ⓓ
4 Ⓕ Ⓖ Ⓗ Ⓙ	14 Ⓕ Ⓖ Ⓗ Ⓙ	24 Ⓕ Ⓖ Ⓗ Ⓙ	34 Ⓕ Ⓖ Ⓗ Ⓙ
5 Ⓐ Ⓑ Ⓒ Ⓓ	15 Ⓐ Ⓑ Ⓒ Ⓓ	25 Ⓐ Ⓑ Ⓒ Ⓓ	35 Ⓐ Ⓑ Ⓒ Ⓓ
6 Ⓕ Ⓖ Ⓗ Ⓙ	16 Ⓕ Ⓖ Ⓗ Ⓙ	26 Ⓕ Ⓖ Ⓗ Ⓙ	36 Ⓕ Ⓖ Ⓗ Ⓙ
7 Ⓐ Ⓑ Ⓒ Ⓓ	17 Ⓐ Ⓑ Ⓒ Ⓓ	27 Ⓐ Ⓑ Ⓒ Ⓓ	37 Ⓐ Ⓑ Ⓒ Ⓓ
8 Ⓕ Ⓖ Ⓗ Ⓙ	18 Ⓕ Ⓖ Ⓗ Ⓙ	28 Ⓕ Ⓖ Ⓗ Ⓙ	38 Ⓕ Ⓖ Ⓗ Ⓙ
9 Ⓐ Ⓑ Ⓒ Ⓓ	19 Ⓐ Ⓑ Ⓒ Ⓓ	29 Ⓐ Ⓑ Ⓒ Ⓓ	39 Ⓐ Ⓑ Ⓒ Ⓓ
10 Ⓕ Ⓖ Ⓗ Ⓙ	20 Ⓕ Ⓖ Ⓗ Ⓙ	30 Ⓕ Ⓖ Ⓗ Ⓙ	40 Ⓕ Ⓖ Ⓗ Ⓙ

RAW SCORES		SCALE SCORES		DATE TAKEN:
ENGLISH	_____	ENGLISH	_____	
MATHEMATICS	_____	MATHEMATICS	_____	ENGLISH/WRITING _____
READING	_____	READING	_____	
SCIENCE	_____	SCIENCE	_____	_____
				COMPOSITE SCORE

Refer to the Scoring Worksheet on page 150 for help in determining your Raw and Scale Scores.

You may wish to remove these sample answer document pages to respond to the practice ACT Writing Test.

Begin WRITING TEST here.

_____

_____

_____

_____

_____

_____

_____

_____

_____

_____

_____

_____

_____

_____

_____

_____

_____

_____

_____

_____

_____

_____

_____

_____

_____

_____

If you need more space, please continue on the next page.

1

Do not write in this shaded area.

WRITING TEST

If you need more space, please continue on the back of this page.

2

Do not write in this shaded area.

WRITING TEST

If you need more space, please continue on the next page.

3

PLEASE DO NOT WRITE IN THIS AREA.

WRITING TEST

_____

_____

_____

_____

_____

_____

_____

_____

_____

_____

_____

_____

_____

_____

_____

_____

_____

_____

_____

_____

_____

_____

_____

_____

_____

_____

_____

STOP here with the Writing Test.

4

1 ■ ■ ■ ■ ■ ■ ■ ■ 1

ENGLISH TEST

45 Minutes—75 Questions

DIRECTIONS: In the passages that follow, some words and phrases are underlined and numbered. In the answer column, you will find alternatives for the words and phrases that are underlined. Choose the alternative that you think is best, and fill in the corresponding bubble on your answer sheet. If you think that the original version is best, choose "NO CHANGE," which will always be either answer choice A or F. You will also find questions about a particular section of the passage, or about the entire passage. These questions will be identified by either an underlined portion or by a number in a box. Look for the answer that clearly expresses the idea, is consistent with the style and tone of the passage, and makes the correct use of standard written English. Read the passage through once before answering the questions. For some questions, you should read beyond the indicated portion before you answer.

PASSAGE I

A Blessing in Disguise

Last spring, I <u>had been</u> fortunate to be chosen to
₁
participate in an exchange study program. In my

application essay, I was careful to express how much I

wanted to see France. I suppose my excitement really

came through in my words. Once I knew that I was going,

all I could think about was the fun of foreign travel and

making all sorts of new and interesting friends. While

traveling was inspiring and meeting people was exciting,

nothing about my semester in France was what I expected.

The moment I arrived in Paris, I was greeted by a nice

French <u>couple who</u> would become my host parents. The
₂
bit of French I had taken in high school began

<u>pouring from my mouth. Speaking</u> the language would
₃
only become more natural over the course of the semester.

At the airport, we all got into the couple's little two-door

hatchback and began the journey to their townhouse in the

suburbs. We talked the whole way there, getting to know

one another bit by bit. Everyday thereafter, I <u>eat</u> breakfast
₄

1. **A.** NO CHANGE
   B. will be
   C. was
   D. have been

2. **F.** NO CHANGE
   G. couple that
   H. couple, Jean and Christine
   J. couple, in a few hours

3. **A.** NO CHANGE
   B. pouring from my mouth, speaking
   C. pouring from my mouth speaking
   D. pouring from my mouth by speaking

4. **F.** NO CHANGE
   G. was eating
   H. began to eat
   J. would eat

GO ON TO THE NEXT PAGE.

1 ■ ■ ■ ■ ■ ■ ■ ■ **1**

with the two of them, <u>so</u> we'd all go our separate ways for
5
the day. In the evening, my host mother would make

delicious dinners for the three of us. My entire experience

was joyous and exhilarating until I received some shocking

news from my program coordinator: there had been a

death in my <u>host parents</u> extended family. They had to
6

travel outside France for several <u>weeks, so tending</u> to all
7
the business that arises from an unforeseen death. That

afternoon, I had to move out of one family's house and

into another so I'd have to <u>repack my suitcases.</u>
8
The exchange coordinator told me I'd have a roommate

this time and asked whether I could share a bedroom with

an <u>English speaker or someone who didn't speak English.</u>
9
To avoid the temptation to speak my native language,

I asked not to be placed with an English-speaking

roommate. When I got to my new room, I introduced

myself to my new roommate Paolo, a Brazilian the same

age as I, <u>whom</u> I was surprised to find playing one of my
10
favorite CDs on the stereo!

<u>In just a few hours, we knew we'd be</u>
11
<u>attached at the hip for the rest of the term.</u>
11
    I left France with many stories, so when people ask me

what my favorite part of the trip was, they are always

surprised to hear me <u>talk, about my Brazilian friend Paolo,</u>
12
and the scores of weekdays in class, weeknights on the

town, and weekends exploring France we enjoyed together.

---

5. **A.** NO CHANGE
     B. since
     C. therefore
     D. then

6. **F.** NO CHANGE
     G. host parent's
     H. host parents'
     J. host's parents

7. **A.** NO CHANGE
     B. weeks to tend
     C. weeks, tended
     D. weeks

8. **F.** NO CHANGE
     G. which would probably be about the same size.
     H. which I hope would be closer to the supermarket.
     J. OMIT the underlined portion and end the sentence with a period.

9. **A.** NO CHANGE
     B. English speaker and one who was not.
     C. English speaker or a person, not an English speaker.
     D. English speaker.

10. **F.** NO CHANGE
     G. which
     H. that
     J. he who

11. Given that all the choices are true, which one provides the most relevant information with regard to the narrator's friendship with Paolo?
     A. NO CHANGE
     B. He hadn't heard of a lot of my CDs, though.
     C. We didn't have a lot of classes together, but at least we liked the same music.
     D. I didn't speak Portuguese, so it took some time to start to understand each other.

12. **F.** NO CHANGE
     G. talk about my Brazilian friend Paolo
     H. talk about my Brazilian friend, Paolo,
     J. talk, about my Brazilian friend Paolo,

GO ON TO THE NEXT PAGE.

1 ▪ ▪ ▪ ▪ ▪ ▪ ▪ ▪ 1

<u>I love people, how they end up being so similar, but are</u>
<u>   13</u>

<u>so different.</u> The most <u>valuable</u> lesson I gained from
<u>   13   14</u>
studying in France wasn't just to respect the French people

but to respect all people, for your next best friend could be

just a continent away. ⬛15⬛

13. A. NO CHANGE
B. I love how people seem so different and are so similar.
C. People seem so different, so I love how they end up being so similar.
D. I love how people can seem so different, but end up being so similar.

14. Which of the choices would be most appropriate here?
F. NO CHANGE
G. enjoyable
H. fun
J. supportive

15. Which of the following sentences, if inserted here, would best conclude the essay as well as maintain the positive tone established earlier in the essay?
A. France is an interesting place once you grasp the language.
B. I would recommend an exchange program to anyone who wants to experience foreign cultures.
C. High school is going to be quite boring now, especially since my new friend Paolo won't be there.
D. It will be nice to graduate at the end of this year.

PASSAGE II

My Favorite Lunch Spot

A few blocks south of the <u>apartment, I'm renting,</u> Joe's
<u>   16</u>
Lunch Bucket serves up amazing sandwiches. The owner

runs the place, so he stays open as late as he has

customers, usually until some time after midnight. The

restaurant <u>is</u> at the end of an alley, and if you sit on the last
<u>   17</u>
stool by the window, you can see the big public

<u>fountain, in</u> the adjacent square. There are usually swarms
<u>   18</u>
of children and teenagers milling around the area; no one

really enforces the curfew, especially in the summer when

the nights are warm and families stroll around the shops

and public spaces downtown.

[1] Joe has a menu stuck to the front window with

masking tape that is yellowed and cracked from years in

the sun. [2] Never mind the dingy interior, noisy kitchen,

and lack of parking. [3] I just go there for the food.

16. F. NO CHANGE
G. apartment I'm renting
H. apartment I'm renting,
J. apartment, I'm renting

17. A. NO CHANGE
B. was located
C. had been
D. will be

18. F. NO CHANGE
G. fountain in
H. fountain in,
J. fountain; in

GO ON TO THE NEXT PAGE.

1 ■ ■ ■ ■ ■ ■ ■ ■ **1**

[4] I've never stopped to read it and, as far as I can tell, neither have the other regulars. [5] I like to sit at the bar along the window and relax with the <u>sinfully deliciousness</u>
19
of Joe's Special Rueben. [6] <u>Newcomers to Joe's who</u>
20
<u>have never seen his creations</u> marvel at the stack of
20
corned beef and <u>sauerkraut; spilling</u> from the bread onto
21
my paper plate. 22

Joe's is my home away from home. The sign outside is
23
hardly eye-catching and the restaurant always appears to be dimly lit, but one can't help noticing the large smiley face decal affixed to the front door that reads "Keep Smiling!" The sandwiches certainly make me smile, but I can't say they do the same for Joe himself. His constant ugly expression <u>belies, the</u> care that he takes with his
24
meats, breads, and cheeses. So, too, does his quirky restaurant. The counters are dented and scratched from years of knife abuse. The old refrigerator case
<u>clicks and whines</u> constantly. As I savor my sandwich, my
25
gaze always drifts toward the caulk along the window panes, once white, which is slowly deteriorating with the rest of the place. In fact, I've often thought to offer Joe my painting services in exchange for some sustenance. 26

19. **A.** NO CHANGE
    B. sinfully delicious
    C. sinful deliciousness
    D. sinful delicious

20. **F.** NO CHANGE
    G. Newcomers to Joe's
    H. Newcomers to Joe's who need a menu to order
    J. People who've never had the pleasure of a Joe's sandwich

21. **A.** NO CHANGE
    B. sauerkraut, spilling
    C. sauerkraut, spilling,
    D. sauerkraut spilling

22. For the sake of logic and coherence, Sentence 4 of this paragraph should be placed:
    F. where it is now.
    G. before Sentence 1.
    H. after Sentence 2.
    J. after Sentence 1.

23. Which choice most effectively guides the reader from the preceding paragraph into this new paragraph?
    A. NO CHANGE
    B. Joe takes good care of his property.
    C. May be Joe learned his sandwich secrets at culinary school.
    D. Good food is the key to Joe's success.

24. **F.** NO CHANGE
    G. belies that the
    H. belies, and the
    J. belies the

25. **A.** NO CHANGE
    B. clicks to whine
    C. clicking and whining
    D. click and whine

26. At this point, the writer wants to add a sentence that would further describe the condition of the restaurant. Which of the following sentences would best accomplish this?
    F. Regardless of the appearance of the place, I still enjoy my delicious sandwich.
    G. I would like to see who his maintenance man is.
    H. If I had a restaurant, I'd make sure it was clean.
    J. People seem to ignore the building, though.

GO ON TO THE NEXT PAGE.

1 ■ ■ ■ ■ ■ ■ ■ ■ 1

The food is, after all, the only charm this little place needs.

A lot of people pay daily visits to the sandwich shop.

I know <u>much</u> of their faces by now, but I could more
₂₇
easily recall their tastes in sandwiches. Older people like

the classics—chicken salad, corned beef, and the like. [28]
Kids come in after school for grilled cheeses or Joe's

tuna salad. <u>Back home, as I am reminiscing on this place,</u>
₂₉
<u>I picture all these people with their favorite meals.</u>
₂₉
Perhaps it's the familiarity that makes Joe's my favorite

sandwich shop. I know that I can come in whenever I

please and someone would look away from a savory

sandwich and offer a friendly hello. It's nice to know that

Joe's Lunch <u>Bucket. And</u> its neighborly ambience are just
₃₀
a short walk away.

27. A. NO CHANGE
B. many
C. mostly
D. none

28. The writer is considering deleting the following phrase from the preceding sentence:

chicken salad, corned beef, and the like.

If the writer were to make this deletion, the essay would primarily lose:
F. foreshadowing of the conclusion.
G. irrelevant information.
H. specific descriptive material.
J. an understatement of important information.

29. A. NO CHANGE
B. When I am back home and reminiscing, I picture all of these people with their favorite meals.
C. Back home, I picture all these people with the favorite meals when I reminisce.
D. Reminiscing back home makes me picture all these people with their favorite meals.

30. F. NO CHANGE
G. Bucket, and
H. Bucket and
J. Bucket;

PASSAGE III

Slowly Spanning the Straits

The Straits of Mackinac, located between Lake Huron

and Lake Michigan, divide Michigan's Upper and Lower

Peninsulas. Native Americans in the former wilderness

territory <u>know</u> how to paddle between several islands to
₃₁
make their way across the Straits. Settlers in the

<u>eighteenth, and nineteenth,</u> centuries crossed the Straits by
₃₂

ferry. However, ferries soon <u>prove</u> to be costly in both lives
₃₃

31. A. NO CHANGE
B. knew
C. have known
D. knows

32. F. NO CHANGE
G. eighteenth, and nineteenth
H. eighteenth and nineteenth
J. eighteenth and nineteenth,

33. A. NO CHANGE
B. proved
C. proves
D. have proven

GO ON TO THE NEXT PAGE.

1 ■ ■ ■ ■ ■ ■ ■ ■ **1**

and money. By the 1880s, the Michigan Legislature had
begun discussing the idea of building a bridge to span the,
<u>34</u>

Strait noting the success of the newly-built Brooklyn
<u>35</u>
Bridge. However, many hurdles stood in the way.
<u>35</u>
    During the late nineteenth century, the Legislature heard
plans for an elaborate system of bridges and causeways
that would use three islands as intermediate points.

However, no action was ever taken <u>on the project.</u> In the
<u>36</u>
1920s, an assembly ordered resumption of ferry service

between the <u>peninsulas; so</u> within five years, Governor
<u>37</u>

Fred Green felt <u>there great cost</u> warranted investigation of
<u>38</u>
the bridge idea once again. The State Highway Authority
concluded that a bridge could be built for around
$30 million.

    In the 1930s, The Mackinac Bridge Authority twice
sought federal funding for construction of the bridge, but
was denied each time. Even so, a route was plotted and
careful study of the lakebed and the rock below began.
Any progress, <u>however, that</u> was put on hold for the
<u>39</u>
duration of World War II, and it was not until 1950 that
funds were fully invested in the bridge project.

    Construction of the Mackinac Bridge finally began in
1954. It would become a crowning achievement for design
engineer David Steinman and, for years, would be

34. F. NO CHANGE
    G. Giving up by the 1880s
    H. Until the 1880s
    J. In terms of the 1880s

35. The writer is considering deleting the underlined por-
    tion from the sentence. If the writer were to delete this
    phrase, the essay would primarily lose:
    A. a minor detail in the essay's opening paragraph.
    B. an explanation of the impetus for discussion of a
       potential bridge.
    C. the writer's opinion about the historical signifi-
       cance of the Mackinac Bridge.
    D. an indication of Michigan's desire to keep pace
       with the transportation development taking place in
       New York City.

36. F. NO CHANGE
    G. for the project
    H. by the project
    J. of the project

37. A. NO CHANGE
    B. peninsulas so
    C. peninsulas, but
    D. peninsulas; and

38. F. NO CHANGE
    G. their great cost
    H. it's great cost
    J. its great cost

39. A. NO CHANGE
    B. however that
    C. however
    D. however,

GO ON TO THE NEXT PAGE.

1 ▪ ▪ ▪ ▪ ▪ ▪ ▪ ▪ 1

the longest suspension bridge in the world. [40] U.S. Steel Company received the contract to build the massive steel superstructure. It was a two-and-a-half year ordeal that cost the state more than $44 million and cost five men

their lives. On November 1, 1957, the Mackinac Bridge, in spite of decades of problems, opened to traffic. Those who did not know the history of the project were elated by the bridge's "on schedule" completion.

Today, the Mackinac Bridge is as solid as ever. In 1998 it collected its 100 millionth toll. It will continue to serve

drivers and highway travelers well into the future and

stand as a monument to Michigan's perseverance.

40. If the writer were to delete the preceding sentence, the paragraph would primarily lose:
F. an explanation of how the Mackinac Bridge was erected.
G. details about the significance of the Mackinac Bridge.
H. background information on the history of building bridges.
J. biographical information about David Steinman.

41. A. NO CHANGE
B. On November 1, 1957, the Mackinac Bridge opened, in spite of decades of problems, to traffic.
C. The Mackinac Bridge opened to traffic, in spite of decades of problems, on November 1, 1957.
D. In spite of decades of problems, the Mackinac Bridge opened to traffic on November 1, 1957.

42. F. NO CHANGE
G. Since,
H. Meanwhile,
J. Historically,

43. A. NO CHANGE
B. highway drivers and travelers
C. drivers—and highway travelers—
D. highway travelers

44. Which of the following alternatives to the underlined portion would be LEAST acceptable in terms of the context of this sentence?
F. mark the union of Michigan's two peninsulas.
G. serve as a symbol of suspension bridges around the world.
H. provide an image of strength and grace to all who cross it.
J. pay tribute to the progress of a great state.

Question 45 asks about the preceding passage as a whole.

45. Suppose the writer had intended to write a brief essay that describes the entire process of designing and building the Mackinac Bridge. Would this essay successfully fulfill the writer's goal?
A. Yes, because it offers such details as the material of the superstructure, the identity of the designer, and the cost of construction.
B. Yes, because it explains in detail each step in the design and construction of the bridge.
C. No, because it focuses primarily on the difficulty and delay in seeing construction of a bridge across the Strait come to fruition.
D. No, because it is primarily a historical essay about the motivation behind the bridge project.

GO ON TO THE NEXT PAGE.

1 ■ ■ ■ ■ ■ ■ ■ ■ 1

> The following paragraphs may or may not be in the most logical order. You may be asked questions about the logical order of the paragraphs, as well as where to place sentences logically within any given paragraph.

Care with Cards

[1]

Does anyone have a real hobby anymore? I must admit I was disheartened when my brother, younger by 10 years, didn't want to go into the sports card shop with me. We went to a department store instead. Every boy
$\quad$ 46

which I have known as a kid had a box in his
$\quad$ 47

room, brimming, with cards. Some boys were into
$\quad$ 48
basketball and football cards, but my passion was for baseball cards. I couldn't believe the shocked look on my brother's face when he saw some of the expensive offerings in the shop's window display. He just couldn't appreciate the history behind the cards and the care taken to preserve them over the decades. For him, no piece of cardboard <u>are</u> worth any sum of money. He would rather
$\quad$ 49
have a video screen to distract him.

[2]

[1] I appreciate the arguments in favor of television,
$\quad$ 50
video games, and other electronic entertainment.
$\quad$ 50

46. **F.** NO CHANGE
G. We decided to go to a department store instead, to look for shoes.
H. (We were in the mall to do some shoe shopping.)
J. OMIT the underlined portion.

47. **A.** NO CHANGE
B. whom I knew
C. I knew
D. OMIT the underlined portion.

48. **F.** NO CHANGE
G. room, brimming
H. room brimming
J. room brimming,

49. **A.** NO CHANGE
B. has
C. was
D. could of been

50. Which choice would most effectively and appropriately lead the reader from the topic of Paragraph 1 to that of Paragraph 2?
F. NO CHANGE
G. Electronic forms of entertainment involve the creative mind instead of the organized, mathematical mind.
H. I find nothing entertaining about television, video games, and other electronic entertainment.
J. Baseball cards decreased in popularity while electronic entertainment has increased.

GO ON TO THE NEXT PAGE.

1 ■ ■ ■ ■ ■ ■ ■ ■ ■ 1

[2] The technology is dynamic <u>and, for the most part,</u> engaging. [3] There's indeed something for everyone.
51

[4] I also believe, however, that these new forms of entertainment have taken time away from "unplugged" fun. [5] <u>A good hands-on hobby should be an important</u>
52
<u>part of any childhood.</u> [6] Instead of simple story books,
52
toddlers have interactive learning computers that read for them. [7] When children aren't watching satellite television, they have console games to entertain them.

[8] It seems to me that more and more of the joys of childhood are being lost to the allure of the video screen.

[3]

Building a sports card collection is a rewarding endeavor for children and adults <u>alike that is fun for everyone.</u> It
53
teaches quality lessons, such as patience and organization. For young fingers, it develops a careful touch. I remember how hard I tried to slide each card into a plastic sleeve without damaging the delicate corners of the card. Nearly <u>all</u> weekend, there was a card show at the local mall where
54
I learned to bargain and trade for all the cards that I needed to fill the gaps in my collection. Although I very much enjoyed spending time alone looking at the cards, <u>I often shared</u> the experience with others. Card collecting
55

is a social activity <u>too encouraging</u> the old and young to
56
swap cards and stories. Today's electronic entertainment, however, keeps people apart and does little to benefit developing minds. The video screen silences spectators as it holds their attention <u>to the screen.</u> Television and video
57
games deliver instant gratification. Tune a channel or insert a disc and off you go. Hours and hours of sedentary

---

51. Which of the following alternatives to the underlined portion would be LEAST acceptable?
  A. and, generally,
  B. but, thoroughly
  C. and, therefore,
  D. and, as such,

52. For the sake of logic and coherence of Paragraph 2 this sentence should be:
  F. placed where it is now.
  G. placed after Sentence 1.
  H. placed after Sentence 7.
  J. OMITTED, because the paragraph focuses only on electronic forms of entertainment.

53. A. NO CHANGE
  B. alike.
  C. alike, which can benefit both groups.
  D. alike that want a wholesome hobby.

54. F. NO CHANGE
  G. each and every
  H. every
  J. every unique

55. A. NO CHANGE
  B. we often shared
  C. I often share
  D. I then shared

56. F. NO CHANGE
  G. too, encouraging
  H. too; encouraging
  J. too, by encouraging

57. A. NO CHANGE
  B. at the screen.
  C. for the screen.
  D. OMIT the underlined portion and end the sentence with a period.

GO ON TO THE NEXT PAGE.

1 ■ ■ ■ ■ ■ ■ ■ ■ **1**

satisfaction are at their fingertips!
                    58

[4]

I am concerned that this trend toward electronics will
lead to less physical activity and make the fun in life
effortless and instant available. The younger generation
                    59
needs to know that pleasure can also come from a hobby
that demands patience, care, hard work, and concentration.

58. F. NO CHANGE
    G. your
    H. one's
    J. people's

59. A. NO CHANGE
    B. instants
    C. instantly
    D. more instant

Question 60 asks about the preceding passage as a whole.

---

60. Suppose the writer had chosen to write an essay that
    indicates that sports card collecting is superior to
    electronic entertainment. Would this essay fulfill the
    writer's goal?
    F. No, because the writer admits that electronic enter-
       tainment has become more popular than sports card
       collecting.
    G. No, because the writer states that electronic enter-
       tainment is dynamic and engaging.
    H. Yes, because the writer claims that, unlike elec-
       tronic entertainment, sports card collecting teaches
       valuable life skills such as organization and care-
       ful handling of fragile items, and also provides a
       medium for social interaction.
    J. Yes, because the writer suggests that any hands-on
       hobby is better than watching television.

PASSAGE V

> The following paragraphs may or may not be in the most
> logical order. You may be asked questions about the log-
> ical order of the paragraphs, as well as where to place
> sentences logically within any given paragraph.

Spies Online

[1]

People who choose to use a personal computer to
connect to the Internet should know the risks that this
poses. Most computer users have some experience with
slow computers, unexplainable program crashes, and
indecipherable warnings about missing system files. These
same computer users are more likely to wait, until
                                          61

61. A. NO CHANGE
    B. wait, until,
    C. wait until,
    D. wait until

GO ON TO THE NEXT PAGE.

1 ■ ■ ■ ■ ■ ■ ■ ■ 1

these problems get too bad to manage. They would buy a new system entirely before trying to fix their current one. Online, the biggest threat is spyware, which is crippling unsecured computers and data networks around the world.

[2]

Like a computer virus, a spyware program is not purely malicious. The developer of the spyware program stands to gain from installing it on your computer, often just in information, but usually financially, too. These programs may monitor your online activity and track your keystrokes and buying habits. This data is sold to marketing agencies for demographic research, and to more unscrupulous firms that will bombard you with email solicitations and sales calls. Not all spyware; however has legitimate commerce behind it.

[3]

Both computer viruses and spyware can cause problems. Other programs show up as system messages, luring unaware users to click their way into corrupting their own operating systems and revealing sensitive personal information. Not only do these programs cause a depletion of system resources, but they waste time and test the nerves of even the most patient user.

[4]

There are plenty of solutions designed to eliminate the spyware problem. The first step is to rid your computer of any unwanted programs. Detection utilities that detect spyware are widely available, many at no cost,

---

62. **F.** NO CHANGE
    G. spyware, which crippling
    H. spyware, and it's crippled by
    J. spyware, and its crippled

63. **A.** NO CHANGE
    B. As with
    C. Unlike
    D. Comparable to

64. **F.** NO CHANGE
    G. except
    H. always
    J. instead of

65. **A.** NO CHANGE
    B. spyware, however,
    C. spyware, however
    D. spyware however

66. Which choice is the most effective first sentence of Paragraph 3?
    F. NO CHANGE
    G. Among the most serious spyware programs are those called "keystroke loggers."
    H. Most people don't know their computers are infected with spyware.
    J. Due to unsecured internet connections, spyware is far more prevalent than computer viruses.

67. **A.** NO CHANGE
    B. initiate depletion of system resources,
    C. lead to depleting system resources,
    D. deplete system resources,

68. **F.** NO CHANGE
    G. Detection utilities
    H. Spyware can be found by detection utilities that
    J. Detection utilities that find spyware

GO ON TO THE NEXT PAGE.

1 ■ ■ ■ ■ ■ ■ ■ 1

that scans the computer for undesirable programs and

<u>then removes them.</u> Once this is accomplished, the utilities
     69

monitor the system constantly to prevent any new

installation of spyware. It is important to understand how

your computer <u>protects</u> and to keep your software updated.
                     70

[5]

Good web surfing habits are essential, too. Avoid web

sites you don't trust. <u>Spyware originates from many
                            71

kinds of web sites.</u> Go online <u>never</u> without a firewall and
     71   72

active virus and spyware protection. Remember that a

computer is just a machine. If you turn it on and never

touch <u>it, it</u> will likely remain fast and reliable. It is
       73

generally what the user does to the computer that affects it.

---

69. **A.** NO CHANGE
    B. that scan the computer for undesirable programs and remove them.
    C. that scan the computer for undesirable programs and removes them.
    D. that scans the computer for undesirable programs then removing them.

70. **F.** NO CHANGE
    G. has been protected
    H. protects them
    J. is protected

71. In this paragraph, the writer intends to recommend a number of sound web surfing habits. This is to be the second recommendation. Given that all of the choices are true, which one would best accomplish the writer's intention?
    A. NO CHANGE
    B. Don't buy anything online from a store with no physical address.
    C. Shut down your computer when you aren't using it.
    D. Know the various names of spyware programs.

72. The best placement for the underlined portion would be:
    F. where it is now.
    G. after the word *Go*.
    H. after the word *firewall*.
    J. at the beginning of the sentence.

73. **A.** NO CHANGE
    B. it
    C. it, while it
    D. it, it,

Questions 74 and 75 ask about the preceding passage as a whole.

---

74. Upon reviewing this essay and realizing that some information has been left out, the writer composes the following sentence, incorporating that missing information:

    If you own a computer, it is vital to understand it, for noxious software is becoming increasingly sophisticated and infectious.

    The most logical and effective place to add this sentence would be after the last sentence of Paragraph:
    F. 2.
    G. 3.
    H. 4.
    J. 5.

GO ON TO THE NEXT PAGE.

1 ■ ■ ■ ■ ■ ■ ■ ■ 1

75. Suppose the writer had decided to write an essay discussing the moral and ethical consequences of programming spyware to illicitly collect private information. Would this essay successfully fulfill the writer's goal?

A. Yes, because the essay explains the moral and ethical consequences when spyware is installed on a computer.

B. Yes, because the essay details the process of ridding a computer of spyware, which helps the reader to understand the consequences of programming spyware.

C. No, because the essay does not explain how to program spyware, so the reader has no basis for making a moral or ethical judgment.

D. No, because the essay limits itself to a brief description of spyware and the basic precautions to be taken against it.

END OF THE ENGLISH TEST.
STOP! IF YOU HAVE TIME LEFT OVER, CHECK YOUR WORK ON THIS SECTION ONLY.

2 △ △ △ △ △ △ △ △ **2**

MATHEMATICS TEST

60 Minutes—60 Questions

DIRECTIONS: Solve each of the problems in the time allowed, then fill in the corresponding bubble on your answer sheet. Do not spend too much time on any one problem; skip the more difficult problems and go back to them later.

You may use a calculator on this test. For this test you should assume that figures are NOT necessarily drawn to scale, that all geometric figures lie in a plane, and that the word *line* is used to indicate a straight line.

---

1. In the standard (x,y) coordinate plane, point X has coordinates $(-4,0)$ and point Y has coordinates $(0,-8)$. What are the coordinates of the midpoint of $\overline{XY}$?
   A. $(-6,-1)$
   B. $(-2,-4)$
   C. $(0,2)$
   D. $(2,4)$
   E. $(6,-1)$

2. Given right triangle $\triangle MNO$ below, how many units long is $\overline{NO}$?

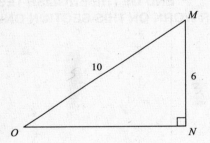

   F. $2\sqrt{2}$
   G. 4
   H. 6
   J. $\sqrt{60}$
   K. 8

3. A distance in meters, M, can be approximated by multiplying a distance in yards, Y, by 1.0936. Which of the following expresses this approximation method? (Note: The symbol $\approx$ means "is approximately equal to.")

   A. $M \approx \dfrac{Y}{1.0936}$

   B. $M \approx \dfrac{1.0936}{Y}$

   C. $M \approx Y(1.0936)$
   D. $M \approx Y + 1.0936$
   E. $M \approx Y(1.0936Y)$

DO YOUR FIGURING HERE.

GO ON TO THE NEXT PAGE.

2   **2**

DO YOUR FIGURING HERE.

4. Seth has 4 plaid shirts and 5 solid-colored shirts hanging together in a closet. In his haste to get ready for work, he randomly grabs 1 of these 9 shirts. What is the probability that the shirt Seth grabs is plaid?

   F. $\dfrac{1}{5}$

   G. $\dfrac{1}{4}$

   H. $\dfrac{4}{9}$

   J. $\dfrac{1}{9}$

   K. $\dfrac{4}{5}$

5. The daily totals of enrollments at Sunnyside Summer Camp last Monday through Saturday were 17, 19, 23, 14, 25, and 28. What was the average number of enrollments per day?

   A. 126
   B. 28
   C. 21
   D. 18
   E. 14

6. In the figure showing $\triangle PQR$ below, line l is parallel to line m. Which one of the following angles must be congruent to $\angle y$?

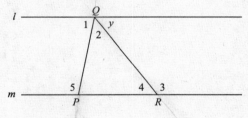

   F. $\angle 1$
   G. $\angle 2$
   H. $\angle 3$
   J. $\angle 4$
   K. $\angle 5$

7. A carton of paper is priced at $27.00 now. If the paper goes on sale for 25% off the current price, what will be the sale price of the carton?

   A. $6.75
   B. $20.25
   C. $22.00
   D. $26.75
   E. $33.75

GO ON TO THE NEXT PAGE.

2 △ △ △ △ △ △ △ △ **2**

8. What is the slope of any line parallel to the line $2x - 3y = 7$?
   F. -3
   G. $-\dfrac{2}{3}$
   H. $\dfrac{2}{3}$
   J. 2
   K. 3

DO YOUR FIGURING HERE.

9. Andrew won a cash prize on a game show. Andrew paid taxes of 30% on the original cash prize and had \$28,000 remaining. How much was the original cash prize?
   A. \$19,600
   B. \$28,300
   C. \$36,400
   D. \$40,000
   E. \$84,000

10. Melissa had 3 fewer apples than Marcia. Then, she gave 2 apples to Marcia. Now how many fewer apples does Melissa have than Marcia?
    F. 0
    G. 2
    H. 3
    J. 5
    K. 7

11. What is the value of $|5 - a|$ if $a = 9$?
    A. -14
    B. -4
    C. 4
    D. 9
    E. 14

12. For all m and n, $(3m + n)(m^2 - n) = ?$
    F. $3m^3 + 2m^2 - 2n$
    G. $m^3 - 2n^2$
    H. $2m^2 - n - n^2$
    J. $3m^2 + 3mn - 2n^2$
    K. $3m^3 - 3mn + m^2n - n^2$

13. For all x, $13 - 2(x + 5) = ?$
    A. $-2x + 3$
    B. $11x + 55$
    C. $13 + 10x$
    D. $23 - 2x$
    E. $23 + 2x$

14. $(n^7)^{11}$ is equivalent to:
    F. n^{77}
    G. n^{18}
    H. $11n^4$
    J. $11n^7$
    K. $77n$

GO ON TO THE NEXT PAGE.

2 △ △ △ △ △ △ △ △ **2**

15. What is the 217th digit after the decimal point in the repeating decimal $0.\overline{3456}$?
    A. 0
    B. 3
    C. 4
    D. 5
    E. 6

16. The perimeter of a square is 48 centimeters. What is its area, in square centimeters?
    F. 12
    G. 96
    H. 144
    J. 192
    K. 2,304

17. What is the product of the 2 solutions of the equation $x^2 + 3x - 21 = 0$?
    A. −63
    B. −21
    C. −20
    D. 20
    E. 21

18. Which of the following expressions is a polynomial factor of $a^{16} - 16$?
    F. $a^4 - 4$
    G. $a^4 + 4$
    H. $a^4 + 2$
    J. $a + 2$
    K. $a - 2$

19. When $n = \frac{1}{4}$, what is the value of $\frac{2n - 5}{n}$?
    A. 18
    B. 9
    C. −3
    D. −9
    E. −18

20. A proofreader can read 40 pages in one hour. How many pages can this proofreader read in 90 minutes?
    F. 45
    G. 60
    H. 150
    J. 360
    K. 940

DO YOUR FIGURING HERE.

GO ON TO THE NEXT PAGE.

2   **2**

DO YOUR FIGURING HERE.

21. The area of a parallelogram may be found by multiplying the base by the height. What is the area, in square inches, of the parallelogram below?

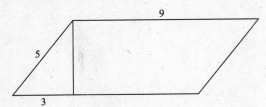

A. 27
B. 36
C. 45
D. 48
E. 81

22. For a certain quadratic equation, $ax^2 + bx + c = 0$, the 2 solutions are $x = \dfrac{3}{4}$ and $x = -\dfrac{2}{5}$. Which of the following could be factors of $ax^2 + bx + c$?

 F. $(4x - 3)$ AND $(5x + 2)$
 G. $(4x - 2)$ AND $(5x + 3)$
 H. $(4x + 2)$ AND $(5x - 3)$
 J. $(4x + 3)$ AND $(5x - 2)$
 K. $(4x + 3)$ AND $(5x + 2)$

23. All sides of a rhombus are the same length, as shown below.

If one diagonal is 12 inches long and the other is 32 inches long, how many inches long, to the nearest hundredth of an inch, is a side of the rhombus?

A. 8.54
B. 17.09
C. 34.17
D. 35.78
E. 48.00

24. A rectangular parking lot that is 3 feet longer than it is wide has an area of 550 square feet. How many feet long is the parking lot?

 F. 19
 G. 20
 H. 22
 J. 25
 K. 28

GO ON TO THE NEXT PAGE.

2 △ △ △ △ △ △ △ △ **2**

25. In the standard (x, y) coordinate plane, what is the slope of the line joining the points $(3,7)$ and $(4,-8)$?
  A. -15

  B. -1

  C. $-\dfrac{1}{7}$

  D. $\dfrac{21}{32}$

  E. 15

26. Which of the following is the solution set of $x + 2 > -4$?
  F. $\{x: x < -6\}$
  G. $\{x: x > -6\}$
  H. $\{x: x < -2\}$
  J. $\{x: x > 2\}$
  K. $\{x: x < 6\}$

27. What is the center of the circle with equation $(x - 3)^2 + (y + 3)^2 = 4$ in the standard (x, y) coordinate plane?
  A. $(3,3)$
  B. $(3,-3)$
  C. $(\sqrt{3},-\sqrt{3})$
  D. $(-3,3)$
  E. $(-\sqrt{3},\sqrt{3})$

28. In the standard (x, y) coordinate plane, what is the length of the line segment that has endpoints $(-3,4)$ and $(5,-6)$?
  F. 9
  G. $2\sqrt{41}$
  H. 18
  J. $20\sqrt{2}$
  K. 40

29. A triangle has sides of length 4.7 meters and 9 meters. Which of the following CANNOT be the length of the third side, in meters?
  A. 5
  B. 7
  C. 8
  D. 11
  E. 14

30. If $\dfrac{n^x}{n^y} = n^2$ for all $n \neq 0$, which of the following must be true?
  F. $x + y = 2$
  G. $x - y = 2$
  H. $x \times y = 2$
  J. $x \div y = 2$
  K. $\sqrt{xy} = 2$

DO YOUR FIGURING HERE.

GO ON TO THE NEXT PAGE.

2 △ △ △ △ △ △ △ △ **2**

31. In the standard (x, y) coordinate plane, what is the y-intercept of the line given by the equation $3x + 5y = 8$?

A. 3

B. $\dfrac{5}{3}$

C. $\dfrac{8}{5}$

D. $-\dfrac{3}{5}$

E. -3

32. There are 16 ounces in one pound. If 3.4 pounds of beef cost \$4.95, what is the cost per ounce, to the nearest cent?

F. \$0.09

G. \$0.31

H. \$1.05

J. \$1.46

K. \$10.99

33. $\left(\dfrac{1}{2}\right)^2 + \left(\dfrac{1}{3}\right)^2 + \left(\dfrac{1}{4}\right)^2 = ?$

A. $\dfrac{1}{29}$

B. $\dfrac{3}{29}$

C. $\dfrac{61}{144}$

D. $\dfrac{15}{32}$

E. 9

34. One route along flat terrain from Hermansville to Melville is to drive straight north from Hermansville for 120 miles to Jamestown, then, at Jamestown, to drive straight west for 80 miles to Melville. If a straight, flat road existed between Hermansville and Melville, approximately how many miles long would it be?

F. 200

G. 144

H. 100

J. 98

K. 40

35. In order to clean her aquarium, Stephanie must remove half of the water. The aquarium measures 30 inches long, 16 inches wide, and 12 inches deep. The aquarium is currently completely full. What volume of water, in cubic inches, must Stephanie remove?

A. 1,440

B. 2,880

C. 4,320

D. 5,760

E. 7,200

GO ON TO THE NEXT PAGE.

36. The bowling league selects its 4 officers by first selecting the president, then the vice president, then the secretary, then the treasurer. If there are 40 bowlers who are eligible to hold office and no member can hold more than one office, which of the following gives the number of different possible results of the election?

  F. 37^4
  G. 39^4
  H. 40^4
  J. $39 \times 38 \times 37 \times 36$
  K. $40 \times 39 \times 38 \times 37$

37. The points R (2,2) and S (6,3) in the standard (x,y) coordinate plane below are 2 vertices of triangle RST, which has a right angle at S. Which of the following could be the third vertex, T?

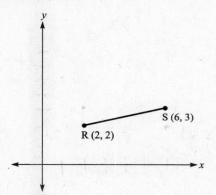

  A. (5,7)
  B. (5,−5)
  C. (4,6)
  D. (4,9)

  E. $\left(4, \dfrac{9}{2}\right)$

38. What value of x will satisfy the equation $0.2(x - 2,700) = x$?

  F. −675
  G. −540
  H. 0
  J. 540
  K. 675

39. If $0° \leq x \leq 90°$ and $\tan x = \dfrac{15}{8}$, then $\cos x = ?$

  A. $\dfrac{8}{17}$

  B. $\dfrac{15}{17}$

  C. $\dfrac{17}{8}$

  D. $\dfrac{17}{15}$

  E. $\dfrac{8}{15}$

GO ON TO THE NEXT PAGE.

DO YOUR FIGURING HERE.

40. A square pool with an area of 81 square feet is to be placed entirely within a circular enclosure with a radius of 10 feet. Tiles will be laid within the entire enclosure around the pool (but not under it). What is the approximate area, in square feet, of the enclosure that will be tiled?

   F. 81
   G. 233
   H. 315
   J. 396
   K. Cannot be determined without knowing the exact placement of the pool.

41. In the standard (x,y) coordinate plane, which of the following lines goes through $(3,4)$ and is parallel to $y = 2x + 2$?

   A. $y = \dfrac{1}{2}x + 2$
   B. $y = 2x - 2$
   C. $y = 2x + 4$
   D. $y = 2x + 10$
   E. $y = 3x + 2$

42. In the figure below, $\tan \varphi = ?$

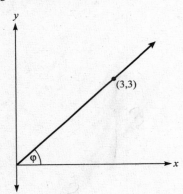

   F. $\dfrac{1}{\sqrt{2}}$
   G. $\sqrt{2}$
   H. 1
   J. 3
   K. $3\sqrt{2}$

43. Which of the following operations will produce the smallest result when substituted for the blank in the expression: $\dfrac{2}{3}$ _____ $- 3$?

   A. plus
   B. minus
   C. multiplied by
   D. divided by
   E. averaged with

GO ON TO THE NEXT PAGE.

2 △ △ △ △ △ △ △ △ 2

DO YOUR FIGURING HERE.

44. The value of b that will make $\dfrac{b}{3}+2 = \dfrac{1}{4}$ a true statement lies between which of the following numbers?
    F. −4 and −6
    G. −1 and −3
    H. −1 and 1
    J. 1 and 3
    K. 3 and 5

45. What is the solution set of $|3a - 2| \leq 7$?
    A. $\{a: a \leq 3\}$
    B. $\left\{a: -\dfrac{5}{3} \leq a \leq 3\right\}$
    C. $\left\{a: -\dfrac{5}{3} \geq a \geq 3\right\}$
    D. $\left\{a: -\dfrac{5}{3} \leq a \geq 3\right\}$
    E. $\left\{a: -\dfrac{5}{3} \geq a \leq 3\right\}$

46. When measured from a point on the ground that is a certain distance from the base of a cell phone tower, the angle of elevation to the top of the tower is 41°, as shown below. The height of the cell phone tower is 200 feet. What is the distance, in feet, to the cell phone tower?

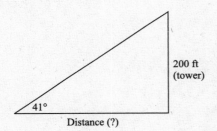

200 ft
(tower)

41°

Distance (?)

    F. $200\ \tan 41°$
    G. $200\ \sin 41°$
    H. $200\ \cos 41°$
    J. $200\ \sec 41°$
    K. $200\ \cot 41°$

47. For the area of a square to triple, the new side lengths must be the length of the old sides multiplied by:
    A. $\sqrt{3}$
    B. 3
    C. 4
    D. $2\sqrt{3}$
    E. 9

GO ON TO THE NEXT PAGE.

2   **2**

48. The volume of a cube is given by the formula s^3, where s is the length of a side. If a cube has a volume of 64, and the length of each side is halved, the new cube's volume will be:

F. 3
G. 6
H. 8
J. 16
K. 32

49. In the parallelogram below, lengths are given in inches. What is the area of the parallelogram, in square inches?

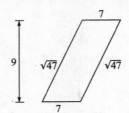

A. $\sqrt{94}$
B. $7\sqrt{47}$
C. 49
D. 63
E. $16\sqrt{47}$

50. If $8a^6b^3 < 0$, then which of the following CANNOT be true?

F. $b < 0$
G. $b > 0$
H. $a = b$
J. $a < 0$
K. $a > 0$

51. If $\log_4 x = 3$, then $x = ?$

A. $\dfrac{1}{\log_{12}}$
B. $4\log^3$
C. 12
D. 64
E. 81

DO YOUR FIGURING HERE.

GO ON TO THE NEXT PAGE.

2 △ △ △ △ △ △ △ △ **2**

52. If a system of 2 linear equations in 2 variables has NO solution, and 1 of the equations is graphed in the (x,y) coordinate plane below, which of the following *could* be the equation of the other line?

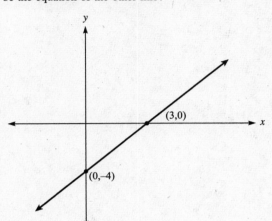

F. $y = -2$

G. $y = -\dfrac{1}{4}x + 2$

H. $y = -2x - 4$

J. $y = \dfrac{4}{3}x + 2$

K. $y = 4x - 4$

53. In a game, 80 marbles numbered 00 through 79 are placed in a box. A player draws 1 marble at random from the box. Without replacing the first marble, the player draws a second marble at random. If both marbles drawn have the same ones digit (that is, both marbles have a number ending in 0, 1, 2, 3, etc.), the player is a winner. If the first marble drawn is numbered 35, what is the probability that the player will be a winner on the next draw?

A. $\dfrac{1}{79}$

B. $\dfrac{7}{80}$

C. $\dfrac{7}{79}$

D. $\dfrac{1}{10}$

E. $\dfrac{8}{79}$

DO YOUR FIGURING HERE.

GO ON TO THE NEXT PAGE.

2 △ △ △ △ △ △ △ △ **2**

54. In the standard (x,y) coordinate plane, what is the equation of the line that passes through the origin and the point $(3,4)$?

F. $y = \dfrac{1}{4}x + \dfrac{3}{4}$

G. $y = \dfrac{1}{4}x - \dfrac{1}{3}$

H. $y = \dfrac{4}{3}x$

J. $y = \dfrac{1}{2}x + \dfrac{3}{4}$

K. $y = \dfrac{9}{4}x$

55. The measure of the vertex angle of an isosceles triangle is $(a + 30)°$. The base angles each measure $(2a - 15)°$. What is the measure in degrees of one of the base angles?

A. $36°$
B. $45°$
C. $57°$
D. $66°$
E. $90°$

56. What is the smallest possible value for the product of 2 integers that differ by 7?

F. 8
G. 0
H. -6
J. -10
K. -12

57. Three distinct lines, all contained within a plane, separate that plane into distinct regions. What are all of the possible numbers of distinct regions of the plane that could be separated by any such three lines?

A. 4, 6, 7
B. 4, 5, 6
C. 3, 5, 7
D. 3, 5, 6
E. 3, 4, 5

DO YOUR FIGURING HERE.

GO ON TO THE NEXT PAGE.

2 △ △ △ △ △ △ △ △ **2**

58. Given the vertices of parallelogram *QRST* in the standard (x, y) coordinate plane below, what is the area of triangle *QRS*, in square units?

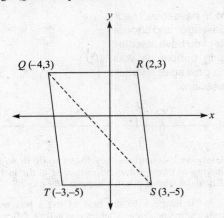

F. 24
G. 28
H. 48
J. 60
K. 80

59. The first and second terms of a geometric sequence are *a* and *ab*, in that order. What is the 643rd term of the sequence?
A. $(ab)^{642}$
B. $(ab)^{643}$
C. $a^{642}b$
D. $a^{643}b$
E. ab^{642}

60. Points *A*, *B*, and *C* are three distinct points that lie on the same line. If the length of *AB* is 19 meters and the length of *BC* is 13 meters, then what are all the possible lengths, in meters, for *AC*?
F. 6 only
G. 32 only
H. 6 and 32 only
J. Any number less than 32 or greater that 6
K. Any number greater than 32 or less than 6

DO YOUR FIGURING HERE.

END OF THE MATHEMATICS TEST.
STOP! IF YOU HAVE TIME LEFT OVER, CHECK YOUR WORK ON THIS SECTION ONLY.

3 ██ **3**

READING TEST

35 Minutes—40 Questions

DIRECTIONS: This test includes four passages, each followed by ten questions. Read the passages and choose the best answer to each question. After you have selected your answer, fill in the corresponding bubble on your answer sheet. You should refer to the passages as often as necessary when answering the questions.

PASSAGE I
PROSE FICTION: *The Summer Sandwich Club*

Maxwell was one of those kids I know I will remember for the rest of my life. I first met Max three summers ago when he showed up at the park on the first day of camp with his mother Katherine. After a brief
5 good morning, he went off to play with the rest of the five and six year olds who I would be counseling for the next several weeks. As his mother walked back to her car, I couldn't help but notice that she looked as though she had just finished running a marathon; however, that
10 thought left my mind soon after she drove away, as I was surrounded by the smiling faces of thirty brand new campers.

The summer started off great, and Max and I hit it off right away; he looked up to me as an older brother,
15 and I thought he was a great little kid. There were a few things that stuck out in my mind as odd, though, like when he would complain of being hungry an hour or so after lunch at least once or twice a week. By the third week of camp, I decided that it was something
20 I needed to investigate, and during lunch time I went over to his table and asked if I could sit next to him. He giggled and said, "Sure Jake," feeling special that I would want to spend my lunch break with him. His lunch consisted of a bag of potato chips, a can of soda,
25 and a chocolate bar—hardly a healthy meal for a five year old. I offered him half of my sandwich and his eyes lit up like it was his birthday.

That afternoon, when Katherine came to pick Max up from the park, I pulled her aside to discuss the lunch
30 issue.

"Katherine, Maxwell needs to have a healthy lunch." She looked down at the ground.

"What do you mean, Jake?"

"I mean Max can not keep eating junk food
35 every day."

"Oh. That. I'm sorry about that. It's just that I work back-to-back jobs every night and barely make it home in time to get him out of bed and dressed before camp starts in the morning. His babysitter is supposed
40 to pack Max's lunch for him at night when she puts him to bed. We have had a couple of new babysitters

lately, and sometimes they forget to do it, so I end up having to throw something together at the last minute. I'll make sure it doesn't happen any more."

45 "It happens to the best of us; I just wanted to make sure you knew what he was eating. After a couple days of him being hungry I got worried and wondered who was making his lunch for him. See you tomorrow morning then."

50 Several days later I expected to see Max eating a sandwich went I went over to him at lunchtime. His lunch once again consisted entirely of junk food. Something had to change; at the very least he needed to be eating much less sugar.

55 "Katherine," I called to his mother as she stepped out of her car that afternoon. I really had no idea what I was supposed to say. It was quite a predicament. "We really need to fix this problem with Max's lunch."

"Jake, I know, it's just that the house payment was
60 due yesterday, and I haven't had the, uh, time to get to the grocery store," she trailed off. "Things are just a little hard for us right now."

She was obviously self-conscious at the moment, and I felt bad for having brought it up again. I told
65 her that I had a plan, and not to worry about it. After explaining what I meant, the look on her face was one of relief and thanks, and she and Max headed home for the day.

For the rest of the summer, I spent my lunches
70 with Max and his friends, having meetings of what we called the "Sandwich Club": every day I would bring a couple of extra sandwiches, and anybody who wanted to try one could have some. Max never seemed to care what kind of sandwiches I brought to the club, but just
75 giggled and smiled up at me every afternoon.

At the end of the summer, I got a letter from Katherine, thanking me for being so kind to she and Max. I wrote back telling her that I could hardly wait until the next meeting of the "Sandwich Club," and to
80 tell Max that I said hello.

For the next two years, the "Sandwich Club" had regular meetings, Monday-Friday at noon, all summer long. After that, Max and his mother moved to be closer to his grandparents, and I went back to having my lunch

GO ON TO THE NEXT PAGE.

3 ▬▬▬▬▬▬▬▬▬▬▬▬▬▬▬▬▬▬▬▬▬ **3**

85 with the rest of the staff. But for those few years, the "Summer Sandwich Club" brought joy to one camp counselor and many young campers.

1. When Jake says, "It happens to the best of us," he is primarily saying that:
   A. he understands that sometimes things happen that are beyond our control.
   B. Katherine is a perfect parent, and he is surprised that Max is unhappy.
   C. Max is a picky eater and would not eat a healthy lunch anyway.
   D. Max is his favorite camper, despite the problems faced by Max's mother.

2. It can be reasonably inferred from the conversations with Jake, that Katherine:
   F. is a stay-at-home-mother.
   G. does not care about her son.
   H. works two jobs to make ends meet.
   J. believes that junk food is healthy.

3. The idea that Jake's mother is trying her best to take care of her son is least supported by which of the following quotations from the passage?
   A. "It's just that I work back-to-back jobs every night and barely make it home in time to get him out of bed and dressed before camp starts in the morning."
   B. "Katherine, Maxwell needs to have a healthy lunch."
   C. "Things are just a little hard for us right now."
   D. "I'll make sure it doesn't happen any more."

4. As it is used in line 57 the word *predicament* most nearly means:
   F. joke.
   G. solution.
   H. complaint.
   J. challenge.

5. It can be inferred from the passage that Jake is:
   A. Max's older brother.
   B. dissatisfied with his job.
   C. a good influence on Max.
   D. someone Max barely knows.

6. The passage makes it clear that the "Sandwich Club":
   F. lasted as long as Max was a camper.
   G. met only when it rained.
   H. was an insult to Katherine.
   J. was Max's favorite part of camp.

7. You may reasonably infer from the details in the passage that Katherine and Max:
   A. dislike Jake.
   B. are very wealthy.
   C. do not trust other people.
   D. have little money.

8. Katherine can most accurately be characterized as:
   F. indifferent and withdrawn.
   G. caring but distracted.
   H. cruel and arrogant.
   J. friendly but aloof.

9. The word *issue*, as it is used in line 30, most nearly means:
   A. publication.
   B. incident.
   C. idea.
   D. problem.

10. The title, "The Summer Sandwich Club," combined with details presented in the passage imply that:
    F. everyone loves sandwiches.
    G. Jake only eats sandwiches in the summer.
    H. children should join clubs to make friends.
    J. the club was created because of Max.

GO ON TO THE NEXT PAGE.

3 ▰▰▰▰▰▰▰▰▰▰▰▰▰▰▰▰▰▰▰▰▰▰▰ **3**

PASSAGE II
SOCIAL SCIENCE: *Lewis and Clark Go West*

Over two hundred years ago, at the request of President Jefferson, the corps of volunteers for "North Western Discovery" set off under the command of Meriwether Lewis and William Clark to find the fastest
5   water route across North America. The path they were to carve out would be the first of its kind; they were setting a course through the territory of potentially dangerous Indian tribes and ferocious animals. None but the fearless and inventive, the most resourceful and
10 curious, would dare to undertake such a venture. In 1803, virtually no one had attempted to cross the stretch of land between the mighty Mississippi and the vast Pacific Ocean using only water routes. All of the wonders of those states in the West are, in part, the result
15 of this expedition. These intrepid pioneers, especially Lewis and Clark, deserve to be remembered now some two centuries after their courageous journey into the unknown lands west of the Mississippi. The rolling hills of the breadbasket, the ski-resorts in the snow-
20 capped Rocky Mountains, and the lush, fertile valleys of the coast echo all those involved.

After receiving wilderness training in Washington D.C., Meriwether Lewis set out on July 5, 1803, picked up guns at Harpers Ferry, Virginia, and then moved to
25 Pittsburgh to pick up a 55-foot keelboat. Floating it down the Ohio, he met with Clark in Indiana, who took over command of the boat and crew, while Lewis then rode on to get supplies in St. Louis. Months later, in May, the entire party gathered in St. Louis. The
30 forty-some men were to travel from there to the Pacific Ocean in only the keelboat and two smaller boats, all of which were moved by sails, towropes, poles, or oars.

The beginning of their journey was a voyage of confirmation; traders had gathered information of
35 various possible water routes to the Pacific, and Lewis and Clark's job was to confirm the truth of such reports and observe anything else of importance along the way. They also catalogued new species of plants and animals which they encountered, and worked toward peace with
40 several Indian tribes. History tells us that the few messages the men were able to send back told of their health and high spirits. They were all eager to explore just what might lie beyond the Mississippi.

Despite having adequate supplies and equipment,
45 including guns, the men's journey was still a dangerous one. They were traversing the wild and until this point, the only other individuals to have crossed it were fur traders and trappers. It was largely Indian territory and although most tribes, such as the Otos, the
50 Missouris, and the Mandans were friendly, the Sioux and the Blackfeet tried to impede the group's progress on more than one occasion. Illness claimed the life of one man early, but despite the strenuous pace of the expedition, there were no further losses.

55 Throughout it all, including long winters and the harsh conditions of wildness living, the travelers continued to forge west in search of an efficient trade route using only the rivers. In September of 1806, some three years after they started on their voyage, Lewis, Clark,
60 and their team made it to the Pacific Ocean. Relying on

the Missouri and Columbia rivers as their main "highways," and taking the help of friendly Indian tribes whenever they could, the expedition was a success, and served as an example for all manner of westward
65 expansion.

Despite the success of their expedition, proving that there was indeed a water route from the Mississippi River to the Pacific Ocean, future travelers to the West found faster passage on land, utilizing the Oregon
70 Trail. Keelboats were eventually replaced by covered wagons and trains, and America pushed ever onward into the West. The settlers who came after Lewis and Clark went forward with blind-devotion knowing then that it could be done. The initial breakthrough into that
75 unknown land was all that the country really needed. From there on out, the rest was history.

11. One of the main points that the author seeks to make in the passage is that westward expansion:
   A. was never attempted prior to the Lewis and Clark expedition.
   B. was a challenging but important aspect of the growth of the United States.
   C. led to the discovery of many new and dangerous Indian tribes.
   D. resulted in the development of the corps of volunteers for "North Western Discovery."

12. The focus of the passage can best be summarized as a study of both the:
   F. Lewis and Clark Expedition and the characteristics of the United States in the early 1800s.
   G. history of Midwest development and the Lewis and Clark Expedition.
   H. Lewis and Clark Expedition and the legendary Northwest Passage.
   J. losses and difficulties faced by the Lewis and Clark Expedition.

13. According to the information presented in the passage, which of the following best describes the relationship between the Lewis and Clark Expedition and the settlers who came after them?
   A. Everyone to follow the Expedition used Lewis and Clark's water route.
   B. The settlers who went west after the Expedition were much more cautious.
   C. Both the Lewis and Clark expedition and the future settlers suffered great losses.
   D. The Lewis and Clark Expedition gave others confidence to head West.

14. According to the passage, the motivation for the Lewis and Clark Expedition was to:
   F. make money.
   G. catalog the animals of North America.
   H. discover a water route to the Pacific.
   J. reach the Rocky Mountains.

GO ON TO THE NEXT PAGE.

3 ███████████████████████████████████ **3**

15. As it is used in the 2nd paragraph (lines 22–32), the word *party* most nearly means:
A. a joyous celebration.
B. a group of people setting out on a trip.
C. a segment of the population.
D. a meeting to discuss business matters.

16. As it is depicted in the passage, the initial mood of the Lewis and Clark expedition can best be described as:
F. hopelessly discouraged.
G. eagerly determined.
H. remarkably cautious.
J. overtly happy.

17. It can be inferred that the word *forge* as it is used in Paragraph 5 (lines 55–65) refers to:
A. creating new tools out of metal.
B. searching for food.
C. continuing a journey.
D. crossing a river on foot.

18. According to the passage, which of the following were the primary dangers faced by the Lewis and Clark expedition?
F. Illness and lack of motivation.
G. Fast moving water.
H. Wagons that fell apart.
J. Conflicts with the indigenous people.

19. As it relates to the passage, all of the following were methods used to move the boats EXCEPT:
A. man power.
B. wind power.
C. rowing power.
D. steam power.

20. According to the passage, in the early part of their journey members of the Lewis and Clark Expedition were doing all of the following EXCEPT:
F. receiving wilderness training.
G. cataloguing new species of plants and animals.
H. confirming possible water routes across the continent.
J. sending back messages regarding their status.

GO ON TO THE NEXT PAGE.

3 ██████████████████████████████████ **3**

PASSAGE III
HUMANITIES: *Colorful Reflections on Fairfield Porter*

My first encounter with the international artist and art critic Fairfield Porter was actually through the poetry of his wife, Anne (Channing) Porter. While both grew to become quite celebrated in their crafts,
5 Fairfield's story is unique.

Born into an affluent, artistic family in 1907, the boy who was to one day become a renowned artist and respected art critic showed a comparative lack of artistic ability when seen next to his siblings. While
10 his older brother Eliot took to photography, Fairfield Porter, despite being remarkably intelligent, appeared to be lacking any natural artistic talents. It seemed that, although a member of a family full of artists, his true skill lay in the critiquing of others' artistry. This
15 was evidenced in his second year at Harvard by Fairfield's decision to pursue art history as his major field of study. After studying at Harvard under Arthur Pope and then traveling briefly through Europe, Fairfield came back to the United States to further his education at
20 the Art Students League in New York City. There he became acquainted with the famed photographer Alfred Stieglitz—the work of whom is said to have positively influenced Fairfield's paintings to some degree.

Between the years 1931 and 1932, Fairfield spent
25 the majority of his time in Italy learning to appreciate and critique the works of the great Renaissance painters. His training came from both direct study under world-famous art historian Bernard Berenson, and from countless hours spent in museums and
30 galleries observing the greatest pieces of Italian art.

Following his marriage to Anne upon his return from Italy, Fairfield spent the better part of the next two decades developing his skills as a painter while caring for his autistic son. During this period his meetings with
35 the French Intimist painter Willem De Kooning would prove to have a profound effect on his later works. Porter was the first to publicly acclaim the work of Kooning.

In fact, what made Porter so famous was his knack
40 for responding directly to an artist's work. He found fault with the common "talk based" criticism that spoke to art only in reference to its past or to some vague theoretical framework; such criticism attempted to shape the future of art and was far too biased for Porter.
45 His time as an art critic for such publications as *Art News* and *The Nation* ended, however, in 1961 when he decided to pursue a full-time painting career.

The other side of his fame, his uncommon approach to painting, is just as important to the
50 understanding of Fairfield Porter's contributions to the world of art. His personal philosophy comes from a blending of two views; art should be personal, emotional, and representative of its subject, while at the same time be boldly colorful, expressive, and gener-
55 ally abstract. Drawing on his vast knowledge of art history, especially the styles of French Intimism, Porter fused these two feelings to create a powerful, emotive collection of paintings about families, individuals, and the home, as well as moving nature scenes such as

60 *The Door to the Woods* (1971) and *Maine – Toward the Harbor* (1967).

When he died in 1975, on a morning walk along the ocean, he left the world as one of the most respected art critics in the past century. On top of that, his work
65 as a painter is still viewed within the art community as amazingly distinctive and especially representative of his life. It is sad to say that now, however, some thirty years after his death, he is still virtually unknown outside of art circles. This remarkably insightful, artic-
70 ulate, creative individual needs to be discovered by the common man and revered for his continuing influence on the artists of today. The words of this intellectual were some of the best and most honest critiques of art ever spoken.

21. The main purpose of the passage can best be described as an attempt to:
   A. explain Porter's renowned ability to candidly address artists' works.
   B. illustrate the influence several renowned artists had on the works of Porter.
   C. appraise Porter's unusual methods of painting and critiquing artwork.
   D. chronicle Porter's life, particularly the events and beliefs that shaped his career.

22. The author's attitude towards the subject of the passage can best be characterized as:
   F. detached interest.
   G. amused tolerance.
   H. warm appreciation.
   J. deep abhorrence.

23. As described in the passage, Porter's method of criticizing art can best be summarized by which of the following statements?
   A. Porter's criticisms were frank and forthright, and were based solely on his evaluation of the piece of art that he was appraising.
   B. Porter criticized art based on the context of the painting and conceptual structures that he found most useful in his evaluations.
   C. Porter's critiques were comparable to those of Bernard Berenson, who greatly influenced Porter's outlook on art.
   D. Porter targeted his criticisms at helping artists by attempting to influence their forthcoming works.

24. Porter's painting style can be described by all of the following EXCEPT:
   F. stirring.
   G. vivid.
   H. trite.
   J. individualistic.

3 ████████████████████████████████ **3**

25. Without the first paragraph, the passage would lose:
- **A.** an overview of the passage as a whole.
- **B.** a brief introduction and transition into the topic.
- **C.** important detail that later becomes relevant to the passage.
- **D.** an explanation of the logic behind the author's viewpoint.

26. In line 11, the statement "despite being remarkably intelligent" is intended to:
- **F.** call attention to the fact that although Porter was a well-respected art critic, he failed to impress his college professors.
- **G.** communicate to the reader that Porter's lack of a formal education did not detract from his ability to critique art.
- **H.** emphasize to the reader that Porter's high level of intelligence was not related to his artistic ability.
- **J.** inform the reader that Porter's position as an art critic was so difficult that it challenged his intellect.

27. The word *revered* in line 71 most nearly means:
- **A.** trusted.
- **B.** depreciated.
- **C.** reminiscent.
- **D.** honored.

28. According to the passage, when did Fairfield Porter become serious about becoming an artist?
- **F.** Immediately upon his return from Italy.
- **G.** While he was studying at the Art Students League.
- **H.** Just before his death in 1975.
- **J.** Approximately thirty years after he returned from Italy.

29. The third paragraph states that, during 1931 and 1932, Fairfield Porter was:
- **A.** continuing his training as an art critic.
- **B.** the greatest art critic in Italy.
- **C.** planning his marriage to Anne Channing.
- **D.** training to become a Renaissance painter.

30. The author uses the phrase "other side of his fame" (line 48) most likely in order to:
- **F.** suggest that Fairfield Porter was better known as an artist than as an art critic.
- **G.** indicate that Fairfield Porter was both a renowned art critic and painter.
- **H.** show that Fairfield Porter was not aware of his popularity as a painter.
- **J.** suggest that other art critics of the time were more famous than was Fairfield Porter.

GO ON TO THE NEXT PAGE.

3 ███████████████████████████████████ **3**

PASSAGE IV

NATURAL SCIENCE: *This passage discusses some of the controversy surrounding the existence of dark matter in the universe.*

Dark matter in the universe is believed by some scientists to be a substance that is not readily observable because it does not directly refract light or energy. Its existence can only be deduced because of the effect that
5 it has on surrounding matter. In fact, some members of the scientific community have argued that dark matter does not actually exist. Others, however, believe in its existence, in part because the scientific community does not have a complete understanding of gravita-
10 tional science. On the other hand, some would argue that it is the understanding of gravitational science that leads most scientists to believe in the existence of dark matter, because without dark matter, there are many cosmological phenomena that are difficult to explain.
15 For example, dark matter in the universe may have a peculiar effect on the Milky Way galaxy. Some scientists believe that the interaction between dark matter and other smaller, nearby galaxies is causing the Milky Way galaxy to take on a warped profile. It has
20 been asserted that not only does dark matter exist, it may also be responsible for the Milky Way's unusual shape. The interaction referenced involves two smaller galaxies near the Milky Way, called Magellanic Clouds, moving through an enormous amount of dark matter,
25 which, in effect, enhances the gravitational pull that the two Magellanic Clouds could have on the Milky Way and other surrounding bodies. Without the existence of the dark matter, the Magellanic Clouds would not have sufficient mass to have such a strong effect on the bend
30 of the Milky Way galaxy.
The strongest evidence for the validity of this hypothesis rests in Newtonian physics, and the hypothesis that anything with mass will exert a gravitational pull. The Milky Way and other galaxies with pecu-
35 liar warped shapes are being molded by a gravitational force. However, there is nothing readily observable with sufficient mass that could cause such a high level of distortion via gravitational pull in the vicinity of the Milky Way. Therefore, something that is not easily
40 observed must be exerting the necessary force to create the warped shape of the galaxy.
Aaron Romanowsky and several colleagues have questioned the effect that dark matter might have on galaxies. They point to the existence of several ellipti-
45 cal galaxies surrounded by very little dark matter as evidence that dark matter is not, in fact, the cause of the warped galaxies. While they do not claim that their findings should be interpreted to conclude that dark matter does not exist, they apparently believe
50 that the results of their studies cast doubt on some of the conventional theories of galaxy formation and manipulation.
Several models constructed by researchers from the University of California at Berkeley, however,
55 point to the idea that dark matter is the most likely explanation for the distorted shape of the Milky Way and other galaxies. Using computer models, they have mapped the likely interactions between certain galaxies and the surrounding dark matter, and those models
60 have shown not only the possibility that dark matter is responsible for the warped shape of the Milky Way, but that the relationship between the dark matter and the Magellanic Clouds is dynamic; the movement of the clouds through the dark matter seems to create a
65 wake that enhances their gravitational influence on the Milky Way.

31. As it is used in line 14, the term *phenomena* most nearly means:
   A. occurrences.
   B. problems.
   C. attitudes.
   D. surprises.

32. The passage states that some members of the scientific community are reluctant to believe in the existence of dark matter because:
   F. there is absolutely no evidence for the existence of dark matter.
   G. no one understands how to apply gravitational science.
   H. dark matter cannot be directly observed.
   J. dark matter has little effect on surrounding matter.

33. What does the passage offer as evidence for the existence of dark matter?
   A. A complete understanding of gravitational science.
   B. The enormous mass of Magellanic Clouds.
   C. The shape of the Milky Way galaxy.
   D. A photograph taken with the aid of a refracting telescope.

34. According to the passage, what is Aaron Romanowsky's theory regarding dark matter?
   F. It cannot be conclusively proven that dark matter affects the shape and formation of galaxies.
   G. The discovery of certain galaxies disproves the theory that dark matter exists in the universe.
   H. Computer models suggest that dark matter is responsible for warped galaxies.
   J. Dark matter has no effect at all on the shape of a galaxy.

GO ON TO THE NEXT PAGE.

3 ████████████████████████████████ **3**

35. The last paragraph supports the general hypothesis provided earlier in the passage that:
A. the effect of Magellanic Clouds on galaxies is enhanced by dark matter.
B. computer models are necessary for an understanding of gravitational science.
C. dark matter has little to no effect on the formation of certain cosmological phenomena.
D. the shape of the Milky Way galaxy can be deduced by observing the matter surrounding it.

36. The main purpose of the third paragraph is to point out that:
F. dark matter was first discovered by applying Newtonian physics.
G. different viewpoints exist regarding gravitational science.
H. galaxies with peculiar shapes could not exist in the presence of dark matter.
J. scientific theories provide support for the existence of dark matter in the universe.

37. The word *conventional* in line 51 most nearly means:
A. easily understood.
B. formally disputed.
C. strictly interpreted.
D. generally accepted.

38. Which one of the following is NOT mentioned in the passage as a scientific theory regarding dark matter?
F. The existence of dark matter cannot be proved by direct observation.
G. Dark matter may be responsible for the shape of the Milky Way.
H. It is certain that dark matter has no influence on surrounding celestial bodies.
J. Magellanic Clouds require the presence of dark matter in order to influence the shape of galaxies.

39. According to the passage, dark matter cannot be readily detected because:
A. dark matter does not actually exist.
B. most of the dark matter in the universe is hidden behind galaxies.
C. it does not directly interact with light or energy.
D. it has no effect on the surrounding matter.

40. The passage supports which of the following statements about dark matter?
F. Its existence is inferred by some researchers based on observations of cosmological bodies composed of ordinary matter.
G. Its existence has been conclusively proven by computer models.
H. If it does not exist, the universe is largely empty.
J. Its presence is readily observable to researchers who completely understand how to apply gravitational science.

END OF THE READING TEST.
STOP! IF YOU HAVE TIME LEFT OVER, CHECK YOUR WORK ON THIS SECTION ONLY.

4 ○ ○ ○ ○ ○ ○ ○ ○ ○ **4**

SCIENCE REASONING TEST

35 Minutes—40 Questions

DIRECTIONS: This test includes seven passages, each followed by several questions. Read the passage and choose the best answer to each question. After you have selected your answer, fill in the corresponding bubble on your answer sheet. You should refer to the passages as often as necessary when answering the questions. You may NOT use a calculator on this test.

PASSAGE I

A researcher has conducted two experiments to test the rate of pinecone production in the *Pinus palustris Miller* (a type of pine tree).

Experiment 1

P. palustris Miller seeds were collected from 5 different populations (A1, A2, A3, A4, A5) each of which was from a different site (S1, S2, S3, S4, S5).

The seeds were grown under controlled conditions in a greenhouse. 300 of these seedlings from each population were chosen at random. Each set of seedlings was divided into 30 groups with 10 seedlings in each group. The seedlings were planted in marked cylindrical containers which were then placed at each of the 5 sites. Figure 1 shows the procedure for A1.

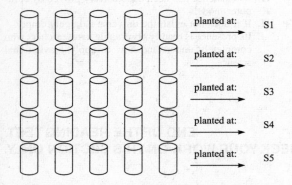

planted at: S1
planted at: S2
planted at: S3
planted at: S4
planted at: S5

Figure 1   25 Cups containing a total of 250 A1 seedlings

Table 1 shows the number of pinecones that were produced on each tree.

The researchers also collected data on the root structure of the trees. From the information they collected they came up with the following formula relating the root structure in inches to the number of pinecones produced:

number of pinecones $= 0.037 + 0.147$ (root thickness)

Statistical analysis indicated that this equation was accurate.

Table 1					
	Pinecones produced per tree				
Site	A1	A2	A3	A4	A5
S1	2.1	7.1	12.0	2.4	3.1
S2	3.9	2.5	8.5	6.2	6.4
S3	0.4	6.7	3.1	9.3	7.2
S4	5.2	2.1	2.9	0.2	4.5
S5	1.8	6.3	0.9	3.7	8.5

Experiment 2

P. palustris Miller seeds were collected and grown in the same manner as in Experiment 1. When the seeds had grown into seedlings, 150 containers were prepared with 5 A1 seedlings and 5 seedlings from either A2, A3, A4 or A5. Seven containers for each of the 4 combinations were planted at each site.

Table 2 shows how many pinecones were produced on each A1 plant.

Table 2				
	Pinecones produced per A1 tree when planted with			
Site	A2	A3	A4	A5
S1	5.7	3.2	6.7	3.5
S2	3.2	1.7	4.3	5.2
S3	9.6	8.4	0.8	7.0
S4	4.2	3.2	1.3	0.2
S5	4.9	6.1	6.1	3.9

GO ON TO THE NEXT PAGE.

1. In Experiment 1, trees from A5 produced more pinecones than did trees from A4 at which of the following sites?
   A. S4 only
   B. S1 and S5 only
   C. S1, S2, S4, and S5 only
   D. S1, S2, S3, S4, and S5 only

2. In Experiment 1, A1 trees produced the largest number of pinecones at which of the following sites?
   F. S1
   G. S3
   H. S4
   J. S5

3. The procedures utilized in Experiment 2 were repeated, except that only 25 containers were planted at a sixth site (S6). The results appear in Table 3.

Table 3				
	Pinecones produced per A1 tree when planted with			
Site	A2	A3	A4	A5
S6	4.1	6.4	1.9	0.3

Based on these data, one should conclude that A1 trees produced more pinecones at S6 than at which of the following sites in Experiment 2?
   A. S1
   B. S3
   C. S4
   D. S5

4. A student wanted to produce the greatest number of pinecones from 6 A1 trees, using the procedures from Experiment 2. Which plants and site should the A1 trees be combined with to achieve the desired results?
   F. A4 and S1
   G. A2 and S3
   H. A3 and S2
   J. A5 and S5

5. In which of the following ways was Experiment 2 different from Experiment 1?
   A. Experiment 2 included trees from more than 1 population.
   B. Experiment 2 combined trees from more than 1 species.
   C. Experiment 2 trees were planted at all 5 sites.
   D. Experiment 2 trees were planted at only 1 site.

6. In Experiment 2, how many seedlings were planted in each container?
   F. 6
   G. 8
   H. 10
   J. 12

GO ON TO THE NEXT PAGE.

4 ◯ ◯ ◯ ◯ ◯ ◯ ◯ ◯ **4**

PASSAGE II

Researchers conducted trials on a certain prescription drug delivered in immediate-release capsules and extended-release capsules.

Figure 1 shows the mean concentration (nanograms per milliliter [ng/mL]) of the two active ingredients of the prescription drug in patients' blood plasma over time (hr).

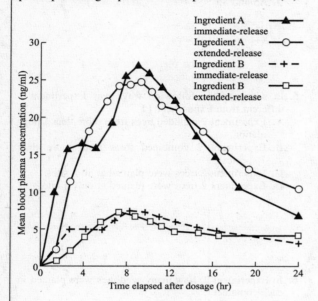

Figure 1

In clinical trials of the prescription drug, subjects given the prescription drug were interviewed at regular intervals about the symptoms the prescription drug is meant to relieve. After each interview, the subjects were assigned a symptom score. A high symptom score corresponds to high intensity of symptoms, and a low symptom score indicates low intensity of symptoms. Figure 2 shows the mean symptom score over time (hr) for subjects who took the prescription drug.

In the clinical trials, some subjects were given the prescription drug and some subjects were given a placebo (an inactive pill). Table 1 shows the percentage of subjects from both groups who reported various adverse side effects.

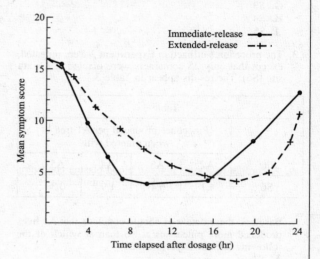

Figure 2

Table 1			
Body system	Side effect	Prescription drug group (%)	Placebo group (%)
General	Feeling of weakness	6	5
	Headache	26	14
Digestive system	Loss of appetite	32	5
	Diarrhea	8	0
	Dry mouth	31	5
	Nausea	14	0
Nervous system	Anxiety	7	4
	Dizziness	9	0
	Insomnia	25	11
	Irritability	11	4
Cardiovascular system	Rapid heart rate	10	2
Nutritional	Weight gain	15	0

GO ON TO THE NEXT PAGE.

7. According to Figure 1, 16 hours after taking the extended-release form of the prescription drug, the difference in mean blood plasma concentration between Ingredient A and Ingredient B is closest to:
   A. 7 ng/ml.
   B. 9 ng/ml.
   C. 11 ng/ml.
   D. 16 ng/ml.

8. Based on the data in Figures 1 and 2, the researchers should make which of the following conclusions about the overall change in mean blood plasma concentration and mean symptom score over time following dosage?
   F. Both mean blood plasma concentration and mean symptom score increase then decrease.
   G. Both mean blood plasma concentration and mean symptom score decrease then increase.
   H. Mean blood plasma concentration increases then decreases, and mean symptom score decreases then increases.
   J. Mean blood plasma concentration decreases then increases, and mean symptom score increases then decreases.

9. According to Figure 1, mean blood plasma concentration of Ingredient A administered in immediate-release form increases most during which of the following time periods?
   A. From the moment of dosage to 3 hours after dosage.
   B. From 3 hours after dosage to 10 hours after dosage.
   C. From 10 hours after dosage to 14 hours after dosage.
   D. From 14 hours after dosage to 24 hours after dosage.

10. Which of the following conclusions about adverse side effects caused by the prescription drug is consistent with the results shown in Table 1?
    F. Results from the placebo group most question the number of instances of feeling of weakness caused by the prescription drug.
    G. Results from the placebo group most question the number of instances of insomnia caused by the prescription drug.
    H. Results from the placebo group least question the number of instances of anxiety caused by the prescription drug.
    J. Results from the placebo group least question the number of instances of irritability caused by the prescription drug.

11. The symptom score of a clinical trial subject given the extended-release form of the prescription drug remained unchanged for 8 hours. Based on Figure 2, the 8-hour period most likely began:
    A. 3 hours after dosage.
    B. 5 hours after dosage.
    C. 9 hours after dosage.
    D. 14 hours after dosage.

GO ON TO THE NEXT PAGE.

4 ○ ○ ○ ○ ○ ○ ○ ○ **4**

PASSAGE III

The atmosphere is made up of 4 distinct layers: the troposphere, stratosphere, mesosphere, and thermosphere. Different types of clouds form in the different layers depending on the pressure in the atmosphere and the ambient temperature. The cloud types include nimbus, stratus, cumulus, and cirrus. Figure 1 shows the location of the

barriers of the atmosphere when the temperature and pressure are at an ideal condition for cloud formation. It also shows the different types of clouds formed at the different levels. Note: Clouds are formed mostly of water crystals, but can also contain particles of rock and dust.

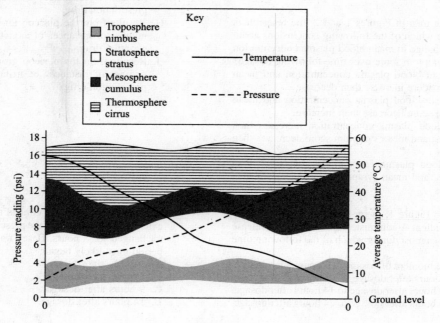

Figure 1

12. According to Figure 1, the atmospheric layer with the greatest range in pressure is the:
   F. mesosphere.
   G. thermosphere.
   H. stratosphere.
   J. troposphere.

13. Which of the following statements about the formation of cumulus clouds is supported by the data presented in Figure 1? Cumulus clouds typically form in:
   A. pressures between 8 and 12 psi and at an average temperature of 35°C.
   B. pressures between 12 and 16 psi and at an average temperature of 22°C.
   C. a pressure of 4 psi and at average temperatures between 12°C and 22°C.
   D. a pressure of 18 psi and at average temperatures between 50°C and 60°C.

14. According to Figure 1, as pressure within the atmospheric layers increases, temperature within the atmospheric layers:
   F. increases only.
   G. decreases only.
   H. increases up to 6 psi, then decreases.
   J. decreases up to 10 psi, then increases.

15. According to the information given in Figure 1, clouds within the stratosphere are most likely formed:
   A. under a pressure of 4 psi and 20°C.
   B. under a pressure of 10 psi and 30°C.
   C. over a pressure of 12 psi and 40°C.
   D. over a pressure of 14 psi and 50°C.

16. If a pressure of 7 psi were sustained within the atmosphere, according to Figure 1, which of the following types of clouds would likely form?
   F. Cirrus
   G. Cumulus
   H. Nimbus
   J. Stratus

GO ON TO THE NEXT PAGE.

4 ○ ○ ○ ○ ○ ○ ○ ○ ○ 4

PASSAGE IV

Because fish live in water they are exposed to any bacteria that exist in the water. Table 1 lists the habitat choices of 7 species of fish in a local pond and the fish's ability to combat the effects of the bacteria found in the water.

Table 1			
Fish species	Relative ability to combat bacteria	Habitat	Exposure to waterborne bacteria
A	<0.2	Shallow water with plants	None
B	<0.3	Shallow water with no plants	Low
C	0.2	Shallow water with no plants	Low
D	0.3	Deep water with no plants	Moderate
E	0.4	Shallow water with plants	High
F	0.6	Shallow water with plants	High
G	1.3	Shallow water with plants	High

Figure 1 shows the percent of fish that survive to adulthood in the lab for the 7 species, after exposure to water with bacteria present or exposure to water with the bacteria removed.

Figure 2 shows predicted bacteria levels over time in 4 geographic regions with fish populations.

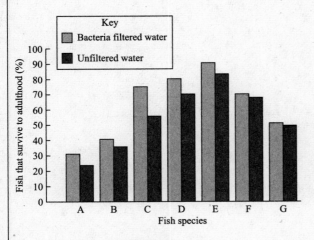

Figure 1

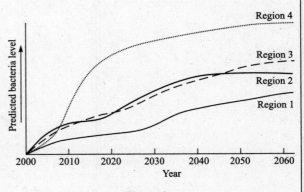

Figure 2

4 ◯ ◯ ◯ ◯ ◯ ◯ ◯ ◯ ◯ **4**

17. Based on the information in Figure 1, fish from which species are most likely to survive prolonged exposure to bacteria?
   A. Species A
   B. Species B
   C. Species D
   D. Species E

18. According to the data in Figure 1, which species showed the greatest difference between the percent of fish that survived to adulthood after exposure to unfiltered water, and the percent of fish that survived to adulthood after exposure to filtered water?
   F. Species A
   G. Species C
   H. Species E
   J. Species G

19. Researchers recently discovered a new species of fish that lives in deep water without plants. Based on the data in Table 1, the researchers would predict that this species' relative ability to combat bacteria is most likely:
   A. high.
   B. moderate.
   C. low.
   D. nonexistent.

20. According to the information in Table 1, for all the species shown, as the exposure to bacteria increases, the relative ability to combat the bacteria generally:
   F. decreases only.
   G. increases only.
   H. decreases, then increases.
   J. increases, then decreases.

21. Based on the data in Table 1 and Figure 1, fish that had the lowest percent of individuals survive to adulthood when exposed to bacteria tend to:
   A. live in shallow water without plants.
   B. live in shallow water with plants.
   C. live in deep water without plants.
   D. live in deep water with plants.

4 ○ ○ ○ ○ ○ ○ ○ ○ ○ **4**

PASSAGE V

While digging in a remote site in Africa, paleontologists discovered a collection of fossilized dinosaur bones. The bones were dated back to the Jurassic period, and have been confirmed to be from a dinosaur known as a velociraptor. Two paleontologists discuss the finding.

Paleontologist 1

Once the well-preserved bones are assembled it is clear that they are velociraptor bones from the Jurassic period. The bones are long in the arms, indicating that the velociraptor was definitely capable of flight. You can see that there are cuts within the arm/wing bones of this dinosaur, indicating that it was caught while in flight. Perhaps it was attempting an escape from a more predatory dinosaur, such as tyrannosaurus rex. It is obvious from the body structure of the velociraptor that it was an effective hunter and predator. It was most likely quick to swoop in on its prey and was more than able to carry the prey away on its own. The form and function of the velociraptor has been misunderstood until this important discovery. The condition of these bones offers a clear picture of the way in which the velociraptor lived.

Paleontologist 2

Indeed, the velociraptor bones are in excellent condition. The long arm bones are indicative of the dinosaur's ability to scavenge prey and fend off larger predators. The cuts within the arm bones show that the velociraptor often stole its meals—the marks resemble defense wounds, perhaps from forcing other would-be scavengers away from the free meal. The structure of the velociraptor's feet indicates that it was a fast runner and was able to maneuver well through the high trees and undergrowth. This would certainly have allowed the velociraptor to quickly escape predators and possibly arrive at a kill-site before other larger dinosaurs, such as tyrannosaurus rex, descended upon the leftovers. The bones that were discovered answer many questions about the velociraptor, but they also bring up many new issues to consider.

22. Paleontologist 1's viewpoint contains the basic assumption that the velociraptor must have been:
    F. unknown until the discovery of these bones.
    G. an ineffective hunter.
    H. previously mischaracterized.
    J. unable to escape large predators.

23. Paleontologist 1 would most likely state that the cuts on the velociraptor bones were the result of:
    A. failed attempts to fly.
    B. fending off a competing scavenger.
    C. an attack by a larger predator.
    D. mistakes made in assembling the bones.

24. Suppose that the fossilized remains of another dinosaur species with long arm bones were discovered, and scientists determined that this dinosaur lived at the same time as the velociraptor. According to the passage, Paleontologist 2 would most likely conclude that:
    F. the new dinosaur could fly.
    G. the new dinosaur could be a scavenger.
    H. the new dinosaur could not escape from predators.
    J. the new dinosaur could swoop in on its prey.

25. Paleontologist 2's viewpoint regarding the velociraptor as a scavenger was based on the dinosaur's:
    A. strong musculature.
    B. excellent condition.
    C. long arm bones.
    D. ability to fly.

26. Paleontologist 1 would most likely support which of the following statements about the lifestyle of the velociraptor?
    F. The velociraptor was a predatory dinosaur capable of flight, and is only now being understood.
    G. The velociraptor was a dinosaur who scavenged other dinosaurs' kills.
    H. The velociraptor was a fast runner that could easily out-maneuver its predators in order to survive.
    J. The velociraptor was hunted by many other dinosaurs during its time on Earth.

27. Assuming all are true, both paleontologists would most likely agree with which of the following facts concerning the velociraptor?
    A. It was threatened by larger dinosaurs, such as tyrannosaurus rex.
    B. It was unable to sustain flight.
    C. It was not built for speed, and therefore, could not easily fend for itself.
    D. It was not an effective hunter.

28. Both Paleontologists 1 and 2 would most likely agree with which of the following statements about the discovery of the velociraptor bones? The bones:
    F. did not clarify any assumptions about the velociraptor.
    G. provided some useful information regarding the velociraptor.
    H. could not be assembled properly due to the poor condition in which they were found.
    J. completely altered both paleontologist's viewpoints regarding the velociraptor.

GO ON TO THE NEXT PAGE.

4 ○ ○ ○ ○ ○ ○ ○ ○ ○ **4**

PASSAGE VI

The peaks of mountains often lose sediment due to wind erosion. Figure 1 shows mountain peak compositions, mountain heights, in meters (m), and the net change in meters (m), in mean peak height (MPH) from 1910 to 1970 along a section of the Rocky Mountains. A net negative change in MPH indicates a net loss of sediment and a net positive change in MPH indicates a gain of sediment.

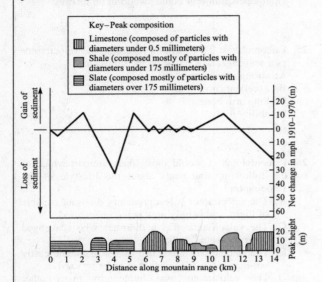

Figure 1

Table 1 shows the percentage of a year that horizontal sections of a mountain are exposed to wind.

Table 1	
Peak section height (m)	Percentage of the year that peak section is exposed to wind
0.0–0.5	1.1
0.5–1.0	3.1
1.0–1.5	7.2
1.5–2.0	10.5
2.0–2.5	14.2
2.5–3.0	19.4
3.0–3.5	23.7
3.5–4.0	29.3
4.0–4.5	37.4
4.5–5.0	42.3
5.0–5.5	48.0
Note: Heights are measured from mean (average) sea level.	

Figure 2 shows Peak C and D erosion rates, in m/y, as they relate to percentage of a year that mountain peak section is exposed to wind.

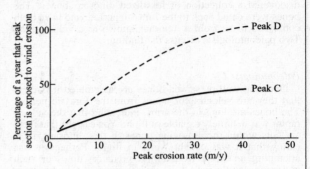

Figure 2

29. According to Figure 1, at a distance of 9 km along the mountain range, peaks of what composition are present, if any?
   A. Peaks of slate
   B. Peaks of shale
   C. Peaks of limestone
   D. No peaks are present

30. According to the information in Figure 1, which of the following properties was used to distinguish the various materials that compose the peaks in the study area?
   F. Particle size
   G. Particle clarity
   H. Particle color
   J. Particle density

31. Based on the information listed in Table 1, a peak section with a height of 5.5–6.0 m would be exposed to wind approximately what percentage of a year?
   A. 22%
   B. 39%
   C. 48%
   D. 53%

32. According to Figures 1 and 2, the difference between Peak C and Peak D erosion rates could best be explained as a difference in the:
   F. heights of the two peaks.
   G. force of the winds on the two peaks.
   H. composition of the two peaks.
   J. annual snowfall on the two peaks.

GO ON TO THE NEXT PAGE.

33. According to Table 1, which of the following figures best represents the relationship between the height of a peak section and the percentage of a year that peak section is exposed to wind erosion?

A.

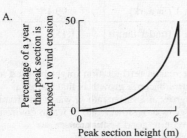

B.

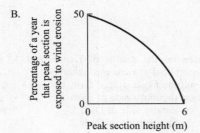

C.

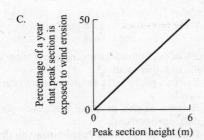

D.

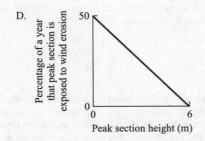

34. According to information in the passage, wind erosion often results in:

F. an increase in the percentage of a mountain peak that is exposed to snow.

G. a reduction in the overall surface area of mountain peaks.

H. a higher number of slate and shale deposits on mountain peaks.

J. a lower number of record snowfalls each year.

GO ON TO THE NEXT PAGE.

PASSAGE VII

A biologist investigated some of the environmental factors that could influence the growth of certain types of bacteria. The following experiments were conducted at a constant temperature, and no sample was tested more than once.

Experiment 1

Ten samples of bacteria were placed in each of 2 Petri dishes, the bottoms of which were each half moist and half dry. The dishes were covered with Petri dish lids. Dish 1 was placed in a darkened area and Dish 2 was placed in a lighted area. After 2 hours the location of bacterial growth in each dish was recorded (Table 1).

Table 1		
	Dry side	Moist side
Dish 1 (in dark)	1	9
Dish 2 (in light)	2	8

Experiment 2

Ten samples of bacteria were placed in each of 2 Petri dishes. The dishes were covered with Petri dish lids. Dish 1 was placed in a darkened area and Dish 2 was placed directly under a 25-watt incandescent lamp, creating a warm, lighted environment. After 2 hours the amount of bacterial growth in each dish was recorded and compared to the amount of growth in a control sample that was placed in a Petri dish and left in a regularly lighted area (Table 2).

Table 2	
	Growth proportional to control
Dish 1 (in dark)	0.93
Dish 2 (under lamp)	1.06

Experiment 3

Ten samples of bacteria were placed in each of 2 Petri dishes. Four different environments were created in each dish—dry/lighted, dry/dark, moist/lighted, and moist/dark. The bottoms of the Petri dishes were each half moist and half dry. The dishes were covered with Petri dish lids. Dish 1 was placed in a darkened area and Dish 2 was placed directly under a 25-watt incandescent lamp, creating a warm, lighted environment. After 2 hours the amount of bacterial growth in each dish was recorded and compared to the amount of growth in a control sample that was placed in a Petri dish and left in a regularly lighted area (Table 3).

Table 3		
	Growth proportional to control	
	Moist side	Dry side
Dish 1 (in dark)	0.99	0.53
Dish 2 (under lamp)	1.15	0.67

35. One reason refrigeration might be used as a means to control bacteria growth is that bacteria:
A. grow at a faster rate in warm environments.
B. grow at a slower rate in warm environments.
C. require good ventilation.
D. prefer dry environments.

36. Based on the results of Experiment 3, the greatest proportional growth was observed:
F. on the moist side of Dish 1.
G. on the moist side of Dish 2.
H. on the dry side of Dish 1.
J. on the dry side of Dish 2.

37. Which of the following conclusions is supported by the results of Experiment 1?
A. Bacteria prefer light environments to dark environments.
B. Bacteria exhibit an equal preference for light and dark environments.
C. Bacteria prefer moist environments to dry environments, regardless of lighting conditions.
D. Bacteria exhibit an equal preference for dry and moist environments.

38. One criticism of these experiments might be that the presence of more than one sample of bacteria in each Petri dish might have had an effect on the results. Which of the following changes in experimental design could be made to counter this criticism?
F. Use additional species of bacteria in each test.
G. Use only bacteria that was taken directly from nature and not generated in a lab.
H. Place each sample in a separate Petri dish.
J. Vary the size of the starting sample.

GO ON TO THE NEXT PAGE.

4 4

39. Bacteria are known to exist on nearly every surface of the world. On the basis of the experimental results, which of the following environments would provide the conditions best suited for a high growth rate?
  A. The surface of a desert rock.
  B. The bottom of a Great Lake.
  C. The surface of Antarctic ice sheet.
  D. Beneath a rock in a tropical forest.

40. In the 3 experiments, the environmental factors that could influence growth were evaluated by recording data about growth after 2 hours. Because bacteria double population size in short intervals, better information about growth might be achieved by recording data:
  F. after 10 minutes.
  G. at 30-minute intervals for 1 hour.
  H. after 1 hour.
  J. at 10-minute intervals for 2 hours.

END OF THE SCIENCE REASONING TEST.
STOP! IF YOU HAVE TIME LEFT OVER, CHECK YOUR WORK ON THIS SECTION ONLY.

WRITING TEST PROMPT

DIRECTIONS: This test is designed to assess your writing skills. You have 30 minutes to plan and write an essay based on the stimulus provided. Be sure to take a position on the issue and support your position using logical reasoning and relevant examples. Organize your ideas in a focused and logical way, and use the English language to clearly and effectively express your position.

When you have finished writing, refer to the Scoring Rubrics discussed in the Introduction (page 4) to estimate your score.

Some high schools ban students from driving to and from school if they live in an area with bus service. Administrators think this will reduce morning and afternoon traffic accidents and congestions as well as alleviate morning tardiness. Opponents say that a student with a driver's license should have the same right to drive to school as do faculty and staff with licenses. Some students say that while they are technically inside the boundary for bus service, walking to and from the bus stop every day is a major inconvenience.

In your opinion, should high schools ban students' commuting to reduce traffic and tardiness problems?

In your essay, take a position on this question. You may write about one of the points of view mentioned above, or you may give another point of view on this issue. Use specific examples and reasons for your position.

English Test

1. C	21. D	41. D	61. D
2. F	22. J	42. F	62. F
3. A	23. D	43. D	63. C
4. J	24. J	44. G	64. F
5. D	25. A	45. C	65. B
6. H	26. F	46. J	66. G
7. B	27. B	47. C	67. D
8. J	28. H	48. H	68. G
9. D	29. B	49. C	69. B
10. F	30. H	50. F	70. J
11. A	31. B	51. B	71. B
12. G	32. H	52. H	72. J
13. D	33. B	53. B	73. A
14. F	34. F	54. H	74. J
15. B	35. B	55. A	75. D
16. H	36. F	56. G	
17. A	37. C	57. D	
18. G	38. J	58. G	
19. C	39. D	59. C	
20. G	40. G	60. H	

Mathematics Test

1. B	21. B	41. B
2. K	22. F	42. H
3. C	23. B	43. A
4. H	24. J	44. F
5. C	25. A	45. B
6. J	26. G	46. K
7. B	27. B	47. A
8. H	28. G	48. H
9. D	29. E	49. D
10. K	30. G	50. G
11. C	31. C	51. D
12. K	32. F	52. J
13. A	33. C	53. C
14. F	34. G	54. H
15. B	35. B	55. C
16. H	36. K	56. K
17. B	37. A	57. A
18. H	38. F	58. F
19. E	39. A	59. E
20. G	40. G	60. H

Reading Test

1. A	21. D
2. H	22. H
3. B	23. A
4. J	24. H
5. C	25. B
6. F	26. H
7. D	27. D
8. G	28. J
9. D	29. A
10. J	30. G
11. B	31. A
12. F	32. H
13. D	33. C
14. H	34. F
15. B	35. A
16. G	36. J
17. C	37. D
18. J	38. H
19. D	39. C
20. F	40. F

Science Reasoning Test

1. C	21. B
2. H	22. H
3. C	23. C
4. G	24. G
5. A	25. C
6. H	26. F
7. C	27. A
8. H	28. G
9. A	29. B
10. F	30. F
11. D	31. D
12. G	32. F
13. A	33. C
14. G	34. G
15. B	35. A
16. J	36. G
17. D	37. C
18. G	38. H
19. B	39. D
20. G	40. J

■ SCORING GUIDE

Your final reported score is your COMPOSITE SCORE. Your COMPOSITE SCORE is the average of all of your SCALE SCORES.

Your SCALE SCORES for the four multiple-choice sections are derived from the Scoring Table on the next page. Use your RAW SCORE, or the number of questions that you answered correctly for each section, to determine your SCALE SCORE. If you got a RAW SCORE of 60 on the English test, for example, you correctly answered 60 out of 75 questions.

Step 1   Determine your RAW SCORE for each of the four multiple-choice sections:

English   _____

Mathematics   _____

Reading   _____

Science Reasoning   _____

The following Raw Score Table shows the total possible points for each section.

RAW SCORE TABLE	
KNOWLEDGE AND SKILL AREAS	**RAW SCORES**
ENGLISH	75
MATHEMATICS	60
READING	40
SCIENCE REASONING	40
WRITING	12

Multiple-Choice Scoring Worksheet

Step 2 Determine your SCALE SCORE for each of the four multiple-choice sections using the following Scoring Worksheet. Each SCALE SCORE should be rounded to the nearest number according to normal rules. For example, $31.2 \approx 31$ and $31.5 \approx 32$. If you answered 61 questions correctly on the English section, for example, your SCALE SCORE would be 29.

English   _____ × 36 = _____ ÷ 75 = _____
               RAW SCORE

                                                              − 2 (*correction factor)

                                                              SCALE SCORE

Mathematics   _____ × 36 = _____ ÷ 60 = _____
               RAW SCORE

                                                              + 1 (*correction factor)

                                                              SCALE SCORE

Reading   _____ × 36 = _____ ÷ 40 = _____
               RAW SCORE

                                                              + 2 (*correction factor)

                                                              SCALE SCORE

Science Reasoning   _____ × 36 = _____ ÷ 40 = _____
                   RAW SCORE

                                                              + 1.5 (*correction factor)

                                                              SCALE SCORE

    *The correction factor is an approximation based on the average from several recent ACT tests. It is most valid for scores in the middle 50% (approximately 16–24 scale composite score) of the scoring range.

    The scores are all approximate. Actual ACT scoring scales vary from one administration to the next based upon several factors.

    If you take the optional Writing Test, you will need to combine your English and Writing scores to obtain your final COMPOSITE SCORE. Once you have determined a score for your essay out of 12 possible points, you will need to determine your ENGLISH/WRITING SCALE SCORE, using both your ENGLISH SCALE SCORE and your WRITING TEST SCORE. The combination of the two scores will give you an ENGLISH/WRITING SCALE SCORE, from 1 to 36, that will be used to determine your COMPOSITE SCORE mentioned earlier.

    Using the English/Writing Scoring Table, find your ENGLISH SCALE SCORE on the left or right hand side of the table and your WRITING TEST SCORE on the top of the table. Follow your ENGLISH SCALE SCORE over and your WRITING TEST SCORE down until the two columns meet at a number. This number is your ENGLISH/WRITING SCALE SCORE and will be used to determine your COMPOSITE SCORE.

Step 3 Determine your ENGLISH/WRITING SCALE SCORE using the English/Writing Scoring Table on the following page:

        English   _____

        Writing   _____

        English/Writing _____

ENGLISH/WRITING SCORING TABLE

ENGLISH SCALE SCORE	WRITING TEST SCORE											ENGLISH SCALE SCORE
	2	3	4	5	6	7	8	9	10	11	12	
36	26	27	28	29	30	31	32	33	34	32	36	36
35	26	27	28	29	30	31	31	32	33	34	35	35
34	25	26	27	28	29	30	31	32	33	34	35	34
33	24	25	26	27	28	29	30	31	32	33	34	33
32	24	25	25	26	27	28	29	30	31	32	33	32
31	23	24	25	26	27	28	29	30	30	31	32	31
30	22	23	24	25	26	27	28	29	30	31	32	30
29	21	22	23	24	25	26	27	28	29	30	31	29
28	21	22	23	24	24	25	26	27	28	29	30	28
27	20	21	22	23	24	25	26	27	28	28	29	27
26	19	20	21	22	23	24	25	26	27	28	29	26
25	18	19	20	21	22	23	24	25	26	27	28	25
24	18	19	20	21	22	23	23	24	25	26	27	24
23	17	18	19	20	21	22	23	24	25	26	27	23
22	16	17	18	19	20	21	22	23	24	25	26	22
21	16	17	17	18	19	20	21	22	23	24	25	21
20	15	16	17	18	19	20	21	21	22	23	24	20
19	14	15	16	17	18	19	20	21	22	23	24	19
18	13	14	15	16	17	18	19	20	21	22	23	18
17	13	14	15	16	16	17	18	19	20	21	22	17
16	12	13	14	15	16	17	18	19	20	20	21	16
15	11	12	13	14	15	16	17	18	19	20	21	15
14	10	11	12	13	14	15	16	17	18	19	20	14
13	10	11	12	13	14	14	15	16	17	18	19	13
12	9	10	11	12	13	14	15	16	17	18	19	12
11	8	9	10	11	12	13	14	15	16	17	18	11
10	8	9	9	10	11	12	13	14	15	16	17	10
9	7	8	9	10	11	12	13	13	14	15	16	9
8	6	7	8	9	10	11	12	13	14	15	16	8
7	5	6	7	8	9	10	11	12	13	14	15	7
6	5	6	7	7	8	9	10	11	12	13	14	6
5	4	5	6	7	8	9	10	11	12	12	13	5
4	3	4	5	6	7	8	9	10	11	12	13	4
3	2	3	4	5	6	7	8	9	10	11	12	3
2	2	3	4	5	6	6	7	8	9	10	11	2
1	1	2	3	4	5	6	7	8	9	10	11	1

Step 4   Determine your COMPOSITE SCORE by finding the sum of all your SCALE SCORES for each of the four sections: English only (if you do not choose to take the optional Writing Test) *or* English/Writing (if you choose to take the optional Writing Test), Math, Reading, and Science Reasoning, and divide by 4 to find the average. Round your COMPOSITE SCORE according to normal rules. For example, $31.2 \approx 31$ and $31.5 \approx 32$.

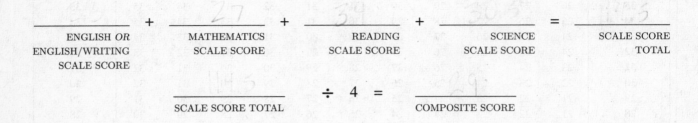

_____	+	____27____	+	____39____	+	___30.5___	=	_____
ENGLISH *OR* ENGLISH/WRITING SCALE SCORE		MATHEMATICS SCALE SCORE		READING SCALE SCORE		SCIENCE SCALE SCORE		SCALE SCORE TOTAL

_____114.5_____   ÷   4   =   _____29_____
SCALE SCORE TOTAL   COMPOSITE SCORE

ANSWERS AND EXPLANATIONS

English Test Explanations

PASSAGE I

1. **The best answer is C.** The narrator was chosen "last spring," which was in the past. Answer choice A is incorrect because the moment the narrator is referring to is relative to the time the narrator wrote the passage, not another time in the past. Answer choices B and D can be eliminated because they are not past tense.

2. **The best answer is F.** The sentence appropriately uses the relative pronoun *who* to introduce the clause that modifies *couple*; this sentence is correct as it is written. The pronoun *who* also functions as the subject of the clause.

3. **The best answer is A.** The sentence represents a clear, complete thought that is grammatically correct. It is correct to begin a new sentence with *speaking*. You can eliminate the other answer choices because either they create incomplete sentences (B), or are otherwise grammatically incorrect.

4. **The best answer is J.** The sentence indicates that eating breakfast with the host family was a routine action in the past. Answer choice J is best because it includes *would*, which suggests repeated eating of breakfast with the couple. You can eliminate answer choice F because it is written in the present tense.

5. **The best answer is D.** The two clauses are unrelated and, therefore, you can connect the two separate ideas by using the word *then*. Answer choices B and C can be eliminated because they express a cause-and-effect relationship that does not fit with the sentence.

6. **The best answer is H.** This question asks you to place the apostrophe correctly in the underlined portion of the sentence. Answer choice H is best because the extended family is that of both parents together. This is made even clearer by the subject *they* in the following sentence.

7. **The best answer is B.** Answer choice B correctly uses the infinitive form *to tend* to explain why the host couple must travel. Choice C is incorrect because inflected forms like *tended* require an expressed subject. Choice D is incorrect because the *to* that follows is realized as a preposition linked

to *travel*. The couple is not physically traveling to the *business*.

8. **The best answer is J.** This question tests your ability to spot relevance. Neither the underlined portion nor the information is answer choice G and H add anything relevant to the sentence. Therefore, it would be best to omit the underlined portion and simply end the sentence with "another."

9. **The best answer is D.** Logically, the question is asking whether the speaker would like to live with someone who speaks English or someone who does not speak English. The term *whether* only requires one side of a two-sided situation (e.g. "I don't know whether she has a roommate," not "I don't know whether she has a roommate or lives by herself.")

10. **The best answer is F.** The word *whom* is an object pronoun, meaning it will occur in object, not subject, position. In this case, it is the object of *find*. Remember, *whom* refers to Paolo, the logical direct object. This becomes clear if you reorder the clause: "I was surprised to *find Paolo* playing one of my favorite CDs on the stereo!"

11. **The best answer is A.** The essay maintains a positive, uplifting tone with regard to the speaker's friendship with Paolo. The other answer choices do not match the tone of the essay.

12. **The best answer is G.** The word *talk* takes a prepositional object starting with *about*; you cannot divide the phrase with a comma. Answer choice H is incorrect because modifiers like "my Brazilian friend" that come before proper names do not need a comma.

13. **The best answer is D.** The sentence is used to describe a faulty or incomplete first impression, then uses *but* to introduce a revision to it. Such clauses introduced by a subordinating conjunction are offset from the first clause of the sentence with a comma.

14. **The best answer is F.** The speaker is summarizing his trip into one important lesson. Answer choices G and H do not represent how meaningful the lesson is to the speaker and answer choice J is awkward as a modifier of *lesson*.

15. The best answer is B. The essay describes an enjoyable friendship between people of two different nationalities that begins in the context of a foreign culture. Answer choices A and C have a negative tone that does not match the rest of the essay. Answer choice D can be eliminated because it is not relevant to the passage.

PASSAGE II

16. The best answer is H. The clause subordinate to *apartment* is *I'm renting* and cannot be divided by a comma. The sentence up to the word *renting* is an adverbial, describing the location of the restaurant, so it must be followed by a comma.

17. The best answer is A. The paragraph is written in present tense. Answer choices B and C are past tense, and imply that the restaurant is not located there anymore. Answer choice D implies that the restaurant is not located there yet.

18. The best answer is G. The prepositional phrase introduced by *in* modifies *fountain* and cannot be divided by a comma. Answer choice J can be eliminated because a semicolon should be used to separate two independent clauses.

19. The best answer is C. Adjectives such as *sinful* modify nouns, such as *deliciousness*, which can be modified by prepositional phrases, such as *of Joe's Special Reuben*. The other answer choices incorrectly pair adjectives, adverbs, and nouns.

20. The best answer is G. This question tests your ability to recognize redundancy in a sentence. *New-comers* implies people who have never seen *his creations*. The other answer choices are redundant.

21. The best answer is D. This question requires you to determine the correct punctuation. No punctuation is necessary between nouns like *sauerkraut* and gerunds like *spilling*, which modify them.

22. The best answer is J. Sentence 4 is about the menu in the window. It should be placed after the sentence that describes the menu. Placing it anywhere else in the paragraph would cause the paragraph not to make sense.

23. The best answer is D. This answer choice describes how the unwelcoming appearance of the restaurant does not reveal the truth about the delicious food. The other answer choices can be eliminated because they are not relevant to the topic of the paragraph.

24. The best answer is J. *Belies* is a transitive verb that takes what follows it as its direct object. A comma

cannot be placed after *belies*; therefore, answer choices F and H can be eliminated. Answer choice G would create a sentence fragment, and can be eliminated.

25. The best answer is A. The verbs must agree with the subject *refrigerator*. Answer choice D is not appropriate when describing a single refrigerator case, and can be eliminated. Answer choice B does not make sense. Answer choice C is not inflected for tense.

26. The best answer is F. This sentence provides a logical transition between the previous sentence, which is about building repair, and the following sentence, which is about how the food is enough to sustain the charm of the restaurant.

27. The best answer is B. *Many* is the appropriate adjective for *"A lot of people"* from the previous sentence. It emphasizes the disparity between the narrator's knowledge of regular customers' faces and the sandwiches they eat. Answer choice A can be eliminated because while *much* can apply to mass nouns (e.g. much trash, much noise), it cannot be used with countable nouns. For those, *many* must be used (e.g. many people, many marbles). Answer choice C is an adverb and would, therefore, be ungrammatical. Answer choice D does not make sense in context.

28. The best answer is H. The phrase describes *the classics*, which by itself may be unclear. Answer choice G can be eliminated because the information is important to your knowledge of what *the classics* are. Answer choices F and J are not supported by the passage.

29. The best answer is B. The information is made clear without the use of excess commas or weak words like *makes* and *this place*. The other answer choices are too wordy or have awkward pauses.

30. The best answer is H. This question requires you to determine the correct punctuation. No punctuation is required between two noun phrases conjoined with *and*.

PASSAGE III

31. The best answer is B. The speaker is talking about Native Americans in the past; therefore, answer choices A, C, and D may be eliminated.

32. The best answer is H. A list of only two items does not need punctuation to separate them; therefore, the other answer choices may be eliminated.

33. The best answer is B. The speaker is talking about the ferries in past tense; therefore, the other answer choices may be eliminated.

34. The best answer is F. The phrase as it is written is clear and concise. Answer choice G is wordy and answer choices H and J do not make sense in the sentence.

35. The best answer is B. The underlined sentence explains that a potential bridge was reasonable because the Brooklyn Bridge was a success. The other answer choices are not supported by the passage.

36. The best answer is F. To "take action on" something is a common idiomatic expression; therefore, the other answer choices may be eliminated.

37. The best answer is C. The second clause describes something that stands in opposition to the first clause; that is, ferry service was resumed, *but* something caused it to stop again. The other answer choices would not link the two clauses correctly.

38. The best answer is J. The possessive form of "it" is "its," without the apostrophe; answer choice H may be eliminated. Here, "its" refers to "ferry service between peninsulas," which is singular; therefore, answer choice G may be eliminated.

39. The best answer is D. The sentence as it is written is a fragment. Simply eliminating "that" after "however" corrects this problem. The word "however," when used in the middle of a sentence must be offset with commas.

40. The best answer is G. The preceding sentence shows the significance of the bridge. Answer choices H and J can be eliminated because they are irrelevant to the topic of the essay. Answer choice F can be eliminated because the sentence does not explain how the bridge was built.

41. The best answer is D. The elements in the sentence are ordered logically. The other answer choices separate elements from each other with use of commas, which make the sentence less clear.

42. The best answer is F. The other answer choices would not make sense with the simple present form "is" used in the sentence.

43. The best answer is D. This question tests your ability to recognize redundancy. *Highway drivers* and *travelers* in this sentence essentially mean the same thing. The other answer choices are redundant.

44. The best answer is G. This answer choice does not fit with the topic of the essay, which is the Mackinac Bridge in the context of Michigan, not the context of the all the world's suspension bridges.

45. The best answer is C. This essay focuses on how the bridge came to be built. Answer choices A and B may be eliminated because the essay does not describe the entire process of building the Mackinac Bridge. Answer choice D may be eliminated because the topic of the essay is not specifically the reason for building the bridge.

PASSAGE IV

46. The best answer is J. The underlined sentence distracts from the intent of the paragraph, and should be omitted. The other answer choices also include information that is irrelevant to the topic of the essay.

47. The best answer is C. The narrator is speaking about his past. Answer choice A is ungrammatical and wordy. Answer C differs from B in that it omits whom, an unnecessary element. Answer D may be eliminated because the sentence would not make sense.

48. The best answer is H. This question requires you to determine the correct punctuation. No punctuation may come between a noun phrase (*box in his room*) and the gerund modifying it (*brimming*).

49. The best answer is C. The simple plural past tense is correct here. *No piece* is a singular subject, and cannot be referred to by answer choice A. Answer choice B would not make sense in the sentence.

50. The best answer is F. In Paragraph 2 the author analyzes the arguments in favor of electronic entertainment and then proposes his counterarguments. Answer choice G can be eliminated because it is irrelevant to the author's argument. Answer choice H is unsupported by the passage and answer choice J does not provide a logical transition from the previous paragraph.

51. The best answer is B. In the sentence, *but* does not correctly conjoin *dynamic* and *engaging*, which are closely related. The other answer choices are equivalent to the underlined sentences and are acceptable.

52. The best answer is H. When placed after Sentence 7, the sentence provides a logical transition to the subsequent paragraph. Answer choices F and

G can be eliminated because their placement would cause the paragraph to be illogical. The assertion in answer choice J is false, and may, therefore, be eliminated.

53. The best answer is B. This question tests your ability to recognize redundancy in a sentence. Answer choice B is the best answer because it avoids redundancy. Answer choices A, C, and D would introduce redundancy.

54. The best answer is H. The answer choice correctly modifies *weekend*. The narrator intends to describe card shows that occurred multiple times over multiple weekends. Answer choice F can be eliminated because it does not accurately convey what the narrator intends to describe.

55. The best answer is A. The sentence describes a habitual action in the past. Answer choice C can be eliminated because it is present tense. Answer choice B can be eliminated because *we* does not make any sense in the sentence.

56. The best answer is G. Adverbials like *too* are separated from the main clause by a comma. The gerund *encouraging* modifies *activity*, so *too* must be followed by a comma as well.

57. The best answer is D. This answer choice eliminates the redundancy. The word *screen* does not need to be repeated because the reader already knows that it is the video screen that silences the spectators.

58. The best answer is G. This answer choice is consistent with the narrator's use of the second person from the preceding sentence. Answer choices F, H, and J can be eliminated because they do not use second person.

59. The best answer is C. The best way to answer this question is to try the answer choices in the sentence. Answer choice C is the best because only adverbs modify adjectives.

60. The best answer is H. The narrator believes video games do not teach the skills card collecting teaches. Showing this in the passage indicates the author finds card collecting superior to electronic entertainment.

PASSAGE V

61. The best answer is D. This question requires you to determine the correct punctuation. In the sentence, *wait* takes a prepositional object headed by *until*, so punctuation must not separate them.

62. The best answer is F. The clause headed by *which* provides descriptive detail about why spyware is a threat. The remaining answer choices are not grammatical.

63. The best answer is C. The writer sets the computer virus in opposition to spyware, to show how the two are unlike each other. The other answer choices compare spyware with a computer virus, which is not the intent of the writer.

64. The best answer is F. The best way to answer this question is to try the answer choices in the sentence. Here, *often* coordinates well with *usually*. Answer choice H can be eliminated because *always* does not make sense with *but*. The other answer choices would not make sense in context.

65. The best answer is B. *However*, when used in the middle of a clause is set apart with commas. The other answer choices can be eliminated because they don't follow this rule.

66. The best answer is G. The paragraph describes some harmful spyware programs. This sentence effectively introduces the topic and links Paragraphs 2 and 3.

67. The best answer is D. This is clear, concise, and in active voice. The other answer choices are wordy.

68. The best answer is G. Answer choice G is the only choice that avoids redundancy. *Detection utilities* suggest that the utilities detect spyware. It is unnecessary to restate the fact that spyware is being detected.

69. The best answer is B. The verbs must agree with the plural subject *Detection utilities*. Answer choice B is the only answer in which *scan* and *remove* correspond with the plural subject.

70. The best answer is J. The writer is using present tense. Answer choices G may be eliminated because it is in past tense. *Computer* is the logical object of *protect*, and therefore, answer choices H and F can be eliminated.

71. The best answer is B. This is the only answer choice that provides a specific sound web surfing habit. Answer choice A is not specific enough to provide you with an example of a habit. Answer choices C and D are irrelevant to the argument the writer is making.

72. The best answer is J. Negative elements appear at the beginning of imperative clauses. *Never* is negative, and therefore, would fit best at the beginning of the sentence.

73. **The best answer is A.** The sentence begins with an "If" clause and ends with a clause describing the result. These two must be separated by a comma and the subject must be repeated. The other answer choices may, therefore, be eliminated.

74. **The best answer is J.** The sentence would provide a logical conclusion to the essay. Answer choices F,

G, and H can be eliminated because if the sentence were placed in one of those paragraphs, it would not support the arguments it followed.

75. **The best answer is D.** Though the author might know how to protect computers from spyware, he makes no reference to its programming or the ethical issues that surround it.

Mathematics Test Explanations

1. The correct answer is B. To find the midpoint of two points, you can take the average of the x and y coordinates. If point X has coordinates $(-4,0)$ and point Y has coordinates $(0,-8)$, then the midpoint is:

$$\left(\frac{(-4+0)}{2}, \frac{(0+-8)}{2}\right)$$

$$\left(\frac{-4}{2}, \frac{-8}{2}\right)$$

$$(-2,-4)$$

2. The correct answer is K. To solve, use the Pythagorean Theorem ($c^2 = a^2 + b^2$). Using values from $\triangle MNO$, you can set up the equation like this:

$$10^2 = 6^2 + NO^2$$

$$100 = 36 + NO^2$$

$$NO^2 = 100 - 36 = 64$$

$$NO = \sqrt{64} = 8$$

3. The correct answer is C. Since a distance in meters, M, can be approximated by multiplying a distance in yards, Y, by 1.0936, it follows that $M \approx Y(1.0936)$.

4. The correct answer is H. Because Seth has 4 plaid shirts and 5 solid-colored shirts, the total number of shirts is $4 + 5 = 9$. Of these 9 shirts, 4 are plaid. Thus the probability that a randomly selected shirt will be plaid is $\frac{4}{9}$.

5. The correct answer is C. Unless otherwise specified, average means "arithmetic mean," which is defined as the sum of a set of values divided by the number of values. Therefore, you can see that the average number of enrollments per day is $\frac{(17 + 19 + 23 + 14 + 25 + 28)}{6} = \frac{126}{6}$, or 21.

6. The correct answer is J. When parallel lines are cut by a transversal (such as segment PR in this problem), "alternate interior angles" are congruent. In this problem, $\angle y$ and $\angle 4$ are alternate interior angles, and so you can conclude that they are congruent.

7. The correct answer is B. The easiest way to solve this problem is to take 25% of the original price and deduct it from the original price. To find 25% of the sale price of the carton of paper, you would multiply $27.00 by 25%, or 0.25. Therefore, the sale price of the carton of paper would be $27.00 - (\$27.00)(0.25) = \$27.00 - \$6.75$, or $20.25.

8. The correct answer is H. To solve this problem, you must recognize that parallel lines always have the same slope. Remember that to find the slope of the line, you have to convert the equation $2x - 3y = 7$ into slope-intercept form ($y = mx + b$, where m is the slope):

$$2x - 3y - 2x = 7 - 2x$$

$$\frac{(-3y)}{3} = \frac{(-2x + 7)}{(-3)}$$

$$y = \frac{-2x}{-3} + \frac{7}{-3}$$

$$y = \frac{2}{3}x - \frac{7}{3}$$

Thus the slope of this line, or any line parallel to it, is $\frac{2}{3}$.

9. The correct answer is D. In order to solve this problem, you must realize that if Andrew had $28,000 remaining after paying 30% in taxes, then the $28,000 constitutes $100\% - 30\%$ or 70% of the original prize, P. Therefore, $0.7P = 28,000$. Dividing by 0.7, you can conclude that the original cash value of the prize was $P = \frac{28,000}{0.7}$, or $40,000.

10. The correct answer is K. To solve this problem, it is useful to assign values to the number of apples that Melissa and Marcia both possess. If Marcia has 10 apples, Melissa has $10 - 3 = 7$ apples. If Melissa gives 2 of her 7 apples to Marcia, Melissa is left with $7 - 2 = 5$ apples. When Marcia receives 2 more apples, she has $10 + 2 = 12$ apples. Since Marcia now has 12 apples and Melissa now has 5 apples, Melissa has $12 - 5 = 7$ fewer apples than Marcia.

11. The correct answer is C. The absolute value of a number is its distance from zero, regardless of whether it is positive or negative. Therefore, the value of $|5 - 9| = |-4| = 4$.

12. The correct answer is K. Since this problem requires you to multiply two binomials, you can utilize the FOIL (First, Outside, Inside, Last) method to multiply the expressions.

$$\text{First: } (3m)(m^2) = 3m^3$$

$$\text{Outside: } (3m)(-n) = -3mn$$

$$\text{Inside: } (n)(m^2) = m^2n$$

$$\text{Last: } (n)(-n) = -n^2$$

Finally, add all these terms up to come up with your final answer. $(3m + n)(m^2 - n) = 3m^3 - 3mn + m^2n - n^2$.

13. **The correct answer is A.** To solve this problem, you must distribute and add like terms, as follows:

$$13 - 2(x + 5) =$$

$$13 - 2x - 10 = 2x + 3$$

14. **The correct answer is F.** Remember that the rule for exponents states that for base number b and exponents x and y, $(b^x)^y = b^{xy}$. Thus, when you apply the numbers from this problem, you find that $(n^7)^{11} = n^{(7)(11)} = n^{77}$.

15. **The correct answer is B.** To solve this problem, recognize that the repeating decimal has four places (0.3456), and that the fourth place is occupied by the number 6. Therefore, every place that is a multiple of 4 will be represented by the number 6. Since 217 is not divisible by 4, you know that the 217th digit cannot be 6; eliminate answer choice E. Because 216 is a multiple of 4, the 216th digit will be 6. Therefore, the 217th digit must be 3, the next digit in the repeating decimal.

16. **The correct answer is H.** If a square has side x, then its perimeter is $4x$; this is because a square is defined as a rectangle where all four sides are of equal length. Since the perimeter of the square is 48, then $48 = 4x$ and $x = \dfrac{48}{4} = 12$. Thus, the length of one side of the square is 12. The area of a square is defined as $(\text{side})^2$; therefore the area of this square is 12^2 or 144.

17. **The correct answer is B.** The easiest way to solve this problem is to remember that when two binomial expressions are multiplied, there is a predictable result. Take the following generalized example: $(x + a)(x - b) = x^2 - bx + ax - ab$. If $x^2 - bx + ax - ab = 0$, then the solutions to the equation are $x = -a$ and $x = b$. The product of the solutions is $-ab$. With this expression, $x^2 + 3x - 21 = 0$, the product of the solutions $(-ab)$ is -21.

18. **The correct answer is H.** Remember that a difference of squares factors easily, such as: $a^2 - b^2 = (a + b)(a - b)$. Using the same technique, you can factor $a^{16} - 16$ into $(a^8 + 4)(a^8 - 4)$. The factor $(a^8 - 4)$ is another difference of squares, so it can be factored further into itself: $(a^8 - 4) = (a^4 + 2)(a^4 - 2)$. Of these factors, only $(a^4 + 2)$ is an answer choice.

19. **The correct answer is E.** Recall that dividing by a fraction is equivalent to multiplying by the reciprocal. When $\dfrac{1}{4}$ is substituted for n in the following expression, $\dfrac{2n - 5}{n}$, the result is:

$$\dfrac{2\left(\frac{1}{4}\right) - 5}{\frac{1}{4}}$$

$$= \left(\dfrac{2}{4} - 5\right)4$$

$$= 2 - 20 = -18$$

20. **The correct answer is G.** Since 90 minutes is equal to 1.5 hours, a proofreader who can read 40 pages in one hour can read $(1.5)(40)$ or 60 pages in 1.5 hours.

21. **The correct answer is B.** The height, h, can be found using the Pythagorean Theorem ($c^2 = a^2 + b^2$):

$$5^2 = 3^2 + h^2$$

$$25 = 9 + h^2$$

$$h^2 = 16, \text{ or } h = 4.$$

Thus, when you multiply the base of the parallelogram by its height, the area of the parallelogram is $9 \times 4 = 36$.

22. **The correct answer is F.** For a certain quadratic equation $ax^2 + bx + c = 0$, if $x = \dfrac{a}{b}$ is a solution, then a possible factor would be $(bx - a)$. Since two solutions for $ax^2 + bx + c = 0$ are $x = \dfrac{3}{4}$ and $x = \dfrac{-2}{5}$, then possible factors are $(4x - 3)$ and $(5x + 2)$.

23. **The correct answer is B.** The diagonals of a rhombus intersect at their midpoints and form right angles as shown below.

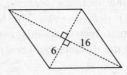

Since the diagonals meet at their midpoints and form right angles, they form a right triangle with legs $\frac{12}{2} = 6$ and $\frac{32}{2} = 16$. To find the length of a side of the rhombus, you can simply use the Pythagorean Theorem and solve where the side of the rhombus, s, is the hypotenuse: $s^2 = 6^2 + 16^2 = 292$; s is approximately equal to 17.09.

24. **The correct answer is J.** If a rectangular parking lot has a length, l, that is 3 feet longer than its width, w, then $l = 3 + w$, or $w = l - 3$. The area of a rectangle is equal to its length times it width, or $A = lw$. Since the area of this parking lot is 550, $lw = 550$. Substituting $(l - 3)$ for

$$550 = l(l - 3) =$$

$$550 = l^2 - 3l$$

$$l^2 - 3l - 550 = 0.$$

To solve for l, factor the quadratic equation to get $(l + 22)(l - 25) = 0$, making $l = -22$ or $l = 25$. Since negative values for length do not make sense in this context, the length is 25.

25. **The correct answer is A.** To find the slope of the line between any two points (x_1, y_1) and (x_2, y_2), you can use the equation $\frac{(y_2 - y_1)}{(x_2 - x_1)}$. Therefore, when you have the points $(3, 7)$ and $(4, -8)$ it follows that the slope of the line joining these points is $\frac{(-8 - 7)}{(4 - 3)} = \frac{-15}{1}$, or -15.

26. **The correct answer is G.** To find the solution set of $x + 2 > -4$, first solve for x by subtracting 2 from both sides. The result is $x > -6$. Thus the solution set is $\{x : x > -6\}$.

27. **The correct answer is B.** To solve this problem, you need to know that the equation of a circle with center (h, k) and radius r is $(x - h)^2 + (y - k)^2 = r^2$. Therefore, the center of the circle in the problem, $(x - 3)^2 + (y + 3)^2 = 4$, is $(3, -3)$.

28. **The correct answer is G.** To find the distance between two points (x_1, y_1) and (x_2, y_2), you can use the distance formula, which is $d = \sqrt{(x_2 - x_1)^2 + (y_2 - y_1)^2}$. The length of the line segment that has endpoints $(-3, 4)$ and $(5, -6)$ will equal the distance between points $(-3, 4)$ and

$(5, -6)$. Therefore, $d =$

$$\sqrt{(5 - (-3))^2 + (-6 - 4)^2}$$

$$= \sqrt{8^2 + 10^2}$$

$$= \sqrt{64 + 100}$$

$$= \sqrt{164}$$

$$= \sqrt{(4)(41)}$$

$$= \sqrt{4}\sqrt{41}$$

$$= 2\sqrt{41}$$

29. **The correct answer is E.** The key to solving this problem is remembering that the triangle inequality states that no one side of a triangle can be greater than the sum of the other two sides. Thus the third side of the triangle in the problem cannot be greater than the sum of the other two sides, 4.7 and 9, which is 13.7. Of the answer choices, only 14 is too large to be a possible value for the third side of the triangle.

30. **The correct answer is G.** To solve this problem, recall that $\frac{n^x}{n^y} = n^{x-y}$. Since it is given in the problem that $\frac{n^x}{n^y} = n^2$, you can conclude that $n^{x-y} = n^2$ and thus $x - y = 2$.

31. **The correct answer is C.** To solve, convert the equation of the line to slope-intercept form ($y = mx + b$, where m is the slope and b is the y-intercept). If $3x + 5y = 8$, then:

$$3x + 5y - 3x = 8 - 3x$$

$$\frac{(5y)}{5} = \frac{(-3x + 8)}{5}$$

$$y = \frac{-3x}{5} + \frac{8}{5}$$

Since the equation $y = \frac{-3x}{5} + \frac{8}{5}$ is in slope-intercept form, the y-intercept is $\frac{8}{5}$.

32. **The correct answer is F.** To find the cost per ounce, first convert 3.4 pounds to ounces. Because there are 16 ounces in a pound, 3.4 pounds is $3.4(16) = 54.4$ ounces. To find cost per ounce, divide the cost in dollars by the number of ounces, or $\frac{\$4.95}{54.4}$ ounces = $0.09 per ounce.

33. **The correct answer is C.** To solve, first square each fraction: $\left(\frac{1}{2}\right)^2 + \left(\frac{1}{3}\right)^2 + \left(\frac{1}{4}\right)^2 = \frac{1}{4} + \frac{1}{9} + \frac{1}{16}$. Remember that to be added, fractions must have a common denominator. In this case, since 4 is a factor of 16, the lowest common denominator is $(9)(16) = 144$. To convert fractions into different denominators, you must multiply the top and bottom of a fraction by the *same* number. If $\frac{1}{4}$ is multiplied by $\frac{36}{36}$, the result is $\frac{36}{144}$. Likewise, multiplying $\frac{1}{9}$ by $\frac{16}{16}$ yields $\frac{16}{144}$, and multiplying $\frac{1}{16}$ by $\frac{9}{9}$ yields $\frac{9}{144}$. Therefore $\frac{1}{4} + \frac{1}{9} + \frac{1}{16} = \frac{36}{144} + \frac{16}{144} + \frac{9}{144} = \frac{(36 + 16 + 9)}{144}$, or $\frac{61}{144}$.

34. **The correct answer is G.** The easiest way to solve this problem is to draw a picture similar to the one below.

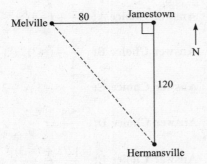

Since the route heads straight north from Hermansville for 120 miles to Jamestown, and then straight west for 80 miles to Melville, the turn at Jamestown creates a right angle. If a straight, flat road existed between Hermansville and Melville, it would form the hypotenuse of a right triangle with legs 80 and 120. Using the Pythagorean Theorem $(c^2 = a^2 + b^2)$, you can see that the distance of this straight route from Hermansville to Melville would be:

$$\sqrt{(120^2 + 80^2)}$$
$$= \sqrt{(14,400 + 6,400)}$$
$$= \sqrt{20,800} \approx 144$$

35. **The correct answer is B.** To solve this problem, calculate the volume of the aquarium and divide by 2. Since volume is equivalent to length × width x height, the volume is $30 \times 16 \times 12$, or 5,760 cubic inches of water. Dividing by two, you see that half of the tank would be 2,880 cubic inches of water.

36. **The correct answer is K.** To solve this problem, you would multiply the number of possibilities in each officer position. Since the league selects its 4 officers by first selecting the president, then the vice president, then the secretary, then the treasurer, there are 40 possibilities for president, 39 possibilities for vice president, 38 possibilities for secretary, and 37 possibilities for treasurer. The total number of different possibilities for the election is therefore $40 \times 39 \times 38 \times 37$.

37. **The correct answer is A.** Because there is a right angle at S, the point T will lie along the line through S that is perpendicular to the segment RS. To solve this problem, find the equation for the line through S that is perpendicular to the segment RS and try each answer choice to find one that lies on the line. Since the line is perpendicular to segment RS, it will have a slope that is the opposite reciprocal of the slope of RS. Since slope is rise/run, the slope of RS is $\frac{(3 - 2)}{(6 - 2)} = \frac{1}{4}$. The slope of a line perpendicular to that is -4. Because a point and the slope of the line are known, the point-slope form of the equation can be utilized. A line through point $(h, -k)$ with slope m has equation $y - k = m(x - h)$. Thus the line through S $(6, -3)$ that is perpendicular to the segment RS has equation $y - 3 = -4(x - 6)$. Distributing and adding like terms, the result is $y = -4x + 27$. Of the answer choices, only the point $(5, 7)$ falls on the line.

38. **The correct answer is F.** To solve the equation $0.2(x - 2,700) = x$, first distribute:

$$0.2x - 540 = x$$
$$-540 = 0.8x$$
$$-675 = x$$

39. **The correct answer is A.** Given that $0° \leq x \leq 90°$ and that $\tan x = \dfrac{15}{8}$, x can be pictured in the right triangle below.

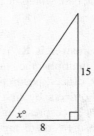

Because tangent is the ratio of the side opposite the angle to the side adjacent to the angle, the legs of the right triangle can be labeled as above. Cosine is the ratio of the side adjacent to the angle to the hypotenuse, which is not given. It is possible to eliminate answer choices in such a manner that it is not necessary to use the Pythagorean Theorem. Since the side adjacent to x is 8, the numerator in $\cos x$ will be 8, eliminating all but answers A and E. Since the legs of the triangle are 8 and 15, the hypotenuse will be longer than either, eliminating answer choice E. Thus $\cos x = \dfrac{8}{17}$.

40. **The correct answer is G.** Since the area of the square pool is given, you must find the area of the circle, with a radius of 10, and subtract the area of the pool. The area of a circle is equal to πr^2, where r is the radius. The area of this circle is $10^2\pi = 100\pi \approx 314$ square feet. Thus the area of the enclosure is approximately $314 - 81 = 233$ square feet.

41. **The correct answer is B.** Remember that all parallel lines have the same slope, so a line parallel to $y = 2x + 2$ will a slope of 2. A quick way to aid you in solving this problem would be to eliminate answer choices that do not have slope 2, so answer choices A and E can be immediately eliminated. Check the point $(3, -4)$ in the remaining answer choices. The only choice that works is $y = 2x - 2$.

42. **The correct answer is H.** Tangent is the ratio of the side opposite to the side adjacent to an angle in a right triangle. Drawing a line that passes through $(3,3)$ and is perpendicular to the x-axis

creates a right triangle, as shown in the figure (see below).

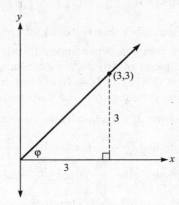

Because point $(3,3)$ is given, both legs of the right triangle have a length of 3. Thus $\tan \varphi = \dfrac{3}{3} = 1$.

43. **The correct answer is A.** To solve, calculate the result for each operation and select the smallest result.

Answer Choice A: $\dfrac{2}{3} + (-3) = -2\dfrac{1}{3}$

Answer Choice B: $\dfrac{2}{3} - (-3) = 3\dfrac{2}{3}$

Answer Choice C: $\dfrac{2}{3} \times -3 = -2$

Answer Choice D: $\dfrac{2/3}{-3} = \dfrac{-2}{9}$

Answer Choice E: $\dfrac{[2/3 + (-3)]}{2} = \dfrac{-7}{6}$

The smallest result is $-2\dfrac{1}{3}$, which was obtained by adding.

44. **The correct answer is F.** To simplify calculations, you can multiply the entire equation by 12 to obtain whole numbers and get $4b + 24 = 3$. Subtracting 24 from both sides yields $4b = -21$. Dividing by 4 yields $b = -\dfrac{21}{4}$, which is a little less than -5. Thus the correct answer will lie between -4 and -6.

45. **The correct answer is B.** To find the solution set for $|3a - 2| \leq 7$, break it up into two separate inequalities: $3a - 2 \leq 7$ and $3a - 2 \geq -7$. Starting with $3a - 2 \leq 7$, solving for a yields $a \leq 3$. With $3a - 2 \geq -7$, solving for a yields $a \geq -\dfrac{5}{3}$. Thus a is between $-\dfrac{5}{3}$ and 3 inclusive.

46. The correct answer is K. Tangent is the ratio of the side opposite to the side adjacent to an angle in a right triangle. If the distance, in feet, to the cell phone tower is x, then $\tan 41° = \dfrac{200}{x}$, or $x = \dfrac{200}{\tan 41°}$. Since $\cot 41° = \dfrac{1}{\tan 41°}$, $x = \dfrac{200}{\tan 41°} = 200 \cot 41°$.

47. The correct answer is A. Since the area of a square is equal to the square of its sides, multiplying the sides by $\sqrt{3}$ will have the effect of multiplying the area by $(\sqrt{3})^2 = 3$.

48. The correct answer is H. In order to solve this problem, you must realize that since the volume of a cube is equal to the cube of its sides, multiplying the length of the sides by $\dfrac{1}{2}$ will have the effect of multiplying the volume by $\left(\dfrac{1}{2}\right)^3 = \dfrac{1}{8}$. The cube in this problem has a volume of 64, so if you halve the length of each side, new cube's volume will be $64\left(\dfrac{1}{8}\right) = 8$.

49. The correct answer is D. The area of a parallelogram is equal to base × height. In the figure, you can see that the base of the parallelogram is 7 and the height of the parallelogram is 9. Thus, the area of the parallelogram is $9 \times 7 = 63$.

50. The correct answer is G. In order for $8a^6b^3$ to be less than zero, either 8 or a^6 or b^3 must be less than zero. However, it is obvious that $8 > 0$ and any number taken to an even power is non-negative. Thus $b^3 < 0$ and in order for that to be true, $b < 0$. Of the answer choices, only $b > 0$ CANNOT be true.

51. The correct answer is D. Logarithms are used to indicate exponents of certain numbers called bases. By definition, $\log_a b = c$, if $a^c = b$. If $\log_4 x = 3$, then $x = 4^3$, or 64.

52. The correct answer is J. In order for a system of 2 linear equations to have no solutions, the graphs of the equations must be parallel. Parallel lines have the same slope. To find the equation whose graph is parallel to the line in the figure, you must find the slope of the line between the points $(0, -4)$ and $(3, -0)$. Since slope is $\dfrac{\text{rise}}{\text{run}}$, the slope is $\dfrac{4}{3}$. The only equation with the correct slope of $\dfrac{4}{3}$ is $y = \dfrac{4}{3}x + 2$.

53. The correct answer is C. Of the 80 marbles, only 8 end in 5. If the first marble is drawn and not replaced, there are 79 marbles left, 7 of which have a ones digit of 5. Thus the probability that the player will be a winner is $\dfrac{7}{79}$.

54. The correct answer is H. To solve this problem, remember that the formula for slope is equal $\dfrac{(y_2 - y_1)}{(x_2 - x_1)}$, where (x_1, y_1) and (x_2, y_2) are two given points on a line. The equation of the line that passes through the origin and the point $(3, 4)$ will have slope $\dfrac{(4 - 0)}{(3 - 0)} = \dfrac{4}{3}$. Since the line passes through the origin, the y-intercept is 0. Thus the correct equation is $y = \dfrac{4}{3}x$.

55. The correct answer is C. To solve this problem, you must remember that in an isosceles triangle, the base angles have the same measure. Since the sum of angles is 180° for all triangles, $180 = (a + 30) + 2(2a - 15)$. Distributing and adding like terms yields

$$180 = (a + 30) + 4a - 30$$
$$180 = 5a$$
$$a = 36$$

Since the base angles are equivalent to $2a - 15$, they equal $2(36) - 15 = 72 - 15$, or 57°.

56. The correct answer is K. The smallest possible value will occur when it is negative. A negative product will result only when one of the numbers is positive and one is negative. The possible pairs are then -1 and 6, -2 and 5, -3 and 4, -4 and 3, -5 and 2, and -6 and 1. Of these pairs, the smallest product is $(-3)(4) = (-4)(3)$, or -12.

57. The correct answer is A. Start by drawing 3 parallel lines.

This creates 4 distinct regions, so the minimum number of distinct regions must be 4. Eliminate answer choices C, D, and E.

Now, try drawing 3 lines in other configurations, and you will see that there will always be either

6 or 7 regions:

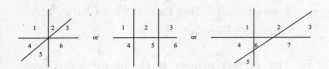

Therefore, the correct answer is 4, 6, or 7 distinct regions, answer choice A.

58. **The correct answer is F.** Remember that the area of a parallelogram is equal to base × height. In this case, the base is $[3 - (-3)]$ or $[2 - (-4)]$, both of which equal 6, and the height is $(3 - (-5)) = 8$. Thus the area is $6 \times 8 = 48$. The area of triangle QRS, $\left[\frac{1}{2}(b)(h)\right]$, is half the area of the parallelogram, or 24.

59. **The correct answer is E.** Refer to the following chart to follow the patter of the sequence.

Term	1	2	'3	4	...	n
Term	a	ab	ab^2	ab^4	...	ab^{n-1}

Since the power of b is one less than the number of term, the nth term will be ab^{n-1}. The 643rd term will then be $ab^{643-1} = ab^{642}$.

60. **The correct answer is H.** Since AB is longer than BC, there are only two possible configurations: B is between A and C or C is between A and B. In the case that B is between A and C, $AC = AB + BC = 19 + 13 = 32$. In the case that C is between A and B, $AC = AB - BC = 19 - 13 = 6$. Therefore, AC can be 6 and 32 only.

Reading Test Explanations

PASSAGE I

1. **The best answer is A.** Jake makes this statement in response to Katherine telling him that she sometimes has to "throw something together at the last minute." This suggests that it does not happen often and is unintentional. The other answer choices are not supported by the passage.

2. **The best answer is H.** During the conversation, Katherine says, "It's just that I work back-to-back jobs every night," and later, "Things are just a little hard for us right now." You can infer that Katherine is working hard and barely getting by.

3. **The best answer is B.** When Jake says, "Katherine, Maxwell needs to have a healthy lunch," he indicates that Max is currently not eating well. This example has nothing to do with how well Katherine takes care of her son, but rather highlights one of the problems she is having in taking care of her son. The other answer choices all make reference to her trying in some way.

4. **The best answer is J.** The word *predicament* is used to indicate Jake's problematic situation with Max's lunches. Based on the context of the paragraph, his situation is somewhat difficult. Therefore, *predicament* most nearly means "challenge," which refers to a difficult task. The other answer choices are not supported by the context of the passage.

5. **The best answer is C.** Throughout the passage, Jake is never referred to as either Max's best friend or his brother, but Jake does know Max; therefore, A, B, and D should be eliminated. He is noted as being Max's camp counselor, and has a good influence on him by encouraging and allowing Max to consume healthier meals. Therefore, answer choice C is correct.

6. **The best answer is F.** At the end of the passage, Jake remarks that the club lasted for two summers, and then Max moved away. This best supports answer choice F. Although answer choice J may appear to be correct because it is implied that Max enjoyed the meetings of the Sandwich Club, the author never defines these meeting as Max's favorite part of camp.

7. **The best answer is D.** At several points in the passage, Katherine refers to how hard it is to find enough money for everything, and how much she has to work to make ends meet. This suggests that Katherine and Max have little money. The other answer choices are not supported by details in the passage.

8. **The best answer is G.** Whenever Jake brings up problems with Katherine, she seems genuinely concerned about Max's well-being. However, because she works so much and has so many other things to get done, her attention is often diverted away from Max. The other answer choices are not supported by the context of the passage.

9. **The best answer is D.** When Jake pulled Katherine aside to discuss the lunch issue, he indicated that Max's lunch is a concern of his, eliminating answer choices A and C. Although answer choice B may appear to be correct, the word "incident" implies a one-time occurrence. Max was consistently bringing unhealthy lunches to camp, therefore answer choice D, "problem," is correct.

10. **The best answer is J.** The passage states that Jake thought of the Sandwich Club because he needed to come up with a solution to help Max eat healthier lunches. The last paragraph also mentions the fact that once Max moved away, the Sandwich Club ended. These facts best support answer choice J. The other answer choices are beyond the scope of the passage.

PASSAGE II

11. **The best answer is B.** The passage states that "None but the fearless and inventive, the most resourceful and curious, would dare to undertake such a venture," which clearly suggests that this was a challenge. The passage later goes on to say that "All of the wonders of those states in the West are, in part, the result of this expedition." This implies that western expansion was important. Answer choice A may appear to be correct; however, the passages tells us that fur traders and trappers had traversed the wilderness to reach the west prior to Lewis and Clark's journey.

12. **The best answer is F.** The passage discusses many aspects of the Lewis and Clark expedition, and mentions several characteristic of the country, describing to the reader that the expedition led to "the unknown lands west of the Mississippi" and that "The path they were to carve out would be the first of its kind." Answer choice H may appear to be correct, however, the passage mentions that the men on the expedition were volunteers for "North Western Discovery," not the "Northwest Passage."

13. **The best answer is D.** The passage states that, "The settlers who came after Lewis and Clark went forward with blind-devotion knowing then that it could be done." This suggests that the Expedition gave other people confidence that they, too, could cross the United States because they knew that it had already been done by other travelers. Answer choice A is incorrect because the passage explicitly states that after Lewis and Clark's historic journey, many people traveled by land. Answer choices B and C are beyond the scope of the passage.

14. **The best answer is H.** The passage explicitly states that the Lewis and Clark expedition was intended to "find the fastest water route across North America." In addition, the passage states that previous to this journey, "virtually no one had attempted to cross the stretch of land between the mighty Mississippi and the vast Pacific Ocean using only water routes." Although Lewis and Clark did catalogue new species of animals on their journey—answer choice G—this was not their primary objective in traveling across the United States.

15. **The best answer is B.** The second paragraph states that, "Months later, in May, the party gathered in St. Louis. The forty-some men were to travel …" Answer choice B best fits the context of the paragraph. The previous statement does not support the idea that party means "a celebration," "a segment of the population," or a "meeting to discuss business," so answer choices A, C, and D can be eliminated.

16. **The best answer is G.** In the third paragraph, the men on the expedition are told to have written of their "health and high spirits." The statement is also made that the men were "all eager to explore," in spite of the potential dangers they faced in their long journey. This best supports answer choice G.

17. **The best answer is C.** It is reasonable to infer that the word "forge," as it is used in the passage – "the travelers continued to *forge* west in search of an efficient trade route using only the rivers"–refers to advancing on a path or journey, answer choice C. The other answer choices do not make sense within the context of the passage.

18. **The best answer is J.** The fourth paragraph mentions that "the Sioux and the Blackfeet tried to impede the group's progress on more than one occasion." This suggests that the Expedition would likely face danger in the form of conflict

with indigenous people, answer choice J. The other answer choices are not supported by details in the passage.

19. **The best answer is D.** As stated in the passage, the men set out on three boats, "all of which were moved by sails, towropes, poles, or oars." These methods involve man power, wind power, or rowing power. Although the passage indicates that steam power eventually replaced the boats, nowhere does it mention that steam power was used on the Expedition.

20. **The best answer is F.** According to the passage, "After receiving wilderness training in Washington D.C., Meriwether Lewis set out …" This indicates that Lewis was the only member of the Expedition to have received wilderness training. All of the other answer choices are mentioned explicitly in the passage as having been done by all members of the Expedition.

PASSAGE III

21. **The best answer is D.** Although the passage discusses Porter's renowned ability to candidly address artists' works, illustrates the influence that several famous artists had on his works, and assesses his unusual methods of painting and critiquing artwork, none of these are the main focus of the passage. Therefore, answer choices A, B, and C can be eliminated. The passage gives a brief summary of Porter's life and discusses all of the above topics as points that shaped his career. This best supports answer choice D.

22. **The best answer is H.** At the end of the passage, the author states that it is sad that Porter "is still virtually unknown outside of art circles," and that "This remarkably insightful, articulate, creative individual needs to be discovered by the common man and revered for his continuing influence on the the artists of today." Clearly, the author thinks very highly of Porter and his works and believes that he deserves to be honored ("revered") for his influence on today's artists. These details best support answer choice H. Answer choice F is incorrect because the author is clearly not "detached," or indifferent. Answer choice G is incorrect because the author is not merely "tolerant," or just able to withstand Porter. Answer choice J is incorrect because the author obviously does not "abhor," or hate, Porter and his works.

23. **The best answer is A.** As stated in the passage, "what made Porter so famous was his knack for

responding directly to an artist's work." Answer choices B and D are incorrect because the passage states that those are the things that Porter did NOT do, for he found criticisms based on those criteria to be insignificant and meaningless. Answer choice C is beyond the scope of the passage; Bernard Berenson's influence on Porter's art critiques is not discussed.

24. **The best answer is H.** Porter's personal philosophy regarding his paintings was that they should be "personal, emotional, and representative of its subject, while at the same time be boldly colorful, expressive, and generally abstract." This description of his works supports all of the answer choices except "trite," answer choice H, which means "ordinary or dull."

25. **The best answer is B.** The first paragraph of the passage simply tells how the author first came to meet Fairfield Porter, and provides a smooth transition into the life of Fairfield Porter. Answer choice A may appear to be correct; however, the author simply tells the reader how he came across Porter; there is no overview of what is to come in the passage. Answer choices C and D are not supported by information found in the passage.

26. **The best answer is H.** The passage states that, "Fairfield Porter, despite being remarkably intelligent, appeared to be lacking any natural artistic talents." Therefore, his high intelligence level was not correlated at all to his level of artistic ability. This best supports answer choice H. Porter's intelligence is not discussed in terms of the criteria listed in answer choices F, G, and J.

27. **The best answer is D.** The author states that, "This remarkably insightful, articulate, creative individual needs to be discovered by the common man and *revered* for his continuing influence on the artists of today." The author is clearly praising Porter and his continuing influence. It makes the most sense that the author believes that Porter should be "honored" for his continuing influence on artists today. The other answer choices do not make sense in the context of the paragraph.

28. **The best answer is J.** It is stated in the passage that Porter was primarily an art critic until "1961 when he decided to pursue a full-time painting career." This was approximately 30 years after he returned from Italy, as he spent time between the years 1931 and 1932 in Italy learning to appreciate and critique artworks. The other answer choices are not supported by details in the passage.

29. **The best answer is A.** As stated in the passage, "Between the years 1931 and 1932, Fairfield spent the majority of his time in Italy learning to appreciate and critique the works of the great Renaissance painters. His training came from both ..." This suggests that Porter was continuing his training as an art critic, answer choice A. The other answer choices are outside the scope of the passage.

30. **The best answer is G.** The passage preceding this phrase discusses Porter's fame as an acclaimed art critic. The passage then goes on to state that, "The other side of his fame, his uncommon approach to painting, is just as important to the understanding of Fairfield Porter's contributions to the world of art." This contrast indicates that Porter was famous both for his criticisms of art, as well as his artwork itself–answer choice G. Answer choice F may appear to be correct, however, the passage does not ever define Porter's level of fame as an artist versus his level of fame as an art critic.

PASSAGE IV

31. **The best answer is A.** The passage states that, "without dark matter, there are many cosmological phenomena that are difficult to explain." In the context of the sentence, it would make the most sense that without dark matter, there would be many "occurrences" or incidents that would be difficult to explain. Answer choice B may appear to be correct; however, the passage does not indicate the nature of the phenomena and whether or not they are problematic.

32. **The best answer is H.** The passage states that, "Dark matter ... is not readily observable because it does not directly refract light or energy. Its existence can only be deduced because of the effect that it has on surrounding matter. In fact, some members of the scientific community have argued that dark matter does not actually exist." This best supports answer choice H. Answer choice F is incorrect because the evidence for the existence of dark matter is its effect on surrounding matter; this discussion of dark matter's effect on surrounding matter also eliminates answer choice J. Answer choice G is not supported by details in the passage.

33. **The best answer is C.** As stated in the passage, "It has been asserted that not only does dark matter exist, it may also be responsible for the Milky Way's unusual shape." The passage then goes on to discuss the way in which dark matter probably affects the shape of the Milky Way. Answer choice

B may appear to be correct; however, the passage does not indicate that the Magellanic Clouds have enormous mass. In fact, the passage explicitly states that "The interaction referenced involves two *smaller* galaxies near the Milky Way, called Magellanic Clouds, moving through an enormous amount of dark matter." Answer choices A and D are not supported by details in the passage.

34. The best answer is F. As stated in reference to Romanowsky's theory, "They point to the existence of several elliptical galaxies surrounded by very little dark matter as evidence that dark matter is not, in fact, the cause of the warped galaxies." By showing galaxies that are similar in shape to the Milky Way but NOT surrounded by enormous amounts of dark matter, the theory illustrates that dark matter may not affect the shape and formation of galaxies, answer choice F. Answer choice G may appear to be correct; however, the passage explicitly states that Romanowsky's theory is not intended "to conclude that dark matter does not exist."

35. The best answer is A. The last paragraph states that "the movement of [the Magellanic] Clouds through the dark matter seems to create a wake that enhances their gravitational influence on the Milky Way." Earlier in the paragraph, when discussing the Magellanic Clouds, the passage states that when a cloud moves through dark matter, it "enhances the gravitational pull that the two Magellanic Clouds could have on the Milky Way and other surrounding bodies." This best supports answer choice A. The other answer choices are not supported by details found in the passage.

36. The best answer is J. The third paragraph discusses the substance of Newton's hypothesis and the consequences that his hypothesis had on the existence of dark matter. When applying this hypothesis, it seems that dark matter must exist: "something that is not easily observed must be exerting the necessary force to create the warped shape of the galaxy." This best supports answer choice J. Answer choice F may appear to be correct; however, it is simply stated that Newtonian physics provide the strongest evidence

for dark matter. It is not stated anywhere in the passage how dark matter was first discovered.

37. The best answer is D. The passage states that "they apparently believe that the results of their studies cast doubt on some of the *conventional* theories of galaxy formation and manipulation." Answer choices A and C do not make sense in the context of the sentence, because if a theory was "easily understood" or "strictly interpreted," there would not be a lot of room for doubt to be cast upon the theory. Answer choice B is incorrect because if a theory was "formally disputed," opposing viewpoints would already exist on that theory. That the result of these studies cast doubt on some "generally accepted" theories makes the most sense; therefore, answer choice D is correct.

38. The best answer is H. There is nothing in the passage to indicate with certainty that dark matter has no influence on surrounding celestial bodies. Although Aaron Romanowsky suggests that dark matter is not responsible for warped galaxies, there is no discussion in the passage to show that he believes dark matter has no influence whatsoever on galaxy shape or other cosmological phenomena. The other answer choices are all mentioned in the passage as scientific theories regarding dark matter.

39. The best answer is C. As stated in the passage, dark matter is "a substance that is not readily observable because it does not directly refract light or energy." This best supports answer choice C. The other answer choices are not supported by details found in the passage.

40. The best answer is F. The passage describes dark matter as surrounding and impacting galaxies composed of common matter, such as the Milky Way. This best supports answer choice F. Answer choice G is incorrect because whether dark matter truly exists is still a topic of debate among scientists. Answer choice H is incorrect because the passage does not provide the magnitude of the amount of dark matter in the universe. Answer choice J is incorrect because dark matter is not directly observable at all; its effect on galaxies is the only proof of its existence.

Science Reasoning Test Explanations

PASSAGE I

1. **The best answer is C.** Table 1 provides information on how many pinecones were produced at each of the six sites. When looking at the A4 and A5 column, the only sites at which A5 trees produced more pinecones per tree than A4 trees were S1, S2, S4, and S5. This best supports answer choice C.

2. **The best answer is H.** The results of Experiment 1 are shown in Table 1. According to these results, the only site at which A1 trees produced more pinecones than the other trees was at S4, answer choice H.

3. **The best answer is C.** According to Table 2, only S4 trees produced fewer pinecones than did the trees at S6. This suggests that A1 trees produced more pinecones at S6 than at S4, because A1 trees were planted with A2, A3, A4, and A5 trees in both experiments.

4. **The best answer is G.** Table 2 provides information on how many pinecones were produced per A1 tree at each of the six sites. To answer the question, you must look at which A1 tree produced the most pinecones. The A1 trees that were planted with seedlings from A2 at S3 produced 9.6 pinecones per tree, more than any other tree on the table. This information best supports answer choice G.

5. **The best answer is A.** To answer this question, you must read the procedures for both Experiment 1 and Experiment 2. In Experiment 2, "150 containers were prepared with 5 A1 seedlings and 5 seedlings from either A2, A3, A4, or A5." This says that, unlike Experiment 1, trees from more than one population were combined in Experiment 2. Therefore, answer choice A is correct.

6. **The best answer is H.** The procedure for Experiment 2 states, "150 containers were prepared with 5 A1 seedlings and 5 seedlings from either A2, A3, A4, or A5." Therefore, 10 seedlings were planted in each container. This data supports answer choice H.

PASSAGE II

7. **The best answer is C.** The point at hr = 16 for the "Ingredient A extended-release" line is at about 15 on the vertical axis. The point at hr = 16 for the "Ingredient B extended-release" line is at about 4 on the vertical axis. Therefore, the difference is about 11.

8. **The best answer is H.** This question can be answered by observing the trends in the Figures or simply thinking critically about how medication generally works. According to Figure 2, it takes a bit of time for the medication to start working, the symptoms decline for a period of time, then, presumably once the medication starts to wear off, the symptoms return. Figure 1 shows that symptom relief is inversely proportional to concentration of the medication in the body.

9. **The best answer is A.** According to Figure 1, the concentration of immediate-release Ingredient A increases most immediately following taking the pill. This is evident by the extended steep upward trend of the line.

10. **The best answer is F.** Table 1 shows that nearly as many subjects given the placebo (5%) reported feelings of weakness as did subjects given the drug (6%). The difference of only 1% shows that there is a high level of uncertainty over whether the drug actually caused the feelings of weakness.

11. **The best answer is D.** Figure 2 reflects the mean (average) symptom score of all the subjects given the drug. To find the 8-hour period of the graph where symptoms scores changed the least, find the 8-hour period of the curve over which slope changes the least. This occurs roughly between hr = 14 and hr = 22.

PASSAGE III

12. **The best answer is G.** By looking at Figure 1, you can determine the range in pressure at which each atmospheric layer can exist. Beginning with answer choice F, calculate the difference between the lowest pressure and the highest pressure at which the atmospheric layer can exist:

   Mesosphere: 14.5 psi − 7.5 psi = 7 psi

   Thermosphere: 17.8 psi − 10.3 psi = 7.5 psi

   Stratosphere: 9.5 psi − 3.8 psi = 5.7 psi

   Troposphere: 5.0 psi − 1.0 psi = 4.0 psi

   The pressure in the thermosphere has the greatest range, answer choice G.

13. **The best answer is A.** To answer this question you need to look at the information on cumulus clouds in Figure 1. Figure 1 suggests that cumulus clouds form in the mesosphere. The mesosphere's

pressure ranges from 8 psi to 12 psi, and the average temperature for this range is 35°C. This information supports answer choice A.

14. **The best answer is G.** The key in Figure 1 includes two lines: temperature and pressure. As the pressure line is increasing (positive slope), the temperature line is decreasing (negative slope). This suggests that as pressure within the atmospheric layer increases, temperature decreases only, answer choice G.

15. **The best answer is B.** Answering this question requires you to look carefully at the range of temperature and pressure combinations at which clouds in the stratosphere form, as shown in Figure 1. Because the clouds here begin to form under 30°C and most are located below a pressure of 10 psi, this combination is correct. The other choices designate ranges of the atmosphere either above or below the stratosphere.

16. **The best answer is J.** At a pressure of 7 psi, Figure 1 shows that cloud formation will most likely occur in the stratosphere. According to Figure 1, clouds that form in the stratosphere are stratus clouds. This information best supports answer choice J.

PASSAGE IV

17. **The best answer is D.** Figure 1 shows the percent of fish that survive after exposure to water with bacteria present. The fish species with the highest percent (85%) of fish that survived after prolonged exposure to bacteria (light gray bar) was fish species E. Answer choice D is correct.

18. **The best answer is G.** To answer this question, you must look at the difference between the light gray and dark gray bars for each species in Figure 1. Answer choice J can be eliminated because the percent of fish that survived with and without exposure to bacteria are almost identical. Species C has the greatest difference in percent between the two, answer choice G.

19. **The best answer is B.** According to Table 1, fish that live in deep water without plants have a moderate ability to combat bacteria.

20. **The best answer is G.** By looking at Table 1, you can see that as you go down the column, the exposure to waterborne bacteria increase. Also as you go down the column, the relative ability to combat bacteria increases. The information supports answer choice G.

21. **The best answer is B.** According to Figure 1, Species A has the lowest percent of fish surviving to adulthood. Table 1 indicates that Species A fish live in shallow water with plants. Therefore, answer choice B is correct.

PASSAGE V

22. **The best answer is H.** This question asks you to identify the assumption that Paleontologist 1 must have made while discussing the finding of the fossilized bones. Answer choice F can be eliminated because the paleontologist refers to the velociraptor as a known dinosaur. Paleontologist 1 says, "The form and function of the velociraptor has been misunderstood until this important discovery." By stating that the dinosaur has been misunderstood, Paleontologist 1 is saying that it has been mischaracterized until now. This statement best supports answer choice H.

23. **The best answer is C.** Paleontologist 1 states, "You can see that there are cuts within the arm/wing bones of this dinosaur, indicating that it was caught while in flight." The paleontologist, then goes on to say, "Perhaps it was attempting an escape from a more predatory dinosaur." This suggests that while trying to escape from a larger predator, the predator caught the velociraptor, answer choice C.

24. **The best answer is G.** According to Paleontologist 2, "long arm bones are indicative of the dinosaur's ability to scavenge prey and fend off larger predators." It makes sense that Paleontologist 2 would conclude that, because the new dinosaur species had long arm bones, it could be a scavenger.

25. **The best answer is C.** According to Paleontologist 2, "The long arm bones are indicative of the dinosaur's ability to scavenge prey and fend off larger predators." This implies that the reason that the velociraptor had long arm bones was to scavenge for food.

26. **The best answer is F.** This question asks you to summarize the main idea of Paleontologist 1's viewpoint. Answer choices G and H can be eliminated because only Paleontologist 2 supports them. Paleontologist 1 says that "the velociraptor was definitely capable of flight" and "the velociraptor has been misunderstood until this important discovery." These two statements support answer choice F.

27. The best answer is A. Both Paleontologists mention the *Tyrannosaurus rex* as a possible threat either to the velociraptor's food source or to its very life. This best supports answer choice A. Answer choices B, C, and D do not support the views of both paleontologists, and therefore, can be eliminated.

28. The best answer is G. By reading the viewpoints of both Paleontologist 1 and Paleontologist 2, you can determine what they thought of the discovery of the velociraptor bones. Answer choices H and J can be eliminated because they are not supported by either passage. Both paleontologists extracted useful information from the discovery of the bones. Therefore, answer choice G is the best answer.

PASSAGE VI

29. The best answer is B. Figure 1 provides information on the compositions of mountain peaks. At a distance of 9 km along the mountain range, the peak composition is shown in the key as shale. This supports answer choice B.

30. The best answer is F. To determine the correct answer, you must look at the key in Figure 1, which shows the different composition of the mountain peaks. It defines limestone as "particles with diameters under 0.5 mm," shale as "composed mostly of particles with diameters under 175 mm," and slate as, "composed mostly of particles with diameters over 175 mm." The only difference between the different compositions is the size of the particle, answer choice F.

31. The best answer is D. As the peak section heights in Table 1 increase, the percentage of the year that peak section is exposed to wind also increases. Since a height of 5.5 m to 6.0 m is higher than the other values in the table, the percentage of the year that the peak section would be exposed to the wind should also be greater than the other values in the table. The only answer choice with a value greater than the other percentages in the table is answer choice D.

32. The best answer is F. Figure 2 shows that Peak D is exposed to wind erosion for a greater percentage of the year than Peak C. Table 1 suggests that the percentage of the peak exposed to wind is directly proportional to peak section height. Therefore, because Peak D is exposed to the wind for longer than Peak C is, Peak D must be

taller than Peak C. This information best supports answer choice F.

33. The best answer is C. Table 1 shows that as the peak section height increases by equal increments, the percentage of the year that peak section is exposed to wind also increases by approximately the same amount. Therefore, the slope of the graph is positive and the graph is a straight line as shown in answer choice C.

34. The best answer is G. The passage states that "the peaks of mountains often lose sediment due to wind erosion." By losing sediment, the mountain peaks are losing mass. This supports answer choice G. Answer choice J can be eliminated because the information is irrelevant to the data presented in the passage.

PASSAGE VII

35. The best answer is A. According to the information in Table 2 and Table 3, the bacteria grew quicker when left under a lamp. This suggests that bacteria grow faster in warm environments, answer choice A. Answer choice C can be eliminated because it is irrelevant to the information presented in the passage.

36. The best answer is G. Table 3 provides information on the proportional growth of bacteria in four different environments. The moist side of Dish 2 produced 1.15 times the amount of bacteria in the control sample, which is more than the other three environments produced when compared to the control sample. This best supports answer choice G.

37. The best answer is C. Table 1 provides the results of Experiment 1. Answer choices A and D can be eliminated because they are not supported by the data. For both dishes, the bacteria growth was greater on the moist side. This information best supports answer choice C.

38. The best answer is H. More than one sample of bacteria was put into each Petri dish. To avoid skewed results, only one sample of bacteria should be placed in each Petri dish. Answer choice H is the best answer. Answer choice J can be eliminated because varying the size of the starting sample would not alter the results.

39. The best answer is D. Both Table 2 and Table 3 show that the bacteria growth rate is highest in moist, warm places. The only answer choice that is both warm and moist is beneath a rock in a tropical forest. The other answer choices can be eliminated because they contain only one or none of the two conditions.

40. **The best answer is J.** According to the question, "bacteria double population size in short intervals." The only answer choice that includes recording data in short intervals is answer choice J.

Writing Test Explanation

Because grading the essay is subjective, we've chosen not to include any "graded" essays here. Your best bet is to have someone you trust, such as your personal tutor, read your essays and give you an honest critique. If you plan on grading your own essays, review the grading criteria and be as honest as possible regarding the structure, development, organization, technique, and appropriateness of your writing. Focus on your weak areas and continue to practice in order to improve your writing skills.

■■■ **ANSWER SHEET**

ACT PRACTICE TEST 3
Answer Sheet

ENGLISH

1 Ⓐ Ⓑ Ⓒ Ⓓ	21 Ⓐ Ⓑ Ⓒ Ⓓ	41 Ⓐ Ⓑ Ⓒ Ⓓ	61 Ⓐ Ⓑ Ⓒ Ⓓ
2 Ⓕ Ⓖ Ⓗ Ⓙ	22 Ⓕ Ⓖ Ⓗ Ⓙ	42 Ⓕ Ⓖ Ⓗ Ⓙ	62 Ⓕ Ⓖ Ⓗ Ⓙ
3 Ⓐ Ⓑ Ⓒ Ⓓ	23 Ⓐ Ⓑ Ⓒ Ⓓ	43 Ⓐ Ⓑ Ⓒ Ⓓ	63 Ⓐ Ⓑ Ⓒ Ⓓ
4 Ⓕ Ⓖ Ⓗ Ⓙ	24 Ⓕ Ⓖ Ⓗ Ⓙ	44 Ⓕ Ⓖ Ⓗ Ⓙ	64 Ⓕ Ⓖ Ⓗ Ⓙ
5 Ⓐ Ⓑ Ⓒ Ⓓ	25 Ⓐ Ⓑ Ⓒ Ⓓ	45 Ⓐ Ⓑ Ⓒ Ⓓ	65 Ⓐ Ⓑ Ⓒ Ⓓ
6 Ⓕ Ⓖ Ⓗ Ⓙ	26 Ⓕ Ⓖ Ⓗ Ⓙ	46 Ⓕ Ⓖ Ⓗ Ⓙ	66 Ⓕ Ⓖ Ⓗ Ⓙ
7 Ⓐ Ⓑ Ⓒ Ⓓ	27 Ⓐ Ⓑ Ⓒ Ⓓ	47 Ⓐ Ⓑ Ⓒ Ⓓ	67 Ⓐ Ⓑ Ⓒ Ⓓ
8 Ⓕ Ⓖ Ⓗ Ⓙ	28 Ⓕ Ⓖ Ⓗ Ⓙ	48 Ⓕ Ⓖ Ⓗ Ⓙ	68 Ⓕ Ⓖ Ⓗ Ⓙ
9 Ⓐ Ⓑ Ⓒ Ⓓ	29 Ⓐ Ⓑ Ⓒ Ⓓ	49 Ⓐ Ⓑ Ⓒ Ⓓ	69 Ⓐ Ⓑ Ⓒ Ⓓ
10 Ⓕ Ⓖ Ⓗ Ⓙ	30 Ⓕ Ⓖ Ⓗ Ⓙ	50 Ⓕ Ⓖ Ⓗ Ⓙ	70 Ⓕ Ⓖ Ⓗ Ⓙ
11 Ⓐ Ⓑ Ⓒ Ⓓ	31 Ⓐ Ⓑ Ⓒ Ⓓ	51 Ⓐ Ⓑ Ⓒ Ⓓ	71 Ⓐ Ⓑ Ⓒ Ⓓ
12 Ⓕ Ⓖ Ⓗ Ⓙ	32 Ⓕ Ⓖ Ⓗ Ⓙ	52 Ⓕ Ⓖ Ⓗ Ⓙ	72 Ⓕ Ⓖ Ⓗ Ⓙ
13 Ⓐ Ⓑ Ⓒ Ⓓ	33 Ⓐ Ⓑ Ⓒ Ⓓ	53 Ⓐ Ⓑ Ⓒ Ⓓ	73 Ⓐ Ⓑ Ⓒ Ⓓ
14 Ⓕ Ⓖ Ⓗ Ⓙ	34 Ⓕ Ⓖ Ⓗ Ⓙ	54 Ⓕ Ⓖ Ⓗ Ⓙ	74 Ⓕ Ⓖ Ⓗ Ⓙ
15 Ⓐ Ⓑ Ⓒ Ⓓ	35 Ⓐ Ⓑ Ⓒ Ⓓ	55 Ⓐ Ⓑ Ⓒ Ⓓ	75 Ⓐ Ⓑ Ⓒ Ⓓ
16 Ⓕ Ⓖ Ⓗ Ⓙ	36 Ⓕ Ⓖ Ⓗ Ⓙ	56 Ⓕ Ⓖ Ⓗ Ⓙ	
17 Ⓐ Ⓑ Ⓒ Ⓓ	37 Ⓐ Ⓑ Ⓒ Ⓓ	57 Ⓐ Ⓑ Ⓒ Ⓓ	
18 Ⓕ Ⓖ Ⓗ Ⓙ	38 Ⓕ Ⓖ Ⓗ Ⓙ	58 Ⓕ Ⓖ Ⓗ Ⓙ	
19 Ⓐ Ⓑ Ⓒ Ⓓ	39 Ⓐ Ⓑ Ⓒ Ⓓ	59 Ⓐ Ⓑ Ⓒ Ⓓ	
20 Ⓕ Ⓖ Ⓗ Ⓙ	40 Ⓕ Ⓖ Ⓗ Ⓙ	60 Ⓕ Ⓖ Ⓗ Ⓙ	

MATHEMATICS

1 Ⓐ Ⓑ Ⓒ Ⓓ Ⓔ	16 Ⓕ Ⓖ Ⓗ Ⓙ Ⓚ	31 Ⓐ Ⓑ Ⓒ Ⓓ Ⓔ	46 Ⓕ Ⓖ Ⓗ Ⓙ Ⓚ
2 Ⓕ Ⓖ Ⓗ Ⓙ Ⓚ	17 Ⓐ Ⓑ Ⓒ Ⓓ Ⓔ	32 Ⓕ Ⓖ Ⓗ Ⓙ Ⓚ	47 Ⓐ Ⓑ Ⓒ Ⓓ Ⓔ
3 Ⓐ Ⓑ Ⓒ Ⓓ Ⓔ	18 Ⓕ Ⓖ Ⓗ Ⓙ Ⓚ	33 Ⓐ Ⓑ Ⓒ Ⓓ Ⓔ	48 Ⓕ Ⓖ Ⓗ Ⓙ Ⓚ
4 Ⓕ Ⓖ Ⓗ Ⓙ Ⓚ	19 Ⓐ Ⓑ Ⓒ Ⓓ Ⓔ	34 Ⓕ Ⓖ Ⓗ Ⓙ Ⓚ	49 Ⓐ Ⓑ Ⓒ Ⓓ Ⓔ
5 Ⓐ Ⓑ Ⓒ Ⓓ Ⓔ	20 Ⓕ Ⓖ Ⓗ Ⓙ Ⓚ	35 Ⓐ Ⓑ Ⓒ Ⓓ Ⓔ	50 Ⓕ Ⓖ Ⓗ Ⓙ Ⓚ
6 Ⓕ Ⓖ Ⓗ Ⓙ Ⓚ	21 Ⓐ Ⓑ Ⓒ Ⓓ Ⓔ	36 Ⓕ Ⓖ Ⓗ Ⓙ Ⓚ	51 Ⓐ Ⓑ Ⓒ Ⓓ Ⓔ
7 Ⓐ Ⓑ Ⓒ Ⓓ Ⓔ	22 Ⓕ Ⓖ Ⓗ Ⓙ Ⓚ	37 Ⓐ Ⓑ Ⓒ Ⓓ Ⓔ	52 Ⓕ Ⓖ Ⓗ Ⓙ Ⓚ
8 Ⓕ Ⓖ Ⓗ Ⓙ Ⓚ	23 Ⓐ Ⓑ Ⓒ Ⓓ Ⓔ	38 Ⓕ Ⓖ Ⓗ Ⓙ Ⓚ	53 Ⓐ Ⓑ Ⓒ Ⓓ Ⓔ
9 Ⓐ Ⓑ Ⓒ Ⓓ Ⓔ	24 Ⓕ Ⓖ Ⓗ Ⓙ Ⓚ	39 Ⓐ Ⓑ Ⓒ Ⓓ Ⓔ	54 Ⓕ Ⓖ Ⓗ Ⓙ Ⓚ
10 Ⓕ Ⓖ Ⓗ Ⓙ Ⓚ	25 Ⓐ Ⓑ Ⓒ Ⓓ Ⓔ	40 Ⓕ Ⓖ Ⓗ Ⓙ Ⓚ	55 Ⓐ Ⓑ Ⓒ Ⓓ Ⓔ
11 Ⓐ Ⓑ Ⓒ Ⓓ Ⓔ	26 Ⓕ Ⓖ Ⓗ Ⓙ Ⓚ	41 Ⓐ Ⓑ Ⓒ Ⓓ Ⓔ	56 Ⓕ Ⓖ Ⓗ Ⓙ Ⓚ
12 Ⓕ Ⓖ Ⓗ Ⓙ Ⓚ	27 Ⓐ Ⓑ Ⓒ Ⓓ Ⓔ	42 Ⓕ Ⓖ Ⓗ Ⓙ Ⓚ	57 Ⓐ Ⓑ Ⓒ Ⓓ Ⓔ
13 Ⓐ Ⓑ Ⓒ Ⓓ Ⓔ	28 Ⓕ Ⓖ Ⓗ Ⓙ Ⓚ	43 Ⓐ Ⓑ Ⓒ Ⓓ Ⓔ	58 Ⓕ Ⓖ Ⓗ Ⓙ Ⓚ
14 Ⓕ Ⓖ Ⓗ Ⓙ Ⓚ	29 Ⓐ Ⓑ Ⓒ Ⓓ Ⓔ	44 Ⓕ Ⓖ Ⓗ Ⓙ Ⓚ	59 Ⓐ Ⓑ Ⓒ Ⓓ Ⓔ
15 Ⓐ Ⓑ Ⓒ Ⓓ Ⓔ	30 Ⓕ Ⓖ Ⓗ Ⓙ Ⓚ	45 Ⓐ Ⓑ Ⓒ Ⓓ Ⓔ	60 Ⓕ Ⓖ Ⓗ Ⓙ Ⓚ

READING

1 (A) (B) (C) (D)	11 (A) (B) (C) (D)	21 (A) (B) (C) (D)	31 (A) (B) (C) (D)
2 (F) (G) (H) (J)	12 (F) (G) (H) (J)	22 (F) (G) (H) (J)	32 (F) (G) (H) (J)
3 (A) (B) (C) (D)	13 (A) (B) (C) (D)	23 (A) (B) (C) (D)	33 (A) (B) (C) (D)
4 (F) (G) (H) (J)	14 (F) (G) (H) (J)	24 (F) (G) (H) (J)	34 (F) (G) (H) (J)
5 (A) (B) (C) (D)	15 (A) (B) (C) (D)	25 (A) (B) (C) (D)	35 (A) (B) (C) (D)
6 (F) (G) (H) (J)	16 (F) (G) (H) (J)	26 (F) (G) (H) (J)	36 (F) (G) (H) (J)
7 (A) (B) (C) (D)	17 (A) (B) (C) (D)	27 (A) (B) (C) (D)	37 (A) (B) (C) (D)
8 (F) (G) (H) (J)	18 (F) (G) (H) (J)	28 (F) (G) (H) (J)	38 (F) (G) (H) (J)
9 (A) (B) (C) (D)	19 (A) (B) (C) (D)	29 (A) (B) (C) (D)	39 (A) (B) (C) (D)
10 (F) (G) (H) (J)	20 (F) (G) (H) (J)	30 (F) (G) (H) (J)	40 (F) (G) (H) (J)

SCIENCE

1 (A) (B) (C) (D)	11 (A) (B) (C) (D)	21 (A) (B) (C) (D)	31 (A) (B) (C) (D)
2 (F) (G) (H) (J)	12 (F) (G) (H) (J)	22 (F) (G) (H) (J)	32 (F) (G) (H) (J)
3 (A) (B) (C) (D)	13 (A) (B) (C) (D)	23 (A) (B) (C) (D)	33 (A) (B) (C) (D)
4 (F) (G) (H) (J)	14 (F) (G) (H) (J)	24 (F) (G) (H) (J)	34 (F) (G) (H) (J)
5 (A) (B) (C) (D)	15 (A) (B) (C) (D)	25 (A) (B) (C) (D)	35 (A) (B) (C) (D)
6 (F) (G) (H) (J)	16 (F) (G) (H) (J)	26 (F) (G) (H) (J)	36 (F) (G) (H) (J)
7 (A) (B) (C) (D)	17 (A) (B) (C) (D)	27 (A) (B) (C) (D)	37 (A) (B) (C) (D)
8 (F) (G) (H) (J)	18 (F) (G) (H) (J)	28 (F) (G) (H) (J)	38 (F) (G) (H) (J)
9 (A) (B) (C) (D)	19 (A) (B) (C) (D)	29 (A) (B) (C) (D)	39 (A) (B) (C) (D)
10 (F) (G) (H) (J)	20 (F) (G) (H) (J)	30 (F) (G) (H) (J)	40 (F) (G) (H) (J)

RAW SCORES	SCALE SCORES	DATE TAKEN:
ENGLISH _____	ENGLISH _____	
MATHEMATICS _____	MATHEMATICS _____	ENGLISH/WRITING _____
READING _____	READING _____	
SCIENCE _____	SCIENCE _____	_____
		COMPOSITE SCORE

Refer to the Scoring Worksheet on page 234 for help in determining your Raw and Scale Scores.

You may wish to remove these sample answer document pages to respond to the practice ACT Writing Test.

Begin WRITING TEST here.

_____
_____
_____
_____
_____
_____
_____
_____
_____
_____
_____
_____
_____
_____
_____
_____
_____
_____
_____
_____
_____
_____
_____
_____

If you need more space, please continue on the next page.

Do not write in this shaded area.

Cut Here

WRITING TEST

_____

_____

_____

_____

_____

_____

_____

_____

_____

_____

_____

_____

_____

_____

_____

_____

_____

_____

_____

_____

_____

_____

_____

_____

_____

_____

_____

_____

If you need more space, please continue on the back of this page.

Do not write in this shaded area.

WRITING TEST

_____

_____

_____

_____

_____

_____

_____

_____

_____

_____

_____

_____

_____

_____

_____

_____

_____

_____

_____

_____

_____

_____

_____

_____

_____

_____

_____

_____

_____

If you need more space, please continue on the next page.

WRITING TEST

_____

_____

_____

_____

_____

_____

_____

_____

_____

_____

_____

_____

_____

_____

_____

_____

_____

_____

_____

_____

_____

_____

_____

_____

_____

_____

STOP here with the Writing Test.

Do not write in this shaded area.

1 ■ ■ ■ ■ ■ ■ ■ ■ 1

ENGLISH TEST

45 Minutes—75 Questions

DIRECTIONS: In the passages that follow, some words and phrases are underlined and numbered. In the answer column, you will find alternatives for the words and phrases that are underlined. Choose the alternative that you think is best, and fill in the corresponding bubble on your answer sheet. If you think that the original version is best, choose "NO CHANGE," which will always be either answer choice A or F. You will also find questions about a particular section of the passage, or about the entire passage. These questions will be identified either by an underlined portion or by a number in a box. Look for the answer that clearly expresses the idea, is consistent with the style and tone of the passage, and makes the correct use of standard written English. Read the passage through once before answering the questions. For some questions, you should read beyond the indicated portion before you answer.

PASSAGE I

> The following paragraphs may or may not be in the most logical order. You may be asked questions about the logical order of the paragraphs, as well as where to place sentences logically within any given paragraph.

Mike and his Cable TV

[1]

My best friend Mike is notorious for ignoring many of the modern conveniences that most people could not live without he'd sooner handwrite anything than sit at a
__1__
computer to type.

He insists that, it would be too much trouble to learn all
__2__
of the functions on a word-processing program. So, I was not the least bit surprised to hear of his disappointment in his evening last Friday. Apparently, he is very excited to
__3__
host some friends from work at his apartment for the first time. Within minutes of their arrival, one of them reached for the television remote and punched in a channel. Alerted by the sound of static from the TV, Mike realized immediately what was happening: the first game of the playoffs was on and he didn't have cable service!

Therefore, he asserts he has no desire to have more than
__4__

1. **A.** NO CHANGE
   B. without, he'd sooner handwrite
   C. without sooner handwriting
   D. without. He'd sooner handwrite

2. **F.** NO CHANGE
   G. insists, that
   H. insists that
   J. insists, that,

3. **A.** NO CHANGE
   B. was
   C. has been
   D. was being

4. **F.** NO CHANGE
   G. Thus, he
   H. Consequently, he
   J. He

GO ON TO THE NEXT PAGE.

1 ■ ■ ■ ■ ■ ■ ■ ■ 1

a few channels to flip through, but I imagine at that moment on Friday evening, he had wished for cable service. [5]

[2]

To help my friend, I said I would look into it for him. I spoke to a sales agent with the cable company about the different packages of channels available to someone living in Mike's apartment building. She started by describing the most premium package, so I quickly interrupted her to say she should begin with the cheapest offer. She insisted that the premium package was amazing, with many extra sports, and movie channels.

I assured her that the cheapest possible option, when she told me it was only $15 per month, would more than suffice, I arranged to have it installed. I knew it would be worth it to Mike.

[3]

[1] During his first few days with cable, Mike has sat in front of his TV; when before he would have been reading a comic book or milling around the apartment. [2] He is fond of animal documentaries and can't believe how many of them he finds every day across the 70 channels. [3] I showed him how to program his VCR to record what he likes.

5. Given that all are true, which of the following additions to the preceding sentence (replacing "cable service") would be most relevant?
   A. cable service to entertain his guests
   B. cable service that was wired into his apartment
   C. cable service with a good remote control
   D. cable service to watch

6. F. NO CHANGE
   G. them
   H. some
   J. cable service

7. A. NO CHANGE
   B. because
   C. due to the fact that
   D. since

8. F. NO CHANGE
   G. sports, and movie, channels.
   H. sports and movie, channels.
   J. sports and movie channels.

9. A. NO CHANGE
   B. I assured her that the cheapest possible option would more than suffice, and when she told me it was only $15 per month, I arranged to have it installed.
   C. I arranged to have installed the cheapest possible option that would more than suffice, which she told me was only $15 per month.
   D. She told me it was only $15 per month, which I assured her would more than suffice as the cheapest possible option, so I arranged to have it installed.

10. F. NO CHANGE
    G. sits
    H. was sitting
    J. sat

11. A. NO CHANGE
    B. TV: when
    C. TV. When
    D. TV when

12. F. NO CHANGE
    G. by programming
    H. a program with
    J. and programmed

GO ON TO THE NEXT PAGE.

1 ■ ■ ■ ■ ■ ■ ■ ■ **1**

[4]

[1] With this discovery of cable television, I suspect Mike might take more kindly to technology in the future. [2] Soon I hope to introduce to him to the Internet and maybe even the cellular phone. [3] <u>I doubt he'll turn out</u>

13

<u>to be a gadget-lover like me someday.</u> ⎙14

13

13. Which of the choices would provide an ending most consistent with the essay as a whole?
   A. NO CHANGE
   B. With time, perhaps he'll learn to embrace modern technology.
   C. I'm not sure if he'd know how to use it, though.
   D. Maybe Mike isn't as behind the times as I once thought.

14. Upon reviewing Paragraph 4 and realizing that some information has been left out, the writer composes the following sentence:

   Little by little, I see him enjoying the pleasures of our digital world.

   The most logical placement for this sentence would be:
   F. before Sentence 1.
   G. after Sentence 1.
   H. after Sentence 2.
   J. after Sentence 3.

Question 15 asks about the preceding passage as a whole.

---

15. The writer is considering deleting Sentence 2 of Paragraph 3. If the writer removed this sentence, the essay would primarily lose:
   A. an interesting detail about how Mike is benefiting from cable television.
   B. details supporting the fact that Mike is inexperienced with cable television.
   C. a humorous blend of descriptive detail and relevant information.
   D. proof that Mike will continue to pay the $15 per month for cable service.

GO ON TO THE NEXT PAGE.

1 ■ ■ ■ ■ ■ ■ ■ ■ 1

PASSAGE II

> The following paragraphs may or may not be in the most logical order. You may be asked questions about the logical order of the paragraphs, as well as where to place sentences logically within any given paragraph.

Ragtime: Uniquely American Music

[1]

Many forms of music have originated in the United
                    16

States, thanks in large part to the nations rich ethnic
                                       17

diversity. It is ragtime that is one form of American music.
                    18
Characterized both by its distinctive African-American

syncopation and conservative European classical structure,

ragtime in its heyday from 1900 to 1918 was enjoyed by
                    19
people of all races and ethnicities.

[2]

Ragtime grew from the marches and jigs popular in the

Northern Black communities of the late 19th century.

Historians consider 1897 the beginning of mature ragtime.

A "rag" can have varied instrumentation; but usually it is
                              20
written for piano. Ragtime songs have a vocal part, but

much of the music makes the piano 21 center stage.

Predating recorded music, ragtime was distributed almost

exclusively as sheet music, which was performed by

amateur pianists in homes and cafés around the country.

For this reason, many consider ragtime to be a form of

classical music. Public performances by ragtime

composers were in short supply, but high demand.

One alternative to seeing a great performance was to hear

the piece on a player piano. The first official ragtime hit

16. F. NO CHANGE
   G. Music forms
   H. One form of music
   J. The form of music that

17. A. NO CHANGE
   B. national
   C. nations'
   D. nation's

18. F. NO CHANGE
   G. Known as ragtime, it is one form of American music.
   H. Ragtime is one such form of American music.
   J. Being one form of American music is ragtime.

19. A. NO CHANGE
   B. ragtime, in its heyday from 1900 to 1918
   C. ragtime, in its heyday, from 1900 to 1918,
   D. ragtime, in its heyday from 1900 to 1918,

20. F. NO CHANGE
   G. instrumentation but
   H. instrumentation, but
   J. instrumentation

21. At this point, the writer is considering adding the following parenthetical phrase:

   –and those who played it –

   Given that it is true, would this be a relevant addition to make here?
   A. Yes, because it helps the reader have a better understanding of the style of music.
   B. Yes, because it provides an important historical detail that is elaborated on later in the paragraph.
   C. No, because this detail is not essential to the meaning of the sentence nor to the content of the paragraph.
   D. No, because the essay only describes the musical form and not its role in American society in the early 20th century.

GO ON TO THE NEXT PAGE.

1 ■ ■ ■ ■ ■ ■ ■ ■ 1

was Scott Joplin's *Maple Leaf Rag*, published in 1899.

America was enthralled by this sophisticated composition.

[3]

[1] Today, Joplin is the most famous figure in ragtime
history. [2] He first showed great musical potential at a
                              _____
                                          22
young age, and when his family moved to a new home in
Texas, his mother worked long hours to earn enough
money to buy a piano for him. [3] His abilities were
noticed by a German piano teacher he gave Joplin free
                                    __
                                    23
lessons and instilled in him good classical technique.

[4] Soon enough, Joplin was a skilled musician and began
studying music composition at George Smith College
                           _____
                                          24
in Sedalia, Missouri. [5] After some years as a traveling
_____
        24

musician, where he eventually settled back in Sedalia and
          _____
           25

became a pianist at several, popular, black men's clubs.
          _____
                              26
[6] It was during this phase of his career that he composed

his *Maple Leaf Rag*, the piano piece that
                     _____
                               27

22. Which of the following alternatives to the underlined
portion would be LEAST acceptable?
F. demonstrated his talent on the piano
G. revealed his musical skills
H. exposed his rhythmic touch
J. played

23. **A.** NO CHANGE
B. who
C. whom
D. that

24. The writer is considering deleting the following clause
from the preceding sentence (placing a period after the
word *composition*):

   at George Smith College in Sedalia, Missouri.

Should the writer make this deletion?
F. Yes, because the information is unrelated to the
topic addressed in this paragraph.
G. Yes, because the information diminishes the impact
of Joplin's natural musical talent on his body of
work.
H. No, because the information explains why Joplin
likely began his career in Sedalia.
J. No, because the information shows that Joplin
was an unremarkable music student who could not
enroll in a more prestigious institution.

25. **A.** NO CHANGE
B. it was there that
C. was where
D. OMIT the underlined portion.

26. **F.** NO CHANGE
G. pianist, at several, popular black men's clubs.
H. pianist at several popular black men's clubs.
J. pianist, at several popular black men's clubs.

27. Given that all of the choices are true, which one would
most effectively tie together the two main subjects of
this essay?
A. NO CHANGE
B. a piano piece most Americans recognize today.
C. his most popular work during his lifetime.
D. the profits from which helped him dedicate more
time to composition instead of performing in clubs.

GO ON TO THE NEXT PAGE.

1 ■ ■ ■ ■ ■ ■ ■ ■ **1**

propelled him, and ragtime itself into
_____
                    27
national prominence. [28]
_____
       27

                    [4]

The ragtime style illustrates how people of diverse

heritage can create unique music that lots of people like.
                                    _____
                                            29
Ragtime gave way to jazz by the 1920s. Audio recording

was becoming popular at the same time. The piano was

no longer required and jazz albums began playing in living

rooms across the country. Like all folk music, though, jazz

pays homage to its predecessor—ragtime—by borrowing

its style, rhythm, and mood.

28. Upon reviewing this paragraph and finding that some
    information has been left out, the writer composes the
    following sentence incorporating that information:

    Connoisseurs of piano music appreciate his com-
    positions for the novel combination of folk
    rhythms and classical harmonies.

    This sentence would most logically be placed after
    Sentence:
    F. 1.
    G. 2.
    H. 5.
    J. 6.

29. **A.** NO CHANGE
    B. everyone likes to listen to.
    C. appeals to a broad audience.
    D. never gets old.

Question 30 asks about the preceding passage as a whole.

30. Suppose the writer's goal had been to write a brief
    essay focusing on the history and development of rag-
    time music. Would this essay successfully fulfill this
    goal?
    F. Yes, because the essay mentions the contributions
    that ragtime music has made to other African-
    American musical traditions.
    G. Yes, because the essay discusses the origins of
    ragtime music and one of its early important
    figures.
    H. No, because the essay refers to other musical forms
    besides ragtime.
    J. No, because the essay focuses on only one ragtime
    musician, Scott Joplin.

PASSAGE III

Sequoia's System of Writing

Although few facts exist regarding the life of the Native
                      _____
                       31
American named Sequoia, the information that is available

articulate and paint a colorful picture of this man
_____
       32

on the plains. Sequoia was born into the Cherokee Nation
_____
     33

31. **A.** NO CHANGE
    B. that exist
    C. are existing
    D. exists

32. **F.** NO CHANGE
    G. paints
    H. articulating and painting
    J. paint articulately

33. **A.** NO CHANGE
    B. of the plains
    C. from and on the plains
    D. on which the plains

GO ON TO THE NEXT PAGE.

1 ■ ■ ■ ■ ■ ■ ■ ■ **1**

in approximately 1770; his <u>mother was</u> a descendant of
        34

many <u>respected</u> Cherokee chiefs. This provided Sequoia
        35
with a secure social stature despite his unknown paternity.

Sequoia's fame comes mainly from his <u>acknowledged</u>
                                        36

development of a written Cherokee language. 37 Over a

period of twelve years, Sequoia developed a *syllabary*

consisting of over eighty characters. Unlike an alphabet,

where each letter represents a basic sound of speech,

a syllabary consists of written characters,

<u>each of which represents a syllable.</u> Remarkably, a person
              38
learning Cherokee using the syllabary is able to read and

write the language in an extremely short period of time

compared to the time it takes someone to master the

English language. <u>Its use</u> among the nation's
                     39

Cherokee people <u>spread quick,</u> and soon Cherokee
                   40

<u>reading materials were being widely published,</u> even
                         41
though other tribes had no written language.

    Religious missionaries quickly realized the advantages

of translating sacred texts into the new Cherokee language,

---

34. **F.** NO CHANGE
   G. mother who was
   H. mother being
   J. mother is

35. **A.** NO CHANGE
   B. respecting
   C. respectably
   D. OMIT the underlined portion.

36. Which choice gives the sense that some of the facts of the story are unsubstantiated?
   F. NO CHANGE
   G. documented
   H. alleged
   J. accounted

37. Assuming that all of the choices are true, which one best links the preceding sentence with the rest of the paragraph?
   A. Sequoia was also known as George Guess, and he frequently interacted with white men.
   B. The Cherokees, like many Native Americans, had primarily used pictographs to communicate.
   C. A syllabary can consist of many different symbols and characters.
   D. Legend reveals that Sequoia was determined to prove that his people could communicate in writing more effectively than could other tribes.

38. **F.** NO CHANGE
   G. that represent one syllable each
   H. that represents a syllable
   J. representing, each one, a syllable

39. **A.** NO CHANGE
   B. It's use
   C. The syllabary's use
   D. Use of it

40. **F.** NO CHANGE
   G. spreads quick
   H. spreads quickly
   J. spread quickly

41. **A.** NO CHANGE
   B. reading materials that were being widely published
   C. had reading materials were widely published
   D. the reading materials, that were being published widely

GO ON TO THE NEXT PAGE.

so Bibles and other religious materials soon
became widespread. Laws were also written using
<u>42</u>
Sequoia's symbols, and the first Native American

newspaper, *The Cherokee Phoenix,* was also launched.

Cherokee history was preserved through new written

records, which included accounts and descriptions of

ceremonial traditions and common customs.

[1] One peculiarity of this new Cherokee language was

that <u>it does not</u> instigate a literary explosion among the
<u>43</u>
Cherokee people. [2] Instead, the syllabary was used

primarily as a recording device. [3] Seemingly, no poetry,

novels, or biographies emerged during that time. [4] The

syllabary elevated the Cherokee nation in the eyes of the

rest of the world, and they became widely regarded as a

learned people as a result. [5] Sequoia's system is still in

use today, and anyone can discover it at a library or a

computer. 44

42. If the writer were to delete the phrase "so Bibles and other religious materials soon became widespread," ending the sentence with "language," the essay would primarily lose a detail that:
 F. enhances the main point of the essay.
 G. helps the reader understand the real purpose of Sequoia's syllabary.
 H. further explains the first part of the same sentence.
 J. adds a humorous element to the essay.

43. A. NO CHANGE
 B. it did not
 C. it might not
 D. it should not

44. Which of the following sequences of sentences makes this paragraph most logical?
 F. NO CHANGE
 G. 1, 3, 2, 4, 5
 H. 3, 4, 2, 1, 5
 J. 4, 3, 1, 2, 5

Question 45 asks about the preceding passage as a whole.

45. Suppose the writer had intended to write a brief introduction to the Cherokee nation of the early United States. Would this essay successfully fulfill this goal?
 A. Yes, because the essay discusses the development of an important part of the Cherokee nation, specifically its written language.
 B. Yes, because Sequoia made a huge contribution to the Cherokee culture.
 C. No, because the essay focuses on one aspect of the Cherokee nation, not on the society as a whole.
 D. No, because the essay does not address any of the most important moments of Cherokee history.

GO ON TO THE NEXT PAGE.

1 ■ ■ ■ ■ ■ ■ ■ ■ 1

PASSAGE IV

Finding My Family Tree

As a boy, I was fortunate to have a close family, all

living in the same town. I saw my grandparents often, and

they'd tell me story after story of a past world and of the

people who dwelled in it.
46

In one summer night I strolled through a thicket with my
47

grandfather, picking up leaves and sticks along the way.

Sometimes I knew from which tree they had fallen, but my

grandpa happily gave me hints for most of them. 48 Bit by

bit, he told me a story about from where he and his family

had come and the acres of woods he had explored as a boy.

My grandfather's immediate family came from Quebec;

his distant relatives hailed from France. He always wanted
49

to take me to his hometown near Montreal, but we hadn't
50

yet had the opportunity. The woods in French Canada,

he said, were hearty and old, all of, the trees were the
51

regrowth from widespread logging over a century ago.

Quebec has a lot of maples, too, and Grandpa explained

how his mother knew how to boil the sap just slowly

enough to make syrup.

46. **F.** NO CHANGE
   G. who, dwelled, in it
   H. who dwelled, in it
   J. who, dwelled in it

47. **A.** NO CHANGE
   B. On one summer night
   C. One summer night,
   D. In one summer night,

48. The writer is considering revising the preceding sentence by deleting the phrase "but my grandpa happily gave me hints for most of them" (placing a period after the word *fallen*). If the writer did this, the paragraph would primarily lose:
   F. information comparing the narrator's knowledge of the woods with that of his grandfather.
   G. details describing the grandfather's lifelong experience with wooded lands.
   H. details describing how the narrator and his grandfather passed the time on their walks in the woods.
   J. details revealing the narrator's fondness of his grandfather through sharing his knowledge of trees.

49. **A.** NO CHANGE
   B. his relatives hailing from distant France
   C. hailing more distant relatives from France
   D. his relatives hailed from France distantly

50. Which of the following alternatives to the underlined portion would NOT be acceptable?
   F. by
   G. outside
   H. about
   J. close to

51. **A.** NO CHANGE
   B. old; all of
   C. old all of
   D. old; all, of

GO ON TO THE NEXT PAGE.

1 ■ ■ ■ ■ ■ ■ ■ ■ 1

When we came in from our walk, Grandpa would
take out one of his dusty shoeboxes from the cellar and sit
down next to me. It amazes me how I've never seen the
same shoebox emerge twice from the attic; his family
records are astounding. In the dusty box were
old sepia photographs of family members

going about their daily business. My great-grandmother

was pictured having kneaded dough in the kitchen.

These edges were splitting on a photograph of boys
skating on a pond, hockey sticks raised in celebration of a
goal. One by one, I felt the emotion captured by these
images, and I got the nagging feeling that I would never
know these people from my family's past. After that day,
I often joined my grandpa to learn about my
French-Canadian ancestry, so that, when he is gone, I will
be the custodian of the stories.

The culmination of our time together was a detailed
family tree, its base formed by our French, ancestors who
first arrived on this continent. Our search for information

uncovered amazing historical documents, as ships'
manifests and handwritten marriage certificates.

If you were lucky, we'd find more than just a name. Dates
recognizing births and deaths were fairly easy to find;
occupations and bits of ancestors' life stories became

---

52. Given that all of the choices are true, which one would most effectively lead the reader from the first sentence of this paragraph to the description that follows in the next two sentences?
  F. NO CHANGE
  G. Maple syrup aside, there are lots of things I like about my family, and my grandpa continued to astound me with his tales.
  H. Grandpa usually has a good story to tell on our walks.
  J. No one else in my family has as much passion for long walks as does my grandpa.

53. Given that all of the choices are true, which one provides information most relevant to the main focus of this paragraph?
  A. NO CHANGE
  B. in suits and dresses.
  C. enjoying a picnic in the country.
  D. with stark expressions that spoke of the toil of farm life generations ago.

54. **F.** NO CHANGE
  G. kneads
  H. kneading
  J. was kneading

55. **A.** NO CHANGE
  B. My edges
  C. The edges
  D. Those edges

56. **F.** NO CHANGE
  G. our French ancestors, whom
  H. our French ancestors whom
  J. our French ancestors who

57. **A.** NO CHANGE
  B. such as
  C. being
  D. as like

58. **F.** NO CHANGE
  G. If we were lucky,
  H. If you are lucky,
  J. If we are lucky,

GO ON TO THE NEXT PAGE.

1 ■ ■ ■ ■ ■ ■ ■ ■ 1

increasing difficult to uncover as we dug deeper
<u>   </u>
                59

into the past. Now, though, we're preserving this history

so that our progeny may learn from these stories

and take comfort in knowing that, though life may end,

<u>photos capture history very well.</u>
                60

59. A. NO CHANGE
    B. increasing and difficult
    C. increasingly difficult
    D. increasing with difficulty

60. The writer wants to balance the statements made in the earlier part of this essay with a related detail that reveals why the narrator wants to preserve this history. Given that all of the choices are true, which one best accomplishes this goal?
    F. NO CHANGE
    G. we can tell our stories through the records of our past.
    H. family goes on forever.
    J. people can reminisce over photo albums and scrapbooks.

PASSAGE V

How Volcanoes Work

What causes the formation of volcanoes? Before

humans understood that the center of the Earth was made

of molten iron, scientific hypotheses pointed to chemical

reactions in superficial layers of magma to explain the

phenomenon. Through modern geology, humans have a

clearer—though hardly complete—understanding of the

mechanism of magma flow, <u>and can</u> analyze the vibrations
                                      61

of the earth to warn of <u>recent</u> eruptions.
                              62

<u>Most volcanoes were being</u> the result of magma flowing
                    63

out of the surface of the earth and hardening, usually near

a subduction zone. As two tectonic plates collide,

<u>one of them is</u> forced under the other, and the seabed rock
              64

melts to form new, low-density magma.

61. A. NO CHANGE
    B. and, can
    C. and can,
    D. and

62. F. NO CHANGE
    G. distant
    H. approximate
    J. impending

63. A. NO CHANGE
    B. Most volcanoes have been
    C. Most volcanoes are
    D. Most volcanoes will be

64. F. NO CHANGE
    G. one of the plates are
    H. one,
    J. one plate, being

GO ON TO THE NEXT PAGE.

1 ■ ■ ■ ■ ■ ■ ■ ■ ■ 1

This <u>magma is red-hot and eventually penetrates unstable</u>
pockets of the Earth's surface. Some magma will succeed

in reaching the surface either to form a new volcano or

<u>adding</u> more mass to an existing one. Not all volcanoes are
formed at continental boundaries, however.

   <u>Hotspot volcanoes form</u> by a different mechanism.
One theory, proposed in the 1960s, seeks to explain

volcanoes such as those that formed the Hawaiian Islands,

which are not at a plate boundary. The probable

explanation is a hotspot, which is a fixed point beneath the

Earth's crust where a narrow plume of magma rises into the

crust and appears at the surface as a continental volcano or

a volcanic island. <u>Chains, of volcanic islands called</u>
<u>archipelagos,</u> provide evidence that the hotspot stays in
place as the tectonic plate passes over it.

   Geologic processes are <u>slow, while</u> research must
include the study of ancient human accounts of eruptions

and layers of rock millions of years old.

<u>In general, eruptions</u> seem to occur every several hundred
or even thousand years, and many volcanoes seem to be

completely dormant, <u>that is unlikely to erupt soon.</u> No one
can say for sure that these volcanoes will not erupt again

in the future, so scientists <u>take serious</u> the study of every
volcano situated where a future eruption could bring

significant human loss and environmental damage.

Predicting volcanic eruptions is not an exact science, and

only within the briefest geological moment can people

<u>warn</u> to evacuate. Through studying the earth's vibrations,
physical deformation, and gas emissions, geologists in

recent decades have made several excellent predictions of

65. Given that all of the choices are true, which one pro-
vides the most logical cause for the action described
in the statement immediately following this underlined
portion?
   A. NO CHANGE
   B. This magma rises
   C. This magma condenses
   D. This magma forms pools

66. **F.** NO CHANGE
   G. adds
   H. add
   J. added

67. **A.** NO CHANGE
   B. Formation of hotspot volcanoes is
   C. There are hotspot volcanoes that forming
   D. In addition, hotspot volcanoes are formed

68. **F.** NO CHANGE
   G. Chains of volcanic islands, called archipelagos,
   H. Chains of volcanic islands called archipelagos
   J. Chains, of volcanic islands, called archipelagos

69. **A.** NO CHANGE
   B. slow, but
   C. slow, so
   D. slow, although

70. **F.** NO CHANGE
   G. Quite regularly, eruptions
   H. Many times, eruptions
   J. Often, eruptions

71. **A.** NO CHANGE
   B. that is, unlikely to erupt soon
   C. that is unlikely, to erupt soon
   D. that, is unlikely to erupt soon

72. **F.** NO CHANGE
   G. taken seriously
   H. seriously taking
   J. take seriously

73. **A.** NO CHANGE
   B. be warning
   C. receive warning
   D. have the warning

GO ON TO THE NEXT PAGE.

1 ■ ■ ■ ■ ■ ■ ■ ■ 1

volcanic eruption, <u>as if</u> at the Philippines' Mount Pinatubo
74
in 1991 and Popocatépetl outside Mexico City in 2000.

Understanding the mechanisms of the earth's interior
and continuing to study volcanoes will advance the
development of reliable early warning systems for
dangerous eruptions. Volcanoes are both feared and
revered for their beauty and awesome destructive power,
<u>but</u> they show that humans have much more to learn about
75
the planet Earth.

74. **F.** NO CHANGE
G. most notably
H. typically
J. characteristically

75. **A.** NO CHANGE
B. seemingly
C. when
D. and

END OF THE ENGLISH TEST.
STOP! IF YOU HAVE TIME LEFT OVER, CHECK YOUR WORK ON THIS SECTION ONLY.

2 △ △ △ △ △ △ △ △ 2

MATHEMATICS TEST

60 Minutes—60 Questions

DIRECTIONS: Solve each of the problems in the time allowed, then fill in the corresponding bubble on your answer sheet. Do not spend too much time on any one problem; skip the more difficult problems and go back to them later.

You may use a calculator on this test. For this test you should assume that figures are NOT necessarily drawn to scale, that all geometric figures lie in a plane, and that the word *line* is used to indicate a straight line.

---

1. The minimum fine for driving in excess of the speed limit is $25. An additional $6 is added to the minimum fine for each mile per hour (mph) in excess of the speed limit. Rachel was issued a $103 fine for speeding in a 55-mph speed limit zone. For driving at what speed, in mph, was Rachel fined?
   A. 48
   B. 52
   C. 62
   D. 68
   E. 78

2. $5x^3 \times 2xy \times 3xy^2$ is equivalent to:
   F. $10x^3y^2$
   G. $10x^5y^3$
   H. $30x^3y^3$
   J. $30x^5y^3$
   K. $30x^5y^2$

3. What is the fourth term in the arithmetic sequence 13, 10, 7, …?
   A. 14
   B. 9
   C. 4
   D. 0
   E. −7

4. When written in symbols, "the product of r and s, raised to the fourth power," is represented as:
   F. r^4s^4
   G. $(r+s)^4$
   H. $(rs)^4$
   J. $\dfrac{r^4}{s^4}$
   K. rs^4

DO YOUR FIGURING HERE.

GO ON TO THE NEXT PAGE.

2 △ △ △ △ △ △ △ △ **2**

5. Which of the following numbers has the digit 5 in the thousandths place?

A. 5,000.00
B. 50.0
C. 0.05
D. 0.005
E. 0.0005

6. Mandy and Jordan each bought some of the same notebooks and the same three-ring binder. Mandy paid $5.85 for 3 notebooks and 1 binder. Jordan paid $4.65 for 2 notebooks and 1 binder. What is the price of one of the notebooks?

F. $2.70
G. $2.25
H. $1.80
J. $1.20
K. $0.75

7. If $mn = k$ and $k = x^2n$, and $nk \neq 0$, which of the following is equal to m?

A. 1
B. $1/x$
C. $\sqrt{x}$
D. x
E. x^2

8. If $7x + 5 = 2x + 9$, then $x = ?$

F. $\dfrac{4}{5}$
G. $1\dfrac{4}{5}$
H. $\dfrac{4}{9}$
J. $1\dfrac{4}{9}$
K. 2

9. What percent of 5 is 7?

A. 14%
B. 35%
C. 71%
D. 140%
E. 157%

DO YOUR FIGURING HERE.

GO ON TO THE NEXT PAGE.

2  **2**

10. If x is a positive real number such that $x^2 = 16$, then $x^3 + \sqrt{x} = ?$

   F. 18

   G. 20

   H. 66

   J. 68

   K. 74

11. $-|-16| - (-16) = ?$

   A. -16

   B. 0

   C. 4

   D. 16

   E. 32

12. A partial deck of cards was found sitting out on a table. If the partial deck consists of 6 spades, 3 hearts, and 7 diamonds, what is the probability of randomly selecting a red card from this partial deck? (Note: diamonds and hearts are considered "red," while spades and clubs are considered "black.")

   F. $\dfrac{9}{16}$

   G. $\dfrac{13}{16}$

   H. $\dfrac{7}{16}$

   J. $\dfrac{3}{8}$

   K. $\dfrac{5}{8}$

13. Which of the following is a simplified form of $4x - 4y + 3x$?

   A. $x(7 - 4y)$

   B. $x - y + 3x$

   C. $-8xy + 3x$

   D. $7x - 4y$

   E. $-4y - x$

DO YOUR FIGURING HERE.

GO ON TO THE NEXT PAGE.

2 △ △ △ △ △ △ △ △ 2

14. Gary has turtles, cats, and birds for pets. The number of birds he has is 4 more than the number of turtles, and the number of cats is 2 times the number of birds. Of the following, which could be the total number of Gary's pets?
    F. 14
    G. 18
    H. 20
    J. 22
    K. 26

15. On a map, 1/4 inch represents 12 miles. If a road is 66 miles long, what is its length, in inches, on the map?
    A. 5 1/2
    B. 5 1/8
    C. 1 1/2
    D. 1 3/8
    E. 7/8

16. If $b = a - 4$, then $(a - b)^3 = $?
    F. 64
    G. 16
    H. −4
    J. −16
    K. −64

17. If g is an integer, which of the following could NOT equal g^2 ?
    A. 0
    B. 1
    C. 4
    D. 8
    E. 9

18. Justin owns 6 different dress shirts, 3 different pairs of pants, and 5 different ties. How many distinct outfits, each consisting of a shirt, a pair of pants, and a tie, can Justin make?
    F. 14
    G. 42
    H. 90
    J. 120
    K. 144

19. An oil refinery produces gasoline from crude oil. For every 10,000 barrels of crude oil supplied, the refinery can produce 6,500 barrels of gasoline. How many barrels of gasoline can be produced from 3,500 barrels of crude oil?
    A. 1,265
    B. 1,750
    C. 2,125
    D. 2,275
    E. 5,385

DO YOUR FIGURING HERE.

GO ON TO THE NEXT PAGE.

2   △ **2**

20. What is the slope of a line that passes through the origin and the point $(-6, 2)$?
    F. 3
    G. 1/3
    H. $-1/3$
    J. -3
    K. -6

21. If $n^x \cdot n^8 = n^{24}$ and $(n^6)^y = n^{18}$, what is the value of $x + y$?
    A. 7
    B. 9
    C. 12
    D. 19
    E. 27

22. What is the slope-intercept form of $9x + 3y - 6 = 0$?
    F. $y = 9x - 6$
    G. $y = 3x + 2$
    H. $y = 3x - 2$
    J. $y = -3x + 2$
    K. $y = -9x + 6$

23. If the volume of a cube is 64, what is the shortest distance from the center of the cube to the base of the cube?
    A. 2
    B. 4
    C. $2\sqrt{4}$
    D. $\sqrt{32}$
    E. 16

24. For the right triangle $\triangle ABC$ shown below, what is $\sin C$?

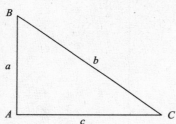

    F. $\dfrac{a}{b}$

    G. $\dfrac{a}{c}$

    H. $\dfrac{b}{a}$

    J. $\dfrac{c}{b}$

    K. $\dfrac{c}{a}$

DO YOUR FIGURING HERE.

GO ON TO THE NEXT PAGE.

DO YOUR FIGURING HERE.

25. What is the area, in coordinate units, of the triangle in the figure below?

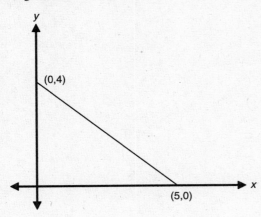

A. 4.5
B. 9.0
C. 10.0
D. 12.5
E. 20.0

26. A shoe store charges $39 for a certain type of sneaker. This price is 30% more than the amount it costs the shoe store to buy one pair of these sneakers. At an end-of-the-year sale, sales associates can purchase any remaining sneakers at 20% off the shoe store's cost. How much would it cost an employee to purchase a pair of sneakers of this type during the sale (excluding sales tax)?
F. $31.20
G. $25.00
H. $24.00
J. $21.84
K. $19.50

27. After excavating a lot, workers removed an estimated 7,000 cubic yards of dirt from the area. If this dirt were spread in an even layer over an empty lot with dimensions 30 yards by 64 yards, about how deep, in yards, would the layer of dirt be?
A. Less than 1
B. Between 1 and 2
C. Between 2 and 3
D. Between 3 and 4
E. More than 4

GO ON TO THE NEXT PAGE.

2   **2**

28. The hypotenuse of the right triangle $\triangle ABC$ shown below is 17 feet long. The cosine of angle C is $\frac{3}{5}$. How many feet long is the segment AC?

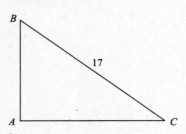

   F. 6
   G. 10.2
   H. 12
   J. 15
   K. 28.3

29. When the choir is arranged in rows of 5 people each, the last row is one person short. When the choir is arranged in rows of 6 people each, the last row is still one person short. What is the least possible number of people in the choir?
   A. 29
   B. 30
   C. 56
   D. 60
   E. 99

30. What is the y-coordinate of the point in the standard (x,y) coordinate plane at which the 2 lines $y = \frac{x}{2} + 3$ and $y = 3x - 2$ intersect?
   F. 5
   G. 4
   H. 3
   J. 2
   K. 1

31. Points B and C lie on segment AD as shown below. Segment AD is 32 units long, segment AC is 23 units long, and segment BD is 27 units long. How many units long, if it can be determined, is segment BC?

   A. 21
   B. 18
   C. 9
   D. 4
   E. Cannot be determined from the given information.

DO YOUR FIGURING HERE.

GO ON TO THE NEXT PAGE.

2   △ △ △ △ △ **2**

32. For all pairs of real numbers M and N where $M = 6N + 5$, $N = ?$

   F. $\dfrac{M}{6} - 5$

   G. $\dfrac{M}{5} + 6$

   H. $6M + 5$

   J. $\dfrac{M - 5}{6}$

   K. $\dfrac{M + 5}{6}$

33. In the figure below, the perimeter of the triangle is $12 + 4\sqrt{3}$ inches. What is the value of x, in inches?

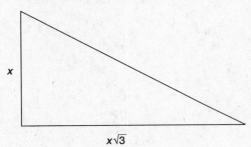

   A. 2
   B. 4
   C. 6
   D. 8
   E. 12

34. In the figure below, $\overline{XY} = \overline{YZ}$. If $a = 40°$, than $\overline{XY} = ?$

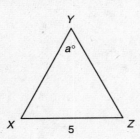

   F. 9.50
   G. 8.75
   H. 7.75
   J. 6.25
   K. 5.50

DO YOUR FIGURING HERE.

GO ON TO THE NEXT PAGE.

2 △ △ △ △ △ △ △ △ **2**

35. In the (x, y) coordinate plane, what is the y-intercept of the line $-9x - 3y = 15$?
   A. -9
   B. -5
   C. -3
   D. 3
   E. 15

36. The product of two integers is between 137 and 149. Which of the following CANNOT be one of the integers?
   F. 15
   G. 13
   H. 11
   J. 10
   K. 7

37. When x is divided by 7, the remainder is 4. What is the remainder when $2x$ is divided by 7?
   A. 1
   B. 4
   C. 5
   D. 7
   E. 8

38. A circle is circumscribed within a square with sides of 12 feet, as shown below. What is the area of the circle, to the nearest square foot?

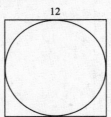

   F. 144
   G. 113
   H. 72
   J. 12π
   K. 3π

39. The average of 7 consecutive numbers is 16. What is the sum of the least and greatest of the 7 integers?
   A. 13
   B. 14
   C. 16
   D. 19
   E. 32

DO YOUR FIGURING HERE.

GO ON TO THE NEXT PAGE.

40. In the figure below, *ABCD* is a trapezoid. Point *E* lies on line *AD*, and angle measures are as marked. What is the measure of angle *BDC*?

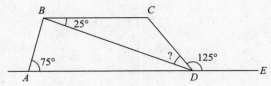

- **F.** 25°
- **G.** 30°
- **H.** 45°
- **J.** 55°
- **K.** 100°

41. For which of the following functions is $f(-5) > f(5)$?
- **A.** $f(x) = 6x^2$
- **B.** $f(x) = 6$
- **C.** $f(x) = 6/x$
- **D.** $f(x) = 6 - x^3$
- **E.** $f(x) = x^6 + 6$

42. For what value of *n* would the following system of equations have an infinite number of solutions?

$$3a + b = 12$$

$$12a + 4b = 3n$$

- **F.** 4
- **G.** 9
- **H.** 16
- **J.** 36
- **K.** 48

43. If *x* and *y* are positive integers such that the greatest common factor of x^2y^2 and xy^3 is 27, then which of the following could *y* equal?
- **A.** 81
- **B.** 27
- **C.** 18
- **D.** 9
- **E.** 3

DO YOUR FIGURING HERE.

GO ON TO THE NEXT PAGE.

2 △ △ △ △ △ △ △ △ **2**

DO YOUR FIGURING HERE.

44. What is the smallest possible integer for which 15% of that integer is greater than 2.3?

F. 3
G. 12
H. 15
J. 16
K. 18

45. What is the distance in the standard (x,y) coordinate plane between the points $(0,1)$ and $(4,4)$?

A. $\sqrt{7}$
B. 3
C. 4
D. 5
E. $\sqrt{27}$

46. The sides of a triangle are 9, 12, and 15 centimeters long. What is the angle between the 2 shortest sides?

F. 180°
G. 90°
H. 60°
J. 45°
K. 30°

47. In the pentagon, shown below, one interior angle measures 40°. What is the total measure of the other 4 interior angles?

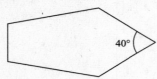

A. 120°
B. 160°
C. 320°
D. 500°
E. 680°

48. For real numbers r and s, when is the equation $|r - s| = |r + s|$ true?

F. Always
G. Only when $r = s$
H. Only when $r = 0$ or $s = 0$
J. Only when $r > 0$ and $s < 0$
K. Never

GO ON TO THE NEXT PAGE.

2 △ △ △ △ △ △ △ △ **2**

DO YOUR FIGURING HERE.

DO YOUR FIGURING HERE.

49. What is the value of $\log_4 64$?
A. 3
B. 4
C. 8
D. 10
E. 16

50. How many different positive three-digit integers can be formed if the three digits 3, 4, and 5 must be used in each of the integers?
F. 6
G. 8
H. 12
J. 15
K. 24

51. Which of the following is the set of all real numbers x such that $x - 3 < x - 5$?
A. The empty set
B. The set containing only zero
C. The set containing all nonnegative real numbers
D. The set containing all negative real numbers
E. The set containing all real numbers

52. What is the slope of a line that is perpendicular to the line determined by the equation $7x + 4y = 11$?
F. -4
G. $-\dfrac{7}{4}$
H. $\dfrac{11}{4}$
J. 4
K. $\dfrac{4}{7}$

53. If each element in a data set is multiplied by 3, and each resulting product is then reduced by 4, which of the following expressions gives the mean of the resulting data set in terms of x?
A. x
B. $3x - 4$
C. $x + \dfrac{4}{3}$
D. $\dfrac{x}{3} + 4$
E. $x + \dfrac{4}{3}$

2 △ △ △ △ △ △ △ △ **2**

54. If $\cos\theta = -\dfrac{3}{5}$ and $\dfrac{\pi}{2} < \theta < \pi$, then $\tan\theta = ?$

   F. $-\dfrac{5}{4}$

   G. $-\dfrac{4}{3}$

   H. $-\dfrac{3}{5}$

   J. $\dfrac{3}{4}$

   K. $\dfrac{4}{3}$

55. The City Council has approved the construction of a circular pool in front of City Hall. The area available for the pool is a rectangular region 12 feet by 18 feet, surrounded by a brick wall. If the pool is to be as large as possible within the walled area, and edge of the pool must be at least 2 feet from the wall all around, how many feet long should the radius of the pool be?

   A. 14
   B. 10
   C. 7
   D. 5
   E. 4

56. Kate rode her bicycle to visit her grandmother. The trip to Kate's grandmother's house was mostly uphill, and took m minutes. On the way home, Kate rode mostly downhill and was able to travel at an average speed twice that of her trip to her grandmother's house. Which of the following expresses the total number of minutes that Kate bicycled on her entire trip?

   F. $3m$

   G. $2m$

   H. $m + \dfrac{1}{2}$

   J. $\dfrac{3m}{2}$

   K. $\dfrac{m}{2}$

57. Let n equal $3a + 2b - 7$. What happens to the value of n if the value of a increases by 2 and the value of b decreases by 1?

   A. It is unchanged.
   B. It decreases by 1.
   C. It increases by 4.
   D. It decreases by 4.
   E. It decreases by 2.

GO ON TO THE NEXT PAGE.

2 △ △ △ △ △ △ △ △ **2**

58. In the figure below, $\triangle ABC$ is a right triangle with legs that measure x and $3x$ inches, respectively. What is the length, in inches, of the hypotenuse?

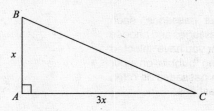

　　F. $\sqrt{10}x$
　　G. $\sqrt{3}x$
　　H. $\sqrt{2}x$
　　J. $2x$
　　K. $4x$

59. If the edges of a cube are tripled in length to produce a new, larger cube, then the larger cube's surface area is how many times larger than the smaller cube's surface area?
　　A. 3
　　B. 9
　　C. 18
　　D. 27
　　E. 54

60. Considering all values of a and b for which $a + b$ is at most 9, a is at least 2, and b is at least -2, what is the minimum value of $b - a$?
　　F. 0
　　G. -7
　　H. -11
　　J. -13
　　K. -15

DO YOUR FIGURING HERE.

END OF THE MATHEMATICS TEST.
STOP! IF YOU HAVE TIME LEFT OVER, CHECK YOUR WORK ON THIS SECTION ONLY.

3 ███████████████████████ **3**

READING TEST

35 Minutes—40 Questions

DIRECTIONS: This test includes four passages, each followed by ten questions. Read the passages and choose the best answer to each question. After you have selected your answer, fill in the corresponding bubble on your answer sheet. You should refer to the passages as often as necessary when answering the questions.

PASSAGE I

PROSE FICTION: *This passage is adapted from* The Story of a Bad Boy *by Thomas Bailey Aldrich © 1869.*

I call my story the story of a bad boy, partly to distinguish myself from those faultless young gentlemen who generally figure in narratives of this kind, and partly because I really was not an angel. I may
5 truthfully say I was an amiable, impulsive lad, and no hypocrite. I didn't want to be an angel; I didn't think the sermons presented to me by the Reverend Hawkins were half so nice as Robinson Crusoe; and I didn't send my pocket-change to the needy, but spent it on
10 peppermint-drops and taffy candy. In short, I was a real human boy, such as you may meet anywhere in New England, and not like the impossible boy in a storybook.

Whenever a new scholar came to our school,
15 I used to confront him at recess with the following words: "My name's Tom Bailey; what's your name?" If the name struck me favorably, I shook hands with the new pupil cordially; but if it didn't, I would turn and walk away, for I was particular on this point. Such
20 names as Higgins, Wiggins, and Spriggins were offensive affronts to my ear; while Langdon, Wallace, Blake, and the like, were passwords to my confidence and esteem.

I was born in Rivermouth almost fifty years
25 ago, but, before I became very well acquainted with that pretty New England town, my parents moved to New Orleans, where my father invested in the banking business. I was only eighteen months old at the time of the move, and it didn't make much difference to me
30 where I was because I was so small; but several years later, when my father proposed to take me North to be educated, I had my own views on the subject. I instantly kicked over the little boy, Sam, who happened to be standing by me at the moment, and, stamping my foot
35 violently on the floor, declared that I would not be taken away to live among a lot of Yankees!

You see I was what is called "a Northern man with Southern principles." I had no recollection of New England: my earliest memories were connected
40 with the South. I knew I was born in the North, but hoped nobody would find it out. I never told my schoolmates I was a Yankee because they talked about the Yankees in such a scornful way it made me feel that it was quite a disgrace not to be born in the South.
45 And this impression was strengthened by Aunt Chloe, who said, "there wasn't no gentlemen in the North no way."

To be frank, my idea of the North was not at all accurate. I supposed the inhabitants were divided into two classes—hunters and schoolmasters. I pictured it to
50 be winter pretty much all the year round. The prevailing style of architecture I took to be log-cabins.

With this picture of Northern civilization in my eye, the reader will easily understand my terror at the bare thought of being transported to Rivermouth to
55 school, and possibly will forgive me for kicking over little Sam, when my father announced this to me. As for kicking little Sam, I always did that, more or less gently, when anything went wrong with me.

My father was greatly perplexed and troubled by
60 this violent outbreak. As little Sam picked himself up, my father took my hand in his and led me thoughtfully to the library. I can see him now as he leaned back in the bamboo chair and questioned me. He appeared strangely puzzled on learning the nature of my
65 objections to going North, and proceeded at once to knock down all my pine log houses, and scatter all the hunters and schoolmasters with which I had populated the greater portion of the Eastern and Middle States.

"Who on earth, Tom, has filled your brain with
70 such silly stories?" asked my father calmly.

"Aunt Chloe, sir; she told me."

My father devoted that evening and several subsequent evenings to giving me a clear and succinct account of New England: its early struggles, its
75 progress, and its present condition—faint and confused glimmerings of which I had obtained at school, where history had never been a favorite pursuit of mine.

I was no longer unwilling to go North; on the contrary, the proposed journey to a new world full of
80 wonders kept me awake nights. Long before the moving day arrived I was eager to be off. My impatience was increased by the fact that my father had purchased for me a fine little Mustang pony, and shipped it to Rivermouth two weeks before the date set for our own
85 journey. The pony completely resigned me to the situation. The pony's name was Gitana, which is the Spanish for "gypsy," so I always called her Gypsy.

GO ON TO THE NEXT PAGE.

Finally the time came to leave the vine-covered mansion among the orange-trees, to say goodbye to
90 little Sam (I am convinced he was heartily glad to get rid of me), and to part with Aunt Chloe. I imagine them standing by the open garden gate; the tears are rolling down Aunt Chloe's cheeks; Sam's six front teeth are glistening like pearls; I wave my hand to him manfully.
95 Then I call out "goodbye" in a muffled voice to Aunt Chloe; they and the old home fade away. I am never to see them again!

1. Which of the following persons mentioned in the passage had the greatest effect on the narrator's negative views of life in the North?
   A. Sam
   B. Aunt Chloe
   C. Tom Bailey
   D. Reverend Hawkins

2. As it is used in line 18, *cordially* most nearly means:
   F. angrily.
   G. strikingly.
   H. sincerely.
   J. offensively.

3. It can reasonably be inferred from the passage that, as compared to most boys in New England, the narrator was:
   A. no better behaved, but no worse behaved.
   B. more angelic and innocent.
   C. less hypocritical but more troublesome.
   D. very different in many ways.

4. According to the passage, which of the following names were acceptable to the narrator?
   I. Higgins
   II. Blake
   III. Wallace
   F. I only
   G. III only
   H. II and III only
   J. I and III only

5. The narrator's initial feeling toward moving to Rivermouth can best be described as:
   A. indifferent, as he was too young to know any better.
   B. reluctant until his father dispelled inaccuracies about life in the North.
   C. apprehensive because he would be forced to leave his pony, Gypsy, behind.
   D. excited until he realized that he would have to part with Aunt Chloe and little Sam.

6. As he is revealed in the conversation he has with his son, the narrator's father can best be characterized as:
   F. understanding and patient.
   G. stern and unforgiving.
   H. proud but uneducated.
   J. ignorant but affectionate.

7. The narrator's point of view is that of:
   A. a young boy.
   B. an adult.
   C. an omniscient observer.
   D. a psychologist.

8. The sixth paragraph suggests that the narrator's relationship with little Sam is primarily characterized by:
   F. the narrator's patience with Sam.
   G. Sam's annoyance with the narrator.
   H. the narrator's abuse of Sam.
   J. Sam's respect for the narrator.

9. It can reasonably be inferred that, when the narrator describes himself as "a Northern man with Southern principles," he means that:
   A. even though he now lives in the South, he has retained and is proud of his Northern heritage.
   B. he is first and foremost a Yankee, as he was born in the North, reluctantly adapting to a Southern lifestyle.
   C. he has successfully reconciled his conflicting allegiances, subscribing to some Northern values and some Southern values.
   D. although he was born in New England he identifies more closely with the way of life and culture of the South.

10. It can reasonably be inferred that the author included the second paragraph to:
    F. support the narrator's assertion that he is a "faultless young gentleman."
    G. show just how much confidence and self-esteem the narrator possesses.
    H. contradict the narrator's belief that he was not a well-behaved, amiable boy.
    J. provide an example of how the narrator is both friendly and fickle.

GO ON TO THE NEXT PAGE.

3   **3**

PASSAGE II
SOCIAL SCIENCE: *This passage is adapted from* The
American Republic: Constitution, Tendencies, and
Destiny *by O.A. Brownson © 1866.*

The ancients summed up the whole of human
wisdom in the maxim "Know Thyself," and certainly
there is for an individual no more important and no
more difficult knowledge, than knowledge of himself.
5 Nations are only individuals on a larger scale. They
have a life, an individuality, a reason, a conscience, and
instincts of their own, and have the same general laws
of development and growth, and, perhaps, of decay,
as the individual man. Equally important, and no less
10 difficult than for the individual, is it for a nation to
know itself, understand its own existence, powers and
faculties, rights and duties, constitution, instincts, tendencies, and destiny. A nation has a spiritual as well
as a material existence, a moral as well as a physical
15 existence, and is subjected to internal as well as external conditions of health and virtue, greatness and
grandeur, which it must in some measure understand
and observe, or become lethargic and infirm, stunted
in its growth, and end in premature decay and death.
20   Among nations, no one has more need of full
knowledge of itself than the United States, and no one
has, to this point, had less. It has hardly had a distinct
consciousness of its own national existence, and has
lived the naive life of the child, with no severe trial,
25 till the recent civil war, to throw it back on itself and
compel it to reflect on its own constitution, its own
separate existence, individuality, tendencies, and end.
The defection of the slaveholding States, and the fearful struggle that has followed for national unity and
30 integrity, have brought the United States at once to
a distinct recognition of itself, and forced it to pass
from thoughtless, careless, heedless, reckless adolescence to grave and reflecting manhood. The nation has
been suddenly compelled to study itself, and from now
35 on must act from reflection, understanding, science,
and statesmanship, not from instinct, impulse, passion, or caprice, knowing well what it does, and why it
does it. The change which four years of civil war have
wrought in the nation is great, and is sure to give it the
40 seriousness, the gravity, and the dignity it has so far
lacked.
Though the nation has been brought to a consciousness of its own existence, it has not, even yet,
attained a full and clear understanding of its own
45 national constitution. Its vision is still obscured by the
floating mists of its earlier morning, and its judgment
rendered indistinct and indecisive by the wild theories
and fancies of its childhood. The national mind has
been quickened, the national heart has been opened,
50 the national disposition prepared, but there remains
the important work of dissipating the mists that still
linger, of brushing away these wild theories and fancies, and of enabling it to form a clear and intelligent
judgment of itself, and a true and just appreciation of
55 its own constitution tendencies.
As the individual states have vindicated their
national unity and integrity, and are preparing to make
a new start in history, nothing is more important than

that they should make that new start with a clear and
60 definite view of their national constitution, and with
a distinct understanding of their political mission in
the future of the world. The citizen who can help his
countrymen to do this will render them an important
service and deserve well of his country, though he may
65 have been unable to serve in her armies and defend
her on the battle-field. The work now to be done by
American statesmen is even more difficult and more
delicate than that which has been accomplished by our
brave armies. As yet the people are hardly better pre-
70 pared for the political work to be done than they were
at the outbreak of the civil war for the military work
they have so nobly achieved. But, with time, patience,
and good-will, the difficulties may be overcome, the
errors of the past corrected, and the government placed
75 on the right track for the future.

11. The author's tone toward the subject of the passage can
best be characterized as:
    A. impassioned.
    B. indifferent.
    C. whimsical.
    D. resigned.

12. The main idea of the passage can best be summarized
by which of the following statements?
    F. The United States will forever be disposed to
       repeating political mistakes of the past.
    G. A country has the responsibility of providing safety
       and stability to its citizens in the form of a national
       constitution.
    H. It is imperative that the United States comprehend
       its identity as a nation, which can be accomplished
       through an understanding of its unique qualities.
    J. The United States is not prepared or able to reunite
       as one nation after the ideological division that
       caused the Civil War.

13. As used in line 24 of the passage, *naive* most nearly
means:
    A. aware.
    B. inexperienced.
    C. difficult.
    D. incapable.

14. According to the passage, what caused the United States
to "pass from thoughtless, careless, heedless, reckless
adolescence to grave and reflecting manhood (lines 31–
33)"?
    F. A difficult and controversial legal trial that captured
       the whole country's attention
    G. The ratification of the final draft of the constitution
    H. International questioning regarding the integrity and
       viability of America's government
    J. The secession of the southern states and the conflict
       that ensued

GO ON TO THE NEXT PAGE.

3 ██ **3**

15. Which of the following statements best summarizes the main point of the first paragraph?
    A. Understanding one's own strengths and weaknesses is a difficult yet important task, not only for individuals, but for nations as a whole.
    B. The spirituality of individuals should be dictated by the nation's government.
    C. Comparing a nation to a person is an inaccurate analogy that only leads to confusion and misrepresentation.
    D. The United States was founded upon a principle of law originating from the ancient world.

16. According to the author, a citizen who helps his countrymen to develop "a distinct understanding of their political mission in the future of the world" (lines 61–62) should be:
    F. enlisted in the military.
    G. ignored.
    H. revered.
    J. tried for treason.

17. According to the last paragraph, what does the author believe will happen if the United States is able to fully understand its own constitution and political duty on a global scale?
    A. Disagreements will be resolved diplomatically, rendering warfare obsolete.
    B. The nation, as a whole, will reconcile its previous missteps and have a more hopeful future.
    C. Citizens will be no more prepared for future conflicts and understanding the past and present of the nation's politics will have no benefit.
    D. The government, realizing the inadequacies of the constitution, will take the necessary steps to improve upon it.

18. As it is used in line 56, the word *vindicated*, in this context, most nearly means:
    F. justified.
    G. weakened.
    H. squandered.
    J. separated.

19. A recurring metaphor the author uses in the piece compares the United States to:
    A. a battlefield, where two separate armies are clashing over political issues.
    B. an ancient sage, who is admired for his great knowledge and wisdom.
    C. a scholar, who is dedicated to the pursuit of higher education.
    D. a man, who begins as an immature child and grows into a wise and experienced adult.

20. According to the passage, what does the author assert will happen to the United States if the nation does not become more aware of itself and its role in the global community?
    F. The country will erupt in a civil war.
    G. Its citizens, no longer having a conscience or moral compass, will rebel against the government.
    H. The nation will become weak, leading to its eventual downfall.
    J. Its strength and power will continue to grow, becoming a global leader in industry.

GO ON TO THE NEXT PAGE.

3 ▬▬▬▬▬▬▬▬▬▬▬▬▬▬▬▬▬▬▬▬▬ **3**

PASSAGE III
HUMANITIES: *William Faulkner: Great Southern Author*

Born in Mississippi in 1897, William Faulkner is touted as the master of such revolutionary literary devices as stream of consciousness, multiple narrations, and time-shifts within a narrative. During a
5 career that spanned more than three decades, Faulkner produced literary works filled with emotional turmoil and unflinching honesty. His unique interpretation of history is highlighted in the symbolism and imagery of his writing. It has also been argued that Faulkner's
10 works are some of the best representations of Southern Gothic literature ever written.

It is clear that Faulkner's Deep South roots greatly influenced his writing. He was a prolific writer whose works both parallel and depart from popular myths of
15 southern culture. Faulkner's remarkable understanding of race relations and his clever satire of Southern characters stemmed from his memories of growing up in rural Mississippi. He set many of his short stories and novels in the fictional Yoknapatawpha County, based
20 on what Faulkner referred to as "my own little postage stamp of native soil," Lafayette County, Mississippi. It was there, immersed in traditional southern lore, that William Faulkner began to write of the great political, social, and economic transformation taking place in the
25 Deep South, depicting traditional society in timeless human dramas.

Faulkner came from an old and relatively prominent Southern family. He grew up surrounded by traditional folklore, family stories, accounts from the
30 Civil War, and lectures about being a Southern gentleman. In his works, Faulkner examined how traditional values and beliefs affected Southern society after the Civil War. Faulkner particularly abhorred the rampant racism and abuse that African Americans suffered in
35 the South. Although Faulkner's novels do not shy away from describing the brutality and anguish that life can bring, his works are filled with profound compassion and humor. Faulkner refused to avoid painful or controversial issues and he was intrigued with understanding
40 human freedom. His work explores, condemns, and analyzes obstructions to human freedom and happiness by examining racism, shame, fear, false pride, and abstract ideals. Much of Faulkner's exploration is done using brilliant symbolism and exquisite dialogue.
45 For example, his novel *The Sound and the Fury*, published in 1929, dealt with the painful demise of a distinguished southern family and demonstrated a rich variety of literary styles, relying most heavily on stream-of-consciousness writing, in which a character's
50 thoughts are conveyed in a manner roughly akin to the way the human mind actually works.

Faulkner's mastery of unique literary styles was formally recognized when, much to his surprise, he was awarded the Nobel Prize for literature in 1949.
55 Always his own harshest critic, William Faulkner considered many of his books failures because they did not live up to his high expectations. However, it is clear that Faulkner's experimental literary techniques simultaneously perplexed and challenged his readers, who were
60 more often than not inspired by his insightful analysis

of the human spirit. Faulkner continued to explore the interconnections between his characters and their counterparts in the real world until his death in 1962.

In the months before his death, Faulkner updated
65 his will, leaving the bulk of his manuscripts to the Faulkner Foundation at the University of Virginia, where he had been appointed its first Writer-in-Residence. While the original documents are protected, electronic versions of the collection are freely available
70 to scholars of great Southern literature and others interested in gaining additional insight into the life's work of a truly revolutionary American author.

21. As it is used in line 22, the word *immersed* most nearly means:
  A. depicted.
  B. submerged.
  C. related.
  D. interpreted.

22. The author describes Faulkner's writing as all of the following EXCEPT:
  F. symbolic.
  G. honest.
  H. malicious.
  J. tumultuous.

23. One of the main ideas of the passage is that:
  A. Faulkner was devoted to his southern roots.
  B. authors employed revolutionary literary devices.
  C. Faulkner was a prominent author with strong convictions.
  D. many of Faulkner's books were considered failures.

24. As it is used in line 33, the word *abhorred* most nearly means:
  F. greatly enjoyed.
  G. strongly disliked.
  H. firmly believed in.
  J. clearly misunderstood.

25. The author suggests which of the following about Faulkner's attitude toward racism in the South?
  A. He felt that racism was a necessary evil.
  B. He hated racism and sought to expose it in his writing.
  C. He shied away from any discussion of racism.
  D. He was not concerned about racism as a social issue.

26. The main emphasis of the fourth paragraph (lines 52–63) is to:
  F. provide support for Faulkner's belief that he was a failed author.
  G. question the claim that Faulkner was a master of unique literary styles.
  H. summarize the value and importance of Faulkner's vision as an author.
  J. sharpen the distinction between Faulkner's different techniques.

GO ON TO THE NEXT PAGE.

3 ▬▬▬▬▬▬▬▬▬▬▬▬▬▬▬▬ **3**

27. With which of the following statements about Faulkner's literary style would the author most likely agree?
   A. It had never been utilized by authors of southern culture.
   B. It was generally less effective than more traditional approaches.
   C. It has often been employed by 20th-century authors.
   D. It was an innovative approach to discussions of social issues.

28. The passage states that *The Sound and the Fury* depicted:
   F. the tragic downfall of a respected family.
   G. the profound rise to freedom of Civil War slaves.
   H. a harsh criticism of William Faulkner.
   J. an inspirational look at southern life.

29. The author uses the term "counterparts" (line 63) most likely in order to:
   A. disprove the theory that fictional characters can be based on real people.
   B. reveal the source of Faulkner's literary methods.
   C. indicate that Faulkner's characters were often based on real people.
   D. cast doubt on the idea that readers often identify with fictional characters.

30. Which of the following best states the main purpose of the passage?
   F. To suggest that some writers are more deserving of major literary awards.
   G. To describe one man's desire to write about important social issues.
   H. To review the use of certain literary devices in best-selling novels.
   J. To illustrate one author's understanding of and commitment to his craft.

3   **3**

PASSAGE IV
NATURAL SCIENCE: *Those Jellystone Bears*

Over the years, there have been countless fans
of the classic Hanna-Barbera cartoon character Yogi
Bear. The cartoon series enjoyed by young and old
alike revolved mostly around the misadventures of this
5 loveable bear and his sidekick Boo-Boo as they
attempted to snag "pic-a-nic" baskets in the made-up
land of Jellystone Park. It's not often that people think
about where the ideas for these cartoons characters
come from, which brings up an interesting point: do
10 bears actually search for food left in picnic baskets
and unattended campsites? Anyone who has watched
an episode of *Yogi Bear* can see that the bears' behavior goes far beyond the limits of what is natural. The
thing which must be explored, then, is which of those
15 humorous antics were license on the part of Hanna-
Barbera, and which were actually based on the bear's
normal behaviors.

Remarkably enough, bears have been known to
seek out food from some unlikely sources, including
20 picnic baskets, on top of their usual diet of berries,
insects, and fish. Bears work throughout the summer
and fall to build up fat stores so as to have energy
enough to last them through their winter hibernations.
Related to this is their need to replenish their depleted
25 reserves when they wake up in the spring. Food is generally scarce in the early spring, and consequently they
will gladly indulge in any foods that are high in proteins or fats. This is the main reason for many incidents
involving bears entering campsites in search of food.

30 Although this behavior may seem strange, it is
no more than the result of nature equipping bears with
a variety of traits that allow them to remain well fed
in increasingly human-populated habitats. Specifically,
the American black bear, *Ursus americanus*, has color
35 vision and has been observed by scientists using its
color vision to distinguish between varying food items
at close range. On top of this, all bears have an acute
sense of smell and can use their especially sensitive lips
to locate food. These sensory talents contribute to the
40 bears' remarkably high intelligence and curiosity, giving them the ability to open closed containers if they
believe food is inside. Their exploratory and naviga-
tional skills are also worthy of note—most bears will
maintain vast territories in order to obtain food from
45 a variety of sources. Bears may even vary their sleep
cycles in areas where there is a large degree of human
activity, either feasting on road-side garbage during the
day or scouring campsites for leftovers at night.

Yet another strange but true comparison is that
50 Yogi and Boo-Boo have developed a social relationship
much like the ones that will form between wild bears
when several animals find themselves sharing a limited
number of food sources. Generally solitary, black bears
will create a hierarchical order in situations where paths
55 cross in pursuit of food, so as to assure that all animals
remain adequately fed. While it is unlikely that any
black bears in nature would actually send a cub after a
camper's lunch, the behavioral relationships that might
inspire the creation of such a story are indeed real.

60 Though many of the features of the comical Yogi
Bear are likely the result of pure imagination, there
is scientific fact behind at least some of his activities.
Despite his apperance as a brown bear, the distinctive
feeding behaviors of the American black bear match
65 remarkably well with the habits of the cartoonish cul-
prit. The uncanny truth behind little known scientific
facts such as these should make everyone think twice
the next time they sit down to watch Saturday morning
cartoons.

31. The main idea of the passage is that:
- **A.** cartoon characters should never be based on real animals.
- **B.** bears have some unique eating habits that are comically portrayed on television.
- **C.** bears are generally solitary creatures, but they sometimes venture into human habitats.
- **D.** there is little scientific data to support the comparison between "Yogi Bear" and the American black bear.

32. The passage states that bears maintain large territories in order to:
- **F.** avoid contact with humans.
- **G.** develop stronger social relationships.
- **H.** ensure that they have enough food.
- **J.** more easily locate abandoned campsites.

33. The passage states that which of the following is a regular staple of a bear's diet?
- **A.** Picnic baskets
- **B.** Garbage
- **C.** Insects
- **D.** Small mammals

34. As it is used in line 37, the word *acute* most nearly means:
- **F.** small.
- **G.** sharp.
- **H.** reduced.
- **J.** abnormal.

GO ON TO THE NEXT PAGE.

3 ███████████████████████████ **3**

35. According to the passage, which of the following traits CANNOT be attributed to bears?
  A. Intelligent
  B. Curiosity
  C. Solitary
  D. Anti-social

36. With which of the following statements would the author most likely agree?
  F. Bears are particularly resourceful.
  G. Bears cannot tolerate human food.
  H. Bears eat voraciously throughout the winter.
  J. Bears have only one method of obtaining food.

37. The author mentions all of the following as potential food sources for bears EXCEPT:
  A. garbage.
  B. general stores.
  C. fish and berries.
  D. unattended campsites.

38. The passage suggests that one of the differences between the American black bear and other bears is the American black bear's:
  F. acute sense of smell.
  G. abnormal sleep patterns.
  H. color vision.
  J. sensitive lips.

39. What is the main idea of the second paragraph (lines 18–29)?
  A. Despite the scarcity of food in the spring, most bears avoid human contact.
  B. Bears must sometimes supplement their regular diets with food found near humans.
  C. Bears engage in strange behaviors to maintain social order.
  D. It is important that humans avoid any contact with bears during the summer and fall.

40. One of the main observations made in the next-to-last paragraph (lines 49–59) is that:
  F. black bears often rely on their cubs to secure food.
  G. black bears will act as a group in order to secure food.
  H. black bears are incapable of securing food without help from humans.
  J. black bears secure food in a manner completely unique to the species.

END OF THE READING TEST.
STOP! IF YOU HAVE TIME LEFT OVER, CHECK YOUR WORK ON THIS SECTION ONLY.

4 ◯ ◯ ◯ ◯ ◯ ◯ ◯ ◯ ◯ **4**

SCIENCE REASONING TEST

35 Minutes—40 Questions

DIRECTIONS: This test includes seven passages, each followed by several questions. Read the passage and choose the best answer to each question. After you have selected your answer, fill in the corresponding bubble on your answer sheet. You should refer to the passages as often as necessary when answering the questions. You may NOT use a calculator on this test.

PASSAGE I

Scientists have observed rapid eutrophication of a local lake, at a rate much higher than that of other lakes in the area. Eutrophication is the aging of a lake, resulting in increased levels of plant life and accumulated sediments, brought on by a build-up of nutrients such as nitrates and phosphates. Rapid eutrophication is harmful, as it leads to the dying off of cold water fish such as trout. Researchers performed the following experiments to determine the possible source of the increased nitrates and phosphates.

Experiment 1

Scientists suspected that one source of nutrients was a feeder stream which intercepts run-off from farmland where pesticides and animal waste are found. Water samples were obtained over several days from that stream (Feeder A) as well as another feeder stream (Feeder B) not near the farm. Results are displayed in Table 1.

Table 1		
Day	Phosphate concentration (mg/L)	Nitrate concentration (mg/L)
Feeder A		
Day 1	20.7	43.2
Day 2	13.2	44.5
Day 3	35.6	41.6
Day 4	42.3	58.0
Feeder B		
Day 1	10.4	13.2
Day 2	11.5	13.4
Day 3	7.9	12.9
Day 4	10.2	11.4

Experiment 2

The scientists also surmised that another possible source of harmful nutrients entering the lake was run-off from a golf course adjacent to the lake where fertilizers were applied. Water samples were obtained from the lake at various distances (0 meters, 100 meters and 200 meters) from the golf course on four successive days, and the levels of chlorophyll, phosphates, and nitrates were measured. The results are depicted in Table 2.

Table 2			
Day	Chlorophyll level (PPB)	Phosphate concentration (mg/L)	Nitrate concentration (mg/L)
0 m			
Day 1	38.9	35.6	52.3
Day 2	39.1	42.3	48.7
Day 3*	38.8	46.9	70.8
Day 4	40.2	57.0	61.6
100 m			
Day 1	30.3	31.8	42.4
Day 2	29.0	29.4	36.6
Day 3*	29.2	30.1	45.2
Day 4	30.4	37.9	44.1
200 m			
Day 1	26.5	25.3	33.9
Day 2	26.8	24.6	33.2
Day 3*	26.4	25.5	34.6
Day 4	27.0	24.2	35.3
Note: *Fertilizer was applied to the golf course on the morning of Day 3.			

GO ON TO THE NEXT PAGE.

4 ○ ○ ○ ○ ○ ○ ○ ○ ○ **4**

1. How do the designs of Experiments 1 and 2 differ in terms of sampling procedure?
   A. In Experiment 1, the lake water was tested, while in Experiment 2 feeder stream water was tested.
   B. In Experiment 2, lake water was tested, while run-off water was tested in Experiment 1.
   C. In Experiment 1, only phosphate concentration was tested, while in Experiment 2, only nitrate concentration was tested.
   D. In Experiment 2, chlorophyll level was tested in addition to phosphates and nitrates, while in Experiment 1, it was not.

2. What was the scientists' hypothesis concerning lake eutrophication in Experiment 1?
   F. Run-off from farmland increases levels of phosphates and nitrates, speeding up the eutrophication process.
   G. Fertilizer used on the golf course increases phosphate and nitrate levels in lake water.
   H. Pesticides and animal waste entering the lake through a feeder stream hinder the eutrophication process.
   J. Increases in phosphate and nitrate concentration lead to more plant and algae growth, increasing chlorophyll levels in the lake.

3. Given the results of Experiments 1 and 2, all of the following would reduce the levels of phosphates and nitrates, and therefore the rate of eutrophication, of the lake EXCEPT:
   A. decreasing the amount of fertilizer used on the lake golf course.
   B. limiting use of pesticides on the farmland on the lake.
   C. increasing the number of farms on the lake.
   D. installing a filtration system to divert run-off from farmlands and the golf course away from the lake.

4. According to Table 2, which of the following statements is NOT true?
   F. Chlorophyll levels increase as distance to the golf course decreases.
   G. Phosphate concentration is unaffected by fertilizer application.
   H. Chlorophyll levels increase sharply the day after application of fertilizer on the golf course.
   J. Nitrate concentration decreases as distance from golf course increases.

5. Scientists suspect that leakage from sewage systems carrying wastewater from the houses on the lake also contributes to nutrient deposit in the lake. In order to test this hypothesis, what should the scientists do next?
   A. Sample groundwater near the sewage systems, testing for phosphate and nitrate content.
   B. Measure the chlorophyll levels at many more locations in the lake.
   C. Test the nutrients in the drinking water of various houses around the lake.
   D. Obtain nutrient content of fertilizer used on residential property.

6. If scientists sampled lake water from a third location 300 meters from the golf course, which of the following would most likely represent the average phosphate level found there?
   F. 35.3 mg/L
   G. 30.6 mg/L
   H. 26.2 mg/L
   J. 20.1 mg/L

GO ON TO THE NEXT PAGE.

PASSAGE II

Students in a science class collected soil samples from various locations in order to analyze the composition of the soil. They measured the percentage of the three types of soil minerals—sand, silt, and clay—in each sample. Their data is presented in Table 1. The students also measured the size of the mineral particles found in the soil samples. The particle size ranges are listed in Table 2.

Table 1			
Soil sample	Sand (%)	Clay (%)	Silt (%)
1	65	10	25
2	10	75	15
3	25	35	40
4	60	20	20
5	55	30	15

Table 2	
Type of mineral particle	Size range of particles (mm)
Sand	2.0–0.06 mm
Silt	0.06–0.002 mm
Clay	less than 0.002 mm

7. According to Table 1, Sample 3 was composed primarily of:
   A. sand and clay.
   B. clay and silt.
   C. silt and sand.
   D. sand only.

8. Based on the data in Table 1, Sample 5 contained:
   F. more sand than silt.
   G. more clay than sand.
   H. less clay than silt.
   J. less sand than silt.

9. Which soil sample is most likely to have an average mineral particle size of 1.3 millimeters?
   A. Sample 2
   B. Sample 3
   C. Sample 4
   D. Sample 5

10. The students collected a sixth soil sample from a location near the location from which they collected Sample 4. Based on information in the passage, this sixth sample would contain mineral particles that were predominantly:
    F. smaller than 0.002 mm.
    G. smaller than 0.06 mm.
    H. larger than 0.06 mm.
    J. larger than 2.0 mm.

11. Sample 2 would most likely, if measured, have an average mineral particle size of:
    A. 1.5 mm.
    B. 1.0 mm.
    C. 0.06 mm.
    D. 0.001 mm.

GO ON TO THE NEXT PAGE.

4 ○ ○ ○ ○ ○ ○ ○ ○ ○ **4**

PASSAGE III

Students debate 4 hypotheses regarding the origin of the asteroid belt located between Mars and Jupiter, based on the following observations.

Observations

Observation 1—If all of the asteroids were gathered together into one object, the diameter of the object formed would be less than half the diameter of Earth's Moon.

Observation 2—The total mass of the asteroid belt is only 4% that of the Moon. One asteroid alone, Ceres, contains $\frac{1}{3}$ of the total mass of the asteroid belt.

Observation 3—Asteroids are largely composed of silicate, with some deposits of iron and nickel, a composition proportionately similar to that of the terrestrial planets. Some asteroids also contain carbon and other elements.

Observation 4—There is a strong orbital resonance (overlapping gravity) with Jupiter in the region of the asteroid belt, which keeps the asteroids in an orbit around the sun.

Observation 5—In reality, asteroids within the belt are very far apart, not clustered together.

Observation 6—Within the early solar system, the velocity of collisions within the region of the asteroid belt was much higher than it is currently.

Hypothesis 1

All of the material that makes up the asteroids in the asteroid belt is similar to that of the material that makes up the terrestrial planets. The velocity of collisions in the early solar system was at one time high enough to break apart planets as they formed. Since one asteroid, Ceres, has $\frac{1}{3}$ the total mass of the belt, the asteroids are most likely the result of a partially formed planet that broke apart and became trapped in an orbit between Mars and Jupiter.

Hypothesis 2

The material that composes the asteroids is similar to that of the terrestrial planets. The belt likely formed during the same time that the planets were forming, and due to the strong orbital resonance with the gas giant Jupiter and high velocity collisions, chunks of the material were pulled away from various planets and trapped within orbit. This also explains the varying composition of the asteroids throughout the belt.

Hypothesis 3

The asteroids could not once have been a planet, because there is not enough material within the entire belt to form a planet-sized object. The lack of material, shown by the total diameter and mass of the objects within the belt, is proof that the asteroids are no more than large particles left over from the formation of the terrestrial planets from a single cloud of material.

Hypothesis 4

The asteroids most likely came from somewhere outside the solar system. As they passed through space at varying intervals, they were trapped by the large orbital resonance of Jupiter and formed a "belt." The vast distances between most of the asteroids in the belt are evidence that they did not come from a singular source, but arrived at different points in the belt's development.

12. According to Hypothesis 2, most of the matter composing the asteroids in the belt came from:
    F. Earth's Moon.
    G. a partially formed planet between Mars and Jupiter.
    H. the same material that composes the terrestrial planets.
    J. a planet outside of Earth's Solar System.

13. Supporters of Hypothesis 1 would most likely agree that, at the time the asteroid belt formed the planets were:
    A. still in the process of forming.
    B. completely formed as they are seen today.
    C. no more than a cloud of material in space.
    D. all the size of asteroids.

14. Suppose that supporters of Hypothesis 2 suggested that the asteroid belt, when it was first formed, contained dense formations of ice and debris slightly bigger than current asteroids. Which of the following statements about the asteroids' composition would be most consistent with their suggestion?
    F. The asteroids' ice content was constant after the belt was formed.
    G. The asteroids' ice content decreased after the belt was formed.
    H. The asteroids' ice content increased slowly after the belt was formed.
    J. The asteroids' ice content increased rapidly after the belt was formed.

GO ON TO THE NEXT PAGE.

15. Hypothesis 3 includes the assertion that the asteroids are made up of particles left over from a single cloud of material. This assertion explains which of the following observations?
  A. Observations 1 and 2
  B. Observation 4 only
  C. Observations 5 and 6
  D. Observation 3 only

16. With which of the following statements would supporters of all four hypotheses agree?
  F. There is not enough scientific data to prove the existence of asteroids.
  G. Asteroids are comprised of the same material as that which comprises Mars.
  H. The asteroid belt lies entirely outside of the solar system.
  J. The objects currently in an orbit between Mars and Jupiter are asteroids.

17. Consider the crust of a terrestrial planet to have a proportion of silicate to iron to nickel of 10,000:100:10. Based on the information in the passage, the ratio of these substances in the composition of an average asteroid is likely to be:
  A. 500:10:1.
  B. 1,000:50:5.
  C. 10,000:100:10.
  D. 10,000:500:50.

18. Which of the following assumptions regarding the asteroid belt's origins is implicit in Hypothesis 1?
  F. The asteroid's composition is identical to that of the Moon.
  G. The asteroids have several different sources of origin.
  H. The asteroid belt is older than Jupiter.
  J. The asteroid belt is younger than Jupiter.

GO ON TO THE NEXT PAGE.

PASSAGE IV

Yeast is a unicellular fungus, and is arguably one of the most important members of the fungus family, primarily because of its involvement in the process of *fermentation*. During this process, yeast breaks down sucrose into alcohol and carbon dioxide. The chemical equation for fermentation is given below. Scientists study how to induce fermentation in yeast most effectively.

$$C_{12}H_{22}O_{11} + H_2O \rightarrow 4C_2H_5OH + 4CO_2$$

Experiment 1

Since yeast needs sucrose to ferment and molasses is 60% sucrose, scientists first study yeast grown in molasses. Five test tubes are filled with .4 grams of yeast and various molasses concentrations. Carbon dioxide levels are measured as an indication of fermentation for each test tube after one day and again after two days. These levels are shown in Table 1.

	Molasses (%)	CO_2 (mm) Day 1	CO_2 (mm) Day 2
		Table 1	
1	6.2	2	9
2	12.5	6	32
3	25	24	78
4	50	69	94
5	100	86	100

Experiment 2

Five different test tubes are filled with .4 grams of yeast and various pure sucrose dilutions. Carbon dioxide levels are then measured as an indication of fermentation after one and two days. These levels are shown in Table 2.

	Sucrose(%)	CO_2 (mm) Day 1	CO_2 (mm) Day 2
		Table 2	
1	60	90	100
2	30	78	100
3	15	40	84
4	7.5	18	43
5	3.25	5	12

Experiment 3

Eight more test tubes were filled with .4 grams of yeast and a 15% sucrose solution. Various combinations of ammonium sulfate, potassium dihydrogen phosphate, minerals, and vitamins were added to the test tubes. Carbon dioxide levels were measured after one and two days. These levels are shown in Table 3.

	Sucrose (%)	Other materials added	CO_2 (mm) Day 1	CO_2 (mm) Day 2
		Table 3		
1	15	$(NH_2)_2SO_4$, KH_2PO_4	19	38
2	15	$(NH_2)_2SO_4$, KH_2PO_4, minerals	28	40
3	15	$(NH_2)_2SO_4$, KH_2PO_4, vitamins	31	52
4	15	$(NH_2)_2SO_4$, KH_2PO_4, minerals, vitamins	100	100
5	15	minerals	3	12
6	15	vitamins	0	9
7	15	minerals, vitamins	0	14
8	15	—	4	5

GO ON TO THE NEXT PAGE.

4

19. Based on Experiment 1, which test tube showed the highest level of fermentation after 1 day?
   A. Test tube 1
   B. Test tube 2
   C. Test tube 4
   D. Test tube 5

20. Which of the following variables was controlled in Experiment 1?
   F. Amount of yeast
   G. Percent of molasses
   H. Percent of sucrose
   J. Carbon dioxide levels

21. Which of the following is a weakness in the design of Experiment 3?
   A. Different amounts of yeast were used in each test tube.
   B. Varying concentrations of sucrose were used.
   C. There was no control group in which the experimental treatment was not applied.
   D. All possible combinations of nutrients were not tested.

22. Which of the following is the most likely reason that a 15% sucrose solution was used in Experiment 3? Results showed that:
   F. in experiment 1, yeast grew most efficiently in a 15% sucrose solution.
   G. yeast produced the most carbon dioxide in a 15% sucrose solution in Experiment 2.
   H. an amount of sucrose greater than 15% did not increase carbon dioxide production in either Experiment 1 or Experiment 2.
   J. a 15% sucrose solution was the minimum concentration needed to produce yeast growth.

23. Based on Experiments 1 and 2, one can infer that, as compared to molasses, pure sucrose:
   A. is more effective at inducing fermentation in yeast.
   B. is less effective at inducing fermentation in yeast.
   C. is exactly as effective at inducing fermentation in yeast.
   D. does not induce fermentation in yeast.

24. In order for scientists to decide which conditions produce the most efficient growth of yeast, which of the following experiments would most likely need to be completed next?
   F. Varying the amount of yeast added to the test tubes and repeating the steps of Experiment 3
   G. Repeating Experiments 1 through 3, measuring for alcohol content rather than carbon dioxide
   H. Measuring yeast growth in a solution of pure water
   J. Testing varying sucrose concentrations with added nutrients of ammonium sulfate, potassium dihydrogen phosphate, minerals, and vitamins in a fourth experiment.

GO ON TO THE NEXT PAGE.

PASSAGE V

Tenebrio molitor is an arthropod insect which, like 90% of all insects, undergoes the process of complete metamorphosis, meaning that it passes through four life stages: egg, larva, pupa, and adult. In the larval stage the insect is commonly known as a mealworm; as a full adult it is a darkling beetle. Figure 1 shows the four stages of the *T. molitor* life cycle (*x*-axis), as well as data for minimum and maximum days spent in each stage of metamorphosis (*y*-axis) for *T. molitor* that were raised by students in a lab.

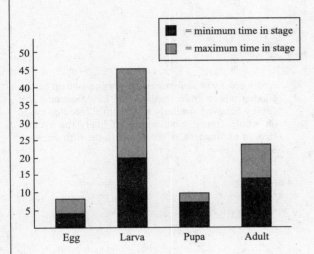

Figure 1

Table 1 includes data recorded for four different colonies of *T. molitor* raised by students in a lab, including the type of food each colony was given, beginning larval length, duration of time in larval and pupal stages, and final adult length. It was decided that the colonies would be given only one type of food source: either a fruit, a vegetable, or one of two whole grains. Apple was chosen as the fruit, carrot for the vegetable, and oats and wheat for the two whole grains.

	Table 1				
Colony	Diet	Avg. larval size (mm)	Avg. duration in larval stage (days)	Avg. duration in pupal stage (days)	Avg. adult size (mm)
1	Apple	25.8	36.9	7.5	19.3
2	Carrot	24.5	39.4	8.4	19.5
3	Oat	24.9	49.1	9.2	20.6
4	Wheat	25.3	57.2	10.8	21.3

GO ON TO THE NEXT PAGE.

25. According to the passage, the *Tenebrio molitor* beetle must spend at least 20 days in what stage of metamorphosis?
   A. Egg stage
   B. Larval stage
   C. Pupal stage
   D. Adult stage

26. According to Table 1, which of the following has no effect on the final adult size of the *Tenebrio molitor* beetle?
   F. Larval size
   G. Duration in larval stage
   H. Duration in pupal stage
   J. Diet

27. A *Tenebrio molitor* specimen has been in the same metamorphic stage for 12 days. According to Figure 1, in which stage is it possible for the specimen to be?
   I. Egg stage
   II. Larval stage
   III. Pupal stage
   IV. Adult stage

   A. II only
   B. I and II only
   C. IV only
   D. II and IV only

28. Which one of the following hypotheses about *Tenebrio molitor* growth is supported by the data presented in Table 1?
   F. Larger larval *T. molitor* yield larger *T. molitor* beetles.
   G. *T. molitor* larvae fed carrots will spend a greater amount of time in the larval stage than those larvae fed apples.
   H. The more time a *T. molitor* spends in the pupal stage, the smaller the adult beetle will be.
   J. Larger *T. molitor* beetles spend less time, on average, in the pupal stage of metamorphosis.

29. A fifth colony of *Tenebrio molitor* was raised on barley, another whole grain, in the same lab. Assuming this colony behaved similarly to the other colonies raised on whole grains, what was most likely the average size, in millimeters, of the adults in the fifth colony?
   A. 17.6
   B. 18.1
   C. 19.2
   D. 20.9

GO ON TO THE NEXT PAGE.

4 ○ ○ ○ ○ ○ ○ ○ ○ **4**

PASSAGE VI

Oil and natural gas stores are formed naturally in reservoirs. However, these reservoirs are not like the giant man-made lakes that might come to mind; they are underground. In fact, a reservoir occurs in a rock that looks on the surface like any other. The oil and gas pool in millions of tiny pores in the rock. Porous rocks include sandstone, limestone, shale, and many more. There are several factors affecting *porosity* (the ability to store fluid in the open spaces located between rock particles). Among these factors are the nature and characteristics of the sand and other sediment that accumulate to form rocks. The sand particle size is not critical to porosity, but the uniformity or sorting of the sand grains greatly effects porosity. Uniform or well-sorted sand will tend to be more porous than poorly sorted sand.

Experiment 1

In a laboratory, a scientist wanted to determine the porosity of 4 samples of different rocks. The scientist recorded the mass of the rock samples prior to the experiment. To measure porosity, the samples were soaked in water and the mass of the samples was recorded periodically. A highly porous rock would have a significant increase in mass the longer it soaked in water, eventually reaching the point at which it could no longer absorb any more water (saturation point). The data was recorded in Table 1.

Table 1				
Sample (volume of sample cm³)				
Time (hr)	Limestone (33 cm³)	Sandstone (27 cm³)	Shale (30 cm³)	Pumice (25 cm³)
0 (starting mass)	27 g	24 g	25 g	34 g
2	29 g	26 g	28 g	35 g
4	30 g	28 g	30 g	36 g
6	31 g	29 g	31 g	37 g
12	32 g	30 g	32 g	38 g
Porosity (%)	15	19	23	12

Experiment 2

Geologists in Arizona were interested in the porosities of different varieties of sandstone. They documented the relationship between porosity, density, sand particle size, and the uniformity or sorting of the sand grains. The geologists found that, in general, neither density nor particle size affected the porosity if the particles were uniform. However, they did find that in samples with a wide variety of particle sizes, the porosity was generally lower. Also, the presence of contaminants such as clay or silt negatively affected the porosity. The geologists recorded their results in the following diagrams.

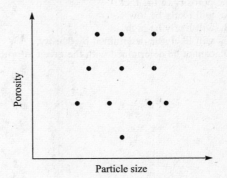

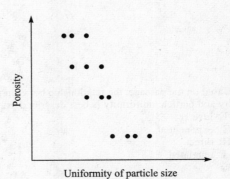

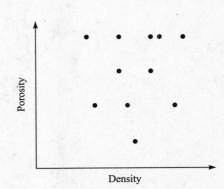

30. Which of the following properties would likely result in a porous rock on the basis of the results of Experiment 2?
   F. High density; small particle size
   G. Uniform particle size; high density
   H. Uniform particle size; low concentration of contaminants
   J. Large particle size; low density

GO ON TO THE NEXT PAGE.

4 ◯ ◯ ◯ ◯ ◯ ◯ ◯ ◯ ◯ **4**

31. If a sample of rock is studied and found to possess medium-sized particles with a high level of uniformity, the porosity of the rock:
   A. will likely be low.
   B. will likely be high.
   C. will likely be determined by density.
   D. cannot be determined with the given information.

32. Based on the passage, the relationship between porosity and particle uniformity is best described as:
   F. inverse.
   G. exponential.
   H. direct.
   J. unrelated.

33. A company wants to investigate the idea of creating a large oil reserve to stockpile oil in case of a shortage. Based on the results of Experiment 1, which of the following rock types would be the best choice for a storage medium?
   A. Limestone
   B. Shale
   C. Sandstone
   D. Granite

34. Which of the following graphs best represents the relationship between time elapsed and saturation of the rocks observed in Experiment 1?

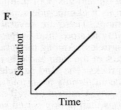

F.

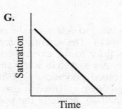

G.

H.

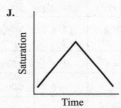

J.

35. Which of the following findings would NOT be consistent with the information provided about rock porosity?
   A. A rock with a low density will always be highly porous.
   B. A rock with uniform particle size will likely be more porous than a rock with varying particle size.
   C. Particle uniformity is a major determining factor of rock porosity.
   D. Rocks can store liquids such as oil and water.

GO ON TO THE NEXT PAGE.

PASSAGE VII

Sedimentary layers form when changes in the environment cause changes in the top soil of the area. As pressure is applied from the additional layers, fossils are formed. Figure 1 shows the different depths and pressure conditions under which different Fauna (categories of fossils) are formed.

A fossil's formation stage (a measure of the age of the fossil) is classified on a scale of early (first recovered) to late (deeply buried). Table 1 lists the grades of Fauna A–I from Figure 1. Figure 2 shows characteristic compounds that may be found in fossils of a given stage.

Table 1	
Fauna	Fossilized stage*
A	Early
B	Late
C	Late
D	Early to moderate
E	Moderate
F	Early
G	Early
H	Late
I	Moderate to late

Note: *Fossilized stage is a measure of the age of the fossil.

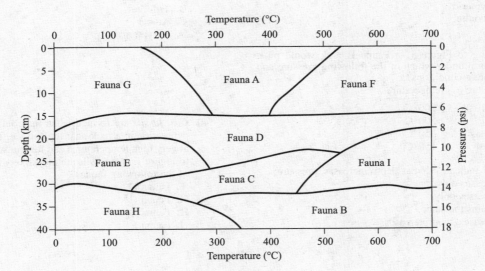

Figure 1

GO ON TO THE NEXT PAGE.

4 ◯ ◯ ◯ ◯ ◯ ◯ ◯ ◯ ◯ **4**

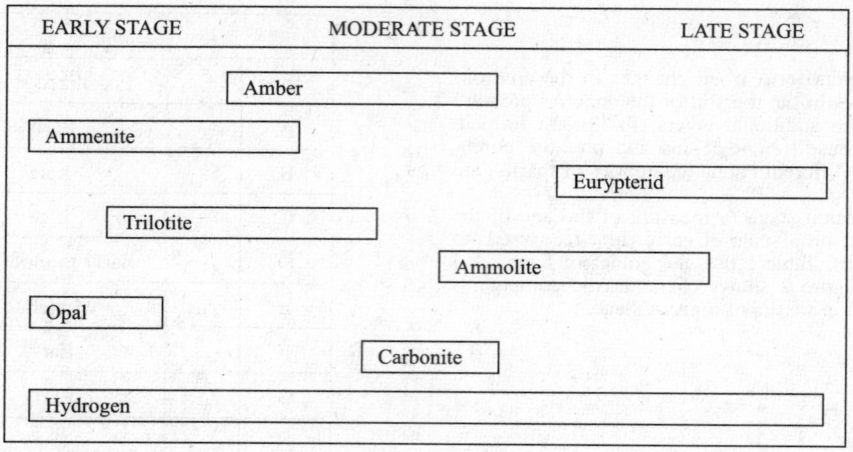

EARLY STAGE	MODERATE STAGE	LATE STAGE

Amber

Ammenite

Eurypterid

Trilotite

Ammolite

Opal

Carbonite

Hydrogen

Figure 2

36. According to Figure 2, which of the following compounds would most typically be found only in rocks at the moderate stage?
   F. Ammoenite
   G. Eurypterid
   H. Carbonite
   J. Clay

37. According to Figure 1, a Fauna H rock would most likely form under which of the following pressure and temperature conditions?

Pressure	Temperature
A. 4 psi	200°C
B. 8 psi	500°C
C. 12 psi	350°C
D. 16 psi	150°C

38. Figure 1 indicates that as depth increases, pressure:
   F. increases only.
   G. decreases only.
   H. remains the same.
   J. decreases, then increases.

39. According to Figure 2, the presence of which of the following compounds in a fossil is the *least* helpful when determining the fossil's stage?
   A. Hydrogen
   B. Trilotite
   C. Amber
   D. Eurypterid

40. *Cast fossils* are formed when material is placed into a depression in a rock near the surface. They are formed at very high temperatures and low pressures. According to Figure 1, cast fossils are most likely formed in which of the following faunas?
   F. Fauna D
   G. Fauna H
   H. Fauna B
   J. Fauna F

END OF THE SCIENCE REASONING TEST.
STOP! IF YOU HAVE TIME LEFT OVER, CHECK YOUR WORK ON THIS SECTION ONLY.

WRITING TEST PROMPT

DIRECTIONS: This test is designed to assess your writing skills. You have 30 minutes to plan and write an essay based on the stimulus provided. Be sure to take a position on the issue and support your position using logical reasoning and relevant examples. Organize your ideas in a focused and logical way, and use the English language to clearly and effectively express your position.

When you have finished writing, refer to the Scoring Rubrics discussed in the Introduction (page 4) to estimate your score.

Some high schools require students and staff to wear name badges any time they are on school property. Some people feel this is an effective measure to take against unauthorized school visitors. Opponents say that so many students will refuse to wear the badge or simply leave it at home that identifying unwanted visitors will be made no easier.

In your opinion, should schools mandate that all students and staff wear a name badge to aid in identifying unaffiliated visitors?

In your essay, take a position on this question. You may write about one of the points of view mentioned above, or you may give another point of view on this issue. Use specific examples and reasons for your position.

▬▬ ANSWER KEY

English Test

1. D	21. B	41. A	61. A
2. H	22. J	42. H	62. J
3. B	23. B	43. B	63. C
4. J	24. H	44. G	64. F
5. A	25. D	45. C	65. B
6. J	26. H	46. F	66. H
7. A	27. A	47. C	67. A
8. J	28. F	48. J	68. H
9. B	29. C	49. A	69. C
10. J	30. G	50. H	70. F
11. D	31. A	51. B	71. B
12. F	32. G	52. F	72. J
13. B	33. B	53. A	73. C
14. G	34. F	54. H	74. G
15. A	35. A	55. C	75. D
16. F	36. H	56. J	
17. D	37. D	57. B	
18. H	38. F	58. G	
19. D	39. C	59. C	
20. H	40. J	60. H	

Mathematics Test

1. D	21. D	41. D
2. J	22. J	42. H
3. C	23. A	43. E
4. H	24. F	44. J
5. D	25. C	45. D
6. J	26. H	46. G
7. E	27. D	47. D
8. F	28. G	48. H
9. D	29. A	49. A
10. H	30. G	50. F
11. B	31. B	51. A
12. K	32. J	52. K
13. D	33. B	53. B
14. H	34. G	54. G
15. D	35. B	55. E
16. F	36. F	56. J
17. D	37. A	57. C
18. H	38. G	58. F
19. D	39. E	59. B
20. H	40. G	60. J

Reading Test		**Science Reasoning Test**	
1. B	21. B	1. D	21. D
2. H	22. H	2. F	22. F
3. A	23. C	3. C	23. A
4. H	24. G	4. H	24. F
5. B	25. B	5. A	25. B
6. F	26. H	6. J	26. F
7. B	27. D	7. B	27. D
8. H	28. F	8. F	28. G
9. D	29. C	9. C	29. D
10. J	30. J	10. H	30. H
11. A	31. B	11. D	31. B
12. H	32. H	12. H	32. H
13. B	33. C	13. A	33. B
14. J	34. G	14. G	34. F
15. A	35. D	15. D	35. A
16. H	36. F	16. J	36. H
17. B	37. B	17. C	37. D
18. F	38. H	18. J	38. F
19. D	39. B	19. D	39. A
20. H	40. G	20. F	40. J

■■■ SCORING GUIDE

Your final reported score is your **COMPOSITE SCORE**. Your **COMPOSITE SCORE** is the average of all of your **SCALE SCORES**.

Your **SCALE SCORES** for the four multiple-choice sections are derived from the Scoring Table on the next page. Use your **RAW SCORE**, or the number of questions that you answered correctly for each section, to determine your **SCALE SCORE**. If you got a **RAW SCORE** of 60 on the English test, for example, you correctly answered 60 out of 75 questions.

Step 1 Determine your RAW SCORE for each of the four multiple-choice sections:

English _____

Mathematics _____

Reading _____

Science Reasoning _____

The following Raw Score Table shows the total possible points for each section.

RAW SCORE TABLE	
KNOWLEDGE AND SKILL AREAS	**RAW SCORES**
ENGLISH	75
MATHEMATICS	60
READING	40
SCIENCE REASONING	40
WRITING	12

Multiple-Choice Scoring Worksheet

Step 2 Determine your SCALE SCORE for each of the four multiple-choice sections using the following Scoring Worksheet. Each SCALE SCORE should be rounded to the nearest number according to normal rules. For example, $31.2 \approx 31$ and $31.5 \approx 32$. If you answered 61 questions correctly on the English section, for example, your SCALE SCORE would be 29.

English _____ × 36 = _____ ÷ 75 = _____
              RAW SCORE   **− 2** (*correction factor)

                                                    _____
                                                    SCALE SCORE

Mathematics _____ × 36 = _____ ÷ 60 = _____
                  RAW SCORE   **+ 1** (*correction factor)

                                                        _____
                                                        SCALE SCORE

Reading _____ × 36 = _____ ÷ 40 = _____
              RAW SCORE   **+ 2** (*correction factor)

                                                    _____
                                                    SCALE SCORE

Science Reasoning _____ × 36 = _____ ÷ 40 = _____
                        RAW SCORE   **+ 1.5** (*correction factor)

                                                            _____
                                                            SCALE SCORE

---

*The correction factor is an approximation based on the average from several recent ACT tests. It is most valid for scores in the middle 50% (approximately 16–24 scale composite score) of the scoring range.

The scores are all approximate. Actual ACT scoring scales vary from one administration to the next based upon several factors.

If you take the optional Writing Test, you will need to combine your English and Writing scores to obtain your final COMPOSITE SCORE. Once you have determined a score for your essay out of 12 possible points, you will need to determine your ENGLISH/WRITING SCALE SCORE, using both your ENGLISH SCALE SCORE and your WRITING TEST SCORE. The combination of the two scores will give you an ENGLISH/WRITING SCALE SCORE, from 1 to 36, that will be used to determine your COMPOSITE SCORE mentioned earlier.

Using the English/Writing Scoring Table, find your ENGLISH SCALE SCORE on the left or right hand side of the table and your WRITING TEST SCORE on the top of the table. Follow your ENGLISH SCALE SCORE over and your WRITING TEST SCORE down until the two columns meet at a number. This number is your ENGLISH/WRITING SCALE SCORE and will be used to determine your COMPOSITE SCORE.

Step 3 Determine your ENGLISH/WRITING SCALE SCORE using the English/Writing Scoring Table on the following page:

English _____

Writing _____

English/Writing _____

ENGLISH/WRITING SCORING TABLE

ENGLISH SCALE SCORE	WRITING TEST SCORE											ENGLISH SCALE SCORE
	2	3	4	5	6	7	8	9	10	11	12	
36	26	27	28	29	30	31	32	33	34	35	36	36
35	26	27	28	29	30	31	31	32	33	34	35	35
34	25	26	27	28	29	30	31	32	33	34	35	34
33	24	25	26	27	28	29	30	31	32	33	34	33
32	24	25	25	26	27	28	29	30	31	32	33	32
31	23	24	25	26	27	28	29	30	30	31	32	31
30	22	23	24	25	26	27	28	29	30	31	32	30
29	21	22	23	24	25	26	27	28	29	30	31	29
28	21	22	23	24	24	25	26	27	28	29	30	28
27	20	21	22	23	24	25	26	27	28	28	29	27
26	19	20	21	22	23	24	25	26	27	28	29	26
25	18	19	20	21	22	23	24	25	26	27	28	25
24	18	19	20	21	22	23	23	24	25	26	27	24
23	17	18	19	20	21	22	23	24	25	26	27	23
22	16	17	18	19	20	21	22	23	24	25	26	22
21	16	17	17	18	19	20	21	22	23	24	25	21
20	15	16	17	18	19	20	21	21	22	23	24	20
19	14	15	16	17	18	19	20	21	22	23	24	19
18	13	14	15	16	17	18	19	20	21	22	23	18
17	13	14	15	16	16	17	18	19	20	21	22	17
16	12	13	14	15	16	17	18	19	20	20	21	16
15	11	12	13	14	15	16	17	18	19	20	21	15
14	10	11	12	13	14	15	16	17	18	19	20	14
13	10	11	12	13	14	14	15	16	17	18	19	13
12	9	10	11	12	13	14	15	16	17	18	19	12
11	8	9	10	11	12	13	14	15	16	17	18	11
10	8	9	9	10	11	12	13	14	15	16	17	10
9	7	8	9	10	11	12	13	13	14	15	16	9
8	6	7	8	9	10	11	12	13	14	15	16	8
7	5	6	7	8	9	10	11	12	13	14	15	7
6	5	6	7	7	8	9	10	11	12	13	14	6
5	4	5	6	7	8	9	10	11	12	12	13	5
4	3	4	5	6	7	8	9	10	11	12	13	4
3	2	3	4	5	6	7	8	9	10	11	12	3
2	2	3	4	5	6	6	7	8	9	10	11	2
1	1	2	3	4	5	6	7	8	9	10	11	1

Step 4   Determine your COMPOSITE SCORE by finding the sum of all your SCALE SCORES for each of the four sections: English only (if you do not choose to take the optional Writing Test) *or* English/Writing (if you choose to take the optional Writing Test), Math, Reading, and Science Reasoning, and divide by 4 to find the average. Round your COMPOSITE SCORE according to normal rules. For example, $31.2 \approx 31$ and $31.5 \approx 32$.

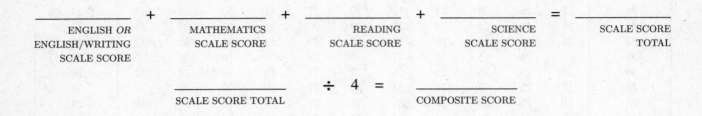

| _____ | + | _____ | + | _____ | + | _____ | = | _____ |
| ENGLISH *OR* ENGLISH/WRITING SCALE SCORE | | MATHEMATICS SCALE SCORE | | READING SCALE SCORE | | SCIENCE SCALE SCORE | | SCALE SCORE TOTAL |

_____   ÷   4   =   _____

SCALE SCORE TOTAL   COMPOSITE SCORE

ANSWERS AND EXPLANATIONS

English Test Explanations

PASSAGE I

1. **The best answer is D.** The contraction *he'd* begins a new, independent clause, which is clear and concise as a separate sentence. Answer choices A and C would make the sentence ungrammatical. Answer choice B would create a run-on sentence.

2. **The best answer is H.** The verb *insists* takes a clause headed by *that* as its object, which may not be separated from the verb with a comma. The other answer choices incorrectly use commas.

3. **The best answer is B.** The sentence should be in past tense, so answer choices A and C may be eliminated. Answer choice D would be ungrammatical in the sentence.

4. **The best answer is J.** There is no cause–effect relationship described between this sentence and the preceding one, so the other answer choices may be eliminated.

5. **The best answer is A.** Unlike the other answer choices, answer choice A describes the primary reason Mike would have wanted cable at the particular moment in the narrative described in the previous sentence.

6. **The best answer is J.** For the sake of clarity, paragraphs are best introduced without the use of pronouns. Furthermore, answer choice G does not agree with the singular noun *cable service*, to which it refers.

7. **The best answer is A.** The underlined portion requires no changes. The word *so* introduces the effect of a cause stated in the first clause. The other answer choices reflect the inverse relationship and would not make sense in context.

8. **The best answer is J.** Nouns conjoined with *and* may not be separated with a comma, as in answer choices F and G, nor may they be separated from the noun with which they form a compound (*channels*), as in answer choices G and H.

9. **The best answer is B.** This list sets the events of the conversation in correct chronological order. The other answer choices are not as clear and concise.

10. **The best answer is J.** The sentence describes a completed event in the past; therefore, the other answer choices may be eliminated.

11. **The best answer is D.** No punctuation is required before the clause that begins with *when*; therefore, the other answer choices may be eliminated.

12. **The best answer is F.** It is correct to use the infinitive *to* followed by the simple verb *program*.

13. **The best answer is B.** It maintains the lighthearted, slightly tongue-in-cheek tone of the passage and makes sense in the paragraph. The other choices may be eliminated for being unrelated and straying from the general tone of the passage.

14. **The best answer is G.** Placing the sentence between Sentence 1 and Sentence 2 provides a logical transition from the former to the latter. The other answer choices would not accomplish this; therefore, they may be eliminated.

15. **The best answer is A.** The Sentence supports the assertion that Mike is profiting from cable service. Answer choices B and D are not supported by the passage. Answer choice C, while possibly true, is not very specific. Moreover, Sentence 2 of Paragraph 3 is not obviously humorous, as answer choice C claims. For these two reasons, answer choice C may be eliminated.

PASSAGE II

16. **The best answer is F.** As it is written, the sentence leads logically to the next sentence, which identifies a single example of a "form of music."

17. **The best answer is D.** The word *nation* refers to a single nation and must be in possessive form in order to modify *rich ethnic diversity*. Answer choice B would create an awkwardly long chain of adjectives before the noun *diversity*.

18. **The best answer is H.** This question tests your ability to express the idea clearly and concisely. The sentence in answer choice H is the most clear and concise among the answer choices.

19. **The best answer is D.** The phrase *in its heyday from 1900 to 1918* is an appositive, which must be separated from the clause with commas.

20. **The best answer is H.** Clauses beginning with *but* must be separated from the main clause with a comma. Only answer choice H uses the correct punctuation. Answer choice F incorrectly uses the semicolon. Answer choice J omits *but*, a critical element in the sentence.

21. **The best answer is B.** The "detail that is elaborated on later in the paragraph" is the fame of a particular ragtime player, Scott Joplin.

22. **The best answer is J.** The other answer choices provide stronger reasons why Joplin's mother would have "worked long hours" to afford a piano. They indicate Joplin was an exceptional talent.

23. **The best answer is B.** The subject pronoun *who* is used to represent human beings in subordinate clauses. Answer choice C is an object pronoun. Answer choice D is a relative pronoun used for non-human things.

24. **The best answer is H.** This detail offers an explanation of why Joplin, though raised in Texas, found fame in Missouri.

25. **The best answer is D.** The sentence needs a main clause, which must begin with a subject. The other answer choices create sentence fragments.

26. **The best answer is H.** When a chain of adjectives modifies a noun in a related way, they are punctuated like a list, e.g. "soft, furry, and lovable rabbit." When the adjectives modify the noun each in a unique way, as in this phrase, they are not punctuated.

27. **The best answer is A.** The sentence, as it is written, ties together the subject of Scott Joplin and the broader subject of ragtime music. The other answer choices emphasize the *Maple Leaf Rag*, which would be left dangling at the end of the paragraph.

28. **The best answer is F.** This sentence describes appealing characteristics of Joplin's music, which supports the assertion made in Sentence 1, that "Joplin is the most famous figure in ragtime history." Sentence 6 makes a similar assertion, but the sentence concerns only one piece specifically, at the time of its creation. On the other hand, answer choice F, like Sentence 1, speaks to modern impressions of Joplin and his work.

29. **The best answer is C.** It uses more descriptive language than the other answer choices, avoiding nonspecific, common words.

30. **The best answer is G.** The essay provides a concise introduction to the birth of ragtime and its most famous composer, which constitute a good introduction to the "history and development" of the musical genre.

PASSAGE III

31. **The best answer is A.** The underlined portion requires no change. It is in simple present tense and third-person plural form to agree with the subject, "few facts." Answer choice B would incorrectly insert "that." Answer choice C has the wrong aspect, which makes it very awkward. Answer choice D is in third-person singular form.

32. **The best answer is G.** Any form of the word "articulate" is awkward and unnecessary. Answer choice G is in the correct form for the simple subject "information" and is clear and concise.

33. **The best answer is B.** Answer choices C and D may be eliminated for their wordiness and awkwardness. Answer choice B reflects the use of "of" that is like "from" in how it introduces one's native land: *man of the North*, *child of the mountains*, etc.

34. **The best answer is F.** It is reasonable to assume that the mother of someone born around 1770 would be deceased, so the past tense is appropriate here. This eliminates answer choice J. A complete sentence is required following a semicolon as it is used here, so answer choices G and H may be eliminated.

35. **The best answer is A.** The notion of respect is a valuable detail, so answer choice D may be eliminated. Among the other answer choices, only answer choice A is an appropriate adjective to modify "Cherokee chiefs."

36. **The best answer is H.** The word "alleged" is similar in meaning to "supposed." This is an example of a word commonly used as an adverb, "allegedly," than as an adjective (e.g., "The defendant allegedly robbed a bank"). Answer choice H is the only one to cast any doubt on the truth of the claims made about Sequoia.

37. **The best answer is D.** This sentence connects the preceding sentence, which simply mentions the belief that Sequoia invented a writing system, with the rest of the paragraph, which details the development of the writing system. It describes why Sequoia chose to create the writing system in the first place.

38. The best answer is F. The underlined portion requires no changes. Answer choices G and H may be eliminated first because a clause introduced by "that" would not follow a comma as it is used here. Answer choice J may be eliminated for awkwardness.

39. The best answer is C. All choices with the pronoun "it" may be eliminated because they would wrongly refer to "the English language," the closest expressed noun.

40. The best answer is J. The sentence should be in past tense, so answer choices G and H may be eliminated. Answer choice J correctly modifies the verb with an adverb, not an adjective, as in answer choice F.

41. The best answer is A. The underlined portion requires no changes. Answer choice B may be eliminated because it would create a sentence fragment. Answer choices C and D would make the sentence ungrammatical.

42. The best answer is H. "Bibles and other religious materials" constitute "sacred texts," which are mentioned earlier in the sentence.

43. The best answer is B. The sentence should explicitly address the past, so the present tense answer choice A and the hypothetical answer choices C and D may be eliminated.

44. The best answer is G. Sentence 3 elaborates on the claim made in Sentence 1, so it should be raised one position in the paragraph. No other changes need to be made to the paragraph, since it flows logically.

45. The best answer is C. The essay is very specific in its scope, so it would not satisfy the requirements of being an "introduction to the Cherokee nation." Answer choice D is incorrect because the passage indeed describes an important part of Cherokee history.

PASSAGE IV

46. The best answer is F. This is a well-formed clause that does not require internal punctuation.

47. The best answer is C. Introductory phrases of time do not require a preposition before them, so answer choice C is the most concise.

48. The best answer is J. This detail is an example of an event that is characteristic of the close relationship between the grandfather and the narrator.

It is consistent with the reminiscent tone of the passage.

49. The best answer is A. Answer choices B and C may be eliminated because a complete sentence is required following the semicolon. Answer choice D may be eliminated because "distant" should modify "relatives."

50. The best answer is H. The only word that is not idiomatic and does not fit the context is "about."

51. The best answer is B. This answer choice forms two closely related complete sentences, which may be joined with a semicolon. The only other acceptable option would be to use a period, but that is not offered among the answer choices.

52. The best answer is F. The next two sentences go into detail about the contents of the shoeboxes. Answer choice G contains an awkward sequence of tenses. The third paragraph describes the activities the author and his grandfather shared after his walks; therefore, answer choices H and J may be eliminated.

53. The best answer is A. The narrator goes on to describe simple photographs of his ancestors' home lives. The other answer choices are not supported by the passage.

54. The best answer is H. A photograph is a kind of timeless representation of something, so the gerund (which bears no tense) correctly follows *pictured*. Here is another example: "At his memorial in Washington, Lincoln is captured *sitting* pensively in a chair."

55. The best answer is C. The definite article "The" is required here because the "edges" have not been previously mentioned; therefore, answer choices A and D may be eliminated. Answer choice B does not make sense in it use of the first-person "my."

56. The best answer is J. The relative subject pronoun *who* joins a noun and a clause to form a complex noun phrase, "our French ancestors who first arrived on this continent." Answer choices G and H incorrectly use the object pronoun *whom*. Answer choice F separates with a comma "French" from the noun it modifies, "ancestors;" therefore, it may be eliminated.

57. The best answer is B. When listing examples, it is appropriate to use "such as." The remaining answer choices are awkward and not grammatical.

58. The best answer is G. The first-person plural subject pronoun "we" correctly refers to the narrator and his grandfather; therefore, answer choices F and H may be eliminated. Answer choice G correctly uses the past tense in agreement with the passage as a whole.

59. The best answer is C. The construction *became* + adjective + infinitive is common. Answer choice D violates this and is awkward. Answer choice B is wordy, and "increasing" does not make sense in context. Answer choice A is wrong because one adjective modifies another; an adverb is required, as in answer choice C.

60. The best answer is H. This answer choice is a clear and concise conclusion. The other answer choices unnecessarily repeat elements from earlier in the sentence and do not capture the essence of the passage as a whole.

PASSAGE V

61. The best answer is A. Answer choice A is best because it leaves "can" in place, which ties together the "understanding" mentioned earlier in the sentence and what it equips scientists to do. Answer choice B and C may be eliminated for incorrectly using the comma.

62. The best answer is J. "Impending" means something similar to *upcoming* and *looming*, which correctly describes the kind of eruptions that demand warning.

63. The best answer is C. The sentence describes the phenomenon of volcanoes generally, so the simple present tense is appropriate. The other answer choices use incorrect verb tense.

64. The best answer is F. The underlined portion requires no changes. Answer choice G is incorrect because it mismatches person between the subject and verb. Answer choices H and J are incorrect because they misuse the comma.

65. The best answer is B. Only answer choice B correctly describes what led the magma to break through the surface of the Earth, as mentioned later in the sentence.

66. The best answer is H. Only answer choice H parallels the uninflected form of the verb *form* that comes before the conjunction *or*.

67. The best answer is A. It is better to write in active voice than it is to write in passive voice. As it is written, the sentence is clear, concise, and in active voice.

68. The best answer is H. The phrase is a complex noun phrase that acts as the subject of the sentence; therefore, no punctuation is needed.

69. The best answer is C. The subordinator "so" correctly indicates the cause–effect relationship between the slowness of geologic processes and the necessity to search for ancient evidence in order to study them.

70. The best answer is F. The author is speaking about all volcanoes, so the introductory phrase "In general" is most appropriate. Furthermore, the other answer choices seem awkward when such a wide range of time is given.

71. The best answer is B. The phrase "that is" is a means to introduce a definition or clarification, and is necessarily set apart from the sentence with commas.

72. The best answer is J. The adverb *seriously* correctly modifies the verb *take*. The sentence as it is written incorrectly uses the adjective *serious* to modify the verb *take*, while answer choices G and H use the wrong form of the verb *take*.

73. The best answer is C. It is most clear and concise. The other answer choices are awkward in context.

74. The best answer is G. The phrase appropriately introduces two famous examples of predictions, which none of the other answer choices do.

75. The best answer is D. The first clause of the sentence (before the comma) is unrelated to the second clause, so the conjunction "and" is most appropriate. Answer choice B would be ungrammatical. Answer choices A and C point to a relationship between the clauses that does not exist.

Mathematics Test Explanations

1. **The correct answer is D.** You are given that Rachel paid a total of $103 for her speeding ticket, and that the basic fine for speeding is $25. This means that Rachel was charged an additional $78 (103 − 25). If the charge for each mile per hour over the speed limit is $6, then Rachel was driving 13 mph over the 55-mph speed limit (78/6 = 13), or 68 mph.

2. **The correct answer is J.** To find the equivalent expression, multiply the constants $(5 \times 2 \times 3)$, combine the x terms $(x^3)(x)(x) = x^{3+1+1} = x^5$ (because when you have a common base you keep the base and add the exponents), and combine the y terms $(y^1)(y^2) = y^{1+2}$, or y^3. The result is $30x^5y^3$.

3. **The correct answer is C.** To solve, determine the pattern in the arithmetic sequence 13, 10, 7, ... The second term, 10, is 3 less than the first term, 13. Likewise, the third term, 7, is three less than the second term, 10. Therefore, the fourth term will be three less than the third term, 7, making it $7 - 3 = 4$.

4. **The correct answer is H.** The product of two numbers is found by multiplying them ($r \times s$ in this case). Raising the product of r and s to the fourth power is represented by $(r \times s)^4$, since you are raising the entire product to the fourth power. Remember that $r \times s$ is equivalent to rs.

5. **The correct answer is D.** To solve this problem, you must remember that if you start at the decimal point and count to the right, the place values are tenths, hundredths, thousandths, ten-thousandths, and so on. Therefore, the decimal 0.005 has the digit 5 in the thousandths place.

6. **The correct answer is J.** To solve this problem, write an equation for the price of all of the notebooks and then solve for the price of one notebook. Make N the price of notebooks and B the price of binders purchased by Mandy and Jordan. If Mandy paid $5.85 for 3 notebooks and 1 binder, the result is $3N + B = 5.85$. Likewise for Jordan, $4.65 for 2 notebooks and 1 binder can be represented in the equation $2N + B = 4.65$.

   Use substitution to solve these equations. Solving Jordan's equation for B yields $B = 4.65 - 2N$. If you substitute $4.6 - 2N$ as B into Mandy's equation, the result is $3N + (4.65 - 2N) = 5.85$. Combining like terms yields $N + 4.65 = 5.85$. If you subtract 4.65 from both sides of the equation, you find that $N = 1.20$. Therefore, the price of one notebook is $1.20.

7. **The correct answer is E.** You are given that $mn = k$ and $k = x^2n$. To solve this problem, first combine the equations into $mn = x^2n$. Then, divide both sides by n to get $m = x^2$.

8. **The correct answer is F.** To solve for x in the equation $7x + 5 = 2x + 9$, you could subtract $2x$ and 5 from both sides of the equation. That results in the equation $5x = 4$. Dividing both sides by 5, the result is $x = \dfrac{4}{5}$.

9. **The correct answer is D.** To find what percent of 5 the number 7 is, you can simply divide 7 by 5 and multiply by 100%, as follows:

$$7/5 = 1.4$$

$$(1.4)(100) = 140\%$$

   Because 7 is greater than 5, you could have eliminated answer choices A, B, and C.

10. **The correct answer is H.** To find what $x^3 + x$ equals, you need to first solve $x^2 = 16$ for x. The solution is the square root of 16, which is 4. Then substituting into the original expression, you get $4^3 + \sqrt{4}$. This expression simplifies to $64 + 2$, or 66.

11. **The correct answer is B.** This question is testing your knowledge of absolute value. The absolute value of -16 is 16. Notice that you must take the negative of the absolute value, or -16. You must then add -16 to 16, which results in 0.

12. **The correct answer is K.** The probability that the card chosen will be red when there are 6 spades, 3 hearts, and 7 diamonds, is the number of favorable outcomes divided by the number of total outcomes. The number of favorable outcomes is 10 because there are 3 hearts and 7 diamonds, which constitute the "red" cards. The total number of outcomes is $6 + 3 + 7 = 16$. Thus the probability of the card being "red" is $\dfrac{10}{16}$, or $\dfrac{5}{8}$ when reduced.

13. **The correct answer is D.** To find a simplified form of $4x - 4y + 3x$, combine like terms (all of the x's and all of the y's) to get $7x - 4y$. Notice that you cannot subtract $4y$ from $4x$ because the variables are different.

14. **The correct answer is H.** To solve this problem, realize that the number of pets that Gary has is determined through relationships between the quantities of the different types of pets: turtles (t), cats (c), and birds (b). Because the number of birds,

b, is 4 more than the number of turtles, *t*, this can be expressed as $b = t + 4$. Also, since the number of cats, *c*, is 2 times the number of birds, this can be expressed as $c = 2b$. You might wish to use a table to show the numerical relationship between the numbers of each pet and the total number of pets, using the answer choices as a guideline:

Number of turtles (*t*)	0	1	2	3	4
Number of birds ($b = t + 4$)	4	5	6	7	8
Number of cats ($c = 2b$)	8	10	12	14	16
TOTAL	12	16	20	24	28

According to this matrix, Gary *could* have a total of 20 pets, but he could not have a total of 14, 18, 22, or 26 pets.

15. The correct answer is D. To solve this equation, first calculate how many 1/4-inch segments there will be. Dividing 66 by 12, you can see that there will be 5.5 1/4-inch segments. Thus, the road's length in inches will be 1/4 + 1/4 + 1/4 + 1/4 + 1/4 + 1/8 = 1 1/4 + 1/8 = 1 3/8.

16. The correct answer is F. To find $(a - b)^3$ given $b = a - 4$, you could solve the equation for $a - b$. By subtracting *b* and −4 from both sides, you get $4 = a - b$. Substituting 4 for $a - b$ in $(a - b)^3$ yields $(4)^3$, or 64.

　　If you got stuck on this one, you could try choosing a specific value for *a*, such as 2. Then $b = -2$ and $(a - b)^3 = (2 + 2)^3 = 4^3$, or 64.

17. The correct answer is D. To solve this problem, you should realize that if *g* is an integer, $\sqrt{g^2}$ would also be an integer. Of the answer choices, only $\sqrt{8}$ is not an integer; in fact, it is an irrational number.

18. The correct answer is H. To find the number of distinct outfits that Justin can make from 6 different dress shirts, 3 different pairs of pants, and 5 different ties, multiply the numbers of the three different components together. Thus there are (6)(3)(5), or 90 distinct outfits that Justin can make.

19. The correct answer is D. To find the number of barrels of gasoline that can be produced from 3,500 barrels of crude oil when, for every 10,000 barrels of crude oil supplied the refinery can produce 6,500 barrels of gasoline, you can set up a proportion with ratios of barrels of gasoline to barrels of crude

oil: $\dfrac{6,500}{10,000} = \dfrac{\text{barrels gasoline}}{3,500}$, resulting in 2,275 barrels of gasoline produced.

20. The correct answer is H. To solve this problem, recall that the formula for finding the slope of a line between the two points (x_1, y_1) and (x_2, y_2) is $(y_2 - y_1)/(x_2 - x_1)$. Also recall that the origin lies at point (0,0). Therefore, the points are (−6,2) and (0,0). You can use either set of points as (x_1, x_2) and (y_1, y_2), as long as you use them consistently within the formula, as follows:

$$(2 - 0)/(-6 - 0) = 2/-6 = -1/3$$

21. The correct answer is D. To solve this problem, remember that, when multiplying the same base number raised to any power, add the exponents. Thus, if $n^x \cdot n^8 = n^{24}$, $x + 8 = 24$, and *x* equals 16. Also, remember that, when raising an exponential expression to a power, multiply the exponent and power. So in $(n^6)^y = n^{18}$, $6y = 18$, and $y = 3$. Therefore, $x + y = 16 + 3$, or 19.

22. The correct answer is J. To find the slope-intercept form of the equation $9x + 3y - 6 = 0$, you could first add 6 and subtract $9x$ from both sides of the equation to get $3y = -9x + 6$. Then, multiply both sides by $\dfrac{1}{3}$ to get $y = -3x + 2$.

23. The correct answer is A. To solve this problem, remember that the volume of a cube is equal to (length)(width)(height) or simply $(\text{side})^3$, since all sides of a cube are equivalent in length. To find the length of one side, find the cube root of 64, which is 4 ($4^3 = 64$). Because all sides of a cube are equal, the shortest distance from the center of the cube to the base of the cube will equal the midpoint of the length of the cube, which is 4/2, or 2.

24. The correct answer is F. The sine (sin) of an acute angle in a right triangle is equivalent to the length of the side opposite the angle over the length of the hypotenuse $\left(\dfrac{\text{opp}}{\text{hyp}}\right)$. To find sin C in $\triangle ABC$, take the length of the opposite side over the length of the hypotenuse, or $\dfrac{a}{b}$.

　　Answer choice G is the tangent $\left(\dfrac{\text{opp}}{\text{adj}}\right)$, H is the cosecant $\left(\dfrac{\text{hyp}}{\text{opp}}\right)$, J is the cosine $\left(\dfrac{\text{adj}}{\text{hyp}}\right)$, and K is the cotangent $\left(\dfrac{\text{adj}}{\text{hyp}}\right)$. If you did not get the correct answer, it would be wise to review trigonometric ratios in a right triangle.

25. The correct answer is C. To solve this problem, remember that the area of a triangle is calculated using the formula A = 1/2(*bh*), where *b* is the base of the triangle and *h* is the height of the triangle. The base of the triangle extends from the origin in the (x, y) coordinate plane, (0,0) to the point (5,0). This means that the base is 5. The height of the triangle extends from the origin in the (x, y) coordinate plane, (0,0) to (0,4). The height of the triangle is 4. Substitute these values into the formula and solve:

$$A = 1/2(bh)$$
$$A = 1/2(5 \times 4)$$
$$A = 1/2(20)$$
$$A = 10$$

26. The correct answer is H. To solve this problem, recognize that the $39 price of the sneakers is 30 percent *more than* the amount it costs the store to purchase one pair of the sneakers. This can be represented as 130%, or 1.3. Thus, the price that the store pays for the sneakers is $39/1.3, or $30. At the end of the year sales associates get 20% off of this $30 price, therefore paying 80% of the price the shoe store pays. The cost to the employees is $30 × 0.80, or $24.

27. The correct answer is D. To find the uniform depth, you would substitute in the formula for volume, V, of a rectangular prism with the height h, length l, and width w, which is $V = lwh$. After substituting you should have 7,000 = 30(64)(h), or 7,000 = 1,920h. Thus $h = \dfrac{7,000}{1,920}$, or about 3.65, which is between 3 and 4.

28. The correct answer is G. To find the length of the segment AC in $\triangle ABC$, where the length of the hypotenuse is 17, and the cosine of $\angle C$ is $\dfrac{3}{5}$, use the definition of cosine: the ratio of the lengths of the adjacent side to the length of the hypotenuse. In $\triangle ABC$ cosine of $\angle C$ is the ratio of the segment AC to the length of the hypotenuse. After substituting the length of the hypotenuse, we get $\dfrac{3}{5} = \dfrac{AC}{17}$, and $AC = \dfrac{(17 \times 3)}{5}$, or 10.2 feet.

29. The correct answer is A. The number of people in the choir is 1 short from being able to be divided evenly by both 5 *and* 6. To find the least possible number of people in the choir, take one less than the lowest number for which 5 and 6 are both

factors. The lowest number for which 5 and 6 are both factors is 30. Thus, the least possible number of people in the choir is $30 - 1 = 29$.

30. The correct answer is G. To find the y-coordinate where the 2 lines $y = \dfrac{x}{2} + 3$ and $y = 3x - 2$ intersect, you could set $\dfrac{x}{2} + 3$ equal to $3x - 2$ because they are both already solved for y. Where they would intersect, their y-coordinates would be equal. To solve $\dfrac{x}{2} + 3 = 3x - 2$, you could add 2 and subtract $\dfrac{x}{2}$ to both sides to get $\dfrac{5x}{2} = 5$, then multiply by $\dfrac{2}{5}$ (the reciprocal of $\dfrac{5}{2}$) to get $x = 2$. Then simply substitute 2 for x into either of the initial equations to get $y = 4$.

31. The correct answer is B. To find the length BC when the length AD is 32 units, the length AC is 23 units, and the length BD is 27 units, and the points are along the segment AD as shown in the problem, you must notice that segment BC is the intersection of segment AC and the segment BD. So, the sum of the lengths AC and BD is the same as the sum of the lengths AD and BC. Using the actual lengths, solve for BC as follows:

$$AC + BD = AD + BC$$
$$23 + 27 = 32 + BC$$
$$50 = 32 + BC$$
$$18 = BC$$

32. The correct answer is J. To solve the equation $M = 6T + 5$ for N you could subtract 5 from both sides to get $M - 5 = 6N$, and then divide by 6 on both sides to get $\dfrac{(M - 5)}{6}$.

33. The correct answer is B. To solve this problem, recognize that the triangle is a "special triangle." A right triangle in which the length of the longer leg is $\sqrt{3}$ times the length of the shorter leg is a $30° - 60° - 90°$ right triangle. Another property of this type of right triangle is that the hypotenuse is 2 times the length of the shorter leg. So, this right triangle has lengths x, $x\sqrt{3}$, and $2x$. The perimeter is the sum of the lengths of the sides. You are given that the perimeter equals $12 + 4\sqrt{3}$. Set the two equations equal and solve for x:

$$12 + 4\sqrt{3} = x + x\sqrt{3} + 2x$$
$$12 + 4\sqrt{3} = 3x + x\sqrt{3}$$

For the right side of the equation to equal the left side of the equation, x must be equal to 4.

34. The correct answer is G. To solve this problem, first recognize that, since $\overline{XY} = \overline{YZ}$, the triangle is isosceles. Because the triangle is isosceles, you know that angles X and Z are congruent and have equal measure. If $a = 40°$, then $180° = 40° + x° + y°$ and $x° + y° = 140°$. Since $x = y$, both angles equal 70°. In triangles, sides have lengths that are proportional to their opposite angles. Because you know that the length of $\overline{XZ}$ is 5, and $\overline{XZ}$ is opposite the 40° angle, you can set up a proportion to find the length of side $\overline{XY}$ using its opposite angle, 70°, as follows:

$$5/40 = \overline{XY}/70$$

$$5 = 40(\overline{XY}/70)$$

$$(5 \times 70) = 40\overline{XY}$$

$$= 350/40 = 8.75$$

35. The correct answer is B. To find the y-intercept of the line $-9x - 3y = 15$, convert the equation to slope-intercept form. To so do, first add $9x$ to both sides to get $-3y = 9x + 15$. Then divide by -3 to get $y = -3x - 5$. Since the slope-intercept form of the equation is $y = -3x - 5$, the slope is -3 and the y-intercept is -5.

36. The correct answer is F. For the product of two integers to lie between 137 and 149, a multiple of both integers must lie between 137 and 149. Of the answer choices, 15 is the only number without a multiple that lies between 137 and 149; $15 \times 9 = 135$, and $15 \times 10 = 150$. Thus, the only number that cannot be one of the integers is 15.

37. The correct answer is A. You are given that x divided by 7 leaves a remainder of 4. The easiest approach to this problem is to assume that 7 goes into x one time, with a remainder of 4. Therefore, x is equal to 11. If $x = 11$, then $2x = 22$. When 22 is divided by 7, the remainder is 1.

38. The correct answer is G. Recall that the area of a circle with radius r is πr^2. The radius of the circle can be found by taking half of the distance across the circle, which in this case is also equal to half of the length of the side of the square. Thus the area of the square is $\pi 6^2 =$ about 113 square feet. If you selected answer choice A you found the area of the square.

39. The correct answer is E. You can apply common sense to solve this problem. If the average of 7 consecutive integers is 16, it would make sense that the middle number is 16 (this assumption only holds because there are an odd number of integers and because the integers are consecutive). Thus, the list of consecutive integers is 13, 14, 15, <u>16</u>, 17, 18, 19. The sum of the first and last integers is $13 + 19 = 32$.

40. The correct answer is G. To find the measure of $\angle BDC$ in the figure, it is helpful to recognize that the sides BC and AD are parallel (definition of trapezoid) and are connected by the transversal BD. $\angle CBD$ and $\angle ADB$ are alternate interior angles, and thus are equal and both measure 25°. Because A, D, and E all lie along the same line, $\angle ADE = 180°$. Because $\angle ADE$ is made up of $\angle ADB$, $\angle BDC$, and $\angle CDE$, you know that the measures of these three angles add up to 180°. If x is the unknown angle measure, then $25° + x + 125° = 180°$; thus x is equal to 30°.

41. The correct answer is D. To solve this problem, first eliminate answer choices that yield equal values for $f(-5)$ and $f(5)$. These include answer choices in which the functions have even powers of x such as answer choice A, where $f(x) = 6x^2$, answer choice B, where $f(x) = 6$, and answer choice E, where $f(x) = x^6 + 6$. Now, substitute -5 and 5 into the remaining answer choices:

Answer choice C: $f(x) = 6/x$. When x is -5, $f(x) = -6/5$, and when x is 5, $f(x) = 6/5$. Therefore, $f(5)$ is greater than $f(-5)$ and answer choice C is incorrect.

Answer choice D: $f(x) = 6 - x^3$. When $x = -5$, $f(x) = 6 - (-125)$ or 131, and when x is 5, $f(x) = 6 - 125$, or -116. Therefore, $f(-5)$ is greater than $f(5)$.

42. The correct answer is H. Systems of equations have an infinite number of solutions when the equations are equivalent. In order for the two equations to be equivalent, the constants and coefficients must be proportional. If the entire equation $3a + b = 12$ is multiplied by 4, the result is $4(3a + b) = 4(12)$, or $12a + 4b = 48$. Thus in order for the two equations to be equivalent, $3n = 48$, or $n = 16$.

43. The correct answer is E. You could take a "brute-force" approach and test all the given values of y and see if you could find an x that worked. For example, if $y = 9$, then the two numbers are $x^2 \times 9^2$ and $x \times 9^3$. You can see that 9^2 is a factor of these 2 numbers, so 27 cannot be the greatest common factor.

It might be more efficient to be more general and avoid testing all 5 values of x. Notice that xy^2

is a common factor of both x^2y^2 and xy^3. Because it is a factor, xy^2 must also be a factor of 27. Well, 27 factors as 3×3^2, so it seems natural to see if $x = 3$ and $y = 3$ are possible solutions. In this case the two numbers from the problem are $3^2 \times 3^2$ and $3^3 \times 3$ and the greatest common factor is $3 \times 3^2 = 27$, so it works.

44. **The correct answer is J.** To solve this problem, make x the smallest possible integer for which 15% of x is greater than 2.3. Then, set up the following inequality: $0.15x > 2.3$. Divide both sides by 0.15 to get $x > 15.333$, repeating. The smallest integer greater than the repeating decimal 15.333 is 16.

45. **The correct answer is D.** To find the distance between 2 points in the standard (x, y) coordinate plane you can use the distance formula $d = \sqrt{[(x_2 - x_1)^2 + (y_2 - y_1)^2]}$. Calculate the distance as follows:

$$\sqrt{[(4-1)^2 + (4-0)^2]} = \sqrt{(3^2 + 4^2)} = \sqrt{25} = 5.$$

46. **The correct answer is G.** A triangle with sides 9, 12, and 15 centimeters long has sides in the ratio of 9:12:15, which simplifies to 3:4:5. Recall that a $3 - 4 - 5$ triangle is a special case because it is known to be a right triangle. Any triangle with sides in the same ratio is also a right triangle. Thus, there is a right angle between the smaller sides.

47. **The correct answer is D.** The sum of the interior angles of a pentagon is $(5 - 2)(180°)$, or $540°$. Thus, the total of the other 4 angles is $540° - 40°$, or $500°$.

48. **The correct answer is H.** To solve this problem, it might be helpful to use test values for r and s and systematically try the scenario presented in each answer choice. The equation $|r - s| = |r + s|$ is true only when $r = 0$ or $s = 0$.

49. **The correct answer is A.** Logarithms are used to indicate exponents of certain numbers called bases. By definition, $\log_a b = c$, if $a^c = b$. To solve, let $\log_4 64 = x$; therefore, $64 = 4^x$. Because $4^3 = 64$, $x = 3$.

50. **The correct answer is F.** To solve, write out every possible three-digit integer: 345, 354, 435, 453, 534, and 543; six different positive three-digit numbers can be formed, answer choice F.

51. **The correct answer is A.** To find the real numbers x such that $x - 3 < x - 5$, you could subtract x from both sides. The result is $-3 < -5$, and because

that inequality is never true, there is no solution for x. The solution set is the empty set. If you chose an incorrect answer you might have thought that a negative value for x might reverse the inequality, which is not the case.

52. **The correct answer is K.** Perpendicular lines have slopes that are opposite reciprocals. To find the slope of a line perpendicular to $7x + 4y = 11$, first find the slope by converting the equation to slope-intercept form, then take the opposite reciprocal. To do so, first subtract from both sides to get $4y = -7x + 11$. Next, divide both sides by 4 to get $y = -\frac{7x}{4} + \frac{11}{4}$. Since the slope in this line is $-\frac{7}{4}$, the slope of a line perpendicular to that is $\frac{4}{7}$.

53. **The correct answer is B.** For the sake of simplicity, let every element in the original set have the value x. If each element in the set is multiplied by 3, and then reduced by 4, each element then has the value $3x - 4$. In a set where each value is $3x - 4$, the mean is $3x - 4$.

54. **The correct answer is G.** One way to find $\tan \theta$ given that $\cos \theta = -\frac{3}{5}$ and $\frac{\pi}{2} < \theta < \pi$, is to first find $\sin \theta$, then find $\frac{\sin \theta}{\cos \theta}$ (which is equivalent to $\tan \theta$). To find $\sin \theta$, use the identity $\sin^2 \theta + \cos^2 \theta = 1$ and the fact that $\sin \theta > 1$ in Quadrant II ($\frac{\pi}{2} < \theta < \pi$ would place the angle in Quadrant II). Substituting you get $\sin^2 \theta + \left(-\frac{3}{5}\right)^2 = 1$, or $\sin^2 \theta + \frac{9}{25} = 1$. After subtracting $\frac{9}{25}$, you get $\sin^2 \theta = \frac{16}{25}$. After taking the square root of both sides, you get $\sin \theta = \pm\frac{4}{5}$. Because $\sin \theta > 1$ in Quadrant II, $\sin \theta = \frac{4}{5}$. Substituting into $\frac{\sin \theta}{\cos \theta}$ gives you $\frac{(4/5)}{(-3/5)}$, which equals $-\frac{4}{3}$.

Another way you could solve this problem would be to construct a right triangle with leg 3 and hypotenuse 5. By virtue of the Pythagorean Theorem, the missing side of the right triangle is 4 units long. From this triangle, knowing that $\text{tangent} = \frac{\text{opposite}}{\text{adjacent}}$, you can get $\tan \theta = \frac{4}{3}$. Then by using the fact that $\frac{\pi}{2} < \theta < \pi$, you could infer that $\tan \theta$ was negative.

55. The correct answer is E. First, draw the picture of the circular pool according to the information given in the problem, where the distance from the edge of the pool to the edge of the long side of the rectangular region is 2 feet. The distance from the edge of the pool to the edge of the sin short side of the rectangular region can be anything greater than 2, but it is not necessary to know this distance to solve the problem:

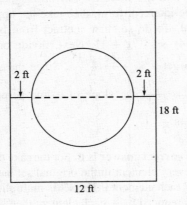

Now you can determine the diameter of the circular pool. The diameter is the maximum distance from one point on a circle to another (the dashed line). Since the short side of the rectangular region is 12 feet, and the distance from the edge of the circular pool to each edge of the long sides of the rectangular region is set at 2 feet, the diameter of the circle must be 12 feet – 2(2 feet), or 12 feet – 4 feet, or 8 feet. The question asks for the radius of the pool, which is $\frac{1}{2}$ of the diameter, or 4.

56. The correct answer is J. According to the problem, Kate traveled distance d in m minutes on the way to her grandmother's house, and she traveled distance d in $\frac{1}{2}m$ minutes (because she went twice as fast, it took her half as long) on the way back. The total number of minutes traveled would be equal to the number of minutes Kate traveled to her grandmother's house and back:

$$1m + \frac{1m}{2}$$
$$= \frac{2m}{2} + \frac{1m}{2}$$
$$= \frac{3m}{2}$$

57. The correct answer is C. To solve this problem, replace the a and b in $3a + 2b - 7$ with $a + 2$ and $b - 1$. The result is $3(a + 2) + 2(b - 1) - 7$. Distribute to get $3a + 6 + 2b - 2 - 7 = 3a + 2b - 3$. Comparing $3a + 2b - 7$ and $3a + 2b - 3$, it is apparent that the value of n increases by 4 if the value of a increases by 2 and the value of b decreases by 1.

58. The correct answer is F. To solve, use the Pythagorean Theorem. The hypotenuse, c, is related to the legs x and $3x$ by the equation $c^2 = x^2 + (3x)^2$, which is equivalent to $x^2 + 9x^2$, or $10x^2$. Since $c^2 = 10x^2$, $c = \sqrt{(10x^2)}$, or $\sqrt{10}x$.

59. The correct answer is B. Let the length of the edge of the smaller cube be s. The surface area is then $6s^2$. If the length of the edges are tripled, then s is replaced by $3s$, making the surface area $6(3s)^2 = (9)6s^2$, or 9 times larger than the initial surface area.

60. The correct answer is J. The first step in solving this problem is to rewrite the information in mathematical terms, as follows:

$a + b$ is at most 9 means that $a + b \leq 9$
a is at least 2 means that $a \geq 2$
b is at least -2 means that $b \geq -2$

Given the information above, the value of $b - a$ will be least when b is at its minimum value of -2. In that case, since $a + b \leq 9$, then $a + (-2) \leq 9$, and $a \leq 11$. Therefore, at its minimum, $b - a$ is equivalent to $-2 - 11$, or -13.

Reading Test Explanations

PASSAGE I

1. **The best answer is B.** The passage states that the narrator's (Tom's) feelings about life in the North were "strengthened by Aunt Chloe, who said, "there wasn't no gentlemen in the North no way." Also, when confronted by his father, who asked him where he had heard such inaccurate things about the North, Tom replied, "'Aunt Chloe, sir; she told me.'" This best supports answer choice B.

2. **The best answer is H.** The author says that if the name of a new pupil struck Tom favorably, he would, in turn, shake the student's hand *cordially*. This has pleasant connotations since, again, Tom only cordially shook the hands of those whose names he saw favorably. Answer choices F, G, and J can be eliminated since they all have negative connotations. Answer choice H, "sincerely," makes the most sense in the context of the passage.

3. **The best answer is A.** In the first paragraph, the narrator describes himself as "a real human boy, such as you may meet anywhere in New England." This implies that he is the same as any other boy found in New England at the time; therefore, he was neither better nor worse behaved than other boys his age. This supports answer choice A.

4. **The best answer is H.** In the second paragraph, the narrator describes meeting new classmates. He states "such names as Higgins, Wiggins, and Spriggins were offensive affronts to my ear," while the names "Langdon, Wallace, Blake, and the like, were passwords to my confidence and esteem." Therefore, Blake and Wallace would be acceptable to him, but Higgins would not be acceptable.

5. **The best answer is B.** When first told by his father that he was going back to school in Rivermouth, Tom resolved that he "would not be taken away to live among a lot of Yankees!" Also, later in the passage he reports feeling "terror at the bare thought of being transported to Rivermouth to school." However, after his father talks to him about how life really was in the North, Tom "was no longer unwilling to go North." This best supports answer choice B.

6. **The best answer is F.** Tom's father shows his patience and understanding through the manner in which he handles Tom's ridiculous misconceptions about moving North. The passage states that Tom's father asked him "calmly"

about who told him such silly stories, and that his father "devoted that evening and several subsequent evenings" to explaining to Tom the true history and present happenings of life in Northern states.

7. **The best answer is B.** In the second paragraph, the narrator states that he "was born in Rivermouth almost fifty years ago." Answer choice A may appear to be correct, but the narrator is telling a story from his adult perspective about his boyhood.

8. **The best answer is H.** In the sixth paragraph, the narrator describes kicking Sam upon finding out that his father wanted to move the narrator back to Rivermouth. In the last sentence of the sixth paragraph, the narrator states "as for kicking little Sam, I always did that . . . when anything went wrong with me." The author takes out his negative feelings on Sam by kicking him and thereby abusing him, answer choice H.

9. **The best answer is D.** The narrator states in the second paragraph that he was born in New England but moved to New Orleans when just an infant. In the next paragraph he states, "I had no recollection of New England: my earliest memories were connected with the South;" and that even though he was born a Yankee, "hoped nobody would find it out," indicating that he adapted to a Southern lifestyle to the point that his Northern heritage was not obvious to anyone else.

10. **The best answer is J.** In the first paragraph the narrator states that he was an "amiable, impulsive lad," meaning that he was friendly, yet fickle. The second paragraph details an example of his amicability—he was eager to introduce himself to new students on the playground—and also his fickleness—if the boy had the wrong last name, Tom was not interested in being his friend anymore.

PASSAGE II

11. **The best answer is A.** The author uses strong language throughout the piece; for example, saying there is "no more important" and "no more difficult" knowledge than that of the self, and that a consequence of a nation not understanding its own being will result in "decay and death." Since *impassioned* means "with strong feeling," answer choice A is best.

12. **The best answer is H.** The passage states that it is important for a nation "to know itself,

understand its own existence, powers and faculties, rights and duties, constitution, instincts, tendencies, and destiny." Later in the passage the author states that the nation must still undertake the important task of gaining an "appreciation of its own constitution tendencies." This best supports answer choice H.

13. **The best answer is B.** The author is comparing America to a child, lacking the experience and knowledge that could be gained from "severe trial." Because of this, answer choice C may appear to be correct, but once placed into context—America has lived the *difficult* life of a child—it no longer makes sense. *Naive* means "lacking experience, wisdom, or judgment," so the best synonym for naive in this context is *inexperienced*.

14. **The best answer is J.** The passage contains the statement, "The defection of the slaveholding States, and the fearful struggle that has followed for national unity and integrity, have ... forced it to pass from ... adolescence to ... manhood." Because this is referring to the Civil War, or the secession of the Southern states and the ensuing conflict, answer choice J is best.

15. **The best answer is A.** The first paragraph states that, in response to the introduction of the maxim of "know thyself," "there is for an individual no more important and no more difficult knowledge, than knowledge of himself." The paragraph goes on to say that a nation is just like an individual in that respect, and that failure to understand its existence will lead to its ultimate undoing. This best supports answer choice A.

16. **The best answer is H.** The author contends that "the citizen who can ... do this will render them an important service and deserve well of his country." Since *revered* means "praised," this is the best answer choice.

17. **The best answer is B.** The author states that "with time, patience, and good-will, the difficulties may be overcome, the errors of the past corrected, and the Government placed on the right track for the future." This indicates that though there have been troubles and errors, the nation will eventually reconcile its past mistakes and have a better and brighter future, answer choice B.

18. **The best answer is F.** The passage claims that the United States is "preparing to make a new start in history" with its "national unity and integrity" intact after the challenge of the Civil War. Since

vindicated means, in this context, "defended or proved worthy of," "justified" is the best answer.

19. **The best answer is D.** The author asserts that the United States has "lived the naive life of the child," but the Civil War has "forced it to pass from ... adolescence to ... reflecting manhood." This best supports answer choice D.

20. **The best answer is H.** It is indicated in the passage that a nation has many aspects of itself to "understand and observe," and if it does not, it will "become lethargic and infirm ... and end in premature decay and death." Since lethargic means "lacking energy" and infirm means "weak or debilitated," the best answer choice is H. Answer choice J may appear to be correct if you did not read the question carefully and realize that the question is asking what will happen if the nation does NOT become more aware of itself and its role in the global community.

PASSAGE III

21. **The best answer is B.** The passage states that Faulkner began writing in Lafayette County, Mississippi, where he was "immersed" in southern lore. Because the sentence is describing Faulkner himself, not his writing, it makes the most sense that he was "submerged" in traditional southern lore. Within the context of the sentence, it does not make logical sense that Faulkner would be "depicted" or "interpreted" in southern lore, nor does it make sense that he was "related" in southern lore.

22. **The best answer is H.** In paragraph one, the author states "Faulkner produced literary works filled with emotional turmoil and unflinching honesty. His unique interpretation of history is highlighted in the symbolism and imagery of his writing." These two sentences describe symbolism, honesty, and turmoil. Nowhere in the passage is it written that Faulkner's works were considered to be malicious.

23. **The best answer is C.** The passage repeatedly makes reference to Faulkner's "clever satire of Southern characters," and his willingness to face the "brutality and anguish that life can bring." These statements show his strong convictions. Other portions of the passage talk of his prominence as an author, such as winning the Nobel Prize or mastering various literary techniques. These sentiments best support answer choice C.

While answer choice A may seem correct as the passage talks of how his "Deep South roots greatly influenced his writing," this does not necessarily mean that he stayed true to those roots.

24. **The best answer is G.** The passage discusses how Faulkner abhorred "rampant racism and abuse," and later that he "condemns ... obstructions to human freedom." Together these statements carry the connotation of a strong dislike for injustice, which best supports answer choice G.

25. **The best answer is B.** The passage talks of how Faulkner "abhorred" racism, which indicates a strong dislike. It further speaks of how he "refused to avoid painful or controversial issues," and it states that he "condemns, and analyzes obstructions to human freedom and happiness by examining racism." Both of these statements support the idea that he hated racism and worked to expose it, along with other difficult and controversial topics concerning life in the South.

26. **The best answer is H.** The fourth paragraph begins by stating that Faulkner "was awarded the Nobel Prize." Later in the paragraph it mentions that many of his readers, when encountering his "experimental literary techniques," "were more often than not inspired by his insightful analysis of the human spirit." These statements reflect the author's intent to emphasize the importance of Faulkner's work and mastery of various styles. The other answer choices are not supported by the passage.

27. **The best answer is D.** The first sentence of the passage calls Faulkner's literary devices "revolutionary." In the third paragraph the author speaks specifically of Faulkner's literary style, saying they included "brilliant symbolism and exquisite dialogue." At the end of that paragraph the author talks of how one technique Faulkner used, stream-of-consciousness, conveyed a character's thoughts "in a manner roughly akin to the way the human mind actually works." Along with references throughout the passage to the sharp social commentary within Faulkner's work, these statements suggest that the author feels they were a new take on discussing social issues, best supporting answer choice D.

28. **The best answer is F.** Within the third paragraph, *The Sound and the Fury* is referred to as "the painful demise of a distinguished southern family." This most closely matches the tragic downfall of a respected family in both tone and

scope. The other answer choices do not contain anything attributed to that novel by the passage.

29. **The best answer is C.** The end of the third paragraph speaks of the connection between Faulkner's "characters and their counterparts in the real world." This statement implies a linkage between the characters within Faulkner's work and real individuals who exist outside of it. Answer choice C is best supported by that information.

30. **The best answer is J.** The passage repeatedly discusses the literary devices, some of which Faulkner invented, that are central to his craft. He clearly understands what he is doing. Additionally, he is described by the author as being "his own harshest critic"; Faulkner "considered many of his books failures because they did not live up to his high expectations." This speaks directly to his commitment to the craft of writing.

PASSAGE IV

31. **The best answer is B.** The passage begins by connecting the character Yogi Bear and his pursuit of picnic baskets to the idea of real bears gathering food. It continues by stating that, "remarkably enough, bears have been known to seek out food from some unlikely sources" and later speaks of another behavior in which "bears may even vary their sleep cycles." These unique feeding mannerisms are the focus of the passage, and connecting them to a cartoon character leads to a comic portrayal on television. The other answer choices are not supported by the passage.

32. **The best answer is H.** Near the end of the third paragraph it states that bears "maintain vast territories in order to obtain food from a variety of sources." That behavior best supports the idea that they are employing several methods so as to ensure that they have enough food, answer choice H.

33. **The best answer is C.** A close examination of the second paragraph will reveal that although bears will feast on picnic baskets if necessary, it is "on top of their usual diet of berries, insects, and fish." Of those three items, insects are the only available answer choice.

34. **The best answer is G.** In the third paragraph, especially the line following the mention of an acute sense of smell, the passage states, "these sensory talents contribute to the bears' remarkably high intelligence and curiosity, giving them the

ability to open closed containers if they believe food is inside." This connection between closed containers and a sense of smell implies that the bears' sense of smell is very accurate, or sharp. Words such as small, reduced, or abnormal do not fit with an idea of specificity.

35. **The best answer is D.** The passage refers to bears as being intelligent and curious in the third paragraph, when speaking of their sensory abilities contributing to their "remarkably high intelligence and curiosity." The fourth paragraph states that bears are "generally solitary." Solitary does not mean anti-social, as the passage then goes on to explain their feeding relationships with other bears.

36. **The best answer is F.** Throughout the passage the author refers to the feeding habits of bears as being varied and discusses a variety of methods that they use to secure food, such as keeping vast territories, varying their sleep cycles, and creating a hierarchical order. These behaviors are somewhat outside the norm of typical animal behavior, so the author would likely call them resourceful. The other answer choices are not supported by the passage.

37. **The best answer is B.** In the second paragraph, "berries, insects, and fish" are mentioned as the usual bear diet. The end of that paragraph also speaks of campsites as potential feeding grounds. The end of the third paragraph says bears vary their sleep cycles to allow for "feasting on road-side garbage during the day." Although the passage mentions building up "fat stores," it does not suggest that general stores are potential food sources for bears.

38. **The best answer is H.** The third paragraph states specifically that the American black bear "has color vision." The other traits, an acute sense of smell, abnormal sleep patterns, and sensitive lips are used to refer to bears in general, but not mentioned in conjunction with a specific species of bear.

39. **The best answer is B.** The paragraph begins by stating that picnic baskets are eaten by bears "on top of their usual diet," and concludes by saying that the main reason bears wander into campsites looking for food is that it is "generally scarce in the early spring, and consequently they will gladly indulge in any foods that are high in proteins or fats." These two ideas encapsulate the main idea of bears needing to sometimes add human food to their regular diets in order to maintain a healthy weight when food is hard to find.

40. **The best answer is G.** When describing cooperation to procure food, the paragraph mentions that "black bears will create a hierarchical order in situations where paths cross in pursuit of food, so as to assure that all animals remain adequately fed." This statement clearly supports the idea that black bears act as a group, answer choice G.

Science Reasoning Test Explanations

PASSAGE I

1. **The best answer is D.** One difference between Table 1 and Table 2 is that Table 1 only includes phosphate and nitrate concentrations, whereas Table 2 includes phosphate, nitrate, and chlorophyll levels. This information best supports answer choice D. Answer choices A, B, and C can be eliminated because they are not supported by the data.

2. **The best answer is F.** According to Experiment 1, "Scientists suspected that one source of nutrients was a feeder stream which intercepts run-off from farmland where pesticides and animal waste are found." This information suggests that the scientists believed that the high rate of eutrophication was caused by the run-off from the farmland, which best supports answer choice F. Answer choice G and J can be eliminated because they contain information not present in Experiment 1. Answer choice H is incorrect because scientists believed that the eutrophication process was accelerated, not hindered, by farmland run-off.

3. **The best answer is C.** The best way to answer this question is by the process of elimination. Experiment 2 suggests that one of the reasons for the high eutrophication rate was the fertilizers used on a nearby golf course. According to the results of Experiment 2, if the amount of fertilizer used was decreased, the concentration of phosphates and nitrates would also be decreased. Answer choice A can be eliminated.

    Experiment 1 suggests that the reason for the high eutrophication rate is the use of pesticides on the farmland near the lake. If the use of pesticides was decreased, the eutrophication rate would likely decrease as well. Answer choice B can be eliminated.

    Increasing the number of farms on the lake could lead to increased fertilizer and animal waste entering the lake, which would **not** reduce eutrophication; answer choice C is correct.

    A filtration system would filter out the harmful nutrients and limit their concentration in the lake. Answer choice D can be eliminated.

4. **The best answer is H.** Table 2 shows the chlorophyll, phosphate, and nitrate concentrations at three distances from the lake on different days. According to the passage, fertilizer was applied on day three. On day four, the chlorophyll levels increased only slightly. This information best

supports answer choice H. The remaining answer choices are all true based on the data in Table 2.

5. **The best answer is A.** The question says, "Scientists suspect that leakage from sewage systems carrying wastewater from the houses on the lake also contributes to nutrient deposits in the lake." This suggests that the groundwater around the sewage systems contains the harmful nutrients phosphate and nitrate. In order to test this, you would want to test for phosphate and nitrate in samples of groundwater near the sewage system, answer choice A. The other answer choices are not relevant to the question.

6. **The best answer is J.** Table 2 shows the concentration of phosphate from different days at 0 meters, 100 meters, and 200 meters away from the golf course. To answer this question, you must find the average phosphate concentrations from each distance, as follows:

$$0 \text{ m}: \left(\frac{35.6+42.3+46.9+57.0}{4}\right)=45.45 \text{ mg/L}$$

$$100 \text{ m}: \left(\frac{31.8+29.4+30.1+37.9}{4}\right)=32.30 \text{ mg/L}$$

$$200 \text{ m}: \left(\frac{25.3+24.6+25.5+24.2}{4}\right)=24.9 \text{ mg/L}$$

As the distance away from the golf course increases, the phosphate concentration decreases. The only answer choice with a concentration less than 24.9 mg/L is answer choice J.

PASSAGE II

7. **The best answer is B.** Table 1 provides information on the percentage of different minerals in the soil samples. Soil sample 3 was composed of 25% sand, 35% clay, and 40% silt. Clay and silt made up most of this soil sample; therefore answer choice B is correct.

8. **The best answer is F.** Looking at the last row in Table 1, you can see the percentage of three different minerals in Sample 5. Sample 5 is made up of 55% sand, 30% clay, and 15% silt. In this sample, there is more sand (55%) than silt (15%). This information supports answer choice F.

9. **The best answer is C.** Table 2 provides information on the size range of the three different mineral particles that were tested for in the soil. An average mineral particle size of 1.3 millimeters lies within the range 2.0–0.06 millimeters, the size range for sand. Table 1 provides information

on the composition of the different soil samples. Out of Samples 2, 3, 4 and 5, Sample 4 has the highest percent composition of sand (60%). This information best supports answer choice C.

10. **The best answer is H.** The sixth soil sample was collected from a location near sample 4. According to Table 1, Sample 4 is composed mostly of sand (60%). Sand, according to Table 2, ranges in size from 0.06 to 2.0 millimeters. Therefore, most of the mineral particles would be larger than 0.06 mm, answer choice H.

11. **The best answer is D.** According to Table 1, Sample 2 is made mostly of clay (75%). Table 2 shows that clay particles are less than 0.002 millimeters in size. The only answer choice with a size of less than 0.002 millimeters is answer choice D.

PASSAGE III

12. **The best answer is H.** According to Hypothesis 2, "The material that composes the asteroids is similar to that of the terrestrial planets." This information best supports answer choice H. Answer choices F and J can be eliminated because they contain information not discussed in Hypothesis 2.

13. **The best answer is A.** According to Hypothesis 1, "The velocity of collisions in the early solar system was at one time high enough to break apart planets as they formed." This suggests that the asteroid belt formed when the planets were forming, answer choice A. Answer choice C can be eliminated because it is irrelevant to Hypothesis 1.

14. **The best answer is G.** The question states that the asteroid belt "contained dense formations of ice and debris slightly bigger than current asteroids." If the formations were larger than they are presently, they would have had to decrease after the asteroid belt was formed, which best supports answer choice G.

15. **The best answer is D.** Observation 3 states "Asteroids are largely composed of silicate, with some deposits of iron and nickel" and, "Some asteroids also contain carbon and other elements." This is the only observation that discusses the material composition of the asteroids, as it relates to the composition of the terrestrial planets.

16. **The best answer is J.** Hypotheses 1, 2, 3, and 4 indicate that the material located near Jupiter's orbit, inside the Kuiper belt, are asteroids. Therefore, supporters of all four hypotheses would most likely agree with answer choice J.

17. **The best answer is C.** According to Observation 3, "Asteroids are largely composed of silicate, with some deposits of iron and nickel, a composition proportionately similar to that of the terrestrial planets." This suggests that the composition of the asteroids is the same as that of the terrestrial planets. The correct answer is answer choice C, which has the same proportion as the question.

18. **The best answer is J.** The best way to answer this question is to plug each statement into the hypothesis to see if it fits with the information presented. Answer choice F and G can be eliminated, because their topics are not talked about in Hypothesis 1, which says, "the asteroids are most likely the result of a partially formed planet that broke apart and became trapped in an orbit between Mars and Jupiter." In order for the asteroid to become trapped in an orbit between Mars and Jupiter, both Mars and Jupiter must have already formed. This information supports answer choice J.

PASSAGE IV

19. **The best answer is D.** You are given that CO_2 is a by-product of the fermentation process. Therefore, the test tube with the highest level of fermentation after 1 day will be the test tube with the highest CO_2 level after 1 day.

20. **The best answer is F.** In Experiment 1, "Five test tubes are filled with 0.4 grams of yeast and various molasses concentrations." In every test tube, there were 0.4 grams of yeast, meaning the amount of yeast was controlled.

21. **The best answer is D.** The best way to answer this question is by the process of elimination. Answer choice A is incorrect because 0.4 grams of yeast were added to each of the eight test tubes. Answer choice B is incorrect because a 15% sucrose solution was added to each test tube. Answer choice C is incorrect because the experimental treatment was not applied in test tube 8. Only answer choice D represents a weakness in the design of the experiment, as different nutrient combinations could yield different results.

22. **The best answer is F.** Table 1 shows that yeast produced the greatest carbon dioxide levels when grown in a 15% sucrose solution. The other answer choices are not supported by the data.

23. **The best answer is A.** You are given that CO_2 is a by-product of the fermentation process.

While Experiment 1 used molasses, Experiment 2 used pure sucrose dilutions, which yielded higher overall CO_2 levels in each test tube. The data suggest that pure sucrose is more effective at inducing fermentation in yeast than is molasses.

24. **The best answer is F.** In Experiments 1, 2, and 3, the amount of yeast was controlled. In order to determine which conditions produce the most efficient growth of yeast, scientists should vary the amount of yeast in the experiment, answer choice F. Answer choice J can be eliminated because this experiment has already been completed. Answer choices G and H are not supported by the information presented in the passage.

PASSAGE V

25. **The best answer is B.** Figure 1 shows the four life stages of the *Tenebrio molitor* beetle. According to the graph, the beetle spends at least 20 days in the larval stage.

26. **The best answer is F.** According to Table 1, the average larval sizes of the four colonies vary, as do the average adult sizes of the four colonies. Because there is no direct relationship between larval size and the adult size, the larval size must not have any effect on the final adult size of the beetle, answer choice F.

27. **The best answer is D.** According to Figure 1, the maximum time that the *Tenebrio molitor* beetle can be in the egg stage is approximately 7.5 days. The maximum time the beetle can be in the pupa stage is approximately 10 days. Therefore, the beetle specimen cannot be in either of these two stages, so eliminate answer choices A and B. The beetle can be in either the larval or adult stage, answer choice D.

28. **The best answer is G.** According to Table 1, *T. molitor* larvae that are fed carrots spend an average of 39.4 days in the larval stage, whereas *T. molitor* larvae that are fed apples spend an average of 36.9 days in the larval stage. The other answer choices are not supported by the data in Table 1.

29. **The best answer is D.** To answer this question, you must consider the information in Table 1. The question says to assume the fifth colony behaved similarly to the other colonies raised on whole grains. This implies that you must average the size of the adult beetles that were fed oat and wheat

as follows: $\dfrac{(20.6 + 21.3)}{2} = 20.95$ millimeters. Answer choice D is closest to this answer and is, therefore, the correct answer choice.

PASSAGE VI

30. **The best answer is H.** According to Experiment 2, "in samples with a wide variety of particle sizes, the porosity was generally lower. Also, the presence of contaminants such as clay or silt negatively affected the porosity." This information suggests that a rock with uniform particle sizes and a low concentration of contaminants will have a high porosity percentage, as indicated in answer choice H. Answer choices F, G, and J can be eliminated because the experiment states "neither density nor particle size affected the porosity."

31. **The best answer is B.** The results of Experiment 2 show that as the uniformity of the particle size increases, so does the porosity. In other words, there is a direct relationship between uniformity and porosity. The results also show that particle size has little to do with porosity, so this information can be ignored. If a sample rock has a high level of uniformity, the porosity of the rock will likely be high, answer choice B.

32. **The best answer is H.** The results of Experiment 2 show that as the particle uniformity increases, so does the porosity of the rock. This relationship is best described as direct, answer choice H.

33. **The best answer is B.** Table 1 shows the results of Experiment 1. If the company wants to create a large oil reserve, it is best to choose a rock with a high porosity, so more oil can be stored in the rock. The rock type with the highest porosity in Experiment 1 was shale (23%).

34. **The best answer is F.** The data in Table 1 shows that as time increases, each of the rock samples increases in weight, suggesting that the samples continue to absorb water as they soak. According to the passage, rocks become fully saturated when they can no longer absorb any more water. Therefore, there is a direct relationship between time and saturation, which is indicated by the graph in answer choice F.

35. **The best answer is A.** The results from Experiment 2 show that density does not affect the porosity of the rock. Therefore, answer choice A is not consistent with the data presented.

PASSAGE VII

36. The best answer is H. According to Figure 2, the only compound that is only located in the moderate stage is carbonite, answer choice H. Answer choice J can be immediately eliminated because hydrogen is found in fossils at all stages.

37. The best answer is D. To answer this question, you must locate the Fauna H area on Figure 1. Fauna H forms at a range of 0–350°C and 14–18 psi. The only answer choice that falls within this range is answer choice D. Notice that you only had to observe the pressure conditions to locate the correct answer.

38. The best answer is F. In Figure 1, as the depth increases (going down the left side of the graph), pressure also increases (going down the right side of the graph); this information best supports answer choice F.

39. The best answer is A. Figure 2 shows the characteristic compounds that may be found in fossils at a given stage. Hydrogen appears in fossils at all stages, and therefore, will not be helpful in determining a fossil's stage; this information best supports answer choice A.

40. The best answer is J. *Cast fossils* are formed at high temperature and low pressures. According to Figure 1, the different faunas that form under these conditions are Faunas G, A, and F. The only one of these faunas that is listed in the answer choices is Fauna F, answer choice J.

Writing Test Explanation

Because grading the essay is subjective, we've chosen not to include any "graded" essays here. Your best bet is to have someone you trust, such as your personal tutor, read your essays and give you an honest critique. If you plan on grading your own essays, review the grading criteria and be as honest as possible regarding the structure, development, organization, technique, and appropriateness of your writing. Focus on your weak areas and continue to practice in order to improve your writing skills.

■■■ **ANSWER SHEET**

ACT PRACTICE TEST 4
Answer Sheet

ENGLISH

1 Ⓐ Ⓑ Ⓒ Ⓓ	21 Ⓐ Ⓑ Ⓒ Ⓓ	41 Ⓐ Ⓑ Ⓒ Ⓓ	61 Ⓐ Ⓑ Ⓒ Ⓓ
2 Ⓕ Ⓖ Ⓗ Ⓙ	22 Ⓕ Ⓖ Ⓗ Ⓙ	42 Ⓕ Ⓖ Ⓗ Ⓙ	62 Ⓕ Ⓖ Ⓗ Ⓙ
3 Ⓐ Ⓑ Ⓒ Ⓓ	23 Ⓐ Ⓑ Ⓒ Ⓓ	43 Ⓐ Ⓑ Ⓒ Ⓓ	63 Ⓐ Ⓑ Ⓒ Ⓓ
4 Ⓕ Ⓖ Ⓗ Ⓙ	24 Ⓕ Ⓖ Ⓗ Ⓙ	44 Ⓕ Ⓖ Ⓗ Ⓙ	64 Ⓕ Ⓖ Ⓗ Ⓙ
5 Ⓐ Ⓑ Ⓒ Ⓓ	25 Ⓐ Ⓑ Ⓒ Ⓓ	45 Ⓐ Ⓑ Ⓒ Ⓓ	65 Ⓐ Ⓑ Ⓒ Ⓓ
6 Ⓕ Ⓖ Ⓗ Ⓙ	26 Ⓕ Ⓖ Ⓗ Ⓙ	46 Ⓕ Ⓖ Ⓗ Ⓙ	66 Ⓕ Ⓖ Ⓗ Ⓙ
7 Ⓐ Ⓑ Ⓒ Ⓓ	27 Ⓐ Ⓑ Ⓒ Ⓓ	47 Ⓐ Ⓑ Ⓒ Ⓓ	67 Ⓐ Ⓑ Ⓒ Ⓓ
8 Ⓕ Ⓖ Ⓗ Ⓙ	28 Ⓕ Ⓖ Ⓗ Ⓙ	48 Ⓕ Ⓖ Ⓗ Ⓙ	68 Ⓕ Ⓖ Ⓗ Ⓙ
9 Ⓐ Ⓑ Ⓒ Ⓓ	29 Ⓐ Ⓑ Ⓒ Ⓓ	49 Ⓐ Ⓑ Ⓒ Ⓓ	69 Ⓐ Ⓑ Ⓒ Ⓓ
10 Ⓕ Ⓖ Ⓗ Ⓙ	30 Ⓕ Ⓖ Ⓗ Ⓙ	50 Ⓕ Ⓖ Ⓗ Ⓙ	70 Ⓕ Ⓖ Ⓗ Ⓙ
11 Ⓐ Ⓑ Ⓒ Ⓓ	31 Ⓐ Ⓑ Ⓒ Ⓓ	51 Ⓐ Ⓑ Ⓒ Ⓓ	71 Ⓐ Ⓑ Ⓒ Ⓓ
12 Ⓕ Ⓖ Ⓗ Ⓙ	32 Ⓕ Ⓖ Ⓗ Ⓙ	52 Ⓕ Ⓖ Ⓗ Ⓙ	72 Ⓕ Ⓖ Ⓗ Ⓙ
13 Ⓐ Ⓑ Ⓒ Ⓓ	33 Ⓐ Ⓑ Ⓒ Ⓓ	53 Ⓐ Ⓑ Ⓒ Ⓓ	73 Ⓐ Ⓑ Ⓒ Ⓓ
14 Ⓕ Ⓖ Ⓗ Ⓙ	34 Ⓕ Ⓖ Ⓗ Ⓙ	54 Ⓕ Ⓖ Ⓗ Ⓙ	74 Ⓕ Ⓖ Ⓗ Ⓙ
15 Ⓐ Ⓑ Ⓒ Ⓓ	35 Ⓐ Ⓑ Ⓒ Ⓓ	55 Ⓐ Ⓑ Ⓒ Ⓓ	75 Ⓐ Ⓑ Ⓒ Ⓓ
16 Ⓕ Ⓖ Ⓗ Ⓙ	36 Ⓕ Ⓖ Ⓗ Ⓙ	56 Ⓕ Ⓖ Ⓗ Ⓙ	
17 Ⓐ Ⓑ Ⓒ Ⓓ	37 Ⓐ Ⓑ Ⓒ Ⓓ	57 Ⓐ Ⓑ Ⓒ Ⓓ	
18 Ⓕ Ⓖ Ⓗ Ⓙ	38 Ⓕ Ⓖ Ⓗ Ⓙ	58 Ⓕ Ⓖ Ⓗ Ⓙ	
19 Ⓐ Ⓑ Ⓒ Ⓓ	39 Ⓐ Ⓑ Ⓒ Ⓓ	59 Ⓐ Ⓑ Ⓒ Ⓓ	
20 Ⓕ Ⓖ Ⓗ Ⓙ	40 Ⓕ Ⓖ Ⓗ Ⓙ	60 Ⓕ Ⓖ Ⓗ Ⓙ	

MATHEMATICS

1 Ⓐ Ⓑ Ⓒ Ⓓ Ⓔ	16 Ⓕ Ⓖ Ⓗ Ⓙ Ⓚ	31 Ⓐ Ⓑ Ⓒ Ⓓ Ⓔ	46 Ⓕ Ⓖ Ⓗ Ⓙ Ⓚ
2 Ⓕ Ⓖ Ⓗ Ⓙ Ⓚ	17 Ⓐ Ⓑ Ⓒ Ⓓ Ⓔ	32 Ⓕ Ⓖ Ⓗ Ⓙ Ⓚ	47 Ⓐ Ⓑ Ⓒ Ⓓ Ⓔ
3 Ⓐ Ⓑ Ⓒ Ⓓ Ⓔ	18 Ⓕ Ⓖ Ⓗ Ⓙ Ⓚ	33 Ⓐ Ⓑ Ⓒ Ⓓ Ⓔ	48 Ⓕ Ⓖ Ⓗ Ⓙ Ⓚ
4 Ⓕ Ⓖ Ⓗ Ⓙ Ⓚ	19 Ⓐ Ⓑ Ⓒ Ⓓ Ⓔ	34 Ⓕ Ⓖ Ⓗ Ⓙ Ⓚ	49 Ⓐ Ⓑ Ⓒ Ⓓ Ⓔ
5 Ⓐ Ⓑ Ⓒ Ⓓ Ⓔ	20 Ⓕ Ⓖ Ⓗ Ⓙ Ⓚ	35 Ⓐ Ⓑ Ⓒ Ⓓ Ⓔ	50 Ⓕ Ⓖ Ⓗ Ⓙ Ⓚ
6 Ⓕ Ⓖ Ⓗ Ⓙ Ⓚ	21 Ⓐ Ⓑ Ⓒ Ⓓ Ⓔ	36 Ⓕ Ⓖ Ⓗ Ⓙ Ⓚ	51 Ⓐ Ⓑ Ⓒ Ⓓ Ⓔ
7 Ⓐ Ⓑ Ⓒ Ⓓ Ⓔ	22 Ⓕ Ⓖ Ⓗ Ⓙ Ⓚ	37 Ⓐ Ⓑ Ⓒ Ⓓ Ⓔ	52 Ⓕ Ⓖ Ⓗ Ⓙ Ⓚ
8 Ⓕ Ⓖ Ⓗ Ⓙ Ⓚ	23 Ⓐ Ⓑ Ⓒ Ⓓ Ⓔ	38 Ⓕ Ⓖ Ⓗ Ⓙ Ⓚ	53 Ⓐ Ⓑ Ⓒ Ⓓ Ⓔ
9 Ⓐ Ⓑ Ⓒ Ⓓ Ⓔ	24 Ⓕ Ⓖ Ⓗ Ⓙ Ⓚ	39 Ⓐ Ⓑ Ⓒ Ⓓ Ⓔ	54 Ⓕ Ⓖ Ⓗ Ⓙ Ⓚ
10 Ⓕ Ⓖ Ⓗ Ⓙ Ⓚ	25 Ⓐ Ⓑ Ⓒ Ⓓ Ⓔ	40 Ⓕ Ⓖ Ⓗ Ⓙ Ⓚ	55 Ⓐ Ⓑ Ⓒ Ⓓ Ⓔ
11 Ⓐ Ⓑ Ⓒ Ⓓ Ⓔ	26 Ⓕ Ⓖ Ⓗ Ⓙ Ⓚ	41 Ⓐ Ⓑ Ⓒ Ⓓ Ⓔ	56 Ⓕ Ⓖ Ⓗ Ⓙ Ⓚ
12 Ⓕ Ⓖ Ⓗ Ⓙ Ⓚ	27 Ⓐ Ⓑ Ⓒ Ⓓ Ⓔ	42 Ⓕ Ⓖ Ⓗ Ⓙ Ⓚ	57 Ⓐ Ⓑ Ⓒ Ⓓ Ⓔ
13 Ⓐ Ⓑ Ⓒ Ⓓ Ⓔ	28 Ⓕ Ⓖ Ⓗ Ⓙ Ⓚ	43 Ⓐ Ⓑ Ⓒ Ⓓ Ⓔ	58 Ⓕ Ⓖ Ⓗ Ⓙ Ⓚ
14 Ⓕ Ⓖ Ⓗ Ⓙ Ⓚ	29 Ⓐ Ⓑ Ⓒ Ⓓ Ⓔ	44 Ⓕ Ⓖ Ⓗ Ⓙ Ⓚ	59 Ⓐ Ⓑ Ⓒ Ⓓ Ⓔ
15 Ⓐ Ⓑ Ⓒ Ⓓ Ⓔ	30 Ⓕ Ⓖ Ⓗ Ⓙ Ⓚ	45 Ⓐ Ⓑ Ⓒ Ⓓ Ⓔ	60 Ⓕ Ⓖ Ⓗ Ⓙ Ⓚ

READING

1 (A)(B)(C)(D)	11 (A)(B)(C)(D)	21 (A)(B)(C)(D)	31 (A)(B)(C)(D)
2 (F)(G)(H)(J)	12 (F)(G)(H)(J)	22 (F)(G)(H)(J)	32 (F)(G)(H)(J)
3 (A)(B)(C)(D)	13 (A)(B)(C)(D)	23 (A)(B)(C)(D)	33 (A)(B)(C)(D)
4 (F)(G)(H)(J)	14 (F)(G)(H)(J)	24 (F)(G)(H)(J)	34 (F)(G)(H)(J)
5 (A)(B)(C)(D)	15 (A)(B)(C)(D)	25 (A)(B)(C)(D)	35 (A)(B)(C)(D)
6 (F)(G)(H)(J)	16 (F)(G)(H)(J)	26 (F)(G)(H)(J)	36 (F)(G)(H)(J)
7 (A)(B)(C)(D)	17 (A)(B)(C)(D)	27 (A)(B)(C)(D)	37 (A)(B)(C)(D)
8 (F)(G)(H)(J)	18 (F)(G)(H)(J)	28 (F)(G)(H)(J)	38 (F)(G)(H)(J)
9 (A)(B)(C)(D)	19 (A)(B)(C)(D)	29 (A)(B)(C)(D)	39 (A)(B)(C)(D)
10 (F)(G)(H)(J)	20 (F)(G)(H)(J)	30 (F)(G)(H)(J)	40 (F)(G)(H)(J)

SCIENCE

1 (A)(B)(C)(D)	11 (A)(B)(C)(D)	21 (A)(B)(C)(D)	31 (A)(B)(C)(D)
2 (F)(G)(H)(J)	12 (F)(G)(H)(J)	22 (F)(G)(H)(J)	32 (F)(G)(H)(J)
3 (A)(B)(C)(D)	13 (A)(B)(C)(D)	23 (A)(B)(C)(D)	33 (A)(B)(C)(D)
4 (F)(G)(H)(J)	14 (F)(G)(H)(J)	24 (F)(G)(H)(J)	34 (F)(G)(H)(J)
5 (A)(B)(C)(D)	15 (A)(B)(C)(D)	25 (A)(B)(C)(D)	35 (A)(B)(C)(D)
6 (F)(G)(H)(J)	16 (F)(G)(H)(J)	26 (F)(G)(H)(J)	36 (F)(G)(H)(J)
7 (A)(B)(C)(D)	17 (A)(B)(C)(D)	27 (A)(B)(C)(D)	37 (A)(B)(C)(D)
8 (F)(G)(H)(J)	18 (F)(G)(H)(J)	28 (F)(G)(H)(J)	38 (F)(G)(H)(J)
9 (A)(B)(C)(D)	19 (A)(B)(C)(D)	29 (A)(B)(C)(D)	39 (A)(B)(C)(D)
10 (F)(G)(H)(J)	20 (F)(G)(H)(J)	30 (F)(G)(H)(J)	40 (F)(G)(H)(J)

RAW SCORES	**SCALE SCORES**	DATE TAKEN:
ENGLISH _____	ENGLISH _____	
MATHEMATICS _____	MATHEMATICS _____	ENGLISH/WRITING _____
READING _____	READING _____	
SCIENCE _____	SCIENCE _____	_____ **COMPOSITE SCORE**

Refer to the Scoring Worksheet on page 314 for help in determining your Raw and Scale Scores.

You may wish to remove these sample answer document pages to respond to the practice ACT Writing Test.

Cut Here

Begin WRITING TEST here.

If you need more space, please continue on the next page.

Do not write in this shaded area.

WRITING TEST

If you need more space, please continue on the back of this page.

Do not write in this shaded area.

Cut Here

WRITING TEST

If you need more space, please continue on the next page.

PLEASE DO NOT WRITE IN THIS AREA.

WRITING TEST

_____

_____

_____

_____

_____

_____

_____

_____

_____

_____

_____

_____

_____

_____

_____

_____

_____

_____

_____

_____

_____

_____

_____

_____

_____

STOP here with the Writing Test.

1 ■ ■ ■ ■ ■ ■ ■ ■ 1

ENGLISH TEST

45 Minutes—75 Questions

DIRECTIONS: In the passages that follow, some words and phrases are underlined and numbered. In the answer column, you will find alternatives for the words and phrases that are underlined. Choose the alternative that you think is best, and fill in the corresponding bubble on your answer sheet. If you think that the original version is best, choose "NO CHANGE," which will always be either answer choice A or F. You will also find questions about a particular section of the passage, or about the entire passage. These questions will be identified either by an underlined portion or by a number in a box. Look for the answer that clearly expresses the idea, is consistent with the style and tone of the passage, and makes the correct use of standard written English. Read the passage through once before answering the questions. For some questions, you should read beyond the indicated portion before you answer.

PASSAGE I

On the Road Again

We drive across the country the way most people might go from home to work and back again to home. I guess you could call us nomads, except for the fact that our trips

have become fairly regular, mostly to Las Vegas, Nevada,

than back to New York, our home for the past 35 years.

My husband and I are retired high school teachers, which means that we have plenty of time to travel. Three of our five children now live west of the Mississippi River. All of our grandchildren live in New York, and we have two large dogs. Therefore, staying in Las Vegas for more than three consecutive weeks is generally enjoyable. And so, we find ourselves back on the road time and time again.

Las Vegas had become our sunshine sanctuary; we have become completely fed up with New York's cold and gloomy winters and are determined to spend as much time

1. **A.** NO CHANGE
   B. to home
   C. back home again
   D. back

2. **F.** NO CHANGE
   G. fair and regular
   H. regularly fair
   J. regular to fair

3. **A.** NO CHANGE
   B. then
   C. and than
   D. and then we go

4. **F.** NO CHANGE
   G. to be traveling
   H. for us to travel
   J. OMIT the underlined portion

5. Which choice would best help establish that the narrator has good reasons for driving back and forth across the country?
   A. NO CHANGE
   B. simplistic
   C. not viable
   D. quite easy

6. **F.** NO CHANGE
   G. became
   H. has became
   J. has become

GO ON TO THE NEXT PAGE.

1 ■ ■ ■ ■ ■ ■ ■ ■ ■ **1**

as possible in the warm sunny West. Moreover, we have
<u>warm sunny</u>
    7

extended family in Nevada, Arizona, Colorado, and

California, so vacationing in Las Vegas makes a lot of

sense for us.

[1] <u>So</u> we have two adopted <u>dogs, both of which are</u>
    8   9

<u>shelter mutts,</u> flying is not an option; we want the dogs
    9

with us and we want to avoid paying boarding fees.

[2] And so, here we are, for the second time this month,

trekking home with our dogs in our extended-cab truck.

[3] Hunter, a lab and spaniel mix, fills his limited space on

the back bench seat, and Lizzie, our elderly pooch, <u>lying</u>
    10

on her special blanket on the floor. [4] They are quiet; they

know the drill. [5] Every few hours they get to jump out of

the truck and sniff out the newest stop. [11]

    Thus far, we <u>have past</u> the Hoover Dam, climbed the
                 12

mountains of Flagstaff, Arizona, crossed the high deserts

of New Mexico and the Texas panhandle, paid <u>our toll's</u> in
                                    13

Oklahoma, and looped around St. Louis, Missouri. After

26 hours on the road, we are a mere seven hours from

home; this will be one of our fastest trips, thanks to

pre-packed turkey sandwiches, fewer stops for gas, good

weather, and audio books.

    The landscape in Missouri is surprisingly snow-free for

the month of January, but the sky is becoming predictably

thick with gray clouds. I'm mentally preparing myself for

---

7. A. NO CHANGE
    B. warm, and, sunny
    C. warm, sunny
    D. warm; sunny

8. F. NO CHANGE
    G. Because
    H. In spite of the fact that
    J. Due to the fact of the matter

9. A. NO CHANGE
    B. dogs both of which are shelter mutts,
    C. dogs both, of which, are shelter mutts
    D. dogs both of which are shelter mutts

10. F. NO CHANGE
    G. lay
    H. lies
    J. was lying

11. For the sake of logic and coherence, Sentence 5 should
    be placed:
    A. where it is now.
    B. before Sentence 1.
    C. after Sentence 3.
    D. after Sentence 2.

12. F. NO CHANGE
    G. are passing
    H. will be past
    J. have passed

13. A. NO CHANGE
    B. our tolls
    C. our tolls,
    D. our tolls'

GO ON TO THE NEXT PAGE.

1 ■ ■ ■ ■ ■ ■ ■ ■ 1

a sunless New York sky during our week at home. [14] But that's okay; it will just reinforce for me the purpose of getting right back on the road in seven days to head back to sunny Las Vegas.

14. The writer is considering deleting the preceding sentence. If the sentence was deleted, the essay would primarily lose:
   F. the writer's focus of the entire essay.
   G. the gravity of the situation that is being discussed in the essay.
   H. a reinforcement of the reason the writer doesn't mind her constant travels.
   J. detail that reiterates why the narrator does not like to live in New York.

> Question 15 asks about the preceding passage as a whole.

15. Suppose the writer had chosen to write a travel article about Las Vegas, Nevada. Would this essay fulfill the writer's goal?
   A. Yes, because the writer expounds on the beautiful weather of Las Vegas and the surrounding areas.
   B. Yes, because the writer clearly gives reasons for leaving New York to go to Las Vegas.
   C. No, because the writer likes Las Vegas only for the warm, sunny weather.
   D. No, because the essay is a personal account of a trip to Las Vegas, and does not highlight any particular features about the city.

PASSAGE II
Listening to a Different Language

Dog obedience training is an important undertaking when <u>one acquires</u> a new dog. This is particularly
                16
important if the dog owner is a social person or plans to

interact with other dogs and <u>the</u> owners. One problem,
                17
however, is that obedience training <u>was</u> a form of one-way
                18
communication from the owner to the dog. Many owners fail to consider that the animal actually communicates back.

Carefully watching a <u>dog</u> movements and facial
                19
expressions reveals a great deal about what a dog is thinking. A dog's forehead, for example, may wrinkle

16. F. NO CHANGE
   G. one's acquiring
   H. one who acquires
   J. it acquires

17. A. NO CHANGE
   B. their
   C. there
   D. they're

18. F. NO CHANGE
   G. can sometimes becoming
   H. is
   J. sometimes is becoming

19. A. NO CHANGE
   B. dogs
   C. dogs'
   D. dog's

GO ON TO THE NEXT PAGE.

1 ■ ■ ■ ■ ■ ■ ■ ■ ■ **1**

when the dog is <u>confused</u> or waiting for a signal from its
20

owner. When the dog wants to play, it might pull <u>the</u> lips
21
back slightly, showing its teeth in a "smile." A relaxed dog

might let its tongue loll out of its mouth, creating a look of

contentment on its face. [22]

Other forms of body language <u>can also indicate</u> which
23
emotion a dog is experiencing. For example, if its ears are

raised, it is probably absorbing the sounds around it.

Shifting its ears back flat against its head demonstrates

submission or fear. [24] A high, wagging tail shows that the

dog is happy and ready to play. If the wagging tail is held

low and taut, however, the dog is probably on guard and

may be ready to pounce. When it feels threatened or

indicates submissiveness, the dog might tuck its tail

between its legs, crouch down, and then roll over onto its

back. <u>Body language and even vocalizations are good</u>
25
<u>indicators of a dog's emotions.</u>
25
[1] While most dogs are capable of learning a variety of

human words and physical <u>signals; training</u> a dog becomes
26
much easier when the owner tries to discern its unique

communication signals. [2] As an owner begins tuning in

20. **F.** NO CHANGE
    G. confusing
    H. confused by some
    J. confused with

21. **A.** NO CHANGE
    B. its
    C. its'
    D. their

22. The author is considering deleting the previous sentence. If the sentence were deleted, the essay would primarily lose:
    F. an example of how a dog communicates with its owner.
    G. support for the author's suggestions regarding the importance of obedience training.
    H. an irrelevant detail.
    J. an important fact about dog anatomy.

23. **A.** NO CHANGE
    B. can do the indicating of
    C. shall be indicative of
    D. can show by indicating

24. Given that all of the following are true, which one, if added here, would provide the most effective support for the statements made in the preceding sentence?
    F. The dog's owner should immediately try to determine what the dog is responding to.
    G. Dogs are often fearful of unusual or unfamiliar situations and people.
    H. It is important to have a dog's hearing assessed by a veterinarian and to check the ears frequently for mites or ticks.
    J. Many purebred dogs have their ears trimmed or clipped in a particular manner to suit their breed.

25. Given that all of the choices are true, which one would most effectively conclude this paragraph?
    A. NO CHANGE
    B. Smaller dogs generally have a higher-pitched bark, while a larger dog usually vocalizes with a much louder and deeper tone.
    C. A yip or whimper indicates some type of pain or discomfort, while a deep bark probably shows more dominance and assertiveness and may be a signal of danger.
    D. Part of obedience training is teaching a dog when it is appropriate to bark and when it isn't.

26. **F.** NO CHANGE
    G. signals, training
    H. signals training
    J. signals and training

GO ON TO THE NEXT PAGE.

1 ■ ■ ■ ■ ■ ■ ■ ■ 1

to his or her dog's body language, he or she may find that the dog responds to movements in addition to verbal commands. [3] For example, when teaching a dog to "come," the owner might find it more effective to crouch down, the owner's back to the dog as its name is called. [4] The dog will interpret this behavior in a more positive light than if the owner leans forward and yells at it to "come." [5] To a dog, a crouching position is more welcoming than a forward-lean, which a dog naturally finds threatening. [6] Dog owners should always have small treats on hand to reward their dog when it obeys a command. [27]

The bottom line, is that there is a great deal more
                          28

involved in communicating with a canine than just
            29
teaching it to come, stay, heel, and fetch. To attain a

strong, two-way relationship, it is best with remembering
                                    30
the importance of non-verbal communication.

27. Which of the following sentences in this paragraph is LEAST relevant to the main focus of the essay and therefore should be deleted?
   A. Sentence 3
   B. Sentence 4
   C. Sentence 5
   D. Sentence 6

28. F. NO CHANGE
   G. line is
   H. line; is
   J. line: is

29. A. NO CHANGE
   B. by communication with
   C. to communicating with
   D. with communication in

30. F. NO CHANGE
   G. best remembering
   H. remembering
   J. best to remember

PASSAGE III

Playing with Piñatas

   While the history of the piñata is somewhat murky. Most scholars believe that the piñata originated in
   31
China and later became popular in Europe. Some historians believe that the modern version of the piñata was created centuries ago in China, where most of them
                                          32
were made to resemble animals. These animal figures were covered with colorful paper and filled with seeds, rather

31. A. NO CHANGE
   B. murky; most
   C. murky most
   D. murky, most

32. F. NO CHANGE
   G. in which most
   H. where, the most
   J. so that most

GO ON TO THE NEXT PAGE.

1 ■ ■ ■ ■ ■ ■ ■ ■ **1**

than candy or toys <u>as is customary today</u>. Once the seeds
₃₃
were spilled, they were gathered and burned as a ritualistic

practice. The ashes of the seeds <u>were in keeping</u> until the
₃₄
end of the year and were thought to bring good luck to

their owners.

  <u>The Italian, explorer, Marco Polo,</u> is probably
₃₅
responsible for bringing the Chinese piñata to Europe. The

piñata quickly became associated with religious

ceremonies and was also used in celebrations. ☐36 Often,

the piñata was made into the shape of a star, which

represented the Star of Bethlehem. During this time in

Italy, the piñata was often made of fragile clay

<u>that broke easily.</u> In fact, the Italian word *pignatta*
₃₇

translates to "fragile pot." The <u>clay pots would be hung</u>
₃₈
from a tree or a pole and a stick would be used to hit the

pot until it broke. The broken pots <u>dispensed of tiny</u>
₃₉
treasures that would fall to the ground, where eager

children and adults would quickly gather them up.

<u>With colorful ribbons and paper, these clay pots could be</u>
₄₀
<u>unadorned or decorated.</u>
₄₀

  In the United States, <u>piñatas'</u> are generally made either
₄₁
of papier-mache or a cardboard-type material. American

piñatas come in almost every shape and design imaginable.

33. A. NO CHANGE
  B. like they do today
  C. which is the standard customary way today
  D. OMIT the underlined portion.

34. F. NO CHANGE
  G. were kept
  H. by being kept
  J. are keeping

35. A. NO CHANGE
  B. The Italian explorer Marco Polo
  C. The Italian explorer, Marco Polo
  D. The Italian explorer, Marco Polo,

36. At this point, the author is considering adding the
  following sentence:

  Europeans celebrate many historic events.

  Would this be a logical and relevant addition to
  the essay?
  F. Yes, because Europeans use piñatas during their
  celebrations.
  G. Yes, because historic events are important.
  H. No, because the essay focuses on piñatas, not on
  historic events.
  J. No, because the essay does not say that Europeans
  use piñatas.

37. A. NO CHANGE
  B. breaking easily
  C. that was easy to break
  D. OMIT the underlined portion.

38. F. NO CHANGE
  G. clay pots, would be hung
  H. clay pots would have been hanging
  J. clay pots, hanging

39. A. NO CHANGE
  B. dispensed
  C. dispensing
  D. dispense

40. F. NO CHANGE
  G. With colorful ribbons and paper, these clay pots
  could be unadorned or decorated.
  H. These clay pots could be unadorned or decorated
  with colorful ribbons and paper.
  J. With colorful ribbons these clay pots could be
  unadorned or decorated with paper.

41. A. NO CHANGE
  B. piñata's
  C. piñatas
  D. piñata

GO ON TO THE NEXT PAGE.

1 ■ ■ ■ ■ ■ ■ ■ ■ **1**

Every holiday has their own host of possible choices and
42

themes. In America, baseball bats are the preferred tool
43
used to break open the piñata. In general, using a baseball

bat should make it simple to break open the piñata, laden
44
with pounds of candy and toys; however, each person

attempting the feat is first blind-folded and then spun

around several times, which presents a challenge.

Onlookers will generally try to help the participant by

offering suggestions, but the audience most enjoys
45
watching the blindfolded person swing mightily at nothing
45
but thin air. Everyone wins when the broken piñata spills

its contents, and onlookers scramble to collect the fun

surprises.

42. **F.** NO CHANGE
    G. its
    H. they're
    J. it's

43. **A.** NO CHANGE
    B. In America baseball bats
    C. In America baseball, bats,
    D. In America, baseball, bats

44. Which of the following alternatives would NOT be
    appropriate?
    F. filled
    G. packed
    H. loaded
    J. barren

45. **A.** NO CHANGE
    B. but the audience watching the blindfolded person
       most enjoys
    C. watching the blindfolded person, but the audience
       most enjoys
    D. most enjoyed by the audience is watching the
       blindfolded person

PASSAGE IV

A Gift From the Heart

Contrary to advertisements seen on television, read,
46

in magazines, or heard on the radio, having spent a lot
46   47
of money on a gift for a friend or loved one is totally
47

unnecessary. Many people collect photos or mementos
48
from special events, trips, or celebrations throughout their

lives, throwing them in a drawer or cardboard box

somewhere, intending to sort them out later. It seems,

though, that "later" never comes. So, the next time

you're ready to plop down a plastic credit card for a silk
49
scarf or pair of leather gloves for that special someone

46. **F.** NO CHANGE
    G. television read in magazines
    H. television; read in magazines
    J. television, read in magazines,

47. **A.** NO CHANGE
    B. having to spend a lot of money
    C. to have to spend a lot of money
    D. spending a lot of money

48. **F.** NO CHANGE
    G. Many people, collect
    H. Many people collecting
    J. Many people, who collect

49. **A.** NO CHANGE
    B. your ready
    C. you, will be ready
    D. you, being ready,

GO ON TO THE NEXT PAGE.

1 ▪ ▪ ▪ ▪ ▪ ▪ ▪ ▪ 1

whom you care about, consider sorting through that junk
                 50

drawer filled of trinkets and special photos.
         51

[1] For example, you can decorate an inexpensive

picture frame with colorful buttons for your seamstress

mother, or you can use nuts and bolts for your
                52

workshop-crazed brother. [2] Shadow boxes are also a

wonderful way to display several objects from a single

special event, such as a wedding. [3] Inserting a

special photo of you and that certain someone will

create a gift that will be treasured forever. [4] Take the

original wedding invitation, a candy favor, and
                                            53

a dried flower from the table centerpiece, a napkin,

or anything else that you can gather from
                                    54

the wedding. [55]

When you have many photos and mementos, making a
                                      56

photo album or scrapbook for a friend or family member.

Today, the options for embellishing your book

are near to be endless. Entering a scrapbooking store can
57

make your head spin. If some happens to you on your first
              58

scrapbooking venture, consider taking an introductory

---

50. **F.** NO CHANGE
    G. who is important to you
    H. who means a lot to you
    J. OMIT the underlined portion.

51. **A.** NO CHANGE
    B. filled with
    C. full with
    D. filling with

52. **F.** NO CHANGE
    G. you can also use
    H. use
    J. also you can use

53. **A.** NO CHANGE
    B. or
    C. as well as
    D. OMIT the underlined portion.

54. **F.** NO CHANGE
    G. gather or take from
    H. get together and take
    J. gather up and take with you

55. Which of the following sequences of sentences makes
    this paragraph most logical?
    A. NO CHANGE
    B. 1, 3, 2, 4
    C. 2, 3, 4, 1
    D. 1, 2, 4, 3

56. **F.** NO CHANGE
    G. mementos, make
    H. mementos make,
    J. mementos to make

57. **A.** NO CHANGE
    B. are near endless
    C. are nearly to be endless
    D. are nearly endless

58. **F.** NO CHANGE
    G. when it
    H. this
    J. so

GO ON TO THE NEXT PAGE.

1 ■ ■ ■ ■ ■ ■ ■ ■ 1

class, which many stores offer. <u>Of course, you will</u>
₅₉
<u>have a much better idea of which scrapbook supplies</u>
₅₉
<u>to buy when the class ends.</u>
₅₉

Pictures or books that can be enjoyed over and over again are one-of-a-kind, original gifts. There is nothing like receiving a gift that comes straight from the heart. Such gifts help people recall happy times and solidify the bond between the giver and the receiver. ⑥⓪

59. Given that all of the choices are true, which one would best conclude the paragraph while providing the reader with the most specific and detailed information about why store owners offer introductory classes?
A. NO CHANGE
B. Most craft stores publish detailed class schedules with a plethora of sessions from which to choose.
C. If you enroll in an instructional class at a craft store, you might receive discounts or coupons to use at local businesses.
D. There you will learn how to use pinking shears, picture cut-outs, lettering, and stickers.

60. At this point, the writer is considering adding the following sentence:

Many people enjoy original gifts.

Should the writer make this addition here?
F. Yes, because it reiterates the notion that gift-giving is a rewarding experience.
G. Yes, because no gift is as good as a homemade gift.
H. No, because the writer is giving a personal opinion contrary to the rest of the essay.
J. No, because it is redundant information.

PASSAGE V

> The following paragraphs may or may not be in the most logical order. You may be asked questions about the logical order of the paragraphs, as well as where to place sentences logically within any given paragraph.

Strides Toward Safety

[1]

Automotive engineers all over the world are responsible for designing and <u>redesigning, special</u> features for the
₆₁
newest car models. These engineers also know that it is necessary to consider safety issues in all new designs. Statistics consistently indicate that car <u>accidents occur</u>
₆₂
<u>more often</u> during the night than during the day. These
₆₂

statistics <u>takes into account</u> that there are fewer drivers on
₆₃
the road at night.

61. **A.** NO CHANGE
B. redesigning; special
C. redesigning: special
D. redesigning special

62. Given that all of the choices are true, which one would provide the most detailed and relevant information at this point in the essay?
F. NO CHANGE
G. accidents occur more frequently
H. accidents can
J. accidents occur about three times more often

63. **A.** NO CHANGE
B. take into account
C. taken into account for
D. taking into account

GO ON TO THE NEXT PAGE.

1 ■ ■ ■ ■ ■ ■ ■ ■ 1

[2]

64 One such design employs headlights that swivel back and forth, allowing the driver to see the road ahead more

clearly by illumination of the sides of the road better than
            65

traditional headlamps. Automatic high-beam headlights is
                                                        66
another innovative design that could improve the driver's

reaction time. All cars have been equipped with high-beam

headlight switches for many years, most drivers do not use
            67

their high-beams even when they would provide a great
                                68
deal more light on the road. Switching back and forth from

high-beam to low-beam lights

proving to be a nuisance to many drivers, especially when
69
another car is coming straight towards them. Therefore,

some car manufacturers now provide a system whereby a

device detects when the high-beams should be on and

when they should be off, and the change is made

automatically.

[3]

[1] Two other systems that are being developed to
                                              70
potentially increase safety on the road at night, the NIR
                    70
(or Near-Infrared) system and the FIR (or Far-Infrared)

system. [2] In the NIR system, an infrared light is emitted

from the front of the vehicle when nearby objects such as

64. Which of the following sentences would most effectively introduce the subject of this paragraph and act as a transition from the preceding paragraph?
  F. In an effort to improve driver and pedestrian safety, auto engineers often come up with ingenious designs.
  G. Headlights are probably the single most important feature of a car for night driving, so they should always be kept in proper working order.
  H. Car manufacturers compete on a daily basis to find the brightest and most accomplished design engineers.
  J. Some of the designs that car engineers come up with are beyond futuristic.

65. A. NO CHANGE
  B. and they illuminate
  C. by illuminating
  D. and, in addition, they illuminate

66. F. NO CHANGE
  G. are
  H. they are
  J. were

67. A. NO CHANGE
  B. switches for many years;
  C. switches for many years
  D. switches, for many years

68. F. NO CHANGE
  G. it
  H. doing so
  J. by doing it, it

69. A. NO CHANGE
  B. prove
  C. will prove
  D. proves

70. F. NO CHANGE
  G. Two other systems are being developed that will potentially make driving at night safer:
  H. Two other systems are being developed which will potentially increase night safety on the road,
  J. There are two other systems being developed on the road for night safety that will potentially increase driving safety, these being

GO ON TO THE NEXT PAGE.

1 ■ ■ ■ ■ ■ ■ ■ ■ **1**

animals or people are detected. [3] Images will display on
a screen in front of the driver who can then respond
appropriately. [4] The FIR system measures the heat
radiation of nearby objects and flashes the images on the
driver's screen. [72] [5] Even as car makers work diligently

to improve safety on the road particularly during dangerous
nighttime driving, no device can replace the vigilance and
skill of the driver. [6] More advanced technologies might
improve safety, but the person in the driver's seat plays the
most critical role in reducing night-driving incidents.

71. **A.** NO CHANGE
    B. are displayed
    C. displayed
    D. are displaying

72. For the sake of the logic and coherence of this
    paragraph, Sentence 5 should be placed:
    F. after Sentence 1.
    G. after Sentence 6.
    H. before Sentence 4.
    J. before Sentence 3.

73. **A.** NO CHANGE
    B. road particularly, during,
    C. road particularly during,
    D. road, particularly during

74. **F.** NO CHANGE
    G. safety, but, the
    H. safety but the
    J. safety but, the

Question 75 asks about the preceding passage as a whole.

---

75. The writer wishes to add the following sentence in
    order to show that car manufacturers are concerned
    with safety issues.

    While many of these accidents are related to driver
    fatigue and drunk driving, the inherent hazards
    of driving in the dark are important factors to be
    considered in any design initiative.

    The new sentence would best support and be placed:
    A. at the beginning of the essay.
    B. at the end of Paragraph 1.
    C. at the end of Paragraph 2.
    D. at the end of Paragraph 3.

END OF THE ENGLISH TEST.
STOP! IF YOU HAVE TIME LEFT OVER, CHECK YOUR WORK ON THIS SECTION ONLY.

2 △ △ △ △ △ △ △ △ **2**

MATHEMATICS TEST

60 Minutes—60 Questions

DIRECTIONS: Solve each of the problems in the time allowed, then fill in the corresponding bubble on your answer sheet. Do not spend too much time on any one problem; skip the more difficult problems and go back to them later.

You may use a calculator on this test. For this test you should assume that figures are NOT necessarily drawn to scale, that all geometric figures lie in a plane, and that the word *line* is used to indicate a straight line.

DO YOUR FIGURING HERE.

1. One foot is equivalent to approximately 0.3048 meters. If a building is 65-feet long, what is the length of the building in meters, to the nearest tenth?
   A. 19.8
   B. 31.1
   C. 65.3
   D. 198.1
   E. 213.3

2. To keep up with rising costs, a carpenter needs to increase his $30.00 per hour rate by 18%. What will be his new hourly rate?
   F. $30.18
   G. $31.80
   H. $35.40
   J. $38.00
   K. $48.00

3. Contributions to the school dance fund are made by each of 4 student groups according to the table below.

Student group	A	B	C	D
Contribution in dollars	25	40	30	15

   What is the average dollar amount of the contributions made by the 4 student groups?
   A. $110.00
   B. $55.00
   C. $35.00
   D. $27.50
   E. $22.50

4. Bus X travels 40 miles per hour for 2 hours; Bus Y travels 60 miles per hour for $1\frac{1}{2}$ hours. What is the difference, in miles, between the number of miles traveled by Bus X and the number of miles traveled by Bus Y?
   F. 10
   G. 20
   H. 50
   J. 80
   K. 90

GO ON TO THE NEXT PAGE.

2   △ △ **2**

5. Which of the following is a value of r for which $(r + 2)(r - 3) = 0$?
  A. 6
  B. 0
  C. −2
  D. −3
  E. −6

6. In the parallelogram $PQRS$ shown below, PS is 7 centimeters long. If the parallelogram's perimeter is 40 centimeters, how many centimeters long is PQ?

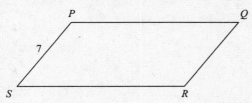

  F. 49
  G. 21
  H. 13
  J. 10
  K. 5.7

7. In the standard (x, y) coordinate plane, if the x-coordinate of each point on a line is 5 more than half the y-coordinate, what is the slope of the line?
  A. −5
  B. $-\dfrac{1}{2}$
  C. $\dfrac{1}{2}$
  D. 2
  E. 5

8. A rectangular garden has a length of x and a width of y. The garden has its length reduced by 3 feet and its width extended by 2 feet. What is the area of the new garden?
  F. $x + y$
  G. $(x - 3)(y - 2)$
  H. $(x + 3)(y + 2)$
  J. $(x - 3)(y + 2)$
  K. $(x + 3)(y - 2)$

9. If $x = 3yz^2$, what is y in terms of x and z?
  A. $\dfrac{x}{3z^2}$
  B. $3xz^2$
  C. $\left(\dfrac{1}{3}\right)xz^2$
  D. $\dfrac{z^2 y}{3x}$
  E. $\dfrac{\sqrt{x}}{3z}$

DO YOUR FIGURING HERE.

GO ON TO THE NEXT PAGE.

2   △ △ △ **2**

10. In the figure below, what is the measure of $\angle\alpha$?

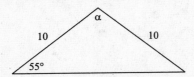

   F. $20°$
   G. $55°$
   H. $70°$
   J. $75°$
   K. $110°$

11. Which of the following is the product of $(3x^2 - 1)(x^2 - 4)$?
   A. $3x^4 + 13x^2 + 4$
   B. $3x^4 + 5$
   C. $3x^4 - 13x^2 + 4$
   D. $3x^4 - 12x^2 + 4$
   E. $3x^4 + 12x^2 + 4$

12. In the standard (x, y) coordinate plane, if a square has the vertices $(-2,-3)$, $(2,-3)$, and $(2,1)$, what is the set of coordinates for the final vertex?
   F. $(2,-1)$
   G. $(1,-2)$
   H. $(-1,2)$
   J. $(-2,-1)$
   K. $(-2,1)$

13. Reduce $\dfrac{x^8 y^{12}}{x^4 y^3 z^2}$ to its simplest terms.
   A. $\dfrac{x^2 y^4}{z^2}$

   B. $\dfrac{x^4 y^9}{z^2}$

   C. $x^4 y^9 z^2$

   D. $x^2 y^{12} z^2$

   E. $\dfrac{x^2 y^9}{z^2}$

14. Which of the following is a value of n that satisfies $\log_n 64 = 2$?
   F. 4
   G. 6
   H. 8
   J. 12
   K. 32

DO YOUR FIGURING HERE.

GO ON TO THE NEXT PAGE.

2 △ △ △ △ △ △ △ △ 2

15. A survey is conducted among 700 high-school students to see who their favorite college basketball teams are. If 250 students like the Hawks, 200 students like the Vikings, 50 students like the Bears, and the remaining students like the Warriors, approximately what percentage of the 700 high school students answered that the Warriors were their favorite team? (round to the nearest tenth of a percentage point)

A. 14.3%
B. 28.6%
C. 42.9%
D. 56.2%
E. 78.6%

DO YOUR FIGURING HERE.

16. If $x^2 = 36$ and $y^2 = 81$, which of the following CANNOT be the value of $x + y$?

F. -15
G. -3
H. 0
J. 3
K. 15

17. A system of linear equations is shown below.

$$4y = 3x + 12$$

$$-4y = -3x - 8$$

Which of the following describes the graph of this system of linear equations in the standard (x, y) coordinate plane?

A. Two parallel lines with negative slope
B. Two parallel lines with positive slope
C. A single line with negative slope
D. A single line with positive slope
E. Two perpendicular lines

18. $\dfrac{-6}{|-3|} = ?$

F. -3
G. -2
H. 0
J. 2
K. 9

19. What are the values for a that satisfy the equation $(a + y)(a + z) = 0$?

A. $-y$ and $-z$
B. $-y$ and z
C. $-yz$
D. y and $-z$
E. y and z

GO ON TO THE NEXT PAGE.

2   **2**

20. In the circle shown below, C is the center and lies on segments $\overline{AE}$ and $\overline{BF}$. Which of the following statements is NOT true?

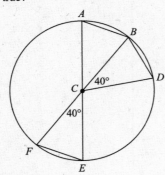

DO YOUR FIGURING HERE.

   F. $\angle BAC$ measures $70°$
   G. $\overline{AB}$ is parallel to $\overline{EF}$
   H. $\overline{AB} \cong \overline{BD}$
   J. $\angle BCE \cong \angle DCF$
   K. $\overline{CF} \cong \overline{EF}$

21. What is the slope of the line given by the equation $21x - 3y + 18 = 0$?
   A. -7
   B. -3
   C. $\dfrac{6}{7}$
   D. $\dfrac{7}{6}$
   E. 7

22. Which of the following is the least common denominator for the expression below?

$$\frac{1}{a^2 \times b \times c} + \frac{1}{b^2 \times c} + \frac{1}{b \times c^2}$$

   F. $b \times c$
   G. $a \times b \times c$
   H. $a^2 \times b \times c$
   J. $a^2 \times b^2 \times c^2$
   K. $a^2 \times b^4 \times c^5$

23. What number can you add to the numerator and denominator of $\dfrac{5}{8}$ to get $\dfrac{1}{2}$?
   A. -5
   B. -3
   C. -2
   D. 0
   E. 1

GO ON TO THE NEXT PAGE.

2 △ △ △ △ △ △ △ △ **2**

DO YOUR FIGURING HERE.

24. If $x + y = 13$ and $2y = 16$, what is the value of x?
  F. 4
  G. 5
  H. 7
  J. 8
  K. 9

25. If the inequality $|m| > |n|$ is true, then which of the following must be true?
  A. $m = n$
  B. $m \neq n$
  C. $m < n$
  D. $m > n$
  E. $m > 0$

26. Given that $y - 5 = \dfrac{1}{2}x + 1$ is the equation of a line, at what point does the line cross the x axis?
  F. -15
  G. -12
  H. 1
  J. 4
  K. 6

Use the following information to answer Questions 27 and 28.

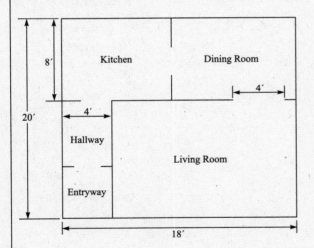

The figure above shows the plan for the ground floor of a townhouse. The thickness of the walls should be ignored when answering the questions. The dimensions shown are in feet, and each region is rectangular.

27. What is the area, in square feet, of the living room?
  A. 360
  B. 280
  C. 216
  D. 168
  E. 120

GO ON TO THE NEXT PAGE.

2 △ △ △ △ △ △ △ △ **2**

28. What is the perimeter, in feet, of the ground floor of the townhouse?

F. 76
G. 80
H. 92
J. 180
K. 360

---

29. Three years ago, the population of a certain species of bird was calculated at 20 birds per acre. This year, a biologist recorded a total of 47 birds in an area equal to 3.25 acres. By about what percentage has the bird population in the biologist's sample decreased over the last 3 years, to the nearest tenth?

A. 14.7%
B. 27.7%
C. 38.3%
D. 42.6%
E. 72.3%

30. A right triangle that has sides measured in the same unit of length is shown below. For any such triangle, $(\tan \alpha)(\sin \beta)$ is equivalent to:

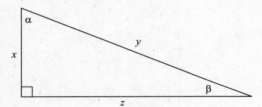

F. $\dfrac{x}{z}$

G. $\dfrac{x^2}{z^2}$

H. $\dfrac{z}{y}$

J. $\dfrac{z}{y^2}$

K. $\dfrac{z^2}{x}$

31. For all $x > 0$, $\dfrac{1}{x} + \dfrac{3}{4} = $?

A. $\dfrac{3}{4x}$

B. $\dfrac{4}{4x}$

C. $\dfrac{4 + 3x}{4x}$

D. $\dfrac{4}{4 + x}$

E. $\dfrac{4 + 3x}{4 + x}$

DO YOUR FIGURING HERE.

GO ON TO THE NEXT PAGE.

2   △ △ △ △ **2**

32. If $\cos A = \dfrac{4}{5}$, and $\sin A = \dfrac{3}{5}$, then $\tan A = ?$

  F. $\dfrac{3}{4}$

  G. $\dfrac{3}{5}$

  H. $\dfrac{4}{5}$

  J. $\dfrac{4}{3}$

  K. $\dfrac{12}{5}$

33. In the (x, y) coordinate plane, what is the y-intercept of the line $5x + 3y = 8$?

  A. $\dfrac{8}{3}$

  B. 3

  C. $\dfrac{5}{3}$

  D. $\dfrac{3}{5}$

  E. $-\dfrac{5}{3}$

34. If $\dfrac{a^x}{a^y} = a^4$ for all $a \neq 0$, which of the following must be true?

  F. $\sqrt{xy} = 4$
  G. $x \times y = 4$
  H. $x + y = 4$
  J. $x - y = 4$
  K. $x \div y = 4$

35. In a certain music store, CDs were put on display and assigned prices for May. Each month after that, the price was 20% less than the price for the previous month. If the price of a CD was d dollars in May, what was the price in August?

  A. $0.2d$
  B. $0.3d$
  C. $0.512d$
  D. $0.64d$
  E. $0.8d$

36. If $|5 - 2x| > 5$, which of the following is a possible value of x?

  F. 2
  G. 3
  H. 4
  J. 5
  K. 6

DO YOUR FIGURING HERE.

GO ON TO THE NEXT PAGE.

2 △ △ △ △ △ △ △ △ **2**

37. What value of t will satisfy the equation $0.1(t + 3,420) = t$?
    A. $-3,420$
    B. -313.64
    C. 313.64
    D. 342
    E. 380

38. What is the slope of any line parallel to the y-axis in the (x, y) coordinate plane?
    F. -1
    G. 0
    H. 1
    J. Undefined
    K. Cannot be determined from the given information

39. Which one of the following lines has the smallest slope?
    A. $y = x + 6$
    B. $y = 2x + 10$
    C. $y = \dfrac{1}{2}x - 1$
    D. $5y = 15x + 4$
    E. $7y = 3x - 7$

40. Amy can run 3.5 miles in x minutes. At that pace, how many minutes would it take her to run 10.5 miles?
    F. $10.5x$
    G. $7x$
    H. $4x$
    J. $3.5x$
    K. $3x$

41. A certain rectangle is 5 times as long as it is wide. Suppose the length and width are both tripled. The perimeter of the second rectangle is how many times as large as the perimeter of the first rectangle?
    A. 3
    B. 5
    C. 6
    D. 12
    E. 15

42. If r and s are constants and $x^2 + rx + 12$ is equivalent to $(x + 3)(x + s)$, what is the value of r?
    F. 3
    G. 4
    H. 7
    J. 12
    K. Cannot be determined from the given information

DO YOUR FIGURING HERE.

GO ON TO THE NEXT PAGE.

2   △ △ △ △ **2**

43. For what value of b would the following system of equations have an infinite number of solutions?

$$3x + 5y = 27$$

$$12x + 20y = 3b$$

A. 9
B. 27
C. 36
D. 81
E. 126

44. Which of the following calculations will yield an even integer for any integer a?

F. $2a^2 + 3$
G. $4a^3 + 1$
H. $5a^2 + 2$
J. $6a^4 + 6$
K. $a^6 - 3$

45. What is the solution set of $|3a - 3| \geq 12$?

A. $a \geq 5$ and $a \leq -5$
B. $a \geq 5$ and $a \leq -3$
C. $a \geq -5$ and $a \leq 5$
D. $a \geq -5$ and $a \leq 3$
E. $a \leq 5$ and $a \geq -5$

46. What is $\cos \dfrac{5\pi}{12}$ given that $\dfrac{5\pi}{12} = \dfrac{\pi}{4} + \dfrac{\pi}{6}$ and that $\cos(\alpha + \beta) = (\cos\alpha)(\cos\beta) - (\sin\alpha)(\sin\beta)$? (Note: You may use the following table of values.)

θ	$\sin\theta$	$\cos\theta$
$\dfrac{\pi}{6}$	$\dfrac{1}{2}$	$\dfrac{\sqrt{3}}{2}$
$\dfrac{\pi}{4}$	$\dfrac{\sqrt{2}}{2}$	$\dfrac{\sqrt{2}}{2}$
$\dfrac{\pi}{3}$	$\dfrac{\sqrt{3}}{2}$	$\dfrac{1}{2}$

F. $\dfrac{1}{4}$

G. $\dfrac{1}{2}$

H. $\dfrac{\sqrt{6} - \sqrt{2}}{4}$

J. $\dfrac{\sqrt{3} - \sqrt{2}}{2}$

K. $\dfrac{\sqrt{6} + 2}{4}$

DO YOUR FIGURING HERE.

GO ON TO THE NEXT PAGE.

2   △ △ △ △ **2**

47. If $y \neq z$, what are the real values of x that make the following inequality true?

$$\frac{xy - xz}{3y - 3z} < 0$$

A. All negative real numbers
B. All positive real numbers
C. $-\frac{1}{3}$ only
D. $\frac{1}{3}$ only
E. 3 only

48. The perimeter of a square is 36 units. How many units long is the diagonal of the square?
 F. 8
 G. $9\sqrt{2}$
 H. 16
 J. 18
 K. $18\sqrt{3}$

49. What is the equation of the circle in the standard (x, y) coordinate plane that has a radius of 4 units and the same center as the circle determined by $x^2 + y^2 - 6y + 4 = 0$?
A. $x^2 + y^2 = -4$
B. $(x + 3)^2 + y^2 = 16$
C. $(x - 3)^2 + y^2 = 16$
D. $x^2 + (y + 3)^2 = 16$
E. $x^2 + (y - 3)^2 = 16$

50. A rectangular kitchen is 8 feet longer than it is wide. Its area is 240 square feet. How long, in feet, is it?
 F. 12
 G. 16
 H. 20
 J. 24
 K. 30

51. What is the slope of a line that is parallel to the line determined by the equation $5x - 4y = 8$?
A. -4
B. $-\frac{5}{4}$
C. $\frac{5}{4}$
D. 2
E. 4

52. If $3^{8x} = 81^{3x-2}$, what is the value of x?
 F. -2
 G. 0
 H. 2
 J. 3
 K. 4

DO YOUR FIGURING HERE.

GO ON TO THE NEXT PAGE.

2   △ △ **2**

53. The picture shown below has a uniform frame-width of $\frac{5}{8}$ inches. What is the approximate area, in square inches, of the viewable portion of the picture?

18 inches

30 inches

- **A.** 426.25
- **B.** 481.56
- **C.** 510.40
- **D.** 510.75
- **E.** 540.00

54. A horse eats 12 bales of hay in 5 days. At this rate, how many bales of hay does the horse eat in $5 + x$ days?

- **F.** $12 + \dfrac{12x}{5}$
- **G.** $12 + \dfrac{x}{5}$
- **H.** $\dfrac{12}{5} + \dfrac{12}{5x}$
- **J.** $\dfrac{12}{5} + \dfrac{x}{5}$
- **K.** $\dfrac{12}{5} + x$

55. When graphed in the standard (x, y) coordinate plane, the lines $x = -5$ and $y = x - 5$ intersect at what point?

- **A.** $(-5, -10)$
- **B.** $(-5, -5)$
- **C.** $(-5, 0)$
- **D.** $(0, -5)$
- **E.** $(0, 0)$

56. Which of the following expresses the number of miles a runner must travel in a 4-lap race where the course is a circle of radius m miles?

- **F.** $4m$
- **G.** $4\pi m$
- **H.** $4\pi m^2$
- **J.** $8\pi m$
- **K.** $16\pi m$

DO YOUR FIGURING HERE.

GO ON TO THE NEXT PAGE.

2 △ △ △ △ △ △ △ △ **2**

57. For some real number n, the graph of the line $y = (n + 1)x + 6$ in the standard (x, y) coordinate plane passes through $(4,8)$. What is the value of n?

A. $-\dfrac{3}{2}$

B. $-\dfrac{1}{2}$

C. $\dfrac{1}{2}$

D. $\dfrac{3}{2}$

E. 2

58. A computer repair person charges $50.00 per hour, plus an additional mileage fee. The charge for mileage varies directly with the square root of the number of miles traveled. If one hour plus 25 miles traveled costs $140.00, what is the total amount charged for one hour plus 36 miles traveled?

F. $218.00
G. $196.92
H. $179.60
J. $158.00
K. $143.60

59. In the right triangle below, $YZ = 10$ units, and $XZ = 4$ units. What is sin Z?

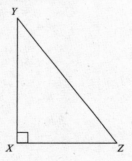

A. $\dfrac{4}{10}$

B. $\dfrac{10}{2\sqrt{21}}$

C. $\dfrac{2\sqrt{21}}{10}$

D. $\dfrac{10}{4}$

E. $\dfrac{4}{2\sqrt{21}}$

DO YOUR FIGURING HERE.

GO ON TO THE NEXT PAGE.

2 △ △ △ △ △ △ △ △ **2**

60. A triangle, $\triangle ABD$, is reflected across the line $y = x$ to have the image $\triangle A'B'D'$ in the standard (x, y) coordinate plane: thus A reflects to A'. The coordinates of point A are (m, n). What are the coordinates of point A'?

F. $(-m, n)$

G. $(m, -n)$

H. $(-m, -n)$

J. (n, m)

K. Cannot be determined from the given information.

DO YOUR FIGURING HERE.

END OF THE MATHEMATICS TEST.

STOP! IF YOU HAVE TIME LEFT OVER, CHECK YOUR WORK ON THIS SECTION ONLY.

3

READING TEST

35 Minutes—40 Questions

DIRECTIONS: This test includes four passages, each followed by ten questions. Read the passages and choose the best answer to each question. After you have selected your answer, fill in the corresponding bubble on your answer sheet. You should refer to the passages as often as necessary when answering the questions.

PASSAGE I
PROSE FICTION: *Football Failures*

A cold wind soothed the faces of the sweaty men huddled on the muddy field. The team stared at the goal line and focused on the game-ending, season-defining play in front of them. Dusty air filled their lungs with
5   each deep heave they mustered.

For almost two hours the men had battled their opponents on the barren football field. Joe, the center, could see the coach describing the play to a younger player. He was one of the grunts, a lineman, big and tall
10 and eager to push open gaps for the backs. The under-classman's labored jog back to the huddle mirrored every man's fatigue.

The quarterback confirmed the play and articulated it to his team. Joe saw his mouth move but could
15 not hear the words; nonetheless, he knew his blocking assignment. The hiss of the crowd muffled all sound on the field. Suddenly, Joe picked a voice out of the din, and turned his attention to his good friend Mark. "This is it guys," Mark was yelling. "We've been practicing
20 for four months this season and for three more years before that. It's time we score and take home a win. Let's get it done!" They all clasped hands to break the huddle and returned to their individual concentration.

Time seemed to drag as the team marched back
25 to the line of scrimmage. Joe glared at his opponents, pleased by the heavy clouds of vapor billowing from their mouths. Exhaustion was written on their faces and in their twitchy movements on the line. He turned his head toward the place in which he wanted to force
30 a gap, then to the defensive end who stood fast with his hands on his knees, gaze fixed on the ground. Joe smiled inwardly; he knew his team had beaten the other with physical play and superior endurance. Time froze as he prepared to snap the ball.
35 Joe leaned over carefully and clutched the moist leather ball. His teammates cautiously took their places right and left, lining up as in countless practice drills, in perfect order. Like clockwork, too, was each man's thorough examination of the opposing force, scanning
40 back and forth for a gap or a weak player, feeling the opponents' stares in return. Joe felt the quarterback crouch behind him. The passer's booming voice still did not register with Joe, but instinct told him what he needed to know. Three staccato hikes later, he snapped

45 the ball with speed and hurled himself towards the first defender.

Joe felt the crunch of pads and brought his forearm under the other man's shoulder pads. Lifting with his arms and legs, he threw the lesser player onto his back.
50 The meager lineman lay stunned for a moment, which greatly amused Joe, assuming the two yards he had sent his man back was more than enough to free the rusher to enter the endzone. This lucid moment lasted but a split second before Joe again lunged toward an upright
55 opponent.

Joe turned abruptly at the sound of a whistle and strained to find the scoring rusher. Something was wrong. Joe's teammates stood stunned, staring at the pile of defensive players who had fallen on their
60 running back. Referees began pulling men off the heap. With only a few men left on the ground, Joe could see the ball, still in the backfield, and in the arms of an opponent. He heard his coach from the sideline: "Fumble? Are you kidding me? I can't believe you
65 guys!"

His men had turned over possession of the ball, and time ran out on the game. "We had them beat, you know," Mark hissed to Joe as they walked slowly off the field. "They were dead tired. We should have
70 won the game." Their one chance was gone and now they had to endure the other team's celebration on the field. Joe's team never liked losing, but having come so close to a victory that day meant their last-minute defeat would be especially disappointing.

1. Joe would most likely agree with which of the following statements about the relationship between the players on his team?
   A. The players take the game very seriously and spend little time interacting with one another.
   B. Most of the players are excellent friends and maintain a lively atmosphere on the field.
   C. The players work very hard at a common goal and provide support for one another to achieve it.
   D. The players react poorly to their coach's hostile yelling and find strength in their shared objection.

GO ON TO THE NEXT PAGE.

3 ████████████████████████████████████ **3**

2. Joe can most accurately be characterized as:
F. self-assured and presumptuous.
G. confident but dismayed.
H. amiable but reserved.
J. engrossed and dedicated.

3. Which of the following statements does NOT describe one of Joe's reactions to the events of the final play of the game?
A. He glanced around, shocked.
B. He lunged at his opponents in a blind rage.
C. He commiserated with Mark.
D. He trudged off the field with his teammates.

4. The main point of the first paragraph is that:
F. football is a game whose players can get very dirty.
G. the players have all worked hard to arrive at a crucial point in the game.
H. the long fall sports season can include some cold-weather days.
J. cool grass fields are ideal surfaces for football games.

5. The main point of the last paragraph is that Joe feels:
A. sad as usual about the loss.
B. frustrated by his teammates' lackluster performance during the final play.
C. guilty that he and his teammates let down the coach.
D. dejected by the loss of this important game.

6. According to the passage, when Joe observes the opposing defensive line, Joe feels:
F. surprised at their resilience so late in the game.
G. quietly pleased by their signs of weakness.
H. apprehensive about their alignment.
J. pensive over the strategy of the defense.

7. Which of the following statements most accurately expresses Mark's feelings after the loss?
A. Mark was disappointed by the loss, but saw the circumstances that led to it.
B. Mark rejected the loss and held to the belief that they had won.
C. Mark denied the loss at first, but was convinced by Joe that it was legitimate.
D. Mark is angered by his team's failure to defeat an inferior team.

8. It can logically be inferred from the passage that the reason the players join hands at the end of a huddle is because:
F. such a ritual draws attention to the quarterback, who must announce the play.
G. the team must have the right number of players to execute the play.
H. it reinforces the notion of team purpose and mutual reliance essential to game play.
J. it alerts players who cannot hear the quarterback to the end of the huddle.

9. A reasonable conclusion Joe draws about his first block is that the block:
A. was particularly effective, leaving ample room for the rusher to score.
B. was insufficient to make a gap for the rusher, who ended up fumbling the football.
C. was clearly illegal, evident in the way Joe's thrust sent the opponent onto his back.
D. was not included in the original play.

10. According to the passage, the reason the final play of the game is crucial to the success of the entire season is that:
F. no game had yet been so closely contested.
G. pride is at stake during important goal line plays.
H. the game comes late in the season after many weeks of preparation.
J. the defending team appeared fatigued and easy to beat.

GO ON TO THE NEXT PAGE.

3   **3**

PASSAGE II
SOCIAL SCIENCE: *American Influences Abroad*

A tourist walks along a muddy Indonesian street looking for a souvenir that represents the local culture. He stops by a small street vendor to look at the goods for sale. What he sees shocks him: T-shirts and posters
5 promoting American football, basketball, and baseball teams, brand-name American food and drink, and an assortment of other items of Americana.

Although this example may seem surprising, it is a reality in many countries. American culture has infil-
10 trated many nations around the world that Americans generally consider the most exotic. In these places, the importation of American culture—be it by consumer goods, media, or otherwise—is affecting indigenous peoples and their traditions.
15 The presence of American culture in other countries receives mixed reactions. Some people praise American business or simply find the so-called invasion innocuous. American logos appear in quite unexpected places, embodying the ubiquitous American symbols
20 worldwide. The presence of such American food and retail goods in a foreign market might indicate that the companies producing them are eager to support the local economy. American corporate confidence in a country's markets can boost additional foreign
25 investment. In many cases, the populations of developing countries and highly industrialized and modern nations have embraced Americana.

Many other people reject what has been called American "cultural imperialism." Some sociologists,
30 anthropologists, and cultural experts lament the steady decline of distinct national, ethnic, and cultural identities as omnipresent American influences overpower ancient traditions and beliefs.

For example, Mexico and the United States have
35 often had a tense relationship unhelped by the language barrier. Regardless, there has been an overwhelming influx of American ideas and products into Mexico. Look to the typical Mexico tourist resort. Only about fifty years ago the sleepy towns were still untouched by
40 commercial development. They held their local culture close. Now, however, grand international hotels tower above the traditional colonial architecture. A walk down a main thoroughfare in a tourist town could reveal a plethora of American businesses. The local cantinas
45 and native boutiques are losing the battle against large American corporations.

Despite these issues, however, many other experts have applauded the spread of American institutions across the world. They point to jobs created, as well
50 as the modernization of infrastructure that comes with American commerce. They explain that these things will help bring lesser-developed nations into the modern world and help to decrease poverty and other social ailments. In fact, many of the jobs offered by
55 American companies pay handsomely compared to the local market's average wage.

Furthermore, some experts point to Japan as a prime example of where American involvement has been beneficial. After helping to rebuild the country
60 both politically and economically after World War II,

America left a pervasive cultural footprint on the country. Although the Japanese people have embraced many American concepts and products, they have maintained a distinct culture that is rich in the traditions of the past
65 but open to Western ideas.

American commercial and cultural expansion abroad has created both benefits and problems. In many places, there is still no clear picture of the future effects of Americana.

11. According to the first paragraph, the tourist was shocked because:
A. he could not find any souvenirs.
B. he expected to find souvenirs that reflected the local culture.
C. he did not realize that the shops would be so small.
D. he had never before been to Indonesia.

12. As it is used in line 19, the word *ubiquitous* most nearly means:
F. very expensive.
G. supportive.
H. far-reaching.
J. localized.

13. According to the passage, some people reject Americana because:
A. it boosts foreign investment in local economies.
B. it modernizes the infrastructure of aging communities.
C. it pays wages that local businesses cannot compete with.
D. it dilutes indigenous cultures.

14. According to the passage, the spread of American influences resulted in which of the following in certain foreign countries?
  I. Increased number of jobs
  II. Modernized infrastructure
  III. Decline in tourism
F. I only
G. II only
H. I and II only
J. II and III only

GO ON TO THE NEXT PAGE.

3

3

15. The passage suggests that tourist resorts in Mexico:
- **A.** remain unaffected by American influences.
- **B.** are struggling to maintain their cultural identity.
- **C.** can only benefit from the influence of American ideas.
- **D.** have never been so popular with Americans.

16. The passage indicates about America's influence on Japanese culture that it:
- **F.** was detrimental to the Japanese economy.
- **G.** led to a harmonious blend of American and Japanese ideas.
- **H.** had no direct effect on Japanese politics.
- **J.** put Japan at a distinct disadvantage in relation to other Asian countries.

17. It can reasonably be inferred from the passage that, if American cultural influences continue to infiltrate foreign markets, those markets:
- I. will experience unlimited economic growth.
- II. will not be able to maintain their unique identities.
- III. could either benefit from or be harmed by such influences.
- **A.** I only
- **B.** II only
- **C.** III only
- **D.** I and II only

18. As it is used in line 30, the word *lament* most nearly means:
- **F.** embrace.
- **G.** enjoy.
- **H.** deny.
- **J.** regret.

19. According to the passage, the Indonesian street vendor sold:
- **A.** American sports memorabilia.
- **B.** only goods manufactured in Indonesia.
- **C.** souvenirs unsuitable for Americans.
- **D.** trinkets imported from the surrounding countries.

20. It can be reasonably inferred from the last paragraph that:
- **F.** American expansion abroad continues to benefit some nations.
- **G.** American expansion abroad will likely decline in the future.
- **H.** American expansion abroad causes more problems than it solves.
- **J.** American expansion abroad will not be supported by either Japan or Mexico.

3 ████████████████████████████████ **3**

PASSAGE III
HUMANITIES: *Artistic Styles Explored*

Many of us have looked at a great work of art and wondered how a person is able to paint or draw something so lifelike and emotive. We see the mas-
5 terpieces of painters such as Monet or Picasso and wonder what stirred these men to put brush to canvas so delicately. Most of an artist's greatness lies in his or her natural ability and practice of technique, but other factors affect the work an artist produces. The trained eye knows that even the smallest of details can have a
10 powerful impact on the meaning of an artist's work.

A formal style is among the most apparent traits of a work of art. One of the first popular styles was known as Realism. Paintings from this school focused on depicting real life unembellished with fanciful notions
15 or feelings. Realism traces its roots to ancient Rome, where artists attempted to depict their leaders in ways that did not glamorize or gloss over unattractive physical attributes. This approach became unpopular after a while for many different reasons, but was revived
20 during the Renaissance. For the next several centuries, Western artists attempted to portray life as realistically as possible.

In the late 19th century, a rebellion against Realism arose in response to the rigidity and staleness some
25 saw in the style. As a result, many artists began paint-
ing in the Impressionist style, which allowed for more creativity. Monet and Manet, two prominent painters, used this style of painting, characterized by its subtle use of light and color to create a dreamlike quality in
30 scenes of the natural world.

Impressionist painters use small brush strokes with unmixed primary colors to simulate reflected light. The result is a picture that appears hazy, leaving a general "impression" upon the viewer. The large number
35 of young painters who took up Impressionism resulted in it being a very vigorous and contentious school of thought. Impressionistic style is still popular with both art collectors and museum-goers.

Several new styles grew out of the Impressionist
40 movement that actually rejected all or some of the beliefs held by Impressionists. Some of these styles became schools of thought in their own right, while others simply existed as one artist's trademark way of painting. Post-Impressionism is one example of a style
45 that grew out of the naturalistic form of Impression-
ism. Post-Impressionism uses form and color to reflect art in a more personal and subjective way than did its predecessor.

Another style that grew out of Impressionism was
50 Pointillism. Georges Seurat led this movement, which emphasized the application of paint in small dots and brush strokes to create the effect of blending and luminosity.

Vincent Van Gogh, a well-known artist, adapted
55 Impressionism to his own unique method. Although a real school of thought never followed his style of painting, he is nonetheless regarded as a brilliant painter for his use of bold, bright colors and even larger and bolder brush strokes.

60 Many other styles of painting evolved from the first descendants of Impressionism. Cubism, Abstract Art, Expressionism, Abstract Expressionism, Modernism, and a host of other styles have all expanded the range of acceptable artistic expression and allowed
65 artists to explore new and creative ways in which to express themselves and their points of view. Each style has distinct ways of interpreting the world and depicting it in art. Although some have similarities, they all are unique and distinguishable from one another. For
70 example, one tableau may reflect the world through rigid geometric figures while another may show life in smooth black curves.

One consequence of the spread of different artistic styles is the wide variety of art people enjoy today.
75 While some favor one style over another, it is important that these styles coexist, because a variety of techniques and opinions is the ideal environment for the evolution of art.

21. As it is used in line 3, the word *emotive* most nearly means:
A. inciting to action.
B. expressing emotion.
C. inducing impassiveness.
D. defining artistry.

22. The author mentions all of the following as adaptations of Impressionism EXCEPT:
F. Modernism.
G. Cubism.
H. Realism.
J. Expressionism.

23. The author suggests that Realists were most interested in depicting:
A. ancient Romans as glamorous figures.
B. people and places as they actually appeared.
C. unattractive physical attributes of Western artists.
D. the dreamlike quality of the real world.

24. The main emphasis of the second paragraph (lines 11–22) regarding the Realist approach is that:
F. despite fluctuations in its popularity, it is an endur-
ing style.
G. it regained popularity during the Renaissance.
H. it was the only formal style of painting in ancient Rome.
J. while it was popular during the Renaissance, it fell out of favor shortly thereafter.

3 ▌▌ **3**

25. Which of the following best states the main point of the passage?
    A. Painters must adapt to a changing world.
    B. Artistic styles have evolved over the years.
    C. Some styles of painting are more popular than others.
    D. Artists often change their styles based on popular demand.

26. As it is used in line 43, the phrase "artist's trademark" most nearly means:
    F. prime example.
    G. legal background.
    H. formal training.
    J. unique style.

27. The passage suggests that Impressionist painters:
    A. rejected Realism.
    B. were unpopular.
    C. embraced Realism.
    D. were rigid and stale.

28. The author claims that Impressionism:
    F. was unable to expand the range of artistic expression.
    G. was the precursor of both Realism and Pointillism.
    H. paved the way for many other creative artistic styles.
    J. evolved from other styles, such as Abstract Art and Cubism.

29. The author of the passage indicates that Post-Impressionism, as compared to Impressionism, is:
    A. more personal.
    B. less subjective.
    C. less natural.
    D. more vigorous.

30. According to the passage, artists rebeled against Realism because:
    F. it used light and color to embellish the real world.
    G. it traced its roots to ancient Rome.
    H. it glossed over the true feelings of the artists.
    J. it did not allow for freedom of artistic expression.

GO ON TO THE NEXT PAGE.

3 ▓▓▓▓▓▓▓▓▓▓▓▓▓▓▓▓▓▓▓▓▓▓▓▓▓ **3**

PASSAGE IV

NATURAL SCIENCE: *Heredity and Gene-linkage: A Possible Relationship*

The ability of every organism on earth to reproduce is the hallmark of life. Reproduction can be either asexual, involving a single parent, or sexual, involving two parents. Sexual reproduction begets offspring that
5 inherit half of their genes from each parent. This transmission of genes from one generation to the next is called *heredity*.

Each hereditary unit, the *gene*, contains specific encoded information that translates into an organism's
10 inherited traits. Inherited traits range from hair color, to height to susceptibility to disease. Genes are actually segments of the *DNA* molecule, and it is the precise replication of DNA that produces copies of genes that can be passed from parents to offspring.
15 DNA is subdivided into *chromosomes* that each include hundreds or thousands of genes. The specific traits or characteristics of each offspring depend on the arrangement and combination of the chromosomes supplied by both parents.
20 Genes located on the same chromosome tend to be inherited together. Transmission of these so-called linked genes can affect the inheritance of two different characteristics. Thomas Hunt Morgan was the first biologist to associate specific genes with specific
25 chromosomes. In the early 20th century, Morgan selected a species of fruit fly, *Drosophila melanogaster*, on which to study his genetic theory. The fruit fly is a prolific breeder, producing hundreds of offspring in a single mating. In addition, the fruit fly has only four
30 pairs of easily distinguishable chromosomes, making it the ideal experimental organism. Soon after Morgan commenced working with *Drosophila*, he began to notice variations in certain traits.

For example, Morgan noticed that the natural
35 characteristics of *Drosophila* included gray bodies and normal wings. However, mutant examples of these characteristics sometimes appeared; these flies had black bodies, and much smaller, vestigial wings. Morgan crossed female flies that appeared normal, but
40 carried the mutant genes, with males that exhibited the mutations. He expected the offspring to include equal numbers of gray flies with normal wings, black flies with vestigial wings, gray flies with vestigial wings, and black flies with normal wings. What he found was
45 a disproportionate number of gray flies with normal wings and black flies with vestigial wings, which suggested to him that the genes for body color and wing size are transmitted together from parents to offspring because they are located on the same chromosome and
50 must be somehow linked.

Additional research conducted by Morgan on *D. melanogaster* demonstrated that many, often spontaneous mutations occur across generations. These observations, together with the results of experiments
55 carried out to test his theory on linked genes, led Morgan to postulate that the location of the genes on the chromosomes contributes to the likelihood of any given gene being transmitted from parent to offspring. This theory of linear arrangement, along with Morgan's

60 other important contributions to the field of genetics, led to his being awarded the Nobel Prize in Physiology or Medicine in 1933.

Current research exploring the significance of linked genes reveals that many factors affect the trans-
65 mission of certain traits from parents to offspring. The location of genes on a particular chromosome is but one of a multitude of determinants involved in whether or not a characteristic will be inherited.

31. The main idea of the passage is that:
  A. fruit flies are excellent experimental organisms.
  B. chromosomes contain many different genes.
  C. the position of genes on a given chromosome can affect the inheritance of certain traits.
  D. linked genes are primarily responsible for all of the mutations associated with body color and wing shape.

32. The passage states that a hereditary unit is called:
  F. a chromosome.
  G. a gene.
  H. an organism.
  J. a characteristic.

33. The passage states that all of the following are examples of inherited traits EXCEPT:
  A. hair color.
  B. molecules.
  C. height.
  D. disease susceptibility.

34. As it is used in line 28, the word *prolific* most nearly means:
  F. easily distinguishable.
  G. characteristically ideal.
  H. clearly superior.
  J. highly productive.

GO ON TO THE NEXT PAGE.

3 ████████████████████████████████████ **3**

35. According to the passage, asexual reproduction involves:
   A. two parents.
   B. either one or two parents.
   C. one parent.
   D. no parents.

36. With which of the following statements would the author most likely agree?
   F. There is still much to learn about the way in which genes are transmitted.
   G. It is no longer necessary to study the effects of linked genes.
   H. The *Drosophila melanogaster* is the best organism on which to experiment for all genetic research.
   J. All genes that are located on the same chromosome are somehow linked.

37. What, according to the passage, was the primary reason that Thomas Hunt Morgan chose to experiment on *Drosophila melanogaster*?
   A. It had many easily distinguishable chromosomes.
   B. It was able to produce many offspring in a short period of time.
   C. It exhibited many different mutations.
   D. It was the only organism that had linked genes.

38. The passage suggests that mutant genes:
   F. are always apparent in an organism's physical characteristics.
   G. can sometimes be suppressed, causing the organism to appear normal.
   H. are never transmitted from parent to offspring.
   J. can clearly be seen on the chromosomes on which they are located.

39. What is the main idea of the last paragraph?
   A. Current research into the effects of linked genes is insufficient.
   B. The location of genes on a chromosome is not important to the transmission of genetic material from parent to offspring.
   C. Certain characteristics will never be inherited, due to their association with linked genes.
   D. The transmission of genetic material is affected by more than simply the location of genes on a chromosome.

40. According to the passage, if the genes for blue eyes and brown hair are located on the same chromosome:
   F. none of the offspring will have both blue eyes and brown hair.
   G. all of the offspring will have both blue eyes and brown hair.
   H. both of the traits are considered mutations.
   J. a certain number of offspring will inherit both traits.

END OF THE READING TEST.
STOP! IF YOU HAVE TIME LEFT OVER, CHECK YOUR WORK ON THIS SECTION ONLY.

4 ◯ ◯ ◯ ◯ ◯ ◯ ◯ ◯ ◯ **4**

SCIENCE REASONING TEST

35 Minutes—40 Questions

DIRECTIONS: This test includes seven passages, each followed by several questions. Read the passage and choose the best answer to each question. After you have selected your answer, fill in the corresponding bubble on your answer sheet. You should refer to the passages as often as necessary when answering the questions. You may NOT use a calculator on this test.

PASSAGE I

A number of different chemical elements are essential for the survival and growth of plants. The *macronutrients*—those nutrients required in the greatest quantity—are nitrogen, phosphorus, and potassium. These macronutrients are only available in the soil and generally come from the decay of other plants. To enrich the soil and make more of these essential nutrients available, many people use fertilizers to supply plants with the nutrients they need to grow faster. Two botanists discuss whether inorganic or organic fertilizers are most optimal for plant growth.

Botanist 1

In addition to carbon, hydrogen, and oxygen available in the water and the air, and other micronutrients, such as sulfur, calcium, and magnesium, plants also need the macronutrients nitrogen, phosphorus, and potassium to thrive. The best way to supply the soil, and thus the plants, with the proper macronutrients is to apply organic fertilizers, as opposed to commercial inorganic fertilizers. Organic nutrients include cow, poultry, horse, and sheep manures. Green manure—a crop that is grown for a specific period of time, then plowed and incorporated into the soil—and compost can also be used. Organic fertilization mimics the natural breakdown of organic material into nutrients for which the plants can use. In other words, organic fertilizer provides a naturally slow release of nutrients as the organic material breaks down in the soil, reducing the likelihood of over-fertilization. Organic fertilizers also improve soil structure in the long term and improve the ability of sandy soils to hold water, which is immensely important in arid climates. Commercial inorganic fertilizers, on the other hand, are often applied too heavily, damaging the roots of the plants. Inorganic fertilizers can also cause chemical imbalances in the soil because they can build up a toxic concentration of salts in the soil.

Botanist 2

Plant growth and survival depends on an adequate supply of essential nutrients that cannot always be found in the soil. Inorganic commercial fertilizers have many benefits over organic fertilizers. The elements in inorganic fertilizers have been thoroughly measured and tested, insuring that each application provides the appropriate amount of nutrients to the plants, as opposed to the highly variable, and often unknown, nutrient content of organic fertilizers. Organic fertilizers are usually lower in nutrient content than inorganic fertilizers, requiring more of the organic material to be applied to achieve the same level of nutrient delivery acquired from the application of smaller amounts of inorganic material. In addition, characteristics of organic fertilizer require application well in advance of need to ensure that the materials have broken down and can be used by the plant. Inorganic fertilizers, however, once applied, offer immediate availability of nutrients to plants for use. The likelihood of nitrogen depletion is another disadvantage of organic fertilizers. Organic material can cause a temporary depletion of nitrogen in the soil and therefore in the plants that depend on it. Inorganic fertilizer use does not present this problem.

1. According to the passage, plants need the most of which of the following to grow and survive?
   A. Oxygen
   B. Fertilizer
   C. Micronutrients
   D. Macronutrients

2. Which of the following can be inferred from Botanist 2's viewpoint about organic fertilizers?
   F. It is impossible to determine the proper amount of inorganic fertilizer to apply.
   G. The levels of essential macronutrients are closer to those that occur naturally.
   H. Organic fertilizers are useless in achieving and promoting plant growth.
   J. Organic fertilizers can reduce the amount of necessary nutrients in the soil.

GO ON TO THE NEXT PAGE.

4 ○ ○ ○ ○ ○ ○ ○ ○ **4**

3. Botanist 2 would most likely agree with which of the following statements made by Botanist 1?
   A. Inorganic fertilizers can create imbalances in the soil.
   B. Organic fertilizer slowly releases nutrients into the soil.
   C. Organic fertilizer should be used in place of inorganic fertilizers.
   D. Inorganic fertilizer is the best source of micronutrients.

4. Which of the following best describes the difference between the two botanists' opinions?
   F. The effects of putting additional macronutrients in the soil.
   G. The amount of fertilizer that should be applied.
   H. The type of fertilizer that is most beneficial to plant growth.
   J. The type of fertilizer that behaves most like natural nutrient-rich soil.

5. According to Botanist 1, all of the following are true of organic fertilizer EXCEPT:
   A. organic fertilizer is safer for the plant in terms of over-application of fertilizer.
   B. soil quality is slowly improved over time with the use of organic fertilizer.
   C. organic fertilizers are less likely than inorganic fertilizers to burn the roots of plants.
   D. less organic fertilizer can be applied to achieve the same results as those achieved with an inorganic fertilizer.

6. With which of the following statements would both botanists likely agree?
   F. Soil quality does not need to be considered if a nitrogen-rich fertilizer is used to compensate for nutrients not found in the soil.
   G. Plants require some additional nutrients to reach optimal growth if the nutrients are not available in the soil.
   H. Plants need only the macronutrients nitrogen, potassium, and phosphorus in order to survive.
   J. The amount of water, oxygen, and other micronutrients available to plants is less important if the proper amount of fertilizer is applied.

7. Which of the following can be inferred from the passage about inorganic fertilizers?
   A. If improperly applied, they are less likely than organic fertilizers to damage crops.
   B. Regardless of their application, they are less effective than organic fertilizers.
   C. If properly applied, they take longer to act than organic fertilizers and are similarly effective.
   D. If properly applied, they are faster acting than organic fertilizers and are just as effective.

GO ON TO THE NEXT PAGE.

4 ○ ○ ○ ○ ○ ○ ○ ○ ○ 4

PASSAGE II

Certain species of flowers attract more bees than others with the scent of their pollen. The pollen is found on a structure within the flower called the *anther*, which is located on top of another structure called the *stamen*. Flowers typically have multiple anthers and stamens.

Bees carry the pollen from the flowers on their legs. The bees move from flower to flower while collecting pollen. Some of the pollen falls from their legs as they land on another flower. This depositing of pollen causes cross-pollination to occur (fertilization of the other flowers). Three studies were conducted to study this process.

Study 1

For two flower species (A and B), pollen quantity per anther in milligrams (mg), anther quantity per flower in number, and percentage of stamens covered with pollen were recorded (see Table 1).

Table 1			
Flower species	Pollen quantity (mg) per anther	Anther quantity per flower	Stamens covered with pollen (%)
A	4.9	12	27
B	7.6	19	27

Study 2

Three study sites were established to determine the pollen collection rate of one species of bee for the flowers used in Study 1. In Site 1, Species A flowers were absent. In Site 2, Species B flowers were absent. In Site 3, both Species A and B flowers were absent.

Two pollen containers were placed at each site: one containing 50 mg Species A pollen and one containing 50 mg Species B pollen. The containers were left in place for 36 hours and the amount of pollen that was taken from the containers was measured. The results are recorded in Table 2.

Table 2			
Site	Flower species absent	Amount of Pollen (mg) removed from dishes containing pollen from:	
		Species A	Species B
1	A	26	13
2	B	12	35
3	A and B	2	4

Study 3

The researchers hand-pollinated flowers from a third species, Species C. They also observed the Species C plants being cross-pollinated by the bees in the area. All flowers were observed for 2 years. The scientists recorded the results in Table 3.

Table 3		
Cross-pollination of Species C flowers	Results from:	
	Hand-pollinated flowers	Bee-pollinated flowers
Flowers that reproduced	31	12
Flowers reproducing after 1 year	10	34
Flowers reproducing after 2 years	8	15
Total flowers produced after 2 years	50	43

8. Based on the results of Study 3, one could generalize that compared to flowers pollinated by hand, flowers pollinated by bees resulted in:
   F. an overall increase in flower production.
   G. an overall decrease in flower production.
   H. increased number of flowers still reproducing after 2 years.
   J. decreased number of flowers still reproducing after 2 years.

9. Which of the following variables was controlled in the design of Study 2?
   A. The amount of pollen placed at each site
   B. The level of pollen on each flower
   C. The total amount of pollen removed by the bees from each site
   D. The number of bees present at each site

10. According to the results of the studies, Species A and Species B are most similar in that their:
    F. percentage of stamens covered with pollen is equivalent.
    G. anther quantity per flower is equivalent.
    H. pollen quantity per anther is equivalent.
    J. rate of cross-pollination after 2 years is equivalent.

GO ON TO THE NEXT PAGE.

11. In Study 2, Site 3 was used to study the:
   A. pollen preference when Species A flowers only were present.
   B. pollen preference when both Species A and Species B flowers were missing.
   C. pollen preference when Species B flowers only were missing.
   D. pollen preference when both Species A and Species B flowers were present.

12. Which of the following is a weakness in the design of Study 2?
   F. Some species of flowers were not at both sites.
   G. Some species of bees were not present at both sites.
   H. The pollen could have been taken away by something other than bees.
   J. The containers did not hold enough pollen for accurate measurements.

13. The results of Study 2 suggest that which of the following factors most affects the flower preference of bees?
   A. Level of pollen count on the stamen.
   B. Location of the particular flower species within the area.
   C. Type of a particular flower species available in the area.
   D. Number of anthers on a flower.

4 ◯ ◯ ◯ ◯ ◯ ◯ ◯ ◯ ◯ **4**

PASSAGE III

A scientist wanted to observe the effects of altitude on the respiratory system of mammals. Four different species of mammals were placed in a chamber that underwent gradual changes in pressure (measured in atmospheres, or atm) to simulate the atmosphere at high altitudes. After 5 minutes at each atmospheric pressure tested, the average number of

breaths per minute (*respiratory rate*) was determined for each of the 4 mammals while they remained at rest. The data from the experiment are shown in the following graph. (Note: Larger animals typically have slower respiratory rates. Higher respiratory rates indicate rapid breathing, a sign of distress in some mammals.)

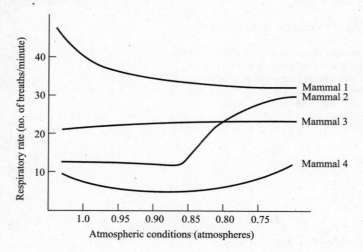

Figure 1

14. What is the relationship between respiratory rate and atmospheric pressure for Mammal 2?
    F. Decreases in pressure decrease the respiratory rate.
    G. Decreases in pressure increase the respiratory rate.
    H. Pressure changes have no effect on the respiratory rate.
    J. Increases in pressure increase the respiratory rate.

15. At approximately which pressure, in atmospheres, did Mammals 2 and 3 have the same respiratory rate?
    A. 1.0
    B. 0.95
    C. 0.80
    D. 0.75

16. Further measurements showed that Mammal 4 used significantly more oxygen per minute than Mammal 2. This would be consistent with the data from the graph if:
    F. Mammal 4 was in a warmer environment than Mammal 2.
    G. Mammal 4 was significantly larger than Mammal 2.
    H. Mammal 2 was significantly larger than Mammal 4.
    J. Mammals 2 and 4 were the same weight.

17. A higher respiratory rate causes mammals to have a higher metabolic rate. Which of the mammals would have a higher metabolic rate at a pressure of 1.0 atm than at .80 atm?
    A. 1 only
    B. 2 only
    C. 4 only
    D. 1 and 4 only

18. Based on the data in the graph, which of the mammals might be native to higher-altitude environments (meaning that they are more comfortable at higher altitudes than at lower altitudes)?
    F. 1 only
    G. 2 only
    H. 3 only
    J. 4 only

GO ON TO THE NEXT PAGE.

4 ○ ○ ○ ○ ○ ○ ○ ○ ○ **4**

PASSAGE IV

The *photoelectric effect* is the emission of electrons from matter upon the absorption of electromagnetic radiation, such as ultraviolet radiation or X-rays. Electromagnetic radiation is made up of *photons*, which can be considered finite packets of energy at various levels. Photons have properties attributed to both particles and waves. This phenomenon is known as the *wave-particle duality*.

The photoelectric effect is especially noticeable when dealing with metals. When a metallic surface is exposed to electromagnetic radiation that is above the minimum energy threshold (which is specific to the type of surface and material), photons are absorbed and electrons are emitted. No electrons are emitted for radiation with energy frequencies below that of the threshold, as the electrons are unable to gain sufficient energy to overcome the attractive forces within the metal. A scientist wishing to measure the photoelectric effect so as to further understand the nature of photons conducted the following experiments.

Experiment 1

Wishing to measure the energy required to produce the photoelectric effect on a surface of a sheet of copper, the scientist directed a beam of radiation at different frequencies (energies)—measured in Hertz (Hz)—onto the surface. After 5 minutes, the charge—measured in volts (V)—of the sheet of metal was recorded. This was done because if electrons were emitted from the surface, the metal would take on a positive charge. The results were recorded in Table 1.

Table 1	
Frequency of radiation (Hertz)	Charge on the sheet of copper (volts)
10^{14}	0
10^{15}	+0.001
10^{16}	+0.224
10^{17}	+0.239

Experiment 2

Solar cells used to generate electricity are based on the concept of the photoelectric effect; however, the goal of the cell is to capture the emitted electron and create an electric current. The scientist measured the effects of different frequencies (in Hz) of radiation on the current (in V) generated by a certain solar cell. The results were recorded in Table 2.

Table 2	
Frequency of radiation (Hertz)	Voltage of electric current (volts)
10^{14}	0.02
10^{15}	0.15
10^{16}	0.95
10^{17}	1.25

19. A scientist predicts that in years to come the earth's atmosphere will become much less effective at shielding the surface from radiation of higher frequencies. If this prediction is correct, which of the following is most likely to happen based on results of the experiments?
    A. The photoelectric effect on metals exposed to the sun will be less evident.
    B. The photoelectric effect on metals exposed to the sun will be more evident.
    C. Solar cells will gradually become less effective at producing electricity.
    D. Fewer photons will be emitted by particular metals.

20. Suppose that the rate of the photoelectric effect is directly proportional to the surface area of the metal exposed. Using a larger sheet of copper metal in Experiment 1 would most likely have affected the results in what way?
    F. The frequency of radiation would have increased.
    G. The charge on the sheet would have decreased.
    H. The charge on the sheet would have increased.
    J. The charge on the sheet would have stayed the same.

21. Which of the following procedures would result in the most accurate values for the effect of frequency of radiation on the photoelectric effect (Experiment 1)?
    A. Test a variety of metals once each and record the trends.
    B. Test a single metal many times and record the trends.
    C. Test a variety of metals each at different frequencies of radiation and record the trends.
    D. Test different sized samples of a variety of metals many times each, systematically varying the frequency, and record the trends.

GO ON TO THE NEXT PAGE.

22. Suppose a scientist wanted to measure the effect of the atmosphere on the photoelectric effect. The scientist could learn most by doing which of the following?
    F. Setting up on the earth's surface a sheet of metal and a detector to measure the metal's charge.
    G. Setting up in orbit around the earth a sheet of metal and a detector to measure the metal's charge
    H. Placing radioactive materials close to a sheet of metal and a detector to measure the metal's charge.
    J. Setting up on the earth's surface and in space in orbit around the earth sheets of metal and detectors to measure the metal's charge.

23. Which of the following assumptions did the scientist probably make in choosing these experiments to test the nature of photons?
    A. The photoelectric effect will occur regardless of the energy of the radiation present.
    B. Radiation will not have an effect on inanimate objects.
    C. Because photons are finite quantities of energy, only photons with high enough frequency will emit electrons.
    D. Doubling the frequency of radiation will result in doubling the emission of electrons by various metals.

24. Do the results of the experiments help to explain the nature of photons as finite packets of energy at various levels?
    F. Yes, because the experiments illustrate how solar panels can produce more electricity when exposed to higher frequencies of radiation.
    G. Yes, because the experiments illustrate how higher frequency radiation (photons with higher energy levels) causes emission of electrons, which require a minimum energy to escape the surface of the metal.
    H. No, because the experiments illustrate how higher frequency radiation (photons with higher energy levels) does not cause increased emission of electrons.
    J. No, because there is no relation between the energy level of photons and the rate of photoelectric emission of electrons.

GO ON TO THE NEXT PAGE.

4 ○ ○ ○ ○ ○ ○ ○ ○ ○ 4

PASSAGE V

Gregor Mendel is known for his work in genetics. He is credited with discovering how traits (characteristics) are passed from one generation to the next. After his observations of inherited traits, Mendel concluded that each organism carries two sets of information about a certain trait. If the two sets differ about the same trait, one set dominates the other. That way, information can be passed on through the generations, even if the trait is not expressed.

It has since been determined that the presence of certain traits is attributed to *genes*, and the different forms that genes can take, known as *alleles*. Dominant alleles (D) produce dominant characteristics; recessive alleles (d) produce recessive charactersitics. Dominant alleles are expressed whenever present (DD, Dd) but recessive alleles are expressed only when the dominant allele is absent (dd).

A study was done in which the independence of two traits was tested. In this study, a rabbit with long black hair was mated with a rabbit with short white hair. The dominant trait for hair length is short (H). The dominant trait for hair color is black (B). If the two initial rabbits (level 1 in the figure below) are *homozygous* for their traits, meaning that the two alleles for each trait are the same, breeding them will result in offspring that have both a dominant and recessive allele for each trait. Such a pairing of alleles is known as *heterozygous*. If, as in level 2 of the figure, two heterozygous rabbits are bred, the chart (level 3) contains all the possibilities for their offspring.

Dominant Traits	Recessive Traits
– Black color (BB)	– White color (bb)
– Short hair (HH)	– Long hair (hh)

Level 1: Long hair (hh) × Short hair (HH)
　　　　Black (BB)　　　　White (bb)

⇩

Level 2: Short hair (Hh)　Short hair (Hh)
　　　　Black (Bb)　　　　Black (Bb)

Level 3:　　　　Hh Bb × Hh Bb

	HB	Hb	hB	hb
HB	HHBB	HHBb	HhBB	HhBb
Hb	HHBb	HHbb	HhBb	Hhbb
hB	HhBB	HhBb	hhBB	hhBb
hb	HhBb	Hhbb	hhBb	hhbb

Length	Color
□ = short	black
▢ = short	white
▨ = long	black
■ = long	white

25. In the figure above, each numbered level represents:
   A. different generations.
   B. different members of the same generation.
   C. which rabbits have dominant alleles.
   D. which rabbits have recessive alleles.

26. Which of the following statements best explains the observation that offspring of the two rabbits in level 1 must have short black hair?
   F. If parents have a certain trait, their offspring must also possess the same trait.
   G. There is a 75% chance that the offspring will have short, black hair.
   H. Because offspring receive one allele per trait from each parent, the only possible outcome of the mixing is to have one dominant and one recessive allele for each trait.
   J. Because offspring receive one allele per trait from each parent, the recessive alleles are not transmitted to the offspring.

27. What is the probability that offspring of the level 2 rabbits will have white hair?
   A. 75%
   B. 25%
   C. 6.25%
   D. 0%

28. If several pairs of heterozygous rabbits were mated (as in level 2), what would be the expected ratio for the traits of the offspring (express as a ratio of short black hair: long black hair: short white hair: long white hair)?
   F. 16:4:4:1
   G. 16:3:3:1
   H. 9:4:4:1
   J. 9:3:3:1

29. Which of the following statements might be a reasonable generalization made after examining this study?
   A. If heterozygous rabbits with opposite traits are bred, the recessive traits will not be visible in the immediate generation, but may be visible in the second generation.
   B. If heterozygous rabbits with opposite traits are bred, the recessive traits might be visible in the immediate generation, but will not be visible in the second generation.
   C. If heterozygous rabbits with opposite traits are bred, the recessive traits will be visible in the immediate generation and in the second generation.
   D. If heterozygous rabbits with opposite traits are bred, the recessive traits will not at all be visible in future generations because they are overcome by the dominant traits.

GO ON TO THE NEXT PAGE.

4 ⚪ ⚪ ⚪ ⚪ ⚪ ⚪ ⚪ ⚪ 4

PASSAGE VI

A *chemical bond* is the physical phenomenon of chemical substances being held together by attraction of atoms to each other through both sharing and exchanging of electrons or electrostatic forces. *Bond energy* is a measure of bond strength in a chemical bond. For example, the carbon—hydrogen (C–H) bond energy is the energy change involved with breaking up the bond between the carbon and hydrogen atoms. Bonds with a higher energy release more energy when they form, and are considered to be more stable (less reactive).

When reacting with nonmetals, hydrogen forms *covalent* bonds, meaning that the bonded atoms share electrons with each other. Figure 1 shows the bond energies and distances for bonds involving hydrogen and nonmetals (H–X). The chart is arranged by period (rows of periodic table); in addition, the values for group 17 (column 17 on the periodic table) are compared.

Bond	Energy (kJ/mol)	Length (pm)
Period 1		
H–H	436	74
Period 2		
H–B	391	119
H–C	413	109
H–N	393	101
H–O	460	96
H–F	568	92
Period 3		
H–P	326	144
H–S	366	134
H–Cl	432	127
Period 4		
H–Se	279	146
H–Br	366	141
Group 17		
H–F	568	92
H–Cl	432	127
H–Br	366	141
H–I	298	161

Figure 1

Bond length is the distance between two bonded atoms in a molecule. Bond lengths are measured in molecules by means of X-ray diffraction. A set of two atoms sharing a bond is unique going from one molecule to the next. For example, the oxygen to hydrogen bond in water is different from the oxygen to hydrogen bond in alcohol. It is, however, possible to make generalizations when the general structure is the same. Figure 2 relates bond energy to bond length for H–X bonds between hydrogen and nonmetals. The elements in each period or group are connected by a line (with the exception of the first, which contains only hydrogen).

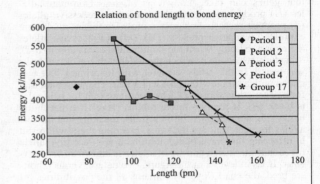

Figure 2

---

30. Suppose a certain experiment calls for a very stable substance with bond energy greater than 420 kJ/mol. Which of the following pairs of elements in a compound would yield a stable enough substance?
 F. H and C
 G. H and O
 H. H and P
 J. H and S

31. Generally speaking, the higher the bond energy, the more stable the bond is. The three *most* stable bonds shown in Figure 1 are:
 A. H–F, H–Cl, H–Br
 B. H–F, H–N, H–H
 C. H–F, H–O, H–H
 D. H–H, H–O, H–Cl

32. Which of the following substances would have the highest sum of bond energies (for example, H_2O has two H–O bonds) ?
 F. H_2O
 G. H_2S
 H. NH_3
 J. H_3Cl

GO ON TO THE NEXT PAGE.

33. Based on observations from Figures 1 and 2, which of the following statements is the best assessment of the data?
    A. Hydrogen H–X bond energies decrease along a group and bond lengths increase along a group.
    B. Hydrogen H–X bond energies increase along a group and bond lengths increase along a group.
    C. Hydrogen H–X bond energies decrease along a group and bond lengths decrease along a group.
    D. Hydrogen H–X bond energies decrease across a period and increase along a group.

34. Which of the following is the correct order for increasing bond lengths for bonds between these pairs of elements: H–O, H–S, H–Se?
    F. H–Se > H–S > H–O
    G. H–S > H–O > H–Se
    H. H–S < H–O < H–Se
    J. H–O < H–S < H–Se

PASSAGE VII

The growth rate of trees can be determined by counting concentric growth bands present in the trunks. This is called *dendrochronology*. Because *dendrochronology* is not completely accurate on its own, it is often combined with a process called *cross dating*, whereby band-growth characteristics across many samples from a homogeneous area (area of similar environmental conditions) are matched. It is believed that variation in the bands is due to some variation in environmental conditions, such as annual rainfall, when the bands were formed. During years with less rain, fewer bands will be formed, and the bands will be narrower than the bands formed during years with heavier rainfall. Heavier rainfall typically results in faster growth.

Researchers applied this information to white oak trees at three separate sites and tabulated the following data. At least 50 trees of varying ages were sampled from each site.

Table 1		
Site	Average number of growth bands per year	Average size of growth bands (mm)
1	11	2
2	15	4
3	20	12

35. Based on the observed trend in the data, which of the following statements is true?
    A. Site 1 received a higher average annual rainfall than Site 2.
    B. Site 2 received a higher average annual rainfall than Site 3.
    C. Site 3 received a higher average annual rainfall than Site 2.
    D. Site 1 received a higher average annual rainfall than Site 3.

36. On the basis of the tabulated data, one would conclude that the trees at Site 1, as compared to the trees at Site 2:
    F. experienced faster growth.
    G. experienced slower growth.
    H. experienced the same growth rate.
    J. are not homogenous.

37. Which of the following graphs best represents the data presented in the table?

A.
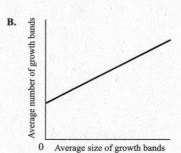

B.
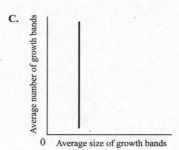

C.
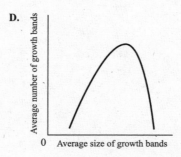

D.
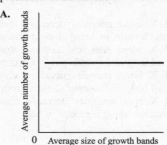

GO ON TO THE NEXT PAGE.

4 ◯ ◯ ◯ ◯ ◯ ◯ ◯ ◯ **4**

38. Based on the passage, the average annual rainfall was most likely highest at which site?
 F. Site 1
 G. Site 2
 H. Site 3
 J. It cannot be determined from the information in the passage.

39. According to the passage, cross dating is applied in order to:
 A. improve the accuracy of determining the growth rate of trees.
 B. predict the amount of rainfall any given area will receive.
 C. decrease the number of trees that are required to be studied.
 D. reduce the number of bands formed during years with heavy rainfall.

40. Trees from another site, Site 4, were sampled and found to have an average of 13 growth bands per year. According to the tabulated data, the average size of these growth bands, in millimeters, is most likely:
 F. less than 2.
 G. between 2 and 4.
 H. between 4 and 12.
 J. greater than 12.

END OF THE SCIENCE REASONING TEST.
STOP! IF YOU HAVE TIME LEFT OVER, CHECK YOUR WORK ON THIS SECTION ONLY.

WRITING TEST PROMPT

DIRECTIONS: This test is designed to assess your writing skills. You have 30 minutes to plan and write an essay based on the stimulus provided. Be sure to take a position on the issue and support your position using logical reasoning and relevant examples. Organize your ideas in a focused and logical way, and use the English language to clearly and effectively express your position.

When you have finished writing, refer to the Scoring Rubrics discussed in the Introduction (page 4) to estimate your score.

Many high schools have a police liaison officer who works full-time with the student body and the administration to combat drugs, violence, and other criminal issues within the school buildings. Supporters of the liaison program feel that the officers are beneficial as an active crime deterrent and first response to incidents within the schools. Opponents say a single officer in each building cannot effectively manage crime in the schools and that police resources are better spent in neighborhoods with more pressing needs.

In your opinion, should a police liaison officer be assigned to every public high school? In your essay, take a position on this question. You may write about one of the points of view mentioned above, or you may give another point of view on this issue. Use specific examples and reasons for your position.

![] **ANSWER KEY**

English Test

1. D	21. B	41. C	61. D
2. F	22. F	42. G	62. J
3. B	23. A	43. A	63. B
4. F	24. G	44. J	64. F
5. C	25. A	45. A	65. C
6. J	26. G	46. J	66. G
7. C	27. D	47. D	67. B
8. G	28. G	48. F	68. H
9. A	29. A	49. A	69. D
10. H	30. J	50. J	70. G
11. A	31. D	51. B	71. B
12. J	32. F	52. H	72. G
13. B	33. A	53. D	73. D
14. H	34. G	54. F	74. F
15. D	35. B	55. D	75. B
16. F	36. H	56. G	
17. B	37. D	57. D	
18. H	38. F	58. H	
19. D	39. B	59. A	
20. F	40. H	60. J	

Mathematics Test

1. A	21. E	41. A
2. H	22. J	42. H
3. D	23. C	43. C
4. F	24. G	44. J
5. C	25. B	45. B
6. H	26. G	46. H
7. D	27. D	47. A
8. J	28. F	48. G
9. A	29. B	49. E
10. H	30. H	50. H
11. C	31. C	51. C
12. K	32. F	52. H
13. B	33. A	53. B
14. H	34. J	54. F
15. B	35. C	55. A
16. H	36. K	56. J
17. B	37. E	57. B
18. G	38. J	58. J
19. A	39. E	59. C
20. K	40. K	60. J

Reading Test

1. C	21. B
2. J	22. H
3. B	23. B
4. G	24. G
5. D	25. B
6. G	26. J
7. D	27. A
8. H	28. H
9. A	29. A
10. H	30. J
11. B	31. C
12. H	32. G
13. D	33. B
14. H	34. J
15. B	35. C
16. G	36. F
17. C	37. B
18. J	38. G
19. A	39. D
20. F	40. J

Science Reasoning Test

1. D	21. D
2. J	22. J
3. B	23. C
4. H	24. G
5. D	25. A
6. G	26. H
7. D	27. B
8. H	28. J
9. A	29. C
10. F	30. G
11. B	31. C
12. H	32. J
13. C	33. A
14. G	34. J
15. C	35. C
16. G	36. G
17. D	37. B
18. J	38. H
19. B	39. A
20. H	40. G

■ SCORING GUIDE

Your final reported score is your COMPOSITE SCORE. Your COMPOSITE SCORE is the average of all of your SCALE SCORES.

Your SCALE SCORES for the four multiple-choice sections are derived from the Scoring Table on the next page. Use your RAW SCORE, or the number of questions that you answered correctly for each section, to determine your SCALE SCORE. If you got a RAW SCORE of 60 on the English test, for example, you correctly answered 60 out of 75 questions.

Step 1   Determine your RAW SCORE for each of the four multiple-choice sections:

English   _____

Mathematics   _____

Reading   _____

Science Reasoning   _____

The following Raw Score Table shows the total possible points for each section.

RAW SCORE TABLE	
KNOWLEDGE AND SKILL AREAS	**RAW SCORES**
ENGLISH	75
MATHEMATICS	60
READING	40
SCIENCE REASONING	40
WRITING	12

Multiple-Choice Scoring Worksheet

Step 2 Determine your SCALE SCORE for each of the four multiple-choice sections using the following Scoring Worksheet. Each SCALE SCORE should be rounded to the nearest number according to normal rules. For example, $31.2 \approx 31$ and $31.5 \approx 32$. If you answered 61 questions correctly on the English section, for example, your SCALE SCORE would be 29.

English _____ $\times$ **36** = _____ $\div$ **75** = _____
RAW SCORE
                                                                    $-\,2$ (*correction factor)

_____
SCALE SCORE

Mathematics _____ $\times$ **36** = _____ $\div$ **60** = _____
RAW SCORE
                                                                    $+\,1$ (*correction factor)

_____
SCALE SCORE

Reading _____ $\times$ **36** = _____ $\div$ **40** = _____
RAW SCORE
                                                                    $+\,2$ (*correction factor)

_____
SCALE SCORE

Science Reasoning _____ $\times$ **36** = _____ $\div$ **40** = _____
RAW SCORE
                                                                    $+\,1.5$ (*correction factor)

_____
SCALE SCORE

*The correction factor is an approximation based on the average from several recent ACT tests. It is most valid for scores in the middle 50% (approximately 16–24 scale composite score) of the scoring range.

The scores are all approximate. Actual ACT scoring scales vary from one administration to the next based upon several factors.

If you take the optional Writing Test, you will need to combine your English and Writing scores to obtain your final COMPOSITE SCORE. Once you have determined a score for your essay out of 12 possible points, you will need to determine your ENGLISH/WRITING SCALE SCORE, using both your ENGLISH SCALE SCORE and your WRITING TEST SCORE. The combination of the two scores will give you an ENGLISH/WRITING SCALE SCORE, from 1 to 36, that will be used to determine your COMPOSITE SCORE mentioned earlier.

Using the English/Writing Scoring Table, find your ENGLISH SCALE SCORE on the left or right hand side of the table and your WRITING TEST SCORE on the top of the table. Follow your ENGLISH SCALE SCORE over and your WRITING TEST SCORE down until the two columns meet at a number. This number is your ENGLISH/WRITING SCALE SCORE and will be used to determine your COMPOSITE SCORE.

Step 3 Determine your ENGLISH/WRITING SCALE SCORE using the English/Writing Scoring Table on the following page:

English _____

Writing _____

English/Writing _____

ENGLISH/WRITING SCORING TABLE

ENGLISH SCALE SCORE	WRITING TEST SCORE											ENGLISH SCALE SCORE
	2	3	4	5	6	7	8	9	10	11	12	
36	26	27	28	29	30	31	32	33	34	32	36	36
35	26	27	28	29	30	31	31	32	33	34	35	35
34	25	26	27	28	29	30	31	32	33	34	35	34
33	24	25	26	27	28	29	30	31	32	33	34	33
32	24	25	25	26	27	28	29	30	31	32	33	32
31	23	24	25	26	27	28	29	30	30	31	32	31
30	22	23	24	25	26	27	28	29	30	31	32	30
29	21	22	23	24	25	26	27	28	29	30	31	29
28	21	22	23	24	24	25	26	27	28	29	30	28
27	20	21	22	23	24	25	26	27	28	28	29	27
26	19	20	21	22	23	24	25	26	27	28	29	26
25	18	19	20	21	22	23	24	25	26	27	28	25
24	18	19	20	21	22	23	23	24	25	26	27	24
23	17	18	19	20	21	22	23	24	25	26	27	23
22	16	17	18	19	20	21	22	23	24	25	26	22
21	16	17	17	18	19	20	21	22	23	24	25	21
20	15	16	17	18	19	20	21	21	22	23	24	20
19	14	15	16	17	18	19	20	21	22	23	24	19
18	13	14	15	16	17	18	19	20	21	22	23	18
17	13	14	15	16	16	17	18	19	20	21	22	17
16	12	13	14	15	16	17	18	19	20	20	21	16
15	11	12	13	14	15	16	17	18	19	20	21	15
14	10	11	12	13	14	15	16	17	18	19	20	14
13	10	11	12	13	14	14	15	16	17	18	19	13
12	9	10	11	12	13	14	15	16	17	18	19	12
11	8	9	10	11	12	13	14	15	16	17	18	11
10	8	9	9	10	11	12	13	14	15	16	17	10
9	7	8	9	10	11	12	13	13	14	15	16	9
8	6	7	8	9	10	11	12	13	14	15	16	8
7	5	6	7	8	9	10	11	12	13	14	15	7
6	5	6	7	7	8	9	10	11	12	13	14	6
5	4	5	6	7	8	9	10	11	12	12	13	5
4	3	4	5	6	7	8	9	10	11	12	13	4
3	2	3	4	5	6	7	8	9	10	11	12	3
2	2	3	4	5	6	6	7	8	9	10	11	2
1	1	2	3	4	5	6	7	8	9	10	11	1

Step 4   Determine your COMPOSITE SCORE by finding the sum of all your SCALE SCORES for each of the four sections: English only (if you do not choose to take the optional Writing Test) *or* English/Writing (if you choose to take the optional Writing Test), Math, Reading, and Science Reasoning, and divide by 4 to find the average. Round your COMPOSITE SCORE according to normal rules. For example, 31.2 ≈ 31 and 31.5 ≈ 32.

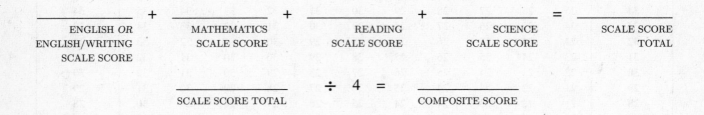

_____ + _____ + _____ + _____ = _____

ENGLISH *OR*   MATHEMATICS   READING   SCIENCE   SCALE SCORE

ENGLISH/WRITING   SCALE SCORE   SCALE SCORE   SCALE SCORE   TOTAL

SCALE SCORE

_____   ÷ 4 =   _____

SCALE SCORE TOTAL   COMPOSITE SCORE

ANSWERS AND EXPLANATIONS

English Test Explanations

PASSAGE I

1. **The best answer is D.** The sentence is clearest and most concise when the word *back* is inserted in place of the underlined portion. Answer choices A, B, and C are either awkward or redundant.

2. **The best answer is F.** This sentence is best as written. The word *fairly* is correctly used as an adverb to further modify the adjective *regular*, which modifies the noun *trips*. Answer choice G is not correct because the word *fair* is being used as an adjective to describe the trips, when it should be used to modify the adjective *regular*. Answer choice H is incorrect because it reverses the words, thereby changing the meaning of the sentence. It is not best to use *regular* because the context of the sentence indicates that the trips were *mostly* between Las Vegas and New York, so answer choice J is incorrect.

3. **The best answer is B.** The context of the sentence indicates that first the author goes to Las Vegas, "then" the author returns home to New York. It is not appropriate to use "than" to indicate a progression in time, so answer choices A and C are incorrect. Answer choice D is wordy and is not as clear and effective as answer choice B.

4. **The best answer is F.** The sentence is best as it is written. It clearly indicates that because the author and her husband are retired, they have sufficient time to travel. Answer choices G and H are wordy and are not as clear and effective as answer choice F. Omitting the underlined portion would result in some ambiguity within the sentence: you do not know for what the author and her husband have plenty of time.

5. **The best answer is C.** According to the passage, the fact that the author's grandchildren live in New York combined with the fact that she has two dogs makes it difficult for her to stay for any longer than three weeks in Las Vegas. These responsibilities require her to be at home in New York most of the time. Therefore, it would not be viable for her to stay longer than a few weeks at a time in Las Vegas.

6. **The best answer is J.** The paragraph is written in the present tense, so it is necessary to use the present tense verb *has*. Answer choices F and G use the past tense, so they are incorrect. It is never correct to use the helping verb *has* with the simple past tense verb *became*, so answer choice H is incorrect.

7. **The best answer is C.** If two adjectives modify a noun in the same way, they are called coordinate adjectives. It is necessary to separate coordinate adjectives, such as *warm* and *sunny* with a comma. You could also insert the coordinate conjunction *and*, but you should not use any commas if you do so; therefore, answer choice B is incorrect. A semicolon should be used to separate two related main clauses, so answer choice D is incorrect.

8. **The best answer is G.** The subordinating conjunction *because* clearly indicates that the dogs are the reason that the author cannot fly to Las Vegas. The subordinating conjunction *so* is used to indicate a consequence, and if it is used here, it creates an incomplete sentence; eliminate answer choice F. Answer choice H is a preposition phrase that does not correctly express the idea that having the dogs prevents the author from flying to Las Vegas, so it is incorrect. While answer choice J expresses essentially the same idea as answer choice G, it is wordy and awkward and should be eliminated.

9. **The best answer is A.** It is necessary to use commas to set off parenthetical expressions within a sentence. Because the phrase "both of which are shelter mutts" is not essential to the meaning of the sentence, it is considered a parenthetical, or non-restrictive phrase. A nonrestrictive phrase can be omitted from the sentence without changing the meaning of the sentence.

10. **The best answer is H.** The sentence is written in the present tense, so it is necessary to use the present tense verb *lies*. In addition, the sentence indicates that only one dog *lies* on a blanket on the floor.

11. **The best answer is A.** It is best to leave Sentence 5 where it is in the paragraph. The paragraph describes the behavior of the dogs as they travel with the author, and the sequence of events is clearly indicated without changing the order of the sentences.

PRACTICE TEST 4 ANSWERS AND EXPLANATIONS

318

12. **The best answer is J.** The passage is written primarily in the present perfect tense so it is necessary to use the present perfect form of the verb *have passed*. The word *past* indicates "the time before the present," and is not a verb that suggests movement. Therefore, eliminate answer choices F and H. Answer choice G is incorrect because it uses the present participle *passing*, which suggests that the action is currently taking place.

13. **The best answer is B.** The context of the sentence indicates that the author paid multiple tolls, so the plural form of the word is correct. The tolls do not possess anything, so it is not necessary to use an apostrophe; eliminate answer choices A and D. Answer choice C includes an extraneous comma, so it is incorrect. Because the phrase "in Oklahoma" is necessary to the meaning of the sentence, it should not be set off by commas.

14. **The best answer is H.** The preceding sentence reads, "I'm mentally preparing myself for a sunless New York sky during our week at home." This sentence and the final sentence of the passage suggest that the author enjoys her visits to "sunny Las Vegas" and is glad for the chance to escape the "sunless New York sky." The sentence reinforces the author's decision to travel back and forth from New York to Nevada.

15. **The best answer is D.** The tone and context of the passage clearly indicate that it is a personal account of the author's travels to and from Nevada. Therefore, it would not fulfill an assignment to write a travel article about Las Vegas, Nevada.

PASSAGE II

16. **The best answer is F.** The indefinite pronoun *one* is used to indicate any of the possible people who acquire a new puppy or dog. Because *one* is a collective pronoun, it is considered a singular pronoun, so the correct verb to use is "acquires." You do not need the pronoun *who* in the sentence, so eliminate answer choice H. It is not correct to use the pronoun *it* refer to people, so eliminate answer choice J.

17. **The best answer is B.** By using the article *the*, the sentence does not clearly indicate to whom the pets belong. The context of the sentence shows that the pets belong to the *dog owners* so it is correct to use the plural pronoun *their*. The word "there" indicates a place, so eliminate answer choice C. The word *they're* is the conjunction of *they* and *are*, so eliminate answer choice D.

18. **The best answer is H.** The sentence is written in the present tense, so it is necessary to use the present tense verb *is*. As it is written, the sentence suggests that the problem will be *become* evident in the future, so eliminate answer choice F. Answer choice G is incorrect because it uses the participle *becoming*; answer choice J is awkward.

19. **The best answer is D.** The sentence discusses the "movements and facial expressions" of "a dog," which means that you should use the singular possessive *dog's*.

20. **The best answer is F.** The sentence is best as it is written. Answer choice G is incorrect because he participle *confusing* suggests that the dog's actions are not clear to the owner, which does not fit the context of the sentence. Answer choice H is incorrect because use of the preposition *by* suggests that the dog finds "waiting for a signal" to be confusing, which is not supported by the context. Answer choice J is incorrect for the same reason; in addition, it is not idiomatic to say "confused with" unless you are making a comparison.

21. **The best answer is B.** Since the sentence refers to a single dog—*the dog*—it is correct to use the singular possessive *its*. As it is written, the sentence is unclear as to whom or what the *lips* belong. It is never correct to use the plural possessive *its,'* because *it* is a singular pronoun. Therefore, answer choice C is incorrect. Answer choice D is incorrect because the sentence refers to a single dog.

22. **The best answer is F.** The paragraph describes several ways that a dog will communicate non-verbally with its owner. The description of a relaxed dog letting "its tongue loll out of its mouth" is another example of this type of communication.

23. **The best answer is A.** This question tests your ability to convey the intended idea clearly and effectively. The simplest way to show that other forms of body language exist is to say "can also indicate." The other answer choices are wordy and awkward and are not appropriate for standard written English.

24. **The best answer is G.** The preceding sentence describes how a dog owner might recognize when his or her dog is being aggressive or fearful. Answer choice G offers a reason for this behavior.

25. **The best answer is A.** The main focus of the paragraph is additional forms of body language that a dog might exhibit when attempting to communicate. Therefore, the best concluding sentence will refer to and generalize the main idea. Only answer

choice A does this. The other answer choices are too specific and offer additional forms of communication.

26. **The best answer is G.** You should use a comma to separate elements that introduce and modify a sentence. The phrase "While most dogs are capable of learning" is an introductory clause that should be followed by a comma. Answer choice F is incorrect because a semicolon should be used to separate two independent clauses. Answer choices H and J are incorrect because it is necessary to use a comma to separate an introductory clause from the rest of the sentence. In addition, answer choice J creates an incomplete sentence.

27. **The best answer is D.** The main focus of the paragraph is on learning to understand a dog's body language and using that knowledge to more effectively train the dog. The sentence that mentions offering a dog treats is least relevant—it does not add any information that is necessary to the flow or structure of the paragraph. While Sentence 6 is not entirely unrelated to the topic, of the answer choices, it is the least relevant to the paragraph.

28. **The best answer is G.** According to the conventions of standard written English, you should never separate a subject from its verb with any sort of punctuation. Therefore, it is incorrect to place a comma, a semicolon, or a colon between *The bottom line*—the subject—and *is*—the verb.

29. **The best answer is A.** The ACT rewards active voice. Therefore, it is better to use the verb *communicating* as opposed to the noun *communication* in this sentence; eliminate answer choices B and D. It is idiomatic to say *involved in*, whereas *involved to* is not correct in standard written English.

30. **The best answer is J.** The ACT rewards active voice. Therefore, it is best to say *to remember*; the other answer choices are not as good because they are written in the passive voice.

PASSAGE III

31. **The best answer is D.** You should use a comma to separate elements that introduce and modify a sentence. The phrase "While the history of the piñata is somewhat murky" is an introductory clause that should be followed by a comma. Answer choice A is incorrect because it creates an incomplete sentence. Answer choice B is incorrect because a semicolon should separate two independent clauses.

Answer choice C is incorrect because you must use a comma to separate an introductory clause from the rest of the sentence.

32. **The best answer is F.** The word *where* correctly indicates that most of the piñatas were made in China. Because China is a place, it is better to say *where* than *in*, so answer choice G is incorrect. Answer choice H is incorrect because it includes an extraneous comma. The coordinate conjunction *so* indicates that China is the reason that most piñatas were made to resemble animals, which does not make sense.

33. **The best answer is A.** The underlined portion clearly and effectively indicates that the current custom of filling piñatas with candy or toys differs from the original custom of filling the piñatas with seeds. Answer choice B is incorrect because it includes the ambiguous pronoun *they*. Answer choice C is redundant—it is not necessary to use both *standard* and *customary* in the sentence because the words are synonyms. If you omit the underlined portion, you lose the comparison between the original custom and the current custom.

34. **The best answer is G.** The sentence is written in the past tense so you must use the past tense verb *were kept*. Answer choice H is incorrect because, while it uses the past tense verb *kept*, it creates an incomplete sentence.

35. **The best answer is B.** No commas are necessary to set off a person's name from a clause when the title of occupation precedes the name: for example, President Abraham Lincoln.

36. **The best answer is H.** The paragraph focuses specifically on the piñata and its use in European celebrations. The sentence that the author is considering adding does not offer anything relevant to the main idea of the paragraph.

37. **The best answer is D.** The phrase "that broke easily," while not grammatically incorrect, is redundant. Something that is fragile, by definition, breaks easily. Therefore, answer choices B and C are also redundant, and it would be best to omit the underlined portion.

38. **The best answer is F.** The sentence is describing an event as it might have taken place in the past. Therefore, it is appropriate to use the auxiliary verb *would be* with the past tense verb *hung*. It is not necessary to use any punctuation in the underlined portion.

39. The best answer is B. The past tense verb *dispensed* effectively indicates that the tiny treasures came from the pot after it was broken. The phrase *dispensed with* refers to getting rid of or doing away with something, which does not fit the context.

40. The best answer is H. Only answer choice H uses the active voice to clearly indicate that either the pots could be unadorned, or they could be decorated with ribbons and paper. The other answer choices are in the passive voice and are awkward.

41. The best answer is C. The sentence is discussing more than one piñata, so the plural form *piñatas* is correct. The "s" apostrophe means plural possession, and the apostrophe "s" means singular possession; possession is not indicated by the context of the sentence, so answer choices A and B are incorrect.

42. The best answer is G. The singular subject *every* needs the singular pronoun *its*. The word *it's* is the conjunction of *it is*.

43. The best answer is A. The phrase "In America" is an introductory clause that must be followed by a comma.

44. The best answer is J. The context of the sentence indicates that the piñatas are filled with candy and toys; in fact, the sentence says *pounds*, which can be interpreted as a large quantity. Because *barren* means *empty*, it would not be an appropriate alternative.

45. The best answer is A. As it is written, the underlined portion clearly and effectively shows what the audience most enjoys doing: "watching the blindfolded person swing mightily at nothing but thin air." It is in the active voice and is free from ambiguity. The other answer choices are either in the passive voice or do not make sense.

PASSAGE IV

46. The best answer is J. If a list contains three or more items, it is necessary to separate those items with commas. It is not appropriate to include a comma between the verb *read* and the prepositional phrase *in magazines*, so answer choice F is incorrect. Answer choice G does not include any of the necessary separating commas, so it is incorrect. A semicolon should be used to separate items in a list that follows a colon, so the use of a semicolon in answer choice H is incorrect.

47. The best answer is D. This sentence requires the use of the participle *spending* in order to accurately show that the spending takes place after the watching, reading, and hearing of the advertisements. The helping verb *having* suggests that the spending occurs first, which does not make sense. Answer choice D is the most simple and clear selection.

48. The best answer is F. The underlined portion is best as it is written. It is not appropriate to use a comma to separate a subject from its verb, so answer choice G is incorrect. Both answer choices H and J create an incomplete sentence that lacks a main verb.

49. The best answer is A. The underlined portion correctly uses the contraction of *you are*, whereas answer choice B incorrectly uses the possessive pronoun *your*. The other answer choices are awkward and contain extraneous commas.

50. The best answer is J. The underlined portion is redundant, because the sentence already indicates that the person is *special*. Therefore, the best thing to do is to omit the underlined portion. Because all of the answer choices are grammatically correct and express the same idea, you should be able to quickly recognize the redundancy.

51. The best answer is B. This question tests your ability to recognize idiom. In standard written English it is appropriate to use the phrase *filled with*.

52. The best answer is H. Because the sentence uses the pronoun *you* earlier in the sentence, it is not necessary to restate the pronoun later in the sentence. It is clear that *you* are performing both actions—decorating a picture frame and using nuts and bolts.

53. The best answer is D. The coordinate conjunction *and* is not necessary at this point in the sentence. The sentence presents a list of items that could be used in a shadow box, and *a dried flower* is an item that falls in the middle of the list. Therefore, no additional language is necessary.

54. The best answer is F. In order to avoid redundancy and wordiness, it is best to simply say *gather from*. This clearly and effectively expresses the idea.

55. The best answer is D. Sentence 1 is an appropriate introductory sentence because it includes the transitional phrase *For example*, and then goes on to give examples of how to create a handmade gift from someone's trinkets or other personal items. Sentence 2 directly follows with yet another example. Sentence 4 would best follow sentence 2, because it provides details on how to make a shadow box. Finally, sentence 3 is best as the last sentence because it effectively concludes the topic discussed in the paragraph.

56. **The best answer is G.** The sentence as it is written is an incomplete sentence that lacks a main verb. Answer choice G is correct because it is necessary to use a comma to separate an introductory clause from the rest of the sentence. Answer choice H has the comma after the verb, which is incorrect.

57. **The best answer is D.** It is best to use the adverb *nearly* to modify the adjective *endless*. Answer choice D is best because it does not include the extraneous verb *to be*.

58. **The best answer is H.** To identify more effectively exactly what is happening, it is better to use the specific pronoun *this*. The pronoun *it* is rather ambiguous, and the coordinate conjunction *so* is not appropriate.

59. **The best answer is A.** The student benefits by learning about scrapbooking and the store benefits be receiving customer patronage. The other answer choices offer support for why a patron would take a class, but not for why a store owner would offer such a class.

60. **The best answer is J.** The notion that original, hand-made pictures or books will be enjoyed is stated previously in the paragraph. Therefore, it is not necessary or relevant to mention it again. The other answer choices are not supported by the essay.

PASSAGE V

61. **The best answer is D.** No punctuation is necessary in this sentence. A good rule of thumb is to use a comma wherever you would naturally pause in a sentence. Because there are no natural pauses in this sentence, you don't need a comma. Answer choice B is incorrect because a semicolon should be used to separate two independent clauses. Answer choice C is incorrect because a colon should generally be used to introduce a list.

62. **The best answer is J.** Answer choice J is best because it indicates not only that accidents occur more frequently, but how many times more frequently they occur. This is more detailed and relevant than the information contained in the other answer choices.

63. **The best answer is B.** The plural subject *These statistics* requires the plural verb *take*. The other answer choices use the wrong verb form or tense.

64. **The best answer is F.** The sentence in answer choice F introduces the idea of *ingenious designs* which are then discussed in the paragraph. Answer choice G does not provide an effective transition, and answer choice H is irrelevant to the topic of the paragraph. Answer choice J is incorrect because the focus of the passage is safety.

65. **The best answer is C.** In order to maintain parallelism within the sentence, it is necessary to use *illuminating* to match the verb *allowing*.

66. **The best answer is G.** The plural noun *headlights* requires the plural verb *are*.

67. **The best answer is B.** You should use a semicolon to separate two independent but related clauses. A comma is insufficient and creates a comma splice, so answer choice A is incorrect. Answer choices C in incorrect because it does not include any punctuation. Answer choice D is incorrect because it is not correctly punctuated.

68. **The best answer is H.** By using the verb phrase *doing so*, answer choice H clearly and effectively indicates that using the high-beams would provide more light. Answer choice F is incorrect because the pronoun *they* is ambiguous—it is unclear whether the antecedent is *high-beams* or *drivers*. Answer choice G is incorrect for a similar reason— the pronoun *it* is ambiguous. Answer choice J is awkward and contains an ambiguous pronoun.

69. **The best answer is D.** It is best to say *switching proves* because *switching* is singular. The other answer choices include incorrect verb tense and aspect.

70. **The best answer is G.** It is appropriate to use a colon to introduce a list of items. Answer choice F is incorrect because it creates an incomplete sentence. Answer choice H is incorrect because it includes a comma splice. Answer choice J is incorrect because it is awkward and wordy.

71. **The best answer is B.** To clearly indicate that the images are displayed on a screen after the images are detected, it is best to use the phrase *are then displayed*. The images themselves do not display; rather, they are displayed, so answer choices A and C are incorrect.

72. **The best answer is G.** Sentence 5 should be the last sentence of the paragraph because it effectively

concludes the topic of the paragraph, and most logically follows sentence 6.

73. The best answer is D. The phrase "particularly during dangerous nighttime driving" is a nonrestrictive clause, which should be set off with commas. Only answer choice D correctly places a comma between *road* and *particularly*.

74. The best answer is F. Use a comma with a coordinating conjunction to separate main clauses within

a sentence. A coordinating conjunction connects words, phrases, or clauses that are of equal importance in the sentence.

75. The best answer is B. Paragraph 1 states that more accidents occur at night than in the daytime. The new sentence uses the possessive determiner *these*, which takes the mention of night accidents as its antecedent from earlier in the paragraph.

Mathematics Test Explanations

1. **The correct answer is A.** You are given that one foot is approximately 0.3048 meters. Therefore, a building that is 65 feet long will be 65(0.3048), or 19.8 meters long.

2. **The correct answer is H.** To calculate the new hourly rate, multiply the current rate by 18%, or 0.18, its decimal equivalent, and add the result to the current rate:

$$30(0.18) + 30 = 30 + 5.40, \text{ or } \$35.40$$

3. **The correct answer is D.** To find the average, divide the sum of the contributions by the number of contributions, as follows:

$$\frac{(25 + 40 + 30 + 15)}{4} = \frac{110}{4} = 27.50$$

4. **The correct answer is F.** To find the difference in the distance traveled, first find the distance traveled by each bus. Distance equals rate multiplied by time. Since Bus X travels 40 miles per hour for 2 hours, it traveled $40(2) = 80$ miles. Likewise, since Bus Y travels 60 miles per hour for $1\frac{1}{2}$ hours, it traveled $60(1.5) = 90$ miles. Therefore, the difference is $90 - 80$, or 10 miles.

5. **The correct answer is C.** The expression $(r + 2)(r - 3)$ will equal zero when either $r + 2$ or $r - 3$ equals zero. Thus $r = -2$ or $r = 3$.

6. **The correct answer is H.** The perimeter is the distance around the parallelogram. In parallelograms, opposing sides have equal lengths. If PS is 7 cm long, so is QR. Also, PQ and SR will have the same length. Set the length of PQ and SR to l, and solve.

$$7 + 7 + l + l = 40$$

$$14 + 2l = 40$$

$$14 + 2l = 40$$

$$l = \frac{26}{2}, \text{ or } 13.$$

7. **The correct answer is D.** If the x-coordinate of each point on a line is 5 more than half the y-coordinate, then $x = \frac{y}{2} + 5$. To find the slope

of the line, solve for y and put the equation in slope-intercept form ($y = mx + b$, where m is the slope). To do so, first subtract 5 from both sides, then multiply the entire equation by 2 to get $y = 2x - 10$. The slope is 2.

8. **The correct answer is J.** You are given that a rectangular garden has a length of x and a width of y, and has its length reduced by 3 feet and its width extended by 2 feet. Therefore, the length becomes $x - 3$ and its width becomes $y + 2$. The area of the new garden is then $(x - 3)(y + 2)$.

9. **The correct answer is A.** To get y in terms of x and z, solve $x = 3yz^2$ for y, as shown below:

$$x = 3yz^2$$

$$\frac{x}{3z^2} = y, \text{ or } y = \frac{x}{3z^2}$$

10. **The correct answer is H.** The triangle pictured is isosceles, meaning that the two angles opposite the sides that have equal length have equal measure. Since the sum of the interior angles of a triangle is 180°, the measure of $\angle \alpha$ is $180° - 2(55°)$, or $180° - 110°$, which is 70°.

11. **The correct answer is C.** To solve this problem, distribute using the FOIL method, as follows:

$$(3x^2 - 1)(x^2 - 4)$$

First: $3x^4$
Outside: $-12x^2$
Inside: $-x^2$
Last: 4

Combine like terms and simplify to get $3x^4 - 13x^2 + 4$.

12. **The correct answer is K.** To solve this problem it might be helpful to draw a picture like the one below.

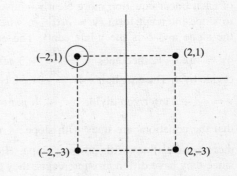

Since the figure is a square, the placement of the missing point becomes clear: the upper left corner. The point will share the same x-coordinate as $(-2,-2)$ and the same y-coordinate as $(2,1)$, making its coordinates $(-2,1)$.

13. **The correct answer is B.** To reduce the expression, recall that when two numbers that consist of the same base raised to a power are divided, you should subtract the exponents. Thus $\dfrac{x^8}{x^4} = x^{8-4} = x^4$. Likewise, the expression $\dfrac{(x^8 y^{12})}{(x^4 y^3 z^2)} = \dfrac{(x^{8-4} y^{12-3})}{z^2}$, which is equivalent to $\dfrac{x^4 y^9}{z^2}$.

14. **The correct answer is H.** Logarithms are used to indicate exponents of certain numbers called bases. By definition, $\log_a b = c$, if $a^c = b$. Therefore, $\log_n 64 = 2$ implies that $64 = n^2$. Thus $n = 8$.

15. **The correct answer is B.** To find the percentage of the 700 high-school students who answered that the Warriors were their favorite team, divide the number of students who answered Warriors by 700 and multiply by 100%. To find the number of students who answered Warriors, add the total number of students who answered that they liked a different team and subtract that quantity from 700. Thus the percentage of students who answered Warriors is $\dfrac{(700 - (250 + 200 + 50))}{700} \times 100\%$, or $\dfrac{(700 - 500)}{700} \times 100\%$, which is $\dfrac{200}{700} \times 100\%$, or approximately 28.6%.

16. **The correct answer is H.** If $x^2 = 36$ and $y^2 = 81$, then $x = \pm 6$ and $y = \pm 9$. There are then 4 possible combinations of $x + y$: $6 + 9$, $-6 + 9$, $6 + (-9)$, and $-6 + (-9)$, which have values 15, 3, -3, and -15, respectively. Therefore, the value of $x + y$ cannot be 0.

17. **The correct answer is B.** To see the properties of each linear equation more clearly, convert each to slope-intercept form ($y = mx + b$, where m is the slope and b is the y-intercept). The equation $4y = 3x + 12$ becomes $y = \dfrac{3x}{4} + 3$ after you divide by 4. The equation $-4y = -3x - 8$ becomes $y = \dfrac{3x}{4} + 2$ after you divide by -4. It is now clear that the equations are lines with slope $\dfrac{3}{4}$, making them parallel lines with positive slope. However, since they have different y-intercepts, they are two distinct lines.

18. **The correct answer is G.** The absolute value of any number is non-negative. Since $|-3| = 3$, the value of $\dfrac{-6}{|-3|} = \dfrac{-6}{3}$, or -2.

19. **The correct answer is A.** In order for the expression $(a + y)(a + z)$ to equal zero, either $a + y = 0$ or $a + z = 0$. Thus either $a = -y$ or $a = -z$.

20. **The correct answer is K.** The statement that CF is congruent to EF is not true because $\triangle CEF$ is an isosceles triangle in which CE and CF are equal. Since the triangle is isosceles, $\angle CFE$ is congruent to $\angle CEF$, and they have measure 70°. In a triangle, the length of a side is proportional to the measure of the angle opposite it. Since the measure of the angle opposite EF is only 40° while the measure of the angle opposite CF is 70°, EF must be shorter than CF.

21. **The correct answer is E.** To find the slope, convert the equation $21x - 3y + 18 = 0$ to slope-intercept form ($y = mx + b$, where m is the slope and b is the y-intercept). To do so, first subtract 18 and $21x$ from both sides to get $-3y = -21x - 18$. Then divide both sides by -3 to get $y = 7x + 6$. Therefore the slope is 7.

22. **The correct answer is J.** The least common denominator (LCD) is actually the least common multiple of the three denominators. To find the LCD, first find the greatest common factor of the denominators. In this case, each denominator contains either a, b, or both b and c, so those are the factors that they have in common. The values that remain in the three denominators represent what they don't have in common, and are the least common multiples of each denominator. To find the least common multiple, otherwise known as the least common denominator (LCD), simply multiply the least common multiples of each denominator together, to get $a^2 \times b^2 \times c^2$.

23. **The correct answer is C.** To solve this problem, go through and try each answer choice to see which one has the desired result. The correct answer is -2 because adding negative 2 is the same as subtracting 2: $\dfrac{(5-2)}{(8-2)} = \dfrac{3}{6}$, or $\dfrac{1}{2}$.

24. **The correct answer is G.** To solve this problem, first solve the equation $2y = 16$ for y to get $y = 8$. Then substitute $y = 8$ into the equation $x + y = 13$ to get $x + 8 = 13$, making $x = 5$.

25. **The correct answer is B.** One possible method of solving this problem is to systematically eliminate wrong answer choices. It is given that $|m| > |n|$.

Assuming that statement is true, then m cannot equal n because if $m = n$, then $|m| = |n|$; eliminate answer choice A. Pick numbers for the variables to more clearly see the relationships, as follows:

> **Answer choice B:** When $m = 3$ and $n = 2$, $|m| > |n|$ is true. Likewise, when $m = -3$ and $n = -2$, $|m| > |n|$ is true. Therefore, answer choice B is correct.
>
> **Answer choice C:** When $m = 2$ and $n = 3$, $|m| > |n|$ is not true, so answer choice C is incorrect.
>
> **Answer choice D:** When $m = 3$ and $n = -4$, $|m| > |n|$ is not true, so answer choice D is incorrect.
>
> **Answer choice E:** Because you are not given any information about n, you cannot determine a relationship, so answer choice E is incorrect.

26. **The correct answer is G.** A graph crosses the x-axis at the point when $y = 0$. Given that $y - 5 = \frac{1}{2x} + 1$, let $y = 0$ such that $-5 = \frac{1}{2x} + 1$. Subtracting 1 from both sides yields $-6 = \frac{1}{2x}$. Multiplying by 2 yields $-12 = x$.

27. **The correct answer is D.** To calculate the area of the living room, first calculate its dimensions. The length of the living room is $18'$ less the width of the hallway, which is $4'$, making it $18 - 4 = 14'$. The width of the living room is $20'$ less the width of the kitchen, which is $8'$, making it $20 - 8 = 12'$. Thus the area of the living room is $14' \times 12' = 168$ square feet.

28. **The correct answer is F.** The perimeter is equal to the distance around an object. To calculate the perimeter of the ground floor of the townhouse, add the sides. The perimeter of the ground floor of the townhouse is $2(20') + 2(18')$, or $40' + 36'$, which is $76'$.

29. **The correct answer is B.** This question asks you to calculate the percentage by which the population has decreased. First, determine the number of birds that you would expect to find in your sample area if the population density had not changed. Multiply the population density 3 years ago (20 birds) by the size of the sample area (3.25 acres):

$$20 \times 3.25 = 65$$

You would expect to find 65 birds in your sample area if there had been no change in population density.

Next, subtract the actual number of birds recorded in the sample area (47) from the expected number of birds (65):

$$65 - 47 = 18$$

There are 18 fewer birds in the sample area than what you would expect to find. Since you are asked to calculate the percentage decrease, set up a proportion:

18 birds is to 65 birds as x percent is to 100 percent.

$$\frac{18}{65} = \frac{x}{100}.$$

Cross-multiply and solve for x:

$$65x = 1,800$$
$$x = \frac{1,800}{65}$$
$$x = 27.69$$

Since the problem asks for an answer to the nearest tenth, round to 27.7. According to the study, the population density of the particular bird that you are studying has decreased by approximately 27.7%.

Answer choice C could be obtained if you found the difference between the number of birds expected (65) and the number of birds recorded (47), then divided by the number of birds recorded (47) to get a percent. Answer choice D is the percentage that the number of birds per acre 3 years ago (20) is of the number of birds recorded in 3.5 acres this year (47).

30. **The correct answer is H.** To find the product $(\tan \alpha)(\sin \beta)$, break up $\tan \alpha$ and $\sin \beta$ to their ratios. The ratio $\tan \alpha$ is the side opposite α divided by the side adjacent to α: $\frac{z}{x}$. The ratio $\sin \beta$ is the side opposite β divided by the hypotenuse: $\frac{x}{y}$. The product $(\tan \alpha)(\sin \beta)$ is, therefore, $\left(\frac{z}{x}\right)\left(\frac{x}{y}\right) = \frac{z}{y}$.

31. **The correct answer is C.** In order to add $\frac{1}{x} + \frac{3}{4}$, the fractions must have a common denominator. To achieve a common denominator, multiply $\frac{1}{x}$ by $\frac{4}{4}$ and $\frac{3}{4}$ by $\frac{x}{x}$ to get $\frac{4}{4x} + \frac{3x}{4x}$, which equals $\frac{(4 + 3x)}{4x}$.

32. The correct answer is F. To solve this problem, it may be helpful to draw a picture in which one angle of a right triangle is labeled A, as shown below:

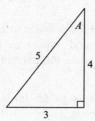

Because $\cos A = \dfrac{4}{5}$, let the side adjacent to angle A be 4 and the hypotenuse be 5. Likewise, since $\sin A = \dfrac{3}{5}$, let the side opposite angle A be 3 and the hypotenuse be 5. It follows then that $\tan A =$ side opposite divided by side adjacent, or $\dfrac{3}{4}$.

33. The correct answer is A. To solve this problem, convert $5x + 3y = 8$ to the slope-intercept form, $y = mx + b$, where m is the slope and b is the y-intercept. To do so, first subtract $5x$ from both sides to get $3y = -5x + 8$. Dividing the entire equation by 3 yields $y = -\dfrac{5x}{3} + \dfrac{8}{3}$. Thus $\dfrac{8}{3}$ is the y-intercept.

34. The correct answer is J. To divide $\dfrac{a^x}{a^y}$, subtract the exponents. Thus $\dfrac{a^x}{a^y} = a^{x-y}$. If $\dfrac{a^x}{a^y} = a^4$, then $a^{x-y} = a^4$, making $x - y = 4$.

35. The correct answer is C. Between May and August, there were 3 price decreases (in June, July, and August). If the price was decreased by 20%, then the resulting price was 80% of the previous month's price. Thus, in June the price was $0.8d$; in July the price was $0.8(0.8d)$; in August the price was $0.8(0.8(0.8d))$, which is equivalent to $(0.8)^3 d$, or $0.512d$.

36. The correct answer is K. Given that $|5 - 2x| > 5$, then either $5 - 2x > 5$ or $5 - 2x < -5$. In the case that $5 - 2x > 5$, $-2x > 0$ making $x < 0$ (when you divide by a negative number remember to switch the direction of the inequality). In the case that $5 - 2x < -5$, then $-2x < -10$ making $x > 5$. Thus the range for x is $x < 0$ or $x > 5$. Of the answer choices, only 6 fits into the range for x.

37. The correct answer is E. To solve this problem, first distribute then combine like terms. Distribute

0.1 as follows:

$$0.1(t + 3,420) = t$$
$$0.1t + 342 = t.$$
$$342 = 0.9t.$$
$$t = \frac{342}{0.9} = 380$$

38. The correct answer is J. Any line parallel to the y-axis is a vertical line. Vertical lines have slopes that are undefined. Remember that the definition of slope is rise/run; vertical lines have no run and thus dividing rise by run is dividing by 0, making the quotient undefined.

39. The correct answer is E. To find which equation has the smallest slope, first convert any equations to slope intercept form ($y = mx + b$, where m is the slope and b is the y-intercept) if they are not already in that form. In choice E, dividing both sides of $7y = 3x - 7$ by 7 yields $y = \dfrac{3x}{7} - 1$, which has a slope of $\dfrac{3}{7}$. When compared to the other slopes, $\dfrac{3}{7}$ is the smallest (the next closest is $\dfrac{1}{2}$, which is only slightly larger than $\dfrac{3}{7}$).

40. The correct answer is K. Let the number of minutes it would take Amy to run 10.3 miles be y. If she ran at the same pace for 10.5 mile as she did for 3.5 miles, then the rates in miles per minute would be equal, making $\dfrac{3.5}{x} = \dfrac{10.5}{y}$. Since the question asks for the number of minutes it would take Amy to run 10.5 miles, solve $\dfrac{3.5}{x} = \dfrac{10.5}{y}$ for y. To do so, first invert both sides of the equation to get $\dfrac{x}{3.5} = \dfrac{y}{10.5}$. Then multiply both sides by 10.5 to get $y = \dfrac{10.5x}{3.5}$, or $3x$.

41. The correct answer is A. Regardless of the dimensions of a rectangle, tripling the length and width will always have the effect of tripling the perimeter because perimeter is directly proportional to length and width ($P = 2l + 2w$).

42. The correct answer is H. To solve this problem, multiply the expression $(x + 3)$ by $(x + s)$ to get $x^2 + 3x + sx + 3s$. You are given that $x^2 + rx + 12$ is equivalent to $x^2 + 3x + sx + 3s$.

Therefore, $3s$ is equal to 12, making s equal to 4. It is also apparent that $3x + sx$ is equivalent to rx.

Set the quantities equal and solve for r, as follows:

$$rx = 3x + sx$$
$$rx = x(3 + s)$$
$$r = 3 + s$$

Because $s = 4$, r must equal 7.

43. The correct answer is C. Systems of equations have an infinite number of solutions when the equations are equivalent (*i.e.* they graph the same lane). In order for the two equations to be equivalent, the constants and coefficients must be proportional. If the entire equation $3x + 5y = 27$ is multiplied by 4, the result is $4(3x + 5y) = 4(27)$, or $12x + 20y = 108$. Thus, in order for the two equations to be equivalent, $3b = 108$, or $b = 36$.

44. The correct answer is J. Any integer when multiplied by an even integer results in an even integer. Also, the addition of any two even integers yields another even integer. Thus, regardless of the value of a or the power of a, multiplying by an even integer and adding an even integer will yield an even integer. This only occurs in the calculation $6a^4 + 6$.

45. The correct answer is B. To solve this problem, remember that $|3a - 3| \geq 12$ is equivalent to $3a - 3 \geq 12$ or $3a - 3 \leq -12$. Adding 3 to both sides and dividing by 3 yields $a \geq 5$ or $a \leq -3$.

46. The correct answer is H. To find $\cos \dfrac{5\pi}{12}$ using $\cos(\alpha + \beta) = (\cos \alpha)(\cos \beta) - (\sin \alpha)(\sin \beta)$ given that $\dfrac{5\pi}{12} = \dfrac{\pi}{4} + \dfrac{\pi}{6}$, you can first substitute $\dfrac{\pi}{4}$ for α and $\dfrac{\pi}{6}$ for β and get $\cos\left(\dfrac{\pi}{4} + \dfrac{\pi}{6}\right) = \left(\cos \dfrac{\pi}{4}\right)\left(\cos \dfrac{\pi}{6}\right) - \left(\sin \dfrac{\pi}{4}\right)\left(\sin \dfrac{\pi}{6}\right)$. Using the table of values to substitute into that equation, you get $\cos \dfrac{5\pi}{12} = \left(\dfrac{\sqrt{2}}{2}\right)\left(\dfrac{\sqrt{3}}{2}\right) - \left(\dfrac{\sqrt{2}}{2}\right)\left(\dfrac{1}{2}\right)$, or $\dfrac{(\sqrt{6} - \sqrt{2})}{4}$.

47. The correct answer is A. To solve this problem, factor out the x in the numerator of the fraction and the 3 in the denominator to get $\dfrac{(xy - xz)}{(3y - 3z)} = \dfrac{x(y - z)}{3(y - z)}$. Since the quantity $y - z$ is on the top and bottom, it cancels out, leaving $\dfrac{x}{3}$. Since

$\dfrac{(xy - xz)}{(3y - 3z)} < 0$, it follows that $\dfrac{x}{3} < 0$. Multiplying both sides of the inequality by 3 yields $x < 0$. Thus x can be any number less than 0 (all negative numbers).

48. The correct answer is G. If the perimeter of a square is 36 units, then each side is 9 (since perimeter in a square is $4(s)$ where s is the length of a side). To find the length of the diagonal, you can use the Pythagorean Theorem because the diagonal is the hypotenuse of a right triangle with legs of length 9. Thus $d^2 = 9^2 + 9^2$, or $81 + 81$, which equals $2(81)$, and $d = \sqrt{(2(81))}$, or $\sqrt{2}\sqrt{81}$, which is $9\sqrt{2}$.

49. The correct answer is E. A circle with center (h, k) and radius r has equation $(x - h)^2 + (y - k)^2 = r^2$. In order to determine the equation of the circle in the standard (x, y) coordinate plane that has a radius of 4 units and the same center as the circle determined by $x^2 + y^2 - 6y + 4 = 0$, first determine the center of the circle defined by $x^2 + y^2 - 6y + 4 = 0$ by converting the equation to the standard form for a circle (complete the square):

$$x^2 + y^2 - 6y + 4 = 0$$
$$x^2 + y^2 - 6y + 9 + 4 - 9 = 0$$
(no net change in value)
$$x^2 + (y^2 - 6y + 9) + 4 - 9 = 0 \quad \text{(regroup)}$$
$$x^2 + (y - 3)^2 + -5 = 0 \quad \text{(factoring)}$$
$$x^2 + (y - 3)^2 = 5$$

Thus the center of the circle is $(0,3)$. A circle that has a radius of 4 units and the same center has the equation $x^2 + (y - 3)^2 = 16$.

50. The correct answer is H. A rectangular kitchen that is 8 feet longer than it is wide with width w would have length $l = w + 8$, or $w = l - 8$. Since the area $A = 240 = lw$, substitute $w = l - 8$ into $240 = lw$ to get $240 = l(l - 8) = l^2 - 8l$, or $l^2 - 8l - 240 = 0$. To find l, factor $l^2 - 8l - 240 = 0$ into $(l + 12)(l - 20) = 0$. Thus $l = -12$ (which doesn't make sense because a kitchen cannot have a negative length), or $l = 20$.

51. The correct answer is C. Parallel lines have equal slopes. To find the slope of a line that is parallel to the line determined by the equation $5x - 4y = 8$, put the equation in slope-intercept form ($y = mx + b$). To do so, first subtract $5x$ from both sides to get $-4y = -5x + 8$. Then divide by -4 to get $y = \dfrac{5x}{4} - 2$. Thus the slope is $\dfrac{5}{4}$.

52. The correct answer is H. To solve this problem, recall that $81 = 3^4$. Then $81^{3x-2} = (3^4)^{3x-2} = 3^{4(3x-2)}$. Further, if $3^{8x} = 81^{3x-2}$, then $3^{8x} = 3^{4(3x-2)}$ and $8x = 4(3x - 2)$, $12x - 8$. Subtracting $8x$ from both sides and adding 8 to both sides yields $4x = 8$, or $x = 2$.

53. The correct answer is B. Since the width of the frame is $\frac{5}{8}$ or 0.625 inches, the length of the viewable portion is $30 - 2(0.625) = 28.75$ inches and the width is $18 - 2(0.625) = 16.75$ inches. Thus, the area is $28.75 \times 16.75 = 481.56$ square inches.

54. The correct answer is F. If a horse eats 12 bales of hay in 5 days, the average rate is $\frac{12}{5}$ bales per day. At this rate, the number of bales of hay that the horse eats in $5 + x$ days is the 12 bales for the 5 days plus $\frac{12}{5}$ bales per day after that, or $\left(\frac{12}{5}\right)x$. Thus the total is $12 + \left(\frac{12}{5}\right)x$, or $12 + \frac{(12x)}{5}$.

55. The correct answer is A. To solve this problem, substitute the equation $x = -5$ into $y = x - 5$ to find the y-coordinate at which the lines $x = -5$ and $y = x - 5$ intersect (the x-coordinate is -5 because it is given that $x = -5$). Thus $y = (-5) - 5 = -10$. The point of intersection is $(-5, -10)$.

56. The correct answer is J. The number of miles a runner must travel in a 4-lap race where the course is a circle of radius m miles will be equal to 4 times the circumference of the circle. Since circumference is $2\pi r$, where r is the radius, the circumference is $2\pi m$. Since it is a 4-lap race, the total number of miles traveled is $4(2\pi m)$, or $8\pi m$.

57. The correct answer is B. Given that the graph of the line $y = (n + 1)x + 6$ in the standard (x,y) coordinate plane passes through $(4,8)$, plug in the values of the point $(4,8)$ into the equation and solve for n. Substituting $(4,8)$ into $y = (n+1)x+6$ yields $8 = (n+1)(4)+6 = 4n+10$. To solve $8 = 4n+10$, subtract 10 from both sides and divide by 4 to get $n = -\frac{1}{2}$.

58. The correct answer is J. You are given that a computer repair person charges $50.00 per hour, plus an additional mileage fee which varies directly with the square root of the number of miles traveled. Therefore, the total fee can be expressed as $50h + k\sqrt{m}$, where h is the number of hours worked, m is the number of miles traveled, and k is some constant. Since one hour plus 25 miles traveled costs $140, 140 = 50 + k\sqrt{25} = 50 + 5k$. Since $140 = 50 + 5k$, $k = 18$. The total amount charged for one hour plus 36 miles traveled is $50+18\sqrt{36} = 50 + 18(6) = 50 + 108 = \$158.00$.

59. The correct answer is C. Since $\sin Z$ is the ratio of the side opposite the angle to the hypotenuse, the side opposite Z, which is XY, must be determined. To do so, apply the Pythagorean Theorem, as follows:

$$10^2 = XY^2 + 4^2$$
$$XY^2 = 100 - 16 = 84$$
$$XY = \sqrt{84} = \sqrt{((21)(4))} = \sqrt{21}\sqrt{4}, \text{ or } 2\sqrt{21}.$$

Since $\sin Z$ is the ratio of the side opposite the angle to the hypotenuse, $\sin Z = \frac{2\sqrt{21}}{10}$

60. The correct answer is J. The image of a point (x, y) reflected across the line $y = x$ will have coordinates (y, x). If the coordinates of point A are (m, n), then the coordinates of point A' are (n, m).

Reading Test Explanations

PASSAGE I

1. **The best answer is C.** The passage provides several interpersonal and physical examples of teammates working together for their goal of winning the game. Mark's quotation is an example of encouragement. The narrator describes the role of linemen in pushing back the defense for the running back. The other answer choices are not supported by the passage.

2. **The best answer is J.** The passage gives details about the almost meditative quality of Joe's preparation for the snap of the football. According to the passage, "instinct told him what he needed to know." *Engrossed* is the quality of being deeply involved in something. The narrator uses rich descriptions of the rituals of the football play to emphasize the players' dedication to the game.

3. **The best answer is B.** The passage discusses Joe's surprise at the final outcome of the game. He first saw what had happened, before it truly sank in that the game had been lost. This correlates with answer choice A. The passage then goes on to state that "'We had them beat, you know,' Mark hissed to Joe as they walked slowly off the field." This illustrates both commiseration with Mark, and that he may have been "trudging" off the field in walking slowly with his teammates. The only answer choice not supported by details in the passage is answer choice B. Nowhere in the passage does it state that Joe attacked his opponents following the game.

4. **The best answer is G.** The first paragraph provides details on the setting that reinforce the intensity of the game so far. "A cold wind soothed the faces" indicates the faces are hurt or uncomfortable. The third sentence describes breathing dirty air. The word "muster" implies considerable effort on the part of the lungs. The phrases "game-ending" and "season-defining" indicate the team is at a crucial moment in the game.

5. **The best answer is D.** The last sentence of the passage describes how the loss is particularly devastating because of how close Joe's team came to winning on the final play. The other choices are not supported by the passage.

6. **The best answer is G.** Details in paragraphs 4 and 5 describe Joe's careful analysis of the defense made prior to the start of the play. The sentence "Joe glared at his opponents, pleased ..." is the best example to support answer choice G. The next sentence provides further evidence.

7. **The best answer is D.** Mark's quotation from the last paragraph shows that the other team was more fatigued at the end of the game than was his team. The sentence "'We should have won the game'" shows that Mark believed the team was prepared to win but failed.

8. **The best answer is H.** The last sentence of paragraph 3 describes the hand clasping, which immediately follows Mark's statement of encouragement to his teammates. These two events come at the end of the huddle before the play. The purpose of the huddle is to establish the play and, hence, the upcoming roles of the individual players. The hand-clasping ritual seems to tie the team back together momentarily before they must break apart to perform their individual tasks during the play.

9. **The best answer is A.** The passage describes Joe being pleased by the block and "assuming" it had sent his man back "more than enough to free the rusher to enter the endzone." This best supports answer choice A.

10. **The best answer is H.** Mark's quotation in paragraph 3 is an example of the magnitude of the game (and so, the final play) in the context of a season that includes "practicing for four months." Mark even alludes to the success of the final play reflecting the quality of the team developed over four years.

PASSAGE II

11. **The best answer is B.** The first paragraph states that the tourist was "looking for a souvenir that represents the local culture." However, when he stopped to browse at a small street vendor, he was shocked to see a plethora of American items. This best supports answer choice B. The other answer choices are not supported by the context of the passage.

12. **The best answer is H.** As written in the passage, "American logos appear in quite unexpected places, embodying the *ubiquitous* American symbols worldwide." Because American symbols appear in unexpected places worldwide, it makes the most sense that these symbols would be described as "far-reaching." Answer choice F is incorrect; the price of these symbols is not mentioned anywhere in the passage. Answer choice G does not make sense in the context of the passage. Answer choice J does not make sense because if American symbols were localized, they would be found solely in America.

13. The best answer is D. It is stated in the passage that those people who reject Americana do so because they "lament the steady decline of distinct national, ethnic, and cultural identities as omnipresent American influences overpower ancient traditions and beliefs."

14. The best answer is H. The passage explicitly states that jobs have been created due to the spread of American influence, and that with American commerce comes the modernization of infrastructure. The passage does not state that declines in tourism result from the spread of American influences, but rather that American businesses are quickly spreading to tourist areas abroad.

15. The best answer is B. When the passage states that "The local cantinas and native boutiques are losing the battle against large American corporations," it is clear that these places are straining to even stay in business and retain their cultural uniqueness versus the American businesses that are invading the resort towns. The other answer choices are not supported by details in the passage.

16. The best answer is G. The passage states that Japan is a "prime example of where American involvement has been beneficial," and that "America left a pervasive cultural footprint on the country" while maintaining "a distinct culture that is rich in the traditions of the past." This clearly indicates that American influence was beneficial to Japan and that a well-balanced mix of American and Japanese culture ensued. This best supports answer choice G. The other answer choices are beyond the scope of the passage.

17. The best answer is C. The passage illustrates both a country that has been helped by American influence (Japan) and a country whose native businesses are suffering due to American influence (Mexico). It is unclear what will happen if American cultural influences continue to penetrate foreign markets. Answer choice B may appear to be correct; however, the example of America's influence on Japan negates this option.

18. The best answer is J. Paragraph 3 discusses those people who are rejecting "American 'cultural imperialism,'" and states that these people "*lament* the steady decline of distinct national, ethnic, and cultural identities as omnipresent American influences overpower ancient traditions and beliefs." Because these people are rejecting this spread of American influence, it does not make sense that they would embrace or enjoy the loss of other cultures. It also does not make sense that they would deny the steady decline of distinct national cultures, as it is

something that is obviously occurring. To "regret" is to express grief over or be unhappy with. The passage illustrates that the people who are rejecting American cultural imperialism are unhappy with its consequences.

19. The best answer is A. As stated in the passage, "What he sees shocks him: T-shirts and posters promoting American football, basketball, and baseball teams." This clearly illustrates the fact that the street vendor was selling American sports memorabilia. The other answer choices are not supported by details in the passage.

20. The best answer is F. The last paragraph of the passage states that many benefits and problems are created by American commercial and cultural expansion abroad. While there are some drawbacks to American expansion, there are still gains. This best supports answer choice F. Answer choice H may appear to be correct; however, the last paragraph does not clarify whether problems from American expansion in the future will be greater than benefits.

PASSAGE III

21. The best answer is B. The passage asks "how a person is able to paint or draw something so lifelike and *emotive*," and marvels at "what stirred these men to put brush to canvas so delicately." "Emotive" means "causing strong feelings," which is also a synonym for "stirring." This is the most logical choice based on the context of the passage.

22. The best answer is H. Realism is noted in the passage as one of the first formal styles of art, preceding Impressionism. The passage later states that among the styles of painting evolving from Impressionism were "Cubism, Abstract Art, Expressionism, Abstract Expressionism, Modernism, and a host of other styles . . ." Realism is the only style of art not mentioned in this list.

23. The best answer is B. As stated in the passage, Realist painters "focused on depicting real life unembellished with fanciful notions or feelings." This correlates with answer choice B. Answer choice C may appear to be correct because the passage makes note of unattractive physical attributes. However, the passage simply states that artists simply did not "gloss over" unattractive physical attributes of their subjects; artists portrayed their subjects as they actually looked. Unattractive features were not the focus of Realist artists.

24. The best answer is G. The passage clearly states that though Realism fell out of favor for a while, it was "revived during the Renaissance," and remained popular for several centuries thereafter. This best supports answer choice G. The other answer choices are not supported by details found in the second paragraph.

25. The best answer is B. The passage begins with one of the first popular formal styles of art. The passage then goes on to describe different styles of art that have evolved over time. This best supports answer choice B. Answer choice A is incorrect because the passage does not discuss the changing world and how painters related to it. Answer choice C is incorrect because the passage only mentions the popularity of Realism falling and rising again; the passage does not discuss the popularity of other styles of painting. Answer choice D is incorrect because the passage does not discuss artists adapting to popular demand.

26. The best answer is J. The passage states that while some styles of art that grew out of Impressionism became their own schools of thought, others were simply an "artist's trademark way of painting." In this context, speaking of styles of art, it makes the most sense that an "artist's trademark" would be his or her own "unique style." Although answer choice F, "prime example," may appear to be correct, the author is discussing different styles of art, not just one specific piece of art. Answer choices G and H do not make sense in the context of the passage.

27. The best answer is A. As stated in the passage, the Impressionist movement was a "rebellion against Realism," which came as a result of "the rigidity and staleness some saw in the style." The rigidity and staleness are referring to the Realist style of painting, not the Impressionist style of painting. Therefore, answer choice A is correct.

28. The best answer is H. The author lists many styles that evolved from Impressionism; these details correlate best with answer choice H. Answer choice F is incorrect because Impressionism greatly expanded the range of artistic expression through the many styles of art that developed as a result of the movement. Answer choice G is incorrect because Realism was a precursor to Impressionism, not vice versa. Likewise, answer choice J is incorrect because Abstract Art and Cubism were predecessors of Impressionism, not vice versa.

29. The best answer is A. The passage states that "Post-Impressionism uses form and color to reflect art in a more personal and subjective way than did its predecessor." This correlates best with answer choice A. The other answer choices are not mentioned in the passage as describing Post-Impressionism in comparison to Impressionism.

30. The best answer is J. As stated in the passage, "a rebellion against Realism arose in response to the rigidity and staleness some saw in the style." The author goes on to say that many artists began to paint in the Impressionist style because it "allowed for more creativity." These facts best support answer choice J. Although Realism could trace its roots to ancient Rome—answer choice G—this was not the reason that artists rebelled against Realism.

PASSAGE IV

31. The best answer is C. The primary focus of the passage is on gene linkage; what it is and how it works. The other answer choices are too specific and do not adequately express the overall main idea of the passage.

32. The best answer is G. The passage states that "Each hereditary unit, the *gene*, contains specific . . ." This clearly shows us that in this passage, a hereditary unit is referred to as a gene.

33. The best answer is B. The passage lists hair color, height, and susceptibility to disease all as inherited traits. Therefore, answer choice B is correct. The passage tells us that genes are found on segments of the DNA molecule, not that molecules are examples of inherited traits.

34. The best answer is J. The passage describes the fruit fly as a "*prolific* breeder, producing hundreds of offspring in a single mating." The word "prolific" means "productive and fertile," which best correlates with answer choice J. This makes the most sense in the context of the passage; if fruit flies produce so many offspring in a single mating they are clearly highly productive breeders. The other answer choices do not fit the context of the sentence as well.

35. The best answer is C. According to the first paragraph, asexual reproduction involves a single parent.

36. The best answer is F. The last paragraph of the passage indicates that current research is exploring the fact that "many factors affect the transmission of certain traits from parents to offspring." The passage goes on to state the location of genes is "but one of a multitude of determinants involved in whether or not a characteristic will be inherited."

These facts suggest that research is ongoing, and that there are still many questions regarding the transmission of genes from one generation to the next. This best correlates with answer choice F.

37. **The best answer is B.** After stating the Morgan chose to experiment on *Drosophila melanogaster*, the passage cites a reason for this choice: "The fruit fly is a prolific breeder, producing hundreds of offspring in a single mating." This best corresponds with answer choice B. Although answer choice A may appear to be correct because fruit flies have easily distinguishable chromosomes, fruit flies have only four pairs of chromosomes, not "many."

38. **The best answer is G.** As stated in paragraph 4, Morgan bred "female flies that appeared normal, but carried the mutant genes." This tells us that the female flies held the mutant genes, yet did not appear to be mutated. This statement is best supported by answer choice G. The other answer choices are not supported by the context of the passage.

39. **The best answer is D.** The last paragraph discusses the "many factors" that affect the transmission of traits, as well as the "multitude of determinants" that determine whether a characteristic will be inherited. These statements indicate that there are many components that affect genetic transmission, which is most consistent with answer choice D. The other answer choices are not supported by the information found in the last paragraph.

40. **The best answer is J.** To answer this question, a parallel must be drawn between the logic used in the passage and the question at hand. As written in the passage "the genes for body color and wing size are transmitted together from parents to offspring because they are located on the same chromosome and must be somehow linked." Therefore, if the genes for blue eyes and brown hair are found on the same chromosome, these two traits would be inherited together. Because the passage also states that combinations from both parents were present, it can be concluded that a certain number of offspring would inherit both blue eyes and brown hair, but a certain number of offspring would receive the eye and hair color of the other parent. This best correlates with answer choice J.

Science Reasoning Test Explanations

PASSAGE I

1. **The best answer is D.** Passage 1 defines macronutrients as "those nutrients required in the greatest quantity." This definition implies that plants need macronutrients more than any other element to grow and survive.

2. **The best answer is J.** Botanist 2 says, "Organic material can cause a temporary depletion of nitrogen in the soil," which suggests that when organic fertilizers are used over time, the nitrogen in the soil will be depleted. This information best supports answer choice J, because nitrogen is mentioned as a necessary nutrient.

3. **The best answer is B.** Botanist 2 states, "characteristics of organic fertilizer require application well in advance of need to ensure that the materials have broken down and can be used by the plant." The botanist is implying that the materials in organic fertilizer require a long time to be broken down and supply nutrients to the plants. This suggests the correct answer is answer choice B.

4. **The best answer is H.** The introductory material states, "Two botanists discuss whether inorganic or organic fertilizers are most optimal for plant growth"; this best supports answer choice H. The other answer choices are not supported by the passage.

5. **The best answer is D.** The best way to answer this question is by the process of elimination. Botanist 1 says, "organic fertilizer provides a naturally slow release of nutrients as the organic material breaks down in the soil, reducing the likelihood of over-fertilization." Answer choice A is true, and, therefore, incorrect. This botanist also says, "Organic fertilizers also improve soil structure in the long term," and this proves answer choice B to be incorrect. The statement "Commercial inorganic fertilizers, on the other hand, are often applied to heavily, damaging the roots of the plants," suggests that, although inorganic fertilizers damage the roots of plants, organic fertilizers do not. Answer choice C can be eliminated. Botanist 1 does not directly discuss the amount of organic fertilizer to use, so answer choice D is best.

6. **The best answer is G.** Both botanists are discussing the use of organic and inorganic fertilizers as a means to "enrich the soil and make more of these essential nutrients available." This implies that plants require essential nutrients for optimal growth, some of which can be supplied by fertilizer.

Answer choice F is incorrect because plants require nutrients other than nitrogen to survive. Answer choice H is not supported by information in the passage. Answer choice J is incorrect because water is not provided by fertilization.

7. **The best answer is D.** Both botanists discuss the fact that organic fertilizers, because of their break down process, have a slow release of nutrients. This implies that inorganic fertilizers can supply nutrients to the plants at a faster rate. In addition, Botanist 2 states "Inorganic fertilizers . . . offer immediate availability of nutrients . . .," which best supports answer choice D.

PASSAGE II

8. **The best answer is H.** Table 3 shows that compared to flowers pollinated by hand, flowers pollinated by bees had a greater number of flowers reproducing after 2 years (15). The other answer choices are not supported by the data.

9. **The best answer is A.** According to Study 2, "Two pollen containers were placed in each site: one containing 50 mg Species A pollen and one containing 50 mg Species B pollen." This means that the amount of pollen placed at each site remained consistent in the study. Answer choices B and C are not supported by the data. Answer choice D can be eliminated because this information was not discussed in the study.

10. **The best answer is F.** The information needed to answer this question is located in Table 1. The best way to answer the question is to read the answer choices and then verify if they are true according to the tables. According to Table 1, the percentage of stamen number covered with pollen is 27% for both flower species A and B, which best supports answer choice F.

11. **The best answer is B.** According to Study 2, flower Species A and B were absent at site 3. This implies that site 3 was used to determine the pollen preference when both Species A and B flowers were missing, answer choice B.

12. **The best answer is H.** According to Study 2, "The containers were left in place for 36 hours and the amount of pollen that was taken from the containers was recorded." This does not take into consideration other insects that could have removed pollen from the containers. This information best supports answer choice H. While it is true that some species of flowers were not at both sites, this was a necessary variable in the experiment, and is not considered a weakness in the experimental design.

13. **The best answer is C.** Table 2 shows the results of Study 2. By reading the table, you can see that the amount of pollen removed from the pollen dishes was greater for the flower species that was absent at each site. This implies that an important factor affecting the flower preference of bees is which flower species is available in an area. Answer choices A and D can be eliminated because the information was not discussed in Study 2.

PASSAGE III

14. **The best answer is G.** According to Figure 1, for Mammal 2, as the atmospheric pressure decreases (going to the right along the *x*-axis), the respiratory rate increases, which best supports answer choice G.

15. **The best answer is C.** Mammals 2 and 3 had the same respiratory rate when the two lines representing each mammal crossed on Figure 1. This overlap occurred when the atmospheric pressure was at approximately 0.80 atm, answer choice C.

16. **The best answer is G.** The note in Passage III says, "Larger animals typically have slower respiratory rates." Since larger animals need more oxygen, the note implies that larger animals take in more oxygen with each breath compared to smaller animals. This would allow them to take a fewer number of breaths per minute, but still get the oxygen they need to survive. In Figure 1, Mammal 4's respiratory rate is consistently lower than Mammal 2's respiratory rate. The only way Mammal 4 could take in significantly more oxygen per minute than Mammal 2 and still have a lower respiratory rate is if Mammal 4 was significantly larger than Mammal 2.

17. **The best answer is D.** If a higher respiratory rate causes mammals to have a higher metabolic rate, mammals that had a higher respiratory rate at a pressure of 1.0 atm and 0.80 atm would have a higher metabolic rate at these two pressures. According to Figure 1, Mammal 1 has a higher respiratory rate at 1.0 atm than at 0.80 atm, so eliminate answer choices B and C. Because Mammal 4's respiratory rate is slightly higher at 1.0 atm, answer choice D must be correct.

18. **The best answer is J.** Mammal 4 is the only mammal, according to Figure 1, that has a low respiratory rate at higher atmospheric pressures. According to the passage, a high respiratory rate (rapid breathing) can be a sign of distress in some animals. This suggests that Mammal 4 is more comfortable (has a low respiratory rate) at higher altitudes, answer choice J.

PASSAGE IV

19. **The best answer is B.** The question states, "the earth's atmosphere will become less effective at shielding the surface from radiation of higher frequencies." If the atmosphere is less effective at shielding higher frequency radiation, surfaces on earth will be exposed to more radiation at higher frequencies. This will cause surfaces to emit more electrons, thus, making the photoelectric effect on metals more evident, which best supports answer choice B.

20. **The best answer is H.** If the rate of the photoelectric effect is directly proportional to the surface area of the metal exposed, by exposing more metal (using a larger sheet of metal) the photoelectric effect will increase. An increase in the photoelectric effect means the charge on the sheet will increase, answer choice H. Answer choice F can be eliminated because the frequency of radiation is irrelevant to this question. The remaining answer choices are not supported by the data.

21. **The best answer is D.** Answer choice D is correct because it tests different metals and their sizes with different frequencies of radiation many times. The other answer choices only account for one variable, and, therefore, are not thorough enough. Answer choice A can be eliminated because experiments should always be repeated more than once to obtain accurate results.

22. **The best answer is J.** If a scientist wanted to measure the effect of the atmosphere on the photoelectric effect, he or she would have to test the photoelectric effect in more than one atmosphere. The only answer choice that tests the photoelectric effect in more than one atmosphere— the earth's surface and outer space—is answer choice J. Answer choice H can be eliminated because the test does not rely on the atmosphere for results.

23. **The best answer is C.** Passage IV states: "No electrons are emitted for radiation with energy frequencies below that of the threshold, as the electrons are unable to gain sufficient energy to overcome attractive forces within the metal." Therefore, the scientist must have assumed that only photons with high enough frequency will emit electrons.

24. The best answer is G. According to the results of Experiments 1 and 2, as the frequency of radiation increased, so did the electron emission (which required a high photon energy). This supports the definition of photons as finite packets of energy at various levels because higher frequency radiation caused the emission of electrons.

PASSAGE V

25. The best answer is A. Each level in the figure represents a generation of rabbits. Level 1 is the first mating, or first generation. Level 2—the second generation—represents the offspring of level 1. Level 3 represents the offspring of level 2.

26. The best answer is H. Passage V implies that each offspring will receive one allele from each parent and, "Dominant alleles are expressed whenever present but recessive alleles are expressed only when the dominant allele is absent." Out of the two parents in level 1, one parent is homozygous for at least one trait, meaning the offspring will only show dominant traits. This information best supports answer choice H.

27. The best answer is B. Figure 1 shows the different possible outcomes for the alleles of the offspring of the level 2 rabbits. The offspring will have white hair if they receive the recessive allele, b, from both parents. Out of the possible outcomes (16), this occurs 4 times. The correct answer is 25%, answer choice B.

28. The best answer is J. By looking at Figure 1, you can determine the ratio for the traits of the offspring of the level 2 parents. Out of the 16 possibilities, short black hair occurs 9 times, long black hair occurs 3 times, short white hair occurs 3 times, and long white hair occurs 1 time. This suggests the ratio would be 9:3:3:1, answer choice J.

29. The best answer is C. If heterozygous rabbits are bred (level 2), it is possible for the recessive traits to be visible in the immediate generation, because it is possible for an offspring to receive two recessive alleles. This is also true for future generations, making answer choice C the best answer.

PASSAGE VI

30. The best answer is G. According to Figure 1, the only pair of elements in the answer choices with a bond energy greater than 420 kJ/mol is H and O (460 kJ/mol), answer choice G.

31. The best answer is C. To answer this question, you must look at Figure 1 to determine which 3 pairs of

elements have the highest bond strength. Element pairs H—F (568 kJ/mol), H—O (460 kJ/mol), and H—H (436 kJ/mol) have the highest bond strengths in the table, and are therefore, the most stable bonds, which best supports answer choice C.

32. The best answer is J. To answer this question you must determine the sum of the bond energies for each answer choice, as shown below:

F. H_2O has two H–O bonds: $(460 \times 2) =$ 920 kJ/mol

G. H_2S has two H–S bonds: $(366 \times 2) =$ 732 kJ/mol

H. NH_3 has three H–N bonds: $(393 \times 3) =$ 1,179 kJ/mol

J. H_3Cl has three H–Cl bonds: $(432 \times 3) =$ 1,296 kJ/mol

The substance with the highest sum of bond energies is H_3Cl, answer choice J.

33. The best answer is A. To answer this question correctly, you must pay attention to the headings in Figure 1. According to Group 17 in Figure 1, the group bond energy decreases as bond length increase. This information best supports answer choice A.

34. The best answer is J. To answer this question, you must look at the bond lengths between the given pairs of elements in Figure 1. The bond lengths for H–O, H–S and H–Se are 96 pm, 134 pm, and 146 pm, respectively. Therefore, the order of their bond lengths in increasing order is H–O < H–S < H–Se, or answer choice J.

PASSAGE VII

35. The best answer is C. Passage VII says, "During years with less rain, fewer bands will be formed, and the bands will be more narrow than the bands formed during years with heavier rainfall." This suggests that trees in areas with more rainfall will have more bands per year and a larger size of growth bands than trees in areas with less rainfall. Site 3's trees had an average of 20 growth bands per year that were 12 mm, which is more than Site 2's trees (15 bands per year at 4 mm).

36. The best answer is G. According to the results of the experiment, trees at Site 1 had smaller and fewer growth bands than trees at Site 2. This implies that the Site 1 trees did not grow as fast as Site 2 trees.

37. The best answer is B. According to the results of the experiment, as the average size of the growth bands increases (going down the table), the average number of growth bands per year also increases. This causes the slope of a number versus size graph to be positive, which is indicated in answer choice B. Answer choice C can be eliminated because this graph shows that all sites had the same size of growth bands, which is not supported by the data. Likewise, the other answer choices are incorrect.

38. **The best answer is H.** The passage implies that trees that receive a heavier rainfall will form larger and more bands. According to the results of the experiment, Site 3 had the largest average number of growth bands per year (20) and the largest average size of growth bands (12 mm). This information supports answer choice H.

39. **The best answer is A.** Passage VII says that *dendrochronology* helps to determine the growth rate of trees but, "Because *dendrochronology* is not completely accurate on its own, it is often combine with a process called cross dating." This implies that cross dating is applied in order to improve the accuracy of determining the growth rate of trees.

40. **The best answer is G.** The question states that trees from Site 4 were found to have an average of 13 growth bands per year, in between Site 1's trees (11 bands) and Site 2's trees (15 bands). This suggests that the trees from Site 4 will have an average size of growth bands that falls between the trees of Site 1 and 2. The average size of growth bands for trees from Site 1 is 2 mm and the average size of growth bands for trees from Site 2 is 4 mm. Therefore, the trees from Site 4 can be estimated to have an average size of growth bands between 2 and 4 mm.

Writing Test Explanation

Because grading the essay is subjective, we've chosen not to include any "graded" essays here. Your best bet is to have someone you trust, such as your personal tutor, read your essays and give you an honest critique. If you plan on grading your own essays, review the grading criteria and be as honest as possible regarding the structure, development, organization, technique, and appropriateness of your writing. Focus on your weak areas and continue to practice in order to improve your writing skills.

■■■ **ANSWER SHEET**

ACT PRACTICE TEST 5
Answer Sheet

ENGLISH

1 (A)(B)(C)(D)	21 (A)(B)(C)(D)	41 (A)(B)(C)(D)	61 (A)(B)(C)(D)
2 (F)(G)(H)(J)	22 (F)(G)(H)(J)	42 (F)(G)(H)(J)	62 (F)(G)(H)(J)
3 (A)(B)(C)(D)	23 (A)(B)(C)(D)	43 (A)(B)(C)(D)	63 (A)(B)(C)(D)
4 (F)(G)(H)(J)	24 (F)(G)(H)(J)	44 (F)(G)(H)(J)	64 (F)(G)(H)(J)
5 (A)(B)(C)(D)	25 (A)(B)(C)(D)	45 (A)(B)(C)(D)	65 (A)(B)(C)(D)
6 (F)(G)(H)(J)	26 (F)(G)(H)(J)	46 (F)(G)(H)(J)	66 (F)(G)(H)(J)
7 (A)(B)(C)(D)	27 (A)(B)(C)(D)	47 (A)(B)(C)(D)	67 (A)(B)(C)(D)
8 (F)(G)(H)(J)	28 (F)(G)(H)(J)	48 (F)(G)(H)(J)	68 (F)(G)(H)(J)
9 (A)(B)(C)(D)	29 (A)(B)(C)(D)	49 (A)(B)(C)(D)	69 (A)(B)(C)(D)
10 (F)(G)(H)(J)	30 (F)(G)(H)(J)	50 (F)(G)(H)(J)	70 (F)(G)(H)(J)
11 (A)(B)(C)(D)	31 (A)(B)(C)(D)	51 (A)(B)(C)(D)	71 (A)(B)(C)(D)
12 (F)(G)(H)(J)	32 (F)(G)(H)(J)	52 (F)(G)(H)(J)	72 (F)(G)(H)(J)
13 (A)(B)(C)(D)	33 (A)(B)(C)(D)	53 (A)(B)(C)(D)	73 (A)(B)(C)(D)
14 (F)(G)(H)(J)	34 (F)(G)(H)(J)	54 (F)(G)(H)(J)	74 (F)(G)(H)(J)
15 (A)(B)(C)(D)	35 (A)(B)(C)(D)	55 (A)(B)(C)(D)	75 (A)(B)(C)(D)
16 (F)(G)(H)(J)	36 (F)(G)(H)(J)	56 (F)(G)(H)(J)	
17 (A)(B)(C)(D)	37 (A)(B)(C)(D)	57 (A)(B)(C)(D)	
18 (F)(G)(H)(J)	38 (F)(G)(H)(J)	58 (F)(G)(H)(J)	
19 (A)(B)(C)(D)	39 (A)(B)(C)(D)	59 (A)(B)(C)(D)	
20 (F)(G)(H)(J)	40 (F)(G)(H)(J)	60 (F)(G)(H)(J)	

MATHEMATICS

1 (A)(B)(C)(D)(E)	16 (F)(G)(H)(J)(K)	31 (A)(B)(C)(D)(E)	46 (F)(G)(H)(J)(K)
2 (F)(G)(H)(J)(K)	17 (A)(B)(C)(D)(E)	32 (F)(G)(H)(J)(K)	47 (A)(B)(C)(D)(E)
3 (A)(B)(C)(D)(E)	18 (F)(G)(H)(J)(K)	33 (A)(B)(C)(D)(E)	48 (F)(G)(H)(J)(K)
4 (F)(G)(H)(J)(K)	19 (A)(B)(C)(D)(E)	34 (F)(G)(H)(J)(K)	49 (A)(B)(C)(D)(E)
5 (A)(B)(C)(D)(E)	20 (F)(G)(H)(J)(K)	35 (A)(B)(C)(D)(E)	50 (F)(G)(H)(J)(K)
6 (F)(G)(H)(J)(K)	21 (A)(B)(C)(D)(E)	36 (F)(G)(H)(J)(K)	51 (A)(B)(C)(D)(E)
7 (A)(B)(C)(D)(E)	22 (F)(G)(H)(J)(K)	37 (A)(B)(C)(D)(E)	52 (F)(G)(H)(J)(K)
8 (F)(G)(H)(J)(K)	23 (A)(B)(C)(D)(E)	38 (F)(G)(H)(J)(K)	53 (A)(B)(C)(D)(E)
9 (A)(B)(C)(D)(E)	24 (F)(G)(H)(J)(K)	39 (A)(B)(C)(D)(E)	54 (F)(G)(H)(J)(K)
10 (F)(G)(H)(J)(K)	25 (A)(B)(C)(D)(E)	40 (F)(G)(H)(J)(K)	55 (A)(B)(C)(D)(E)
11 (A)(B)(C)(D)(E)	26 (F)(G)(H)(J)(K)	41 (A)(B)(C)(D)(E)	56 (F)(G)(H)(J)(K)
12 (F)(G)(H)(J)(K)	27 (A)(B)(C)(D)(E)	42 (F)(G)(H)(J)(K)	57 (A)(B)(C)(D)(E)
13 (A)(B)(C)(D)(E)	28 (F)(G)(H)(J)(K)	43 (A)(B)(C)(D)(E)	58 (F)(G)(H)(J)(K)
14 (F)(G)(H)(J)(K)	29 (A)(B)(C)(D)(E)	44 (F)(G)(H)(J)(K)	59 (A)(B)(C)(D)(E)
15 (A)(B)(C)(D)(E)	30 (F)(G)(H)(J)(K)	45 (A)(B)(C)(D)(E)	60 (F)(G)(H)(J)(K)

READING

1 Ⓐ Ⓑ Ⓒ Ⓓ	11 Ⓐ Ⓑ Ⓒ Ⓓ	21 Ⓐ Ⓑ Ⓒ Ⓓ	31 Ⓐ Ⓑ Ⓒ Ⓓ
2 Ⓕ Ⓖ Ⓗ Ⓙ	12 Ⓕ Ⓖ Ⓗ Ⓙ	22 Ⓕ Ⓖ Ⓗ Ⓙ	32 Ⓕ Ⓖ Ⓗ Ⓙ
3 Ⓐ Ⓑ Ⓒ Ⓓ	13 Ⓐ Ⓑ Ⓒ Ⓓ	23 Ⓐ Ⓑ Ⓒ Ⓓ	33 Ⓐ Ⓑ Ⓒ Ⓓ
4 Ⓕ Ⓖ Ⓗ Ⓙ	14 Ⓕ Ⓖ Ⓗ Ⓙ	24 Ⓕ Ⓖ Ⓗ Ⓙ	34 Ⓕ Ⓖ Ⓗ Ⓙ
5 Ⓐ Ⓑ Ⓒ Ⓓ	15 Ⓐ Ⓑ Ⓒ Ⓓ	25 Ⓐ Ⓑ Ⓒ Ⓓ	35 Ⓐ Ⓑ Ⓒ Ⓓ
6 Ⓕ Ⓖ Ⓗ Ⓙ	16 Ⓕ Ⓖ Ⓗ Ⓙ	26 Ⓕ Ⓖ Ⓗ Ⓙ	36 Ⓕ Ⓖ Ⓗ Ⓙ
7 Ⓐ Ⓑ Ⓒ Ⓓ	17 Ⓐ Ⓑ Ⓒ Ⓓ	27 Ⓐ Ⓑ Ⓒ Ⓓ	37 Ⓐ Ⓑ Ⓒ Ⓓ
8 Ⓕ Ⓖ Ⓗ Ⓙ	18 Ⓕ Ⓖ Ⓗ Ⓙ	28 Ⓕ Ⓖ Ⓗ Ⓙ	38 Ⓕ Ⓖ Ⓗ Ⓙ
9 Ⓐ Ⓑ Ⓒ Ⓓ	19 Ⓐ Ⓑ Ⓒ Ⓓ	29 Ⓐ Ⓑ Ⓒ Ⓓ	39 Ⓐ Ⓑ Ⓒ Ⓓ
10 Ⓕ Ⓖ Ⓗ Ⓙ	20 Ⓕ Ⓖ Ⓗ Ⓙ	30 Ⓕ Ⓖ Ⓗ Ⓙ	40 Ⓕ Ⓖ Ⓗ Ⓙ

SCIENCE

1 Ⓐ Ⓑ Ⓒ Ⓓ	11 Ⓐ Ⓑ Ⓒ Ⓓ	21 Ⓐ Ⓑ Ⓒ Ⓓ	31 Ⓐ Ⓑ Ⓒ Ⓓ
2 Ⓕ Ⓖ Ⓗ Ⓙ	12 Ⓕ Ⓖ Ⓗ Ⓙ	22 Ⓕ Ⓖ Ⓗ Ⓙ	32 Ⓕ Ⓖ Ⓗ Ⓙ
3 Ⓐ Ⓑ Ⓒ Ⓓ	13 Ⓐ Ⓑ Ⓒ Ⓓ	23 Ⓐ Ⓑ Ⓒ Ⓓ	33 Ⓐ Ⓑ Ⓒ Ⓓ
4 Ⓕ Ⓖ Ⓗ Ⓙ	14 Ⓕ Ⓖ Ⓗ Ⓙ	24 Ⓕ Ⓖ Ⓗ Ⓙ	34 Ⓕ Ⓖ Ⓗ Ⓙ
5 Ⓐ Ⓑ Ⓒ Ⓓ	15 Ⓐ Ⓑ Ⓒ Ⓓ	25 Ⓐ Ⓑ Ⓒ Ⓓ	35 Ⓐ Ⓑ Ⓒ Ⓓ
6 Ⓕ Ⓖ Ⓗ Ⓙ	16 Ⓕ Ⓖ Ⓗ Ⓙ	26 Ⓕ Ⓖ Ⓗ Ⓙ	36 Ⓕ Ⓖ Ⓗ Ⓙ
7 Ⓐ Ⓑ Ⓒ Ⓓ	17 Ⓐ Ⓑ Ⓒ Ⓓ	27 Ⓐ Ⓑ Ⓒ Ⓓ	37 Ⓐ Ⓑ Ⓒ Ⓓ
8 Ⓕ Ⓖ Ⓗ Ⓙ	18 Ⓕ Ⓖ Ⓗ Ⓙ	28 Ⓕ Ⓖ Ⓗ Ⓙ	38 Ⓕ Ⓖ Ⓗ Ⓙ
9 Ⓐ Ⓑ Ⓒ Ⓓ	19 Ⓐ Ⓑ Ⓒ Ⓓ	29 Ⓐ Ⓑ Ⓒ Ⓓ	39 Ⓐ Ⓑ Ⓒ Ⓓ
10 Ⓕ Ⓖ Ⓗ Ⓙ	20 Ⓕ Ⓖ Ⓗ Ⓙ	30 Ⓕ Ⓖ Ⓗ Ⓙ	40 Ⓕ Ⓖ Ⓗ Ⓙ

RAW SCORES	**SCALE SCORES**	DATE TAKEN:
ENGLISH _____	ENGLISH _____	
MATHEMATICS _____	MATHEMATICS _____	ENGLISH/WRITING _____
READING _____	READING _____	
SCIENCE _____	SCIENCE _____	_____
		COMPOSITE SCORE

Refer to the Scoring Worksheet on page 398 for help in determining your Raw and Scale Scores.

You may wish to remove these sample answer document pages to respond to the practice ACT Writing Test.

Begin WRITING TEST here.

_____
_____
_____
_____
_____
_____
_____
_____
_____
_____
_____
_____
_____
_____
_____
_____
_____
_____
_____
_____
_____
_____
_____
_____
_____
_____
_____
_____

If you need more space, please continue on the next page.

1

Cut Here

WRITING TEST

If you need more space, please continue on the back of this page.

2

WRITING TEST

_____

_____

_____

_____

_____

_____

_____

_____

_____

_____

_____

_____

_____

_____

_____

_____

_____

_____

_____

_____

_____

_____

_____

_____

_____

_____

_____

_____

If you need more space, please continue on the next page.

Cut Here

WRITING TEST

STOP here with the Writing Test.

4

1 ■ ■ ■ ■ ■ ■ ■ ■ 1

ENGLISH TEST

45 Minutes—75 Questions

DIRECTIONS: In the passages that follow, some words and phrases are underlined and numbered. In the answer column, you will find alternatives for the words and phrases that are underlined. Choose the alternative that you think is best, and fill in the corresponding bubble on your answer sheet. If you think that the original version is best, choose "NO CHANGE," which will always be either answer choice A or F. You will also find questions about a particular section of the passage, or about the entire passage. These questions will be identified by either an underlined portion or by a number in a box. Look for the answer that clearly expresses the idea, is consistent with the style and tone of the passage, and makes the correct use of standard written English. Read the passage through once before answering the questions. For some questions, you should read beyond the indicated portion before you answer.

PASSAGE I

The following paragraphs may or may not be in the most logical order. You may be asked questions about the logical order of the paragraphs, as well as where to place sentences logically within any given paragraph.

Michigan's Mesmeric Stone

Some residents of Michigan would probably be surprised and shocked to learn that, during the Devonian
                     ―――――――――――
                            1
Age, 350 million years ago, this northern state was located near the earth's equator. At that time, Michigan was hidden underneath by a warm body of water. It was this
――――――――――――
        2
marine environment that eventually produced Michigan's unique rock formation known as the Petoskey stone.

The light brown Petoskey stone is easily distinguished from other stones having its pattern of numerous and
                      ――――
                        3
contiguous six-sided cells. These cells were once the living coral that was present during the Devonian Age, which slow became petrified into rock that was then gradually
―――――――――
    4
carried north by the slow movement of glaciers. Petoskey stones can vary in appearance, largely due to the content of each coral cell. Most Petoskey stones contain high levels

1. **A.** NO CHANGE
   B. saddened
   C. surprised
   D. disappointed

2. **F.** NO CHANGE
   G. submerged and under
   H. hidden beneath
   J. completely and totally submerged by

3. **A.** NO CHANGE
   B. by
   C. because
   D. from

4. **F.** NO CHANGE
   G. as slow as
   H. slowly became
   J. slow to become

GO ON TO THE NEXT PAGE.

1 ■ ■ ■ ■ ■ ■ ■ ■ **1**

of calcite, but some also contain quartz, pyrite, silica, and
                       5
other minerals. Because of this variety in makeup,

polishing a Petoskey stone can either be a fairly simple

task or one that highly requires a high level of skill and
                     6
patience.

[1] Some rock collectors might be fortunate to find a

Petoskey stone that has been naturally polished by

wind; sand; and water. [2] In many cases, though, the
     7
stones are not exposed to the elements, so some hard labor

might be necessary to produce a smooth, shiny surface that

displays the stones' unique pattern. [3] Despite this, the
                                            8
calcite contained in Petoskey stone is highly conducive to

hand polishing; it is soft enough to give way to sandpaper,
     9
yet strong enough to accept the polishing compound that is

usually applied once all the scratch marks have been

carefully sanded away. [4] It is important to take time to

remove all of the scratches, then they will be present in the
                               10
finished stone along with the coral fossils. [11]

For the serious rock enthusiast, investing in an electric

rock tumbler is a good way to simplify the process of

rock-polishing. Simply place the collected rocks into the

paint-can sized canister, add polishing compound, and push

the button. This begins a long rotation process whereby the

stones are abraded until they have a smooth, glossy finish.
   12

5. Which choice would best help to establish that
   Petoskey stones can vary from one another?
   A. NO CHANGE
   B. but contain some
   C. which predominantly possess
   D. and also include

6. F. NO CHANGE
   G. requires a level of high
   H. requires a high level
   J. required a high level

7. A. NO CHANGE
   B. wind and sand
   C. wind sand
   D. wind, sand,

8. F. NO CHANGE
   G. Fortunately,
   H. Still,
   J. Nevertheless,

9. A. NO CHANGE
   B. hand polishing, it
   C. hand polishing being it
   D. hand polishing it

10. F. NO CHANGE
    G. whereas
    H. otherwise
    J. and

11. For the sake of logic and coherence, Sentence 2 should
    be placed:
    A. where it is now.
    B. before Sentence 1.
    C. after Sentence 3.
    D. after Sentence 4.

12. F. NO CHANGE
    G. stones' are
    H. stone's are
    J. stones, are

GO ON TO THE NEXT PAGE.

1 ■ ■ ■ ■ ■ ■ ■ ■ 1

One advantage of using a rock tumbler instead of hand polishing the stones <u>are that</u> the tumbler can do the work
₁₃
while you scout for more stones to put in it!

Petoskey stones are often difficult to find, depending on the season of the year. Generally, early spring will bring in a new crop of stones after the ice has melted and the stones have been pushed to the shorelines of the northern Great Lakes. ⑭ A good rain will highlight the Petoskey stone's coral pattern, making it easier to spot in the sand. Of course, you can always find Petoskey stones in tourist shops throughout the northern part of the state, but it is much more fun and satisfying to locate one yourself as you walk along the beautiful beaches of Michigan.

13. **A.** NO CHANGE
    B. is that
    C. can be
    D. is so

14. The writer is considering deleting the preceding sentence. If the sentence were deleted, the essay would primarily lose:
    F. the introduction to the essay.
    G. a summary of the preceding paragraph.
    H. an important detail supporting a main idea.
    J. the conclusion to the essay.

> Question 15 asks about the preceding passage as a whole.

15. Suppose the writer had chosen to write an essay about living near the Great Lakes. Would this essay fulfill the writer's goal?
    A. Yes, because this essay refers to Michigan and the Great Lakes several times throughout the text.
    B. Yes, because the writer makes it clear that Petoskey stones are unique to that area of the country.
    C. No, because the writer discusses only the state of Michigan and not the Great Lakes in general.
    D. No, because the essay is primarily about the Petoskey stone and not about living near the Great Lakes.

GO ON TO THE NEXT PAGE.

1 ■ ■ ■ ■ ■ ■ ■ ■ ■ **1**

PASSAGE II

Summer Creatures

The day was hot and sultry, but the cool of the evening approaches as the sun hides itself behind the horizon. Each of us has pulled a lawn chair <u>onto</u> the expansive wooden
16

deck and <u>have settled in</u> for the show. No one says a word.
17
A slight rustling in the thicket of maidenhair ferns off in

the distance <u>can resonate</u>; something is either bedding
18
down or emerging for an evening hunt. A similar sound is

barely audible just in front of <u>us, and we</u> remain silent and
19
attentive.

Suddenly, loud clucking penetrates the silence,

<u>followed by</u> more feverish clucking and chirping, some of
20
it loud and commanding, some more soothing and

calming. These are the sounds of wild turkey hens coming

in to roost, <u>sounding off on</u> safety issues and weather
21
predictions. They cluck and rustle as they roam through

the woods, final destination unknown. Here and there, a

chickadee, finch, or red-headed woodpecker flies overhead

toward a cozy nest. <u>The sky</u> darkens and the last diurnal
22
winged creature takes to its bed, the evening air begins

16. **F.** NO CHANGE
    G. over
    H. by
    J. upon

17. **A.** NO CHANGE
    B. settled in
    C. has settled in
    D. have been settled in

18. **F.** NO CHANGE
    G. resonated
    H. resonates
    J. can be resonating

19. Which of the following alternatives to the underlined portion would NOT be acceptable?
    A. us. We
    B. us—we
    C. us; we
    D. us we

20. **F.** NO CHANGE
    G. following by
    H. followed with
    J. following

21. At this point, the writer wants to liken the wild turkeys to people. Which choice would most effectively accomplish this purpose?
    A. NO CHANGE
    B. clucking and chirping over
    C. fluffing their feathers over
    D. making noise about

22. **F.** NO CHANGE
    G. (Do NOT begin a new paragraph) Which the sky
    H. (Begin a new paragraph) The sky
    J. (Begin a new paragraph) As the sky

GO ON TO THE NEXT PAGE.

1 ■ ■ ■ ■ ■ ■ ■ ■ 1

to welcome its nocturnal flyers, namely fruit bats and night owls. The frenetic bats dart back and forth, high and low, as they began filling their bellies with mosquitoes and other insects. Occasionally an owl will let out its soft "hoo-hoo." This single call is enough to please the small crowd on the deck.

23

We begin to hear more rustling that seems much louder than before. As the evening light darkens, the field creatures become braver and bolder, their vision becoming more acute as ours fades with the disappearing light.

It is almost completely dark now, aside from the massive blanket of stars that lingers over our heads. ☐24 It is dizzying to look up and focus on individual stars, and equally disabling to scan the entire sky and take it in all at once. We still say nothing, except for an occasional whisper of "Did you hear that?" or "Wow." The reverence is clear, the quiet awe palpable.

[1] Suddenly, we hear a single coyote howl way off in the distance, low and slightly tentative, followed shortly by another coyote baying, this time louder and more insistent. [2] We had been told that coyotes live here, but now we knew for sure. [3] The darkness falls all around us and the baying and howling grow louder. [4] Are the coyotes coming closer, or does sound become clearer as the night enfolds us? [5] It is difficult to know for sure: but each subsequent "oowww–ooooh" brings us

25
25
25
25
26

23. A. NO CHANGE
   B. they have begun
   C. they begin
   D. they are beginning

24. Given that all of the following are true, which sentence, if added here, would provide the most effective support for the statements made regarding the night sky?
   F. The moon is not out tonight, so the stars shine ever more brightly and the Milky Way appears ethereal and primordial.
   G. The cloud cover overhead makes the night seem that much darker.
   H. The night air is beginning to have the hint of a chill and we begin thinking about our warm blankets inside the cabin.
   J. The clear sky finds it difficult to give way to the dark shadows of the night.

25. Given that all of the choices are true, which one would most effectively introduce the subject of this paragraph and maintain the tone of the essay?
   A. NO CHANGE
   B. Coyotes are rarely seen during the day as they prefer to do their hunting in the dark of the night.
   C. The lights in the cabin seem to beckon to us.
   D. Of all the sounds we hear, the howling of the coyote seems to be the most endearing.

26. F. NO CHANGE
   G. sure but
   H. sure; but
   J. sure, but

GO ON TO THE NEXT PAGE.

1 ■ ■ ■ ■ ■ ■ ■ ■ 1

closer to moving inside the warm cabin. [27] We are

calm; but ready to give the night back to its rightful
‾‾‾‾
28

owners. Our skin has cooled from the day's heat and we
‾‾‾‾‾‾
29
have had our bedtime story. Just as we sense that the time

has come to slip inside, the unmistakable flash of a

streaking meteor is catching our eyes and we jerk our
‾‾‾‾‾‾‾‾‾‾‾‾‾‾
30
heads upwards, just in time to see the shooting star fade

into the blackness. It is time to say goodnight.

27. Which of the following sentences in this paragraph is
LEAST relevant to the main focus of the essay and,
therefore, could be deleted?
A. Sentence 1
B. Sentence 2
C. Sentence 3
D. Sentence 4

28. F. NO CHANGE
G. calm but
H. calm, but
J. calm. But

29. A. NO CHANGE
B. has been cooled
C. got cooled
D. cooled

30. F. NO CHANGE
G. caught our eyes
H. catches our eye
J. has caught our eyes

PASSAGE III

> The following paragraphs may or may not be in the most
> logical order. You may be asked questions about the log-
> ical order of the paragraphs, as well as where to place
> sentences logically within any given paragraph.

Adventures in Australian English

"Have a gander! Some mozzies landed in the barbie,

right on the chook! We'll have to get take-away!"

Translation: "Look! Some mosquitoes have been landed in
‾‾‾‾‾‾‾‾‾‾‾‾‾‾
31
the barbecue, right on the chicken! We'll have to get

carry-out!"

Such is the colorful lilt of Australian English, which is

as unique and distinctive as Australia itself. From

Australia's beginnings as an English penal colony in the
‾‾‾‾‾‾‾‾‾‾‾‾‾‾
32
late 1700s to its later incarnation as a land of opportunity,

the country continues to be influenced by outside forces,
‾‾‾‾‾‾‾‾‾‾‾‾‾‾
33
which included the American military during World

War II. As a result, the Australian language is a rather

clever, often humorous blend of both British and American

31. A. NO CHANGE
B. had landed
C. landed
D. are landing

32. F. NO CHANGE
G. Australia's first beginnings
H. the first beginnings of Australia began
J. Australia's first beginning

33. A. NO CHANGE
B. by being influenced by
C. the influence of
D. to being influenced by

GO ON TO THE NEXT PAGE.

1 ■ ■ ■ ■ ■ ■ ■ ■ **1**

versions of English. American television also played a major role in the Americanization of Australian English, often causing <u>Australian's</u> to replace British words with
₃₄
their American counterparts, such as the American word *truck* replacing the British word *lorry*.

There are three main <u>principal</u> types of Australian
₃₅
English, although they overlap quite a bit. "General

Australian English" is spoken by <u>the majority of native</u>
₃₆
<u>Australians,</u> and emphasizes shorter vowel sounds
₃₆

<u>and have</u> fewer variations in diction. "Broad Australian"
₃₇
is more prevalent outside of the island's major cities.

The <u>lesser common</u> dialect of Australian English is the
₃₈
"cultivated" form, which is spoken by about 10 percent of the Australian population. Many Australians consider the cultivated form to be <u>too</u> haughty and snobbish.
₃₉

<u>Vast majority of Australians</u> reject that particular variety.
₄₀
Australian English vocabulary also varies from one region to another. For example, in New South Wales, a bathing suit may be called a *swimmer* or a *tog*, while in other areas it is referred to as a *bather*. A ten-ounce drinking glass may be called a *pot*, *handle*, *middy*, *ten*, or *schooner*, depending on the region of the country.

<u>Additionally, the word *footy* can refer</u> to Australian
₄₁
football or rugby.

Australian English has other distinctive traits, such as a propensity toward more vivid expressions like *mangy maggot* or *bloody grub* used to signify unlikable people. Australians also frequently shorten English words, then

34. **F.** NO CHANGE
    G. Australians
    H. Australians'
    J. Australian

35. **A.** NO CHANGE
    B. and principal
    C. principally
    D. OMIT the underlined portion.

36. Which choice best gives the sense that "General Australian English" is the most prevalent form used in Australia?
    F. NO CHANGE
    G. people in Australia
    H. Australians
    J. those native to Australia

37. **A.** NO CHANGE
    B. but have
    C. so has
    D. and has

38. **F.** NO CHANGE
    G. least of all common
    H. less common
    J. least common

39. **A.** NO CHANGE
    B. to
    C. so
    D. far to

40. **F.** NO CHANGE
    G. Vast majority of English Australians
    H. The vast majority of Australians
    J. Majority of the Australians

41. **A.** NO CHANGE
    B. The word *footy*, additionally, can refer
    C. Referring to the word *footy* can additionally refer
    D. Additionally, in reference to the word *footy*, it refers

GO ON TO THE NEXT PAGE.

1 ■ ■ ■ ■ ■ ■ ■ ■ **1**

add an "o" or "ie" to the end, thus producing a diminutive form. [42] Examples are *servo*, which means service station, and *ambo*, which means ambulance or the person who drives one.

[1] In 1981, the Macquarie Dictionary of Australian

English has been published by Macquarie Library Pty,
          ‾‾‾‾‾‾‾‾‾‾‾‾‾‾
                    43
Ltd., in association with the Linguistics Department of Macquarie University in Sydney. [2] Subsequent editions have included encyclopedic entries and more extensive word and phrase origins. [3] Over time, Australian schools, businesses, and legal systems have adopted the Macquarie Dictionary, although it is difficult to keep up with the country's ever-changing adaptations caused by outside (particularly American) influences. [4] As some Australians would say, the Macquarie Dictionary has *Buckley's* of keeping up with modern times! [44]

42. If the writer were to delete the phrase "adding an 'o' or 'ie' to the end" (ending the sentence with the word *form*), the essay would primarily lose a detail that:
   F. is necessary in order to understand the beginning of the sentence.
   G. gives an example of the humor that is often associated with Australian English.
   H. contradicts the references to the Americanization of Australian English.
   J. is necessary to explain the examples that are given in the next sentence.

43. A. NO CHANGE
   B. was published
   C. were published
   D. is published

44. Which of the following sequences of sentences makes this paragraph most logical?
   F. NO CHANGE
   G. 1, 3, 2, 4
   H. 1, 2, 4, 3
   J. 1, 4, 2, 3

Question 45 asks about the preceding passage as a whole.

45. Suppose the writer had intended to write a travel magazine article that would prepare a visitor for a trip to Australia. Would this essay successfully fulfill this goal?
   A. Yes, because the essay describes the nuances of Australian English, which is the main language spoken in Australia.
   B. Yes, because the writer gives specific examples of word usage and vocabulary commonly used in Australia.
   C. No, because the essay only addresses the language used in Australia and does not mention other aspects of the country and its people.
   D. No, because the essay mainly discusses Australia from an historical perspective.

GO ON TO THE NEXT PAGE.

1 ■ ■ ■ ■ ■ ■ ■ ■ 1

PASSAGE IV

> The following paragraphs may or may not be in the most logical order. You may be asked questions about the logical order of the paragraphs, as well as where to place sentences logically within any given paragraph.

"Eye" Can See You!

Imagine, if you can, sticking a clear, semi-rigid dime into each of your eyes. As a ninth-grader in the early 60s,
                    46

that's what I felt I will be doing with my first pair of
                    47
contact lenses. In those days, wearing contact lenses

was, truly a novelty. "Hard lenses," as they are called, is
      48
an apt description of those things, and equally so of the

frustration they cause in the pursuit of clear vision.

I was diagnosed in third grade as being near-sighted
                    49
and astigmatic. My teacher had noticed that something was
  49
wrong because I stood about a foot away from a classroom

projection screen in order to read the captions on the

science slides. In those days, we learned through a
                               50
sequence of picture slides the teacher would narrate, kind

of like a rudimentary computer presentation. While most
          51
students thrilled to see the teacher dim the lights and fire

up the projector, I was sunk in my seat to avoid her
                    52
attention once the time inevitably came to read aloud the

fine print so fuzzy in the distance.

[1] When I was finally fitted with my first glasses at age

eight, I remember thinking how cheated I had been in my

young life; I had no idea that most people could see as

clearly as I began to that day! [2] It was dizzying walking

out of the optometrist's office. [3] Objects were suddenly

46. **F.** NO CHANGE
    G. both of
    H. two of
    J. OMIT the underlined portion

47. **A.** NO CHANGE
    B. was doing
    C. had done
    D. would do

48. **F.** NO CHANGE
    G. was truly, a novelty
    H. was truly a novelty
    J. was, truly a, novelty

49. **A.** NO CHANGE
    B. as near-sighted in the third grade and diagnosed with astigmatism
    C. diagnosed in the third grade with an astigmatism and also nearsightedness
    D. near-sighted as a diagnosis, with astigmatism

50. **F.** NO CHANGE
    G. learn
    H. we have learned
    J. we were learning

51. Which of the alternatives would be LEAST appropriate and relevant to the essay?
    A. NO CHANGE
    B. primitive
    C. simple
    D. complicated

52. **F.** NO CHANGE
    G. had sunk
    H. had sank
    J. sank

GO ON TO THE NEXT PAGE.

1 ■ ■ ■ ■ ■ ■ ■ ■ **1**

more rigid and linear; colors seemed more intense and striking. [4] For eight years, everything around me had been one big blur and I hadn't a clue! [5] I felt so alive! [6] My eyeglasses became a sort of lifeline, the first thing I put on and the last thing I took off every day. ⑸⑶

Although they represent a less dramatic change, my first contact lenses six years later at once again sharpened my
⁵⁴
focus and heightened my senses. Wearing contact lenses, however, took some adjustment; several weeks were required to build calluses on the underside of each eyelid. Putting those saucers in each eye also proved a challenge. Regardless, the old lenses were much thicker than today's
⁵⁵
contact lenses.

While applying the lenses to each eye was difficult, they were easy to pop out, especially when you least
⁵⁶
expected them to. There is nothing like fishing a contact lens out of a toilet bowl or gingerly using the stopper to
⁵⁷
retrieve a lens from the wall of the bathroom sink drain. I probably lost and found at least a dozen lenses in the first two years of wearing them. Since I was virtually blind without my contacts, my immediate reaction was always to cry out for help in locating the missing lens.

I can still remember one day sitting in the back row in algebra class surrounded by several classmates. I glanced up quickly at the teacher when, in a flash, out came a lens. I could sense it falling to the tile floor certainly in the path
⁵⁸
of some kid's foot. I tried working my way to the floor

53. Which of the following sequences of sentences makes this paragraph most logical?
A. NO CHANGE
B. 1, 3, 2, 4, 5, 6
C. 2, 3, 4, 1, 5, 6
D. 1, 4, 2, 3, 5, 6

54. F. NO CHANGE
G. later than
H. later
J. OMIT the underlined portion

55. A. NO CHANGE
B. Again,
C. Unfortunately,
D. However,

56. F. NO CHANGE
G. those lenses were easy to pop out
H. they popped out easily
J. the lenses also popped out easily

57. A. NO CHANGE
B. while
C. whereas
D. and

58. F. NO CHANGE
G. floor, certainly
H. floor; certainly
J. floor, but certainly

GO ON TO THE NEXT PAGE.

1 ■ ■ ■ ■ ■ ■ ■ ■ 1

as discreetly as possible, <u>palms down.</u> Suddenly, my
                              59
chair's metal legs slipped a few inches on the waxy floor

and I landed right on top of my precious lens with a thud,

crushing it to oblivion. I had gotten my new contacts only

three days earlier. How would I explain this to my mother?

She had already questioned my maturity for months before

buying me this latest pair. ⑥₀

59. Given that all of the choices are true, which one would
best conclude the sentence while providing the reader
with the most vivid image of how the writer searched
for his lost contact lens?
   A. NO CHANGE
   B. moving towards where I thought the last contact
would be.
   C. without anyone noticing.
   D. patting the linoleum in wide sweeps.

60. At this point, the writer is considering adding the
following sentence:

> In the end, my mother understood the delicate
> nature of wearing contact lenses, and within days
> I was again able to see clearly with my new lenses.

Should the writer make this addition here?
   F. Yes, because it tells the reader the real reason why
the author is upset about breaking her contact lens.
   G. Yes, because it effectively concludes the essay
while maintaining the tone of the essay.
   H. No, because the author explains throughout the
essay that she preferred wearing eyeglasses.
   J. No, because the author is not really near-sighted.

PASSAGE V

> The following paragraphs may or may not be in the most
> logical order. You may be asked questions about the log-
> ical order of the paragraphs, as well as where to place
> sentences logically within any given paragraph.

Graphic Artists: Art Meets Technology

[1]

"Many graphic artists who obtained their training 15 to

20 years ago will have a problem finding work if they

haven't learned to use computer software to create their

<u>art."</u> declares Sue Mauro, publicist for a U.S. hotel chain.
 61

In fact, successful businesses often rely on the creativity
                                              62
and talent of graphic artists to create and produce
                    62
images and text in the form of digital media,
                       62
print, films, packaging, and signage.
         62

61. **A.** NO CHANGE
   B. art,"
   C. art"
   D. art!"

62. Given that all of the choices are true, which one would
provide the most detailed and relevant information at
this point in the essay?
   F. NO CHANGE
   G. Many young people are seeking degrees in the field
of graphic arts.
   H. Finding a college that offers a strong graphic arts
program can often be a challenge.
   J. The field of graphic arts has changed considerably
due to advanced technology.

GO ON TO THE NEXT PAGE.

1 ■ ■ ■ ■ ■ ■ ■ ■ 1

[2]

Mauro's comment <u>was also</u> applicable to the creation
　　　　　　　　63
of animated films.

[64] Flip-books are a perfect basic example of early

animation; each drawing in the book has a slight

variation from the preceding drawing. When the pages

are flipped in rapid <u>succession; an</u> action scene unfolds
　　　　　　　　　　65
over a few seconds. Traditional animated films are

based on this same principle, <u>although</u> their production
　　　　　　　　　　　　　　66
is much more complicated and time-consuming. In

traditional film animation, several drawings are

meticulously applied to <u>cels. Sheets</u> of clear plastic.
　　　　　　　　　　67

<u>As a result,</u> the entire series of cels is photographed in
　68
succession, creating a long, moving cartoon story.

Layering cels allows objects that remain stationary to

reappear so that only the moving parts must be redrawn.

[3]

[1] This old way of creating <u>animated moving</u> films is
　　　　　　　　　　　　　　　69
known as traditional ink-and-paint and has given way to

today's digital ink-and-paint. [2] In the digital

ink-and-paint process, the hand drawings are scanned and

digitized. [3] <u>The rest of the production of the film takes
　　　　　　　　　　　　　　　70
place through the use of the computer rather than being
　　　　　　70
applied to individual cels.</u> [4] This method has greatly
　70

63. **A.** NO CHANGE
B. is to be
C. was
D. is also

64. Which of the following sentences would most effectively introduce the subject of this paragraph and act as a transition from the preceding paragraph?
F. Film animation began as a series of pictures that simulated motion when shown together rapidly.
G. Flip-books were a popular 'toy' in the 1950s.
H. Some graphic artists have no interest in creating motion pictures and are focusing instead on print media, such as that used in advertising.
J. Film animation has changed dramatically over the past several decades.

65. **A.** NO CHANGE
B. succession an
C. succession-an
D. succession, an

66. **F.** NO CHANGE
G. therefore
H. because
J. and in contrast

67. **A.** NO CHANGE
B. cels; or sheets
C. cels, or sheets
D. cels, which like sheets

68. **F.** NO CHANGE
G. Consequently,
H. Therefore,
J. Eventually,

69. **A.** NO CHANGE
B. animated
C. animatedly moving
D. animated and moving

70. **F.** NO CHANGE
G. The rest of the balance of the production takes place by using the computer instead of applying the artwork to the cels.
H. The balance of the production is done through the use of computer software instead of using acetate cels.
J. The film is then produced using a computer rather than the plastic cels.

GO ON TO THE NEXT PAGE.

1 ■ ■ ■ ■ ■ ■ ■ ■ 1

decreased the amount and length of time that it takes to
_____
                    71

create a whole film, and has allowed animators, from
                                                                  _____
                                                                         72
all over the world, to contribute to a single film's
_____
       72
production. [5] With more advanced technologies,

animators can even draw their original pictures on a

graphics tablet that enters the data directly into a computer.

[6] Once the outline of the drawing is complete, it is rather

simple to add color. [7] In addition, it is easier to make

changes than it is with traditional ink-and-paint. [8] Digital

animation also produces an entirely different look to the

finished product, and graphic art has always depended on
_____
          73

fresh, new looks to grab viewers' attention. [74]

[4]

Though some graphic artists resist change, those who

delve into this new technological world often find a way to

become comfortable with the marriage of art and

technology. The bottom line is that working with

technology may be the only way to remain in their chosen

field.

71. A. NO CHANGE
  B. length of time, as well as the amount,
  C. length and amount and time
  D. time

72. F. NO CHANGE
  G. animators from all over the world,
  H. animators, from all over the world
  J. animators from all over the world

73. Which of the following alternatives to the underlined portion would NOT be acceptable?
  A. product—graphic art
  B. product; graphic art
  C. product, graphic art
  D. product. Graphic art

74. For the sake of the logic and coherence of this paragraph, Sentence 5 should be placed:
  F. where it is now.
  G. before Sentence 3.
  H. before Sentence 4.
  J. after Sentence 7.

Question 75 asks about the preceding passage as a whole.

75. The writer wishes to add the following sentence in order to emphasize the influence of technology in jobs related to graphic arts:

  Most graphic artists start out as traditional artists, and many are discovering that their natural talent is no longer enough to survive in this highly competitive field.

  The new sentence would best support and be placed at the beginning of Paragraph:
  A. 1
  B. 2
  C. 3
  D. 4

END OF THE ENGLISH TEST.
STOP! IF YOU HAVE TIME LEFT OVER, CHECK YOUR WORK ON THIS SECTION ONLY.

2 △ △ △ △ △ △ △ △ **2**

MATHEMATICS TEST

60 Minutes—60 Questions

DIRECTIONS: Solve each of the problems in the time allowed, then fill in the corresponding bubble on your answer sheet. Do not spend too much time on any one problem; skip the more difficult problems and go back to them later.

You may use a calculator on this test. For this test you should assume that figures are NOT necessarily drawn to scale, that all geometric figures lie in a plane, and that the word *line* is used to indicate a straight line.

---

1. Which of the following lists all the positive factors of 32?
   A. 1, 32
   B. 2, 16
   C. 2, 4, 8, 16
   D. 2, 4, 8, 16, 32
   E. 1, 2, 4, 8, 16, 32

2. All CDs are equally priced. If 8 CDs cost $76.00, what is the cost of 1 CD?
   F. $0.10
   G. $2.05
   H. $7.60
   J. $9.50
   K. $10.50

3. $2x^2 \times 3x^2y^2 \times 5x^2y$ is equivalent to:
   A. $30x^8y^3$
   B. $30x^8y^2$
   C. $30x^6y^3$
   D. $11x^8y^3$
   E. $11x^6y^2$

4. What is the value of the expression $10(100x - 10,000) + 100$ when $x = 250$?
   F. 2,500
   G. 150,100
   H. 160,000
   J. 210,000
   K. 300,100

5. $4a^3 \times 5a^8 = ?$
   A. $9a^5$
   B. $9a^{11}$
   C. $9a^{24}$
   D. $20a^{11}$
   E. $20a^{24}$

DO YOUR FIGURING HERE.

GO ON TO THE NEXT PAGE.

2 △ △ △ △ △ △ △ △ 2

6. In the figure shown below, $AD = 16$, $ED = 11$, and AE is congruent to CD. What is the length of AB?

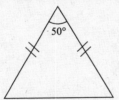

DO YOUR FIGURING HERE.

   F. 5
   G. $5\sqrt{2}$
   H. 6
   J. $11\sqrt{2}$
   K. 25

7. Which of the following numbers is the least in value?
   A. 0.02×10^4
   B. 0.2×10^3
   C. 2.0×10^{-2}
   D. 20.0×10^2
   E. 0.002×10^5

8. The isosceles triangle below has one angle measure as shown. What is the measure of each of the other angles?

50°

   F. 30°
   G. 45°
   H. 50°
   J. 65°
   K. 130°

9. The sum of the real numbers a and b is 13. Their difference is 5. What is the value of ab?
   A. 5
   B. 8
   C. 18
   D. 36
   E. 65

10. 37 is what percent of 144, to the nearest percent?
   F. 26%
   G. 37%
   H. 44%
   J. 74%
   K. 107%

GO ON TO THE NEXT PAGE.

2   △ **2**

Use the following information to answer Questions 11–12.

The Moondance Riding Academy held its annual horse show for 3 days. The total amount collected in entry fees for the 3 days was $1,450. The amount collected, in dollars, is shown for each of the 3 days in the bar graph below:

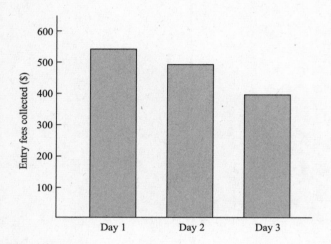

DO YOUR FIGURING HERE.

11. Approximately what percent of the money collected from entry fees over the 3 days was collected on Day 2?
   A. 29%
   B. 34%
   C. 38%
   D. 66%
   E. 90%

12. The mean amount collected per day during the 3-day period is what, to the nearest dollar?
   F. $300
   G. $483
   H. $577
   J. $1,450
   K. $4,350

13. For all n, $(3n + 5)^2 = ?$
   A. $6n^2 + 15n + 10$
   B. $6n^2 + 30n + 25$
   C. $9n^2 + 6n + 10$
   D. $9n^2 + 15n + 25$
   E. $9n^2 + 30n + 25$

GO ON TO THE NEXT PAGE.

2 △ △ △ △ △ △ △ △ **2**

14. A certain brand of cereal costs $3.25 per box before sales tax is added. When you buy 5 or more boxes of this cereal you receive 1 additional box for free. What is the average cost per box of cereal for 6 boxes before sales tax is added?

 F. $2.17
 G. $2.71
 H. $2.80
 J. $3.25
 K. $3.79

15. Rana and Tom own a pizza shop, which offers 3 kinds of cheese, 4 kinds of meat toppings, and 5 kinds of vegetable toppings. Each type of pizza on the menu has a combination of exactly 3 ingredients: 1 cheese, 1 meat, and 1 vegetable. How many types of pizzas are possible?

 A. 12
 B. 24
 C. 36
 D. 50
 E. 60

16. On the real number line, what is the midpoint of -3 and 11?

 F. -5
 G. 0
 H. 4
 J. 7
 K. 14

17. Which real number satisfies $(2^n)(8) = 16^3$?

 A. 3
 B. 4
 C. 6
 D. 9
 E. 12

18. If $f(x) = -3x^2 - 8$, then $f(-4) = ?$

 F. -56
 G. -40
 H. 8
 J. 24
 K. 40

DO YOUR FIGURING HERE.

GO ON TO THE NEXT PAGE.

19. A clock tower casts a 150-foot shadow on level ground, as shown below. The angle of elevation from the tip of the shadow to the top of the tower is 40°. To the nearest tenth of a foot, what is the height of the clock tower?

DO YOUR FIGURING HERE.

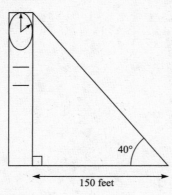

40°

← 150 feet →

(Note: $\cos 40° = \sin 50° \approx 0.77$

$\cos 50° = \sin 40° \approx 0.64$

$\tan 50° \approx 1.19$

$\tan 40° \approx 0.84$)

A. 194.8
B. 178.5
C. 150.0
D. 126.0
E. 115.5

20. If $4(x - 2) + 5x = 3(x + 3) - 11$, then $x = ?$
 F. −3
 G. −1
 H. 0
 J. 1
 K. 2

21. What is the least common multiple of 40, 70, and 60?
 A. 240
 B. 420
 C. 840
 D. 1,680
 E. 168,000

22. If $4\frac{2}{5} = a - 1\frac{2}{3}$, then $a = ?$

 F. $\frac{95}{15}$

 G. $\frac{91}{15}$

 H. $\frac{41}{15}$

 J. $\frac{27}{8}$

 K. $\frac{17}{8}$

GO ON TO THE NEXT PAGE.

2 △ △ △ △ △ △ △ **2**

DO YOUR FIGURING HERE.

23. A system of linear equations is shown below.

$$4y - 2x = 8$$
$$4y + 2x = 8$$

Which of the following describes the graph of this system of linear equations in the standard (x, y) coordinate plane?
A. A single line with positive slope
B. A single line with negative slope
C. Two distinct intersecting lines
D. Two parallel lines with positive slope
E. Two parallel lines with negative slope

24. A house painter charges $24.00 per hour for a painting job that requires more than 5 hours to complete. For any job requiring 5 hours or less, the house painter charges a flat fee of $100. If n represents the number of hours the job requires, which of the following expressions gives the charge, in dollars, for a job requiring more than 5 hours to complete?
F. 124.0
G. $-24n + 100$
H. $24n - 100$
J. $24n$
K. $24n + 100$

25. The average (arithmetic mean) of a and b is 6 and the average of a, b, and c is 11. What is the value of c?
A. 21
B. 17
C. 13
D. 8
E. 5

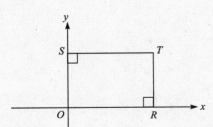

26. In the figure above, $OS = ST$ and the coordinates of T are $(k, 5)$. What is the value of k?
F. −5
G. −3
H. −2
J. 0
K. 5

GO ON TO THE NEXT PAGE.

2   **2**

27. At a summer camp, one boy and one girl will be selected to lead the weekly activities. If there are 130 boys and 145 girls at the camp, how many different 2-person combinations of 1 boy and 1 girl are possible?

   A. 15
   B. 275
   C. 550
   D. 9,425
   E. 18,850

28. If 3 times a number x is added to 12, the result is negative. Which of the following gives the possible value(s) for x?

   F. All $x > 4$
   G. All $x < -4$
   H. 36 only
   J. 4 only
   K. 0 only

29. The figure below shows 2 tangent circles such that the 9-inch diameter of the smaller circle is equal to the radius of the larger circle. What is the approximate area, in square inches, of the shaded region?

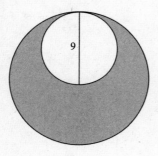

   A. 28.27
   B. 56.55
   C. 63.62
   D. 190.74
   E. 254.47

30. $(x^3 + 2x^2 + 3x - 2) - (2x^3 - x^2 - 4)$ is equivalent to:

   F. $-x^3 + x^2 + 3x - 6$
   G. $-x^3 + 3x^2 + 3x + 2$
   H. $2x^3 - 2x^2 + 3x - 2$
   J. $2x^6 + x^4 + 3x - 6$
   K. $2x^6 + 3x^4 + 3x + 2$

DO YOUR FIGURING HERE.

GO ON TO THE NEXT PAGE.

2 △ △ △ △ **2**

x	0	1	2	3
$f(x)$	−6	−5	−2	3

DO YOUR FIGURING HERE.

31. The table above gives values of the quadratic function f for selected values of x. Which of the following defines the quadratic function f?

A. $f(x) = x^2 - 6$
B. $f(x) = x^2 + 6$
C. $f(x) = 2x^2 - 10$
D. $f(x) = 2x^2 - 6$
E. $f(x) = 2x^2 - 7$

32. What is the median of the following 6 test scores?

  64, 72, 85, 80, 72, 89

F. 64
G. 72
H. 76
J. 77
K. 82.5

33. For all numbers x and y, let the operation ¤ be defined as $x \, ¤ \, y = 2xy - 4x$. If a and b are positive integers, which of the following can be equal to zero?
  I. $a \, ¤ \, b$
  II. $(a - b) \, ¤ \, b$
  III. $b \, ¤ \, (a - b)$

A. I only
B. II only
C. III only
D. I and II only
E. I, II, and III

34. In the figure shown below, the measure of $\angle SRT$ is $(x + 15)°$ and the measure of $\angle SRU$ is 90°. What is the measure of $\angle TRU$?

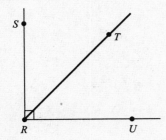

F. $(105 + x)°$
G. $(105 - x)°$
H. $(75 + x)°$
J. $(75 - x)°$
K. $(x - 75)°$

GO ON TO THE NEXT PAGE.

2   △ △ △ △ △ **2**

35. $(6a - 12) - (4a + 4) = ?$
   A. $2(a + 2)$
   B. $2(a + 4)$
   C. $2(a - 2)$
   D. $2(a - 4)$
   E. $2(a - 8)$

36. In the standard (x, y) coordinate plane below, the points $(0,2)$, $(8,2)$, $(3,6)$, and $(11,6)$ are the vertices of a parallelogram. What is the area, in square units, of the parallelogram?

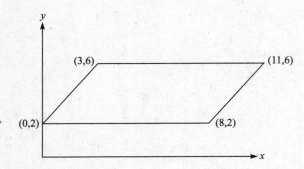

   F. $6\sqrt{2}$
   G. 16
   H. 32
   J. 56
   K. 88

37. Which of the following equations expresses z in terms of x for all real numbers x, y, and z, such that $x^5 = y$ and $y^3 = z$?
   A. $z = x$
   B. $z = \dfrac{3}{5}x$
   C. $z = 3x^5$
   D. $z = x^8$
   E. $z = x^{15}$

38. Which of the following statements is NOT true about the geometric sequence 36, 18, 9, ...?
   F. The fourth term is 4.5.
   G. The sum of the first five terms is 69.75.
   H. Each consecutive term is $\dfrac{1}{2}$ of the previous term.
   J. Each consecutive term is evenly divisible by 3.
   K. The common ratio of consecutive terms is 2:1.

GO ON TO THE NEXT PAGE.

2 △ △ △ △ △ △ △ △ 2

39. For right triangle *ABC* with dimensions in centimeters as given below, what is tan *C*?

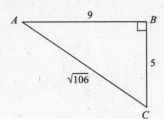

A. $\dfrac{5}{9}$

B. $\dfrac{5}{\sqrt{106}}$

C. $\dfrac{9}{\sqrt{106}}$

D. $\dfrac{\sqrt{106}}{9}$

E. $\dfrac{9}{5}$

40. The area of a trapezoid is found by using the equation $\frac{1}{2}h(b_1 + b_2)$, where *h* is the height and b_1 and b_2 are the lengths of the bases. What is the area of the trapezoid shown below?

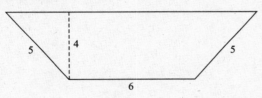

F. 18
G. 20
H. 24
J. 30
K. 36

41. The diagonal of a rectangular garden is 15 feet, and one side is 9 feet. What is the perimeter of the garden?

A. 135
B. 108
C. 68
D. 48
E. 42

DO YOUR FIGURING HERE.

GO ON TO THE NEXT PAGE.

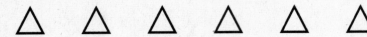

2 △ △ △ △ △ △ △ △ **2**

42. $\left(\dfrac{1}{3}a - b\right)^2 = ?$

   F. $\dfrac{1}{9}a^2 + b^2$

   G. $\dfrac{1}{9}a^2 - \dfrac{2}{3}ab + b^2$

   H. $\dfrac{1}{3}a^2 - \dfrac{2}{3}ab + b^2$

   J. $a^2 + b^2$

   K. $a^2 - \dfrac{1}{3}ab + b^2$

43. Which of the following inequalities defines the solution set for the inequality $23 - 6x \geq 5$?
   A. $x \geq -3$
   B. $x \geq 3$
   C. $x \geq 6$
   D. $x \leq 3$
   E. $x \leq -6$

44. What is the approximate distance between the points $(4, -3)$ and $(-6, 5)$ in the standard (x, y) coordinate plane?
   F. 8.92
   G. 12.81
   H. 16.97
   J. 17.95
   K. 19.22

45. The ratio of x to z is 3 to 5, and the ratio of y to z is 1 to 5. What is the ratio of x to y?
   A. 5:3
   B. 5:1
   C. 3:1
   D. 1:3
   E. 1:1

46. If $\tan \alpha = \dfrac{x}{y}$, $x > 0$, $y > 0$, and $0 < \alpha < \dfrac{\pi}{2}$, then what is $\cos \alpha$?

   F. $\dfrac{\sqrt{x^2 + y^2}}{y}$

   G. $\dfrac{y}{\sqrt{x^2 + y^2}}$

   H. $\dfrac{x}{\sqrt{x^2 + y^2}}$

   J. $\dfrac{y}{x}$

   K. $\dfrac{x}{y}$

GO ON TO THE NEXT PAGE.

2   **2**

47. In the figure below, *FGHJ* is a square and *Q*, *R*, *S*, and *T* are the midpoints of its sides. If $\overline{GH} = 10$ inches, what is the area of *QRST*, in inches?

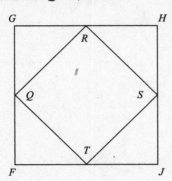

DO YOUR FIGURING HERE.

A. 100
B. 50
C. 25
D. 20
E. $5\sqrt{2}$

48. In △ *XYZ* below, $\overline{XZ}$ is $\frac{7}{8}$ of *h*, the length of the altitude. What is the area of △ *XYZ* in terms of *h*?

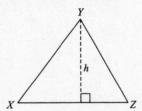

F. $\frac{7h}{8}$

G. $\frac{7h^2}{8}$

H. $\frac{7h}{16}$

J. $\frac{7h^2}{16}$

K. $\frac{7h^2}{12}$

49. On Friday, a computer was priced at $800. On the following Wednesday, the price was reduced by 15%. On the following Friday, the price was further reduced by 20%. What percent of the original price was the final price?
A. 82.5
B. 68
C. 65
D. 35
E. 32

GO ON TO THE NEXT PAGE.

2 △ △ △ △ △ △ △ △ **2**

DO YOUR FIGURING HERE.

50. If $ghjk = 24$ and $ghkl = 0$, which of the following must be true?
    - F. $g > 0$
    - G. $h > 0$
    - H. $j = 0$
    - J. $k = 0$
    - K. $l = 0$

51. Given the vertices of parallelogram *FGHJ* in the standard (x, y) coordinate plane below, what is the area of triangle *GHJ*, in square units?

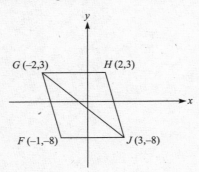

- A. 11
- B. 15
- C. 22
- D. 44
- E. 88

52. If X, Y, and Z are real numbers, and $XYZ = 1$, then which of the following conditions must be true?
    - F. $XZ = \dfrac{1}{Y}$
    - G. X, Y, and $Z > 0$
    - H. Either $X = 1$, $Y = 1$, or $Z = 1$
    - J. Either $X = 0$, $Y = 0$, or $Z = 0$
    - K. Either $X < 1$, $Y < 1$, or $Z < 1$

53. In the standard (x,y) coordinate plane, the y-intercept of the line $6x + 2y = 14$ is?
    - A. -6
    - B. -3
    - C. 2
    - D. 7
    - E. 14

54. The average of a set of six integers is 38. When a seventh number is included in the set, the average of the set increases to 47. What is the seventh number?
    - F. 38
    - G. 47
    - H. 101
    - J. 228
    - K. 329

GO ON TO THE NEXT PAGE.

2 △ △ △ △ △ △ △ △ **2**

55. The area of a rectangular kitchen is 80 square feet. If the length of the floor is 4 feet less than four times the width, what is the width of the floor in feet?

A. 4
B. 5
C. 8
D. 16
E. 17

56. For every cent increase in price of a pound of apples, the grocery store sells 25 fewer pounds per day. The grocery store normally sells 800 pounds of apples per day at $1.09 per pound. Which of the following expressions represents the number of pounds of apples sold per day if the cost is increased by $3x$ cents per pound of apples?

F. $(1.09 + 3x)(800 - 75x)$
G. $800 - 25x$
H. $800 - 75(1.09)x$
J. $800 + 75x$
K. $800 - 75x$

57. Jason has been hired to build a circular wading pool in his neighbor's backyard. The rectangular backyard measures 60 feet wide by 50 feet long. Jason's neighbors want the pool to be as large as possible, with the edge of the pool at least 8 feet from the edge of the backyard all around. How long should the radius of the pool be, in feet?

A. 8
B. 17
C. 22
D. 34
E. 44

58. If $f(x) = x^2 + 3$, then $f(x + y) = ?$

F. $x^2 + 2xy + y^2 + 3$
G. $x^2 + 2xy + y^2$
H. $x^2 + 2xy + 3$
J. $x^2 + 3 + y$
K. $x^2 + y^2$

DO YOUR FIGURING HERE.

GO ON TO THE NEXT PAGE.

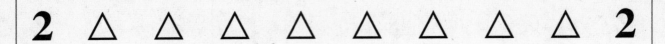

2 △ △ △ △ △ △ △ △ **2**

59. In a game, 84 marbles numbered 00 through 83 are placed in a box. A player draws 1 marble at random from the box. Without replacing the first marble, the player draws a second marble at random. If both marbles drawn have the same tens digit (that is, both marbles are numbered between 00 and 09, or 10 and 19, or 20 and 29, etc.), the player is a winner. If the first marble Dave draws is numbered 23, what is the probability that Dave will be a winner on the next draw?

A. $\dfrac{9}{84}$

B. $\dfrac{74}{83}$

C. $\dfrac{9}{83}$

D. $\dfrac{75}{84}$

E. $\dfrac{10}{83}$

60. What is the smallest possible value for the product of 2 real numbers that differ by 6?

F. -9
G. -8
H. -5
J. 0
K. 7

DO YOUR FIGURING HERE.

END OF THE MATHEMATICS TEST.
STOP! IF YOU HAVE TIME LEFT OVER, CHECK YOUR WORK ON THIS SECTION ONLY.

3   3

READING TEST

35 Minutes—40 Questions

DIRECTIONS: This test includes four passages, each followed by ten questions. Read the passages and choose the best answer to each question. After you have selected your answer, fill in the corresponding bubble on your answer sheet. You should refer to the passages as often as necessary when answering the questions.

PASSAGE I

PROSE FICTION: *The Lessons of Wilderness Living*

Members of modern society are fortunate to enjoy many conveniences once unheard of or reserved for the elite. Imagine, if you can, only one day without running water. It strains the mind to think of all the daily rituals
5 one would have to change if the tap suddenly went dry. People today take electricity for granted, too. Lately, I've realized that while reliance on modern technology can improve the efficiency and quality of life, it also keeps people from learning meaningful lessons
10 about living with the earth. The conservation ethics that I gained this summer while working at a hunting lodge I could not have learned elsewhere.

The lodge is located on a massive, little known lake in northern Canada, closer to the Arctic Circle than
15 it is to the U.S. border. Every spring, the lodge reopens to welcome scores of dedicated anglers itching to dip a line in the nearby pristine creeks. By summer, the small lodge fills to capacity with eager hunters. On the guided treks, these men and women primarily chase
20 migratory birds and caribou, but I have seen plenty of other unique game come back to the lodge kitchen for preparation. Every hunter agrees that what one finds at the lodge is a truly luxurious hunting experience. Many people are surprised to find the lodge is totally
25 self-sufficient, with the exception of the food staples it receives by small airplane. For a whole season, I was "off the grid," totally dependent on the lodge to provide me with heat, light, water, and sanitation.

When I asked the owner why he built his
30 modern-looking log lodge so far beyond the reach of civilization, he replied, "I didn't really like hunting anywhere the sewer line ran." *Or electricity or telephone or the water main*, I thought to myself. The boss is a peculiar man, but I see why he had no reservations
35 about setting up shop so deep in the wilderness. He had learned to love it years ago when he was an elite mountain soldier in the army. He always mentioned that life wasn't as difficult in the sub-arctic wilderness as people think. Of course, he had a lodge to run, and
40 not everyone was as hardy as he. His creative solutions to the lack of infrastructure are impressive.

The first necessity of employees and guests is clean water for cooking, eating, and washing. A nearby creek feeds a large pump that draws the water through a
45 particulate filter and into a large holding tank. A much smaller pipe takes some of this water through a series of purification devices. Inside, every sink has three taps: two blue and one red. Guests are used to the blue ones, drinkable hot and cold water, but the red one
50 always requires an explanation. My contribution over the summer was to design a sign for each sink explaining the ways one could use the unpurified water from the red tap that came directly from the holding tank. Showering and cleaning are the most important uses,
55 but "red" water is also useful for the garden or to give to the dogs.

The roof of the lodge is layered with solar cells to take advantage of the bright, clear summer sky. On average, the 10-room lodge can generate the
60 same amount of power as a conventional two-bedroom apartment uses. Naturally, this poses challenges. The biggest conservation measure I could see was total lack of electronics, with the exception of the computer in the back office, which I've never seen turned on. The
65 ceiling of every room has a large skylight, eliminating the need for electric light during the day. At night, a limited set of high-efficiency fluorescent bulbs illuminates the corridors and public spaces. Staff is equipped with flashlights for use in closets, outside, or in other
70 unlit spaces. Interestingly, the low lighting seems to foster an "early to bed, early to rise" mentality among the guests, who always rave about how rested they feel after a week's stay.

Guests and staff alike stay warm with heavy
75 woolen blankets, or, as my boss once quipped, "personal insulating devices." A full-circle fireplace in the center heats the main space. Smoke floats up the chimney while the heavy stainless steel hood reflects heat to all corners of the room. When guests close their
80 room doors at night, they can barely hear the high-speed electric impellers that draw warmth from the fire into the rooms.

The lodge is a model of efficiency in an often-unforgiving territory. My summer there taught me to
85 budget more carefully my consumption of water and power. It is such discipline that will be necessary in the future when costs of these commodities might be so high that civilization can no longer take their abundance for granted.

GO ON TO THE NEXT PAGE.

3   **3**

1. Which of the following disadvantages of modern utilities is best supported by the details in the passage?
   A. Public water and electricity are currently very expensive.
   B. Utility commodities might eventually run out.
   C. Public utility lines reinforce the divide between densely populated cities and sparse wilderness.
   D. Municipal water and electricity are taken for granted, so most people never learn to live without them.

2. One can reasonably infer from the passage that a person who were to drink from a red tap would most likely:
   F. prefer cooler water.
   G. have to become accustomed to water with added chlorine or fluoride.
   H. be disappointed by the low pressure.
   J. risk falling ill from waterborne pathogens.

3. Given the way he is presented in the passage, the boss of the lodge can best be described as:
   A. sheltered and timid.
   B. vain and insincere.
   C. eccentric and enterprising.
   D. brash and calculating

4. The narrator's comment about "luxurious" hunts (lines 22–23) refers to trips that:
   F. provide amenities such as gourmet food.
   G. are all-inclusive, where no one need bring personal equipment.
   H. expose hunters to an unusual variety of game.
   J. educate guests on arctic ecology as they hunt.

5. The second and third paragraphs suggest that, if not for the need to host a variety of guests, the boss would prefer:
   A. a lodge closer to city services.
   B. a more modest lodge with fewer creature comforts.
   C. a large hunting estate with modern improvements.
   D. a wilderness skills training facility.

6. Which of the following conclusions about the relationship between the narrator and the boss is best supported by the details in the passage?
   F. The narrator does not fully grasp the boss's rationale for having such an isolated lodge, but admires his ingenuity nonetheless.
   G. The boss largely ignores the narrator and the rest of the workforce, focusing instead on the guests, but the narrator does not resent him for it.
   H. The boss is very shy and the narrator obliges him with privacy.
   J. The narrator is an inquisitive person whose frequent questions irritate the boss.

7. What does the narrator suggest is a central characteristic of modern society's water and power consumption?
   A. Temperance
   B. Resourcefulness
   C. Exorbitance
   D. Caution

8. As it is used in line 27, the word *grid* most likely means:
   F. roadway system.
   G. map.
   H. utility system.
   J. populated land.

9. The boss would most likely agree with which of the following characterizations of his lodge?
   A. It is rustic, unrefined, and occasionally uncomfortable.
   B. It retains its wilderness charm in spite of concessions to some modern conveniences.
   C. It establishes an oasis in the barren North for guests demanding luxury.
   D. It focuses on premium lodging, with some guests choosing to participate in guided hunts.

10. It is most reasonable to infer from the passage that the creeks near the lodge are pristine because:
    F. they teem with fish.
    G. the lodge only draws water from one of them.
    H. civilization is not present to alter or pollute them.
    J. many specialty fishes can be readily caught in their waters.

GO ON TO THE NEXT PAGE.

3

3

PASSAGE II
SOCIAL SCIENCE: *A Cure for Polio*

In the early twentieth century, no other disease caused as much fear and anxiety in the United States as *paralytic poliomyelitis*. *Paralytic poliomyelitis*, more commonly known as polio, was a particularly
5 devastating disease because of its effect on children. Many children stricken with polio became permanently confined to wheelchairs or died at a very early age.

It was during the summer of 1916 that Americans first realized that polio was a threatening and
10 deadly disease. As a virus, polio seemed to spread most quickly and easily during the summer months. Throughout that fateful summer, New York City experienced a polio epidemic that killed 9,000 people and left 27,000 paralyzed.

15 Even though polio was not a new disease, medical experts around the turn of the century were still uncertain about how to prevent it. While it is difficult to determine polio's first appearance in history, various accounts of lameness and paralysis suggest that polio
20 can be traced back to early Egypt. It was probably not until 1908, when two Austrian physicians identified the submicroscopic virus, that scientists began to have an accurate understanding of the disease. Until 1908, conditions such as overheating, chilling, and
25 even teething were thought to cause polio's symptoms. Some scientists and doctors even believed that diseases such as whooping cough and pneumonia were the cause of polio.

For many decades, polio research centered on
30 treating symptoms as well as developing a vaccine to prevent polio. There was no known cure for people already infected with polio, so doctors focused on managing the disease's debilitating effects. Scientists and doctors concentrated on making the polio patient
35 more comfortable and preventing fatalities. During the 1920s, the *iron lung* became a common device used to assist polio patients in breathing. When using the iron lung, patients would lie in a metal, human-sized tank for long periods of time. Sometimes, polio patients
40 would have to continue this treatment their entire lives. Serum therapy was also attempted. During this type of treatment, polio victims would receive doses of serum extracted from polio-recovered monkeys, humans, and even horses. After nearly 20 years of research and trials,
45 serum therapy was finally abandoned and deemed unsuccessful.

In the medical field, other debates occurred regarding the proper treatment of polio patients. Initially, it was thought that diseased limbs should be
50 immobilized and even placed in casts. In addition, polio patients were prescribed complete bed rest. However, other theories suggested that paralyzed arms and legs should be wrapped in hot compresses and exercised regularly to prevent muscular atrophy. This
55 latter approach soon became typical protocol because it seemed to relieve some pain and discomfort.

During World War II, the effort to cure and prevent polio in the United States was stalled because medical researchers became more involved with military issues
60 and diseases overseas. However, at the end of the War,

as numerous troops returned home and polio epidemics once again increased, attention was turned back to this dreaded disease. Finally, a breakthrough occurred during the early 1950s when a medical researcher named
65 Jonas Salk developed an effective vaccine using the tissue culture method. Salk discovered that injecting elements of the dead poliovirus into healthy patients was effective, because vaccinated patients would build antibodies against the dead virus. These acquired
70 antibodies prevented any future infection.

Later, another medical researcher named Albert Sabin developed an even easier method of distributing the vaccine. Sabin's vaccine became known as the oral polio vaccine. This innovation eliminated the use of
75 needles; the vaccine was administered by mouth. Children had no difficulty tolerating the vaccine because it was infiltrated into a sugar cube. By 1955, the Salk vaccination trials were deemed successful. The government quickly established a program to administer
80 vaccines to everyone in the country. By the early 1960s, the oral Sabin vaccine replaced the Salk injections. The Sabin vaccine was a live, attenuated virus that provided longer-lasting effects. By 1964, only 121 cases of polio were reported. This was a dramatic decrease from the
85 58,000 cases reported in 1952.

While the scourge of polio is well under control in the United States, it is still a dangerous disease worldwide. Polio is especially a threat in more remote and undeveloped countries. In addition, 500,000 Americans
90 continue to live with the effects of childhood polio infections that began decades ago.

---

11. According to the passage, the most significant effects of the polio epidemic in America were on:
- **A.** the development of government programs.
- **B.** children stricken with the disease.
- **C.** the medical community that attempted to cure polio.
- **D.** public involvement in promoting the vaccine.

12. As it is used in the passage (line 33) the word *debilitating* most nearly means:
- **F.** invigorating.
- **G.** crippling.
- **H.** coercing.
- **J.** revitalizing.

13. According to the information presented in the passage, what would likely have happened if the iron lung had not been invented?
- **A.** Some polio patients would have perished more quickly.
- **B.** Paralysis in children would have worsened.
- **C.** Patients would not have received proper bed rest.
- **D.** Muscular atrophy would not have been prevented.

GO ON TO THE NEXT PAGE.

3   **3**

14. According to the passage, why did medical research first focus on the treatment of polio's symptoms, instead of the disease itself?
  F. Scientists and medical experts did not understand the cause of polio.
  G. A cure for the debilitating disease had recently been discovered.
  H. Funds were not available from the government to develop a cure for polio.
  J. Medical researchers were fearful of working with the poliovirus.

15. As it is used in the fifth paragraph, the phrase "became typical protocol" implies that:
  A. the most common practice for treating polio became widely accepted.
  B. medical experts debated with scientists regarding the proper treatment of polio.
  C. doctors and scientists had yet to discover an effective polio treatment.
  D. there was no consistent or widespread treatment for those infected with polio.

16. Based on the passage, the author's discussion of the poliovirus emphasizes the:
  F. consequential debate about dead versus live viruses for vaccines.
  G. competition among medical researchers to develop a cure.
  H. complexity of the disease and the difficulty in discovering a cure.
  J. lack of understanding in the medical community about curing diseases.

17. The information in the passage primarily suggests that:
  A. the Salk vaccine was not truly successful.
  B. Salk and Sabin had strong disagreements over a polio cure.
  C. the Salk vaccine paved the way for the Sabin oral vaccine.
  D. the use of a live virus is always better in developing a vaccine.

18. It can be reasonably inferred that the author would probably consider which of the following to be most similar to the discussion of polio in the passage?
  F. Malnutrition and starvation in developing countries.
  G. Researching and developing a cure for cancer.
  H. Obesity in the United States.
  J. Social security deficits leading to poverty.

19. According to the passage, which of the following is NOT true regarding polio?
  A. One of the most incapacitating effects of polio was the fact that it made it difficult to breathe properly.
  B. Whooping cough and pneumonia were both thought to be caused by polio infection.
  C. The season and time of year seemed to have an impact on the spread of the crippling disease.
  D. Children seemed to bear the brunt of the attack of the poliovirus.

20. Based on the overall tone of the passage, which of the following statements best summarizes the author's perspective on the effects of the American polio epidemic of the early 1900s?
  F. There is virtually no residual evidence of the epidemic today.
  G. Polio continues to be a silent threat to American children.
  H. The cure for polio may be temporary and prove ineffective in the future.
  J. Thousands of Americans continue to live with the effects of polio.

GO ON TO THE NEXT PAGE.

3

3

PASSAGE III
HUMANITIES: *Mythology of the Chinese Zodiac*

Everyday, one takes for granted the ease of finding
out what date it is. This is simplified to such a great
degree by following the Gregorian calendar, based on
the solar cycle, which keeps track of 365.25 days
5 each year. This has not always been the case, however. In ancient China, the calendar was based on the
lunar cycle, and consisted of a repeating twelve-year
sequence, each named for a different animal.

The origin of the twelve animals is mythological,
10 with the story being passed down from generation to
generation. A common telling of the tale recounts a
celebration to honor the Jade Emperor; all of the animals were expected to pay tribute to him on the night
of the New Year and the first twelve to arrive would
15 receive a great distinction.

In order to reach the Emperor's Palace, the animals were required to cross a fast-moving river. The
cunning rat arrived first, climbed atop the ox, who was
a much stronger swimmer than the rat, and jumped off
20 of the ox right before reaching shore, so as to win the
race. The ox received second place, followed shortly
thereafter by the tiger – the strength of both animals
allowed them to finish quickly. The rabbit followed,
with his agility, by jumping from stone to stone across
25 the river. Next came the mighty and majestic dragon,
who flew across the river. When asked why he was
not first, he replied that he needed to make rain for
the people of Earth and was thus delayed. His kindness earned him the fifth place in the cycle. During the
30 dragon's explanation there was a galloping sound, sig-
naling the arrival of the horse. Suddenly, hidden coiled
around the leg of the horse, appeared the snake – nearly
as cunning as the rat – who darted in front of the horse
taking sixth place. The horse settled for seventh, just
35 as a raft reached the shore with three more animals.
The sheep (eighth), the monkey (ninth), and the rooster
(tenth) had worked together to build a raft and traverse
the river using their combined efforts. For this show
of teamwork they were rewarded in the order that they
40 stepped off of the raft. Next to arrive was the dog, who
was met with questioning looks. Supposedly the best
swimmer, the dog's lateness was due to his taking a
bath in the refreshing waters of the river. His vanity
nearly cost him the race. Lastly was the lazy pig, who
45 stopped on the other side of the river for a feast before
a attempted to cross, and was so weighed down by its
meal that it arrived only moments before the Emperor
declared the race to be finished.

Missing from this list of animals is the cat. Sadly,
50 he was a victim of the rat's cunning; the day before the
race the rat informed the cat that he would awaken him
prior to the race, so as to allow the cat to rest and save
its strength for the race. The day of the race arrived,
and the cat continued to sleep while the rat took his
55 spot atop the ox. When the cat awoke, the race was
finished, and it has hated the rat for what it did ever
since.

Beyond the twelve-year distinctions that the animals of the Zodiac lend to the calendar, there is an
60 additional ten-year overlay of five elements: water,
wood, fire, metal, and earth. Each of these elements
occurs two years in a row, in balance with the Yang and
Yin, the governing forces of all things. Even numbered
years are considered Yang, and odd numbered years
65 are considered Yin. When all factors are combined, a
sixty-year repeating calendar results, the current cycle
of which began in 1984.

Despite its complexity, the Calendar is followed
to a certain degree, and the Chinese New Year is
70 celebrated by many. Primary among the great astrological purposes to the Zodiac is the common belief that
the animal that governs the time of a person's birth will
influence that person's personality for life. Whether or
not that is true is a matter of debate that is sure to
75 continue for many years to come.

21. The passage primarily emphasizes the idea that:
   A. the animals that are included in the Chinese Zodiac
      calendar all had to find ways to reach the Emperor's
      Palace.
   B. the Chinese Zodiac calendar is correct in the long
      run, but somewhat distorted on a year-to-year basis.
   C. the Chinese Zodiac calendar is surrounded by myths
      and legends that still permeate Chinese society
      today.
   D. according to the Chinese Zodiac, the animal one
      is born under will directly influence that person's
      personality.

22. The passage begins with the phrase "Everyday, one
    takes for granted the ease of finding out what date it is"
    primarily to:
   F. draw the distinction between the ease of today's
      Gregorian calendar and the complexity of the
      Chinese Zodiac calendar.
   G. emphasize to the reader how effortless it is to use the
      Chinese Zodiac calendar to determine the current
      date.
   H. inform the reader that using a solar cycle to create
      a calendar is the simplest way to discern what the
      current date is.
   J. downplay the fact that the Chinese Zodiac calendar
      has a varying number of days each year while the
      Gregorian calendar does not.

23. In the context of the passage, the phrase "His vanity
    nearly cost him the race," suggests that the dog:
   A. felt that the water was so refreshing, he had no
      choice but to bathe in it whether it lost him the race
      or not.
   B. intended to look his best and be his cleanest when he
      reached the palace, in order to honor the Emperor.
   C. forgot that he was in a race to reach the Emperor's
      Palace until he saw the pig approaching the river-
      bank.
   D. prioritized his egotistical impulses over his desire to
      reach the Emperor's Palace on time.

GO ON TO THE NEXT PAGE.

3 ▮▮▮▮▮▮▮▮▮▮▮▮▮▮▮▮▮▮▮▮▮▮▮▮▮ **3**

24. As it is used throughout the passage, the word *cunning* most nearly means:
- **F.** ingenuity.
- **G.** dependability.
- **H.** apprehension.
- **J.** tolerance.

25. According to the passage, which of the following would NOT be a possible year of the Chinese Zodiac?
- **A.** Wood, Yang, dragon, 3028
- **B.** Yin, fire, pig, 3029
- **C.** Rat, earth, Yang, 3052
- **D.** Metal, Yin, tiger, 3030.

26. The narrator uses the example of the cat in the passage (lines 49–57) most likely in order to:
- **F.** accentuate the fact that many animals strove to earn the Emperor's distinction but only a select few attained it.
- **G.** highlight the fact that the rat was very shrewd and was only out for himself in the race to the Emperor's Palace.
- **H.** offer proof that the cat was one of the most indolent animals and therefore did not deserve the Emperor's great distinction.
- **J.** provide proof that, in actuality, the ox preferred the companionship of the rat to that of the cat.

27. It can be inferred from the passage that the Emperor most highly valued what traits among the animals?
- **A.** Deceitfulness and compassion.
- **B.** Goodwill and narcissism.
- **C.** Generosity and unanimity.
- **D.** Gluttony and collaboration.

28. According to the passage, all of the following are true regarding the animals that reached the Emperor's Palace EXCEPT:
- **F.** the rabbit was very nimble in crossing the river and made it across quite easily.
- **G.** the tiger's vigor allowed him to swim across the river effortlessly.
- **H.** the snake wound himself around the dragon's leg to reach the end of the race.
- **J.** the pig narrowly reached the end of the race to the Emperor's Palace.

29. As it is used in line 9, the word *mythological* most closely means:
- **A.** legitimate.
- **B.** bona fide.
- **C.** ludicrous.
- **D.** legendary.

30. It can be reasonably inferred from the passage's last sentence that the narrator:
- **F.** believes that the Chinese Zodiac influences the personality of those who believe in the astrology of the Chinese Zodiac system.
- **G.** does not have a rigid stance on the multitude of elements composing the Chinese Zodiac calendar and how these elements affect people.
- **H.** thinks that calendars are too intricate to ever fully grasp how and when the days of each year occur.
- **J.** is undecided as to whether or not the Chinese Zodiac system really has an effect on the calendar year.

GO ON TO THE NEXT PAGE.

3   **3**

PASSAGE IV
NATURAL SCIENCE: *The Eating Habits of Related Primates*

Scientists know very little about the eating habits of our ancestors who lived over two and a half million years ago. To solve this problem, scientists have started examining chimpanzees' hunting behavior and diet to
5 find clues about our own prehistoric past.

It is not difficult to determine why studying chimpanzees might be beneficial. Modern humans and chimpanzees are actually very closely related. Experts believe that chimpanzees share about 98.5 percent of
10 our DNA sequence. If this is true, humans are more closely related to chimpanzees than to any other animal species.

In the early 1960s, Dr. Jane Goodall began studying chimpanzees in Tanzania. Before the 1960s,
15 scientists believed that chimpanzees were strict vegetarians. It was Goodall who first reported that meat was a natural part of the chimpanzee diet. In fact, Goodall discovered that chimpanzees are actually very proficient hunters. Individual chimpanzees have been
20 known to hunt and eat more than 150 small animals each year. Among the chimpanzees' favorite prey are the red colobus monkey, feral pig, and various small antelope species. The red colobus monkey is one of the most important animals in the chimpanzees' diet. In one
25 notable study, the red colobus monkey accounted for more than 80 percent of the animals eaten by one group of chimpanzees.

Despite these findings, scientists still maintain that chimpanzees are mostly fruit-eating creatures. In fact,
30 meat composes only about 3 percent of the chimpanzee diet. This is substantially less than the quantity of meat consumed by the average human. Studies show that chimpanzees do most of their hunting in the dry season. August and September appear to be the most popular
35 months for hunting. During the dry season, food shortages in the forest cause the chimpanzees' body weight to drop. Consequently, chimpanzees supplement their diets with meat. During the height of the dry season, the estimated meat intake is about 65 grams of meat per day
40 for adult chimpanzees. This is comparable to the quantity of meat eaten by modern human societies whose members forage when other food sources are scarce. The chimpanzees' eating habits also closely resemble those of the early human hunter-gatherers.

45 Humans and chimpanzees are the only members of the Great Ape family that hunt and eat meat on a regular basis. However, like chimpanzees, humans are not truly carnivorous creatures. In fact, most ancient humans ate a diet composed mostly of plants, and even
50 modern humans are considered omnivores because they eat fruits, vegetables, and meat.

Most people assume that food choices are based solely on nutritional costs and benefits. Although it is clear that the hunting habits of chimpanzees are
55 guided mostly by nutritional needs, some aspects of the chimpanzees' behavior are not well explained by nutrition alone. Researchers suggest that chimpanzees might hunt for social gain. For instance, a male chimpanzee might try to demonstrate his competence to other male

60 chimpanzees by killing prey. Chimpanzees may also use meat as a political tool to punish rivals and reward friends. However, a study also shows that female chimpanzees that receive large portions of meat after a hunt have healthier and stronger offspring. This indicates
65 that there might be reproductive benefits to eating meat as well.

The information that scientists have been able to gather regarding chimpanzee hunting behavior is shedding some light on the eating habits of our ancestors.
70 Further investigation is needed, however, to provide stronger evidence regarding this aspect of man's prehistoric past.

---

31. The main purpose of the passage is to:
  - **A.** explore biological and physiological similarities between humans and chimpanzees.
  - **B.** examine the hunting behavior and diet of chimpanzees and compare them to similar human activity.
  - **C.** discuss the health benefits of hunting and eating meat while simultaneously predicting the effect of these behaviors on chimpanzee offspring.
  - **D.** bring attention to the pioneering research of Dr. Jane Goodall in Tanzania.

32. It can be inferred from the passage that chimpanzees:
  - **F.** find that the red colobus monkey is the easiest prey to hunt.
  - **G.** only hunt when no other plant food is available.
  - **H.** hunt only during the dry season when other food sources are scarce.
  - **J.** vary their diet depending on environmental factors.

33. According to the passage, the word *proficient* (line 19) most nearly means:
  - **A.** skilled.
  - **B.** individual.
  - **C.** incompetent.
  - **D.** important.

34. According to the passage, which of the following statements regarding the eating habits of chimpanzees is true?
  - **F.** Chimpanzee eating habits cannot be studied in the wild.
  - **G.** Chimpanzee eating habits are directly influenced by social factors.
  - **H.** It is not possible to determine the exact diet of chimpanzees.
  - **J.** Chimpanzee eating habits are not related to those of humans.

GO ON TO THE NEXT PAGE.

3 ███████████████████████████████████████ **3**

35. Based on the context of the passage, the author most likely makes the comparison between chimpanzees and humans (lines 45–51) in order to suggest that:

A. chimpanzees are more similar to early humans than to modern humans.

B. studies of chimpanzees will contribute to an understanding of early humans.

C. early hunter-gatherers typically ate more meat than did chimpanzees.

D. data collected on chimpanzees cannot be applied to the study of humans.

36. As it is used in the passage, the word *forage* (line 42) most nearly means:

F. consume meats.

G. alter their diets.

H. search for food.

J. lose weight.

37. According to the passage, Dr. Jane Goodall's research was important because:

A. Dr. Goodall was the first scientists to study chimpanzees in their natural habitat.

B. Dr. Goodall discovered previously undocumented chimpanzee behavior.

C. Dr. Goodall had always argued that chimpanzees were actually carnivorous creatures.

D. Dr. Goodall discovered that red colobus monkeys make up 80% of chimpanzees' diets.

38. It can be inferred from the passage that ancient humans and chimpanzees:

F. share a DNA structure that is more similar than that of any two other animals.

G. only ate meat when fruit, grains, and vegetables were not available.

H. differ from other related species.

J. hunted for social gain and prestige in their communities.

39. According to the passage, chimpanzees hunt primarily because of:

A. increased numbers of red colobus monkeys.

B. food shortages during the dry season.

C. their DNA sequence.

D. their preference for meat over plants.

40. In the context of the passage, the tone in lines 52–66 can best be described as:

F. affectionate.

G. humorous.

H. somber.

J. informational.

END OF THE READING TEST.

STOP! IF YOU HAVE TIME LEFT OVER, CHECK YOUR WORK ON THIS SECTION ONLY.

4 ○ ○ ○ ○ ○ ○ ○ ○ ○ 4

SCIENCE REASONING TEST

35 Minutes—40 Questions

DIRECTIONS: This test includes seven passages, each followed by several questions. Read the passage and choose the best answer to each question. After you have selected your answer, fill in the corresponding bubble on your answer sheet. You should refer to the passages as often as necessary when answering the questions. You may NOT use a calculator on this test.

PASSAGE I

Researchers have noticed sudden decay in limestone grave markers in a cemetery downwind from a coal-burning power plant. Two studies were conducted to examine this decay process.

Study 1

A key mineral component of limestone is *feldspar*, which is also abundant in ground soil. Feldspar, as it weathers and decays, breaks down into another mineral, *kaolinite*. The weathering process is often expedited by moisture from rain and humidity. Researchers measured the levels of feldspar and kaolinite in the soil of the cemetery and other

locations at specific distances from the cemetery before and after rain showers. The results are shown in Table 1. (Note: The soil sample sizes were the same for each location tested.)

Study 2

The researchers believe that the emissions from the nearby power plant are somehow affecting the decay of the limestone. Levels of common gases – carbon dioxide (CO_2), oxygen (O_2), nitrogen dioxide (NO_2), and sulfur (S) – in the atmosphere were tested at the cemetery and other locations at specific distances from both the cemetery and the power plant. Measurements in parts per million (ppm) were recorded in Table 2.

Table 1				
	Before rain		After rain	
Distance from cemetery (m)	Amount of feldspar in the soil (g/ft³)	Amount of kaolinite soil (g/ft³)	Amount of feldspar in the soil (g/ft³)	Amount of kaolinite in the soil (g/ft³)
0	26.3	13.7	25.2	14.6
125	29.1	12.9	28.5	13.7
225	29.9	12.4	29.6	12.6
325	30.8	12.1	30.7	12.2
425	32.4	11.5	32.3	11.6

Table 2					
Distance from power plant (m)	Distance from cemetery (m)	CO_2 levels (ppm)	O_2 levels (ppm)	NO_2 levels (ppm)	S levels (ppm)
0	125	7	3	13	26
100	225	8	5	10	22
200	325	10	12	9	17
300	425	11	14	5	10
400	525	13	17	3	5

GO ON TO THE NEXT PAGE.

1. Which of the following factors was varied in Study 1?
   A. Distance from power plant
   B. Size of soil sample
   C. Distance from cemetery
   D. Common gas levels

2. Carbon monoxide is another gaseous byproduct associated with coal-burning power plants. If carbon monoxide levels behave like the sulfur gas levels in Study 2, one would expect that carbon monoxide levels:
   F. would increase as distance from power plant increases.
   G. would be higher when O_2 levels are higher.
   H. would decrease as distance from power plant increases.
   J. would be lower when NO_2 levels are higher.

3. According to Study 1, *kaolinite* levels are highest at what distance from the cemetery?
   A. >400 meters
   B. Between 200 and 400 meters
   C. Between 100 and 300 meters
   D. <100 meters

4. According to the results of Study 2, as distance from the power plant decreases:
   F. sulfur levels decrease.
   G. sulfur and NO_2 levels increase.
   H. NO_2 and O_2 levels decrease.
   J. CO_2 and O_2 levels increase.

5. According to the results of Study 1, as distance from the cemetery increases, feldspar decay:
   A. increases only.
   B. is not affected.
   C. is reversed.
   D. decreases only.

GO ON TO THE NEXT PAGE.

4 ◯ ◯ ◯ ◯ ◯ ◯ ◯ ◯ **4**

PASSAGE II

Coronary heart disease affects millions of people worldwide each year. It is the end result of a build up of plaque (cholesterol) on the interior walls of the arteries that supply the muscle of the heart. Most individuals with coronary heart disease show no evidence of disease for decades as the disease progresses before the first onset of symptoms, often a "sudden" heart attack. After decades of building up on the artery walls, the plaque may reduce the blood flow to the heart muscle. There are several hypotheses that have been proposed to explain the causes of plaque build-up leading to coronary heart disease.

Behavioral Hypothesis

The primary causes of coronary heart disease are behavioral factors such as diet, risky behaviors, and level of physical activity. Coronary heart disease is associated with smoking, obesity, *hypertension* (chronic high blood pressure) and a lack of vitamin C. According to one study, individuals who consume large amounts of saturated fats and trans-fats have high levels of cholesterol and are at higher levels of risk for heart disease. Vegetarians have been shown to have a 24% reduced risk of heart disease due to dietary modifications alone. In addition, extra weight is thought to lead to higher total cholesterol levels, high blood pressure, and an increased risk of coronary heart disease. Obesity increases the chances of developing other risk factors for heart disease, especially high blood pressure, high blood cholesterol, and diabetes. Smoking is also a major cause of heart disease as it puts individuals at higher risk of developing a number of chronic disorders. Furthermore, people who are not physically active have a greater risk of heart attack than do people who exercise regularly. Exercise burns calories, helps to control cholesterol levels and diabetes, and may lower blood pressure. Exercise also strengthens the heart muscle and makes the arteries more flexible.

Familial Hypothesis

Coronary heart disease is genetically inherited, meaning it tends to run in families. For example, people whose parents or siblings had a heart or circulatory problem before the age of 55 are at greater risk for heart disease than someone who does not have that family history. Risk factors (including hypertension, diabetes, and obesity) may also be passed from one generation to another. Studies have determined that the single greatest indicator of risk for coronary heart disease is family history. Other studies have shown isolated populations to be significantly more or less susceptible to coronary heart disease than is the general population. Isolated populations share the same *gene pool* (a set of genetic traits found within a population), which supports the proposition that family history is the primary cause and indicator of the disease.

6. To accept the evidence presented in the Familial Hypothesis, one must assume that all members of a population sharing the same gene pool have:
   F. a varied family history.
   G. a common family history.
   H. a history of high risk for heart disease.
   J. a history of low risk for heart disease.

7. One advantage of the Behavioral Hypothesis is that it best explains why heart disease is more common in which of the following groups?
   A. Isolated populations.
   B. Smokers.
   C. Individuals with a family history of heart disease.
   D. Vegetarians.

8. According to the Familial Hypothesis, individuals whose parents or siblings had a heart or circulatory problem before the age of 55 are:
   F. members of an isolated population.
   G. at a lower risk for heart disease than someone who does not have that family history.
   H. at a higher risk for heart disease than someone who does not have that family history.
   J. at the same risk for heart disease as someone who does not have that family history.

9. Which of the following is a criticism that supporters of the Behavioral Hypothesis would make of the Familial Hypothesis?
   A. Behaviors and dietary norms are passed down between generations.
   B. Obesity is not related to being at risk for heart disease.
   C. Exercise is not related to being at risk for heart disease.
   D. Family history is the single greatest indicator of risk for heart disease.

10. How would supporters of the Behavioral Hypothesis explain the studies cited in the Familial Hypothesis regarding isolated populations?
    F. A common gene pool does not indicate familial ties.
    G. All members in an isolated population are at a high level of risk for heart disease.
    H. Members within isolated populations rarely behave in a similar manner.
    J. Members within isolated populations often behave in a similar manner.

GO ON TO THE NEXT PAGE.

11. Assume that increased cholesterol levels result in increased risk for coronary heart disease. How would supporters of the Familial Hypothesis explain the study cited in the Behavioral hypothesis?

A. Family history is a major factor in developing hypertension.

B. A common gene pool determines heart disease risk level.

C. Behaviors and dietary norms are passed down from family members.

D. Family history is a major factor in determining cholesterol levels.

12. The Behavior Hypothesis and the Familial Hypothesis are similar in that they both:

F. name family history as the greatest factor of risk for heart disease.

G. name diet as the greatest factor of risk for heart disease.

H. cite hypertension, cholesterol, and obesity as major risk indicators.

J. promote a vegetarian diet.

GO ON TO THE NEXT PAGE.

PASSAGE III

A scientist tested the ability of 5 newly engineered drugs to kill penicillin-resistant bacteria.

Experiment 1

Equal numbers of penicillin-resistant bacteria were put into flasks containing 10.0 milliliters of a nutrient medium. The flasks were incubated for 1 hour at 37°C with different concentrations of the 5 drugs shown in Table 1. A control consisted of bacteria incubated in the medium without any drugs. The bacteria were washed to remove residual drug traces and grown on nutrient agar plates for 7 days. During this time, the bacteria reproduced, forming colonies, which were then counted at the end of the seventh day. Plates with more colonies were assumed to have more live bacteria at the end of the 1-hour incubation period. Table 1 shows the number of colonies counted. The drug-free control showed 50 colonies at the end of 7 days.

Table 1				
Drug	Drug concentration (mM)			
	5	10	15	25
	Number of colonies:			
R	41	26	9	0
S	42	29	12	2
T	45	35	20	5
U	47	38	21	6
V	50	40	22	7

Notes: *mM is micromolar
Numbers of colonies are averages for 5 replicates (identical samples).

Experiment 2

Bacteria were handled as described in Experiment 1 with two exceptions: all drugs were tested at the same concentration and the incubation time of each culture was varied. Table 2 shows the number of colonies counted for Experiment 2.

Table 2				
Drug	Incubation time (h)			
	1	6	12	24
	Number of colonies:			
R	22	8	2	0
S	39	12	4	1
T	40	15	6	2
U	41	18	7	3
V	45	22	9	5
None	50	50	50	50

Note: Numbers of colonies are averages for 7 replicates (identical samples).

Experiment 3

Permeability coefficients measure a drug's ability to break through the cell membrane of a bacterium. The larger the permeability coefficient, the faster the drug is able to transfer through the membrane. The molecular mass, in atomic mass units (amu), and permeability coefficient, in centimeters per second (cm/s) of the 5 drugs at 37°C were measured. The results are shown in Table 3.

Table 3		
Drug	Molecular mass (amu)	Permeability coefficient (cm)
R	455	10^{-7}
S	470	10^{-8}
T	485	10^{-5}
U	500	10^{-10}
V	515	10^{-11}

GO ON TO THE NEXT PAGE.

13. Based on Experiment 1, at a concentration of 10 mM, which drug was most effective at killing bacteria?
  A. Drug R
  B. Drug S
  C. Drug T
  D. Drug V

14. Based on the results of Experiment 3, which drug enters bacteria cells most quickly?
  F. Drug R
  G. Drug S
  H. Drug T
  J. Drug V

15. If Experiment 2 were repeated with Drug U and an incubation time of 3 hours, the number of colonies counted would most likely be:
  A. more than 50.
  B. between 41 and 50.
  C. between 18 and 41.
  D. fewer than 18.

16. Which of the following statements best describes the relationship between the molecular mass and the permeability coefficient of the drugs, as shown in Experiment 3?
  F. As the molecular mass decreases, the permeability coefficient increases.
  G. As the molecular mass increases, the permeability coefficient increases.
  H. As the molecular mass decreases, the permeability coefficient remains constant.
  J. As the molecular mass increases, the permeability coefficient remains constant.

17. Which of the following statements best describes the relationship between incubation time and number of live bacteria in Experiment 2?
  A. As incubation time increases, the number of live bacteria increases only.
  B. As incubation time increases, the number of live bacteria decreases only.
  C. As incubation time increases, the number of live bacteria quickly increases, then slowly decreases.
  D. As incubation time increases, the number of live bacteria quickly decreases, then slowly increase.

18. In Experiment 1, what was the relationship between drug concentration and the drug's effectiveness in killing penicillin-resistant bacteria?
  F. Based on Experiment 1, there is no relationship between drug concentration and drug effectiveness.
  G. Some of the drugs were most effective at the lowest concentration used while others were most effective at the highest concentration used.
  H. All 5 drugs were most effective at the highest concentration used.
  J. All 5 drugs were most effective at the lowest concentration used.

19. The experimental procedures used in Experiment 1 and 2 differed in that in Experiment 1:
  A. incubation time was held constant, while drug concentration was varied.
  B. incubation time was varied, while drug concentration was held constant.
  C. incubation time and drug concentration were both held constant.
  D. incubation time and drug concentration were both varied.

GO ON TO THE NEXT PAGE.

4 ○ ○ ○ ○ ○ ○ ○ ○ ○ **4**

PASSAGE IV

Large lakes have their own climate that differs from the climate in adjacent forest and sand dune areas. A scientist performed the following studies to learn more about lake climates.

Study 1

A remote site in a rural area was selected where a large body of water was located next to a vast stretch of sand dunes. After both the lake and the sand dunes had been exposed to full sunlight for 8 hours, air temperature readings, in degrees Celsius (°C), were taken at the surface every 30 meters (m) across the water and sand, starting above the deepest part of the lake, and moving toward a point on the shoreline. The results are shown in Figure 1.

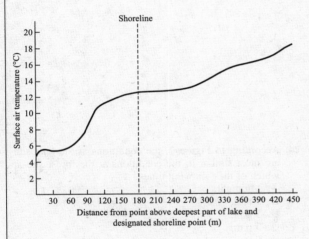

Figure 1

Study 2

Air temperatures were recorded hourly over a 24-hour period at 3 sites: above the deepest part of a large body of water (the lake site), an adjacent sand dune site, and a nearby forest site. Temperatures were recorded on 30 consecutive days during the summer and 30 consecutive days during the winter. Each hourly temperature was averaged for the season. The results are shown in Figure 2.

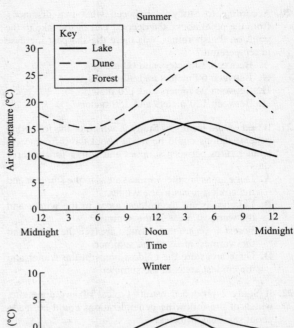

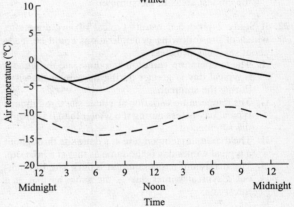

Figure 2

GO ON TO THE NEXT PAGE.

20. According to Study 1, between what two distances, from the point above the deepest part of the lake to the point on the shoreline, was there the sharpest increase in temperature?
   F. Between 30 meters and 60 meters
   G. Between 60 meters and 90 meters
   H. Between 90 meters and 120 meters
   J. Between 120 meters and 150 meters

21. Based on the results of Study 2, which of the following generalizations could be made about the difference in temperatures between summer and winter for the three sites?
   A. Dune areas are the warmest areas in the summer and the coldest areas in the winter.
   B. Lake areas are the coldest areas in the winter and the warmest areas in the summer.
   C. Forest areas are the warmest areas in the winter and the warmest areas in the summer.
   D. Dune areas are the coldest areas in the winter and the coldest areas in the summer.

22. If Study 2 produced results typical of any dune site, which of the following generalizations could be made about seasonal climates?
   F. The temperature variation at a dune site throughout a typical day is greater during the winter than it is during the summer.
   G. The temperature variation at a dune site throughout a typical day is less during the winter than it is during the summer.
   H. The maximum temperature at a dune site throughout a typical winter day is the same as that at a lake site.
   J. The maximum temperature at a dune site throughout a typical winter day is the same as that at a forest site.

23. According to Study 2, the temperature difference between the forest and dune sites at 9 p.m. on a typical summer day is approximately:
   A. 0°C.
   B. 5°C.
   C. 8°C.
   D. 15°C.

24. According to Figure 2, the conditions at the lake site are most similar to the conditions at the forest site at which of the following times?
   F. Midnight
   G. 9 a.m.
   H. 3 p.m.
   J. 9 p.m.

GO ON TO THE NEXT PAGE.

4 ○ ○ ○ ○ ○ ○ ○ ○ ○ **4**

PASSAGE V

Horses are susceptible to hoof infections that can seriously impair the horses' ability to walk. Horse breeders routinely administer dietary supplements in addition to the horses' regular feed in order to prevent these infections. A side effect of one of the these supplements – supplement X – is increased urination, which can sometimes lead to dehydration in the animal.

Twenty (20) adult horses, each weighing approximately 1,000 pounds, were randomly selected and assigned to two groups of 10 horses each. Group R received dietary supplement X while Group S received a placebo (a substance containing no supplement). Each horse in both groups received the same amount of feed and water each day. The horses were placed in individual stalls for 7 days, during which time their urine output was measured. The results are shown in Table 1.

Table 1		
	Group R	Group S
Average urine output per horse (gallons):		
Day 1	1.8	2.1
Day 2	1.9	2.0
Day 3	2.0	1.8
Day 4	2.2	1.9
Day 5	2.5	1.8
Day 6	2.6	2.0
Day 7	2.8	1.9

25. Which of the following generalizations best fits the results of the study?
   A. The effects of dietary supplement X on urinary output cannot be immediately detected.
   B. Dietary supplements should be administered over time in order to be effective.
   C. Dietary supplement X has no effect on urinary output in horses.
   D. The horses in Group R urinated less frequently than did the horses in Group S.

26. In order to best determine the effects of dietary supplement X in this experiment, one should examine:
   F. the type of feed that each horse was given.
   G. the amount of feed that each horse was given.
   H. the urinary output over time of each horse.
   J. the average urinary output of a third group.

27. Based on the information in Table 1, on which day did the control group have the highest urinary output?
   A. Day 7
   B. Day 4
   C. Day 3
   D. Day 1

28. During the study, several of the horses in Group R began showing signs of dehydration. According to the passage, what is the most likely cause of this?
   F. The low urinary output of the horses in Group R.
   G. The amount of water that the horses in Group R were given.
   H. The high urinary output of the horses in Group R.
   J. The lack of supplements in the diet of the horses in Group R.

29. Which of the following statements is supported by the data presented in Table 1?
   A. Urinary output increased over time for Group S only.
   B. Urinary output increased over time for Group R only.
   C. Urinary output increased over time for neither Group R or Group S.
   D. Urinary output increased over time for both Group R and Group S.

30. Do the results of the study show that dietary supplement X could cause dehydration in horses?
   F. Yes, because the urinary output increased over time in the group that received the supplement.
   G. Yes, because the control group maintained a relatively constant urinary output.
   H. No, because the urinary output stayed the same over time in the group that received the supplement.
   J. No, because the urinary output of the control group was not adequately measured.

GO ON TO THE NEXT PAGE.

4 ○ ○ ○ ○ ○ ○ ○ ○ ○ **4**

PASSAGE VI

People use many different chemicals each day for common household tasks such as cleaning and food preparation. Since the inception of consumer protection laws, chemicals come with toxicity warning labels, directions about proper use, and cautions about the hazards of improper use. Some household chemicals can be quite dangerous, especially when mixed together. One such example is the reaction that occurs when mixing household bleach (NaOCl) with ammonia (NH_3). The by-products of the reaction vary depending on the concentrations of the reactants. The following experiments were conducted to determine the levels at which certain by-products resulted from mixing bleach and ammonia.

Experiment 1

A known by-product of the reaction of bleach and ammonia is chlorine gas (Cl_2). Chlorine gas has an intensely disagreeable suffocating odor, and is very poisonous. To determine the quantities of bleach and ammonia that, when mixed together, produce chlorine gas, a varying quantity of bleach was added to eight different ammonia–water solutions and the resulting chlorine gas from each mixture was collected and measured. A solution of 1.0 mole (mol) of NH_3 in 1 kg of water was used in each trial. A certain quantity of NaOCl was added to each of the solutions; the amount added was gradually increased for each trial. The amount of chlorine gas produced in each trial was recorded and graphed in Figure 1.

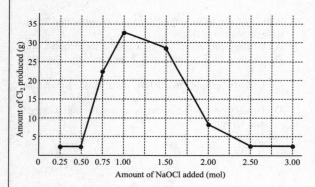

Figure 3

Experiment 2

Another known by-product of the reaction of bleach and ammonia is nitrogen trichloride (NCl_3). Nitrogen trichloride is a yellow, oily, pungent-smelling liquid, often found as a by-product of chemical reactions between nitrogen-containing compounds and chlorine. It is highly explosive. To determine the quantities of bleach and ammonia that, when mixed together, produce NCl_3, again a varying quantity of bleach was added to eight different ammonia–water solutions and the resulting NCl_3 from each mixture was measured. A solution of 1.0 mole (mol) of NH_3 in 1 kg of water was used in each trial. A certain quantity of NaOCl was added to each solution; the quantity added was gradually increased for each trial. The amount of nitrogen trichloride produced in each trial was recorded in see Table 1.

Table 1		
Trial	NaOCl level (mol)	Amount of NCl_3 produced (mol)
1	0.50	0.01
2	1.00	0.03
3	1.50	0.04
4	2.00	0.06
5	2.50	0.44
6	3.00	0.98
7	3.50	1.00
8	4.00	1.00

Experiment 3

In yet another reaction, bleach and ammonia combined under certain conditions produce a compound known as chloramine. Chloramine (NH_2Cl) is a toxic substance commonly used in low concentrations as a disinfectant in municipal water systems as an alternative to chlorination. To determine the mixture of bleach and ammonia at which NH_2Cl is produced, a varying amount of ammonia was added to eight different bleach–water solutions and the resulting chlorine gas from each mixture was collected and measured. A solution of 1.0 mole (mol) of NaOCl in 1 kg of water was used in each trial. A certain quantity of NH_3 was added to each solution; the quantity of ammonia added was gradually increased for each trial. The amount of chloramine produced in each trial was recorded in Table 2.

Table 2		
Trial	NH_3 level (mol)	Amount of NH_2Cl produced (mol)
1	0.50	0.05
2	1.00	0.08
3	1.50	0.11
4	2.00	0.14
5	2.50	0.17
6	3.00	0.21
7	3.50	0.23
8	4.00	0.25

GO ON TO THE NEXT PAGE.

4 ○ ○ ○ ○ ○ ○ ○ ○ **4**

31. Which of the following is the most likely reason that amounts greater than 3.00 mol of bleach were not tested in Experiment 1? The results showed that:
    A. amounts less than 3.00 mol of bleach increased the amount of chlorine gas produced.
    B. when more bleach was added the mixture became too volatile.
    C. adding more bleach no longer increased the level of ammonia.
    D. amounts greater than 1.00 mol of bleach decreased the amount of chlorine gas produced.

32. Based on the results of Experiment 3, as the NH_3 level increased from 0.50 to 4.00 mol, the greatest increase in the amount of NH_2Cl produced occurred:
    F. between the trials of 0.50 and 1.00 mol of NH_3.
    G. between the trials of 1.50 and 2.00 mol of NH_3.
    H. between the trials of 2.50 and 3.00 mol of NH_3.
    J. between the trials of 3.50 and 4.00 mol of NH_3.

33. If a ninth trial were conducted in Experiment 3, adding 1.25 mol of NH_3 to the bleach–water solution, the amount of NH_2Cl produced would be closest to:
    A. 0.06 mol.
    B. 0.10 mol.
    C. 0.12 mol.
    D. 0.16 mol.

34. Each of the following is a by-product resulting from mixing bleach and ammonia EXCEPT:
    F. Cl_2
    G. NCl_3
    H. $NaOCl$
    J. NH_2Cl

35. The production of a certain plastic calls for a mixture of bleach and ammonia. However, the presence of chlorine gas is highly undesirable. Based on the results of Experiments 1, 2, and 3, which of the following specifications should be chosen?
    A. Minimum of 2.00 mol $NaOCl$ and maximum 1.00 mol NH_3
    B. Minimum of 1.00 mol $NaOCl$ and maximum 1.00 mol NH_3
    C. Exactly of 1.50 mol NH_3 and exactly 1.50 mol $NaOCl$
    D. Exactly of 1.00 mol NH_3 and exactly 1.50 mol $NaOCl$

36. In Experiment 2, different quantities of $NaOCl$ were added to the ammonia solution resulting in the production of nitrogen trichloride. The amounts of nitrogen trichloride produced for 3.00, 3.50, and 4.00 mol of $NaOCl$ added were approximately the same. Which of the following best explains why the production of NCl_3 was limited, based on this observation and the results of the experiment?
    F. $NaOCl$ absorbs the extra NH_3.
    G. The amount of chlorine gas produced slows the reaction.
    H. $NaOCl$ binds with the H_2O in the solution and causes the reaction rate to decrease.
    J. The amount of NH_3 available for reaction is limited, and once used up, the reaction stops.

GO ON TO THE NEXT PAGE.

4 ○ ○ ○ ○ ○ ○ ○ ○ **4**

PASSAGE VII

Water pressure influences the rate at which water flows. As water pressure increases, so does the rate of flow. Water pressure can be defined as the amount of force that the water exerts on the container it is in. The more water that is in the container, the greater the water pressure will be. Some students conducted the following experiment:

Experiment

Students used tacks to punch holes in an empty plastic 2-liter bottle. The students created 4 holes, each 1-inch apart, from top to bottom. The tacks were left in each hole as the hole was created. The bottle was filled to the top with water and placed on a table. An 8 × 9-inch pan with a piece of blotting paper was placed lengthwise in front of the bottle. A ruler was placed in the pan to measure the spot at which the water stream touched the paper (range of water stream). The students removed the tack nearest the top of the bottle and marked the spot where the water stream touched the paper (range of water stream). The tack was then replaced, the bottle was filled to the top, and the next tack was removed. The spot where the water stream touched the paper was measured. Rate of flow was indicated by the length of the water stream. This procedure was repeated a total of 4 times, once for each tack. The results are recorded in Table 1 below.

Table 1		
Tack	Position of Tack in the bottle	Approximate range of water stream (inches)
1	First (top)	2.3
2	Second	4.2
3	Third	4.7
4	Fourth (bottom)	5.5

37. Based on Table 1, water pressure is greatest:
  A. at the top of the full container.
  B. at the bottom of the full container.
  C. when the water stream is 4.2 inches long.
  D. when the water stream is 4.7 inches long.

38. Which of the following is an assumption that the students made prior to beginning the experiment?
  F. Water pressure has no effect on the water stream produced.
  G. The rate of flow cannot be accurately determined using tacks and plastic bottles.
  H. The rate of flow corresponds directly to the water stream produced.
  J. Water pressure and rate of flow are the two most important characteristics of water.

39. Based on the results of the experiment, removing Tack 3:
  A. created a 4.7 inch water stream.
  B. caused the bottle to empty more quickly than did removing Tack 4.
  C. increased the total water pressure in the bottle.
  D. created a 5.5 inch water stream.

40. Suppose that the students removed the tacks in order, replaced each tack after measuring the water stream, but did not re-fill the bottle after removing and replacing each tack. According to the passage, the water stream would most likely:
  F. be identical to the first experiment.
  G. increase for each tack removed.
  H. be less than or equal to the previous tack removed.
  J. decrease at first and then increase.

END OF THE SCIENCE REASONING TEST.
STOP! IF YOU HAVE TIME LEFT OVER, CHECK YOUR WORK ON THIS SECTION ONLY.

WRITING TEST PROMPT

DIRECTIONS: This test is designed to assess your writing skills. You have 30 minutes to plan and write an essay based on the stimulus provided. Be sure to take a position on the issue and support your position using logical reasoning and relevant examples. Organize your ideas in a focused and logical way, and use the English language to clearly and effectively express your position.

When you have finished writing, refer to the Scoring Rubrics discussed in the Introduction (page 4) to estimate your score.

Presently in the United States, it is illegal to intentionally disrupt many kinds of radio transmissions, including those for cellular telephone service. Organizations such as places of worship, public schools, and movie theaters, are calling for exceptions to be made to the law in cases where placing and receiving telephone calls has proven annoying to others. However, some people argue that they are entitled to the cellular service they pay for no matter where they may be, that telephone courtesy should remain a personal responsibility, and that cellular users rely on uninterrupted service in case of emergencies at work or at home.

In your opinion, should cellular signal disruptors be allowed in places where phone calls are perceived as annoying?

In your essay, take a position on this question. You may write about either one of the two points of view given, or you may present a different point of view on this question. Use specific reasons and examples to support your opinion.

ANSWER KEY

English Test

1. C	21. A	41. A	61. B
2. H	22. J	42. J	62. F
3. B	23. C	43. B	63. D
4. H	24. F	44. G	64. F
5. A	25. A	45. C	65. D
6. H	26. J	46. F	66. F
7. D	27. B	47. B	67. C
8. G	28. G	48. H	68. J
9. A	29. A	49. A	69. B
10. H	30. H	50. F	70. J
11. A	31. C	51. D	71. D
12. F	32. F	52. J	72. J
13. B	33. A	53. D	73. C
14. H	34. G	54. H	74. G
15. D	35. D	55. C	75. D
16. F	36. F	56. H	
17. C	37. D	57. A	
18. H	38. J	58. G	
19. D	39. A	59. D	
20. F	40. H	60. G	

Mathematics Test

1. E	21. C	41. E
2. J	22. G	42. G
3. C	23. C	43. D
4. G	24. J	44. G
5. D	25. A	45. C
6. G	26. K	46. G
7. C	27. E	47. B
8. J	28. G	48. J
9. D	29. D	49. B
10. F	30. G	50. K
11. B	31. A	51. C
12. G	32. H	52. F
13. E	33. E	53. D
14. G	34. J	54. H
15. E	35. E	55. B
16. H	36. H	56. K
17. D	37. E	57. B
18. F	38. J	58. F
19. D	39. E	59. C
20. J	40. K	60. F

Reading Test		**Science Reasoning Test**	
1. D	21. C	1. C	21. A
2. J	22. F	2. H	22. G
3. C	23. D	3. D	23. C
4. H	24. F	4. G	24. H
5. B	25. D	5. D	25. A
6. F	26. G	6. G	26. H
7. C	27. C	7. B	27. D
8. H	28. H	8. H	28. H
9. B	29. D	9. A	29. B
10. H	30. G	10. J	30. F
11. B	31. B	11. D	31. D
12. G	32. J	12. H	32. H
13. A	33. A	13. A	33. B
14. F	34. H	14. F	34. H
15. A	35. B	15. C	35. A
16. H	36. H	16. F	36. J
17. C	37. B	17. B	37. B
18. G	38. J	18. H	38. H
19. B	39. B	19. A	39. A
20. J	40. J	20. H	40. H

▬▬ SCORING GUIDE

Your final reported score is your COMPOSITE SCORE. Your COMPOSITE SCORE is the average of all of your SCALE SCORES.

Your SCALE SCORES for the four multiple-choice sections are derived from the Scoring Table on the next page. Use your RAW SCORE, or the number of questions that you answered correctly for each section, to determine your SCALE SCORE. If you got a RAW SCORE of 60 on the English test, for example, you correctly answered 60 out of 75 questions.

Step 1 Determine your RAW SCORE for each of the four multiple-choice sections:

English   _____

Mathematics   _____

Reading   _____

Science Reasoning   _____

The following Raw Score Table shows the total possible points for each section.

RAW SCORE TABLE	
KNOWLEDGE AND SKILL AREAS	**RAW SCORES**
ENGLISH	75
MATHEMATICS	60
READING	40
SCIENCE REASONING	40
WRITING	12

Multiple-Choice Scoring Worksheet

Step 2 Determine your SCALE SCORE for each of the four multiple-choice sections using the following Scoring Worksheet. Each SCALE SCORE should be rounded to the nearest number according to normal rules. For example, $31.2 \approx 31$ and $31.5 \approx 32$. If you answered 61 questions correctly on the English section, for example, your SCALE SCORE would be 29.

English   _____ $\times$ 36 = _____ $\div$ 75 = _____
                              RAW SCORE -2 (*correction factor)

                                                                                                              _____
                                                                                                              SCALE SCORE

Mathematics   _____ $\times$ 36 = _____ $\div$ 60 = _____
                              RAW SCORE $+1$ (*correction factor)

                                                                                                              _____
                                                                                                              SCALE SCORE

Reading   _____ $\times$ 36 = _____ $\div$ 40 = _____
                              RAW SCORE $+2$ (*correction factor)

                                                                                                              _____
                                                                                                              SCALE SCORE

Science Reasoning _____ $\times$ 36 = _____ $\div$ 40 = _____
                              RAW SCORE $+1.5$ (*correction factor)

                                                                                                              _____
                                                                                                              SCALE SCORE

---

*The correction factor is an approximation based on the average from several recent ACT tests. It is most valid for scores in the middle 50% (approximately 16–24 scale composite score) of the scoring range.

The scores are all approximate. Actual ACT scoring scales vary from one administration to the next based upon several factors.

If you take the optional Writing Test, you will need to combine your English and Writing scores to obtain your final COMPOSITE SCORE. Once you have determined a score for your essay out of 12 possible points, you will need to determine your ENGLISH/WRITING SCALE SCORE, using both your ENGLISH SCALE SCORE and your WRITING TEST SCORE. The combination of the two scores will give you an ENGLISH/WRITING SCALE SCORE, from 1 to 36, that will be used to determine your COMPOSITE SCORE mentioned earlier.

Using the English/Writing Scoring Table, find your ENGLISH SCALE SCORE on the left or right hand side of the table and your WRITING TEST SCORE on the top of the table. Follow your ENGLISH SCALE SCORE over and your WRITING TEST SCORE down until the two columns meet at a number. This number is your ENGLISH/WRITING SCALE SCORE and will be used to determine your COMPOSITE SCORE.

Step 3 Determine your ENGLISH/WRITING SCALE SCORE using the English/Writing Scoring Table on the following page:

English   _____

Writing   _____

English/Writing   _____

ENGLISH/WRITING SCORING TABLE

ENGLISH SCALE SCORE	WRITING TEST SCORE											ENGLISH SCALE SCORE
	2	3	4	5	6	7	8	9	10	11	12	
36	26	27	28	29	30	31	32	33	34	32	36	36
35	26	27	28	29	30	31	31	32	33	34	35	35
34	25	26	27	28	29	30	31	32	33	34	35	34
33	24	25	26	27	28	29	30	31	32	33	34	33
32	24	25	25	26	27	28	29	30	31	32	33	32
31	23	24	25	26	27	28	29	30	30	31	32	31
30	22	23	24	25	26	27	28	29	30	31	32	30
29	21	22	23	24	25	26	27	28	29	30	31	29
28	21	22	23	24	24	25	26	27	28	29	30	28
27	20	21	22	23	24	25	26	27	28	28	29	27
26	19	20	21	22	23	24	25	26	27	28	29	26
25	18	19	20	21	22	23	24	25	26	27	28	25
24	18	19	20	21	22	23	23	24	25	26	27	24
23	17	18	19	20	21	22	23	24	25	26	27	23
22	16	17	18	19	20	21	22	23	24	25	26	22
21	16	17	17	18	19	20	21	22	23	24	25	21
20	15	16	17	18	19	20	21	21	22	23	24	20
19	14	15	16	17	18	19	20	21	22	23	24	19
18	13	14	15	16	17	18	19	20	21	22	23	18
17	13	14	15	16	16	17	18	19	20	21	22	17
16	12	13	14	15	16	17	18	19	20	20	21	16
15	11	12	13	14	15	16	17	18	19	20	21	15
14	10	11	12	13	14	15	16	17	18	19	20	14
13	10	11	12	13	14	14	15	16	17	18	19	13
12	9	10	11	12	13	14	15	16	17	18	19	12
11	8	9	10	11	12	13	14	15	16	17	18	11
10	8	9	9	10	11	12	13	14	15	16	17	10
9	7	8	9	10	11	12	13	13	14	15	16	9
8	6	7	8	9	10	11	12	13	14	15	16	8
7	5	6	7	8	9	10	11	12	13	14	15	7
6	5	6	7	7	8	9	10	11	12	13	14	6
5	4	5	6	7	8	9	10	11	12	12	13	5
4	3	4	5	6	7	8	9	10	11	12	13	4
3	2	3	4	5	6	7	8	9	10	11	12	3
2	2	3	4	5	6	6	7	8	9	10	11	2
1	1	2	3	4	5	6	7	8	9	10	11	1

Step 4   Determine your **COMPOSITE SCORE** by finding the sum of all your **SCALE SCORES** for each of the four sections: English only (if you do not choose to take the optional Writing Test) *or* English/Writing (if you choose to take the optional Writing Test), Math, Reading, and Science Reasoning, and divide by 4 to find the average. Round your COMPOSITE SCORE according to normal rules. For example, $31.2 \approx 31$ and $31.5 \approx 32$.

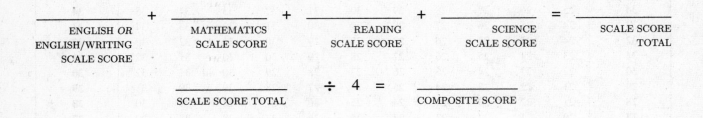

| _____ | + | _____ | + | _____ | + | _____ | = | _____ |
| ENGLISH *OR* ENGLISH/WRITING SCALE SCORE | | MATHEMATICS SCALE SCORE | | READING SCALE SCORE | | SCIENCE SCALE SCORE | | SCALE SCORE TOTAL |

_____   ÷ 4 =   _____
SCALE SCORE TOTAL   COMPOSITE SCORE

■ ANSWERS AND EXPLANATIONS

English Test Explanations

PASSAGE I

1. The best answer is C. The words *surprised* and *shocked* both have the same meaning. To avoid redundancy, you should use only one of them in the sentence. Eliminate answer choice A. One would also not be *saddened* or *disappointed* to learn about Michigan's location 350 million years ago. Eliminate answer choices B and D.

2. The best answer is H. Only answer choice H clearly indicates in a clear and concise manner that Michigan was covered by water. The other answer choices are awkward.

3. The best answer is B. The word *because* creates an incomplete sentence. The word *from* implies that the stone and its pattern are two separate entities. *By* is the only answer choice that makes it clear that the stone is easily identified through recognition of its pattern.

4. The best answer is H. The passage tells us the cells turned into rock over time. The phrase *as slow as* suggests a comparison, which there is not. *Slow to* is in the present tense, but the passage is written in the past tense. *Slowly* is the only answer choice that properly modifies the verb *becoming*.

5. The best answer is A. This question asks you to decide which phrase indicates that the Petoskey stones can differ from each other. The phrase *but some also contain* highlights the fact that while the stones are high in calcite, the elements that they contain can vary. All other answer choices imply that the stones always contain these varied elements.

6. The best answer is H. This sentence is written in the present tense; eliminate answer choice J. The question requires you to correctly place the modifier *high* or *highly*. Answer choice H, *requires a high level*, is the most concise and correct answer.

7. The best answer is D. The items in a list must be separated by commas, so there should be a comma after *wind* and a comma after *sand*.

8. The best answer is G. This sentence elaborates on the *hard labor* the preceding sentences mention. To say that the stones are *conducive* to polishing means that they are easy to polish, making *Fortunately* the appropriate introductory word.

9. The best answer is A. The semicolon is the appropriate punctuation mark between two closely related sentences.

10. The best answer is H. The correct word is the conjunctive adverb *otherwise*, which properly introduces what will occur if some action is not taken.

11. The best answer is A. Sentence 2 describes the case opposite to that in Sentence 1; therefore, Sentence 2 should follow Sentence 1. The word *though* signals that the sentence presents some information that counters a preceding statement.

12. The best answer is F. The phrase is correct as written, with the noun in plural non-possessive form and no punctuation between subject and verb.

13. The best answer is B. The verb must agree with the simple subject *advantage*, which is singular; this eliminates answer choice A. The clausal predicate that comes after *is* requires *that* to be grammatical; therefore, answer choices C and D may be eliminated.

14. The best answer is H. The sentence is evidence of the claim made in the first sentence of the paragraph, which asserts that Petoskey stone availability fluctuates over the course of the year.

15. The best answer is D. The essay is clearly about a particular kind of rock. No details are given about living near the Great Lakes.

PASSAGE II

16. The best answer is F. The underlined portion is clear and precise. The remaining answer choices are not idiomatic.

17. The best answer is C. The simple subject of the sentence is *each*, which is singular; this eliminates answer choices A and D. Answer choice B, "settled into," is not idiomatic in this sentence.

18. The best answer is H. The simple present-tense form of this answer choice parallels the verb form of the previous sentence. Answer choice F may be grammatical, but should be eliminated for being in passive voice.

19. The best answer is D. The word *us* ends the first clause and *we* begins the next one; therefore, some conjunction or punctuation is necessary to separate them.

20. The best answer is F. The phrase *followed by* is a common introductory phrase, therefore, the other answer choices may be eliminated.

21. The best answer is A. The phrasal verb *sound off* means "express one's opinion vigorously." This is the most humanlike of the answer choices.

22. The best answer is J. This sentences follows logically from the previous one, which describes daytime-flying animals. Additionally, a new subtopic is being introduced, so it is appropriate to begin a new paragraph.

23. The best answer is C. The simple present-tense form coincides with the same form in the previous clause: *dart*.

24. The best answer is F. This sentence develops the idea of "the massive blanket of stars" presented in the previous sentence.

25. The best answer is A. The passage maintains a pattern of vivid descriptions of natural sounds and surroundings. This sentence follows that pattern better than the other choices.

26. The best answer is J. A subordinate clause introduced by *but* must be preceded by a comma.

27. The best answer is B. Sentence 2 strays from the pattern of vivid descriptions of sights, sounds, and emotions that is maintained throughout the passage.

28. The best answer is G. Two opposing adjectives divided by *but* do not require punctuation to separate them. This rule also applies with *yet*. For example: "a fun but exhausting afternoon on the lake," and "The experience was silly yet rewarding."

29. The best answer is A. The skin in question is still cool, so the present perfect form is appropriate here, and no changes are required.

30. The best answer is H. This verb should be in simple present-tense form to match the same form of *jerk* later in the sentence.

PASSAGE III

31. The best answer is C. The best clue is in the Australian version at the beginning of the passage,

where the simple past tense form "landed" is also used.

32. The best answer is F. The sentence is best as it is written. The other answer choices have clear redundancies; the notion of a *beginning* implies it is the *first* of a course of actions.

33. The best answer is A. The verb *continue*, as it is used here, takes an infinitive verb ("to be") as its complement; this eliminates the other answer choices.

34. The best answer is G. The word is used to mean all of the Australian people, so it should be in plural, non-possessive form.

35. The best answer is D. The word *principal* has nearly the same meaning as *main*, so it is redundant and may be eliminated.

36. The best answer is F. The word *majority* means a group more than half of the whole. This indicates that the dialect is "the most prevalent form," as the question asks.

37. The best answer is D. The subject of the clause in *General Australian English*, which is singular; this eliminates answer choices A and B. Answer choice C may be eliminated because the clause on *diction* (word choice) does not detract from the claim that the dialect has different vowel sounds.

38. The best answer is J. The paragraph defines dialects of Australian English in order of prevalence; therefore, the *cultivated* form of Australian English is the *least* spoken. In fact, the passage cites a figure of 10% of the population.

39. The best answer is A. The word *too* is an adverb; the other answer choices are not. Adjectives like *haughty* and *snobbish* must be modified by adverbs. Answer choice C is an adverb, but the word *too* more clearly proves why many Australians object to the *cultivated* dialect.

40. The best answer is H. *The vast majority* is a common expression. An article such as *the* or *a* may never be omitted; therefore, the other answer choices may be eliminated.

41. The best answer is A. As it is written, the sentence is clear and concise. The other answer choices are awkward.

42. The best answer is J. This detail identifies the phenomenon for which examples are given in the next sentence. The other choices are not supported by the passage.

43. The best answer is B. The act of publication occurred in the past and is finished; therefore, the simple past-tense form is required. The simple subject *Dictionary* is singular, so answer choice C may be eliminated.

44. The best answer is G. Flipping Sentences 2 and 3 allows the paragraph to flow more logically. Sentence 3 describes the implementation of and subsequent problems with the Macquarie Dictionary. Sentence 2 describes the publisher's reaction to the problems.

45. The best answer is C. The essay is about Australian language exclusively. No other topics are addressed that would be important information for a tourist, so the passage would not serve well as the article the question describes.

PASSAGE IV

46. The best answer is F. As it is written, the sentence correctly matches singular *dime* with *each* eye. Answer choice G could only be correct if the sentence described instead putting dimes (plural) in "your eyes." Obviously, one dime could not be set into two eyes at once.

47. The best answer is B. The sentence is clear that the act of putting in contacts occurred regularly and in the past. The past progressive (e.g. "I was studying"), sometimes called the past continuous, is appropriate here.

48. The best answer is H. There should not be punctuation between a verb (*was*), and its modifier (*truly*), and its predicate (*a novelty*). Adding commas breaks up the natural rhythm of the sentence and makes it awkward to read.

49. The best answer is A. As it is written, the sentence is clearest and most concise. The other answer choices incorrectly associate *in the third grade* with only one of the two diagnoses.

50. The best answer is F. The learning described in the sentence is in the past and completed, so the simple past form is appropriate.

51. The best answer is D. The other answer choices suit the tone of the passage, which describes early, hard-to-manage lens technology. Commenting on the simplicity or primitiveness of a slide presentation helps reinforce the notion of the difference between modern technology and that of the 1960s, the time of the author's childhood.

52. The best answer is J. The sentence describes a simple habitual action in the past; therefore, the simple past is the most appropriate of the answer choices. Answer choice H is actually an incorrect pair of the auxiliary verb *had* with the simple past form of *sink*, which is *sank*.

53. The best answer is D. Sentence 1 introduces the paragraph by mentioning the author's first experience with eyeglasses. Sentence 4 comes next because it is a logical exclamation to include about never having had clear vision. Sentences 2, 3, and 5, in that order, describe the first sensations of going outside with new glasses. Sentence 6 tells the ultimate effect that the glasses had on the author, so it naturally concludes the paragraph.

54. The best answer is H. The word *later* is part of the phrase *six years later* and must be included. The *than* in answer choice G is incorrect because no comparison of time is being made within the sentence.

55. The best answer is C. The best introductory word is *unfortunately* because the sentence defines the undesirable feature of the lenses—their thickness— that caused all the troubles the author describes earlier in the paragraph. The other answer choices do not reflect the relationship between lens thickness and the author's problems.

56. The best answer is H. The author did not intend to have the lenses pop out, so answer choices F and G may be eliminated. Answer choice J is not the best answer because a pronoun could take the place of *the lenses* and *also* does not clearly link to anything in context.

57. The best answer is A. The correct conjunction in the case is *or* because the author is proposing two alternative illustrations of the same annoyance of retrieving a lost lens in the bathroom. The other answer choices would indicate the two events are more closely linked to each other.

58. The best answer is G. The prepositional phrase introduced by *certainly* is further detail added to the lens' *falling*, so it must be separated from preceding prepositional phrase with a comma.

59. The best answer is D. This answer choice is the strongest detail in support of how helpless the author is to see when missing a contact lens.

60. The best answer is G. The sentence provides a response to the rhetorical question posed previously. The passage shows how the author recovered from numerous vision-correction setbacks, so this sentence maintains that pattern.

PASSAGE V

61. The best answer is B. Quotations are set apart from the short clause that defines the speaker with a comma (e.g. "Joe says, 'I like cheese,'" *or* " 'Go home,' cried Martha.") An exclamation point may be used when the sentence warrants it; this sentence does not, since it is not an unusually excited utterance.

62. The best answer is F. The preceding sentence is a quotation from a corporate publicist. This sentence should be relevant to her concerns. The other answer choices too broadly address the field of graphic arts.

63. The best answer is D. The sentence should mean that *Mauro's comment* is relevant to animation in general, not limited to some time period in the past. This eliminates answer choice C. The *also* in answer choice D is important for tying the previous comment on *business* with the upcoming mention of *animated films*.

64. The best answer is F. This sentence essentially defines the earliest animation as a kind of flip-book, which is the subject of the next sentence.

65. The best answer is D. This adverbial phrase (*When the pages are flipped in rapid succession*) begins the sentence and so should be separated from the main clause (*an action scene unfolds . . .*) with a comma.

66. The best answer is F. The conjunctive adverb *although* is the best choice because it is used to lessen the degree of a preceding claim. Here, the complication and time requirements of *traditional animated films* takes away from the assertion that the production is based on the same principle as flip-books.

67. The best answer is C. The phrase *or sheets of clear plastic* describes the *cels*. It is correct to use a comma to separate a modifying clause from the noun that it modfies. A period or a semicolon should be used to separate two independent clauses, so answer choices A and B are incorrect.

Answer choice D creates an incomplete sentence, so it should be eliminated.

68. The best answer is J. The context of the paragraph indicates that certain events happen in order: first the drawings are applied to cels, and eventually those cels are photographed in succession to create a movie. Only answer choice J expresses this idea. Answer choices F, G, and H can be eliminated because they mean essentially the same thing and cannot all be correct.

69. The best answer is B. The word *animated* means *moving*, so to avoid redundancy, one should be eliminated. Only answer choice B is free from redundancy.

70. The best answer is J. Only answer choice J clearly and concisely expresses the intended idea. The other answer choices are awkward.

71. The best answer is D. It is not necessary to use both amount and time in the same sentence. To avoid redundancy and wordiness, select one or the other. Answer choice D is clear and concise.

72. The best answer is J. The phrase *animators from all over the world* is a complex noun phrase that must not be broken up with commas, as in answer choices F and H, nor separated from the sentence with a comma, as in answer choice G.

73. The best answer is C. A comma cannot be the only element separating two independent clauses. A dash, semicolon, or period may be used.

74. The best answer is G. Describing data entry on a graphic's tablet corresponds to the mention of scanning hand-drawn images into a computer describes in Sentence 2. Sentence 3 introduces the description of the computer-side editing process, so Sentence 5 could come before it.

75. The best answer is D. This sentence is a good introductory statement for Paragraph 4, in which artists' adaptation to technological change is addressed.

Mathematics Test Explanations

1. **The correct answer is E.** The positive factors of 32 include all of the positive integers that divide evenly into 32. Don't get confused between *positive* integers (which include 1) and *even* integers.

2. **The correct answer is J.** If all CDs are equally priced and 8 CDs cost $76.00, then the cost of 1 CD is $\frac{\$76.00}{8}$, or $9.50.

3. **The correct answer is C.** To multiply these quantities, first group like terms:

$$2x^2 \times 3x^2y^2 \times 5x^2y = (2 \times 3 \times 5)(x^2x^2x^2)(y^2y).$$

To multiply the same base, add the exponents: $(2 \times 3 \times 5)(x^2x^2x^2)(y^2y) = 30x^6y^3$.

4. **The correct answer is G.** To solve this problem, substitute the value 250 for x in the expression $10(100x - 10,000) + 100$, as follows:

$$10(100(250) - 10,000) + 100 =$$
$$10(25,000 - 10,000) + 100 =$$
$$10(15,000) + 100 =$$
$$150,000 + 100 = 150,100.$$

5. **The correct answer is D.** To solve this problem, recall that when two numbers that consist of the same base and different exponents are multiplied together, you keep the base and add the exponents. Because multiplication is commutative, the expression $4a^3 \times 5a^8$ can be written as $4 \times 5 \times a^8 \times a^3$, or $20a^{8+3}$, which equals $20a^{11}$. You can eliminate answer choice A, B, and C because they add the coefficients instead of multiplying them.

6. **The correct answer is G.** To solve this problem, first note that AB is the hypotenuse of a right triangle with legs AE and BE, then apply the Pythagorean Theorem. According to the figure, E is between A and D, which means that $AD = AE + ED$, or $AE = AD - ED$. It is given that $AD = 16$ and $ED = 11$, therefore $AE = 16 - 11$, or 5. Also according to the figure, you can reasonably assume that BE and CD have the same length, and since AE is congruent to CD, the segments BE and CD have a length of 5 as well. Thus, AB is the hypotenuse of a right triangle with legs of 5, making $AB^2 = 5^2 + 5^2 = 25 + 25$, or 50. Since $AB^2 = 50$, $AB = \sqrt{50} = \sqrt{(25 \times 2)} = \sqrt{25}\sqrt{2}$, or $5\sqrt{2}$.

7. **The correct answer is C.** Recall that in scientific notation $2.0 \times 10^2 = 2.0 \times 100 = 200$ and $2.0 \times 10^{-2} = 2.0 \times 0.01 = 0.02$. To solve this problem, determine the decimal value of each answer choice by changing the scientific notation to decimals:

A. $0.02 \times 10^4 = 0.02 \times 10,000 = 200$
B. $0.2 \times 10^3 = 0.2 \times 1000 = 200$
C. $2.0 \times 10^{-2} = 2.0 \times 0.01 = 0.02$
D. $20.0 \times 10^2 = 20.0 \times 100 = 2000$
E. $0.002 \times 10^5 = 0.002 \times 100,000 = 200$

Thus $2.0 \times 10^{-2} = 2.0 \times 0.01 = 0.02$ is the number that is least in value.

8. **The correct answer is J.** Since the triangle is isosceles, the base angles will have the same measure, x. Since the sum of the angles in a triangle is $180°$, $50 + 2x = 180$, making $x = \frac{(180 - 50)}{2} = \frac{130}{2}$, or $65°$.

9. **The correct answer is D.** If the sum of the real numbers a and b is 13, then $a + b = 13$. If the difference between a and b is 5, then $|a - b| = 5$. Think of the difference as the positive distance between a and b on the number line. Solve the first equation for a, as follows:

$$a + b = 13$$
$$a = 13 - b$$

Now, substitute $13 - b$ for a in the second equation and solve for b:

$$|13 - b - b| = 5$$
$$|13 - 2b| = 5$$
$$|-2b| = 8$$
$$|-b| = 4$$
$$b = 4$$

Now substitute b in the first equation to get $a + 4 = 13$, so $a = 9$. If $a = 9$ and $b = 4$, $ab = 36$.

10. **The correct answer is F.** To find what percent 37 is of 144, divide 37 by 144 and multiply by 100%:

$$\frac{37}{144} \approx 0.26$$
$$0.26 \times 100\% = 26\%.$$

11. **The correct answer is B.** To solve this problem, divide the amount collected on Day 2 (about $500 according to the graph) by the total collected, $1,450, and multiply by 100%:

$$\frac{500}{1450} \times 100\% \approx 34\%.$$

12. The correct answer is G. To solve this problem, divide the total amount collected by the number of days:

$$\frac{1450}{3} = \text{about } \$483 \text{ per day.}$$

13. The correct answer is E. To solve, use the FOIL (First, Outside, Inside, Last) method for binomial multiplication to expand $(3n+5)^2$. It may be helpful to picture $(3n + 5)^2$ as $(3n + 5)(3n + 5)$. Using the FOIL method, $(3n+5)(3n+5)$ becomes $9n^2+15n+15n+25$, which can be reduced to $9n^2 + 30n + 25$.

14. The correct answer is G. To solve this problem, first find the cost of 5 boxes of cereal, then divide that total by 6. Since each box costs \$3.25, the cost for 5 boxes is $5(3.25)$, or \$16.25. Since each additional box is free, the average cost per box for the 6 boxes is $\dfrac{\$16.25}{6}$, or \$2.71.

15. The correct answer is E. To solve this problem, multiply the number of possibilities for each option. Since there are 3 kinds of cheese, 4 kinds of meat toppings, and 5 kinds of vegetable toppings and each type of pizza on the menu has a combination of exactly 3 ingredients: 1 cheese, 1 meat, and 1 vegetable, the total number of pizza types that are possible is $3 \times 4 \times 5 = 60$.

16. The correct answer is H. To find the midpoint on a number line, take the average of the two points. The average of -3 and 11 is $\dfrac{(-3 + 11)}{2} = \dfrac{8}{2}$, or 4, answer choice H. This is the same as applying the midpoint formula, which, given two points on a line, can be expressed as $\left(\dfrac{[x_1 + x_2]}{2}, \dfrac{[y_1 + y_2]}{2}\right)$.

17. The correct answer is D. To solve this problem, recall that $b^x b^y = b^{x+y}$ and $(b^x)^y = b^{xy}$. Given $(2^n)(8) = 16^3$, it will be helpful for this problem to think of 8 as 2^3 and 16 as 2^4. Thus $(2^n)(8) = (2^n)(2^3) = 2^{n+3}$, and $16^3 = (2^4)^3 = 2^{12}$. Since $(2^n)(8) = 16^3$, it follows that $2^{n+3} = 2^{12}$ and that $n + 3 = 12$. Therefore $n = 12 - 3 = 9$.

18. The correct answer is F. To solve this problem, substitute -4 for x in the expression $-3x^2 - 8$, as follows (remember to keep track of the negative signs!):

$$-3(-4)^2 - 8$$
$$= -3(16) - 18$$
$$-48 - 8 = -56$$

If you did not keep track of the negative signs, you would most likely arrive at one of the incorrect answer choices.

19. The correct answer is D. To solve this problem, let the height of the clock tower be x. Using the fact that the figure shown forms a right triangle with legs 150 and x, the height of the clock tower can be calculated using the trigonometric ratio tangent. Because the tangent of an angle is the ratio of the side opposite an angle to the side adjacent to the angle, $\tan 40° = \dfrac{x}{150}$. In the problem it is given that $\tan 40° \approx 0.84$, making $0.84 = \dfrac{x}{150}$, or $x = 150(0.84) = 126.0$. The height of the clock tower is therefore 126.0 feet.

20. The correct answer is J. To solve this problem, first distribute and combine like terms before attempting any algebra:

$$4(x - 2) + 5x = 3(x + 3) - 11$$
$$4x - 8 + 5x = 3x + 9 - 11$$
$$9x - 8 = 3x - 2$$
$$6x = 6$$
$$x = 1$$

21. The correct answer is C. To solve this problem, start by finding the least common multiple of 60 and 70, which is 420. However, 420 is not a multiple of 40. Next try 2×420, which is 840. The number 840 is still a multiple of 60 and 70 and is also a multiple of 40. Another possible strategy for this problem would be to start with the smallest answer choice (you are asked for the least common multiple) and stop when you find an answer choice that is evenly divisible by 40, 60, and 70.

22. The correct answer is G. Given that $4\dfrac{2}{5} = a - 1\dfrac{2}{3}$, $a = 4\dfrac{2}{5} + 1\dfrac{2}{3}$. To solve this problem, convert the mixed numbers to fractions with 15 as the common denominator. The quantity $4\dfrac{2}{5}$ is also written $\dfrac{22}{5}$. To convert $\dfrac{22}{5}$ so that its denominator is 15, multiply it by $\dfrac{3}{3}$ to get $\dfrac{66}{15}$. Likewise, the quantity $1\dfrac{2}{3}$ can be written as $\dfrac{5}{3}$. To convert $\dfrac{5}{3}$ so that its denominator is 15, multiply it by $\dfrac{5}{5}$ to get $\dfrac{25}{15}$. Therefore $a = 4\dfrac{2}{5} + 1\dfrac{2}{3}$, or $\dfrac{66}{15} + \dfrac{25}{15}$, which equals $\dfrac{(66 + 25)}{15}$, or $\dfrac{91}{15}$.

23. The correct answer is C. To solve this problem, it would be helpful to make the properties of both lines more evident by converting them to slope-intercept form ($y = mx + b$, where m is the slope and b is the y-intercept). To start, adding $2x$ to both sides and dividing both sides of the equation $4y - 2x = 8$ by 4 yields $y = \frac{x}{2} + 2$. Similarly, subtracting $2x$ from both sides and dividing both sides of the equation $4y + 2x = 8$ by 4 yields $y = -\frac{x}{2} + 2$. The relationship between $y = \frac{x}{2} + 2$ and $y = -\frac{x}{2} + 2$ is that they are lines that share the same y-intercept, yet they have opposite slopes $\left(\frac{1}{2} \text{ and } -\frac{1}{2}\right)$. Therefore these are two distinct intersecting lines.

24. **The correct answer is J.** Since the house painter charges $24.00 per hour for a painting job that requires more than 5 hours to complete and n represents the number of hours the job requires, the charge, in dollars, for a job requiring more than 5 hours to complete can be expressed as $(24.00)(n)$, or $24n$. This problem tested your ability to disregard irrelevant information.

25. **The correct answer is A.** To solve this problem, first recognize that $\frac{a + b}{2} = 6$, which means that $a + b = 12$. Also, $\frac{a + b + c}{3} = 11$, which means that $a + b + c = 33$. Therefore, $12 + c = 33$, so c must equal $33 - 12$, or 21.

26. **The correct answer is K.** Because the figure is a square ($OS = ST$), the x-coordinate must be the same number of units as the y-coordinate. Also, since T is in Quadrant I, the x-coordinate must be positive. Eliminate answer choices A, B, and C. Since the y-coordinate is 5, the x-coordinate, k, must also be 5.

27. **The correct answer is E.** To solve this problem, multiply the number of possibilities for each option. Since there are 130 boys and 145 girls at the camp, the number of 2-person combinations of 1 boy and 1 girl that are possible is $(130)(145) = 18,850$.

28. **The correct answer is G.** To solve this problem, write a mathematical expression for the phrase in the problem. Because when 3 times a number x is added to 12 the result is negative, $3x + 12 < 0$. To solve for x, subtract 12 from both sides and divide by 3 to get $x < -4$.

29. **The correct answer is D.** To solve this problem, calculate the areas of the circles and subtract the area of the smaller circle from the area of the larger circle. Since the 9-inch diameter of the smaller

circle is equal to the radius of the larger circle, the area of the larger circle is $\pi(9)^2 = 81\pi$. Since the diameter of the smaller circle is 9 inches, its radius is $\frac{9}{2} = 4.5$ inches. The area of the smaller circle is then $\pi(4.5)^2 = 20.25\pi$. The area of the shaded region is therefore $(81 - 20.25)\pi$, or 60.75π, which is approximately equal to 190.76. Remember that π is approximately equal to 3.14.

30. **The correct answer is G.** To solve this problem, distribute the -1 and add like terms. After distributing, the expression $(x^3 + 2x^2 + 3x - 2) - (2x^3 - x^2 - 4)$ becomes $x^3 + 2x^2 + 3x - 2 - 2x^3 + x^2 + 4$. Combining like terms yields $-x^3 + 3x^2 + 3x + 2$.

31. **The correct answer is A.** To solve this problem, substitute the given values for x into each function to see if you get the correct value for $f(x)$. Answer choice A is correct because for each of the four given x values, $x^2 - 6$ yields the correct $f(x)$ values.

32. **The correct answer is H.** The median is the middle value of a list of values that are in ascending or descending order. First, put the test scores in order: 64, 72, 72, 80, 85, 89. Because there are six values, the median will be the average of the middle two values: $\frac{72 + 80}{2} = \frac{152}{2}$, or 76.

33. **The correct answer is E.** To solve this problem, substitute a for x and b for y and set it equal to zero: $2ab - 4a = 0$. Factor out $2a$: $2a(b - 2) = 0$. Since a cannot equal zero (it must be positive), then $(b - 2) = 0$. Solving for b gives you $b = 2$. Since b is an integer, Roman Numeral I can equal 0. Eliminate answer choices B and C. Substitute $(a - b)$ for x and b for y and set it equal to zero: $2(a - b)b - 4(a - b) = 0$. Factor out $2(a - b)$: $2(a - b)(b - 2) = 0$. This is true if $a = b$ or if $b = 2$. Since a or b can be an integer, Roman Numeral II can equal 0. Eliminate answer choice A. Substitute b for x and $(a - b)$ for y and set it equal to zero: $2b(a - b) - 4b = 0$. Factor out $2b$: $2b[(a - b) - 2] = 0$. Since b cannot equal zero (it must be positive), then $(a - b - 2) = 0$. Solving for a gives you $a = b + 2$, which can be an integer. Solving for b gives you $b = 2 - a$, which can be an integer. So, Roman Numeral III can equal 0. Eliminate answer choice D. Each of the Roman Numerals can be equal to zero.

34. **The correct answer is J.** According to the figure, it is clear that $\angle SRT$ and $\angle TRU$ are complementary (they add up to 90°). Therefore, since $m\angle SRT + m\angle TRU = 90°$ and since $m\angle SRT = (x + 15)°$,

$(x+15)° + m\angle TRU = 90°$. Thus $m\angle TRU = 90° - (x+15)°$, or $(75-x)°$.

35. **The correct answer is E.** To solve this problem, combine like terms, keeping track of the negatives. The expression $(6a - 12) - (4a + 4)$ becomes $6a - 12 - 4a - 4$, which can be simplified to $2a - 16$. The coefficient 2 can be factored out of both terms to get $2(a - 8)$.

36. **The correct answer is H.** The area of a parallelogram is bh, where b is the length of the base and h is the height perpendicular to the bases. The length of the base can be determined by subtracting the x-coordinates of the points that determine the bases: $8 - 0 = 11 - 3 = 8$ units long. The height, since it is the height perpendicular to the bases, can be determined by subtracting the y-coordinates of the points: $6 - 2 = 4$. Therefore the area is $bh = (8)(4)$, or 32.

37. **The correct answer is E.** To solve this problem, substitute $x^5 = y$ for y in $y^3 = z$. The equation $y^3 = z$ becomes $(x^5)^3 = z$, or $z = x^{15}$, answer choice E.

38. **The correct answer is J.** To solve this problem, systematically evaluate each answer choice for correctness. From the sequence 36, 18, 9, …, it is clear that each term is $\frac{1}{2}$ of the preceding term; eliminate answer choice H. The fourth term is $\frac{9}{2}$, or 4.5 and the fifth term is $\frac{4.5}{2}$, or 2.25, so eliminate answer choices F and G. While the first three terms are evenly divided by 3, the fourth and fifth (and any term following) are not evenly divisible by 3, so answer choice J is correct.

39. **The correct answer is E.** Recall that the tangent of an angle in a right triangle is the ratio of the side opposite the angle to the side adjacent to the angle. From the figure shown of $\triangle ABC$, the side opposite angle C is 9 and the side adjacent to C is 5. Therefore $\tan C = \frac{9}{5}$.

40. **The correct answer is K.** To solve this problem, first determine the length of the top base using the Pythagorean theorem. Since the height is 4 and the length of one of the diagonal sides is 3, the length of the other leg of the triangle is 3. The top base equals the length of the bottom base plus twice the leg of the triangle just calculated. Thus the length of the top base is $6 + 2(3) = 12$. Using the formula for the area of a trapezoid, $\frac{1}{2}h(b_1 + b_2), A = \frac{1}{2}(4)(6 + 12)$, or 36.

41. **The correct answer is E.** To solve this problem, it might be helpful to draw a picture, as shown below:

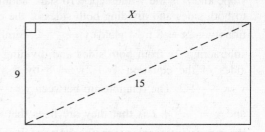

If a rectangular garden has a side of 9 feet and a diagonal of 15 feet, it forms a right triangle with leg 9 and hypotenuse 15. According to the Pythagorean Theorem, the length of the other leg, x, can be determined using the following equation:

$$15^2 = 9^2 + x^2$$
$$x^2 = 225 - 81$$
$$x^2 = 144$$
$$x = 12$$

The perimeter of the rectangle is therefore $2(9) + 2(12)$, or 42.

42. **The correct answer is G.** To solve this problem, use the FOIL (First, Outside, Inside, Last) method for binomial multiplication to expand $\left(\frac{1}{3}a - b\right)^2$. It may be helpful to picture $\left(\frac{1}{3}a - b\right)^2$ as $\left(\frac{1}{3}a - b\right)\left(\frac{1}{3}a - b\right)$. Using the FOIL method, $\left(\frac{1}{3}a - b\right)\left(\frac{1}{3}a - b\right)$ becomes $\left(\frac{1}{9}\right)a^2 - \left(\frac{1}{3}\right)ab - \left(\frac{1}{3}\right)ab + b^2 = \left(\frac{1}{9}\right)a^2 - \left(\frac{2}{3}\right)ab + b^2$.

43. **The correct answer is D.** To solve this problem, first subtract 23 from both sides of $23 - 6x \geq 5$ to get $-6x \geq -18$. Then divide both sides of the inequality by -6 (flip the direction of the inequality when dividing by a negative number) to get $x \leq 3$.

44. **The correct answer is G.** To solve this problem, use the distance formula which states that for any two points (x_1, y_1) and (x_2, y_2), the distance between them, d, is given by $d = \sqrt{[(x_2 - x_1)^2 + (y_2 - y_1)^2]}$. Therefore the distance between $(4, -3)$ and $(-6, 5)$ is $\sqrt{[(4 - (-6))^2 + (-3 - 5)^2]} = \sqrt{(10^2 + 8^2)}$,

which equals $\sqrt{164}$, or about 12.81. Another way to look at this problem would be to draw a picture and use the Pythagorean Theorem to find the hypotenuse of the triangle that is formed from the given points.

45. The correct answer is C. If the ratio of x to z is 3 to 5, and the ratio of y to z is 1 to 5, then $\dfrac{x}{z} = \dfrac{3}{5}$ and $\dfrac{y}{z} = \dfrac{1}{5}$. The ratio $\dfrac{x}{y} = \left(\dfrac{x}{z}\right)/\left(\dfrac{y}{z}\right) = \left(\dfrac{3}{5}\right)\left(\dfrac{1}{5}\right) = \dfrac{3}{1}$. Thus, the ratio of x to y is 3:1.

46. The correct answer is G. To solve this problem, it might be helpful to draw a picture in which α is an angle in a right triangle with side opposite of length x and side adjacent of length y, as shown below:

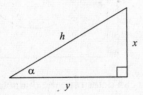

The hypotenuse, h, of this triangle can be determined using the Pythagorean Theorem, as follows:

$$h^2 = x^2 + y^2$$
$$h = \sqrt{(x^2 + y^2)}$$

Since cosine is the ratio of the side adjacent to the hypotenuse, $\cos \alpha = \dfrac{y}{\sqrt{(x^2 + y^2)}}$.

47. The correct answer is B. To find the area of $QRST$, first determine the length of its sides. To do so, use the fact that right triangles exist in every corner of $FGHJ$ with legs that are equal to half the length of a side of $FGHJ$, and with hypotenuse equal to the length of a side of $QRST$. Since the length of a side of $FGHJ$ is 10, the legs of the triangles have length 5. Using the Pythagorean Theorem, the length of the hypotenuse, h, is expressed by $h^2 = 5^2 + 5^2 = 25 + 25 = 50; h = \sqrt{50}$. Since the length of the hypotenuse is equal to the length of a side of $QRST$, the area of $QRST$ is $(\sqrt{50})^2$, or 50.

48. The correct answer is J. Since $XZ = \dfrac{7}{8}h$ and the area of a triangle is $\dfrac{1}{2}bh$, then the area of this triangle is $\dfrac{1}{2}\left(\dfrac{7}{8}h\right)h$, or $\dfrac{7}{16}h^2$, answer choice J.

49. The correct answer is B. If a price is reduced by 15%, then 85% of the original price is retained.

Likewise, if a price is reduced by 20%, then 80% of the original price is retained. If a price is reduced by 15% and then again by 20%, the percent of the original price that remains is $(85\%)(80\%) = (0.85)(0.80)$, or 0.68, which is equivalent to 68%.

50. The correct answer is K. Since $ghjk = 24$, none of these variables (g, h, j, or k) can equal 0. If one of them did equal 0, their product would also be 0. Thus, eliminate answer choices C and D. If g and h were both negative, their product would still be positive and therefore, you can eliminate answer choices A and B. Since $ghkl = 0$ and g, h, and k cannot equal 0, l must equal 0.

51. The correct answer is C. The area of a triangle is $\dfrac{1}{2}(bh)$, where b is the base, and h is the height. You can determine the base by measuring the distance along the x-axis, and you can determine the height by measuring the distance along the y-axis:

The distance between -1 and 3 on the x-axis is 4 units; likewise, the distance between -2 and 2 on the x-axis is 4 units. The length of the base is 4.

The distance between -8 and 3 on the y-axis is 11. The height is 11.

Now plug these values into the formula for the area of a triangle:

$$A = \dfrac{1}{2}(bh)$$

$$A = \dfrac{1}{2}(4 \times 11)$$

$$A = \dfrac{1}{2}(44) = 22.$$

52. The correct answer is F. If $XYZ = 1$, then Z cannot equal 0. If Z (or X or Y, for that matter) were 0, then XYZ would equal 0. Both sides of the equation can be divided by Y, which gives you $XZ = \dfrac{1}{Y}$, answer choice F. Answer choice G is incorrect because two of the values *could* be -1. Answer choice H is incorrect because two of the values *could* be fractions and the third value *could* be a whole number, that, when multiplied by the fractions give you 1. Answer choices J and K are incorrect because you have already determined that none of the values can be equal to zero.

53. The correct answer is D. The slope-intercept form of a line is $y = mx + b$, where m is the slope and b is the y-intercept. Put the equation given in the problem in the slope-intercept form:

$$6x + 2y = 14$$

$$2y = -6x + 14$$

$$y = -3x + 7$$

The y-intercept is 7.

54. **The correct answer is H.** If the average of six integers is 38, then the total must be 6×38, or 228. If the average of seven integers is 47, then the total must be 7×47, or 329. Since you are adding a seventh integer to the set, the value of the seventh integer will be the difference between 329 and 228: $329 - 228 = 101$.

55. **The correct answer is B.** The area of a rectangle is calculated by multiplying the width by the length ($w \times l$). You are given that the length is 4 feet less than four times the width. Set the width equal to w; the length is then $4w - 4$. Plug these values into the equation for the area of a rectangle:

$$(w)(4w - 4) = 80$$

$$4w^2 - 4w = 80$$

Put this equation into the quadratic form and factor to find the solutions for w:

$$4w^2 - 4w - 80 = 0$$

$$4(w^2 - w - 20) = 0$$

$$4(w + \_\_\_)(w - \_\_\_) = 0$$

$$4(w + 4)(w - 5) = 0$$

$$(w + 4) = 0; w = -4$$

$$(w - 5) = 0; w = 5$$

Since the width of a room cannot have a negative value, the width must be 5.

56. **The correct answer is K.** The problem asks for an expression that represents the *number* of pounds of apples sold, not the *cost* of the pounds of apples sold. Therefore, answer choices F and H can be eliminated because they include reference to the cost per pound of apples ($1.09). The problem states that fewer pounds per day are sold when the price is increased, so the correct expression cannot be J, which shows an increase from the 800 pounds of apples that the grocery store normally sells. Since we are given that the store sells 25 less for every cent increased, then for $3x$ cents increased, the store will sell $25(3x)$, or $75x$ less apples.

57. **The correct answer is B.** First, draw the picture of the wading pool according to the information given in the problem, where the distance from the edge of the pool to the edge of the long side of the rectangular region is 8 feet. The distance from the edge of the pool to the edge of the short side of the rectangular region can be anything greater than 8, but it is not necessary to know this distance to solve the problem:

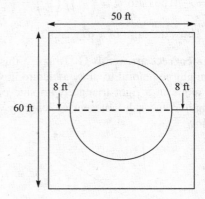

Now you can determine the diameter of the circular pool. The diameter is the maximum distance from one point on a circle to another (the dashed line) through the center of the circle. Since the short side of the rectangular region is 50 feet, and the distance from the edge of the circular pool to each edge of the long sides of the rectangular region is set at 8 feet, the diameter of the circle must be 50 feet − 2(8 feet), or 50 feet − 16 feet, or 34 feet. The question asks for the radius of the pool, which is $\frac{1}{2}$ of the diameter. $34 \div 2 = 17$.

58. **The correct answer is F.** To answer this questions, substitute $(x + y)$ for x in the equation and solve using the FOIL method, as follows:

$$(x + y)^2 + 3$$

$$(x + y)(x + y) + 3$$

$$x^2 + xy + xy + y^2 + 3$$

$$x^2 + 2xy + y^2 + 3$$

59. **The correct answer is C.** The rules of the game state that a player is a winner if two marbles drawn have the same tens digit. The player has already drawn the marble numbered 23, which has a 2 in the tens digit. In order to win, the player must draw another marble with a 2 in the tens digit. The possible winning marbles are 20, 21, 22, 24, 25, 26, 27, 28, and 29. Therefore, the player has nine chances to draw a winning marble. Since he has already

drawn one of the 84 marbles and did not put it back, he has nine chances out of 83 to draw a winning marble. The probability is $\frac{9}{83}$.

60. **The correct answer is F.** If 2 numbers, x and y, differ by 6, that means that $x - y = 6$. Multiplying the two numbers, $(x)(y)$, will yield the product. Solve the first equation for x.

$$x - y = 6$$
$$x = y + 6$$

Substitute the result for x in the second equation.

$$(y + 6)y$$

Since one of the answer choices must be the solution to that equation, plug in the answer choices,

starting with the smallest value (note that the answer choices are in ascending order):

$$(y + 6)y = -9$$
$$y^2 + 6y + 9 = 0$$
$$(y + 3)^2 = 0$$
$$y = -3$$

Now, substitute -3 for y in the first equation and solve for x:

$$x - (-3) = 6$$
$$x = 3$$

Since $(x)(y) = (3)(-3) = -9$ is the smallest value given as an answer, answer choice F must be correct.

Reading Test Explanations

PASSAGE I

1. **The best answer is D.** The first paragraph discusses the fact that people today are "fortunate to enjoy many conveniences once unheard of or reserved for the elite," and then goes on to declare that people take water and electricity for granted. These details best support answer choice D. Answer choice A may appear to be correct; however, the passages states the it is "in the future" when the prices of these commodities will be so high that people can no longer take their quantity and use for granted.

2. **The best answer is J.** The passage indicates that water from the blue tap is "drinkable hot and cold water," while water from the red tap is "unpurified" and not meant for consumption by humans. If the water from the red tap is unpurified and not drinkable, it makes the most sense that those who drank it would run the risk of falling ill from waterborne pathogens – answer choice J. Answer choice G may appear to be correct; however, water with added chlorine and fluoride is water that has been purified. As indicated by the passage, water from the red tap is not purified.

3. **The best answer is C.** In the passage, the author states that "The boss is a peculiar man," and that "His creative solutions to the lack of infrastructure are impressive." This indicates that the boss is both eccentric and enterprising. The other answer choices are beyond the scope of the passage and not supported by descriptions of the boss of the lodge.

4. **The best answer is H.** The passage states that though the hunters often return with "migratory birds and caribou," the narrator has seen "plenty of other unique game come back to the lodge kitchen for preparation." This indicates that an unusual variety of game exists in the woods surrounding the lodge, answer choice H. Answer choices F, G, and J are all statements made without supporting details to back them up present in the passage.

5. **The best answer is B.** The second paragraph discusses the many hunters who voyage to the lodge every summer, and the fact that the lodge is almost totally self-sufficient. The third paragraph discusses the boss' desire to situate himself so deeply into the wilderness and his hardiness. These facts all support answer choice B. Answer choices A and C are incorrect because they indicate that the boss would like a more modern, less remote hunting lodge, when he clearly enjoys being beyond the

reach of civilization. Answer choice D is beyond the scope of the passage; nowhere in the passage is a wilderness skills training facility mentioned.

6. **The best answer is F.** In the passage, the narrator asks the boss what the rationale is behind constructing his lodge so far out in the wilderness, and the narrator continues on to describe the boss as a "peculiar man." These statements indicate that the narrator does not fully comprehend the extreme isolation of the lodge. The narrator goes on to describe the boss as having impressive "creative solutions to the lack of infrastructure." This implies that the narrator respects the resourcefulness, or ingenuity, of the boss. These facts best correlate with answer choice F.

7. **The best answer is C.** Modern society's consumption of water and power is described as being taken for granted and presumed. This implies that society does not value water and power as much as they should, nor do they take conservation efforts that they could. "Exorbitance" means "excessiveness and wastefulness," which makes the most sense in the context of the passage.

8. **The best answer is H.** The author follows his statement that he was "off the *grid*" with the fact that he was fully dependent on the lodge to give him "heat, light, water, and sanitation." All of these provisions are components of utility systems—answer choice H. Therefore, though the word "grid" could refer to any of the answer choices, answer choice H makes the most sense in the context of the passage.

9. **The best answer is B.** Throughout the passage, the lodge is described as being extremely rustic. However, it is mentioned that a computer is present in the back office, and that at night "a limited set of high-efficiency fluorescent bulbs illuminates the corridors and public spaces." This best corresponds with answer choice B; even though the lodge is rustic and has a wilderness charm, some modern conveniences help it remain habitable.

10. **The best answer is H.** The passage discusses the fact that the lodge is situated "deep in the wilderness," "far beyond the reach of civilization." The fact that the lodge is far from civilization correlates best with answer choice H, which states that civilization is not present to alter or pollute the rivers. Answer choice F is incorrect because the passage indicates neither the quantity of fish in the creeks, nor the effect that would have on the cleanliness of the creeks. Likewise, answer choice J is incorrect because the types of fish caught in the creek are not mentioned. Although answer choice G is mentioned

in the passage, its relevance to the cleanliness of the creeks is not drawn and therefore is incorrect.

PASSAGE II

11. The best answer is B. As stated in the passage, polio was a "particularly devastating disease because of its effect on children. Many children stricken with polio became permanently confined to wheelchairs or died at a very early age." The effects of this disease on children were clearly devastating and far-reaching. Although there were effects on the medical community because its members were desperately searching for a cure, the effects on children were much more extensive and severe. Answer choices A and D do not make sense within the context of the passage.

12. The best answer is G. The passage speaks of "managing the disease's *debilitating* effects," which, according to the passage, included difficulty breathing, paralysis, and potential death. These effects all can best be described as "crippling," answer choice G. Answer choices F and J do not make sense; they both imply that the effects of the disease brought strength and vitality to patients with polio. Answer choice H is incorrect because "coercing" means "forcing to think or act in some way." This does not make sense in the context of the passage.

13. The best answer is A. According to the passage, the iron lung assisted patients in breathing, and some patients "would have to continue this treatment their entire lives." This suggests that if the iron lung was not in existence, or if the patients did not continue iron lung therapy, that they may have not have survived for nearly as long with their disease. This best correlates with answer choice A. Answer choices B and C are outside the context of the passage; neither is associated with the iron lung in the passage. Answer choice D refers to the exercising of paralyzed arms and legs, not the iron lung.

14. The best answer is F. The passage states that "conditions such as overheating, chilling, and even teething were thought to cause polio's symptoms. Some scientists and doctors even believed that diseases such as whooping cough and pneumonia were the cause of polio." The passage goes on to say that "For many decades, polio research centered on treating symptoms …" Clearly, scientists and doctors did not have a clear picture as to the cause of polio. This best supports answer choice F.

15. The best answer is A. The fifth paragraph gives two treatments that were used in handling polio patients and says that the "latter approach soon *became typical protocol* because it seemed to relieve some pain and discomfort," referring to the exercising of the paralyzed limbs of polio patients. This suggests that exercising soon became the most commonly practiced treatment for polio patients, which best correlates with answer choice A. Answer choices B, C, and D do not make sense within the context of the passage.

16. The best answer is H. Throughout the passage, the author discusses the difficulties that medical researchers had in finding a cure for polio, and many of the different attempts made at treating the inexplicable disease. This best correlates with answer choice H. Answer choice G may appear to be correct; however, nowhere in the passage does it mention that doctors and researchers were competing to find a cure; all those who were studying polio were working towards the same goal. Likewise, answer choice J may appear to be correct because the medical community did have trouble understanding how to cure polio. However, answer choice J is too broad in stating that the medical community as a whole lacks understanding about curing diseases in general.

17. The best answer is C. The passage discusses Salk's breakthrough vaccine and its effectiveness and then goes on to state that "Later, another medical researcher named Albert Sabin developed an even easier method of distributing the vaccine." This suggests that Sabin had developed an easier method of distributing Salk's vaccine. This best supports answer choice C. Answer choice A may appear to be correct because Sabin's vaccine was easier to distribute than Salk's. However, Salk's vaccine was indeed successful in curing polio, it merely was not as easy to distribute as Sabin's.

18. The best answer is G. Cancer is very similar today to what polio was in the early 20th century. Like polio, cancer has many crippling effects and for most types of cancer, there is still no known cure despite the many attempts of medical researchers. Therefore, G is the best answer choice. Answer choices F and H are epidemics like polio, but neither is a strictly medical condition and both can be cured. Answer choice J is outside the context of the passage.

19. The best answer is B. As stated in the passage, "Some scientists and doctors even believed that diseases such as whooping cough and pneumonia were the cause of polio." Therefore, whooping cough and pneumonia were thought to trigger polio, not to be the result of polio. Answer choices A, C, and D are all supported by details found in the passage.

20. **The best answer is J.** The author states in the last sentence of the passage that "500,000 Americans continue to live with the effects of childhood polio infections that began decades ago." These people still are feeling the consequences of a disease that was prevalent years and years ago, answer choice J. Answer choice F directly contradicts the author's final statement in the passage. Answer choice G is incorrect because an effective cure has been found for polio; therefore, children are not at risk for infection of the disease. Answer choice H is outside the context of the passage.

PASSAGE III

21. **The best answer is C.** All four answer choices are mentioned directly or indirectly throughout the passage. However, you must decide between which answer choices are supporting details and which answer choice is the main idea of the passage. Answer choice C best encompasses the whole of the passage by including both past myths and present times, both of which are discussed throughout the passage. Answer choices A, B, and D are all true, but are not the main focus of the passage.

22. **The best answer is F.** Following this statement, the passage reads "This is simplified to such a great degree by following the Gregorian calendar." Therefore, the phrase mentioning ease of finding out the date is referring to the Gregorian calendar. The passage goes on to state that "This has not always been the case, however," referring to the ancient Chinese Zodiac calendar. These facts best support answer choice F.

23. **The best answer is D.** "Vanity" is an "extreme interest in one's own appearance and achievements." Thus, the dog was more interested in how he looked than in his performance in the race, causing him to stop and bathe in the river. Answer choice D best summarizes this, in saying that the dog prioritized his selfish whims over his wish to reach the Emperor's Palace in time. Although answer choice B may appear to be correct, vanity refers to self-interest, not the interests of others. Therefore, the dog was taking a bath for his own benefit and not that of the Emperor.

24. **The best answer is F.** Both the rat and the snake are described as "cunning" when participating in the race. Both animals used their cleverness and

creativity to make it to the finish line before other animals; the rat climbed atop the ox to cross the river and jumped ahead of him to reach the finish line and the snake coiled itself around the horses leg and jumped ahead at the last moment to beat the horse. This best suggests that "cunning" refers to the "ingenuity," or the "cleverness and creativity," of the rat and the snake – answer choice F. These animals were certainly not "dependable," in reference to the cat and rat incidence. They also did not appear to be "apprehensive" or "nervous and worried" about making it to the finish line on time. Likewise, it does not make sense within the context of the passage that the rat and the snake were "tolerant" or "understanding and patient."

25. **The best answer is D.** As stated in the passage, "Even numbered years are considered Yang, and odd numbered years are considered Yin." The only answer choice that does not correctly pair even numbered year with Yang and odd numbered year with Yin is answer choice D, stating that 3030 would be a year of Yin.

26. **The best answer is G.** The passage states that the cat "was a victim of the rat's cunning." This once again implies the craftiness of the rat in assuring himself and himself alone a place among those animals that received the Emperor's great distinction. This best corresponds with answer choice G. The passage does not indicate what or how many other animals in all strove to earn the Emperor's great distinction; therefore, answer choice F is incorrect. Answer choice H is incorrect because although the cat slept through the race, there is no evidence that he was "indolent," or lazy. Answer choice J is beyond the scope of the passage; no reference is made to which animal's companionship the ox preferred.

27. **The best answer is C.** The dragon was delayed in crossing the finish line because he needed to make rain for the people and "His kindness earned him the fifth place in the cycle." The sheep, monkey, and rooster all worked together to cross the river and "For this show of teamwork they were rewarded in the order that they stepped off of the raft." These are the only animals who are described as being "rewarded" with a place in the cycle, thus it can be concluded that the emperor most values "generosity," or "kindness," and "unanimity," or "unity and teamwork." Answer choice B may appear to be correct because "goodwill" is a synonym for "kindness"; however, "narcissism" is a symbol for vanity; the vain dog was not rewarded with his place among the

12 animals but merely earned it by reaching the finish line in time.

28. **The best answer is H.** As stated in the passage, "Suddenly, hidden coiled around the leg of the horse, appeared the snake." The snake was coiled around the leg or the horse, not the leg of the dragon. Therefore, answer choice H is correct. All of the other answer choices can be found within the passage.

29. **The best answer is D.** The passage states that the "origin of the 12 animals is *mythological*, with the story being passed down from generation to generation." The story of the 12 animals is clearly not based on actual fact, so answer choices A and B can immediately be eliminated. "Legitimate" and "bona fide" are both synonyms for "genuine" and "true." Answer choice C is incorrect because the word has "ludicrous" has negative connotations, meaning "ridiculously absurd." Answer choice D, "legendary," makes the most sense within the context of the passage. If something is "legendary," such as the tale of the 12 animals, it is "an ancient or traditional story lacking actual historical basis."

30. **The best answer is G.** The last sentence of the paragraph is referring to the second-to-last sentence of the paragraph, which states "Primary among the great astrological purposes to the Zodiac is the common belief that the animal that governs the time of a person's birth will influence that person's personality for life." The author is indecisive as to whether this statement is true or not, leading the reader to believe that the author has not taken a side in the debate over the accuracy of the Chinese Zodiac and its influence on personality. This best corresponds with answer choice G. Answer choice J may appear to be correct; however, the last sentence is referring to the Zodiac's influence over people's personalities, not the calendar year.

PASSAGE IV

31. **The best answer is B.** The passage discusses first the diet and hunting behaviors of chimpanzees, and then moves on to briefly discuss similar human activity in diet and early human hunting and gathering. This is the overall focus of the passage, which most closely corresponds with answer choice B. Answer choice A may appear to be correct; however, the passage solely discusses diet and hunting habits; the passage does not go into depth about biological and physiological similarities between humans and chimpanzees.

32. **The best answer is J.** As stated in the passage, "chimpanzees do most of their hunting in the dry season." The passage also notes that chimpanzees supplement their diet with meat when food shortages occur in the forest, particularly during dry season. Although answer choices G and H may appear to be correct, they are not inclusive of all of the environmental factors that play a role in the hunting habits of chimpanzees. Thus, answer choice J is correct. Answer choice F is incorrect because although the red colobus monkey is noted as "one of the most important animals in the chimpanzees' diet," the relative ease of hunting the red colobus monkey is not specified.

33. **The best answer is A.** It is noted in the passage that "chimpanzees are actually very *proficient* hunters," and that "Individual chimpanzees have been known to hunt and eat more than 150 small animals each year." Answer choice A–"skilled"–makes the most logical sense within the context of the passage. The sheer number of animals that chimpanzees can successfully hunt each year tells you that they are competent at hunting and can find plenty of prey to supplement their diet each year.

34. **The best answer is H.** The passage indicates that chimpanzees prey on many different kinds of small animals and that the amount of meat that they consume varies each year with environmental factors. Not only this, but chimpanzees' diets can vary due to social and reproductive factors. This information best supports answer choice H; the exact diet of chimpanzees cannot be determined. Answer choice A is incorrect because the study in the passage was done in the wild. Answer choice G is incorrect because the passage clearly states "Although it is clear that the hunting habits of chimpanzees are guided mostly by nutritional needs … chimpanzees might hunt for social gain." It is a possibility that chimpanzees' eating habits could be influenced by social factors, but not a given fact.

35. **The best answer is B.** The passage states that "It is not difficult to determine why studying chimpanzees might be beneficial. Modern humans and chimpanzees are actually very closely related. Experts believe that chimpanzees share about 98.5% of our DNA sequence," which best supports answer choice B.

36. **The best answer is H.** As stated in the passage, "This is comparable to the quantity of meat eaten by modern human societies whose members *forage* when other food sources are scarce." This sentence indicates that these humans looked for other sources of food, such as meat, when their normal

food sources were in short supply. This corresponds with answer choice H, "search for food."

37. The best answer is B. The passage states that "It was Goodall who first reported that meat was a natural part of the chimpanzee diet. In fact, Goodall discovered that chimpanzees are actually very proficient hunters." This tells us that Goodall was the first scientist to discover previously undocumented chimpanzee behavior, and that chimpanzees were actually not vegetarians. Answer choice D might appear to be correct; however, the passage refers to the colobus monkey information as being found in "one notable study," not the study of Dr. Goodall.

38. The best answer is J. According to the passage, humans and chimpanzees share many biological and social qualities. The passage states "Researchers suggest that chimpanzees might hunt for social gain." You can infer then, that ancient humans also hunted for social gain and prestige in their communities. The other answer choices are not supported by information in the passage.

39. The best answer is B. As stated in the passage, "During the dry season, food shortages in the forest cause the chimpanzees' body weight to drop. Consequently, chimpanzees supplement their diets with meat." This best corresponds with answer choice B. Answer choices A, C, and D are not supported by details found within the passage.

40. The best answer is J. The lines in the question stem refer to the sixth paragraph, which focuses on a discussion of food choices among chimpanzees. The paragraph is strictly informational, and does not express any emotion.

Science Reasoning Test Explanations

PASSAGE I

1. **The best answer is C.** In Study 1 the "Researchers measured the levels of feldspar and kaolinite in the soil of the cemetery and other locations at specific distances from the cemetery." This states that the distances from the cemetery where the measurements were taken was varied. Answer choices A and D can be eliminated because these factors were not tested in Study 1. Answer choice B can be eliminated because Study 1 states: "The soil sample sizes were the same for each location tested."

2. **The best answer is H.** The results from Study 2 are shown in Table 2. As the distance from the power plant increases, the sulfur levels decrease. If carbon monoxide behaves similarly to sulfur, one would expect the carbon monoxide levels to decrease as the distance from the power plant increases.

3. **The best answer is D.** The results from Study 1 are shown in Table 1. As the distance from the cemetery increases, the amount of kaolinite in the soil decreases both before and after the rain. This means that the highest levels of kaolinite are found in soil that is closest to the cemetery, which corresponds with answer choice D (less than 100 meters from the cemetery).

4. **The best answer is G.** Table 2 shows that as the distance from the power plant decreases (moving up the table), the levels of sulfur and NO_2 increase. Answer choice H can be eliminated because NO_2 and O_2 do not behave similarly.

5. **The best answer is D.** Feldspar decay decreases as the amount of feldspar in the soil increases. According to Table 1 as the distance from the cemetery increases (going down the column), the amount of feldspar in the soil increases. Therefore, the feldspar decay is decreasing.

PASSAGE II

6. **The best answer is G.** The Familial Hypothesis says, "Isolated populations share the same *gene pool*, which supports the proposition that familial history is the primary cause and indicator of the disease." This suggests that within the same gene pool there is a common family history.

7. **The best answer is B.** The Behavioral Hypothesis talks about why smokers are at a greater risk of developing coronary heart disease, while the Familial Hypothesis does not.

8. **The best answer is H.** According to the Familial Hypothesis, "people whose parents or siblings had a heart or circulatory problem before the age of 55 are at greater risk for heart disease than someone who does not have that family history."

9. **The best answer is A.** The Familial Hypothesis supporters say that risk of heart disease is higher for people in the same gene pool. The Behavioral Hypothesis supporters, however, would say that the reason heart problems run in families is because behaviors (such as smoking, dietary norms, and exercise habits) are passed down from generation to generation through the course of habit. If parents tend to consume large amounts of saturated fats and trans-fats, their offspring will be likely to do the same because they have grown up in an environment where this is normal.

10. **The best answer is J.** The Behavioral Hypothesis supporters believe that the primary causes of coronary heart disease are behavioral factors. They would react to the isolated population studies by saying that members within isolated populations often behave in a similar manner, including having the same diet and engaging in similar physical activities. This would mean that the cause of higher or lower risks of heart disease is not because of familial ties, but because of behavioral factors.

11. **The best answer is D.** Familial Hypothesis supporters believe that the primary cause of coronary heart disease is family history. These supporters would address the study that said high cholesterol levels increase the risk of heart disease by explaining that cholesterol levels are mainly determined by family history. Therefore, family history is still the main cause of coronary heart disease. Answer choice A can be eliminated because hypertension is irrelevant to the question.

12. **The best answer is H.** Both the Familial Hypothesis and the Behavioral Hypothesis cite hypertension, cholesterol, and obesity as major risk indicators, answer choice H. The other answer choices can be eliminated because the information is only cited in one of the two hypotheses.

PASSAGE III

13. **The best answer is A.** According to Table 1, at a drug concentration of 10 mM, Drug R had the least number of bacteria colonies (26), which means that Drug R was most effective at killing bacteria.

14. **The best answer is F.** Experiment 3 states: "The larger the permeability coefficient, the faster the

drug is able to transfer through the membrane." The drug with the largest permeability coefficient, according to Table 3, is Drug R.

15. The best answer is C. According to Table 2, Drug U had 41 colonies at an incubation time of 1 hour and 18 colonies at an incubation time of 6 hours. At an incubation of 3 hours (in between 1 and 6 hours), the number of colonies counted would most likely be in between 18 and 41 colonies.

16. The correct answer F. According to Table 3, as the molecular mass increases, the permeability coefficient decreases. Therefore, as the molecular mass decreases, the permeability coefficient increases, answer choice F. Answer choices H and J can be eliminated because the permeability coefficient does not remain constant while the molecular mass changes.

17. The best answer is B. According to Table 2, as incubation time increases, the number of colonies counted decreases. This means that as time passes, fewer bacteria remain alive, which best supports answer choice B.

18. The best answer is H. Table 1 shows the results of Experiment 1. In the table, as the drug concentration increased, the number of colonies for every drug decreased, which means that the drug's effectiveness increased. This information best supports answer choice H.

19. The best answer is A. In Experiment 1, "The flasks were incubated for 1 hour at 37°C with different concentrations of the 5 drugs," but in Experiment 2, "the incubation time of each culture was varied." This indicates that in Experiment 1, the incubation time was held constant, while the drug concentration was varied, answer choice A.

PASSAGE IV

20. The best answer is H. According to Figure 1, the greatest increase in temperature occurs between 90 meters and 120 meters (approximately 7°C to approximately 11°C).

21. The best answer is A. The results of Study 2 are shown in Figure 2. According to this figure, during the summer, dunes were the warmest. During the winter, dunes were the coldest.

22. The best answer is G. According to the results of Study 2, during the summer the dunes range in temperature from 15°C to 27.5°C and during

the winter the dunes range from −14°C to −9°C. Therefore, the temperature range is smaller throughout a typical day during the winter.

23. The best answer is C. According to the passage, at 9 p.m. on a typical summer day, the dune temperature is approximately 22.5°C. At the same time, the forest temperature is approximately 14.5°C. Because 22.5 − 14.5 = 8.0°C, answer choice C is correct.

24. The best answer is H. According to Figure 2, during the summer, the lake and forest temperatures are the same (the two lines cross) at about 6 a.m. and 3 p.m. During the winter, the lake and forest temperatures are the same at about 3 a.m. and 3 p.m. Therefore, the temperatures are the same during the summer and winter at 3 p.m., answer choice H.

PASSAGE V

25. The best answer is A. According to the results of the experiment, the increase in urine output caused by the dietary supplement X could not be immediately detected. On Days 1 and 2, the horses that received a placebo had a greater average urine output than Group R. It does not become apparent until Day 3 that the dietary supplement is steadily increasing the urine output of the Group R horses.

26. The best answer is H. In order to best determine the effects of dietary supplement X in this experiment, one should examine the urinary output over time of each horse. This would provide more information on the effects of dietary supplement X on each horse.

27. The best answer is D. Table 1 shows the control group (Group S) having the highest average urine output per horse on Day 1 (2.1 gallons).

28. The best answer is H. Passage V states: "A side effect of one of these supplements – supplement X – is increased urination, which can sometimes lead to dehydration in the animal." This suggests that the reason several horses began showing signs of dehydration is because of their high urinary output. Answer choice G can be eliminated because this information was not discussed in the passage.

29. The best answer is B. Table 1 shows that over the course of the seven days, the urinary output for each horse in Group R increased, but the urinary output for Group S remained about the same, which best supports answer choice A.

30. **The best answer is answer choice F.** Over time, the urinary output for the group that received the supplement increased. According to the passage, increased urination can sometimes lead to dehydration, which supports the statement that dietary supplement X could cause dehydration in horses. Answer choice H can be eliminated because the table suggests this answer choice is false.

PASSAGE VI

31. **The best answer is D.** The graph shows the chlorine gas levels decreasing after 1.00 mole of bleach was added. Because the chlorine levels continued to decrease as bleach was added, it was unnecessary to proceed further. The other answer choices are not supported by the data.

32. **The best answer is H.** The results of Experiment 3 are shown in Table 2. According to the table, when 2.50 moles of NH_3 were added to the $NaOCl$ solution, 0.17 moles of NH_2Cl were produced. When 3.00 moles of NH_3 were added, 0.21 moles were produced, resulting in a 0.04 mole increase in NH_2Cl.

33. **The best answer is B.** In Experiment 3, when 1.00 mole of NH_3 was added to the solution, 0.08 moles of NH_2Cl were produced. When 1.50 moles of NH_3 were added, 0.11 moles were produced. If 1.25 moles of NH_3 were added to the $NaOCl$ solution, the amount of NH_2Cl produced would likely be in between 0.08 and 0.11 moles.

34. **The best answer is H.** According to the passage, bleach is chemically known as $NaOCl$; therefore, $NaOCl$ is *not* a by-product.

35. **The best answer is A.** According to the results of Experiment 1 (the only experiment that looked at chlorine gas as a product), either less than 0.50 mol or more than 2.00 mol of $NaOCl$ added to 1.00 mol of NH_3 produced the lowest amounts of chlorine gas. This information suggests that in order to pro-

duce the least amount of chlorine gas, a minimum of 2.00 mol of $NaOCl$ and a maximum of 1.00 mol NH_3 should be chosen.

36. **The best answer is J.** In Experiment 2, $NaOCl$ was added to a constant concentration of NH_3. At first, an increase in the amount of $NaOCl$ added led to an increase in the amount of NCl_3 produced. After 3.00 moles of $NaOCl$ were added, however, the amount of NCl_3 remained relatively constant. This is most likely because after all of the NH_3 is used in a reaction between $NaOCl$, there is no NH_3 remaining to continue the reaction. There is nothing in the passage to support the other answer choices.

PASSAGE VII

37. **The best answer is B.** Passage VII states: "As water pressure increases, so does the rate of flow." Because the "rate of flow was indicated by the water stream," and the water stream was greatest at the 4th tack (bottom of the bottle), the water pressure is greatest at the bottom of the full container.

38. **The best answer is H.** In order for this experiment to be accurate, the students must have assumed that the rate of flow corresponds directly to the water stream produced. Otherwise, the water stream would supply no useful information.

39. **The best answer is A.** According to the results of the experiment, when Tack 3 was removed, the water stream produced was approximately 4.7 inches long. Answer choice B can be eliminated because this information was not discussed in the experiment.

40. **The best answer is H.** Not refilling the bottle would cause the water pressure at each hole to be the same or less than the previous hole; and therefore, the water streams would each be the same or less than those produced by the previous hole.

Writing Test Explanation

Because grading the essay is subjective, we've chosen not to include any "graded" essays here. Your best bet is to have someone you trust, such as your personal tutor, read your essays and give you an honest critique. If you plan on grading your own essays, review the grading criteria and be as honest as possible regarding the structure, development, organization, technique, and appropriateness of your writing. Focus on your weak areas and continue to practice in order to improve your writing skills.

ACT PRACTICE TEST 6
Answer Sheet

ENGLISH

1 Ⓐ Ⓑ Ⓒ Ⓓ	21 Ⓐ Ⓑ Ⓒ Ⓓ	41 Ⓐ Ⓑ Ⓒ Ⓓ	61 Ⓐ Ⓑ Ⓒ Ⓓ
2 Ⓕ Ⓖ Ⓗ Ⓙ	22 Ⓕ Ⓖ Ⓗ Ⓙ	42 Ⓕ Ⓖ Ⓗ Ⓙ	62 Ⓕ Ⓖ Ⓗ Ⓙ
3 Ⓐ Ⓑ Ⓒ Ⓓ	23 Ⓐ Ⓑ Ⓒ Ⓓ	43 Ⓐ Ⓑ Ⓒ Ⓓ	63 Ⓐ Ⓑ Ⓒ Ⓓ
4 Ⓕ Ⓖ Ⓗ Ⓙ	24 Ⓕ Ⓖ Ⓗ Ⓙ	44 Ⓕ Ⓖ Ⓗ Ⓙ	64 Ⓕ Ⓖ Ⓗ Ⓙ
5 Ⓐ Ⓑ Ⓒ Ⓓ	25 Ⓐ Ⓑ Ⓒ Ⓓ	45 Ⓐ Ⓑ Ⓒ Ⓓ	65 Ⓐ Ⓑ Ⓒ Ⓓ
6 Ⓕ Ⓖ Ⓗ Ⓙ	26 Ⓕ Ⓖ Ⓗ Ⓙ	46 Ⓕ Ⓖ Ⓗ Ⓙ	66 Ⓕ Ⓖ Ⓗ Ⓙ
7 Ⓐ Ⓑ Ⓒ Ⓓ	27 Ⓐ Ⓑ Ⓒ Ⓓ	47 Ⓐ Ⓑ Ⓒ Ⓓ	67 Ⓐ Ⓑ Ⓒ Ⓓ
8 Ⓕ Ⓖ Ⓗ Ⓙ	28 Ⓕ Ⓖ Ⓗ Ⓙ	48 Ⓕ Ⓖ Ⓗ Ⓙ	68 Ⓕ Ⓖ Ⓗ Ⓙ
9 Ⓐ Ⓑ Ⓒ Ⓓ	29 Ⓐ Ⓑ Ⓒ Ⓓ	49 Ⓐ Ⓑ Ⓒ Ⓓ	69 Ⓐ Ⓑ Ⓒ Ⓓ
10 Ⓕ Ⓖ Ⓗ Ⓙ	30 Ⓕ Ⓖ Ⓗ Ⓙ	50 Ⓕ Ⓖ Ⓗ Ⓙ	70 Ⓕ Ⓖ Ⓗ Ⓙ
11 Ⓐ Ⓑ Ⓒ Ⓓ	31 Ⓐ Ⓑ Ⓒ Ⓓ	51 Ⓐ Ⓑ Ⓒ Ⓓ	71 Ⓐ Ⓑ Ⓒ Ⓓ
12 Ⓕ Ⓖ Ⓗ Ⓙ	32 Ⓕ Ⓖ Ⓗ Ⓙ	52 Ⓕ Ⓖ Ⓗ Ⓙ	72 Ⓕ Ⓖ Ⓗ Ⓙ
13 Ⓐ Ⓑ Ⓒ Ⓓ	33 Ⓐ Ⓑ Ⓒ Ⓓ	53 Ⓐ Ⓑ Ⓒ Ⓓ	73 Ⓐ Ⓑ Ⓒ Ⓓ
14 Ⓕ Ⓖ Ⓗ Ⓙ	34 Ⓕ Ⓖ Ⓗ Ⓙ	54 Ⓕ Ⓖ Ⓗ Ⓙ	74 Ⓕ Ⓖ Ⓗ Ⓙ
15 Ⓐ Ⓑ Ⓒ Ⓓ	35 Ⓐ Ⓑ Ⓒ Ⓓ	55 Ⓐ Ⓑ Ⓒ Ⓓ	75 Ⓐ Ⓑ Ⓒ Ⓓ
16 Ⓕ Ⓖ Ⓗ Ⓙ	36 Ⓕ Ⓖ Ⓗ Ⓙ	56 Ⓕ Ⓖ Ⓗ Ⓙ	
17 Ⓐ Ⓑ Ⓒ Ⓓ	37 Ⓐ Ⓑ Ⓒ Ⓓ	57 Ⓐ Ⓑ Ⓒ Ⓓ	
18 Ⓕ Ⓖ Ⓗ Ⓙ	38 Ⓕ Ⓖ Ⓗ Ⓙ	58 Ⓕ Ⓖ Ⓗ Ⓙ	
19 Ⓐ Ⓑ Ⓒ Ⓓ	39 Ⓐ Ⓑ Ⓒ Ⓓ	59 Ⓐ Ⓑ Ⓒ Ⓓ	
20 Ⓕ Ⓖ Ⓗ Ⓙ	40 Ⓕ Ⓖ Ⓗ Ⓙ	60 Ⓕ Ⓖ Ⓗ Ⓙ	

MATHEMATICS

1 Ⓐ Ⓑ Ⓒ Ⓓ Ⓔ	16 Ⓕ Ⓖ Ⓗ Ⓙ Ⓚ	31 Ⓐ Ⓑ Ⓒ Ⓓ Ⓔ	46 Ⓕ Ⓖ Ⓗ Ⓙ Ⓚ
2 Ⓕ Ⓖ Ⓗ Ⓙ Ⓚ	17 Ⓐ Ⓑ Ⓒ Ⓓ Ⓔ	32 Ⓕ Ⓖ Ⓗ Ⓙ Ⓚ	47 Ⓐ Ⓑ Ⓒ Ⓓ Ⓔ
3 Ⓐ Ⓑ Ⓒ Ⓓ Ⓔ	18 Ⓕ Ⓖ Ⓗ Ⓙ Ⓚ	33 Ⓐ Ⓑ Ⓒ Ⓓ Ⓔ	48 Ⓕ Ⓖ Ⓗ Ⓙ Ⓚ
4 Ⓕ Ⓖ Ⓗ Ⓙ Ⓚ	19 Ⓐ Ⓑ Ⓒ Ⓓ Ⓔ	34 Ⓕ Ⓖ Ⓗ Ⓙ Ⓚ	49 Ⓐ Ⓑ Ⓒ Ⓓ Ⓔ
5 Ⓐ Ⓑ Ⓒ Ⓓ Ⓔ	20 Ⓕ Ⓖ Ⓗ Ⓙ Ⓚ	35 Ⓐ Ⓑ Ⓒ Ⓓ Ⓔ	50 Ⓕ Ⓖ Ⓗ Ⓙ Ⓚ
6 Ⓕ Ⓖ Ⓗ Ⓙ Ⓚ	21 Ⓐ Ⓑ Ⓒ Ⓓ Ⓔ	36 Ⓕ Ⓖ Ⓗ Ⓙ Ⓚ	51 Ⓐ Ⓑ Ⓒ Ⓓ Ⓔ
7 Ⓐ Ⓑ Ⓒ Ⓓ Ⓔ	22 Ⓕ Ⓖ Ⓗ Ⓙ Ⓚ	37 Ⓐ Ⓑ Ⓒ Ⓓ Ⓔ	52 Ⓕ Ⓖ Ⓗ Ⓙ Ⓚ
8 Ⓕ Ⓖ Ⓗ Ⓙ Ⓚ	23 Ⓐ Ⓑ Ⓒ Ⓓ Ⓔ	38 Ⓕ Ⓖ Ⓗ Ⓙ Ⓚ	53 Ⓐ Ⓑ Ⓒ Ⓓ Ⓔ
9 Ⓐ Ⓑ Ⓒ Ⓓ Ⓔ	24 Ⓕ Ⓖ Ⓗ Ⓙ Ⓚ	39 Ⓐ Ⓑ Ⓒ Ⓓ Ⓔ	54 Ⓕ Ⓖ Ⓗ Ⓙ Ⓚ
10 Ⓕ Ⓖ Ⓗ Ⓙ Ⓚ	25 Ⓐ Ⓑ Ⓒ Ⓓ Ⓔ	40 Ⓕ Ⓖ Ⓗ Ⓙ Ⓚ	55 Ⓐ Ⓑ Ⓒ Ⓓ Ⓔ
11 Ⓐ Ⓑ Ⓒ Ⓓ Ⓔ	26 Ⓕ Ⓖ Ⓗ Ⓙ Ⓚ	41 Ⓐ Ⓑ Ⓒ Ⓓ Ⓔ	56 Ⓕ Ⓖ Ⓗ Ⓙ Ⓚ
12 Ⓕ Ⓖ Ⓗ Ⓙ Ⓚ	27 Ⓐ Ⓑ Ⓒ Ⓓ Ⓔ	42 Ⓕ Ⓖ Ⓗ Ⓙ Ⓚ	57 Ⓐ Ⓑ Ⓒ Ⓓ Ⓔ
13 Ⓐ Ⓑ Ⓒ Ⓓ Ⓔ	28 Ⓕ Ⓖ Ⓗ Ⓙ Ⓚ	43 Ⓐ Ⓑ Ⓒ Ⓓ Ⓔ	58 Ⓕ Ⓖ Ⓗ Ⓙ Ⓚ
14 Ⓕ Ⓖ Ⓗ Ⓙ Ⓚ	29 Ⓐ Ⓑ Ⓒ Ⓓ Ⓔ	44 Ⓕ Ⓖ Ⓗ Ⓙ Ⓚ	59 Ⓐ Ⓑ Ⓒ Ⓓ Ⓔ
15 Ⓐ Ⓑ Ⓒ Ⓓ Ⓔ	30 Ⓕ Ⓖ Ⓗ Ⓙ Ⓚ	45 Ⓐ Ⓑ Ⓒ Ⓓ Ⓔ	60 Ⓕ Ⓖ Ⓗ Ⓙ Ⓚ

READING

1 Ⓐ Ⓑ Ⓒ Ⓓ	11 Ⓐ Ⓑ Ⓒ Ⓓ	21 Ⓐ Ⓑ Ⓒ Ⓓ	31 Ⓐ Ⓑ Ⓒ Ⓓ
2 Ⓕ Ⓖ Ⓗ Ⓙ	12 Ⓕ Ⓖ Ⓗ Ⓙ	22 Ⓕ Ⓖ Ⓗ Ⓙ	32 Ⓕ Ⓖ Ⓗ Ⓙ
3 Ⓐ Ⓑ Ⓒ Ⓓ	13 Ⓐ Ⓑ Ⓒ Ⓓ	23 Ⓐ Ⓑ Ⓒ Ⓓ	33 Ⓐ Ⓑ Ⓒ Ⓓ
4 Ⓕ Ⓖ Ⓗ Ⓙ	14 Ⓕ Ⓖ Ⓗ Ⓙ	24 Ⓕ Ⓖ Ⓗ Ⓙ	34 Ⓕ Ⓖ Ⓗ Ⓙ
5 Ⓐ Ⓑ Ⓒ Ⓓ	15 Ⓐ Ⓑ Ⓒ Ⓓ	25 Ⓐ Ⓑ Ⓒ Ⓓ	35 Ⓐ Ⓑ Ⓒ Ⓓ
6 Ⓕ Ⓖ Ⓗ Ⓙ	16 Ⓕ Ⓖ Ⓗ Ⓙ	26 Ⓕ Ⓖ Ⓗ Ⓙ	36 Ⓕ Ⓖ Ⓗ Ⓙ
7 Ⓐ Ⓑ Ⓒ Ⓓ	17 Ⓐ Ⓑ Ⓒ Ⓓ	27 Ⓐ Ⓑ Ⓒ Ⓓ	37 Ⓐ Ⓑ Ⓒ Ⓓ
8 Ⓕ Ⓖ Ⓗ Ⓙ	18 Ⓕ Ⓖ Ⓗ Ⓙ	28 Ⓕ Ⓖ Ⓗ Ⓙ	38 Ⓕ Ⓖ Ⓗ Ⓙ
9 Ⓐ Ⓑ Ⓒ Ⓓ	19 Ⓐ Ⓑ Ⓒ Ⓓ	29 Ⓐ Ⓑ Ⓒ Ⓓ	39 Ⓐ Ⓑ Ⓒ Ⓓ
10 Ⓕ Ⓖ Ⓗ Ⓙ	20 Ⓕ Ⓖ Ⓗ Ⓙ	30 Ⓕ Ⓖ Ⓗ Ⓙ	40 Ⓕ Ⓖ Ⓗ Ⓙ

SCIENCE

1 Ⓐ Ⓑ Ⓒ Ⓓ	11 Ⓐ Ⓑ Ⓒ Ⓓ	21 Ⓐ Ⓑ Ⓒ Ⓓ	31 Ⓐ Ⓑ Ⓒ Ⓓ
2 Ⓕ Ⓖ Ⓗ Ⓙ	12 Ⓕ Ⓖ Ⓗ Ⓙ	22 Ⓕ Ⓖ Ⓗ Ⓙ	32 Ⓕ Ⓖ Ⓗ Ⓙ
3 Ⓐ Ⓑ Ⓒ Ⓓ	13 Ⓐ Ⓑ Ⓒ Ⓓ	23 Ⓐ Ⓑ Ⓒ Ⓓ	33 Ⓐ Ⓑ Ⓒ Ⓓ
4 Ⓕ Ⓖ Ⓗ Ⓙ	14 Ⓕ Ⓖ Ⓗ Ⓙ	24 Ⓕ Ⓖ Ⓗ Ⓙ	34 Ⓕ Ⓖ Ⓗ Ⓙ
5 Ⓐ Ⓑ Ⓒ Ⓓ	15 Ⓐ Ⓑ Ⓒ Ⓓ	25 Ⓐ Ⓑ Ⓒ Ⓓ	35 Ⓐ Ⓑ Ⓒ Ⓓ
6 Ⓕ Ⓖ Ⓗ Ⓙ	16 Ⓕ Ⓖ Ⓗ Ⓙ	26 Ⓕ Ⓖ Ⓗ Ⓙ	36 Ⓕ Ⓖ Ⓗ Ⓙ
7 Ⓐ Ⓑ Ⓒ Ⓓ	17 Ⓐ Ⓑ Ⓒ Ⓓ	27 Ⓐ Ⓑ Ⓒ Ⓓ	37 Ⓐ Ⓑ Ⓒ Ⓓ
8 Ⓕ Ⓖ Ⓗ Ⓙ	18 Ⓕ Ⓖ Ⓗ Ⓙ	28 Ⓕ Ⓖ Ⓗ Ⓙ	38 Ⓕ Ⓖ Ⓗ Ⓙ
9 Ⓐ Ⓑ Ⓒ Ⓓ	19 Ⓐ Ⓑ Ⓒ Ⓓ	29 Ⓐ Ⓑ Ⓒ Ⓓ	39 Ⓐ Ⓑ Ⓒ Ⓓ
10 Ⓕ Ⓖ Ⓗ Ⓙ	20 Ⓕ Ⓖ Ⓗ Ⓙ	30 Ⓕ Ⓖ Ⓗ Ⓙ	40 Ⓕ Ⓖ Ⓗ Ⓙ

RAW SCORES | **SCALE SCORES** | DATE TAKEN:

ENGLISH _____ | ENGLISH _____

MATHEMATICS _____ | MATHEMATICS _____ | ENGLISH/WRITING _____

READING _____ | READING _____

SCIENCE _____ | SCIENCE _____

_____ **COMPOSITE SCORE**

Refer to the Scoring Worksheet on page 482 for help in determining your Raw and Scale Scores.

Begin WRITING TEST here.

If you need more space, please continue on the next page.

1

WRITING TEST

If you need more space, please continue on the back of this page.

2

WRITING TEST

If you need more space, please continue on the next page.

3

Cut Here

WRITING TEST

_____

_____

_____

_____

_____

_____

_____

_____

_____

_____

_____

_____

_____

_____

_____

_____

_____

_____

_____

_____

_____

_____

_____

_____

_____

_____

_____

_____

STOP here with the Writing Test.

1 ■ ■ ■ ■ ■ ■ ■ ■ ■ 1

ENGLISH TEST

45 Minutes—75 Questions

DIRECTIONS: In the passages that follow, some words and phrases are underlined and numbered. In the answer column, you will find alternatives for the words and phrases that are underlined. Choose the alternative that you think is best, and fill in the corresponding bubble on your answer sheet. If you think that the original version is best, choose "NO CHANGE," which will always be either answer choice A or F. You will also find questions about a particular section of the passage, or about the entire passage. These questions will be identified either by an underlined portion or by a number in a box. Look for the answer that clearly expresses the idea, is consistent with the style and tone of the passage, and makes the correct use of standard written English. Read the passage through once before answering the questions. For some questions, you should read beyond the indicated portion before you answer.

PASSAGE I

> The following paragraphs may or may not be in the most logical order. You may be asked questions about the logical order of the paragraphs, as well as where to place sentences logically within any given paragraph.

The Reappearance of the Ivory-billed Woodpecker

[1]

In the spring of 1999, a university student—also an avid
        $\overline{}$
            1
hunter—stalked wild turkeys in the woods of Louisiana's

Pearl River Wildlife Management Area. Turkey license in

hand, he did not expect to discover a far more rarer bird,
                                   $\overline{}$
                                                  2
one that had been declared extinct in 1994. The student's
$\overline{}$
        2
report of seeing a pair of ivory-billed woodpeckers

eventually leading to an exhaustive search for the
$\overline{}$
          3
supposedly lost species in the vast 35,000-acre wilderness.

[2]

Extensive logging and unregulated hunting in the 1800s

decimated the population of the ivory-billed woodpecker

in the native habitat of the Southeastern United States.
  $\overline{}$
  4

By the 1920s, the species, which is the ivory-billed
                  $\overline{}$
                            5
woodpecker, had been given up as extinct. By 1938,
$\overline{}$
        5
however, around 20 individuals were known to exist in an

1. **A.** NO CHANGE
   B. spring, of 1999, a university
   C. spring of 1999 a university
   D. spring of 1999; a university

2. **F.** NO CHANGE
   G. a bird that was even more rare, and also one that was
   H. a far more rare bird that had been
   J. a bird, which was far rarer, and that had been

3. **A.** NO CHANGE
   B. would eventually lead
   C. was leading eventually
   D. was eventually lead

4. **F.** NO CHANGE
   G. their
   H. its
   J. a

5. **A.** NO CHANGE
   B. the species, ivory-billed woodpeckers
   C. ivory-billed woodpeckers, the species,
   D. the species

GO ON TO THE NEXT PAGE.

1 ■ ■ ■ ■ ■ ■ ■ ■ ■ 1

isolated tract of old-growth forest in Louisiana. Despite

pleas from four state governments and the National

Audubon Society, logging began in the forest, and by 1944
                                    6
the last known ivory-billed woodpecker had disappeared

from the ruined habitat. The only evidence of the

species survival before its rediscovery at the end of the
        7
century was an unconfirmed recording of its distinctive

call made in Texas in 1967.

[3]

[1] New hope of finding an ivory-billed woodpecker

arose from the 1999 sighting. [2] This hope led a team
                                                8
of biologists to conduct an extensive search for the
                                    8
elusive bird in 2002. [3] Evidence of active woodpeckers
        8
was found in markings and large cavities in tree

trunks. [4] They made a sound recording originally

believed to be the distinctive double-tap sound of the

elusive bird; but determined it later it was likely the
        9
echoes from a gunshot. [5] In the end, existence of the

ivory-billed woodpecker could not be proven. [10]

[4]

[1] Subsequent deployment of remote listening devices

and motion-sensing cameras finally gave scientists the

evidence they needed to confirm existence of the

bird, so then in 2004, a large woodpecker was videotaped.
        11

[2] Its wings, flight, and plumage were cited as evidence
          12
that the bird was indeed an ivory-billed woodpecker.

[3] Furthermore, the Arkansas researchers noted evidence

of active woodpeckers in markings on trees, and they also

documented several bird sightings.

6. **F.** NO CHANGE
   G. Society, logging began in the forest; and
   H. Society, logging began, in the forest and,
   J. Society logging, began, in the forest, and

7. **A.** NO CHANGE
   B. species' survival
   C. survival of the species
   D. surviving species'

8. Which of the alternatives best provides new, specific information about the search for the ivory-billed woodpecker?
   F. NO CHANGE
   G. A group of biologists searched the woods where the ivory-billed woodpecker had been spotted for almost a month in 2002.
   H. After hearing of the sighting in 1999, Louisiana State University's biologists spent time searching for the ivory-billed woodpecker.
   J. In 2002, biologists from Louisiana State University spent nearly a month in the Pearl River Wildlife Management Area searching for the bird.

9. **A.** NO CHANGE
   B. bird, but later determined
   C. bird but determined later that
   D. bird. Later determined,

10. Which of the following sequences of sentences will make Paragraph 3 most logical?
    F. NO CHANGE
    G. 1, 2, 5, 3, 4
    H. 2, 1, 5, 3, 4
    J. 1, 2, 4, 3, 5

11. **A.** NO CHANGE
    B. bird, in 2004
    C. bird. In 2004
    D. bird. It was in 2004

12. **F.** NO CHANGE
    G. wings, flight and plumage
    H. wings flight and plumage
    J. wings, flight, and plumage,

GO ON TO THE NEXT PAGE.

1 ■ ■ ■ ■ ■ ■ ■ ■ 1

[4] <u>Fearing birdwatchers flooding</u>, further searches were
₁₃
conducted in secret, as was the rush by the privately funded
Nature Conservancy to purchase potential woodpecker
habitat in the Arkansas wilderness. [5] Additional audio
evidence was gathered to support the claim of the bird's
existence, and in 2005, a detailed report of the findings
was published in a major scientific journal. [6] While there
remain skeptics, the ornithology community now generally
<u>accepted</u> the existence of the ivory-billed woodpecker.
₁₄
[7] As such, it is no longer considered extinct, but rather
extremely endangered.

13. A. NO CHANGE
   B. The birdwatchers flooding was a fear
   C. Fearing a flood of birdwatchers
   D. The fear of flooding birdwatchers

14. F. NO CHANGE
   G. accepts
   H. is accepting of
   J. accepting

15. The writer wants to add the following sentence to Paragraph 4:

   Approximately 15 sightings were reported in early 2004, all possibly of the same bird.

   This sentence would most logically be placed:
   A. before Sentence 1.
   B. before Sentence 2.
   C. after Sentence 2.
   D. after Sentence 3.

PASSAGE II

A Medical Journal

Working as an editor for my university's medical
journal is very <u>demanding, and my</u> fellow editors and
₁₆

<u>I spent</u> long hours year-round maintaining the various parts
₁₇
of the publication.

<u>In late summer,</u> the editorial board reconvenes in
₁₈
anticipation of the new fall semester. We develop a formal

16. Which of the following alternatives would NOT be an acceptable way to write the sentence?
   F. NO CHANGE
   G. demanding, my
   H. demanding. My
   J. demanding; my

17. A. NO CHANGE
   B. I am spending
   C. I, spending
   D. I spend

18. F. NO CHANGE
   G. In late summer, consequently, the
   H. However, in late summer the
   J. Later in the summer, as a result, the

GO ON TO THE NEXT PAGE.

1 ■ ■ ■ ■ ■ ■ ■ ■ 1

call for papers <u>nationwide research institutions are</u>
                                    19
<u>distributed to</u>, from which we gather a wide variety of
      19
papers and reports dealing with all areas of medicine,

human biology, and public health. <u>Researchers, and</u>
                                                        20
<u>authors,</u> are notified of our calls for papers through our
    20
web site, e-mail list, and the flyers that we mail.

   <u>They all receive submissions</u> by the end of October
                    21
every year. Editors read each work carefully over the

following <u>month and submit</u> their critiques to the other
                      22
members of the board.

   <u>They always get</u> as many bad papers as good ones.
          23

[24] Those we have trouble deciphering are

<u>immediately declining</u>, and if the formatting is poor,
          25
we insist on a revised copy from the author. The editors

agree that each paper must reflect the professional

standards of the journal and the medical community.

<u>For instance,</u> they choose those works that they feel
      26
provide the most beneficial information for the journal's

readers. Despite this policy, disagreements can still occur.

19. **A.** NO CHANGE
    B. to which nationwide research institutions we distribute
    C. that we distribute to research institutions nationwide
    D. that are distributing nationwide to research institutions

20. **F.** NO CHANGE
    G. Researchers, and authors
    H. Researchers and authors
    J. Researchers and authors,

21. **A.** NO CHANGE
    B. All submissions we receive
    C. All the submissions received
    D. We receive all submissions

22. **F.** NO CHANGE
    G. month, and are submitting
    H. month; submitting
    J. month and then they submit

23. **A.** NO CHANGE
    B. There always are either
    C. Always, they get
    D. There are always

24. At this point, the writer is considering adding the following sentence:

    Some of the papers even come hand-written, which makes it hard to tell the good from the bad.

    Would this be a logical and relevant addition to the essay?
    F. Yes, because it serves to establish the tone for the remainder of the passage.
    G. Yes, because it provides additional details regarding the journal submissions.
    H. No, because the passage does not discuss the relevance of the form of the submitted papers.
    J. No, because it is ambiguous whether hand-writing a paper is a good or bad thing.

25. **A.** NO CHANGE
    B. immediately declined
    C. declining immediately
    D. immediate declined

26. **F.** NO CHANGE
    G. In fact,
    H. Moreover,
    J. However,

GO ON TO THE NEXT PAGE.

1 ■ ■ ■ ■ ■ ■ ■ ■ ■ **1**

With passion, editors argue often for their choices.
                              27

By January, we have enough content to fill three

monthly issues of the journal. Once we finalize the

layout, we send all three issues to the print shop. When the
        28

pallet-loads of journals arrive in our office, we hire some

undergraduates to address, sort, and bundle them for

mailing. In the intervening time, the editorial board meets
                                                    29

again to plan the next three issues and to call for more

papers. The sixth and final issue of the year appears in

June, and once all work is done, we take off to enjoy a few

months of vacation, well-earned.
                  30

27. A. NO CHANGE
B. Passionately and fervently, editors often argue for their choices.
C. Editors often argue passionately for their choices.
D. For their choices, editors argue passionately and often.

28. F. NO CHANGE
G. layout, we're sending
H. layout we send
J. layout we just send

29. A. NO CHANGE
B. meet
C. meeting
D. has been meeting

30. F. NO CHANGE
G. well-earned vacation.
H. vacation, that is well-earned.
J. vacation earned well.

PASSAGE III

> The following paragraphs may or may not be in the most logical order. You may be asked questions about the logical order of the paragraphs, as well as where to place sentences logically within any given paragraph.

Maria Montessori's Method

[1]

At the end of the 19th century, Maria Montessori

became Italys' first modern woman physician. Early in her
          31

career, she struggled to advance by the male-dominated
                              32

profession. As a member of the University of Rome

faculty, she was assigned to the city's insane asylums to

experiment with the patients' capacity to learn: a task
                                          33

considered menial by medical professionals at the time.

31. A. NO CHANGE
B. the Italian
C. Italys
D. Italy's

32. F. NO CHANGE
G. for a
H. in the
J. due to their

33. A. NO CHANGE
B. learn, a
C. learn a
D. learn

GO ON TO THE NEXT PAGE.

1 ■ ■ ■ ■ ■ ■ ■ ■ 1

Although her education was in the science of the human
body, her interaction with mentally-disabled children drew
$\overline{34}$
her to study the processes of the mind and, specifically,

how children learn. By 1906, she had resigned from the
$\overline{35}$
university to pursue a career in child education.

[2]

[1] Her observation of these children inspired her life's
work in teaching and the pursuit of progressive educational
restructuring. [2] With the first children that were
$\overline{36}$
working class, numbering sixty, Montessori established a
$\overline{36}$
"children's house" in Rome to foster an environment
ideally suited for child development. [3] Her efforts led her
students—even those with supposed learning
disabilities—to excel at standardized examinations. [4] In
the children's house, Montessori realized how
ready children learn from their environment. [38]
$\overline{37}$

[3]

At its core, the Montessori Method is a theory of
$\overline{39}$

child development. Comparison of a child's development
$\overline{39}$ $\overline{40}$
to universal standards and norms is discouraged, since it is

34. At this point, the writer would like to provide specific information about Montessori's education. Which alternative does that best?
 F. NO CHANGE
 G. anatomy and physiology
 H. the way the human body works
 J. science

35. A. NO CHANGE
 B. the method by which children learn
 C. children learning
 D. a child's ways to learn

36. F. NO CHANGE
 G. She got her first sixty children that were working-class, and
 H. Starting with sixty working-class children,
 J. She had sixty working-class children first, so

37. A. NO CHANGE
 B. children, readily
 C. children ready
 D. readily children

38. For the sake of logic and coherence, Sentence 1 should be placed:
 F. where it is now.
 G. after Sentence 2.
 H. after Sentence 3.
 J. after Sentence 4.

39. At this point, the writer would like to provide the reader with a more specific definition of the Montessori Method. Assuming all are true, which of the following does that best?
 A. NO CHANGE
 B. a philosophy of teaching.
 C. a means of fostering development and learning in children.
 D. a style of teaching utilized in many school districts.

40. F. NO CHANGE
 G. childs' development
 H. developing child
 J. child that is developing

GO ON TO THE NEXT PAGE.

1 ■ ■ ■ ■ ■ ■ ■ ■ 1

believed that children naturally develop in <u>different ways, and acquire skills,</u> at different times. Acknowledging
₄₁

this, a Montessori educator closely <u>observed</u> the child and
₄₂
provides him or her with the tools necessary for independent learning. Adults avoid giving criticism for mistakes and rewards for successes. The goal of these steps is to ease the child into an environment of learning without fear. Self-learning and self-correction are the fundamental processes of the Montessori Method, <u>considering</u> Maria Montessori showed will foster a lifelong
₄₃
love of learning and joy in the pursuit of one's goals.

[4]

Today, children are taught with the Montessori Method in <u>schools both public and private</u> in the United States and
₄₄
many countries around the world. With increasing pressure on schools to provide quality education to a growing population, Montessori's visionary ideas of teaching self-reliance and love of learning continue to gain popularity. [45]

41. A. NO CHANGE
  B. different ways and acquire skills
  C. different ways, and acquire, skills
  D. different ways; and acquire skills

42. F. NO CHANGE
  G. is observing
  H. observes
  J. can observe

43. A. NO CHANGE
  B. though
  C. despite
  D. which

44. F. NO CHANGE
  G. schools, both public, and private,
  H. both public and private schools
  J. public schools and private schools both,

45. Suppose the writer were to eliminate Paragraph 4. This omission would cause the essay as a whole to lose primarily:
  A. relevant details about the current development and utilization of Montessori education.
  B. irrelevant details about the past development and utilization of Montessori education.
  C. information that distracts from the essay's primarily biographical tone.
  D. a conclusion that reiterates the main purpose of the passage.

GO ON TO THE NEXT PAGE.

1 ■ ■ ■ ■ ■ ■ ■ ■ 1

PASSAGE IV

> The following paragraphs may or may not be in the most logical order. You may be asked questions about the logical order of the paragraphs, as well as where to place sentences logically within any given paragraph.

The Paris Metro

[1]

If you ever travel to Europe, you will likely want to visit the monuments and museums of Paris, one of the most beautiful cities in the world. You immerse yourself in art,
46
architecture, and the history of Western civilization.

The cultural treasures of France's capital are awe-inspiring,
47
but the most amazing thing about visiting Paris is the ease with which you can tour the city using the extensive subway network, in which the French call the
48
Métropolitain, or simply the Metro.

[2]

The Metro was constructed in anticipation of the 1900 World Fair. Additional tunnels were excavated over the following three decades making the Metro one of the
49
world's most extensive and most patronized subway systems. Second in size only to the New York City subway, the Metros stations throughout Paris.
50

[51] Paris does have buses and taxis, but nothing is faster or more convenient than catching a subway train. Not just a useful resource for Parisians, the Metro is ideal for

46. **F.** NO CHANGE
    G. You will
    H. You were going to
    J. OMIT the underlined portion.

47. **A.** NO CHANGE
    B. France's capital has cultural treasures, they are awe-inspiring
    C. The awe-inspiring treasures of France's capital
    D. The treasures of France's capital that inspire awe

48. **F.** NO CHANGE
    G. network that being which
    H. network, what
    J. network;

49. **A.** NO CHANGE
    B. decades—making
    C. decades, making
    D. decades; making

50. **F.** NO CHANGE
    G. Metros'
    H. Metro is
    J. Metro has

51. At this point in the paragraph, the writer wishes to emphasize the expansiveness of the Metro system and the coverage that it provides. Which of the following sentences does that best?
    A. Each station serves a multitude of travelers.
    B. Sometimes, you have to walk as far as nine or ten blocks to get to the nearest Metro station.
    C. If you cannot read or understand French, you might have a hard time navigating yourself from station to station.
    D. You cannot walk anywhere along the streets of Paris without encountering a staircase that descends to a Metro station.

GO ON TO THE NEXT PAGE.

1 ■ ■ ■ ■ ■ ■ ■ ■ **1**

tourist travel (no matter what country you are from!).
                        _____
                                    52
All major sites in the city have a nearby station, most

named by the attraction they are near. For example, the
_____
   53
Louvre-Rivoli Station drops you off next door to the

famous museum, and the Pont Neuf Station is at the foot of

the famous bridge across the River Seine. I love the feeling

of going underground at one attraction and coming back to
        _____
                           54
the surface in another famous place. The Metro is also fast,

with a train arriving at the station every few minutes.

Best of all, tourists can buy a day pass for unlimited

Metro trips, or a single ticket if just one trip is needed.

Swiping your ticket once and you may enter the network,
_____
   55
including all transfers between lines. [56]

[3]

I would much rather use the Metro than rent a car

in Paris. Beyond the stresses of city driving, and parking,
                                    _____
                                            57
and the high cost of fuel in Europe, the Metro keeps you
_____
   57
from ever getting lost. You can wander to your heart's

content, discovering the corners of Paris tourists rarely see.

Metro travel couldn't be easier!

[4]

People are accustomed generally to making
       _____
                  58
transportation arrangements ahead of time when traveling

to a new place. What I admire about the Paris Metro is the

52. F. NO CHANGE
G. (your country of origin aside)
H. (even if you are not French!)
J. OMIT the underlined portion.

53. A. NO CHANGE
B. named for
C. naming
D. names are

54. F. NO CHANGE
G. underground at one attraction, coming up
H. underground at one attraction, and come
J. underground at one attraction, and coming

55. A. NO CHANGE
B. You swiped
C. Swipe
D. You will swipe

56. The writer wishes to add a relevant example to Paragraph 2 without straying from the purpose of informing the reader as to how advantageous using the Metro is. Which of the following alternatives does that best?
F. I once made a trip from the end of one line to the end of another, with three transfers in between. I can't imagine how expensive such a taxi ride would have been!
G. I always purchase a day pass for unlimited trips. When I am in Paris, I want to cram as much sightseeing as possible into my schedule.
H. I once accidentally got on a train going the wrong direction, but I simply transferred trains and was on my way to the Notre Dame.
J. If you buy an unlimited day pass, be careful not to lose it. If you do, you will be forced to purchase a whole new ticket!

57. A. NO CHANGE
B. driving parking and the
C. driving, parking and the
D. driving, parking, and the

58. F. NO CHANGE
G. are generally accustomed
H. generally can be accustomed
J. generally accustom

GO ON TO THE NEXT PAGE.

1 ■ ■ ■ ■ ■ ■ ■ ■ **1**

incredible freedom of movement that <u>it provides.</u>
                                        59

As soon as you arrive at the airport, you can buy a pass

and head underground. The monuments and museums of

Paris are amazing, but I am equally impressed by how easy

and cheap it is to travel between them beneath the city.

PASSAGE V
Peat: an Ancient and Modern Fuel

For the country of Ireland, peat is

<u>an abundant and plentiful</u> natural resource that has been
            61
heating stoves and homes since the 8th century. The soft

organic material lies in huge <u>bogs. Across</u> 17 percent of
                                  62
the Irish countryside. The plant, fungus, and animal

detritus that composes peat is kept from fully decomposing

<u>among</u> the acidic environment of these marshlands. When
  63

peat is <u>harvested, it</u> can be dried and compressed to form a
           64
solid fuel. Ancient inhabitants of Ireland relied on this

combustible material in areas of the island where trees

were scarce. Even today, stacks of freshly dug peat can be

seen <u>dryer</u> in rural Irish villages. Peat remains as useful as
       65

59. A. NO CHANGE
B. provided by the Paris Metro.
C. the Paris Metro provides.
D. providing it.

> Question 60 asks about the preceding passage as a whole.

60. The writer wishes to include the following sentence in the essay:

> When you've had your fill, you can simply stride right into the nearest Metro station, look at the map, and head straight for home.

This sentence will fit most smoothly and logically into Paragraph:
F. 1, before the last sentence.
G. 2, after the last sentence.
H. 3, before the last sentence.
J. 4, before the last sentence.

61. A. NO CHANGE
B. a plentifully abundant
C. an abundant
D. an abundant plentifully

62. F. NO CHANGE
G. bogs across
H. bogs—across
J. bogs: across

63. A. NO CHANGE
B. for
C. in
D. with

64. F. NO CHANGE
G. harvested. It
H. harvested; it
J. harvested it

65. A. NO CHANGE
B. drying
C. as dry
D. dry

GO ON TO THE NEXT PAGE.

1 ■ ■ ■ ■ ■ ■ ■ ■ **1**

ever for heat production and soil enrichment. <u>Using</u>
₆₆
<u>millions of stacks of dried peat each year,</u> Ireland still
₆₆
generates 13 percent of its power from peat-fired turbines.

Prior to the advent of heavy farming machinery, peat
farmers plowed trenches throughout a virgin bog to drain
the peat, <u>which consist of about</u> 95-percent water.
₆₇
Following the several years that it took for the peat to dry
sufficiently, farmers would undertake the arduous task of
hand-carving peat blocks from the earth. Today, the Irish
peat industry is overseen by the state-owned company
Bord Na <u>Móna. Which</u> produces over four million metric
₆₈
tons of peat every year. About three-quarters is used for

domestic energy <u>production, while the remainder is</u>
₆₉
processed for horticultural applications.

Modern peat harvesting is a four-stage process. First,
large tractors mill a thin layer of peat over a large area of
bog. Over the next several days, <u>a machine called a harrow</u>
₇₀
passes over the milled peat, turning the crop several times
to expedite drying. During the next step, a ridging machine
passes over the dry peat, channeling it into straight rows
ready for collection. Finally, the harvester <u>past</u> its large
₇₁

vacuum over the ridges, <u>drawing the peat</u> into a large
₇₂
collection bin. The peat is then taken to processing
facilities where it is further dried for briquette production
or use in power plants.

66. Which of the following alternatives provides the contrast most appropriate and relevant to the essay?
 F. NO CHANGE
 G. Although the majority of its use is in smaller towns,
 H. Even though no other countries use peat as a heat source,
 J. In spite of modern coal, natural gas, and hydro-electric technologies,

67. A. NO CHANGE
 B. which consisted of about
 C. that is about
 D. consistent with about

68. F. NO CHANGE
 G. Móna; which
 H. Móna which
 J. Móna, which

69. Which of the following is NOT an acceptable way to write this sentence?
 A. production; the remainder
 B. production. The remainder
 C. production, the remainder
 D. production, and the remainder

70. F. NO CHANGE
 G. a harrow
 H. a machine that they call a harrow
 J. a harrow, the machine type used,

71. A. NO CHANGE
 B. passed
 C. passing
 D. passes

72. F. NO CHANGE
 G. the harvester draws the peat
 H. the peat is drawn by the harvester
 J. and peat draws

GO ON TO THE NEXT PAGE.

With <u>the</u> history of abundance and renewability as
  73

a fuel and nutrient source, <u>peat remains an essential</u>
                                                74

<u>part of Irish culture.</u>
        74

73. **A.** NO CHANGE
    B. it's
    C. its
    D. OMIT the underlined portion.

74. The writer wants to link the essay's opening and concluding sentences. Which one of the following alternatives to the underlined portion most successfully achieves this effect?
    F. peat will surely remain a part of Irish culture for generations to come.
    G. the renewability of peat will surely make peat last as a power source for a long time to come.
    H. modern peat harvesting has greatly simplified the collection and utilization of peat.
    J. peat is not as useful today as it was centuries ago.

Question 75 asks about the preceding passage as a whole.

75. Suppose the writer had been assigned to write a brief essay on the evolution of power sources. Would this essay successfully fulfill the requirements?
    A. Yes, because it describes an alternative power source not usually considered by essayists.
    B. Yes, because the writer describes clearly the historical development of peat.
    C. No, because Ireland is a historically unimportant country in the development of power sources.
    D. No, because the writer only focuses on the evolution of a single power source from one specific country.

END OF THE ENGLISH TEST.
STOP! IF YOU HAVE TIME LEFT OVER, CHECK YOUR WORK ON THIS SECTION ONLY.

2 △ △ △ △ △ △ △ △ 2

MATHEMATICS TEST

60 Minutes—60 Questions

DIRECTIONS: Solve each of the problems in the time allowed, then fill in the corresponding bubble on your answer sheet. Do not spend too much time on any one problem; skip the more difficult problems and go back to them later. You may use a calculator on this test.

For this test you should assume that figures are NOT necessarily drawn to scale, that all geometric figures lie in a plane, and that the word *line* is used to indicate a straight line.

---

1. The lowest temperature on a winter morning was −7°F. Later the same day the temperature reached a high of 21°F. By how many degrees Fahrenheit did the temperature increase?
   A. 32
   B. 28
   C. 21
   D. 14
   E. 7

2. Disregarding sales tax, how much will you save when you buy a $12.00 video that is on sale for 20% off?
   F. $0.24
   G. $0.48
   H. $1.20
   J. $2.40
   K. $3.60

3. As part of a school report on the cost of gasoline, Raquel wants to find the average cost of purchasing a gallon of regular unleaded gasoline from local gas stations. She surveys 4 stations and finds the cost per gallon of regular unleaded gas from the 4 stations to be $2.45, $2.50, $2.49, and $2.56, respectively. Using this data, what is the average cost of purchasing one gallon of regular unleaded gasoline from these 4 gas stations?
   A. $2.55
   B. $2.53
   C. $2.50
   D. $2.49
   E. $2.45

4. What is the volume, in cubic inches, of a cube whose edges each measure 5 inches in length?
   F. 15
   G. 25
   H. 50
   J. 125
   K. 500

5. If $3(a - 6) = -21$, then $a = ?$
   A. −9
   B. $-\dfrac{3}{2}$
   C. −1
   D. $\dfrac{7}{3}$
   E. 5

DO YOUR FIGURING HERE.

GO ON TO THE NEXT PAGE.

2 △ △ △ △ △ △ △ △ **2**

6. The price of a cantaloupe is directly proportional to its weight. If a cantaloupe that weighs 3.0 pounds costs $3.87, approximately how much will a 2.25-pound cantaloupe cost?
   F. $2.90
   G. $2.65
   H. $2.25
   J. $1.87
   K. $1.29

7. In the figure below, D is a point on segment AB, and the segment CD is perpendicular to the segment AB. Based on this information, which of the following conclusions can be made?

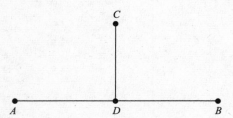

   A. Point C is equidistant from A to B.
   B. Segments AD and DB are equal in length.
   C. The segment CD bisects the segment AB.
   D. Angle CDA is larger than angle CDB.
   E. Angle CDA is congruent to angle CDB.

8. If $6x - 5 = 3x - 16$, then $x = ?$
   F. -11
   G. -7
   H. $-\dfrac{11}{3}$
   J. $\dfrac{11}{3}$
   K. 7

9. Which of the following is always equal to $y(3 - y) + 5(y - 7)$?
   A. $8y - 35$
   B. $8y - 7$
   C. $-y^2 + 8y - 7$
   D. $-y^2 + 8y - 35$
   E. $8y^3 - 35$

DO YOUR FIGURING HERE.

GO ON TO THE NEXT PAGE.

2 △ △ △ △ △ △ △ △ **2**

10. The figure below shows part of a circle whose circumference is 40. If arcs of length 4 and length s continue to alternate around the entire circle so that there are 8 arcs of each length, what is the degree measure of each of the arcs of length s?

DO YOUR FIGURING HERE.

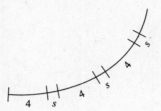

F. 6°
G. 9°
H. 12°
J. 18°
K. 36°

11. In a poll, 44 people were in favor of constructing a new high school, 58 were against it, and 8 people had no opinion. What fraction of those people polled were in favor of constructing a new high school?

A. $\dfrac{1}{9}$

B. $\dfrac{1}{5}$

C. $\dfrac{2}{5}$

D. $\dfrac{3}{5}$

E. $\dfrac{4}{9}$

12. On the line segment below, the ratio of lengths AB to BC is 1:4. What is the ratio of AB to AC?

F. 1:5
G. 1:4
H. 1:3
J. 5:1
K. Cannot be determined from the given information

13. If a board 9 feet 6 inches in length is cut into 2 equal parts, what will be the length of each part?
A. 3 feet 8 inches
B. 4 feet 5 inches
C. 4 feet 8 inches
D. 4 feet 9 inches
E. 5 feet 2 inches

GO ON TO THE NEXT PAGE.

14. The speed of a car exceeds twice the speed of a truck by 15 mph. If t is the speed of the truck, which of the following expresses the speed, in miles per hour, of the car?

  F. $t + 15$
  G. $t + 30$
  H. $t - 30$
  J. $2t + 15$
  K. $2t + 30$

15. The circle shown below has a radius of 5 meters, and the length of chord XY is 8 meters. If C marks the center of the circle, what is the length, in meters, of segment CZ?

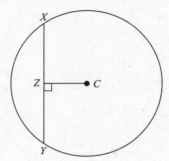

  A. $2\sqrt{3}$
  B. 3
  C. $\sqrt{13}$
  D. 5
  E. 9

16. What is the value of the expression $2x^3 - x^2 + 3x + 5$ for $x = -2$?

  F. -21
  G. -13
  H. 8
  J. 11
  K. 21

17. What is the next term after $-\dfrac{1}{3}$ in the geometric sequence $9, -3, 1, -\dfrac{1}{3}, \ldots$?

  A. $-\dfrac{1}{9}$
  B. 0
  C. $\dfrac{1}{9}$
  D. $\dfrac{1}{6}$
  E. $\dfrac{1}{3}$

DO YOUR FIGURING HERE.

GO ON TO THE NEXT PAGE.

2 △ △ △ △ △ △ △ △ △ **2**

18. On the blueprint for Roger's house, $\frac{1}{4}$ inch represents an actual length of 1 foot. What is the area, in square feet, of Roger's rectangular living room, which is 3 inches by $4\frac{1}{4}$ inches on the blueprint?

F. 51
G. 104
H. 144
J. 204
K. 244

19. If $m > 0$ and $n < 0$, then $m - n$:
   A. is always positive.
   B. is always negative.
   C. is always zero.
   D. cannot be zero, but can be any real number other than zero.
   E. can be any real number.

20. If $x + \frac{2}{3} = \frac{8}{21}$, then $x = ?$

   F. $-\frac{8}{21}$

   G. $-\frac{2}{7}$

   H. $-\frac{1}{21}$

   J. $\frac{1}{21}$

   K. $\frac{2}{7}$

21. What is the slope of the line given by the equation $3x + 4y = -12$?
   A. -3

   B. $-\frac{4}{3}$

   C. $-\frac{3}{4}$

   D. $\frac{3}{4}$

   E. 4

22. The length of a side of a square is represented as $(3x - 2)$ inches. Which of the following general expressions represents the area of the square, in square inches?
   F. $12x - 8$
   G. $9x^2 - 4$
   H. $9x^2 - 6x + 4$
   J. $9x^2 - 12x - 4$
   K. $9x^2 - 12x + 4$

23. Which of the following is a polynomial factor of $x^2 - 2x - 24$?
   A. $x - 4$
   B. $x + 4$
   C. $x + 6$
   D. $6 - x$
   E. x

DO YOUR FIGURING HERE.

GO ON TO THE NEXT PAGE.

2 △ △ △ △ △ △ △ △ **2**

DO YOUR FIGURING HERE.

24. In the equation $r = \dfrac{4}{(2 + k)}$, k represents a positive integer. As k gets larger without bound, the value of r:
 F. gets closer and closer to 4.
 G. gets closer and closer to 2.
 H. gets closer and closer to 0.
 J. remains constant.
 K. gets larger and larger.

25. While doing research on the climates of South American countries, Andrea notices that all of the temperatures are given in degrees Celsius. Because she is not as familiar with the Celsius temperature scale, it is difficult for her to know whether a location with an average temperature of 25°C has a warm climate. Fahrenheit, F, and Celsius, C, are related by the formula $F = \left(\dfrac{9}{5}\right)C + 32$.
What is the temperature in degrees Fahrenheit of the location with an average temperature of 25°C?
 A. 103
 B. 88
 C. 83
 D. 77
 E. 69

26. The length of a rectangle is 5 inches longer than its width. If the perimeter of the rectangle is 38 inches, what is the width, in inches?
 F. 5
 G. 7
 H. 12
 J. 17
 K. 28

27. What are all the solutions for x if $3x^2 - 2x - 21 = 0$?
 A. $x = -21$ only
 B. $x = -7$ or $x = 3$
 C. $x = -3$ or $x = \dfrac{7}{3}$
 D. $x = -\dfrac{7}{3}$ or $x = 3$
 E. $x = -3$ or $x = 7$

28. In Sulema's geography class, all tests count equally. So far, Sulema has taken 2 of the 3 tests in geography this marking period and earned scores of 88% and 79%, respectively. What is the minimum score Sulema needs on the third test to have a test average of 87%?
 F. 99%
 G. 94%
 H. 91%
 J. 87%
 K. 84%

29. If, a, b, and c are positive integers such that $a^b = m$ and $c^{2b} = n$, then $mn = ?$
 A. $(ac^2)^b$
 B. $(ac)^{3b}$
 C. $2(ac)^b$
 D. ac^{2b}
 E. $a^b c$

GO ON TO THE NEXT PAGE.

2 △ △ △ △ △ △ △ △ **2**

30. What is the area, in square inches, of a circle with a diameter equal to 12 inches?

F. 144
G. 36
H. 12π
J. 36π
K. 144π

DO YOUR FIGURING HERE.

31. In Mrs. Hartley's foreign language class, students must take both a written exam and an oral exam. In the past, 85% of her students passed the written exam and 70% of those who passed the written exam also passed the oral exam. Based on these figures, about how many students in a random group of 100 students would you expect to pass both exams?

A. 85
B. 78
C. 70
D. 65
E. 60

32. If $\sin A = \dfrac{3}{5}$, then which of the following could be $\tan A$?

F. $\dfrac{1}{4}$
G. $\dfrac{3}{4}$
H. 1
J. $\dfrac{4}{3}$
K. 4

33. If x is any number other than 3 and 6, then $\dfrac{(x-3)(x-6)}{(3-x)(x-6)} = ?$

A. 18
B. 1
C. 0
D. -1
E. -18

34. $\sqrt{27} + \sqrt{48} = ?$

F. $5\sqrt{3}$
G. $7\sqrt{3}$
H. $3\sqrt{3} + 3\sqrt{4}$
J. $12\sqrt{3}$
K. $3 + 4\sqrt{3}$

35. $\triangle ABC$ is similar to $\triangle XYZ$. AB is 5 inches long, BC is 8 inches long, and AC is 3 inches long. If the longest side of $\triangle XYZ$ is 20 inches long, what is the perimeter, in inches, of $\triangle XYZ$?

A. 16
B. 28
C. 40
D. 64
E. 88

GO ON TO THE NEXT PAGE.

2   2

36. Sides $\overline{AB}$, $\overline{BC}$, $\overline{CD}$, and $\overline{DA}$ of square $ABCD$ are broken up by points W, X, Y, and Z as shown below. If $\overline{AB}$ is 6 inches long, what is the area, in square inches, of the shaded region?

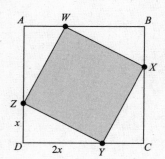

F. 36
G. 32
H. 20
J. 16
K. 12

37. In the figure below, AC is the diameter of the circle, B is a point on the circle, AB is congruent to BC, and D is the midpoint of AC. What is the degree measure of angle ABD?

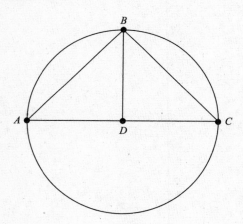

A. 30°
B. 45°
C. 60°
D. 90°
E. Cannot be determined from the given information

DO YOUR FIGURING HERE.

GO ON TO THE NEXT PAGE.

38. In the standard (x,y) coordinate plane, what are the coordinates of the midpoint of a line segment with endpoints $(-1,3)$ and $(2,5)$?

F. $(1,8)$

G. $(3,2)$

H. $\left(\dfrac{3}{2},1\right)$

J. $\left(\dfrac{1}{2},4\right)$

K. $\left(\dfrac{3}{2},4\right)$

39. Maria posted a time of 37 minutes and 29 seconds for a 5-mile running course. About how many miles per hour did she average during the run?

A. 12

B. 10

C. 8

D. 7

E. 5

40. For the 2 functions $f(x)$ and $g(x)$, tables of values are shown below. What is the value of $g(f(-1))$?

x	$f(x)$		x	$g(x)$
-3	-6		1	0
-1	2		2	3
1	-3		3	8
3	9		4	15

F. -3

G. 0

H. 2

J. 3

K. 8

41. For positive real numbers x, y, and z, which of the following expressions is equivalent to $x^{\frac{1}{2}}y^{\frac{3}{4}}z^{\frac{5}{8}}$?

A. $\sqrt[4]{xy^3z^5}$

B. $\sqrt[8]{x^2y^3z^5}$

C. $\sqrt[8]{x^4y^3z^5}$

D. $\sqrt[8]{x^4y^6z^5}$

E. $\sqrt[14]{xy^3z^5}$

DO YOUR FIGURING HERE.

GO ON TO THE NEXT PAGE.

2   △ △ **2**

42. The formula for the area of a trapezoid is $A = \frac{1}{2}h(b_1 + b_2)$, where b_1 and b_2 are the lengths of the two parallel sides and h is the height. Which of the following is an expression for b_1?

F. $\dfrac{2A}{h} - b_2$

G. $\dfrac{2A}{h + b_2}$

H. $\dfrac{2h}{A - b_2}$

J. $2(Ah - b_2)$

K. $\dfrac{1}{2}Ah + b_2$

43. The line graphed below shows the predicted gasoline use for a certain truck. Which of the following is the closest estimate of this truck's predicted rate of gasoline use, in miles per gallon?

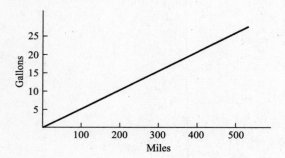

A. 25
B. 20
C. 16
D. 10
E. 8

GO ON TO THE NEXT PAGE.

2 △ △ △ △ △ △ △ △ **2**

44. The graph of $y = ax^2 + bx + c$ in the standard (x,y) coordinate plane is shown below. When $y = 0$, which of the following best describes the solution set for x?

DO YOUR FIGURING HERE.

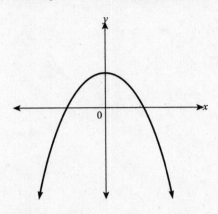

   F. 2 imaginary solutions
   G. 1 double imaginary solution
   H. 1 real and 1 imaginary solution
   J. 1 double imaginary solution
   K. 2 real solutions

45. If $|x| = x + 12$, then $x = $?
   A. -12
   B. -6
   C. 0
   D. 6
   E. 12

46. What fraction lies exactly halfway between $\frac{1}{3}$ and $\frac{1}{2}$?
   F. $\frac{3}{8}$
   G. $\frac{11}{24}$
   H. $\frac{5}{12}$
   J. $\frac{1}{6}$
   K. $\frac{2}{5}$

47. When entering information about the budget of her charity ball, Laura records an expense of $20.00. However, Laura accidentally enters the $20.00 as income instead of an expense. The balance of the charity ball budget now shows:
   A. $40 less than it should.
   B. $20 less than it should.
   C. the correct amount.
   D. $20 more than it should.
   E. $40 more than it should.

GO ON TO THE NEXT PAGE.

2 △ △ △ △ △ △ △ △ **2**

48. Rebecca is trying to schedule volunteers to help at a school carnival. There are 5 one-hour shifts to be filled by 5 different volunteers. If each shift must have one and only one volunteer, how many different arrangements can the schedule have?
    F. 5
    G. 20
    H. 25
    J. 50
    K. 120

49. In the standard (x,y) coordinate plane, what is the distance between the points $(4,-7)$ and $(-1,5)$?
    A. 5
    B. 12
    C. 13
    D. 20
    E. 26

50. A formula for the volume, V, of a right circular cylinder is $V = \pi r^2 h$, where r is the radius and h is the height. If a tanker truck has a tank as shown below with a diameter of 3 meters and a length of 10 meters and is filled with water, then the weight, in pounds, of the water cargo is: (Note: 1 cubic meter of water weighs approximately 2,205 pounds.)

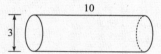

    F. less than 75,000.
    G. between 125,000 and 175,000.
    H. between 175,000 and 225,000.
    J. between 225,000 and 275,000.
    K. more than 275,000.

51. In the figure below, line AB is parallel to the base of the triangle and creates a smaller triangle inside of the original triangle. If the lengths of segments are as shown and the smaller triangle has an area of 8 cm^2, what is the area, in centimeters, of the original triangle?

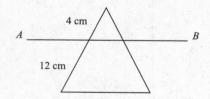

    A. 16
    B. 24
    C. 32
    D. 64
    E. 128

GO ON TO THE NEXT PAGE.

2 △ △ △ △ △ △ △ △ **2**

52. The figure below is a regular hexagon. What is the measure of one of the interior angles of the hexagon?

   F. 108°
   G. 120°
   H. 135°
   J. 150°
   K. 720°

53. It is estimated that, from the beginning of 1993 to the end of 1997, the average number of CDs bought by teenagers increased from 7 per year to 15 per year. During the same time period, the average number of video games purchased by teenagers increased from 6 per year to 18 per year. Assuming that in each case the rates or purchase are the same, in what year did teenagers buy the same average number of CDs and video games?
   A. 1993
   B. 1994
   C. 1995
   D. 1996
   E. 1997

54. If $x^2 - 45b^2 = 4xb$, what are the 2 solutions for x in terms of b?
   F. $15b$ or $-3b$
   G. $5b$ or $-9b$
   H. $15b$ or $3b$
   J. $45b$ or $-4b$
   K. $9b$ or $-5b$

55. Which of the following is (are) equivalent to the mathematical operation $a(b - c)$ for all real numbers a, b, and c?
   I. $ca - ba$
   II. $ab - ac$
   III. $(b - c)a$
   A. II only
   B. I and II only
   C. I and III only
   D. II and III only
   E. I, II and III

DO YOUR FIGURING HERE.

GO ON TO THE NEXT PAGE.

PRACTICE TEST 6 MATHEMATICS TEST

2 △ △ △ △ △ △ △ △ **2**

56. For values of x where $\sin x$, $\cos x$, and $\tan x$ are all defined, $\dfrac{(\cos x)}{(\tan x)(\sin x)} = ?$

   F. $\dfrac{\cos^2 x}{\sin^2 x}$

   G. $\tan^2 x$

   H. 1

   J. $\sin^2 x$

   K. $\sec x$

57. If a is inversely proportional to b and $a = 36$ when $b = 12$, what is the value of a when $b = 48$?

   A. 0

   B. $\dfrac{1}{3}$

   C. $\dfrac{1}{4}$

   D. 4

   E. 9

58. For which of the following values of c will there be 2 distinct real solutions to the equation $5x^2 + 16x + c = 0$?

   F. 3

   G. 12

   H. 14

   J. 15

   K. 20

59. If the volume of a cube is 64, what is the shortest distance from the center of the cube to the base of the cube?

   A. 2

   B. 4

   C. $2\sqrt{4}$

   D. $\sqrt{32}$

   E. 16

60. What is the slope of a line that is perpendicular to the line determined by the equation $5x + 8y = 17$?

   F. -3

   G. $-\dfrac{5}{8}$

   H. $\dfrac{17}{8}$

   J. $\dfrac{3}{17}$

   K. $\dfrac{8}{5}$

DO YOUR FIGURING HERE.

END OF THE MATHEMATICS TEST.
STOP! IF YOU HAVE TIME LEFT OVER, CHECK YOUR WORK ON THIS SECTION ONLY.

3   3

READING TEST

35 Minutes—40 Questions

DIRECTIONS: This test includes four passages, each followed by ten questions. Read the passages and choose the best answer to each question. After you have selected your answer, fill in the corresponding bubble on your answer sheet. You should refer to the passages as often as necessary when answering the questions.

PASSAGE I
PROSE FICTION: *Extreme Dad*

As I was growing up, each autumn brought with it the excitement of a new school year and new friends. However, I did not look forward to the inevitable question young boys pose to one another: "What does your
5 dad do?" Some people cannot remember being asked that question in school, but it bears special weight for me. My father is recently retired from his career as a Hollywood stunt performer. When I was a child, he would do more death-defying tricks in a week than I'm
10 sure I will ever do in my lifetime. My father's extreme career and energetic lifestyle made him the coolest dad in town, and I had to live up to him.

For American boys, no piece of plywood is safe; it has "ramp" written all over. We would prop some
15 plywood up on a cinderblock and see how high it could launch us on a bike or skates. That was sufficiently fun for years, but eventually my father's reputation caught up with me. Soon, my friends wanted to go bigger with the idea of a homemade launch pad. They urged
20 me to seek my father's help. At first, I resisted, since I didn't want to start a trend of hair-raising stunts on my neighborhood street. Who knows what the old lady across the street would think?

As it turned out, my father was more eager than
25 I was to introduce some stunts to my group of friends. Instead of building a giant ramp, he suggested, why not build a platform high in the ponderosa pine tree out back from which we could rappel to the ground? It sounded crazy to me, but I yielded to my father.
30 He loved the cliché appeasement, "Trust me; I'm a professional." So, that afternoon, my friends, father, and I piled in the truck and headed for the lumberyard. By this time, I was starting to warm to the idea of a rappelling platform in my backyard. My friends could
35 hardly contain their excitement. After all, they were about to do something crazy under the supervision of a real stuntman!

My father cruised the aisles at the lumberyard with amazing deftness and efficiency. As he waited for some
40 plywood to be cut, he filled his cart with all kinds of materials that little boys love: nails, screws, glue, chain, cable, nuts, and bolts. This would be the first time my friends and I had built anything out of shiny, new parts. No doubt this would be the most awesome
45 stunt in town!

When we returned home, we unloaded all of the supplies near the base of the tree. Looking up the trunk, my friends and I realized we had a lot of cool building materials but no way to get them up the tree.
50 At that moment, my dad emerged from the garage. "Here's the last piece." He held a climbing harness and rope in his hands. "Now I'm going to go up there and build the structure, then two of you can come up and help with the rigging." For the next hour, we sat
55 in stunned silence. My father threw one end of his rope around an upper limb, secured it, and started the slow process of drawing on the two mechanical ascenders. Before long, he had reached the notch in the tree, braced himself, and sent down a length of cord to us.
60 "Put a quarter-inch bit in the drill and send it up," he cried. We prepared the drill and tied it to the line. My father hoisted it and bored the boltholes into the tree. We repeated this process with two-by-fours, bolts, nuts, and finally the plywood square that would become
65 the platform. My father built it with lightning speed. One of my friends gaped at how quickly my father could drive screws. Before long, Dad called down saying everything was finished and ready for "preliminary testing." I didn't know what he meant by that. "Stand
70 back, guys," my dad called. We hastily obliged. My father, already standing on the platform, looked strangely comfortable so high in the ponderosa tree. Granted, he was still in his harness roped to the tree, but nerves have a funny way of ignoring appeals to logic.
75 Satisfied with his handiwork, my dad began bouncing lightly on the balls of his feet. The platform didn't budge. Next, he started jumping up and down violently. This shook the platform and made the tree sway, but everything seemed soundly built and tightly secured.
80 "All right, now we learn to rappel."

My father slid down his rope and called us to join him in the attic of the garage. I had only seen what was up there a few times, and it mostly bored me. Behind an old armoire, though, was a dusty black trunk that
85 I had never seen before. My father began pulling ropes and harnesses from it, then carabiners and rappelling devices. We eagerly grabbed the equipment and took it to the backyard. My father fit us for the harnesses and began an impromptu lesson on the critical safety rules
90 of climbing and rappelling.

In a few hours and after a little practice off the roof of the house, we were all ready to tackle the huge tree in the back yard.

GO ON TO THE NEXT PAGE.

3   **3**

1. The passage establishes that the narrator and his father have all of the following traits in common EXCEPT:
   A. an innate desire for danger.
   B. a taste for exhilarating activities.
   C. a pleasant attitude toward others.
   D. an awareness of the fun that boys like to have.

2. Which of the following is NOT an accurate description of the passage?
   F. A story about boys who endeavor to perform stunts and are helped by a professional.
   G. A glimpse at one boy's change from being hesitant about to being proud of his father's occupation.
   H. A look at how a group of boys had a great time, despite some early misgivings.
   J. A portrait of a boy struggling to overcome the popularity of his father.

3. In both the first paragraph (lines 1–12) and the second paragraph (lines 13–23) the author is portraying a narrator who:
   A. feels compelled to act differently from his father to avoid earning his negative reputation.
   B. acts without caution in dangerous situations.
   C. hesitates to involve his father in activities involving his friends.
   D. loathes the reputation that precedes his father.

4. At the time of writing the story, the narrator is:
   F. an adult reflecting on a difficult period he had as a youth.
   G. a youth describing an example of the adventures he has with his father.
   H. an adolescent analyzing how his father embarrasses him.
   J. an adult reminiscing fondly about a childhood memory.

5. The passage states that the narrator had to cope with his father's reputation as:
   A. famously daring and socially engaging.
   B. severe and unyielding to the narrator's wishes.
   C. incorrigibly unmindful of the narrator and the narrator's friends' activities in the neighborhood.
   D. prone to reckless stunts and outlandish behavior.

6. Which of the following statements best describes the way the fourth paragraph (lines 38–45) functions in the passage as a whole?
   F. It reveals the reason for the narrator's qualms about asking his father for help, as expressed in the second paragraph.
   G. It details the mundane task of shopping for materials, which includes waiting for lumber to be cut and finding the appropriate hardware.
   H. It shows the reader that as the plan to build the rappelling platform was moving forward, the narrator was warming to it.
   J. It divides the passage into two parts, one about the narrator's relationship with his father and the other about tree climbing and rappelling.

7. The statement "eventually my father's reputation caught up with me" (lines 17–18) functions in the passage to support the narrator's view that:
   A. his father's lifestyle made keeping boyhood friends difficult.
   B. his father's unusual career pulled him into uncommon adventures.
   C. his friends would have stopped building ramps if his father was not a stunt performer.
   D. his father disapproved of untrained boys performing stunts on bikes and skates.

8. It can reasonably be inferred from the passage as a whole that the narrator views his father's reputation as one that developed:
   F. to a degree that was exceptional even in the Hollywood stunt community, but not in his residential neighborhood.
   G. to a degree that was common among all professionals in the area and, therefore, unremarkable.
   H. to a lesser degree than those of the narrator's friends' fathers, in spite of a clear status disparity between his family and theirs.
   J. to a degree that was based on his years of performing film stunts professionally, establishing his popularity with neighborhood youth.

9. As it is used in line 54, *rigging* most nearly means:
   A. platform bracing.
   B. branch trimming.
   C. nuts and bolts.
   D. rope system.

10. The narrator can most accurately be characterized as:
   F. anxious and uncertain.
   G. level-headed but fun-loving.
   H. strong-willed but compassionate.
   J. creative and enthusiastic.

GO ON TO THE NEXT PAGE.

3   **3**

PASSAGE II
SOCIAL SCIENCE: *The Gunpowder Plot*

Remember, remember the 5th of November,
The gunpowder treason and plot.
I know of no reason why gunpowder treason
Should ever be forgot.

5   This famous children's poem speaks directly to
the Gunpowder Plot of 1605 in which a group of
Roman Catholic coconspirators attempted to blow up
Westminster Palace during the formal opening of
Parliament. King James I of England (James VI
10 of Scotland) was in attendance to address the joint
assembly of the House of Lords and the House of
Commons. The failed bomb plot certainly could have
killed the King and potentially the rest of the English
Legislature; it would have been a near-complete
15 removal of the aristocracy. Guy Fawkes was instrumen-
tal in the final stages of the plot, but was apprehended
just prior to completing his work. Shortly thereafter,
Fawkes and his coconspirators were put to death for
treason and attempted murder. It has been said by
20 many—quite tongue-in-cheek—that Guy Fawkes was
the only man ever to enter Parliament with honest
intentions.
       The plot, masterminded by Robert Catesby, had
surprising origins. He and Guy Fawkes, along with
25 several other Roman Catholics, were thought to be
denouncers of the king's own Church of England.
Consequently, they risked civil and criminal penalties.
In realizing that Spain, at the time a great Catholic
world power, was involved in too many wars to help
30 the cause of English Catholics, Catesby decided that
unless something was done from within, nothing would
likely change.
       Luck smiled upon the plotters when they stumbled
upon a cellar for rent beneath the House of Lords; the
35 original plan, to dig a mineshaft beneath Westminster,
proved remarkably difficult, the rock and debris
requiring removal in secret. Being able to rent a cellar under Parliament expedited their efforts immensely,
allowing them to fill the cellar with 1,800 pounds of
40 gunpowder.
       The one crucial flaw in the plot, though, was
that several conspirators had scruples over the potential
for harm to other Catholics likely to be in attendance
during the opening address. One of the men wrote
45 a letter of warning to Lord Monteagle, a fellow
Catholic, who received it on October 26. Learning
about the letter the following day, several conspirators wished to abort the plan, yet the decision was
made to continue when Guy Fawkes confirmed that
50 nothing within the cellar had been discovered. Despite
Fawkes' confidence, Lord Monteagle took the letter
seriously, and tasked the secretary of state with completing a search of all spaces beneath Westminster.
Early in the morning on November 5, Fawkes was
55 apprehended in the cellar. Over the next few days,
he was tortured until he confessed the identities of
the other individuals who contributed to the plot.
On January 31, 1606, each man convicted of treason
was taken to Old Palace Yard to be hanged, drawn,

60 and quartered—this most exotic form of execution was
intended as a lesson to the public: treason would not
be tolerated under any circumstances.
       Currently, on November 5 of each year, British
children burn effigies of Fawkes and recite the
65 renowned poem as a way of remembering this influential figure of the past. Guy Fawkes Day serves as a
chilling reminder to everyone, not just the British, that
if pressed hard enough, an individual will press back.
No brutal threat can stop the most committed believer
70 from rising in defense of his beliefs.

11. One of the points the author seeks to make in the
passage is that some English Roman Catholics in 1605:
A. were convicted of treason for supporting the king.
B. sought religious freedom by rebelling against the
current regime.
C. were forced into hiding by the powerful religious
minority behind the monarchy.
D. gained notoriety by conspiring against the Roman
Catholic church.

12. The author asserts that the Gunpowder Plot coconspi-
rators were generally:
F. capable and sufficiently covert.
G. inept but sufficiently covert.
H. capable but insufficiently covert.
J. inept and insufficiently covert.

13. The author uses the description of the modern Guy
Fawkes Day to point out that some acts are:
A. too powerful to let their lessons fade into history.
B. so powerful that adults must make light of them for
their children's sake.
C. more powerful for people today than they were at
the time they occurred.
D. so powerful that children must be reminded of their
depravity.

14. When the author asserts that Guy Fawkes had *honest
intentions* (lines 21–22), he most likely means that
members of parliament are:
F. not concerned about their perception among the
people.
G. too detached from average citizens to provide effective leadership.
H. prepared to surrender power to religious minorities.
J. prone to exploiting their power by being deceitful.

GO ON TO THE NEXT PAGE.

3 ████████████████████████████████ **3**

15. According to the passage, when are citizens most pressed to act against the government?
   A. When parliament meets in joint session
   B. When there is collusion between the monarch and the judiciary
   C. When personal beliefs are threatened
   D. When there are bad economic times

16. As it is used in line 60, the word *exotic* means:
   F. alluring.
   G. mysterious.
   H. unusual.
   J. foreign.

17. According to the passage, under which of the following government actions would an uprising most likely occur?
   A. Government troops are given permission to conduct unwarranted searches of suspected dissidents.
   B. An average-looking murder suspect at-large prompts police to round up for interrogation anyone who looks like the perpetrator.
   C. Sales and income tax rates are raised sharply at the same time due to budget shortfalls.
   D. Chocolate, gold, and other precious commodities are strictly rationed during wartime.

18. The passage makes the claim that brutal threats from the government are not a solution to the risk of public rebellion because:
   F. harsh punishment of dissenters only breeds further contempt.
   G. there will always be certain individuals who risk the punishment to overthrow a government.
   H. weapons of assassination are too easily concealed to provide reasonable security for government officials.
   J. often the inciting rebels are impossible to locate.

19. As it is used in lines 33–34, the phrase *stumbled upon* most nearly means:
   A. discovered.
   B. tripped over.
   C. walked on.
   D. sought.

20. The *mineshaft* in line 35 refers to:
   F. a tunnel dug to facilitate extraction of a particular mineral.
   G. a metaphorical deep pit from which nothing can climb out.
   H. an underground space to be filled with explosives.
   J. a crawlspace to permit clandestine observation of Parliament.

GO ON TO THE NEXT PAGE.

3

3

PASSAGE III

HUMANITIES: *Tennessee Williams: Celebrated Southern Gothic Writer*

American literature encompasses many unique styles and genres, including Southern Gothic. As its name implies, the literature reflects life in the American South. It maintains some of the characteristics of
5 Gothic writing, such as use of the supernatural or the ironic; however, Southern Gothic does not focus on creating tension and suspense as do other Gothic genres. Instead, its storylines examine Southern people and their postbellum social structure.
10 Writers in the genre generally spurn the pre-Civil-War stereotype of the plantation gentleman and the glamorous Southern belle. Instead, the authors develop characters that are sinister or reclusive and not particularly pleasant on the surface. Nevertheless, these
15 characters usually have redeeming qualities that allow and encourage the reader to sympathize with their situations and dilemmas. It is through these immoral and unhappy personalities that the Southern Gothic writer is able to present and explore moral issues of the
20 American South, such as slavery and bigotry, without blatant accusations.

Many American authors are known for their Southern Gothic style. Playwright Tennessee Williams (1911–1983) is among the most celebrated. Williams'
25 long list of plays and novels include the Pulitzer Prize winning stage dramas *A Streetcar Named Desire* (1948) and *Cat on a Hot Tin Roof* (1955). Williams' characters are known to be modeled directly on members of his own family. For instance, it is speculated that
30 the pitiable character Laura in *The Glass Menagerie* (1944) is modeled after Williams' mentally disabled sister Rose. In the same play, Amanda Wingfield is said to mirror Williams' own mother. Williams even portrays himself in *Suddenly, Last Summer* (1958) and
35 *The Glass Menagerie*. His adult life, plagued with depression and alcoholism, appears to play out in his embroiled characters.

If Tennessee Williams was a tormented man, it was due in no small part to his troubled family.
40 As a seven-year-old in Mississippi, Williams contracted diphtheria and remained housebound for two years. His mother, fearing for Tennessee's mental wellbeing, pushed him toward creative arts during his period of illness. It was she who bought him a typewriter at age 13,
45 which he heartily accepted.

Having already moved once, the Williams family eventually relocated to St. Louis, where Tennessee's increasingly abusive father Cornelius squeaked out a living as a traveling shoe salesman. Tennessee's
50 mother Edwina was a genteel sort prone to smothering. The most traumatic event in the young writer's life, however, occurred when his sister Rose, described as a slender, refined beauty, was diagnosed with schizophrenia.
55 Various treatments were unsuccessful during Rose's years of residence in mental asylums. In 1943, the Williams parents consented to the now-defunct prefrontal lobotomy in an effort to treat her schizophrenia. The operation was ruinous and Rose lay vegetative

60 for the rest of her life. The fallout came when Tennessee blamed his parents for authorizing the operation. In the 1960s, he wrestled with the notion that he, too, would go insane. A decade of depression took hold. He would, at least nominally, overcome it, but
65 Tennessee Williams' family life would haunt him the rest of his days.

21. The main purpose of the passage can best be described as an effort to:
   A. explain how and why Tennessee Williams' life suited writing in the Southern Gothic style.
   B. illustrate what the South was like at the time Tennessee Williams was writing his body of work.
   C. discuss how Tennessee Williams' life changed during his youth and young adulthood.
   D. describe the different elements of Southern Gothic style present in Tennessee Williams' works.

22. The author's attitude toward the subject of the passage can best be characterized as:
   F. amused tolerance.
   G. detached interest.
   H. warm appreciation.
   J. mild skepticism.

23. It can be reasonably inferred that the author believes Tennessee Williams' first great success came from a play published in:
   A. 1944.
   B. 1948.
   C. 1955.
   D. 1958.

24. According to the sixth paragraph (lines 55–66), compared to modern standards of medicine, the prefrontal lobotomy is described as:
   F. more apt to produce symptom improvement, but at unacceptable risk to the patient.
   G. more apt to cause discomfort to the patient, but in exchange for reduced mental anguish.
   H. less apt to diminish schizophrenia, and likely to incapacitate the patient.
   J. less apt to treat mental disease, but with very manageable side effects.

GO ON TO THE NEXT PAGE.

3 ██ **3**

25. As described in the passage, the effect Tennessee's family had on him can best be summarized by which of the following statements?
   A. His family's impact can be safely overlooked because many other authors with less traumatic pasts have written in the Southern Gothic style.
   B. His family gave Tennessee his sense of melancholy, which faded in his prosperous later years.
   C. His family problems directly influenced his decades of writing and left Tennessee conflicted and distraught.
   D. The destruction of the Williams family caused Tennessee's plays to turn to darker themes that did not appeal well to audiences.

26. When the author states that Southern Gothic literature does not make "blatant accusations" (line 21), he most likely means that the genre avoids:
   F. defending the abolition of slavery and other social reforms in the postbellum South.
   G. explicitly stating who among the characters are racist or otherwise morally corrupted.
   H. addressing any social problems in the South, preferring that the reader juxtapose his own opinion with the facts of the plot.
   J. righteous characters who overtly decry bigoted behavior of other characters.

27. The passage indicates that Tennessee Williams' creative streak began because:
   A. he was trapped in an abusive household where his only refuge was in the fantasies he wrote.
   B. he was tortured by his sister's condition and took to writing as a way of searching for an explanation for her decline.
   C. he was severely ill as a boy and his mother took care to engage him in creative pursuits when he could not be physically active.
   D. he was inspired by the success of other family members and wished to capture the feeling in prose.

28. According to the author, the primary characteristic of the Southern Gothic genre is that it:
   F. indirectly uses distant or malevolent characters to raise issues of social justice.
   G. incorporates the haunting religious themes of traditional Gothic literature into 20th-century Southern society.
   H. is the first American genre to be able to set aside the issue of slavery.
   J. carefully avoids volatile characters, in spite of plots set in tumultuous time periods.

29. The author calls some of Tennessee Williams' characters "embroiled" in line 37 most likely because they:
   A. exist in the sultry Southern climate at a time where dress was uncomfortably conservative.
   B. seem doomed to create continual problems for themselves.
   C. deal with daunting personal problems or overwhelming moral quandaries.
   D. bear a larger-than-life aesthetic that makes their words and deeds uniquely impactful.

30. The "social structure" mentioned in line 9 most directly refers to what the author sees as:
   F. the remnants of racism and inequality in Southern culture following the end of slavery.
   G. the unspoken disparity between rich landowners and poor farmhands at the turn of the 20th century.
   H. the uncommon compassion and hospitality for which the South has become famous.
   J. the system of vigilante justice that arose as a consequence of inadequate policing following the Civil War.

GO ON TO THE NEXT PAGE.

3   **3**

PASSAGE IV
NATURAL SCIENCE: *Michigan's Beloved Songbird*

Sometimes an object in nature is so rare that it escapes mention in nature books. Such is the case with the delightful Kirtland's warbler, a plump, yellow-breasted bird that can be found nesting almost
5 exclusively in the northern half of Michigan's Lower Peninsula. Although this bird migrates to the Bahamas for the winter, Michigan is its natural habitat. Unfortunately, so few Kirtland's warblers exist that the species is classified endangered. The remaining Kirtland's
10 warblers now enjoy living in stands of young Jack pines located in protected Michigan forests.

Interestingly, the Kirtland's warbler nests on the ground in the jack pine forests, and not in the trees themselves. Male warblers generally return to
15 Michigan in May to spend the summer. Females arrive as the males stake out territory and choose a suitable nesting area. At the completion of the long journey from the Bahamas to Michigan, female warblers begin to collect leaves and grass to build their nests. During
20 this process, the female warblers' mates provide food. Eventually, female Kirtland's warblers each lay four to five speckled eggs. The eggs hatch in two to three weeks, and both the male and female warblers tend to the chicks. Five weeks after they hatch, the fledglings
25 are prepared to survive on their own.

Kirtland's warblers are extremely fastidious about their habitat. This is probably why these birds have become endangered. Kirtland's warblers insist on living in expansive areas of Jack pine forest rooted in
30 *Grayling sand*, which percolates quickly to prevent flooding of nests built on or near the ground. Grayling sand also supports the type of plant material that the warblers prefer for their diet and nest building.

If not for ongoing human conservation efforts,
35 this special habitat and this rare bird would probably not exist today. As the massive 19th-century logging boom faded in Michigan, natural forest fires increased, fueled by the burgeoning undergrowth. Jack pine numbers increased dramatically, since the tree depends on
40 regular fires to expose the seeds within its tough cones. The early 1900s, though, saw natural fires suppressed by new forest management policies and, consequently, Jack pine forests quickly diminished. This greatly reduced the number of nesting areas available for the
45 Kirtland's warbler.

To correct this problem, Jack pine areas are currently managed on a rotating basis. This ensures an appropriate number of nesting sites, which encourages warblers to return and reproduce annually. The
50 protected Jack pine forests are also home to the white-tailed deer, the black bear, the Eastern bluebird, the upland sandpiper, and the snowshoe hare. Unfortunately, for the Kirtland's warbler, the brown-headed cowbird is also prevalent in these woods. This brood
55 parasite is well known for its tendency to steal the nests of other birds by replacing the original bird's eggs with its own eggs. When the chicks are hatched, the warblers raise the young cowbirds as their own. This, of course, negatively impacts the population of
60 the Kirtland's warbler. Studies have shown that when a cowbird lays one egg in a warbler's nest, generally only one to three warbler chicks will survive. If two or more cowbird chicks survive in a single warbler nest, none of the warblers will survive. To combat this dilemma,
65 government programs have been established to trap and eradicate cowbirds that attempt to nest in the warblers' habitat. These efforts have greatly improved the survival and proliferation of the Kirtland's warbler over the past few decades.

70 The male Kirtland's warbler is prized as a songbird, emitting a persistent, melodic song audible up to a quarter-mile away. For researchers, counting these songs becomes important during mating season, since saving the warbler from extinction demands an annual
75 census of the population to ensure that conservation measures are effective.

Debates periodically surface over whether to replace the robin with the Kirtland's warbler as Michigan's state bird. Admirers of the Kirtland's
80 warbler argue that it is strictly a Michigan bird. Supporters of the robin point out that the Kirtland's warbler is only present in Michigan for, at most, half of the year. Perhaps this debate will continue until more residents have a chance to see the beautiful and elusive
85 Kirtland's warbler, which calls Michigan home.

---

31. In the context of the passage as a whole, it is most reasonable to infer that the phrase "jack pine areas are currently managed on a rotating basis" (lines 46–47) means that:
  A. resources are limited, so work must be done on one small section of forest at a time.
  B. forests are occasionally burned to encourage new tree growth.
  C. lumber is harvested only as fast as tree re-growth permits.
  D. efforts to restore the Kirtland's warbler habitat are detrimental to other species.

32. The passage suggests that the population of the Kirtland's warbler declined in the past because forest management policies:
  F. failed to account for unforeseen ecological consequences of fire prevention.
  G. permitted excessive logging of nesting trees.
  H. aimed to eliminate the jack pine.
  J. catered exclusively to the powerful industrial establishment.

GO ON TO THE NEXT PAGE.

3   **3**

33. What does the passage offer as evidence that Kirtland's warblers have environmental sensitivities?
   A. Cowbird eggs incubating at the expense of warbler eggs
   B. Males and females arriving in Michigan at different times of year
   C. Long period during which hatchlings need to stay in the nest
   D. Nests requiring an uncommon environment

34. It can be inferred that the author feels Michigan, not the Bahamas, is the Kirtland's warbler's natural habitat because the birds:
   F. inhabit very specific parts of Michigan.
   G. migrate from the tropics a great distance to summer in Michigan.
   H. are protected by endangered species laws in the United States.
   J. mate and raise offspring in Michigan.

35. According to the passage, what is the reason jack pine forests declined in the early 1900s?
   A. Logging in the 1800s decimated mature jack pines, which produce hearty seeds.
   B. Logging in the 1800s left room for low-growing shrubs that accelerated the spread of many forest fires.
   C. Forest management focused on eradication of the wildfires necessary for jack pine proliferation.
   D. Forest management placed a higher value on some trees than others.

36. What does the author suggest in lines 54–55 by stating that the cowbird is a "brood parasite?"
   F. The cowbird exploits the nesting instincts of the Kirtland's warbler.
   G. The cowbird feeds on the eggs of Kirtland's warblers.
   H. The cowbird shows wanton disregard for the survival of the Kirtland's warbler.
   J. The cowbird's appearance is marked by unappealing plumage.

37. The passage states that the habitat needs of the Kirtland's warbler, as compared to those of other birds, are:
   A. less specific.
   B. more specific.
   C. equally specific.
   D. little understood.

38. According to the passage, which of the following correctly states the relationship of the Jack pine to fire?
   F. Fire is the mechanism by which cones release their seeds.
   G. Fire stimulates the jack pine to produce seed-bearing cones.
   H. Fire destroys small, weak trees, leaving room for jack pine seeds to grow to maturity.
   J. Fire expands through jack pine forests particularly fast.

39. The author states that the main reason for the Kirtland's warbler's decline is:
   A. its rapid life cycle.
   B. cowbird infestations.
   C. strain on its habitat.
   D. logging of jack pines in the past.

40. As it is used in lines 30–32, the term *Grayling sand* most nearly means:
   F. grey or silver soil, which is rich in ore deposits.
   G. highly permeable soil suitable for some vegetation.
   H. nutrient-poor sandy soil that occurs along salt water beaches.
   J. dry riverbed soil that once supported a population of Grayling fish.

END OF THE READING TEST.
STOP! IF YOU HAVE TIME LEFT OVER, CHECK YOUR WORK ON THIS SECTION ONLY.

4 ○ ○ ○ ○ ○ ○ ○ ○ ○ 4

SCIENCE REASONING TEST

35 Minutes—40 Questions

DIRECTIONS: This test includes seven passages, each followed by several questions. Read the passages and choose the best answer to each question. After you have selected your answer, fill in the corresponding bubble on your answer sheet. You should refer to the passages as often as necessary when answering the questions. You may NOT use a calculator on this test.

PASSAGE I

Amino acids are considered the building blocks of *protein* in the body. Amino acids combine with each other to form chains called *peptides*, which then combine to form proteins. The human body requires twenty different amino acids, whose combinations produce every essential protein in the body. When amino acids form peptides, the *residue* is what is left after the amino acid sheds a molecule of water (a hydrogen ion from one end and a hydroxide ion from the other end). The *reaction rate* is the factor by which the protein is able to build itself up through the combination of peptides. Figures 1–3 show the effects that changes in temperature, water volume, and residue concentration have on the rate of reaction of residue when Amino Acids A and B are present. Figure 4 shows the effects that changes in the concentrations of Amino Acids A and B have on the rates of reaction in residue solutions of the same concentration.

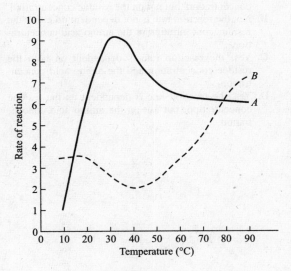

Figure 1

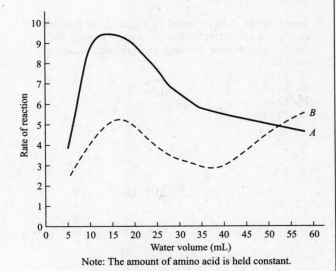

Note: The amount of amino acid is held constant.

Figure 2

GO ON TO THE NEXT PAGE.

○ ○ ○ ○ ○ ○ ○ ○ ○

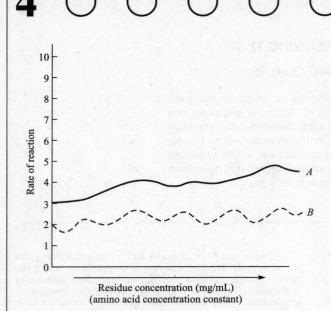

Figure 3

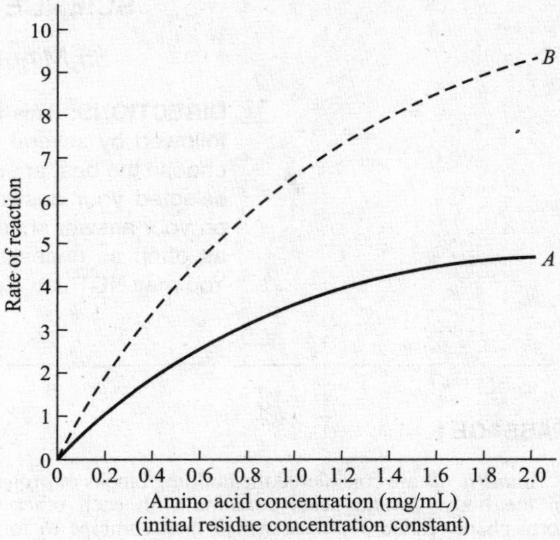

Figure 4

1. According to Figure 2, Amino Acid A has the highest reaction rate at a water volume closest to:
   A. 0
   B. 4
   C. 12
   D. 20

2. Based on the data presented in Figure 2, at approximately which of the following water volumes does Amino Acid A have the same reaction rate as Amino Acid B?
   F. 30 mL
   G. 40 mL
   H. 50 mL
   J. 60 mL

3. A researcher claims that the reaction rate of Amino Acid B is dependent on both residue concentration and amino acid concentration. Do the data in Figures 3 and 4 support this claim?
   A. No, the reaction rate is dependent on the amino acid concentration, but not on the residue concentration.
   B. No, the reaction rate is not dependent on either the residue concentration or the amino acid concentration.
   C. Yes, the reaction rate is dependent on both the residue concentration and the amino acid concentration.
   D. Yes, the reaction rate is dependent on the residue concentration, but not on the amino acid concentration.

4. A researcher claims that under the conditions used to determine the data for Figure 4, the reaction rate for Amino Acid A at any given concentration will always be greater than the reaction rate for Amino Acid B at the same concentration. Do the data support this conclusion?

   F. No, Amino Acid A has a lower reaction rate at all given residue concentrations tested.

   G. No, Amino Acid A has a lower reaction rate at all given amino acid concentrations tested.

   H. Yes, Amino Acid A has a higher reaction rate at all given reside concentrations tested.

   J. Yes, Amino Acid A has a higher reaction rate at all given amino acid concentrations tested.

5. The figure below shows the relative reaction rates for *alanine*, an amino acid found in DNA, and *glycine* an amino acid found in the muscles.

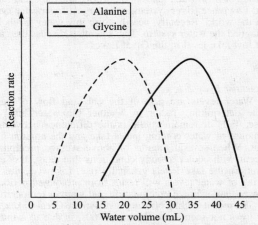

Note: The amount of amino acid is held constant.

Based on this figure, one would best conclude that compared to the water volume at the peak reaction rate of amino acids in DNA, the water volume at the peak reaction rate of amino acids in the muscles:

   A. is higher.

   B. is lower.

   C. is the same.

   D. cannot be measured.

4 ○ ○ ○ ○ ○ ○ ○ ○ 4

PASSAGE II

The Great Lakes are a group of five large lakes located in the United States and Canada. They make up the largest group of fresh water lakes in the world, and the Great Lakes-St. Lawrence River system is the largest freshwater system in the world. Recently, near-historic low water levels have plagued the water system. Two scientists discuss the causes of low lake level in the Great Lakes.

Scientist 1

Water levels are part of the ebb and flow of nature. The determining factor in whether the water level will rise, fall, or remain stable is the difference between the amount of water coming into a lake and the amount going out. When several months of above-average precipitation occur with cooler, cloudy conditions that cause less evaporation, the lake levels gradually rise. Likewise, the lowering of water levels will result from prolonged periods of lower-than-average precipitation and warmer temperatures.

The recent decline of water levels in the Great Lakes, now at lows not seen since the mid-1960s, is due to a number of causes. Higher degrees of evaporation from warmer than usual temperatures in recent years, a series of mild winters, and below-average snow pack in the Lake Superior basin all contribute to the phenomenon. Since precipitation, evaporation, and runoff are the major factors affecting the water supply to the lakes, levels cannot be controlled or accurately predicted for more than a few weeks into the future. Further, the influence of human regulation on lake levels is inconsequential. Because water is added through snow and rain and taken away through evaporation, nature has most of the control over lake levels.

Scientist 2

Several human activities have affected levels and flow of the water in the Great Lakes. For example, structures have been built to regulate the outflows of both Lake Superior and Lake Ontario. Lake Superior has been regulated since 1921 as a result of hydroelectric and navigation developments in the St. Mary's River, such as the Soo Locks. Lake Ontario has been regulated since 1960 after completion of the St. Lawrence Seaway and Power Project. Diversions bring water into, and take water out of, the Great Lakes. Many such diversions were constructed for hydropower generation and logging. For example, the Lake Michigan diversion at Chicago moves water out of Lake Michigan and into the Mississippi River for domestic, navigation, hydroelectric, and sanitation purposes.

In addition, the St. Clair and Detroit rivers have been dredged and modified. This has caused some drop in the levels of Lake Michigan and Lake Huron. Channel and shoreline modifications in connecting the channels of the Great Lakes have affected lake levels and flows as well, because the infilling of shoreline areas can reduce the flow carrying-capacity of the river. Further, the extensive use of groundwater deposited in massive aquifers (underground layers of water-bearing permeable rock) in the Midwest has affected the lake levels. Vast quantities of water deposited in aquifers surrounding the Great Lakes are taken to population centers outside of the Great Lakes' watershed (region of land whose water drains into a specified body of water). Thus, the water in the lakes is not replenished.

6. Which of the following best describes the major point of difference between the scientists' viewpoints?
   F. The major contributing factor of low lake levels.
   G. The effects of water use on the environment.
   H. The effects of reduced lake levels.
   J. The major function of the Great Lakes.

7. With which of the following statements would both scientists likely agree?
   A. The probability of lake level fluctuation is small.
   B. Human activity is largely responsible for the changes in lake levels.
   C. Recent trends show that the lake levels are decreasing.
   D. The decreased lake levels are not a major concern.

8. Which of the following statements best describes how Scientist 1 would explain why human interference is of little importance in determining lake levels?
   F. Aquifer use has little effect on lake levels.
   G. Rivers flowing into the Great Lakes raise the water levels in the lakes.
   H. Dredging or widening rivers can cause reductions in water levels in the lakes.
   J. Lake levels are mainly controlled by nature and not manipulated by humans.

9. According to Scientist 2, human activity diverts lake waters, thus:
   A. decreasing the density of the water in the lakes.
   B. reducing the amount of water in the lakes.
   C. increasing the amount of water in the lakes.
   D. changing the weather patterns.

GO ON TO THE NEXT PAGE.

4 〇 〇 〇 〇 〇 〇 〇 〇 〇 **4**

10. Scientist 1's viewpoint would most likely be *weakened* by which of the following statements?

  F. Lake level fluctuation has severe consequences for coastal communities.

  G. Studies have shown precipitation and evaporation levels to be stable for the last 50 years.

  H. Studies detailing aquifer use announce a dramatic increase in volume in the last 5 years.

  J. Recreational boating releases thousands of gallons of petroleum-based chemicals into the water system each year.

11. Scientist 2 claims that all of the following are human activities that are decreasing lake levels EXCEPT:

  A. destruction of watershed tributaries.

  B. diversions for domestic, navigation, hydroelectric, and sanitation purposes.

  C. dredging and modification of rivers.

  D. infilling of shoreline areas.

12. How would the effect of the use of aquifer water differ from that described by Scientist 2 if all of the water taken from aquifers that surrounds the Great Lakes was used *within* the Great Lakes' watershed? The use of aquifer water would:

  F. continue to cause decreases in lake levels.

  G. have little or no effect on lake levels.

  H. have an increased effect on receding lake levels.

  J. increase levels of pollution within the watershed region.

GO ON TO THE NEXT PAGE.

4 ○ ○ ○ ○ ○ ○ ○ ○ ○ 4

PASSAGE III

Students conducted an experiment to determine the insulating properties of certain materials. In each trial, "blankets" made of different materials of different thicknesses were wrapped around an aluminum capsule filled with 0.250 L of water at a known initial temperature, T_i, and placed into an oven preheated to a certain temperature.

Heat was transferred through the insulating materials from the oven to the water inside the capsule. After 5 minutes, the temperature of the water inside the capsule, T_f, was recorded. The heat flow, measured in joules per second (J/s), is shown in Table 1.

(Note: In each trial, the same size and shape of aluminum capsule were used. One trial was done with no insulation around the aluminum capsule.)

						Table 1
Trial	Insulating material	Thickness of insulator (in.)	T_i (°C)	T_f (°C)	Temp of oven (°C)	Heat flow (J/s)
1	Fiberglass	1.0	70	43	25	−94
2	Fiberglass	1.0	90	63	45	−94
3	Fiberglass	0.5	20	36	75	56
4	Fiberglass	1.0	20	31	75	38
5	Fiberglass	1.5	20	28	75	32
6	Cellulose	1.0	20	37	75	59
7	Cellulose	1.5	20	33	75	45
8	Asbestos	1.0	20	30	75	31
9	Asbestos	1.5	20	27	75	24
10	Rubber	0.5	20	57	75	129
11	Rubber	1.0	20	52	75	112
12	Aluminum	****	20	70	75	174

13. According to the information provided, heat flowed from the water in the capsule at temperature T_i to the surrounding oven in which of the following trials?
   A. Trial 1
   B. Trial 5
   C. Trial 9
   D. Trial 12

14. The best insulators are those that are the poorest heat conductors. According to Trials 3 through 11, which of the following materials would likely provide the best insulation between a room and the outdoors?
   F. Aluminum
   G. Cellulose
   H. Fiberglass
   J. Rubber

15. According to Table 1, which of the following combinations of insulating material and insulator thickness resulted in the greatest heat flow?
   A. Fiberglass, 1.5 in
   B. Fiberglass, 1.0 in
   C. Cellulose, 1.5 in
   D. Cellulose, 1.0 in

GO ON TO THE NEXT PAGE.

4 ○ ○ ○ ○ ○ ○ ○ ○ ○ **4**

16. Materials differ in their *thermal conductivity*: the higher the thermal conductivity, the greater the heat flow through the corresponding thickness of the insulating material. According to Trials 4 through 11, which of the following statements about relative thermal conductivities is NOT true?

   F. Fiberglass has a higher thermal conductivity value than asbestos.
   G. Rubber has a higher thermal conductivity value than cellulose.
   H. Cellulose has a lower thermal conductivity value than fiberglass.
   J. Fiberglass has a lower thermal conductivity value than rubber.

17. Trials 3 and 5 provide evidence that heat flow depends on which of the following factors?

   A. Type of insulating material.
   B. Temperature of oven.
   C. Contact area.
   D. Thickness of insulating material.

4 ○ ○ ○ ○ ○ ○ ○ ○ ○ **4**

PASSAGE IV

A group of students conducted several experiments using a variety of nonstick cookware, a spring scale, and several different weighted objects. Their goal was to determine which brand of cookware products had the best nonstick surface by measuring the *coefficient of static friction*, which is a measure of how resistant a stationary object is to movement.

Experiment 1

A student connected the spring scale to a weighted object that was placed inside a piece of nonstick cookware as shown in Figure 1.

The students planned to calculate the coefficient of static friction by determining the force required to disturb an object from rest. During the experiment, one student anchored the nonstick cookware be holding tightly to the handle while the other student attached a weighted, smooth steel object to the spring scale. The student pulled on the spring until the object began to move. A third student recorded the force in newtons, N, indicated on the spring scale at the moment the object began to move across the nonstick surface.

This procedure was repeated for 3 different brands of cookware; each brand of cookware was tested with various weighted objects. The coefficient of static friction was calculated by dividing the average force required to move the object by its weight (mass × g, the gravitational constant). The results are shown in Table 1.

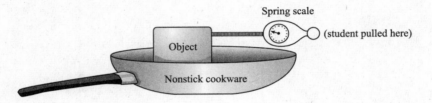

Figure 1

			Force (N) to move object				Coefficient of static friction (force/weight)
Cookware brand	Mass of weighted object (g)	Weight of object (N)	Trial 1	Trial 2	Trial 3	Average	
A	50	0.49	0.026	0.031	0.027	0.028	0.057
	150	1.47	0.074	0.085	0.081	0.080	0.054
	250	2.45	0.139	0.137	0.129	0.135	0.055
B	50	0.49	0.027	0.031	0.029	0.029	0.059
	150	1.47	0.087	0.091	0.092	0.090	0.061
	250	2.45	0.149	0.150	0.144	0.147	0.060
C	50	0.49	0.025	0.023	0.024	0.024	0.048
	150	1.47	0.074	0.070	0.072	0.072	0.049
	250	2.45	0.128	0.126	0.121	0.125	0.051

Table 1

GO ON TO THE NEXT PAGE.

4 ○ ○ ○ ○ ○ ○ ○ ○ ○ **4**

Experiment 2

The students performed an experiment similar to Experiment 1, except three different brands of cooking spray were applied to the same cookware surface before the weights were put in place. The results are shown in Table 2.

Cooking spray brand	Mass of weighted object (g)	Weight of object (N)	Force (N) to move object				Coefficient of static friction (force/weight)
			Trial 1	Trial 2	Trial 3	Average	
X	50	0.49	0.019	0.021	0.023	0.021	0.043
	150	1.47	0.064	0.064	0.061	0.063	0.043
	250	2.45	0.111	0.107	0.106	0.108	0.044
Y	50	0.49	0.019	0.015	0.020	0.018	0.037
	150	1.47	0.057	0.056	0.055	0.056	0.038
	250	2.45	0.087	0.089	0.088	0.088	0.036
Z	150	1.47	0.064	0.069	0.071	0.068	0.046
	250	2.45	0.118	0.116	0.120	0.118	0.048

Table 2

18. The results of the 2 experiments support the conclusion that as the weight of an object increases, the average force required to move it from rest generally:
   F. decreases.
   G. increases.
   H. varies, with no particular trend.
   J. remains constant.

19. If Experiment 1 was repeated for Brand B cookware with a 200 gram mass, the average force needed to disturb the object from rest would be closest to:
   A. 0.03 N.
   B. 0.06 N.
   C. 0.12 N.
   D. 0.18 N.

20. Based on the results of Experiments 1 and 2, which of the following combinations would result in the surface with the *least* coefficient of static friction?
   F. Cookware brand A and cooking spray brand X.
   G. Cookware brand B and cooking spray brand Y.
   H. Cookware brand C and cooking spray brand Y.
   J. Cookware brand C and cooking spray brand Z.

21. Which brand(s) of cooking spray was/were tested with only 2 different weights in Experiment 2?
   A. Brand Y only.
   B. Brand Z only.
   C. Brands X and Y only.
   D. Brands X and Z only.

22. According to the passage, for the students to accurately measure the coefficient of static friction, which force would have to be overcome?
   F. The weight of the object.
   G. The force between the spring scale and the object.
   H. The force of applying the cooking spray to the surface.
   J. The force required to disturb the object from rest.

23. The students' instructor gave them one piece of nonstick cookware and asked them to identify the brand. The students repeated the procedures followed in Experiment 1 and obtained average forces of 0.088 N for the 150 gram object and 0.149 N for the 250 gram object. Which of the following brands would most likely have produced these results?
   A. Brand B only.
   B. Brand C only.
   C. Brand A and C only.
   D. Brand B and C only.

GO ON TO THE NEXT PAGE.

PASSAGE V

Aphids are small plant-eating insects known to feed on rosebushes. In the cultivation of roses, certain pesticides are often applied when the presence of aphids is detected. However, sometimes the flowers that are treated with the pesticides are not as vibrant or fragrant as those that did not receive the pesticide treatment. Two experiments were conducted to study the effects of certain pesticides on rosebushes.

Experiment 1

A gardener filled 125 pots with Soil Type 1. No pesticide was added to the soil in 25 pots. The other pots were divided into four groups of 25 and the soils in each group were treated with 5, 15, 25, or 35 parts per million (ppm) of either Pesticide A or Pesticide B. All other factors were held constant. Fully grown rosebushes with buds but no flowers were planted after the pesticide was placed in the soil. After 30 days the rosebushes were uprooted, sun-dried, and the total number of petals produced by the bushes was counted. The results are shown in Table 1.

Experiment 2

Experiment 1 was repeated with 100 pots of Soil Type 1 and 100 pots of Soil Type 2. The same pesticide doses and type and number of rosebushes were used. All other factors were held constant. After 30 days the rosebushes were uprooted and weighed. The results are shown in Table 2.

Information on the composition of the two soil types used is given in Table 3.

Table 3			
Solid type	pH level	Organic matter (%)	Clay (%)
1	4.1	3.0	12.5
2	3.9	6.5	6.3

Table 1		
Pesticide dose (ppm)	Number of petals	
	Pesticide A	Pesticide B
5	12	15
15	2	7
25	9	14
35	5	7
None	14	14

Table 2				
Pesticide dose (ppm)	Average weight of rosebush (oz)			
	Soil type 1		Soil type 2	
	Pesticide A	Pesticide B	Pesticide A	Pesticide B
5	47.5	51.4	52.7	61.2
15	37.1	42.3	40.3	51.7
25	27.5	32.9	31.1	40.3
35	19.7	22.1	23.6	29.7
Note: Average plant weight with untreated Soil Type 1 was 42.1 oz; average plant weight with untreated Soil Type 2 was 24.7 oz.				

GO ON TO THE NEXT PAGE.

24. Which of the following sets of rosebushes served as the control in Experiment 1?
   F. Rosebushes grown in soil with no pesticide added
   G. Rosebushes grown in soil treated with 15 ppm of Pesticide A
   H. Rosebushes grown in soil treated with 15 ppm of Pesticide B
   J. Rosebushes grown in soil treated with 35 ppm of Pesticide A

25. Which of the following, if true, best explains why the pesticides were applied to the soil as opposed to being placed directly on the rosebushes?
   A. Pesticides are never applied to the soil when treating aphids or other pests.
   B. Aphids are not affected when a pesticide is applied directly to the soil.
   C. The experiments were testing how water levels affect growth patterns.
   D. Rosebushes generally die when pesticides are applied to them directly.

26. Assume that there is a direct correlation between plant weight and the number of petals on the flowers. If a rosebush was grown in Soil Type 2, one would predict that the number of petals would be *lowest* under which of the following conditions?
   F. Pesticide B at 35 ppm.
   G. Pesticide A at 35 ppm.
   H. Pesticide B at 25 ppm.
   J. Pesticide A at 15 ppm.

27. Assume that a rosebush was grown in soil treated with varying doses of a third pesticide (Pesticide C). Based on the results of the experiments, what prediction, if any, about the effect of Pesticide C on the growth of this rosebush can be made?
   A. Pesticide C would have no impact on the growth of the rosebushes.
   B. Pesticide C would interfere with the growth of these rosebushes by making them smaller.
   C. Pesticide C would interfere with the growth of these rosebushes by making them less fragrant.
   D. No prediction can be made on the basis of the results.

28. The results of Experiment 2 indicate that, at every pesticide dose, average plant weight was *lowest* under which of the following conditions?
   F. Pesticide B and Soil Type 1
   G. Pesticide A and Soil Type 1
   H. Pesticide B and Soil Type 2
   J. Pesticide A and Soil Type 2

GO ON TO THE NEXT PAGE.

4 ○ ○ ○ ○ ○ ○ ○ ○ **4**

PASSAGE VI

Dopamines serve as *enhancers* or *catalysts* (a substance that initiates or increases the rate of impulses during a chemical reaction, but is not depleted during the process) to certain reactions involved in the activity of human thought. The dopamine *intropin* is involved in the stimulation of the neurotransmitters in the brain when thought is initiated. A student investigated the effects of dopamine activity on a specific neurotransmitter.

Experiment 1

To each of 10 test tubes, 7 milliliters (mL) of a *peptide* (a neurotransmitter) solution was added. Two mL of an intropin solution was added to each of Tubes 1–9. Tube 10 received 2 mL of water without intropin. The tubes were then stirred at a constant rate in water baths at various temperatures and incubated (heated) from 0 to 15 minutes (min). At the end of the incubation period, 0.3 mL of NaCl solution was added to each tube. The NaCl stopped the reaction between the intropin and the peptide. The *precipitates*, solids formed in a solution during a chemical reaction, which in this case were caused by the reaction of NaCl and the peptide, were removed from the tubes and dried. The masses of the precipitates, in milligrams (mg), were measured to determine the relative amount of enhancer that remained in the tube. The results are shown in Table 1.

Experiment 2

Peptide solution (8 mL) was added to an additional 8 test tubes to which 2 mL of intropin solution was then added. The tubes were incubated at 10 degrees Celsius and stirred at a constant rate for 15 min. The effect of acidity on the neurotransmitter was observed by varying the acidity levels (using the pH scale). The relative amount of neurotransmitter present in each tube was determined in the same manner as Experiment 1, by adding NaCl solution to each test tube. The results are in shown in Table 2.

Table 2		
Test tube	pH	Mass of precipitate (mg)
11	2.0	2.5
12	5.0	2.7
13	6.0	2.9
14	7.0	3.0
15	8.0	6.2
16	9.0	4.1
17	12.0	3.8
18	13.0	3.6

Table 1				
Test tube	Temperature of water bath (°C)	Amount of intropin (mL)	Incubation time (min)	Mass of precipitate (mg)
1	25	2.0	0	4.3
2	25	2.0	5	3.9
3	25	2.0	10	2.8
4	25	2.0	15	1.7
5	30	2.0	5	3.6
6	30	2.0	10	2.5
7	30	2.0	15	1.4
8	35	2.0	5	1.8
9	35	2.0	10	1.3
10	35	0	15	0.2

GO ON TO THE NEXT PAGE.

29. In Experiment 1, which of the following conditions allowed for the large amount of precipitate in Tube 1?
    A. Lack of intropin.
    B. Higher temperature.
    C. Lack of water.
    D. Shorter incubation period.

30. In which of the following ways did the designs of Experiments 1 and 2 differ?
    F. A larger volume of the peptide solution was used in Experiment 2 than in Experiment 1.
    G. The temperature was held constant in Experiment 1 and varied in Experiment 2.
    H. No NaCl was added after incubation in Experiment 2, but it was in Experiment 1.
    J. The remaining fluid level was measured in Experiment 1 but not in Experiment 2.

31. Which of the following hypotheses about the effects of pH on intropin activity is best supported by the results of Experiment 2? As the pH of the solutions increases from 2 to 13, the effectiveness of intropin:
    A. increases only.
    B. decreases only.
    C. increases, then decreases.
    D. remains the same.

32. Suppose that NaCl had been added immediately to Tube 5 with no incubation period. Based on the results from Experiment 1, the best prediction about the amount of precipitate (in mg) formed would be:
    F. 4.1
    G. 3.5
    H. 2.1
    J. 1.4

33. According to Table 1, which of the following combinations of water bath temperature and incubation time yielded the greatest amount of precipitate?
    A. 25°C, 5 min
    B. 25°C, 10 min
    C. 35°C, 5 min
    D. 35°C, 10 min

34. According to the results of both experiments, one can predict that the LEAST amount of precipitate would be formed if tubes were incubated for 15 min under which of the following conditions?
    F. 20°C at pH of 2.0
    G. 20°C at pH of 6.0
    H. 30°C at pH of 2.0
    J. 30°C at pH of 6.0

GO ON TO THE NEXT PAGE.

4 ○ ○ ○ ○ ○ ○ ○ ○ ○ **4**

PASSAGE VII

Several scientists considered some different environmental factors and their influence on the growth of certain bacteria. The following experiments used *Salmonella* bacteria to measure the effect of pH levels, nutrients, and temperature on the number of bacteria produced within a given time period.

Experiment 1

A known quantity of *Salmonella* bacteria was placed in each of 3 Petri dishes with the same nutrient concentration at the same temperature. The pH level of each nutrient concentration in each dish was varied according to Table 1. On the pH scale, 7 represents neutral, values less than 7 indicate an acid, and values greater than 7 indicate a base. The lids of the Petri dishes were replaced after the bacteria were added and the dishes were left alone. After 6 hours, the percent growth of *Salmonella* bacteria was recorded (Table 1).

Table 1		
Dish	pH level	Growth (%)
1	5	90
2	7	81
3	9	43

Experiment 2

A known quantity of *Salmonella* bacteria was placed in each of 3 Petri dishes with different nutrient concentrations in the form of organic compounds. The temperature and pH level (neutral 7) were held constant in each sample. The lids of the Petri dishes were replaced after the bacteria were added and the dishes were left alone. After 6 hours, the percent growth of *Salmonella* bacteria was recorded (Table 2).

Table 2			
Dish	Organic compound	Dry weight (%)	Growth (%)
1	Carbon	50	37
	Oxygen	20	
	Nitrogen	15	
2	Carbon	25	16
	Oxygen	10	
	Nitrogen	7	
3	Carbon	12.5	8
	Oxygen	5	
	Nitrogen	20	

Experiment 3

A known quantity of *Salmonella* bacteria was placed in each of 3 Petri dishes at different temperatures. The pH level and nutrient concentrations were held constant. The lids of the Petri dishes were replaced after the bacteria were added and the dishes were left alone. After 6 hours, the percent growth of *Salmonella* bacteria was recorded (Table 3).

Table 3		
Dish	Temperature (°C)	Growth (%)
1	10	13
2	40	83
3	90	24

35. According to Table 1, what might best contribute to the growth of *Salmonella* bacteria?
   A. A pH level above 9
   B. A pH level below 5
   C. A pH level near 7
   D. A pH level near 5

36. According to the results of the three experiments, which combination of the three factors studied would be expected to produce the highest percent growth?
   F. pH level of 5, organic compound in Dish 2, temperature of 40°C
   G. pH level of 7, organic compound in Dish 2, temperature of 10°C
   H. pH level of 5, organic compound in Dish 1, temperature of 40°C
   J. pH level of 9, organic compound in Dish 1, temperature of 90°C

37. Which of the following conclusions is strengthened by the results of Experiment 1?
   A. *Salmonella* bacteria reproduce most efficiently in an acidic environment.
   B. *Salmonella* bacteria reproduce most efficiently in a neutral environment.
   C. *Salmonella* bacteria cannot reproduce in a basic environment.
   D. *Salmonella* bacteria cannot reproduce in an acidic environment.

GO ON TO THE NEXT PAGE.

4 ○ ○ ○ ○ ○ ○ ○ ○ **4**

38. Bacteria will generally reproduce until all of the nutrients available have been depleted. How could the experiment be altered to maximize the length of time that bacteria will reproduce?
    F. Change the observation time from 6 hours to 12 hours.
    G. Regularly re-supply each group of bacteria with unlimited nutrients.
    H. Increase the rate of growth by decreasing the pH levels.
    J. Do not test the effect of different nutrient combinations on growth.

39. Which of the following was the independent variable in Experiment 3?
    A. pH level
    B. temperature
    C. organic compound
    D. percent growth

40. The experiments recorded the percent growth that occurred over a 6-hour period. Bacteria often reproduce at a rate that drastically varies from one stage to the next. The best way to study the different stages of growth would be to record the percent growth:
    F. after 2 hours only.
    G. after 4 hours, then again after 6 hours.
    H. after 8 hours only.
    J. every 15 minutes for 3 hours.

END OF THE SCIENCE REASONING TEST.
STOP! IF YOU HAVE TIME LEFT OVER, CHECK YOUR WORK ON THIS SECTION ONLY.

WRITING TEST PROMPT

DIRECTIONS: This test is designed to assess your writing skills. You have 30 minutes to plan and write an essay based on the stimulus provided. Be sure to take a position on the issue and support your position using logical reasoning and relevant examples. Organize your ideas in a focused and logical way, and use the English language to clearly and effectively express your position.

When you have finished writing, refer to the Scoring Rubrics discussed in the Introduction (page 4) to estimate your score.

In some school districts, policy makers are expanding the radius around the school that does not receive bus service. As a result, more students must walk, bicycle, or seek alternative transportation to and from school every day. People who support the measure feel that it is a practical solution to alleviate pressure on school budgets, and, coincidentally, encourage more exercise. Opponents say transportation costs will simply be forced upon the students who no longer receive bus transportation, since they will most likely begin driving personal vehicles to school or receiving rides from others.

In your opinion, should school districts limit bus service either to save costs or to promote exercise?

In your essay, take a position on this question. You may write about either one of the two points of view given, or you may present a different point of view on this question. Use specific reasons and examples to support your opinion.

■■■ **ANSWER KEY**

English Test

1. A	21. D	41. B	61. C
2. H	22. F	42. H	62. G
3. B	23. D	43. D	63. C
4. H	24. G	44. H	64. F
5. D	25. B	45. A	65. B
6. F	26. H	46. G	66. J
7. B	27. C	47. A	67. B
8. J	28. F	48. H	68. J
9. B	29. A	49. C	69. C
10. J	30. G	50. J	70. G
11. C	31. D	51. D	71. D
12. F	32. H	52. J	72. F
13. C	33. B	53. B	73. C
14. G	34. G	54. F	74. F
15. D	35. A	55. C	75. D
16. G	36. H	56. F	
17. D	37. D	57. D	
18. F	38. J	58. G	
19. C	39. C	59. A	
20. H	40. F	60. H	

Mathematics Test

1. B	21. C	41. D
2. J	22. K	42. F
3. C	23. B	43. B
4. J	24. H	44. K
5. C	25. D	45. B
6. F	26. G	46. H
7. E	27. D	47. E
8. H	28. G	48. K
9. D	29. A	49. C
10. G	30. J	50. G
11. C	31. E	51. C
12. F	32. G	52. G
13. D	33. D	53. B
14. J	34. G	54. K
15. B	35. C	55. D
16. F	36. H	56. F
17. C	37. B	57. E
18. J	38. J	58. F
19. A	39. C	59. A
20. G	40. J	60. K

Reading Test

1. A	21. A
2. J	22. G
3. C	23. B
4. J	24. H
5. A	25. C
6. H	26. J
7. B	27. C
8. J	28. F
9. D	29. C
10. G	30. F
11. B	31. B
12. H	32. F
13. A	33. D
14. J	34. J
15. C	35. C
16. H	36. F
17. A	37. B
18. G	38. F
19. A	39. C
20. H	40. G

Science Reasoning Test

1. C	21. B
2. H	22. J
3. A	23. A
4. G	24. F
5. A	25. D
6. F	26. G
7. C	27. D
8. J	28. G
9. B	29. D
10. G	30. F
11. A	31. C
12. G	32. F
13. A	33. A
14. H	34. H
15. D	35. D
16. H	36. H
17. D	37. A
18. G	38. G
19. C	39. B
20. H	40. J

SCORING GUIDE

Your final reported score is your COMPOSITE SCORE. Your COMPOSITE SCORE is the average of all of your SCALE SCORES.

Your SCALE SCORES for the four multiple-choice sections are derived from the Scoring Table on the next page. Use your RAW SCORE, or the number of questions that you answered correctly for each section, to determine your SCALE SCORE. If you got a RAW SCORE of 60 on the English test, for example, you correctly answered 60 out of 75 questions.

Step 1 Determine your RAW SCORE for each of the four multiple-choice sections:

English _____

Mathematics _____

Reading _____

Science Reasoning _____

The following Raw Score Table shows the total possible points for each section.

RAW SCORE TABLE	
KNOWLEDGE AND SKILL AREAS	**RAW SCORES**
ENGLISH	75
MATHEMATICS	60
READING	40
SCIENCE REASONING	40
WRITING	12

Multiple-Choice Scoring Worksheet

Step 2 Determine your SCALE SCORE for each of the four multiple-choice sections using the following Scoring Worksheet. Each SCALE SCORE should be rounded to the nearest number according to normal rules. For example, $31.2 \approx 31$ and $31.5 \approx 32$. If you answered 61 questions correctly on the English section, for example, your SCALE SCORE would be 29.

English _____ × 36 = _____ ÷ 75 = _____
RAW SCORE   − 2 (*correction factor)

_____
SCALE SCORE

Mathematics _____ × 36 = _____ ÷ 60 = _____
RAW SCORE   + 1 (*correction factor)

_____
SCALE SCORE

Reading _____ × 36 = _____ ÷ 40 = _____
RAW SCORE   + 2 (*correction factor)

_____
SCALE SCORE

Science Reasoning _____ × 36 = _____ ÷ 40 = _____
RAW SCORE   + 1.5 (*correction factor)

_____
SCALE SCORE

*The correction factor is an approximation based on the average from several recent ACT tests. It is most valid for scores in the middle 50% (approximately 16–24 scale composite score) of the scoring range.

The scores are all approximate. Actual ACT scoring scales vary from one administration to the next based upon several factors.

If you take the optional Writing Test, you will need to combine your English and Writing scores to obtain your final COMPOSITE SCORE. Once you have determined a score for your essay out of 12 possible points, you will need to determine your ENGLISH/WRITING SCALE SCORE, using both your ENGLISH SCALE SCORE and your WRITING TEST SCORE. The combination of the two scores will give you an ENGLISH/WRITING SCALE SCORE, from 1 to 36, that will be used to determine your COMPOSITE SCORE mentioned earlier.

Using the English/Writing Scoring Table, find your ENGLISH SCALE SCORE on the left or right hand side of the table and your WRITING TEST SCORE on the top of the table. Follow your ENGLISH SCALE SCORE over and your WRITING TEST SCORE down until the two columns meet at a number. This number is your ENGLISH/WRITING SCALE SCORE and will be used to determine your COMPOSITE SCORE.

Step 3   Determine your ENGLISH/WRITING SCALE SCORE using the English/Writing Scoring Table on the following page:

English   _____

Writing   _____

English/Writing   _____

ENGLISH/WRITING SCORING TABLE

ENGLISH SCALE SCORE	WRITING TEST SCORE											ENGLISH SCALE SCORE
	2	3	4	5	6	7	8	9	10	11	12	
36	26	27	28	29	30	31	32	33	34	32	36	36
35	26	27	28	29	30	31	31	32	33	34	35	35
34	25	26	27	28	29	30	31	32	33	34	35	34
33	24	25	26	27	28	29	30	31	32	33	34	33
32	24	25	25	26	27	28	29	30	31	32	33	32
31	23	24	25	26	27	28	29	30	30	31	32	31
30	22	23	24	25	26	27	28	29	30	31	32	30
29	21	22	23	24	25	26	27	28	29	30	31	29
28	21	22	23	24	24	25	26	27	28	29	30	28
27	20	21	22	23	24	25	26	27	28	28	29	27
26	19	20	21	22	23	24	25	26	27	28	29	26
25	18	19	20	21	22	23	24	25	26	27	28	25
24	18	19	20	21	22	23	23	24	25	26	27	24
23	17	18	19	20	21	22	23	24	25	26	27	23
22	16	17	18	19	20	21	22	23	24	25	26	22
21	16	17	17	18	19	20	21	22	23	24	25	21
20	15	16	17	18	19	20	21	21	22	23	24	20
19	14	15	16	17	18	19	20	21	22	23	24	19
18	13	14	15	16	17	18	19	20	21	22	23	18
17	13	14	15	16	16	17	18	19	20	21	22	17
16	12	13	14	15	16	17	18	19	20	20	21	16
15	11	12	13	14	15	16	17	18	19	20	21	15
14	10	11	12	13	14	15	16	17	18	19	20	14
13	10	11	12	13	14	14	15	16	17	18	19	13
12	9	10	11	12	13	14	15	16	17	18	19	12
11	8	9	10	11	12	13	14	15	16	17	18	11
10	8	9	9	10	11	12	13	14	15	16	17	10
9	7	8	9	10	11	12	13	13	14	15	16	9
8	6	7	8	9	10	11	12	13	14	15	16	8
7	5	6	7	8	9	10	11	12	13	14	15	7
6	5	6	7	7	8	9	10	11	12	13	14	6
5	4	5	6	7	8	9	10	11	12	12	13	5
4	3	4	5	6	7	8	9	10	11	12	13	4
3	2	3	4	5	6	7	8	9	10	11	12	3
2	2	3	4	5	6	6	7	8	9	10	11	2
1	1	2	3	4	5	6	7	8	9	10	11	1

Step 4   Determine your COMPOSITE SCORE by finding the sum of all your SCALE SCORES for each of the four sections: English only (if you do not choose to take the optional Writing Test) *or* English/Writing (if you choose to take the optional Writing Test), Math, Reading, and Science Reasoning, and divide by 4 to find the average. Round your COMPOSITE SCORE according to normal rules. For example, 31.2 ≈ 31 and 31.5 ≈ 32.

_____ + _____ + _____ + _____ = _____

ENGLISH *OR*	MATHEMATICS	READING	SCIENCE	SCALE SCORE
ENGLISH/WRITING	SCALE SCORE	SCALE SCORE	SCALE SCORE	TOTAL
SCALE SCORE				

_____   ÷   4   =   _____

SCALE SCORE TOTAL   COMPOSITE SCORE

ANSWERS AND EXPLANATIONS

English Test Explanations

PASSAGE I

1. **The best answer is A.** The comma is needed to separate the introductory clause from the main clause. The date does not have to be separated by two commas, and a semicolon would indicate two complete sentences.

2. **The best answer is H.** "Far more rarer" is redundant. Remember that the ACT rewards conciseness. In addition, to form the comparative, either add the word "more" or add the "-er," not both. Always choose the grammatically correct response with the fewest words—in this case, answer choice H. Answer choice G is awkward and wordy.

3. **The best answer is B.** The gerund "leading" does not bear tense and so cannot be the main verb of the sentence. In this case, the sentence needs a form of the future tense because the search would occur after the student's report. Answer choice C, "was leading," is in the past. Answer choice D, "was lead," could never be correct because the past form of "lead" is "led" and the passive voice does not make sense here.

4. **The best answer is H.** The sentence would be improved with a definite pronoun to identify the habitat. Answer choices F and J are indefinite, and therefore should be eliminated. "Its" is correct because "woodpecker" is singular. Answer choice G is correspondingly incorrect because "their" is plural.

5. **The best answer is D.** The subject of the passage and of the paragraph is the ivory-billed woodpecker. It's the only "species" designated as such. Therefore, it's redundant to combine "species" with "ivory-billed woodpecker" in this sentence. The ACT values conciseness. Always choose the least-wordy option that is grammatically correct.

6. **The best answer is F.** In this sentence, it is necessary to use commas to set off the introductory phrase and the two independent clauses. Answer choices H and J use commas to separate short phrases that are not full clauses. Semicolons are used between independent clauses not linked by a conjunction, so answer choice G would be correct if there was no conjunction, "and." Therefore, the sentence is best as it stands.

7. **The best answer is B.** Because "species" ends in an "s," an apostrophe can simply be added to the end of the word without adding another "s" to create possession. Answer choice C is too wordy. Answer choice D is wrong for two reasons: first, "species" has to modify "survival," not the other way around, and second, in this example "species" should not be possessive.

8. **The best answer is J.** Answer choice H is incorrect because the passage already states that the most recent sighting was in 1999. The rest of the sentence is too vague to answer the question. Answer choice G does not make clear if the month in 2002 was when the biologists searched the woods or when the bird was spotted again. While answer choice F is grammatically correct and offers new information, choice J adds the most specific details to the passage.

9. **The best answer is B.** A comma is used before a coordinating conjunction joining independent clauses in a sentence. Therefore, answer choice B is correct, and answer choice C is incorrect. Answer choice A adds an extra "it" to the sentence and uses a semicolon where a comma is needed. The clause "later determined," in answer choice D, does not make sense.

10. **The best answer is J.** The topic of the paragraph is the new search for the ivory-billed woodpecker. The search is instigated by the 1999 sighting, so Sentence 1 should remain first. Sentence 2 introduces the search and should continue to follow Sentence 1. The conjunction "though" in Sentence 3, however, indicates a contrast that only makes sense if it comes after the lack of evidence cited in Sentence 4. The fifth sentence starts with the phrase, "In the end," and should remain last.

11. **The best answer is C.** Answer choices A and D are too wordy. Answer choice B is more concise, but would need a semicolon to separate the clauses because they form two complete sentences. Answer choice C uses a period to separate the sentences and is the best answer choice.

12. **The best answer is F.** Commas should be used to separate the elements in a series, but it is not necessary to put a comma between the last element in the series and the following verb. So, answer choices H and J are incorrect. A comma should come between the second to last element and the conjunction, so answer choice G is incorrect.

13. **The best answer is C.** The idea here is that researchers feared a sudden influx of birdwatchers drawn by the new sightings. The only selection that matches that meaning is answer choice C.

14. **The best answer is G.** The word "accepts" makes the most sense in the sentence because it clearly and simply indicates present tense. The phrase "is accepting of" may appear to be correct, but it is rather awkward and would be more appropriate if it referred to evidence of the birds rather than their actual existence.

15. **The best answer is D.** Sentence 3 discusses "sightings" by researchers in Arkansas. This would lead easily to information about those sightings, like the "15 sightings" mentioned in the extra sentence. Sentences 1 and 2 could refer to multiple video tapings, but the tapings are from motion-sensing cameras and are different from personal sightings. Therefore, the best place for the new sentence is after Sentence 3, answer choice D.

PASSAGE II

16. **The best answer is G.** This sentence is made up of two complete clauses that could both stand independently. Therefore, answer choices H and J would be acceptable ways to write the sentence. Answer choice H makes two complete sentences separated by a period, while J uses a semicolon to separate them. Answer choice F, "no change," is also acceptable because the conjunction "and" follows the comma. Answer choice G, however, is not acceptable because it uses a comma without a conjunction to join two complete thoughts. This is called a "comma splice," and it is grammatically incorrect.

17. **The best answer is D.** The sentence is written in the present tense, and therefore, the correct form of the verb is "spend." Answer choice B is also wrong because the sentence has a compound subject ("editors and I") which requires a plural verb form ("are" instead of "am"). Answer choice C is incorrect because it leaves the clause without a main verb.

18. **The best answer is F.** The passage is acceptable as it stands because it doesn't need a causal connection between the end of the first paragraph and the beginning of the second. In other words, the editorial board doesn't reconvene in the summer as a result of the editors' long hours, so it's unnecessary to say "consequently" or "as a result," as in answer choices G and J. "However" (answer choice H) is also unnecessary because there's no contrast.

19. **The best answer is C.** The sentence needs a relative clause to explain what is done with the call for papers. In this case, the clause needs a subject and a verb in the present tense. Answer choice D lacks a subject. Answer choice B is not in standard English word order (i.e. subject, verb, object). And finally, the phrase "nationwide research institutions" in answer choices A and C implies that each institution exists nationwide (as opposed to, say, a state university). Only answer choice C is complete and grammatically correct.

20. **The best answer is H.** "Researchers and authors" forms a compound subject. A compound subject requires a plural verb, which this sentence has. It does not need any commas, however, so the correct answer is answer choice H.

21. **The best answer is D.** This sentence needs a main clause that contains a subject, verb, and object. Answer choices B and C would leave an incomplete sentence. Answer choice A has an unclear antecedent—that is, the sentence does not make clear who is meant by "they." Only answer choice D is clear and grammatically correct.

22. **The best answer is F.** This sentence has two parallel subordinate clauses. Each clause should have the same structure, so the editors should "read" and "submit" each work. Answer choices G and J change the form of the second verb. Answer choice H is incorrect because, as it stands, the second clause is not a complete sentence and cannot be set apart by a semicolon.

23. **The best answer is D.** The sentence as it stands (answer choice F) is grammatically correct. The next sentence begins with the pronoun "those" that refers back to the subject of the previous sentence. In answer choices A and C, the subject is the editors. In answer choice D, the subject is the paper submissions, which is a better match for what comes next. Answer choice B is too wordy and the word "either" is unnecessary.

24. **The best answer is G.** The added sentence would be helpful because it would clarify how a paper might be indecipherable. This is why answer choice G is correct and answer choice J is incorrect. The form of the papers is relevant (answer choice H) because papers can be returned to the author if the formatting is poor. Answer choice F is incorrect because the new sentence does not change or establish the tone—the first sentence has

already done that by introducing the possibility of bad papers.

25. The best answer is B. The clause needs a finite verb, not a participle. This eliminates answer choices A and C. Answer choice D is incorrect because a verb should be modified by an adverb ("immediately"), not an adjective ("immediate").

26. The best answer is H. Answer choices F and G are essentially interchangeable. They both imply that the most beneficial information for the journal's readers is an example of the professional standards of the journal. Therefore, it is best to eliminate both choices. Answer choice J implies a contrast between the beneficial information and the professional standards. This does not make sense within the passage. Answer choice H, however, suggests that the professional standards refer, at least in part, to the format and presentation mentioned earlier, while the beneficial information is an additional requirement for publication. This makes the best sense in context.

27. The best answer is C. The simplest option is often the best. In this case, answer choice C has the fewest clauses and the simplest structure. It is grammatically correct and not redundant.

28. The best answer is F. Adverbial clauses, like the one that starts this sentence, need to be separated from the main clause by a comma. This eliminates answer choices H and J. The phrase, "once we finalize," indicates a single action that should be followed by another single action to keep parallel structure. The phrase, "we're sending," implies repeated or continuing action. Therefore, answer choice G is incorrect. Answer choice F has a comma after "layout," and "send" is parallel in construction with "finalize," so this is the best answer choice.

29. The best answer is A. The verb "meets" indicates that the action is taking place in the present, while the journals are being prepared to mail. Answer choice B is incorrect because the noun phrase "editorial board" is singular, and so requires a singular verb. Both answer choices C and D create incomplete sentences.

30. The best answer is G. In standard English, adjectives typically go before the nouns they modify. In this case, "well-earned" modifies "vacation," and so answer choice G is correct. The other choices are incorrect or simply awkward.

PASSAGE III

31. The best answer is D. "Italy," as it is used here, needs to be put in the possessive. Because the country is singular and does not end in an "s," the correct form is "Italy's."

32. The best answer is H. The passage states that Montessori was Italy's first modern woman physician. That implies she was trying to advance *within* the profession (answer choice H). Answer choice F would imply that the male physicians were helping her, which is contrary to the statement that she struggled. Answer choice G would imply that she was trying to promote the profession and not her own career, which is not supported by the rest of the passage. In answer choice J, the pronoun does not appear to refer to anything.

33. The best answer is B. A colon is used to introduce an explanatory phrase if the first part of the sentence creates a sense of anticipation about what follows. This sentence does not do that, so answer choice A is incorrect. However, the addition does provide important information about why Montessori was sent there, so it would be wrong to eliminate it as in answer choice D. The additional information is in a subordinate clause and so needs a comma to separate it from the rest of the sentence. Answer choice B is correct.

34. The best answer is G. The passage makes a distinction between Montessori's training and the processes of the mind. Only answer choice G, "anatomy and physiology," makes this distinction clear. Answer choices F, H, and especially J are broad and could include study of the mind. They do not make a clear distinction and are incorrect.

35. The best answer is A. This clause is specifying Montessori's studies in the processes of the mind. It needs to be an example of a process. Answer choices C and D put the emphasis on the children, not on the way they learn. Answer choice B has the right emphasis, but it is unnecessarily wordy.

36. The best answer is H. The main clause in this sentence begins with "Montessori established a 'children's house.'" What comes before is an adverbial clause that needs to be separated from the main clause by a comma. This eliminates answer choices G and J, which were also wordy and awkward. Answer choice F is also wordy and difficult to follow. Answer choice H makes clear that Montessori had sixty children from the working class when she established her house.

37. **The best answer is D.** The word "ready" actually refers to *how* the children learn, and so it modifies the verb "learn" not the noun "children." Therefore, it should be in the form of an adverb, "readily." That eliminates answer choices A and C. There is no natural pause between "children" and "readily" and no grammatical need to put a comma, so answer choice B is incorrect.

38. **The best answer is J.** Sentence 2 establishes the topic of the paragraph: Montessori's experiences in her "children's house." Sentences 3 and 4 give examples of what she learned. Sentence 1 describes how these specific experiences influenced her subsequent work. Therefore, sentence 1 should conclude the paragraph and be put after Sentence 4.

39. **The best answer is C.** By mentioning both development and learning, answer choice C combines the information in answer choices A and B. Therefore, it is more complete and specific than either of them. Answer choice D introduces the idea of school districts, which does not belong in this passage.

40. **The best answer is F.** The topic of the sentence is development, not children. This means the child's development is supposed to be compared to standards and norms, not the child in general. This eliminates answer choices H and J. Answer choice G places the apostrophe in the wrong place. The correct placement is used in answer choice F.

41. **The best answer is B.** This sentence has a compound verb: the subject "children" is shared by "develop" and "acquire." Commas are not used to separate compound verbs. (Consider the related rule about compound subjects: *Bill, and I went to the store* is clearly incorrect.) This eliminates answer choices A and C. Meanwhile, semicolons are used to separate two complete sentences. The final clause is not a complete sentence (it lacks a subject), so answer choice D is incorrect.

42. **The best answer is H.** To maintain parallel construction with the verb form "provides," use the present tense "observes."

43. **The best answer is D.** The second clause in this sentence is a relative clause. That means it is a subordinate clause that behaves like an adjective in that it helps describe a noun phrase. In this case, the noun phrase is the fundamental processes of the Montessori Method. The subsequent clause provides more information about that noun phrase and so acts like an adjective. Relative clauses are

introduced by relative pronouns. The only choice of a relative pronoun is "which," answer choice D.

44. **The best answer is H.** In simple sentences, standard English usually puts the adjective in front of its noun. While answer choice F is not grammatically incorrect, it does not match the straightforward style of the rest of the passage. Answer choice G has unnecessary commas, while J is awkward and too wordy.

45. **The best answer is A.** The fourth paragraph shifts the passage from a historical discussion of how Montessori developed her method to a description of how Montessori's method is used by schools today. This eliminates answer choice B, which talks about past development, and answer choice D, which ignores the shift in topic. Answer choice C is wrong because a discussion of Montessori's current significance shows her importance to her field, which helps justify a biography of her in the first place. That leaves answer choice A, which is correct.

PASSAGE IV

46. **The best answer is G.** The verb "immerse" needs to agree with the preceding verb "want" in order to maintain parallel construction. The verb "want" is actually "will . . . want" and is in the future tense. Therefore, answer choice G, which creates "you will immerse," is the correct answer.

47. **The best answer is A.** The underlined portion forms a clause that contrasts ("but") Paris' awe-inspiring cultural treasures with the ease of travel on the Metro. Answer choice A works grammatically because it creates two independent clauses separated by a comma. To be correct, answer choice B would need a period or a semicolon after "treasures" because "France's capital has cultural treasures" is a complete sentence. Both answer choices C and D are noun phrases in need of a verb to make sense.

48. **The best answer is H.** The underlined section introduces a nonrestrictive relative clause, which means it contributes information about what is referenced (the subway) without restricting the reference. In this case, the clause tells the reader the name of the subway system but does not distinguish it, say from subways in other cities. Nonrestrictive relative clauses are introduced by "wh"-relative pronouns (who, which, etc.) and are frequently

separated from the rest of the sentence by a comma. Answer choice G is awkward and ungrammatical. Answer choice F uses the wrong pronoun, while answer choice J would only be correct if the final clause were a complete sentence.

49. The best answer is C. The gerund "making" marks the beginning of a descriptive phrase that needs to be set apart by some form of punctuation. A dash indicates a sharp break in the continuity of the sentence. A semicolon indicates the start of a new complete sentence. Neither of these occur in this sentence, so a comma is the best choice.

50. The best answer is J. The sentence needs a main verb, and "has" fits the sense well. While it is possible to contract the subject/verb "Metro has" to "Metro's," the apostrophe is in the wrong place in answer choice G and missing in answer choice F. Answer choice H is incorrect because the Metro is more than just stations; it is a system of travel.

51. The best answer is D. Answer choice D illustrates how easy it is to access the Metro from anywhere in Paris. This would provide a good example of the Metro system's expansiveness and coverage. Answer choice B would contradict the desired emphasis. While answer choice A would indicate the Metro is popular, it doesn't provide proof that the stations are numerous. Answer choice C is irrelevant.

52. The best answer is J. The phrase "ideal for tourist travel" is all-encompassing. It could be modified by a phrase that restricts the ideal (for example, "unless you don't speak French"), but none of the choices does that. Therefore, it is best to omit the underlined portion altogether.

53. The best answer is B. Answer choice B correctly states that the stations took their names from the adjacent attractions. Answer choice A implies that the attractions named the stations, which would be impossible because the attractions are inanimate. Answer choice C implies the opposite, which is also impossible. Answer choice D makes no sense.

54. The best answer is F. Here, we have a compound adjective. The author loves the feeling of going underground and coming back to the surface. The going and coming should not be separated by a comma. "Coming" should also remain the gerund form to maintain parallel construction with "going."

55. The best answer is C. The verb "to swipe" should be in the imperative form because the author is giving a directive. The imperative form of "to swipe" is "swipe."

56. The best answer is F. Answer choice F emphasizes how a rider can utilize the full extent of the Metro at a very reasonable price. This definitely illustrates a tremendous advantage to using the subway system. Answer choice H does this, too, but to a lesser extent. Answer choice G is even more vague, and therefore, less acceptable as an answer choice. Answer choice J points out a disadvantage to using the Metro and should be eliminated.

57. The best answer is D. Commas are used to separate words or phrases in a series of three or more items. ACT style always uses a comma between the second-to-last item and the conjunction (usually "and"). Answer choices B and C do not have enough commas, while answer choice A adds an unnecessary "and" before "parking."

58. The best answer is G. In standard written English, the modifier usually goes before whatever it is modifying. Here, "generally" modifies the adjective "accustomed" and so should go before it. The main verb "to be" should also agree in tense with the other main verbs. The other verbs are in the present tense, so this sentence should use the form "are." Both of these points support answer choice G. Because "accustomed" is an adjective, there is no need to change its spelling, answer choice J.

59. The best answer is A. The author tells the reader that the Metro provides incredible freedom of movement. Because it's clear that the author is talking about the Metro, it is redundant to use the phrase "Paris Metro" again, as in answer choices B and C. Answer choice B could also only be correct if the relative pronoun "that" were removed. Answer choice D would leave a clause that reads "that providing it." This doesn't make sense because it needs something to come next. Therefore, answer choice D should be eliminated.

60. The best answer is H. Paragraph 3 talks about the ease of traveling around the city and the joys of finding new places. The new sentence continues the idea of easy traveling but adds the delight of returning to a familiar place. This completes the circuit of a day and leads smoothly to the last sentence: "Metro travel couldn't be easier!"

PASSAGE V

61. The best answer is C. *Plentiful* and *abundant* are synonyms. Therefore, it is redundant to use both of them in this sentence. Answer choice D is also grammatically incorrect.

62. The best answer is G. This sentence contains only one clause. Therefore, it is unnecessary to divide it with punctuation of any kind. The remaining answer choices imply strong divisions that are not supported by the structure of the sentence.

63. The best answer is C. Here it is necessary to choose the correct preposition to introduce the rest of the prepositional phrase, "the acidic environment of these marshlands." The preposition "in" suggests location—that the stuff that makes up peat is kept from decomposing because it is in the acidic environment. "With" would suggest accompaniment—that the stuff is sitting in the bog alongside the acidic environment, which is not correct. "For" is incorrect because it suggests that some other agent is preventing decomposition to maintain an acidic environment. Finally, "among" would only be used if there was a plural object in the prepositional phrase.

64. The best answer is F. "When peat is harvested" is an introductory clause. It should be separated from the main clause by a comma. A period or semicolon, as in answer choices G and H, would mean that it is a complete sentence.

65. The best answer is B. Choosing the proper verb form depends on understanding the sense of the sentence. Something is happening to the peat in the Irish villages. Peat is dug out of wet marshlands and used as fuel. It makes sense that at some point freshly dug peat has to dry out. This process would have to occur over time, so the correct verb form would use the participle "drying" to indicate action over time. This is called the progressive aspect.

66. The best answer is J. The passage's main idea is the use of peat as a fuel source. The most appropriate and relevant contrast would be in direct opposition to that main idea. Answer choice F talks about the amount of peat used, while Answer choices G and H state where it is used. These are details that add to the main idea, not contrast with it. Only answer choice J offers alternatives to peat as a fuel source. Therefore, answer choice J is the correct answer.

67. The best answer is B. First, the verb in this clause refers to the peat, which is singular. Therefore, the verb form must agree with a singular subject. That eliminates answer choice A. Also, the verb needs to be in the past tense to be consistent with "plowed" in the preceding clause.

68. The best answer is J. The underlined section introduces a nonrestrictive relative clause, which means it contributes information about what is referenced (Bord Na Móna) without restricting the reference. In this case, the clause tells the reader the output of the company but does not distinguish it, say, from the output of other companies. Nonrestrictive relative clauses are introduced by "wh"-relative pronouns (who, which, etc.) and are separated from the rest of the sentence by a comma. The relative clause is not a complete sentence, so answer choices F and G could never be correct.

69. The best answer is C. Answer choice C has what is known as a "comma splice." This means that the sentence is composed of two complete sentences joined together by a comma with no separating preposition or conjunction. Answer choice A has the adverb conjunction "while" after the comma, and answer choice D has the word "and." Both choices are grammatically correct and acceptable. Answer choice B simply separates the two sentences, and so it, too, is acceptable.

70. The best answer is G. Answer choice G is the most concise option. It is also consistent with "ridging machine" used later in the paragraph. In fact, none of the equipment is defined or described in any detail. Therefore, "harrow machine" fits best with the language of the paragraph.

71. The best answer is D. The correct form of the verb is "passes" to stay consistent with the rest of the paragraph. The word "passes" is used several times in the paragraph, and this sentence gives no reason to change tenses.

72. The best answer is F. Answer choices G and H would create a comma splice by combining two complete sentences with only a comma. Answer choice F uses the passive form of the verb "to draw" to correctly describe the harvester as putting the peat into a collection bin. Answer choice J is incorrect because it uses the active form of the verb. This implies that the peat is putting something into the bin, which does not make any sense in the context of the paragraph.

73. The best answer is C. The phrase "the history" is too vague. The sentence would have better clues for the reader with a pronoun referring to the sentence's subject, "peat." The correct pronoun is "its." Answer choice B, "it's," is a contraction of "it is." The verb is not necessary here, and answer choice B is incorrect.

74. **The best answer is F.** The passage puts peat in the context of Ireland from the very beginning. Peat is not just a resource, it is an *Irish* resource. Answer choice F is the only choice that acknowledges peat's role in Irish culture. Therefore, it provides the best link between the opening and closing sentences.

75. **The best answer is D.** An essay on the evolution of power sources suggests that the topic would have some breadth. In other words, it would cover more than one type of power source and more than one country. This passage only describes one power source and locates that source in only one country. Therefore, answer choice D is correct.

Mathematics Test Explanations

1. **The correct answer is B.** To find how many degrees Fahrenheit the temperature increased, you need to find the range between the highest and lowest temperature for the day. To do so, subtract the lowest temperature from the highest temperature: $21 - (-7) = 21 + 7 = 28$ degrees Fahrenheit. If you chose D, you may have forgotten that subtracting a negative number is the same thing as adding that number.

2. **The correct answer is J.** To find how much money you save when you buy a $12 video that is on sale for 20% off, you should find 20% of $12. To do so, multiply $12 by 20%, or 0.20; $(\$12)(0.20) = \$2.40$.

3. **The correct answer is C.** To compute the average of the four prices per gallon of gasoline, add the four prices and divide that sum by the number of prices, which in this case is four: $\dfrac{\$2.45 + \$2.50 + \$2.49 + \$2.56}{4} = \dfrac{10}{4}, \$2.50$.

4. **The correct answer is J.** The volume of a cube is calculated by multiplying the length by the width by the height. Because each side of a cube is congruent, simply calculate $(\text{side})^3$. Therefore, the volume is 5^3, or 125.

5. **The correct answer is C.** Given that $3(a-6) = -21$:

$$\frac{3(a-6)}{3} = \frac{-21}{3}$$

$$(a-6) + 6 = -7 + 6$$

$$a = -1$$

6. **The correct answer is F.** When a cantaloupe weighing 3.0 pound cantaloupe costs $3.87, you can find the cost of a 2.25-pound cantaloupe by setting up a proportion, or by finding the cost per pound and then multiplying by the weight. To solve with a proportion, let x be the cost of the 2.25 pound cantaloupe. Thus $\dfrac{x}{2.25} = \dfrac{\$3.87}{3.0}$; solving for x yields $x = \dfrac{\$3.87 \times 2.25}{3.0} = \$2.90$.

To solve by finding the per pound rate, divide $3.87 by 3.0 to find the cost per pound in the first cantaloupe, and then multiply that rate by 2.25 pounds, the weight of the second cantaloupe:

$$\frac{\$3.87}{3.0} \text{ pounds} = \$1.29 \text{ per pound}$$

$$(\$1.29 \text{ per pound})(2.25 \text{ pounds})$$

$$= \$2.90$$

7. **The correct answer is E.** Remembering that perpendicular lines form right angles, the angles CDA and CDB both measure 90° and thus are equal in measure, answer choice E. From the figure it may appear as if segments AD and DB are equal in length, but that cannot be determined based solely on the information given in the problem.

8. **The correct answer is H.** To solve this problem, since the equations equal each other, you must combine like terms and solve for x:

$$6x - 5 = 3x - 16$$

$$6x - 5 - 3x = 3x - 16 - 3x$$

$$3x - 5 + 5 = -16 + 5$$

$$\frac{3x}{3} = -\frac{11}{3}$$

$$x = -\frac{11}{3}$$

9. **The correct answer is D.** To solve this problem, you must distribute correctly and remember the proper signs. When you distribute $y(3-y)+5(y-7)$, you arrive at $3y - y^2 + 5y - 35$. Once you add like terms, you get $-y^2 + 8y - 35$.

10. **The correct answer is G.** First, find the value of s. Since there are 8 arcs of each length, it follows that there are 8 arcs of length $(4 + s)$. Since the circumference is 40, then $8(4 + s) = 40$. Solve for s: $32 + 8s = 40$ and $s = 1$. Now that you know the value of each length, you can solve for the degree measure of each of the arcs of length s. You know that the entire circle has 360°. You also know that the length of the smaller arc (s) is $\dfrac{1}{4}$ the length of the larger arc. Therefore, you can set up the following equation: $8x + 8\dfrac{1}{4}x = 360°$, where x is the degree measure corresponding to each arc of length 4 and $\dfrac{1}{4}x$ is the degree measure corresponding to each arc of length $s = 1$. Now you have $8x + 8\dfrac{1}{4}x$, or $8x + 2x$, which is $10x = 360°$. So $x = 36°$. Recall that x is the degree measure corresponding to each arc of length 4. The degree measure corresponding to each arc of length s is $\dfrac{1}{4}x$; $\dfrac{1}{4}(36) = 9°$.

11. The correct answer is C. To solve this problem, divide the number of those people in favor of constructing a new high school by the total number of people polled and simplify, as follows:

$$44 \div (44 + 58 + 8) = 44/110 = 2/5$$

12. The correct answer is F. To determine the ratios, it is helpful to assign numerical values to the lengths of the segments. In this case, since the ratio of AB to BC is 1:4, let AB have a length of 1 and BC have a length of 4. Since $AC = AB + BC$, it can be given a length of 5. Therefore, the ratio of lengths AB to AC is 1:5.

13. The correct answer is D. To find half of 9 feet 6 inches, recall that there are 12 inches in a foot. Therefore, 9 feet 6 inches is equal to $9(12) + 6 = 114$ inches. Half of 114 inches is 57 inches, which is equivalent to 4 feet 9 inches $[4(12) + 9 = 57]$.

14. The correct answer is J. If t is the speed of the truck, then twice the speed of the truck can be written as $2t$. If the speed of the car exceeded twice the speed of the truck by 15 mph, the car's speed was $2t + 15$.

15. The correct answer is B. If the length of the chord XY is 8, then the length of the segment XZ is 4. The right triangle XCZ has a hypotenuse of 5 (equal to the radius), leg of 4, and second leg equal to the length of segment CZ. To find the length of segment CZ you can use the Pythagorean Theorem for a right triangle ($c^2 = a^2 + b^2$ where c is the hypotenuse and a and b are legs):

$$5^2 = 4^2 + CZ^2$$
$$CZ^2 = 5^2 - 4^2$$
$$CZ^2 = 25 - 16$$
$$CZ^2 = 9$$
$$CZ = 3$$

16. The correct answer is F. To find the value of the expression $2x^3 - x^2 + 3x + 5$ for $x = -2$, simply substitute -2 into the expression wherever there is an x, as follows:

$$2(-2)^3 - (-2)^2 + 3(-2) + 5$$
$$2(-8) - (4) + 3(-2) + 5$$
$$2(-8) - 4 + (-6) + 5$$

Recall that when taking negative numbers to odd powers, they retain their negative sign; however, when negative numbers are taken to even powers, they become positive. Thus the expression $2(-8) - 4 + (-6) + 5$ is equivalent to $-16 - 4 - 6 + 6 = 21$.

17. The correct answer is C. To find the next term in the geometric sequence, recall that when looking at a geometric sequence, the nth term can be written (for some base number b) as b^n. This sequence is decreasing in magnitude, thus the absolute value of b is less than 1. It also alternates signs, which indicates that b is negative. At this point, mathematical intuition might suggest trying $b = -\dfrac{1}{3}$, and then calculating for what value of n the terms in the given sequence correspond (see table).

Table 1					
n	1	2	3	4	5
nth term	9	-3	1	$-\dfrac{1}{3}$	$\dfrac{1}{9}$
	$\left(-\dfrac{1}{3}\right)^{-2}$	$\left(-\dfrac{1}{3}\right)^{-1}$	$\left(-\dfrac{1}{3}\right)^{0}$	$\left(-\dfrac{1}{3}\right)^{1}$	$\left(-\dfrac{1}{3}\right)^{2}$

18. The correct answer is J. Since $\dfrac{1}{4}$ inch on the blueprint represents an actual length of 1 foot, 1 inch on the blue print represents an actual length of 4 feet. When the room is 3 inches by $4\dfrac{1}{4}$ inches on the blueprint, it is actually $4(3)$ feet by $4\left(4\dfrac{1}{4}\right)$ feet. Because the room is rectangular, the area is equal to length times width, so the area is $4(3) \times 4\left(4\dfrac{1}{4}\right) = 12 \times 17 = 204$ square feet.

19. The correct answer is A. Although the exact values of m and n are not known, it can be determined that the difference of m and n is always positive. This is true because subtracting a negative number is the same as adding the positive. Since $n < 0$, subtracting the negative n will always be a net addition to the value of m, which is a positive number to begin with. Therefore, answer choice A is correct.

20. The correct answer is G. To solve the equation $x + \dfrac{2}{3} = \dfrac{8}{21}$ for x, subtract $\dfrac{2}{3}$ from both sides.

Doing so will yield $x = \dfrac{8}{21} - \dfrac{2}{3}$. Fractions must have common denominators in order to be added or subtracted from one another. To obtain a common denominator in this problem, you can multiply $\dfrac{2}{3}$ by $\dfrac{7}{7}$ $\left(\text{multiplying by } \dfrac{7}{7} \text{ is like multiplying by 1, thus it does not change the value of the fraction}\right)$. $\dfrac{2}{3} \times \dfrac{7}{7} = \dfrac{14}{21}$. The equation is now $x = \dfrac{8}{21} - \dfrac{14}{21} = \dfrac{-6}{21}$, which reduces to $\dfrac{-2}{7}$.

21. **The correct answer is C.** The line $3x + 4y = -12$ is given in standard form. To find the slope, convert the equation into slope-intercept form ($y = mx + b$, where m is the slope and b is the y-intercept):

$$(3x + 4y) - 3x = -12 - 3x$$

$$\frac{(4y)}{4} = \frac{(-3x - 12)}{4}$$

$$y = \left(\frac{-3}{4}\right)x - 3$$

Since the equation is now in slope-intercept form, it is easy to see that the slope is $\dfrac{-3}{4}$.

22. **The correct answer is K.** A square with sides $(3x - 2)$ inches would have an area of $(3x - 2)(3x - 2)$ square inches. Use the "FOIL" method to multiply all terms in the equation:

First: $(3x)(3x) = 9x^2$

Outside: $(3x)(-2) = -6x$

Inside: $(-2)(3x) = -6x$

Last: $(-2)(-2) = 4$

Adding all of these terms yields the expression $9x^2 - 6x - 6x + 4$. After combining like terms, the expression is $9x^2 - 12x + 4$.

23. **The correct answer is B.** To solve this problem it is necessary to factor the polynomial $x^2 - 2x - 24$. In this case, since the final term is negative, you know that when this equation is factored, one sign will be positive and the other will be negative. Further, since the term is -24, the numbers in the problem will be factors of 24. The factors of 24 are 1 and 24, 2 and 12, 3 and 8, or 4 and 6. It is logical to look for the factors that have a difference of 2 because of the $-2x$ term in the original polynomial. In this case, 4 and 6 are the only factors of 24 that have a difference of 2. Because the term $-2x$ is negative, the logical expression is $(x + 4)(x - 6)$. Therefore, $x + 4$ is the correct answer choice.

24. **The correct answer is H.** As k gets larger and larger without bound, the expression $\dfrac{4}{(2 + k)}$ becomes 4 divided by an increasingly large number. For example, think about the trend between the following fractions: $\dfrac{4}{100}, \dfrac{4}{10,000}, \dfrac{4}{1,000,000}$, ... Looking at it this way, you can see that the expression for r gets closer and closer to zero.

25. **The correct answer is D.** To convert 25°C to degrees Fahrenheit using the formula $F = \left(\dfrac{9}{5}\right)C + 32$, simply substitute 25 for C in the formula:

$$\left(\frac{9}{5}\right)25 + 32 = 77°F$$

26. **The correct answer is G.** In a rectangle with length l which is 5 inches longer than the width w, the relation between the sides is $l = w + 5$. Since perimeter, which is the distance around, can be written as twice the length plus twice the width, $38 = 2l + 2w$. In order to solve for width w, use the equation $l = w + 5$ to substitute into the perimeter equation:

$$38 = 2(w + 5) + 2w$$

$$38 = 2w + 10 + 2w$$

$$38 - 10 = 4w + 10 - 10$$

$$\frac{28}{4} = \frac{4w}{4}$$

$$w = 7$$

27. **The correct answer is D.** For the equation $3x^2 - 2x - 21 = 0$, all solutions of x can be found by either factoring or by using the quadratic formula $\left[x = \dfrac{(-b \pm \sqrt{(b^2 - 4ac)})}{2a}\right]$ for quadratic equations $ax^2 + bx + c = 0$. In this case, since the final term is negative, you know that when this equation is factored, one sign will be positive and the other will be negative. Knowing that the factors of 21 are 1 and 21 and 3 and 7, you can guess and check your answers with relative ease. In this case, the correct answer is $(3x + 7)(x - 3) = 0$.

Solve for x: $x = \dfrac{-7}{3}$ or $x = 3$.

28. **The correct answer is G.** A good way to go about solving this problem is to think of the tests as each having a value of 100 points, making the total of all 3 tests worth 300 points. In order to average 87% overall, Sulema would then need to score 87% of the 300 points, or 300(0.87), or 261 points. By scoring 88% and 79% on her previous tests, she has already obtained 88 + 79, or 167 points. Thus Sulema must score 261 − 167, or 94 points on the third test, which is equivalent to 94%.

29. **The correct answer is A.** If $a^b = m$ and $c^{2b} = n$, then $mn = (a^b)(c^{2b})$. Because a and c are not necessarily the same number, you cannot simply add the exponents. The only legitimate answer choice that further manipulates the expression $(a^b)(c^{2b})$ factors out the b exponent and places it outside a set of parentheses. Thus $(a^b)(c^{2b}) = (a^b c^{2b}) = (ac^2)^b$.

30. **The correct answer is J.** A circle with diameter 12 inches has a radius of 6 inches. The area of a circle is $A = \pi r^2$, where r is the radius. Thus, the area of this circle is $A = \pi (6^2) = 36\pi$ square inches.

31. **The correct answer is E.** The percent of students who pass both exams is (85%)(70%), or 0.85×0.70, which is 0.595. In a sample of 100, 100×0.595, or 59.5 (roughly 60) students would be expected to pass both exams.

32. **The correct answer is G.** Given that $\sin A = \dfrac{3}{5}$, you might want to draw a picture like the one below to illustrate the situation.

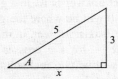

In this case, the ratio of the side opposite angle A to the hypotenuse is $\dfrac{3}{5}$. To find $\tan A$, the length of the other leg is needed. This can be obtained using the Pythagorean Theorem, or by knowing that this is a special 3–4–5 right triangle. According to the Pythagorean Theorem (in a right triangle with sides a, b, and c, where c is the hypotenuse, $c^2 = a^2 + b^2$), $5^2 = 3^2 + x^2$, where x is the length

of the unknown leg. Solve for x:

$$x^2 = 5^2 - 3^2$$

$$x^2 = 25 - 9$$

$$x^2 = 16$$

$$x = 4$$

Once the length of the third leg is obtained, $\tan A = \dfrac{\text{opposite}}{\text{adjacent}} = \dfrac{3}{4}$.

33. **The correct answer is D.** To solve $\dfrac{[(x-3)(x-6)]}{[(3-x)(x-6)]}$ for any x other than 3 or 6, first try to cancel any possible quantities. In this case, $(x - 6)$ appears in both the numerator and the denominator, so it can be canceled out of the equation. The new equation is then $\dfrac{(x-3)}{(3-x)}$. You also must realize that $(3 - x)$ can be written as $-1(x - 3)$. Thus the remaining expression is:

$$\frac{(x-3)}{(-1(x-3))}$$

$$-1 \times \frac{(x-3)}{(x-3)}$$

$$-1 \times 1 = -1$$

34. **The correct answer is G.** The first step in solving this problem is to factor $\sqrt{27}$ and $\sqrt{48}$:

$$\sqrt{27} = \sqrt{9} \times \sqrt{3} = 3\sqrt{3}$$

$$\sqrt{48} = \sqrt{16} \times \sqrt{3} = 4\sqrt{3}$$

Now, you can add the simplified numbers; thus $\sqrt{27} + \sqrt{48} = 3\sqrt{3} + 4\sqrt{3}$, or $7\sqrt{3}$.

35. **The correct answer is C.** When AB is 5 inches long, BC is 8 inches long, and AC is 3 inches long, $\triangle ABC$ has a perimeter of $5 + 8 + 3 = 16$. To find the perimeter of $\triangle XYZ$ when its longest side is 20, you can set up proportions to find the lengths of the sides, since the sides of similar triangles are in proportion to each other. In this case, you can take the proportion of the longest sides, 20:8, and apply it to the perimeter p:

$$\frac{20}{8} = \frac{p}{16}$$

$$p = \frac{20 \times 16}{8} = 40$$

36. The correct answer is H. When square $ABCD$ is divided as shown, each of the small triangles has legs of length 2 and 4. They also happen to be right triangles, because each shares one angle with the corner of the large square, which are right angles. To solve for the area of the shaded region, you can use the Pythagorean Theorem to calculate the length of the side of the shaded square. Alternatively, you can find the area of one triangle, quadruple that value, and subtract it from the area of square $ABCD$, which is 6^2, or 36 square inches.

The area of a triangle is equal to $\frac{1}{2}$(base)(height). In a right triangle, either leg will work as the value for the base or the height, so the area of one triangle is $A = \frac{1}{2}(2)(4) = 4$. The area of the 4 triangles together, then, is 4×4, or 16. Thus the area of the shaded region is $36 - 16$, or 20.

37. The correct answer is B. Since AC is the diameter of the circle, and D is the midpoint of AC, D is the center of the circle. Thus the distance from D to any point on the circle is equal to the radius, r. Since B is a point on the circle, the distance BD is equal to r. Since A is a point on the circle, the distance AD is also equal to r. Further, since AB is congruent to BC, the segment AB is perpendicular to the segment AD, thus the measure of angle ADB is 90°. In the triangle ABD, two sides are equal to r, thus the triangle is isosceles with one of the angles equal to 90°. The other two angles are then equal in measure and add up to 90°. Therefore, angle ABD has a measure of 45°.

38. The correct answer is J. To solve this problem, recall that the midpoint formula for points (x_1, y_1) and (x_2, y_2) is $\left(\dfrac{(x_1 + x_2)}{2}, \dfrac{(y_1 + y_2)}{2} \right)$. Therefore, for points $(-1, 3)$ and $(2, 5)$, the midpoint is $\left(\dfrac{(-1 + 2)}{2}, \dfrac{(3 + 5)}{2} \right) = \left(\dfrac{1}{2}, \dfrac{8}{2} \right)$, or $\left(\dfrac{1}{2}, 4 \right)$.

39. The correct answer is C. Maria ran 5 miles in 37 minutes 29 seconds, which is about 37.5 minutes. To solve for miles per hour, first calculate how long it took Maria to travel one mile. $\dfrac{37.5 \text{ minutes}}{5 \text{ miles}} = \dfrac{7.5 \text{ minutes}}{\text{mile}}$, or 1 mile in 7.5 minutes. To convert this into miles per hour, simply multiply by the number of minutes there are in one hour: $\left(\dfrac{60 \text{ minutes}}{1 \text{ hour}} \right) \times \left(\dfrac{1 \text{ mile}}{7.5 \text{ minutes}} \right) = 8$ miles per hour.

40. The correct answer is J. To find $g(f(x))$ using the values of the functions $f(x)$ and $g(x)$ as given in the tables, think of $g(f(x))$ as applying the function g to $f(x)$. So, first find $f(x)$ for $x = -1$; $f(-1) = 2$. Then, find $g(x)$ for $x = 2 : g(2) = 3$.

41. The correct answer is D. To find an equivalent expression for $x^{\frac{1}{2}} y^{\frac{3}{4}} z^{\frac{5}{8}}$, it is important to be familiar with exponent rules. For example, $x^{\frac{2}{3}} = (x^2)^{\frac{1}{3}} = \sqrt[3]{x^2}$. The first step in this problem would be to "pull out" a common multiple from the exponents. To better see this, it might be helpful to convert all of the exponents into a common denominator: $x^{\frac{1}{2}} y^{\frac{3}{4}} z^{\frac{5}{8}} = x^{\frac{4}{8}} y^{\frac{6}{8}} z^{\frac{5}{8}}$. In this case, you can see that $\frac{1}{8}$ is the common multiple: $x^{\frac{4}{8}} y^{\frac{6}{8}} z^{\frac{5}{8}} = (x^4 y^6 z^5)^{\frac{1}{8}}$. Further, $(x^4 y^6 z^5)^{\frac{1}{8}}$ can be written as $\sqrt[8]{x^4 y^6 z^5}$.

42. The correct answer is F. To solve $A = \dfrac{1}{2} h(b_1 + b_2)$ for b_1, divide both sides by h and multiply both sides by 2. The remaining equation is $2\dfrac{A}{h} = b_1 + b_2$. Then simply subtract b_2 from both sides of the equation to get $b_1 = 2\dfrac{A}{h} - b_2$.

43. The correct answer is B. To find the rate of gasoline use, which translates into miles per gallon, divide the number of miles traveled by the number of gallons of gasoline used. In this case, you can see that the graph goes through the point (100,5), (200,10) and so on. Based on this information, the rate would be $\dfrac{100 \text{ miles}}{5 \text{ gallons}}$, or 20 miles per gallon.

44. The correct answer is K. In a graph, the values at which $y = 0$ will be where the graph of a function crosses the x-axis. As seen in the figure, the graph of $y = ax^2 + bx + c$ crosses the x-axis twice; thus there will be two real solutions for the equation $0 = ax^2 + bx + c$. Imaginary solutions would apply if the graph did not cross the x-axis at any point.

45. The correct answer is B. Recall that $|x|$ means "absolute value of x," which is the magnitude of a number, regardless of its sign. For instance $|-2| = |2| = 2$. In the case of this problem, the equation $|x| = x + 12$ can be broken into 2 related sub-equations: $x = x + 12$ and $-x = x + 12$. When

$x = x + 12$, the equation does not make sense because if you subtract x from both sides, $0 = 12$ remains, which obviously is false. With the other sub-equation, $-x = x + 12$, you can subtract an x from both sides to get $-2x = 12$. Dividing by -2, you arrive at $x = -6$.

46. **The correct answer is H.** To solve this problem, convert $\frac{1}{3}$ and $\frac{1}{2}$ to fractions with a common denominator, such that $\frac{1}{3} = \frac{2}{6}$ and $\frac{1}{2} = \frac{3}{6}$. The halfway point will be somewhere between $\frac{2}{6}$ and $\frac{3}{6}$. From there, you can increase the magnitude of the denominator so that a halfway point between the numerators is more evident. $\frac{1}{3} = \frac{2}{6} = \frac{4}{12}$ and $\frac{1}{2} = \frac{3}{6} = \frac{6}{12}$. Thus the halfway point is between $\frac{4}{12}$ and $\frac{6}{12}$, which is $\frac{5}{12}$.

47. **The correct answer is E.** Because Laura recorded the $20 as income, the balance of the budget would appear to be $20 higher than it should be. However, because the $20 was an expense, once the $20 was deducted from the income statement and then deducted again from the expense report, the balance would appear to be $40 more than it should.

48. **The correct answer is K.** Think of each shift as a spot to be filled: __×__×__×__×__. In each spot there are only a certain number of available workers. For example, the first spot can have any of the 5 volunteers working, leaving 4 possible workers for the next shift, and so on. Therefore, the number of possible arrangements of volunteers is $5 \times 4 \times 3 \times 2 \times 1 = 5!$, or 120.

49. **The correct answer is C.** To find the distance between points $(4,-7)$ and $(-1,5)$ in the standard (x,y) coordinate plane, use the distance formula $d = \sqrt{[(x_2 - x_1)^2 + (y_2 - y_1)^2]}$ as follows:

$$\sqrt{(-1 - 4)^2 + (5 + 7)^2}$$

$$\sqrt{(-5)^2 + (12)^2} = \sqrt{169}$$

$$\sqrt{169} = 13$$

Another way to look at this problem would be to draw a picture (as below). Then you can use the

Pythagorean Theorem to find the hypotenuse of the triangle that is formed from those points.

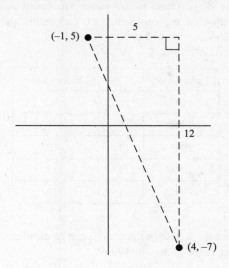

50. **The correct answer is G.** The diameter of the cylinder is 3 meters. Therefore, the radius is 1.5 meters. Using the formula for the volume of a right circular cylinder, $V = \pi r^2 h$ with h equal to the length 10 meters, $V = \pi (1.5)^2 (10)$, or approximately 70.65 cubic meters. Since water weighs about 2,205 pounds per cubic meter, the weight of the water cargo is $2,205 \times 70.65$, or about 156,000 pounds.

51. **The correct answer is C.** Since the two lines are parallel, the two triangles are similar and share the same constant ratio. The smaller triangle has one side with a length of 4 cm, and the larger triangle has one side with a length of $4 + 12$, or 16 cm. The legs of the triangles have a ratio of 4:16, which can be reduced to 1:4. The ratio of 1:4 also extends to the area of the triangles. You are given that the smaller triangle has an area of 8cm^2. The larger triangle has an area that is 4 times larger, so the area of the larger triangle is $4 \times 8 = 32$ cm^2.

52. **The correct answer is G.** To solve for the total measure of all interior angles of a regular polygon, use the formula $(n-2)(180°)$ where n is the number of vertices of the polygon. A regular hexagon has 6 vertices, so the total measure of all interior angles is $(6 - 2)(180) = (4)(180) = 720°$. Since there are six interior angles, each one is $\frac{720°}{6} = 120°$.

53. **The correct answer is B.** The best way to solve this problem is to set up a table indicating the time

period in years and the number of both CDs and video games purchased during the years given. The rate of purchase is the same, so, based on information in the problem, you can fill in the table below.

Time period	CDs	Video games
1993	7	6
1994	9	9
1995	11	12
1996	13	15
1997	15	18

Teenagers bought the same average number of CDs and video games in 1994.

54. **The correct answer is K.** The first step in answering this question is to set $x^2 - 45b^2 = 4xb$ equal to zero, by isolating all of the terms on the left side:

$$x^2 - 4xb - 45b^2 = 0$$

The next step is to factor the equation and set each group equal to 0 in order to solve for x:

$$(x + 5b)(x - 9b) = 0$$

$$x + 5b = 0, \text{ so } x = -5b$$

$$x - 9b = 0, \text{ so } x = 9b$$

The two solutions for x are $-5b$ or $9b$.

55. **The correct answer is D.** This question tests your ability to recognize and apply the distributive property of multiplication. According to the distributive property, for any numbers a, b, and c, $a(b - c) = ab - ac$.

$a(b - c) = ab - ac$, which is NOT equivalent to

$ca - ba$, so Roman Numeral I is incorrect; eliminate answer choices B, C, and E.

$ab - ac$, so Roman Numeral II is correct.

$(b - c)a$, so Roman Numeral III is also correct.

Since II and III are equivalent to $a(b - c)$, answer choice D is correct.

56. **The correct answer is F.** By definition, the tangent of any angle is the $\dfrac{\sin}{\cos}$. Therefore, $\dfrac{(\cos x)}{(\tan x)(\sin x)}$ is equal to $\dfrac{\cos x}{\frac{(\sin x)}{(\cos x)}(\sin x)}$. Multiply both the numerator and denominator by $\cos x$ to get $\dfrac{\cos^2 x}{\sin^2 x}$.

57. **The correct answer is E.** By definition, if a and b are inversely proportional, then $a_1 b_1 = a_2 b_2$. Therefore, $(36)(12) = (48)a$. Solve for a as follows:

$$(36)(12) = (48)a$$

$$432 = 48a$$

$$9 = a$$

58. **The correct answer is F.** The best way to solve this problem is to plug in the answer choices for c, and factor the equation, starting with answer choice F:

$$5x^2 + 16x + 3 = 0$$

$$(5x + 1)(x + 3) = 0$$

$$5x + 1 = 0, x = \dfrac{-1}{5}$$

$$x + 3 = 0; x = -3$$

Answer choice F gives you 2 distinct solutions for x, so you do not need to try the remaining answer choices. Using the quadratic formula to solve the other choices will not give you real solutions.

59. **The correct answer is A.** To solve this problem, you must realize that the volume of a cube is equal to (length)(width)(height) or simply (side)^3, since all sides of a cube are equivalent in length. To find the length of one side, find the cube root of 64, which is 4. $(4^3 = 64)$ Because all sides of a cube are equal, the shortest distance from the center of the cube to the base of the cube will equal the midpoint of the length of the cube, which is $\dfrac{4}{2}$, or 2.

60. **The correct answer is K.** The line $5x + 8y = 17$ is given in standard form. You should find the slope of this line by converting the equation into

slope-intercept form ($y = mx + b$, where m is the slope and b is the y-intercept):

$$5x + 8y = 17$$
$$8y = -5x + 17$$
$$y = \frac{-5x}{8} + \frac{17}{8}$$

Since the equation is now in slope-intercept form, it is easy to see that the slope of the line is $\frac{-5}{8}$. The slope of a line perpendicular to the line with a slope of $\frac{-5}{8}$ is $\frac{8}{5}$, answer choice K (remember that perpendicular lines have negative reciprocal slopes).

Reading Test Explanations

PASSAGE I

1. **The best answer is A.** In the second paragraph, the narrator states, "I didn't want to start a trend of hair-raising stunts," but his father continues with his plan for a rappelling platform anyway.

2. **The best answer is J.** The passage focuses on the fun that the narrator, his father, and his friends had while building a rappelling platform, even though there was some hesitation on the part of the narrator. Only the first paragraph details the narrator's father's popularity, and nothing in the passage suggests that the narrator is "struggling" with it.

3. **The best answer is C.** The first and second paragraph demonstrate that the narrator is more timid than his father when it comes to exhilarating stunts. The narrator is not sure whether he wants to bring his friends to his father for ideas.

4. **The best answer is J.** The first sentence of the passage establishes a timeframe that reveals the narrator is no longer a child: "As I was growing up, . . ." Therefore eliminate answer choices G and H. The tone of the passage is positive so answer choice J is best.

5. **The best answer is A.** The last sentence of the first paragraph describes the narrator's father's "extreme career and energetic lifestyle." Answer choice D might seem correct, although the passage notes that the narrator's father was once a Hollywood stuntman, indicating that he would be trained in safety procedures, some of which arise during his "impromptu lesson on the critical safety rules."

6. **The best answer is H.** In the paragraph, the author describes the pleasure of following his father around the lumberyard, as well as the anticipation of what all the "shiny, new parts" would serve to build, which best supports answer choice H.

7. **The best answer is B.** After this sentence, the rest of the passage describes how the narrator's friends convinced him to consult his father for advice on a bigger, bolder stunt. This information suggests that this uncommon adventure, at least, was the result of the narrator's father's unusual occupation.

8. **The best answer is J.** According to the passage, "My father is recently retired from his career as a Hollywood stunt performer. When I was a child, he would do more death-defying tricks in a week than I'm sure I will ever do in my lifetime. My father's extreme career and energetic lifestyle made him the coolest dad in town, and I had to live up to him," which best supports answer choice J.

9. **The best answer is D.** The word "rigging" is a well-known sailing term, referring to the ropes and pulleys used with the sails. By extension, any support system of ropes or similar lines—such as the one required for rappelling—could be called "rigging." The other answer choices are mentioned in the passage, but do not have the same meaning as "rigging."

10. **The best answer is G.** The passage states that "At first, I resisted, since I didn't want to start a trend of hair-raising stunts on my neighborhood street. Who knows what the old lady across the street would think?" Answer choice G is the best choice because while the passage focuses on a fun experience that the narrator had with his friends, it also describes his apprehension to do anything that could be unreasonably dangerous or disruptive to the neighborhood.

PASSAGE II

11. **The best answer is B.** The passage states that Robert Catesby, Guy Fawkes, and several other Roman Catholics "were thought to be denouncers of the king's own Church of England," and they "decided that unless something was done from within, nothing would likely change." These statements suggest that some English Roman Catholics did not agree with the king and rebelled against him, seeking their own religious freedom. The other answer choices are not supported by the passage.

12. **The best answer is H.** The passage asserts that the plan was carefully conceived and well executed, except just before the planned detonation, when a conflicted conscience led one conspirator to reveal the plan to a government official, which best supports answer choice H.

13. **The best answer is A.** The last paragraph states that "Guy Fawkes Day serves as a chilling reminder" for British people. Answer choice D seems plausible, but the passage does not indicate that modern British citizens find fault with (i.e., consider depraved) Fawkes' reaction to the king's policy governing religion.

14. **The best answer is J.** The phrase "tongue-in-cheek" implies humor at the expense of members

of parliament. Skepticism of the true motives of legislators is evident in the passage.

15. The best answer is C. The final two sentences of the passage state that "an individual will press back … in defense of his beliefs." This best supports answer choice C.

16. The best answer is H. The execution was meant to teach a lesson to the public. The king wanted to make a powerful statement against treason, so he chose an "unusual" punishment to shock the masses. The word "exotic" can refer to something that is "unusual" or "unexpected," so it is the best choice here.

17. The best answer is A. As Fawkes and his Catholic cohorts saw it, the king was unreasonably treading on their right to practice their own religion. In the second paragraph, the author asserts that the Church of England was "the king's own," insinuating that it held political sway. Hence, answer choice A is correct because it represents an action of government taken to preserve its power. The other choices reflect government actions taken for the common good.

18. The best answer is G. The passage implies that although the threat of punishment may deter most people from action, "no brutal threat can stop the most committed believer," which best supports answer choice G.

19. The best answer is A. The passage states that the conspirators were lucky to find a cellar space beneath Westminster Palace. A physical sense of "stumbled upon," as in answer choices B and C does not make sense in context. Answer choice D is incorrect because the decision to seek something seems unrelated to luck.

20. The best answer is H. According to the passage, the conspirators were preparing an explosion underneath the floor of Parliament in order to maximize destruction. The "mineshaft" refers to the actual space to be filled with explosives.

PASSAGE III

21. The best answer is A. The first two paragraphs describe the qualities of Southern Gothic literature. The rest of the passage relates Tennessee Williams' tumultuous life story, explaining in the process how the author's family members inspired several of the his characters, which best supports answer choice A.

22. The best answer is G. The passage maintains an even, analytical tone, meaning the author does not attempt to persuade the reader to feel a certain way about the facts of Williams' life; the author is interested in William's life, but remains detached, or apart, from it. The other answer choices suggest emotions that are not indicated by the tone of the passage.

23. The best answer is B. The year of publication of Williams' plays mentioned in the passage are (in order of appearance) 1948, 1955, 1944, and 1958. The passage states that the play from 1948, *A Streetcar Named Desire*, won a Pulitzer Prize, perhaps the most prestigious literary award in the United States.

24. The best answer is H. The prefrontal lobotomy is described as a "now-defunct" ("outdated") procedure that was "ruinous" ("destructive") to Rose, rendering her a vegetable. The other choices hint at some benefit to the procedure, but the passage asserts that no good to Rose nor to the Williams family came from the treatment.

25. The best answer is C. The third paragraph describes how Williams used family members as models for his characters. The final paragraph details how emotionally damaged he was for the rest of his life. This best supports answer choice C. Answer choice D may be distracting, but the fact that Williams is "among the most celebrated" of Southern Gothic playwrights proves that his work did indeed appeal to his audience.

26. The best answer is J. The phrase "blatant accusations" refers to transparent rhetoric that might come from a character taking a stand on the "moral issues" of the past. The richness of Southern Gothic literature is due in part to the absence of overt commentary on such subjects. The reader is left to infer the morality in the prose from the actions of the characters. The word "overtly" refers to something that is open and obvious.

27. The best answer is C. The passage states that Williams' "mother … pushed him toward creative arts during his period of illness." He "heartily accepted" her gift of a typewriter. These statements best support answer choice C.

28. The best answer is F. According to the passage, Southern Gothic literature "reflects life in the American South. It maintains some of the characteristics of Gothic writing, such as use of the supernatural or the ironic; however, Southern Gothic does not focus on creating tension and suspense as do other Gothic genres." In addition, the passage states that "that the Southern Gothic writer is able to present and explore moral issues of the American South, such as slavery and bigotry . . ." These statements best support answer choice F.

29. The best answer is C. A person "depressed and fighting alcoholism" can be said to be "embroiled" in personal problems. As for Williams' characters, which are characteristic of Southern Gothic style, they are brooding and often uninviting, and it is through them that "moral quandaries" (ethical dilemmas) are analyzed.

30. The correct answer is F. The word "postbellum" means, in general, "post-war," but it is usually restricted to mean "post-Civil-War." With the end of the Civil War came the end of slavery, but antebellum, or pre-war attitudes of "racism and inequality" persisted, which are what Williams' characters struggle to reconcile. This best supports answer choice F.

PASSAGE IV

31. The best answer is B. According to the passage, jack pine "depends on regular fires to expose the seeds within its tough cones." It is likely that any management of the forests would include periodic, supervised burning in order to encourage new growth.

32. The best answer is F. The passage states that, "The early 1900s, though, saw natural fires suppressed by new forest management policies and, consequently, jack pine forests quickly diminished." These fire prevention policies stopped all fires, most likely because of the destructive threat they pose to land, buildings, and infrastructure. An unforeseen consequence ("externality") was the depletion of fire-dependent jack pines, which constitute the exclusive habitat of the Kirtland's warbler.

33. The best answer is D. The passage states that the warblers are "extremely fastidious [picky] about their habitat." Subsequent paragraphs describe historical strain on Jack pine forests which host the birds. Answer choices B and C are never said to be detrimental to the success of the bird. Answer choice A, while detrimental, is coincidental to the birds' renewed proliferation among the

jack pines. The principal reason that the bird is endangered is the widespread decline of suitable habitat.

34. The best answer is J. The passage states that the Kirtland's warbler "migrates to the Bahamas for the winter." This suggests a temporary stay, much like how people in the United States may winter in Florida, but still call their northern residence home. The warbler engages in its most complex behavior while in Michigan (i.e., building nests and mating), which best supports answer choice J.

35. The best answer is C. According to the passage, forest policy at the turn of the century dictated that all fires should be prevented; as a result, Jack pines, which require fire to reproduce, suffered, which best supports answer choice C.

36. The best answer is F. The word "brood" describes the group of eggs a bird raises at one time. Thus a "brood parasite" is an organism that preys on the nestling of another bird.

37. The best answer is B. The fact that the passage claims that Kirtland's warblers are "fastidious about their habitat" indicates that their habitat requirements are uncommonly rigid as compared to other birds, which best supports answer choice B.

38. The best answer is F. The passage states "the tree depends on regular fires to expose the seeds within its tough cones." This indicates the cones are ready prior to the fire, eliminating answer choice G. Answer choices H and J are not supported by the passage.

39. The best answer is C. The Jack pine problem is cited as the major contributing factor to Kirtland's warbler decline. These trees are the bird's habitat. Answer choice D might appear to be correct, but the logging of jack pines is not cited as a reason for the widespread depletion of the tree; fire prevention is.

40. The best answer is G. The word "percolates" means "drains" in the context of soil, indicating it is "permeable." This is important to prevent flooding of nests. The passage continues by indicating that Grayling sand supports the plants that the Kirtland's warbler requires.

Science and Reasoning Test Explanations

PASSAGE I

1. **The best answer is C.** According to Figure 2, Amino Acid A (the solid line) has the highest rate (on the y-axis) at a water volume between 10 mL and 15 mL. This volume is closest to answer choice C, 12 mL.

2. **The best answer is H.** Amino Acid A and Amino Acid B have the same reaction rate when the two lines cross on the graph. This happens at a water volume of approximately 50 mL.

3. **The best answer is A.** Figure 3 shows that the reaction rate of Amino Acid B is not dependent on the residue concentration. Figure 4 shows that the reaction rate of Amino Acid B is dependent on the amino acid concentration. Therefore, the figures do not support the researcher's claims that the reaction of Amino Acid B is dependent on both concentrations.

4. **The best answer is G.** According to Figure 4, Amino Acid A always has a lower rate of reaction than Amino Acid B. This does not support the researcher's claims that the reaction rate for Amino Acid A at any given concentration will always be greater than Amino Acid B for the same concentration. Answer choices F and H can be eliminated because the effect of residue concentrations on the rate of reaction is not shown in Figure 4.

5. **The best answer is A.** According to the figure, the water volume of peak reaction rates for amino acids in the muscles (glycine) is higher (35 mL) than that of amino acids in DNA (alanine–20 mL).

PASSAGE II

6. **The best answer is F.** Scientist 1 discusses nature as the major factor contributing to the low lake levels. Scientist 2 discusses human activities as the major contributing factor. This is the major difference between the scientists' viewpoints. Answer choices G and H can be eliminated because the scientists do not discuss the effects of the water or lake levels.

7. **The best answer is C.** The two scientists are discussing the causes of low lake levels in the Great Lakes. This implies that both scientists agree that recent trends show that the lake levels are decreasing. Answer choice B can be eliminated because only Scientist 2 supports this viewpoint.

8. **The best answer is J.** Scientist 1 says, "the influence of human regulation on lake levels is inconsequential. Because water is added through snow and rain and taken away through evaporation, nature has most of the control over lake levels." The scientist believes that the lake levels are mainly controlled by nature, and human manipulation does not interfere. Answer choices F and H can be eliminated because only Scientist 2 discusses this information.

9. **The best answer is B.** Scientist 2 talks about a number of ways that human activity causes the Great Lakes' water levels to decrease. Activities such as the Lake Michigan diversion at Chicago, the dredging and modifying of the St. Clair and Detroit rivers, and channeling and shore lining modifications in connecting the channels of the Great Lakes have all contributed to the low lake levels. This information best supports answer choice B.

10. **The best answer is G.** If studies have shown precipitation and evaporation levels to be stable for the last 50 years, Scientist 1's viewpoint would be weakened. This is because Scientist 1 says a recent increase in evaporation has contributed to lower lake levels: "The recent decline of water levels in the Great Lakes, now at lows not seen since the mid-1960s, is due to a number of causes. High degrees of evaporation from warmer than usual temperatures in recent years . . ." Because this statement would be disproved, the scientist's viewpoint would be weakened.

11. **The best answer is A.** The best way to answer this question is by the process of elimination. Answer choice B is incorrect because the passage says, "the Lake Michigan diversion at Chicago moves water out of Lake Michigan and into the Mississippi River for domestic, navigation, hydroelectric, and sanitation purposes." Answer choice C is incorrect because the passage states "the St. Clair and Detroit rivers have been dredged and modified. This has caused some drop in the levels of Lake Michigan and Lake Huron." Answer choice D is incorrect because the passage says, "the infilling of shoreline areas can reduce the flow carrying capacity of the river." Answer choice A is correct because it is the only answer choice that is not discussed by Scientist 2.

12. **The best answer is G.** If the water deposited in aquifers surrounding the Great Lakes was used within the Great Lakes' watershed, the water would be cycling through the Great Lakes, and no water would be taken outside of the cycle. Thus, this would have little or no effect on lake levels, answer choice G.

PASSAGE III

13. The best answer is A. If heat were to flow from the water in the capsule to the surrounding oven, the heat flow would be negative because the water is losing energy. The only trial in which this occurred is Trial I, answer choice A (Trial 1: -94 J/s).

14. The best answer is H. If the best insulators are those that are the poorest heat conductors, material with the lowest heat flow are the best insulators. Of the four answer choices, fiberglass has the lowest heat flow, so it is the best insulator.

15. The best answer is D. According to Table 1, heat flowed at a rate of 59 J/s when 1.0 inch of cellulose was used as an insulator. This is the greatest flow rate among the combinations shown in the answer choices.

16. The best answer is H. The thermal conductivity for fiberglass at 1.0 in. and 1.5 in. is 38 J/s and 32 J/s, respectively. The thermal conductivity for cellulose at 1.0 in. and 1.5 in. is 59 and 45 J/s, respectively. The results show that cellulose has a higher conductivity than fiberglass and proves answer choice H is NOT true. Therefore, answer choice H is the correct answer.

17. The best answer is D. Trials 3 and 5 both had the same insulation material, initial temperature, and oven temperature; however, they had different heat flows. The only condition that was varied between the two trials was the thickness of the insulator. This suggests that heat flow depends on the thickness of the insulating material, answer choice D.

PASSAGE IV

18. The best answer is G. According to Tables 1 and 2, as the weight of the object increases (going down the column) for each brand, the average force required to move the object also increases. In other words, there is a direct relationship.

19. The best answer is C. Table 1 shows that for brand B cookware, when the mass of the weighted object was 150 g and 250 g, the average force required to move the object was 0.090 N and 0.147 N, respectively. Because 200 g is in between 150 g and 250 g, you would expect the force needed to move an object that has a mass of 200 g to be between 0.090 and 0.147 N. Answer

choice C (0.12 N) is the only answer choice within this range.

20. The best answer is H. The results from Table 1 show that brand C cookware has the smallest coefficient of static friction. The results from Table 2 show that brand Y cooking spray has the smallest coefficient of static friction. This information suggests that these two brands, if combined, would result in the surface with the least coefficient of static friction.

21. The best answer is B. Table 2 shows the results of Experiment 2. In the table, brands X and Y were both tested with 50 g, 150 g, and 250 g objects. Brand Z, however, was only tested with 150 g and 250 g objects. Answer choice B is correct because only brand Z cooking spray was tested with only 2 different weights in Experiment 2.

22. The best answer is J. The Experiment states: "The students planned to calculate the coefficient of static friction by determining the force required to disturb an object from rest." Answer choice H can be eliminated because the coefficient of static friction could be determined in both experiments, but cooking spray was only used in Experiment 2.

23. The best answer is A. According to Table 1, brand B cookware had an average force of 0.090 N for the 150 g weight and 0.147 N for the 250 g weight. These results are the closest to the results the students obtained when their instructor gave them the new piece of nonstick cookware.

PASSAGE V

24. The best answer is F. In Experiment 1, the control group (the group that the results are compared to) included the rosebushes that were grown in soil with no pesticide added.

25. The best answer is D. The best way to answer this question is by the process of elimination. Answer choices A and B are incorrect because they contradict information in the passage. Answer choice C is incorrect because this explanation is irrelevant to the topic of the passage. Answer choice D is the correct answer because if rosebushes generally die when pesticides are applied to them directly, it would make sense to apply to the pesticides to the soil.

26. **The best answer is G.** If there is a direct correlation between plant weight and the number of petals on the flowers, the lower the average weight of the rosebush, the lower the number of petals. A rosebush grown in Soil Type 2 would have the lowest number of petals with Pesticide A at 35 ppm (23.6 oz).

27. **The best answer is D.** If Pesticide C was used to treat a rosebush, no prediction could be made on the basis of the previous results because no information about Pesticide C was given. Answer choice C can be eliminated because the fragrance of the flowers was not tested in this experiment.

28. **The best answer is G.** The results of Experiment 2 are shown in Table 2. According to the table, the average weight of the rosebush was lowest in every row for Soil Type 1 and Pesticide A.

PASSAGE VI

29. **The best answer is D.** According to Table 1, the mass of the precipitate in Test Tube 1 was 4.3 mg. The difference between this test tube and the other test tubes is that it had a shorter incubation time (0 min) than other test tubes at the same temperature water bath.

30. **The best answer is F.** In Experiment 1, "7 milliliters of a *peptide* (a neurotransmitter) solution was added." In Experiment 2 "8 mL of peptide solution was added" to the test tubes. One difference between the two experiments is the amount of peptide solution used. A larger volume of the peptide solution was used in Experiment 2, answer choice F.

31. **The best answer is C.** According to Table 2, as the pH level increases (going down the table), the mass of the precipitate first increases from 2.5 mg to 6.2 mg and then starts to decrease. This information best supports answer choice C. Answer choice D can be eliminated because the masses of the precipitates in Table 2 do not remain constant.

32. **The best answer is F.** According to Table 1, the masses of the precipitate for Test Tube 1 (incubation period 0 min) and Test Tube 2 (incubation period 5 min) were 4.3 mg and 3.9 mg, respectively. If Tube 5 is incubated for 5 min and has a mass precipitate of 3.6 mg, the mass is just below that of Tube 2 for the same incubation period. It could be predicted that if Tube 5 were not incubated, the mass of its precipitate would equal 4.1 mg, just below that of Tube 1's mass.

33. **The best answer is A.** According to Table 1, 3.9 mg of precipitate was collected from Test tube 2 at a temperature of 25°C after a 5-minute incubation period. This is the greatest amount of precipitate yielded among the combinations shown in the answer choices.

34. **The best answer is H.** To answer this question, you must look at the results in Tables 1 and 2. According to Table 1, the mass of the precipitate is the least for test tubes with an incubation period of 15 min for 30°C (1.4 mg). According to Table 2, the mass of the precipitate is least for the test tube with a pH of 2.0. Therefore, if combined, these two conditions would likely produce the lease amount of precipitate.

PASSAGE VII

35. **The best answer is D.** According to Table 1, *Salmonella* bacteria had the greatest percent growth at a pH level of 5. This information suggests a pH level near 5 might best contribute to the growth of the bacteria.

36. **The best answer is H.** To answer this question you must look at the results shown in all of the tables and choose the conditions that create the greatest percent growth of bacteria. In Table 1, a pH level of 5 created the highest percent growth (81%) of the bacteria. In Table 2, the organic compound in Dish 1 created the greatest percent growth (37%) of the bacteria. In Table 3, a temperature of 40°C created the greatest percent growth (83%) bacteria. By combining these three conditions you would expect to get the greatest percent growth.

37. **The best answer is A.** Table 1 shows that the *Salmonella* bacteria reproduced most efficiently in a pH of 5 (acidic). A conclusion stating that *Salmonella* bacteria reproduce most efficiently in an acidic environment would reaffirm the results of Experiment 1.

38. **The best answer is G.** To maximize the length of time that bacteria will reproduce, the bacteria should be provided an unlimited supply of nutrients. In order to make sure the nutrients are not depleted, the bacteria groups must be regularly resupplied with unlimited nutrients, answer choice G.

39. **The best answer is B.** In a scientific experiment, the independent variable is the factor that is changed by the experimenter during the experiment. In Experiment 3, the temperature was changed; each dish had a different temperature. The factor being studied or observed, in this case the percent of the growth, is the dependent variable. Whether it changes depends on the manipulation of one or more independent variables.

40. **The best answer is J.** Answer choice J is the best answer because it is the only answer choice that tests the bacteria at intervals. Because bacteria reproduce at a rate that varies from one stage to the next, by testing at 15-min intervals you could study the different stages of growth most effectively.

Writing Test Explanation

Because grading the essay is subjective, we've chosen not to include any "graded" essays here. Your best bet is to have someone you trust, such as your personal tutor, read your essays and give you an honest critique. If you plan on grading your own essays, review the grading criteria and be as honest as possible regarding the structure, development, organization, technique, and appropriateness of your writing. Focus on your weak areas and continue to practice in order to improve your writing skills.

■■ ANSWER SHEET

ACT PRACTICE TEST 7
Answer Sheet

ENGLISH

1 (A)(B)(C)(D)	21 (A)(B)(C)(D)	41 (A)(B)(C)(D)	61 (A)(B)(C)(D)
2 (F)(G)(H)(J)	22 (F)(G)(H)(J)	42 (F)(G)(H)(J)	62 (F)(G)(H)(J)
3 (A)(B)(C)(D)	23 (A)(B)(C)(D)	43 (A)(B)(C)(D)	63 (A)(B)(C)(D)
4 (F)(G)(H)(J)	24 (F)(G)(H)(J)	44 (F)(G)(H)(J)	64 (F)(G)(H)(J)
5 (A)(B)(C)(D)	25 (A)(B)(C)(D)	45 (A)(B)(C)(D)	65 (A)(B)(C)(D)
6 (F)(G)(H)(J)	26 (F)(G)(H)(J)	46 (F)(G)(H)(J)	66 (F)(G)(H)(J)
7 (A)(B)(C)(D)	27 (A)(B)(C)(D)	47 (A)(B)(C)(D)	67 (A)(B)(C)(D)
8 (F)(G)(H)(J)	28 (F)(G)(H)(J)	48 (F)(G)(H)(J)	68 (F)(G)(H)(J)
9 (A)(B)(C)(D)	29 (A)(B)(C)(D)	49 (A)(B)(C)(D)	69 (A)(B)(C)(D)
10 (F)(G)(H)(J)	30 (F)(G)(H)(J)	50 (F)(G)(H)(J)	70 (F)(G)(H)(J)
11 (A)(B)(C)(D)	31 (A)(B)(C)(D)	51 (A)(B)(C)(D)	71 (A)(B)(C)(D)
12 (F)(G)(H)(J)	32 (F)(G)(H)(J)	52 (F)(G)(H)(J)	72 (F)(G)(H)(J)
13 (A)(B)(C)(D)	33 (A)(B)(C)(D)	53 (A)(B)(C)(D)	73 (A)(B)(C)(D)
14 (F)(G)(H)(J)	34 (F)(G)(H)(J)	54 (F)(G)(H)(J)	74 (F)(G)(H)(J)
15 (A)(B)(C)(D)	35 (A)(B)(C)(D)	55 (A)(B)(C)(D)	75 (A)(B)(C)(D)
16 (F)(G)(H)(J)	36 (F)(G)(H)(J)	56 (F)(G)(H)(J)	
17 (A)(B)(C)(D)	37 (A)(B)(C)(D)	57 (A)(B)(C)(D)	
18 (F)(G)(H)(J)	38 (F)(G)(H)(J)	58 (F)(G)(H)(J)	
19 (A)(B)(C)(D)	39 (A)(B)(C)(D)	59 (A)(B)(C)(D)	
20 (F)(G)(H)(J)	40 (F)(G)(H)(J)	60 (F)(G)(H)(J)	

MATHEMATICS

1 (A)(B)(C)(D)(E)	16 (F)(G)(H)(J)(K)	31 (A)(B)(C)(D)(E)	46 (F)(G)(H)(J)(K)
2 (F)(G)(H)(J)(K)	17 (A)(B)(C)(D)(E)	32 (F)(G)(H)(J)(K)	47 (A)(B)(C)(D)(E)
3 (A)(B)(C)(D)(E)	18 (F)(G)(H)(J)(K)	33 (A)(B)(C)(D)(E)	48 (F)(G)(H)(J)(K)
4 (F)(G)(H)(J)(K)	19 (A)(B)(C)(D)(E)	34 (F)(G)(H)(J)(K)	49 (A)(B)(C)(D)(E)
5 (A)(B)(C)(D)(E)	20 (F)(G)(H)(J)(K)	35 (A)(B)(C)(D)(E)	50 (F)(G)(H)(J)(K)
6 (F)(G)(H)(J)(K)	21 (A)(B)(C)(D)(E)	36 (F)(G)(H)(J)(K)	51 (A)(B)(C)(D)(E)
7 (A)(B)(C)(D)(E)	22 (F)(G)(H)(J)(K)	37 (A)(B)(C)(D)(E)	52 (F)(G)(H)(J)(K)
8 (F)(G)(H)(J)(K)	23 (A)(B)(C)(D)(E)	38 (F)(G)(H)(J)(K)	53 (A)(B)(C)(D)(E)
9 (A)(B)(C)(D)(E)	24 (F)(G)(H)(J)(K)	39 (A)(B)(C)(D)(E)	54 (F)(G)(H)(J)(K)
10 (F)(G)(H)(J)(K)	25 (A)(B)(C)(D)(E)	40 (F)(G)(H)(J)(K)	55 (A)(B)(C)(D)(E)
11 (A)(B)(C)(D)(E)	26 (F)(G)(H)(J)(K)	41 (A)(B)(C)(D)(E)	56 (F)(G)(H)(J)(K)
12 (F)(G)(H)(J)(K)	27 (A)(B)(C)(D)(E)	42 (F)(G)(H)(J)(K)	57 (A)(B)(C)(D)(E)
13 (A)(B)(C)(D)(E)	28 (F)(G)(H)(J)(K)	43 (A)(B)(C)(D)(E)	58 (F)(G)(H)(J)(K)
14 (F)(G)(H)(J)(K)	29 (A)(B)(C)(D)(E)	44 (F)(G)(H)(J)(K)	59 (A)(B)(C)(D)(E)
15 (A)(B)(C)(D)(E)	30 (F)(G)(H)(J)(K)	45 (A)(B)(C)(D)(E)	60 (F)(G)(H)(J)(K)

READING

1 Ⓐ Ⓑ Ⓒ Ⓓ	11 Ⓐ Ⓑ Ⓒ Ⓓ	21 Ⓐ Ⓑ Ⓒ Ⓓ	31 Ⓐ Ⓑ Ⓒ Ⓓ
2 Ⓕ Ⓖ Ⓗ Ⓙ	12 Ⓕ Ⓖ Ⓗ Ⓙ	22 Ⓕ Ⓖ Ⓗ Ⓙ	32 Ⓕ Ⓖ Ⓗ Ⓙ
3 Ⓐ Ⓑ Ⓒ Ⓓ	13 Ⓐ Ⓑ Ⓒ Ⓓ	23 Ⓐ Ⓑ Ⓒ Ⓓ	33 Ⓐ Ⓑ Ⓒ Ⓓ
4 Ⓕ Ⓖ Ⓗ Ⓙ	14 Ⓕ Ⓖ Ⓗ Ⓙ	24 Ⓕ Ⓖ Ⓗ Ⓙ	34 Ⓕ Ⓖ Ⓗ Ⓙ
5 Ⓐ Ⓑ Ⓒ Ⓓ	15 Ⓐ Ⓑ Ⓒ Ⓓ	25 Ⓐ Ⓑ Ⓒ Ⓓ	35 Ⓐ Ⓑ Ⓒ Ⓓ
6 Ⓕ Ⓖ Ⓗ Ⓙ	16 Ⓕ Ⓖ Ⓗ Ⓙ	26 Ⓕ Ⓖ Ⓗ Ⓙ	36 Ⓕ Ⓖ Ⓗ Ⓙ
7 Ⓐ Ⓑ Ⓒ Ⓓ	17 Ⓐ Ⓑ Ⓒ Ⓓ	27 Ⓐ Ⓑ Ⓒ Ⓓ	37 Ⓐ Ⓑ Ⓒ Ⓓ
8 Ⓕ Ⓖ Ⓗ Ⓙ	18 Ⓕ Ⓖ Ⓗ Ⓙ	28 Ⓕ Ⓖ Ⓗ Ⓙ	38 Ⓕ Ⓖ Ⓗ Ⓙ
9 Ⓐ Ⓑ Ⓒ Ⓓ	19 Ⓐ Ⓑ Ⓒ Ⓓ	29 Ⓐ Ⓑ Ⓒ Ⓓ	39 Ⓐ Ⓑ Ⓒ Ⓓ
10 Ⓕ Ⓖ Ⓗ Ⓙ	20 Ⓕ Ⓖ Ⓗ Ⓙ	30 Ⓕ Ⓖ Ⓗ Ⓙ	40 Ⓕ Ⓖ Ⓗ Ⓙ

SCIENCE

1 Ⓐ Ⓑ Ⓒ Ⓓ	11 Ⓐ Ⓑ Ⓒ Ⓓ	21 Ⓐ Ⓑ Ⓒ Ⓓ	31 Ⓐ Ⓑ Ⓒ Ⓓ
2 Ⓕ Ⓖ Ⓗ Ⓙ	12 Ⓕ Ⓖ Ⓗ Ⓙ	22 Ⓕ Ⓖ Ⓗ Ⓙ	32 Ⓕ Ⓖ Ⓗ Ⓙ
3 Ⓐ Ⓑ Ⓒ Ⓓ	13 Ⓐ Ⓑ Ⓒ Ⓓ	23 Ⓐ Ⓑ Ⓒ Ⓓ	33 Ⓐ Ⓑ Ⓒ Ⓓ
4 Ⓕ Ⓖ Ⓗ Ⓙ	14 Ⓕ Ⓖ Ⓗ Ⓙ	24 Ⓕ Ⓖ Ⓗ Ⓙ	34 Ⓕ Ⓖ Ⓗ Ⓙ
5 Ⓐ Ⓑ Ⓒ Ⓓ	15 Ⓐ Ⓑ Ⓒ Ⓓ	25 Ⓐ Ⓑ Ⓒ Ⓓ	35 Ⓐ Ⓑ Ⓒ Ⓓ
6 Ⓕ Ⓖ Ⓗ Ⓙ	16 Ⓕ Ⓖ Ⓗ Ⓙ	26 Ⓕ Ⓖ Ⓗ Ⓙ	36 Ⓕ Ⓖ Ⓗ Ⓙ
7 Ⓐ Ⓑ Ⓒ Ⓓ	17 Ⓐ Ⓑ Ⓒ Ⓓ	27 Ⓐ Ⓑ Ⓒ Ⓓ	37 Ⓐ Ⓑ Ⓒ Ⓓ
8 Ⓕ Ⓖ Ⓗ Ⓙ	18 Ⓕ Ⓖ Ⓗ Ⓙ	28 Ⓕ Ⓖ Ⓗ Ⓙ	38 Ⓕ Ⓖ Ⓗ Ⓙ
9 Ⓐ Ⓑ Ⓒ Ⓓ	19 Ⓐ Ⓑ Ⓒ Ⓓ	29 Ⓐ Ⓑ Ⓒ Ⓓ	39 Ⓐ Ⓑ Ⓒ Ⓓ
10 Ⓕ Ⓖ Ⓗ Ⓙ	20 Ⓕ Ⓖ Ⓗ Ⓙ	30 Ⓕ Ⓖ Ⓗ Ⓙ	40 Ⓕ Ⓖ Ⓗ Ⓙ

RAW SCORES	**SCALE SCORES**	DATE TAKEN:
ENGLISH _____	ENGLISH _____	
MATHEMATICS _____	MATHEMATICS _____	ENGLISH/WRITING _____
READING _____	READING _____	
SCIENCE _____	SCIENCE _____	
		_____
		COMPOSITE SCORE

Refer to the Scoring Worksheet on page 568 for help in determining your Raw and Scale Scores.

You may wish to remove these sample answer document pages to respond to the practice ACT Writing Test.

Cut Here

Begin WRITING TEST here.

If you need more space, please continue on the next page.

Do not write in this shaded area.

WRITING TEST

If you need more space, please continue on the back of this page.

Do not write in this shaded area.

WRITING TEST

If you need more space, please continue on the next page.

Cut Here

WRITING TEST

_____

_____

_____

_____

_____

_____

_____

_____

_____

_____

_____

_____

_____

_____

_____

_____

_____

_____

_____

_____

_____

_____

_____

_____

_____

_____

STOP here with the Writing Test.

4

1 ■ ■ ■ ■ ■ ■ ■ ■ ■ 1

ENGLISH TEST

45 Minutes—75 Questions

DIRECTIONS: In the passages that follow, some words and phrases are underlined and numbered. In the answer column, you will find alternatives for the words and phrases that are underlined. Choose the alternative that you think is best, and fill in the corresponding bubble on your answer sheet. If you think that the original version is best, choose "NO CHANGE," which will always be either answer choice A or F. You will also find questions about a particular section of the passage, or about the entire passage. These questions will be identified either by an underlined portion or by a number in a box. Look for the answer that clearly expresses the idea, is consistent with the style and tone of the passage, and makes the correct use of standard written English. Read the passage through once before answering the questions. For some questions, you should read beyond the indicated portion before you answer.

PASSAGE I

An Island Speaks

For some, backpacking is the ultimate vacation. The wilderness has a way of cleansing the spirit. What was once <u>a tedious, tiring activity, for me, is</u> now an essential
₁
part of my summer recreation. My passion for backpacking took hold many years ago when I crossed paths <u>with a hiker in the backcountry of Isle Royale National Park.</u>
₂

<u>The excitement in his eyes needless to say was infectious</u>
₃
as he gazed out over Lake Superior. "By the shores of Gitche Gumee,/By the shining Big-Sea-Water,/Stood the wigwam of Nokomis,/Daughter of the Moon, Nokomis." He continued with more verses. "Have you read Longfellow's *Song of Hiawatha*?" <u>he asked, inquiring me.</u>
₄

I had not. "Read it," he replied, "and <u>you have felt the</u>
₅
passion that the native people had for this lake, this land. It was their lifeblood." I understood what he meant. In the wilderness both physical and spiritual sustenance can be

1. **A.** NO CHANGE
   B. for me, a tedious and tiring activity is
   C. a tedious, tiring activity for me is
   D. a tedious and tiring activity for me, is

2. **F.** NO CHANGE
   G. in the backcountry, with a hiker, of Isle Royale National Park
   H. with the backcountry of Isle Royale National Park, with a hiker
   J. in Isle Royale National Park (the backcountry) with a hiker

3. **A.** NO CHANGE
   B. excitement in his eyes was
   C. excitement in his eyes—needless to say—was
   D. excitement in his eyes, I considered to be

4. **F.** NO CHANGE
   G. he asked inquiring me
   H. he asked
   J. he asked of me

5. **A.** NO CHANGE
   B. you would feel
   C. you felt
   D. you will feel

GO ON TO THE NEXT PAGE.

1 ■ ■ ■ ■ ■ ■ ■ ■ 1

found, so every step along the trail brings you, closer to
peace. My goal in backpacking is no longer the destination.

However, like the people in Longfellow's epic, I now seek
harmony with the Earth through immersion in its scenic
riches.

    After many summers on the trail, I've established my
preferred routine. I rise and retire with the sun. Sunrises

and sunsets are time with calm reflection. After breakfast
and before dinner, I slowly walk around the area near my
tent, taking note of the plants, animals, and minerals that
surround me. If I'm lucky, there is a creek, or a pond, to
discover. Sometimes I find a fallen log or a huge boulder
perfect for sitting upon and reflecting. In these times I
surrender myself to the wilderness, allowing the sights,
sounds, and smells to pass through me. ⑪

    Sometimes what I write in the wilderness is poetry,
other time's it's prose. Years later I can look at my
notepads to stir up vivid memories of my travels. This

creative process has made backpacking more than
immeasurably rewarding. The backcountry stimulates both
my primal instincts and high levels of creativity.

6. F. NO CHANGE
    G. brings you closer, to peace.
    H. brings you closer to peace.
    J. brings, you closer, to peace.

7. A. NO CHANGE
    B. Now, like
    C. Occasionally, like
    D. Like

8. F. NO CHANGE
    G. preference
    H. preferential
    J. preferring

9. A. NO CHANGE
    B. are times for
    C. times are for
    D. are for time of

10. F. NO CHANGE
    G. lucky, there is a creek or a pond
    H. lucky, there is a creek, or a pond
    J. lucky there is a creek, or a pond,

11. Which of the following sentences, if added here, would
    best strengthen the tone of the essay while providing a
    transition into the next paragraph?
    A. I once sat on the bank of a small creek for nearly
       an entire day; I became so absorbed in my own
       musings that I completely lost all track of time.
    B. I sometimes speculate about how much my sur-
       roundings have changed over time. Did a native
       person sit on this same boulder watching the
       sunrise, much like I am today?
    C. I often find the sights around me to be the most
       thought provoking. A single autumn leaf changing
       from green to crimson inspires awe and wonder
       in me.
    D. In silence, I ponder the natural system at play, and
       in occasional moments of lucidity, words pour from
       my brain to my hand to my notepad.

12. F. NO CHANGE
    G. times'
    H. times
    J. time

13. A. NO CHANGE
    B. immeasurable
    C. immeasurably more
    D. highly immeasurably

GO ON TO THE NEXT PAGE.

1 ■ ■ ■ ■ ■ ■ ■ ■ 1

Nowhere else do I feel as rawly human. When others snap
                                                    14

photographs, I write. Therefore, a picture isn't worth a
                              15
thousand words. A journal of reflections imbued with

nature's spectacle is far more valuable.

African Dogs

When I was preparing for my two-week vacation to

southern Africa, I realized that the continent would be like

nothing ever that I'd seen, never having left
         16

North America. I wanted to explore the urban's streets as
                                        17
well as the savannah; it's always been my goal to have

experiences while on vacation that most

tourists fail to find. Upon my arrival in Africa, the amiable
      18
people there welcomed me with open arms. Despite the

warmth of these people, I discovered that our cultural

differences were stunning and made for plenty of laughter

and confusion. What's funny now, though, more than ever,

is how ridiculous I must have seemed to the people of one

village when I played with their dog. [19]

When I walk the streets of my hometown now, I often

find myself staring at all the dogs and dog-owners on the

sidewalk. The owner smiles and stares at the animal,

panting excitedly in anticipation of the next stimulus along
20

the path. Dog's owners love to believe their animal is
          21
smart, while people who've never owned a dog tend to

14. F. NO CHANGE
  G. others snapped
  H. other's snap
  J. other's are snapping

15. A. NO CHANGE
  B. (Do NOT begin a new paragraph) For me,
  C. (Begin a new paragraph) Finally,
  D. (Begin a new paragraph) Nevertheless,

16. F. NO CHANGE
  G. I'd ever seen
  H. I'd ever saw
  J. I'd seen ever

17. A. NO CHANGE
  B. urban streets'
  C. urbans streets
  D. urban streets

18. F. NO CHANGE
  G. tourist's fail finding
  H. failing tourists find
  J. tourists are failing to find

19. Which of the following sentences, if added here, would
  most effectively introduce the subject of the remainder
  of the essay?
  A. Like my dog at home, their dog was a German
     Shepherd and Golden Retriever mix.
  B. Apparently, the role of dogs in America is nothing
     like it is in the third world.
  C. Their dog had never played fetch before, so I tried
     to teach it how to play.
  D. Dog lovers like myself always stop and play with
     the dogs that they cross paths with.

20. F. NO CHANGE
  G. and pants
  H. which pants
  J. who panted

21. A. NO CHANGE
  B. Dog owner's
  C. Dogs owner
  D. Dog owners

GO ON TO THE NEXT PAGE.

1 ■ ■ ■ ■ ■ ■ ■ ■ **1**

believe the opposite. [22] Perhaps Americans enjoy dogs for

just that sort of ignorant bliss. With a little training, dogs
                                            23
won't bark, bite, or use the sofa as a toilet, but they will

provide years of unconditional affection and loyalty, plus

the occasional lame-brained escapade at which human

onlookers can laugh.

　　If a dog happens to live on the urban streets of
                       24

southwest Africa, they soon learn to deal with a
                        25

starkly different reality than that of the American pooch.
          26
As I saw it, the relationship between a typical African and

his dog is one of mutualism. [27] I say tangible because the

African sees himself as the dominant creature not to be

bothered by the dog but nevertheless responsible for
                        28
providing for it. Hence, attempts at behavior training are

rare on African dogs. Instead, a villager seizes power with

a chunk of scrap meat and a bowl of water. The dog soon

learns to quit yapping and biting at the hand that feeds

him. Never does the villager speak to the animal. I'm not
                        29
even sure such dogs get names. Their behavior becomes

interestingly balanced, however, much to the surprise of

22. The writer wants to add a quote here that would fur-
    ther exemplify what he believes are the attitudes of
    Americans who have never owned a pet. Which of the
    following would most effectively accomplish this?
    F. "Look John, your dog just fell asleep with his head
       on my leg."
    G. "John, I think your dog has fleas. He won't stop
       scratching and biting himself."
    H. "John, your dog is standing in front of the mirror
       and barking at himself again."
    J. "Where did your dog go John? I can't find him
       anywhere."

23. Which of the choices would NOT be acceptable here?
    A. With some training
    B. After minimal training
    C. If they are trained a little
    D. With less training

24. F. NO CHANGE
    G. happen
    H. happening
    J. happened

25. A. NO CHANGE
    B. it soon learns
    C. they soon learned
    D. it soon was learning

26. F. NO CHANGE
    G. reality that is differently stark
    H. differently stark reality
    J. different reality that is stark

27. In order to emphasize the visibility of the typical
    African's relationship with his dog, the author intends
    to add the word "tangible" to the preceding sen-
    tence. The word would most effectively serve the
    above-stated purpose if added:
    A. before the word *typical*.
    B. before the word *African*.
    C. before the word *dog*.
    D. before the word *mutualism*.

28. F. NO CHANGE
    G. dog; but
    H. dog, but
    J. dog—but

29. A. NO CHANGE
    B. It never occurs that the villager speaks to the
       animal.
    C. By the villager, the animal is never spoken to.
    D. The villager speaks never to the animal.

GO ON TO THE NEXT PAGE.

1 ■ ■ ■ ■ ■ ■ ■ ■ 1

the compassionate American dog lover. I believe that the secret to the villager's success after so little effort is providing for the dog's physical needs.

Without the man the dog eats no meat so the dog reveres
                                                         30
the man. Perhaps tomorrow the dog will eat another's scraps. Soon, the animal becomes tame, well-mannered community property that keeps the rodent population down and the children company.

30. F. NO CHANGE
   G. Without the man, the dog eats no meat, so
   H. Without the man, the dog eats no meat, so,
   J. Without the man the dog, eats no meat, so,

PASSAGE III

Need for Speed

As an avid skier and inline skater, I thought I had already achieved some incredible downhill speeds. On a recent trip to Quebec City, nevertheless, my concept of how fast
                         31
humans can move was radically altered. It was Carnaval season, the time when people from across the province and the world flocking to the old walled city for two weeks of
                 32
food, drink, revelry, and winter sports. Normally, I go to Carnaval looking for the rare thrill, all the better if it requires a helmet and my signature on a release of liability.

This time for me, it was full-contact downhill
                                              33

ice-skating. [34]
     33
The course looked a lot like a bobsled run. From the top of the mountain a sturdy metal chute descended that wound left and right on its way down. About eight inches of icepack covered the metal surface, which was wetted twice daily to maintain an ideal slickness. If by the time you reach the end of the chute you still haven't regained your footing, there's a line of meter-thick foam padding to
                                                            35
absorb your crash.

31. A. NO CHANGE
   B. thus
   C. therefore
   D. though

32. F. NO CHANGE
   G. flock
   H. flocked by
   J. are flocking

33. A. NO CHANGE
   B. It was full-contact for me this time, I was ice-skating downhill.
   C. Ice-skating downhill this time for me, it was full-contact.
   D. This time, I was full-contact ice-skating downhill.

34. At this point, the author wants to add a sentence to the paragraph that further illustrates his adventurous nature. Which of the options does this best?
   F. I certainly didn't know what I had signed up for!
   G. Downhill ice-skating sounded much more exciting than normal ice-skating!
   H. I could easily have been injured, but the thrill I got was worth the risk!
   J. I normally wouldn't sign up for such a thing, but anything goes at Carnaval!

35. A. NO CHANGE
   B. footing; there's a line of meter-thick foam padding
   C. footing there's a line of meter-thick foam padding,
   D. footing; there's a line of meter-thick foam padding,

GO ON TO THE NEXT PAGE.

1 ■ ■ ■ ■ ■ ■ ■ ■ 1

The thrill seeker in me was chomping at the bit to try out this new sport. I signed up and put on my helmet. The organizer quickly looked me over shooting me a sarcastic
                                                    36

grin. Smiling back and giving him a brief nod, I mounted
                                    37
the chair lift for the top of the mountain and prepared to watch the few heats that came before mine.

The first heat of the day went smooth and gave me a
                                    38
good idea of what was permitted and what was against the rules, as well as good and bad technique on the chute. Professionals were what the first five racers looked like.
                                    39
They calmly and silently approached the starting line, which was at the head of a 20-meter flat strip of ice that racers use to gain speed before entering the downhill section. The starting gun rang out and a few men began with powerful strides, landing them at the head of the pack. When they all entered the chute, their striding stopped and the physical contact began. This is the time I
                                                    40
learned that full hockey-style body checks are perfectly legal, as one competitor veered sharply to his left, knocking the smallest racer up and over the wall of the chute and into the meters-deep powdery snow that lined the outside of the chute. Racing continued with countless
                                    41
rounds of hip checks and slippery maneuvers. By the end of the race, only three men were on their feet—it was a photo finish. As the large digital-display on both ends of
                42
the run showed that the men had approached speeds of sixty miles per hour.

Luckily, they seeded me in a heat with four other first-timers. When the starting gun sounded, I was quickly off to the pack's head. I shot down the track surprisingly
                                    43
smoothly when I suddenly realized I had no competition.

---

36. **F.** NO CHANGE
   G. and shoots
   H. and shooting
   J. and shot

37. Which of the following choices most appropriately characterizes the attitude of the organizer of the race?
   A. NO CHANGE
   B. His lack of confidence notwithstanding
   C. Assured by his enthusiasm
   D. With his exuberance empowering me

38. **F.** NO CHANGE
   G. went smoother
   H. went smoothly
   J. went smoothing

39. **A.** NO CHANGE
   B. The first five racers looked like professionals.
   C. Looking like professionals, the first five racers.
   D. They looked like professionals, the first five racers.

40. **F.** NO CHANGE
   G. Now is when
   H. When
   J. OMIT the underlined portion.

41. **A.** NO CHANGE
   B. Racing continuing
   C. Continuing racing
   D. Racing continues

42. **F.** NO CHANGE
   G. finish and so the
   H. finish, therefore the
   J. finish! The

43. **A.** NO CHANGE
   B. packs head
   C. head of the pack
   D. head pack

GO ON TO THE NEXT PAGE.

1 ■ ■ ■ ■ ■ ■ ■ ■ 1

I looked back and saw the other four skaters splayed out on the ice sliding helplessly toward the finish line. 44

44. Which of the following statements, if added here, would best conclude the essay?
   F. The next person to cross the finish line did so nearly forty seconds after I did.
   G. I was much better at downhill ice-skating than I thought I would be.
   H. I would be the clear winner of that heat and planned to celebrate my victory on the town that night.
   J. I would have lost if I hadn't been placed in a heat of inexperienced racers!

Question 45 asks about the preceding passage as a whole.

45. Suppose the writer had been asked to write a brief essay discussing extreme sports. Would this essay successfully fulfill the requirements?
   A. No, because the author simply gives a description of a single extreme sport that he personally has participated in.
   B. No, because the author does not discuss extreme sports, but rather his desire for speed.
   C. Yes, because the author gives an in-depth description of the extreme sport of downhill ice-skating.
   D. Yes, because the writer details his own personal experiences in extreme sports.

PASSAGE IV

The Joy of Sailing

Pictures and postcards of the Caribbean do not lie; the shining water with every shade of aquamarine, from pale
——46——
pastel green to deep emerald and navy. The ocean

hypnotizes with it's glassy vastness. A spell is set upon the
             ——47——

soul and a euphoric swell rises to the corners of the mouth
                                 ——48——
pushing up. One sailing trip in particular brings back fond
——48——
memories.

On this beautiful day, my good friends and I joined a more experienced crew and sailed blissfully from one cay to another. We were incredibly happy to be sailing
                    ——49——
through the cays. As boating novices, my friends and I
         ——49——
were in charge of spotting the light areas of the seafloor

46. **F.** NO CHANGE
   G. water there shone
   H. water shining
   J. water there shines

47. **A.** NO CHANGE
   B. its
   C. the
   D. its'

48. **F.** NO CHANGE
   G. to push up the corners of the mouth
   H. pushing the corners of the mouth up
   J. to the mouth to push up the corners

49. **A.** NO CHANGE
   B. Because we were sailing through the cays, we were content.
   C. Sailing through the cays brought us much delight.
   D. OMIT the underlined portion.

GO ON TO THE NEXT PAGE.

1 ■ ■ ■ ■ ■ ■ ■ ■ 1

that signaled dangerous reefs. Ocean reefs have the potential to rupture the hull of any sailboat that passes over them, so while the electronic depth sounder is an indispensable tool, it is always helpful to find a reef ahead of time so that it can be more easily avoided. [50] All at once, a smooth sail can turn into complete pandemonium

as the captain at the wheel begins yell directions to the first
                                   ‾‾‾
                                    51
mate, who quickly begins struggling with the sails and

rigging. Generally, the wind continues offers of resistance.
                                       ‾‾‾‾‾‾‾‾‾
                                          52
This makes the first mate's struggle more demanding and outright frightening to the less experienced boaters on board. This mad yelling and steering, along with the raucous flapping of the sails go on for several minutes
            ‾‾‾‾‾‾‾‾‾‾‾‾‾‾‾‾‾‾‾‾‾‾‾‾‾‾‾‾‾
                          53
before all is right again and the boat settles into its new

course. With congratulatory smiles,
      ‾‾‾‾‾‾‾‾‾‾‾‾‾‾‾‾‾‾‾‾‾‾‾‾‾‾
                 54
once this has occurred, the captain and first mate acknowledge
‾‾‾
                                 54
each other. We novices, however, are still recovering from
‾‾‾‾‾‾‾‾‾
  54

our terror and wondering to ourselves. "Was all that
                        ‾‾‾‾‾‾‾‾‾‾‾‾‾
                              55
supposed to happen? And they think this is fun?"

 The marina we were heading back toward, the
‾‾‾‾‾‾‾‾‾‾‾‾‾‾‾‾‾‾‾‾‾‾‾‾‾‾‾‾‾‾‾‾‾
                  56
unpredictable wind not only slowed but stopped, and soon the boat did too. After several minutes, the ship's patient crew grudgingly turned on the trolling motor.
                     ‾‾‾‾‾‾‾‾
                       57

50. Given that all are true, which of the following sen-
    tences, if added here, would most effectively introduce
    the new topic of this paragraph?
    F. One aspect of boating that is reserved for the
        experts is tacking, the nautical term for changing
        direction.
    G. The more experienced crew played a larger role in
        maneuvering the boat.
    H. The captain and his first mate served as role models
        for those of us who were inexperienced boaters.
    J. Sailing through the Caribbean is always a nice
        break from the realities of everyday life.

51. **A.** NO CHANGE
    B. yelling
    C. to start yelling
    D. OMIT the underlined portion.

52. **F.** NO CHANGE
    G. offered
    H. to offer
    J. by offering

53. **A.** NO CHANGE
    B. flapping of the sails, can go on
    C. flapping of the sails, went on
    D. flapping of the sails goes on

54. **F.** NO CHANGE
    G. The captain and first mate acknowledge each other
        once this has occurred, with congratulatory smiles.
    H. Once this has occurred, the captain and first
        mate acknowledge each other with congratulatory
        smiles.
    J. The captain and first mate, with congratulatory
        smiles once this has occurred, acknowledge each
        other.

55. **A.** NO CHANGE
    B. to ourselves; "was
    C. to ourselves, "Was
    D. to ourselves "was

56. **F.** NO CHANGE
    G. As we, heading, back towards the marina
    H. The marina was what we were headed toward
    J. As we headed back toward the marina

57. **A.** NO CHANGE
    B. turns on
    C. is turning on
    D. will turn on

GO ON TO THE NEXT PAGE.

1 ■ ■ ■ ■ ■ ■ ■ ■ 1

Unfortunately, the motor wouldn't start and so we lay

adrift at sea, no land in sight, just waiting. It was late

afternoon when I began to recognize the panic that was

rising in my throat. Eventually, the ship's captain got the
                        58
engine running and we slowly trolled back to our cozy

slip. The sails were up and the little motor hummed along.

From the shore, we may have looks like we were
                              59

actually sailing. 60

58. F. NO CHANGE
　　G. Therefore
　　H. Since then
　　J. Because of this

59. A. NO CHANGE
　　B. looked
　　C. been looking
　　D. had looks

60. The writer is considering adding the following sentence:

> Of course we weren't, and I admit that I was thrilled to see that the beautiful wind-powered craft could take on a motor in a pinch.

Would this sentence be a relevant addition at this point in the essay, and why?
　　F. Yes, because it illustrates another emotion the author felt while aboard the sailboat.
　　G. No, because it contains information that detracts from the focus of this paragraph.
　　H. Yes, because it effectively provides a conclusion to the paragraph that would otherwise be absent.
　　J. No, because it is unclear what the author means by the phrase "I know better."

PASSAGE V

> The following paragraphs may or may not be in the most logical order. You may be asked questions about the logical order of the paragraphs, as well as where to place sentences logically within any given paragraph.

History of the Louvre

[1]

The Louvre, in Paris, France, is one of the largest

museums in the world. It has almost 275,000 works of art,

which are displayed in over 140 exhibition rooms. The

Louvre contains some of the most famous works of art in

the history of the world including the *Mona Lisa* by
                          61
Leonardo DaVinci and the *Venus de Milo* by Michelangelo.

61. A. NO CHANGE
　　B. world, including
　　C. world; including
　　D. world: including

GO ON TO THE NEXT PAGE.

1 ■ ■ ■ ■ ■ ■ ■ ■ 1

[2]

The Louvre is ordinarily celebrated for its vast collection of artwork, and also it has a long and interesting history as a building. It was originally a fort built by King Phillip sometime around 1200 A.D. In the 1300s, it became a royal residence for Charles V, who had it renovated to accommodate his lavish taste. While he did have his own collection of art there, everything was dispersed when he died.

[3]

This majestic building remained empty until 1527, when Francois I decided then he wanted it for his private residence. Francois I was a collector of early Italian Renaissance art when he moved into the Louvre, and already owned the *Mona Lisa*, as well as paintings by Titian and Raphael. However, he would not move into the Louvre until it was completely renovated and made even more efficient

than being during the reign of Charles V.

[4]

[1] Unfortunately, Francois I died before the work was completed, but they continued until the death of the head architect. [2] After the passing of both the King and his architect, several generations of French royalty lived in the sprawling palace until Louis XIV, the last of the monarchs to call the Louvre home, left in 1682. [3] The art collection grew from about 200 paintings to about 2,500 works of art from 1643 to 1715.

62. **F.** NO CHANGE
    G. artwork it also
    H. artwork but also it
    J. artwork, but it also

63. **A.** NO CHANGE
    B. taste: while
    C. taste. Thus
    D. taste, thus

64. **F.** NO CHANGE
    G. which
    H. than
    J. that

65. **A.** NO CHANGE
    B. *Mona Lisa*, paintings by Titian, and paintings by Raphael.
    C. *Mona Lisa*, paintings by Titian, and Raphael.
    D. *Mona Lisa*, Titian, and Raphael.

66. Which of these choices would be most consistent with the way the Louvre is portrayed in the essay, while reflecting the fact that it was being renovated for a king?
    F. NO CHANGE
    G. grandiose
    H. unpretentious
    J. monotonous

67. **A.** NO CHANGE
    B. than it had been
    C. then it would have been
    D. then it will be

68. **F.** NO CHANGE
    G. he
    H. it had
    J. the work

69. **A.** NO CHANGE
    B. From about 200 paintings in 1643 to about 2,500 works of art in 1715 grew its art collection.
    C. Its art collection grew from about 200 paintings in 1643 to about 2,500 works of art in 1715.
    D. Starting in 1643, its art collection grew from about 200 paintings to about 2,500 works of art over the course of seventy-two years.

GO ON TO THE NEXT PAGE.

[4] It was a hub of creativity and elites, until the public
70
began to be admitted in 1749. [5] The Louvre, however,

was far from abandoned. [6] For about 30 years after

Louis XIV's death in 1715, the Louvre became the home

of assorted artists and intellectuals. 71̄

[5]

72̄ Napoleon plundered art from all over the world and

added it to the Louvre's collection. He also hired laborers

to construct several wings to accommodate his ballooning

collection. After Napoleon's demise, the original owners

reclaimed much of the plundered artwork.

[6]

During the last 100 years, art academies have been

established at the Louvre, and some of the artwork has

been moved by specialized museums. Changes are
73

continually being made to the Louvre, although it remains
74

a marvelous place to visit and viewing some of the most
75
glorious works of art of all time.

70. **F.** NO CHANGE
G. elitists
H. elitism
J. elite

71. Which of the following sentence sequences will make Paragraph 4 most logical?
A. NO CHANGE
B. 1, 2, 5, 6, 3, 4
C. 1, 2, 4, 5, 3, 6
D. 2, 1, 6, 3, 5, 4

72. Which of the following would best introduce the information in the paragraph that follows?
F. Throughout the French Revolution and the years dominated by Napoleon, the art collection in the Louvre grew immensely.
G. In 1799, Napoleon Bonaparte staged a coup, which installed the French Consulate, successfully setting the stage for his dictatorship.
H. Many leaders of France during the seventeenth and eighteenth centuries had a vested interest in the Louvre, and therefore made sure to contribute to its collection.
J. In 1805, Napoleon constructed the *Arc de Triomphe du Carrousel* at the entrance of the Louvre to commemorate his victories and provide an entrance to the palatial gardens.

73. **A.** NO CHANGE
B. moved to
C. moved where
D. moved for

74. Which of the following choices would NOT be acceptable?
F. NO CHANGE
G. Louvre; it
H. Louvre, yet it
J. Louvre. While it

75. **A.** NO CHANGE
B. view of some of
C. view some of
D. OMIT the underlined portion.

END OF THE ENGLISH TEST.
STOP! IF YOU HAVE TIME LEFT OVER, CHECK YOUR WORK ON THIS SECTION ONLY.

2 △ △ △ △ △ △ △ △ 2

MATHEMATICS TEST

60 Minutes—60 Questions

DIRECTIONS: Solve each of the problems in the time allowed, then fill in the corresponding bubble on your answer sheet. Do not spend too much time on any one problem; skip the more difficult problems and go back to them later.

You may use a calculator on this test. For this test you should assume that figures are NOT necessarily drawn to scale, that all geometric figures lie in a plane, and that the word *line* is used to indicate a straight line.

---

1. Which point in the standard (x,y) coordinate plane below has the coordinates $(2,-5)$?

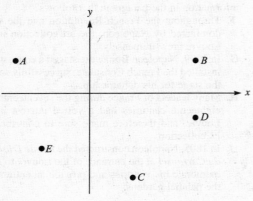

    A. *A*
    B. *B*
    C. *C*
    D. *D*
    E. *E*

2. Assume that the statements in the box below are true.

> All students who attend Tarrytown High School have a student ID.
> Amelia does not attend Tarrytown High School.
> Carrie has a student ID.
> Traci has a student ID.
> Joseph attends Grayson High School.
> Michael is a high school student who attends Tarrytown High School.

    Considering only the statements in the box, which of the following statements must be true?
    F. Michael has a student ID.
    G. Amelia is not a high school student.
    H. Carrie attends Tarrytown High School.
    J. Traci attends Tarrytown High School.
    K. Joseph does not have a student ID.

DO YOUR FIGURING HERE.

GO ON TO THE NEXT PAGE.

2   **2**

DO YOUR FIGURING HERE.

3. The balance of Juan's savings account quadrupled during the year. At the end of the year, Juan withdrew $300, and the resulting balance was $400. What was the balance in the account before it quadrupled?
   A. $100
   B. $175
   C. $300
   D. $350
   E. $700

4. For what value of a is the equation $3(a + 5) - a = 23$ true?
   F. 9
   G. 8
   H. 5
   J. 4
   K. 2

5. On the real number line below, numbers decrease in value from right to left, and Y is positive. The value of X must be:

left ————•————•————→ right
                 X Y

   A. positive.
   B. negative.
   C. greater than Y.
   D. less than Y.
   E. between 0 and Y.

6. In $\triangle ABC$ below, $AB \cong BC$, and the measure of $\angle B$ is 55°. What is the measure of $\angle C$?

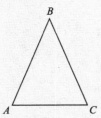

   F. 27.5°
   G. 55°
   H. 62.5°
   J. 125°
   K. Cannot be determined from the given information

7. If $3(x - 2) = -7$, then $x =$?
   A. 3
   B. 1
   C. $\dfrac{1}{3}$
   D. $-\dfrac{1}{3}$
   E. $-\dfrac{5}{3}$

GO ON TO THE NEXT PAGE.

2 △ △ △ △ △ △ △ △ **2**

8. Which of the following is a factor of the polynomial $x^2 + 3x - 18$?
   F. $x - 6$
   G. $x - 12$
   H. $x - 18$
   J. $x + 3$
   K. $x + 6$

9. A line in the standard (x, y) coordinate plane is parallel to the x-axis and 5 units below it. Which of the following is an equation of this line?
   A. $y = -5$
   B. $x = -5$
   C. $y = -5x$
   D. $y = x - 5$
   E. $x = y - 5$

10. $\dfrac{2r}{3} + \dfrac{4s}{5}$ is equivalent to:
    F. $\dfrac{2r + 4s}{8}$
    G. $\dfrac{2r + 4s}{15}$
    H. $\dfrac{2(r + 2s)}{15}$
    J. $\dfrac{(10r + 12s)}{15}$
    K. $\dfrac{2(10r + 12s)}{15}$

11. A pie recipe calls for $\dfrac{1}{3}$ cup sugar to make one 9-inch pie. According to this recipe, how many cups of sugar should be used to make three 9-inch pies?
    A. $\dfrac{1}{9}$
    B. $\dfrac{2}{3}$
    C. 1
    D. $1\dfrac{1}{9}$
    E. 3

12. $|5 - 3| - |2 - 6| = ?$
    F. -4
    G. -2
    H. 2
    J. 4
    K. 6

DO YOUR FIGURING HERE.

GO ON TO THE NEXT PAGE.

2   **2**

13. If Ryan traveled 20 miles in 4 hours and Jeff traveled twice as far in half the time, what was Jeff's average speed, in miles per hour?
   A. 80
   B. 40
   C. 20
   D. 10
   E. 5

14. If $x = -5$, what is the value of $2x^2 + 6x$?
   F. -80
   G. -20
   H. 5
   J. 20
   K. 50

15. For what value of a is $b = 4$ a solution to the equation $b - 2 = ab + 16$?
   A. -3.5
   B. -1.5
   C. 0
   D. 3.5
   E. 7

16. In the figure below, S and T are points on RU. What is the ratio of the area of square $STVX$ to the area of parallelogram $RUVY$?

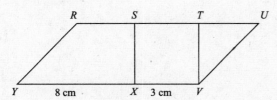

   F. 3:8
   G. 1:11
   H. 3:11
   J. 9:11
   K. 3:24

DO YOUR FIGURING HERE.

GO ON TO THE NEXT PAGE.

DO YOUR FIGURING HERE.

17. If $f(x) = 2x^2 - 6x + 7$, then $f(-3) = ?$
   A. 7
   B. 18
   C. 25
   D. 36
   E. 43

18. A map is drawn so that 1.2 inches represents 50 miles. About how many miles do 1.4 inches represent?
   F. 54
   G. 58
   H. 65
   J. 70
   K. 100

19. $(5x^3 + 3xz^2 - 17z) - (4xz^2 + 5z - 2x^3) = ?$
   A. $7x^3 - xz^2 - 22z$
   B. $7x^3 - xz^2 - 12z$
   C. $3x^3 - xz^2 - 12z$
   D. $3x^3 + 7xz^2 - 22z$
   E. $3x^3 + 7xz^2 - 12z$

20. In the standard (x,y) coordinate plane shown below, what is the distance on the y-axis, in units, from point A to point B?

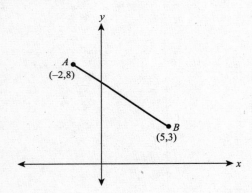

   F. -3
   G. -5
   H. 3
   J. 5
   K. 11

21. Which of the following is NOT a solution of $(x - 5)(x - 3)(x + 3)(x + 9) = 0$?
   A. 5
   B. 3
   C. -3
   D. -5
   E. -9

22. If $0 < pr < 1$, then which of the following CANNOT be true?
   F. $p < 0$ and $r < 0$
   G. $p < -1$ and $r < 0$
   H. $p < -1$ and $r < -1$
   J. $p < 1$ and $r < 1$
   K. $p < 1$ and $r > 0$

GO ON TO THE NEXT PAGE.

2 △ △ △ △ △ △ △ △ **2**

23. If $n = 10$, then which of the following represents 552?
   A. $5n + 2$
   B. $5n^2 + 2$
   C. $5n^2 + 5n + 2$
   D. $5n^3 + 5n + 2$
   E. $5n^4 + 5n + 2$

24. What is the value of b in the solution to the system of equations below?
$$3a - b = 18$$
$$a + 3b = -4$$
   F. -10
   G. -3
   H. 3
   J. 6
   K. cannot be determined with the given information

25. Which of the following is an equivalent form of $x + x(x + x + x)$?
   A. $5x$
   B. $x^2 + 3x$
   C. $3x^2 + x$
   D. $5x^2$
   E. $x^3 + x$

26. Due to inflation, a refrigerator that formerly sold for $450 now sells for 7% more. Which of the following calculations gives the current cost, in dollars, of the refrigerator?
   F. $450 + 7$
   G. $450 + 450(0.07)$
   H. $450 + 450(0.7)$
   J. $450 + 450(7)$
   K. $450(0.07)$

27. In a 3-dimensional (x, y, z) space, the set of all points 5 units from the x-axis is:
   A. a line.
   B. 2 parallel lines.
   C. a circle.
   D. a sphere.
   E. a cylinder.

28. An overlay of an accessibility ramp of a building is placed on the standard (x, y) coordinate plane so that the x-axis aligns with the horizontal. The line segment representing the side view of the ramp goes through the points $(-2, -1)$ and $(16, 2)$. What is the slope of the accessibility ramp?
   F. -3
   G. $-\dfrac{1}{3}$
   H. $-\dfrac{1}{6}$
   J. $\dfrac{1}{6}$
   K. $\dfrac{1}{14}$

DO YOUR FIGURING HERE.

GO ON TO THE NEXT PAGE.

2   △ △ △ **2**

DO YOUR FIGURING HERE.

29. The number 0.002 is 100 times as large as which of the following numbers?
A. 0.000002
B. 0.00002
C. 0.0002
D. 0.02
E. 0.2

30. The volume, V, of a sphere is determined by the formula $V = \dfrac{4\pi r^3}{3}$, where r is the radius of the sphere. What is the volume, in cubic inches, of a sphere with a diameter 12 inches long?
F. 48π
G. 72π
H. 288π
J. 864π
K. 2304π

31. Which of the following is equal to $\dfrac{\left(\dfrac{1}{3} - \dfrac{1}{4}\right)}{\left(\dfrac{1}{3} + \dfrac{1}{4}\right)}$?

A. $-\dfrac{1}{7}$

B. $\dfrac{1}{7}$

C. $\dfrac{1}{12}$

D. $\dfrac{7}{12}$

E. $\dfrac{12}{7}$

32. One traffic light flashes every 6 seconds. Another traffic light flashes every 9 seconds. If they flash together and you begin counting seconds, how many seconds after they flash together will they next flash together?
F. 6
G. 9
H. 18
J. 36
K. 54

33. If $\sqrt{2x} + 5 = 9$, then $x = ?$
A. −4
B. 2
C. 4
D. 8
E. 16

GO ON TO THE NEXT PAGE.

2 △ △ △ △ △ △ △ △ **2**

34. In the figure below, what is the sum of *p* and *q*?

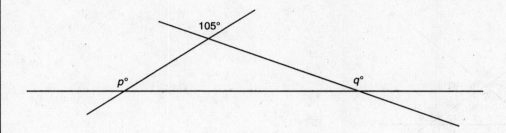

F. 75°
G. 150°
H. 180°
J. 285°
K. 360°

35. How many ordered pairs (x, y) of real numbers will satisfy the equation $5x - 7y = 13$?
A. 0
B. 1
C. 2
D. 3
E. Infinitely many

36. How many different positive 3-digit integers can be formed if the three digits 3, 4, and 5 must be used in each of the integers?
F. 6
G. 7
H. 8
J. 9
K. 12

GO ON TO THE NEXT PAGE.

2   △ △ △ **2**

37. Each of the 3 lines crosses the other 2 lines as shown below. Which of the following relationships, involving angle measures (in degrees) *must* be true?

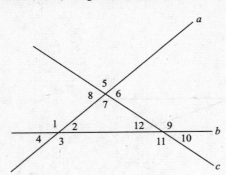

    I. $m\angle 2 + m\angle 7 + m\angle 12 = 180°$
    II. $m\angle 4 + m\angle 5 + m\angle 10 = 180°$
    III. $m\angle 3 + m\angle 8 + m\angle 11 = 180°$

A. I only
B. II only
C. III only
D. I and II only
E. I, II, and III

38. If $x^2 - y^2 = 49$ and $x - y = 7$, then $x =$?
  F. 14
  G. 7
  H. 4
  J. −4
  K. −7

39. For $a \neq 0$, $\dfrac{a^9}{a^3}$ is equivalent to:
  A. 1
  B. 3
  C. a^3
  D. a^4
  E. a^6

GO ON TO THE NEXT PAGE.

2 △ △ △ △ △ △ △ △ **2**

40. The polygon below was once a rectangle with sides 10 and 14 before a triangle was cut off. What is the perimeter, in inches, of this polygon?

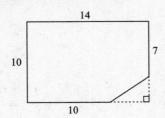

F. 54
G. 48
H. 46
J. 41
K. 36

DO YOUR FIGURING HERE.

41. A circle in the standard (x, y) coordinate plane has center $(-4, 5)$ and radius 5 units. Which of the following equations represents this circle?
A. $(x - 4)^2 - (y + 5)^2 = 5$
B. $(x - 4)^2 + (y + 5)^2 = 5$
C. $(x - 4)^2 - (y + 5)^2 = 25$
D. $(x + 4)^2 + (y - 5)^2 = 25$
E. $(x + 4)^2 - (y - 5)^2 = 25$

42. For the triangle shown below, what is the value of $\tan x$?

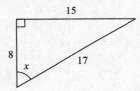

F. $\dfrac{8}{15}$

G. $\dfrac{8}{17}$

H. $\dfrac{15}{8}$

J. $\dfrac{15}{17}$

K. $\dfrac{17}{8}$

43. You have enough material to build a fence 120-feet long. If you use it all to enclose a square region, how many square feet will you enclose?
A. 900
B. 480
C. 240
D. 120
E. 60

GO ON TO THE NEXT PAGE.

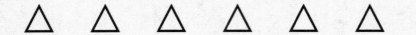

2 △ △ △ △ △ △ △ △ **2**

44. For what nonzero whole number k does the quadratic equation $y^2 + 2ky + 4k = 0$ have exactly one real solution for y?

  F. 8
  G. 4
  H. 2
  J. −4
  K. −8

45. In △ABC below, points B, D, and C are collinear. Segment AB is perpendicular to segment BC, and segment AD bisects angle BAC. If the measure of angle DCA is 60°, what is the measure of angle ADB?

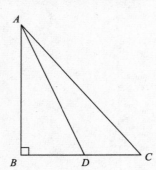

  A. 15°
  B. 45°
  C. 60°
  D. 75°
  E. 105°

46. For all $x > 4$, $\dfrac{4x - x^2}{x^2 - 2x - 8} = ?$

  F. $-\dfrac{x}{x + 2}$

  G. $\dfrac{x}{x - 2}$

  H. $\dfrac{1}{x + 2}$

  J. $-\dfrac{1}{8}$

  K. $\dfrac{1}{8}$

DO YOUR FIGURING HERE.

GO ON TO THE NEXT PAGE.

2   **2**

47. If the circumference of a circle is $\frac{4}{3}\pi$ inches, how many inches long is its radius?

   A. $\frac{3}{4}$

   B. $\frac{3}{2}$

   C. $\frac{2}{3}$

   D. $\sqrt{\frac{4}{3}}$

   E. $\frac{4\sqrt{3}}{3}$

48. If the function f satisfies the equation $f(x+y) = f(x) + f(y)$ for every pair of real numbers x and y, what is (are) the possible value(s) of $f(1)$?

   F. Any real number
   G. Any positive real number
   H. 0 and 1 only
   J. 0 only
   K. 1 only

49. The area of the trapezoid below is 24 square inches, the altitude is 3 inches, and the length of one base is 5 inches. What is the length, b, of the other base, in inches?

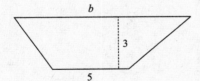

   A. 3
   B. 8
   C. 11
   D. 13
   E. 16

50. If a, b, and c are consecutive positive integers and $2^a \times 2^b \times 2^c = 512$, then $2^a + 2^b + 2^c = ?$

   F. 6
   G. 9
   H. 14
   J. 16
   K. 28

GO ON TO THE NEXT PAGE.

2   **2**

51. If 30% of x equals 60% of y, which of the following expresses y in terms of x ?

   A. $y = 33\%$ of x

   B. $y = 50\%$ of x

   C. $y = 66\%$ of x

   D. $y = 150\%$ of x

   E. $y = 200\%$ of x

52. For which values of x will $3(x + 4) \geq 9(4 + x)$?

   F. $x \leq -4$

   G. $x \geq -4$

   H. $x \geq -16$

   J. $x \leq 4$

   K. $x \leq -16$

53. If $x = 6a + 3$ and $y = 9 + a$, which of the following expresses y in terms of x?

   A. $y = x + 51$

   B. $y = 7x + 12$

   C. $y = 9 + x$

   D. $y = \dfrac{57 + x}{6}$

   E. $y = \dfrac{51 + x}{6}$

54. ABCD is a trapezoid that is bisected by line PQ, which is parallel to lines AB and DC. If the length of line DP is 8 units, the length of line PA is 12 units, and the length of line AB is 36 units, what is the length of PQ?

   F. 8

   G. 9

   H. 12

   J. 16

   K. 24

55. The total weekly profit p, in dollars, from producing and selling x units of a certain product is given by the function $p(x) = 225x - (165x + c)$, where c is a constant. If 75 units were produced and sold last week for a profit of $3,365, what is the value of c?

   A. $-1,135$

   B. -745

   C. $1,135$

   D. $4,500$

   E. $9,010$

DO YOUR FIGURING HERE.

GO ON TO THE NEXT PAGE.

2 △ △ △ △ △ △ △ **2**

56. In the figure below, sin α =?

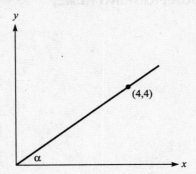

F. $\dfrac{1}{2}$

G. $\dfrac{\sqrt{3}}{2}$

H. 1

J. $\dfrac{\sqrt{2}}{2}$

K. $\dfrac{\sqrt{2}}{4}$

57. For all real integers, which of the following is *always* an even number?

    I. $x^3 + 4$
    II. $2x + 4$
    III. $2x^2 + 4$

A. I only
B. II only
C. III only
D. I and II only
E. II and III only

GO ON TO THE NEXT PAGE.

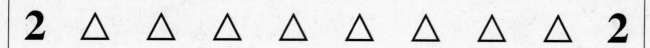

2 △ △ △ △ △ △ △ △ 2

DO YOUR FIGURING HERE.

58. Carol has an empty container and puts in 6 red chips. She now wants to put in enough white chips so that the probability of drawing a red chip at random from the container is $\frac{3}{8}$. How many white chips should she put in?
    F. 3
    G. 6
    H. 8
    J. 10
    K. 16

59. A wheel 27 inches in diameter rolls along a line. How many inches does the wheel roll along the line in 32 revolutions?
    A. 27π
    B. 32π
    C. 432π
    D. 864π
    E. $1,728\pi$

60. For any real number a, the equation $|x - 2a| = 5$. On a number line, how far apart are the 2 solutions for x?
    F. $2a$
    G. $5 + 2a$
    H. $10a$
    J. 5
    K. 10

END OF THE MATHEMATICS TEST.
STOP! IF YOU HAVE TIME LEFT OVER, CHECK YOUR WORK ON THIS SECTION ONLY.

3 ▬▬▬▬▬▬▬▬▬▬▬▬▬▬▬▬▬ **3**

READING TEST

35 Minutes—40 Questions

DIRECTIONS: This test includes four passages, each followed by ten questions. Read the passages and choose the best answer to each question. After you have selected your answer, fill in the corresponding bubble on your answer sheet. You should refer to the passages as often as necessary when answering the questions.

PASSAGE I

PROSE FICTION: *This passage is adapted from Susan Coolidge's novel,* What Katy Did © 1872.

The September sun was glinting cheerfully into a pretty bedroom furnished with blue. It danced on the glossy hair and bright eyes of two girls, who sat together hemming ruffles for a white muslin dress. The
[5] half-finished skirt of the dress lay on the bed, and as each crisp ruffle was completed, the girls added it to the snowy heap, which looked like a drift of transparent clouds or a pile of foamy white of egg beaten stiff enough to stand alone.
[10] These girls were Clover and Elsie Carr, and it was Clover's first evening dress for which they were hemming ruffles. It was nearly two years since a certain visit made by Johnnie to Inches Mills and more than three since Clover and Katy had returned home from
[15] the boarding school at Hillsover.
Clover was now eighteen. She was a very small Clover still, but it would have been hard to find anywhere a prettier little maiden than she had grown to be. Her skin was so exquisitely fair that her arms and
[20] wrists and shoulders, which were round and dimpled like an infant's, seemed cut out of daisies or white rose leaves. Her thick, brown hair waved and coiled gracefully about her head. Her smile was peculiarly sweet, and the eyes, always Clover's chief beauty,
[25] had still that pathetic look which made them quite irresistible to anyone with a tender or sympathetic heart.
Elsie, who adored Clover, considered her as beautiful as girls in books, and was proud to be permitted
[30] to hem ruffles for the dress in which she was to burst upon the world. Though, as for that, not much "bursting" was possible in the village of Burnet, where tea parties of a middle-aged description, and now and then a mild little dance, rep-resented "gaiety" and
[35] "society." Girls "came out" very much as the sun comes out in the morning—by slow degrees and gradual approaches, with no particular one moment which could be fixed upon as having been the climax of the joyful event.

[40] "There," said Elsie, adding another ruffle to the pile on the bed, "there's the fifth done. It's going to be ever so pretty, I think. I'm glad you had it all white; it's a great deal nicer."

"Cecy wanted me to have a blue bodice and sash,"
[45] said Clover, "but I wouldn't. Then she tried to persuade me to get a long spray of pink roses for the skirt."

"I'm so glad you didn't! Cecy was always crazy about pink roses. I only wonder she didn't wear them when she was married!"

[50] Yes, the excellent Cecy, who at thirteen had announced her intention to devote her whole life to teaching Sunday School, visiting the poor, and setting a good example to her more worldly contemporaries, had actually forgotten these fine resolutions, and before
[55] she was twenty had become the wife of Sylvester Slack, a young lawyer in a neighboring town! Cecy's wedding and wedding clothes, and Cecy's house furnishing, had been the great excitement of the preceding year in Burnet; and a fresh excitement had come since in the
[60] shape of Cecy's baby, now about two months old, and named 'Katherine Clover,' after her two friends. This made it natural that Cecy and her affairs should still be of interest in the Carr household, and Johnnie, at the time we write of, was paying her a week's visit.

[65] "She *was* rather wedded to them," went on Clover, pursuing the subject of the pink roses. "She was almost vexed when I wouldn't buy the spray. But it cost lots, and I didn't want it at all, so I stood firm. Besides, I always said that my first party dress should be plain
[70] white. Girls in novels always wear white to their first balls and fresh flowers are a great deal prettier, anyway, than the artificial ones. Katy says she'll give me some violets to wear."

"Oh, will she? That will be lovely!" cried the ador-
[75] ing Elsie. "Violets look just like you, somehow. Oh, Clover, what sort of a dress do you think I shall have when I grow up and go to parties and things? Won't it be awfully interesting when you and I go out to choose it?" Clover's smile beamed.

1. When Clover says "She *was* rather wedded to them," (line 65) she is expressing her belief that:

A. Cecy was married when she wore pink roses.

B. Cecy's husband presented her with pink roses on their wedding day.

C. Cecy seemed to have a sentimental attachment to pink roses.

D. Cecy believed that pink roses must only be worn at one's wedding.

GO ON TO THE NEXT PAGE.

3 ██ **3**

2. It can be reasonably inferred from the context of the passage that Cecy is:
   F. a sister of Clover and Elsie.
   G. a dear friend of Clover.
   H. a middle-aged acquaintance of the Carr family.
   J. approximately the same age as Elsie.

3. The fact that Clover is preparing to attend a milestone event can best be exemplified by which of the following quotations from the passage?
   A. "I always said that my first party dress should be plain white."
   B. "with no particular one moment which could be fixed upon as having been the climax of the joyful event."
   C. "Oh, Clover, what sort of a dress do you think I shall have when I grow up and go to parties and things?"
   D. "and was proud to be permitted to hem ruffles for the dress in which she was to burst upon the world."

4. As it is used in Paragraph 3, the phrase "the eyes, always Clover's chief beauty, had still that pathetic look" most nearly means that:
   F. Clover was beautiful with the exception of her pitiable eyes.
   G. Clover's eyes aroused a feeling of compassion.
   H. people often felt sorry for Clover when they looked into her eyes.
   J. Clover had pretty eyes but very poor vision.

5. According to the passage, before Cecy became a lawyer's wife she had intended to devote her life to:
   A. making evening dresses.
   B. designing furniture.
   C. performing good deeds.
   D. writing novels.

6. The passage makes it clear that Clover and Elsie:
   F. rarely have the chance to spend time together.
   G. often avoid spending time with Cecy.
   H. take pleasure in each other's company.
   J. are completely independent of their parents.

7. In the third paragraph (lines 16–27) the appearance of Clover's arms is compared to:
   A. those of a pretty maiden.
   B. those of a baby.
   C. a wedding dress.
   D. those of her sister Elsie.

8. Details in the passage suggest that Clover:
   F. is aware of how beautiful the townspeople perceive her to be.
   G. is about to get married to Johnnie.
   H. is jealous of her friend Cecy's wedding clothes.
   J. did not want to use the flowers that Cecy was suggesting.

9. The passage indicates that Elsie's feelings towards Clover can best be described as:
   A. admiring.
   B. objective.
   C. malevolent.
   D. predictable.

10. It can be reasonably inferred from the last paragraph of the passage that:
    F. Clover and Elsie are very close in age.
    G. Elsie is more interested in the dress than Clover is.
    H. Clover and Elsie needed to hurry to finish sewing the skirt.
    J. Elsie values the opinions of her sister.

GO ON TO THE NEXT PAGE.

3 ██ **3**

PASSAGE II
SOCIAL SCIENCE: *Adam Smith and the "Invisible Hand" Doctrine*

In *An Inquiry into the Nature and Causes of the Wealth of Nations*, Scottish economist Adam Smith asserts the power of the "invisible hand," the notion that a society benefits from people acting in their
5   own self-interest, without regard to community service. Wrote Smith, "It is not from the benevolence of the butcher, the brewer, or the baker, that we can expect our dinner, but from their regard to their own interest." So, the butcher does not cut meat because the
10 community desires it, but rather because it is a means to earn money. Smith points out that in the absence of fraud and deception, a mercantile transaction must benefit both parties. The buyer of a steak values the steak more than his money, while the butcher values
15 the money more than the steak.

The "invisible hand" is harshly criticized by parties who argue that untempered self-interest is immoral and that charity is the superior vehicle for community improvement. Some of these people, though, fail to
20 recognize several important aspects of Smith's concept. First, he was not declaring that people should adopt a pattern of overt self-interest, but rather that people already act in such a way. Second, Smith was not arguing that all self-interest is positive for society;
25 he simply did not agree that it was necessarily bad. Standing as a testament to his benevolence, Smith bequeathed much of his wealth to charity.

Additionally, the "invisible hand" has come to stand for the resilience of the market after apparently
30 ruinous circumstances. Smith posited that markets naturally recover without intervention on the part of government or similar regulatory bodies. For example, should a product be in excess production, its price in the market would fall, providing incentive for the public to
35 purchase it, thus reducing the stock. This kind of reaction leads to the "natural price" of a good or service, which, Smith believed, was the production cost plus a reasonable profit. This idea would become central to the doctrine of the *laissez-faire* economists several
40 generations later.

Adam Smith's *Wealth of Nations* was written for the masses and is generally accepted as the first treatise on economics. For these reasons, the book is thoroughly studied; for the theory within, Smith's magnum
45 opus remains controversial. It stresses low government intervention and personal action as the roots of a prosperous market. As societies balance the question of whether and how to manipulate their markets, Smith presents a valuable warning, saying of man, "he intends
50 only his own gain, and he is in this, as in many other cases, led by an invisible hand to promote an end which was no part of his intention."

11. As it is used in the passage (lines 44–45), the phrase *magnum opus* most nearly means:
   A. crowning achievement.
   B. manuscript.
   C. attitude.
   D. community improvement.

12. According to the passage, the main focus of Smith's "invisible hand" theory is:
   F. community.
   G. self-interest.
   H. society.
   J. benevolence.

13. According to the description of the "invisible hand" theory in the passage, what would happen in the market if there were a shortage of a product?
   A. Stock of the product would be reduced.
   B. The price of the product would rise.
   C. The product would become more profitable.
   D. The public would have little incentive to purchase the product.

14. According to the information presented in the passage, which of the following best describes Adam Smith's view of the relationship between a baker and the community?
   F. The baker bakes bread to increase his wealth and also because the community desires bread.
   G. The baker values his trade as a baker; the community members value their own personal wealth.
   H. The baker and the community both see money as the key commodity in any mercantile transaction.
   J. The baker bakes in order to increase his wealth; the community members value the baker's bread more than their money.

15. All of the following are assertions made in of Smith's *Wealth of Nations* EXCEPT:
   A. people naturally base their actions on what will be most beneficial to themselves.
   B. markets adjust to change naturally, without assistance from the government.
   C. the natural prices of objects should include profuse amounts of profit.
   D. all transactions that occur have some benefit to each party involved in the transaction.

16. Which of the following is a basis upon which some criticize Smith's *Wealth of Nations*?
   F. Market prices should not include profit.
   G. Commercial transactions need to benefit both participants.
   H. Falling market prices reduce the stock of products that have excess production.
   J. Exorbitant self-interest is unethical.

GO ON TO THE NEXT PAGE.

3   **3**

17. It can be inferred that the word *benevolence*, as it is used in line 6, primarily refers to:
  A. a penchant for performing generous acts.
  B. formal or obligatory politeness.
  C. having a stubborn disposition.
  D. the requisite giving of payments or gifts.

18. It can be inferred from Smith's quotation at the end of the passage ("He intends … intention.") that Smith believes that:
  F. people do not want an "invisible hand" controlling their actions.
  G. the "invisible hand" deters people from following their selfish interests.
  H. individuals acting selfishly can unwittingly create an outcome that is beneficial to others.
  J. no single person intends to be selfish, but every person is.

19. As described in the passage, Smith's theory of "natural price" is vital to the theory of:
  A. charitable organizations.
  B. self-interest, without regard to community service.
  C. *laissez-faire* economics.
  D. mercantile transactions absent of fraud.

20. Based on the passage as a whole, which of the following would most likely approximate Smith's views on competition in the marketplace?
  F. Competition is a good thing because it keeps prices for goods and services low for the consumer.
  G. The government should try to eliminate competition because people make purchases based on self-interest.
  H. Competition is positive, for it causes profit margins to increase and thereby increases market prices.
  J. The government should foster competition in order to boost the country's economy in times of recession.

GO ON TO THE NEXT PAGE.

3 ▬▬▬▬▬▬▬▬▬▬▬▬▬▬▬▬ 3

PASSAGE III
HUMANITIES: *Michael Nyman: Minimalist Composer*

Many people take classical music to be the realm of the symphony orchestra or smaller ensembles of orchestral instruments. Even more restrictive is the mainstream definition of "classical," which only
[5] includes the music of generations past that has seemingly been pushed aside by such contemporary forms of music as jazz, rock, and rap. In spite of its waning limelight, however, classical music occupies an enduring niche in Western culture, always the
[10] subject of experimentation on the part of composers and performers.

Of the various schools of composition that emerged in the 20th century, Minimalism remains one of the most influential. English composer Michael
[15] Nyman has emerged as one of the great writers, conductors, and performers of experimental and often minimalist pieces of music. In fact, it was he who coined the term "Minimalism," in a review of another composer's work. Nyman's compositions vary greatly
[20] in mood and orchestration, but generally reflect the characteristic tenets of minimalist fare; composer-author David Cope defines these as silence, conceptual forms, brevity, continuity, and strong patterns.

A 1976 commission led Nyman to form what
[25] he once called "the loudest unamplified street band" possible. Eventually coined the Michael Nyman Band, his group comprised several saxophonists and some players of ancient string and woodwind instruments of various medieval-sounding names. When Nyman set
[30] to developing material for his band, he implemented piano segments for himself, a rich string section, and eventually, amplification of all the instruments. In this setting, the composer honed his style of deliberate melodies, malleable rhythms, and precise ensemble
[35] playing. Nyman's popularity grew within classical circles. He would often profit from it, accepting commissions from celebrated orchestras, choreographers, vocalists, and string groups. These works, though, would not reach his largest audience.

[40] Nyman will be remembered by the masses for his stunning film scores. His most famous achievement was the music for *The Piano* (1993), winner of the Cannes Film Festival's prestigious Palme d'Or award for best picture. In the U.S., the film was nominated for
[45] six Academy Awards, and won three. However, a nomination was not even granted to Nyman's soundtrack for the Best Score award. Despite this oversight, the soundtrack remains among the bestselling film music recordings of all time. Its grace is achieved through
[50] skillful use of the piano to replace the female lead's voice, which is absent throughout the film. Similarly emotive is Nyman's composition for *Gattaca* (1997), a film that tells the tale of a world obsessed with highly sophisticated bioengineering, which creates a society
[55] woefully stratified according to genetic purity. Nyman layers repetitive melodies played on string instruments to create an atmosphere of soaring highs tempered with sorrow, but these melodies overcome hopeless melancholy to finish on an uplifting note. The austere
[60] blues and greens of the film's cinematography blend with Nyman's round melodies to impose a trance on the audience, infusing a cold future reality with vivid romance.

Following Nyman's snub by the Academy, the
[65] composer admitted the critics tend to look down their noses at his work. He concedes that giving a sold-out performance at a major concert hall does little to impress them. According to Nyman, there will always be some stuffed shirts anxious to cry foul at
[70] the new and different. Though rarely awarded for his many accomplishments, Nyman certainly remains an important figure in the innovation of classical music and represents a substantial reason for its persistent popularity.

21. One of the main arguments the author is trying to make in the passage is that:
 A. until recently, classical music had been fading in popularity among Western societies.
 B. Michael Nyman has produced much important music, but remains underappreciated.
 C. modern classical music is changing the way in which artists interpret the world.
 D. *The Piano* gained widespread popularity because of Michael Nyman's impressive soundtrack.

22. Considering the information given in the first two paragraphs (lines 1–23), which of the following is the most accurate description of modern classical music?
 F. It lacks the intellectual richness of classical music from earlier periods.
 G. It has not progressed since the emergence of Minimalism.
 H. It shares audiences with other forms of music, but has not stopped evolving.
 J. It has become more of an artistic medium than it had been historically.

23. As it is used in the passage, "fare" (line 21) most nearly means:
 A. a fee paid to attend a minimalist concert.
 B. Michael Nyman's ability to write minimalist music.
 C. the collection of minimalist music.
 D. a feeling evoked by minimalist music.

24. Which of the following statements from the passage is an acknowledgment by the author that the Michael Nyman Band enjoys limited popularity?
 F. "English composer Michael Nyman has emerged as one of the great writers, conductors, and performers of experimental and often minimalist pieces of music" (lines 14–17).
 G. "Nyman's compositions vary greatly in mood and orchestration" (lines 19–20).
 H. "These works, though, would not reach his largest audience" (lines 38–39).
 J. "Despite this oversight, the music remains among the bestselling film music recordings of all time" (lines 47–49).

3　　　　　　　　　　　　　　　　　　　　　　　　**3**

25. The author claims Michael Nyman used the music for *Gattaca* "to impose a trance on the audience" (lines 61–62) because:
    A. it reverberates with layers of emotional string melodies.
    B. it features sorrowful melodies instead of uplifting ones.
    C. it reflects the harsh reality of the world portrayed in the film.
    D. it dulls the raw emotion caused by the futuristic crisis in the film.

26. When the author says that Michael Nyman is "rarely rewarded" (line 70), he most likely means that Nyman:
    F. lacks the musical merit to deserve critical acclaim.
    G. produces obscure music that fails to appeal to a modern audience.
    H. gives many long recitals throughout the year.
    J. deserves praise, but does not receive enough of it.

27. The author implies by the phrase "snub by the Academy" (line 64) that Michael Nyman:
    A. did not deserve to win an Academy Award nomination.
    B. prepared a superficial composition for *The Piano*.
    C. considers the score for *The Piano* his crowning achievement.
    D. deserved an Academy Award nomination, but was denied one.

28. According to the passage, by considering classical music only a historical form of music, many people lose the sense that:
    F. playing unamplified, traditional instruments remains an enriching enterprise.
    G. classical music has never disappeared, but rather has evolved with the times.
    H. Michael Nyman is a valuable contributor to Western music.
    J. classical music is the highest form of recorded music.

29. The second paragraph (lines 12–23) states that, at the time of Michael Nyman's emergence as a composer, Minimalism was:
    A. in a period of stylistic turmoil.
    B. an ancient practice in classical music.
    C. a young musical style.
    D. invented by Michael Nyman.

30. When the author says that "austere blues and greens of the film's cinematography blend with Nyman's round melodies" (lines 59–61), he most likely means that the film:
    F. presents a conflicting viewpoint to the audience.
    G. tempers its severe elements with appeals to human emotion.
    H. juxtaposes ugliness with whimsy.
    J. is really a tongue-in-cheek commentary on the progress of science.

GO ON TO THE NEXT PAGE.

3 ███████████████████████████████████ **3**

PASSAGE IV

NATURAL SCIENCE: *The Great Pyramid at Giza: Its Composition and Structure*

The Great Pyramid at Giza is arguably one of the most fascinating and contentious piece of architecture in the world. In the 1980s, researchers began focusing on studying the mortar from the pyramid, hoping it
5　would reveal important clues about the pyramid's age and construction. Instead of clarifying or expunging older theories about the Great Pyramid's age, the results of the study left the researchers mystified.

Robert J. Wenke from the University of
10　Washington received authorization to collect mortar samples from some of the famous ancient construction sites. Among these sites was the Great Pyramid. The mortar that Wenke discovered was formed by particles of pollen, charcoal, and other organic matter. By using
15　radiocarbon dating, scientists were able to make some disconcerting discoveries. After adjusting the data, the mortar revealed that the pyramid must have been built between 3100 BC and 2850 BC with an average date of 2977 BC. This discovery was controversial because
20　these dates claimed that the structure was built over 400 years earlier than most archaeologists originally believed it had been constructed.

Furthermore, archaeologists discovered something even more anomalous. Most of the mortar samples
25　collected appeared to be little more than processed gypsum with traces of sand and limestone. The sand and limestone found in the gypsum were not added but were actually contaminants of the processed gypsum. The mortar used to build the Great Pyramid is of an
30　unknown origin. It has been analyzed repeatedly and its chemical composition has been established. However, even using modern techniques, scientists have been unable to reproduce it. The gypsum mortar is stronger than the stone on the pyramid and the mortar is still
35　intact today, thousands of years after the pyramid was built. This mortar was not used to bond the heavy stone blocks together like cement mortar does with modern bricks. Instead, the gypsum mortar's role was to buffer the joints and to reduce friction as the enormous blocks
40　were put into place.

Examining the mortar from the Great Pyramid assists scientists in making inferences about Egypt's past. Researchers questioned why the Egyptian builders would choose to use gypsum mortar over lime mortar.
45　Egypt had numerous limestone mines that could have been used to create a more durable lime mortar. Despite the abundance of lime, there is no evidence of lime mortar being used in Egypt until 2500 years after the pyramids were built. Researchers then began to deter-
50　mine why the more water-soluble gypsum would have been preferred. They discovered that gypsum would have been easier to mine than limestone. In addition, the Egyptian builders discovered that when gypsum is heated to approximately 265 degrees Fahrenheit, some
55　of the moisture is excluded. When the processed gypsum is mixed with water again, the resulting substance is used for the mortar.

Despite having significant mineral resources, Egypt has few natural fuels available. The 265 degree
60　Fahrenheit temperatures needed to process the gypsum and turn it into mortar can be achieved with the heat of an open fire. On the other hand, to make lime mortar, extremely high temperatures of around 1800 degrees Fahrenheit are needed. Most historians conjecture that
65　the high heat needed to process limestone is the reason lime mortar was not used. The shortage of natural fuel sources would most likely have made the creation of lime mortar highly uneconomical.

31. From the author's reference to the Great Pyramid at Giza as both "fascinating and contentious," (line 2) it can be inferred that the Great Pyramid is seen as both:
  A. captivating and flawless.
  B. placid and disputable.
  C. intriguing and controversial.
  D. monotonous and statuesque.

32. According to the passage, the mortar used to build the Great Pyramid included all of the following EXCEPT:
  F. charcoal.
  G. processed limestone.
  H. pollen.
  J. processed gypsum.

33. The passage indicates that, unlike gypsum, limestone:
  A. needs extremely high temperatures to be transformed into mortar.
  B. would have been very easy for ancient Egyptians to mine.
  C. was not nearly as resilient as gypsum.
  D. was very soluble when mixed with water.

34. Which of the following was NOT a use of the mortar used in constructing the Great Pyramid?
  F. Assisting in the placement of stone blocks
  G. Shielding the joints of the heavy stone blocks
  H. Adhering heavy stone blocks together
  J. Diminishing friction between the stone blocks

35. It may be reasonably inferred from the passage that for those studying ancient pyramids:
  A. radiocarbon dating is a relatively simple method to find an exact date of construction.
  B. analyzing the chemical composition of a building material allows scientists to recreate the material being evaluated.
  C. there is typically a very large gap between the conclusions of scientific researchers and those of archaeologists.
  D. when conclusive facts are not available, researchers must sometimes speculate about the nature of certain findings.

GO ON TO THE NEXT PAGE.

3   **3**

36. The passage indicates that the type of mortar used in the construction of ancient Egyptian pyramids was affected by:
  F. the durability of the mortar.
  G. the amount of mineral resources available.
  H. the inferences drawn by the researchers.
  J. the natural fuel sources available.

37. As it is used in line 6, the word *expunging* most nearly means:
  A. eliminating.
  B. restoring.
  C. devising.
  D. obscuring.

38. Previous to the research discussed in the passage, it was believed that the Great Pyramid was constructed in approximately what year?
  F. 3377 BC
  G. 2977 BC
  H. 2577 BC
  J. 2177 BC

39. The passage indicates that researchers believed that examination of the mortar would reveal information regarding the Great Pyramid's:
  A. natural fuel sources.
  B. construction.
  C. durability.
  D. constant temperature.

40. According to the passage, which of the following is a reason that gypsum was used to create mortar instead of limestone?
  F. Gypsum is more water-soluble than limestone.
  G. Gypsum is less complicated to mine than limestone.
  H. Gypsum is sturdier than limestone.
  J. Gypsum is more costly to mine than limestone.

END OF THE READING TEST.
STOP! IF YOU HAVE TIME LEFT OVER, CHECK YOUR WORK ON THIS SECTION ONLY.

SCIENCE REASONING TEST

35 Minutes—40 Questions

DIRECTIONS: This test includes seven passages, each followed by several questions. Read the passages and choose the best answer to each question. After you have selected your answer, fill in the corresponding bubble on your answer sheet. You should refer to the passages as often as necessary when answering the questions. You may NOT use a calculator on this test.

PASSAGE I

Friction is the resistance to the movement of one object past another object with which the first object is in contact. A group of students performed several experiments using rectangular blocks of various materials and a smooth inclined plane 2 meters in length. To compare how different materials are affected by friction, the blocks were placed at the top of the plane and released to travel the 2-meter distance. The time in seconds (s) that it took for each block to reach the end of the inclined plane was recorded.

Experiment 1

The group of students wanted to know which materials moved down the plane in the shortest amount of time. The students used blocks of wood, steel, aluminum, glass, plastic, and concrete. The dimensions of each block were the same, the volume of each block remained constant, and the mass of the blocks was varied. The incline of the plane was set at 45° for each trial. The students conducted 3 trials for each material, and recorded the results in Table 1.

Experiment 2

The students conducted a similar experiment as in Experiment 1 to test the effect of volume on the time that it took for the blocks to move down the inclined plane. The results are shown in Table 2.

Table 2					
Block material	Volume of block (cm³)	Mass of block (g)	Time (s)		
			Trial 1	Trial 2	Trial 3	Average
Wood	2,725	1,500	1.70	1.72	1.65	1.69
Steel	190	1,500	1.32	1.28	1.33	1.31
Aluminum	550	1,500	1.36	1.38	1.37	1.37
Glass	750	1,500	1.30	1.32	1.29	1.30
Plastic	1,150	1,500	1.44	1.41	1.44	1.43
Concrete	650	1,500	2.47	2.41	2.53	2.47

Experiment 3

Objects can be rated according to their ability to move efficiently. The students created a scale from 5 to 30 (least to most resistant to motion due to friction) and tested four objects of a known rating. Three trials were conducted for each object, using the same methods as in Experiment 1. The results are shown in Table 3.

Table 3				
Object rating	Time (s)			
	Trial 1	Trial 2	Trial 3	Average
5	1.05	1.08	1.08	1.07
9	1.26	1.28	1.33	1.29
13	1.45	1.44	1.34	1.42
19	1.76	1.82	1.79	1.79

Table 1					
Block material	Volume of block (cm³)	Mass of block (g)	Time (s)		
			Trial 1	Trial 2	Trial 3	Average
Wood	750	412	1.65	1.67	1.60	1.64
Steel	750	5,850	1.34	1.30	1.35	1.33
Aluminum	750	2,025	1.36	1.32	1.37	1.35
Glass	750	1,875	1.27	1.31	1.29	1.29
Plastic	750	975	1.40	1.40	1.43	1.41
Concrete	750	1,725	2.47	2.51	2.65	2.54

GO ON TO THE NEXT PAGE.

1. If Experiment 1 were repeated with a plane length of 4 meters, the movement time for the wood block, in seconds, would be closest to:
   A. 2.31
   B. 1.64
   C. 1.32
   D. 0.64

2. What value would the plastic object used in Experiment 2 likely have on the scale described in Experiment 3?
   F. Less than 5
   G. Between 5 and 9
   H. Between 9 and 13
   J. Between 13 and 19

3. A furniture maker wants to build a chair whose legs can move more easily across a smooth wooden floor. Based on Experiment 3, which of the following object ratings should the chair material have to best accomplish that goal?
   A. 5
   B. 9
   C. 13
   D. 19

4. In which of the following ways are the designs of Experiments 1 and 2 different?
   F. In Experiment 1 mass was held constant, while in Experiment 2 it varied.
   G. In Experiment 1 volume varied, while in Experiment 2 it was held constant.
   H. In Experiment 1 volume was held constant, while in Experiment 2 mass was varied.
   J. In Experiment 1 volume was held constant, while in Experiment 2 mass was held constant.

5. Based on the assumption that the loss in speed that is due to friction is responsible for longer travel times down the inclined plane, which of the following lists of objects used in Experiment 2 is in order of increasing loss of speed due to friction?
   A. Plastic, aluminum, wood, concrete
   B. Glass, aluminum, wood, concrete
   C. Aluminum, steel, wood, concrete
   D. Concrete, wood, glass, aluminum

6. Based on the results of Experiments 1 and 2, as the volume of the blocks increased, the average time it took each block to move down the inclined plane:
   F. increased only.
   G. decreased only.
   H. increased for some blocks and decreased for other blocks.
   J. remained the same.

GO ON TO THE NEXT PAGE.

PASSAGE II

The Earth's magnetic field is one of its most significant natural phenomena. For centuries, the field has been used to aid navigation and exploration, and has been vital to many major discoveries. The magnetic field of the Earth extends several thousands of miles into space. It has the effect of shielding the Earth from solar wind, protecting the planet from dangerous high-energy particles and radiation. The exact source of the Earth's magnetic field is not certain. The following two Scientists attempt to explain the phenomenon.

Scientist 1

The Earth's magnetic field is similar to that of a bar magnet tilted 11 degrees from the spin axis of the Earth. The magnetic field of a bar magnet, or any other type of permanent magnet, is created by the coordinated motions of electrons within iron atoms. It is widely accepted that the Earth's core consists of metals. The inner core is 70% as wide as the moon and consists of a solid iron ball, which would exhibit properties of *ferromagnetism* (the natural magnetic tendency of iron). The core has its own rotation and is surrounded by a "sea" of molten rock. The magnetic field grows and wanes, and the Earth's poles drift and occasionally flip as the rotation of the core changes. The poles of the magnetic field have "flipped" many times due to the fluctuations in the rotation of the solid inner core. Other fluctuations in the magnetic field that can occur on a daily basis are largely the result of interference by solar wind.

Scientist 2

The Earth's magnetic field is attributed to a *dynamo effect* of circulating electric current in the molten outer core. Electric currents cause magnetic fields; therefore, the circulating electric currents in the Earth's molten metallic core are the origin of the magnetic field. When conducting fluid flows across an existing magnetic field, electric currents are induced, creating another magnetic field. When this magnetic field reinforces the original magnetic field, a *dynamo* is created which sustains itself.

Sitting atop the hot, iron inner core, the Earth's molten outer core churns and moves. The outer core also has cyclones or whirlpools powered by the Coriolis effects of Earth's rotation. These complex and unpredictable motions generate the fluctuating magnetic field. The outer core is seething, swirling, and turbulent, which has been detected by the constant changes and reversals in polarity throughout the planet's history. Further, iron has a special characteristic. When it is hotter than 1043 K, its Curie temperature, iron loses its magnetic properties. Therefore the Earth's magnetic field is caused not by magnetised iron deposits, but mostly by electric currents in the liquid outer core.

7. Which of the following statements about the Earth's core was implied by Scientist 2?
   A. The Earth's inner core is a rotating mass of iron.
   B. The Earth's inner core is solely responsible for the magnetic field.
   C. The Earth's core is iron and possesses properties similar to a bar magnet.
   D. The Earth's core has a temperature above 1043 K.

8. A scientific article stated, "Since 1848, when the strength of the Earth's magnetic field was first measured, the field has lost 10% of its strength." Which of the scientists' viewpoints, if any, is (are) in agreement with this statement?
   F. Scientist 1 only.
   G. Scientist 2 only.
   H. Scientist 1 and 2.
   J. Neither Scientist 1 nor 2.

9. Researchers notice that volcanic rocks exhibit regular and predictable variations in their magnetic properties depending on their age. Which of the following statements about the variations would both scientists most likely agree with?
   A. Electric currents, the liquid outer core cause variation in the magnetic properties of volcanic rock.
   B. Solar wind levels at the time the rocks were created determine the magnetic properties of the rock.
   C. The varying magnetic properties of the volcanic rocks are a result of the status of the Earth's fluctuating magnetic field at the time the rocks cooled.
   D. The Earth's magnetic field shields it from solar wind, thereby altering the magnetic properties of volcanic rocks.

10. Scientists 1 and 2 would most likely disagree about which of the following statements?
    F. The strength of the Earth's magnetic field fluctuates over time.
    G. The polarity of the Earth's magnetic field can change over time.
    H. The Earth's inner core is surrounded by a liquid outer core.
    J. The inner core of the Earth possesses magnetic properties.

11. Do the Scientists differ in their description of the Earth's magnetic field?
    A. Yes; Scientist 1 claims that the Earth's magnetic field is significant and Scientist 2 does not.
    B. Yes; Scientist 1 claims that the Earth's magnetic field is created by the coordinated motions of electrons within iron atoms and Scientist 2 does not.
    C. No; both Scientists claim that the Earth's magnetic field is created from the circulating electric currents in the Earth's molten outer core.
    D. No; neither Scientist discusses the Earth's magnetic field in detail.

GO ON TO THE NEXT PAGE.

12. Suppose a new type of sensor was invented that could detect electric currents in the outer core. This new technology would:
   F. be consistent with the view of Scientist 1 only.
   G. be consistent with the view of Scientist 2 only.
   H. be consistent with the view of Scientist 1 and 2.
   J. have no relevance to either scientist's viewpoint.

13. According to Scientist 1, which of the following assumptions about the source of the Earth's magnetic field is a major flaw in Scientist 2's theory?
   A. The iron in the inner core possesses no magnetic properties.
   B. The iron in the liquid outer core possesses ferromagnetic properties.
   C. The outer core can conduct electricity.
   D. The magnetic field shields the Earth from solar wind.

4 ◯ ◯ ◯ ◯ ◯ ◯ ◯ ◯ 4

PASSAGE III

Radioactive decay is a natural process by which an atom of a radioactive *isotope* (chemical element) spontaneously decays into another element. The unstable nucleus disintegrates by emitting alpha or beta particles, or gamma rays. This process changes the composition of the nucleus and continues to take place until a stable nucleus is reached. *Half-life* refers to the amount of time it takes for half (50%) of the atoms in a sample to decay.

Figure 1 shows the decay from Radon 222 to Polonium 218 and other decay products.

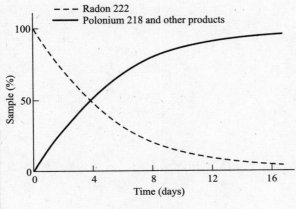

Figure 1

Figure 2 shows the decay from Mercury 206 to Thallium 206 to Lead 206.

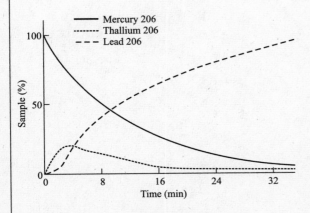

Figure 2

Table 1 shows decay products and associated energy in MeV, million electron volts, and the type of particle emitted from the decay.

Table 1			
Isotope	Decay product	Energy (MeV)	Particle emitted
Radon 222	Polonium 218	5.590	Alpha
Lead 210	Mercury 206	3.792	Alpha
Mercury 206	Thallium 206	1.308	Beta
Thallium 206	Lead 206	1.533	Beta

14. According to Figure 1, what is the approximate half-life of Radon 222?
   F. 2 days
   G. 4 days
   H. 12 days
   J. 16 days

15. Based on the passage, radioactive decay:
   A. is unstable.
   B. does not occur in nature.
   C. is a natural process.
   D. only occurs in half of the atoms.

16. Based on Table 1, what is the relationship between decay energy and the type of particle emitted?
   F. Beta particles tend to have higher decay energies.
   G. Alpha particles tend to have lower decay energies.
   H. Alpha particles tend to have higher decay energies.
   J. There is no apparent relationship between type of particle and decay energy.

GO ON TO THE NEXT PAGE.

17. When Technetium 98 decays into Ruthenium 98, the decay energy is 1.796 MeV. According to the data in Table 1, the decay particle type is most likely:
  A. an alpha particle.
  B. a beta particle.
  C. similar to that of Radon 222.
  D. gamma ray.

18. According to the passage, approximately when do Radon 222 and Polonium 218 have the same percent of atoms remaining?
  F. On Day 2.
  G. On Day 4.
  H. On Day 8.
  J. On Day 16.

19. What statement best explains the meaning of the shape of the Radon 222 curve in Figure 1 and the Mercury 206 curve in Figure 2?
  A. The rate of decay is erratic.
  B. The rate of decay starts off slowly and then speeds up.
  C. The rate of decay occurs very quickly at first and slows as the number of atoms is reduced.
  D. The rate of decay occurs at a steady rate over time.

GO ON TO THE NEXT PAGE.

PASSAGE IV

When connection to a municipal water system is not feasible, wells are drilled to access ground water. Engineers employed by a company interested in developing a remote plot of land conducted studies to compare the water quality of 2 possible well locations on the land. Water quality is determined by a number of factors, including the levels of nitrates, lead, microbes, pH, "hardness" (calcium carbonate), and alkalinity. The water samples were kept at a constant temperature of 72°F throughout the study. The results in Table 1 show the readings of each test for the two different 100 mL samples of water, as well as the ideal level, or concentration, for each chemical.

Table 1			
Factor	Ideal	Sample 1	Sample 2
Nitrates	<10 mg/L	8 mg/L	7 mg/L
Lead	<0.015 mg/L	0.01 mg/L	0.008 mg/L
Iron	<0.3 mg/L	0.45 mg/L	<0.40 mg/L
pH	6.5–8.5	6.0	7.5
Hardness	80–100 mg/L	40 mg/L	200 mg/L
Alkalinity	200–500 mg/L	120 mg/L	350 mg/L
Total disolved solids	<1,500 mg/L	1,050 mg/L	900 mg/L

The pH scale measures how acidic or basic a substance is on a scale of 0 to 14. Lower numbers indicate increasing acidity and higher numbers indicate increasing basicity. The normal pH level of groundwater systems is between 6 and 8.5. Water with a low pH (<6.5) could be acidic, soft, and corrosive, and could contain elevated levels of toxic metal that might cause premature damage to metal piping. Water with a pH >8.5 could indicate that the water is hard. Hard water does not pose a health risk, but can cause mineral deposits on fixtures and dishes and can have a bad taste and odor.

Alkalinity is the water's capacity to resist decreases in pH level. This resistance is achieved through a process called *buffering* (a buffered solution resists changes in pH until the buffer is used up). Alkalinity of natural water is determined by the soil and bedrock through which it passes. The main sources for natural alkalinity are rocks that contain carbonate, bicarbonate, and hydroxide compounds. These compounds, however, also cause hardness, which is less desirable in a drinking source. To illustrate the affect of alkalinity on pH stability, acid was added to two 100 milliliters sample solutions that initially had a pH of 6.5. The solution in Figure 1A had an alkalinity level of 200 mg/L while the solution in Figure 1B tested at zero alkalinity. The pH of the two solutions was recorded after every addition of acid and the results are shown in the figures below.

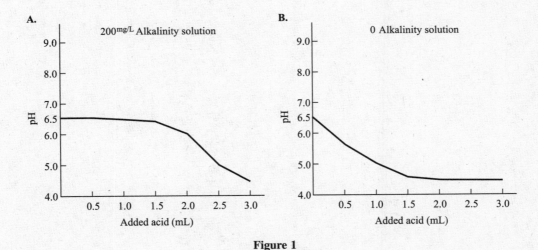

Figure 1

GO ON TO THE NEXT PAGE.

20. Which of the following statements best describes the concentration of lead in Sample 1?

   F. The concentration of lead in Sample 1 is above the ideal level.
   G. The concentration of lead in Sample 1 may be corrosive to surfaces.
   H. The concentration of lead in Sample 1 is at or below the ideal level.
   J. The concentration of lead in Sample 1 is less than the concentration of lead in Sample 2.

21. An ideal alkalinity level prevents pH levels from becoming too low. Which statement is best supported by this fact? When testing drinking water:

   A. an alkalinity test is not necessary.
   B. an alkalinity level above 500 is ideal.
   C. ideal samples will have levels similar to that of Sample 1.
   D. a proper alkalinity level can prevent water from becoming overly corrosive.

22. The test results of Sample 1 indicate that:

   F. the water from Sample 1 is probably balanced and safe.
   G. the water from Sample 1 is too acidic and corrosive.
   H. alkalinity levels are high enough to prevent it from becoming overly acidic.
   J. the water tested in Sample 1 is hard water.

23. Based on the test results, Sample 2 is acceptable as a water source as long as the developers:

   A. are willing to accept high iron levels and hard water.
   B. are willing to accept high lead levels and soft water.
   C. are willing to accept high alkalinity levels and soft water.
   D. treat the water to reduce its corrosive nature.

24. Suppose chemicals could be added to treat the high iron levels in either sample. The chemical additive would be safe to use in Sample 2 and not safe to use in Sample 1 if:

   F. the chemical additive caused a drastic increase in pH levels in unbuffered solutions.
   G. the chemical additive caused an increase in water hardness levels.
   H. the chemical additive caused a decrease in total dissolved solids.
   J. the chemical additive increased the amount of dissolved solids by at least 200 mg/L.

GO ON TO THE NEXT PAGE.

PASSAGE V

Some students performed 3 studies to measure the average speed on a flat surface of a gas-powered golf cart. Each study was conducted on a fair day with no wind. A 500-foot long flat surface was measured, and the cart's travel time was measured from start to finish with a stopwatch. The cart was not modified in any way, the same driver was used each time, and the cart's fuel tank was filled before each trial.

Study 1

The students first drove the cart on a smooth asphalt road. One student drove the cart as the other student started the stopwatch. The student stopped the stopwatch as the cart crossed the 500-foot mark. The students calculated the results of three separate trials and averaged the results (see Table 1).

Table 1		
Trial	Time (s)	Speed (ft/s)
1	34.5	14.2
2	33.4	15.0
3	33.7	14.8
Average	33.9	14.7

Study 2

The students repeated the procedure used in Study 1, except the cart was driven on the fairway (very short, well-groomed grass). The results are shown in Table 2.

Table 2		
Trial	Time (s)	Speed (ft/s)
1	39.4	12.7
2	39.9	12.5
3	38.7	12.9
Average	39.3	12.7

Study 3

The students repeated the procedure used in Study 1, except they drove the cart through the rough (thick, long grass). The results are shown in Table 3.

Table 3		
Trial	Time (s)	Speed (ft/s)
1	52.6	9.5
2	55.4	9.0
3	51.3	9.7
Average	53.3	9.4

25. The highest average speeds resulted from using which surface?
   A. Fairway
   B. Rough
   C. Asphalt
   D. The speeds remained constant.

26. According to Table 1, the average speed for all three trials is:
   F. less than the speed measured in Trial 1.
   G. greater than the speed measured in Trial 3.
   H. greater than the speed measured in Trial 2.
   J. less than the speed measured in Trial 3.

27. According to Tables 1, 2, and 3:
   A. the average speed of the cart in the rough is approximately two-thirds of the average speed of the cart on asphalt.
   B. the average speed of the cart on the fairway is approximately one-third of the average speed of the cart on asphalt.
   C. the average speed of the cart in the rough is approximately two-thirds of the average speed of the cart on the fairway.
   D. the average speed of the cart on asphalt is approximately two-thirds of the average speed of the cart in the rough.

28. According to the passage, which of the following was the independent variable in each of the studies?
   F. The surface upon which the golf cart was driven.
   G. The amount of fuel in the tank of the golf cart.
   H. The average speed of the golf cart.
   J. The number of trials conducted.

29. During which of the following was the average travel time of the car the slowest?
   A. Study 1, Trial 2.
   B. Study 2, Trial 2.
   C. Study 3, Trial 2.
   D. Study 3, Trial 3.

GO ON TO THE NEXT PAGE.

PASSAGE VI

The common grackle is one of the most abundant species of bird in North America. When two male grackles encounter each other, there is often a threat display (a loud, abrasive call). The dominant male usually forces the submissive male to cower and eventually fly away. A biologist conducted two experiments to determine the rank in aggression in male grackles. In the experiments described below, five adult male birds were placed together in a cage and their interactions were observed and recorded.

Experiment 1

To determine what factors might affect aggressiveness, the biologists recorded the sequence in which the birds were placed in the cage, their weight, their ages, and the number of calls each grackle made during the experiment. In addition, the birds were ranked according to their aggressiveness toward each other, from most aggressive (1) to least aggressive (5). The results are shown in Table 1.

			Table 1		
Grackle	Sequence	Body weight (g)	Age in months	Number of calls	Aggression (rank)
A	1st	200	6	17	4
B	2nd	325	18	34	1
C	3rd	300	12	29	2
D	4th	340	24	12	5
E	5th	350	30	24	3

Experiment 2

The male grackles were placed back into the cage in the same sequence as in Experiment 1. The results of all aggressive encounters (number of calls) between pairs of birds were recorded. A bird was declared a "winner" if it forced the other bird, the "loser," to flee from the encounter. Table 2 shows the results of the interactions between the birds. There were no draws (ties) observed.

Table 2						
		Losing grackle				
		A	B	C	D	E
Winning grackle	A	–	0	5	10	10
	B	25	–	15	25	30
	C	20	10	–	20	30
	D	15	0	5	–	15
	E	10	0	0	5	–

Table 3 summarizes the results of all the encounters for each bird.

		Table 3	
Grackle	Wins	Losses	Encounters
A	25	70	95
B	95	10	105
C	80	25	105
D	35	60	95
E	15	75	90

30. Which of the following generalizations about the relationship between body weight and rank is consistent with the experimental results?
   F. The heaviest bird will be the most dominant.
   G. The heaviest bird will be the most submissive.
   H. Body weight has no effect on rank.
   J. The lightest bird will be the most dominant.

31. It was suggested that the more dominant a male grackle is, the more likely it is to mate. Accordingly, one would predict, based on win–loss records, that the grackle with the highest likelihood of mating would be:
   A. Grackle B.
   B. Grackle D.
   C. Grackle C.
   D. Grackle A.

32. A sixth grackle, whose body weight was 330 grams and whose age was 24 months, was added to the experimental cage. It was observed that the bird called a total of 10 times during the experiment. Based on the results of Experiment 1, what would be the rank of the sixth grackle in terms of its aggressiveness?
   F. 3
   G. 4
   H. 5
   J. 6

GO ON TO THE NEXT PAGE.

33. According to the results of Experiments 1 and 2, which of the following factors is (are) related to the dominance of one male grackle over other males?

     I. Age
    II. Body weight
   III. Number of calls

A. I and II only
B. I and III only
C. II only
D. III only

34. One can conclude from the results of Experiment 2 that Grackle C and Grackle A had a total of how many encounters with each other?

 F. 5
 G. 20
 H. 25
 J. 30

35. A criticism of this study is that the order that the grackles were placed in the cage may have affected the aggressiveness of each bird. The best way to refute this criticism would be to:

A. randomize the order before starting the experiments.
B. repeat the experiments several times with different orders each time.
C. place the birds in the cage in order of their age.
D. place the birds in the cage in order of their weight.

GO ON TO THE NEXT PAGE.

4 ◯ ◯ ◯ ◯ ◯ ◯ ◯ ◯ ◯ **4**

PASSAGE VII

In nature, different types of organisms often form *symbiotic* (mutually beneficial) relationships with each other. One such example of this is between certain types of fungi and plants; this relationship is known as a *mycorrhiza*. The association provides the fungus with food through access to sugars from photosynthesis in the plant. In return, the plant gains the use of the fungi's surface area to absorb mineral nutrients from the soil. It is believed that without the assistance of fungi, these plants would not be able to absorb crucial nutrients, including phosphates, from the soil. Two experiments were performed to study the effect that the plant-fungi relationship has on plant growth.

Experiment 1

For 6 weeks, several specimens of three different types of plants, selected from among four different types of plants, were grown in a greenhouse. The average growth of each type of plant was recorded every two weeks. The soil used for the plants was treated to remove any trace of fungi to establish expected growth without the plant-fungi association. The results are shown in Table 1.

Table 1			
Plant type	Average plant growth (in)		
	Week 2	Week 4	Week 6
1	1.2	2.8	3.7
3	0.6	1.7	2.0
4	0.9	2.6	3.5

Experiment 2

In this experiment, several specimens of four different types of plants were grown in a greenhouse for six weeks, and the average growth of each type of plant was recorded every two weeks. This time, however, untreated soil that contained fungi was used. The results are shown in Table 2.

Table 2			
Plant type	Average plant growth (in)		
	Week 2	Week 4	Week 6
1	2.6	3.8	5.1
2	2.9	4.1	5.9
3	1.9	3.3	5.4
4	1.7	3.4	4.9

Information on the plant types used is given in Table 3.

Table 3			
Plant type	Root structure	Native climate type	Leaf type
1	Diffuse	Prairie	Grass-like
2	Taproot	Northern forest	Evergreen needle
3	Taproot	Prairie	Broad
4	Diffuse	Tropical forest	Broad

36. The results of Experiment 1 indicate that during what time frame did all of the plant types studied experience the greatest increase in growth rate?
    F. 0–2 weeks
    G. 2–4 weeks
    H. 4–6 weeks
    J. Cannot be determined from the given information.

37. A plant from which climate type was NOT studied in Experiment 1?
    A. Prairie
    B. Tropical forest
    C. Northern forest
    D. All climate types were studied in Experiment 1.

38. Based on the results of Experiment 1, which plant type experienced the most total growth between Week 2 and Week 6?
    F. Plant Type 1
    G. Plant Type 3
    H. Plant Type 4
    J. Each plant type experienced the same total growth.

GO ON TO THE NEXT PAGE.

4 ◯ ◯ ◯ ◯ ◯ ◯ ◯ ◯ ◯ **4**

39. Based on the experiments, on the growth of which plant type did the presence of fungi in the soil have the greatest effect?
  A. Plant Type 1
  B. Plant Type 3
  C. Plant Type 4
  D. The fungi had the exact same effect on all three plant types

40. Based on the results of Experiments 1 and 2, which of the following statements is most accurate?
  F. The presence of fungi has little or no impact on plant growth.
  G. Removing fungi from soil can help to increase growth in some plants.
  H. The presence of certain fungi in the soil increases plant growth.
  J. Fungi cannot survive in local greenhouses.

**END OF THE SCIENCE REASONING TEST.
STOP! IF YOU HAVE TIME LEFT OVER, CHECK YOUR WORK ON THIS SECTION ONLY.**

WRITING TEST PROMPT

DIRECTIONS: This test is designed to assess your writing skills. You have 30 minutes to plan and write an essay based on the stimulus provided. Be sure to take a position on the issue and support your position using logical reasoning and relevant examples. Organize your ideas in a focused and logical way, and use the English language to clearly and effectively express your position.

When you have finished writing, refer to the Scoring Rubrics discussed in the Introduction (page 4) to estimate your score.

Some high schools in the United States have installed security cameras in various locations throughout the school, including the classrooms. Some educators and parents think that student behavior must be constantly monitored in order to ensure the safety of both teachers and students. Others think that security cameras can create distractions during class and even promote bad behavior in some students.

In your opinion, should high schools install security cameras in the classroom?

In your essay, take a position on this question. You may write about one of the points of view mentioned above, or you may give another point of view on this issue. Use specific examples and reasons for your position.

■ **ANSWER KEY**

English Test

1. C	21. D	41. A	61. B
2. F	22. H	42. J	62. J
3. B	23. D	43. C	63. A
4. H	24. F	44. H	64. J
5. D	25. B	45. A	65. A
6. H	26. F	46. J	66. G
7. D	27. D	47. B	67. B
8. F	28. H	48. G	68. J
9. B	29. A	49. D	69. C
10. G	30. G	50. F	70. H
11. D	31. D	51. B	71. B
12. H	32. G	52. H	72. F
13. C	33. A	53. B	73. B
14. F	34. H	54. H	74. J
15. B	35. A	55. C	75. C
16. G	36. J	56. J	
17. D	37. B	57. A	
18. F	38. H	58. F	
19. B	39. B	59. B	
20. H	40. J	60. H	

Mathematics Test

1. C	21. D	41. D
2. F	22. H	42. H
3. B	23. C	43. A
4. J	24. G	44. G
5. D	25. C	45. D
6. H	26. G	46. F
7. D	27. E	47. C
8. K	28. J	48. F
9. A	29. B	49. C
10. J	30. H	50. K
11. C	31. B	51. B
12. G	32. H	52. F
13. C	33. D	53. E
14. J	34. J	54. K
15. A	35. E	55. C
16. H	36. F	56. J
17. E	37. D	57. E
18. G	38. G	58. J
19. A	39. E	59. D
20. J	40. H	60. K

	Reading Test			**Science Reasoning Test**	
1. C	21. B		1. A	21. C	
2. G	22. H		2. H	22. G	
3. D	23. C		3. A	23. A	
4. G	24. H		4. J	24. F	
5. C	25. A		5. B	25. C	
6. H	26. J		6. J	26. J	
7. B	27. D		7. D	27. A	
8. J	28. G		8. H	28. F	
9. A	29. C		9. C	29. C	
10. J	30. G		10. J	30. H	
11. A	31. C		11. B	31. A	
12. G	32. G		12. G	32. J	
13. B	33. A		13. A	33. D	
14. J	34. H		14. G	34. H	
15. C	35. D		15. C	35. B	
16. J	36. J		16. H	36. G	
17. A	37. A		17. B	37. C	
18. H	38. H		18. G	38. H	
19. C	39. B		19. D	39. B	
20. F	40. G		20. H	40. H	

■■■ SCORING GUIDE

Your final reported score is your COMPOSITE SCORE. Your COMPOSITE SCORE is the average of all of your SCALE SCORES.

Your SCALE SCORES for the four multiple-choice sections are derived from the Scoring Table on the next page. Use your RAW SCORE, or the number of questions that you answered correctly for each section, to determine your SCALE SCORE. If you got a RAW SCORE of 60 on the English test, for example, you correctly answered 60 out of 75 questions.

Step 1 Determine your RAW SCORE for each of the four multiple-choice sections:

English   _____

Mathematics   _____

Reading   _____

Science Reasoning   _____

The following Raw Score Table shows the total possible points for each section.

RAW SCORE TABLE	
KNOWLEDGE AND SKILL AREAS	**RAW SCORES**
ENGLISH	75
MATHEMATICS	60
READING	40
SCIENCE REASONING	40
WRITING	12

Multiple-Choice Scoring Worksheet

Step 2 Determine your SCALE SCORE for each of the four multiple-choice sections using the following Scoring Worksheet. Each SCALE SCORE should be rounded to the nearest number according to normal rules. For example, $31.2 \approx 31$ and $31.5 \approx 32$. If you answered 61 questions correctly on the English section, for example, your SCALE SCORE would be 29.

English _____ × 36 = _____ ÷ 75 = _____
                 RAW SCORE   **− 2** (*correction factor)

                                                                                                                 _____
                                                                                                                 SCALE SCORE

Mathematics _____ × 36 = _____ ÷ 60 = _____
                      RAW SCORE   **+ 1** (*correction factor)

                                                                                                                 _____
                                                                                                                 SCALE SCORE

Reading _____ × 36 = _____ ÷ 40 = _____
                 RAW SCORE   **+ 2** (*correction factor)

                                                                                                                 _____
                                                                                                                 SCALE SCORE

Science Reasoning _____ × 36 = _____ ÷ 40 = _____
                            RAW SCORE   **+ 1.5** (*correction factor)

                                                                                                                 _____
                                                                                                                 SCALE SCORE

*The correction factor is an approximation based on the average from several recent ACT tests. It is most valid for scores in the middle 50% (approximately 16–24 scale composite score) of the scoring range.

The scores are all approximate. Actual ACT scoring scales vary from one administration to the next based upon several factors.

If you take the optional Writing Test, you will need to combine your English and Writing scores to obtain your final COMPOSITE SCORE. Once you have determined a score for your essay out of 12 possible points, you will need to determine your ENGLISH/WRITING SCALE SCORE, using both your ENGLISH SCALE SCORE and your WRITING TEST SCORE. The combination of the two scores will give you an ENGLISH/WRITING SCALE SCORE, from 1 to 36, that will be used to determine your COMPOSITE SCORE mentioned earlier.

Using the English/Writing Scoring Table, find your ENGLISH SCALE SCORE on the left or right hand side of the table and your WRITING TEST SCORE on the top of the table. Follow your ENGLISH SCALE SCORE over and your WRITING TEST SCORE down until the two columns meet at a number. This number is your ENGLISH/WRITING SCALE SCORE and will be used to determine your COMPOSITE SCORE.

Step 3   Determine your ENGLISH/WRITING SCALE SCORE using the English/Writing Scoring Table on the following page:

       English   _____

       Writing   _____

       English/Writing   _____

ENGLISH/WRITING SCORING TABLE

ENGLISH SCALE SCORE	WRITING TEST SCORE											ENGLISH SCALE SCORE
	2	**3**	**4**	**5**	**6**	**7**	**8**	**9**	**10**	**11**	**12**	
36	26	27	28	29	30	31	32	33	34	32	36	**36**
35	26	27	28	29	30	31	31	32	33	34	35	**35**
34	25	26	27	28	29	30	31	32	33	34	35	**34**
33	24	25	26	27	28	29	30	31	32	33	34	**33**
32	24	25	25	26	27	28	29	30	31	32	33	**32**
31	23	24	25	26	27	28	29	30	30	31	32	**31**
30	22	23	24	25	26	27	28	29	30	31	32	**30**
29	21	22	23	24	25	26	27	28	29	30	31	**29**
28	21	22	23	24	24	25	26	27	28	29	30	**28**
27	20	21	22	23	24	25	26	27	28	28	29	**27**
26	19	20	21	22	23	24	25	26	27	28	29	**26**
25	18	19	20	21	22	23	24	25	26	27	28	**25**
24	18	19	20	21	22	23	23	24	25	26	27	**24**
23	17	18	19	20	21	22	23	24	25	26	27	**23**
22	16	17	18	19	20	21	22	23	24	25	26	**22**
21	16	17	17	18	19	20	21	22	23	24	25	**21**
20	15	16	17	18	19	20	21	21	22	23	24	**20**
19	14	15	16	17	18	19	20	21	22	23	24	**19**
18	13	14	15	16	17	18	19	20	21	22	23	**18**
17	13	14	15	16	16	17	18	19	20	21	22	**17**
16	12	13	14	15	16	17	18	19	20	20	21	**16**
15	11	12	13	14	15	16	17	18	19	20	21	**15**
14	10	11	12	13	14	15	16	17	18	19	20	**14**
13	10	11	12	13	14	14	15	16	17	18	19	**13**
12	9	10	11	12	13	14	15	16	17	18	19	**12**
11	8	9	10	11	12	13	14	15	16	17	18	**11**
10	8	9	9	10	11	12	13	14	15	16	17	**10**
9	7	8	9	10	11	12	13	13	14	15	16	**9**
8	6	7	8	9	10	11	12	13	14	15	16	**8**
7	5	6	7	8	9	10	11	12	13	14	15	**7**
6	5	6	7	7	8	9	10	11	12	13	14	**6**
5	4	5	6	7	8	9	10	11	12	12	13	**5**
4	3	4	5	6	7	8	9	10	11	12	13	**4**
3	2	3	4	5	6	7	8	9	10	11	12	**3**
2	2	3	4	5	6	6	7	8	9	10	11	**2**
1	1	2	3	4	5	6	7	8	9	10	11	**1**

Step 4   Determine your COMPOSITE SCORE by finding the sum of all your SCALE SCORES for each of the four sections: English only (if you do not choose to take the optional Writing Test) *or* English/Writing (if you choose to take the optional Writing Test), Math, Reading, and Science Reasoning, and divide by 4 to find the average. Round your COMPOSITE SCORE according to normal rules. For example, 31.2 ≈ 31 and 31.5 ≈ 32.

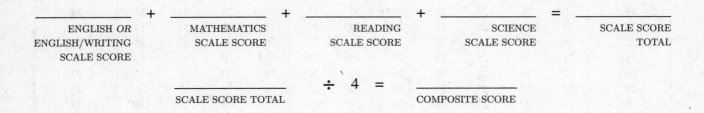

ENGLISH *OR*   MATHEMATICS   READING   SCIENCE   SCALE SCORE
ENGLISH/WRITING   SCALE SCORE   SCALE SCORE   SCALE SCORE   TOTAL
SCALE SCORE

_____ ÷ 4 = _____
SCALE SCORE TOTAL   COMPOSITE SCORE

▬▬ ANSWERS AND EXPLANATIONS

English Test Explanations

PASSAGE I

1. The best answer is C. It is necessary to include a comma between "tedious" and "tiring" because they are coordinate adjectives—they modify the same noun. Answer choice A is incorrect because it includes two additional and unnecessary commas.

2. The best answer is F. The sentence is clear as it is written. The other answer choices would be very awkward to read.

3. The best answer is B. This question relies on your ability to recognize wordiness. The phrase "needless to say" adds little to the meaning to the sentence and interrupts the natural rhythm of the clause.

4. The best answer is H. This question relies on your ability to recognize redundancy. "Asking" is equivalent to "inquiring," so answer choices F and G may be eliminated. Between answer choices H and J, answer choice H is better because it omits the unnecessary phrase "of me," further eliminating wordiness.

5. The best answer is D. The future tense is necessary because the feeling of passion the hiker asserts will come only after reading the book.

6. The best answer is H. The verb "brings" requires a direct object (what is being brought) and a prepositional element (where the direct object is being brought). The pronoun "you" and the phrase "closer to peace" are the constituents of the verb form "bring"; no commas are necessary within the clause.

7. The best answer is D. The preceding sentence identifies what is "no longer" the case. It would make sense that the next sentence describes what is true currently. Answer choices B and D may appear to be equally appropriate, except answer choice B must be eliminated because "now" appears again later in the sentence.

8. The best answer is F. Placement before a noun indicates that the word must be an adjective, eliminating answer choices G and J.

9. The best answer is B. The word "time" should refer to "sunrises and sunsets," so the plural "times"

is more appropriate; therefore, answer choices A and D may be eliminated. Answer choice C does not have correct word order, so it may be eliminated.

10. The best answer is G. Nouns conjoined with "or," as in the underlined portion, stand on equal footing. They should not have any intervening commas.

11. The best answer is D. The word "notepad" implies writing, which is the subject of the next paragraph. As a description of how moments of literary creativity arise for the author, this answer choice would provide a good transition between paragraphs.

12. The best answer is H. The phrase "other times" means "on other occasions." Among the answer choices, only H is acceptable because it is plural and lacks the possessive apostrophe.

13. The best answer is C. Answer choice A may be eliminated for wordiness. Answer choice B is an adjective, so it cannot modify a verb; eliminate it. Answer choices C and D would both be grammatical, but answer choice C would form a less awkward chain of modifiers.

14. The best answer is F. The word "others" is a noun meaning "other people;" eliminate answer choices H and J. As the passage in written in present tense, the past tense answer choice G may be eliminated.

15. The best answer is B. This sentence is simply a response to the preceding sentence, which identifies some people's preferred activity. The introductory phrase "For me" is a natural fit for a sentence about the author's opposing view.

PASSAGE II

16. The best answer is G. The word "ever" is best placed between auxiliary and participle; eliminate answer choice J. The word "saw" is the simple past form of "see," not the participle; therefore, answer choice H may be eliminated.

17. The best answer is D. The word "urban" is an adjective and should modify the noun "streets." Answer choices A and B contain an incorrect possessive form. Answer choice C may be eliminated because adjectives do not take the pluralizing "s" before nouns.

18. The best answer is F. The next-best answer choice would be J because both answer choices F and J have appropriate meaning and word order; however, answer choice J may be eliminated because the clause refers to vacation in general, so it must be written in simple present tense.

19. The best answer is B. The next two paragraphs explore the differences between dogs in America and dogs in Africa. Answer choice B provides a general introduction to what is coming up in the essay.

20. The best answer is H. The dog is panting, not the owner, so answer choices F and G may be eliminated. The sentence is in simple present tense, so answer choice H is best.

21. The best answer is D. "Dog owners" is a compound noun and the subject of the sentence. The other answer choices incorrectly contain possessive markers on one or both parts of the compound.

22. The best answer is H. The preceding sentence asserts people who have never owned a dog think dogs are not smart. Only answer choice H reveals naïveté on the part of the animal.

23. The best answer is D. To get a dog to improve behavior, it is logical that more training is needed, not less.

24. The best answer is F. The sentence addresses a general situation and makes sense in the simple present tense. Answer choice F is the third-person singular simple present form of "happen," and agrees with the subject "a dog."

25. The best answer is B. This clause should parallel the previous clause's logical subject ("a dog" becomes "it") and tense; therefore, the other answer choices may be eliminated.

26. The best answer is F. "Stark" is an adjective commonly used with "differences" in order to emphasize the degree of difference. Here, "starkly" (adv.) modifies "different" (adj.), so answer choice F is best. The other answer choices have awkward word order.

27. The best answer is D. "Mutualism" is a kind of symbiotic relationship that exists in nature. To say that "mutualism" between person and dog is tangible means that the exchange of benefits between the two is outwardly apparent. Inserting "tangible" before "mutualism" is supported by the rest of the paragraph, which details exactly how the human and dog profit from each other's presence.

28. The best answer is H. The "but" heads information that is part of the clause. Answer choice F may be eliminated because a comma is necessary before "but." Answer choice G may be eliminated because the semicolon divides only full independent clauses. Answer choice J may be eliminated because the dash is used to give special emphasis to something, which is not appropriate here.

29. The best answer is A. Answer choices B and C may be eliminated first because they are very awkward. Answer choice D, while less awkward, should be eliminated, too, because the placement of "never" after the verb is less acceptable than the placement of "never" at the beginning of the sentence, as in answer choice A.

30. The best answer is G. A single comma preceding "so" is all that is necessary. No comma is necessary after "so" when it introduces an action resulting from some pre-existing condition (e.g., "It rained, so I stayed home."); therefore, answer choices H and J may be eliminated.

PASSAGE III

31. The best answer is D. This sentence states something that seems at odds with the preceding sentence. Only "though," answer choice D, reflects this relationship.

32. The best answer is G. "Carnaval season" indicates that the event comes around at least once a year. The verb "flock" should be in simple present tense to reflect how the clause is a general statement.

33. The best answer is A. The sentence is clearest as written. Answer choices B and C are comma-spliced run-on sentences. The subject-predicate pair in answer choice D does not make sense.

34. The best answer is H. Reminding the reader of the dangers the author likes to face emphasizes his "adventurous nature," as the question puts it. The other answer choices do not seem well-matched to the "extreme" theme the author maintains throughout the passage.

35. The best answer is A. The major clue here is the initial "If" clause in the sentence. It must be followed by a comma, then a second clause; the other answer choices may be eliminated.

36. The best answer is J. Answer choice F has correct word order, but a comma would be necessary before the gerund "shooting." The best alternative is answer choice J because it uses the conjunction "and," which does not require a preceding comma, and maintains past tense from the preceding clause.

37. **The best answer is B.** The "sarcastic grin" from the preceding sentence surely indicates that the race organizer has his doubts about the author's fitness for the activity, but is willing to let him try it nonetheless. Only answer choice B reflects this attitude.

38. **The best answer is H.** The verb "went" may only be modified by an adverb, so the other answer choices should be eliminated.

39. **The best answer is B.** Answer choice C may be eliminated for being a sentence fragment. The other answer choices are grammatical, but answer choice B is clearest because it is in conventional word order and has active voice.

40. **The best answer is J.** The phrase "This is the time" is wordy; eliminate answer choice F. The preceding sentence does a satisfactory job of defining the time frame. No words are required before the main clause "I learned … legal"; therefore, answer choices G and H may be eliminated.

41. **The best answer is A.** Here, "Racing" is the subject of the sentence, so answer choice C may be eliminated. Since the race took place in the past, answer choice A is appropriate.

42. **The best answer is J.** Because that the race result was so close, the mention of a photo finish seems an appropriate place for an exclamation point. Answer choice F leaves a sentence fragment at the end of the paragraph. Answer choices G and H may be eliminated because they incorrectly link the two clauses, which are not related conceptually.

43. **The best answer is C.** The noun phrase "head of the pack" is a common colloquialism and should not be rephrased.

44. **The best answer is H.** This answer choice ties the events of the author's heat with the overarching concept of his penchant for thrill seeking. Surely, the author would celebrate a successful slide down the chute.

45. **The best answer is A.** An "essay discussing extreme sports" would have to include information on several extreme sports. This essay only mentions one.

PASSAGE IV

46. **The best answer is J.** What follows a semi-colon dividing a sentence must be a well-formed clause, containing minimally a subject and a verb. Answer choice J correctly uses "the water" as a subject and "shines" as the appropriate simple present tense verb. Answer choice G would make a well-formed clause, but the past tense is not appropriate for giving a description of a place that is unlikely to be affected by time (like the color of the water).

47. **The best answer is B.** The possessive form of the pronoun "it" is "its." Note the lack of apostrophe, which contradicts the normal rule of adding apostrophe + "s" to singular nouns to create possessive forms.

48. **The best answer is G.** The sentence means to say that the "euphoric swell" is responsible for pushing up "the corners of the mouth" of some hypothetical visitor to the Caribbean. Answer choice G uses conventional word order and is clearest and most concise.

49. **The best answer is D.** The verb phrase from the previous sentence, "sailed blissfully from one cay to another," means exactly what this sentence does. For the sake of brevity, it may be omitted.

50. **The best answer is F.** This paragraph describes the chaotic scene of a sailing crew effecting a change of direction. Answer choice F alludes to this fact by saying that tacking is "reserved for the experts."

51. **The best answer is B.** A verb in infinitive or gerund form would be appropriate here. Answer choice A lacks "to" before the verb in order to form the infinitive. Answer choice C may be eliminated because "start" is redundant with "begins." Answer choice D is not appropriate because omitting the mention of yelling takes away from the chaotic scene the author is trying to create.

52. **The best answer is H.** For the sake of clarity and brevity, the simple infinitive form should be used here.

53. **The best answer is B.** A clause introduced by a subordinating conjunctive adverb such as "along with" must be set apart from the sentence with commas. Eliminate answer choices A and D. Answer choice C is incorrect because the past tense verb "went" is not appropriate.

54. **The best answer is H.** This answer choice uses conventional word order and is clearest and most concise.

55. The best answer is C. Introducing speech or inner monologue requires a comma before the direct quotation. Furthermore, if the quotation is a complete sentence, the first word of it should be capitalized as usual.

56. The best answer is J. The subject "the unpredictable wind" introduces the main clause, so what comes before it should anticipate that. Answer choices F and H fail to do this, and answer choice G is ungrammatical; they all may be eliminated.

57. The best answer is A. This sentence is part of the narrative of the author's trip, so it should be in past tense; eliminate the other answer choices.

58. The best answer is F. The preceding two sentences identify that the boat lay adrift at sea for some time before the motor was started. The introductory word "Eventually," answer choice F, is most appropriate.

59. The best answer is B. This sentence is part of the narrative of the author's trip, so it should be in past tense; eliminate answer choices A and C. Answer choice D may be eliminated because it does not make sense in context.

60. The best answer is H. The sentence gives the author's ultimate reaction to the absence of wind at the end of his sailing trip. It provides a conclusion to the details of the paragraph.

PASSAGE V

61. The best answer is B. In general, details introduced by the word "including" must be set apart from the clause with a comma.

62. The best answer is J. A subordinate clause headed by "but" or "and" must be set apart from the main clause with a comma. Eliminate answer choice H. Answer choice G would create a run-on sentence; eliminate it. Answer choice J is the best fit for the sentence because the adverb "ordinarily" describes a general condition that the clause with "but" is going to counter. Careful reading will reveal that "but" (answer choice J) is preferable to "and" (answer choice F) in the sentence.

63. The best answer is A. These two sentences are independent thoughts and cannot be separated with a colon or a comma; eliminate answer choices B and D. The adverb "thus" normally introduces the consequence of some pre-stated condition. The two sentences addresses by the questions do not have that relationship.

64. The best answer is J. If a clause comes after a form of the verb "decide," either the complementizer "that" or a null (absent) complementizer must precede the clause.

65. The best answer is A. Answer choice B may be eliminated for wordiness. Answer choice C may be eliminated for the lack of a conjunction between any of the elements of the list, as well as incorrect use of the comma after "Titian." The "*Mona Lisa*" is a painting and "Titian" and "Raphael" are artists, so answer choice D does not make sense.

66. The best answer is G. At the beginning of the paragraph, the Louvre is described as "majestic." Certainly, a the French king would want a palace to match his extensive art collection. The other answer choices do not reflect this, so they may be eliminated.

67. The best answer is B. Charles V is mentioned earlier in the passage as a previous resident of the Louvre. Answer choice B describes a durative condition—how nice the palace was—in the past.

68. The best answer is J. It is generally inappropriate to begin a paragraph with a sentence that uses one or more pronouns; therefore, answer choice J would create the clearest sentence.

69. The best answer is C. This sentence pairs the number of works of art with the corresponding year and represents the clearest word order among all the choices.

70. The best answer is H. The concept of "elitism" matches best with "creativity" because they are both human qualities. The other answer choices are words for certain kinds of people and would not be a good fit in the conjoined phrase.

71. The best answer is B. The preceding paragraph focuses on Francois 1 and his renovation of the Louvre. Therefore, Sentence 1 is a good transition between the third and fourth paragraphs. Eliminate answer choice D, which places Sentence 2 first. The three remaining answer choices (A, B, and C) all put Sentence 2 in the second position, so look at whether Sentence 3, Sentence 4, or Sentence 5 should follow Sentence 2. Because Sentence 2 mentions that royalty lived in the sprawling palace (the Louvre), Sentence 3, which discusses the art collection, seems out of place. Eliminate answer choice A. Sentence 5 effectively joins Sentence 2 and 6 by indicating that after Louis XIV left, many more people lived in the palace. Sentences 3 and

4 chronologically follow Sentence 6, which makes answer choice B the most logical selection.

72. **The best answer is F.** The "ballooning collection" mentioned in this paragraph supports inserting an introductory sentence like answer choice F at the head of the paragraph. None of the other answer choices are supported by evidence in the paragraph.

73. **The best answer is B.** The correct idiomatic phrase is "moved to," which indicates where the artwork has been moved.

74. **The best answer is J.** Answer choice J creates two incomplete sentences, so it would not be acceptable. The remaining answer choices are grammatically correct, and do not change the meaning of the paragraph.

75. **The best answer is C.** The verb should match the unconjugated form of "visit" before the conjunction "and;" eliminate answer choice A. Answer choice B shows "view" as a noun, so it may be eliminated. Answer choice D may be eliminated since it would leave "and" without a second part.

Mathematics Test Explanations

1. **The correct answer is C.** Since the point $(2,-5)$ has a positive x-coordinate, it will have a placement to the right of the y-axis. Similarly, since the point has a negative y-coordinate, it will have a placement below the x-axis. Of the possible points, only C and D fit such a description. Of the two points, C appears to have a y-coordinate with greater magnitude than its x-coordinate, which would correspond to the point $(2,-5)$.

2. **The correct answer is F.** To solve this problem, systematically assess each answer choice and eliminate incorrect choices. Of the choices, only the statement that "Michael has a student ID" must be true because it is given that "Michael is a high school student who attends Tarrytown High School" and "All students who attend Tarrytown High School have a student ID."

3. **The correct answer is B.** When Juan withdrew $300, the resulting balance was $400, making the balance of the account before withdrawal $400 + $300, or $700. Since the balance of Juan's savings account quadrupled during the year, the balance, b, in the account before it quadrupled is represented by $4b = 700$. Therefore $b = \dfrac{700}{4}$, or $175.

4. **The correct answer is J.** To find the value of a such that the equation $3(a + 5) - a = 23$ is true, solve $3(a + 5) - a = 23$ for a:

$$3a + 15 - a = 23$$
$$2a + 15 = 23$$
$$2a = 8$$
$$a = 4$$

5. **The correct answer is D.** It is given that on the number line, numbers decrease in value from right to left, meaning that numbers on the right are greater than numbers on the left. Since no indication of the location of 0 is given in the picture, no assumption about negative or positive can be made. Simply because numbers on the right are greater than numbers on the left and Y is to the right of X, Y must be greater than X. Put another way, X must be less than Y, answer choice D.

6. **The correct answer is H.** To solve this problem, use the fact that since $AB \cong BC$, triangle ABC is isosceles. In isosceles triangles, the angles opposite equal sides have equal measure. In this triangle, since angles A and C are opposite sides AB and BC, they have equal measure. Because the sum of the angles in a triangle is always $180°$, the sum of the measures of angles A and C is $180°$ less the measure of angle B, or $180° - 55° = 125°$. Therefore, since angles A and C have equal measure, they both equal $\dfrac{125°}{2} = 62.5°$.

7. **The correct answer is D.** To solve for x, distribute the 3 in the equation $3(x - 2) = -7$ to get $3x - 6 = -7$. Adding 6 to both sides of the equation yields $3x = -1$, or $x = -\dfrac{1}{3}$.

8. **The correct answer is K.** To solve this problem, factor the polynomial $x^2 + 3x - 18$. To do so, think of $x^2 + 3x - 18$ as $(x + ?)(x - ?)$. To fill in the question marks, find two numbers that multiply to equal -18 and add up to 3. One such pair of numbers is 6 and -3. To check, make sure that $(x + 6)(x - 3) = x^2 + 3x - 18$, which it does. Of the answer choices, only $(x + 6)$ is a factor.

9. **The correct answer is A.** A line parallel to the x-axis is horizontal. Horizontal lines have the equation $y = b$, where b is a constant, and represents the y-intercept. Therefore, a line in the standard (x, y) coordinate plane is parallel to the x-axis and 5 units below it will have the equation $y = -5$.

10. **The correct answer is J.** To solve this problem, first find the common denominator, and then add the fractions. In the case of $\dfrac{2r}{3} + \dfrac{4s}{5}$, the common denominator is 3×5, or 15. To convert $\dfrac{2r}{3}$, multiply by $\dfrac{5}{5}$ to get $\dfrac{10r}{15}$. To convert $\dfrac{4s}{5}$, multiply by $\dfrac{3}{3}$ to get $\dfrac{12s}{15}$. The sum is therefore $\dfrac{10r}{15} + \dfrac{12s}{15} = \dfrac{(10r + 12s)}{15}$.

11. **The correct answer is C.** If a pie recipe calls for $\dfrac{1}{3}$ cup sugar to make one 9-inch pie, making three 9-inch pies will require $3\left(\dfrac{1}{3}\right)$, or 1 cup of sugar.

12. **The correct answer is G.** To solve this problem, first perform the subtractions and then evaluate the absolute values:

$$|5 - 3| - |2 - 6|$$
$$|2| - |-4|$$
$$2 - 4 = -2$$

13. **The correct answer is C.** Since Jeff traveled twice as far as Ryan in half the time, Jeff traveled 40 miles in 2 hours. Jeff's average speed is equivalent to 40 miles ÷ 2 hours, or 20 miles per hour.

14. **The correct answer is J.** To solve this problem, substitute -5 for x in the expression $2x^2 + 6x$:

$$2(-5)^2 + 6(-5)$$

$$2(25) - 30$$

$$50 - 30 = 20$$

15. **The correct answer is A.** To solve this problem, substitute 4 for b in the equation $b - 2 = ab + 16$:

$$4 - 2 = 4a + 16$$

$$2 - 16 = 4a + 16 - 16$$

$$\frac{(-14)}{4} = \frac{(4a)}{4}$$

$$a = -\frac{14}{4} = -3.5$$

16. **The correct answer is H.** Recall that the area of a parallelogram is equivalent to base × height. Since $STVX$ is a square, all sides of $STVX$ will be equal. Likewise, since the height of the parallelogram is equal to the height of the square, the height of the parallelogram is 3. The area of the square $STVX$ is $3^2 = 9$. The area of the parallelogram is therefore $(8 + 3)(3) = (11)(3)$, or 33. Thus the ratio of the area of square $STVX$ to the area of parallelogram $RUVY$ is 9:33, or 3:11.

17. **The correct answer is E.** To solve this problem, substitute -3 for x in $2x^2 - 6x + 7$:

$$2(-3)^2 - 6(-3) + 7$$

$$2(9) - (-18) + 7$$

$$18 + 18 + 7 = 43$$

18. **The correct answer is G.** To solve this problem, set up a proportion between the length in inches and the length in miles represented. Let the x be the number of miles represented by 1.4 inches. Since 1.2 inches represents 50 miles, $\frac{50}{1.2} = \frac{x}{1.4}$. Multiplying both sides of the proportion by 1.4 yields $x = \frac{(50)(1.4)}{1.2} \approx 58$ miles.

19. **The correct answer is A.** To solve this problem, distribute the -1 and combine like terms, as follows:

$$(5x^3 + 3xz^2 - 17z) - (4xz^2 + 5z - 2x^3)$$

$$5x^3 + 3xz^2 - 17z - 4xz^2 - 5z + 2x^3$$

$$(5x^3 + 2x^3) + (3xz^2 - 4xz^2) + (-17z - 5z)$$

$$7x^3 - xz^2 - 22z$$

20. **The correct answer is J.** The distance on the y-axis from point A to point B is the difference in the y-coordinates of points A and B. Since point A is $(-2,8)$ and point B is $(5,3)$, the distance in the y-direction is $8 - 3 = 5$.

21. **The correct answer is D.** The solutions of $(x - 5)(x - 3)(x + 3)(x + 9) = 0$ are the values of x that make the product $(x - 5)$ $(x - 3)(x + 3)(x + 9)$ equal to zero. Such values of x will be the values that make any one of the four parts of $(x - 5)(x - 3)(x + 3)(x + 9)$ equal to zero, which would be 5, 3, -3, and -9. Of the answer choices, only -5 is not a value of x such that $(x - 5)(x - 3)(x + 3)(x + 9) = 0$.

22. **The correct answer is H.** At first glance, you might think that you don't have enough information to solve this problem. However, if you recognize that pr must be a positive fraction since it lies between 0 and 1, you can work your way through the answer choices and eliminate those that could be true:

Answer choice F: If both p and r were less than 0, their product would be positive. It's possible for pr to be a positive fraction, because both p and r could be negative fractions, so eliminate answer choice F.

Answer choice G: If p were -1 and r were also a negative number, their product would be positive. It's possible for pr to be a positive fraction, because r could be a negative fraction, so eliminate answer choice G.

Answer choice H: If both p and r were less -1, then pr would be greater than 1, so this statement cannot be true, and answer choice H is correct.

Answer choice J: If both p and r were less than 1, their product could be positive. It's possible for pr to be a positive fraction, because both p and r could be negative fractions, so eliminate answer choice J.

Answer choice K: If p were less than 1, p could be a positive fraction. If r were greater than 0, it would be a positive number, and it's possible for pr to be a positive fraction; eliminate answer choice K.

23. **The correct answer is C.** To solve this problem, recall that $10^2 = 100$. Therefore since $n = 10$, $n^2 = 100$. The number 552 can be broken up into $500 + 50 + 2$, which can be written as $5(100) + 5(10) + 2$. Again, since $n = 10$ and $n^2 = 100, 5(100) + 5(10) + 2 = 5n^2 + 5n + 2$.

24. **The correct answer is G.** To solve this problem, add the two equations, or multiples of them, so that cancellation occurs and you can solve for the b variable. If the equation $a + 3b = -4$ is multiplied by -3, the result is $-3a - 9b = 12$. The addition of $-3a - 9b = 12$ to the second equation is shown below:

$$3a - b = 18$$

$$-3a - 9b = 12$$

$$-10b = 30$$

By canceling out the a terms, you can solve for b:

$$b = \frac{30}{-10} = -3.$$

25. **The correct answer is C.** To solve this problem, first combine like terms. The expression $x + x(x + x + x)$ becomes $x + x(3x)$. Multiplying the second term yields $x + 3x^2$.

26. **The correct answer is G.** Since the refrigerator that sold for $450 now sells for 7% more, the current price is $450 + (7\% \text{ of } \$450)$, or $450+450(0.07)$. Remember that 0.07 is the decimal equivalent of 7%.

27. **The correct answer is E.** The set of all points 5 units from the x-axis in 3-dimensional space can be likened to the set of all points 5 units from the x-axis in 2-dimensional space, which are two lines. Revolving such lines about the x-axis creates a tube-like shape that is a cylinder.

28. **The correct answer is J.** To solve this problem, calculate the slope of the ramp in the same manner as calculating the slope of a line through the points $(-2,-1)$ and $(16,2)$. Slope is defined as $\frac{\text{rise}}{\text{run}}$, or $\frac{\text{change in } y}{\text{change in } x}$, therefore $(-2,-1)$ and $(16,2)$

the equation is:

$$\frac{(2+1)}{(16+2)} = \frac{3}{18}$$

$$\frac{3}{18} = \frac{1}{6}$$

29. **The correct answer is B.** To solve this problem, express the number 0.002 in scientific notation, which is 2×10^{-3}, because the decimal point moved 3 places to the right. If the number 10^{-3} is 100 times larger than some number x, then:

$$10^{-3} = 100x, \text{ or } x = \frac{10^{-3}}{100}$$

$$\frac{10^{-3}}{10^2} = 10^{-3-2}$$

$$10^{-3-2} = 10^{-5}$$

$$10^{-5}$$

Therefore, 2×10^{-3} is 100 times larger than 2×10^{-5} which equals 0.00002 because you must move the decimal point 5 places to the right.

30. **The correct answer is H.** If a sphere has a diameter of 12, then its radius is 6. A sphere with radius 6 has volume $V = \frac{4\pi r^3}{3} = \frac{4\pi(6)^3}{3} = \frac{4\pi(216)}{3} = \frac{864\pi}{3}$, or 288π.

31. **The correct answer is B.** To solve this problem, first establish a common denominator and add the terms in the numerator and. For the numerator, the common denominator of $\frac{1}{3} - \frac{1}{4}$ is 12. $\frac{1}{3} = \frac{4}{12}$ and $\frac{1}{4} = \frac{3}{12}$. The result is $\frac{1}{3} - \frac{1}{4} = \frac{4}{12} - \frac{3}{12} = \frac{1}{12}$. Likewise, for the denominator, the common denominator of $\frac{1}{3} + \frac{1}{4}$ is 12. $\frac{1}{3} = \frac{4}{12}$ and $\frac{1}{4} = \frac{3}{12}$, which makes $\frac{1}{3} + \frac{1}{4} = \frac{4}{12} + \frac{3}{12} = \frac{7}{12}$. The quotient $\frac{(1/3 - 1/4)}{(1/3 + 1/4)}$ equals $\frac{(1/12)}{(7/12)}$, or $\left(\frac{1}{12}\right)\left(\frac{12}{7}\right)$, which equals $\frac{1}{7}$.

32. **The correct answer is H.** To solve this problem, find the least common multiple of 6 and 9. The correct answer is 18 because $6 \times 3 = 18$ and $9 \times 2 = 18$.

33. **The correct answer is D.** To solve this problem, first subtract 5 from both sides of $\sqrt{2x} + 5 = 9$

to get $\sqrt{2x} = 4$. Squaring both sides of $\sqrt{2x} = 4$ yields $2x = 16$, or $x = 8$.

34. **The correct answer is J.** To solve this problem, set up three other variables, x, y, and z. Let x be the supplement of angle p. Let y be the supplement of angle q. Let z be the angle opposite of the 105° angle, so $z = 105°$. With these new variables, you know that $p = 180 - x$ and $q = 180 - y$. This means that $p + q = (180 - x) + (180 - y)$, which simplifies to $360 - (x+y)$. You can see that the three lines form a triangle and that one of the angles is 105°. That means that the other two angles, x and y must have a sum of $180 - 105$, or 75°. Thus, if $x+y = 75°$, then $p+q = 360 - (x+y)$, or $360 - 75$, which is 285°.

35. **The correct answer is E.** The equation $5x - 7y = 13$ defines a line. Since there are an infinite number of points in a line, there are an infinite number of ordered pairs (x, y) of real numbers that satisfy the equation $5x - 7y = 13$.

36. **The correct answer is F.** To easily solve this problem, write out every possible three-digit integer: 345, 354, 435, 453, 534, and 543; six different positive three-digit numbers can be formed.

37. **The correct answer is D.** To solve this problem, recognize that any three angles that are part of a triangle add to 180°. Relationship I: $\angle 2$, $\angle 7$, and $\angle 12$ make up the three angles within the triangle pictured, therefore $m\angle 2 + m\angle 7 + m\angle 12 = 180°$. Relationship II: using the property that vertical angles are congruent $\angle 4 \cong \angle 2, \angle 5 \cong \angle 7$, and $\angle 10 \cong \angle 12$, therefore $m\angle 4 + m\angle 5 + m\angle 10 = 180°$. Relationship III: two of these angles in this relationship are clearly greater than 90° each, thus $m\angle 3 + m\angle 8 + m\angle 11 > 180°$. Therefore the only relationships that must be true are I and II.

38. **The correct answer is G.** To solve for x, substitute $y = x - 7$ into the equation $x^2 - y^2 = 49$ (Since $x - y = 7, y = x - 7$):

$$x^2 - (x - 7)^2 = 49$$

$$x^2 - (x^2 - 14x + 49) = 49$$

$$x^2 - x^2 + 14x - 49 = 49$$

$$14x - 49 = 49$$

$$14x = 98$$

$$x = 7$$

39. **The correct answer is E.** The expression $\frac{a^9}{a^3}$ is simplified by subtracting the exponents to get $\frac{a^9}{a^3} = a^{9-3} = a^6$.

40. **The correct answer is H.** To solve this problem, first determine the length of the unknown side of the polygon. To do so, use the fact that the piece cut off was a right triangle. The unknown side is the hypotenuse of the triangle with legs $14 - 10 = 4$ and $10 - 7 = 3$. Use the Pythagorean Theorem to calculate the length of the hypotenuse (the unknown side of the polygon):

$$4^2 + 3^2 = c^2$$

$$16 + 9 = c^2$$

$$25 = c^2$$

$$c = 5$$

The length of the unknown side is 5. Therefore the perimeter of the entire polygon is $14 + 10 + 10 + 7 + 5 = 46$.

41. **The correct answer is D.** To solve this problem, you must recall that a circle with center (h, k) and radius r has the equation $(x - h)^2 + (y - k)^2 = r^2$. A circle that has center $(-4, 5)$ and radius 5 units would therefore have an equation $(x + 4)^2 + (y - 5)^2 = 25$.

42. **The correct answer is H.** The tangent of an angle is the ratio of the side opposite the angle to the side adjacent to the angle. The side opposite angle x is 15 and the side adjacent is 8, making $\tan x = \frac{15}{8}$.

43. **The correct answer is A.** Enclosing a square region with 120 feet of fence would make each side of the square $\frac{120}{4}$, or 30 feet. Therefore, the number of square feet enclosed is the area of the region, which would be 30^2, or 900 square feet.

44. **The correct answer is G.** To solve this problem, recall that a quadratic equation has exactly one real solution when the solution is a "double zero." Such an equation would have the factored form of $(y + b)^2 = 0$, where b is a real number. When you expand the equation, it becomes $(y + b)^2$ is $y^2 + 2by + b^2$. The equation $y^2 + 2ky + 4k = 0$ has a similar form; however, in order for the term $4k$ to represent b^2, k must equal 4.

45. The correct answer is D. If the measure of angle DCA is 60°, then the measure of angle BCA is 60° as well. Because the angles in a triangle have the sum of 180°, angle BAC is $180 - 90 - 60$, or 30°. Because the segment AD bisects angle BAC, angle BAD is equivalent to angle DAC, which is $\dfrac{30°}{2}$, or 15°. Further, since the triangle ABD is a right triangle, the measure of angle $ADB = 180 - 90 - 15$, or 75°.

46. The correct answer is F. To solve this problem, factor the numerator and denominator. Factoring the numerator $4x - x^2$ yields $x(4 - x)$. Factoring the denominator $(x^2 - 2x - 8)$ yields $(x + 2)$ $(x-4)$. Thus the expression $\dfrac{(4x - x^2)}{(x^2 - 2x - 8)}$ becomes $\dfrac{x(4 - x)}{(x + 2)(x - 4)}$. The expression $(4 - x)$, when -1 is factored out, equals $-(x - 4)$. Therefore $\dfrac{x(4 - x)}{(x + 2)(x - 4)} = \dfrac{-x(x - 4)}{(x + 2)(x - 4)}$, which can be simplified to $\dfrac{-x}{x + 2}$.

47. The correct answer is C. To solve this problem, recall that circumference is $2\pi r$, where r is the radius. If a circle has a circumference of $\left(\dfrac{4}{3}\right)\pi$, then $\left(\dfrac{4}{3}\right)\pi = 2\pi r$. Therefore, $2r = \dfrac{4}{3}$, or $r = \dfrac{2}{3}$.

48. The correct answer is F. If the function f satisfies the equation $f(x + y) = f(x) + f(y)$ for every pair of real numbers x and y, then f is a linear function. For some unknown linear function f, the value of $f(1)$ can be any real number (think of all the possible lines that can be drawn).

49. The correct answer is C. To solve this problem, use the formula for the area of a trapezoid, $\dfrac{1}{2}h(b_1 + b_2)$, where h is the altitude (height) and b_1 and b_2 are the bases. In this case, the altitude (height) is 3 and one of the bases is 5. Because the area is known to be 24, the other base can be determined by using the equation $24 = \left(\dfrac{1}{2}\right)(3)(b + 5)$. Dividing both sides of the equation by $\dfrac{3}{2}$ (or multiplying both sides of the equation by $\dfrac{2}{3}$) yields $16 = b + 5$, or $b = 11$.

50. The correct answer is K. To solve this problem, it might be helpful to make a list of the powers of 2: $2^1 = 2$, $2^2 = 4$, $2^3 = 8$, $2^4 = 16$, $2^5 = 32$, and so on. Select consecutive values from this list and

multiply them, starting with the values that make the most sense. For example, you know that $2 \times 4 \times 8$ will be less than 512, so try $4 \times 8 \times 16$, which does equal 512. Now, add those same terms: $4 + 8 + 16 = 28$.

51. The correct answer is B. You are given that 30% of x equals 60% of y, which can be expressed mathematically as $0.3x = 0.6y$. To express y in terms of x, solve for y, as follows:

$$0.3x = 0.6y$$
$$0.3x/0.6 = y$$
$$0.5x = y$$

This is equivalent to the expression $y = 50\%$ of x.

52. The correct answer is F. To answer this question, solve the inequality for x, as follows:

$$3(x - 4) \geq 9(4 + x)$$
$$3x + 12 \geq 36 + 9x$$
$$-6x \geq 24$$
$$x \leq -4$$

Remember that the direction of the sign in an inequality switches when dividing by a negative number.

53. The correct answer is E. The first step in solving this problem is to solve $x = 6a + 3$ for a:

$$x = 6a + 3$$
$$x - 3 = 6a$$
$$\dfrac{x - 3}{6} = a$$

Now you can substitute $\dfrac{x - 3}{6}$ for a in the second equation, and solve for y:

$$y = 9 + a$$
$$y = 9 + \dfrac{(x - 3)}{6}$$
$$y = \dfrac{54}{6} + \dfrac{x - 3}{6}$$
$$y = \dfrac{54 + x - 3}{6}$$
$$y = \dfrac{51 + x}{6}$$

54. **The correct answer is K.** In a trapezoid, the bases are parallel, so $AB||DC$. You are given that $PQ||AB||DC$. By definition, the ratio of the length of DP to the length of PA is the same as the ratio of PQ to AB. In other words:

$$\frac{DP}{PA} = \frac{PQ}{AB}$$

Substitute the lengths that are given for DP, PA, and AB and solve for PQ:

$$\frac{8}{12} = \frac{PQ}{36}$$

$$36 \times \frac{8}{12} = PQ$$

$$3 \times 8 = PQ$$

$$24 = PQ$$

55. **The correct answer is C.** To solve this problem, substitute the given values into the given equation:

$$3365 = 225(x) - (165x + c)$$

You know that 75 units were sold, so set x equal to 75 and solve for c:

$$3365 = 225(75) - (165(75) + c)$$

$$3365 = 16875 - (12375 + c)$$

$$3365 = 16875 - 12375 - c$$

$$3365 - 4500 = -c$$

$$1135 = c$$

56. **The correct answer is J.** The sine of any acute angle is calculated by dividing the length of the side opposite to the acute angle by the hypotenuse ($\sin = \frac{opp}{hyp}$). It may help you to draw a diagram to solve this problem, as shown below:

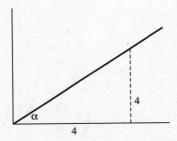

Use the Pythagorean Theorem to calculate the length of the hypotenuse.

$$a^2 + b^2 = c^2$$

$$4^2 + 4^2 = c^2$$

$$16 + 16 = c^2$$

$$32 = c^2$$

$$\sqrt{32} = c$$

$$\sqrt{16}\sqrt{2} = c$$

$$4\sqrt{2} = c$$

So, the sine of angle α is $\frac{4}{4\sqrt{2}}$, which can be reduced to $\frac{1}{\sqrt{2}}$. Recall that roots should be elimnated from denominators: $\frac{1}{\sqrt{2}} \frac{(\sqrt{2})}{(\sqrt{2})} = \frac{\sqrt{2}}{2}$.

57. **The correct answer is E.** Integers can be even or odd, and positive or negative. Pick real numbers to substitute into the expressions in each Roman Numeral, then eliminate any Roman Numerals that do not always yield and odd number.
Whenever a number is multiplied by 2, the result is always even. Thus, II and III are true; answer choice E is correct.

58. **The correct answer is J.** Probability refers to the likelihood of something happening. How many white chips should Carol put into the container so that she is likely to draw 3 red chips every eight draws? Try the answer choices.

F: If she puts in 3 white chips, then the probability of drawing a red chip is 6 (red chips) out of 9 (total chips). Eliminate answer choice F.

G: If she puts in 6 white chips, then the probability of drawing a red chip is 6 (red chips) out of 12 (total chips). Eliminate answer choice G.

H: If she puts in 8 white chips, then the probability of drawing a red chip is 6 (red chips) out of 14 (total chips). Eliminate answer choice H.

J: If she puts in 10 white chips, then the probability of drawing a red chip is 6 (red chips) out of 16 (total chips), which is equivalent to 3 out of 8, or $\frac{3}{8}$. She should add 10 white chips.

59. **The correct answer is D.** When a wheel makes one revolution that means that it goes completely around one time. The distance one time around a wheel is equal to the wheel's circumference.

A wheel is a circle, and the formula for the circumference of a circle is $C = 2\pi r$. If the diameter of the wheel is 27, then one time around, or one revolution, of the wheel is equal to 27, which is equal to $2r$. So, the circumference of the wheel is $2r\pi$, or, 27π. Since the wheel made 32 revolutions, multiply 32 by 27π to get 864π.

60. **The correct answer is K.** The absolute value of a number is indicated when a number is placed within two vertical lines. Absolute value can be defined as the numerical value of a real number without regard to its sign. This means that the absolute value of 10, $|10|$, is the same as the absolute value of -10, $|-10|$, in that they both equal 10. If the absolute value of $x-2a = 5$, then $x-2a$ must also equal -5. If $x - 2a = 5$, then $x = 2a + 5$. If $x - 2a = -5$, then $x = 2a - 5$. These equations are represented on the number line as follows:

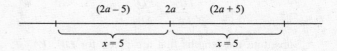

So, the distance apart on the number line is $5 + 5$, or 10.

Reading Test Explanations

PASSAGE I

1. **The best answer is C.** Although the statement in the question uses the word "wedded," it does not simply mean "marriage;" wedded also means "closely dedicated or attached to." In this statement, Clover is implying that Cecy had an attachment or affection for pink roses, answer choice C. Answer choices A, B, and D can be eliminated because there is no reference to an actual wedding when Clover says "She *was* rather wedded to them." Clover is simply referring to Cecy's fondness for pink roses.

2. **The best answer is G.** Cecy and Clover's relationship can be implied when the passage writes that the name of Cecy's baby was "'Katherine Clover,' after her two friends." This distinguishes Clover as a close friend of Cecy, answer choice G. Answer choice F may appear to be correct; however, when the passage identifies Clover as a friend of Cecy, it is clear that they are not sisters.

3. **The best answer is D.** This statement indicates that Elsie is pleased to be sewing ruffles onto the skirt in which her sister Clover is about "to burst upon the world." The fact that Clover is preparing to "burst upon the world" tells us that Clover is attending a sort of coming-of-age or milestone event. Answer choice A simply discusses Clover's visions of her first party dress. Answer choice B is incorrect because although it discusses girls "coming out," it does not specifically refer to Clover. Answer choice C is incorrect because Elsie is dreaming of her future, which has little to do with Clover's upcoming milestone event.

4. **The best answer is G.** This statement indicates that Clover's eyes were always her most notable source of beauty; therefore, answer choice F can be immediately eliminated. The passage states that Clover's eyes, with their pathetic look, "made them quite irresistible to anyone with a tender or sympathetic heart." This indicates that her eyes were compelling to kind and compassionate people, which best correlates with answer choice G. Answer choices H and J are not supported by details found in the passage.

5. **The best answer is C.** The passage states that, "Yes, the excellent Cecy, who at thirteen had announced her intention to devote her whole life to teaching Sunday school, visiting the poor, and setting a good example to her more worldly contemporaries, had actually forgotten these fine resolutions, and before she was twenty had become the wife of Sylvester Slack, a young lawyer in a neighboring town!" This information best supports answer choice C.

6. **The best answer is H.** According to the passage, Elsie "adored Clover," which suggests that she enjoyed spending time with her sister. The context of the passage indicates that both girls enjoyed the pleasure of each other's company. The other answer choices are not supported by the passage.

7. **The best answer is B.** The passage states that "her arms and wrists and shoulders ... were round and dimpled like an infant's." The other answer choices are not supported by the passage.

8. **The best answer is J.** The passage mentions several times that Cecy was trying to convince Clover to use a spray of pink roses on her dress. When Clover is discussing the type of flowers to use, she states that she wouldn't use the spray of pink roses because "it cost lots, and I didn't want it at all ... fresh flowers are a great deal prettier, anyway, than the artificial ones." This clearly indicates that Clover did not want to follow her friend Cecy's advice on what type of flowers to use on her dress. The other answer choices are not supported by details found in the passage.

9. **The best answer is A.** As stated in the passage, "Elsie, who adored Clover, considered her as beautiful as girls in books." Later in the passage, Elsie is described as "the adoring Elsie." This best correlates to answer choice A, "admiring," which is a synonym for "adoring." The other answer choices are not supported by descriptions of Elsie's feelings towards Clover.

10. **The best answer is J.** In the last passage, Elsie expresses her approval of Clover's flower choice and how "lovely" she thinks that they will be. Elsie also discusses the dress that she will wear when she is old enough to "go to parties and things," and how it will be "interesting" when both Clover and herself go to pick it out. These facts both indicate that Elsie is both interested in and appreciative of Clover's opinion, answer choice J. Answer choice F is incorrect because the last paragraph highlights the fact that Clover is of age to attend parties and the like, while Elsie is not.

PASSAGE II

11. The best answer is A. In reference to Smith's *Wealth of Nations*, "the book is thoroughly studied; for the theory within, Smith's *magnum opus* remains controversial." The phrase "magnum opus" means "a great work or masterpiece," which makes sense in the context of the passage since Smith's *Wealth of Nations* is portrayed as being a far-reaching economic treatise that is studied by the masses.

12. The best answer is G. The passage states that "Adam Smith asserts the power of the 'invisible hand,' the notion that a society benefits from people acting in their own self-interest, without regard to community service." This corresponds with answer choice G. The other answer choices are not supported by details found in the passage.

13. The best answer is B. The passage discusses Smith's theory of markets and the "natural price" of goods and services, stating that "For example, should a product be in excess production, its price in the market would fall." If a decrease in market price is caused by having too much of a product, you can safely assume that an increase in market price would be caused by a shortage in production of a product. Therefore, answer choice B is the best choice. Answer choice A is incorrect because the passage states that stock is reduced if a product is in excess production, not during a shortage of that product. Answer choice C may appear to be correct; however, Smith's theory states that "natural prices" include a "reasonable profit" but does not indicate whether profit margins fluctuate with excesses/shortages of products.

14. The best answer is J. The passage tells you that "the butcher does not cut meat because the community desires it, but rather because it is a means to earn money ... The buyer of a steak values the steak more than his money, while the butcher values the money more than the steak." Applying this to the baker, you can infer that the baker bakes in order to earn money and that the community members value the bread more than their money. This corresponds with answer choice J. All of the other answer choices contradict the example set forth in the butcher illustration.

15. The best answer is C. The passage states that Smith believed that the "natural price" of goods and services should equal "the production cost plus a reasonable profit." Since "profuse" means "extravagant or excessive," Adam Smith would not see a profuse amount of profits as being "reasonable."

Therefore, answer choice C is correct. All of the other answer choices are supported by details found in the passage.

16. The best answer is J. Those people who criticize the *Wealth of Nations* "argue that untempered self-interest is immoral," or in other words, excessive self-interest is corrupt or unethical, answer choice J. The other answer choices are beyond the scope of the passage and are not illustrated as being reasons for criticisms of Adam Smith's *Wealth of Nations*.

17. The best answer is A. According to the passage, "Standing as a testament to his *benevolence*, Smith bequeathed much of his wealth to charity." "Benevolence" is a "tendency to perform kind or charitable acts," which best supports answer choice A. Answer choices B and D can be eliminated because it is implied that Smith voluntarily donated much of his wealth; the words "obligatory" and "requisite" imply that Smith was required to donate his money. Answer choice C does not make sense within the context of the passage.

18. The best answer is H. Smith's quotation begins by stating that man "intends only his own gain," which insinuates that people are naturally selfish and are out for their own interests. This eliminates answer choice J. The quotation continues on to say that man is "led by an invisible hand to promote an end which was no part of his intention." This statement tells you that people are led towards unintentionally fulfilling certain objectives by the "invisible hand." This suggests that the "invisible hand" directs the actions of selfish individuals and creates an outcome—one that ultimately benefits society—not anticipated by the individual. Answer choice G may appear to be correct, but the quotation does not indicate that the "invisible hand" discourages people from following their selfish interests; it merely says that the hand promotes some actions that are unintentional for man.

19. The best answer is C. When discussing the theory of natural price, the passage states that "This idea would become central to the doctrine of the *laissez-faire* economists several generations later." This supports answer choice C. The other answer choices are not supported by the passage.

20. The best answer is F. Answer choices G and J can be eliminated immediately; Smith was an advocate for "low government intervention" and believed that markets recover from recession "without intervention on the part of government or similar regulatory bodies." Answer choice F is the best answer choice because in a competitive market, there are many options for comparable products. This can be paralleled to Smith's hypothesis on excessive production of products—the more available a product is, the lower its market price falls. Therefore, competition would be a good thing for consumers in keeping prices reasonably low.

PASSAGE III

21. The best answer is B. The closing sentence of the passage states that "Though rarely awarded for his many accomplishments, Nyman certainly remains an important figure in the innovation of classical music and represents a substantial reason for its persistent popularity." This conveys both the sense that Nyman has produced important music and the fact that Nyman is underappreciated because he is "rarely rewarded." Answer choice A may appear to be correct; however, the passage states that "in spite of its waning limelight …" This indicates that the fading popularity of classical music is still occurring, and is not a thing of the past.

22. The best answer is H. The first paragraph states that classical music has been "pushed aside by such contemporary forms of music as jazz, rock, and rap." This describes the other types of music with which classical music has come to share an audience. The first paragraph also states that classical music is "always the subject of experimentation on the part of composers and performers," and the passage also mentions the "various schools of composition that emerged in the 20th century." This provides basis for the fact that classical music has not stopped evolving, and these points together provide the best support for answer choice H.

23. The best answer is C. The passage states that "Nyman's compositions vary greatly in mood and orchestration, but generally reflect the characteristic tenets of minimalist *fare*." The context of that statement suggests that Nyman's compositions typically reflect the style of the collection of minimalist music. The other answer choices are not supported by the passage.

24. The best answer is H. Answer choice H states that "These works, though, would not reach his largest audience," indicating that the works of Nyman's band were not largely popular. Nyman's popularity came later with his score for *The Piano*. Answer choice J may appear to be correct; however, answer choice J calls attention to the high point in Nyman's commercial success, not the fact that his popularity is limited.

25. The best answer is A. The passage states that Nyman "layers repetitive melodies … to create an atmosphere of soaring highs tempered with sorrow." It was these emotional melodies that were said to put the audience into a trance, answer choice A. Answer choice B is incorrect because Nyman including "soaring highs," and finished the film "on an uplifting note." Likewise, the other answer choices are not supported by the passage.

26. The best answer is J. The author describes Nyman as "one of the great writers, conductors, and performers" of his type of music; the author also describes Nyman's film scores as "stunning." The author also identifies the score to *The Piano* as being one of the best-selling film musical recordings ever. Answer choices F and G can be eliminated because the author has clearly distinguished Nyman as worthy of critical acclaim, and the fact that his score to *The Piano* has been so successful proves that his music does appeal to modern audiences. Answer choice J makes the most sense within the context of the passage.

27. The best answer is D. The word "snub" means "to rebuff or refuse to acknowledge," and the author describes the score to *The Piano* in a very positive light. From this, you can infer that although the author believed that Nyman's work was very good and deserving of an Academy Award nomination, Nyman was not so well received by the Academy. The other answer choices are not supported by the context of the passage.

28. The best answer is G. The passage states that "In spite of its waning limelight, however, classical music occupies an enduring niche in Western culture, always the subject of experimentation on the part of composers and performers." This assertion highlights both the fact that classical music has never disappeared, and the fact that classical music is always changing and evolving due to the ceaseless experimenting of composers and performers. Although answer choice H may appear to be correct, this choice focuses only on the music of Michael Nyman and not classical music as a whole.

29. The best answer is C. It is stated in the passage that Michael Nyman "emerged as" one of the great originators of "experimental and often minimalist pieces of music." The passage goes on to state that it was Nyman himself "who coined the term 'Minimalism.'" This indicates that Minimalism was still very new when Nyman emerged as a composer, being that it had not even been formally named yet. However, although Nyman gave a formal name to the musical style, he did not create this musical style. Therefore, answer choice D is not the correct answer.

30. The best answer is G. The passage states that "Nyman layers repetitive melodies played on string instruments to create an atmosphere of soaring highs tempered with sorrow, but these melodies overcome hopeless melancholy to finish on an uplifting note. The austere blues and greens of the film's cinematography blend with Nyman's round melodies to impose a trance on the audience, infusing a cold future reality with vivid romance." The word "austere" means "stark" or "severe." The statements suggests that the severity of the film's cinematography blended with Nyman's softer, "rounder" melodies to appeal to the audience's sense of romance. The other answer choices are not supported by the passage.

PASSAGE IV

31. The best answer is C. "Fascinating" and "intriguing" are synonyms of one another, both meaning "interesting or exciting." Likewise, "contentious" and "controversial" are synonyms of one another, both meaning "causing disagreement." Answer choices A, B, and D do not have pairs of words that mean the same thing as "fascinating" and "contentious."

32. The best answer is G. The passage states that mortar used in the construction of the Great Pyramid was found to be formed of "particles of pollen, charcoal, and other organic matter," and that most of the mortar collected was made of "processed gypsum with traces of sand and limestone." Answer choice G, processed limestone, is the only material not explicitly listed as composing the mortar of the Great Pyramid.

33. The best answer is A. The passages tells you that gypsum needs a temperature of 265 degrees Fahrenheit to be turned into mortar; on the other hand, "to make lime mortar, extremely high temperatures of around 1800 degrees Fahrenheit are needed." This best supports answer choice A. Answer choices B, C, and D are not supported by details found in the passage.

34. The best answer is H. The passage states that the gypsum mortar used in constructing the Great Pyramid "was not used to bond the heavy stone blocks together." This fact supports answer choice H. The passage also goes on to state, "The gypsum mortar's role was to buffer the joints and to reduce friction as the enormous blocks were put into place." This tells you that answer choices F, G,

and J all were uses of the mortar when constructing the Great Pyramid.

35. The best answer is D. Throughout the passage, there are several references to researchers not having conclusive facts and making the best hypotheses they can regarding their findings. For example, the fourth paragraph begins with the statement "Examining the mortar from the Great Pyramid assists scientists in making inferences about Egypt's past," and goes on to discuss the conclusions researchers drew based on the findings that they had discovered. Answer choice A may appear to be correct; however, the information given on radiocarbon dating does not provide an exact date of construction. Rather, scientists had to conjecture about the precise date the Pyramid was built, which supports answer choice D. Answer choice B is incorrect because the passage states that after analysis of the gypsum mortar, "even using modern techniques, scientists have been unable to reproduce it." Answer choice C is beyond the scope of the passage; there is no evidence that the conclusions of scientific researchers and archaeologists usually vary.

36. The best answer is J. The passage states that Egypt "has few natural fuels available," and goes on to say that "The shortage of natural fuel sources would most likely have made the creation of lime mortar highly uneconomical." This best supports answer choice J. It is stated in the passage that limestone was both more durable and more abundant than gypsum, thus answer choices F and G can be eliminated. The inferences drawn by the researchers are irrelevant to the choice of material that the Egyptians used in constructing the pyramids; therefore, answer choice H is also incorrect.

37. The best answer is A. The passage states that "Instead of clarifying or *expunging* older theories about the Great Pyramid's age, the results of the study left the researchers mystified." The word "expunge" means "to get rid of or remove," so within the context of the passage, the results of the study did not clarify or eliminate any older theories about the Great Pyramid, answer choice A.

38. The best answer is H. The passage states that from radiocarbon dating, it was found that the average date of construction for the Great Pyramid was 2977 BC. The passage goes on to state that this discovery was disputed because this date asserted that the Pyramid was built "over 400 years earlier than most archaeologists originally believed." If archaeologists believed the Pyramid to have been constructed 400 years after 2977 BC, the original date of construction was, therefore, assumed to be approximately 2577 BC.

39. The best answer is B. As stated in the passage, "researchers began focusing on studying the mortar from the pyramid, hoping it would reveal important clues about the pyramid's age and construction." This supports answer choice B. The topics of the other answer choices are discussed throughout the passage; however, these topics are not the chief topics the researchers were looking to learn from studying the mortar.

40. The best answer is G. The passage states that the gypsum "would have been easier to mine than limestone." This best correlates with answer choice G. Answer choice F may appear to be correct; however, the passage does not discuss whether a more water-soluble material would be advantageous when making mortar.

Science Reasoning Test Explanations

PASSAGE I

1. The best answer is A. If Experiment 1 were repeated with a length of 4 m, the movement time for the wood block would be expected to be greater than the time measured for 2 m (1.64 s). The only answer choice with a time greater than this is answer choice A (2.31 s).

2. The best answer is H. According to Table 2, the plastic object in Experiment 2 took an average of 1.41s to move down the inclined plane. This time is closest to the average time of 1.42 s in Table 3. The object rating of the object with an average time of 1.42 s is 13. Because the plastic object's time is just below the time in Table 3, it would most likely have an object rating of between 9 and 13, answer choice H.

3. The best answer is A. The students rated objects on a scale from 5 (least friction) to 30 (most friction). In order for the chair to move more easily across a floor, the material must have a low friction rating. Therefore, a material with an object rating of 5 (the least amount of friction) would move most easily across a floor.

4. The best answer is J. In Experiment 1, the volume of each of the blocks of material was 750 cm^3. In Experiment 2, the mass of each of the blocks of material was 1500 g. The difference between the two experiments is that, in Experiment 1 volume was held constant, while in Experiment 2 mass was held constant. The correct answer is answer choice J.

5. The best answer is B. If the loss in speed due to friction leads to longer travel time down the inclined plane, to rank objects in order of increasing loss in speed due to friction you must rank them in order of increasing time. Answer choice B is correct because glass (1.31 s) < aluminum (1.35 s) < wood (1.69 s) < concrete (2.47 s).

6. The best answer is H. To answer this question compare the average times listed for each block in Tables 1 and 2. When the volume is increased, the average time goes up for some blocks and down for others.

PASSAGE II

7. The best answer is D. Scientist 2 states that when iron is "hotter than 1043K, its Curie temperature, iron loses its magnetic properties." The scientist is implying that the Earth's core has a temperature above 1043K; therefore, it has lost its magnetic properties and cannot cause the Earth's magnetic fields. Answer choice B can be eliminated because this is the viewpoint of Scientist 1 only.

8. The best answer is H. Scientist 1 states: "The magnetic field grows and wanes, and the Earth's poles drift and occasionally flip as the rotation of the core changes." Scientist 2 states that the molten outer core and the Coriolis effects "generate the fluctuating magnetic field." Both scientists address the Earth's changing magnetic field and, therefore, are in agreement with the statement in the question.

9. The best answer is C. Both scientists talk about the fluctuations in Earth's magnetic field. They would both agree with answer choice C because it describes the varying magnetic properties in volcanic rocks as the result of the fluctuations they have talked about. Answer choices B and D can be eliminated because solar wind is only discussed by Scientist 1. Answer choice A supports Scientist 2 only.

10. The best answer is J. According to Scientist 1, "The inner core … consists of a solid iron ball, which would exhibit properties or *ferromagnetism* …" Scientist 2, on the other hand, suggests that the core is too hot to maintain its magnetic properties. This information best supports answer choice J.

11. The best answer is B. According to Scientist 1, the coordinated motions of electrons within iron atoms create the Earth's magnetic field. According to Scientist 2, the Earth's magnetic field is created from the circulating electric currents in the Earth's molten outer core.

12. The best answer is G. Scientist 2 says, "The Earth's magnetic field is attributed to a *dynamo effect* of circulating electric current in the molten outer core." If a new type of sensor detected electric currents in the outer core, the new technology would be consistent with the view of Scientist 2. Scientist 1, however, does not talk about the outer core.

13. The best answer is A. Scientist 2 says that the Earth's inner core does not influence the Earth's magnetic field because iron loses its magnetic properties at high temperatures (reached by the inner core). This contradicts what Scientist 1 says, so it is likely that Scientist 1 would consider this a flaw in Scientist 2's theory.

PASSAGE III

14. The best answer is G. According to Figure 1, 50% (half) of the Radon 222 sample is left after 4 days.

15. The best answer is C. Passage III states: "Radioactive decay is a natural process by which an atom of a radioactive isotope spontaneously decays into another element."

16. The best answer is H. According to Table 1, the energies associated with alpha particle emission were 5.590 MeV and 3.792 MeV. The energies associated with beta particle emission were 1.308 MeV and 1.533 MeV—lower than that of the alpha particle emission.

17. The best answer is B. The decay energy of 1.796 MeV is closest to the decay energies in Table 1 associated with beta particles (1.308 and 1.533 MeV). Therefore, the particle most likely emitted is a beta particle. Answer choice D can be eliminated because Table 1 provides no information about gamma rays.

18. The best answer is G. The isotopes will have the same percent of atoms remaining at the point at which the lines associated with each isotope cross. Based on Figure 1, Radon 222 and Polonium 218 cross at about Day 4.

19. The best answer is D. Because the shape of the curves in Figures 1 and 2 are unvarying parabolas, it is clear that the decay rate of these two elements is constant over time.

PASSAGE IV

20. The best answer is H. According to Table 1, the ideal lead level is below 0.015 mg/L. Sample 1 has a lead level of 0.01 mg/L, which is at the ideal lead level.

21. The best answer is C. The passage explains, "Water with a low pH (<6.5) could be acidic, soft, and corrosive." If an ideal alkalinity level prevents pH levels from becoming too low, it will also prevent water from becoming overly corrosive. Answer choice B can be eliminated because the ideal alkalinity level shown in Table 1 is between 200 and 500 mg/L.

22. The best answer is G. Table 1 shows that Sample 1's water had a pH of 6.0. Because the ideal pH level is between 6.5 and 8.5, the water in Sample 1 is too acidic, and therefore, too corrosive. Answer choice H can be eliminated because the alkalinity level of Sample 1 was below the ideal level.

23. The best answer is A. According to Table 1, Sample 2 water has the ideal levels of all of the tested factors except iron and hardness. The water tested above the ideal level for both of these factors. This water would be acceptable as long as the developers are willing to accept high iron levels and hard water. Answer choices B and C can be eliminated because only Sample 1 contained soft water.

24. The best answer is F. Sample 2 has an ideal level of alkalinity and can effectively buffer the water. Sample 1, however, has a level of alkalinity below the ideal and is susceptible to changes in pH. If the chemical additive caused a drastic increase in pH levels in un-buffered solutions, Sample 1's pH level would be unsafe but Sample 2 would be unaffected.

PASSAGE V

25. The best answer is C. The average speed on asphalt was 14.7 ft/s, which is higher than the other surfaces.

26. The best answer is J. According to Table 1, the average speed on asphalt was 14.7 ft/s, which is less than the 14.8 ft/s speed measured in Trial 3.

27. The best answer is A. To answer this question, you must solve each answer choice and see which answer is correct.

A: $14.8 \left(\dfrac{2}{3} \right) = 9.87$ ft/s (speed in the rough)

B: $14.8 \left(\dfrac{1}{3} \right) = 4.93$ ft/s (speed on the fairway)

C: $12.7 \left(\dfrac{2}{3} \right) = 8.47$ ft/s (speed in the rough)

D: $9.4 \left(\dfrac{2}{3} \right) = 6.27$ ft/s (speed on asphalt)

Therefore, the average speed of the cart in the rough is approximately two-thirds of the average speed of the cart on asphalt, answer choice A.

28. The best answer is F. In a scientific experiment or study, the independent variable is the factor that is changed by the experimenter. Each study was conducted using a different surface, so the surface upon which the golf cart was driven was the independent variable. The factor being studied or observed is the dependent variable. Whether it changes depends on the manipulation of one or more independent variables.

29. The best answer is C. The slowest travel of all of the studies and trials was recorded in Table 3, Trial 2: 55.4 seconds.

PASSAGE VI

30. The best answer is H. According to the information in Table 1, Grackle E (the heaviest bird at 350 g) was ranked 3rd—right in the middle—in aggressiveness. In addition, Table 3 indicates that Grackle A, the lightest bird, had more wins and fewer losses than did Grackle E, which would suggest that Grackle A is more aggressive than Grackle E. The data best supports the idea that body weight has no effect on aggression, answer choice H.

31. The best answer is A. Table 3 shows each of the grackles' win–loss records. The grackle with the highest win–loss record was Grackle B (95–10). This information would suggest Grackle B would have the highest likelihood of mating, answer choice A.

32. The correct answer is J. To solve this problem, compare the values given with the values listed in Table 1. Based on those values, the sixth grackle is most similar to Grackle D, which had an aggression rank of 5. However, because the sixth grackle had fewer calls, it would be less aggressive, and so would likely have a lower rank.

33. The best answer is D. According to Experiments 1 and 2, in general, the more calls a grackle makes, the higher the aggression ranking and the more times the grackle wins. This information suggests the number of calls is related to the dominance of one male grackle over other males.

34. The best answer is H. Table 2 shows the number of times each grackle won over another grackle. According to the table, Grackle A won over Grackle C a total of 5 times. Grackle C won over Grackle A 20 times. This information suggests the two birds encountered each other $20 + 5 = 25$ times.

35. The best answer is B. In order to refute the criticism that the order the grackles were placed in the cage may have affected the aggressiveness of each bird, the experiment should be repeated several times with different orders each time. Answer choice A seems plausible, but even though the order is randomized, it might still affect aggressiveness. By repeating the experiment several times, the criticism will be overcome.

PASSAGE VII

36. The best answer is G. To answer this question, you must look at Table 1 and determine the amount of growth for each week.

Plant type 1: Week 0–2: $1.2 - 0 = 1.2$ in.
Week 2–4: $2.8 - 1.2 = 1.6$ in.
Week 4–6: $3.7 - 2.8 = 1.1$ in.

Plant type 3: Week 0–2: $0.6 - 0 = 0.6$ in.
Week 2–4: $1.7 - 0.6 = 1.1$ in.
Week 4–6: $2.0 - 1.7 = 0.3$ in.

Plant type 4: Week 0–2: $0.9 - 0 = 0.9$ in.
Week 2–4: $2.6 - 0.9 = 1.5$ in.
Week 4–6: $3.5 - 2.6 = 0.9$ in.

In all three plant types, the greatest growth occurred between Weeks 2 and 4.

37. The best answer is C. In Experiment 1, Plant type 2 was not studied. According to Table 3, Plant type 2 is from the Northern Forest.

38. The best answer is H. To answer this question, find the difference in growth between Week 1 and Week 6 for each plant type:

Plant type 1: $3.7 - 1.2 = 2.5$
Plant type 3: $2.0 - 0.6 = 1.4$
Plant type 4: $3.5 - 0.9 = 2.6$

Answer choice J can be eliminated because each plant had a different amount of growth.

39. The best answer is B. To answer this question, you must look at the different in growth between the plants in Tables 1 and 2.

Plant type 1: $5.1 - 3.7 = 1.4$ in.
Plant type 3: $5.4 - 2.0 = 3.4$ in.
Plant type 4: $4.9 - 3.5 = 1.4$ in.

Fungi had the greatest affect on Plant type 3.

40. The best answer is H. According to Tables 1 and 2, Plants 1, 3, and 4 all grew more when the fungi present in the soil. This information suggests that the presence of certain fungi in the soil increases plant growth.

Writing Test Explanation

Because grading the essay is subjective, we've chosen not to include any "graded" essays here. Your best bet is to have someone you trust, such as your personal tutor, read your essays and give you an honest critique. If you plan on grading your own essays, review the grading criteria and be as honest as possible regarding the structure, development, organization, technique, and appropriateness of your writing. Focus on your weak areas and continue to practice in order to improve your writing skills.

ACT PRACTICE TEST 8
Answer Sheet

ENGLISH

1 Ⓐ Ⓑ Ⓒ Ⓓ	21 Ⓐ Ⓑ Ⓒ Ⓓ	41 Ⓐ Ⓑ Ⓒ Ⓓ	61 Ⓐ Ⓑ Ⓒ Ⓓ
2 Ⓕ Ⓖ Ⓗ Ⓙ	22 Ⓕ Ⓖ Ⓗ Ⓙ	42 Ⓕ Ⓖ Ⓗ Ⓙ	62 Ⓕ Ⓖ Ⓗ Ⓙ
3 Ⓐ Ⓑ Ⓒ Ⓓ	23 Ⓐ Ⓑ Ⓒ Ⓓ	43 Ⓐ Ⓑ Ⓒ Ⓓ	63 Ⓐ Ⓑ Ⓒ Ⓓ
4 Ⓕ Ⓖ Ⓗ Ⓙ	24 Ⓕ Ⓖ Ⓗ Ⓙ	44 Ⓕ Ⓖ Ⓗ Ⓙ	64 Ⓕ Ⓖ Ⓗ Ⓙ
5 Ⓐ Ⓑ Ⓒ Ⓓ	25 Ⓐ Ⓑ Ⓒ Ⓓ	45 Ⓐ Ⓑ Ⓒ Ⓓ	65 Ⓐ Ⓑ Ⓒ Ⓓ
6 Ⓕ Ⓖ Ⓗ Ⓙ	26 Ⓕ Ⓖ Ⓗ Ⓙ	46 Ⓕ Ⓖ Ⓗ Ⓙ	66 Ⓕ Ⓖ Ⓗ Ⓙ
7 Ⓐ Ⓑ Ⓒ Ⓓ	27 Ⓐ Ⓑ Ⓒ Ⓓ	47 Ⓐ Ⓑ Ⓒ Ⓓ	67 Ⓐ Ⓑ Ⓒ Ⓓ
8 Ⓕ Ⓖ Ⓗ Ⓙ	28 Ⓕ Ⓖ Ⓗ Ⓙ	48 Ⓕ Ⓖ Ⓗ Ⓙ	68 Ⓕ Ⓖ Ⓗ Ⓙ
9 Ⓐ Ⓑ Ⓒ Ⓓ	29 Ⓐ Ⓑ Ⓒ Ⓓ	49 Ⓐ Ⓑ Ⓒ Ⓓ	69 Ⓐ Ⓑ Ⓒ Ⓓ
10 Ⓕ Ⓖ Ⓗ Ⓙ	30 Ⓕ Ⓖ Ⓗ Ⓙ	50 Ⓕ Ⓖ Ⓗ Ⓙ	70 Ⓕ Ⓖ Ⓗ Ⓙ
11 Ⓐ Ⓑ Ⓒ Ⓓ	31 Ⓐ Ⓑ Ⓒ Ⓓ	51 Ⓐ Ⓑ Ⓒ Ⓓ	71 Ⓐ Ⓑ Ⓒ Ⓓ
12 Ⓕ Ⓖ Ⓗ Ⓙ	32 Ⓕ Ⓖ Ⓗ Ⓙ	52 Ⓕ Ⓖ Ⓗ Ⓙ	72 Ⓕ Ⓖ Ⓗ Ⓙ
13 Ⓐ Ⓑ Ⓒ Ⓓ	33 Ⓐ Ⓑ Ⓒ Ⓓ	53 Ⓐ Ⓑ Ⓒ Ⓓ	73 Ⓐ Ⓑ Ⓒ Ⓓ
14 Ⓕ Ⓖ Ⓗ Ⓙ	34 Ⓕ Ⓖ Ⓗ Ⓙ	54 Ⓕ Ⓖ Ⓗ Ⓙ	74 Ⓕ Ⓖ Ⓗ Ⓙ
15 Ⓐ Ⓑ Ⓒ Ⓓ	35 Ⓐ Ⓑ Ⓒ Ⓓ	55 Ⓐ Ⓑ Ⓒ Ⓓ	75 Ⓐ Ⓑ Ⓒ Ⓓ
16 Ⓕ Ⓖ Ⓗ Ⓙ	36 Ⓕ Ⓖ Ⓗ Ⓙ	56 Ⓕ Ⓖ Ⓗ Ⓙ	
17 Ⓐ Ⓑ Ⓒ Ⓓ	37 Ⓐ Ⓑ Ⓒ Ⓓ	57 Ⓐ Ⓑ Ⓒ Ⓓ	
18 Ⓕ Ⓖ Ⓗ Ⓙ	38 Ⓕ Ⓖ Ⓗ Ⓙ	58 Ⓕ Ⓖ Ⓗ Ⓙ	
19 Ⓐ Ⓑ Ⓒ Ⓓ	39 Ⓐ Ⓑ Ⓒ Ⓓ	59 Ⓐ Ⓑ Ⓒ Ⓓ	
20 Ⓕ Ⓖ Ⓗ Ⓙ	40 Ⓕ Ⓖ Ⓗ Ⓙ	60 Ⓕ Ⓖ Ⓗ Ⓙ	

MATHEMATICS

1 Ⓐ Ⓑ Ⓒ Ⓓ Ⓔ	16 Ⓕ Ⓖ Ⓗ Ⓙ Ⓚ	31 Ⓐ Ⓑ Ⓒ Ⓓ Ⓔ	46 Ⓕ Ⓖ Ⓗ Ⓙ Ⓚ
2 Ⓕ Ⓖ Ⓗ Ⓙ Ⓚ	17 Ⓐ Ⓑ Ⓒ Ⓓ Ⓔ	32 Ⓕ Ⓖ Ⓗ Ⓙ Ⓚ	47 Ⓐ Ⓑ Ⓒ Ⓓ Ⓔ
3 Ⓐ Ⓑ Ⓒ Ⓓ Ⓔ	18 Ⓕ Ⓖ Ⓗ Ⓙ Ⓚ	33 Ⓐ Ⓑ Ⓒ Ⓓ Ⓔ	48 Ⓕ Ⓖ Ⓗ Ⓙ Ⓚ
4 Ⓕ Ⓖ Ⓗ Ⓙ Ⓚ	19 Ⓐ Ⓑ Ⓒ Ⓓ Ⓔ	34 Ⓕ Ⓖ Ⓗ Ⓙ Ⓚ	49 Ⓐ Ⓑ Ⓒ Ⓓ Ⓔ
5 Ⓐ Ⓑ Ⓒ Ⓓ Ⓔ	20 Ⓕ Ⓖ Ⓗ Ⓙ Ⓚ	35 Ⓐ Ⓑ Ⓒ Ⓓ Ⓔ	50 Ⓕ Ⓖ Ⓗ Ⓙ Ⓚ
6 Ⓕ Ⓖ Ⓗ Ⓙ Ⓚ	21 Ⓐ Ⓑ Ⓒ Ⓓ Ⓔ	36 Ⓕ Ⓖ Ⓗ Ⓙ Ⓚ	51 Ⓐ Ⓑ Ⓒ Ⓓ Ⓔ
7 Ⓐ Ⓑ Ⓒ Ⓓ Ⓔ	22 Ⓕ Ⓖ Ⓗ Ⓙ Ⓚ	37 Ⓐ Ⓑ Ⓒ Ⓓ Ⓔ	52 Ⓕ Ⓖ Ⓗ Ⓙ Ⓚ
8 Ⓕ Ⓖ Ⓗ Ⓙ Ⓚ	23 Ⓐ Ⓑ Ⓒ Ⓓ Ⓔ	38 Ⓕ Ⓖ Ⓗ Ⓙ Ⓚ	53 Ⓐ Ⓑ Ⓒ Ⓓ Ⓔ
9 Ⓐ Ⓑ Ⓒ Ⓓ Ⓔ	24 Ⓕ Ⓖ Ⓗ Ⓙ Ⓚ	39 Ⓐ Ⓑ Ⓒ Ⓓ Ⓔ	54 Ⓕ Ⓖ Ⓗ Ⓙ Ⓚ
10 Ⓕ Ⓖ Ⓗ Ⓙ Ⓚ	25 Ⓐ Ⓑ Ⓒ Ⓓ Ⓔ	40 Ⓕ Ⓖ Ⓗ Ⓙ Ⓚ	55 Ⓐ Ⓑ Ⓒ Ⓓ Ⓔ
11 Ⓐ Ⓑ Ⓒ Ⓓ Ⓔ	26 Ⓕ Ⓖ Ⓗ Ⓙ Ⓚ	41 Ⓐ Ⓑ Ⓒ Ⓓ Ⓔ	56 Ⓕ Ⓖ Ⓗ Ⓙ Ⓚ
12 Ⓕ Ⓖ Ⓗ Ⓙ Ⓚ	27 Ⓐ Ⓑ Ⓒ Ⓓ Ⓔ	42 Ⓕ Ⓖ Ⓗ Ⓙ Ⓚ	57 Ⓐ Ⓑ Ⓒ Ⓓ Ⓔ
13 Ⓐ Ⓑ Ⓒ Ⓓ Ⓔ	28 Ⓕ Ⓖ Ⓗ Ⓙ Ⓚ	43 Ⓐ Ⓑ Ⓒ Ⓓ Ⓔ	58 Ⓕ Ⓖ Ⓗ Ⓙ Ⓚ
14 Ⓕ Ⓖ Ⓗ Ⓙ Ⓚ	29 Ⓐ Ⓑ Ⓒ Ⓓ Ⓔ	44 Ⓕ Ⓖ Ⓗ Ⓙ Ⓚ	59 Ⓐ Ⓑ Ⓒ Ⓓ Ⓔ
15 Ⓐ Ⓑ Ⓒ Ⓓ Ⓔ	30 Ⓕ Ⓖ Ⓗ Ⓙ Ⓚ	45 Ⓐ Ⓑ Ⓒ Ⓓ Ⓔ	60 Ⓕ Ⓖ Ⓗ Ⓙ Ⓚ

READING

1 Ⓐ Ⓑ Ⓒ Ⓓ	11 Ⓐ Ⓑ Ⓒ Ⓓ	21 Ⓐ Ⓑ Ⓒ Ⓓ	31 Ⓐ Ⓑ Ⓒ Ⓓ
2 Ⓕ Ⓖ Ⓗ Ⓙ	12 Ⓕ Ⓖ Ⓗ Ⓙ	22 Ⓕ Ⓖ Ⓗ Ⓙ	32 Ⓕ Ⓖ Ⓗ Ⓙ
3 Ⓐ Ⓑ Ⓒ Ⓓ	13 Ⓐ Ⓑ Ⓒ Ⓓ	23 Ⓐ Ⓑ Ⓒ Ⓓ	33 Ⓐ Ⓑ Ⓒ Ⓓ
4 Ⓕ Ⓖ Ⓗ Ⓙ	14 Ⓕ Ⓖ Ⓗ Ⓙ	24 Ⓕ Ⓖ Ⓗ Ⓙ	34 Ⓕ Ⓖ Ⓗ Ⓙ
5 Ⓐ Ⓑ Ⓒ Ⓓ	15 Ⓐ Ⓑ Ⓒ Ⓓ	25 Ⓐ Ⓑ Ⓒ Ⓓ	35 Ⓐ Ⓑ Ⓒ Ⓓ
6 Ⓕ Ⓖ Ⓗ Ⓙ	16 Ⓕ Ⓖ Ⓗ Ⓙ	26 Ⓕ Ⓖ Ⓗ Ⓙ	36 Ⓕ Ⓖ Ⓗ Ⓙ
7 Ⓐ Ⓑ Ⓒ Ⓓ	17 Ⓐ Ⓑ Ⓒ Ⓓ	27 Ⓐ Ⓑ Ⓒ Ⓓ	37 Ⓐ Ⓑ Ⓒ Ⓓ
8 Ⓕ Ⓖ Ⓗ Ⓙ	18 Ⓕ Ⓖ Ⓗ Ⓙ	28 Ⓕ Ⓖ Ⓗ Ⓙ	38 Ⓕ Ⓖ Ⓗ Ⓙ
9 Ⓐ Ⓑ Ⓒ Ⓓ	19 Ⓐ Ⓑ Ⓒ Ⓓ	29 Ⓐ Ⓑ Ⓒ Ⓓ	39 Ⓐ Ⓑ Ⓒ Ⓓ
10 Ⓕ Ⓖ Ⓗ Ⓙ	20 Ⓕ Ⓖ Ⓗ Ⓙ	30 Ⓕ Ⓖ Ⓗ Ⓙ	40 Ⓕ Ⓖ Ⓗ Ⓙ

SCIENCE

1 Ⓐ Ⓑ Ⓒ Ⓓ	11 Ⓐ Ⓑ Ⓒ Ⓓ	21 Ⓐ Ⓑ Ⓒ Ⓓ	31 Ⓐ Ⓑ Ⓒ Ⓓ
2 Ⓕ Ⓖ Ⓗ Ⓙ	12 Ⓕ Ⓖ Ⓗ Ⓙ	22 Ⓕ Ⓖ Ⓗ Ⓙ	32 Ⓕ Ⓖ Ⓗ Ⓙ
3 Ⓐ Ⓑ Ⓒ Ⓓ	13 Ⓐ Ⓑ Ⓒ Ⓓ	23 Ⓐ Ⓑ Ⓒ Ⓓ	33 Ⓐ Ⓑ Ⓒ Ⓓ
4 Ⓕ Ⓖ Ⓗ Ⓙ	14 Ⓕ Ⓖ Ⓗ Ⓙ	24 Ⓕ Ⓖ Ⓗ Ⓙ	34 Ⓕ Ⓖ Ⓗ Ⓙ
5 Ⓐ Ⓑ Ⓒ Ⓓ	15 Ⓐ Ⓑ Ⓒ Ⓓ	25 Ⓐ Ⓑ Ⓒ Ⓓ	35 Ⓐ Ⓑ Ⓒ Ⓓ
6 Ⓕ Ⓖ Ⓗ Ⓙ	16 Ⓕ Ⓖ Ⓗ Ⓙ	26 Ⓕ Ⓖ Ⓗ Ⓙ	36 Ⓕ Ⓖ Ⓗ Ⓙ
7 Ⓐ Ⓑ Ⓒ Ⓓ	17 Ⓐ Ⓑ Ⓒ Ⓓ	27 Ⓐ Ⓑ Ⓒ Ⓓ	37 Ⓐ Ⓑ Ⓒ Ⓓ
8 Ⓕ Ⓖ Ⓗ Ⓙ	18 Ⓕ Ⓖ Ⓗ Ⓙ	28 Ⓕ Ⓖ Ⓗ Ⓙ	38 Ⓕ Ⓖ Ⓗ Ⓙ
9 Ⓐ Ⓑ Ⓒ Ⓓ	19 Ⓐ Ⓑ Ⓒ Ⓓ	29 Ⓐ Ⓑ Ⓒ Ⓓ	39 Ⓐ Ⓑ Ⓒ Ⓓ
10 Ⓕ Ⓖ Ⓗ Ⓙ	20 Ⓕ Ⓖ Ⓗ Ⓙ	30 Ⓕ Ⓖ Ⓗ Ⓙ	40 Ⓕ Ⓖ Ⓗ Ⓙ

RAW SCORES	SCALE SCORES	DATE TAKEN:
ENGLISH _____	ENGLISH _____	
MATHEMATICS _____	MATHEMATICS _____	ENGLISH/WRITING _____
READING _____	READING _____	
SCIENCE _____	SCIENCE _____	_____
		COMPOSITE SCORE

Refer to the Scoring Worksheet on page 656 for help in determining your Raw and Scale Scores.

You may wish to remove these sample answer document pages to respond to the practice ACT Writing Test.

Begin WRITING TEST here.

_____
_____
_____
_____
_____
_____
_____
_____
_____
_____
_____
_____
_____
_____
_____
_____
_____
_____
_____
_____
_____
_____
_____
_____
_____
_____
_____
_____
_____
_____

If you need more space, please continue on the next page.

1

Do not write in this shaded area.

WRITING TEST

If you need more space, please continue on the back of this page.

Do not write in this shaded area.

Cut Here

WRITING TEST

If you need more space, please continue on the next page.

PLEASE DO NOT WRITE IN THIS AREA.

WRITING TEST

_____

_____

_____

_____

_____

_____

_____

_____

_____

_____

_____

_____

_____

_____

_____

_____

_____

_____

_____

_____

_____

_____

_____

_____

_____

_____

_____

STOP here with the Writing Test.

1 ■ ■ ■ ■ ■ ■ ■ ■ 1

ENGLISH TEST

45 Minutes—75 Questions

DIRECTIONS: In the passages that follow, some words and phrases are underlined and numbered. In the answer column, you will find alternatives for the words and phrases that are underlined. Choose the alternative that you think is best, and fill in the corresponding bubble on your answer sheet. If you think that the original version is best, choose "NO CHANGE," which will always be either answer choice A or F. You will also find questions about a particular section of the passage, or about the entire passage. These questions will be identified either by an underlined portion or by a number in a box. Look for the answer that clearly expresses the idea, is consistent with the style and tone of the passage, and makes the correct use of standard written English. Read the passage through once before answering the questions. For some questions, you should read beyond the indicated portion before you answer.

PASSAGE I

The Deer Fence

A family emergency took us across the country for several weeks during the spring of that year. We had left
₁
our first vegetable garden in the midst of early growing season, a time when careful monitoring of emerging seeds
₂
is essential to ensure their vitality. Only a serious family matter would have as an instigation for such a departure.
₃

We arrived home three weeks later to witness an
₄
incredible transformation upon our return. Not only had the
₅
broccoli stalks and scarlet radishes come to bear fruit, but

1. **A.** NO CHANGE
   B. a
   C. this
   D. OMIT the underlined portion.

2. The writer would like to emphasize how critical her direct involvement is to the success of her garden. Given that all the choices are true, which one best accomplishes the writer's goal?
   F. NO CHANGE
   G. plenty of sunshine for
   H. abundant rainfall for
   J. casual observance of

3. **A.** NO CHANGE
   B. instigates
   C. instigating
   D. instigated

4. **F.** NO CHANGE
   G. by witnessing
   H. for the witnessing of
   J. to the witness of

5. **A.** NO CHANGE
   B. when we got back
   C. after our arrival
   D. OMIT the underlined portion.

GO ON TO THE NEXT PAGE.

1 ■ ■ ■ ■ ■ ■ ■ ■ 1

they are the local deer population had decided to make a
                                6
meal of our freshly sprouted crop. Deer do not use a

freshly sharpened kitchen knife to remove delicious

morsels from their stems. Rather, the animals gnaw and

shred at the plants with their vegetarian teeth, leaving a

mess of rejected foliage, hoof prints, and raw vegetable

soup. 7

Our four-foot twig garden fence suddenly appeared

comical and humorously purely decorative. There was
                         8
obviously a lack of real deterring qualities, that needed to
                                    9
be remedied quickly. Even though we were now back

home to stand guard, our absence had inadvertently

established our kitchen garden as a food plot for the

nearby wildlife. Deer are typically night eaters, and we

weren't about to change our own sleeping patterns to

accommodate them! Stopping the deer would

require a concerted, multi-pronged approach.
                  10

6. **F.** NO CHANGE
   G. the local deer population, they
   H. the local deer population
   J. they

7. The writer is considering deleting the phrase "leaving a mess of rejected foliage, hoof prints, and raw vegetable soup" from the preceding sentence. Should the phrase be kept or deleted?
   A. Kept, because it emphasizes both the destructiveness of deer and the importance of protecting a garden.
   B. Kept, because it is relevant to the essay's focus on the construction of the deer fence.
   C. Deleted, because it distracts the reader from the description of the deer fence.
   D. Deleted, because this level of detail is not consistent with the essay's discussion of protecting a garden from deer.

8. **F.** NO CHANGE
   G. decorative, yet funny.
   H. purely decorative and humorous.
   J. purely decorative.

9. **A.** NO CHANGE
   B. deterring qualities, which
   C. deterring, qualities, which
   D. deterring, qualities that

10. The writer would like to indicate that protecting the garden from future destruction will be time-consuming and must be well planned. Given that all choices are true, which one best accomplishes the writer's goal?
    F. NO CHANGE
    G. not be easy.
    H. take some time.
    J. require a team effort.

GO ON TO THE NEXT PAGE.

1 ■ ■ ■ ■ ■ ■ ■ ■ 1

Following a tedious journey to the local hardware store,
we assembled our army's ammunition: 350 feet of chicken
wire; a box of four-inch screws; neon-orange plastic
ribbon; and a heavy duty staple gun. Unrolling a 350-foot
roll of chicken wire is no easy task. Constructing the
bottom tier of the fence was just as daunting; one person
unrolled the four-foot wide tube while another person
followed behind, stapling the chicken wire to the existing
fence posts. Tackling the second row was another story
altogether. Since our original posts were a mere four feet
high, each post needed a four-foot extension attached to it,
followed by another round of chicken wire.

After hours of back-breaking work, we stood back to
admire this new fence. The big test would come when
darkness fell. Deer can and will leap over an eight-foot
barrier if necessary, but our saving grace would be the
intimidation factor of our new fence, with its metallic
outline glinting in the moonlight and neon-orange tags
flapping in the wind. Swift and beautiful leapers,
the newness and appearance of the enclosure should
nonetheless serve to frighten away our backyard deer.
It has been two months since the transformation of our
little twig-fenced garden into a chicken-wired vegetable

prison. Each night we sit down to the likes of delicious
sweet corn, baked zucchini, tomato and cucumber salad,
and snap beans. No broccoli or radishes this year, but we're
already discussing the blueberry bushes and strawberry
plants for next year. First, though, we will give some
serious thought to the black bears that live in our woods.

11. Which of the following alternatives to the underlined portion would NOT be acceptable?
   A. After
   B. Soon after
   C. Followed by
   D. Returning from

12. Which of the following alternatives to the underlined portion would NOT be acceptable?
   F. also daunting
   G. as daunting a venture
   H. daunting as well
   J. just for daunting

13. Given that all the choices are true, which one provides the most specific detail and maintains the style and tone of the essay?
   A. NO CHANGE
   B. our newly erected, sturdy fortress.
   C. the taller enclosure.
   D. the rectangular area enclosed by a chicken-wire fence attached to posts.

14. F. NO CHANGE
   G. Swift and beautiful leapers, the deer in our back-yard should nonetheless be frightened away by the newness and appearance of the enclosure.
   H. While they are swift and beautiful leapers, the newness and appearance of the enclosure should nonetheless serve to frighten away the deer in our backyard.
   J. While they are swift and beautiful leapers, nonetheless the newness and appearance of the enclosure should frighten away the deer in our backyard.

15. A. NO CHANGE
   B. for the likes of
   C. by the likes of
   D. at the likes of

GO ON TO THE NEXT PAGE.

1 ■ ■ ■ ■ ■ ■ ■ ■ ■ **1**

PASSAGE II

A Flute in the Forest

A quiet walk along a forest path during an early spring
dusk <u>surprisingly</u> revealed an unexpected gift of nature.
16
The sound of a flute seemed to float from the tallest trees
in the near distance. This flute song was like none ever
made by man. Our guide quickly raised his hand in a
signal for us to stop and remain still, and then whispered
these simple words: "Wood Thrush." <u>Truly,</u> any attempts to
17
describe this spectacular birdsong with words does a grave
injustice to its unique vocalizations.

The Wood Thrush is a rather plain, brown, robin-like
bird. Its most distinctive features are its white spotted
chest and pinkish legs. Viewing these birds can be
especially <u>difficult, as</u> they enjoy perching on the tallest
18
branch that is still able to offer seclusion among its leaves
and twigs. Binoculars are a must. With each Wood Thrush
song, a birdwatcher is able to track the bird's location.
Because it is a migratory bird, early spring is generally the
first opportunity to observe the Wood Thrush in the United
States. 19 A mixed forest is its preferred habitat, one with
both deciduous and evergreen trees of varying heights.
Interestingly, while the Wood Thrush enjoys singing from

the tallest branches, <u>it's</u> nest is often found much closer to
20
the ground.

16. **F.** NO CHANGE
    G. by chance
    H. unwittingly
    J. OMIT the underlined portion.

17. Which of the following alternatives to the underlined
    portion would NOT be acceptable?
    A. Really,
    B. Precisely,
    C. Honestly,
    D. Surely,

18. **F.** NO CHANGE
    G. difficult; as
    H. difficult as,
    J. difficult. As

19. The writer is considering deleting the first part of the
    preceding sentence, so that the sentence would read:

    Early spring is generally the first opportunity to
    observe the Wood Thrush in the United States.

    If the writer were to make this change, the essay would
    primarily lose:
    A. details that indicate to the reader what will eventu-
    ally happen.
    B. the contrast between the appearance of the Wood
    Thrush and the appearance of other forest birds.
    C. an example of one of the features that makes the
    Wood Thrush such a special bird.
    D. an indication of why bird watchers will usually see
    the Wood Thrush only during certain times of the
    year.

20. **F.** NO CHANGE
    G. its
    H. they're
    J. their

GO ON TO THE NEXT PAGE.

1 ■ ■ ■ ■ ■ ■ ■ 1

[1] <u>As the birds</u> settle into their spring nesting areas, the
                21
race to find a mate starts in earnest. [2] Fortunately for
bird lovers, this is when the male Wood Thrush begins
perfecting his song as he attempts to attract a willing
female. [3] Starting in the late evening, just as dusk begins
to encompass the landscape and most other birds have
quieted down, the Wood Thrush tentatively begins his
symphony of love. [4] <u>His songs come in distinct parts,</u>
                                              22
and he can sometimes even sing two sweet notes
simultaneously. [5] His concert generally lasts for a full
half hour, and he completes more than 100 songs in that
time. [6] With each song, the listener <u>begins to hear</u> this
                                               23
fancy flutist working on new combinations of notes,
extending a particular collection of chords, and changing
pitch and volume at will. [7] Abruptly, the singing stops,

<u>indicating that</u>
       24

the bird's pure exhaustion. [25]

---

21. Which of the following alternatives to the underlined portion would NOT be acceptable?
   A. While the birds
   B. The birds
   C. Once the birds
   D. When the birds

22. **F.** NO CHANGE
   G. His songs, come in distinct parts
   H. His songs come, in distinct parts,
   J. His songs, come in, distinct parts,

23. Which of the following alternatives to the underlined portion would NOT be acceptable?
   A. can hear
   B. starts hearing
   C. begins by hearing
   D. hears

24. **F.** NO CHANGE
   G. indicates
   H. indicating
   J. so indicates

25. Upon reviewing this paragraph and realizing that some information has been left out, the writer composes the following sentence:

   > All of these songs play an important role in the male bird's attempt to secure a mate, and the female Wood Thrush hears subtle nuances that escape the human ear.

   This sentence should most logically be placed after Sentence:
   A. 1.
   B. 2.
   C. 6.
   D. 7.

GO ON TO THE NEXT PAGE.

1 ■ ■ ■ ■ ■ ■ ■ ■ **1**

Following a long rest, the male Wood Thrush awakens
<u>   </u>
                                                                    26
to begin his quest anew. Early in the morning, before the
<u>   </u>
        26

other forest birds awaken, the Wood Thrush <u>by starting</u> his
                                                                                    27
melody all over again, waking the world up to another

long and <u>harmonious musical arrangement.</u> It seems
                                    28
unimaginable that more than one such display is necessary

to attract an interested partner, but the songs continue for

the entire spring and even into the summer months. One

can only determine that the Wood <u>Thrush chosen</u> female
                                                                    29
and subsequent offspring are begging him

<u>for to keep singing.</u> As poet Henry David Thoreau wrote,
<u>   </u>
                30
the Wood Thrush "alone declares the immortal wealth and

vigor that is in this forest."

26. Given that all the choices are true, which one most
    effectively introduces the information in this para-
    graph?
    F. NO CHANGE
    G. Subsequently, the male Wood Thrush requires
       several hours of sleep each night.
    H. By this time, many other forest birds have settled
       in for the night.
    J. It is hard to believe that the male Wood Thrush
       attracts only one mate with his beautiful songs.

27. A. NO CHANGE
    B. had started
    C. will have started
    D. will start

28. Which choice provides the most specific and precise
    information?
    F. NO CHANGE
    G. solitary tune.
    H. beautiful song.
    J. sweet sound.

29. A. NO CHANGE
    B. Thrush chooses
    C. Thrush's chose
    D. Thrush's chosen

30. F. NO CHANGE
    G. to keep singing.
    H. by keeping singing.
    J. in keeping with singing.

GO ON TO THE NEXT PAGE.

1 ■ ■ ■ ■ ■ ■ ■ ■ ■ 1

PASSAGE III

The following paragraphs may or may not be in the most logical order. Each paragraph is numbered in brackets, and Question 45 will ask you to choose where Paragraph 4 should most logically be placed.

Sacajawea: Girl Guide

[1]

Probably one of the most well-known members of the Shoshone Indian tribe, Sacajawea may have been Americas 31 first introduction to the plight of the working mother. As depicted in numerous works of art, photos, and statues, Sacajawea is most famous for accompanying Lewis and 32 Clark on their expedition to the Pacific Ocean. From early April of 1805 until the summer of 1806, the 17-year-old Sacajawea and her infant son rode horseback across mountains and rivers from North Dakota to the west coast. She demonstrated a sense of calm and quiet determination throughout the trip, as reflected in their journals kept by 33 the other members of the tireless group.

She was always described as being helpful and unobtrusive, caring for her child while at times aiding the party in obtaining supplies and finding easier pathways through treacherous territory. [34]

31. A. NO CHANGE
B. America
C. America's
D. Americas'

32. Which of the following alternatives to the underlined portion would NOT be acceptable?
F. achieved fame for accompanying
G. being famous for accompanying
H. became famous for accompanying
J. is best remembered for accompanying

33. A. NO CHANGE
B. her
C. those
D. OMIT the underlined portion.

34. At this point, the writer is considering adding the following true statement:

Clark was primarily responsible for calculating the daily distances traveled by the team.

Should the writer add this sentence here?
F. Yes, because it shows how meticulous Lewis and Clark were in their measurements.
G. Yes, because it is necessary to understanding the essay as a whole.
H. No, because it provides information that is included previously in the essay.
J. No, because it would distract readers from the main topic of the essay.

GO ON TO THE NEXT PAGE.

1 ■ ■ ■ ■ ■ ■ ■ ■ **1**

[2]

Sacajawea's early life was traumatic; she was stolen as a
young girl from her Shoshone home by a rival tribe. Soon
after, however, French-Canadian Toussaint Charbonneau
bought Sacajawea and made her his wife. At age 16, she
gave birth to her son and with her husband, son,
and the Lewis and Clark party, her trek began shortly
thereafter.
While historians often refer to Sacajawea as an official
guide for this expedition, she was only included on
it's roster because she was married to Charbonneau, a
well-known fur trapper. Along the way, because of her
familiarity with her homeland, she was able to serve as
both an interpreter and an aid for finding shortcuts and
easier routes.

[3]

At one point on this historic journey, Sacajawea
is reunited with her Shoshone home and family. Although
she found that most – believe it or not – of her
immediate family members had perished, her surviving
brother, Cameahwait, had become the chief of the
Shoshone tribe. Sacajawea was able to negotiate with her
brother for horses and supplies, as well as for a map and
guide so that they could press forward with their
mission. [41]

35. Which of the following alternatives to the underlined
portion would NOT be acceptable?
   A. traumatic. She
   B. traumatic, she
   C. traumatic, in part because she
   D. traumatic, partly because she

36. Which choice provides the most logical arrangement
of the parts of this sentence?
   F. NO CHANGE
   G. her trek began shortly thereafter with her husband,
son, and the Lewis and Clark party westward.
   H. began her trek shortly thereafter westward with her
husband, son, and the Lewis and Clark party.
   J. shortly thereafter began her trek westward with her
husband, son, and the Lewis and Clark party.

37. A. NO CHANGE
   B. its roster
   C. its' roster
   D. their roster,

38. F. NO CHANGE
   G. is being reunited
   H. has been reunited
   J. was reunited

39. A. NO CHANGE
   B. most – amazingly enough – of her immediate
family
   C. most of (she could not believe it) her immediate
family
   D. most of her immediate family

40. F. NO CHANGE
   G. supplies. In addition to
   H. supplies. As well as
   J. supplies, in addition to,

41. If the writer were to delete the last part of the preceding
sentence (ending the sentence with a period after the
word *guide*), the paragraph would primarily lose:
   A. support for the essay's point about Sacajawea's
importance to the continuation of the expedition.
   B. a direct link to the first paragraph.
   C. a humorous description of Sacajawea's negotiating
skills.
   D. an extensive digression about Sacajawea's relationship with her brother and other members of her
family.

GO ON TO THE NEXT PAGE.

1 ■ ■ ■ ■ ■ ■ ■ ■ 1

[4]

Controversy surrounds the end of Sacajawea's life.
Some historians list the year of 1812 as the year she died
at the age of 25. Shoshone history, however, records
Sacajawea as living the remainder of her life on the
reservation where she was born and dying there at age 97.

[5]

Many of the personal narratives of this momentous trip
refer to Sacajawea's demeanor and the oftentimes subtle
role she played in the trip's success. One such account
describes a river crossing in which Sacajawea's boat nearly
capsized during a storm. As the boat tipped onto its side,
Sacajawea carefully and calmly began retrieving the many
books and precious instruments that fell into them.
Fortunately, the items had been wrapped in waterproof
material and remained intact. The group was convinced
that all would have been lost had it not been for
Sacajawea's methodical and composed actions.

[6]

Despite the questions surrounding her death, there is no
question that Sacajawea left her mark on American history.

42. F. NO CHANGE
    G. one year of
    H. the time of
    J. OMIT the underlined portion.

43. A. NO CHANGE
    B. it.
    C. the water.
    D. OMIT the underlined portion.

44. Given that all the choices are true, which one most
effectively concludes and summarizes the essay?
    F. NO CHANGE
    G. Expert guide and negotiator, Sacajawea appeared
to live a long and prosperous life.
    H. In addition to her navigational skills, Sacajawea
was undeniably a great mother.
    J. Despite the drama of her early life, Sacajawea
remained calm and collected.

Question 45 asks about the preceding passage as a whole.

45. For the sake of the logic and coherence of the essay,
Paragraph 4 should be placed:
    A. where it is now.
    B. after Paragraph 1.
    C. after Paragraph 2.
    D. after Paragraph 5.

GO ON TO THE NEXT PAGE.

1 ■ ■ ■ ■ ■ ■ ■ ■ **1**

PASSAGE IV

Puzzling Numbers

The Japanese number game Sudoku has taken the world

<u>with</u> storm. While crossword puzzles seem to be the game
46

of choice, <u>they need</u> only sit in an airport or doctor's office
47

in any city to see how Sudoku is slowly overtaking the

popular word game.

In the most common game of Sudoku, the player is

faced with a nine-by-nine space grid with a total of

81 spaces. The solution to the puzzle requires a number,

one through nine, to be placed in each box. [48] Each

number must appear only once in each row and only once

in each column. A Sudoku puzzle will begin with a few

digits already in place. The solver's <u>task, is</u> to figure out
49

which numeral belongs in the remaining empty spaces.

While being a math whiz is no requirement for this

seemingly simple process, a level of logic and reasoning <u>is</u>
50

necessary in order to choose the correct number for each

space. As with most such activities, practice makes perfect

with Sudoku. The puzzles that seem impossible at first

glance <u>eventual become</u> more manageable.
51

46. **F.** NO CHANGE
    G. by
    H. of
    J. OMIT the underlined portion.

47. **A.** NO CHANGE
    B. one needs
    C. it needs
    D. which need

48. The writer is considering deleting the preceding sentence. Should this sentence be kept or deleted?
    F. Kept, because the reader needs to understand the process by which he or she can solve the puzzle.
    G. Kept, because it helps the reader visualize the solution to a specific puzzle in a magazine.
    H. Deleted, because it is not relevant to the preceding sentence.
    J. Deleted, because it is unnecessarily wordy.

49. **A.** NO CHANGE
    B. task; is
    C. task is
    D. task – is

50. **F.** NO CHANGE
    G. are
    H. were
    J. is being

51. **A.** NO CHANGE
    B. became eventual
    C. eventually becoming
    D. eventually become

GO ON TO THE NEXT PAGE.

1 ■ ■ ■ ■ ■ ■ ■ ■ 1

The name Sudoku is derived from the phrase *single number* in the Japanese language. Nevertheless, its definition refers to the placement or allotment of a single
                                                                                      52

number. This puzzle is aptly named, since the misplacement of a single number spells the beginning of an incorrect solution. For this reason, Sudoku
                          53

should have been played using a pencil with a good eraser.
54

It is nearly impossible to discern which number the solver has placed incorrectly once an error is discovered. If you
                                        55
don't have a pencil, use a pen to write the digit as a series of light dots. This way, should you make a mistake, you
                                                           56
can retrace your steps to locate and correct the original errant placement.

There are certain strategies involved in solving a Sudoku puzzle, including the process of elimination. For example, if a row of nine spaces already has the number 4, that row cannot contain another 4. This goes for columns as well. The solver can use these clues and a bit of deduction to limit the possible combinations of numbers. By attacking the puzzle using logic, you can turn the process into an
                    57
amusing challenge rather than an impossible task.

52. **F.** NO CHANGE
    G. Specifically,
    H. Ultimately,
    J. Largely,

53. Which of the following alternatives to the underlined portion would be LEAST acceptable?
    A. named because
    B. named, as
    C. named, while
    D. named;

54. **F.** NO CHANGE
    G. should be
    H. should being
    J. should of been

55. **A.** NO CHANGE
    B. that number
    C. a number
    D. number

56. Which choice fits most specifically with the information at the end of this sentence?
    F. NO CHANGE
    G. if you want to
    H. time permitting
    J. with your pen

57. **A.** NO CHANGE
    B. logic, and
    C. logic, so
    D. logic

GO ON TO THE NEXT PAGE.

1 ■ ■ ■ ■ ■ ■ ■ ■ 1

[1] The origin of Sudoku is attributed to Leonhard Euler, the Swiss mathematician who <u>sometimes</u> developed the game Magic Squares in 1783. [2] In fact, Euler's game was
₅₈
actually based on a game derived from Chinese folklore. [3] The primary difference between Magic Squares and Sudoku is that Euler's game has no grid dividing the puzzle and it is somewhat easier to solve, since there are multiple possibilities for a solution. [4] In true Sudoku, each puzzle has only one solution. [5] The puzzle's difficulty varies according to the number of digits that are initially provided. [6] When faced with a puzzle with only one 3 provided, for example, you can be sure that it will be more difficult to solve than a puzzle that already has half of the numbers placed in the correct boxes. 59

One has only to examine a local newspaper to ascertain the popularity of this addictive brain teaser. Where comics and crossword puzzles reign supreme, it is often easy to locate a grid of spaces and numbers tucked off in a corner, or even sitting boldly next to the time-honored crossword.

58. The best placement for the underlined portion would be:
   F. where it is now.
   G. before the word *origin*.
   H. before the word *attributed*.
   J. before the word *Swiss*.

59. If the writer were to divide the preceding paragraph into two shorter paragraphs in order to differentiate between the origin and evolution of the game and the difficulty of playing the game, the new paragraph should begin with Sentence:
   A. 2.
   B. 3.
   C. 4.
   D. 6.

Question 60 asks about the preceding passage as a whole.

60. If the writer were to delete the final paragraph from the essay, which of the following would be lost?
   F. A detailed description of where to find Sudoku games.
   G. A comment on the similarities between Sudoku and crossword puzzles.
   H. A reference to the opening paragraph's mention of Sudoku's popularity.
   J. A plea to the reader to avoid Sudoku because of its addictive nature.

GO ON TO THE NEXT PAGE.

1 ■ ■ ■ ■ ■ ■ ■ ■ 1

PASSAGE V

Early Communication

Most new parents find that their biggest problem is determining what their babys cries mean. Sometimes the <u>cries seem to sound alike,</u> and other times they are as
₆₁
different as night and day. Yet, what do they mean? Recent studies have shown that babies do have unique cries to identify their <u>needs, and</u> interpreting a baby's vocalizations
₆₂
is not as difficult as it may seem.

Perhaps the biggest hurdle in making sense of an infant's

sounds is the parent's own anxiety and <u>being confused.</u>
₆₃
With a little study and patience, parents can fine-tune their listening skills and sidestep their frustrations.

Movement is another way that infants communicate. For many years, scientists have been able to interpret various messages by filming a sequence of movements and then playing <u>those</u> back in slow motion. Three-month-olds who
₆₄
appear to be flailing their arms around randomly are often reaching for something specific, perhaps a toy or a familiar face. Even the youngest infants will move their heads toward a familiar voice, often producing the first glimmer of a smile, clearly communicating <u>happiness, and, comfort.</u>
₆₅

As the baby grows, new utterances emerge that often
<u>sounds</u> random and nonsensical.
₆₆

61. A. NO CHANGE
    B. babies cries
    C. baby's cries
    D. babys cry's

62. Which of the following alternatives to the underlined portion would NOT be acceptable?
    F. needs. Interpreting
    G. needs; interpreting
    H. needs, so
    J. needs, interpreting

63. A. NO CHANGE
    B. confusion.
    C. to be confused.
    D. for confusing.

64. F. NO CHANGE
    G. them
    H. the film
    J. that

65. A. NO CHANGE
    B. happiness, and comfort.
    C. happiness and, comfort.
    D. happiness and comfort.

66. F. NO CHANGE
    G. sound
    H. sounding
    J. sounded

GO ON TO THE NEXT PAGE.

1 ■ ■ ■ ■ ■ ■ ■ ■ 1

More than likely, however, these noises actually mean something to the baby. An acute observer can often quickly interpret the child's utterances and reinforce the development of language, whereas a parent who does not
                                    67
pay attention could miss an attempt at communication from her baby. It is easy to imagine how much faster language development will come when a one-year-old feels success and positive reinforcement in his attempts to communicate. Conversely, not being understood can easily
                    68
create frustration and reactive responses, perhaps partially explaining the onset of the "terrible twos."

　　Many parents find that sign language can be a valuable tool for the emerging orator who is just learning to speak.
                                    69
A nine-month-old seems to have an easier time mimicking less precise hand movements that she observes than vocalizing the complexities of consonants and vowel sounds. A small repertoire of such hand movements can greatly diminish the anxiety-producing challenge of communicating hunger, tiredness, thirst, and the like.
                                    70
Often, as parents demonstrate a sign to their baby, they will vocalize the word for that sign over and over. Eventually, as the child uses the sign successfully, she will begin to mimic the word that seems to go with it, and eventually drop the use of her hands. [71]

---

67. Which of the following alternatives to the underlined portion would NOT be acceptable?
- **A.** language, while
- **B.** language;
- **C.** language, but
- **D.** language, being

68. **F.** NO CHANGE
- **G.** Therefore,
- **H.** Consequently,
- **J.** Likewise,

69. **A.** NO CHANGE
- **B.** whose speech is just developing
- **C.** who is on the verge of speaking
- **D.** OMIT the underlined portion

70. Given that all the choices are true, which one most specifically and vividly describes the needs of the child?
- **F.** NO CHANGE
- **G.** his needs.
- **H.** what he wants.
- **J.** his desires to his parents.

71. The writer is considering deleting the following phrase from the preceding sentence (and revising the capitalization accordingly):

　　Eventually, as the child uses the sign successfully,

Should this phrase be kept or deleted?
- **A.** Kept, because it clarifies how the proper use of signs can reinforce language development.
- **B.** Kept, because it provides specific details about the signs that parents use to teach their children to speak.
- **C.** Deleted, because it contradicts the preceding paragraph, which makes it clear that children do not use movement to communicate.
- **D.** Deleted, because this information is provided later in the paragraph.

GO ON TO THE NEXT PAGE.

1 ■ ■ ■ ■ ■ ■ ■ ■ **1**

Long before a young <u>distinct</u> child is able to speak
                          72
words, his ability to understand the speech of others is

developing. Before a child can say "mama" or "dada," he

may easily be able <u>follow</u> a command such as "Give me
                       73
the ball" or "Get your blanket." As the toddler learns the

names of objects, people, and actions, a vocabulary

explosion begins to occur. [74] Most people believe

communication begins when the child is able to use

language to express an idea or feeling. <u>By comparison,</u>
                                              75
communication has been going on for much longer.

Language development will come sooner and easier if

parents respond more consistently to their infant's

communication efforts from day one.

72. The best placement for the underlined portion
would be:
  F. where it is now.
  G. after the word *speak*.
  H. after the word *speech*.
  J. after the word *developing*.

73. A. NO CHANGE
     B. by following
     C. to follow
     D. following

74. The writer is considering deleting the following clause
from the preceding sentence (revising the capitalization
accordingly):

  As the toddler learns the names of objects, people,
  and actions,
Should this clause be kept or deleted?
  F. Kept, because it clarifies for the readers that toddlers can only learn to speak if they are given
commands.
  G. Kept, because it makes the connection between
understanding what others are saying and learning
how to speak.
  H. Deleted, because it contradicts the essay's main
point by implying that toddlers cannot communicate effectively with their parents.
  J. Deleted, because it misleads the readers into thinking that the paragraph is about baby names rather
than language development.

75. A. NO CHANGE
     B. In truth,
     C. On the other hand,
     D. Despite this,

END OF THE ENGLISH TEST.
STOP! IF YOU HAVE TIME LEFT OVER, CHECK YOUR WORK ON THIS SECTION ONLY.

2 △ △ △ △ △ △ △ △ 2

MATHEMATICS TEST

60 Minutes—60 Questions

DIRECTIONS: Solve each of the problems in the time allowed, then fill in the corresponding bubble on your answer sheet. Do not spend too much time on any one problem; skip the more difficult problems and go back to them later. You may use a calculator on this test. For this test you should assume that figures are NOT necessarily drawn to scale, that all geometric figures lie in a plane, and that the word *line* is used to indicate a straight line.

1. $|9 - 5| - |5 - 9| = ?$
   A. -8
   B. -6
   C. -4
   D. 0
   E. 8

2. An editor charges $30 for each hour he works on a book project, plus a flat $25 editing fee. How many hours of work are included in a $190 bill for a book project?

   F. $3\frac{2}{5}$
   G. 4
   H. $5\frac{1}{2}$
   J. $6\frac{1}{3}$
   K. 7

3. Runner A averages 5 miles per hour, and Runner B averages 6 miles per hour. At these rates, how much longer does it take Runner A than Runner B to run 15 miles?
   A. .5 hour
   B. 1 hour
   C. 1.5 hours
   D. 2.5 hours
   E. 3 hours

4. $x^2 + 60x + 54 - 59x - 82x^2$ is equivalent to:
   F. $-26x^2$
   G. $-26x^6$
   H. $-81x^2 + x + 54$
   J. $-81x^2 - x + 54$
   K. $-83x^2 - x - 54$

DO YOUR FIGURING HERE.

GO ON TO THE NEXT PAGE.

2   **2**

5. The figure below is composed of square *ABDE* and equilateral triangle *BCD*. The length of line segment *AE* is 18 centimeters. What is the perimeter of *ABCDE*, in centimeters?

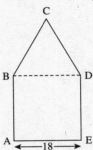

   A. 48
   B. 54
   C. 72
   D. 90
   E. 106

6. The expression $(6n - 5)(n + 4)$ is equivalent to:
   F. $6n^2 - 20$
   G. $6n^2 - 19n - 20$
   H. $6n^2 - 29n - 20$
   J. $6n^2 + 19n$
   K. $6n^2 + 19n - 20$

7. Blair expects an increase of 3% in her current annual salary of $42,000. What would her new annual salary be?
   A. $42,003
   B. $42,126
   C. $43,260
   D. $45,000
   E. $54,600

8. The 6 consecutive integers below add up to 513.

$$n - 2$$
$$n - 1$$
$$n$$
$$n + 1$$
$$n + 2$$
$$n + 3$$

What is the value of n?
   F. 48
   G. 53
   H. 64
   J. 85
   K. 86

DO YOUR FIGURING HERE.

GO ON TO THE NEXT PAGE.

2 △ △ △ △ △ △ △ △ **2**

9. In the standard (x, y) coordinate plane, point B with coordinates (5,6) is the midpoint of AC, and A has coordinates (6,7). What are the coordinates of C?
   A. (11,13)
   B. (7,8)
   C. (4,5)
   D. (5.5,6.5)
   E. (−4,−8)

10. Rectangle $PQRS$ lies in the standard (x, y) coordinate plane so that its sides are not parallel to the axes. What is the product of the slopes of all four sides of rectangle $PQRS$?
    F. −2
    G. −1
    H. 0
    J. 1
    K. 2

11. If Tom traveled 45 miles in 12 hours and Jim traveled four times as far in one-third the time, what was Jim's average speed, in miles per hour?
    A. 5
    B. 15
    C. 30
    D. 45
    E. 90

12. Given the triangle shown below with exterior angles that measure $a°$, $b°$, and $c°$ as shown, what is the sum of a, b, and c?

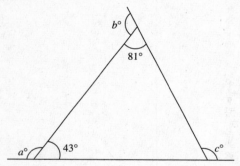

    F. 180
    G. 236
    H. 261
    J. 360
    K. Cannot be determined from the given information

GO ON TO THE NEXT PAGE.

2 △ △ △ △ △ △ △ △ 2

Use the following information to answer Questions 13 – 15.

A poll of 200 students was taken before Center High School changed the name of its mascot. All 200 students indicated which 1 of the 4 mascot names they would vote for. The results of the poll are given in the table below.

Mascot name	Number of students
Spartans	30
Lions	40
Gophers	80
Knights	50

13. What percent of the students polled chose Spartans in the poll?
   A. 40%
   B. 30%
   C. 25%
   D. 20%
   E. 15%

14. If the information in the table were converted to a pie chart, then the central angle of the sector for Lions would measure how many degrees?
   F. 144°
   G. 108°
   H. 72°
   J. 54°
   K. 45°

15. If the poll is indicative of how the 3,000 students at Center High School will actually vote, which of the following is the best estimate of the number of votes Knights will receive?
   A. 50
   B. 200
   C. 525
   D. 750
   E. 900

DO YOUR FIGURING HERE.

GO ON TO THE NEXT PAGE.

2 △ △ △ △ △ △ △ △ **2**

16. The total surface area of the rectangular solid shown below is the sum of the areas of the 6 sides. What is the solid's total surface area, in square inches?

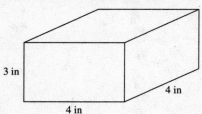

3 in

4 in

4 in

F. 18
G. 36
H. 48
J. 80
K. 96

17. Which of the following is the slope of a line parallel to the line $y = \frac{2}{5}x + 7$ in the standard (x, y) coordinate plane?

A. -7

B. $-\frac{5}{2}$

C. $\frac{2}{5}$

D. 2

E. $\frac{5}{2}$

18. A circular lamp base has a radius of 2.5 inches. When placed on a flat table, approximately how much area does the lamp base cover, in square inches?

F. 5.00
G. 6.25
H. 15.70
J. 19.63
K. 25.00

19. What is the largest integer less than $\sqrt{42}$?

A. 3
B. 6
C. 7
D. 9
E. 23

DO YOUR FIGURING HERE.

GO ON TO THE NEXT PAGE.

2   △ **2**

DO YOUR FIGURING HERE.

20. Amanda plans to paint the 4 walls of her bedroom with 1 coat of paint. The walls are rectangular, and each wall measures 12 feet by 14 feet. She will not paint either the 3-foot-by-4-foot rectangular window in her bedroom or the 3-foot-by-7-foot rectangular bedroom door. Amanda knows that each gallon of paint covers between 350 and 400 square feet. If only 1-gallon cans of paint are available, which of the following is the minimum number of cans of paint Amanda needs to buy to paint her bedroom walls?

  F. 1
  G. 2
  H. 3
  J. 4
  K. 5

21. For all $x > 0$, the expression $\dfrac{3x^3}{3x^9}$ equals:

  A. x^{-6}
  B. x^3
  C. x^6
  D. x^{12}
  E. x^{27}

22. What values of a are solutions for $a^2 + 2a = 8$?

  F. 6 and 8
  G. 0 and 2
  H. -2 and 4
  J. -2 and 0
  K. -4 and 2

23. In the square graphed below, what is the slope of line segment AC?

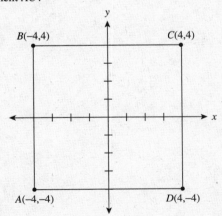

  A. 4
  B. 2
  C. 1
  D. -1
  E. -4

GO ON TO THE NEXT PAGE.

24. The fixed costs of printing a certain textbook are $900.00 per week. The variable costs are $1.50 per textbook. Which of the following expressions can be used to model the cost of printing t textbooks in 1 week?

  F. $901.50t$
  G. $150t - \$900.00$
  H. $\$900.00t + \$1.50$
  J. $\$900.00 - \$1.50t$
  K. $\$900.00 + \$1.50t$

25. In the figure shown below, the perimeter of the triangle is $15 + 5\sqrt{3}$. What is the value of x?

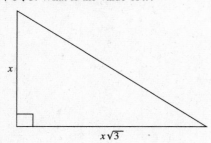

  A. 2
  B. 3
  C. 4
  D. 5
  E. 6

26. If $\dfrac{4\sqrt{9}}{y\sqrt{11}} = \dfrac{4\sqrt{9}}{11}$, then $y = ?$

  F. 1
  G. $\sqrt{11}$
  H. 11
  J. 22
  K. 36

27. Casey has buckets of 3 different sizes. The total capacity of 12 of the buckets is g gallons, the total capacity of 8 buckets of another size is g gallons, and the total capacity of 4 buckets of the third size is also g gallons. In terms of g when $g > 0$, what is the capacity, in gallons, of each of the smallest-sized buckets?

  A. $\dfrac{g}{12}$

  B. $\dfrac{g}{8}$

  C. $\dfrac{g}{4}$

  D. $12g$
  E. $8g$

DO YOUR FIGURING HERE.

GO ON TO THE NEXT PAGE.

2 △ △ △ △ △ △ △ △ **2**

28. What is the area of a circle that has a circumference of $.5\pi$?
    F. 0.0625π
    G. 0.10π
    H. 0.25π
    J. 25π
    K. 625π

29. Cube X has an edge length of 2 inches. Cube Y has an edge length triple that of Cube X. What is the volume, in cubic inches, of Cube Y?
    A. 6
    B. 12
    C. 36
    D. 72
    E. 216

30. A formula used to compute the current value of an investment account is $A = P(1 + r)^n$, where A is the current value, P is the amount deposited, r is the rate of interest for 1 compounding period, expressed as a decimal, and n is the number of compounding periods. Which of the following is closest to the value of an investment account after 3 years if $8,000 is deposited at 5% annual interest compounded annually?
    F. $8,400
    G. $9,261
    H. $15,730
    J. $25,200
    K. $33,463

31. A right circular cylinder is shown below, with dimensions given in inches. What is the total surface area of the cylinder, in square inches?
    (Note: The total surface area of a cylinder is given by $2\pi r^2 + 2\pi rh$, where r is the radius and h is the height.)

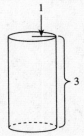

    A. 3π
    B. 5π
    C. 6π
    D. 8π
    E. 11π

32. Given $f(x) = 3x + 5$ and $g(x) = x^2 - x + 7$, which of the following is an expression for $f(g(x))$?
    F. $3x^2 - 3x + 26$
    G. $3x^2 - 3x + 12$
    H. $x^2 - x + 12$
    J. $9x^2 + 25x + 27$
    K. $3x^2 + 21$

DO YOUR FIGURING HERE.

GO ON TO THE NEXT PAGE.

33. The table below shows the total number of touchdowns scored in each of 16 football games during a regular season. What is the average number of touchdowns scored per game, to the nearest tenth?

Total number of touchdowns in a game	Number of games with this total
0	2
1	3
2	3
3	5
4	2
5	1

  A. 2.6
  B. 2.3
  C. 2.0
  D. 1.5
  E. 0.9

34. In the triangles shown below, what is the average of angles $a, b, c, d,$ and e?

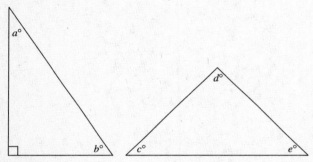

  F. 30°
  G. 45°
  H. 54°
  J. 60°
  K. 72°

35. $(4x^4)^4$ is equivalent to:
  A. x
  B. $16x^8$
  C. $16x^{16}$
  D. $256x^8$
  E. $256x^{16}$

36. Which of the following is equivalent to the inequality $3x - 6 > 6x + 9$?
  F. $x > -5$
  G. $x < -5$
  H. $x > -2$
  J. $x < 3$
  K. $x > 3$

DO YOUR FIGURING HERE.

GO ON TO THE NEXT PAGE.

2 △ △ △ △ △ △ △ △ **2**

37. In the xy-coordinate system, $(\sqrt{5}, s)$ is one of the points of intersection of the graphs $y = 2x^2 + 6$ and $y = -4x^2 + m$, where m is a constant. What is the value of m?

A. 30
B. 33
C. 36
D. 39
E. 42

38. For right triangle XYZ below, what is $\cos \angle Z$?

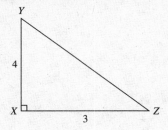

F. $\dfrac{4}{3}$

G. $\dfrac{5}{4}$

H. $\dfrac{3}{4}$

J. $\dfrac{3}{5}$

K. Cannot be determined from the given information

39. Which of the following statements is NOT true about the arithmetic sequence 16, 11, 6, 1, …?

A. The fifth term is -4.
B. The sum of the first 5 terms is 30.
C. The seventh term is -12.
D. The common difference of consecutive integers is -5.
E. The sum of the first 7 terms is 7.

40. If there are 6×10^{14} oxygen molecules in a volume of 3×10^7 cubic meters, what is the average number of oxygen molecules per cubic meter?

F. 2×10^5
G. 2×10^7
H. 2×10^{21}
J. 18×10^7
K. 18×10^{21}

GO ON TO THE NEXT PAGE.

2   **2**

41. The lengths of the sides of right triangle *ABC* are shown in the figure below. What is the cotangent of ∠*B*?

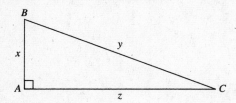

A. $\dfrac{x}{y}$

B. $\dfrac{x}{z}$

C. $\dfrac{y}{z}$

D. $\dfrac{z}{x}$

E. $\dfrac{z}{y}$

42. What rational number is halfway between $\dfrac{1}{6}$ and $\dfrac{1}{2}$?

F. $\dfrac{1}{8}$

G. $\dfrac{1}{4}$

H. $\dfrac{1}{3}$

J. $\dfrac{2}{3}$

K. $\dfrac{3}{2}$

43. If $|6 - 2x| > 9$, which of the following is a possible value of *x*?

A. -2
B. -1
C. 0
D. 4
E. 7

GO ON TO THE NEXT PAGE.

2   △ △ △ △ **2**

44. A square and a regular pentagon have equal perimeters. If the pentagon has sides of length 12, what is the area of the square?

F. 30
G. 48
H. 60
J. 225
K. 244

45. A classroom has 10 tables that will seat up to 4 students each. If 20 students are seated at tables, and NO tables are empty, what is the greatest possible number of tables that could be filled with students?

A. 5
B. 3
C. 2
D. 1
E. 0

46. If $x < y$, then $|x - y|$ is equivalent to which of the following?

F. $x + y$
G. $-(x + y)$
H. $\sqrt{x - y}$
J. $x - y$
K. $-(x - y)$

47. The trapezoid below is divided into 2 triangles and 1 rectangle. Lengths are given in centimeters. What is the combined area, in square centimeters, of the 2 shaded triangles?

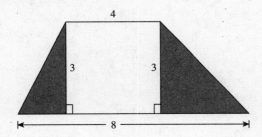

A. 18
B. 12
C. 9
D. 6
E. 4

GO ON TO THE NEXT PAGE.

48. In the figure below, all line segments are either horizontal or vertical, and the dimensions given are in feet. What is the perimeter, in feet, of the figure?

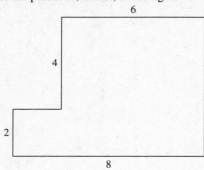

   F. 20
   G. 24
   H. 26
   J. 28
   K. 32

49. If c is directly proportional to s^2 and $c = \dfrac{7}{16}$ when $s = \dfrac{1}{4}$, what is the value of s when $c = 175$?
   A. 2
   B. 3
   C. 4
   D. 5
   E. 6

50. If the value, to the nearest thousandth, of $\cos \alpha$ is -0.385, which of the following could be true about α?
   F. $\dfrac{2\pi}{3} \le \alpha \le \pi$

   G. $\dfrac{\pi}{2} \le \alpha \le \dfrac{2\pi}{3}$

   H. $\dfrac{\pi}{3} \le \alpha \le \dfrac{\pi}{2}$

   J. $\dfrac{\pi}{6} \le \alpha \le \dfrac{\pi}{3}$

   K. $0 \le \alpha \le \dfrac{\pi}{6}$

51. An integer from 10 through 99, inclusive, is to be chosen at random. What is the probability that the number chosen will have 0 as at least 1 digit?
   A. $\dfrac{2}{90}$

   B. $\dfrac{1}{10}$

   C. $\dfrac{9}{89}$

   D. $\dfrac{10}{89}$

   E. $\dfrac{9}{100}$

DO YOUR FIGURING HERE.

GO ON TO THE NEXT PAGE.

2   **2**

52. A 12-centimeter-by-16-centimeter rectangle is inscribed in a circle as shown below. What is the area of the circle, in square centimeters?

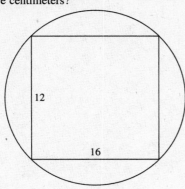

   F. 5π
   G. 14π
   H. 25π
   J. 100π
   K. 192π

53. If $\log_a x = n$ and $\log_a y = p$, then $\log_a (xy)2 =?$
   A. np
   B. $2np$
   C. $4np$
   D. $n + p$
   E. $2(n + p)$

54. For every positive 2-digit number, a, with units digit x and tens digit y, let b be the 2-digit number formed by reversing the digits of a. Which of the following expressions is equivalent to $a - b$?
   F. 0
   G. $9x - y$
   H. $9y - x$
   J. $9(x - y)$
   K. $9(y - x)$

55. If $f(a) = a^2 - 2$, then $f(a + b) =?$
   A. $a^2 + b^2$
   B. $a^2 - 2 + b$
   C. $a^2 + b^2 - 2$
   D. $a^2 + 2ab + b^2$
   E. $a^2 + 2ab + b^2 - 2$

56. In the complex numbers, where $i^2 = -1$, $\dfrac{1}{(1 + i)} \times$

   $\dfrac{(1 - i)}{(1 - i)} =?$
   F. $i - 1$
   G. $1 + i$
   H. $1 - i$
   J. $\dfrac{(1 - i)}{2}$
   K. $\dfrac{(1 + i)}{2}$

GO ON TO THE NEXT PAGE.

2 △ △ △ △   △ △ △ △ **2**

57. Amy's best marathon time decreased by 10% from 2005 to 2006 and by 20% from 2006 to 2007. By what percent did her best marathon time decrease from 2005 to 2007?

   A. 28%
   B. 30%
   C. 50%
   D. 72%
   E. 10%

58. The sum of an infinite geometric sequence series with first term x and common ratio $y < 1$ is given by $\dfrac{x}{(1-y)}$. The sum of a given infinite geometric series is 200, and the common ratio is 0.15. What is the second term of this series?

   F. 199.85
   G. 170
   H. 169.85
   J. 30
   K. 25.5

59. How many different integer values of a satisfy the inequality $\dfrac{1}{11} < \dfrac{2}{a} < \dfrac{1}{8}$?

   A. 1
   B. 2
   C. 3
   D. 4
   E. 5

60. In 3 fair coin tosses, where the 2 outcomes, heads and tails, are equally likely, what is the probability of obtaining exactly 2 heads?

   F. $\dfrac{1}{3}$

   G. $\dfrac{3}{8}$

   H. $\dfrac{1}{2}$

   J. $\dfrac{2}{3}$

   K. $\dfrac{7}{8}$

DO YOUR FIGURING HERE.

END OF THE MATHEMATICS TEST.
STOP! IF YOU HAVE TIME LEFT OVER, CHECK YOUR WORK ON THIS SECTION ONLY.

3 ███ **3**

READING TEST

35 Minutes—40 Questions

DIRECTIONS: This test includes four passages, each followed by ten questions. Read the passages and choose the best answer to each question. After you have selected your answer, fill in the corresponding bubble on your answer sheet. You should refer to the passages as often as necessary when answering the questions.

PASSAGE I

PROSE FICTION: *Silence: A Story of Courage and Healing*

Some say that silence is a great healer. If you'd said that to me two years ago, I wouldn't have agreed. "Silence," I would have argued, "is anything but healing. There is nothing therapeutic about keeping your
5 feelings inside, never talking about what's going on in your life." I now believe that silence is the reward you get from great healing, in addition to being the healer itself. But I didn't know that then.

I had never understood the value of silence.
10 I didn't have to. My family was loud and happy. And why not? Nothing serious ever went wrong—not that we knew about. Sure, my siblings and I always fought noisily until our mom yelled at us to stop. Then we'd shout and complain about injustice, but always, even-
15 tually, hug and make-up. Within the parameters of my innocent world, I knew silence as a lack of something: a lack of noise, a lack of discussion, a lack of feel-
ing, a lack of love. Maybe I was even a little afraid of the emptiness it created—the aural darkness where
20 forgiveness never happened. I thought I knew … I was very wrong.

Jaime entered my life without much fanfare about two years ago. I'll never forget the day I met him. My university required a community service stint to
25 graduate, and I wanted to get it out of the way. I'd heard that the local YMCA was a good resource, and I liked working with little kids. I thought maybe they'd let me teach swimming. So, on a cool October day in the fall of my sophomore year, I made my way to the
30 YMCA looking for easy credits.

I didn't have a car at school until my junior year of college, so if I needed to go anywhere, I would generally catch a ride with a friend or walk. On that particular day, no friend was available and the ten-mile
35 walk was far beyond my dedication to public service. Consequently, I was at the mercy of public transporta-
tion. Thankfully, I'd heard the local bus system was pretty reliable. With the help of the CITA bus line map, I climbed onto Bus Route 3, paid my fifty cents,
40 and scanned for a seat. Buses often have their own

unique demographic: each crowd is unlike any other. On this bus, most everyone was either asleep or totally oblivious. Except for one kid. He wasn't all that big—maybe thirteen years old—and he was seated by
45 himself, farther apart from the other riders than seemed possible in such a crowded space. Unlike the others, his eyes were alert. And they were glued on me.

Normally, I ignore people with such awkward habits. But for some reason, I couldn't stop staring
50 back. Odder still, instead of avoiding him, I found myself passing an empty seat to sit down on the bench beside him. Once I did, he turned to look out the window. That's when the strangeness of it all hit me, and I started to feel a little awkward. I wanted to get back
55 in control of the situation. Trying to be subtle, I looked him over. I noticed some scarring on his hands, and a small gash on his cheek. Suddenly, he turned and looked me in the eye. Expecting him to say something, I just waited, watching. He said nothing. After about
60 fifteen seconds, I couldn't take the silence anymore.

"Hi," I said, trying not to appear as nervous as I felt.

No response. He just kept staring.

"I'm Katie." I added a smile. Again, I received no
65 response. I gave it one more try.

"I've never used the bus system before. It seems pretty reliable. Do you use it a lot?" Silence. My cheery voice sounded out of place. Other people were starting to stare at me. This time I gave up and turned my
70 head toward the front of the bus, trying to ignore the thirteen-year-old staring me down… again. I opened my cell phone to check the time and saw that only two minutes had passed. This was going to be the longest bus ride ever.

75 Then a thin voice cut through the silence.

"I'm Jaime."

My heart skipped a beat. Could it be that my silence was the catalyst for this small victory? By allowing Jaime the room that silence allows to make
80 his own decision about talking to me, I had made a con-
nection. Suddenly, I knew that my long held opinion of silence was forever changed.

GO ON TO THE NEXT PAGE.

3   **3**

1. Which of the following best describes the structure of the passage?
   A. A dialogue between two people in which both relate their reasons for travel in an almost equal amount of detail.
   B. An account of the narrator's perspective of meeting a life-changing new person for the first time.
   C. A character sketch of two people as related by a narrator who knows both of them and their thoughts.
   D. A detailed narration the narrator's community service projects accompanied by a description one of the people she helped.

2. Based on the passage, which of the following statements best describes the overall attitude of the narrator towards the boy?
   F. The boy's quiet, composed behavior challenges the narrator and makes her initially uncomfortable.
   G. The boy's aggressive behavior frightens the narrator and makes her angry.
   H. The boy's friendly demeanor relaxes the narrator and makes her more thoughtful.
   J. The boy's apathy provokes the narrator and makes her wistful, longing for the quiet days of her youth.

3. It can reasonably be inferred from the passage that the narrator had been raised with which of the following attitudes towards silence?
   A. It is pleasant and calming.
   B. It is positive and reaffirming.
   C. It is dangerous and threatening.
   D. It is empty and ominous.

4. According to the narrator, silence is usually characterized by:
   F. forgiveness.
   G. absence.
   H. injustice.
   J. innocence.

5. In relation to the first paragraph's earlier description of silence, the narrator's comments in lines 6–8 primarily serve to:
   A. reveal how silence heals a person.
   B. explain how silence can actually be a positive force.
   C. clarify why the narrator distrusts silence.
   D. suggest that silence is quite overrated.

6. Which of the following statements about the people on the bus is best supported by the passage?
   F. The bus is filled with fascinating people, most of whom you see on every bus ride.
   G. People who ride the bus are always quiet.
   H. You might never see the same people on any given bus ride.
   J. People who take the bus are dull and uninteresting.

7. According to the passage, the main reason the narrator decided to go to the YMCA was that:
   A. her university required community service credits.
   B. she liked to swim.
   C. she was looking for a new job working with children.
   D. she was exploring her new town.

8. Based on the narrator's account, the boy, Jaime, is best described as:
   F. sleepy, yet hostile.
   G. bored and antagonistic.
   H. outgoing and friendly.
   J. aware, yet shy.

9. As it is used in line 15, the word *parameters* most nearly means:
   A. requirements.
   B. variables.
   C. limitations.
   D. attributes.

10. In the passage, the narrator describes her cheery voice as sounding out of place most likely because:
    F. the bus was silent; most of the other passengers were asleep or lost in their own thoughts.
    G. the bus was noisy; most of the other passengers were loudly talking to their neighbors.
    H. the bus was noisy; most of the other passengers were arguing with their neighbors.
    J. the bus was silent; most of the other passengers were watching a scene on the street.

GO ON TO THE NEXT PAGE.

3   **3**

PASSAGE II

SOCIAL SCIENCE: *Julius Caesar and the Fall of the Roman Republic*

Caius Julius Caesar is popularly considered the founder of the Roman Empire, though it would be more accurate to consider his political rise as marking the end of the Roman Republic. The distinction,
5 which some would call insignificant, is more than mere semantics. The founding of the Empire rightly belongs to Caesar's great-nephew, Augustus Caesar, who was adopted by his uncle as his heir. The Republic had been under considerable stress for several years before Caius
10 Julius was born, thus he did not create the fissures that led to the collapse of the Roman Republic, though he did capitalize on them brilliantly. Caius Julius' singular success as a politician and general has guaranteed him a place among the most influential persons in world
15 history.

Rome's social troubles began in a land crisis. Roman armies were traditionally made up of small landholders—farmers who, by law, had to own a minimum number of acres to join the military service.
20 Unfortunately, a series of wars in the late-third and early-second centuries B.C. kept these farmers away from their land, frequently leading to bankruptcy. The small farm plots were taken over by the wealthy upper class, who farmed the plots with slaves won in foreign
25 wars. With no more land to farm, the returning soldiers settled in Rome, where they added to the unemployment dole and increased political instability. Adding to the problem, once the soldiers were landless, they could no longer enlist in the army. This led to a significant
30 problem for military recruitment.

The first notable Romans to address both issues were the reformers known as the Gracchi Brothers. Starting around 133 B.C., the older brother, Tiberius Gracchus, tried to reform the system by proposing to
35 confiscate, or take, public land to distribute to returning soldiers. He hoped this would solve the unemployment crisis and increase the number of men eligible for the army. Unfortunately, the land had been leased, often at very low rates, to wealthy members of the Roman Sen-
40 ate. At this time, Rome was governed by two political bodies: the Senate and the Assembly. The Senate was made up of wealthy landed nobility and was often in conflict with the more populist Assembly. Not surprisingly, the senators bitterly fought government seizure
45 of the land, which they considered their own property. In the end, Tiberius Gracchus was murdered, though the Roman Senate passed a modified version of the Gracchan land laws to quell public outrage. When the younger brother, Gaius Gracchus, began his reforms
50 10 years later, he was able to extend political rights to the lower classes and reduce opportunities for bribery and corruption among the upper classes. He, too, was murdered for pushing the system too far.

The reforms of the Gracchus brothers were soon
55 apparently championed by a new political leader, Gaius Marius, although Marius' real fame came from his military genius—especially after he brutally halted the invasion of German tribes into Italy. He successfully reorganized the Roman military, in the process doing
60 away with the land requirement. Marius also challenged the traditional structure of the army where nobility were regularly given authority over lower-class officers with more experience and ability. Julius Caesar later exploited this reform, promoting officers based on
65 ability not class, to tremendous success in Gaul and elsewhere.

Marius' role as champion of the lower classes was solidified when he opposed the Roman general, Cornelius Sulla. Sulla was allied with the Roman
70 Senate, who feared Marius' ambition and influence with the masses. Sulla believed in strengthening the power of the Senate against the popular Assembly. To this end, he marched his armies against Rome, defeating Marius and establishing himself as Dictator. While
75 Sulla eventually resigned the dictatorship peacefully, he had exiled or killed thousands of political opponents during his reign. Some critics say the real end of the Roman Republic occurred during the struggle between Marius and Sulla.

80 Julius Caesar was related by marriage to both Marius and Sulla. Despite this patrician background, he chose to promote his connections to Marius. Like the Gracchi brothers, Julius Caesar supported the redistribution of public lands to the poor and protected the
85 grain supply (a large part of the unemployment dole). In his armies, he promoted ability before social rank. He was also widely seen to support the middle and lower classes against the privileges of the aristocracy, namely the Senate. The senators saw him as a traitor to
90 their class and, therefore, to the Republic itself. When Julius Caesar was eventually assassinated by a group of senators, the outcry from the general population was completely unanticipated. The resulting political chaos ultimately led to the rise of Augustus Caesar
91 as emperor, effectively ending the Roman Republic forever.

11. The author most nearly characterizes the role Julius Caesar plays in the fall of the Roman Republic as one that:
   A. takes advantage of past conflicts to promote his own ideals.
   B. contradicts the efforts of the Gracchi brothers.
   C. supports the Republic despite its faults.
   D. idealizes the position of the wealthy landed nobility.

12. The main idea of the first paragraph is that the Julius Caesar:
   F. was the founder of the Roman Empire.
   G. was the grand-uncle of Augustus Caesar, who founded the Roman Empire.
   H. exploited the political problems at the end of the Roman Republic for his own gain.
   J. was the most successful Roman politician and general.

GO ON TO THE NEXT PAGE.

3 ████████████████████████████████ **3**

13. The author uses the remark "farmers who, by law, had to own a minimum number of acres to join the military service" (lines 18–19) primarily as an example of:
    A. the kind of useless requirements made by the Roman military.
    B. the ancient Romans' preoccupation with farming.
    C. the clash between ancient Roman agricultural society and the wealthy elite.
    D. the close traditional relationship between farming and military service.

14. The author indicates the common factor leading to the murders of the Gracchus Brothers was:
    F. aristocratic fear of political reform.
    G. mob violence due to political corruption.
    H. aristocratic desire to reform the political system.
    J. the inability of Roman senators to rent cheap land.

15. By his statement in lines 60–63, the author most nearly means that, unlike in past armies, in Marius' army:
    A. soldiers tried to set a precedent for Julius Caesar.
    B. ability meant more than social class.
    C. nobility were often put in charge of lower-class soldiers.
    D. rank was based only on popularity.

16. The author cites all of the following as actions of Cornelius Sulla EXCEPT:
    F. strengthening the power of the Senate against the Assembly.
    G. establishing himself as Dictator.
    H. peacefully resigning his dictatorship.
    J. successfully uniting his allies and opponents during his dictatorship.

17. The author uses the events listed in lines 81–85 primarily to:
    A. show Julius Caesar as a true political reformer, despite his family connections to the aristocracy.
    B. imply that Julius Caesar exploited his political connections for his own gain.
    C. imply that Julius Caesar had no choice but to support his uncle, Marius.
    D. show that the grain supply was an important basis of power in the Roman Republic.

18. The author implies that prominent Roman politicians who tried to limit the aristocratic power of the senators often were:
    F. eventually assassinated.
    B. promoted to Dictator.
    G. exiled to foreign countries.
    H. generals in the Roman army.

19. Which of the following is NOT listed in the passage as a political reform in the Roman Republic?
    A. Redistributing public land to retired soldiers.
    B. Protecting the grain supply for the unemployment dole.
    C. Extending political rights to the lower classes.
    D. Eliminating slavery in the Republic.

20. The author calls which of the following a result of political chaos?
    F. The murder of the Gracchus Brothers.
    G. The rise of Cornelius Sulla as Dictator of Rome.
    H. The rise of Augustus Caesar as Emperor of Rome.
    J. The need for retired soldiers to receive unemployment payments.

3 ████████████████████████████████████ **3**

PASSAGE III
HUMANITIES: *The Táin Bó Culainge: Early Irish Epic*

Ireland has the oldest vernacular literature in Europe. Where other early European authors wrote their literary works in Latin, the Irish began writing down their stories in their own language starting at least
5 as early as the 6th century A.D. and continuing to the modern day. While much of the earliest Irish writing has been lost or destroyed, several manuscripts survive from the late medieval period (12th through 16th centuries). These books usually contain collections of
10 stories, many of which are much older than the books themselves.

One of the most famous of these collections is the epic cycle, *The Táin Bó Culainge*, which in translation means "The Cattle Raid of Cooley." It's often abbre-
15 viated to simply *The Táin*. In its narrowest sense, the raid refers to a series of battles fought by the northern Irish province of Connacht to steal a magic bull from the neighboring province of Ulster. However, the cycle includes many other legends that together tell the
20 national story of the people of Ulster, especially during the reign of the great Ulster king, Conchobor mac Nessa.

According to *The Táin*, Queen Medb of Connacht orders the raid because there are only two magic bulls
25 in all of Ireland, and, as her husband, Aillil, has the first, she determines to acquire the second. Her determination makes more sense when one considers the laws of the time. Wives were considered legal equals to men if they came into their marriage with as much
30 or more property than their husbands. If she had less, the wife would be a legal dependent of her husband and, like a child, would have limited rights of her own. Irish queens were used to having their own political autonomy and making their own political deals. Medb's
35 insistence on equaling the property of her husband was for reasons far more serious than vanity.

During the cattle raid, Medb's forces are joined by Fergus, the former king of Ulster, and his men. The bull is defended by the current king, Conchobor,
40 and the young warrior, Cú Chulainn. The middle of the story tells of how Cú Chulainn single-handedly fends off Medb's army while Conchobor's men struggle against an ancient curse. In the end, many warriors die, both bulls are killed, and peace is re-established
45 between Connacht and Ulster.

Of course, this is merely plot. Thematically, the work explores several great issues that would occupy medieval authors for over six hundred years. One of the most important was the lovers' triangle between
50 the king, the queen, and the warrior hero. Think of the romances of King Arthur, Queen Guinevere, and Sir Lancelot, or those of Tristran, Isolde, and her husband, King Mark. In *The Táin*, Queen Medb takes up with the warrior Fergus, with the approval of her husband,
55 in order to guarantee Fergus' allegiance during the war. Of course, in the early Irish versions, the message is far more subtle than an extramarital affair. According to Irish mythology, Medb was a demigoddess—the personification of power itself. As she herself notes,
60 power never goes long without a suitor. Still, even

Medb's daughter, Finnabair, is tied linguistically to the Arthurian legend: Finnabair and Guinevere are different spellings of the same name.

At least as interesting as the raid itself are the
65 *remscéla* (literally, the "before stories") that tell how the situation for the raid came to be. The *remscéla* tell how the bulls were originally two pig-keepers who knew magic; the stories explain how the Ulstermen came to be cursed with debilitating pain whenever their
70 country was in danger. They explain who Cú Chulainn was and how he got his name. And, most poignantly, the *remscéla* tell how Fergus lost his crown and why he agreed to fight against his countrymen. This last story, told in the tragic legend of Deirdre and the Sons
75 of Usnech, is one of the most striking of all the Irish myths.

Over twelve hundred years old, *The Táin* is certainly an epic work—but epic doesn't necessarily mean "dead." If the images meet a cultural need, they can
80 come back to life as living artistic works. During the English occupation of Ireland and continuing through the Irish Revolution, many artists plumbed the depths of Irish mythology to create what they saw as an image of Ireland free of English cultural repression. Writers
85 still call on *The Táin* for inspiration, just as ancient Irish bards once called on the ghost of Fergus to tell them the true story of the Cattle Raid of Cooley.

---

21. Which of the following statements best expresses the main idea of the passage?
    A. *The Táin* tells the story of Queen Medb and the magic bull of Ulster.
    B. Stories told in the vernacular are much better than stories told in Latin.
    C. *The Táin* is an epic, one of the great national stories of Ireland, which has inspired writers for hundreds of years.
    D. *The Táin* provides an image of Ireland in the late medieval period, before the English occupation.

22. Which of the following questions is NOT answered in the passage?
    F. What is "vernacular literature?"
    G. Why did Queen Medb want the magic bull of Ulster?
    H. What does "*The Táin Bó Culainge*" mean?
    J. How did the warrior, Cú Chulainn, get his name?

23. The passage suggests that one of *The Táin's* most important contributions to Irish literature is that:
    A. it provides an inspirational image of Ireland free of English cultural repression.
    B. it illustrates the political power of women in early European countries.
    C. it personifies the ancient Irish demigods, incorporating them into one literary figure.
    D. it collects several important mythological stories into one book, making them less significant.

GO ON TO THE NEXT PAGE.

3 ▆▆▆▆▆▆▆▆▆▆▆▆▆▆▆▆▆▆▆▆▆▆▆▆ **3**

24. The main function of the second paragraph (lines 12–22) is to:
  F. give a brief description of *The Táin Bó Culainge*.
  G. introduce the Ulster king, Conchobor mac Nessa.
  H. describe Ireland's agrarian society in the early middle ages.
  J. define an "epic cycle."

25. All of the following details are used in the passage to show the range of content in *The Táin* EXCEPT:
  A. the bulls were originally pig-keepers who knew magic.
  B. the Ulstermen were cursed with debilitating pain whenever their country was attacked.
  C. Fergus was once a king of Ulster who lost his crown and subsequently agreed to fight against his old country.
  D. Deirdre was originally promised in marriage to King Conchobor.

26. The last paragraph establishes all of the following about *The Táin* EXCEPT:
  F. *The Táin* is over twelve hundred years old.
  G. once a literary work is dead, it ceases to have any cultural significance.
  H. modern writers use *The Táin* as a source of artistic inspiration.
  J. Irish bards once called on the ghost of Fergus to tell them the true story of *The Táin*.

27. One of the main points in the third paragraph (lines 23–36) is that, under medieval Irish law:
  A. bulls were important instruments of attaining political power.
  B. a king was defined as the local man who had the most cattle.
  C. children had limited legal rights.
  D. women had legal rights equal to men, but only under certain conditions.

28. According to the passage, literary lovers' triangles have included all of the following EXCEPT:
  F. Queen Medb, King Aillil, and Fergus.
  G. Queen Isolde, King Mark, and Sir Tristram.
  H. Queen Guinevere, King Arthur, and Sir Lancelot.
  J. Queen Medb, King Mark, and King Arthur.

29. The author most likely includes the information in lines 60–63 ("Still even Medb's daughter, Finnabair, … same name") to suggest that:
  A. some thematic similarities between the King Arthur story and *The Táin* are very strong.
  B. medieval authors knew that Finnabair and Guinevere were originally the same person.
  C. the King Arthur story is an English version of *The Táin*.
  D. no medieval kings could fully trust their best warriors.

30. Which of the following phrases best describe best describes why Medb wanted the magic bull of Ulster?
  F. Spiteful vanity.
  G. Marital jealousy.
  H. Serious ambition.
  J. Childish determination.

3
3

PASSAGE IV
NATURAL SCIENCE: *A Short History of Homeopathy*

Homeopathy is a system for treating physical disease and other ailments using the theory of treating "like with like." In practice, homeopathic medicine seeks substances that mimic an ailment's symptoms;
5 this sameness is considered "likeness." The substance is then diluted to infinitesimal amounts and administered to the patient in order to cure the problem. Homeopathic treatment is currently in use for everything from cancer to colds and flu, though many
10 scientists remain heavily skeptical about its efficacy.

Homeopathy was developed in the late 18th century by the German medical doctor Samuel Hahnemann. Despite being a physician himself, Hahnemann was deeply skeptical of the medical prac-
15 tices of his time. In general, 18th century medicine was founded on the theory of the four temperaments, or "humors": Choleric, Melancholic, Sanguine, and Phlegmatic. These temperaments were based on the various possible combinations of hot and cold and wet
20 and dry. A choleric, or angry, disposition meant that a person had a constitution that was essentially hot and dry. Phlegmatic, or unemotional, persons were thought to be cold and wet. Melancholy was caused by an excess of cold and dry, whereas Sanguine, or
25 passionate, persons were hot and wet.

Humors theory was first developed by the Greek physician Hippocrates, the founder of western medicine, and later expanded upon by Galen. When a person became ill, doctors believed it was because one
30 or more of the humors had come out of balance. Some of the best treatments were thought to be bloodletting and purgation —the assumption being that these treatments would effectively drain off the excess humors. Other popular treatments included blistering plasters
35 and emetics. Often the treatment proved worse than the disease. Many patients died from excessive blood-loss or were poisoned by unregulated medications. In this environment, Hahnemann's skepticism was well warranted.
40 Hahnemann first stumbled upon his theory when he was investigating a common treatment for malaria, cinchona bark. Modern scientists now know that cinchona bark contains quinine—a substance still used to treat malaria—but at the time, no one knew why
45 the bark was effective. Hahnemann chose to implement the concept of treating "like with like" by testing an undiluted dose of the bark on himself. Finding that he had symptoms similar to those of malaria sufferers, Hahnemann concluded that effective drugs must pro-
50 duce symptoms in healthy people that are similar to those produced by the diseases that the drugs would be expected to treat. Hahnemann further hypothesized that, while undiluted substances would only worsen symptoms in the sick, heavily diluted substances could
55 be effective for a cure. The doctor and his colleagues then proceeded to test a variety of substances to see what symptoms they induced, in the hopes of finding cures for diseases with similar symptoms. Perhaps not surprisingly, Hahnemann's new field of homeopa-
60 thy (i.e. "similar suffering") was met with considerable resistance from doctors comfortable with their usual practices.

In fact, Hahnemann's methodology for scientifically testing potential treatments was remarkably
65 modern. Nevertheless, his conclusions remain extraordinarily controversial. One of the main points of contention involves the standard homeopathic practice of heavy dilution to create the appropriate dose of a substance. Dilution of homeopathic substances
70 happens in stages. Hahnemann had hypothesized that shaking the solution after each dilution would imprint the molecular "memory" of the original substance into the solution, which would allow the diluted dose to be effective without the possibility of overdose or adverse
75 side effects.

Modern scientists have been unable to find any evidence to support the theory of molecular memory. In fact, the idea that diluting a substance makes it stronger runs against the principles of chemistry and physics.
80 Moreover, scientists point to a lack of standardized clinical data on homeopathic treatment. Clinical studies that do show effectiveness indicate that homeopathic cure rates are generally equal to those of placebos.

Today, many conventional medical practitioners
85 generally disregard homeopathy. Homeopathic practitioners are frequently termed quacks by conventional scientists. Nevertheless, homeopathy remains extremely popular both in the United States and abroad. In European countries such as France and England,
90 conventional doctors frequently prescribe homeopathic treatments for common illnesses such as colds and flu. Pharmacists who are trained to answer questions about the homeopathic treatments' use and desired effects then fill the prescriptions.

31. The passage mentions all of the following about the use of homeopathy to treat disease EXCEPT that:
   A. it is used to treat everything from cancer to colds and flu.
   B. it is based on the theory of treating "like with like."
   C. its doses are administered in infinitesimal amounts.
   D. it is scientifically proven to be effective.

32. According to the fifth paragraph (lines 63–75), Hahnemann hypothesized that heavily diluted substances remained effective because:
   F. shaking each dilution imprinted the molecular "memory" of the original substance into the solution.
   G. substances that were too strong often had no effect on the patient.
   H. dilution made the substance more similar to the original disease.
   J. he used modern methodology for testing potential treatments, foregoing any information learned in the past.

GO ON TO THE NEXT PAGE.

3   **3**

33. Hahnemann believed cinchona bark was an effective treatment for malaria because it caused similar symptoms when taken by a healthy person. According to the fourth paragraph, what reason would a modern scientist likely give for using cinchona bark to treat malaria?
A. Recent clinical studies show that traditional medicines can sometimes be as effective as modern medicines.
B. Clinical studies show cinchona bark is an effective treatment for malaria, but only in undiluted doses.
C. Cinchona bark contains quinine, and quinine is known to be an effective treatment for malaria.
D. No modern scientist would recommend using cinchona bark to treat malaria.

34. According to the passage, one of the reasons modern scientists are unable to find evidence to support homeopathic treatment is because:
F. homeopathic cure rates are superior to those of placebos.
G. there is a substantial amount of standardized clinical data on homeopathic treatment.
H. the theory of molecular memory is well-documented.
J. the idea that diluting a substance makes it stronger runs against the principles of chemistry and physics.

35. Information in the last paragraph indicates that:
A. homeopathy should only be used to treat colds and flu.
B. based on clinical studies, conventional scientists are unnecessarily harsh in their judgment of homeopathy.
C. despite a lack of clinical data, homeopathy remains a popular form of treatment, even with doctors and pharmacists.
D. pharmacies are the safest places to buy homeopathic treatments.

36. The passage indicates that, in the Middle Ages, illness was thought to be caused by an imbalance in the "humors" that was best treated by:
F. conditioning exercises to improve balance.
G. sitting in a sauna or steam room.
H. draining off the excess humors.
J. tilting the patient's bed to improve blood flow.

37. According to the passage, a person with a *sanguine* disposition would most likely be which of the following?
A. Hot and dry.
B. Hot and wet.
C. Cold and wet.
D. Cold and dry.

38. As it is used in line 62, the word *practices* most nearly means:
F. exercises.
G. habits.
H. medical offices.
J. methods of treatment.

39. According to the passage, why did Hahnemann use heavily diluted substances to treat patients?
A. Undiluted substances were frequently too expensive for all but the richest patients.
B. He believed undiluted substances would only worsen the patient's symptoms.
C. He believed a patient's memory of treatment was more important than the treatment itself.
D. It allowed him to use several different treatments on a single patient.

40. In the last paragraph, the author expresses which of the following beliefs about homeopathy?
F. Homeopathy is medically unproven and thus practiced only by quacks.
G. Homeopathy is a necessary form of treatment that should be widely used to help the sick.
H. Homeopathy is a controversial form of medical treatment that is frequently used, despite a lack of supporting evidence.
J. Doctors in Europe are in agreement about the effectiveness of homeopathy.

END OF THE READING TEST.
STOP! IF YOU HAVE TIME LEFT OVER, CHECK YOUR WORK ON THIS SECTION ONLY.

4 ◯ ◯ ◯ ◯ ◯ ◯ ◯ ◯ ◯ 4

SCIENCE REASONING TEST

35 Minutes—40 Questions

DIRECTIONS: This test includes seven passages, each followed by several questions. Read the passage and choose the best answer to each question. After you have selected your answer, fill in the corresponding bubble on your answer sheet. You should refer to the passages as often as necessary when answering the questions. You may NOT use a calculator on this test.

PASSAGE I

A *pluvial* lake is an ancient lake with high water levels, generally associated with times of high precipitation. Lake Bonneville was a prehistoric pluvial lake that covered much of North America's Great Basin region during the last ice age (see Figure 1). Most of the territory it covered was in present-day Utah, though parts of the lake extended into present-day Idaho and Nevada. Formed about 32,000 years ago, it existed until about 16,800 years ago, when most of the contents of the lake were released through the Red Rock Pass in Idaho.

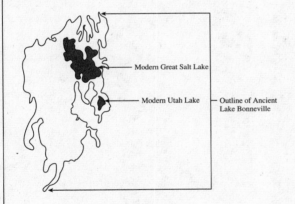

Figure 1

At more than 1,000 feet (305 m) deep and more than 19,691 square miles (50,999.5 km²) in area, Lake Bonneville was nearly as large as Lake Michigan and significantly deeper. Over time, increasing temperatures in North America caused the lake to begin drying up, leaving Great Salt Lake, Utah Lake, Sevier Lake, Rush Lake, and Little Salt Lake as remnants. While each of these lakes is considered a freshwater lake, the salinity levels are higher than normal. Figure 2 shows a cross-section of part of Utah Lake and its sediment and bedrock, with measurements taken at the cities of Genola and Provo and two test sites in between.

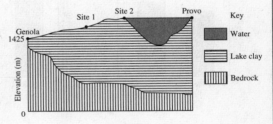

Figure 2

1. According to Figure 2, the lake clay deposit is thinnest at which of the following locations?
   A. Genola
   B. Test Site 1
   C. Test Site 2
   D. Provo

2. According to the passage, Lake Bonneville existed in its entirety for approximately how many years?
   F. 32,000
   G. 16,800
   H. 15,200
   J. Cannot be determined from the given information

3. According to Figure 2, as the thickness of the lake clay increases from Genola to Site 2, the thickness of the bedrock beneath it:
   A. increases.
   B. remains the same.
   C. first increases and then decreases.
   D. decreases.

GO ON TO THE NEXT PAGE.

4. According to Figure 2, which of the following graphs best represents the elevations, in meters above sea level, of the top of the lake clay layer at Test Sites 1 and 2?

F.

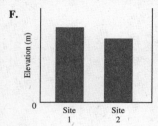

G.

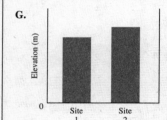

H.

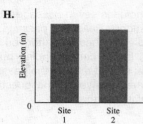

J.

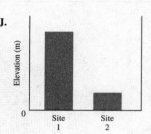

5. Great Salt Lake is fed mainly by 3 tributary rivers that deposit large amounts of minerals into its waters. The lake is salty because it has no outflow for water other than evaporation, which is predominately mineral-free. If local temperatures were to decrease significantly, while freshwater rain were to increase significantly, what would be the likely resulting change to the salinity of the Great Salt Lake?

A. Salinity would decrease.
B. Salinity would increase.
C. Salinity would remain the same.
D. Salinity cannot be predicted.

4 ○ ○ ○ ○ ○ ○ ○ ○ ○ **4**

PASSAGE II

The order *Lepidoptera* includes butterflies and moths. Table 1 is a key for identifying some Lepidoptera in North America.

Table 1			
Step	Trait	Appearance	Result
1	Body	Slim	Go to Step 2
		Fuzzy	Go to Step 3
2	Upper side of wings	Orange with black markings	*Agraulis vanillae*
		Yellow with markings	Go to Step 4
3	Upper side of wings	Brown	Go to Step 5
		Yellow	Go to Step 7
4	Underside of wings	Silver markings	Go to Step 6
		Green marbling	*Anthocharis cethura*
5	Hindwings*	Pronounced spot on wings	Go to Step 8
		No pronounced markings	*Citheronia sepulcralis*
6	Silver markings	Round and elongated	*Speyeria coronis*
		Triangular	*Speyeria zerene*
7	Underside of body	No prominent markings	*Eacles imperialis*
		Prominent brown bands	*Eacles oslari*
8	Wingspan	5–8 cm	*Automeris io*
		10–15 cm	*Antheraea polyphemus*

*The hindwings are the pair of wings farthest from the head of the butterfly or moth.

GO ON TO THE NEXT PAGE.

4 ◯ ◯ ◯ ◯ ◯ ◯ ◯ ◯ ◯ **4**

Table 2 describes 4 Lepidoptera that were seen in North America.

Table 2	
Lepidoptera	Traits
W	• Fuzzy body • Upper side of wings yellow • Prominent brown bands on the underside
X	• Slim body • Upper side of wings orange with black markings • 7.2 cm
Y	• Slim body • Upper side of wings yellow with markings • Silver, triangular-shaped markings on the underside of wings
Z	• Fuzzy body • Upper side of wings yellow • No prominent markings on the underside of body • 9.7 cm

6. Table 1 is used to identify animals that belong to which of the following groups?
   F. Birds
   G. Reptiles
   H. Insects
   J. Mammals

7. Based on the information provided, the Lepidoptera listed in Table 1 that is most closely related to *Agraulis vanillae* most likely has which of the following characteristics?
   A. Fuzzy body.
   B. Wings are orange with black markings.
   C. Hindwings have pronounced spots.
   D. Green marbling on underside of wings.

8. Based on Table 1, which of the following traits of Lepidoptera Y indicates that it is NOT a *Speyeria coronis*?
   F. Slim body.
   G. Yellow upper side of wings, with markings.
   H. Triangular, silver markings on the underside of wings.
   J. Round, elongated silver markings on the underside of wings.

9. The results from Table 1 for Lepidoptera W and Lepidoptera Z first diverge at which of the following steps?
   A. Step 1.
   B. Step 3.
   C. Step 7.
   D. Step 8.

10. According to Table 1, *Automeris io* and *Antheraea polyphemus* both have which of the following traits?
    F. Pronounced spot on hindwings.
    G. Round markings on the underside of body.
    H. A wingspan of 5–8 cm.
    J. Slim bodies.

GO ON TO THE NEXT PAGE.

4 ○ ○ ○ ○ ○ ○ ○ ○ ○ 4

PASSAGE III

A mercury thermometer, at an initial temperature of 20°C, was placed in 40°C water, and the temperature registered by the thermometer was recorded over time. This procedure was repeated using water samples at 50°C and 60°C (see Figure 1). Next, the same thermometer, at an initial temperature of 60°C, was placed in an air sample at 50°C, and the temperature registered by the thermometer was recorded over time. This procedure was repeated using air samples at 30°C and 40°C (see Figure 2).

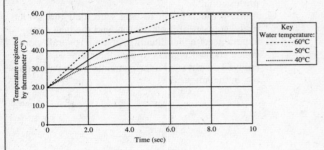

Figure 1

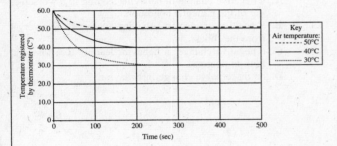

Figure 2

(Note: Assume that the temperatures of the water and air samples did not change during the measurements.)

11. Based on Figure 1, at 3.0 sec, the thermometer reading in the 40°C water most likely was closest to which of the following?
    A. 47°C.
    B. 42°C.
    C. 36°C.
    D. 31°C.

12. According to Figure 2, for an air temperature of 30°C, over which of the following time intervals was the thermometer reading changing most rapidly?
    F. 0–100 sec.
    G. 100–200 sec.
    H. 200–300 sec.
    J. 300–400 sec.

13. When the thermometer was in the 40°C water, in the time interval between 0 sec and 2 sec, approximately how rapidly, in °C/sec, was the temperature registered by the thermometer changing?
    A. 1°C/sec.
    B. 5°C/sec.
    C. 10°C/sec.
    D. 40°C/sec.

14. Based on Figure 2, if the thermometer, at an initial temperature of 60°C, had been placed in an air sample at 20°C, how long would it most likely have taken the thermometer reading to reach 20°C?
    F. Less than 10 sec.
    G. Between 10 and 50 sec.
    H. Between 50 and 100 sec.
    J. Greater than 100 sec.

15. According to the passage, at which of the following did the thermometer register the highest reading?
    A. Water temperature 60°, 4.0 sec.
    B. Water temperature 60°, 2.0 sec.
    C. Water temperature 50°, 4.0 sec.
    D. Water temperature 50°, 2.0 sec.

GO ON TO THE NEXT PAGE.

4 ○ ○ ○ ○ ○ ○ ○ ○ **4**

PASSAGE IV

Clinical research has become an important element in the development of modern medicine. Perhaps one of the most widely-debated issues in today's clinical research is the use of *placebos*, treatments believed to be biologically ineffective but used anyway for psychological or experimental purposes; an example of a placebo is a sugar pill, which contains no medication. In the realm of clinical research, placebos are used to establish a control group within the pool of research participants. A certain percentage of research patients are administered the test treatment, and another percentage is administered a placebo treatment. Patients are not informed of which percentage they are a part.

For various reasons, the use of placebos in clinical research is a controversial issue. Two scientists debate whether the use of placebos is a good or bad practice in research.

Scientist 1

Placebos are an important aspect of clinical research for many reasons. Not only do they establish a control group for the test treatment in question, but they also help address the issue of mind over matter, which is an important issue when working towards treatment for a particular illness. The body is a powerful life force, with natural recuperative abilities. A placebo encourages such recuperation.

Placebos also address the psychological aspect of illness. Because patients are unaware of whether they are receiving treatment or a placebo, the possibility of receiving treatment often provides patients with a psychological boost. The use of placebos addresses the question of whether a person's positive attitude may be important in recovery from illness. As a result, the placebo effect—a change in the patient's condition due to the idea of treatment, rather than its biological effectiveness—may be a measurable change in behavior as a result of the belief in treatment.

For both their physical and psychological benefits, placebos should be used in clinical research.

Scientist 2

There are many reasons why placebos shouldn't be used in clinical research. For example, placebos encourage deception in the doctor-patient relationship. Because this relationship is crucial to the confidence of both the doctor and the patient, and therefore the overall success of the patient's involvement in a study, placebos not only deceive patients, but can also have an adverse affect on research results. Placebos also violate patients' autonomy, or their right to choose treatment. While they can choose to be involved in a study, patients are unable to select their own course of treatment because it chosen for them.

Some argue that the placebo is worth its implementation in order to evaluate for the occurrence of the placebo effect. However, such action may skew the results of the study. For example, placebo-related changes could be over-estimated. Different illnesses, by definition, will react differently to the placebo. For example, in the instance of chronic pain or mood disorders, it's possible for patients to show spontaneous improvement. The placebo effect can also result from

contact with doctors or a respected professional. Patients are vulnerable to their environment, which significantly affects the psychological results of the placebo.

Due to its capability to skew research results, the placebo shouldn't be used in clinical research.

16. Which of the following is most consistent with the reasons supporting the use of placebos in clinical research? Many patients administered a placebo during a study:
    F. found it very difficult to trust their various medical professionals.
    G. found it much easier to deal with their illness due to the support of their doctors and medical team.
    H. experienced a heightening in their overall confidence and willingness to beat their illnesses.
    J. enjoyed no physical improvements while participating in the study.

17. According to Scientist 1's viewpoint, the placebo effect often reveals in the patient:
    A. a negative change in behavior leading to a worsening of the patient's condition.
    B. a positive change in behavior leading to recovery from the illness.
    C. a negative change in behavior leading to a loss of faith in doctors.
    D. no discernable change in behavior.

18. According to the passage, both Scientists agree that:
    F. the implementation of the placebo is worthwhile for the evaluation of the placebo effect.
    G. the use of placebos can cause the placebo effect in patients.
    H. few patients experience any sort of a response to placebos.
    J. placebos are valuable for both their physical and psychological effects on the body.

19. According to Scientist 2's viewpoint, which of the following observations provides the strongest argument against using placebos in clinical research?
    A. The fact that patients sometimes deceive researchers
    B. The danger of adverse reactions to sugar pills
    C. The potential to skew the results of the research
    D. The possibility that patients might choose ineffective treatments

GO ON TO THE NEXT PAGE.

4 ◯ ◯ ◯ ◯ ◯ ◯ ◯ ◯ **4**

20. An evaluation of several placebo-using studies found that those patients who were involved were not only very trusting of their doctors and medical teams, but they were also more willing to communicate the various effects the treatment was having on them. This finding contradicts evidence stated in which viewpoint?
   F. Scientist 1's viewpoint, because the patients had a positive relationship with their doctors.
   G. Scientist 1's viewpoint, because use of the placebos discouraged the medical team from obtaining accurate results.
   H. Scientist 2's viewpoint, because placebos are a critical component in any clinical study.
   J. Scientist 2's viewpoint, because the placebo studies encouraged rather than discouraged communication between doctors and patients.

21. Scientist 1's viewpoint implies that Scientist 2's viewpoint would be *weakened* by which of the following observations?
   A. All patients in a control group recover less quickly than the patients receiving medical treatment.
   B. Some patients seem to benefit from choosing their own treatments.
   C. A patient who learns that she has been given a placebo becomes ill.
   D. A patient who is given a sugar pill develops new symptoms due to an allergic reaction to the pill.

22. Which of the following assumptions about the use of placebos is implicit in Scientist 1's viewpoint?
   F. Placebos are more cost-effective than other research tools.
   G. Placebos are significantly more difficult to administer than real medications.
   H. Real experimental medications are often dangerous to patients.
   J. The use of placebos is safe for most patients.

GO ON TO THE NEXT PAGE.

PASSAGE V

Near the end of the 19th century, British engineer Osborne Reynolds ran a set of experiments to observe and predict the transition between *laminar* (steady) and turbulent flow of a liquid through a pipe. In Reynolds' experiments, dye was forced through a liquid to show visually when the flow changed from laminar to turbulent. Laminar flow is common only in cases in which the flow channel is relatively small, the fluid is moving slowly, and its *viscosity* (the degree to which a fluid resists flow under an applied force) is relatively high. In turbulent flow, the speed of the fluid at any given point is continuously undergoing changes in both magnitude and direction. Reynolds demonstrated that the transition from laminar to turbulent flow in a pipe depends upon the value of a mathematical quantity equal to the velocity of flow (V) times the diameter of the tube (D) times the mass density (ρ) of the fluid divided by its absolute viscosity (μ). The "Reynolds number," as it is called, is determined by the following equation:

$$R = \frac{\rho VD}{\mu}$$

Several students designed similar experiments to observe flow rates of different liquids. To conduct the experiments, the students were given the following apparatus:

- Liquid supply tank with clear test section tube and 'bell mouth' entrance
- 1 Rotameter to measure the velocity of flow (flow rate)
- Tap water
- Motor oil
- 4, 10-ft long smooth pipes of various diameters: 0.25-inch, 0.50-inch, 0.75-inch, 1.0-inch

Figure 1 illustrates an approximation of the set-up of each experiment.

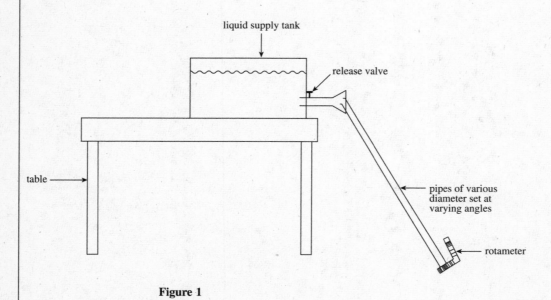

Figure 1

GO ON TO THE NEXT PAGE.

4 ◯ ◯ ◯ ◯ ◯ ◯ ◯ ◯ ◯ **4**

Figure 2 shows approximate viscosities of the water and motor oils used in the experiments.

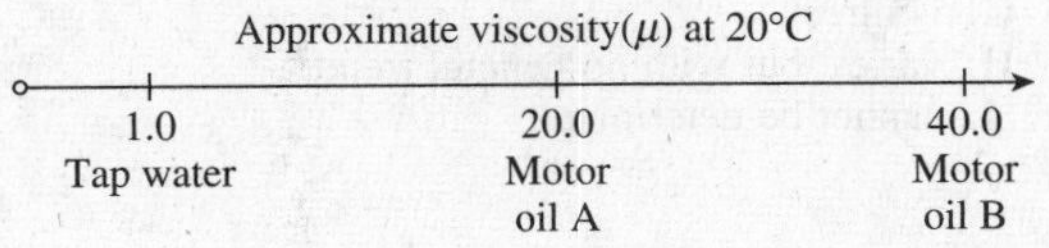

Approximate viscosity(μ) at 20°C

1.0	20.0	40.0
Tap water	Motor oil A	Motor oil B

Figure 2

Experiment 1

In Experiment 1, students began with a pipe of diameter 0.25 inches. The pipe was set first at a 15° angle and tap water was released steadily from the tank into the pipe. The velocity of flow (V) was measured. The pipe was then set at a 30° angle, a 45° angle, and a 60° angle, water was released steadily from the tank into the pipe, and the velocity of flow was measured. The process was then repeated for each diameter of pipe using the same amount of water each time. All data were recorded in Table 1. Temperature of the water was held constant at 20°C.

Table 1		
D (in)	Angle of pipe	V(ft/s)
0.25	15°	2.0
	30°	4.0
	45°	6.5
	60°	8.0
0.50	15°	5.0
	30°	9.0
	45°	12.5
	60°	15.0
0.75	15°	8.0
	30°	12.5
	45°	16.0
	60°	20.0
1.00	15°	10.5
	30°	15.0
	45°	18.5
	60°	25.0

Experiment 2

In the second experiment, the tap water was replaced by Motor Oil A and the processes were repeated. The results are given in Table 2.

Table 2		
D (in)	Angle of pipe	V(ft/s)
0.25	15°	1.0
	30°	2.5
	45°	4.0
	60°	6.5
0.50	15°	3.0
	30°	5.5
	45°	7.0
	60°	9.5
0.75	15°	5.0
	30°	7.5
	45°	9.0
	60°	12.5
1.00	15°	7.0
	30°	10.5
	45°	12.0
	60°	18.5

GO ON TO THE NEXT PAGE.

Experiment 3

In a third experiment, the tap water was replaced by Motor Oil B and the processes were repeated.

Table 3		
D (in)	Angle of pipe	V(ft/s)
0.25	15°	.50
	30°	.75
	45°	1.0
	60°	3.0
0.50	15°	1.0
	30°	2.0
	45°	3.5
	60°	5.0
0.75	15°	2.5
	30°	4.0
	45°	6.5
	60°	10.5
1.00	15°	3.0
	30°	5.5
	45°	8.0
	60°	12.5

23. Information in the passage and the results of the experiments indicate which of the following? Compared to tap water, Motor Oil A:
   A. has a lower viscosity.
   B. has a higher viscosity.
   C. has an overall higher flow rate.
   D. does not exhibit laminar flow.

24. Based on Experiment 1, the relationship between the angle of the pipe and the velocity of flow:
   F. is indirect.
   G. is direct.
   H. varies, but with no general trend.
   J. cannot be determined.

25. According to the passage, laminar flow was *most* likely to be observed under which of the following conditions?
   A. Experiment 1, pipe diameter of 0.50 in, pipe angle of 45°.
   B. Experiment 3, pipe diameter of 0.50 in, pipe angle of 15°.
   C. Experiment 1, pipe diameter of 1.0 in, pipe angle of 30°.
   D. Experiment 3, pipe diameter of 1.0 in, pipe angle of 60°.

26. Which of the following conclusions is best supported by information in the passage? As viscosity increases:
   A. laminar flow decreases.
   B. velocity of flow increases.
   C. velocity of flow decreases.
   D. laminar flow cannot be measured.

27. In Experiment 1, at a 30° angle, flow rate would most likely have been approximately 6.0 ft/s for which new pipe diameter?
   A. 0.4 in
   B. 0.6 in
   C. 0.8 in
   D. 1.2 in

28. All of the experimental factors were identical EXCEPT:
   F. the length of the pipes.
   G. the amount of liquid released into each pipe.
   H. the type of liquid used.
   J. the apparatus used to measure flow rate.

GO ON TO THE NEXT PAGE.

PASSAGE VI

Certain preservatives known as *sulfites* are often added to fruit products to keep the fruit fresher longer. Use of sulfites is controversial because studies have linked sulfites to severe reactions in some asthmatics. Students performed 2 experiments to measure sulfite levels.

Experiment 1

Four solutions, each containing a different amount of sulfite dissolved in H_2O were prepared. A coloring agent was added that binds with sulfite to form a red compound that strongly absorbs light of a specific wavelength, and each solution was diluted to 100 mL. A *blank* solution was prepared in the same manner, but no sulfite was added. A *colorimeter* (a device that measures how much light of a selected wavelength is absorbed by a sample) was used to measure the *absorbance* of each solution. The absorbances were corrected by subtracting the absorbance of the blank solution from each reading (see Table 1 and Figure 1).

Table 1		
Concentration of SO_3^{-2}(ppm*)	Measured absorbance	Corrected absorbance
0.0	0.130	0.000
1.0	0.283	0.153
2.0	0.432	0.302
4.0	0.730	0.600
8.0	1.350	1.220
*ppm is parts per million		

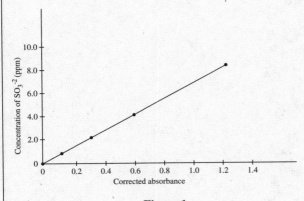

Figure 1

Experiment 2

A 100 g fruit sample was ground in a food processor with 50 mL of H_2O and the mixture was filtered. The food processor and remaining fruit were then washed with H_2O, these washings were filtered, and the liquid was added to the sample solution. The coloring agent was added and the solution was diluted to 100 mL. The procedure was repeated for several fruits, and the absorbances were measured (see Table 2).

Table 2		
Fruit	Corrected absorbance	Concentration of SO_3^{-2}(ppm)
craisins	0.668	4.4
prunes	0.562	3.7
banana chips	0.031	0.2
raisins	0.941	6.2
dried apricots	0.774	5.1

29. Based on the results of Experiment 1, if the concentration of sulfite in a solution is doubled, then the corrected absorbance of the solution will approximately:
    A. remain the same.
    B. halve.
    C. double.
    D. quadruple.

30. A sample of dried pineapple was also measured in Experiment 2 and its corrected absorbance was determined to be 0.603. Which of the following correctly lists prunes, apricots, and dried pineapple in *decreasing* order of sulfite concentration?
    F. Prunes, dried apricots, dried pineapple.
    G. Dried pineapple, apricots, prunes.
    H. Prunes, dried pineapple, dried apricots.
    J. Dried apricots, dried pineapple, prunes.

31. Based on the results of Experiment 1, if a solution with a concentration of 1.5 ppm sulfite had been tested, the corrected absorbance would have been closest to which of the following values?
    A. 0.160
    B. 0.240
    C. 0.300
    D. 0.360

GO ON TO THE NEXT PAGE.

32. If Experiments 1 and 2 were repeated using a different coloring agent that produces a different color when it binds with sulfite, which of the following changes in procedure would be necessary?

   F. The new coloring agent should be added to the blank solution, but not to the sample solutions.

   G. Both of the coloring agents should be added to the blank solution and to all of the samples.

   H. The absorbance of the blank solution made with the new coloring agent should be added to the measured absorbances.

   J. The colorimeter should be set to measure at a different wavelength of light.

33. Based on the results of Experiments 1 and 2, if the measured absorbances for the fruits tested in Experiment 2 were compared with their corrected absorbances, the measured absorbances would be:

   A. higher for all of the fruits tested.

   B. lower for all of the fruits tested.

   C. lower for some of the fruits tested, higher for others.

   D. the same for all of the fruits tested.

34. If some of the water-soluble contents found in all of the fruits tested in Experiment 2 absorbed light of the same wavelength as the compound formed with sulfite and the coloring agent, how would the measurements have been affected? Compared to the actual sulfite concentrations, the sulfite concentrations apparently measured would be:

   F. higher.

   G. lower.

   H. the same.

   J. higher for some of the fruits, lower for others.

GO ON TO THE NEXT PAGE.

PASSAGE VII

The molar heat of fusion is the amount of heat necessary to melt (or freeze) 1.00 mole of a substance at its melting point at a constant pressure. The molar heat of fusion for water is 6.02 kilojoules per mole (kJ/mol).

The equation for molar heat of fusion is:

$$q = \Delta H_{fus}(\text{mass/molar mass})$$

In this equation, q is the total amount of heat involved, ΔH_{fus} represents the molar heat of fusion (this value is a constant for a given substance), and (mass/molar mass) represents the number of moles of a given substance.

The following table lists molar heats of fusion, boiling points, and melting points for several elements.

Element	Melting point (°C)	Boiling point (°C)	ΔH_{fus} (kJ/mol)
Calcium	839.00	1,484.00	8.54
Silver	961.92	2,212.00	11.30
Iron	1,535.00	2,750.00	13.80
Nickel	1,453.00	2,732.00	17.46
Note: measured at a pressure of 1 atmosphere (atm).			

35. According to the passage, ΔH_{fus} of water:
   A. is less than ΔH_{fus} of calcium.
   B. is greater than ΔH_{fus} of calcium.
   C. is greater than ΔH_{fus} of nickel.
   D. cannot be determined.

36. The energy required to melt 1.00 mole of iron at 1,535°C and constant pressure of 1 atm is:
   F. 6.02 kJ.
   G. 8.54 kJ.
   H. 13.80 kJ.
   J. 2,750.00 kJ.

37. According to the table, as the energy required to melt 1 mole of the given elements increases, the melting points:
   A. increase only.
   B. decrease only.
   C. increase then decrease.
   D. neither increase nor decrease.

38. The boiling point of potassium is 759.90°C. If potassium follows the general pattern of the other elements in the table, its heat of fusion would be:
   F. below 8 kJ/mol.
   G. between 8 and 11 kJ/mol.
   H. between 11 and 14 kJ/mol.
   J. between 14 and 18 kJ/mol.

39. Molar heat of fusion is directly related to the strength of the forces that hold molecules together; strong forces make it difficult for molecules to break away into the liquid or gaseous phase. Data in the table support the conclusion that those forces are stronger in:
   A. calcium than in silver.
   B. silver than in nickel.
   C. iron than in calcium.
   D. iron than in nickel.

40. It was hypothesized that the heat of fusion will increase as the boiling point increases. Based on the data in the table, which of the following pairs of elements support(s) this hypothesis?
   I. Nickel and iron
   II. Water and calcium
   III. Silver and iron
   F. I only
   G. III only
   H. II and III only
   J. I, II, and III

END OF THE SCIENCE REASONING TEST.
STOP! IF YOU HAVE TIME LEFT OVER, CHECK YOUR WORK ON THIS SECTION ONLY.

WRITING TEST PROMPT

DIRECTIONS: This test is designed to assess your writing skills. You have 30 minutes to plan and write an essay based on the stimulus provided. Be sure to take a position on the issue and support your position using logical reasoning and relevant examples. Organize your ideas in a focused and logical way, and use the English language to clearly and effectively express your position.

When you have finished writing, refer to the Scoring Rubrics discussed in the Introduction (page 4) to estimate your score.

Some public high schools have started to offer single-sex education, meaning that boys and girls are taught separately in classes such as chemistry and mathematics. Those in favor believe that, as long as the educational opportunities are equal, separation of the sexes is the best method because there are fewer distractions. They argue that, in separated classes, students are less likely to act out gender stereotypes. Those opposed reply that separate is never equal. They believe that single-sex education is a recipe for gender discrimination. In your opinion, should public high schools offer single-sex education?

In your essay, take a position on this question. You may write about either one of the two points of view given, or you may present a different point of view on this question. Use specific reasons and examples to support your position.

ANSWER KEY

English Test

1. C	21. B	41. A	61. C
2. F	22. F	42. J	62. J
3. D	23. C	43. C	63. B
4. F	24. H	44. F	64. H
5. D	25. C	45. D	65. D
6. H	26. F	46. G	66. G
7. A	27. D	47. B	67. D
8. J	28. F	48. F	68. F
9. B	29. D	49. C	69. D
10. F	30. G	50. F	70. F
11. C	31. C	51. D	71. A
12. J	32. G	52. G	72. G
13. B	33. D	53. C	73. C
14. G	34. J	54. G	74. G
15. A	35. B	55. A	75. B
16. J	36. J	56. F	
17. B	37. B	57. A	
18. F	38. J	58. H	
19. D	39. D	59. C	
20. G	40. F	60. H	

Mathematics Test

1. D	21. A	41. B
2. H	22. K	42. H
3. A	23. C	43. A
4. H	24. K	44. J
5. D	25. D	45. B
6. K	26. G	46. K
7. C	27. A	47. D
8. J	28. F	48. J
9. C	29. E	49. D
10. J	30. G	50. G
11. D	31. D	51. B
12. J	32. F	52. J
13. E	33. B	53. E
14. H	34. H	54. J
15. D	35. E	55. E
16. J	36. G	56. J
17. C	37. C	57. A
18. J	38. J	58. K
19. B	39. C	59. D
20. G	40. G	60. G

Reading Test

1. B	21. C
2. F	22. J
3. D	23. A
4. G	24. F
5. B	25. D
6. H	26. G
7. A	27. D
8. J	28. J
9. C	29. A
10. F	30. H
11. A	31. D
12. H	32. F
13. D	33. C
14. F	34. J
15. B	35. C
16. J	36. H
17. A	37. B
18. F	38. J
19. D	39. B
20. H	40. H

Science Reasoning Test

1. A	21. A
2. H	22. J
3. D	23. B
4. G	24. G
5. A	25. B
6. H	26. C
7. B	27. A
8. H	28. H
9. C	29. C
10. F	30. J
11. C	31. B
12. F	32. A
13. B	33. A
14. J	34. F
15. A	35. A
16. H	36. H
17. B	37. C
18. G	38. F
19. C	39. C
20. J	40. H

▬▬ SCORING GUIDE

Your final reported score is your COMPOSITE SCORE. Your COMPOSITE SCORE is the average of all of your SCALE SCORES.

Your SCALE SCORES for the four multiple-choice sections are derived from the Scoring Table on the next page. Use your RAW SCORE, or the number of questions that you answered correctly for each section, to determine your SCALE SCORE. If you got a RAW SCORE of 60 on the English test, for example, you correctly answered 60 out of 75 questions.

Step 1 Determine your RAW SCORE for each of the four multiple-choice sections:

English   _____

Mathematics   _____

Reading   _____

Science Reasoning   _____

The following Raw Score Table shows the total possible points for each section.

RAW SCORE TABLE	
KNOWLEDGE AND SKILL AREAS	**RAW SCORES**
ENGLISH	75
MATHEMATICS	60
READING	40
SCIENCE REASONING	40
WRITING	12

Multiple-Choice Scoring Worksheet

Step 2 Determine your SCALE SCORE for each of the four multiple-choice sections using the following Scoring Worksheet. Each SCALE SCORE should be rounded to the nearest number according to normal rules. For example, $31.2 \approx 31$ and $31.5 \approx 32$. If you answered 61 questions correctly on the English section, for example, your SCALE SCORE would be 29.

English _____ $\times$ **36** = _____ $\div$ **75** = _____
RAW SCORE

$\underline{-2}$ (*correction factor)

_____
SCALE SCORE

Mathematics _____ $\times$ **36** = _____ $\div$ **60** = _____
RAW SCORE

$\underline{+1}$ (*correction factor)

_____
SCALE SCORE

Reading _____ $\times$ **36** = _____ $\div$ **40** = _____
RAW SCORE

$\underline{+2}$ (*correction factor)

_____
SCALE SCORE

Science Reasoning _____ $\times$ **36** = _____ $\div$ **40** = _____
RAW SCORE

$\underline{+1.5}$ (*correction factor)

_____
SCALE SCORE

*The correction factor is an approximation based on the average from several recent ACT tests. It is most valid for scores in the middle 50% (approximately 16–24 scale composite score) of the scoring range.

The scores are all approximate. Actual ACT scoring scales vary from one administration to the next based upon several factors.

If you take the optional Writing Test, you will need to combine your English and Writing scores to obtain your final COMPOSITE SCORE. Once you have determined a score for your essay out of 12 possible points, you will need to determine your ENGLISH/WRITING SCALE SCORE, using both your ENGLISH SCALE SCORE and your WRITING TEST SCORE. The combination of the two scores will give you an ENGLISH/WRITING SCALE SCORE, from 1 to 36, that will be used to determine your COMPOSITE SCORE mentioned earlier.

Using the English/Writing Scoring Table, find your ENGLISH SCALE SCORE on the left or right hand side of the table and your WRITING TEST SCORE on the top of the table. Follow your ENGLISH SCALE SCORE over and your WRITING TEST SCORE down until the two columns meet at a number. This number is your ENGLISH/WRITING SCALE SCORE and will be used to determine your COMPOSITE SCORE.

Step 3 Determine your ENGLISH/WRITING SCALE SCORE using the English/Writing Scoring Table on the following page:

English _____

Writing _____

English/Writing _____

ENGLISH/WRITING SCORING TABLE

ENGLISH SCALE SCORE	WRITING TEST SCORE											ENGLISH SCALE SCORE
	2	3	4	5	6	7	8	9	10	11	12	
36	26	27	28	29	30	31	32	33	34	32	36	36
35	26	27	28	29	30	31	31	32	33	34	35	35
34	25	26	27	28	29	30	31	32	33	34	35	34
33	24	25	26	27	28	29	30	31	32	33	34	33
32	24	25	25	26	27	28	29	30	31	32	33	32
31	23	24	25	26	27	28	29	30	30	31	32	31
30	22	23	24	25	26	27	28	29	30	31	32	30
29	21	22	23	24	25	26	27	28	29	30	31	29
28	21	22	23	24	24	25	26	27	28	29	30	28
27	20	21	22	23	24	25	26	27	28	28	29	27
26	19	20	21	22	23	24	25	26	27	28	29	26
25	18	19	20	21	22	23	24	25	26	27	28	25
24	18	19	20	21	22	23	23	24	25	26	27	24
23	17	18	19	20	21	22	23	24	25	26	27	23
22	16	17	18	19	20	21	22	23	24	25	26	22
21	16	17	17	18	19	20	21	22	23	24	25	21
20	15	16	17	18	19	20	21	21	22	23	24	20
19	14	15	16	17	18	19	20	21	22	23	24	19
18	13	14	15	16	17	18	19	20	21	22	23	18
17	13	14	15	16	16	17	18	19	20	21	22	17
16	12	13	14	15	16	17	18	19	20	20	21	16
15	11	12	13	14	15	16	17	18	19	20	21	15
14	10	11	12	13	14	15	16	17	18	19	20	14
13	10	11	12	13	14	14	15	16	17	18	19	13
12	9	10	11	12	13	14	15	16	17	18	19	12
11	8	9	10	11	12	13	14	15	16	17	18	11
10	8	9	9	10	11	12	13	14	15	16	17	10
9	7	8	9	10	11	12	13	13	14	15	16	9
8	6	7	8	9	10	11	12	13	14	15	16	8
7	5	6	7	8	9	10	11	12	13	14	15	7
6	5	6	7	7	8	9	10	11	12	13	14	6
5	4	5	6	7	8	9	10	11	12	12	13	5
4	3	4	5	6	7	8	9	10	11	12	13	4
3	2	3	4	5	6	7	8	9	10	11	12	3
2	2	3	4	5	6	6	7	8	9	10	11	2
1	1	2	3	4	5	6	7	8	9	10	11	1

Step 4 Determine your COMPOSITE SCORE by finding the sum of all your SCALE SCORES for each of the four sections: English only (if you do not choose to take the optional Writing Test) *or* English/Writing (if you choose to take the optional Writing Test), Math, Reading, and Science Reasoning, and divide by 4 to find the average. Round your COMPOSITE SCORE according to normal rules. For example, $31.2 \approx 31$ and $31.5 \approx 32$.

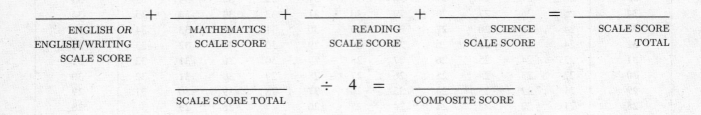

_____ + _____ + _____ + _____ = _____

ENGLISH *OR*   MATHEMATICS   READING   SCIENCE   SCALE SCORE

ENGLISH/WRITING   SCALE SCORE   SCALE SCORE   SCALE SCORE   TOTAL

SCALE SCORE

_____ ÷ 4 = _____

SCALE SCORE TOTAL   COMPOSITE SCORE

ANSWERS AND EXPLANATIONS

English Test Explanations

PASSAGE I

1. **The best answer is C.** The modifier *that* should be used to reference a specific year; because the actual year is not stated in the passage, the underlined portion should be changed to *this*, which clarifies the sentence and provides context. It is not appropriate here to use the article *a* before the noun *year*, so eliminate answer choice B. Omitting the underlined portion creates an incomplete sentence, so eliminate answer choice D.

2. **The best answer is F.** The adjective *careful* correctly modifies the verb phrase *monitoring of*. This choice also indicates the writer's direct involvement—answer choices G and H are not controlled by the writer, and answer choice J does not indicate any action on the part of the writer.

3. **The best answer is D.** It is correct to use the past tense verb *instigated* to match the tense used throughout the paragraph.

4. **The best answer is F.** This sentence is correct as written. It is in the active voice and correctly uses the infinitive *to witness*. Answer choice G suggests that witnessing the transformation was the method by which the author arrived home, which doesn't make sense. Answer choices H and J are awkward and do not effectively convey the intended idea.

5. **The best answer is D.** The phrase *upon our return* is redundant because the writer has already stated that they had arrived back home. Answer choices B and C are also redundant for the same reason.

6. **The best answer is H.** The phrase *the local deer population* correctly identifies the subject of the clause. The pronoun *they* is an unnecessary addition in both answer choices F and G. In answer choice J, *they* would have referred logically to the plants, which doesn't make sense.

7. **The best answer is A.** The focus of the paragraph is the condition of the vegetable garden. The writer is painting a detailed picture of the garden, so the level of detail is appropriate. The construction of the garden fence comes later and is irrelevant at this point, which eliminates answer choices B and C.

8. **The best answer is J.** The writer's use of the word *comical* conveys the idea of humor. Only answer choice J adds to that idea without being redundant, while also being grammatically correct.

9. **The best answer is B.** The phrase *needed to be remedied immediately* is a nonrestrictive clause. This means it could be eliminated from the sentence and the sentence would still make sense. Nonrestrictive clauses take the pronoun *which*. Answer choice C is wrong because *deterring* modifies *qualities* and therefore should not be separated from it by a comma.

10. **The best answer is F.** Answer choice F implies sophistication and detailed preparation, both of which indicate time-consuming planning. Answer choices G, H, and J are vague. They add very little to communicate the writer's message.

11. **The best answer is C.** Answer choices A, B, and D all indicate a sequence of time where the writer first goes to the hardware store and then arranges her tools, which she logically implies were purchased at the store. Answer choice C reverses the sequence and, therefore, doesn't make sense.

12. **The best answer is J.** Answer choices F, G, and H convey the same idea of a difficult task. While some are wordier than absolutely necessary, all three are grammatically correct. Answer choice J, however, is neither grammatically correct, nor idiomatic.

13. **The best answer is B.** Only answer choice B matches the tone of the rest of the passage, while providing the same degree of description. Answer choice D is too wordy and awkward, while answer choices A and C do not provide the level of detail offered in the rest of the passage.

14. **The best answer is G.** The descriptive clause *swift and beautiful leapers* should refer to the subject of the sentence. Only answer choice G has the subject *deer*. In the other choices, the subject is *the newness and appearance of the enclosure*, which cannot be modified by the clause *swift and beautiful leapers*.

15. **The best answer is A.** This question really asks which preposition should follow *we sit down*. A person sits down *to* eat something—in this case, a variety of vegetables. Simplifying the sentence allows you to hear the correct idiomatic form.

PASSAGE II

16. The best answer is J. The idea of surprise is already expressed by the word *unexpected*. Therefore, *surprisingly* is redundant and should be omitted.

17. The best answer is B. The adverb *truly* is used here as an interjection to express wonder. Answer choice B changes the tone to something more objectively descriptive. Because of this change, the choice is NOT acceptable.

18. The best answer is F. The clause that begins *as they enjoy* is not a complete sentence. Therefore, answer choices G and J should be eliminated. Answer choice H places a comma after *as*, which breaks up its clause. However, the phrase *Viewing these birds can be difficult* is a complete thought and can be separated from the following clause by a comma.

19. The best answer is D. The beginning of this paragraph focuses on a physical description of the Wood Thrush and where it likes to perch. Without the information about migration, a reader might assume these details explain when the bird is seen in the United States. This would be misleading, because the real explanation is the bird's migration pattern. Therefore, D is the correct answer choice.

20. The best answer is G. The singular possessive pronoun refers back to a singular subject: *the Wood Thrush*. Therefore, answer choices H and J are incorrect. The word *it's* is a contraction of *it is*, so answer choice F is incorrect.

21. The best answer is B. This introductory clause needs a preposition to indicate duration of time. Answer choices A, C, and D all have prepositions that place the action of nesting in a temporal sequence. Only answer choice B lacks the preposition, which makes the clause awkward and incomplete.

22. The best answer is F. The underlined portion is a complete thought. This means it does not require commas to separate its ideas. Answer choice H places too much emphasis on *in distinct parts*, which is not supported by the focus of the sentence.

23. The best answer is C. The writer wants to give the idea of the listener learning new things about the Wood Thrush's song *over time*. All of the answer choices have a sense of duration *except* answer choice C. Answer choice C implies that the listener learns something at the beginning of the song only; the learning process does not continue as the song continues. Therefore, answer choice C is the correct answer choice.

24. The best answer is H. The underlined portion introduces a subordinate clause that explains the action of the main clause (i.e. the bird has stopped singing because it's exhausted). All of the answer choices could be used in a subordinate clause, but, apart from answer choice H, they would need additional words to make grammatical sense. For example, answer choice J would have to read: *and so indicates* in order to make sense. Answer choice H contains a participle clause that stands on its own. The addition of the relative pronoun *that* (answer choice F) is unnecessary.

25. The best answer is C. The added sentence gives more detail about the songs that the writer begins to describe in sentences 4 through 6. Therefore, answer choices A and B are too early in the paragraph to be correct. By sentence 7, the topic has shifted to why the songs have ended. Only sentence 6 (answer choice C) places the additional information in the correct context with other details about the Wood Thrush songs.

26. The best answer is F. In the next paragraph, the writer describes the bird's continuing urge to sing, even after each act exhausts him. Only answer choice F introduces that idea to the reader. The other answer choices are either irrelevant, like answer choice H, or mis-focused, like answer choices G and J.

27. The best answer is D. The underlined portion is in the main clause of the sentence and needs an active verb. Because the writer is using the present tense, only answer choice D, *will start*, is consistent. Answer choices B and C are forms of the past tense. Answer choice A is a participle and would only be appropriate in a subordinate clause.

28. The best answer is F. The phrase *harmonious musical arrangement* is the most specific and precise because it gives the most detail about the sound itself. The other answer choices are vague and less descriptive.

29. The best answer is D. The *chosen female and subsequent offspring* belong to the Wood Thrush male. Therefore, the possessive form needs to be used. Answer choices B and C are incorrect because *chosen* is an adjective modifying *female*, indicating that the female is the Thrush's mate; the verb phrase, *are begging*, comes later.

30. The best answer is G. The subordinate clause describes what the female and offspring are begging the male to do. Consequently, the infinitive clause *to keep singing* is correct. Answer choice H implies that the female and offspring are the ones singing. Answer choices F and J are awkward and grammatically incorrect.

PASSAGE III

31. The best answer is C. The singular noun *America* must be in the possessive form.

32. The best answer is G. The underlined portion contains the sentence's main verb. Answer choices F, H, and J all have active voice verbs that would be acceptable in the passage. Answer choice G has only an *–ing* participle, *being*, which doesn't work as a main verb, and is NOT acceptable.

33. The best answer is D. The writer explains that other members of the group wrote the journals. Therefore, no modifier is necessary before the word *journals*, and answer choice D is correct.

34. The best answer is J. The addition is not necessary because it is off topic. Both the preceding paragraph and the following paragraph focus on Sacajawea's life and personality. Clark's role may be true and interesting, but it doesn't really clarify Sacajawea's role. Instead, the addition distracts the reader from Sacajawea's contribution and is unnecessary.

35. The best answer is B. The original sentence contains two complete thoughts with two main verbs. Connecting these two clauses with a comma is called a comma splice and is grammatically incorrect. Answer choice A creates two separate sentences, which is acceptable. Answer choices C and D turn the second half of the sentence into a subordinate clause, which can be separated from a main clause by a comma.

36. The best answer is J. The most logical arrangement would place the two verbs close together so that the reader could easily follow the action. Therefore, answer choices G, H, and J are all preferable to F. Adjectives should also be placed close to the noun they modify. Therefore, answer choice J is better than G and H because *westward* is kept closest to *trek* in answer choice J. While H does keep the two verbs the closest, its construction is too awkward to be the best answer choice.

37. The best answer is B. *Its* is a possessive pronoun modifying *roster*, but refers back to the singular noun *expedition*. *It's* is a contraction of the subject/verb *it is*, which makes no sense here. Answer choice D is incorrect because it includes an extraneous comma and *their* is plural. Because it is a singular pronoun, *its'* does not exist in correct English.

38. The best answer is J. The simple past tense *was reunited* is consistent with the tense used in the rest of the passage.

39. The best answer is D. The interjections in answer choices A, B, and C do not add necessary information to the passage. More importantly, they are too casual and do not match the academic tone of the rest of the passage.

40. The best answer is F. Only answer choice F is grammatically correct. Answer choices G and H are wrong because they create incomplete sentences. Answer choice J places an unnecessary comma after *in addition to*, which makes it grammatically incorrect.

41. The best answer is A. The best answer choice is A because the final clause directly explains why her successful negotiations were important. While the whole sentence is consistent with the first paragraph, the final clause does not provide a direct link, so answer choice B is not correct. The clause is not humorous (answer choice C) or a lengthy description of Sacajawea's family (answer choice D).

42. The best answer is J. Because *1812* is directly followed by the phrase *as the year she died*, answer choices F and H are redundant. Answer choice G does not make sense.

43. The best answer is C. The sentence has to specify what the books and instruments were falling into, so answer choice D is incorrect. The pronouns in answer choices A and B are unclear referents. Only answer choice C correctly explains where the books and instruments were going.

44. The best answer is F. Only answer choice F accurately summarizes the main idea of the passage. Answer choice G is incorrect because it focuses on a detail, and it also contradicts the passage, which claims Sacajawea's lifespan is controversial. Answer choice H also focuses on a detail: Sacajawea's role as mother. While the passage does mention Sacajawea's calm manner several times (answer choice J), her demeanor is only important because it enabled her to be an important influence on American history.

45. The best answer is D. Answer choice D is correct because it places the information about the end of Sacajawea's life at the end of the passage. This way, the passage presents its information in a consistently chronological fashion. It also leads nicely into the last paragraph, which refers to the controversy introduced in Paragraph 4.

PASSAGE IV

46. The best answer is G. To take something *by storm* is an idiomatic expression meaning to overcome suddenly and with great force. None of the other answer choices make sense in this context.

47. The best answer is B. The underlined portion contains the main verb of the sentence. Therefore, answer choice D is incorrect because it contains a relative pronoun, which would make the phrase a relative clause. Answer choices A and C are vague – the reader does not know who is doing the needing. Answer choice B, however, contains a pronoun that means "anyone." This makes perfect sense in the context of the sentence.

48. The best answer is F. The sentence in question is important because it explains how to play the game of Sudoku, and Sudoku is the subject of the passage. Answer choice G is incorrect because it does not provide a solution to any particular game. Answer choices H and J are incorrect because the sentence is both relevant and to the point.

49. The best answer is C. In this sentence, *the solver's task* is the subject and *is* is the main verb. It is unnecessary to separate them with any punctuation.

50. The best answer is F. The subject here is *a level*, which is singular. Therefore, answer choices G and H, which use plural verbs, are incorrect. Answer choice F is also correct because it uses the present indicative *is*.

51. The best answer is D. In this sentence, *become* is the main verb and is modified by the adverb *eventually*. Answer choices A and B use the incorrect form of the adverb. Answer choice C turns *become* into the gerund *becoming*, which is incorrect for a main verb in a main clause.

52. The best answer is G. Here the underlined word serves as a connector between this sentence and the preceding sentence. This sentence gives specific details refining the ideas of the previous one. Therefore, answer choice G is best. Answer choice F suggests contrast that is inappropriate in this context. Answer choice H suggests consequence. Answer choice J is too vague and doesn't make sense here.

53. The best answer is C. The subordinate clause explains why the puzzle is aptly named. Answer choices A, B, and D all contain the idea of explanation, and therefore would be appropriate alterna-

tives. Answer choice C suggests a contrast, which doesn't make sense in this context.

54. The best answer is G. The underlined verb needs to be in the present tense to be consistent with the rest of the passage. Answer choice J contains a mistaken form of *should have*, which is never correct English.

55. The best answer is A. The modifier *which* correctly specifies that the writer is referring to a unique, but unspecified, number. *That* is inappropriate because it would indicate that the writer had a specific number in mind, so eliminate answer choice B. The article *a* is too vague, and doesn't give any direction to the reader, so eliminate answer choice C. Omitting the modifier creates an awkward sentence, so eliminate answer choice D.

56. The best answer is F. This choice introduces the idea of a hypothetical mistake that the reader can then correct. This makes logical sense within the scope of the paragraph, which focuses on making mistakes while playing Sudoku. Answer choice G does not give a reason for the correction; therefore, it's unclear and should be eliminated. The same is true of answer choice J. Answer choice H introduces a time constraint that is not supported by the passage.

57. The best answer is A. Introductory dependent clauses must be separated from the main clause by a comma. Therefore, answer choice D should be eliminated. The preposition and participle (*By attacking*) also make the conjunctions *and* and *so* unnecessary. Therefore, answer choices B and C should be eliminated.

58. The best answer is H. The underlined word *sometimes* introduces the idea of irregularity. Euler was not occasionally Swiss nor did he invent Sudoku only on certain days, so answer choices F and J can be eliminated. On the other hand, it makes logical sense that only some people credit Euler with inventing the game. Therefore, answer choice H is the best answer.

59. The best answer is C. The beginning of this paragraph focuses on Euler's game and its relationship to Sudoku. However, with Sentence 4, the writer shifts focus to just Sudoku and the ways it challenges players. Therefore, answer choice C is the best answer because it recognizes this shift in focus.

60. The best answer is H. The beginning sentence of this paragraph ties the topic of the passage back to the introductory paragraph. Therefore, answer choice H is best. The writer does not make explicit comparisons between Sudoku and crossword puzzles, so answer choice G can be eliminated. The writer also repeatedly encourages readers to try Sudoku, not to avoid it, so answer choice J can be eliminated. Answer choice F should be eliminated because the writer only hints at where Sudoku puzzles are located in a newspaper.

PASSAGE V

61. **The best answer is C.** In this example, *baby* is modifying *cries* and should be in the possessive.

62. **The best answer is J.** In this sentence, the two clauses contain two grammatically complete ideas. They can be made into two separate sentences as in answer choices F and G, or they can be connected by a conjunction as in answer choice H. Answer choice J, however, connects two complete sentences with a comma. This is called a "comma splice" and it is grammatically incorrect.

63. **The best answer is B.** This question tests parallel construction. Because *anxiety* is a noun, the idea that is linked to it should also be a noun in order to stay consistent. Therefore, answer choice B *confusion* is the best answer. The other answer choices are verbs.

64. **The best answer is H.** This choice clearly indicates what is being played back in slow motion (the film). Good writing is clear and not ambiguous. The remaining answer choices are awkward and unclear.

65. **The best answer is D.** A list of only two items, in this case *happiness and comfort*, does not need to be separated by commas. Therefore, answer choice D is the best answer.

66. **The best answer is G.** In this example, *sound* refers back to the plural noun phrase *new utterances*, so answer choice F can be eliminated. Because *sound* is the main verb in a relative clause, answer choice H should be eliminated. Finally, to stay consistent with the rest of the passage, *sound* needs to be in the present tense, so answer choice H can be eliminated.

67. **The best answer is D.** In this sentence, the two clauses contain two grammatically complete ideas. They can be made into two separate sentences joined by a semicolon as in answer choice B, or

they can be connected by a conjunction as in answer choices A and C. Answer choice D is grammatically unacceptable.

68. **The best answer is F.** This sentence contrasts the results of failure to communicate with the results of success in the previous sentence. Therefore, answer choice F is the best answer because it is the only answer choice that indicates contrast. The other answer choices indicate causation (answer choices G and H) or comparison (answer choice J).

69. **The best answer is D.** The adjective *emerging* tells the reader that the child is just learning to talk. Therefore, any additional statement of that idea is redundant. Answer choice D is the best answer because the underlined passage is unnecessary.

70. **The best answer is F.** This is the only answer choice that lists specific needs. The other answer choices are not detailed and should be eliminated.

71. **The best answer is A.** The phrase explains the causal relationship between sign language and verbal language development. It does not provide any specific detail about individual signs, so answer choice B can be eliminated. The phrase does not contradict other information in the passage, so answer choice C can be eliminated. Finally, the phrase is already at the end of the paragraph, so answer choice D can be eliminated.

72. **The best answer is G.** The underlined word *distinct* is an adjective; it can't modify a verb, therefore answer choice J is incorrect. Also, in English, adjectives almost always come before the noun they modify. Since *distinct* correctly modifies *words*, answer choice G is the best answer. Answer choices F and H don't make sense.

73. **The best answer is C.** The verb phrase *may be able* must be followed by an infinitive verb, so answer choice C is the best answer. The other answer choices don't make grammatical sense.

74. **The best answer is G.** The section links the child's ability to follow commands to her own language acquisition. Answer choice F should be eliminated because the author doesn't say commands are the *only* way children learn language—in fact, the section on sign language would contradict this idea. Answer choice H is also contradicted by the passage and should be eliminated. Answer choice J should be eliminated because baby names are not mentioned at all.

75. The best answer is B. This sentence stands in contrast to the sentence before it by correcting the mistaken idea of *most people*. The underlined phrase should introduce that concept of contrast and correction; therefore, answer choice A should be eliminated. Answer choice C has the idea of contrast but implies that the two ideas are equally correct, so it should be eliminated. Answer choice D is similar to answer choice C. Only answer choice B clarifies the logical relationship between the two sentences, and is the best answer.

Mathematics Test Explanations

1. **The correct answer is D.** To solve this problem, first perform the operations within the absolute value signs, and then perform the subtraction, as follows:

$$|9 - 5| - |5 - 9|$$
$$= |4| - |-4|$$
$$= 4 - 4 = 0$$

2. **The correct answer is H.** To solve this problem, first subtract the flat fee from the total bill:

$$190 - 25 = 165$$

The editor billed $165 for his hourly work. Now, simply divide 165 by 30 to determine the number of hours he worked:

$$165 \div 30 = 5.5, \text{ or } 5\frac{1}{2}$$

3. **The correct answer is A.** The first step in solving this problem is to calculate the time it takes each runner to run 15 miles. Use the Distance = Rate × Time formula, as follows (because you are calculating the time, use the variable x):

A (5 mph)	B (5 mph)
$D = (r)(t)$	$D = (r)(t)$
$15 = 5x$	$15 = 6x$
$x = 3$	$x = 2.5$

Runner A takes 3 hours and Runner B takes 2.5 hours to run 15 miles. Therefore, it takes Runner A half an hour $(3 - 2.5 = 0.5)$ longer to run 15 miles.

4. **The correct answer is H.** To solve this problem, add or subtract like terms, as follows:

$$x^2 + 60x + 54 - 59x - 82x^2$$
$$= (-82x^2 + x^2) + (60x - 59x) + 54$$
$$= -81x^2 + x + 54$$

5. **The correct answer is D.** The perimeter is the distance around an object. You are given that the figure is composed of a square, which has congruent sides, and an equilateral triangle, which has congruent sides. You are also given that the length of one side of the square is 18 cm, which means that the length of each of the remaining sides is also 18. Therefore, the perimeter of $ABCDE$ is $18 \times 5 = 90$.

6. **The correct answer is K.** To solve this problem, use the FOIL method, as follows:

$$(6n - 5)(n + 4)$$

First terms: $6n^2$

Outside terms: $24n$

Inside terms: $-5n$

Last terms: -20

Now, put the like terms in order and simplify:

$$6n^2 + 24n - 5n - 20$$
$$= 6n^2 + 19n - 20$$

7. **The correct answer is C.** A quick way to solve this problem is to multiply Blair's current salary by 1.03, which will yield her new salary with a 3% raise (remember, the decimal equivalent of 3% is .03):

$$42,000 \times 1.03 = 43,260$$

You could also multiply Blair's current salary by .03, then add the result to her current salary:

$$42,000 \times .03 = 1,260$$
$$42,000 + 1,260 = 43,260$$

8. **The correct answer is J.** One way to solve this problem is to simply set up the equation and solve for n, as follows:

$$(n - 2) + (n - 1) + n + (n + 1)$$
$$+ (n + 2) + (n + 3) = 513$$
$$6n - 2 + (-1) + 1 + 2 + 3 = 513$$
$$6n - 3 + 6 = 513$$
$$6n + 3 = 513$$
$$6n = 510$$
$$n = 85$$

9. **The correct answer is C.** One way to solve this problem is to sketch the (x, y) coordinate plane and plot the given points, as shown below:

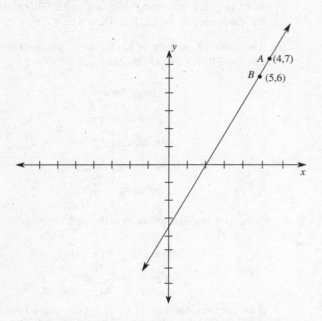

A quick glance at the figure and the answer choices should indicate that point C would likely have coordinates (4,5) because none of the other options match the figure. Use the midpoint formula to calculate the coordinates, as follows:

$$5 = \frac{(6+x)}{2} \qquad 6 = \frac{(7+y)}{2}$$
$$10 = 6 + x \qquad 12 = 7 + y$$
$$4 = x \qquad\qquad 5 = y$$

10. **The correct answer is J.** Since the figure is a rectangle, the adjacent sides are perpendicular. Perpendicular lines have slopes that are negative reciprocals of each other, meaning that the product of their slopes is -1. Since there are four lines and four perpendicular angles, the product of the slopes is $(-1) \times (-1) \times (-1) \times (-1) = 1$.

11. **The correct answer is D.** You are given that Tom traveled 45 miles in 12 hours and that Jim traveled four times as far in one-third the time. That means that Jim traveled 45×4, or 180 miles in $12 \times (\frac{1}{3})$, or 4 hours. Therefore, Jim traveled $\frac{180}{4}$, or 45 miles per hour.

12. **The correct answer is J.** If you recognized that a, b, and c are supplementary to the interior angles of the triangle, you could have quickly arrived at the correct answer: $a + c = 180$; $a + b = 180$;

$b + c = 180$; therefore, $a + b + c = 360$. You could also have calculated the sum of a, b, and c by first finding their values. Because 2 of the interior angles total 124 (43 + 81), the third angle must measure $180 - 124 = 56$. Therefore, angle c must measure $180 - 56 = 124$, angle a must measure $180 - 43 = 137$, and angle b must measure $180 - 81 = 99$. The sum is $137 + 99 + 124 = 360$.

13. **The correct answer is E.** According to the information given in the table, 30 students voted for the name Spartans. Therefore, 30 out of 200 students voted for Spartans. Because you are looking for a percentage, set up a proportion and solve for x, as follows:

$$\frac{30 \text{ students}}{200 \text{ students}} = \frac{x \text{ percent}}{100 \text{ percent}}$$
$$3,000 = 200x$$
$$15 = x$$

14. **The correct answer is H.** According to the information given in the table, 40 students voted for the name Lions. Therefore, 40 out of 200 students voted for Lions. First, calculate the percentage of the whole pie chart represented by Lions by setting up a proportion and solving for x, as follows:

$$\frac{40 \text{ students}}{200 \text{ students}} = \frac{x \text{ percent}}{100 \text{ percent}}$$
$$4,000 = 200x$$
$$20 = x$$

You now know that 20% of the students voted for Lions. Because there are 360° in a circle, find 20% of 360:

$$360 \times 0.2 = 72$$

15. **The correct answer is D.** According to the information given in the table, 50 students voted for the name Knights. Therefore, 50 out of 200 students polled voted for Knights. First, calculate the percentage of those students polled who voted for Knights by setting up a proportion and solving for x, as follows:

$$\frac{50 \text{ students}}{200 \text{ students}} = \frac{x \text{ percent}}{100 \text{ percent}}$$
$$5,000 = 200x$$
$$25 = x$$

You now know that 25% of the students polled voted for Lions. You are given that there are 3,000 students at Center High School, so find 25% of 3,000:

$$3000 \times 0.25 = 750$$

16. **The correct answer is J.** To solve this problem, calculate the area of the sides:
Top/Bottom:

$$4 \times 4 = 16$$
$$2(16) = 32$$

Sides:

$$3 \times 4 = 12$$
$$4(12) = 48$$

$32 + 48 = 80$, the total surface area.

17. **The correct answer is C.** In the equation of a line, $y = mx + b$, m is the slope. Recall that parallel lines have the same slope. Therefore, because the slope of the given line is $\frac{2}{5}$, the slope of any line parallel to that line will also have a slope of $\frac{2}{5}$.

18. **The correct answer is J.** To solve this problem, use the formula for the area of a circle: $A = \pi r^2$. Substitute 2.5 for the radius and solve (remember that $\pi \cong 3.14$):

$$r = 2.5$$
$$A = \pi(2.5)^2$$
$$A = \pi(6.25)$$
$$A \cong 19.625 \cong 19.63$$

19. **The correct answer is B.** To quickly solve this problem, recall the perfect squares that are closest to $\sqrt{42}$:

$$\sqrt{36} = 6$$
$$\sqrt{49} = 7$$

Because the question asks for the largest integer *less* than $\sqrt{42}$, the correct answer must be 6.

20. **The correct answer is G.** The first step in solving this problem is to calculate the total surface area of Amanda's room. Each wall measures 12 by 14, so each wall has an area of $12 \times 14 = 168$. There are 4 walls, so the total area is $168 \times 4 = 672$. Now, subtract the area that will not be painted: $3 \times 4 = 12$

for the window, and $3 \times 7 = 21$ for the door; $168 - 12 - 21 = 639$. Because Amanda needs to cover 639 square feet, and each can of paint covers 350 to 400 square feet, she will need a minimum of 2 cans of paint.

21. **The correct answer is A.** To answer this question, remember that when you divide exponential values with the same base you must subtract the exponents. Simplify the expression as follows:

$$\frac{3x^3}{3x^9}$$
$$= \frac{x^3}{x^9}$$
$$= x^{-6}$$

22. **The correct answer is K.** To solve this problem, factor the quadratic equation as follows:

$$a^2 + 2a - 8 = 0$$
$$(a + 4)(a - 2) = 0$$
$$a + 4 = 0 \quad a - 2 = 0$$
$$a = -4 \quad a = 2$$

The values of a are -4 and 2.

23. **The correct answer is C.** Calculate the slope by finding the change in y-values over the change in x-values using the coordinates for points A and C:

$$\frac{4 - (-4)}{4 - (-4)} = \frac{8}{8} = 1$$

24. **The correct answer is K.** You are given that the fixed costs are $900, which means that the cost of printing will be $900 *plus* the cost of printing each textbook. The cost of printing each textbook is determined by multiplying the number of textbooks, t, by the cost per textbook, $1.50. Therefore, the cost of printing each textbook is $1.50t$, and the cost of printing t textbooks in one week is $900 + 1.50t$.

25. **The correct answer is D.** A right triangle in which the length of the longer leg is $\sqrt{3}$ times the length of the shorter leg is a 30°–60°–90° right triangle. Another property of this type of right triangle is that the hypotenuse is 2 times the length of the shorter leg. So, this right triangle has lengths x, $x\sqrt{3}$, and $2x$. Its perimeter is $x + x\sqrt{3} + 2x = 15$, or $3x + x\sqrt{3} = 15 + 5\sqrt{3}$. Subtract $5\sqrt{3}$ from both sides to get $3x = 15$; $x = 5$.

26. **The correct answer is G.** To solve this problem, note that the numerators are equivalent. Because

this is an equation where the fractions are equal to one another, the denominators must also be equivalent. Set up an equation for the denominators and solve for y as follows:

$$y\sqrt{11} = \sqrt{11}$$
$$y = 11/\sqrt{11}$$
$$y^2 = (\frac{11}{\sqrt{11}})^2$$
$$y^2 = \frac{121}{11} = 11$$
$$y = \sqrt{11}$$

You could also have quickly arrived at the correct answer by noticing that $\sqrt{11} \times \sqrt{11} = 11$, so y must equal $\sqrt{11}$.

27. **The correct answer is A.** To solve this problem, first determine the size of each bucket. Because the total capacity of 12 buckets is g gallons, each bucket can hold $(\frac{1}{12})g$, or $\frac{g}{12}$ gallons. Because the total capacity of 8 buckets is g gallons, then each of those buckets can hold $(\frac{1}{8})g$, or $\frac{g}{8}$ gallons. If the total capacity of 4 buckets is g gallons, then each bucket is $(\frac{1}{4})g$, or $\frac{g}{4}$ gallons. Therefore, the capacity of the smallest buckets is $\frac{g}{12}$.

28. **The correct answer is F.** To solve this problem, remember that the formula for the circumference of a circle is $C = 2\pi r$, and the formula for the area of a circle is $A = \pi r^2$, where r is the radius. You are given that the circumference is $.5\pi$. Calculate the value of r as follows:

$$2\pi r = 0.5\pi$$
$$r = 0.25$$

Now, substitute 0.25 into the formula for the area and solve:

$$A = \pi r^2$$
$$= \pi (0.25)^2$$
$$= 0.0625\pi$$

29. **The correct answer is E.** The volume of a cube is calculated by multiplying the length $\times$ width $\times$ height. You are given that Cube X has an edge length of 2. Because Cube Y has an edge length triple that of Cube X, the volume of Cube Y is $6 \times 6 \times 6$, or $6^3 = 216$ cubic inches.

30. **The correct answer is G.** To solve this problem, substitute the given values into the formula as follows:

$$A = 8,000(1 + 0.05)^3$$
$$= 8,000(1.157625)$$
$$= 9,261$$

31. **The correct answer is D.** To solve this problem, substitute the given values into the formula as follows:

$$S = 2\pi r^2 + 2\pi rh$$
$$= 2\pi(1)^2 + 2\pi(1)(3)$$
$$= 8\pi$$

32. **The correct answer is F.** To solve this problem, substitute the given values into the function as follows:

$$f(x) = 3x + 5 \quad \text{and} \quad g(x) = x^2 - x + 7$$

Therefore, $f(g(x)) = f(x^2 - x + 7)$. Substitute $x^2 - x + 7$ for x and solve:

$$f(g(x)) = 3(x^2 - x + 7) + 5$$
$$= 3x^2 - 3x + 21 + 5$$
$$= 3x^2 - 3x + 26$$

33. **The correct answer is B.** To solve this problem, first calculate the total number of touchdowns as follows:

2 games with 0 touchdowns = 0 touchdowns

3 games with 1 touchdown = 3 touchdowns

3 games with 2 touchdowns = 6 touchdowns

5 games with 3 touchdowns = 15 touchdowns

2 games with 4 touchdowns = 8 touchdowns

1 games with 5 touchdowns = 5 touchdowns

$0 + 3 + 6 + 15 + 8 + 5 = 37$ touchdowns

Now, calculate the average number of touchdowns per game. You are given that there were 16 games, so the average is $37 \div 16 = 2.3125$, rounded to the nearest tenth is 2.3.

34. **The correct answer is H.** To solve this problem, first calculate the total measure of all the angles. The first triangle is a right triangle, which means that $a + b = 90°$. The sum of the interior angles of any triangle is 180°, so $c + d + e = 180°$. The total measure of the angles, then, is $90° + 180°$, or 270°. Calculate the average: $270° \div 5 = 54°$.

35. **The correct answer is E.** Because the entire value $4x^4$ is being raised to the 4th power, you must multiply the exponents: $4 \times 4 = 16$, so $(x4)^4 = x^{16}$. Therefore, you can eliminate answer choices A, B, and D. Next, you must raise 4 to the 4th power: $4^4 = 256$, and the correct answer is $256x^{16}$.

36. **The correct answer is G.** Inequalities can be solved like equations, by isolating the variable on one side. Remember, though, that when you multiply an inequality by a negative number, you must reverse the sign:

$$3x - 6 > 6x + 9$$
$$-3x > 15$$
$$x < -5$$

37. **The correct answer is C.** To find the point of intersection, set the equations equal to each other: $2x^2 + 6 = -4x^2 + m$. Add $4x^2$ to both sides: $6x^2 + 6 = m$. Since the x-coordinate of the point of intersection is $\sqrt{5}$, then $6(\sqrt{5})^2 + 6 = m$ and $m = 36$.

38. **The correct answer is J.** The first step in solving this problem is to calculate the length of the hypotenuse. If you recognize that this is a special triangle, you know that the hypotenuse is 5. You could also let the answer choices guide you, since they each include some combination of 3, 4, and 5. Otherwise, use the Pythagorean theorem, as follows:

$$a^2 + b^2 = c^2$$
$$3^2 + 4^2 = c^2$$
$$9 + 16 = c^2$$
$$25 = c^2$$
$$c = 5$$

Next, recall that cosine is equal to the length of the adjacent side over the length of the hypotenuse. Therefore, $\cos \angle Z$ is $\frac{3}{5}$.

39. **The correct answer is C.** The best way to solve this problem is to use the process of elimination. Remember that you are looking for the answer that is NOT true! First, determine the common difference of the sequence: $16 + (-5) = 11$; $11 + (-5) = 6$; $6 + (-5) = 1$. The common difference is -5, so eliminate answer choice D. Now, consider each of the remaining answer choices:

Answer choice A: The common difference is -5, so the fifth term is $1 + (-5) = -4$; eliminate answer choice A.

Answer choice B: The sum of the first five terms is $16 + 11 + 6 + 1 + -4 = 30$; eliminate answer choice B.

Answer choice C: If the fifth term is -4, the sixth term is $-4 + (-5) = -9$, and the seventh term is $-9 + (-5) = -14$. Answer choice C is correct because it is NOT true.

40. **The correct answer is G.** The first step in solving this problem is to recognize that the average will be equivalent to the volume divided by the number of oxygen molecules. Set up the fraction and solve, keeping in mind that when you divide exponential values with the same base you subtract the exponents:

$$\frac{6 \times 10^{14}}{3 \times 10^7} = 2 \times 10^7$$

41. **The correct answer is B.** Cotangent is defined by the length of the adjacent side over the length of the opposite side. Therefore, the cotangent of $\angle B$ is $\frac{x}{z}$.

42. **The correct answer is H.** A rational number is any number that can be written as a ratio; in other words, a fraction. So simply determine the fraction that is exactly halfway between $\frac{1}{6}$ and $\frac{1}{2}$. One way to do this is to find the average, as follows:

$$\frac{\left(\frac{1}{2} + \frac{1}{6}\right)}{2} = \frac{2}{6} = \frac{1}{3}$$

Another way to solve this problem is to find the Lowest Common Denominator (LCD):

$$\frac{1}{2} = \frac{3}{6}, \text{ so the LCD is 6.}$$

The value that is halfway between $\frac{1}{6}$ and $\frac{3}{6}$ is $\frac{2}{6}$, which is equivalent to $\frac{1}{3}$.

43. **The correct answer is A.** This problem tests your knowledge of absolute values and inequalities. The inequality $|6-2x|>5$ can be written as two separate inequalities: $6 - 2x > 9$ *or* $6 - 2x < -9$. Because the original inequality was a greater than, the word in between the two new inequalities must be "or." This means that $6 - 2x > 9 = -2x > 3 = x < -\frac{3}{2}$, *or* that $6 - 2x < -9 = -2x < -15 = x > \frac{15}{2}$. (Remember to reverse your inequality when multiplying or dividing by negative numbers.) The only answer choice that fits one of the inequalities is -2, which is less than $-\frac{3}{2}$. There are no answer choices that are greater than $\frac{15}{2}$.

44. **The correct answer is J.** A regular pentagon (5-sided figure) is a pentagon with equal sides and equal angles. If each side of the pentagon has a length of 12, its perimeter is 60. For the square to have a perimeter of 60, each side of the square must have a length of 15. If each side of the square has length of 15, its area is 225.

45. **The correct answer is B.** You are given that no table can be empty, which means that there must be at least one student seated at each table. There are 20 students in all and 10 tables, so if one student is seated at each table, you have accounted for 10 students. Now simply fill tables with the remaining 10 students until no students remain:

> Table 1 already has 1 student; add 3 more so that it is filled. You now have 7 more students to seat.
> Table 2 already has 1 student; add 3 more so that it is filled. You now have 3 more students to seat.
> Table 3 already has 1 student; add the 3 remaining students so that it is filled.

You have accounted for all of the students and have filled 3 tables. You cannot fill more than 3 tables with students while leaving no tables empty.

46. **The correct answer is K.** One way to solve this problem is to pick numbers for x and y. You are given that $x < y$, so make $x = 2$ and $y = 3$.

Now, substitute those values into the absolute value given: $|x - y| = |2 - 3| = |-1| = 1$.
Now, substitute the values into each answer choice. The answer choice that yields a value of 1 will be correct:

> **Answer choice F:** $2 + 3 = 5$; eliminate answer choice F.
> **Answer choice G:** $-(2 + 3) = -5$; eliminate answer choice G.
> **Answer choice H:** $\sqrt{2} - 3 \neq 1$; eliminate answer choice H.
> **Answer choice J:** $2 - 3 = -1$; eliminate answer choice J
> **Answer choice K:** $-(2 - 3) = -(-1) = 1$. Answer choice K is correct. For any values of x and y when $x < y$, $|x - y| = -(x - y)$.

47. **The correct answer is D.** You can solve this problem by first calculating the area of the trapezoid. Use the formula $A = \frac{1}{2}(b_1 + b_2)h$:

$$A = \frac{1}{2}(4 + 8)3$$

$$A = \frac{1}{2}(12)3$$

$$A = \frac{1}{2}(36)$$

$$A = 18$$

Next, calculate the area of the rectangle: $3 \times 4 = 12$. Because the shaded regions comprise the difference between the area of the trapezoid and the area of the rectangle, the area of the shaded regions is $18 - 12 = 6$.

48. **The correct answer is J.** To solve this problem, find the missing side lengths. Because the lengths 2 and 4 make up the entire left vertical side of the figure, you can deduce that the entire right vertical side of the figure will be $2 + 4 = 6$. Likewise, because the entire bottom horizontal side of the figure is 8, you can deduce that the missing horizontal length will be 2, because $8 - 6 = 2$. Therefore, the perimeter of the figure is $6 + 6 + 8 + 8 = 28$.

49. **The correct answer is D.** Since c is directly proportional to s^2, then $c = as^2$, for some constant a. Given that $c = \frac{7}{16}$ when $s = \frac{1}{4}$, you can solve for a, as follows:

$$\frac{7}{16} = a\left(\frac{1}{4}\right)^2$$

$$\frac{7}{16} = \left(\frac{1}{16}\right)a$$

$$a = 7$$

You now know that $a = 7$, and $c = as^2$. Substitute 175 for c and 7 for a and solve for s, as follows:

$$175 = 7s^2$$

$$25 = s^2$$

$$s = 5$$

50. **The correct answer is G.** You must know something about the values of cosine functions at certain values of α to answer this question correctly. Work through each of the answer choices, as follows:

Answer choice F: $(\frac{2\pi}{3} \leq \alpha \leq \pi)$ When α is $\frac{2\pi}{3}$, $\cos \alpha = -\frac{1}{2}$; when α is π, $\cos \alpha = -1$. The value -0.385 is not between $-\frac{1}{2}$ and -1, so eliminate answer choice F.

Answer choice G: $(\frac{\pi}{2} \leq \alpha \leq \frac{2\pi}{3})$ When α is $\frac{\pi}{2}$, $\cos \alpha = 0$; when $\alpha \frac{2\pi}{3}$, $\cos \alpha = -\frac{1}{2}$. The value -0.385 is between 0 and $-\frac{1}{2}$, so answer choice G is correct.

51. **The correct answer is B.** The first step in solving this problem is to determine how many integers between 10 and 99, inclusive, will have 0 as at least one digit, as follows:

10, 20, 30, 40, 50, 60, 70, 80, 90

There are 9 integers that will have 0 as at least one digit. Next, because there are a total of 90 numbers in the given range, the probability of choosing one of those 9 numbers is $\frac{9}{90}$, which simplifies to $\frac{1}{10}$.

52. **The correct answer is J.** The first step in solving this problem is to calculate the diameter of the circle, which corresponds to the diagonal of the rectangle. Use the Pythagorean Theorem to determine the length of the diagonal:

$$12^2 + 16^2 = c^2$$

$$144 + 256 = c^2$$

$$400 = c^2$$

$$20 = c$$

To find the area of the circle, you need the radius, which is equal to one-half the diameter, or 10. The formula for the area of a circle is $A = \pi r^2$, so the area is $\pi r^2 = 100\pi$.

53. **The correct answer is E.** By definition, $\log_a(xy)^2 = 2\log_a(xy) = 2(\log_a x + \log_a y)$. Because you are given that $\log_a x = n$ and $\log_a y = p$, the correct answer is $2(n + p)$.

54. **The correct answer is J.** You are given that a is a number with units digit x and tens digit y. Therefore, x is equivalent to 10 times y, and $a = xy = 10x + y$. You are given that b is formed by reversing the digits of a. Therefore, $b = yx = 10y + x$. Set up an equation and solve for $a - b$ as follows:

$$a - b = (10x + y) - (10y + x)$$

$$= 10x + y - 10y - x$$

$$= 9x - 9y$$

$$= 9(x - y)$$

55. **The correct answer is E.** To solve this problem, substitute $a + b$ for a in $(a^2 - 2)$ as follows:

$$(a^2 - 2)$$

$$= (a + b)^2 - 2$$

$$= (a + b)(a + b) - 2$$

$$= a^2 + ab + ab + b^2 - 2$$

$$= a^2 + 2ab + b^2 - 2$$

56. **The correct answer is J.** To solve this problem, cross multiply and make the necessary substitution, as follows:

$$\frac{1}{(1 + i)} \times \frac{(1 - i)}{(1 - i)}$$

$$= \frac{1(1 - i)}{(1 + i)(1 - i)}$$

$$= \frac{1 - i}{1 - i^2}$$

$$= \frac{1 - i}{1 - (-1)}$$

$$= \frac{1 - i}{2}$$

57. **The correct answer is A.** To solve this problem, let t be Amy's time in 2005. Because her time decreased by 10% in 2006, her time in 2006 was $(.9)t$. Her time in 2007 would be $.8(.9t) = .72t$, which means that her time in 2007 was 72% of her time in 2005, so her time decreased by 28%.

58. **The correct answer is K.** According to the question stem, the sum of the sequence is given by

PRACTICE TEST 8 ANSWERS AND EXPLANATIONS

$\dfrac{x}{(1-y)}$. Therefore, sum $= \dfrac{x}{(1-y)}$. To solve this problem, first substitute the given values into the equation and solve for x:

$$200 = \frac{x}{(1-0.15)}$$

$$200 = \frac{x}{0.85}$$

$$170 = x$$

The first term of the sequence, x, is 170. To find the value of the second term, multiply 170 by the common ratio, 0.15: $170 \times 0.15 = 25.5$.

59. **The correct answer is E.** You are asked for integer values of a, which means that a must be a whole number. The first step will be to change $\dfrac{1}{11}$ to $\dfrac{2}{22}$ and $\dfrac{1}{8}$ to $\dfrac{2}{16}$; now it is easy to see that if $\dfrac{2}{a}$ is between $\dfrac{2}{22}$ and $\dfrac{2}{16}$, a can be equal to 21, 20, 19, 18, or 17.

60. **The correct answer is G.** In 3 fair coin tosses, there are exactly 8 equally likely outcomes: HHH, HHT, HTH, HTT, THH, THT, TTH, and TTT. Of these 8 outcomes, 3 include exactly 2 heads, so the probability of obtaining exactly 2 heads is $\dfrac{3}{8}$.

Reading Test Explanations

PASSAGE I

1. **The best answer is B.** The narrator begins by describing how silence was a concept unfamiliar to her. It made her uncomfortable: "I knew silence as a lack of something." The passage concludes by showing that her silence on the bus allowed Jaime to gather the courage to speak to the narrator, and that this experience had changed her long held opinion of silence.

2. **The best answer is F.** The tone of the passage indicates that the narrator is initially uncomfortable with silence in general. When the narrator sat next to Jaime, his quietness made her "feel a little awkward." This information best supports answer choice F.

3. **The best answer is D.** According to the passage, the narrator "never understood the value of silence." She considered silence "a lack of something," and goes on to say that, "maybe I was even a little afraid of the emptiness it created—the aural darkness where forgiveness never happened." These details best support answer choice D.

4. **The best answer is G.** The passage states that, "I knew silence as a lack of something." It goes on to say about silence that the narrator was "a little afraid of the emptiness it created." In addition, once the narrator encounters Jaime, he did not speak for several minutes. These details best support answer choice G.

5. **The best answer is B.** The narrator says that she didn't believe in silence as a healer before she met Jaime. However, the lines referenced in the question indicate a change of heart that is best expressed in answer choice B.

6. **The best answer is H.** According to the passage, "Buses often have their own unique demographic: each crowd is unlike any other." This best supports answer choice H.

7. **The best answer is A.** According to the passage, "My university required a community service stint to graduate ... I'd heard that the local YMCA was a good resource ... I made my way to the YMCA looking for easy credits." These statements best support answer choice A.

8. **The best answer is J.** The passage states that, "his eyes were alert. And they were glued on me." These statements indicate that Jaime was alert, not sleepy or bored, so eliminate answer choices F and G. Because Jaime didn't speak to the narrator

for several minutes, he could be described as shy, but he certainly could not be described as outgoing; eliminate answer choice H.

9. **The best answer is C.** The passage states that, "Within the parameters of my innocent world, I knew silence as a lack of something." This, along with other sentiments expressed by the author, suggests that the author's view of silence was limited or restricted. The other answer choices are not supported by the context.

10. **The best answer is F.** The passage states that, "On this bus, most everyone was either asleep or totally oblivious." This detail best supports answer choice F.

PASSAGE II

11. **The best answer is A.** As stated in the first paragraph of the passage, "The Republic had been under considerable stress for several years before Caius Julius was born, thus he did not create the fissures that led to the collapse of the Roman Republic, though he did capitalize on them brilliantly." This sentence indicates that Julius Caesar used conflicts of the past to enhance and promote his own power.

12. **The best answer is H.** The passage states that, "Caius Julius Caesar is popularly considered the founder of the Roman Empire, though it would be more accurate to consider his political rise as marking the end of the Roman Republic." From this statement, one can assume that because Caesar's political rise marked the end of the Roman Empire, Caesar exploited the political problems of the Roman Empire in order to gain power. The other answer choices do not reflect the main idea of the paragraph.

13. **The best answer is D.** The passage states, "Roman armies were traditionally made up of small land-holders." This statement, along with the phrase in the question stem, indicates that unless a farmer owned a certain amount of land, he could not join the military, thereby establishing a close traditional relationship between farming and military service.

14. **The best answer is F.** As indicated by the passage, aristocratic fear of political reform was the reasoning behind the brothers' murders. Tiberius Gracchus was murdered over his determination to rid the Roman Empire of the military enrollment land requirement, while his brother, Gaius Gracchus, also caused trouble due to his rebellious ideas. "When the younger brother, Gaius Gracchus, began his reforms 10 years later, he was

able to extend political rights to the lower classes and reduce opportunities for bribery and corruption among the upper classes. He, too, was murdered for pushing the system too far." This information best supports answer choice F.

15. **The best answer is B.** As stated in the passage, "Marius also challenged the traditional structure of the army where nobility were regularly given authority over lower-class officers with more experience and ability." This indicates that Marius saw more value in ability than social class.

16. **The best answer is J.** The passage states, "Sulla was allied with the Roman Senate, who feared Marius' ambition and influence with the masses. Sulla believed in strengthening the power of the Senate against the popular Assembly. To this end, he marched his armies against Rome, defeating Marius and establishing himself as Dictator. While Sulla eventually resigned the dictatorship peacefully, he had exiled or killed thousands of political opponents during his reign." Answers F, G, and H are all found within the passage. Answer choice J is the only answer not found within the passage.

17. **The best answer is A.** The last paragraph of the passage opens by contrasting Julius Caesar's ties to aristocracy to his actions as a reformer. As indicated by the passages, Julius Caesar supported many ideas that were exactly the opposite of what his family ties desired. This contrast helps to illustrate that Julius Caesar was a true political reformer.

18. **The best answer is F.** Throughout the passage the author cites the actions of several different reformers, including Julius Caesar as well as the Gracchi brothers. Every reformer detailed by the author was assassinated. Because the author includes the stories and outcomes of these reformers, one can infer that many Roman reformers were eventually assassinated.

19. **The best answer is D.** The passage states, "Like the Gracchi brothers, Julius Caesar supported the redistribution of public lands to the poor and protected the grain supply (a large part of the unemployment dole). In his armies, he promoted ability before social rank. He was also widely seen to support the middle and lower classes against the privileges of the aristocracy, namely the Senate." Answer choices A, B, and C are all political reforms mentioned by the passage.

20. **The best answer is H.** The passage closes with the following statement in regard to the aftermath of

Julius Caesar's assassination; "The resulting political chaos ultimately led to the rise of Augustus Caesar as emperor, effectively ending the Roman Republic forever." The other answer choices are not supported by the passage.

PASSAGE III

21. **The best answer is C.** The passage states in the last paragraph that *The Táin* is an epic of great value. "If the images meet a cultural need, they can come back to life as living artistic works. During the English occupation of Ireland through the Irish Revolution, many artists plumbed the depths of Irish mythology to create what they saw as an image of Ireland free of English cultural repression. Writers still call on *The Táin* for inspiration, just as ancient Irish bards once called on the ghost of Fergus to tell them the true story of the Cattle Raid of Cooley." The passage makes it clear that the epic is of significant value to Irish history.

22. **The best answer is J.** The passage answers the questions presented in answer choices F, G, and H. The question regarding vernacular literature is answered with the following: "Ireland has the oldest vernacular literature in Europe. Where other early European authors wrote their literary works in Latin, the Irish began writing down their stories in their own language starting at least as early as the 6th century A.D. and continuing to the modern day." Vernacular language is defined by the passage as stories written down in one's native language. In regard to Queen Medb's desire to acquire a magic bull, her "insistence on equaling the property of her husband was for reasons far more serious than vanity… Wives were considered legal equals to men if they came into their marriage with as much or more property than their husbands. If she had less, the wife would be a legal dependent of her husband and, like a child, would have limited rights of her own." Finally, the passage explains that *The Táin Bó Culainge* means "The Cattle Raid of Cooley." Answer choice J is the only question not answered by information in the passage.

23. **The best answer is A.** In regard to why the epic plays an important role in Irish literature, the passage states, "During the English occupation of Ireland through the Irish Revolution, many artists plumbed the depths of Irish mythology to create what they saw as an image of Ireland free of English cultural repression." This information best supports answer choice A.

24. The best answer is F. The second paragraph serves to describe The Cattle Raid of Cooley. In its narrowest sense, the raid refers to a series of battles fought by the northern Irish province of Connacht to steal a magic bull from the neighboring province of Ulster. However, the cycle includes many other legends that together tell the national story of the people of Ulster, especially during the reign of the great Ulster king, Conchobor mac Nessa.

25. The best answer is D. Of the four answer choices, A, B, and C can all be found in the passage. "The *remscéla* tell how the bulls were originally two pig-keepers who knew magic; the stories explain how the Ulstermen came to be cursed with debilitating pain whenever their country was in danger. They explain who Cú Chulainn was and how he got his name. And, most poignantly, the *remscéla* tell how Fergus lost his crown and why he agreed to fight against his countrymen. This last story, told in the tragic legend of Deirdre and the Sons of Usnech, is one of the most striking of all the Irish myths." Answer choice D is the only choice not mentioned by the passage.

26. The best answer is G. As stated in the last paragraph of the passage, "Over twelve hundred years old, *The Táin* is certainly an epic work—but epic doesn't necessarily mean "dead." If the images meet a cultural need, they can come back to life as living artistic works … Writers still call on *The Táin* for inspiration, just as ancient Irish bards once called on the ghost of Fergus to tell them the true story of the Cattle Raid of Cooley." Not only does this segment of the passage establish answer choices F, H, and J as elements of *The Táin,* but it also states that an epic isn't dead, as long as it still has cultural significance.

27. The best answer is D. In an effort to explain why Queen Medb wanted a magic bull, the passage states the following: "Wives were considered legal equals to men if they came into their marriage with as much or more property than their husbands. If she had less, the wife would be a legal dependent of her husband and, like a child, would have limited rights of her own. Irish queens were used to having their own political autonomy and making their own political deals." This information best supports answer choice D.

28. The best answer is J. When speaking of love triangles, the passage gives the following as examples, "Think of the romances of King Arthur, Queen Guinevere, and Sir Lancelot, or those of Tristran, Isolde, and her husband, King Mark. In *The Táin,*

Queen Medb takes up with the warrior Fergus, with the approval of her husband, in order to guarantee Fergus' allegiance during the war."

29. The best answer is A. As indicated by the passage, there are strong thematic similarities between the King Arthur story and *The Táin*. Specifically, the passage states, "Still, even Medb's daughter, Finnabair, is tied linguistically to the Arthurian legend: Finnabair and Guinevere are different spellings of the same name." This statement is used to further support the passages earlier tie between the two stories; "Thematically, the work explores several great issues that would occupy medieval authors for over six hundred years. One of the most important was the lovers' triangle between the king, the queen, and the warrior hero. Think of the romances of King Arthur, Queen Guinevere, and Sir Lancelot, or those of Tristran, Isolde, and her husband, King Mark." These statements best support answer choice A.

30. The best answer is H. The passage explains that Medb's dedication to acquiring one of the two magic bulls of Ulster was because not only did her husband have the other magic bull, but if she acquired a bull as well, she would attain the same level of political power as her husband. Otherwise, she would be at his mercy. Due to these circumstances, Medb was very ambitious in her pursuits. The other answer choices are not supported by the passage.

PASSAGE IV

31. The best answer is D. Of the four answer choices, choices A, B, and C can all be found in the first paragraph of the passage. This passage reads, "Homeopathy is a system for treating physical disease and other ailments using the theory of treating "like with like." In practice, homeopathic medicine seeks substances that mimic an ailment's symptoms; this sameness is considered "likeness." The substance is then diluted to infinitesimal amounts and administered to the patient in order to cure the problem. Homeopathic treatment is currently in use for everything from cancer to colds and flu, though many scientists remain heavily skeptical about its efficacy." Not only is answer choice D not mentioned in this paragraph, but the passage indicates that, "Modern scientists have been unable to find any evidence to support the theory of molecular memory," which is the opposite of the statement asserted by answer choice D.

32. The best answer is F. The passage states that, "Hahnemann had hypothesized that shaking the solution after each dilution would imprint the molecular "memory" of the original substance into the solution, which would allow the diluted dose to be effective without the possibility of overdose or adverse side effects." This information best supports answer choice F.

33. The best answer is C. As stated in the passage, "Hahnemann first stumbled upon his theory when he was investigating a common treatment for malaria, cinchona bark. Modern scientists now know that cinchona bark contains quinine—a substance still used to treat malaria—but at the time, no one knew why the bark was effective." This information best supports answer choice C.

34. The best answer is J. The passage states, "Modern scientists have been unable to find any evidence to support the theory of molecular memory. In fact, the idea that diluting a substance makes it stronger runs against the principles of chemistry and physics." Based on this information, one can infer that modern doctors are unable to find evidence to support homeopathic treatment because the theory of molecular memory is contrary to the principles of chemistry and physics.

35. The best answer is C. The last paragraph of the passage states, "Today, many conventional medical practitioners generally disregard homeopathy. Homeopathic practitioners are frequently termed quacks by conventional scientists. Nevertheless, homeopathy remains extremely popular both in the United States and abroad. In European countries such as France and England, conventional doctors frequently prescribe homeopathic treatments for common illnesses, such as colds and flu. Pharmacists who are trained to answer questions about the homeopathic treatments' use and desired effects

then fill the prescriptions." Based on this information, one can conclude that, although there is a lack of clinical data, homeopathy remains a popular form of treatment, even among doctors and pharmacists.

36. The best answer is H. As is explained by the passage, "When a person became ill, doctors believed it was because one or more of the humors had come out of balance. Some of the best treatments were thought to be bloodletting and purgation—with the assumption being that these treatments would effectively drain off the excess humors." This information best supports answer choice F.

37. The best answer is B. As described in the second paragraph of the passage, "... Sanguine, or passionate, persons were hot and wet."

38. The best answer is J. The fourth paragraph of the passage states that, "Perhaps not surprisingly, Hahnemann's new field of homeopathy (i.e. "similar suffering") was met with considerable resistance from doctors comfortable with their usual practices." As it is used in this sentence, one can infer that *practices* most closely means the various treatments employed by doctors of Hahnemann's era. This information best supports answer choice J.

39. The best answer is B. The fourth paragraph of the passage explains, "Hahnemann further hypothesized that, while undiluted substances would only worsen symptoms in the sick, heavily diluted substances could be effective for a cure." This information best supports answer choice B.

40. The best answer is H. The last paragraph of the passage explains that homeopathy is a controversial form of medical treatment. "Nevertheless, homeopathy remains extremely popular both in the United States and abroad." This information best supports answer choice H.

Science Reasoning Test Explanations

PASSAGE I

1. **The correct answer is A.** In Figure 2, lake clay is indicated by the horizontal stripes. Of the 4 areas listed (Genola, Site 1, Site 2, and Provo) the lake clay deposit is thinnest at Genola.

2. **The correct answer is H.** The passage states that Lake Bonneville was formed "about 32,000 years ago" and that "it existed until about 16,800 years ago." Therefore, you can determine that it existed in its entirety for approximately $32,000 - 16,800 = 15,200$ years.

3. **The correct answer is D.** To answer this question, look at the relationship between the area marked by horizontal stripes (lake clay) and the area marked by vertical stripes (bedrock). As the lake clay gets thicker, the bedrock below it gets thinner. Therefore, the thickness of the bedrock decreases.

4. **The correct answer is G.** According to Figure 2, both Site 1 and Site 2 are situated atop the lake clay layer, with Site 2 at a slightly higher elevation than Site 1. The only graph that shows Site 2 at a higher elevation is answer choice G.

5. **The correct answer is A.** The passage states that, "Over time, increasing temperatures in North America caused the lake to begin drying up, leaving Great Salt Lake … the salinity levels are higher than normal." You can deduce from this statement that rising temperatures led to increased water evaporation, which led to increased salinity levels. Therefore, a decrease in temperature and an increase in freshwater rainfall would likely lead to *decreased* salinity levels in Great Salt Lake.

PASSAGE II

6. **The correct answer is H.** You are given that "The order *Lepidoptera* includes butterflies and moths. Table 1 is a key for identifying some Lepidoptera in North America." Because butterflies and moths are not birds, reptiles, or mammals, they must be insects. Even though you might never have seen the word *Lepidoptera* before, you can still correctly answer the question because the term is defined for you.

7. **The correct answer is B.** To answer this question, find *Agraulis vanillae* on Table 1. According to Table 1, the upper side of *Agraulis vanillae* wings is orange with black markings. This species does not have a fuzzy body—Table 1 indicates that you

should skip to Step 3 if the insect has a fuzzy body, bypassing *Agraulis vanillae* completely. Likewise, the features mentioned in answer choices C and D are located after *Agraulis vanillae* on the table.

8. **The correct answer is H.** To answer this question, find the listed traits of lepidoptera *Y* in Table 2, and apply them to the steps in Table 1. Table 2 indicates that lepidoptera *Y* has a slim body; therefore, go to Step 2 and eliminate answer choice F. Table 2 indicates that lepidoptera *Y* has yellow wings with markings on the upper side, so go to Step 4 and eliminate answer choice G. Table 2 indicates that lepidoptera *Y* has silver markings, so go to Step 6. Because the silver markings of *Speyeyria coronis* are round and elongated and lepidoptera *Y* has triangular shaped silver markings, you can deduce that lepidoptera *Y* is not a *Speyeyria coronis*.

9. **The correct answer is C.** To answer this question, evaluate each of the answer choices and eliminate those that are incorrect:
   Answer choice A: Step 1—According to Table 2, both *W* and *Z* have a fuzzy body; eliminate answer choice F.
   Answer choice B: Step 3—According to Table 2, both *W* and *Z* have wings with yellow on the upper side; eliminate answer choice G.
   Answer choice C: Step 7—According to Table 2, *W* has prominent brown bands on its underside, and *Z* has no prominent markings on its underside. Therefore, Step 7 is where they first diverge.

10. **The correct answer is F.** To answer this question, first notice that *Automeris io* and *Antheraea polyphemus* are both listed in Step 8. According to Table 1, to get to Step 8 the lepidoptera must have pronounced spots on their hindwings. Note that the lepidoptera in the question have different wingspans, so answer choice H is incorrect. Also, by moving directly to Step 8, Steps 6 and 7 are skipped, so eliminate answer choice G. The only way to get to Step 5 is to have a fuzzy body, so eliminate answer choice J.

PASSAGE III

11. **The correct answer is C.** According to Figure 1, the dotted line represents a water temperature of 40°. Even though 3.0 seconds is not listed on the graph, you can determine that it is halfway between 2.0 and 4.0 seconds; at 3.0 seconds, the dotted line is at approximately 36°.

12. **The correct answer is F.** According to Figure 2, the dotted line represents an air temperature of 30°. During the interval from 0–100 seconds, the dotted

line moves rapidly down and to the right, showing a significant drop in temperature. The dotted line begins to level off shortly after 100 seconds, indicating a stable temperature from about 200 seconds forward.

13. **The correct answer is B.** To answer this question, look at Figure 1. Between 0 and 2 seconds, the thermometer in the 40° water registered a temperature increase from 20° to 30°. Therefore, during the 2-second interval the temperature increased 10°, and the increase in temperature per second was 5°.

14. **The correct answer is J.** You are given that a thermometer at an initial temperature of 60° was placed in air samples at 30°, 40°, and 50°. According to Figure 2, it took approximately 200 seconds for the temperature to stabilize at 30°. You can hypothesize that, if the 60° thermometer was placed in a colder air sample, it would take more than 200 seconds for the temperature to stabilize.

15. **The correct answer is A.** To answer this question, look at Figure 1. The dashed line represents 60° and the solid line represents 50°. The dashed line is always higher than the solid line, so eliminate answer choices C and D. According to the figure, at 4.0 seconds the thermometer in the 60° water registered a temperature of about 48°, which is higher than the temperature recorded after 2.0 seconds (about 38°).

PASSAGE IV

16. **The correct answer is H.** Scientist 1 supports the use of placebos in clinical research. According to Scientist 1, placebos "help address the issue of mind over matter, which is an important issue when working towards treatment for a particular illness." In addition, Scientist 1 states that, "… the possibility of receiving treatment often provides patients with a psychological boost." These statements best support answer choice H.

17. **The correct answer is B.** Scientist 1 states that, "… the possibility of receiving treatment often provides patients with a psychological boost. The use of placebos addresses the question of whether a person's positive attitude may be important in recovery from illness." These statements best support answer choice B.

18. **The correct answer is G.** Both Scientists address the use of placebos in clinical research; Scientist 1 supports the use of placebos while Scientist 2 argues against the use of placebos. Both

Scientists discuss the placebo effect as a possible result of using placebos in clinical research. Therefore, the only statement that both Scientists would agree with is answer choice G.

19. **The correct answer is C.** Scientist 2 states that, "Due to its capability to skew research results, the placebo shouldn't be used in clinical research."

20. **The correct answer is J.** Scientist 2 believes that the use of placebos encourages deception in the doctor-patient relationship, which suggests that the use of placebos would lead to less positive communication between the patients and their doctors. Because the finding indicates that the opposite is true—in fact, that the patients were very trusting of their doctors and freely communicated with them—Scientist 2's viewpoint would be weakened.

21. **The correct answer is A.** Scientist 1 states that placebos "establish a control group for the test treatment in question …" If an observation were made suggesting that patients in a control group—the group receiving the placebo—did not recover as quickly as patients who received the medical treatment, Scientist 2's viewpoint against the use of placebos would be weakened. According to Scientist 2, "placebo-related changes could be over-estimated. Different illnesses, by definition, will react differently to the placebo." The observation in answer choice A would support using placebos to help determine the efficacy of a given medical treatment.

22. **The correct answer is J.** Because Scientist 1 believes that using placebos is beneficial in clinical research, Scientist 1 must assume that the use of placebos is safe for most patients. None of the other answer choices are supported by the passage.

PASSAGE V

23. **The correct answer is B.** According to Figure 2, tap water has a viscosity of approximately 1.0, while Motor Oil A has a viscosity of approximately 20.0. Additionally, the results of Experiments 1 and 2 show that the general flow rate of Motor Oil A is lower than that of tap water.

24. **The correct answer is G.** The results of Experiment 1 show that, as the angle of the pipe increases, the velocity of flow increases as well. Therefore, there is a direct relationship.

25. **The correct answer is B.** According to the passage, "Laminar flow is common only in cases in which the flow channel is relatively small, the fluid

is moving slowly, and its *viscosity* (the degree to which a fluid resists flow under an applied force) is relatively high." This information best supports answer choice B, because the pipe diameter is small, the fluid is moving slowly, and Motor Oil B has the highest viscosity of the liquids tested.

26. **The correct answer is C.** According to the passage, Motor Oil B has the highest viscosity, followed by Motor Oil A, followed by tap water. The tables indicate that Motor Oil B has the slowest flow rates, Motor Oil A has slightly faster flow rates, and tap water has the fastest flow rates, overall. This information best supports answer choice C.

27. **The correct answer is A.** According to Table 1, the flow rate of a pipe at a 30° angle with a diameter of 0.25 was 4.0 ft/s, while the flow rate of a pipe at a 30° angle with a diameter of 0.50 was 9.0 ft/s. Therefore, a pipe with a diameter between 0.25 and 0.50 would likely have a flow rate between 4.0 ft/s and 9.0 ft/s. Only answer choice A fits within these parameters.

28. **The correct answer is H.** The three experiments varied only in the type of liquid being used—tap water, Motor Oil A, or Motor Oil B. All of the other factors listed were identical in each experiment.

PASSAGE VI

29. **The correct answer is C.** Both Table 1 and Figure 1 indicate that, as the concentration of sulfite is doubled, the corrected absorbance approximately doubles; 2 is 1 doubled, and 0.302 is approximately 0.153 doubled.

30. **The correct answer is J.** To answer this question, look at Table 2. You are given that dried pineapple measures 0.603, which is higher than prunes; therefore, eliminate answer choices F and H. The order of decreasing concentration is: dried apricots at 0.774; dried pineapple at 0.603; and prunes at 0.562.

31. **The correct answer is B.** According to Table 1, a sulfite concentration of 1.5, which is halfway between 1.0 and 2.0, would have a corrected absorbance about halfway between 0.153 and 0.302.

32. **The correct answer is J.** According to the passage, a colorimeter is a device that measures how much light of a selected wavelength is absorbed. Because different colors have different wavelengths, the colorimeter needs to be adjusted to read at its

maximum capacity. The other answer choices are not supported by the passage.

33. **The correct answer is A.** According to Table 1, all of the measured absorbances are higher than the corrected absorbances for the fruits tested. Likewise, the sulfite concentration has a direct relationship with the corrected absorbance in both Table 1 and Table 2. This information best supports answer choice A.

34. **The correct answer is F.** You are given that *additional* contents in the fruits are absorbing light, which means that the apparent absorbance reading will be higher.

PASSAGE VII

35. **The correct answer is A.** The passage states that the molar heat of fusion (ΔH_{fus}) of water is 6.02. This value is less than the molar heat of fusion of calcium.

36. **The correct answer is H.** According to the passage, molar heat of fusion (ΔH_{fus}) is "the amount of heat necessary to melt (or freeze) 1.00 mole of a substance at its melting point at a constant pressure." The table indicates that the molar heat of fusion for iron is 13.8 kJ/mol.

37. **The correct answer is C.** According to the passage, molar heat of fusion (ΔH_{fus}) is "the amount of heat necessary to melt (or freeze) 1.00 mole of a substance at its melting point at a constant pressure." The table shows that molar heat of fusion and melting point both increase for calcium, silver, and iron, but the melting point decreases as the molar heat of fusion continues to increase for nickel. This best supports answer choice C.

38. **The correct answer is F.** The table shows that, in general, higher boiling points result in a higher molar heat of fusion. Therefore, because the boiling point for potassium is lower than the boiling point for calcium, it is likely that the molar heat of fusion for potassium will be lower than the molar heat of fusion for calcium.

39. **The correct answer is C.** You are given that the molar heat of fusion is directly related to the strength of the forces that hold molecules together; therefore, higher molar heats of fusion will indicate stronger bonds between molecules. Iron has a higher molar heat of fusion than calcium, so the

forces holding molecules together will be stronger in iron than in calcium.

40. The correct answer is H. To answer this question, compare the boiling points and molar heats of fusion for each of the pairs of elements:

   I. Nickel and iron—the boiling point of iron is higher than the boiling point of nickel, but the molar heat of fusion is lower for iron than it is for nickel. Roman numeral I does *not*

support the hypothesis, so eliminate answer choices F and J.

   II. Water and calcium—the boiling point of water is lower than the boiling point of calcium, and the molar heat of fusion is lower for water than it is for calcium. Roman numeral II supports the hypothesis, so eliminate answer choice G.

The process of elimination leaves you with answer choice H, but if you evaluate Roman numeral III you will see that it also supports the hypothesis.

Writing Test Explanation

Because grading the essay is subjective, we've chosen not to include any "graded" essays here. Your best bet is to have someone you trust, such as your personal tutor, read your essays and give you an honest critique. If you plan on grading your own essays, review the grading criteria and be as honest as possible regarding the structure, development, organization, technique, and appropriateness of your writing. Focus on your weak areas and continue to practice in order to improve your writing skills.

ANSWER SHEET

ACT PRACTICE TEST 9
Answer Sheet

ENGLISH

1 (A)(B)(C)(D)	21 (A)(B)(C)(D)	41 (A)(B)(C)(D)	61 (A)(B)(C)(D)
2 (F)(G)(H)(J)	22 (F)(G)(H)(J)	42 (F)(G)(H)(J)	62 (F)(G)(H)(J)
3 (A)(B)(C)(D)	23 (A)(B)(C)(D)	43 (A)(B)(C)(D)	63 (A)(B)(C)(D)
4 (F)(G)(H)(J)	24 (F)(G)(H)(J)	44 (F)(G)(H)(J)	64 (F)(G)(H)(J)
5 (A)(B)(C)(D)	25 (A)(B)(C)(D)	45 (A)(B)(C)(D)	65 (A)(B)(C)(D)
6 (F)(G)(H)(J)	26 (F)(G)(H)(J)	46 (F)(G)(H)(J)	66 (F)(G)(H)(J)
7 (A)(B)(C)(D)	27 (A)(B)(C)(D)	47 (A)(B)(C)(D)	67 (A)(B)(C)(D)
8 (F)(G)(H)(J)	28 (F)(G)(H)(J)	48 (F)(G)(H)(J)	68 (F)(G)(H)(J)
9 (A)(B)(C)(D)	29 (A)(B)(C)(D)	49 (A)(B)(C)(D)	69 (A)(B)(C)(D)
10 (F)(G)(H)(J)	30 (F)(G)(H)(J)	50 (F)(G)(H)(J)	70 (F)(G)(H)(J)
11 (A)(B)(C)(D)	31 (A)(B)(C)(D)	51 (A)(B)(C)(D)	71 (A)(B)(C)(D)
12 (F)(G)(H)(J)	32 (F)(G)(H)(J)	52 (F)(G)(H)(J)	72 (F)(G)(H)(J)
13 (A)(B)(C)(D)	33 (A)(B)(C)(D)	53 (A)(B)(C)(D)	73 (A)(B)(C)(D)
14 (F)(G)(H)(J)	34 (F)(G)(H)(J)	54 (F)(G)(H)(J)	74 (F)(G)(H)(J)
15 (A)(B)(C)(D)	35 (A)(B)(C)(D)	55 (A)(B)(C)(D)	75 (A)(B)(C)(D)
16 (F)(G)(H)(J)	36 (F)(G)(H)(J)	56 (F)(G)(H)(J)	
17 (A)(B)(C)(D)	37 (A)(B)(C)(D)	57 (A)(B)(C)(D)	
18 (F)(G)(H)(J)	38 (F)(G)(H)(J)	58 (F)(G)(H)(J)	
19 (A)(B)(C)(D)	39 (A)(B)(C)(D)	59 (A)(B)(C)(D)	
20 (F)(G)(H)(J)	40 (F)(G)(H)(J)	60 (F)(G)(H)(J)	

MATHEMATICS

1 (A)(B)(C)(D)(E)	16 (F)(G)(H)(J)(K)	31 (A)(B)(C)(D)(E)	46 (F)(G)(H)(J)(K)
2 (F)(G)(H)(J)(K)	17 (A)(B)(C)(D)(E)	32 (F)(G)(H)(J)(K)	47 (A)(B)(C)(D)(E)
3 (A)(B)(C)(D)(E)	18 (F)(G)(H)(J)(K)	33 (A)(B)(C)(D)(E)	48 (F)(G)(H)(J)(K)
4 (F)(G)(H)(J)(K)	19 (A)(B)(C)(D)(E)	34 (F)(G)(H)(J)(K)	49 (A)(B)(C)(D)(E)
5 (A)(B)(C)(D)(E)	20 (F)(G)(H)(J)(K)	35 (A)(B)(C)(D)(E)	50 (F)(G)(H)(J)(K)
6 (F)(G)(H)(J)(K)	21 (A)(B)(C)(D)(E)	36 (F)(G)(H)(J)(K)	51 (A)(B)(C)(D)(E)
7 (A)(B)(C)(D)(E)	22 (F)(G)(H)(J)(K)	37 (A)(B)(C)(D)(E)	52 (F)(G)(H)(J)(K)
8 (F)(G)(H)(J)(K)	23 (A)(B)(C)(D)(E)	38 (F)(G)(H)(J)(K)	53 (A)(B)(C)(D)(E)
9 (A)(B)(C)(D)(E)	24 (F)(G)(H)(J)(K)	39 (A)(B)(C)(D)(E)	54 (F)(G)(H)(J)(K)
10 (F)(G)(H)(J)(K)	25 (A)(B)(C)(D)(E)	40 (F)(G)(H)(J)(K)	55 (A)(B)(C)(D)(E)
11 (A)(B)(C)(D)(E)	26 (F)(G)(H)(J)(K)	41 (A)(B)(C)(D)(E)	56 (F)(G)(H)(J)(K)
12 (F)(G)(H)(J)(K)	27 (A)(B)(C)(D)(E)	42 (F)(G)(H)(J)(K)	57 (A)(B)(C)(D)(E)
13 (A)(B)(C)(D)(E)	28 (F)(G)(H)(J)(K)	43 (A)(B)(C)(D)(E)	58 (F)(G)(H)(J)(K)
14 (F)(G)(H)(J)(K)	29 (A)(B)(C)(D)(E)	44 (F)(G)(H)(J)(K)	59 (A)(B)(C)(D)(E)
15 (A)(B)(C)(D)(E)	30 (F)(G)(H)(J)(K)	45 (A)(B)(C)(D)(E)	60 (F)(G)(H)(J)(K)

READING

1 Ⓐ Ⓑ Ⓒ Ⓓ	11 Ⓐ Ⓑ Ⓒ Ⓓ	21 Ⓐ Ⓑ Ⓒ Ⓓ	31 Ⓐ Ⓑ Ⓒ Ⓓ
2 Ⓕ Ⓖ Ⓗ Ⓙ	12 Ⓕ Ⓖ Ⓗ Ⓙ	22 Ⓕ Ⓖ Ⓗ Ⓙ	32 Ⓕ Ⓖ Ⓗ Ⓙ
3 Ⓐ Ⓑ Ⓒ Ⓓ	13 Ⓐ Ⓑ Ⓒ Ⓓ	23 Ⓐ Ⓑ Ⓒ Ⓓ	33 Ⓐ Ⓑ Ⓒ Ⓓ
4 Ⓕ Ⓖ Ⓗ Ⓙ	14 Ⓕ Ⓖ Ⓗ Ⓙ	24 Ⓕ Ⓖ Ⓗ Ⓙ	34 Ⓕ Ⓖ Ⓗ Ⓙ
5 Ⓐ Ⓑ Ⓒ Ⓓ	15 Ⓐ Ⓑ Ⓒ Ⓓ	25 Ⓐ Ⓑ Ⓒ Ⓓ	35 Ⓐ Ⓑ Ⓒ Ⓓ
6 Ⓕ Ⓖ Ⓗ Ⓙ	16 Ⓕ Ⓖ Ⓗ Ⓙ	26 Ⓕ Ⓖ Ⓗ Ⓙ	36 Ⓕ Ⓖ Ⓗ Ⓙ
7 Ⓐ Ⓑ Ⓒ Ⓓ	17 Ⓐ Ⓑ Ⓒ Ⓓ	27 Ⓐ Ⓑ Ⓒ Ⓓ	37 Ⓐ Ⓑ Ⓒ Ⓓ
8 Ⓕ Ⓖ Ⓗ Ⓙ	18 Ⓕ Ⓖ Ⓗ Ⓙ	28 Ⓕ Ⓖ Ⓗ Ⓙ	38 Ⓕ Ⓖ Ⓗ Ⓙ
9 Ⓐ Ⓑ Ⓒ Ⓓ	19 Ⓐ Ⓑ Ⓒ Ⓓ	29 Ⓐ Ⓑ Ⓒ Ⓓ	39 Ⓐ Ⓑ Ⓒ Ⓓ
10 Ⓕ Ⓖ Ⓗ Ⓙ	20 Ⓕ Ⓖ Ⓗ Ⓙ	30 Ⓕ Ⓖ Ⓗ Ⓙ	40 Ⓕ Ⓖ Ⓗ Ⓙ

SCIENCE

1 Ⓐ Ⓑ Ⓒ Ⓓ	11 Ⓐ Ⓑ Ⓒ Ⓓ	21 Ⓐ Ⓑ Ⓒ Ⓓ	31 Ⓐ Ⓑ Ⓒ Ⓓ
2 Ⓕ Ⓖ Ⓗ Ⓙ	12 Ⓕ Ⓖ Ⓗ Ⓙ	22 Ⓕ Ⓖ Ⓗ Ⓙ	32 Ⓕ Ⓖ Ⓗ Ⓙ
3 Ⓐ Ⓑ Ⓒ Ⓓ	13 Ⓐ Ⓑ Ⓒ Ⓓ	23 Ⓐ Ⓑ Ⓒ Ⓓ	33 Ⓐ Ⓑ Ⓒ Ⓓ
4 Ⓕ Ⓖ Ⓗ Ⓙ	14 Ⓕ Ⓖ Ⓗ Ⓙ	24 Ⓕ Ⓖ Ⓗ Ⓙ	34 Ⓕ Ⓖ Ⓗ Ⓙ
5 Ⓐ Ⓑ Ⓒ Ⓓ	15 Ⓐ Ⓑ Ⓒ Ⓓ	25 Ⓐ Ⓑ Ⓒ Ⓓ	35 Ⓐ Ⓑ Ⓒ Ⓓ
6 Ⓕ Ⓖ Ⓗ Ⓙ	16 Ⓕ Ⓖ Ⓗ Ⓙ	26 Ⓕ Ⓖ Ⓗ Ⓙ	36 Ⓕ Ⓖ Ⓗ Ⓙ
7 Ⓐ Ⓑ Ⓒ Ⓓ	17 Ⓐ Ⓑ Ⓒ Ⓓ	27 Ⓐ Ⓑ Ⓒ Ⓓ	37 Ⓐ Ⓑ Ⓒ Ⓓ
8 Ⓕ Ⓖ Ⓗ Ⓙ	18 Ⓕ Ⓖ Ⓗ Ⓙ	28 Ⓕ Ⓖ Ⓗ Ⓙ	38 Ⓕ Ⓖ Ⓗ Ⓙ
9 Ⓐ Ⓑ Ⓒ Ⓓ	19 Ⓐ Ⓑ Ⓒ Ⓓ	29 Ⓐ Ⓑ Ⓒ Ⓓ	39 Ⓐ Ⓑ Ⓒ Ⓓ
10 Ⓕ Ⓖ Ⓗ Ⓙ	20 Ⓕ Ⓖ Ⓗ Ⓙ	30 Ⓕ Ⓖ Ⓗ Ⓙ	40 Ⓕ Ⓖ Ⓗ Ⓙ

RAW SCORES		SCALE SCORES		DATE TAKEN:
ENGLISH	_____	ENGLISH	_____	
MATHEMATICS	_____	MATHEMATICS	_____	ENGLISH/WRITING _____
READING	_____	READING	_____	
SCIENCE	_____	SCIENCE	_____	_____
				COMPOSITE SCORE

Refer to the Scoring Worksheet on page 744 for help in determining your Raw and Scale Scores.

You may wish to remove these sample answer document pages to respond to the practice ACT Writing Test.

Cut Here

Begin WRITING TEST here.

If you need more space, please continue on the next page.

Do not write in this shaded area.

WRITING TEST

If you need more space, please continue on the back of this page.

2

WRITING TEST

If you need more space, please continue on the next page.

3

Cut Here

WRITING TEST

_____

_____

_____

_____

_____

_____

_____

_____

_____

_____

_____

_____

_____

_____

_____

_____

_____

_____

_____

_____

_____

_____

_____

_____

STOP here with the Writing Test.

4

1 ■ ■ ■ ■ ■ ■ ■ ■ 1

ENGLISH TEST

45 Minutes—75 Questions

DIRECTIONS: In the passages that follow, some words and phrases are underlined and numbered. In the answer column, you will find alternatives for the words and phrases that are underlined. Choose the alternative that you think is best, and fill in the corresponding bubble on your answer sheet. If you think that the original version is best, choose "NO CHANGE," which will always be either answer choice A or F. You will also find questions about a particular section of the passage, or about the entire passage. These questions will be identified by either an underlined portion or by a number in a box. Look for the answer that clearly expresses the idea, is consistent with the style and tone of the passage, and makes the correct use of standard written English. Read the passage through once before answering the questions. For some questions, you should read beyond the indicated portion before you answer.

PASSAGE I

Lil' Lou

The old cedar chest hadn't been opened nor its contents examined in years, maybe even a decade or more. My grandmother had asked me to help her sort through some of her old belongings, giving me a rare opportunity to hear some of her stories from long ago and, consequently, revealing my own personal history. Grandma had been widowed long ago, and I knew very little about my grandfather other than what a wonderful man he had been. This was the recurring description of my grandfather whenever his name was mentioned to anyone
                                    1
who had known him: the person would slowly move his lowered head from side to side and softly mutter, "A wonderful man … he was a wonderful man."

[1] That afternoon, I found myself standing in front of the chest with my grandmother by my side. [2] Grandma had been putting off opening the chest, which was sure
                                    2
to be an emotional experience. [3] She knew better than
                                    2
anyone else that vast memories

1. **A.** NO CHANGE
   B. grandfather whenever his name should have been mentioned
   C. grandfather whenever his name being mentioned
   D. grandfather. Whenever his name was mentioned

2. Given that all of the choices are true, which one provides a detail that best leads into the description that follows in this paragraph?
   F. NO CHANGE
   G. which had been purchased from an old catalog long ago.
   H. which was made of cedar and redwood.
   J. which was kept locked to protect the contents from mice.

GO ON TO THE NEXT PAGE.

1 ■ ■ ■ ■ ■ ■ ■ ■ **1**

were stored in this treasure, trove, and the mere opening of
                        _____
                             3
its lid would stir up a flood of happiness and grief,

spinning and growing like a hurricane out of control. [4]

Truth be told, the kind of help my grandmother needed
_____
           4
when opening the chest was more likely emotional than

physical. [5] I was ready and eager, and with my help as a

buffer, Grandma was ready, too. ⑤

The moment the air hit the wooden box interior, a
                            _____
                                   6
strong waft of cedar scent made its way to our noses.

My grandmother having explained that the source of this
               _____
                     7
forest-like aroma made it possible for the artifacts inside

the chest to remain intact, with no moth holes or tattered

fabric. Sure enough, as my grandmother lifted the first

item out of its tomb, I could see that the garment was very

old, but at the same time it appeared very new. It was my

grandfather's wool flying jacket from World War II.

Grandma hugged it to her chest for several moments

before holding it out in front of her, as if she could see my

grandfather wearing it. I simply sat and watched, waiting

for her to tell me about it and about him.

      Grandpa had been a pilot during the war, flying what
                                      _____
                                           8
was known as a Stinson L-5 Sentinel. Besides, when
                                      _____
                                           9

3. A. NO CHANGE
   B. treasure trove, and, the
   C. treasure trove, and the
   D. treasure trove and, the

4. Which of the following alternatives to the underlined
   portion would NOT be acceptable?
   F. If the truth were told, the kind of help
   G. Truth be told, the sort of help
   H. Truth be told, the kind of type of help
   J. To tell the truth, the kind of help

5. Which of the following sentences in this paragraph
   is LEAST relevant to the purpose of describing the
   narrator's actions and, therefore, could be deleted?
   A. Sentence 1
   B. Sentence 2
   C. Sentence 3
   D. Sentence 4

6. F. NO CHANGE
   G. wooden box's interior
   H. wooden boxes interior
   J. wooden boxes' interior

7. A. NO CHANGE
   B. explains
   C. explained
   D. was explaining

8. F. NO CHANGE
   G. war which was flying
   H. war he was flying
   J. war flying

9. A. NO CHANGE
   B. After all, when
   C. Instead, when
   D. When

GO ON TO THE NEXT PAGE.

1 ■ ■ ■ ■ ■ ■ ■ ■ 1

Grandpa first decided to fly, his dream had been to man
bomber planes; he desperately wanted to be on the
frontline of the air defense. After taking the appropriate
instruction, he was removed from the bombing corps
because of his imperfect eyesight, and his dream was
shattered. For Grandma, this was her dream come true;
Grandpa's chances of returning home safely to his
<u>new wife, and, daughter</u> were much higher
　　10

with <u>their</u> new designation as a
　11

liaison pilot. ⑫

　　As my grandmother told my grandfather's story, she
mindlessly examined his jacket, putting her hand down
one sleeve, turning to see its back, and sticking her fingers
into each lined pocket. Tucked into the breast pocket of
my grandfather's heavy flight jacket was a small black and
white photo. It was my grandfather standing in front of his
<u>large plane</u>, his "Lil' Lou," which was painted on the
　13
plane's nose, along with a happy little pink rabbit with a
bright orange carrot. I knew instantly that the L-5's
nickname was a loving reference to my grandmother,

<u>whose</u> given name was Louise.
　14

10. **F.** NO CHANGE
　　G. new wife and daughter
　　H. new wife, and daughter
　　J. new wife and daughter,

11. **A.** NO CHANGE
　　B. it's
　　C. its
　　D. his

12. Which of the following true statements, if added at
　　the beginning of this paragraph would most effectively
　　introduce readers to the information presented in the
　　paragraph?
　　F. Good eyesight has always been an essential quality
　　　　in a bomber pilot.
　　G. Men have always had their dreams of glory, and
　　　　my grandfather was no different.
　　H. My grandfather joined the army soon after my
　　　　mother was born.
　　J. My great-grandparents were pacifists, but that
　　　　hadn't stopped my grandfather from enlisting.

13. Given that all the choices are true, which one provides
　　information that is most relevant at this point in the
　　essay?
　　A. NO CHANGE
　　B. pride and joy
　　C. bomber
　　D. war plane

14. **F.** NO CHANGE
　　G. who's
　　H. her
　　J. by her

GO ON TO THE NEXT PAGE.

1 ■ ■ ■ ■ ■ ■ ■ ■ 1

Question 15 asks about the preceding passage as a whole.

15. Suppose the writer's goal had been to write a brief essay on the historical significance of air support in World War II. Would this essay successfully accomplish this goal?
   A. Yes, because it describes the different types of air support used by the military in World War II.
   B. Yes, because it explains the importance of liaison pilots to the overall military effort.
   C. No, because it focuses instead on the personal significance of an individual World War II pilot.
   D. No, because it fails to describe the relationship between the narrator's grandparents.

PASSAGE II

The Fruit of the Vine

It is difficult to imagine a human diet without tomatoes in some form, whether a fresh tomato right off the vine or in a spaghetti sauce over pasta. Having become a staple of the American kitchen, tomatoes are even when out of season and of inferior quality.
                                                                    16

During the growing season, tomatoes of every variety abound in grocery stores, roadside stands, and even on tables in front of peoples' homes. With tomatoes so readily
                                                                    17
available during the growing season, it's easy to run out of things to do with them. ⬚18 Luckily, there are

16.   F. NO CHANGE
   G. Tomatoes have become a staple of the American kitchen,
   H. With tomatoes becoming a staple of the American kitchen,
   J. While tomatoes have become a staple of the American kitchen,

17.   A. NO CHANGE
   B. grocery stores roadside stands and even on tables in front of peoples' homes.
   C. grocery stores, roadside stands and, even on tables in front of peoples' homes.
   D. grocery stores, roadside stands and, even, on tables in front of peoples' homes.

18. If the writer were to delete the phrase "With tomatoes so readily available during the growing season" from the preceding sentence, the paragraph would primarily lose:
   F. a detail that more fully explains why a reader would need more tomato recipes.
   G. information that explains why the writer likes tomatoes.
   H. a comparison between tomatoes and other summer produce.
   J. nothing at all, since the details about the availability of tomatoes is irrelevant to the paragraph.

GO ON TO THE NEXT PAGE.

1 ■ ■ ■ ■ ■ ■ ■ ■ 1

some <u>plenty</u> ways to use and enjoy this surplus of fresh
<u>　　　</u>
19

tomatoes. <u>While all are delicious, recipes for using</u>
　　　　　　　　　　　　　　　　20
<u>fresh tomatoes</u> range from a basic tomato salad (sliced
20

tomatoes with oil and vinegar) to complicated sauces

requiring hours to simmer and stew. Many cooks prefer to

peel and deseed the <u>tomatoes, while</u> using them in a
　　　　　　　　　　　21

cooking recipe. Peeling can be <u>easily accomplished</u> by first
　　　　　　　　　　　　　　　　22
scoring one end of the tomato with a sharp knife, making a

small crosshatch, and then dropping the fruit into boiling

water for approximately 30 seconds. <u>Whomever chooses</u>
　　　　　　　　　　　　　　　　　　23
this method should be careful not to splash the hot water

when placing the tomato into the pot. After the time is up,

the cook can use tongs to remove the tomato from the

boiling water and set it aside. <u>Waiting until it is</u>
　　　　　　　　　　　　　　　　24
<u>cool enough to handle.</u> The skin can then be easily
　　　24
removed with a sharp kitchen knife, and the tomato's seeds

can be collected in a strainer. This is an important step,

<u>as the tomato may still be very hot.</u>
　　　25

　　　Even green tomatoes harvested before the first frost can

be ripened indoors or used in a green tomato <u>recipe, green</u>
　　　　　　　　　　　　　　　　　　　　　　26

19. A. NO CHANGE
　　B. plenty of
　　C. plenty with
　　D. OMIT the underlined portion.

20. Given that all the choices are true, which one provides
　　the best transition by providing specific information?
　　F. NO CHANGE
　　G. Especially, recipes for using fresh tomatoes
　　H. Even though recipes for using fresh tomatoes
　　J. Some recipes for using fresh tomatoes

21. A. NO CHANGE
　　B. tomatoes and
　　C. tomatoes, and
　　D. tomatoes before

22. F. NO CHANGE
　　G. easy; accomplish
　　H. easily accomplishing
　　J. easily accomplish

23. A. NO CHANGE
　　B. Whoever chooses
　　C. Whomever chose
　　D. Whoever chose

24. F. NO CHANGE
　　G. aside. Until it is cooling enough to handle.
　　H. aside until it is cool enough to handle.
　　J. aside. Just until it is cool enough to handle.

25. Given that all the choices are true, which one concludes
　　this paragraph with a point most consistent with other
　　points made in this paragraph?
　　A. NO CHANGE
　　B. as the tomato seeds can be used to grow new plants.
　　C. as tomato seeds can be very slippery when they are
　　　　wet.
　　D. as tomato seeds can sometimes add a bitter taste to
　　　　a tomato dish.

26. F. NO CHANGE
　　G. recipe green
　　H. recipe. Green
　　J. recipe, while green

GO ON TO THE NEXT PAGE.

1 ■ ■ ■ ■ ■ ■ ■ ■ ■ 1

tomatoes placed on a kitchen shelf will ripen nicely in just a short amount of time. Once a tomato is <u>a bright red color, it</u> can be used for cooking or stored for later use. A fresh tomato won't last long, even in the refrigerator, so it's best to decide early on which tomatoes should become salsa or sauce and which should be served raw in a salad or sandwich. 28

There is truly only one way to eat a fresh tomato and experience its ultimate taste. Go into a garden, pluck a tomato off the vine, brush off any dirt, and then eat it like an apple. The Italians may have rejected the tomato when it was first introduced to their diets, believing it to be poisonous, but it certainly didn't take <u>one</u> long to incorporate this delicious fruit into nearly every homemade dish. Biting into a freshly picked, red tomato irrefutably explains why.

27. **A.** NO CHANGE
    B. a bright, red, color, it
    C. a bright red color it
    D. a bright, red, color it

28. The writer is considering revising the phrase "which tomatoes should become salsa or sauce and which should be served raw in a salad or sandwich" in the preceding sentence to read:

    which tomatoes should be prepared or cooked in a salsa or sauce and which should be left in their natural raw state, but sliced in a salad or sandwich.

    F. Make the revision, because it adds details that clarify the point being made in this sentence.
    G. Make the revision, because it emphasizes how important it is to choose fresh vegetables.
    H. Keep the phrase as it is, because it's specific, whereas the proposed revision is ambiguous.
    J. Keep the phrase as it is, because it's shorter and more concise than the proposed revision.

29. **A.** NO CHANGE
    B. it
    C. anyone
    D. them

Question 30 asks about the preceding passage as a whole.

30. Suppose the writer's goal had been to describe the many ways tomatoes can be used in modern cuisine. Does this essay successfully accomplish this goal?
    F. Yes, because it describes many different tomato dishes and encourages the reader to try them.
    G. Yes, because it makes a distinction between ancient and modern attitudes towards the tomato.
    H. No, because it discusses tomatoes in a more general sense and includes other pieces of information.
    J. No, because it only discusses cooking techniques and does not mention specific recipes.

GO ON TO THE NEXT PAGE.

1 ■ ■ ■ ■ ■ ■ ■ ■ **1**

PASSAGE III

> The following paragraphs may or may not be in the most
> logical order. Each paragraph is numbered in brack-
> ets, and Question 45 will ask you to choose where
> Paragraph 3 should most logically be placed.

Modern Dentistry

[1]

Only two or three generations ago, a painful toothache
often resulted in an equally painful extraction, permanently
leaving an empty hole where an incisor or molar had once
been. Aging often meant eventually losing each tooth, one
by one, as decay or breakage took its toll. Many people
ended up in the same position as when their lives
began, gumming their food instead of chewing it.

[2]

It wasn't until the early 1960s that dentistry began
looking the way it does today, with its sterile tools, modern
equipment, and new techniques.
Disposable needles that can be tossed in the trash, first
introduced during World War II, and a better understanding
of bacteria and the spread of diseases provided for a much
more sterile environment than before. Tools that were not
disposable were sterilized with the use of an autoclave,
which became a required piece of equipment in any
dentist's office. [35] The autoclave, or sterilizer, first
invented by Charles Chamberland in 1879, is a pressurized
container that heats the water inside it above the boiling
point, effectively sterilizing any steel instruments inside by

31. A. NO CHANGE
  B. a gaping
  C. somewhat of a
  D. OMIT the underlined portion.

32. F. NO CHANGE
  G. began; gumming
  H. began. Gumming
  J. began gumming

33. A. NO CHANGE
  B. However, it
  C. For example, it
  D. In the meantime, it

34. F. NO CHANGE
  G. Disposable needles designed to be thrown away
  H. Disposable needles that can be tossed out
  J. Disposable needles

35. The writer is considering deleting the phrase "which
became a required piece of equipment in any dentist's office" from the preceding sentence (ending the
sentence with *autoclave*). Should the phrase be kept or
deleted?
  A. Kept, because it emphasizes the universal importance of the device in modern dentistry.
  B. Kept, because it clarifies the term *autoclave* and
contributes to the logic of the paragraph.
  C. Deleted, because the paragraph has already stated
that modern dentist offices had become more
sterile.
  D. Deleted, because it draws attention away from teeth
and places it on equipment.

GO ON TO THE NEXT PAGE.

1 ■ ■ ■ ■ ■ ■ ■ ■ 1

using the heat to kill the viruses and bacteria on the instruments. [36] Today, most dentists use as many disposable tools and materials as possible in an effort to squelch the spread of any viruses or bacteria. Most dental workers will even wear facemasks over their mouths and

use plastic gloves as they <u>worked</u> on a patient.
                                    37

[3]

In many ways, today's dentists have an easier task before them as the profession has evolved and materials and procedures have improved. <u>On the other hand the constant changes</u> being made in the
                                    38
dental profession require a dentist to both learn about and incorporate the changes into his or her own practice. <u>Looking back</u> at the last 50 years of this evolution
                    39
demonstrates that making these changes

<u>can be a daunting challenge.</u>
                    40

[4]

High speed drills have replaced the foot pump operation of older drills, and more effective water coolers and suction tools have replaced the cruder prototypes used in the early 1900s. The cuspidor has gone mostly by the wayside, replaced by a suction device that the dentist's assistant uses to remove rinse-water or tooth fragments from the patient's mouth. X-ray equipment has also greatly improved over the past several <u>decades; X-ray</u>
                                                    41

36. The writer is considering deleting the phrase "by using the heat to kill the viruses and bacteria on the instruments" from the preceding sentence (and placing a period after the word *inside*). Should the phrase be kept or deleted?
  F. Kept, because it clarifies the claim made in first part of the sentence.
  G. Kept, because it strengthens the paragraph's focus on viruses and bacteria.
  H. Deleted, because the essay is mainly about dentistry, not spreading diseases.
  J. Deleted, because the phrase fails to add new or useful information.

37. A. NO CHANGE
  B. work
  C. have worked
  D. working

38. F. NO CHANGE
  G. On the other hand; the constant changes
  H. On the other hand, the constant changes
  J. On the other hand, the constant changes,

39. A. NO CHANGE
  B. In looking back
  C. While looking back
  D. Whereas looking back

40. Given that all the choices are true, which one best clarifies the distinction between today's dentists and the ones of 50 years ago?
  F. NO CHANGE
  G. pushes today's dentists to the limits of their training.
  H. is difficult.
  J. involves all aspects of dentistry.

41. A. NO CHANGE
  B. decades, X-ray
  C. decades X-ray
  D. decades, and making X-ray

GO ON TO THE NEXT PAGE.

1 ■ ■ ■ ■ ■ ■ ■ ■ 1

machines are now much safer and easier to operate, as well as more compact in size. The dental chair has also undergone radical changes over the years, <u>because it would allow</u> greater comfort for the patient and
42
easier access for the dentist.

[5]

Dental procedures and techniques likewise improved dramatically during the second half of the twentieth <u>century after 1950.</u> New anesthetic methods add to patient
43
comfort, an essential component in any successful dental procedure. The physician can choose from a variety of numbing options, depending on the patient and the procedure being done. Preserving teeth, rather than simply extracting them when damaged, is the goal of most dentists today. <u>Dental amalgams, silicates, and gold and</u>
44
<u>porcelain crowns have all become easier to work with</u>
44
<u>and are much more durable.</u>
44

42. **F.** NO CHANGE
    G. since it allows for
    H. allowing
    J. which would be allowing

43. **A.** NO CHANGE
    B. century, after 1950.
    C. century, after 1950 and later.
    D. century.

44. Given that all the choices are true, which one concludes the paragraph with a precise and detailed description that relates to the main topic of the essay?
    F. NO CHANGE
    G. Sunny smiles and happy patients are finally brightening dentist offices across the country.
    H. Over time, even more improvements can be expected.
    J. Hardly any patients need dentures anymore.

Question 45 asks about the preceding passage as a whole.

45. For the sake of the logic and coherence of this essay, Paragraph 3 should be placed:
    A. where it is now.
    B. after Paragraph 1.
    C. after Paragraph 4.
    D. after Paragraph 5.

GO ON TO THE NEXT PAGE.

1 ■ ■ ■ ■ ■ ■ ■ ■ **1**

English Art

Our Advanced English teacher Mr. Peale; decided to end
the semester with a unique and unexpected challenge. He
wanted each of us to find a picture of a famous oil
painting that we especially liked and bring it to school.
We were certain he was going to have us write something

about our pictures, so we all happily shared: our Picassos,
Van Goghs, and Cezannes in class the next day. Then the
surprise announcement came. We were each to attempt to
copy our picture onto a full-sized canvas using real oil
paints and brushes. The brushes were not real boar
bristles, but Mr. Peale said they would work just as well.

I will never forget how terribly insecure I felt as I began
my painting. As I secretly glanced looking at others
around me, my anxiety and self-doubt only seemed

to grow. It appears to me that my peers were not only
brilliant English students but accomplished artists as well!
Mr. Peale walked around the classroom and suddenly
became an art instructor as he loudly proclaimed to the
other students what an excellent job they were doing. I felt
quite tentative and barely had a mark on my own canvas. I
was way out of my element!

[1] Mr. Peale finally walked over to me and I silently
gulped. [2] He said very little about my attempts, which
was both a blessing and a curse. ⁵³ [3] His lack of
comment kept me from turning beet red, yet his quiet

46. F. NO CHANGE
G. teacher Mr. Peale—
H. teacher, Mr. Peale
J. teacher, Mr. Peale,

47. A. NO CHANGE
B. painting, that we especially liked, and
C. painting that we especially liked, and
D. painting, that we especially liked, and,

48. F. NO CHANGE
G. shared
H. shared,
J. share

49. A. NO CHANGE
B. Did I mention this wasn't an art class?
C. I had chosen a French impressionist.
D. DELETE the underlined portion.

50. F. NO CHANGE
G. glanced looking at others around me on all sides
H. glanced around me
J. glanced at others surrounding me

51. A. NO CHANGE
B. appeared
C. appearing
D. has appeared

52. Which of the following alternatives to the underlined portion would be LEAST acceptable?
F. declared
G. announced
H. affirmed
J. published

53. If the writer were to delete the phrase "which was both a blessing and a curse" from the preceding sentence (ending the sentence with *attempts*), the essay would primarily lose:
A. a relevant description of the writer's attitude towards her English teacher.
B. information about the writer's attitude towards Impressionist art.
C. the suggestion that the writer was feeling ambivalent about her teacher's response to her painting.
D. a fact about the writer's skill as a painter.

GO ON TO THE NEXT PAGE.

1 ■ ■ ■ ■ ■ ■ ■ ■ 1

demeanor clearly told me that he was unimpressed with my torturous efforts. [4] He continued past me to the next student, which, to me, was an obvious message that I was completely hopeless as an artist. [5] I had been so reluctant to begin my painting, despite my love for the artist's rendering of a beautiful bronze, pink, and yellow sunset and a single leafless tree in the foreground. [6] Something snapped inside me as Mr. Peale announced that we were done for the day, and we would continue this week-long project the tomorrow. [7] I could hardly wait to get back there and work on my masterpiece. 54

By the end of this odd assignment, I was actually

thrilled with that being which I had reproduced. While my
                    ———————————
                         55
painting wasn't as dramatic as many of my classmates', and it didn't look exactly like its original, I did feel I had captured its essence. 56

54. For the sake of the logic and coherence of this paragraph, Sentence 3 should be placed:
   F. where it is now.
   G. before Sentence 1.
   H. before Sentence 2.
   J. after Sentence 5.

55. A. NO CHANGE
    B. the painting of which
    C. what
    D. that

56. At this point, the writer is considering adding the following true statement:

   It had a certain beauty and serenity about it that the photo had emitted to me from the beginning.

   Should the writer make this addition here?

   F. Yes, because it provides details about the essence of the painting and explains reasons behind its value to the writer.
   G. Yes, because it provides important information about the original artist's style of painting.
   H. No, because it does not provide a direct connection between the original artwork and the writer's reproduction.
   J. No, because it is already clear from the essay why her reproduction was valuable to the writer.

GO ON TO THE NEXT PAGE.

1 ■ ■ ■ ■ ■ ■ ■ ■ 1

The painting is actually hanging on my wall for years
57
afterwards. I had moved past my fears and lack of

self-confidence and allowed myself to explore the space of

the canvas, the enticing oil colors, and a variety of brush

strokes. I actually felt that somewhat inside of me there
58
was an artist.

To this day, I have no idea what Mr. Peale's intention

was when he asked his English students to reproduce a

famous oil painting. Was he merely trying to fill up the end

of the semester by keeping us preoccupied with busywork
59
while he sat at his desk and red-lined the novelettes we

had written earlier in the semester? Or was he challenging

our self-importance as Advanced English students, trying

to knock us down a peg or two? I do know what I will
60
still think about what that assignment taught me about
60
myself: the absolute beauty of surrendering to the

possibilities in life, and that for a small moment, I too was

an artist.

57. **A.** NO CHANGE
    B. The painting actually hung on my wall
    C. I was actually hanging by the painting
    D. The painting was actually hung by me on my wall

58. **F.** NO CHANGE
    G. somewhere
    H. even though
    J. throughout

59. **A.** NO CHANGE
    B. keeping us busy and preoccupied with unimportant tasks
    C. keeping us preoccupied
    D. maintaining our preoccupation

60. **F.** NO CHANGE
    G. that I am still full of thought
    H. that which I still think
    J. that I still think

GO ON TO THE NEXT PAGE.

1 ■ ■ ■ ■ ■ ■ ■ ■ 1

PASSAGE V

Coffee in the Shade

Who would have thought that there was any connection between a cup of coffee and a bird, butterfly, or even a bat? Such seems to be the case, however, as methods for
<u>61</u>
cultivating coffee plants have gradually changed over the past 30 to 40 years. Coffee plants were first discovered growing naturally, in Africa; hundreds of years ago. The
<u>62</u>
plants grew under a wide canopy of forests, which protected the coffee plants' tender leaves from the burning sun. As coffee was introduced to other country, growers
<u>63</u>
would naturally attempt to simulate the plants' preferred

natural habitat. Nevertheless, coffee plantations all over the
<u>64</u>
world could be found growing successfully in the shade of tall trees. These trees provided more than shade for coffee plants; so they were also home and protection for
<u>65</u>
many species of birds, reptiles, insects, and other plants.

Over the past several decades, growers were developing
<u>66</u>

a new kind of coffee plant, one which is not only tolerant
<u>67</u>
of the sun but thrives in open sunlight. Sun-grown coffee
<u>67</u>
produced as much as three times the yield of shade-grown

coffee in the same amount with time and space.
<u>68</u>

Consequently, the high demand for coffee throughout the
<u>69</u>
world makes the sun-grown method of coffee production

appear to be the best method.

61. A. NO CHANGE
B. however; as
C. however. As
D. however as,

62. F. NO CHANGE
G. naturally in Africa
H. naturally; in Africa,
J. naturally: in Africa

63. A. NO CHANGE
B. other countries
C. other countries'
D. other countries,

64. F. NO CHANGE
G. Despite this,
H. As a result,
J. Even more so,

65. A. NO CHANGE
B. coffee plants; they
C. coffee plants, they
D. coffee plants that they

66. F. NO CHANGE
G. growers, by developing
H. growers developed
J. by growers was developed

67. Which of the following alternatives to the underlined portion would NOT be acceptable?
A. tolerates the sun and even thrives
B. is able to tolerate the sun and thrive
C. is not only tolerant of the sun however thrives
D. does not merely tolerate the sun but thrives

68. F. NO CHANGE
G. amounting to
H. amount for
J. amount of

69. A. NO CHANGE
B. Since
C. However,
D. Furthermore,

GO ON TO THE NEXT PAGE.

1 ■ ■ ■ ■ ■ ■ ■ ■ ■ 1

[1] It has been discovered, however, that there are some unanticipated consequences to using this newer method of growing coffee. [2] First, there might be a chance of rain,

70

often washing away the soil's nutrients and minerals.

[3] Ornithologists who are discovering alarming decreases

71

in some species of songbirds that migrate to the northern United States. [4] This necessitates an increased use of fertilizers and additives, which is labor-intensive and liable to create health risks. [5] Second, as forests are taken

72

down to make way for sun-grown coffee plants, native and

migratory birds, as well as many other fauna and flora, no

73

longer have a home. [6] This is threatening many species, and the effect is now being examined and recorded.

[7] Finally, more pesticides and insecticides are used in the sun-grown method, all of which take their toll on both the environment and the long-term health of the coffee plants themselves. [74]

Today, shade-grown coffee is more difficult to find and thus more costly. Sitting out on the patio with a morning cup of coffee may soon be a much quieter experience in some locations due to the decimation of certain local songbird species. As more people recognize the connection

75

between coffee production and the environment, perhaps they will be willing to pay the higher prices, encouraging growers to return to the more natural method of producing this world-wide staple.

70. Given that all the choices are true, which one would add the most effective visual detail to the description provided in the second part of this sentence?
F. NO CHANGE
G. the lack of tree cover leaves the land open to pounding rainfall,
H. the land is vulnerable to rain,
J. rain often falls,

71. A. NO CHANGE
B. who discovered
C. are discovering
D. discovered

72. Which of the following alternatives to the underlined portion would NOT be acceptable?
F. when
G. since
H. because
J. therefore

73. A. NO CHANGE
B. birds as well as many other fauna and flora
C. birds, as well as many other fauna, and flora
D. birds, as well as many other fauna, and flora,

74. For the sake of the logic and coherence of this paragraph, Sentence 3 should be placed:
F. where it is now.
G. before Sentence 2.
H. before Sentence 5.
J. before Sentence 7.

75. A. NO CHANGE
B. As more and more people together recognize
C. As more people as one group recognize
D. As lots more people who think recognize

END OF THE ENGLISH TEST.
STOP! IF YOU HAVE TIME LEFT OVER, CHECK YOUR WORK ON THIS SECTION ONLY.

2 △ △ △ △ △ △ △ △ **2**

MATHEMATICS TEST

60 Minutes—60 Questions

DIRECTIONS: Solve each of the problems in the time allowed, then fill in the corresponding bubble on your answer sheet. Do not spend too much time on any one problem; skip the more difficult problems and go back to them later. You may use a calculator on this test.

For this test you should assume that figures are NOT necessarily drawn to scale, that all geometric figures lie in a plane, and that the word line is used to indicate a straight line.

DO YOUR FIGURING HERE.

1. One pound is equivalent to 16 ounces. If a book weighs 1.5 pounds, how many ounces, to the nearest tenth, does the book weigh?
   A. 10.7
   B. 17.5
   C. 24.0
   D. 61.5
   E. 165.0

2. Which of the following expressions is equivalent to $(3x + 4)(x - 5)$?
   F. $3x^2 + 9x - 9$
   G. $3x^2 + 9x + 20$
   H. $3x^2 - 19x - 9$
   J. $3x^2 - 11x - 20$
   K. $3x^2 + 20x - 20$

3. Let a function of 2 variables be defined by $f(a, b) = ab - (a - b)$. What is the value of $f(8,9)$?
   A. 89
   B. 73
   C. 71
   D. 34
   E. 0

4. What is 1/5 of 16% of $24,000?
   F. $160
   G. $768
   H. $3,840
   J. $4,032
   K. $7,500

5. If $5x + 5 = 25 + 3x$, then $x =$?
   A. 2.5
   B. 10
   C. 20
   D. 50
   E. 62.5

GO ON TO THE NEXT PAGE.

2   **2**

6. In parallelogram *ABCD* shown below, *AB* is 7 inches long. If the parallelogram's perimeter is 46 inches, how many inches long is *AD*?

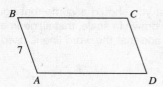

   F. $6\frac{1}{2}$
   G. 16
   H. 28
   J. 39
   K. 49

DO YOUR FIGURING HERE.

7. $|14| \times |-2| =$?
   A. -28
   B. -16
   C. -12
   D. 16
   E. 28

8. In the figure below, *X* and *Y* lie on the sides of $\triangle ABC$, and $\overline{XY}$ is parallel to $\overline{AB}$. What is the measure of $\angle C$?

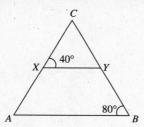

   F. 120°
   G. 90°
   H. 80°
   J. 60°
   K. 40°

9. If $x = -3$ and $y = 2$, then $x^3 y + xy^3 =$?
   A. 78
   B. 30
   C. -6
   D. -30
   E. -78

GO ON TO THE NEXT PAGE.

2 △ △ △ △ △ △ △ △ **2**

10. Two professors were hired to begin work at the same time. Professor A's contract called for a starting salary of \$50,000 with an increase of \$1,500 after each year of employment. Professor B's contract called for a starting salary of \$42,000 with an increase of \$2,800 after each year of employment. If y represents the number of full years of employment (that is, the number of yearly increases each professor has received), which of the following equations could be solved to determine the number of years until B's yearly salary equals A's yearly salary?

   F. $50,000 + 1,500y = 42,000 + 2,800y$
   G. $50,000 + 2,800y = 42,000 + 1,500y$
   H. $1,500y + 2,800y = y$
   J. $1,500y + 2,800y = 42,000$
   K. $1,500y + 2,800y = 50,000$

11. If $W = XYZ$, then which of the following is an expression for Z in terms of W, X, and Y?

   A. $\dfrac{XY}{W}$

   B. $\dfrac{W}{XY}$

   C. WXY
   D. $W - XY$
   E. $W + XY$

12. Two whole numbers have a greatest common factor of 8 and a least common multiple of 48. Which of the following pairs of whole numbers will satisfy the given conditions?

   F. 4 and 9
   G. 5 and 10
   H. 10 and 16
   J. 14 and 20
   K. 16 and 24

13. A rope 55 feet long is cut into two pieces. If one piece is 23 feet longer than the other, what is the length, in feet, of the shorter piece?

   A. 2
   B. 16
   C. 23
   D. 32
   E. 51

DO YOUR FIGURING HERE.

GO ON TO THE NEXT PAGE.

2 △ △ △ △ △ △ △ △ **2**

14. If $(x + r)^2 = x^2 + 22x + r^2$ for all real numbers x, then $r =$?

F. 11
G. 22
H. 44
J. 88
K. 176

DO YOUR FIGURING HERE.

15. Jenny ran $3\frac{1}{3}$ miles on Saturday and $2\frac{4}{5}$ miles on Sunday. The total distance, in miles, Jenny ran during those 2 days is within which of the following ranges?

A. At least $6\frac{1}{2}$ and less than $6\frac{2}{3}$

B. At least $6\frac{1}{3}$ and less than $6\frac{1}{2}$

C. At least 6 and less than $6\frac{1}{3}$

D. At least $5\frac{2}{3}$ and less than 6

E. At least $5\frac{1}{2}$ and less than $5\frac{2}{3}$

16. A car leaves a parking lot and travels directly north for 6 miles. It then turns and travels 8 miles east. How many miles is the car from the parking lot?

F. 6
G. 8
H. 10
J. 14
K. 68

17. In the standard (x,y) coordinate plane, how many times does the graph of $(x + 1)(x - 2)(x + 3)(x + 4)$ intersect the x-axis?

A. 1
B. 4
C. 6
D. 10
E. 24

18. Marcia's horse's rectangular corral is 50 feet wide by 125 feet long. Marcia wants to increase the area by 1,850 square feet by increasing the width and length by the same amount. What will be the new dimensions (width by length), in feet?

F. 55 by 130
G. 60 by 135
H. 65 by 135
J. 65 by 140
K. 70 by 145

19. The lengths of the sides of a triangle are 3 consecutive even integers. If the perimeter of the triangle is 48 inches, what is the length, in inches, of the longest side?

A. 12
B. 14
C. 16
D. 18
E. 24

GO ON TO THE NEXT PAGE.

2   **2**

20. In the standard (x,y) coordinate plane, what is the slope of the line with equation $4y - 6x = 8$?

   F. $-\dfrac{3}{2}$

   G. -6

   H. $\dfrac{3}{2}$

   J. 3

   K. 6

21. In the right triangle shown below, which of the following statements is true about $\angle X$?

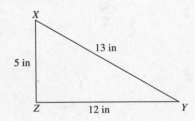

   A. $\cos X = \dfrac{13}{5}$

   B. $\sin X = \dfrac{12}{13}$

   C. $\tan X = \dfrac{5}{12}$

   D. $\cos X = \dfrac{12}{5}$

   E. $\sin X = \dfrac{13}{12}$

Use the following information to answer Questions 22–24.

Quadrilateral $QRST$ is shown below in the standard (x,y) coordinate plane. For this quadrilateral, $QT = 5$, $RS = \sqrt{34}$, $ST = 3$, and $RQ = 6$, all in coordinate units.

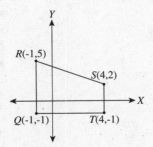

DO YOUR FIGURING HERE.

GO ON TO THE NEXT PAGE.

2 △ △ △ △ △ △ △ △ **2**

22. What is the length of QS in coordinate units?
   F. $\sqrt{34}$
   G. $\sqrt{10}$
   H. $\sqrt{8}$
   J. 8
   K. 4

23. Which of the following are the coordinates of the image of R under a 90° counterclockwise rotation about the origin?
   A. $(5,-1)$
   B. $(1,5)$
   C. $(1,-5)$
   D. $(-1,-5)$
   E. $(-5,-1)$

24. Which of the following is closest to the perimeter of quadrilateral $QRST$, in coordinate units?
   F. 26.0
   G. 22.5
   H. 19.8
   J. 15.0
   K. 14.0

25. If 5 times a number x is subtracted from 15, the result is negative. Which of the following gives the possible value(s) for x?
   A. All $x < 3$
   B. All $x > 3$
   C. 10 only
   D. 3 only
   E. 0 only

26. The temperature, t, in degrees Fahrenheit, in a certain city on a certain spring day satisfies the inequality $|t - 34| \leq 40$. Which of the following temperatures, in degrees Fahrenheit, is NOT in this range?
   F. 74
   G. 16
   H. 0
   J. -6
   K. -8

27. What is the slope-intercept form of $10x - y - 8 = 0$?
   A. $y = -2x$
   B. $y = -10x - 8$
   C. $y = -10x + 8$
   D. $y = 10x - 8$
   E. $y = 10x + 8$

GO ON TO THE NEXT PAGE.

2 △ △ △ △ △ △ △ △ △ **2**

28. A chord 32 centimeters long is 6 centimeters from the center of a circle, as shown below. What is the radius of the circle, to the nearest tenth of a centimeter?

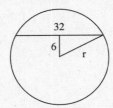

    F. 5.3
    G. 13.9
    H. 17.1
    J. 26.0
    K. 38.0

29. What is the least common multiple of 3, $4a$, $5b$, and $6ab$?
    A. $15ab$
    B. $60ab$
    C. $60a^2b$
    D. $120ab$
    E. $120a^2b$

30. What is the y-coordinate of the point in the standard (x,y) coordinate plane at which the 2 lines $y = 3x + 4$ and $y = 2x + 6$ intersect?
    F. 1
    G. 2
    H. 4
    J. 6
    K. 10

31. For $x^2 \neq 169$, $\dfrac{(x-13)^2}{x^2-169} = ?$

    A. $\dfrac{1}{13}$

    B. $-\dfrac{1}{13}$

    C. $\dfrac{1}{(x+13)}$

    D. $\dfrac{1}{(x-13)}$

    E. $\dfrac{(x-13)}{(x+13)}$

32. If $n = m + 2$, then $(m - n)^4 = ?$
    F. 16
    G. 8
    H. 1
    J. -8
    K. -16

DO YOUR FIGURING HERE.

GO ON TO THE NEXT PAGE.

2 △ △ △ △ △ △ △ △ **2**

33. The larger of two numbers exceeds twice the smaller number by 9. The sum of twice the larger and 5 times the smaller number is 74. If a is the smaller number, which equation below determines the correct value of a?
    A. $5(2a + 9) + 2a = 74$
    B. $5(2a - 9) + 2a = 74$
    C. $(4a + 9) + 5a = 74$
    D. $2(2a + 9) + 5a = 74$
    E. $2(2a - 9) + 5a = 74$

34. When $x/y = 4$, $x^2 - 12y^2 =$?
    F. 0
    G. $4y^2$
    H. $-4y^2$
    J. $-8y^2$
    K. $4y$

35. The ratio of the side lengths for a triangle is exactly 15:14:12. In a second triangle similar to the first, the longest side is 10 inches long. To the nearest tenth of an inch, what is the length of the shortest side of the second triangle?
    A. 6.4
    B. 8.0
    C. 9.3
    D. 12.0
    E. Cannot be determined from the given information

36. If a and b are positive integers such that the greatest common factor of a^2b^2 and ab^3 is 45, then which of the following could b equal?
    F. 3
    G. 5
    H. 9
    J. 15
    K. 45

37. The costs of carriage rides of different lengths, given in half miles, are shown in the table below:

Number of half miles	5	6	7	10
Cost	$8.00	$8.50	$9.00	$10.50

Each cost consists of a fixed charge and a charge per half mile. What is the fixed charge?
    A. $0.50
    B. $1.00
    C. $5.50
    D. $5.00
    E. $1.50

GO ON TO THE NEXT PAGE.

2   △ △ △ △ **2**

38. The hypotenuse of right triangle *ABC* shown below is 16 inches long. The sine of angle *A* is $\frac{3}{5}$. About how many inches long is $\overline{BC}$?

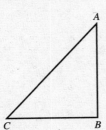

F. 8.0
G. 9.6
H. 12.4
J. 14.3
K. 15.6

39. A circle in the standard (x, y) coordinate plane has center $(12, -5)$ and radius 4 coordinate units. Which of the following is an equation of the circle?
A. $(x - 12)^2 + (y - 5)^2 = 4$
B. $(x - 12)^2 - (y + 5)^2 = 4$
C. $(x - 12)^2 - (y - 5)^2 = 8$
D. $(x - 12)^2 + (y - 5)^2 = 16$
E. $(x - 12)^2 + (y + 5)^2 = 16$

40. What is the largest integer value of *t* that satisfies the inequality $\frac{24}{30} > \frac{t}{24}$?
F. 30
G. 19
H. 18
J. 10
K. 8

41. What is the distance in the standard (x, y) coordinate plane between the points $(5, 5)$ and $(1, 0)$?
A. $\sqrt{26}$
B. $\sqrt{41}$
C. 4
D. 6
E. 16

DO YOUR FIGURING HERE.

GO ON TO THE NEXT PAGE.

2   △ **2**

42. In the figure below, *LMNO* is a trapezoid, *P* lies on *LO*, and angle measures are as marked. What is the measure of angle *MON*?

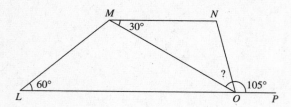

DO YOUR FIGURING HERE.

    F. 15°
    G. 25°
    H. 30°
    J. 35°
    K. 45°

43. In $\triangle ABC$, $AB \cong AC$ and the measure of $\angle B$ is 34°. What is the measure of $\angle A$?
    A. 34°
    B. 56°
    C. 68°
    D. 73°
    E. 112°

44. In a certain budget, 30% of the money goes toward housing costs, and, of that portion, 20% goes toward rent. If the amount of money that goes toward rent is $630, what is the total amount of the budget?
    F. $1,680
    G. $2,100
    H. $4,095
    J. $7,560
    K. $10,500

45. What is the matrix product $\begin{bmatrix} 2x \\ 3x \\ 5x \end{bmatrix}$ [1, 0, −1]?

    A. $\begin{bmatrix} 2x & 0 & -2x \\ 3x & 0 & -3x \\ 5x & 0 & -5x \end{bmatrix}$

    B. $\begin{bmatrix} 2x & 0 & -2x \\ 0 & 0 & 0 \\ 10x & 0 & -10x \end{bmatrix}$

    C. [2x 3x 5x]
    D. [9x 0 −9x]
    E. [0]

GO ON TO THE NEXT PAGE.

2 △ △ △ △ △ △ △ △ **2**

46. In the figure below, all line segments are either horizontal or vertical and the dimensions are given in feet. What is the perimeter in feet, of the figure?

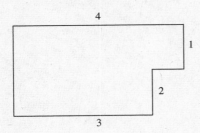

F. 16
G. 14
H. 13
J. 12
K. 10

47. The average of a and b is 6 and the average of a, b, and c is 11. What is the value of c?
A. 21
B. 17
C. 13
D. 8
E. 5

48. The greatest integer of a set of consecutive even integers is 12. If the sum of these integers is 40, how many integers are in this set?
F. 5
G. 6
H. 12
J. 20
K. 40

49. On the number line shown below, t, u, v, w, x, y, and z are coordinates of the indicated points. Which of the following is closest in value to $|w - u|$?

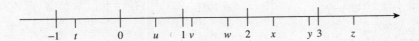

A. t
B. v
C. x
D. y
E. z

DO YOUR FIGURING HERE.

GO ON TO THE NEXT PAGE.

2 △ △ △ △ △ △ △ △ **2**

50. The length of arc *XY* of a circle is equal to $\frac{1}{6}$ of the circumference of the circle. The length of the arc is 7π inches. What is the radius, in inches, of the circle?

  F. 42
  G. 21
  H. 14
  J. 7
  K. 3

51. Let *S* be the set of all integers that can be written as $2n^2 - 6n$, where *n* is a nonzero integer. Which of the following integers is in *S*?

  A. 6
  B. 30
  C. 46
  D. 64
  E. 80

52. Let the function *g* be defined by $g(x) = 3(x^2 - 2)$. When $g(x) = 69$, what is a possible value of $2x - 3$?

  F. -7
  G. -5
  H. 2
  J. 5
  K. 7

53. If $a + b = 25$ and $a > 4$, then which of the following *must* be true?

  A. $a = 22$
  B. $b < 21$
  C. $b > 4$
  D. $b = 0$
  E. $a < 25$

54. If *m*, *n*, and *p* are positive integers such that $m + n$ is even and the value of $(m + n)^2 + n + p$ is odd, which of the following *must* be true?

  F. *m* is odd
  G. *n* is even
  H. *p* is odd
  J. If *n* is even, *p* is odd
  K. If *p* is odd, *n* is odd

DO YOUR FIGURING HERE.

GO ON TO THE NEXT PAGE.

2 △ △ △ △ △ △ △ △ 2

55. A bag contains only quarters, dimes, and nickels. The probability of randomly selecting a quarter is 1/6. The probability of randomly selecting a nickel is 1/4. Which of the following could be the total number of coins in the bag?

A. 15
B. 24
C. 30
D. 32
E. 40

56. In the xy-coordinate system, if (r,s) and $(r+2, s+t)$ are two points on the line defined by the equation $y = 4x+5$, then $t = ?$

F. 4
G. 5
H. 8
J. 9
K. 11

57. In the figure shown below, $s \perp r$ and $x > 90$. Which of the following *must* be true?

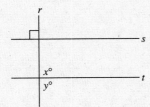

A. $s \, // \, t$
B. $r \perp t$
C. $y = 90$
D. $y > 90$
E. $y < 90$

58. Let $x = 2y + 3z - 5$. What happens to the value of x if the value of y decreases by 1 and the value of z increases by 2?

F. It decreases by 2
G. It is unchanged
H. It increases by 1
J. It increases by 2
K. It increases by 4

DO YOUR FIGURING HERE.

GO ON TO THE NEXT PAGE.

2 △ △ △ △ △ △ △ △ **2**

59. On the cube in the figure shown below, each of the following points is the same distance from R as it is from S EXCEPT:

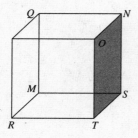

A. M
B. O
C. T
D. Q
E. N

60. In the figure shown below, $\overline{YZ}$ and $\overline{MB}$ intersect at O and $\overline{XO}$ is perpendicular to $\overline{YZ}$. What is the value of $3p + 4s - 2t$?

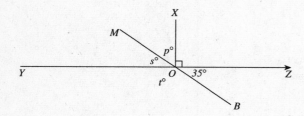

F. $15°$
G. $35°$
H. $55°$
J. $135°$
K. $150°$

DO YOUR FIGURING HERE.

END OF THE MATHEMATICS TEST.
STOP! IF YOU HAVE TIME LEFT OVER, CHECK YOUR WORK ON THIS SECTION ONLY.

3   3

READING TEST

35 Minutes—40 Questions

DIRECTIONS: This test includes four passages, each followed by ten questions. Read the passages and choose the best answer to each question. After you have selected your answer, fill in the corresponding bubble on your answer sheet. You should refer to the passages as often as necessary when answering the questions.

PASSAGE I

PROSE FICTION: *Moving Day*

Two sodas, four candy bars, a packet of trail mix, and one bathroom break later, we'd made it. As far as I was concerned, it was just in time. After spending six hours in the car, my legs were in need of some
5 serious stretching. I opened the door and swung my aching legs over the side of the passenger seat, letting the hot, sticky air hit me like a brick wall. While I'm thankful for the conveniences of the modern car, sometimes even thick, humid air, heavy with pollen
10 and summer sweat, tastes a million times better than stale air conditioning. I could feel my mood begin to improve.

"So, what do you think?"

I turned to look at my husband, John, as he got
15 out of the car, his eyes sparkling as he awaited my response. It was our second trip to the apartment complex in the last three weeks, but this time, there was something different. Three weeks ago, we were simply visitors looking to sign a rental agreement, but now,
20 we were home.

"I like it," I answered, hoping the enthusiasm in my voice would match the sparkle in his eyes. Encouraged, he smiled and turned back to the car.

"We'd better start unloading before it gets too
25 hot," he said.

"Too late. I'm already sweating." I pushed my bangs off my forehead, hoping to prevent my hair from looking absolutely disgusting. John must have noticed, because I caught him looking at me through the rear
30 window.

"Libby, we have an entire car and trailer to unpack. You might as well forget about looking glamorous, at least for now. Besides, it's not like we're back in D.C. No C-Span cameras here!" He chuckled as he
35 said it, but the sparkle had left his eyes.

"Yeah, yeah," I answered, tossing my head as I laughed gamely. I didn't want to lose that sense of optimism—not at the beginning. I stretched my legs out in front of me, hoping it'd make getting out of the
40 car a little bit easier. No such luck. My knees cracked as I stood up, and my calves were tight from the cramped quarters. I'd had no idea my legs would miss the high heels my feet had gladly given up. Suppressing a sigh, I headed towards the trunk to help John unload our life.

45 We each grabbed an armful and headed towards our new apartment, just a few blocks away from the squat, industrial-looking building where John would start teaching. The fall semester was just a few short weeks away. I'd always thought that university
50 buildings were lofty, ivy-covered brick and stone—at least that's what I was used to. Things were certainly different in the Midwest. After transferring some bags from one arm to the other, I managed to get the front door key out of my pocket. By the time I got the door
55 open, I thought John was going to topple right into the apartment.

There's something monumental about taking your first step into a new home. For John and me, it was our first home we had chosen together. Walking through
60 the door, the bags heavy on my arms, I felt like we were starting the first pages in the next chapter of our lives. When John had asked me to marry him and move to Ohio, I'd had no idea what the future held for us. Now, suddenly, I knew the future had begun. And, just
65 as suddenly, I knew it could be anything we wanted it to be.

"Well, this is it," John said.

"Yep. This is it." Looking around the empty apartment, I realized its beige walls were simply a blank
70 canvas waiting for us to fill it. I felt a thrill of real excitement as a slow grin spread across my face. John saw it and started to relax. He leaned against the doorframe and followed me with his eyes as I traced the outline of the room. It would work. Excited to begin,
75 I turned to John.

"Well, are you ready?" I asked.

"I think so. Are you?" he replied.

"Sure am. Let's go."

With that, we dropped our armfuls in the middle of
80 the living room and headed back to the car for another load. We were home.

GO ON TO THE NEXT PAGE.

3 ████████████████████████████████████ **3**

1. The first seven paragraphs establish all of the following about Libby EXCEPT that she:
   A. used to live in Washington, D.C.
   B. was excited about the move from the beginning.
   C. sometimes prefers hot, sticky air to stale air-conditioning.
   D. has just rented a new apartment with her husband, John.

2. According to details in the passage, Libby and John most likely moved into their new apartment:
   F. in early winter.
   G. in late autumn.
   H. in early spring.
   J. in late summer.

3. Compared to John's initial attitude towards arriving at their new home, Libby's initial reaction is best described as:
   A. contrasting; Libby is less enthusiastic about the move.
   B. contrasting; Libby resents moving to Ohio.
   C. similar; Libby is excited to begin a new life.
   D. similar; Libby enjoys long, cross-country trips.

4. Which of the following best describes Libby's reaction to her first steps into her new home?
   F. Total fear.
   G. Mild dread.
   H. Cautious optimism.
   J. Real excitement.

5. According to the passage, John's new workplace is all of the following EXCEPT:
   A. ivy-covered brick and stone.
   B. squat.
   C. industrial-looking.
   D. close to John and Libby's apartment.

6. Which of the following is NOT an accurate description of the passage?
   F. A story about the hardships faced by a young married couple in their first home.
   G. A glimpse into the lives of two young people as they enter a new phase.
   H. A look at how two people with initially divergent viewpoints reach an understanding.
   J. A snapshot of a young couple's journey into a new life together.

7. It is most reasonable to infer from the passage that John would agree with which of the following statements about his wife, Libby?
   A. Libby is an important government legislator.
   B. Libby misses wearing high-heeled shoes.
   C. Libby is somewhat vain.
   D. Libby hates living in Ohio.

8. As it is used in the twelfth paragraph, the statement, "Looking around the empty apartment, I realized its beige walls were simply a blank canvas waiting for us to fill it" primarily supports which of the following points implied by the passage?
   F. John and Libby will need to work hard to make their new life exciting.
   G. John and Libby are starting a new life together filled with exciting potential.
   H. The apartment is not what the couple expected.
   J. The apartment is industrial looking and needs a fresh coat of paint.

9. The primary point of the first paragraph is that:
   A. people often eat junk food on long car trips.
   B. the main character prefers hot weather to cool weather.
   C. the main character is grateful that her long trip has ended.
   D. modern cars have many conveniences, including air conditioning.

10. As it is used in the passage, the phrase *unload our life* (line 44) refers to the:
    F. sense of loss Libby and John feel regarding their move.
    G. many furniture items contained within the car and trailer.
    H. disappointment Libby feels because she had to leave Washington, D.C.
    J. significance of the move from Washington, D.C. to Ohio.

GO ON TO THE NEXT PAGE.

3   3

PASSAGE II

SOCIAL SCIENCE: *Defining the Poverty Line: A Political Question*

Poverty is an enduring problem that must be addressed by all modern societies. In fact, some ethicists say a civilization can be judged by how well it treats its least fortunate. By this measure, the United

5 States has much to be proud of. On a national level, the United States has done remarkable work to decrease the suffering of the poor by subsidizing food, housing, and education, and even by giving money directly to those who need it the most. Still, even in the public sector,

10 projects have to be evaluated to see if they are effective. No one can measure the benefits of aid without defining what poverty is, and when someone has been lifted out of it. This leads to one very political question: How exactly should poverty be measured?

15   The question of poverty is extremely complex. Should it be considered absolute—as a simple matter of the availability of food and shelter—or should it be relative to the goods and services enjoyed by the society as a whole? In other words, if a person can

20 afford a DVD player but not to live in a safe neighborhood, is that person poor? Certainly something as fluid as the economy can affect any number of forces to cause financial suffering—sometimes quite suddenly. Still, according to our federal government, there is

25 a specific measure, the "poverty line," that answers the question. Such a measure was devised in 1963 by government economist Mollie Orshansky, then working for the Social Security Administration under the jurisdiction of the Office of Management and Budget.

30   Orshansky's statistical measurement was one small part of the federal government's plan to attack the difficult national economic conditions that were hurting millions of Americans in the early 1960s. President Lyndon Johnson labeled the plan the government's

35 "War on Poverty," and it led to such national programs as Head Start, VISTA, and the Jobs Corps. Orshansky developed her poverty threshold from a Department of Agriculture study outlining the cost of nutritionally adequate meals.

40   From the Agriculture study, Orshansky took the most economic and healthy meal design she could find. She then estimated statistically that the average American family in the 1950s spent approximately one-third of its household income on food; from there, she

45 multiplied by three the cost of the most economically efficient, nutritional diet. This multiplier effect, in theory, produced the level of pre-tax household income at or below which a family should be considered poor. Orshansky's calculation was distributed for use across

50 the government, and the measure came to be known as the poverty line. It has been scaled every year for inflation, and it is adjustable to household size.

Given the decades-old origins of this measure and the limited data available to Orshansky at the time, it is

55 fair to wonder if her standard is still accurate. Studies show that it is not. While families today spend about 12 percent of their income on food—nowhere near the 33 percent assumed in the 1950s—the cost of important

budget items, such as housing, transportation, and

60 health care, has increased dramatically. Orshansky's poverty measure, which only takes into account the ability of a household to provide itself with food, is missing several essential components to be accurate in modern society. With over $60 billion in federal aid

65 tied each year to this guideline, not to mention an additional $260 billion in Medicaid spending, the fact is many Americans are still falling deeper into poverty and failing to receive the aid they so desperately need and deserve.

70   If reform of the measure of poverty used by society is an obvious need, it remains to be seen why such reform has not been forthcoming. The answer lies in the very politics that caused the measure to be created in the first place. Any change in the measured poverty

75 level of a society is an indicator of economic health within that society, and no president has been willing to increase the perceived amount of poverty for a statistical recalculation, no matter how justified. Indeed, some economists say that updating the poverty measure

80 would increase the number of those considered poor, and therefore eligible for government aid, by as much as 2 percentage points. That may not seem significant, but in real terms it means an additional several million people are living below the "poverty line"—whether

85 we count them or not.

11. In the context of lines 46–51, the statement "the measure came to be known as the poverty line" (line 51) is used to support the idea that:

A. poverty can be measured and defined by a single number.

B. poor neighborhoods in the United States are marked off from richer neighborhoods by a metaphorical "line."

C. inflation and household size are the only variables needed to define poverty.

D. poor people often have to stand in line to receive government support.

12. It can be reasonably inferred from the passage that:

F. being poor means not being able to afford a DVD player.

G. Americans have overcome poverty in recent years.

H. defining poverty is complex and difficult to do.

J. lowering the poverty line would not impact the economic health of the U.S.

13. It can reasonably be inferred from the passage that Orshansky estimated that, in the 1950s, the percentage of income that the average American family spent on non-food items was:

A. less than one-third.

B. one-third.

C. between one-third and two-thirds.

D. approximately two-thirds.

GO ON TO THE NEXT PAGE.

3 ██ **3**

14. Which of the following best expresses the paradox described in the fifth paragraph (lines 53–69)?

    F. Americans today have to spend far less of their income on food, which makes them seem richer by Orshansky's measure, but they have to spend far more on other necessary items, which makes them really much poorer.

    G. Americans today have far more money than they did in the 1950s, which makes them much richer than they used to be.

    H. In America today, ensuring reliable transportation is far more important to families than providing nutritious meals.

    J. Orshansky's economic model neglects to account for the cost of modern technology, but it includes a detailed discussion of the modern economy.

15. According to the passage, the impact of Orshansky's economic model on the distribution of federal aid to the poor is that:

    A. far more federal money is now available to help the poor.

    B. poor people are unaware that they are eligible for $260 billion in Medicaid assistance.

    C. legitimately poor people are not receiving the aid they're entitled to receive from the federal government.

    D. poor people are not receiving government aid because the government does not know where they live.

16. The author traces Orshansky's economic model back to its origins in:

    F. the merger between the Social Security Administration and the Office of Management and Budget.

    G. President Lyndon Johnson's "War on Poverty."

    H. President Lyndon Johnson's Head Start program.

    J. the Civil Rights movement of the early 1960s.

17. The main point of the first paragraph is that:

    A. the United States does an excellent job taking care of its poor.

    B. poverty is an important issue in society, and it must be measured accurately so that aid can be given effectively.

    C. public assistance programs must be eliminated if they are found to be ineffective at alleviating poverty.

    D. poverty is an issue that affects few modern societies.

18. According to the passage, which of the following statements is accurate regarding the percentage of income the average American family spends on food?

    F. The percentage of income the average American family spends on food has increased dramatically since the 1950s.

    G. The average American family now spends most of its money on food.

    H. The percentage of income spent on food has decreased from approximately 33% to approximately 12% since the 1950s.

    J. The percentage of income spent on food has increased from approximately 12% to approximately 33% since the 1950s.

19. The passage implies that no president has been willing to change the poverty measure for all of the following reasons EXCEPT:

    A. no president has been willing to increase the perceived level of poverty.

    B. changing the poverty level will increase the number of people eligible for federal aid.

    C. no president wants to risk making the economy look less healthy.

    D. poverty is an obvious problem and presidents are more concerned with complex problems.

20. According to the passage, Orshansky's role in President Johnson's "War on Poverty" was to:

    F. provide a precise measure of the number of poor who needed help in the early 1960s.

    G. answer critics who complained that the government was not doing enough to help the poor.

    H. provide a precise measure of the number of poor people eligible for Job Corps programs.

    J. support the annual budget of the Social Security Administration.

GO ON TO THE NEXT PAGE.

3   3

PASSAGE III
HUMANITIES: *J.R.R. Tolkien and Me*

John Ronald Reuel Tolkien, better known as J.R.R. Tolkien, was many things in his long life, including philologist, writer, and university professor. Of course, today, most people remember him as the
5 author of *The Lord of the Rings*—a monumental work that became an epic film.

A friend introduced me to Tolkien's writings when I was 10 years old. Aileen gave me a copy of *The Hobbit*, and told me her father was reading *The Lord*
10 *of the Rings* to her and her brother at the dinner table every night after the family had finished eating. I read *The Hobbit* and was hooked. By the time I was 14, I had read every piece of fiction Tolkien had published.

The more I read, the more fascinated I became
15 with not only the world Tolkien had created, but with the man himself. I began to dream of meeting Tolkien. I imagined someday traveling to Oxford University, where he had been a professor of English Language and Literature, and somehow finding the words to tell
20 him how meaningful his writings had been for me.

But, growing up in the Midwest, the possibility of traveling to England seemed very remote. Then I discovered that Tolkien had died years before I'd even started reading *The Hobbit*. I forgot about my dream
25 and got down to the business of school and sports and college applications.

I started college as a chemistry major, but by my sophomore year, I was major-less. Somehow, by my junior year, I was accepted into the Honors
30 English program. This introduced me to the Medieval and Renaissance Collegium (MARC). The director of MARC thought I would be a perfect fit for a new diploma program he was developing—an interim program between undergraduate and graduate work.
35 I applied, was accepted, and found myself faced with my old dream: I was headed to England—to Oxford University, the home of my favorite author!

Oxford isn't set up like most American universities. It's not a single uniform entity. Instead, it's a
40 collection of 39 independent colleges, each with its own internal structure and activities, with an overlying administration that conducts examinations and confers degrees. Tolkien, for example, had been a professor at
45 Merton College. His close friend, C.S. Lewis, taught at Magdalen College (pronounced: Mawdlin). Most students identify with their college, not with the university. This means that pretty much anyone there wearing an Oxford University sweatshirt is a tourist.

50 I loved Oxford. I loved the tiny streets and the way the trees hid the modern shop fronts, showing only the medieval towers from the rolling hills of a nearby park. Even more, I loved the sense of living history—the way the children would play carelessly under towering
55 trees among centuries-old tombstones in the back-yards of churches, or the stories our housekeeper would tell of Lawrence of Arabia's ghost who, apparently, lived in our own quarters. When inexplicable drafts would sweep through my room, our housekeeper swore it was
60 Lawrence. I loved walking every Tuesday on my way to my folklore tutorial, past the pub—The Eagle and

the Child—where Tolkien met with his best friends to discuss their ideas for writing. The sign on the pub allegedly was the inspiration for Bilbo's flight with the
65 Giant Eagles. Best of all, I had a professor who had actually known J.R.R. Tolkien himself.

Sr. Benedicta was a very smart but very kindly, elderly nun. She was no slouch as an academic and had published several highly regarded books in her
70 field. As a colleague, she had spent time with Tolkien when she was newly hired at St. Stephen's College. One day, when she had asked me how I liked studying at Oxford, I decided to tell her about my dream. I told her how, when I was a child, I had wanted so badly
75 to meet Tolkien. I had vividly imagined traveling to Oxford, finding his little cottage, passing through the picket fence, past the rose bushes, to finally knock at the great man's door. I had even imagined him opening it and looking at me. I just could never, ever, think of
80 anything to say that didn't make me feel like a complete idiot.

Sr. Benedicta smiled indulgently at me for a moment, and then said, "He would have encouraged that feeling." Apparently, most people have this
85 impression of Tolkien as a gentle, grandfatherly sort of man, but, unless you were his grandchild, that wasn't actually the case. In person, he was frequently severe and not terribly friendly. I suppose it probably made him a better professor. In the end, I was very glad
90 I finally made my pilgrimage to Oxford, but considered it for the best that I never had a chance to thank J.R.R. Tolkien in person.

21. The point of view from which this passage is narrated is best described as:
   A. an adult reflecting on her youth.
   B. a parent recalling her daughter's travels.
   C. a teenager who aspires to be a writer.
   D. Sr. Benedicta, a nun who worked with J.R.R. Tolkien.

22. Which of the following best summarizes the emotional shift that is presented by the narrator in the passage?
   F. An adult learns that she doesn't have to meet her heroes for them to leave a profound impression on her.
   G. A teenager moves from appreciating fantasy novels to preferring historical fiction.
   H. An adult learns that she prefers to visit distant places rather than merely to read about them.
   J. A teenager learns first-hand that famous authors are frequently unpleasant individuals.

23. J.R.R. Tolkien is presented by the narrator as being:
   A. gentle and grandfatherly.
   B. severe but friendly.
   C. intelligent but caring.
   D. talented but intimidating.

GO ON TO THE NEXT PAGE.

3 ▬▬▬▬▬▬▬▬▬▬▬▬▬▬▬▬▬▬▬▬ **3**

24. In the seventh paragraph, the narrator's attitude towards Oxford is best described as:
   F. exasperated and unimpressed.
   G. fond and appreciative.
   H. overwhelmed and depressed.
   J. disinterested and despondent.

25. In the fourth paragraph, the narrator's attitude toward being unable to meet Tolkien can best be characterized as:
   A. relieved.
   B. morose.
   C. angry.
   D. accepting.

26. It can most reasonably be inferred that by telling Sr. Benedicta about her childhood desire to meet J.R.R. Tolkien, the narrator intends to:
   F. impress her teacher by showing her dedication to Oxford.
   G. illustrate her love of medieval English.
   H. create a connection to her childhood hero by talking about him to a mutual friend.
   J. pass the time of day with an interesting companion.

27. Which of the following best represents the narrator's initial opinions about J.R.R. Tolkien's writings?
   A. The writings were obscure and difficult to follow.
   B. The writings were fascinating and made the narrator want to read more.
   C. The writings were interesting, but there were far too many to read them all.
   D. The most interesting writings were about Oxford, England.

28. When the narrator says, "When inexplicable drafts would sweep through my room, our housekeeper swore it was Lawrence," she means that:
   F. the housekeeper believed that Lawrence of Arabia's ghost haunted the student dorms.
   G. Lawrence of Arabia was the junior housekeeper in charge of student rooms.
   H. the housekeeper was a silly, superstitious woman.
   J. the student dorms were very old and drafty.

29. As it is used in line 68, the phrase "she was no slouch as an academic" most nearly means:
   A. she had excellent posture when teaching.
   B. she had difficulty explaining technical terms.
   C. she was an excellent researcher.
   D. she was new to her field.

30. As it is used in line 39, the word *uniform* most nearly means:
   F. solid.
   G. similar.
   H. unchanging.
   J. consistent.

GO ON TO THE NEXT PAGE.

3 ████████████████████████████████████ 3

PASSAGE IV
NATURAL SCIENCE: *El Niño: A Meteorological Enigma*

Almost any mention of climate change brings thoughts of global warming, complete with mental images of rising seas and melting ice caps. While few reputable scientists contest the reality of global
5 warming, most climatologists are also aware of other powerful meteorological phenomena that shape the weather on a daily, seasonal, or even multi-year basis. In fact, these "background oscillations," or fluctuations, appear to cause major climate shifts every few
10 decades. Among the most influential are the North Pacific Oscillation (NPO), the North Atlantic Oscillation (NAO), the Pacific Decadal Oscillation (PDO), and the El Niño-Southern Oscillation (ENSO). Of these, probably the best-known is the El Niño-Southern
15 Oscillation, popularly called "El Niño."

The term El Niño was first reported in scientific circles in 1892. It originally referred to a local event: an annual, weak, warm ocean current that fishermen discovered along the central western coast
20 of South America. The current was most noticeable around Christmastime, which led to its name because El Niño is Spanish for "little boy" and is frequently used when referring to the Christ Child. (The reverse phenomenon, a cold ocean current, is known by a
25 corresponding term, La Niña, Spanish for "little girl.") Along this area of South America, El Niños reduce the upwelling of cold, nutrient-rich water that sustains large fish populations. Predators such as larger fish and sea birds depend on these populations for survival, as
30 do local fisheries.

As climatology developed as a discipline, scientists discovered that both trends in the current were part of a larger phenomenon affecting global climate patterns, the Southern Oscillation. The definition of
35 El Niño has therefore expanded and continues to change as climate researchers compile more data. Now scientists say that during El Niños, sea-surface temperatures over a large part of the central Pacific climb above normal and stay high for many months. This
40 creates a large pool of warm water that coincides with a change in wind patterns. The shift in wind patterns changes where evaporation takes place. Together, the warm water and shifting wind affect where storms form and where rainfall occurs on a global level.
45 Most of the time, strong El Niños bring wet winters to the Southwestern United States and milder winters to the Midwest. They tend to bring dry conditions to Indonesia and northern Australia. They generally occur every two to seven years. La Niñas usually,
50 but not always, follow El Niños. During La Niñas, water temperatures in the Central Pacific drop below normal, and weather patterns shift in the other direction. Together, the El Niño and La Niña cycles complete the El Niño-Southern Oscillation (ENSO).
55 ENSO weather oscillations are discrete from the NPO, NAO, and PDO weather patterns. This means one oscillation does not cause or usually influence the others. Sometimes, however, the various oscillations "beat" together at the same frequency, causing the

60 fluctuations to be synchronized. When this happens, scientists say the resulting weather can be intensified.

Weather effects can be damaging. The warming patterns of El Niño are one of the leading causes of natural damage to coral reefs, while wider ENSO
65 fluctuations may cause flooding or drought to occur on land. In these cases, extreme shifts can cause economic pressure by disrupting entire fishing industries or damaging crops.

Sometimes, pressure caused by intense weather
70 can have unexpected political effects. Some scientists argue that unusually cold weather brought by a strong El Niño phenomenon caused significant crop damage in 1788–89, which many say contributed to the French Revolution. Other climate researchers claim that strong
75 oscillation coupling, combined with strong El Niños in the late 1930s and early 1940s, led to a profound cold snap in Northern Europe in the middle of the Second World War. The scientists argue that this unexpected cold snap significantly contributed to the failure
80 of Germany to capture Moscow, which changed the course of World War II.

ENSO phenomena, along with the other three oscillations, are separate from those attributed to global warming. The causes are completely independent.
85 However, because El Niño and global warming both can result in strong temperature variability, disruptive rain distribution, and extreme damage to a variety of ecosystems, any synchronicity will be closely observed by scientists seeking to document the total effects
90 of each.

31. The main purpose of the passage is to:
  A. explain the weather pattern known as El Niño and describe its effects.
  B. argue that El Niños are a far more significant source of weather change than global warming.
  C. discuss the four meteorological patterns that form global weather.
  D. describe how scientists study the weather.

32. It can reasonably be inferred from the passage that scientists began to show interest in El Niño weather patterns during which of the following decades?
  F. 1780s
  G. 1890s
  H. 1930s
  J. 1990s

33. As presented in the passage, the statements in lines 49–81 are best characterized as:
  A. facts based on careful historical and scientific documents.
  B. speculation based on rumor and hearsay.
  C. hypotheses supported by evidence.
  D. estimates based on data.

GO ON TO THE NEXT PAGE.

34. The author uses the information in parentheses in lines 23–25 primarily to:
  F. present information related to the topic, but not immediately relevant to the paragraph.
  G. suggest that La Niña is less important than El Niño.
  H. support the use of Spanish terminology in meteorological research.
  J. imply that La Niña phenomena were discovered considerably later than El Niño.

35. Based on the passage, some scientists speculate that when weather oscillations "beat" at the same frequency, the resulting weather:
  A. is frequently neutralized.
  B. is milder than normal.
  C. is unusually cold.
  D. is often intensified.

36. The main purpose of the third paragraph is to:
  F. provide a history of 20th century climatology.
  G. explain why meteorological predictions are often inaccurate.
  H. describe how modern climatologists define El Niño phenomena.
  J. show how climatologists know where rainfall will occur worldwide.

37. Suppose that a scientist was trying to determine if a given year in the past had been an El Niño year. Which of the following would most likely indicate an El Niño weather pattern?
  A. Reports of unusually wet weather in Southern California and reports of drought in Darwin, Australia.
  B. Reports of ice storms in Wisconsin and Michigan.
  C. Reports of flooding in Jakarta, Indonesia and reports of unusually dry weather in Africa.
  D. Reports of drought in New Mexico and Texas.

38. Based on the passage, how should the claim that "pressure caused by intense weather can have unexpected political effects" (lines 69–70) most likely be interpreted?
  F. People are more likely to attend indoor political rallies in poor weather.
  G. Severe weather caused problems that changed the political landscape of modern Europe.
  H. In the 18th century, people frequently blamed their political leadership when weather turned bad.
  J. A series of particularly severe El Niños caused Germany to lose World War II.

39. According to the passage, all of the following are negative consequences of El Niño weather patterns EXCEPT:
  A. damage to coral reefs.
  B. flooding.
  C. drought.
  D. increases in large fish populations.

40. The author makes which of the following comparisons between El Niño and global warming?
  F. El Niño patterns and global warming have nothing to do with one another, and have no effect on global weather.
  G. El Niño patterns and global warming have the same underlying causes.
  H. The effects of El Niño patterns and global warming are easy to confuse.
  J. El Niño patterns and global warming are completely independent, but often have the same effects on global weather.

END OF THE READING TEST.
STOP! IF YOU HAVE TIME LEFT OVER, CHECK YOUR WORK ON THIS SECTION ONLY.

4 ◯ ◯ ◯ ◯ ◯ ◯ ◯ ◯ ◯ **4**

SCIENCE REASONING TEST

35 Minutes—40 Questions

DIRECTIONS: This test includes seven passages, each followed by several questions. Read the passage and choose the best answer to each question. After you have selected your answer, fill in the corresponding bubble on your answer sheet. You should refer to the passages as often as necessary when answering the questions. You may NOT use a calculator on this test.

PASSAGE I

In recent decades, astronomers deduced that there is approximately five times more material in clusters of galaxies than expected based on visible galaxies and hot gas. Most of the material in these galaxies is, in fact, invisible. Since galaxies are the largest structures in the universe held together by gravity, some scientists concluded that most of the matter in the entire universe is invisible. They called this invisible material dark matter. Two scientists offer theories on whether dark matter exists.

Scientist 1

Recent studies by researchers at Northeastern University and the University of Victoria may suggest that dark matter—a substance previously considered viable in light of Newton's theories of gravity—does not actually exist. Dark matter is not readily observable because it does not directly refract light or energy. Its existence could only be deduced because of the perceived gravitational effect that it has on surrounding matter.

This new research is based upon Einstein's theory of general relativity. Although Newtonian physics may provide for the cohesive nature of solar systems, when applied to galaxies the 'numbers' do not add up. Because there is not enough visible matter for the various gravitational equations to balance, dark matter was theorized to make up this deficit. Without a source for the rest of the missing matter, there was previously nothing in Newtonian physics to explain the movement or shape of galaxies.

In terms of general relativity, a galaxy, seen collectively, has its own gravity and essentially drives its own rotation at a constant rate. Aaron Romanowsky of Harvard University and several colleagues point to the existence of several elliptical-shaped galaxies surrounded by very little dark matter as evidence that dark matter is not, in fact, the cause of the warped galaxies. The results of their studies cast doubt on some of the conventional theories of galaxy formation and manipulation.

This theory does not explain everything, such as how large clusters of galaxies are able to bind to one another, but it does allow for already proven equations to explain the motion of galaxies without dark matter.

Scientist 2

Without dark matter, there are many cosmological phenomena that are difficult to explain. Some scientists believe that the interaction between dark matter and other smaller, nearby galaxies is causing the Milky Way galaxy to take on a warped, elliptical profile. This interaction involves two smaller galaxies (called Magellanic Clouds) near the Milky Way, moving through an enormous amount of dark matter, which in effect enhances the gravitational pull that the two Magellanic Clouds could exert on the Milky Way and other surrounding bodies. Computer models from the University of California at Berkeley seem to support this theory. Without the existence of the dark matter, the Magellanic Clouds would not have sufficient mass to have such a strong effect on the bend of the Milky Way galaxy.

The strongest evidence for the validity of this hypothesis rests in Newtonian physics and the hypothesis that anything with mass will exert a gravitational pull. However, there is nothing readily observable in the vicinity of the Milky Way with sufficient mass that could cause such a high level of distortion via gravitational pull.

In addition, theoretical arguments for the existence of dark matter can be made by looking at the cosmic microwave background in the universe. This "leftover" light radiation, emitted only a few hundred thousand years after the formation of the universe, provides information about conditions in the universe on a very large scale. Measurements of cosmic microwave radiation imply the existence of dark matter, although even dark matter cannot solve all of the mysteries of the universe.

1. Which of the following statements is most consistent with Scientist 1's viewpoint?
   A. The application of the theory of general relativity to observed phenomena requires the inclusion of dark matter.
   B. Einstein invented dark matter to cover up deficiencies in his theory of relativity.
   C. Newton's theories are completely dependent upon the proven existence of dark matter in the universe.
   D. New research shows that dark matter is not required to explain astronomers' observations.

GO ON TO THE NEXT PAGE.

4 ◯ ◯ ◯ ◯ ◯ ◯ ◯ ◯ ◯ **4**

2. According to the passage, a similarity between the two viewpoints is that both scientists believe that:
   F. dark matter has little to no effect on galaxy shape.
   G. there are still many unexplained cosmological phenomena.
   H. cosmic microwave radiation suggests the presence of dark matter.
   J. dark matter can be easily observed in the universe.

3. Which of the following best summarizes Scientist 2's position?
   A. The existence of dark matter is a scientific fraud perpetrated by astronomers and physicists.
   B. The existence of dark matter is probable based on currently available evidence.
   C. Dark matter is misnamed because it is visible using modern instruments.
   D. Dark matter is no longer a necessary part of the general theory of relativity.

4. With which of the following statements would both Scientist 1 and Scientist 2 most likely agree?
   F. Astronomical observations of the known universe are of no value when it comes to explaining the shape of the Milky Way.
   G. Warped galaxies are a convenient fiction created by astronomers and physicists.
   H. Newtonian physics can account for the existence of warped galaxies without resorting to dark matter as part of the explanation.
   J. Warped galaxies such as the Milky Way present an astronomical puzzle that is worth investigating.

5. Scientist 2's position would be most weakened by which of the following observations?
   A. The Magellanic Clouds actually move more quickly than previously thought.
   B. The Magellanic Clouds are actually much more massive than previously thought.
   C. The Milky Way is warped more than previously thought.
   D. U.C. Berkeley computer models are much more accurate than previously thought.

6. According to the passage, the main point of the disagreement between Scientist 1 and Scientist 2 is:
   F. the existence of dark matter in the universe.
   G. the source of dark matter in the universe.
   H. the likelihood that Einstein was aware of Newton's theories.
   J. the existence of the Magellanic Clouds near the Milky Way.

7. Scientist 1's position would be most weakened by:
   A. the revelation that Einstein's general theory of relativity is significantly flawed.
   B. the appearance of several newly-discovered warped galaxies similar to the Milky Way.
   C. the discovery that previous estimates of the mass of galaxies were too high.
   D. proof that Einstein was aware of Newton's theories at the time he postulated his general theory of relativity.

GO ON TO THE NEXT PAGE.

PASSAGE II

Asian soybean rust (ASR) is a disease caused by the fungus *Phakospora pachyrhizi*. ASR spreads by windborne spores that infect soybean leaves. As rust lesions mature, they produce thousands of additional spores. Over time, large spore loads build up within fields and across large geographical areas. In 2004, this disease was detected in nine states in the American southwest, and by 2005 it had invaded several other states. ASR can drastically reduce crop yields in areas where it commonly occurs, so monitoring and application of preventive measures such as fungicide will likely be necessary.

Certain fungicides have been tested for their effectiveness against ASR. These fungicides are listed in Table 1. The simplest classification of fungicides divides them into three categories: contact, locally systemic, and systemic. Properties of these fungicide categories are given in Table 2.

Table 1

Fungicide	Category
chlorthalonil	Contact
boscalid	Contact
azoxystrobin	Locally systemic
pyraclostrobin	Locally systemic
myclobutanil	Systemic
tebuconazole	Systemic

Table 2

Fungicide category	Properties
Contact	protectant only; no penetration of leaf tissue; active only on the surface
Locally systemic	absorbed into leaf; does not spread from leaf to which it was applied
Systemic	absorbed into leaf tissue and plant xylem; translocated throughout the plant

ASR infections generally begin in the lower leaf canopy where humidity is higher and leaves stay wet for longer periods. For this reason, the lower soybean leaf canopy is the primary spray target. Both upper and lower leaf surfaces must be sprayed. Coverage as dense as 400 spray droplets per square inch is considered ideal.

The different properties of fungicide types have important implications for spray application. Contact and locally systemic fungicides require better spray coverage than systemic fungicides. Contact fungicides, because they do not penetrate the plant tissue, are more easily washed off the leaf by rain. This results in a shorter residual control period and more frequent re-application of the fungicide.

Tests have shown that fungicides effectiveness varies based on the soybean growth stage at which the fungicide is applied. Figure 1 identifies some of the different stages of soybean growth. Soybean leaves can be infected at any time with ASR. However, research has shown that the most critical time to protect soybean plants with fungicides is from the R1 through R5 growth stages. Fungicide applications should not be initiated after the R5 growth stage (seed development and mature plant).

GO ON TO THE NEXT PAGE.

4 ◯ ◯ ◯ ◯ ◯ ◯ ◯ ◯ ◯ **4**

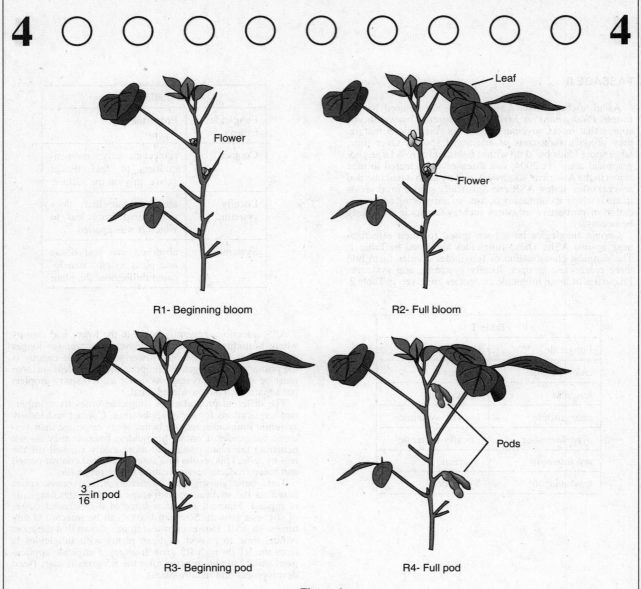

Figure 1

8. According to the passage, which of the following fungicides should be reapplied frequently?
   F. *boscalid*
   G. *azoxystrobin*
   H. *pyraclostrobin*
   J. *tebuconazole*

9. Based on the information provided, during which stage of growth will the application of *chlorthalonil* be least effective?
   A. R1
   B. R3
   C. R6
   D. *Chlorthalonil* should not be applied during any growth stage.

GO ON TO THE NEXT PAGE.

10. A student claimed that, "Application of a systemic fungicide will only prevent the growth of fungi if applied after Growth Stage 5." Does the passage support this claim?

F. No; systemic fungicides are active only on the surface of the leaf.

G. No; fungicides are most effective when applied between Growth Stage 1 and Growth Stage 5.

H. Yes; systemic fungicides are most effective when applied during Growth Stage 6, but not before.

J. Yes; soybean plants can only be infected with ASR late in their development.

11. According to the passage, if fewer than 400 spray droplets per square inch of *tebuconazole* were applied during Growth Stage 2, the chances that the soybean plants would become infected with ASR would most likely:

A. not be affected.

B. decrease only.

C. decrease, then increase.

D. increase only.

12. Equal amounts of *azoxystrobin*, *boscalid*, and *myclobutanil* were applied to three different soybean plants during Growth Stage 3. After 24-hours, each of the plants was sprayed with water. Based on the data, which of the following represents the order, from least effective to most effective, of the fungicides' likelihood of preventing ASR?

F. *myclobutanil, azoxystrobin, boscalid.*

G. *azoxystrobin, boscalid, myclobutanil.*

H. *boscalid, azoxystrobin, myclobutanil.*

J. *myclobutanil, boscalid, azoxystrobin.*

13. According to Figure 1, during which of the following stages in the growth of a soybean plant should fungicide NOT be applied?

A. Beginning flower.

B. Full seed.

C. Full flower.

D. Beginning pod.

GO ON TO THE NEXT PAGE.

PASSAGE III

Echinoderms are defined as any of a variety of invertebrate marine animals characterized by a hard, spiny covering or skin. They have attracted much attention due to their extensive fossil record, ecological importance, and bizarre body forms. Most echinoderms are extinct, but many living representatives still exist. All living echinoderms have an internal skeleton and a central cavity, but the outward appearance can vary significantly. For example, starfish and brittle stars have arms that extend from a central disk; sea lilies have a central stalk, or stem, and resemble flowers; sea cucumbers are wormlike and tend to burrow.

The ways in which echinoderms move and feed are as diverse as their body forms. Table 1 lists certain echinoderms and their methods of locomotion (movement) and feeding.

Table 1		
Echinoderm	Locomotion method	Feeding method
Asteroid (starfish)	"walks" using spines and tube feet	predatory; exudes stomach through mouth to capture prey
Ophiuroid (brittle star)	thrashes and rows its arms	suspension feeder; catches small organisms with its arms
Holothurian (sea cucumber)	contracts and expands body; some use of tube feet	swallows mud and sand; digests organic material and ejects remainder
Crinoid (sea lilies)	swims by raising arms up and down	suspension feeder; fans arms out to catch passing plankton

Table 2 includes examples of echinoderm habitats around the world.

Table 2	
Echinoderm	Habitats
Starfish	rocky shores, sandy areas, waterlogged wood on the deep-sea floor
Brittle star	rocky shores, sandy areas
Sea cucumber	rocky shores, sandy areas, deep ocean trenches
Sea lilies	offshore mud and ooze

GO ON TO THE NEXT PAGE.

14. The echinoderm shown below is most likely a:

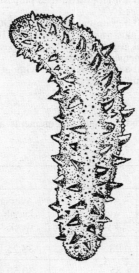

    F. sea lily.
    G. starfish.
    H. sea cucumber.
    J. brittle star.

15. According to Table 1 and Table 2, *crinoids* can be found feeding on plankton:
    A. near the shore.
    B. in deep ocean trenches.
    C. in offshore mud and ooze.
    D. on the deep-sea floor.

16. Based on the data provided in the passage, sea cucumbers most likely burrow in order to:
    F. locate food.
    G. avoid worms.
    H. move offshore.
    J. shed their spines.

17. Suppose scientists discover a new echinoderm that uses its tube feet to move across the deep-sea floor as it hunts for prey. This newly discovered echinoderm can most likely be classified as a(n):
    A. *crinoid.*
    B. *asteroid.*
    C. *ophiunoid.*
    D. *holothurian.*

18. A student hypothesized that large populations of sea cucumbers could greatly alter the physical and chemical composition of the sea floor. Is this hypothesis supported by the data in the passage?
    F. Yes; sea cucumbers often prey upon commercially important organisms, such as oysters.
    G. Yes; sea cucumbers feed by swallowing sediment, extracting organic matter, and ejecting the remainder.
    H. No; sea cucumbers cannot burrow into the sediment, so will not affect the composition of the sea floor.
    J. No; sea cucumbers do not have a viable method of locomotion.

GO ON TO THE NEXT PAGE.

4 ◯ ◯ ◯ ◯ ◯ ◯ ◯ ◯ ◯ **4**

PASSAGE IV

Students wanted to test the effects of nutrition on the growth of guinea pigs. Two experiments were conducted using different feeds and vitamin supplements. For both experiments, four groups of 10 guinea pigs each were given a different type of feed over an 8-week period. Each group received the same quantity of food and was provided with fresh water daily. The guinea pigs were measured and weighed weekly. The guinea pigs in each group had an average starting weight of 50 grams (g) and an average starting length of 20 centimeters (cm).

Experiment 1
Group 1 was fed a high-protein feed (Feed P).
Group 2 was fed a grain-based feed with vitamin supplements (Feed Q).
Group 3 (control group) was fed a grain-based feed without supplements (Feed R).
Group 4 was fed a grain-based feed without supplements plus fruits and vegetables (Feed S).

The results and average measurements are recorded in Table 1 below.

Table 1		
Group	Average weight after 8 weeks (g)	Average length after 8 weeks (cm)
1	93	32.50
2	82	29.00
3	74	25.25
4	76	23.00

Experiment 2
Group 5 was fed a high-protein feed plus fruits and vegetables (Feed V).
Group 6 was fed a grain-based feed with vitamin supplements plus fruits and vegetables (Feed W).
Group 7 (control group) was fed a grain-based feed without supplements (Feed X).
Group 8 was fed a grain-based feed without supplements plus fruits only (Feed Y).

The results and average measurements are recorded in Table 2 below.

Table 2		
Group	Average weight after 8 weeks (g)	Average length after 8 weeks (cm)
5	98	38.25
6	85	30.50
7	75	25.00
8	74	23.25

19. Based on the results of the experiments, which feed resulted in the greatest weight gain?
    A. Feed P.
    B. Feed S.
    C. Feed V.
    D. Feed Y.

GO ON TO THE NEXT PAGE.

4 ○ ○ ○ ○ ○ ○ ○ ○ **4**

20. Based on the results of Experiment 1, the guinea pigs in the group that was fed a grain-based feed with vitamins gained how much weight, on average, during each week of the experiment?
   F. 29 grams.
   G. 11 grams.
   H. 10 grams.
   J. 4 grams.

21. If the students added vitamin supplements to Feed V for a new group (Group 9), what might the result be after 8 weeks?
   A. The guinea pigs in Group 9 would weigh less than those in Group 5.
   B. The guinea pigs in Group 9 would weigh less than those in Group 6.
   C. The guinea pigs in Group 9 would have a greater average length than those in Group 5.
   D. The guinea pigs in Group 9 would have a shorter average length than Group 6.

22. Which of the following statements is true, according to Table 2?
   F. Feed W produces guinea pigs that are almost twice as long as those in the control group.
   G. Feed V produces guinea pigs that weigh three times as much as those in the control group.
   H. Feed Y produces guinea pigs with the greatest average length.
   J. Feed X produces guinea pigs similar to those produced by Feed Y.

23. From the results of the experiments the students would hypothesize that the guinea pigs in Groups 3 and 4 are similar because:
   A. the control group was fed larger quantities of food.
   B. the fruits and vegetables given in Experiment 1 did not have a very high nutritional value.
   C. neither group received enough high-protein food.
   D. the vitamin supplements given in Experiment 2 were more potent than those given in Experiment 1.

24. According to the passage, the guinea pigs in which of the following groups showed the least overall growth?
   F. Group 8.
   G. Group 7.
   H. Group 4.
   J. Group 1.

GO ON TO THE NEXT PAGE.

4 ◯ ◯ ◯ ◯ ◯ ◯ ◯ ◯ ◯ **4**

PASSAGE V

Students studied the effect of temperature on the conversion rates of two organic acids to their corresponding alcohols. The two organic acids studied were lactic acid (LA) and propionic acid (PA). Each acid was mixed with an Ru/C catalyst (to start the conversion) in an aqueous (water) solution. Lactic acid was found to break down into propylene glycol (PG), water, and various carbon side products. Propionic acid was found to break down into 1-propanol (1-PrOH), water, and various carbon side products. For all experiments, temperature was measured in degrees Kelvin (K).

Experiment 1

Students mixed an LA concentration of 0.5 moles (M) in a 50-milliliter (ml) aqueous solution along with a 5% Ru/C catalyst. The temperature was then varied to study the effect on the rate of conversion from lactic acid to PG. The results are shown in Figure 1.

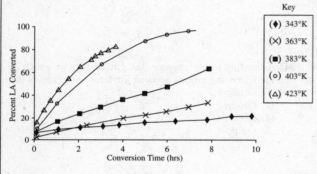

Key
(♦) 343°K
(✕) 363°K
(■) 383°K
(○) 403°K
(△) 423°K

Figure 1

Experiment 2

Students mixed a PA concentration of 0.5 M in a 50 ml aqueous solution along with a 5% Ru/C catalyst. The temperature was then varied to study the effect on the rate of conversion from propionic acid to 1-PrOH. The results are shown in Figure 2.

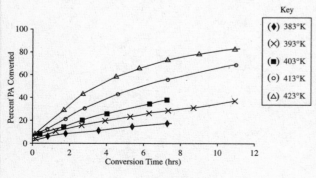

Key
(♦) 383°K
(✕) 393°K
(■) 403°K
(○) 413°K
(△) 423°K

Figure 2

25. According to Figure 1, after two hours at 403°K, the percent of LA converted was closest to which of the following?
 A. 10%.
 B. 50%.
 C. 80%.
 D. 100%.

26. According to Figure 1, at 423°K, the greatest percentage of conversion occurred during which of the following time intervals?
 F. 8 to 10 hours.
 G. 6 to 8 hours.
 H. 2 to 4 hours.
 J. 0 to 2 hours.

27. Which of the following was held constant in each of the experiments?
 A. The amount of catalyst used.
 B. The temperature.
 C. The conversion rates.
 D. The type of acid used.

28. Based on the data in Tables 1 and 2, which of the following best describes the results of the experiments? As conversion time increased, the percent of acid converted:
 F. decreased at some temperatures only until conversion stopped.
 G. increased at some temperatures only until conversion stopped.
 H. decreased at all temperatures until conversion stopped.
 J. increased at all temperatures until conversion stopped.

29. A chemist claimed that the propionic acid conversion rate at 403°K dramatically increases between 8 and 12 hours. Do the results of the experiments support this claim?
 A. No; according to Figure 2, conversion stops after 8 hours and does not reach 100%.
 B. No; according to Figure 1, nearly 100% of the acid has been converted after 8 hours.
 C. Yes; according to Figure 1, there is a significant increase in the conversion rate after 8 hours.
 D. Yes; according to Figure 2, less than 50% of the acid has been converted after 8 hours.

30. Based on the results of Experiment 2, assuming that conversion of PA at 423°K continued until it reached 100%, one could predict that 100% of the PA would be converted during which of the following time intervals?
 F. < 2 hours.
 G. 4 to 6 hours.
 H. 12 to 14 hours.
 J. < 12 hours.

GO ON TO THE NEXT PAGE.

4 ○ ○ ○ ○ ○ ○ ○ ○ ○ 4

PASSAGE VI

Carbon monoxide (CO) is a colorless, odorless gas produced by burning material that contains carbon, such as coal or natural gas. Carbon monoxide is the leading cause of accidental poisoning deaths in America. The Centers for Disease Control estimates that carbon monoxide poisoning claims nearly 500 lives and causes more than 15,000 visits to hospital emergency departments annually. Common household appliances produce carbon monoxide. When not properly ventilated, carbon monoxide emitted by these appliances can build up. The only way to detect carbon monoxide is through testing, using a specialized sensing device.

Gas stoves have been known to emit high levels of carbon monoxide. Average carbon monoxide levels in homes without gas stoves vary from 0.5 to 5.0 parts per million (ppm). Levels near properly adjusted gas stoves are often 5.0 to 15.0 ppm and those near poorly adjusted stoves may be 30.0 ppm or higher. CO levels between 0.5 and 15.0 ppm are considered safe.

Table 1 shows the carbon monoxide levels in ppm for each of five homes, with and without gas stoves.

Table 1	
Home	Carbon monoxide level (ppm)
5	<1.0
4	1.0 to 5.0
3	5.0 to 15.0
2	15.0 to 25.0
1	>25.0

31. According to the passage, which of the following homes listed in Table 1 most likely has a poorly adjusted gas stove?
  A. 5
  B. 4
  C. 3
  D. 1

32. A sensing device was installed in Home 2 to test CO levels. Which of the following is most likely true about the results of the test?
  F. The results indicated below average CO emissions.
  G. The results indicated above average CO emissions.
  H. The results indicated average CO emissions.
  J. The results indicated no CO emissions.

33. According to the passage, which of the following carbon monoxide levels would be considered most harmful?
  A. 40.25 ppm
  B. 12.00 ppm
  C. 6.50 ppm
  D. 0.30 ppm

34. According to the passage, if Home 4 has a gas stove, should it be removed?
  F. Yes, because it is emitting a high level of carbon monoxide.
  G. Yes, because it is not properly adjusted.
  H. No, because carbon monoxide levels in the house are within a safe range.
  J. No, because there is no indication of any carbon monoxide emissions.

35. Suppose a 6th home was tested for carbon monoxide and the results showed a carbon monoxide level of 10.0 ppm. According to the passage, which of the following conclusions can be reached?
  A. The residents of Home 6 are highly susceptible to CO poisoning.
  B. Home 6 has a poorly adjusted gas stove that should be repaired or removed.
  C. The CO levels in Home 6 will not pose any danger to the residents.
  D. The CO sensing device is defective and should be replaced.

GO ON TO THE NEXT PAGE.

4 ○ ○ ○ ○ ○ ○ ○ ○ ○ **4**

PASSAGE VII

Turf grasses are used throughout the United States in many suburban lawns. Kentucky bluegrass is the most common type of turf grass used in the northern part of the United States. To keep lawns green and healthy, many homeowners apply fertilizer up to five times a year. Inorganic fertilizers are becoming more popular, and contain three common elements – nitrogen, phosphorous, and potassium – for the development of plant color, strength, and health. Most turf grass lawns do not use all of the nutrients provided in the fertilizer, which means that much of the nitrogen, phosphorous, and potassium remains in the soil. When water enters the soil, it accumulates a portion of the excess nitrogen from the soil. This water, now termed *leachate*, flows into surrounding waterways. The leaching of high concentrations of nitrogen into natural waterways can throw off the environmental equilibrium of the aquatic ecosystem, often resulting in an increase in plant growth that can have a negative impact on the native fish populations.

A study was performed to examine the degree of nitrogen leaching in Kentucky bluegrass turf; 2 one-acre plots of turf were compared. The scientists conducting the study relied completely on natural rainwater to irrigate the test plots. Each plot received fertilizer applications containing different levels of nitrogen two times per week during the months of April and September for 5 years. The plots had a 5% slope to facilitate leaching; leachate was collected in one-liter jugs. The leachate collected from each plot was measured for nitrogen concentration.

Plot A, received a low nitrogen application, 98 kilograms of N per acre from 2000 to 2004. Plot B, received an initially high nitrogen application, 245 kilograms of N per acre from 2000–2002. In the last year of the study, the amount of nitrogen in the fertilizer was decreased to 196 kilograms of N per acre for Plot B. Table 1 shows the average nitrogen concentration in milligrams per liter (mg/L) in the leachate collected from each plot during each year. Figure 1 shows the percent concentration of nitrogen in the leachate.

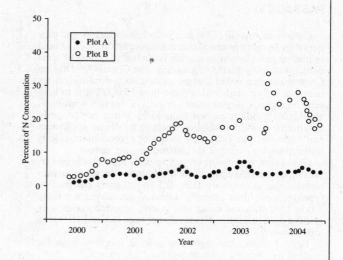

Table 1		
Year	N concentration (mg/L)	
	Plot A	Plot B
2000	2.1	14.7
2001	3.7	18.9
2002	4.8	25.3
2003	6.3	29.7
2004	2.6	11.8

36. According the passage, as the amount of nitrogen in the fertilizer increased, the average amount of nitrogen in the leachate:
   F. decreased only.
   G. increased only.
   H. decreased for several years, then increased.
   J. increased for several years, then decreased.

37. Based on the data in Table 1 and Figure 1, one can conclude that when fertilizer with a low nitrogen concentration is applied, native fish populations in surrounding waterways will most likely:
   A. remain stable.
   B. be reduced by 5%.
   C. be completely decimated.
   D. not have enough food.

38. It was determined that during times of heavy rain, more nitrogen was leached from the soil. Based on the results of the study, which year most likely had times of heavy rain in April and September?
   F. 2000.
   G. 2001.
   H. 2003.
   J. None.

GO ON TO THE NEXT PAGE.

4

39. According to the Environmental Protection Agency, average nitrogen levels in leachate must be less than 10 mg/L to be safe for the environment. Based on this standard and the results of the study, which of the following fertilizer applications is considered safe?

A. 196 kilograms of N per acre.
B. 98 kilograms of N per acre.
C. 245 kilograms of N per acre.
D. None of the tested applications is safe.

40. In 2005, it was found that average nitrogen levels in the leachate from Plot B were 8.2 mg/L. The data from the study supports which of the following conclusions?

F. Kentucky bluegrass should not be used for lawns in suburbs near a public waterway.
G. Once high-nitrogen fertilizer has been applied to a suburban lawn, nitrogen levels in the leachate will remain high, even if low-nitrogen fertilizer is later applied.
H. Following the application of low-nitrogen fertilizers, it will take more than one year to reach safe nitrogen levels in leachate from suburban lawns previously fertilized with high-nitrogen fertilizer.
J. The measurable concentration of nitrogen in leachate from suburban lawns will always be within the range considered safe by the Environmental Protection Agency, as long as irrigation is kept to a minimum.

END OF THE SCIENCE REASONING TEST.
STOP! IF YOU HAVE TIME LEFT OVER, CHECK YOUR WORK ON THIS SECTION ONLY.

WRITING TEST PROMPT

DIRECTIONS: This test is designed to assess your writing skills. You have 30 minutes to plan and write an essay based on the stimulus provided. Be sure to take a position on the issue and support your position using logical reasoning and relevant examples. Organize your ideas in a focused and logical way, and use the English language to clearly and effectively express your position.

When you have finished writing, refer to the Scoring Rubrics discussed in the Introduction (page 4) to estimate your score.

Some educators have recently banned students from exhibiting visible piercings and tattoos on high school property. They feel that body art, as it is called, distracts student attention from the main purpose of high school, which is education. Tattoos and piercings, they argue, can create an atmosphere of intimidation. Others feel that body art, like other art, should be protected under the law as freedom of expression. They argue that students should be allowed to exhibit visible piercings and tattoos on school property as long as the work is not obscene. In your opinion, should students be banned from exhibiting visible piercings and tattoos on school property?

In your essay, take a position on this question. You may write about either one of the two points of view given, or you may present a different point of view on this question. Use specific reasons and examples to support your position.

■ **ANSWER KEY**

English Test

1. A	21. D	41. A	61. A
2. F	22. F	42. H	62. G
3. C	23. B	43. D	63. D
4. H	24. H	44. F	64. H
5. A	25. D	45. D	65. B
6. G	26. H	46. J	66. H
7. C	27. A	47. A	67. C
8. F	28. J	48. G	68. J
9. D	29. D	49. D	69. A
10. G	30. H	50. H	70. G
11. D	31. B	51. B	71. C
12. G	32. F	52. J	72. J
13. B	33. A	53. C	73. A
14. F	34. J	54. F	74. J
15. C	35. A	55. C	75. A
16. G	36. J	56. F	
17. A	37. B	57. B	
18. F	38. H	58. G	
19. B	39. A	59. C	
20. F	40. G	60. J	

Mathematics Test

1. C	21. B	41. B
2. J	22. F	42. K
3. B	23. E	43. E
4. G	24. H	44. K
5. B	25. B	45. A
6. G	26. K	46. G
7. E	27. D	47. A
8. J	28. H	48. F
9. E	29. B	49. B
10. F	30. K	50. G
11. B	31. E	51. E
12. K	32. F	52. K
13. B	33. D	53. B
14. F	34. G	54. J
15. C	35. B	55. B
16. H	36. F	56. H
17. B	37. C	57. E
18. G	38. G	58. K
19. D	39. E	59. E
20. H	40. G	60. F

Reading Test

1. B	21. A
2. J	22. F
3. A	23. D
4. H	24. G
5. A	25. D
6. F	26. H
7. C	27. B
8. G	28. F
9. C	29. C
10. J	30. J
11. A	31. A
12. H	32. G
13. D	33. C
14. F	34. F
15. C	35. D
16. G	36. H
17. B	37. A
18. H	38. G
19. D	39. D
20. F	40. J

Science Reasoning Test

1. D	21. C
2. G	22. J
3. B	23. B
4. J	24. F
5. B	25. B
6. F	26. J
7. A	27. A
8. F	28. J
9. C	29. A
10. G	30. H
11. D	31. D
12. H	32. G
13. B	33. A
14. H	34. H
15. C	35. C
16. F	36. G
17. B	37. A
18. G	38. H
19. C	39. B
20. J	40. H

■■■ SCORING GUIDE

Your final reported score is your COMPOSITE SCORE. Your COMPOSITE SCORE is the average of all of your SCALE SCORES.

Your SCALE SCORES for the four multiple-choice sections are derived from the Scoring Table on the next page. Use your RAW SCORE, or the number of questions that you answered correctly for each section, to determine your SCALE SCORE. If you got a RAW SCORE of 60 on the English test, for example, you correctly answered 60 out of 75 questions.

Step 1 Determine your RAW SCORE for each of the four multiple-choice sections:

English   _____

Mathematics   _____

Reading   _____

Science Reasoning   _____

The following Raw Score Table shows the total possible points for each section.

RAW SCORE TABLE	
KNOWLEDGE AND SKILL AREAS	**RAW SCORES**
ENGLISH	75
MATHEMATICS	60
READING	40
SCIENCE REASONING	40
WRITING	12

Multiple-Choice Scoring Worksheet

Step 2 Determine your SCALE SCORE for each of the four multiple-choice sections using the following Scoring Worksheet. Each SCALE SCORE should be rounded to the nearest number according to normal rules. For example, $31.2 \approx 31$ and $31.5 \approx 32$. If you answered 61 questions correctly on the English section, for example, your SCALE SCORE would be 29.

English _____ × 36 = _____ ÷ 75 = _____

<u>RAW SCORE</u>

$-\,2$ (*correction factor)

_____

SCALE SCORE

Mathematics _____ × 36 = _____ ÷ 60 = _____

<u>RAW SCORE</u>

$+\,1$ (*correction factor)

_____

SCALE SCORE

Reading _____ × 36 = _____ ÷ 40 = _____

<u>RAW SCORE</u>

$+\,2$ (*correction factor)

_____

SCALE SCORE

Science Reasoning _____ × 36 = _____ ÷ 40 = _____

<u>RAW SCORE</u>

$+\,1.5$ (*correction factor)

_____

SCALE SCORE

*The correction factor is an approximation based on the average from several recent ACT tests. It is most valid for scores in the middle 50% (approximately 16–24 scale composite score) of the scoring range.

The scores are all approximate. Actual ACT scoring scales vary from one administration to the next based upon several factors.

If you take the optional Writing Test, you will need to combine your English and Writing scores to obtain your final COMPOSITE SCORE. Once you have determined a score for your essay out of 12 possible points, you will need to determine your ENGLISH/WRITING SCALE SCORE, using both your ENGLISH SCALE SCORE and your WRITING TEST SCORE. The combination of the two scores will give you an ENGLISH/WRITING SCALE SCORE, from 1 to 36, that will be used to determine your COMPOSITE SCORE mentioned earlier.

Using the English/Writing Scoring Table, find your ENGLISH SCALE SCORE on the left or right hand side of the table and your WRITING TEST SCORE on the top of the table. Follow your ENGLISH SCALE SCORE over and your WRITING TEST SCORE down until the two columns meet at a number. This number is your ENGLISH/WRITING SCALE SCORE and will be used to determine your COMPOSITE SCORE.

Step 3 Determine your ENGLISH/WRITING SCALE SCORE using the English/Writing Scoring Table on the following page:

English _____

Writing _____

English/Writing _____

ENGLISH/WRITING SCORING TABLE

ENGLISH SCALE SCORE	WRITING TEST SCORE											ENGLISH SCALE SCORE
	2	3	4	5	6	7	8	9	10	11	12	
36	26	27	28	29	30	31	32	33	34	32	36	36
35	26	27	28	29	30	31	31	32	33	34	35	35
34	25	26	27	28	29	30	31	32	33	34	35	34
33	24	25	26	27	28	29	30	31	32	33	34	33
32	24	25	25	26	27	28	29	30	31	32	33	32
31	23	24	25	26	27	28	29	30	30	31	32	31
30	22	23	24	25	26	27	28	29	30	31	32	30
29	21	22	23	24	25	26	27	28	29	30	31	29
28	21	22	23	24	24	25	26	27	28	29	30	28
27	20	21	22	23	24	25	26	27	28	28	29	27
26	19	20	21	22	23	24	25	26	27	28	29	26
25	18	19	20	21	22	23	24	25	26	27	28	25
24	18	19	20	21	22	23	23	24	25	26	27	24
23	17	18	19	20	21	22	23	24	25	26	27	23
22	16	17	18	19	20	21	22	23	24	25	26	22
21	16	17	17	18	19	20	21	22	23	24	25	21
20	15	16	17	18	19	20	21	21	22	23	24	20
19	14	15	16	17	18	19	20	21	22	23	24	19
18	13	14	15	16	17	18	19	20	21	22	23	18
17	13	14	15	16	16	17	18	19	20	21	22	17
16	12	13	14	15	16	17	18	19	20	20	21	16
15	11	12	13	14	15	16	17	18	19	20	21	15
14	10	11	12	13	14	15	16	17	18	19	20	14
13	10	11	12	13	14	14	15	16	17	18	19	13
12	9	10	11	12	13	14	15	16	17	18	19	12
11	8	9	10	11	12	13	14	15	16	17	18	11
10	8	9	9	10	11	12	13	14	15	16	17	10
9	7	8	9	10	11	12	13	13	14	15	16	9
8	6	7	8	9	10	11	12	13	14	15	16	8
7	5	6	7	8	9	10	11	12	13	14	15	7
6	5	6	7	7	8	9	10	11	12	13	14	6
5	4	5	6	7	8	9	10	11	12	12	13	5
4	3	4	5	6	7	8	9	10	11	12	13	4
3	2	3	4	5	6	7	8	9	10	11	12	3
2	2	3	4	5	6	6	7	8	9	10	11	2
1	1	2	3	4	5	6	7	8	9	10	11	1

Step 4   Determine your COMPOSITE SCORE by finding the sum of all your SCALE SCORES for each of the four sections: English only (if you do not choose to take the optional Writing Test) *or* English/Writing (if you choose to take the optional Writing Test), Math, Reading, and Science Reasoning, and divide by 4 to find the average. Round your COMPOSITE SCORE according to normal rules. For example, $31.2 \approx 31$ and $31.5 \approx 32$.

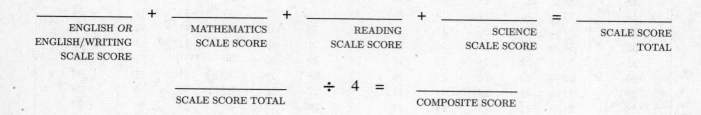

ENGLISH *OR* ENGLISH/WRITING SCALE SCORE	MATHEMATICS SCALE SCORE	READING SCALE SCORE	SCIENCE SCALE SCORE	SCALE SCORE TOTAL

_____   ÷ 4 =   _____

SCALE SCORE TOTAL   COMPOSITE SCORE

ANSWERS AND EXPLANATIONS

English Test Explanations

PASSAGE I

1. **The best answer is A.** The pronoun *this* tells the reader that a description is coming further in the sentence. The sentence as it is written uses the correct verb tense and keeps the entire thought in one sentence; therefore, it's the best answer choice.

2. **The best answer is F.** The paragraph is most concerned with the writer's Grandma and her emotional relationship to the chest. Answer choices G, H, and J all shift attention away from the grandmother's personal response and towards superficial, physical descriptions.

3. **The best answer is C.** The best answer choice correctly uses commas to separate the two clauses. *Treasure* is an adjective modifying *trove*, so there is no need for a comma between them (answer choice A). Answer choices B and D include unnecessary commas after *and*.

4. **The best answer is H.** All of the answer choices have acceptable replacements for the idiomatic saying *truth be told*. However, answer choice H has the phrase *kind of type of*, which is redundant. Therefore, it is not an acceptable replacement.

5. **The best answer is A.** The first sentence sets the stage for the action, but does not give any new information. It could easily be deleted without losing the sense of the story.

6. **The best answer is G.** The object of this sentence is the *interior* of the *wooden box*. Because *wooden box* is singular and possessive, it needs an apostrophe and an s.

7. **The best answer is C.** The story is being told using the simple past tense. Answer choice A creates an incomplete sentence. Answer choice D indicates action over time, which is also not appropriate in this context.

8. **The best answer is F.** The phrase that begins with *flying* is a nonrestrictive clause. That means it could be removed without destroying the meaning of the sentence. Nonrestrictive clauses need to be set off by commas, making answer choice F best.

9. **The best answer is D.** Answer choices A and C imply a contrast that is not supported by the sentence. Answer choice B implies a conclusion that is also not supported. In fact, no connective is needed, and answer choice D is best.

10. **The best answer is G.** The underlined phrase is a list with only two items, and no commas are necessary to separate them from each other. Likewise, because it's a restrictive clause, necessary for the sentence to make sense, it doesn't need commas to separate it from the rest of the sentence.

11. **The best answer is D.** This pronoun properly refers to the writer's grandfather. Therefore answer choice D, *his*, is best.

12. **The best answer is G.** The topic of this paragraph is *dreams*—more specifically, the contrast between the dreams of the writer's grandfather and grandmother. The grandfather's dreams were to be a heroic bomber pilot, while the grandmother wanted him to do something that would keep him safe for his family. Answer choice G best introduces the tension between the two.

13. **The best answer is B.** The writer makes it clear that her grandfather took pride not only in being a pilot, but also in his wife. It would make sense that her grandfather would have a picture of the plane he named after his wife, and that the writer would refer to it as her grandfather's *pride and joy*.

14. **The best answer is F.** Use the possessive relative pronoun to refer to the writer's grandmother.

15. **The best answer is C.** This passage is intensely personal. It doesn't try to place the actions into a larger historical context, and gives very little information about the use of airplanes in World War II. Therefore, answer choices A and B are inappropriate. The passage indicates that the writer's grandparents had a loving relationship, so answer choice D is not best.

PASSAGE II

16. **The best answer is G.** Only answer choice G has a subject (*tomatoes*), verb (*have become*), and object (*a staple*) without being in a dependent clause. The other answer choices lack a main verb and create incomplete sentences.

17. **The best answer is A.** This phrase is a three-item list; each item must be separated by a comma. Answer choices C and D are incorrect because the comma needs to be placed after *stands*, not after *and*.

18. **The best answer is F.** Answer choice G is incorrect because the phrase doesn't do anything to explain anything about the writer. The phrase also doesn't mention other summer produce, so answer choice H is incorrect. The phrase does, however, explain that tomatoes are plentiful during the growing season, which would logically lead to a need for more tomato recipes.

19. **The best answer is B.** The correct idiom is *plenty of*. Omitting the underlined portion, while not grammatically incorrect, would reduce the clarity of the sentence, which focuses on the number of ways to prepare and eat tomatoes.

20. **The best answer is F.** As written, the underlined portion introduces the idea of a contrast between recipes that are universally delicious, but have individual levels of difficulty in preparation. The remaining answer choices are either too vague or awkward.

21. **The best answer is D.** The writer wants to give a sequence of events: first peeling and deseeding, then cooking. Only answer choice D tells the reader precisely which action comes first.

22. **The best answer is F.** The verb here is in the passive voice because the action, *peeling*, is happening *to* the subject. Therefore, the correct form is *accomplished*. Because *accomplished* is a verb, it needs to be modified by the adverb, *easily*.

23. **The best answer is B.** The pronoun *whoever* is the subject of this sentence, so *who* is the correct form. Answer choices A and C use the object form *whom*, and should be eliminated. The passage is written in the present tense, so answer choice B is correct.

24. **The best answer is H.** In this sentence, the phrase surrounding *cool enough to handle* doesn't have a main verb, so it can't stand on its own. This eliminates all choices except answer choice H.

25. **The best answer is D.** The paragraph explains in great detail how to peel and deseed tomatoes. The last sentence tells us this is important, but only answer choice D includes information that tells us why. Answer choices C and D explain why it might be important to use a strainer, but their scope doesn't cover the entire paragraph. Answer choice B introduces a new idea, growing new plants, that is also outside the scope of the paragraph.

26. **The best answer is H.** This sentence is actually two complete sentences. Joining them with a comma, as in answer choice F, is called a "comma splice" and is grammatically incorrect. Answer choice G

creates a run-on sentence. Answer choice J implies a contrast that doesn't make sense in this context.

27. **The best answer is A.** The adjective *bright* modifies *red*, so the words don't need to be separated by a comma. This eliminates answer choices B and D. However, the phrase *Once a tomato...* is a nonrestrictive relative clause and does need to be separated from the main sentence by a comma.

28. **The best answer is J.** The phrase doesn't add significant details or explain why fresh vegetables are important. Therefore, answer choices F and G can be eliminated. Both of the remaining phrases are specific, so answer choice H can be eliminated. Answer choice J is best because the proposed replacement is much wordier than the original without adding anything significant.

29. **The best answer is D.** The pronoun here refers back to the noun *Italians*. Therefore, the plural pronoun, *them*, is best.

30. **The best answer is H.** The key phrase in this question is *modern cuisine*. The essay's focus is much more general than how tomatoes are used in a particular type of cuisine. Therefore, answer choices F and G can be eliminated. The essay does mention specific recipes, so answer choice J can be eliminated. Answer choice H is best because the writer takes a general approach and includes pieces of information like the fact that Italians once thought that tomatoes were poisonous.

PASSAGE III

31. **The best answer is B.** By definition, a *hole* is empty, so the underlined portion, as it is, is somewhat redundant. The adjective that best fits the tone of the paragraph is *gaping*. Omitting the underlined portion eliminates the modifier *a*, creating an awkward, ungrammatical sentence.

32. **The best answer is F.** The phrase beginning with *gumming* is a nonrestrictive relative clause; therefore it needs to be set apart from the main sentence by a comma. The phrase is not a complete sentence, so answer choices G and H should be eliminated.

33. **The best answer is A.** This paragraph introduces a new idea: the tools and techniques of modern dentistry. No connective to the previous paragraph is necessary, so answer choice A is best. Answer choices C and D are incorrect because they imply continuity with the previous paragraph. Answer choice B implies a level of contrast that isn't necessary.

34. The best answer is J. Answer choices F, G, and H are all redundant. By definition, a disposable needle is one that can be disposed of. Answer choice J has the all the information needed; therefore, it's the best answer.

35. The best answer is A. The focus of this paragraph is equipment; therefore, answer choice A is best because it describes the widespread use of autoclaves in modern dentistry. Answer choice B should be eliminated because the phrase does not further define the term *autoclave*. Answer choice C is incorrect because the phrase helps explain *how* the offices had become more sterile. Answer choice D can be eliminated because the focus of the paragraph is not on teeth.

36. The best answer is J. The sentence already tells the reader that the equipment uses heat to sterilize the equipment. Therefore, the phrase beginning *by using the heat* is redundant.

37. The best answer is B. The verb *work* has to be in the present tense to match the rest of the paragraph. Therefore, answer choices A and C can be eliminated. Answer choice D would need the auxiliary verb *are* to be correct.

38. The best answer is H. The contrast *on the other hand* needs to be separated from the main sentence by a comma. The phrase, *constant changes*, however, is the subject of the main clause and doesn't need a comma. This phrase is also followed by a restrictive relative clause, which requires no comma.

39. The best answer is A. Answer choices C and D imply a contrast with the previous sentence, and so can be eliminated. Answer choice B makes the phrase a separate clause. Answer choice A is correct because the phrase is part of a noun phrase that acts as the subject of the sentence and doesn't need a conjunction.

40. The best answer is G. All of the answer choices offer some added detail. However, answer choices F, H, and J are too vague. Only answer choice G gives a detail that improves the reader's understanding of the challenges faced by modern dentists as opposed to those of 50 years ago.

41. The best answer is A. This sentence is really two complete sentences, and therefore needs to be separated by a period or a semicolon. Answer choice B creates a comma splice, answer choice C creates a run-on sentence, and answer choice D creates a long, incomplete sentence.

42. The best answer is H. Answer choices F, G, and J are either too wordy or grammatically incorrect. Answer choice H is both succinct and grammatically correct, so it is best.

43. The best answer is D. The phrase *after 1950* means the same thing as *second half of the twentieth century*. So, answer choices A, B, and C are all redundant. Answer choice D is best because it has all the information necessary without repeating itself.

44. The best answer is F. The tone of the passage is scientific and dispassionate. Answer choice G, therefore, should be eliminated because it has the wrong tone. Answer choice H is too vague, and answer choice J is off topic. Answer choice F explains precise ways in which dentistry has improved over the past 50 years, which relates directly back to the main topic of the essay.

45. The best answer is D. Paragraph 3 does not contain detailed information about dental practices, as do Paragraphs 2 and 4. Instead, it's more of a summary of the changes in dentistry over time. Therefore, the best place for it is at the end of the essay, which makes answer choice D best.

PASSAGE IV

46. The best answer is J. Here, *Mr. Peale* is a type of nonrestrictive clause modifying *our Advanced English teacher*, and should be separated by commas from the rest of the sentence.

47. The best answer is A. *That we especially liked* is a restrictive relative clause. That means, if it were removed, the basic sense of the sentence would change. Restrictive relative clauses do not take commas, so answer choices B and D can be eliminated. The final clause is not independent, so it does not take a comma. This eliminates choice C.

48. The best answer is G. Because the list of painters is the object of the verb *shared*, a colon is incorrect; eliminate answer choice F. Commas are not used to begin lists, so eliminate answer choice H. Answer Choice J, *share*, is in the wrong tense.

49. The best answer is D. The topic of this paragraph is to introduce a day when the writer had to reproduce a famous painting in her English class. Answer choices A and C provide specific details that are not followed up in the next paragraph. Therefore, they are off topic and should be eliminated. Answer choice B does not have the right tone and is also off topic. The best choice is to delete the sentence altogether because it is irrelevant.

50. **The best answer is H.** Answer choices F, G, and J are redundant. Answer choice H, however, contains all the necessary information without any extra words.

51. **The best answer is B.** The passage has been written in the past tense. Therefore, answer choices A and C can be eliminated. Answer choice D doesn't make grammatical sense, so it should be eliminated.

52. **The best answer is J.** The word *proclaimed* means to state loudly and with assurance. Answer choices F, G, and H are all close synonyms. Answer choice J, however, indicates that Mr. Peale put his thoughts in writing, which is not an acceptable alternative.

53. **The best answer is C.** The writer's phrase is not directed at either her teacher or Impressionist art. So, answer choices A and B can be eliminated. She is instead commenting on how his response made her feel—which was ambivalent.

54. **The best answer is F.** The subject of Sentence 3 is Mr. Peale's lack of comment. It would not make sense to place the sentence before Sentence 2 because that's where the writer gives that information. So, eliminate answer choices G and H. By Sentence 4, Mr. Peale has moved on, so eliminate answer choice J. Answer choice F makes the most logical sense.

55. **The best answer is C.** Answer choices A and B are unnecessarily wordy. Answer choice D implies a relative clause that isn't there. Answer choice C is grammatically correct and concise.

56. **The best answer is F.** The proposed sentence needs to link the idea that the writer had captured the essence of the original painting and that she valued her reproduction enough to hang it on her wall, even though it wasn't terribly dramatic. The proposed sentence does this by emphasizing that the reproduction had captured the parts of the original most valued by the writer: its beauty and serenity.

57. **The best answer is B.** The correct sentence needs to be in the past tense, to stay consistent with the rest of the essay and use of active voice. So, answer choice A can be eliminated. Answer choice C doesn't make grammatical sense. Answer choice D has the awkward and unnecessary phrase *by me*, so it also can be eliminated.

58. **The best answer is G.** Answer choice F implies a conditional state not supported by the sentence. Answer choice H implies a contrast not supported by the sentence. Answer choice J does not make

sense. Only answer choice G provides an appropriate adverb.

59. **The best answer is C.** Answer choices A and B are wordier versions of answer choice C, so they can be eliminated. Answer choice D doesn't make sense and can be eliminated.

60. **The best answer is J.** Answer choice F is in the future tense, so eliminate it. Answer choices G and H are awkward and wordy, so eliminate them. Answer choice J is concise and grammatically correct.

PASSAGE V

61. **The best answer is A.** The conjunction *however* needs to be separated from the rest of the sentence by commas. Answer choices B and C create incomplete sentences.

62. **The best answer is G.** The phrase *in Africa* is a restrictive clause that should not be separated from the rest of the sentence by punctuation.

63. **The best answer is D.** The use of the modifier *other* instead of *another* tells the reader that the noun *countries* needs to be plural. Additionally, the introductory clause must be separated by a comma from the main clause. Answer choice C uses a comma correctly, but it incorrectly includes the plural possessive form of the noun.

64. **The best answer is H.** The conjunction here needs to connect this sentence to the previous one by suggesting that this sentence offers an example. Answer choices F and G imply a contrast to the previous sentence. Answer choice J implies a comparative. Only answer choice H correctly implies that the tall trees on plantations around the world assisted in the growth of coffee plants by simulating their preferred habitats.

65. **The best answer is B.** The two phrases are each complete sentences and must be joined by either a semicolon or some form of end punctuation. Answer choice C creates a "comma splice" by using a comma to join two independent clauses.

66. **The best answer is H.** This paragraph is written in the present tense. Therefore, the simple past tense is correct. Answer choice H is also in the active voice, making it the best choice.

67. **The best answer is C.** The sense of the phrase is that the new plants are sun-tolerant *and also* able to thrive in open sunlight. All of the choices have this sense of continuity except answer choice C.

68. **The best answer is J.** The phrase *amount of* is idiomatic and should be used here. The remaining answer choices are not idiomatic.

69. **The best answer is A.** The conjunction here needs to give the sense of result or conclusion. Answer choices B and C imply contrast. Answer choice D implies continuity, but not result.

70. **The best answer is G.** The key to this question is *effective visual detail*. Answer choice G offers the most precise detail because it specifies that the ground protection is from *trees* and that the rainfall is *pounding*.

71. **The best answer is C.** Because *ornithologists* is the subject of the sentence and *discover* is the verb, the relative pronoun *who* is unnecessary. Therefore, answer choices A and B can be eliminated. Answer choice D is in the past tense, while the rest of the paragraph is in the present tense.

72. **The best answer is J.** The conjunction *as* implies a reason or explanation, or even action over time. Consequently, answer choices F, G, and H would all

be acceptable alternatives. Answer choice J, *therefore*, implies a conclusion or direct result. It is not an acceptable alternative to *as*.

73. **The best answer is A.** The phrase *as well as many other fauna and flora* is a nonrestrictive clause because removing it does not significantly alter the meaning of the sentence. A nonrestrictive clause is separated from the main sentence by commas.

74. **The best answer is J.** Sentence 3 tells the reader about recorded decreases in the songbird population of the northern United States. However, the effect of coffee production on birds is not introduced until Sentence 5. Therefore, Sentence 3 should logically come after Sentence 5, after Sentence 6 most specifically. That makes answer choice J, *before Sentence 7*, the best answer.

75. **The best answer is A.** Answer choice A clearly and concisely states the idea of many people coming to a realization. The other choices state the same idea, but they are grammatically awkward and too wordy or redundant.

Mathematics Test Explanations

1. The correct answer is C. To solve this problem, multiply the number of ounces by the number of pounds:

$$16 \times 1.5 = 24$$

2. The correct answer is J. To solve this problem, use the FOIL method then combine like terms, as follows:

First terms: $3x^2$

Outside terms: $-15x$

Inside terms: $4x$

Last terms: -20

$$3x^2 - 15x + 4x - 20 = 3x^2 - 11x - 20$$

3. The correct answer is B. To solve this problem, substitute 8 for a and 9 for b in the given function and solve, as follows:

$$f(a, b) = ab - (a - b)$$
$$f(8, 9) = (8)(9) - (8 - 9)$$
$$= 72 - (-1)$$
$$= 72 + 1 = 73$$

4. The correct answer is G. To solve this problem, first calculate 16% of 24,000, as follows:

$$24,000 \times .16 = 3,840$$

Next, calculate 1/5 of 3,840, as follows:

$$3,840 \times 1/5$$
$$= 3,840 \div 5 = 768$$

5. The correct answer is B. Solve this problem by isolating x on the left side of the equation. Perform the following operations:

$$5x + 5 = 25 + 3x$$

Subtract $3x$ from both sides:

$$2x + 5 = 25$$

Subtract 5 from both sides:

$$2x = 20$$

Divide both sides by 2:

$$x = 10$$

6. The correct answer is G. Remember that the perimeter is the distance around an object. In this case, because the figure is a parallelogram, its perimeter is twice the sum of the lengths of two adjacent sides. You are given that the length of one side, AB is 7 inches. Set up the following equation with x as the unknown side length, AD:

$$46 = 2(7 + x)$$
$$46 = 14 + 2x$$
$$32 = 2x$$
$$16 = x$$

7. The correct answer is E. To solve this problem, recall that absolute values are always positive. Therefore, you can ignore the negative sign in front of 2 and solve, as follows:

$$|14| \times |-2|$$
$$= 14 \times 2 = 28$$

8. The correct answer is J. To solve this problem you should notice that, because line XY is parallel to line AB, a new triangle, XYC, which is similar to triangle ABC has been created. Therefore, the corresponding angle measures in each triangle will be congruent, which means that angle $A = 40°$. You are given that the measure of angle B is 80°. The sum of the measure of angles in a triangle is 180°, so set up the following equation to solve for the measure of angle C:

$$180° = 40° + 80° + C$$
$$180° = 120° + C$$
$$60° = C$$

9. The correct answer is E. To solve this problem, simply substitute -3 for x and 2 for y in the equation, as follows (carefully track the negative sign!):

$$x^3y + xy^3 = (-3)^3(2) + (-3)(2)^3$$
$$= (-27)(2) + (-3)(8)$$
$$= -54 - 24$$
$$= -78$$

10. The correct answer is F. One way to solve this problem is to draw a chart like the one shown below. You are given that y represents the number of full years of employment. Therefore, the salary increase for each professor should be shown as a coefficient of y:

A	B
$50,000 + 1,500y$	$42,000 + 2,800y$

Now that you know how to calculate each professor's salary after y number of years, set these values equal to each other to come up with the correct equation:

$$50,000 + 1,500y = 42,000 + 2,800y$$

11. **The correct answer is B.** Don't let the fact that there are no numbers in this math problem confuse you! Simply remember that W, X, Y, and Z each represent some number, and perform the correct mathematical operations to isolate Z on one side of the equation, as follows:

$$W = XYZ$$

$$\frac{W}{XY} = Z$$

12. **The correct answer is K.** You are given that both numbers have a factor of 8 and that they both factor into 48 evenly (48 is the least common multiple). Therefore, the following is true:

$$48 = 8 \times a \times b$$

Because $48 = 8 \times 6$, $a \times b$ must equal 6; a could equal 2 and b could equal 3, which means that one of the given numbers has a factor of 2 and the other has a factor of 3. Both numbers have a common factor of 8, so one number could be $8 \times 2 = 16$ and the other number could be $8 \times 3 = 24$.

13. **The correct answer is B.** To solve this problem, set up an equation to determine the length of the shorter piece, substituting x for the unknown, shorter length:

$$x + (x + 23) = 55$$

$$2x + 23 = 55$$

$$2x = 32$$

$$x = 16$$

The problem states that one piece is 23 feet longer than the other piece, which does not necessarily mean that the shorter piece will be 23 feet

long, so answer choice A is incorrect. If you simply subtracted 23 from 55 you would get answer choice D, which is incorrect. This calculation does not account for both lengths of rope. If you divided the original length of the rope (55) by 2, subtracted 23 and rounded up, you would get answer choice E. This is not the correct calculation to perform.

14. **The correct answer is F.** To solve this problem, expand $(x + r)^2$ using the FOIL method:

$$(x + r)^2$$
$$= (x + r)(x + r)$$
$$= x^2 + 2xr + r^2$$

Now, substitute this value for $(x + r)^2$ in the given equation:

$$x^2 + 2xr + r^2 = x^2 + 22x + r^2$$

You can see that $2xr = 22x$, so solve for r, as follows:

$$2xr = 22x$$
$$r = 22x/2x$$
$$r = 11$$

15. **The correct answer is C.** To solve this problem, first find the common denominator, as follows:

$$3\frac{1}{3} + 2\frac{4}{5} = 3\frac{5}{15} + 2\frac{12}{15}$$

Next, add the fractions:

$$3\frac{5}{15} + 2\frac{12}{15}$$
$$= 5\frac{17}{15}$$
$$= 6\frac{2}{15}$$

Now look at the fraction part of this mixed number and work through the answer choices. You know that $\frac{2}{15}$ is less than $\frac{1}{2}$ $(\frac{7.5}{15})$, so eliminate answer choice A. You also know that $\frac{2}{15}$ is less than $\frac{1}{3}$ $(\frac{5}{15})$, so eliminate answer choice B. Because $6\frac{2}{15}$ is greater than 6 but less than

$6\frac{1}{3}$, Jenny's total distance is between 6 and $6\frac{1}{3}$ miles.

16. **The correct answer is H.** To solve this problem, it might be helpful to draw a picture like the one shown next:

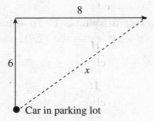

You can see that the route traveled creates a right triangle. Use the Pythagorean Theorem to calculate the distance from the parking lot, as follows:

$$6^2 + 8^2 = x^2$$
$$36 + 64 = x^2$$
$$100 = x^2$$
$$10 = x$$

17. **The correct answer is B.** A line, parabola, and so on will intersect the x-axis when $y = 0$. Therefore, you can set each of the elements given in the question to 0 and solve for x, as follows:

$$(x + 1) = 0, x = -1$$
$$(x - 2) = 0, x = 2$$
$$(x + 3) = 0, x = -3$$
$$(x + 4) = 0, x = -4$$

The graph will cross the x-axis at $-1, 2, -3$, and -4.

18. **The correct answer is G.** To solve this problem, first calculate the new area of Marcia's horse corral:

Initial area $= 50 \times 125 = 6,250$ square feet

New area $= 6,250 + 1,850 = 8,100$ square feet

Now, you can try the answer choices to see which combination of width and length fits the parameters given in the question:

Answer choice F: While these dimensions indicate an increase of 5 feet for both the width and the length, the area does not equal 8,100 ($55 \times 130 = 7,150$ square feet).

Answer choice G: These dimensions reflect an increase of 10 feet for both the width and the length, and the area equals 8,100 ($60 \times 135 = 8,100$ square feet), so this is the correct answer.

19. **The correct answer is D.** To solve this problem, first remember that perimeter is equal to the distance around an object. Therefore, the perimeter of a triangle is simply the sum of the lengths of its sides. You are given that the lengths of the sides of the triangle are 3 consecutive even integers. Set the first length (the shortest side) equal to x, the second length equal to $x + 2$, and the third length (the longest side) equal to $x + 4$. Now, create an equation and solve for x, as follows:

$$x + (x + 2) + (x + 4) = 48$$
$$3x + 6 = 48$$
$$x = 14$$

You now know that the length of the shortest side is 14, so the length of the longest side must be $14 + 4 = 18$.

20. **The correct answer is H.** To solve this problem, put the given equation in the standard form, $y = mx + b$, where m is the slope:

$$4y - 6x = 8$$
$$4y = 6x + 8$$
$$y = \left(\frac{6}{4}\right)x + 2$$
$$y = \left(\frac{3}{2}\right)x + 2$$

Therefore, $m = \frac{3}{2}$.

21. **The correct answer is B.** One way to solve this problem is to use SOH CAH TOA to find the sin, cos, and tan of angle X, as follows:

SOH: sin = opposite/hypotenuse = $\frac{12}{13}$

CAH: cos = adjacent/hypotenuse = $\frac{5}{13}$

TOA: tan = opposite/adjacent = $\frac{12}{5}$

Only answer choice B, $\sin X = \frac{12}{13}$, is a true statement about angle X.

22. **The correct answer is F.** To solve this problem, draw a line from Q to S on the figure, creating right

triangle QST. You are given that the length of QT is 5 and the length of ST is 3. Use the Pythagorean theorem to find the length of QS, the hypotenuse:

$$3^2 + 5^2 = c^2$$
$$9 + 25 = c^2$$
$$34 = c^2$$
$$\sqrt{34} = c$$

23. **The correct answer is E.** To solve this problem, recall that a counterclockwise rotation will move point R to the left about the origin. Therefore, the x-value will be negative, and you can eliminate answer choices A, B, and C. Likewise, a rotation about the origin will move point R from its current location, so the x-value will change, leaving answer choice E as the only option.

24. **The correct answer is H.** Recall that the perimeter is the distance around any object. You are given the side lengths, so start by finding the sum of the given lengths:

$$QT = 5, RS = \sqrt{34}, ST = 3, \text{ and } RQ = 6$$
$$5 + \sqrt{34} + 3 + 6$$
$$= 14 + \sqrt{34}$$

At this point you can safely eliminate answer choices J and K because they are too small. You are asked for an approximation, so you don't actually have to do all the math. The square root of 34 is slightly less than the square root of 36, so the perimeter will be slightly less than $14 + 6 = 20$, leaving you with 19.8 as the only viable option.

25. **The correct answer is B.** To solve this problem, first convert the information in the question into its mathematical equivalent, as follows:

5 times a number $x = 5x$

Subtracting $5x$ from 15 yields a negative result, so

$15 - 5x < 0$.

Now, solve the inequality for x:

$$15 - 5x < 0$$
$$- 5x < -15$$

Divide both sides by -5 and reverse the inequality to get $x > 3$.

26. **The correct answer is K.** One way to solve this problem is to substitute each of the answer choices for t in the inequality to determine which one does NOT work:

Answer choice F: $|74 - 34| = |40| = 40$; $40 \leq 40$, so eliminate answer choice F.

Answer choice G: $|16 - 34| = |-18| = 18$; $18 \leq 40$, so eliminate answer choice G.

Answer choice H: $|0 - 34| = |-34| = 34$; $34 \leq 40$, so eliminate answer choice H.

Answer choice J: $|-6 - 34| = |-40| = 40$; $40 \leq 40$, so eliminate answer choice J.

By the process of elimination, answer choice K must be correct: $|-8 - 34| = |-42| = 42$, which is NOT ≤ 40.

27. **The correct answer is D.** The slope-intercept form of the equation for a line is $y = mx + b$; isolate y on the left side of the equation, as follows:

$$10x - y - 8 = 0$$
$$10x - y = 8$$
$$- y = -10x + 8$$
$$y = 10x - 8$$

28. **The correct answer is H.** As shown in the figure, the radius, r, is the hypotenuse of a right triangle. One leg of the triangle is 6 and the other is half of 32, or 16. Use the Pythagorean theorem to calculate the length of r, as follows:

$$6^2 + 16^2 = r^2$$
$$36 + 256 = r^2$$
$$292 = r^2$$
$$17.08 = r$$

Rounded to the nearest tenth of a centimeter, $r = 17.1$ cm.

29. **The correct answer is B.** Each of the numbers in the values given must divide evenly into the least common multiple. Therefore, you can quickly eliminate answer choice A because 4 does not divide evenly into 15. Next, notice that each of the number values divides evenly into 60, which is less than 120, so eliminate answer choices D and E. Because ab is a smaller multiple than a^2b, and ab divides evenly into the product of all of the given values, answer choice B is the least common multiple of the given values.

30. The correct answer is K. You are given that the two lines intersect at a certain point, which means that the lines cross at the *same* point in the (x,y) coordinate plane, so at that point, the equations of those lines is equal. Set up the following equation and solve for x:

$$3x + 4 = 2x + 6$$
$$x = 2$$

Now, substitute 2 for x in either equation and find y, as follows:

$$y = 3x + 4$$
$$y = 3(2) + 4$$
$$y = 6 + 4 = 10$$

31. The correct answer is E. To solve this problem, first expand the numerator and factor the denominator, then simplify, as follows:

$$\frac{(x-13)(x-13)}{(x-13)(x+13)} = \frac{(x-13)}{(x+13)}$$

32. The correct answer is F. To solve this problem, first recognize that, if $n = m + 2$, then $m - n = -2$. Now, substitute this value into the second expression and solve:

$$(m - n)^4 = (-2)^4 = 16$$

33. The correct answer is D. To solve this problem, first convert the information given into its mathematical equivalent, as follows (use b to represent the larger number):

The larger of two numbers exceeds twice the smaller number by nine: $b = 2a + 9$

The sum of twice the larger and five times the smaller number is 74: $2b + 5a = 74$

Now, simply substitute the value of b into the second equation in order to solve for a:

$$2(2a + 9) + 5a = 74$$

34. The correct answer is G. You are given that $x/y = 4$, so $x = 4y$. Substitute $4y$ for x in the equation and solve, as follows:

$$x^2 - 12y^2$$
$$= (4y)^2 - 12y^2$$
$$= 16y^2 - 12y^2$$
$$= 4y^2$$

35. The correct answer is B. You are given certain ratios in this problem, so you can set up a proportion to find the length of the shortest side of the second triangle. The ratio of the longest sides of both triangles is $\frac{15}{10}$. Set the length of the shortest side of the second triangle to x so that the ratio of the shortest sides of both triangles is $\frac{12}{x}$. Now, set up a proportion, cross-multiply, and solve for x:

$$\frac{15}{10} = \frac{12}{x}$$
$$15x = 120$$
$$x = 8$$

36. The correct answer is F. One way to solve this problem is to recognize that ab^2 is a common factor of a^2b^2 and ab^3. Therefore, it must also be a factor of 45, which can be factored as 5×3^2. Now you can see that b could be 3, and since there can only be one correct answer, F must be it. If you test $a = 5$ and $b = 3$, you see that the greatest common factor of $5^2 \times 3^2$ and 5×3^3 is 5×3^2, which equals 45.

37. The correct answer is C. To solve this problem, set the fixed charge to x and set the number of half-miles to y. Now, select two values from the table to create a set of equations, and solve for x and y, as follows:

$$x + 5y = 8.00$$
$$x + 6y = 8.50$$

The x values will cancel out, leaving $y = 0.50$, which means that the cost per half-mile is \$0.50; eliminate answer choice A. Now, substitute .5 for y in one of the equations to solve for x:

$$x + 5y = 8$$
$$x + 5(.5) = 8$$
$$x = 8 - 2.5 = 5.50$$

38. The correct answer is G. One way to solve this problem is to use SOH CAH TOA for angle A. You are given that the sine of angle A is 3/5, which means that the ratio of the length of the side opposite angle A to the length of the hypotenuse is 3 to 5. So, the ratio 3/5 is equal to the ratio BC/AC. You are given that AC, the hypotenuse, is equal to 16, so now you can set up a proportion, cross-multiply, and solve for BC, as follows:

$$3/5 = BC/AC$$
$$5BC = 3AC$$
$$5BC = 3(16)$$
$$5BC = 48$$
$$BC = 9.6$$

39. **The correct answer is E.** The equation of a circle is $(x - h)^2 + (y - k)^2 = r^2$, where h and k are the x and y-coordinates of the center of the circle and r is the radius. Therefore, the equation of the circle centered at point $(12, -5)$ with a radius of 4 is $(x - 12)^2 + (y + 5)^2 = 16$.

40. **The correct answer is G.** One way to solve this problem is to recognize that, in order for $\frac{24}{30}$ to be greater than $\frac{t}{24}$, t must be less than 24. This is true because any fraction with a denominator larger than or equal to its numerator will always be *less* than a fraction whose numerator is larger than or equal to its denominator. So, $\frac{t}{24}$ is only less than $\frac{24}{30}$ when t is less than 24. Because you are asked for the largest integer value of t and you know that t must be less than 24, the correct answer must be 19. You could also set the values equal to each other, cross-multiply and solve for t, as follows:

$$\frac{24}{30} = \frac{t}{24}$$
$$30t = 576$$
$$t = 19.2$$

The integer value that makes $\frac{24}{30}$ greater than $\frac{t}{24}$, therefore, is 19.

41. **The correct answer is B.** To solve this problem you could either use the distance formula, or sketch a quick figure like the one shown below:

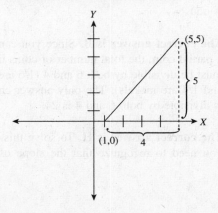

You can see that the distance between the points is the hypotenuse of the right triangle with side lengths of 5 and 4. Use the Pythagorean theorem to solve for the hypotenuse, c:

$$c^2 = 5^2 + 4^2 = 41$$
$$c = \sqrt{41}$$

42. **The correct answer is K.** To solve this problem, recognize that MN is parallel to LO and that these lines are cut by the transversal MO. Therefore, angles OMN and MOL are alternate interior angles and they have the same measure, 30°. Now, because a straight line has 180°, the measure of angle MON must be $180° - 30° - 105° = 45°$.

43. **The correct answer is E.** A good way to solve this problem is to sketch triangle ABC, as shown below:

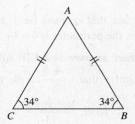

You are given that AB is congruent to AC, and that the measure of angle B is 34°. This means that the measure of angle C is also 34°, and the measure of angle A is $180° - 34° - 34° = 112°$.

44. **The correct answer is K.** To solve this problem, first set the total amount of the budget equal to b. Housing costs are equal to 30 percent of b, or $.3b$. Of this portion, 20 percent, or $.2$, goes toward rent. Therefore, rent, r, is equal to $.2(.3b)$, or $.06b$. You are given that rent, r, equals \$630, so now you can set up an equation and solve for b, as follows:

$$.06b = 630$$
$$b = 630/.06$$
$$b = 10,500$$

45. **The correct answer is A.** To find the matrix product, simply multiply the terms from a row in the first matrix by the corresponding term

from a column in the second matrix, as shown next:

$$2x \times 1 = \mathbf{2x} \quad 2x \times 0 = \mathbf{0} \quad 2x \times -1 = \mathbf{-2x}$$

$$3x \times 1 = \mathbf{3x} \quad 3x \times 0 = \mathbf{0} \quad 3x \times -1 = \mathbf{-3x}$$

$$5x \times 1 = \mathbf{5x} \quad 2x \times 0 = \mathbf{0} \quad 5x \times -1 = \mathbf{-5x}$$

46. The correct answer is G. To solve this problem, you will need to find the two missing dimensions. Sketch the figure as shown below to help visualize the missing dimensions:

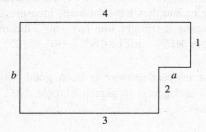

You can see that a must be 1 and b must be 3. Therefore, the perimeter is $4+3+2+1+1+3 = 14$.

47. The correct answer is A. To solve this problem, first recognize that $\dfrac{a+b}{2} = 6$, which means that $a + b = 12$. Also, $\dfrac{a+b+c}{3} = 11$, which means that $a + b + c = 33$. Therefore, $12 + c = 33$, so c must equal $33 - 12$, or 21.

48. The correct answer is F. One quick way to solve this problem is to start with 12 and add each preceding even integer until you get to a sum of 40, and then count the terms:

$$12 + 10 + 8 + 6 + 4 = 40.$$
There are 5 terms in the set.

49. The correct answer is B. The absolute value of any number is positive. Eliminate answer choice A because it is negative. Since w is close to 1.75 on the number line shown, and u is close to 0.6 on the number line shown, the difference of w and u is close to 1.15 on the number line shown. This corresponds to v.

50. The correct answer is G. To solve this problem, you must remember that the formula for the circumference of a circle is $C = 2\pi r$, where r is the radius. You are given that the length of arc XY is 7π, and

that this is 1/6 of the total circumference. Therefore, the circumference must be $6 \times 7\pi = 42\pi$. Substitute this value for C in the equation and solve for r, as follows:

$$42\pi = 2\pi r$$

$$21\pi = \pi r$$

$$21 = r$$

51. The correct answer is E. To solve this problem, start with $n = 1$ until you reach an answer choice: when you reach $n = 8$, you will get $2(8)^2 - 6(8) = 80$, answer choice E.

52. The correct answer is K. To solve this problem, first find the values of x for which $g(x) = 69$ by solving the equation $69 = 3(x^2 - 2)$, as follows:

$$69 = 3(x^2 - 2)$$

$$23 = x^2 - 2$$

$$25 = x^2$$

$$x = 5 \text{ or } x = -5$$

The possible values of $2x - 3$ are therefore 7 or -13, of which 7 is the only available answer choice.

53. The correct answer is B. The correct answer will be the statement that is always true. Because a is greater than 4, and $25 - 4 = 21$, b must always be less than 21.

54. The correct answer is J. You are given that $m + n$ is even and the value of $(m + n)^2$ is also even. However, because $(m + n)^2 + n + p$ is odd, the sum $n + p$ must be odd. A sum of two positive integers is odd only when one is even and one is odd. Therefore, it must be true that if n is even, p is odd.

55. The correct answer is B. Since you cannot have a partial coin, the total number of coins in the bag must be divisible by both 6 and 4 (1/6 are quarters and 1/4 are nickels). The only answer choice that is divisible by both 6 and 4 is 24.

56. The correct answer is H. To solve this problem, you need to recognize that the slope of the line is equal to 4. In the standard equation for a line, $y = mx + b$, m is equivalent to the slope. The slope is equal to the change in y-values over the change in x-values; set up the following equation to solve for t:

$$\text{slope} = (s + t) - s/(r + 2) - r$$
$$4 = t/2$$
$$8 = t$$

57. **The correct answer is E.** You are given that $x > 90$, which means that y must be less than 90, because it is a complimentary angle to x. The sum of complimentary angles is 180. None of the other answer choices must necessarily be true.

58. **The correct answer is K.** You are given that $x = 2y + 3z - 5$. If the value of y decreases by 1, then the new value of y is $y - 1$; if the value of z increases by 2, then the new value of z is $z + 2$. Substitute these values into the original equation to see the effects of the changes on the value of x:

$$x = 2(y - 1) + 3(z + 2) - 5$$
$$x = 2y - 2 + 3z + 6 - 5 = 2y + 3z - 1$$

Therefore, x now equals $2y + 3z - 1$, which is 4 more than $2y + 3z - 5$.

59. **The correct answer is E.** The distance between R and N is the length of a diagonal of the cube, whereas the distance from S to N is the length of a side of the cube. The length of the diagonal is longer than the length of the side. Therefore, the distance from N to R is not the same as the distance as N to S.

60. **The correct answer is F.** Since t is the supplement of the 35 degree angle, $t = 180 - 35$, or $145°$. Because s is the supplement to t, $s = 180 - 145$, or $35°$. Since p is the complement of s, $p = 90 - 35$, or $55°$. Therefore, $3p + 4s - 2t = 3(55) + 4(35) - 2(145) = 165 + 140 - 290 = 15°$.

Reading Test Explanations

PASSAGE I

1. **The best answer is B.** The tone of the first seven paragraphs suggests that Libby is not as excited about the move as is her husband John. The passages states, "… hoping the enthusiasm in my voice would match the sparkle in his eyes" to indicate that Libby was attempting to appear excited for John's sake. The other answer choices are clearly indicated in the first seven paragraphs.

2. **The best answer is J.** The passage states that, "The fall semester was just a few short weeks away." This statement and the mention elsewhere in the passage of the hot weather indicates that it was most likely late summer when the couple moved into their new apartment.

3. **The best answer is A.** According to the passage, Libby initially was less enthusiastic than John about the move, but eventually changed her attitude. The passages states, "… hoping the enthusiasm in my voice would match the sparkle in his eyes" to indicate that Libby was initially attempting to appear excited for John's sake. This information best supports answer choice A.

4. **The best answer is H.** According to the passage, Libby initially was less enthusiastic than John about the move, but eventually changed her attitude. The passage states that, "There's something monumental about your first step into a new home … Now, suddenly, I knew the future had begun … I knew it could be anything we wanted it to be." These statements best support an attitude of cautious optimism. While Libby was not very excited when she first arrived, nothing in the passage suggests that she dreaded the move, so eliminate answer choice G. Likewise, the other answer choices are not supported by details in the passage.

5. **The best answer is A.** The passage states that, "We each grabbed an armful and headed towards our new apartment, just a few blocks away from the squat, industrial-looking building where John would start teaching." This statement best supports answer choice A. While Libby was accustomed to university buildings that were ivy-covered, John's new workplace was different.

6. **The best answer is F.** The passage does not describe the hardships faced by a young couple in their first home. While there is some mention of Libby's initial reservations about moving into the new apartment, there is not enough detail about

any hardships she and John may have faced to support answer choice F as an accurate description of the passage.

7. **The best answer is C.** The question asks about John's perception of his wife. When John says, "Libby, we have an entire car and trailer to unpack. You might as well forget about looking glamorous, at least for now. Besides, it's not like we're back in D.C. No C-Span cameras here!" he is referring to her attempt to fix her hair after the long trip. This suggests that he thought Libby was somewhat vain and too concerned about her appearance. The other answer choices are not supported by the passage.

8. **The best answer is G.** Prior to the lines mentioned in the question, the passage states that Libby "knew it [the future] could be anything we wanted it to be." The passage goes on to state that Libby, "felt a thrill of real excitement" after she looked around the apartment. These statements best support answer choice G.

9. **The best answer is C.** The first two sentences of the first paragraph set the tone for the paragraph; as far as Libby, the main character, was concerned they had made it "just in time." Additionally, after she got out of the car, her mood began to improve, which suggests that being in the car had made her somewhat unhappy. Answer choices A and D are too general and broad, while answer choice B is too specific.

10. **The best answer is J.** The primary focus of the passage is the young couple's move from Washington, D.C. to Ohio, where their lives would be quite different. They packed up the life they had in D.C. and moved it halfway across the country to the Midwest. The statement "unload our life" refers to this significant change.

PASSAGE II

11. **The best answer is A.** According to the passage, there is a "specific measure, the 'poverty line,'" that can be used to determine poverty. Because the passage refers to this line as being a specific measure, answer choice A is best. The other answer choices are not supported by the passage.

12. **The best answer is H.** As stated in the passage, "The question of poverty is extremely complex." Therefore, one can infer that measuring poverty is a difficult task. The other answer choices are not supported by the passage.

13. **The best answer is D.** According to the passage, the average American family in the 1950s "spent approximately one-third of its household income on food." When one subtracts 1/3 from the whole, 2/3 remains. Therefore, the average American family spent 2/3 of their income on non-food items in the 1950s.

14. **The best answer is F.** As stated in the passage, "While families today spend about 12 percent of their income on food—nowhere near the 33 percent assumed in the 1950s—the cost of important budget items, such as housing, transportation, and health care, has increased dramatically. Orshansky's poverty measure, which only takes into account the ability of a household to provide itself with food, is missing several essential components to be accurate in modern society. With over $60 billion in federal aid tied each year to this guideline, not to mention an additional $260 billion in Medicaid spending, the fact is many Americans are still falling deeper into poverty and failing to receive the aid they so desperately need and deserve." This information suggests that Americans are much poorer than they were in the past, which best supports answer choice F.

15. **The best answer is C.** The passage states that, "Orshansky's poverty measure, which only takes into account the ability of a household to provide itself with food, is missing several essential components to be accurate in modern society. With over $60 billion in federal aid tied each year to this guideline, not to mention an additional $260 billion in Medicaid spending, the fact is many Americans are still falling deeper into poverty and failing to receive the aid they so desperately need and deserve." These statements best support answer choice C.

16. **The best answer is G.** As indicated in the passage, "Orshansky's statistical measurement was one small part of the federal government's plan to attack the difficult national economic conditions that were hurting millions of Americans in the early 1960s. President Lyndon Johnson labeled the plan the government's "War on Poverty," and it led to such national programs as Head Start, VISTA, and the Jobs Corps." These statements best support answer choice G.

17. **The best answer is B.** The first paragraph of the passage states that, "Poverty is an enduring problem that must be addressed by all modern societies." It also states that, "projects have to be evaluated to see if they are effective. No one can measure the benefits of aid without defining what poverty is, and when someone has been lifted out of it." Based on this information, one can infer that the paragraph aims to detail the importance of measuring poverty in relation to aid disbursement.

18. **The best answer is H.** The passage states the following information: "While families today spend about 12 percent of their income on food—nowhere near the 33 percent assumed in the 1950s ..." This statement best supports answer choice H.

19. **The best answer is D.** According to the passage, "Any change in the measured poverty level of a society is an indicator of economic health within that society, and no president has been willing to increase the perceived amount of poverty for a statistical recalculation, no matter how justified. Indeed, some economists say that updating the poverty measure would increase the number of those considered poor, and therefore eligible for government aid, by as much as 2 percentage points." Based on this information, answer choices A, B, and C are all reasons why no president is willing to make a poverty level change.

20. **The best answer is F.** As stated in the passage, "Orshansky's statistical measurement was one small part of the federal government's plan to attack the difficult national economic conditions that were hurting millions of Americans in the early 1960s." Specifically, Orshansky worked to formulate a way to define poverty so that the government could help those who met this definition. This information best supports answer choice F.

PASSAGE III

21. **The best answer is A.** This passage is written by someone reflecting on her past. Specifically, the author reflects on both her childhood and her college years. According to this information, answer choices B and C can be eliminated. The author mentions Sr. Benedicta, but the author is not Sr. Benedicta. Therefore, answer choice D can be eliminated, making answer choice A best.

22. **The best answer is F.** Initially, the author discusses her childhood yearning to meet J.R.R. Tolkien. Paragraph 3 details this longing. However, after studying at Oxford as a young adult and experiencing Tolkien's life second-hand, the author realizes that she does not have to meet him to enjoy his writing.

23. The best answer is D. The author begins the passage detailing one of J.R.R. Tolkien's greatest works. "Of course, today, most people remember him as the author of *The Lord of the Rings*—a monumental work that became an epic film." This statement indicates the author's acknowledgement of Tolkien's talent. Later in the passage, when speaking of Tolkien's personality, the author says, "Apparently, most people have this impression of Tolkien's as a gentle, grandfatherly sort of man, but, unless you were his grandchild, that wasn't actually the case. In person, he was frequently severe and not terribly friendly." This statement describes Tolkien's intimidating personality. Together, this information best supports answer choice D.

24. The best answer is G. As stated by the author, "I loved Oxford." Throughout the seventh paragraph of the passage, the author lists several reasons to support this love for the university. The other answer choices are not supported by the tone or details of the passage.

25. The best answer is D. In the fourth paragraph of the passage, the author says, "But, growing up in the Midwest, the possibility of traveling to England seemed very remote. Then I discovered that Tolkien had died years before I'd even started *The Hobbit*. I forgot about my dream and got down to the business of school and sports and college applications." Based on this information, one can infer that the author came to an understanding of her situation.

26. The best answer is H. As stated by the author, "Sr. Benedicta was a very smart but very kindly, elderly nun. She was no slouch as an academic and had published several highly-regarded books in her field. As a colleague, she had spent time with Tolkien when she was newly hired at St. Stephen's College. One day, when she had asked me how I liked studying at Oxford, I decided to tell her about my dream." The author's decision to share this dream was an effort to connect to Tolkien through Benedicta, which best supports answer choice H.

27. The best answer is B. The author begins the passage with the following, "A friend introduced me to Tolkien's writings when I was 10 years old. Aileen gave me a copy of *The Hobbit*, and told me her father was reading *The Lord of the Rings* to her and her brother at the dinner table every night after the family had finished eating. I read *The Hobbit* and was hooked. By the time I was 14, I had read every piece of fiction Tolkien had

published." Based on this information, one can infer that the author very much enjoyed Tolkien's writings and she continued reading his works. This best supports answer choice B.

28. The best answer is F. The author says that she loved "the stories our housekeeper would tell of Lawrence of Arabia's ghost who, apparently, lived in our own quarters. When inexplicable drafts would sweep my room, our housekeeper swore it was Lawrence." One can infer from this statement that the housekeeper thought Lawrence of Arabia's ghost haunted their quarters.

29. The best answer is C. In the passage, the author says that Sr. Benedicta "was no slouch as an academic," followed by the statement that the professor had "published several highly-regarded books in her field." Based on this information, one can infer that Sr. Benedicta was an excellent researcher.

30. The best answer is J. The passage states, "Oxford isn't set up like most American universities. It's not a single uniform entity. Instead, it's a collection of 39 independent colleges, each with its own internal structure and activities, with an overlying administration that conducts examinations and confers degrees." As it is used in this statement, the word *uniform* means consistent.

PASSAGE IV

31. The best answer is A. By reading the passage, one learns about El Niño and its effects. For example, the first paragraph ends with the following statement: "Of these, probably the best-known is the El Niño-Southern Oscillation, popularly called 'El Niño.'" Following this, the article offers details about the oscillation, such as, "Along this area of South America, El Niños reduce the upwelling of cold, nutrient-rich water that sustains large fish populations. Predators such as larger fish and sea birds depend on these populations for survival, as do local fisheries." The passage also details the various political ramifications of El Niño. This information best supports answer choice A.

32. The best answer is G. According to the passage, "The term El Niño was first reported in scientific circles in 1892." Because 1892 is within the 1890s, answer choice G is best.

33. The best answer is C. The paragraph starts with the following: "Sometimes, pressure caused by intense weather can have unexpected political effects." The paragraph then goes on to give examples of how the weather may have caused certain political events, such as the French Revolution and Germany's failure to capture Moscow during WWII. This information best supports answer choice C.

34. The best answer is F. Paragraph 2 of the passage puts the following information in parentheses, "The reverse phenomenon, a cold ocean current, is known by a corresponding term, La Niña, Spanish for 'little girl.'" While this information is interesting and related to the topic, it is not immediately relevant to its surrounding context.

35. The best answer is D. The paragraph states, "Sometimes, however, the various oscillations "beat" together at the same frequency, causing the fluctuations to be synchronized. When this happens, scientists say the resulting weather can be intensified." These details best support answer choice D.

36. The best answer is H. The third paragraph of the passage begins with the following: "As climatology developed as a discipline, scientists discovered that both trends in the current were part of a larger phenomenon affecting global climate patterns, the Southern Oscillation. The definition of El Niño has therefore expanded and continues to change as climate researchers compile more data." The paragraph then goes on to detail the process by which this definition is determined, which best supports answer choice H.

37. The best answer is A. When detailing El Niño, the passage states, "Most of the time, strong El Niños bring wet winters to the Southwestern United States and milder winters to the Midwest. They tend to bring dry conditions to Indonesia and northern Australia." Of the four given answers, answer choice A is most closely related to these weather effects. Because California is in the Southwestern United States, unusually wet weather indicates an El Niño weather pattern. Furthermore, because droughts are reported in Australia, it seems likely that an El Niño oscillation is present. The other answer choices are not supported by the passage.

38. The best answer is G. According to the passage, "Some scientists argue that unusually cold weather brought by a strong El Niño phenomenon caused significant crop damage in 1788–89, which many say contributed to the French Revolution. Other climate researchers claim that strong oscillation coupling, combined with strong El Niños in the late 1930s and early 1940s, led to a profound cold snap in Northern Europe in the middle of the Second World War. The scientists argue that this unexpected cold snap significantly contributed to the failure of Germany to capture Moscow, which changed the course of World War II." This information taken in its entirety best supports answer choice G. Answer choices F and H are not supported by the passage, and, although the passage indicates that some scientists argue that El Niño changed the course of the Second World War, nothing in the passage suggests that Germany would have won had it not been for El Niño.

39. The best answer is D. According to the passage, "Weather effects can be damaging. The warming patterns of El Niño are one of the leading causes of natural damage to coral reefs, while wider ENSO fluctuations may cause flooding or drought to occur on land. In these cases, extreme shifts can cause economic pressure by disrupting entire fishing industries or damaging crops." Based on this information, damage to coral reefs, flooding, drought, and the disruption of fishing industries and crops are all possible effects of El Niño. Only answer choice D is NOT mentioned specifically in the passage as a negative consequence.

40. The best answer is J. The last paragraph of the passage states that, "ENSO phenomena, along with the other three oscillations, are separate from those attributed to global warming. The causes are completely independent." The passage also indicates that "because El Niño and global warming both can result in strong temperature variability, disruptive rain distribution, and extreme damage to a variety of ecosystems, any synchronicity will be closely observed by scientists seeking to document the total effects of each." Based on this information, once can conclude that, while they are independent of one another, El Niño patterns and global warming have similar effects of global weather, making answer choice J best.

Science Reasoning Test Explanations

PASSAGE I

1. **The correct answer is D.** According to Scientist 1, "Recent studies by researchers at Northeastern University and the University of Victoria may suggest that dark matter … does not actually exist." Additionally, Scientist 1 goes on to say that, "a galaxy, seen collectively, has its own gravity and essentially drives its own rotation at a constant rate." This information best supports answer choice D.

2. **The correct answer is G.** The process of elimination is a good approach to correctly answering this question. Scientist 2 believes that dark matter is responsible for the warped shape of galaxies such as the Milky Way, so eliminate answer choice F. Both scientists conclude that not all questions about the universe have been answered, which supports answer choice G. Only Scientist 2 believes that cosmic microwave radiation suggests the presence of dark matter, and neither scientist believes that dark matter can be easily observed in the universe, so eliminate answer choices H and J.

3. **The correct answer is B.** According to the passage, Scientist 2 believes that dark matter can explain many cosmological phenomena. Therefore, you can eliminate answer choice A. Scientist 2 does not indicate that dark matter is visible using modern instruments, only that its effect on other objects in the universe can be detected; eliminate answer choice C. Scientist 2 does not suggest that dark matter was ever a part of the general theory of relativity, so eliminate answer choice D.

4. **The correct answer is J.** Both scientists mention the existence of warped galaxies in their discussions regarding the existence of dark matter in the universe. Clearly, this phenomenon is critical to their viewpoints, so eliminate answer choices F and G. Scientist 2 references Newtonian physics in order to suggest the existence of dark matter in order to explain the additional gravitational pull needed to account for warped galaxies, so eliminate answer choice H.

5. **The correct answer is B.** According to Scientist 2, "Without the existence of dark matter, the Magellanic Clouds would not have sufficient mass to have such a strong effect on the bend of the Milky Way galaxy." If it were discovered that the Magellanic Clouds are actually more massive than previously thought, Scientist 2's theory

would be weakened. The other answer choices are not supported by the passage.

6. **The correct answer is F.** The main point of difference between the two positions is whether dark matter exists. Scientist 1 believes that it does not, while Scientist 2 believes that it does. The other answer choices are not supported by the passage.

7. **The correct answer is A.** According to Scientist 1, the new research suggesting that dark matter does not actually exist is based upon Einstein's theory of general relativity. If Einstein's theory were flawed, Scientist 1's position would be seriously weakened. The other answer choices are not supported by the passage.

PASSAGE II

8. **The correct answer is F.** According to the passage, "Contact fungicides, because they do not penetrate the plant tissue, are more easily washed off the leaf by rain. This results in a shorter residual control period and more frequent re-application of the fungicide." Table 1 indicates that *boscalid* is a contact fungicide, so it should be applied more frequently than the others listed.

9. **The correct answer is C.** The passage states that, "Fungicide applications should not be initiated after the R5 growth stage." There is nothing in the passage to indicate that *chlorthalonil* should not be applied during any growth stage.

10. **The correct answer is G.** According to the passage, "research has shown that the most critical time to protect soybean plants with fungicides is from the R1 through R5 growth stages. Fungicide applications should not be initiated after the R5 growth stage." This information best supports answer choice G.

11. **The correct answer is D.** According to the passage, "ASR infections generally begin in the lower leaf canopy … Coverage as dense as 400 spray droplets per square inch is considered ideal." Therefore, you can predict that if fewer than 400 droplets of any fungicide were applied, the chances of the plant becoming infected with ASR would increase.

12. **The correct answer is H.** According to Table 2, systemic fungicides are most effective because they are absorbed into the leaf tissue and translocated throughout the plant. Table 1 indicates that *myclobutanil* is a systemic fungicide. Because the question asks you to put the fungicides in order

of increasing effectiveness, *myclobutanil* should be last on the list. Eliminate answer choices F and J. The data indicate that contact fungicides are the least effective and that *boscalid* is a contact fungicide. Therefore, *boscalid* should be first on the list.

13. **The correct answer is B.** According to the passage, "research has shown that the most critical time to protect soybean plants with fungicides is from the R1 through R5 growth stages. Fungicide applications should not be initiated after the R5 growth stage." Because growth stage R6 is characterized by a full seed, fungicide should NOT be applied during the full seed stage.

PASSAGE III

14. **The correct answer is H.** According to the passage, "sea cucumbers are wormlike and tend to burrow." The echinoderm pictured most resembles a worm so it is likely a sea cucumber.

15. **The correct answer is C.** According to Table 1, sea lilies are *crinoids*. Table 2 shows that sea lilies are most likely found in offshore mud and ooze, which best supports answer choice C.

16. **The correct answer is F.** According to Table 1, the feeding method of *halothurian* (sea cucumbers) is to swallow mud and sand; therefore, it is most likely that sea cucumbers burrow into the mud and sand in search of food. The other answer choices are not supported by the passage.

17. **The correct answer is B.** According to Table 1, *asteroids* (starfish) are predatory and use their tube feet to move. Table 2 indicates that starfish can be found on the deep-sea floor. This information best supports answer choice B.

18. **The correct answer is G.** According to the passage, "sea cucumbers are wormlike and tend to burrow." Table 1 indicates that sea cucumbers feed by swallowing mud and sand, digesting any organic material, and ejecting whatever is left over. Sea cucumbers in large numbers could, simply by feeding, alter the physical and chemical composition of the sea floor. The other answer choices are not supported by the data.

PASSAGE IV

19. **The correct answer is C.** The passage states that the average starting weight of the guinea pigs in each group was 50 g. According to Table 2, the guinea pigs in Group 5 had the highest average

weight after 8 weeks (98 g). Guinea pigs in this group were given Feed V.

20. **The correct answer is J.** According to Table 1, the guinea pigs that were fed a grain-based feed with vitamin supplements (Group 2, Feed Q) gained an average of 32 grams over 8 weeks ($82 - 50 = 32$). Therefore, on average, these guinea pigs gained 4 grams per week ($32 \div 8 = 4$).

21. **The correct answer is C.** According to the question, the guinea pigs in Group 9 would receive Feed V (the same as Group 5) and a vitamin supplement. According to Table 2 and the information in the passage, the guinea pigs in Group 5 had the greatest average weight and height after 8 weeks. Additionally, the guinea pigs given a vitamin supplement (like in Group 6) showed more growth than the guinea pigs that did not receive vitamin supplements (such as Groups 7 and 8). Therefore, if Group 9 is given Feed V with vitamin supplements, the guinea pigs will most likely be even larger than those in Group 5, which best supports answer choice C.

22. **The correct answer is J.** The best way to answer this question is to examine each of the answer choices, and eliminate those that are not supported by the data in Table 2.

   Answer choice F: Group 7 is the control group. Group 6 was given Feed W. It is not true that the guinea pigs in Group 6 are twice as long as the guinea pigs in Group 7 so eliminate answer choice F.

   Answer choice G: Group 5 was given Feed V. It is not true that the guinea pigs in Group 5 weigh three times more than the guinea pigs in Group 7, so eliminate answer choice G.

   Answer choice H: Group 8 was given Feed Y; guinea pigs in this group did not have the greatest average length, so eliminate answer choice H.

   Answer choice J is correct, because it is true that the guinea pigs in Group 7, who received Feed X, are similar in both weight and length to the guinea pigs in Group 8, who received Feed Y.

23. **The correct answer is B.** The only difference between Group 3 (the control group) and Group 4 is that the guinea pigs in Group 4 were fed fruits and vegetables in addition to a grain-based feed. The students can hypothesize that those fruits and vegetables must have a relatively low nutritional value, since the guinea pigs in Group 4 did not grow any more than did the guinea pigs in the control group.

24. The correct answer is F. According to the results of the experiments, the guinea pigs in Group 8 gained the least amount of weight ($74 - 50 = 24$ grams) and had the smallest increase in average length ($23.25 - 20 = 3.25$ cm).

PASSAGE V

25. The correct answer is B. To answer this question, find the symbol for 403°K in the key, then find 2 hours on the *x*-axis. Move your finger up from the 2-hour mark until it intercepts the appropriate symbol. You will see that the symbol is at approximately 50% on the *y*-axis.

26. The correct answer is J. To answer this question, find the symbol for 423°K in the key, and then follow its movement on the graph. You will see that conversion stops at 8 hours, so eliminate answer choice F. The line is steepest from 0 to 2 hours, which suggests that this is the period during which most of the conversion took place.

27. The correct answer is A. In each experiment, 5% Ru/C catalyst was used. The temperature was varied in each experiment, and the conversion rates were dependent on the various temperatures. Two different types of acid were used.

28. The correct answer is J. The data in Table 1 and Table 2 indicate a direct relationship between time and percentage of conversion. As time increased, at each temperature the percent of acid converted also increased up to a certain point, at which time conversion stopped.

29. The correct answer is A. The conversion of propionic acid was studied in Experiment 2, the results of which are shown in Table 2. According to Table 2, the conversion of propionic acid at 403°K stops at 8 hours, which does not support the chemist's claim.

30. The correct answer is H. The results of Experiment 2 are shown in Table 2. To answer this question, find the symbol for 423°K in the key, and then follow its movement on the graph. Notice that at 12 hours, the PA is approximately 80% converted. It makes sense that, if the conversion continued, 100% of the acid would be converted sometime between 12 and 14 hours.

PASSAGE VI

31. The correct answer is D. The passage states that, "Levels near properly adjusted gas stoves are often 5.0 to 15.0 ppm and those near poorly adjusted stoves may be 30.0 ppm or higher."

Because Home 1 has CO levels greater than 25.0 ppm, it is the most likely home to have a poorly adjusted gas stove.

32. The correct answer is G. According to Table 1, Home 2 has CO levels between 15.0 and 25.0 ppm. The passage states that average CO levels in homes without gas stoves are between 0.5 and 5.0 ppm, which means the CO levels in Home 2 are above average.

33. The correct answer is A. The passage states that, "Levels near properly adjusted gas stoves are often 5.0 to 15.0 ppm and those near poorly adjusted stoves may be 30.0 ppm or higher. CO levels between 0.5 and 15.0 ppm are considered safe." This information best supports answer choice A. The remaining answer choices indicate safe levels.

34. The correct answer is H. According to Table 1, Home 4 has CO levels between 1.0 and 5.0 ppm. The passage indicates that levels between 0.5 and 15.0 ppm are considered safe. Therefore, the CO levels in Home 4 are not dangerous, so if it has a gas stove, the stove is properly adjusted and does not have to be removed.

35. The correct answer is C. According to the passage, "CO levels between 0.5 and 15.0 ppm are considered safe." Therefore, a CO level of 10.0, as found in Home 6, will not pose any danger to the residents.

PASSAGE VII

36. The correct answer is G. According to the passage, Plot B received applications of high-nitrogen fertilizer, whereas Plot A received applications of low-nitrogen fertilizer. Both Table 1 and Figure 1 indicate that the leachate from Plot B always contained higher average nitrogen levels than the leachate from Plot A. This information best supports answer choice G.

37. The correct answer is A. The passage states that, "The leaching of high concentrations of nitrogen into natural waterways can throw off the environmental equilibrium of the aquatic ecosystem, often resulting in an increase in plant growth that can have a negative impact on the native fish populations." Therefore, if low-nitrogen fertilizer is applied, any leachate into surrounding waterways should have low concentrations of nitrogen, and the native fish populations will not be affected.

38. The correct answer is H. According to Table 1, the average nitrogen concentration in the leachate from both plots during 2003 was higher than in previous or subsequent years. Therefore, more nitrogen was leached from the soil in 2003, suggesting that this year experienced heavy rainfall during the months of the study.

39. The correct answer is B. According to Table 1, only Plot A had average nitrogen concentrations less than 10 mg/L. Because this plot received a fertilizer application containing 98 kilograms of nitrogen per acre, you can conclude that the Environmental Protection Agency would consider this application safe.

40. The correct answer is H. According to the passage, the nitrogen levels in the fertilizer applied to Plot B were reduced in 2004. However, Table 1 shows that the nitrogen concentration in the leachate from Plot B was 11.8 mg/L, which is still considered unsafe. In 2005, the concentration had gone down to a safe 8.2 mg/L. Therefore, you can conclude that it will take more than one year to reach safe nitrogen levels in the leachate. The other answer choices are not supported by the data.

Writing Test Explanation

Because grading the essay is subjective, we've chosen not to include any "graded" essays here. Your best bet is to have someone you trust, such as your personal tutor, read your essays and give you an honest critique. If you plan on grading your own essays, review the grading criteria and be as honest as possible regarding the structure, development, organization, technique, and appropriateness of your writing. Focus on your weak areas and continue to practice in order to improve your writing skills.

ACT PRACTICE TEST 10
Answer Sheet

ENGLISH

1 Ⓐ Ⓑ Ⓒ Ⓓ	21 Ⓐ Ⓑ Ⓒ Ⓓ	41 Ⓐ Ⓑ Ⓒ Ⓓ	61 Ⓐ Ⓑ Ⓒ Ⓓ
2 Ⓕ Ⓖ Ⓗ Ⓙ	22 Ⓕ Ⓖ Ⓗ Ⓙ	42 Ⓕ Ⓖ Ⓗ Ⓙ	62 Ⓕ Ⓖ Ⓗ Ⓙ
3 Ⓐ Ⓑ Ⓒ Ⓓ	23 Ⓐ Ⓑ Ⓒ Ⓓ	43 Ⓐ Ⓑ Ⓒ Ⓓ	63 Ⓐ Ⓑ Ⓒ Ⓓ
4 Ⓕ Ⓖ Ⓗ Ⓙ	24 Ⓕ Ⓖ Ⓗ Ⓙ	44 Ⓕ Ⓖ Ⓗ Ⓙ	64 Ⓕ Ⓖ Ⓗ Ⓙ
5 Ⓐ Ⓑ Ⓒ Ⓓ	25 Ⓐ Ⓑ Ⓒ Ⓓ	45 Ⓐ Ⓑ Ⓒ Ⓓ	65 Ⓐ Ⓑ Ⓒ Ⓓ
6 Ⓕ Ⓖ Ⓗ Ⓙ	26 Ⓕ Ⓖ Ⓗ Ⓙ	46 Ⓕ Ⓖ Ⓗ Ⓙ	66 Ⓕ Ⓖ Ⓗ Ⓙ
7 Ⓐ Ⓑ Ⓒ Ⓓ	27 Ⓐ Ⓑ Ⓒ Ⓓ	47 Ⓐ Ⓑ Ⓒ Ⓓ	67 Ⓐ Ⓑ Ⓒ Ⓓ
8 Ⓕ Ⓖ Ⓗ Ⓙ	28 Ⓕ Ⓖ Ⓗ Ⓙ	48 Ⓕ Ⓖ Ⓗ Ⓙ	68 Ⓕ Ⓖ Ⓗ Ⓙ
9 Ⓐ Ⓑ Ⓒ Ⓓ	29 Ⓐ Ⓑ Ⓒ Ⓓ	49 Ⓐ Ⓑ Ⓒ Ⓓ	69 Ⓐ Ⓑ Ⓒ Ⓓ
10 Ⓕ Ⓖ Ⓗ Ⓙ	30 Ⓕ Ⓖ Ⓗ Ⓙ	50 Ⓕ Ⓖ Ⓗ Ⓙ	70 Ⓕ Ⓖ Ⓗ Ⓙ
11 Ⓐ Ⓑ Ⓒ Ⓓ	31 Ⓐ Ⓑ Ⓒ Ⓓ	51 Ⓐ Ⓑ Ⓒ Ⓓ	71 Ⓐ Ⓑ Ⓒ Ⓓ
12 Ⓕ Ⓖ Ⓗ Ⓙ	32 Ⓕ Ⓖ Ⓗ Ⓙ	52 Ⓕ Ⓖ Ⓗ Ⓙ	72 Ⓕ Ⓖ Ⓗ Ⓙ
13 Ⓐ Ⓑ Ⓒ Ⓓ	33 Ⓐ Ⓑ Ⓒ Ⓓ	53 Ⓐ Ⓑ Ⓒ Ⓓ	73 Ⓐ Ⓑ Ⓒ Ⓓ
14 Ⓕ Ⓖ Ⓗ Ⓙ	34 Ⓕ Ⓖ Ⓗ Ⓙ	54 Ⓕ Ⓖ Ⓗ Ⓙ	74 Ⓕ Ⓖ Ⓗ Ⓙ
15 Ⓐ Ⓑ Ⓒ Ⓓ	35 Ⓐ Ⓑ Ⓒ Ⓓ	55 Ⓐ Ⓑ Ⓒ Ⓓ	75 Ⓐ Ⓑ Ⓒ Ⓓ
16 Ⓕ Ⓖ Ⓗ Ⓙ	36 Ⓕ Ⓖ Ⓗ Ⓙ	56 Ⓕ Ⓖ Ⓗ Ⓙ	
17 Ⓐ Ⓑ Ⓒ Ⓓ	37 Ⓐ Ⓑ Ⓒ Ⓓ	57 Ⓐ Ⓑ Ⓒ Ⓓ	
18 Ⓕ Ⓖ Ⓗ Ⓙ	38 Ⓕ Ⓖ Ⓗ Ⓙ	58 Ⓕ Ⓖ Ⓗ Ⓙ	
19 Ⓐ Ⓑ Ⓒ Ⓓ	39 Ⓐ Ⓑ Ⓒ Ⓓ	59 Ⓐ Ⓑ Ⓒ Ⓓ	
20 Ⓕ Ⓖ Ⓗ Ⓙ	40 Ⓕ Ⓖ Ⓗ Ⓙ	60 Ⓕ Ⓖ Ⓗ Ⓙ	

MATHEMATICS

1 Ⓐ Ⓑ Ⓒ Ⓓ Ⓔ	16 Ⓕ Ⓖ Ⓗ Ⓙ Ⓚ	31 Ⓐ Ⓑ Ⓒ Ⓓ Ⓔ	46 Ⓕ Ⓖ Ⓗ Ⓙ Ⓚ
2 Ⓕ Ⓖ Ⓗ Ⓙ Ⓚ	17 Ⓐ Ⓑ Ⓒ Ⓓ Ⓔ	32 Ⓕ Ⓖ Ⓗ Ⓙ Ⓚ	47 Ⓐ Ⓑ Ⓒ Ⓓ Ⓔ
3 Ⓐ Ⓑ Ⓒ Ⓓ Ⓔ	18 Ⓕ Ⓖ Ⓗ Ⓙ Ⓚ	33 Ⓐ Ⓑ Ⓒ Ⓓ Ⓔ	48 Ⓕ Ⓖ Ⓗ Ⓙ Ⓚ
4 Ⓕ Ⓖ Ⓗ Ⓙ Ⓚ	19 Ⓐ Ⓑ Ⓒ Ⓓ Ⓔ	34 Ⓕ Ⓖ Ⓗ Ⓙ Ⓚ	49 Ⓐ Ⓑ Ⓒ Ⓓ Ⓔ
5 Ⓐ Ⓑ Ⓒ Ⓓ Ⓔ	20 Ⓕ Ⓖ Ⓗ Ⓙ Ⓚ	35 Ⓐ Ⓑ Ⓒ Ⓓ Ⓔ	50 Ⓕ Ⓖ Ⓗ Ⓙ Ⓚ
6 Ⓕ Ⓖ Ⓗ Ⓙ Ⓚ	21 Ⓐ Ⓑ Ⓒ Ⓓ Ⓔ	36 Ⓕ Ⓖ Ⓗ Ⓙ Ⓚ	51 Ⓐ Ⓑ Ⓒ Ⓓ Ⓔ
7 Ⓐ Ⓑ Ⓒ Ⓓ Ⓔ	22 Ⓕ Ⓖ Ⓗ Ⓙ Ⓚ	37 Ⓐ Ⓑ Ⓒ Ⓓ Ⓔ	52 Ⓕ Ⓖ Ⓗ Ⓙ Ⓚ
8 Ⓕ Ⓖ Ⓗ Ⓙ Ⓚ	23 Ⓐ Ⓑ Ⓒ Ⓓ Ⓔ	38 Ⓕ Ⓖ Ⓗ Ⓙ Ⓚ	53 Ⓐ Ⓑ Ⓒ Ⓓ Ⓔ
9 Ⓐ Ⓑ Ⓒ Ⓓ Ⓔ	24 Ⓕ Ⓖ Ⓗ Ⓙ Ⓚ	39 Ⓐ Ⓑ Ⓒ Ⓓ Ⓔ	54 Ⓕ Ⓖ Ⓗ Ⓙ Ⓚ
10 Ⓕ Ⓖ Ⓗ Ⓙ Ⓚ	25 Ⓐ Ⓑ Ⓒ Ⓓ Ⓔ	40 Ⓕ Ⓖ Ⓗ Ⓙ Ⓚ	55 Ⓐ Ⓑ Ⓒ Ⓓ Ⓔ
11 Ⓐ Ⓑ Ⓒ Ⓓ Ⓔ	26 Ⓕ Ⓖ Ⓗ Ⓙ Ⓚ	41 Ⓐ Ⓑ Ⓒ Ⓓ Ⓔ	56 Ⓕ Ⓖ Ⓗ Ⓙ Ⓚ
12 Ⓕ Ⓖ Ⓗ Ⓙ Ⓚ	27 Ⓐ Ⓑ Ⓒ Ⓓ Ⓔ	42 Ⓕ Ⓖ Ⓗ Ⓙ Ⓚ	57 Ⓐ Ⓑ Ⓒ Ⓓ Ⓔ
13 Ⓐ Ⓑ Ⓒ Ⓓ Ⓔ	28 Ⓕ Ⓖ Ⓗ Ⓙ Ⓚ	43 Ⓐ Ⓑ Ⓒ Ⓓ Ⓔ	58 Ⓕ Ⓖ Ⓗ Ⓙ Ⓚ
14 Ⓕ Ⓖ Ⓗ Ⓙ Ⓚ	29 Ⓐ Ⓑ Ⓒ Ⓓ Ⓔ	44 Ⓕ Ⓖ Ⓗ Ⓙ Ⓚ	59 Ⓐ Ⓑ Ⓒ Ⓓ Ⓔ
15 Ⓐ Ⓑ Ⓒ Ⓓ Ⓔ	30 Ⓕ Ⓖ Ⓗ Ⓙ Ⓚ	45 Ⓐ Ⓑ Ⓒ Ⓓ Ⓔ	60 Ⓕ Ⓖ Ⓗ Ⓙ Ⓚ

READING

1 (A) (B) (C) (D)   11 (A) (B) (C) (D)   21 (A) (B) (C) (D)   31 (A) (B) (C) (D)
2 (F) (G) (H) (J)   12 (F) (G) (H) (J)   22 (F) (G) (H) (J)   32 (F) (G) (H) (J)
3 (A) (B) (C) (D)   13 (A) (B) (C) (D)   23 (A) (B) (C) (D)   33 (A) (B) (C) (D)
4 (F) (G) (H) (J)   14 (F) (G) (H) (J)   24 (F) (G) (H) (J)   34 (F) (G) (H) (J)
5 (A) (B) (C) (D)   15 (A) (B) (C) (D)   25 (A) (B) (C) (D)   35 (A) (B) (C) (D)
6 (F) (G) (H) (J)   16 (F) (G) (H) (J)   26 (F) (G) (H) (J)   36 (F) (G) (H) (J)
7 (A) (B) (C) (D)   17 (A) (B) (C) (D)   27 (A) (B) (C) (D)   37 (A) (B) (C) (D)
8 (F) (G) (H) (J)   18 (F) (G) (H) (J)   28 (F) (G) (H) (J)   38 (F) (G) (H) (J)
9 (A) (B) (C) (D)   19 (A) (B) (C) (D)   29 (A) (B) (C) (D)   39 (A) (B) (C) (D)
10 (F) (G) (H) (J)   20 (F) (G) (H) (J)   30 (F) (G) (H) (J)   40 (F) (G) (H) (J)

SCIENCE

1 (A) (B) (C) (D)   11 (A) (B) (C) (D)   21 (A) (B) (C) (D)   31 (A) (B) (C) (D)
2 (F) (G) (H) (J)   12 (F) (G) (H) (J)   22 (F) (G) (H) (J)   32 (F) (G) (H) (J)
3 (A) (B) (C) (D)   13 (A) (B) (C) (D)   23 (A) (B) (C) (D)   33 (A) (B) (C) (D)
4 (F) (G) (H) (J)   14 (F) (G) (H) (J)   24 (F) (G) (H) (J)   34 (F) (G) (H) (J)
5 (A) (B) (C) (D)   15 (A) (B) (C) (D)   25 (A) (B) (C) (D)   35 (A) (B) (C) (D)
6 (F) (G) (H) (J)   16 (F) (G) (H) (J)   26 (F) (G) (H) (J)   36 (F) (G) (H) (J)
7 (A) (B) (C) (D)   17 (A) (B) (C) (D)   27 (A) (B) (C) (D)   37 (A) (B) (C) (D)
8 (F) (G) (H) (J)   18 (F) (G) (H) (J)   28 (F) (G) (H) (J)   38 (F) (G) (H) (J)
9 (A) (B) (C) (D)   19 (A) (B) (C) (D)   29 (A) (B) (C) (D)   39 (A) (B) (C) (D)
10 (F) (G) (H) (J)   20 (F) (G) (H) (J)   30 (F) (G) (H) (J)   40 (F) (G) (H) (J)

RAW SCORES		SCALE SCORES		DATE TAKEN:
ENGLISH	_____	ENGLISH	_____	
MATHEMATICS	_____	MATHEMATICS	_____	ENGLISH/WRITING _____
READING	_____	READING	_____	
SCIENCE	_____	SCIENCE	_____	COMPOSITE SCORE

Refer to the Scoring Worksheet on page 826 for help in determining your Raw and Scale Scores.

You may wish to remove these sample answer document pages to respond to the practice ACT Writing Test.

Cut Here

Begin WRITING TEST here.

If you need more space, please continue on the next page.

Do not write in this shaded area.

WRITING TEST

If you need more space, please continue on the back of this page.

2

Do not write in this shaded area.

Cut Here

WRITING TEST

If you need more space, please continue on the next page.

PLEASE DO NOT WRITE IN THIS AREA.

WRITING TEST

1 ■ ■ ■ ■ ■ ■ ■ ■ 1

ENGLISH TEST

45 Minutes—75 Questions

DIRECTIONS: In the passages that follow, some words and phrases are underlined and numbered. In the answer column, you will find alternatives for the words and phrases that are underlined. Choose the alternative that you think is best, and fill in the corresponding bubble on your answer sheet. If you think that the original version is best, choose "NO CHANGE," which will always be either answer choice A or F. You will also find questions about a particular section of the passage, or about the entire passage. These questions will be identified either by an underlined portion or by a number in a box. Look for the answer that clearly expresses the idea, is consistent with the style and tone of the passage, and makes the correct use of standard written English. Read the passage through once before answering the questions. For some questions, you should read beyond the indicated portion before you answer.

PASSAGE I
Walter Reed's Medical Breakthrough

Just over 100 years ago, one of the most important

medical discoveries, in modern times relieved the suffering
                              1
and saved the lives of untold thousands. This major

breakthrough was the identification of the cause and spread

of the disease *yellow fever*. For several centuries, yellow

fever was a scourge upon societies in various parts of the
        2
world, striking towns and killing thousands of people.

Thanks to the efforts of Major Walter Reed and many
3
courageous volunteers, the mechanisms for contracting and

spreading yellow fever were uncovered.

During Reed's lifetime, it was a common acceptance
                                      4
that yellow fever was spread by contact with infected

items; such as the clothing or blankets of a person with
     5
yellow fever. Some doctors, however, questioned this

notion, as the spread of yellow fever was not consistent

1. **A.** NO CHANGE
   B. discoveries in modern, times
   C. discoveries, in modern times,
   D. discoveries in modern times

2. **F.** NO CHANGE
   G. was in societies as a scourge
   H. was a scourge and also problematic in societies
   J. was annoying

3. **A.** NO CHANGE
   B. In spite of
   C. It was
   D. Regardless of

4. **F.** NO CHANGE
   G. accepted as a common fact
   H. commonly accepted
   J. accepted in a common way

5. **A.** NO CHANGE
   B. items. Such as
   C. items, such as
   D. items such as being

GO ON TO THE NEXT PAGE.

1 ■ ■ ■ ■ ■ ■ ■ ■ ■ **1**

with the spread of other communicable diseases. [6]

Doubts about the accepted theory's of the fever's spread
                                    7
prompted the U.S. Army to assign Reed and several

doctors to the problem. They studied yellow fever in Cuba,

where they were infecting soldiers fighting in the Spanish
      8

American War at a discouraging rate. Acting on a hunch,
                     9
several doctors volunteered to be bitten by mosquitoes; the

volunteers developed yellow fever. This was enough

information to spur General Reed to conduct more

comprehensive experiments, so helping his cause.
                                           10
American and Spanish soldiers were paid to participate in

these experiments, but some participants wanted only to

advance science and refused the money.

The experiments began with the construction of a

building in which men who did not have yellow fever were

housed. These men were placed in contact with clothing

that have been worn by yellow fever victims. Not one of
     11

these men contracted the fever. A second building was
                            12
constructed with two sides separated by

6. Which of the following sentences, if inserted here,
   would be the best example of how yellow fever seemed
   to be spread differently than other communicable
   diseases?
   F. For example, people had no choice but to wear
      clothing and use blankets, so the fever could not
      have spread that way.
   G. For example, sometimes one person would get sick
      in a household, while nobody else in that household
      would get sick.
   H. For example, yellow fever caused a great deal of
      pain in its victims.
   J. For example, some doctors were willing to go
      against what the rest of the medical establishment
      was saying.

7. A. NO CHANGE
   B. theorize
   C. theories'
   D. theories

8. F. NO CHANGE
   G. the disease was
   H. the doctors were
   J. the Army was

9. The writer wants to emphasize how quickly yellow
   fever was infecting the troops in the Spanish American
   War. Which choice does that best?
   A. NO CHANGE
   B. a great
   C. an alarming
   D. a normal

10. F. NO CHANGE
    G. experiments; which helped his cause.
    H. experiments (which helped his cause).
    J. experiments.

11. A. NO CHANGE
    B. had been worn
    C. has been worn
    D. was being worn

12. F. NO CHANGE
    G. fever, while a
    H. fever; and a
    J. fever, a

GO ON TO THE NEXT PAGE.

1 ■ ■ ■ ■ ■ ■ ■ ■ 1

a screen. An infected volunteer lived on one side, and more volunteers lived on the other side, where they were completely protected from mosquitoes. This experiment was repeatable many times, and the volunteers who were
13
protected from mosquitoes never contracted the fever.

[14] As a result of his findings and of the bravery of the volunteers, measures were taken to control the mosquito population and to keep the insects away from people.

Eventually a vaccine was developed, which reduced further
15
the outbreaks of yellow fever incidences.
15

13. **A.** NO CHANGE
    B. repeated
    C. repeating
    D. a repeat

14. Which choice, assuming they are all true, would most logically introduce the final paragraph?
    F. These results convinced Reed that yellow fever was spread by mosquitoes, and not by contact with contaminated materials.
    G. A memorial was built in honor of the volunteers who helped advance the cause of science.
    H. Reed died within a year of making these discoveries, but his contributions to medicine will never be forgotten.
    J. Major Walter Reed not only was crucial to the eradication of yellow fever, but he performed research on typhoid as well.

15. **A.** NO CHANGE
    B. which further reduced the incidence of yellow fever outbreaks.
    C. which is often too expensive for poor residents of tropical countries who are most susceptible to yellow fever.
    D. and it was no longer necessary for people to risk their health and lives to determine the cause and spread of yellow fever.

PASSAGE II

The Giant Panda

[1]

The Giant Panda is one of the best-known and most adored animals in the world. It is a very rare creature and is protected by law in it's native China, where it lives in
16
the bamboo forests and on the mountain slopes.

16. **F.** NO CHANGE
    G. their
    H. there
    J. its

GO ON TO THE NEXT PAGE.

1 ■ ■ ■ ■ ■ ■ ■ ■ **1**

At one time, Giant Pandas lived at lower altitudes, but
17

farming and land development will have pushed the
18
animals high into the mountains. We really know very

little about how wild Pandas live, since so few people have

seen them in their natural habitat.

[2]

In fact, Giant Pandas are by, nature extremely solitary
19
animals, usually avoiding direct contact with other

animals and even going out of their way to avoid other

Giant Pandas. In there dense habitat, the black and white
20
coat of the Giant Pandas may help make them more

conspicuous to each other, which keeps them from

encroaching on their neighbor's territory. Even in captivity
21
where there may be as many as ten to twelve of the

animals occupying the same caged area, rarely will you

see them play with or acknowledge each other. They will

find an unoccupied place in the area and sit down. Content
22
to munch on bamboo or other food items, seemingly

totally oblivious of each other. However, at crucial stages

in their lives, Giant Pandas must give up being loners for a

short time. In the spring, males and females must seek

each other out in order to mate.

[3]

Giant Pandas are known to begin mating when they

reach an age of about six years of age. Mating usually
23

takes place sometime between the months of March, and
24
May. During this brief courtship period, Giant Pandas are
24

17. Which of the choices would be most appropriate here?
   A. NO CHANGE
   B. In the near future,
   C. Suddenly,
   D. Rarely,

18. **F.** NO CHANGE
   G. will push
   H. have pushed
   J. will be pushing

19. **A.** NO CHANGE
   B. are, by nature,
   C. are, by nature
   D. are by nature

20. **F.** NO CHANGE
   G. this dense
   H. they're dense
   J. their dense

21. **A.** NO CHANGE
   B. their neighbor's territory, encroaching upon it.
   C. encroaching, and avoiding their neighbor's territory.
   D. their neighbor's encroaching on their territory.

22. **F.** NO CHANGE
   G. sit down; content
   H. sit down, content
   J. sit down content

23. **A.** NO CHANGE
   B. an age of about six years old.
   C. about six years in their age.
   D. about six years of age.

24. **F.** NO CHANGE
   G. March and May.
   H. March, and, May.
   J. March and, May.

GO ON TO THE NEXT PAGE.

1 ■ ■ ■ ■ ■ ■ ■ ■ 1

highly vocal animals. The males bark, and roar as they try
                                    _____
                                       25

to intimidate each other. The female in a tree perches
                                     _____
                                          26
while the male remains on the ground fending off any

potentially rivals. Female Giant Pandas give birth between
_____
    27
95 and 160 days after mating. Their cubs are born in dens

that they dig in the ground.
          ___
           28

[4]

[29] Therefore, the Giant Panda is always a favorite at any

zoo fortunate enough to have one. Its furry white and

black body makes the Giant Panda appear cuddly and soft.

It has a large, round head and a white face with black

patches around the eyes. Giant Pandas have very thick,

oily, woolly fur that kept them warm in their natural cold,
             _____
                30
wet mountain habitat. Their fur is composed of two types

of hairs: the top layer contains long, thick, coarse hairs,

and a shorter, fine, dense, waterproof fur lies beneath.

While Giant Panda cubs weigh just a few ounces when

they are born, an adult Giant Panda can weigh 200 to

300 pounds and stand five to six feet tall.

25. A. NO CHANGE
B. barking and roaring
C. bark and roar
D. bark, and roaring

26. F. NO CHANGE
G. trees in a perch
H. perching in a tree
J. perches in a tree

27. A. NO CHANGE
B. potential rivals.
C. rivals, potentially.
D. potentially rivalry.

28. F. NO CHANGE
G. it digs
H. the females dig
J. she digs

29. Which of the following offers the best introduction to
Paragraph 4?
A. Due to the elusiveness of this fascinating creature,
many people across the world have never seen a
Giant Panda.
B. The Giant Panda is now considered a true bear.
C. Despite the dwindling natural habitat of the Giant
Panda, scientists still attempt to study the animal
in the wild.
D. The Giant Panda remains a difficult creature to
study in the wild.

30. F. NO CHANGE
G. that keeps
H. that's keeping
J. for to keep

PASSAGE III

Alfred Nobel

How interesting that the Nobel Peace Prize is named for
                                             _____
                                                 31
Alfred Nobel, the inventor of dynamite. A Swedish-born

scientist, Alfred Nobel was the son of Immanuel Nobel,

a brilliant and accomplished engineer. Born in 1833,

31. A. NO CHANGE
B. is named
C. will be named for
D. was named

GO ON TO THE NEXT PAGE.

1 ■ ■ ■ ■ ■ ■ ■ ■ ■ 1

Alfred quickly was following his father's footsteps,
                    ⎯⎯⎯⎯⎯⎯
                         32
latching on to chemistry in particular. He

devotes his energies to developing a myriad of materials
⎯⎯⎯⎯⎯⎯⎯⎯⎯⎯⎯
       33
and substances, patenting over 300 inventions throughout

his lifetime.

   Nobel's work with dynamite was obviously fraught with

risk and danger and, indeed, Nobel lost his younger

brother, Emil, to an explosion in their own laboratory. ⸨34⸩

Nobel knew that nitroglycerin, the basis for dynamite, had

great potential as a useful substance, but he also knew that

a big part of his work must resolve the safety issues in
                                          ⎯⎯⎯⎯⎯⎯
                                               35
addition.
⎯⎯⎯⎯⎯
   35
   (1) Due to more stringent laws enacted in Stockholm

regarding explosive materials, Nobel moved his lab out of
                                                  ⎯⎯⎯⎯
                                                    36
the city and onto a barge in nearby lake. (2) There he
⎯⎯⎯⎯⎯⎯⎯
   36

discovered some way to control how dynamite is
           ⎯⎯⎯⎯⎯⎯
              37
detonated, and, subsequently, patented the blasting cap.

(3) He also figured out how to safely transport

nitroglycerin by converting it from a liquid into a paste.

(4) Once Nobel had a safe, usable product, he established

his company, Nitroglycerin AB, in 1864. (5) In little time,

Nobel dynamite became useful to consumers, but he
⎯⎯⎯⎯⎯⎯⎯⎯⎯⎯
     38
continued to work on many other inventions and products.

(6) Among his many patents were synthetic versions of

32. **F.** NO CHANGE
    G. followed in
    H. was followed by
    J. followed by

33. **A.** NO CHANGE
    B. devotion of his energy
    C. devoted his energies
    D. devoted of his energy

34. The writer wishes to include another example of the dangers of dynamite during Nobel's time. Which of the following true sentences, if inserted here, would best fulfill that goal?
    F. Even today, safety precautions are required when working with dynamite.
    G. Dynamite has many uses, from excavating for natural resources to imploding decayed buildings.
    H. Many other less serious explosions also occurred in Nobel's laboratory, and grave danger was ever-present.
    J. As a volatile liquid substance, nitroglycerin is highly explosive.

35. **A.** NO CHANGE
    B. issues.
    C. issues, also.
    D. issues, too.

36. **F.** NO CHANGE
    G. and took it out of the city
    H. removing it out of the city
    J. from out of the city

37. **A.** NO CHANGE
    B. the way that
    C. a way
    D. how that

38. **F.** NO CHANGE
    G. Nobels' dynamite
    H. Nobel's dynamite
    J. OMIT the underlined portion.

GO ON TO THE NEXT PAGE.

1 ■ ■ ■ ■ ■ ■ ■ ■ **1**

rubber, silk, and leather, all of which are still used today. 39

Nobel was also a scholar <u>who</u> had
                              40

<u>great interest in literature, poetry, and social issues.</u>
                              41

In <u>his will was</u> instructed his estate to
       42

<u>establish annual prizes</u> to be given to outstanding
          43
contributors in the fields of Physics, Chemistry, Medicine,

Literature, and Peace. On December 10 each year,

corresponding to <u>Nobel's date</u> of death, these esteemed
                      44

prizes are awarded to people from <u>over the worldwide.</u>
                                    45

---

39. Which of the following sequence of sentences makes this paragraph most logical?
  A. NO CHANGE
  B. 1, 3, 2, 4, 5, 6
  C. 6, 5, 4, 3, 2, 1
  D. 2, 4, 3, 1, 5, 6

40. F. NO CHANGE
  G. that
  H. which
  J. he

41. Which of the following alternatives to the underlined portion would NOT be acceptable?
  A. much interest in non-scientific areas.
  B. great interest in subjects other than chemistry, his main area of study.
  C. interesting literature, poetry, and social issues.
  D. a healthy interest in other areas, such as literature and poetry.

42. F. NO CHANGE
  G. his, will he
  H. his will he,
  J. his will, he

43. A. NO CHANGE
  B. establish one annual prize
  C. a prized establishment
  D. established prizes

44. F. NO CHANGE
  G. Nobels date
  H. Nobels' date
  J. Nobel's dates

45. A. NO CHANGE
  B. everywhere, worldwide.
  C. all over the world.
  D. OMIT the underlined portion.

PASSAGE IV

Construction Destruction

Watching a local construction project as it unfolds can

evoke <u>a series of many</u> different emotions. A new
        46

subdivision of homes <u>built into</u> a once
                       47

<u>thickly wooded</u> plot of land often devastates the natural
     48
beauty of the entire area. Many builders, however, will

---

46. F. NO CHANGE
  G. a variety of many
  H. many
  J. many series of

47. A. NO CHANGE
  B. building on
  C. built
  D. built on

48. Which choice provides the most detailed image?
  F. NO CHANGE
  G. treed
  H. woodsy
  J. wooded

GO ON TO THE NEXT PAGE.

1 ■ ■ ■ ■ ■ ■ ■ ■ ■ 1

have taken great care to maintain as much of the natural
     49
landscape as possible by keeping mature trees untouched

when possible. Despite this careful attention, construction
    50
damage to existing trees can wreak havoc that only

appears years after the construction is complete.

    Any disruption to a tree's root system, trunk, or main

branches can often be tied to construction. When

considering the large, heavy equipment used at
           51

construction sites, it is easy to understand why they choose
                   52
to flatten the land and start over with new plantings.
During construction, much of the damage to existing trees

occurs beneath the soil, which is why it is often not
             53
detected until much later. If 40 percent or more of a root

system is a loss, the tree will probably die.
   54
    (1) Tree roots typically lie close to the surface of the soil

and extends way beyond the circumference of the tree's
   55
canopy. (2) As the bulldozers, dump trucks, and cement

trucks drives over the soil, they can easily crush the tender
    56
roots below. (3) Compacting soil around the vital roots

with the heavy equipment, may destroy the tree as
         57

49. **A.** NO CHANGE
    B. take great cares
    C. take great care
    D. takes great care

50. **F.** NO CHANGE
    G. as is possible
    H. whenever possible
    J. OMIT the underlined portion.

51. **A.** NO CHANGE
    B. largely heavy
    C. large heavily
    D. heavy, largely

52. **F.** NO CHANGE
    G. some builders
    H. some of them
    J. some

53. **A.** NO CHANGE
    B. they are
    C. its
    D. this damage is

54. **F.** NO CHANGE
    G. can be lost
    H. is lost
    J. is to be lost

55. **A.** NO CHANGE
    B. does extend
    C. extend
    D. will extend

56. **F.** NO CHANGE
    G. drive over
    H. drove over
    J. had driven over

57. **A.** NO CHANGE
    B. equipment may destroy
    C. equipment may destroy,
    D. equipment; may destroy

GO ON TO THE NEXT PAGE.

well, 58 (4) Roots need air pockets around them in order to stay healthy. (5) Also, by adding fill dirt or topsoil, the roots suddenly become buried.

58. The writer wishes to conclude this sentence with a phrase that would continue the explanation of the importance of a tree's root system. Which choice would best accomplish this?
   F. since it is through the roots that a tree receives necessary oxygen, water, and minerals.
   G. since roots are so important to the health of the tree.
   H. since the tree cannot survive with damaged roots.
   J. since roots are only one part of a tree's system.

Questions 59 and 60 ask about the preceding passage as a whole.

59. For the sake of unity and coherence, Sentence 5 of the last paragraph should be placed:
   A. where it is now.
   B. immediately after Sentence 1.
   C. immediately before Sentence 2.
   D. immediately before Sentence 4.

60. Suppose that the writer has intended to write a brief essay discussing ways to prevent tree damage during construction. Does the essay successfully fulfill the assignment?
   F. Yes, because the writer describes how trees are damaged by construction equipment and specifically states ways to prevent the damage.
   G. Yes, because the essay's main focus is preventing tree damage during construction.
   H. No, because the essay focuses only on construction equipment, not on prevention of tree damage.
   J. No, because the essay focuses primarily on how trees can be damaged during construction, not on ways to prevent damage.

Body Armor

If you were an officer of the law or an armed military person, would you prefer to wear a "bullet-proof vest" or "soft body armor" under your <u>suit and uniform</u>?
   61

61. A. NO CHANGE
   B. street clothes
   C. jacket
   D. uniform

<u>Most often the person</u> would probably opt for the
   62
bullet-proof vest, as its name tends to denote a higher level of security. The problem, though, is that no

62. F. NO CHANGE
   G. Most people
   H. Most of all people
   J. Most all persons

GO ON TO THE NEXT PAGE.

1 ■ ■ ■ ■ ■ ■ ■ ■ 1

"bullet-proof vest" is really bullet-proof. In fact, there is
                                    63
no protective clothing currently available that offers

complete protection from firearms.

As weaponry and ammunition have changed through

the centuries; so have the materials from which protective
                 64
clothing is made. During the black powder era of the

1700s, silk was the material of choice to ward off injury or
                     65
death from a black powder ball. Black powder propelled

lead balls were much slower than present-day bullets, and

silk was sometimes fairly effective protection against

weapons at longer ranges. During World War II, the "flak

jacket" was developed as a protective device. Soon, the
                                              66
best this attire could do was to protect the wearer from

shrapnel, not from the bullets themselves. Today's modern
                                           67
protective vests are made from a variety of synthetic

materials, some of which are more with effectiveness than
                                  68
others. The idea is to produce a material that is strong

enough to ward off high-speed bullets yet light enough to

allow for ease of movement. This can be a daunting task

when cost is also considered, ⬜69

Most people have the idea that protective gear causes a

bullet to deflect off of it, almost similar to a Ping-Pong ball
                        70
hitting the lid of a tin can. However, these vests actually

absorb the impact of the bullet spreading its energy around
                               71

63. A. NO CHANGE
B. prevents bullets.
C. isn't really bullet-proof.
D. like those worn by police officers, is really bullet-proof.

64. F. NO CHANGE
G. the centuries,
H. the centuries, so too
J. the centuries so

65. The best placement for the underlined portion would be
A. where it is now.
B. before the word *silk*.
C. at the end of that sentence.
D. after the word *death*.

66. F. NO CHANGE
G. Nevertheless,
H. Unfortunately,
J. Therefore,

67. A. NO CHANGE
B. Today's recent
C. In today's modern times
D. Today's

68. F. NO CHANGE
G. more effective
H. affecting
J. affectively more

69. Which of the following true statements, if added here, would best serve as a further explanation of the idea presented in the preceding sentence?
A. since most heavy materials are too bulky for easy movement.
B. as it takes a great deal of study and research to develop these types of synthetic materials.
C. since this type of material is never inexpensive to develop or produce.
D. as most military personnel and police officers cannot afford to purchase their own equipment.

70. F. NO CHANGE
G. of it. In fact, sort of like
H. of it, almost sort of like
J. it, like

71. A. NO CHANGE
B. bullet, spreading
C. bullet. Spreading
D. bullet; spreading

GO ON TO THE NEXT PAGE.

1 ■ ■ ■ ■ ■ ■ ■ ■ **1**

the body rather than been sustained in a single area.
                                              72

Normally, the layers of the vest's material will stop the
                                              73
bullet from entering the body. However, the vest's

wearer is very likely to sustain bruises

and perhaps even internal injuries.
                              74
    Most police officers and military personnel are happy to

don their protective clothing as they head out on their

assignments. However, they know better than anyone that

their safety and security cannot be entrusting completely to
                                          75
their protective gear.

72. **F.** NO CHANGE
    G. sustaining itself
    H. having been sustained
    J. OMIT the underlined portion.

73. Which choice best shows that body armor does not
always prevent injury or death?
    A. NO CHANGE
    B. In the best-case scenario,
    C. Most of the time,
    D. Almost always,

74. The writer is considering deleting the underlined portion. If the writer chooses to delete this phrase,
the paragraph would primarily lose a statement that
suggests:
    F. wearing protective gear does not necessarily ensure
that there will be a lack of serious injury.
    G. wearing protective clothing ensures that there will
be absolute safety from serious injury.
    H. wearing protective gear always protects the wearer
from death.
    J. a wearer of protective gear will probably only
sustain bruises.

75. **A.** NO CHANGE
    B. trusting
    C. entrusted
    D. by trust

END OF THE ENGLISH TEST.
STOP! IF YOU HAVE TIME LEFT OVER, CHECK YOUR WORK ON THIS SECTION ONLY.

2 △ △ △ △ △ △ △ △ 2

MATHEMATICS TEST

60 Minutes—60 Questions

DIRECTIONS: Solve each of the problems in the time allowed, then fill in the corresponding bubble on your answer sheet. Do not spend too much time on any one problem; skip the more difficult problems and go back to them later. You may use a calculator on this test. For this test you should assume that figures are NOT necessarily drawn to scale, that all geometric figures lie in a plane, and that the word *line* is used to indicate a straight line.

---

1. In triangle *ABC* below, the measure of angle *A* is 20° and the measure of angle *B* is 3 times larger than the measure of angle *C*. What is the measure of angle *B*?

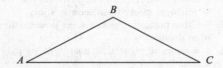

   A. 40°
   B. 60°
   C. 80°
   D. 120°
   E. 160°

2. The 65-member high school band raised money to go on a trip by having a bake sale. If the original cost per band member for the trip is $18.50 and the band members earned a total of $585.00 at the bake sale, how much more money does each band member need in order to pay for the trip?
   F. $9.00
   G. $9.50
   H. $18.50
   J. $46.50
   K. $65.00

3. Fred works at a car wash where he makes $40.00 per day plus $1.75 per car that he washes. Yesterday, Fred made a total of $61.00. How many cars did he wash yesterday?
   A. 10
   B. 12
   C. 17
   D. 20
   E. 34

DO YOUR FIGURING HERE.

GO ON TO THE NEXT PAGE.

2 △ △ △ △ △ △ △ △ **2**

4. Molality, m, tells us the number of moles of solute dissolved in exactly 1 kilogram (kg) of solvent. Molality is represented by the equation, $m = \dfrac{s}{k}$, were s represents the moles of solute and k represents the mass of the solvent in kilograms. A solution is known to have a molality of 0.2 and contain 13 kg of solvent. What is the number of moles of solute contained in the solution?
   F. 0.01
   G. 2.6
   H. 3.2
   J. 26
   K. 32

5. In the figure below, l_1 is parallel to l_2, and l_3 is parallel to l_4. Which of the following angles is NOT equal to angle x?

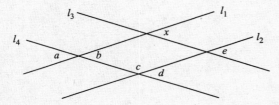

   A. a
   B. b
   C. c
   D. d
   E. e

6. Which of the following is equivalent to 4.2×10^{-5}?
   F. 0.000042
   G. 0.00042
   H. 42,000
   J. 420,000
   K. 4,200,000

7. $3.234 \times 0.01 = ?$
   A. 323.4
   B. 32.34
   C. 3.234
   D. 0.3234
   E. 0.03234

8. For all $x \neq 1$, $\dfrac{x^2 - 2x + 1}{x - 1}$ is equal to ?
   F. 1
   G. $x + 2$
   H. x^2
   J. $\dfrac{x + 2}{x - 1}$
   K. $x - 1$

GO ON TO THE NEXT PAGE.

2   △ △ △ △ **2**

DO YOUR FIGURING HERE.

9. If $9 - x^3 + 2 = 19$, what is the value of x?
- **A.** -2
- **B.** -1
- **C.** 2
- **D.** 3
- **E.** 8

10. In the parallelogram below, what is the measure of $\angle WXY$?

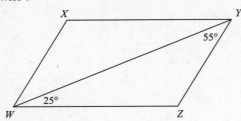

- **F.** $25°$
- **G.** $55°$
- **H.** $65°$
- **J.** $100°$
- **K.** $120°$

11. The graph below represents which of the following inequalities?

- **A.** $x > 1$
- **B.** $x < -1$
- **C.** $x \leq -1$
- **D.** $x \geq -1$
- **E.** $-1 > x > 1$

12. If $93 - x = 342$, then $x =$?
- **F.** -435
- **G.** -249
- **H.** -156
- **J.** 249
- **K.** 435

13. In the figure below, triangles ABC and ABX are both right triangles. If the length of $\overline{AB}$ is 6 units, the length of $\overline{BX}$ is 10 units, and the length of $\overline{XC}$ is 4 units, what is the length of $\overline{BC}$?

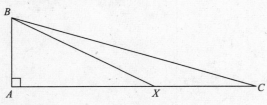

- **A.** $\sqrt{11}$
- **B.** $2\sqrt{3}$
- **C.** $2\sqrt{10}$
- **D.** $2\sqrt{35}$
- **E.** $6\sqrt{5}$

GO ON TO THE NEXT PAGE.

2 △ △ △ △ △ △ △ △ 2

14. A rectangular parking lot has an area 315 square yards. Its length (l) is 3 times its width (w). Which of the following equations could you use to determine the width of the parking lot?

 F. $3w \times w = 315$

 G. $3l \times l = 315$

 H. $w \times 3 = 315$

 J. $w = \dfrac{315}{3}$

 K. $w - 3 = 315$

15. Jordan went for a 3.5-mile jog on Monday that took him 40 minutes. If on Tuesday Jordan jogs at the same rate of speed, how far will he jog in 60 minutes?

 A. 3.5 miles

 B. 4.0 miles

 C. 5.25 miles

 D. 7.0 miles

 E. 7.25 miles

16. A floor has the dimensions shown below. How many square feet of tile are needed to cover the entire floor?

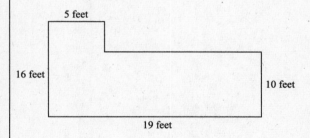

 F. 50

 G. 95

 H. 160

 J. 190

 K. 220

17. There are 32 ounces in a quart. If 2 quarts of milk costs $2.65, what is the cost of milk per ounce, to the nearest cent?

 A. $0.04

 B. $0.08

 C. $0.24

 D. $0.41

 E. $0.64

DO YOUR FIGURING HERE.

GO ON TO THE NEXT PAGE.

2   **2**

18. In the figure below, triangle ABC is a 30–60–90 right triangle. If angle x measures 125°, what is the measure of angle y?

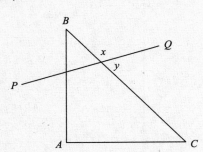

   F. 35°
   G. 45°
   H. 55°
   J. 70°
   K. 90°

19. Given the system of equations below, $x = ?$

$$y + 3x = 9$$

$$2x - \frac{1}{3}y = 6$$

   A. 1
   B. 3
   C. 5
   D. 7
   E. 9

20. $\dfrac{\left(\frac{5}{4}\right)\left(\frac{4}{3}\right)}{\left(\frac{1}{3}\right)\left(\frac{2}{3}\right)} = ?$

   F. $\dfrac{2}{5}$

   G. $\dfrac{7}{15}$

   H. $\dfrac{4}{5}$

   J. $\dfrac{7}{4}$

   K. $\dfrac{15}{2}$

21. For all x, $x^2 - (3x - 2) + 2x(4x - 1) = ?$

   A. $x^2 - 5x - 2$
   B. $9x^2 + 5x - 2$
   C. $9x^2 - 5x + 2$
   D. $8x^2 - 3x$
   E. $9x^2 - 4x + 2$

GO ON TO THE NEXT PAGE.

2 △ △ △ △ △   △   △   △ **2**

DO YOUR FIGURING HERE.

22. For all $x \neq -3$, $\dfrac{x^2 - 6x + 9}{6x - 18} = ?$

    F. $\dfrac{x + 3}{x - 3}$

    G. $\dfrac{x - 3}{6}$

    H. $\dfrac{1}{x - 3}$

    J. $x - 3$

    K. $\dfrac{x}{3}$

23. If $x = 3$ is 1 solution for the equation $2x^2 - 5x - a = 0$, what is the value of a?

    A. -2
    B. 0
    C. 3
    D. 5
    E. 6

24. In the figure below, triangles PQR, PSQ, and QSR are right triangles. If the measure of angle P is 55°, what is the measure of angle R?

    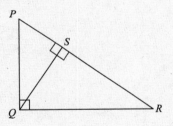

    F. 35°
    G. 45°
    H. 55°
    J. 65°
    I. 75°

25. Daniel is painting a wall in his bedroom. He can cover 36 square feet with 1 gallon of paint. If the wall is 8 feet high and 12 feet long, how many gallons, to the nearest whole gallon, will Daniel need to paint the wall?

    A. 20
    B. 16
    C. 12
    D. 4
    E. 3

GO ON TO THE NEXT PAGE.

2   △ △ △ **2**

26. For all values, x, y, and z, if $x \leq y$ and $y \leq z$, which of the following CANNOT be true?

     I. $x = z$
     II. $x > z$
     III. $x < z$

   F. I only
   G. II only
   H. III only
   J. I and II only
   K. I, II, and III

DO YOUR FIGURING HERE.

27. As shown in the figure below, what is the sine of angle C?

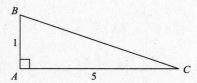

   A. $\dfrac{1}{5}$

   B. $\dfrac{1}{\sqrt{26}}$

   C. $\dfrac{\sqrt{26}}{5}$

   D. 5

   E. $\sqrt{26}$

28. What is the sum of all the solutions to $\dfrac{4x}{x-1} = \dfrac{4x}{2x+2}$?

   F. -3
   G. -2
   H. 2
   J. 5
   K. 8

29. $|-2|^2 + |-5| - 3 = ?$
   A. 0
   B. 6
   C. 8
   D. 10
   E. 13

GO ON TO THE NEXT PAGE.

2 △ △ △ △ △ △ △ △ **2**

30. In the figure below, parallel lines XY and ZW are bisected by line AB. If the lengths of XY, YZ, and ZW are the same, and angle t is 45°, then what is the measure of angle s?

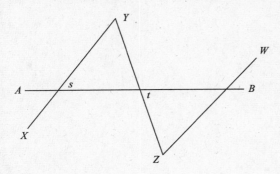

- **F.** 25°
- **G.** 45°
- **H.** 55°
- **J.** 75°
- **K.** 90°

31. If $x^2 - 3 \leq 13$, what is the greatest real value that x can have?
- **A.** 10
- **B.** 5
- **C.** 4
- **D.** 3
- **E.** 0

32. In an isosceles right triangle, the hypotenuse is 12. What is the length of one (1) of the sides?
- **F.** $6\sqrt{2}$
- **G.** $2\sqrt{6}$
- **H.** $2\sqrt{4}$
- **J.** $2\sqrt{3}$
- **K.** $\sqrt{3}$

33. In the standard (x,y) coordinate plane, what is the center of a circle with the equation $(x - 2)^2 + (y + 1)^2 = 4$?
- **A.** $(-2,1)$
- **B.** $(-2,4)$
- **C.** $(2,-1)$
- **D.** $(4,-2)$
- **E.** $(-2,2)$

34. What is the slope of the line determined by the equation $2x - 3y = 6$?
- **F.** -6
- **G.** -3
- **H.** $-\dfrac{3}{2}$
- **J.** $\dfrac{2}{3}$
- **K.** 2

GO ON TO THE NEXT PAGE.

2 △ △ △ △ △ △ △ △ **2**

35. Fifty (50) households were surveyed to determine the number of TVs in each of the households. The number of TVs in each household is shown in the chart below. What is the average number of TVs per household for these 50 households?

No. of TVs in household	2	3	4	5
No. of households	5	20	15	10

A. 1.0
B. 1.3
C. 2.7
D. 3.6
E. 4.2

DO YOUR FIGURING HERE.

36. In the figure below, both circles are centered around X. The length of XY is 2 units and the length of XZ is 6 units. If the smaller circle is cut out of the larger circle, how much of the area, in square units, of the larger circle will remain?

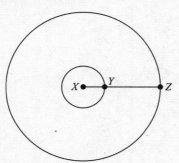

F. 12π
G. 16π
H. 32π
J. 36π
K. 40π

37. In the standard (x,y) coordinate plane, what is the x intercept of a line that has a slope of $\frac{2}{3}$ and passes through the point $(-2,2)$?
A. $(-3,0)$
B. $(-5,0)$
C. $(3,0)$
D. $(0,-2)$
E. $(2,0)$

38. The figure below represents a solution set for which of the following inequalities?

−2

F. $-2x + 12 < x - 2$
G. $4x - 2 \geq 2x - 3$
H. $5x + 5 \geq x$
J. $3x - 1 \leq 5x + 3$
K. $6x - 3 > 3x + 2$

GO ON TO THE NEXT PAGE.

39. What is the slope of the line pictured in the standard (x,y) coordinate plane below that passes through $(1,3)$ and $(5,5)$ in the standard (x,y) coordinate plane?

DO YOUR FIGURING HERE.

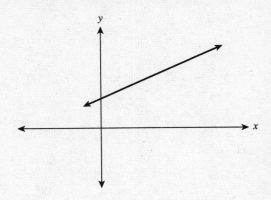

A. -2

B. $-\dfrac{2}{5}$

C. $\dfrac{1}{5}$

D. $\dfrac{1}{2}$

E. $\dfrac{5}{3}$

40. A formula for calculating simple interest is $I = Pr$, were I is the interest earned in dollars, P is the principal or original investment, and r is the fixed rate of interest. If the amount of interest earned is \$2.25 and the interest rate is 3%, what is P?

F. \$6.75

G. \$7.50

H. \$13.30

J. \$67.50

K. \$75.00

41. Three vertices of a rectangle in the standard (x,y) coordinate plane have the coordinates $(-2,3)$, $(4,3)$ and $(4,2)$. What are the coordinates of the fourth vertex?

A. $(-2,-2)$

B. $(3,-3)$

C. $(-3,3)$

D. $(2,-2)$

E. $(-2,2)$

GO ON TO THE NEXT PAGE.

2 △　△　△　△　△　△　△　△　**2**

42. If two lines in the standard (x,y) coordinate plane are perpendicular and the slope of one of the lines is $-\dfrac{5}{7}$, what is the slope of the other line?

F. $\dfrac{7}{5}$

G. $\dfrac{5}{7}$

H. $-\dfrac{5}{7}$

J. $-\dfrac{7}{5}$

K. -5

43. Anne made apple jelly and applesauce out of a bushel of apples. If the number of jars of jelly, j, is 3 less than twice the number of jars of applesauce, a, which expression shows the relationship of jars of jelly, j, to the jars of applesauce, a?

A. $2j = 2a - 3$

B. $j - 3 = 2a$

C. $2j = 3a$

D. $j + 3 = 2a$

E. $ja = 2a$

44. What are the solutions for the equation $3x^2 - 5x + 2 = 0$?

F. $x = -1, x = -\dfrac{3}{2}$

G. $x = 1, x = \dfrac{2}{3}$

H. $x = -5, x = \dfrac{2}{3}$

J. $x = \dfrac{2}{5}, x = 1$

K. $x = -1, x = \dfrac{3}{2}$

45. What is the smallest possible value for a where $y = \sin 2a$ reaches its maximum?

A. $\dfrac{\pi}{4}$

B. $\dfrac{\pi}{2}$

C. π

D. 2π

E. 4π

46. Let $x = 3y - 4z + 7$. What happens to the value of x if the value of y decreases by 2 and the value of z is increased by 1?

F. It increases by 3.

G. It increases by 5.

H. It decreases by 1.

J. It decreases by 10.

K. It is unchanged.

DO YOUR FIGURING HERE.

GO ON TO THE NEXT PAGE.

47. Which of the following represents the values of x that are solutions for the inequality $(x - 1)(4 - x) < 0$?

A. $-\dfrac{1}{4} < x < 1$

B. $x < 1$ or $x > 4$

C. $-1 < x < \dfrac{1}{4}$

D. $-4 < x < 1$

F. $\dfrac{1}{4} < x < 4$

DO YOUR FIGURING HERE.

48. In the figure below, triangle PQR is an isosceles right triangle. What is the ratio of the hypotenuse to the length of PQ?

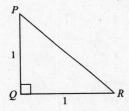

F. $\dfrac{\sqrt{2}}{2}$:1

G. $\dfrac{\sqrt{3}}{3}$:1

H. $\sqrt{2}$:1

J. $\sqrt{3}$:1

K. $2\sqrt{2}$:1

49. If $\tan x = \dfrac{3}{4}$ and $0° \leq x° \leq 90°$, then $\cos x = $?

A. $\dfrac{5}{3}$

B. $\dfrac{4}{3}$

C. $\dfrac{5}{4}$

D. $\dfrac{4}{5}$

E. $\dfrac{3}{5}$

GO ON TO THE NEXT PAGE.

2

DO YOUR FIGURING HERE.

50. For all $a \neq 0$ and $b \neq 0$, $\dfrac{a+b}{b(a+b) - 2a(a+b)} = ?$

F. $\dfrac{1}{b-2}$

G. $\dfrac{1}{2ab}$

H. $\dfrac{1}{a+b}$

J. $\dfrac{1}{b-2a}$

K. $-\dfrac{1}{2b}$

51. In the figure below, $PQRS$ is a rectangle with sides of lengths shown. X is the midpoint of $\overline{SR}$. What is the perimeter of triangle PXQ?

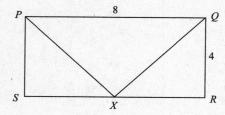

A. 10

B. $4\sqrt{2} + 12$

C. $3\sqrt{2} + 12$

D. $8\sqrt{2} + 8$

E. $4\sqrt{2} + 4$

52. A line in the standard (x,y) coordinate plane has a slope of $\dfrac{2}{3}$ and passes through points $(3,4)$ and $(t,-2)$. What is the value of t?

F. 3

G. 2

H. 0

J. -2

K. -6

53. José is building a scale model of a sailboat, complete with a main sail. The actual sailboat's main sail measures 56 feet high with a base of 32 feet. If the model sailboat's main sail has a base of 8 inches, how tall will the model's main sail be, in inches?

A. 14

B. 28

C. 32

D. 56

E. 112

GO ON TO THE NEXT PAGE.

2   **2**

54. What values of x make the inequality $-5x - 7 > 3x + 1$ true?

F. $x > 1$
G. $x < 8$
H. $x < -1$
J. $x > -4$
K. $x < 2$

55. In the figure below, the lengths of the sides of triangle BAC are as shown. $\overline{BD}$ bisects side $\overline{AC}$. What is the length of DC?

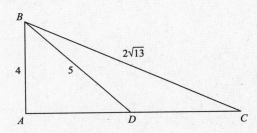

A. $\sqrt{3}$
B. 2
C. 3
D. $2\sqrt{5}$
E. 4

56. Which of the following intervals contains the solution to the equation $x - 2 = \dfrac{2x + 5}{3}$?

F. $-6 < x < 11$
G. $11 \le x < 15$
H. $6 < x \le 10$
J. $-5 < x \le -3$
K. $-11 \le x \le -2$

57. In the figure below, P and Q lie on the circle R, which has a radius of 9. If the angle PRQ is $120°$, what is the area of sector PRQ?

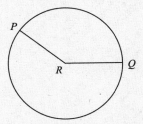

A. 3π
B. 9π
C. 27π
D. 81π
E. 243π

GO ON TO THE NEXT PAGE.

2   **2**

58. Given the graph below in the standard (x,y) coordinate plane, the slope of line a is m_a and the slope of line b is m_b. Which of the following statements about the slope of lines a and b is true?

DO YOUR FIGURING HERE.

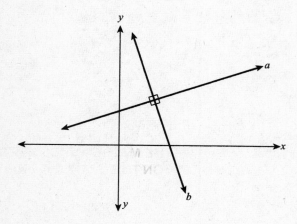

F. $m_a = \dfrac{-1}{m_b}$

G. $m_a + m_b = 0$

H. $-\dfrac{1}{2}m_a = m_b$

J. $m_a - 1 = m_b$

K. $m_a - m_b = 0$

59. If $\cos x = \dfrac{5}{7}$ and $\tan x = \dfrac{4}{5}$, what is $\sin x$?

A. $\dfrac{4}{7}$

B. $\dfrac{7}{9}$

C. $\dfrac{5}{4}$

D. $\dfrac{9}{7}$

E. $\dfrac{7}{5}$

GO ON TO THE NEXT PAGE.

2 △ △ △ △ △ △ △ △ **2**

60. A total of f men went on a fishing trip. Each of the r boats that were used to carry the fishermen could accommodate a maximum number of m passengers. If one boat had 5 open spots and the remaining boats were filled to capacity, which of the following expresses the relationship among f, r, and m?

F. $rm + 5 = f$

G. $rm - 5 = f$

H. $r + m + 5 = f$

J. $rf = m + 5$

K. $rf = m - 5$

DO YOUR FIGURING HERE.

END OF THE MATHEMATICS TEST.

STOP! IF YOU HAVE TIME LEFT OVER, CHECK YOUR WORK ON THIS SECTION ONLY.

3 ▬▬▬▬▬▬▬▬▬▬▬▬▬▬▬▬▬▬▬▬ 3

READING TEST

35 Minutes—40 Questions

DIRECTIONS: This test includes four passages, each followed by ten questions. Read the passages and choose the best answer to each question. After you have selected your answer, fill in the corresponding bubble on your answer sheet. You should refer to the passages as often as necessary when answering the questions.

PASSAGE I

FICTION: *This passage is adapted from* Jane Eyre *by Charlotte Brontë, published in 1897.*

Seeing me, she roused herself: she made a sort of effort to smile, and framed a few words of congratulations; but the smile expired, and the sentence was abandoned unfinished. She put up her spectacles and
5 pushed her chair back from the table.

"I feel so astonished," she began, "I hardly know what to say to you, Miss Eyre. I have surely not been dreaming, have I? Sometimes I half fall asleep when I am sitting alone and fancy things that have never
10 happened. It has seemed to me more than once when I have been in a doze, that my dear husband, who died fifteen years since, has come in and sat down beside me; and that I have even heard him call me by my name, Alice, as he used to do. Now, can you tell me
15 whether it is actually true that Mr. Rochester has asked you to marry him? Don't laugh at me. But I really thought he came in here five minutes ago, and said that in a month you would be his wife."

"He has said the same thing to me," I replied.

20 "He has! Do you believe him? Have you accepted him?"

"Yes."

She looked at me bewildered.

"I could never have thought it. He is a proud man;
25 all the Rochesters were proud: and his father at least, liked money. He, too, has always been called careful. He means to marry you?"

"He tells me so."

She surveyed my whole person: in her eyes I read
30 that they had there found no charm powerful enough to solve the enigma.

"It passes me!" she continued; "but no doubt it is true since you say so. How it will answer I cannot tell: I really don't know. Equality of position and fortune
35 is often advisable in such cases; and there are twenty years of difference in your ages. He might almost be your father."

"No, indeed, Mrs. Fairfax!" I exclaimed, nettled; "he is nothing like my father! No one, who saw us
40 together, would suppose it for an instant. Mr. Rochester looks as young, and is as young, as some men at five and twenty."

"Is it really for love he is going to marry you?" she asked.

45 I was so hurt by her coldness and skepticism, that the tears rose to my eyes.

"I am sorry to grieve you," pursued the widow; "but you are so young, and so little acquainted with men, I wished to put you on your guard. It is an old
50 saying that 'all is not gold that glitters'; and in this case I do fear there will be something found to be different to what either you or I expect."

"Why?—am I a monster?" I said: "Is it impossible that Mr. Rochester should have a sincere affection
55 for me?"

"No: you are very well; and much improved of late; and Mr. Rochester, I dare say, is fond of you. I have always noticed that you were a sort of pet of his. There are times when, for your sake, I have been a little
60 uneasy at his marked preference, and have wished to put you on your guard; but I did not like to suggest even the possibility of wrong. I knew such an idea would shock, perhaps offend you; and you were so discreet, and so thoroughly modest and sensible, I hoped you
65 might be trusted to protect yourself. Last night I cannot tell you what I suffered when I sought all over the house, and could find you nowhere, nor the master either; and then, at twelve o'clock, saw you come in with him."

70 "Well never mind that now," I interrupted impatiently; "it is enough that all was right."

"I hope all will be right in the end," she said: "but, believe me, you cannot be too careful. Try and keep Mr. Rochester at a distance: distrust yourself as well
75 as him. Gentlemen in his station are not accustomed to marry their governesses."

GO ON TO THE NEXT PAGE.

3   **3**

1. When Mrs. Fairfax says, "Gentlemen in his station are not accustomed to marry their governesses," she is expressing her belief that:
   A. Mr. Rochester is incapable of loving Miss Eyre.
   B. Mr. Rochester will treat Miss Eyre like a governess when they are married.
   C. Mr. Rochester may not be sincere about his feeling towards Miss Eyre.
   D. Mr. Rochester may not really have asked Miss Eyre to marry him.

2. It can be reasonably inferred from the conversation that Mrs. Fairfax believes Miss Eyre will:
   F. recognize that Mr. Rochester actually wants to marry Mrs. Fairfax.
   G. marry Mr. Rochester much sooner than originally planned.
   H. no longer desire to marry Mr. Rochester.
   J. potentially regret her decision to agree to marry Mr. Rochester.

3. Mrs. Fairfax's opinion about Miss Eyre and Mr. Rochester's relationship can best be exemplified by which of the following quotations from the passage?
   A. "Mr. Rochester looks as young, and is as young, as some men at five and twenty."
   B. "How it will answer I cannot tell: I really don't know."
   C. "He is a proud man; all the Rochesters were proud."
   D. "But I really thought he came in here five minutes ago, and said that in a month you would be his wife."

4. The phrase "you were so discreet, and so thoroughly modest and sensible" (lines 63–64) is used by Mrs. Fairfax to:
   F. explain why Miss Eyre should not marry Mr. Rochester.
   G. explain why it is likely that Mr. Rochester really does not plan on marrying Miss Eyre.
   H. explain why Mrs. Fairfax had not discussed Mr. Rochester's feelings toward Miss Eyre before.
   J. insult Miss Eyre and let her know that Mrs. Fairfax was disappointed in her.

5. The passage makes it clear that Miss Eyre and Mr. Rochester:
   A. get married.
   B. do not really know each other well enough to become engaged.
   C. will not live happily because they will be shunned by society.
   D. have a relationship that is not typical in their society.

6. In lines 47–52, Mrs. Fairfax compares Miss Eyre and Mr. Rochester's relationship as possibly being similar to:
   F. a mystery that cannot be solved.
   G. an object that appears to be something but really is another thing entirely.
   H. a game used to entertain the innocent and naïve.
   J. a shiny gem that holds more value than it appears to.

7. We may reasonably infer from details in the passage that Miss Eyre and Mrs. Fairfax are alike because they both:
   A. believe that Mr. Rochester should not marry his governess.
   B. believe that Mr. Rochester will break Miss Eyre's heart.
   C. are of the same age and social class.
   D. believe that Mr. Rochester is fond of Miss Eyre.

8. Based on the passage, Miss Eyre's feelings about her relationship with Mr. Rochester can best be described as:
   F. unbelievable.
   G. erratic.
   H. diplomatic.
   J. self-assured.

9. It can be inferred from the passage that Mrs. Fairfax:
   A. does not believe that Mr. Rochester's actions with Miss Eyre are characteristic of him.
   B. does not believe that Miss Eyre's character is good enough for Mr. Rochester.
   C. does not believe that Miss Eyre understands how wealthy and important Mr. Rochester is.
   D. does not believe that Miss Eyre is being honest about her feelings towards Mr. Rochester.

10. Details in the passage suggest that Mrs. Fairfax is uncertain about Miss Eyre and Mr. Rochester's engagement because:
    F. Mrs. Fairfax believes that Miss Eyre is too young to be married.
    G. Mrs. Fairfax does not believe that Miss Eyre really loves Mr. Rochester, due to their twenty-year age difference.
    H. Mrs. Fairfax fears that Miss Eyre will be hurt by her relationship with Mr. Rochester if things do not go as Miss Eyre plans.
    J. Mrs. Fairfax believes that Miss Eyre will not enjoy being both a governess and Mr. Rochester's wife.

GO ON TO THE NEXT PAGE.

3 ██ **3**

PASSAGE II
SOCIAL SCIENCE: *Abraham Lincoln and the American Republic*

Throughout the Abraham Lincoln and Stephen Douglas presidential debates, Stephen Douglas repeatedly criticized Lincoln's "House Divided" speech. In his "House Divided" speech, Lincoln argues that the
5 "Spirit of Nebraska," the alleged right to choose slavery over freedom in territories, had invaded the country and divided it. The North and the South were no longer working together to put slavery on the road to extinction. In fact, by the late 1850s, the South had fully
10 embraced slavery and wanted to expand it. This new attitude toward slavery promoted by Southerners and some Northern Democrats led Lincoln to believe that they wanted to nationalize slavery.

In the Lincoln–Douglas debates, Lincoln stated
15 that the nation was too divided to continue to compromise on slavery. Lincoln began his defense by referring to the actions of the Founding Fathers, who had worked to eradicate slavery. He mentioned the unanimous abolition of the African slave trade, as well as the
20 Northwest Ordinance and the lack of the word *slave* in the Constitution, to show that the Founding Fathers intended slavery to be strangled in the original Southern States. Lincoln argued that the South had moved away from this course of ending slavery. Lincoln
25 also stated that the federal government, through the Missouri Compromise and the Compromise of 1850, had always regulated slavery in the territories. The Missouri Compromise and the Compromise of 1850 were at odds with the new Dred Scott decision, which
30 denied that Congress had a right to exclude slavery in the states. The Dred Scott decision also reinforced the idea that African Americans were not citizens and that slaves could be brought into the North without gaining their freedom. The Dred Scott decision had the
35 effect of undermining Lincoln's Republican platform that wanted to repeal the Kansas/Nebraska Act.

Both in the debates and the "House Divided" speech, Lincoln repeatedly questioned the Democrats' involvement in the Dred Scott decision. Lincoln
40 suggested that a conspiracy may have taken place between President Buchanan, President Pierce, Judge Taney, and other Democrats, like Stephen Douglas. Lincoln used evidence to show that the Democrats seemed to have known that the Dred Scott decision
45 was coming. A key piece of evidence is that the Dred Scott decision was pushed back until after the election of 1856. In addition, the Democrats had drafted legislation in 1850 and 1854 that contained language which seemed to predict that Congress would not be
50 able to exclude slavery in the territories because of Constitutional constraints. The Dred Scott decision cast doubts on the platform of the Democrats. The Democrats had been endorsing a platform of popular sovereignty, which stated that all new states and
55 territories should be able to vote on whether slavery should be allowed within their borders. The Dred Scott decision reaffirmed for the South that slaves

were considered property. Because America's Constitution protects property, exclusion of slavery through
60 unfriendly legislation was unconstitutional.

Lincoln spoke about the Kansas/Nebraska Act and his opinion on the repeal of the Missouri Compromise throughout the debates. He believed that popular sovereignty was contrary to the principle that valued
65 freedom over slavery. The "Spirit of Nebraska" was what prompted Northerners like Douglas to create the Kansas/Nebraska Act that went against the "Spirit of '76," which was the hope of the Founding Fathers that slavery would be strangled within the original
70 southern states over time. Without the majority of public opinion actively opposed to slavery, Lincoln realized that the battle over slavery could not be won.

Tensions had increased dramatically in both the North and the South in the late 1850s. Violence in
75 Kansas had turned neighbor against neighbor, and there were even physical fights breaking out in the Senate. The South had begun to threaten secession with regularity, and many Northerners afraid of disunion were willing to sacrifice freedom to keep the country
80 together.

Lincoln's "House Divided" speech and his arguments in the Lincoln–Douglas debates show that he believed that slavery was threatening to become a national institution. He saw the American public
85 become increasingly indifferent to slavery and believed the people were naive to the Democratic conspiracy. By the late 1850s, Lincoln realized that a serious conflict was imminent. The North and South were drifting further and further apart and their ideologies were
90 becoming more different every year.

11. The function of the first paragraph in relation to the passage as a whole is to:
   A. orient the reader to the subject of Stephen Douglas's policies toward slavery.
   B. explain how slavery had become a national problem in the 1850s.
   C. establish an outline of Lincoln's arguments during his debates with Stephen Douglas.
   D. explain and introduce the different political parties that existed in the 1850s.

12. Which of the following best describes the way the second paragraph (lines 14–36) functions in the passage as a whole?
   F. It presents Lincoln's arguments from an historical perspective and introduces Lincoln's arguments about slavery.
   G. It proves that Lincoln won the presidential debates because he referenced the work of the Founding Fathers to demonstrate his point.
   H. It sheds light on why the South supported slavery and why many Northerners wanted to abolish it.
   J. It diminishes the importance of Lincoln's arguments against the Dred Scott decision, because it referenced the "House Divided" speech instead.

GO ON TO THE NEXT PAGE.

3   **3**

13. It can reasonably be inferred from the passage that, before the Dred Scott decision:
   A. African Americans were considered citizens and slaves simultaneously.
   B. both the Southern states and the Northern states had abolished slavery.
   C. no slaves were brought into the North.
   D. it was unclear whether or not Congress could exclude slavery in the states.

14. The reference to the fights between neighbors in Kansas (lines 74–77) is used to illustrate the point made in the passage that:
   F. the people in Kansas supported Lincoln even though Kansas was considered a slave state.
   G. slavery was becoming a more divisive institution that caused tension between abolitionists and supporters of slavery.
   H. the actions of the Democrats caused pro-slavery feelings to spread into otherwise anti-slave states.
   J. slavery was slowly becoming nationalized by spreading into the newly acquired territories.

15. Information in the fourth paragraph (lines 61–72) establishes that the "Spirit of '76" was:
   A. the desire of the Founding Fathers to eliminate slavery in America at the time the Declaration of Independence was written.
   B. the desire of the Founding Fathers to encourage slavery in the original Southern states with the hope that slavery would die out on its own.
   C. the desire of the Founding Fathers to allow each new state that entered the Union to decide whether or not to allow slavery within its borders.
   D. the desire of the Founding Fathers to create a new nation built on the ideas of freedom, democracy, and liberty for all citizens.

16. Which of the following statements best describes how Lincoln felt the rest of the country was responding to the expansion of slavery?
   F. Lincoln believed that most Southerners wanted to limit slavery to the original Southern states.
   G. Lincoln believed that all of the new territories desired slavery and that the North was unwilling to allow it.
   H. Lincoln believed that the South desired the expansion of slavery in the territories and the North was becoming too indifferent or frightened to challenge the South.
   J. Lincoln believed that most Northerners wanted the territories to have slavery because they felt it would help strangle slavery in the original Southern states.

17. The passage suggests that the Democrats knew the Dred Scott decision was coming because:
   A. the Dred Scott decision was postponed until after the 1856 presidential election.
   B. Stephen Douglas and other Democrats used their influence to manipulate the United State Supreme Court and President Buchanan.
   C. the Dred Scott decision was widely accepted only in the states where the Democratic Party was the majority.
   D. the Dred Scott decision mimicked the platform of the Democratic Party.

18. According to the passage, all of the following were given as reasons by Lincoln as proof that the Founding Fathers endorsed the "Spirit of '76" EXCEPT:
   F. the unanimous abolition of the slave trade.
   G. the lack of the exact word *slave* in the Constitution.
   H. the Northwest Ordinance.
   J. the Declaration of Independence's promise of life, liberty, and the pursuit of happiness.

19. Lincoln's accusation that some Americans wanted to nationalize slavery can be supported by all of the following EXCEPT:
   A. the Dred Scott decision, which supported the idea that Congress cannot exclude slavery in states because of constitutional constraints.
   B. the desire by many in the South for slavery to be allowed to expand in the territories.
   C. the increased popularity of the "Spirit of Nebraska."
   D. the popularity of the Missouri Compromise during the late 1850s.

20. The passage indicates that the late 1850s' Democrats:
   F. were all Southern slaveholders who wanted to expand slavery into the territories.
   G. used legislation in the early 1850s to support their agenda.
   H. had a platform that would require all territories and new states to allow slavery.
   J. supported the "Spirit of '76."

GO ON TO THE NEXT PAGE.

3   **3**

PASSAGE III

HUMANITIES: *This passage is adapted from the Memoirs of Mary Robinson, published in 1895.*

On the day of my first performance, the theatre was crowded with fashionable spectators; the green room and orchestra were thronged with critics. My dress was a pale pink satin, trimmed with crêpe, and
5 richly spangled with silver. My head was ornamented with white feathers and my glorious suit, for the last scene, was white satin and completely plain, except that I wore a veil of the most transparent gauze, which fell quite to my feet from the back of my head, and a
10 string of beads round my waist.

When I approached the side wing my heart throbbed convulsively; I then began to fear that my resolution would fail, and I leaned upon the Nurse's arm, almost fainting. Mr. Sheridan and several other
15 friends encouraged me to proceed; and at length, with trembling limbs and fearful apprehension, I approached the audience.

The thundering applause that greeted me nearly overpowered all my faculties. I stood mute and bending
20 with alarm, which did not subside till I had feebly articulated the few sentences of the first short scene, during the whole of which I had never once ventured to look at the audience.

On my return to the green room, I was again
25 encouraged, as far as my looks were deemed deserving of approval; for of my powers nothing yet could be known, my fears having as it were affected both my voice and action. The second scene being the masquerade, I had time to collect myself. I never shall forget
30 the sensation which rushed through my bosom when I first looked towards the pit. I beheld a gradual ascent of heads. All eyes were fixed upon me, and the sensation they conveyed was awfully impressive.

As I acquired courage, I found the applause
35 augment; and the night was concluded with peals of loud approbation. I was complimented on all sides. I then experienced, for the first time in my life, a pleasure that language could not explain. I heard one of the most fascinating men, and the most distinguished
40 geniuses of the age, honor me with partial admiration.

The second character which I played was Amanda, in *A Trip to Scarborough*. The play was altered from *Vanbrugh's Relapse*; and the audience, supposing it was a new piece, on finding themselves deceived, expressed
45 a considerable degree of disapproval. I was terrified beyond imagination when Mrs. Yates, no longer able to bear the hissing of the audience, quitted the scene, and left me alone to encounter the audience. I stood for some moments as though I had been petrified.
50 Mr. Sheridan, from the side wing, desired me not to quit the boards. The late Duke of Cumberland from the stage box, bade me take courage: "It is not you, but the play, they hiss," said his Royal Highness. I curtsied and that curtsey seemed to electrify the whole house, for a
55 thundering appeal of encouraging applause followed.

The third character I played was Statira, in *Alexander the Great*. Mr. Lacey, then one of the proprietors of Drury Lane Theatre, was the hero of the night, and the part of Roxana was performed
60 by Mrs. Melmoth. Again, I was received with great warmth and approval. My dress was white and blue, made after the Persian costume; and though it was then singular on the stage, I wore neither a hoop nor powder; my feet were bound by richly ornamented sandals, and
65 the whole dress was picturesque and characteristic.

Though I was always received with the most flattering approval, the characters in which I was most popular were Ophelia, Juliet, and Rosalind. Palmira was also one of my most approved representations. The
70 last character that I played was Sir Harry Revel, in Lady Craven's comedy of *The Miniature Picture*; and the epilogue song in *The Irish Widow* was my last farewell to the labor of my profession.

21. Which of the following descriptions most accurately and completely represents this passage?
    A. An actress reminisces about how fame and admiration changed her personality.
    B. An actress gives a complete listing of the characters that she played during her career on stage.
    C. An actress remembers specific performances and reflects on some more memorable performances.
    D. An actress seeks to explain stage fright and how she overcame her fear of performing in front of crowds.

22. All of the following were clearly identified in the passage as plays that the narrator performed in EXCEPT:
    F. *A Trip to Scarborough*
    G. *Alexander the Great*
    H. *The Miniature Picture*
    J. *Vanbrugh's Relapse*

23. As it is used in line 13, the word *resolution* most nearly means:
    A. decision.
    B. pledge.
    C. courage.
    D. devotion.

24. Details in the passage suggest that:
    F. the narrator was not always cast to play female characters.
    G. the narrator preferred masquerade scenes to any other scene.
    H. the narrator believes that no actress can be successful in theater if she has stage fright.
    J. the narrator's stage fright disappeared because she never had to face hostile audiences.

GO ON TO THE NEXT PAGE.

3   **3**

25. It can be most reasonably concluded from the narrator's reference to her performance in *A Trip to Scarborough* that:
  A. the narrator's acting was the cause for disapproval within the crowd.
  B. the narrator did not become nervous in front of a disgruntled audience.
  C. Mrs. Yates was not as successful an actress as the narrator.
  D. the narrator acted in at least one play that was not a completely original work.

26. According to the passage, in which order did the following events occur in the writer's life?

  I. Appearing in *The Miniature Picture*
  II. Playing the character of Statira in *Alexander the Great*
  III. Playing the character of Amanda in *A Trip to Scarborough*
  IV. Being involved in the production of *The Irish Widow*

  F. I, II, III, IV
  G. III, II, I, IV
  H. IV, III, II, I
  J. II, III, IV, I

27. Which of the following best describes the narrator's experience during her first theater performance?
  A. Terrified throughout the entire performance because of the size of the audience
  B. Initially frightened and overwhelmed, but joyful by the end of the performance
  C. Proud of the beauty of her costume and the set of the play, but discouraged by her performance
  D. Upset because of the difficult masquerade scene

28. All of the following are recollections of the narrator's first performance EXCEPT:
  F. the narrator's costumes during this performance were partially made of satin.
  G. Nurse and Mr. Sheridan were present to assist the narrator.
  H. there was a masquerade scene in her first performance.
  J. the narrator received criticism for her opening lines that were delivered feebly.

29. As it is used in the passage, the word *faculties* (line 19) most nearly means:
  A. senses.
  B. determination.
  C. teachers.
  D. emotions.

30. The primary focus of lines 34–40 is:
  F. the narrator's emotions immediately after her first performance.
  G. the opinion of an important gentleman regarding the narrator's performance.
  H. the narrator's elation because she had become famous.
  J. the narrator's own reflections on the quality of her first performance.

GO ON TO THE NEXT PAGE.

3 ▬▬▬▬▬▬▬▬▬▬▬▬▬▬▬▬▬▬▬▬▬▬ **3**

PASSAGE IV

NATURAL SCIENCE: *This passage discusses a disease that is detrimental to certain trees in North America.*

One of the greatest concerns of landscapers is tree disease. Ash trees are among the most common trees in North America, and they are also very susceptible to disease and decline.

5 One cause of decline in ash trees is *ash yellows*. This disease infects mainly white and green ash in the Northern United States. Ash yellows is caused by a *phytoplasma*: virus-like pathogens that are spread by insects. Ash yellows leads to a gradual decline
10 in tree health for about two to ten years before the tree dies. Some common symptoms include short internodes and tufting of foliage at branch ends, pale green or pale yellow leaves, defoliation, and a sparse canopy. Cankers may also form on the branches and trunk.
15 Unsightly "witches' broom" sprouts might appear on the branches, but it is more common for them to appear on the trunk. The trunk may also develop cracks if the tree is infected with ash yellows. Rarely does an ash tree recover from ash yellows. Experts guess that this
20 disease is more common than most homeowners realize because witches' brooms and yellowing are not always visible on the infected trees. Sometimes cankers and cracks are the only signs of the disease.

The term *ash decline* is used to refer to a tree with
25 more than one condition. Ash decline may involve the ash yellows disease or another problem called *verticillium wilt*. Ash decline is often used to describe any decline in health that is unexplainable. Ash decline involves branch tip death, defoliation, and a slow
30 decline over a number of years. Trees with ash decline may appear to recover in the spring and decline again in July and August.

Verticillium wilt on ash can also result in cankers and dieback similar to ash yellows. Trying to diagnose
35 a tree is difficult because symptoms could be caused by a variety of problems. Sick ash trees may suffer from verticillium wilt, ash yellows, environmental stress, or a combination of these ailments.

Ash yellows has been a known disease in the
40 United States since the 1930s. However, the disease was not distinguished from general ash decline involving environmental factors until the 1980s. In the last eighty years, North America has seen a significant decline in some of its ash trees.
45 No single factor has been proven to cause ash decline. Ash yellows and environmental factors may work together to create ash decline. Studies show that ash yellows is often detected where environmental factors like water shortage or insect damage are present.
50 A survey of several Midwestern states found that some ash decline was found to be independent of ash yellows. The droughts in the 1980s may have caused the decline of ash trees in the Midwest. Cold winter temperatures may also play a role in decline.
55 Ash trees are important in the ecology of North American forests. The decline of these trees may have a severe impact on the health of other plant and animal communities. Green ash provides nesting sites for several species of birds and other wild creatures. Insects

60 and fish flourish in the cool waters made possible by the shade of ash trees. Green and white ash are also very popular in landscaping. Their decline could result in reduced property values.

Ash trees also represent a valuable hardwood
65 resource. An estimated 275 million feet of ash lumber is harvested annually. In the Northeastern United States, about 33 percent of the commercial forest area includes ash trees.

There are no known cures for the diseases
70 mentioned. Experts recommend removing very sick trees while keeping healthy trees well watered and fertilized. Dead limbs should also be removed to maintain the health of ash trees.

---

31. According to the passage, many scientists feel that most ash decline is likely caused:
    A. almost exclusively by ash yellows.
    B. by a combination of disease and environmental factors.
    C. by improper watering and fertilization by homeowners.
    D. by a combination of ash yellows and verticillium wilt only.

32. The passage likens verticillium wilt to ash yellows in that:
    F. both diseases share the symptoms of cankers and dieback.
    G. verticillium is likely to be a cause of ash yellows in white and green ash trees.
    H. poor watering and fertilization techniques can cause verticillium wilt and ash yellows.
    J. verticillium wilt and ash yellows were discovered around the same time period and kill a similar number of trees.

33. The difficulty in diagnosing disease in an ash tree is due to all of the following EXCEPT:
    A. similar diseases that have similar symptoms.
    B. some ash trees in decline may be unhealthy due to environmental conditions rather than diseases.
    C. more than one factor could be contributing to an ash tree's decline.
    D. sick ash trees are difficult to test because they decline so rapidly.

34. The passage states that ash yellows is caused by:
    F. insufficient water.
    G. virus-like pathogens.
    H. insects that eat or destroy the leaves of the ash trees.
    J. cankers, witches' broom, and cracking in the tree trunk.

GO ON TO THE NEXT PAGE.

3 ██ **3**

35. According to the passage, the author believes that:
    A. landscapers should never use ash trees in landscaping designs.
    B. ash trees are the most important tree in North America.
    C. ash trees are important because they can provide a home for some wildlife.
    D. ash trees are essential to ecosystems because they lock in heat from the sun to warm shady forests.

36. According to the passage, which of the following is an argument for NOT blaming ash decline solely on ash yellows?
    F. Most ash decline is caused by verticillium wilt, not ash yellows.
    G. A study cited in the passage proves that only environmental factors have impacted ash decline in recent years.
    H. A study mentioned in the passage shows that drought and weather may contribute to ash decline.
    J. verticillium wilt, ash yellows, and environmental conditions all contribute to ash decline equally.

37. As it is used in line 60, the word *flourish* most nearly means:
    A. decorate.
    B. prosper.
    C. decline.
    D. swim.

38. The author would most likely agree with which of the following statements?
    F. It is important for research to continue into a cure for ash yellows.
    G. Ash yellows is not worthy of continued scientific research.
    H. All ash trees in North America will need to be destroyed to stop the spread of disease.
    J. Ash trees are not significant to the good health of plant and animal communities.

39. According to the passage, what is NOT a characteristic of the disease ash yellows?
    A. The pathogens that cause the disease are spread by insects.
    B. It causes a gradual decline in the tree's health.
    C. Its symptoms include a sparse canopy and defoliation.
    D. It turns the leaves of ash trees bright yellow.

40. Which of the following are accurate statements about ash trees, according to the passage?
    I. Ash trees with ash yellows disease are easily cured.
    II. Ash trees infected with ash yellows usually die after having the disease for two to ten years.
    III. Ash trees infected with ash yellows do not usually recover.
    IV. Ash trees infected with ash yellows sometimes appear to recover in the spring.

    F. I, II, III, IV
    G. II and III only
    H. I and IV only
    J. II, III, and IV only

END OF THE READING TEST.

STOP! IF YOU HAVE TIME LEFT OVER, CHECK YOUR WORK ON THIS SECTION ONLY.

4 ◯ ◯ ◯ ◯ ◯ ◯ ◯ ◯ ◯ **4**

SCIENCE REASONING TEST

35 Minutes—40 Questions

DIRECTIONS: This test includes seven passages, each followed by several questions. Read the passages and choose the best answer to each question. After you have selected your answer, fill in the corresponding bubble on your answer sheet. You should refer to the passages as often as necessary when answering the questions. You may NOT use a calculator on this test.

PASSAGE I

Earth's habitability is sustained by the sun. Currently, the sun provides enough light and warmth to maintain temperature conditions that can support life on our planet. It is undisputed that the sun is a star. All stars go through phases where they change in size, temperature, and brightness. Two scientists present their views on how long Earth will remain habitable.

Scientist 1

Earth's sun has another 7 billion years before it enters the Red Giant phase. Currently, Earth could not sustain human life during the Red Giant phase. However, it is important not to believe that human life on Earth will immediately cease to exist as we know it in 7 billion years. Technology has played a huge role in helping humans adapt to conditions on this planet. We humans have 7 billion years to advance technology and find solutions to adapt to the atmospheric changes the Red Giant phase would bring. For instance, creating a large sunshade to protect Earth would allow life to continue even when the sun enters the Red Giant phase. Another solution would be to develop technology that would stir the sun and bring new hydrogen to the sun's core. This would greatly extend the current phase that our sun is in. There is enough time and incentive to discover ways to thwart the natural progress of nature. Therefore, I believe that human life on this planet will exist indefinitely.

Scientist 2

The sun will enter its Red Giant phase in about 7 billion years. However, new models suggest that Earth has less than a billion years before atmospheric carbon dioxide levels drop to levels that can no longer support photosynthesis. This would lead to a dramatic temperature increase. Once Earth's average temperature rises to above 70°C, the oceans will evaporate and Earth's water sources will be almost completely eliminated. One billion years is not long enough for humans to evolve in order to meet large atmospheric and environmental changes, or to develop the technology needed to make Earth habitable. In a billion years, atmospheric changes will eliminate all life on Earth as we know it. Humans need to accept the reality that advanced life flourishes for only a limited period of time. Science fiction–inspired plans to create space colonies or massive sunshades

are unrealistic and will not likely be developed in the next billion years.

1. If the interpretation of Scientist 1 is correct, which of the following generalizations about technology is most accurate?
   A. Technology only develops when there is a dire need for it and plenty of time to conduct experiments.
   B. Some technology can either alter or enhance natural forces.
   C. Technology is solely responsible for making the planet habitable.
   D. Technology can help prevent the sun from changing indefinitely.

2. Studies show that Venus may once have had an atmosphere and environment almost identical to Earth's. Now, Venus has no water on its surface or in its atmosphere. How would Scientist 2 most likely explain the change in Venus's atmosphere and environment?
   F. Venus's living beings were not able to stir the sun to bring new hydrogen to its core.
   G. Venus's sun entered its Red Giant phase much earlier in the planet's development.
   H. The carbon dioxide levels in the atmosphere dropped to levels that no longer supported photosynthesis.
   J. Venus's location to the sun made it more vulnerable to atmospheric and environmental changes.

3. Which of the following does Scientist 1 suggest would postpone the sun reaching its Red Giant phase?
   A. Using technology to create space colonies built from pieces of meteorites
   B. Using technology to create a giant sunshade to protect Earth from the sun
   C. Using technology to change the levels of hydrogen in the sun's core
   D. Using technology to increase the amount of hydrogen in Earth's core

GO ON TO THE NEXT PAGE.

4

4. Scientist 1 suggests that:
  F. humans will always be adapt to any changes in Earth's atmosphere and environment.
  G. the earth will no longer be able to sustain human life in 7 billion years.
  H. sufficient time and incentive are not necessary elements in advancing technology.
  J. creating sunshades would help to increase levels of carbon dioxide in the air, which is important in maintaining life on the planet.

5. The passage argues that Scientists 1 and 2 disagree on:
  A. whether technology will evolve in time to prevent Earth from becoming inhabitable.
  B. whether the sun will ever enter the Red Giant phase.
  C. whether water and a temperate climate are needed for human survival.
  D. whether the technology to create space colonies already exists.

6. The views of both scientists are similar because they both argue that:
  F. humans will be able to exist indefinitely on Earth.
  G. 7 billion years is long enough to create technology that will protect the earth from a changing sun.
  H. the earth is subject to future atmospheric changes.
  J. it might be possible to discover new planets that are able to sustain human life.

7. Which of the following findings, if true, would weaken the arguments of Scientist 2?
  A. The planet Venus was unable to sustain life when atmospheric changes occurred.
  B. Studies have shown that, during prehistoric times, Earth's temperature reached 75° Celsius.
  C. It is impossible to create a space colony large enough to support life for long periods of time.
  D. Recent scientific models have shown that the earth will not be habitable in 1 billion years.

GO ON TO THE NEXT PAGE.

4 ○ ○ ○ ○ ○ ○ ○ ○ ○ **4**

PASSAGE II

Radon is a radioactive gas that occurs naturally in the environment as a result of the decay of uranium. If inhaled into the lungs at high concentrations and over a long period of time, radon gas can increase the chance that an individual will develop lung cancer.

Outdoors, radon levels are rarely high enough to pose a health threat to individuals. Indoors, however, radon is a concern because it can seep into the foundation of a home through the ground and accumulate in areas with little ventilation, where levels can then become threatening. Radon gas can seep from the ground through many different pathways, such as cracks in the basement floor, through drains and sump pumps, or through loose-fitting pipes.

The only way to detect radon levels is through testing, using a specialized sensing device. Radon is colorless and odorless, and the levels are constantly changing from one area to the next and from one day to the next. In addition, radon exposure produces no short-term health symptoms. Therefore, radon levels should be monitored on a regular basis.

Radon potential is an estimate of the radon level of a structure measured in *picocuries* per liter of air (pCi/L). A picocurie is one-trillionth of a Curie (a measurement unit of radioactivity). The Environmental Protection Agency (EPA) assigns each county in the United States to a zone, based on its radon potential. Radon potential is not used to determine which houses should be tested in an area. Instead, levels are used to determine if radon-resistant features should be installed in new structures being built in an area. Table 1 shows the radon levels in pCi/L for each of 3 zones, with areas in Zone 1 indicating a high radon potential, areas in Zone 2 indicating a moderate radon potential, and areas in Zone 3 indicating a low radon potential.

Table 1	
Zone	Radon level (pCi/L)
3	<2
2	2 to 4
1	>4

8. According to the passage, radon levels are tested in indoors because:
   F. radon levels are different in every area, but they are always the same indoors.
   G. radon accumulates in the air inside a home and poses a possible health threat.
   H. radon gas has a strong, unpleasant smell that can only be detected indoors.
   J. radon levels vary from season to season but are similar for most houses.

9. All of the following are mentioned as characteristics of radon that contribute to the importance of continual in-home testing EXCEPT:
   A. radon is colorless and odorless.
   B. radon produces no short-term symptoms.
   C. radon levels vary from day to day.
   D. radon is a naturally occurring radioactive gas.

10. Studies have shown that existing homes in the same neighborhood can have very different radon levels. Are these findings consistent with information presented in the passage?
    F. No, because radon levels cannot be measured in existing homes.
    G. No, because radon seeps into all homes in the same way.
    H. Yes, because the occurrence of radon is very rare.
    J. Yes, because radon levels vary depending on many different factors.

11. According to the passage, which of the following radon levels would be considered most harmful?
    A. 5.2 pCi/L
    B. 4.0 pCi/L
    C. 3.0 pCi/L
    D. 1.9 pCi/L

GO ON TO THE NEXT PAGE.

PASSAGE III

Predation is an interaction between individuals of 2 species in which one is harmed (the prey), and the other is helped (the predator). Predation can occur among plants and animals as well as between plants and animals. Some biologists contend that *herbivores*, or plant eaters, are predators. Table 1 indicates some characteristics and examples of certain predators.

Table 1		
Predator	Characteristics	Examples
Herbivore	Eats plants only, can be very selective in the plants that they eat	Rabbits, deer, some birds, some insects
Carnivore	Eats herbivores and other carnivores	Lions, wolves, some birds, some insects
Parasite	Feeds on another organism's parts, generally without killing the organism	Bacteria, some worms, some plants

Predation is very important in maintaining a natural balance in any given ecosystem. For example, without predators, prey populations tend to grow exponentially. Without prey, predator populations tend to decline exponentially. Predators consume individual members of the prey population, thereby controlling the overall numbers in the ecosystem. The number of prey consumed depends on the number of prey present as well as the number of predators present. The rate of change in the number of prey is a function of the birth of new prey minus the death of other prey, due either to predation or other causes. The death rate is assumed to depend on the number of prey available and the number of predators. The rate of change in the number of predators is a function of the births of new predators—which depends on the number of prey—minus the death of some predators.

Over long periods of time, predator and prey tend to balance each other out. This is called the *predator-prey cycle*. Prey numbers will increase when predator numbers decrease. When the number of prey reaches a certain point, predators will start to increase until they eat enough prey to cause a decline in prey numbers. When this happens, the number of predators will begin to decrease because they can't find enough prey to eat, and the cycle will begin again. Figure 1 represents an example of a *predator-prey cycle*.

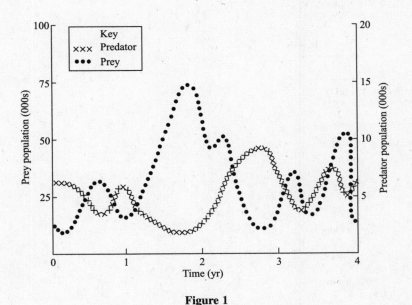

Figure 1

GO ON TO THE NEXT PAGE.

12. Based on information in the passage and in Table 1, an herbivore is:
   F. a predator only.
   G. both a parasite and a predator.
   H. prey only.
   J. both a predator and prey.

13. According to information in the passage, the number of prey consumed in an ecosystem is dependent on:
   A. the natural balance of the ecosystem.
   B. the total number of predators that die because of predation.
   C. the type of parasites available in the ecosystem.
   D. the number of predators present and the number of prey present.

14. Based on Figure 1, during the first year, predator numbers were mostly:
   F. higher than prey numbers.
   G. lower than prey numbers.
   H. equal to prey numbers.
   J. unable to be determined.

15. Studies have shown that a certain species of deer will only eat a specific type of plant found in the deer's natural habitat, and nothing else. Is this finding supported by the information in the passage?
   A. No, because a deer is an herbivore, which means it eats all plants
   B. No, because a deer is a carnivore and does not eat plants
   C. Yes, because a deer is an herbivore, and herbivores can be selective eaters
   D. Yes, because a deer is a prey animal, so it must use caution when eating

16. Based on Figure 1, during which year were the greatest number of prey animals available?
   F. 1
   G. 2
   H. 3
   J. 4

GO ON TO THE NEXT PAGE.

4 ○ ○ ○ ○ ○ ○ ○ ○ ○ 4

PASSAGE IV

The term *weathering* refers to the processes that cause surface rock to disintegrate into smaller particles or dissolve in water. These processes are often slow, taking place over thousands of years. The amount of time that rock has been exposed to the elements (primarily wind and water) influences the degree to which the rock will weather.

Weathering processes are divided into three categories: physical, chemical, and biological.

Table 1 shows some of the factors that contribute to physical weathering.

Table 1	
Physical weathering	
Mechanism	Results
Animals and plants	Animals burrow into the earth, moving rock fragments and sediment. Plant roots have the same effect.
Crystallization	Water evaporates from rock, which leads to the development of salt crystals. The crystals grow, eventually breaking apart the rock.
Temperature variation	Minerals in rocks expand and contract with temperature changes. Repeated expansion and contraction cracks and splits the rocks.
Exfoliation	Exfoliation occurs as slabs of cracked rock slip off other rock, which leads to further erosion.

Chemical weathering occurs when minerals in rock are chemically altered. Table 2 shows some of the factors that contribute to chemical weathering.

Table 2	
Chemical weathering	
Mechanism	Results
Carbonation	Water combines with carbon dioxide to form carbonic acid. The carbonic acid chemically alters the rock, so that it dissolves.
Hydrolysis	Water, usually in the form of rain, disrupts the chemical composition of the minerals, destabilizing the rock.
Hydration	When water combines with compounds in rock, the mineral's grain will be physically altered.
Oxidation	Oxygen combines with compound elements in rock to form oxides and weaken the rock.

Plants and bacteria contribute to biological weathering. The ultimate product of biological agents on rock is soil. Table 3 shows some factors of biological weathering.

Table 3	
Biological weathering	
Mechanism	Results
Lichens	Lichens are rich in chelating agents, which trap elements of the decomposing rock, resulting in etching and grooving.
Bacteria	Alters the acidity of groundwater, which can lead to erosion of the rock.

17. Based on the data in the passage, plants contribute to which of the following types of weathering?
    A. Physical only
    B. Both physical and biological
    C. Biological only
    D. Physical, chemical, and biological

18. According to Table 1, extreme temperature changes can lead to:
    F. increased acidity in groundwater.
    G. the creation of carbonic acid.
    H. the development of salt crystals.
    J. cracked and split rock.

19. A layer of fine sediment mixed with some organic material is found surrounding a rock formation. The most likely cause for this is:
    A. chemical weathering.
    B. exfoliation.
    C. biological weathering.
    D. oxidation.

20. Based on Table 2, the factor that contributes most to the alteration of minerals and rock is:
    F. the acidity level.
    G. the presence of water.
    H. the availability of oxygen.
    J. the mineral composition of the rock.

21. According to Table 3, a chelating agent:
    A. releases elements into the soil.
    B. alters the acidity of groundwater.
    C. dissolves rapidly in water.
    D. traps elements of the decomposing rock.

22. Rainwater is slightly acidic, and it can dissolve many minerals over time. This process is most consistent with the mechanism of:
    F. exfoliation.
    G. oxidation.
    H. hydrolysis.
    J. chelation.

GO ON TO THE NEXT PAGE.

4 ⬤ ◯ ◯ ◯ ◯ ◯ ◯ ◯ ◯ **4**

PASSAGE V

Sea anemones look like plants, but they actually are predatory animals. They are invertebrates, which means that they do not have a skeleton. To protect themselves, they will attach to firm objects on the sea floor, such as rock or coral.

Sea anemones can alter their body shape according to changes in their environment. For example, when ocean currents are strong, the sea anemone will reduce its internal volume in order to decrease the surface area that is exposed to the current. Sea anemones are dependent on water flow for food and nutrients and also for assistance in eliminating waste.

Most anemones share a symbiotic relationship with marine algae called *zooxanthellae*. These are photosynthetic organisms whose waste products are a food source for the sea anemone. The sea anemone also enjoys a mutualistic relationship with the clown fish. This fish is immune to the stinging tentacles of the sea anemone, and it helps the anemone by actually cleaning the tentacles. The cleaning process yields food for the clown fish, while it remains protected from potential predators by the sea anemones stinging tentacles.

Figure 1 shows a cross-section of portions of the internal anatomy of a sea anemone.

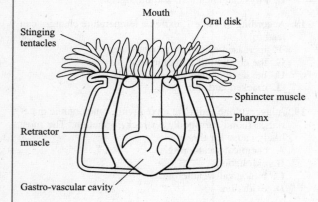

Figure 1

23. According to Figure 1, the sea anemone's mouth is located:
  A. below the pharynx.
  B. at its center.
  C. near its base.
  D. inside the sphincter muscle.

24. According to information in the passage, the sea anemone benefits from the presence of:
  F. both the clown fish and zooxanthellae.
  G. the clown fish only.
  H. zooxanthellae only.
  J. neither the clown fish nor zooxanthellae.

25. Which of the following statements about the sea anemone is supported by the passage? The sea anemone most resembles:
  A. a clown fish.
  B. a flower.
  C. marine algae.
  D. a rock.

26. Suppose that a strong storm stirred up the water in which a sea anemone was living. The sea anemone's response would most likely be:
  F. to expose itself to the strong current.
  G. to seek the protection of a clown fish.
  H. to reduce its internal volume.
  J. to detach itself from the seafloor.

27. As shown in Figure 1, the part of the sea anemone's anatomy that connects its mouth to its gastrovascular cavity is the:
  A. oral disk.
  B. tentacle.
  C. pharynx.
  D. sphincter muscle.

GO ON TO THE NEXT PAGE.

4 ○ ○ ○ ○ ○ ○ ○ ○ ○ **4**

PASSAGE VI

Compost is the name given to a mixture of decaying leaves and other organic material. This mixture is often used as fertilizer. Several students designed experiments to test various types of soil, and various combinations of soil and compost on plant growth.

Experiment 1

The students dug a soil sample from an empty field next to the school. They put soil into 4 different clay pots, and mixed in various amounts of compost so that the volume of soil mixture was the same in each pot. They then planted the same number of radish seeds (4) in each pot. The soil/compost mixtures for each pot are shown in Table 1.

The clay pots were placed next to each other on a windowsill and watered at the same time each day. The students took care to ensure that the pots each received the same amount of sunlight and water each day. After 2 weeks, the students began recording the growth of the radish plants. They continued recording this data for two more weeks. The results are shown in Table 2.

Experiment 2

The students repeated Experiment 1, with the following changes; each pot contained a different soil type, and no compost was used. This experiment was begun at the same time as Experiment 1. The results of Experiment 2 are shown in Table 3.

Table 1	
Soil/compost mixture (Pot #)	% Soil/% compost
1	25%/75%
2	50%/50%
3	75%/25%
4	100% soil

Table 2						
Soil/compost mixture (Pot #)	Average plant height (cm)			Average number of leaves		
	14 days	21 days	28 days	14 days	21 days	28 days
1	4.2	5.3	6.2	3	5.5	8
2	3.8	4.8	5.1	3	4.5	6.5
3	3.3	4.4	4.8	2	4	5.5
4	3.2	4.1	4.4	2	3.5	4.5

Table 3						
Soil type	Average plant height (cm)			Average number of leaves		
	14 days	21 days	28 days	14 days	21 days	28 days
Sand (1)	2.4	2.9	3.4	1	2.5	3.5
Potting soil (2)	3.9	4.7	5.3	3	4	6
Soil from field near the school (3)	3.2	4.2	4.3	2	3.5	4.5
Mixture of sand and potting soil (4)	3.1	3.3	4.2	2	4	5.5

GO ON TO THE NEXT PAGE.

28. Based on the results of Experiment 2, which soil type yielded the most overall growth after 28 days?
  F. Sand
  G. Potting soil
  H. Soil from the field near the school
  J. Mixture of sand and potting soil

29. Based on the results of Experiment 1, which soil/compost mixture yielded the greatest average plant height after the first 2 weeks?
  A. 4
  B. 3
  C. 2
  D. 1

30. Experiment 2 was different from Experiment 1 in that none of the clay pots:
  F. were watered during the first 2 weeks.
  G. contained any compost.
  H. contained any soil.
  J. were placed on the windowsill.

31. The results of Soil Type 3 in Experiment 2 and Pot Number 4 in Experiment 1 were almost identical. This is most likely because:
  A. the same amount of compost was used.
  B. the plants were allowed to grow for 2 more weeks.
  C. the pots were the same size.
  D. the same type of soil was used.

32. In Experiment 2, how many seeds were planted in each clay pot?
  F. 4
  G. 14
  H. 21
  J. Cannot be determined.

33. According to the results of Experiment 1, what percentage of compost yielded the highest average number of leaves?
  A. 100%
  B. 75%
  C. 50%
  D. 25%

GO ON TO THE NEXT PAGE.

4 ○ ○ ○ ○ ○ ○ ○ ○ ○ 4

PASSAGE VII

The Great Lakes—Huron, Ontario, Michigan, Erie, and Superior—form the largest freshwater system in the world. Each of the lakes tends to *stratify*, or form layers of warmer and colder water, depending on the season. This is called *seasonal turnover*. In winter, for example, the coldest water in the lake lies just below the surface ice. The water gets progressively warmer at deeper levels. In spring, the sun melts the ice, and the surface water warms. Because the surface water is still cooler than the layers below, the water at the surface sinks to the bottom of the lake, forcing the cooler water at the bottom of the lake to the surface. This mixing, known as *spring turnover*, eliminates the temperature stratification that was established during the winter. In the absence of this thermal layering, wind continues to mix the water to a greater depth, bringing oxygen (O_2) to the bottom of the lake and nutrients to the surface. This results in a relatively even distribution of O_2 throughout the lake. When summer arrives, the lake again becomes stratified, with warm water at the surface, and cold water at the bottom. A narrow zone of water undergoing rapid temperature changes separates these layers. This zone is called the *thermocline*. Cool, fall temperatures cause the lake water to mix again, until the surface begins to freeze and the winter stratification is reestablished.

The stability of the lake's stratification depends on several factors: the lake's depth, shape, and size, as well as the wind and both the inflow and outflow of lake water. Lakes with a lot of water flowing into and out of them do not develop consistent and lasting thermal stratification.

Figure 1 shows an example of lake stratification during the summer.

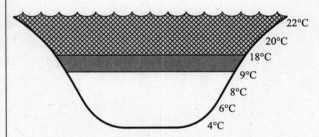

Figure 1   Cross-section of a lake during the summer.

34. According to Figure 1, the temperature of the water below the thermocline is:
   F. higher than the temperature of the water above the thermocline.
   G. equal to the temperature of the water above the thermocline.
   H. lower than the temperature of the water above the thermocline.
   J. equal to the average temperature of the water in the lake.

35. Based on the passage, which of the following best represents O_2 levels in one of the Great Lakes during the spring?

A.

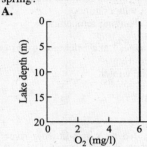

B.

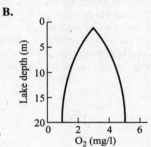

C.

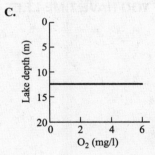

D.

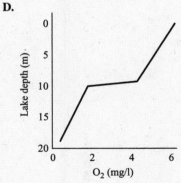

GO ON TO THE NEXT PAGE.

4 ○ ○ ○ ○ ○ ○ ○ ○ ○ **4**

36. According to the passage, the thermocline is:
    F. established during the winter.
    G. responsible for bringing nutrients to the surface.
    H. a zone of constant temperatures.
    J. a zone of rapidly changing temperatures.

37. According to the passage, Lake Michigan experiences thermal stratification during:
    A. the summer and the winter.
    B. the summer only.
    C. the spring and fall.
    D. the spring only.

38. A small, inland lake, fed by a fast-flowing river was found to have very little thermal stratification. Based on the passage, this is most likely because:
    F. not enough water was flowing into the lake.
    G. the inflow of water from the river was too high.
    H. the lake was too shallow to support stratification.
    J. too much water was flowing out of the lake into the river.

39. According to Figure 1, during the summer, as the depth of the lake increases, the temperature of the water:
    A. decreases suddenly, then gradually increases.
    B. increases only.
    C. remains stable.
    D. decreases only.

40. Based on the passage, the stability of thermal stratification depends on all of the following EXCEPT:
    F. the depth of the lake.
    G. seasonal turnover.
    H. the amount of wind.
    J. water inflow.

END OF THE SCIENCE REASONING TEST.
STOP! IF YOU HAVE TIME LEFT OVER, CHECK YOUR WORK ON THIS SECTION ONLY.

WRITING TEST PROMPT

DIRECTIONS: This test is designed to assess your writing skills. You have thirty minutes to plan and write an essay based on the stimulus provided. Be sure to take a position on the issue and support your position using logical reasoning and relevant examples. Organize your ideas in a focused and logical way, and use the English language to clearly and effectively express your position.

When you have finished writing, refer to the Scoring Rubrics discussed in the Introduction (page 4) to estimate your score.

Some high schools in the United States have a policy of random searches of student lockers for illegal items such as drugs and weapons. Some faculty and staff believe that the searches are necessary in order to protect student safety. Other teachers and administrators believe that the searches infringe on students' privacy and that searches should only be conducted when there is a reason to suspect that an individual student may have something illegal in his or her locker. In your opinion, should high schools conduct random searches of student lockers to search for illegal items?

In your essay, take a position on this question. You may write about one of the points of view mentioned above, or you may give another point of view on this issue. Use specific examples and reasons for your position.

ANSWER KEY

English Test

1. D	21. A	41. C	61. D
2. F	22. H	42. J	62. G
3. A	23. D	43. A	63. A
4. H	24. G	44. F	64. H
5. C	25. C	45. C	65. A
6. G	26. J	46. H	66. H
7. D	27. B	47. D	67. D
8. G	28. H	48. F	68. G
9. C	29. A	49. C	69. C
10. J	30. G	50. J	70. J
11. B	31. A	51. A	71. B
12. F	32. G	52. G	72. J
13. B	33. C	53. D	73. B
14. F	34. H	54. H	74. F
15. B	35. B	55. C	75. C
16. J	36. F	56. G	
17. A	37. C	57. B	
18. H	38. H	58. F	
19. B	39. A	59. D	
20. J	40. F	60. J	

Mathematics Test

1. D	21. C	41. E
2. G	22. G	42. F
3. B	23. C	43. D
4. G	24. F	44. G
5. C	25. E	45. A
6. F	26. G	46. J
7. E	27. B	47. B
8. K	28. F	48. H
9. A	29. B	49. D
10. J	30. G	50. J
11. D	31. C	51. D
12. G	32. F	52. K
13. E	33. C	53. A
14. F	34. J	54. H
15. C	35. D	55. C
16. K	36. H	56. G
17. A	37. B	57. C
18. H	38. J	58. F
19. B	39. D	59. A
20. K	40. K	60. G

Reading Test		Science Reasoning Test	
1. C	21. C	1. B	21. D
2. J	22. J	2. H	22. H
3. B	23. C	3. C	23. B
4. H	24. F	4. F	24. F
5. D	25. D	5. A	25. B
6. G	26. G	6. H	26. H
7. D	27. B	7. B	27. C
8. J	28. J	8. G	28. G
9. A	29. A	9. D	29. D
10. H	30. F	10. J	30. G
11. C	31. B	11. A	31. D
12. F	32. F	12. J	32. F
13. D	33. D	13. D	33. B
14. G	34. G	14. F	34. H
15. A	35. C	15. C	35. A
16. H	36. H	16. G	36. J
17. A	37. B	17. B	37. A
18. J	38. F	18. J	38. G
19. D	39. D	19. C	39. D
20. G	40. J	20. G	40. G

▣ SCORING GUIDE

Your final reported score is your COMPOSITE SCORE. Your COMPOSITE SCORE is the average of all of your SCALED SCORES.

  Your SCALED SCORES for the four multiple-choice sections are derived from the Scoring Table on the next page. Use your RAW SCORE, or the number of questions that you answered correctly for each section, to determine your SCALED SCORE. If you got a RAW SCORE of 60 on the English test, for example, you correctly answered 60 out of 75 questions.

Step 1 Determine your RAW SCORE for each of the four multiple-choice sections:

English _____

Mathematics _____

Reading _____

Science Reasoning _____

The following Raw Score Table shows the total possible points for each section.

RAW SCORE TABLE	
KNOWLEDGE AND SKILL AREAS	**RAW SCORES**
ENGLISH	75
MATHEMATICS	60
READING	40
SCIENCE REASONING	40
WRITING	12

Multiple-Choice Scoring Worksheet

Step 2   Determine your SCALED SCORE for each of the four multiple-choice sections using the following Scoring Worksheet. Each SCALED SCORE should be rounded to the nearest number according to normal rules. For example, $31.2 \approx 31$ and $31.5 \approx 32$. If you answered 61 questions correctly on the English section, for example, your SCALED SCORE would be 29.

English   _____ × 36 = _____ ÷ 75 = _____
                          RAW SCORE   − 2 (*correction factor)

                                                                          _____
                                                                          SCALED SCORE

Mathematics   _____ × 36 = _____ ÷ 60 = _____
                          RAW SCORE   + 1 (*correction factor)

                                                                          _____
                                                                          SCALED SCORE

Reading   _____ × 36 = _____ ÷ 40 = _____
                          RAW SCORE   + 2 (*correction factor)

                                                                          _____
                                                                          SCALED SCORE

Science Reasoning   _____ × 36 = _____ ÷ 40 = _____
                          RAW SCORE   + 1.5 (*correction factor)

                                                                          _____
                                                                          SCALED SCORE

*The correction factor is an approximation based on the average from several recent ACT tests. It is most valid for scores in the middle 50% (approximately 16–24 scale composite score) of the scoring range.

The scores are all approximate. Actual ACT scoring scales vary from one administration to the next based upon several factors.

If you take the optional Writing Test, you will need to combine your English and Writing scores to obtain your final COMPOSITE SCORE. Refer to Chapter 7 for guidelines on scoring your Writing Test Essay. Once you have determined a score for your essay out of 12 possible points, you will need to determine your ENGLISH/WRITING SCALED SCORE, using both your ENGLISH SCALE SCORE and your WRITING TEST SCORE. The combination of the two scores will give you an ENGLISH/WRITING SCALED SCORE, from 1 to 36, that will be used to determine your COMPOSITE SCORE mentioned earlier.

Using the English/Writing Scoring Table, find your ENGLISH SCALED SCORE on the left or right hand side of the table and your WRITING TEST SCORE on the top of the table. Follow your ENGLISH SCALED SCORE over and your WRITING TEST SCORE down until the two columns meet at a number. This number is your ENGLISH/WRITING SCALED SCORE and will be used to determine your COMPOSITE SCORE.

Step 3   Determine your ENGLISH/WRITING SCALED SCORE using the English/Writing Scoring Table on the following page:

English   _____

Writing   _____

English/Writing   _____

ENGLISH/WRITING SCORING TABLE

ENGLISH SCALED SCORE	WRITING TEST SCORE											ENGLISH SCALED SCORE
	2	3	4	5	6	7	8	9	10	11	12	
36	26	27	28	29	30	31	32	33	34	32	36	36
35	26	27	28	29	30	31	31	32	33	34	35	35
34	25	26	27	28	29	30	31	32	33	34	35	34
33	24	25	26	27	28	29	30	31	32	33	34	33
32	24	25	25	26	27	28	29	30	31	32	33	32
31	23	24	25	26	27	28	29	30	30	31	32	31
30	22	23	24	25	26	27	28	29	30	31	32	30
29	21	22	23	24	25	26	27	28	29	30	31	29
28	21	22	23	24	24	25	26	27	28	29	30	28
27	20	21	22	23	24	25	26	27	28	28	29	27
26	19	20	21	22	23	24	25	26	27	28	29	26
25	18	19	20	21	22	23	24	25	26	27	28	25
24	18	19	20	21	22	23	23	24	25	26	27	24
23	17	18	19	20	21	22	23	24	25	26	27	23
22	16	17	18	19	20	21	22	23	24	25	26	22
21	16	17	17	18	19	20	21	22	23	24	25	21
20	15	16	17	18	19	20	21	21	22	23	24	20
19	14	15	16	17	18	19	20	21	22	23	24	19
18	13	14	15	16	17	18	19	20	21	22	23	18
17	13	14	15	16	16	17	18	19	20	21	22	17
16	12	13	14	15	16	17	18	19	20	20	21	16
15	11	12	13	14	15	16	17	18	19	20	21	15
14	10	11	12	13	14	15	16	17	18	19	20	14
13	10	11	12	13	14	14	15	16	17	18	19	13
12	9	10	11	12	13	14	15	16	17	18	19	12
11	8	9	10	11	12	13	14	15	16	17	18	11
10	8	9	9	10	11	12	13	14	15	16	17	10
9	7	8	9	10	11	12	13	13	14	15	16	9
8	6	7	8	9	10	11	12	13	14	15	16	8
7	5	6	7	8	9	10	11	12	13	14	15	7
6	5	6	7	7	8	9	10	11	12	13	14	6
5	4	5	6	7	8	9	10	11	12	12	13	5
4	3	4	5	6	7	8	9	10	11	12	13	4
3	2	3	4	5	6	7	8	9	10	11	12	3
2	2	3	4	5	6	6	7	8	9	10	11	2
1	1	2	3	4	5	6	7	8	9	10	11	1

Step 4 Determine your COMPOSITE SCORE by finding the sum of all your SCALED SCORES for each of the four sections: English only (if you do not choose to take the optional Writing Test) *or* English/Writing (if you choose to take the optional Writing Test), Mathematics, Reading, and Science Reasoning, and divide by 4 to find the average. Round your COMPOSITE SCORE according to normal rules. For example, $31.2 \approx 31$ and $31.5 \approx 32$.

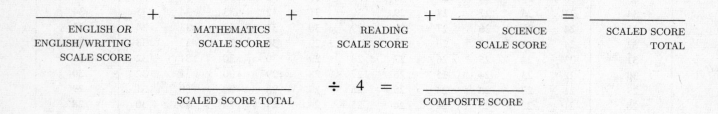

ENGLISH *OR* ENGLISH/WRITING SCALE SCORE	+	MATHEMATICS SCALE SCORE	+	READING SCALE SCORE	+	SCIENCE SCALE SCORE	=	SCALED SCORE TOTAL

SCALED SCORE TOTAL   ÷ 4 =   COMPOSITE SCORE

ANSWERS AND EXPLANATIONS

English Test Explanations

PASSAGE I

1. **The best answer is D.** The question requires you to determine the correct punctuation. A good rule of thumb when it comes to commas is to use them where you would naturally pause when reading a sentence. A comma is not necessary anywhere within the underlined portion of the sentence, so answer choice D is correct.

2. **The best answer is F.** The best way to answer this question is to go through each of the answer choices and determine which of the phrases works best when substituted for the underlined portion of the sentence. Answer choice G can be eliminated because it is awkward and does not make sense. Answer choice H can also be eliminated because it is too wordy. Yellow fever was a serious disease, not just "annoying," so answer choice J can be eliminated because it is not supported by the context of the passage. The sentence is best as it is written.

3. **The best answer is A.** "In spite of" and "regardless of" are prepositional phrases that are not supported by the rest of the sentence. Eliminate answer choices B and D. The sentence no longer makes sense when "it was" is substituted for the underlined portion, so answer choice C can eliminated.

4. **The best answer is H.** The question tests your ability to express the idea clearly and simply. The underlined portion lacks a verb that is parallel to the other verbs used in the sentence. Eliminate answer choice F. Answer choices G and J are wordy and slightly awkward. The phrase "commonly accepted" is clear and concise.

5. **The best answer is C.** The question requires you to correctly punctuate the underlined portion of the sentence. A semicolon should be followed by an independent clause. Since "such as the clothing or blankets …" could not stand alone, answer choice A should be eliminated. Answer choice B creates an incomplete sentence, and answer choice D is awkward and ungrammatical.

6. **The best answer is G.** To answer this question, look for an answer choice that proves that the spread of yellow fever is different from any other disease that is spread by contact with an infected person. Answer choice G is correct because it shows that yellow fever is not spread by direct contact.

7. **The best answer is D.** This question requires you to determine whether to use the plural or possessive form of a word. An apostrophe is used to show possession. Since the "theories" do not possess anything, eliminate answer choices A and C. "Theorize" is a verb that means to "formulate a theory." Eliminate answer choice B. The sentence requires the plural form of "theory," which is "theories," so answer choice D is correct.

8. **The best answer is G.** This question requires you to use specific language. It does not make sense that either the doctors or the Army was infecting soldiers with yellow fever, so eliminate answer choices H and J. Likewise, eliminate answer choice F, because it implies that the doctors were infecting the soldiers.

9. **The best answer is C.** The question requires you to determine which descriptive word best emphasizes how fast yellow fever was infecting soldiers. "Great," "normal," and "discouraging" do not effectively describe the rate of infection, so answer choices A, B, and D can eliminated. "An alarming" rate best emphasizes the rapid spread of yellow fever, and it is idiomatic.

10. **The best answer is J.** The question tests your ability to express the idea clearly and simply, and to identify irrelevant information. "So helping his cause," and "which helped his cause" are both unnecessary and awkward within this sentence. The most clear and simple way to express the sentence is to end it after the word "experiments."

11. **The best answer is B.** The question requires you to determine the correct form of the underlined portion of the sentence. "Materials" is plural, so answer choices C and D can be eliminated because both are in singular form. Since the paragraph discusses events that occurred in the past, answer choice A can also be eliminated, as "have" is present tense.

12. **The best answer is F.** The first two sentences of the paragraph discuss the first part of the experiment. "A second building …" begins the discussion of a

different part of the experiment. The sentence as written makes it clear that the paragraph discusses separate experiments.

13. **The best answer is B.** The question requires you to determine the form of "repeat" that best fits in the context of the sentence. To maintain parallel construction, the past-tense verb "repeated" should be used. This clearly indicates that the experiments were performed "many times." The other answer choices do not make sense when used within the sentence.

14. **The best answer is F.** Paragraph 3 discusses the experiments that were run to test the source of yellow fever. Paragraph 4 explains that the results of the experiments saved many people from yellow fever. Answer choice F is the only selection that successfully links Paragraph 3 to Paragraph 4.

15. **The best answer is B.** This question requires you to express the idea clearly and simply. Only answer choice B clearly identifies the effect of the vaccines on the incidence of yellow fever outbreaks. Answer choice A is awkward, and answer choices C and D are irrelevant.

PASSAGE II

16. **The best answer is J.** The question requires you to determine which form you should use to suggest that the Giant Panda is native to China. "It's" is a contraction for "it is," so answer choice F can be eliminated. The sentence refers to "it," which is singular, so answer choice G can be eliminated. "There" indicates location, not possession, so answer choice H can be eliminated. "Its" is singular and correctly implies that China is the Great Panda's native country.

17. **The best answer is A.** The sentence implies that the Giant Pandas have been pushed from low to high altitudes. In other words, the underlined portion should suggest that the pandas lived at lower altitudes at sometime in the past. The remaining answer choices are not supported by the context the sentence.

18. **The best answer is H.** The sentence requires that the underlined portion refer to an event that has already occurred. "Will push," "will have pushed," and "will be pushing," refer to events that may happen in the future. Answer choice H indicates that the pandas have already been pushed into higher altitudes, which is correct.

19. **The best answer is B.** The phrase "by nature" should be treated as extra information in the sentence. This is called a parenthetical expression, and it should be set off by commas. In other words, there should be a comma before "by" and a comma after "nature."

20. **The best answer is J.** The question requires you to determine the correct way to express that the dense habitat belongs to the Giant Pandas. "There" refers to a location, not possession, so answer choice F can be eliminated. Eliminate answer choice G because it does not make it clear to whom the habitat belongs. "They're" is a contraction of "they are," which does not express possession, so eliminate answer choice H.

21. **The best answer is A.** The question tests your ability to express the idea clearly and simply. The sentence is best as it is written. The other answer choices are awkward, and they do not effectively express the idea that the pandas are able to stay away from one another if they so choose.

22. **The best answer is H.** The question requires you to correctly punctuate the underlined portion of the sentence. The sentence as written makes the second sentence incomplete. Eliminate answer choice F. A semicolon should be followed by an independent clause, so answer choice G can be eliminated. Since answer choice J would create a run-on sentence, it should be eliminated as well.

23. **The best answer is D.** The sentence as it is written is redundant, so answer choice A can be eliminated. Answer choices C and B can also be eliminated because both are awkward. The only selection that is clear and simple is answer choice D.

24. **The best answer is G.** A comma is used to separate the items in a list, but only if the list includes three or more items. No commas are necessary within the underlined portion, so answer choice G is correct.

25. **The best answer is C.** A comma is used to separate the items in a list, but only if the list includes three or more items. No commas are necessary within the underlined portion, so answer choice C is correct.

26. **The best answer is J.** This question tests your ability to express the idea clearly and simply. The first thing you should do is eliminate answer choices F and G because both are awkward. It does not make sense to say "The female perching," so eliminate answer choice H. Only answer choice J effectively indicates what the female is doing and where she is doing it.

27. The best answer is B. The question tests your ability to express the idea clearly and simply. The first step is to recognize that you should use the noun "rivals," not "rivalry." Eliminate answer choice D. Next, the word "potential" is used as an adjective to describe "rivals," it is not used as an adverb (potentially) to describe the action of "fending off," so eliminate answer choices A and C.

28. The best answer is H. The preceding sentence refers to the female pandas only, so the "their" in the next sentence still refers to multiple female pandas. Answer choice F suggest that the cubs dig the dens, which does not make sense. Answer choice G does not refer to multiple females and can be eliminated. "She digs" refers to only one female panda, so answer choice J can also be eliminated.

29. The best answer is A. The first sentence of Paragraph 4 begins with "Therefore" and then suggests that a Giant Panda is a popular display at any zoo. A logical introduction should explain why the Giant Panda is a favorite at any zoo. Answer choice A is correct because it says that most people have never seen the Giant Panda, which is a logical reason as to why the Giant Panda is popular at the zoo.

30. The best answer is G. The question requires you to determine the proper form of the verb "to keep." Since the rest of the sentence is in present tense, the verb should also be in present tense. Therefore, "that keeps" is the best choice. Answer choices H and J are awkward and should be eliminated.

PASSAGE III

31. The best answer is A. The question tests your ability to properly determine the verb tense of the sentence. Although the naming of the Nobel Peace Prize occurred in the past, it is still named after Alfred Nobel, so the verb should be in the present tense. Eliminate answer choice C because it refers to the future, and eliminate answer choice D because it refers to the past. Answer choice B does not make any sense because it does not include "after," which is essential to the sentence. The Nobel Peace Prize is not named Alfred Nobel.

32. The best answer is G. Since the sentence is referring to events that occurred in the past, the verb tense must also be in the past. "Followed" is the correct form of the verb, and Alfred followed "in" his father's footsteps, not "by" them, so answer choice G is correct. It does not make sense that the footsteps followed Alfred, so eliminate answer choice H.

33. The best answer is C. Since the sentence is referring to events that occurred in the past, the verb tense must also be in the past, so eliminate answer choice A. "Devoted" is the correct form of the verb, so eliminate answer choice B. Alfred devoted "his energies," not "of his energies," so answer choice C is correct.

34. The best answer is H. The question requires you to determine which of the answer choices is an example of the "dangers of dynamite during Nobel's time." Answer choice F refers to "today," not Nobel's time, so it can be eliminated. Answer choices G and J can be eliminated because they do not include any examples of the dangers of using dynamite.

35. The best answer is B. This question tests your ability to recognize redundancy. Since the word "also" is used earlier in the sentence, it is not necessary to include it again. Eliminate answer choice C. "In addition" and "too" are synonyms of "also," so eliminate answer choices A and D.

36. The best answer is F. This question tests your ability to express the idea clearly and simply. Eliminate answer choices G and H, because they are wordy and redundant. It is not necessary to include the word "from" in the sentence, so eliminate answer choice J. The sentence as it is written clearly indicates where the lab was moved from (out of the city) and to (onto a barge).

37. The best answer is C. To answer this question correctly, look for the most precise answer choice. Eliminate answer choices B and D, because they do not make sense when inserted into the sentence. The word "some" is too general; based on the context of the sentence, Nobel refined one way, or "a way" to control the detonation of dynamite.

38. The best answer is H. The dynamite belongs to Nobel, so answer choice F can be eliminated because it does not show possession. Now you must decide between "Nobels'" and "Nobel's." Nobel is a single person, so the proper way to show possession is with an apostrophe s. The sentence would no longer makes sense if you omitted, or removed, the underlined portion, so eliminate answer choice J.

39. The best answer is A. The best way to answer this question is to determine which sentence belongs in the first position. Sentence 1 effectively introduces the paragraph, and serves as a good transition from the preceding paragraph. Eliminate answer choices C and D, which do not place Sentence 1 in the first position. Sentence 1 shows where Nobel moved his lab. Sentence 2 states that "there," in that new location, Nobel refined the way in which dynamite is controlled. Therefore, Sentences 2 should follow Sentence 1. Only answer choice A has all of the sentences in the correct order.

40. **The best answer is F.** "Who" is a pronoun that refers to "Nobel." "That" and "which" do not refer to a person, so both answer choices G and H can be eliminated. Answer choice J creates a run-on sentence, so it should be eliminated.

41. **The best answer is C.** The best way to answer this question is to go through each of the answer choices and determine which of the phrases works best when substituted for the underlined portion of the sentence. All of the answer choices make sense and convey the same meaning, except answer choice C. It does not make sense to say that Nobel "had interesting literature, poetry, and social issues."

42. **The best answer is J.** "In his will" is an introductory phrase that must be followed by a comma separating it from the rest of the sentence. Answer choices F, G, and H can all be eliminated because they do not have a comma after "will." Also, only answer choice J makes it clear that, in his will, Nobel instructed his estate to establish the prizes.

43. **The best answer is A.** The sentence makes it clear that more than one prize should be given, so eliminate answer choice B. Nobel's wish was to set up "prizes," not an "establishment," so eliminate answer choice C. Answer choice D does not make sense when inserted into the sentence, so it should also be eliminated.

44. **The best answer is F.** Because the sentence is discussing Nobel's date of death, the singular possessive is correct. Nobel only has one date of death, so eliminate answer choice J.

45. **The best answer is C.** The phrase "all over the world" is idiomatic. This question requires you to express the idea clearly and simply. The sentence as it is written is awkward and does not make sense, so eliminate answer choice A. Answer choice B is redundant and should be eliminated. Omitting, or removing the underlined portion gets rid of information that is essential to the sentence. Eliminate answer choice D.

PASSAGE IV

46. **The best answer is H.** This question tests your ability to recognize redundancy. The word "many" indicates both a "series" or a "variety," so eliminate answer choices F, G, and J because they are redundant. Inserting the word "many" clearly and simply expresses the idea.

47. **The best answer is D.** This question tests your ability to express the idea clearly and simply. The passage discusses the "construction," or "building," of homes. Answer choices A and B are not idiomatic. Answer choice C implies that the subdivision "built" the plot of land, so it should be eliminated.

48. **The best answer is F.** The choice with the most descriptive language will provide the most detailed image. Answer choices G and H are too broad, and they do not include details about how many trees there are on the plot of land. While "tree-filled" is more descriptive, it does not evoke the image of thick woods that the writer is trying to convey.

49. **The best answer is C.** This question tests your ability to express the idea clearly and simply, as well as your ability to select the correct verb form. Since "builders" is plural, you should use the plural verb form "take." Eliminate answer choice D. The word "care" as it is used in the sentence should be singular, not plural, so eliminate answer choice B. Since the paragraph is written in the simple present tense, answer choice C most effectively and accurately expresses the idea.

50. **The best answer is J.** This question tests your ability to recognize redundancy. The writer includes the words "as possible" earlier in the sentence, so it is not necessary to use them again at the end of the sentence. Omitting the underlined portion gets rid of the redundancy created by the other answer choices.

51. **The best answer is A.** This question requires you to punctuate the underlined portion correctly. The words "large" and "heavy" are coordinate adjectives describing the "equipment." It is necessary to separate coordinate adjectives with a comma if you do not use a coordinate conjunction such as "and." Answer choice D uses a comma in the right place, but the word "largely" is not appropriate.

52. **The best answer is G.** This question tests your ability to express the idea clearly. The sentence as it is written includes the ambiguous pronoun "they." It is unclear to whom or to what the pronoun "they"

is referring. Eliminate answer choice F. Likewise, answer choices H and J are ambiguous and unclear, and should be eliminated. Only answer choice G clearly indicates who chooses to flatten the land.

53. **The best answer is D.** This question tests your ability to express the idea clearly. The sentence as it is written includes the ambiguous pronoun "it." It is unclear to whom or to what the pronoun "it" is referring. Eliminate answer choice A. Answer choice C includes the possessive form "its," which is not correct here. Only answer choice D clearly indicates what is not detected until much later.

54. **The best answer is H.** This question tests your ability to express the idea clearly and simply. The context of the sentence suggests that a tree will probably die if 40 percent or more of its root system "is lost." Since the paragraph is written in simple present tense, the best selection is answer choice H.

55. **The best answer is C.** To maintain parallel construction within the sentence, the subject and verb must agree. Since the subject is plural ("tree roots") you must use the plural form of the verb ("extend"). Eliminate answer choices A and B, which include singular verb forms. The paragraph is written in simple present tense, so eliminate answer choice D which includes the future tense of the verb form.

56. **The best answer is G.** To maintain parallel construction within the sentence, the subject and verb must agree. Since the subject is plural ("bulldozers, dump trucks, and cement trucks") you must use the plural form of the verb ("drive"). Eliminate answer choice F. The paragraph is written in the simple present tense, so eliminate answer choice H, which includes the past tense form of the verb, and answer choice J, which includes the past participle form of the verb.

57. **The best answer is B.** This question requires you to punctuate the underlined portion correctly. A good rule of thumb when it comes to commas is to use them where you would naturally pause when reading a sentence. There is no natural pause after the word "equipment" or the word "destroy." Since the idea is that "compacting" the soil "may destroy" the tree, you do not need to separate the clauses with a comma.

58. **The best answer is F.** A detailed explanation of why a tree's root system is so important would best accomplish the goal presented in the question. Answer choices G, H, and J, while correct, are too broad and do not effectively continue the

explanation of the importance of a tree's root system.

59. **The best answer is D.** Since Sentence 4 explains why it is necessary to keep roots from becoming buried, it makes sense that Sentence 5 should be placed immediately before Sentence 4. Placing it elsewhere in the paragraph would not make sense.

60. **The best answer is J.** This question requires you to determine the main idea of the essay. Since the focus is not on ways to prevent damage during construction, eliminate answer choices F and G. The essay focuses primarily on how trees and their root systems can become damaged during construction. Answer choices J best supports this idea.

PASSAGE V

61. **The best answer is D.** This question tests your ability to express the idea clearly and simply. It does not make sense that an officer of the law or an armed military person would be wearing both a suit and a uniform, so eliminate answer choice A. Likewise, eliminate answer choices B and C because they do not effectively convey the connection between an officer of the law or an armed military person, and what those people are likely to be wearing.

62. **The best answer is G.** In this sentence, the word "most" is used to indicate the number of people who might opt for a bullet-proof vest. "Most" should always be used with a plural noun, so eliminate answer choice F. Answer choices H and J are awkward, and do not clearly and simply express the idea, so they should be eliminated as well.

63. **The best answer is A.** This question tests your ability to express the idea clearly and simply. Answer choice B is unclear—prevents bullets from doing what? Therefore, it should be eliminated. Answer choice C creates a double negative, so it should be eliminated. Answer choice D is too wordy and contains irrelevant information, so it should be eliminated as well. The sentence as it is written best conveys the idea that bullet-proof vests aren't actually bullet-proof.

64. **The best answer is H.** This question requires you to punctuate the underlined portion correctly. A good rule of thumb when it comes to commas is to use them where you would naturally pause when reading a sentence. A semicolon should be followed by an independent clause, so eliminate answer choice F. Answer choice G creates an incomplete sentence, and answer choice J creates

a run-on sentence. Both of these choices should be eliminated. Only answer choice H clearly indicates that weaponry, ammunition, and materials have all changed through the centuries.

65. The best answer is A. This question tests your ability to express the idea clearly and simply. Since "silk" is the material being discussed, it makes sense to place the underlined portion directly after the word "silk," as it is written. Placing the underlined portion elsewhere makes the sentence awkward and unclear.

66. The best answer is H. This question requires you to select the best transition between sentences. The word "soon" implies a sense of time that does not fit within the context of the paragraph. Eliminate answer choice F. The paragraph discusses the importance of protecting the wearer from bullets. It makes sense that, because the flak-jacket did *not* protect the wearer from bullets, that the best transition word to use is "unfortunately."

67. The best answer is D. This question tests your ability to recognize redundancy. The word "today" suggests "recent" and "modern," so it is not necessary to include all of those words in the sentence. The most simple way to express the idea is with the word "today's."

68. The best answer is G. The best way to answer this question correctly is to insert the answer choices in the sentence and select the one that makes sense. You must answer the question, "A variety of synthetic materials, some of which are" what? The word "effective" best answers that question. Answer choices F, H, and J are very awkward and do not successfully convey the idea being presented in the sentence.

69. The best answer is C. The preceding sentence discusses the "production" of synthetic materials, so you should look for an answer choice that further explains the production of these materials. Eliminate answer choices A and D because they do not discuss production of material. You must also tie the idea presented in the preceding sentence to the concept of cost, since that is mentioned in the sentence about which you are being asked. Answer choice C does this best.

70. The best answer is J. This question tests your ability to express the idea clearly and simply. In this case, you should try the shortest answer choice to

see if it makes sense and effectively conveys the idea. Answer choices F, G, and H are very wordy and awkward, and they do not express the idea as clearly and simply as does answer choice J.

71. The best answer is B. This question requires you to correctly punctuate the underlined portion. The sentence as it is written is a run-on sentence, so eliminate answer choice A. Answer choice C creates an incomplete sentence, so it should also be eliminated. A semicolon should be followed by an independent clause, so eliminate answer choice D.

72. The best answer is J. This question tests your ability to express the idea clearly and simply, which, in this case, means eliminating answer choices that include irrelevant information. Since the sentence already indicates that the impact is spread around the body, any information about how this is in contrast to the impact being sustained in one area is redundant and irrelevant. Omitting, or removing, the underlined portion keeps the sentence simple, while still effectively expressing the idea.

73. The best answer is B. The question asks you to indicate that body armor does *not* always prevent injury or death. Answer choices A, C, and D suggest that the material in a bullet-proof vest will often or always prevent injury or death. Answer choice B effectively shows that, only under some circumstances, but certainly not always, will body armor prevent injury or death.

74. The best answer is F. The best way to answer this question correctly, is to determine what, if anything, the underlined portion adds to the sentence. The underlined portion includes information that indicates that the bullet-proof-vest wearer could sustain serious injury while wearing the vest. If this information is removed, the paragraph would lose a statement that suggests protective gear does not guarantee or ensure a lack of serious injury. The other answer choices are not supported by the context of the paragraph.

75. The best answer is C. This question requires you to select the correct verb form. The verb "entrust" means to "place trust in," which makes sense based on the context of the paragraph. The idea being conveyed is that police officers and military personal know that their safety cannot be "entrusted" completely to the protective gear that they wear; they must take additional precautions to ensure their safety.

Mathematics Test Explanations

1. **The correct answer is D.** Given that angle A is $20°$ and that angle B is three times larger than angle C, you can set up the following equation. $20° + B + C = 180°$. Since $B = 3C$, you have $20° + 3C + C = 180°$. Combine like terms: $20° + 4C = 180°$. Solve for C: $4C = 160°$; $C = 40°$. If $C = 40°$, then $B = (40°)(3) = 120°$.

2. **The correct answer is G.** The first step is to calculate the total cost of the trip by multiplying the number of people in the band (65) by the cost per member:

   $$65 \times 18.50 = \$1202.50$$

   A total of $\$585.00$ was raised from the bake sale, $\$1202.50 - \$585.00 = \$617.50$, which is the total amount left to earn. That means that each of the 65 members must pay an additional $\dfrac{617.50}{65}$, or $\$9.50$.

3. **The correct answer is B.** To solve this problem, set up an equation showing that Fred's total daily income equals his fixed daily income. ($\$40.00$) + the amount he earns for washing cars. Set the number of cars equal to C: $\$61.00 = \$40.00 + \$1.75C$.

   Solve for C: $\$1.75C = \$21.00$
   $C = 12$

4. **The correct answer is G.** Since you are given the equation for molality, $m = \dfrac{s}{k}$, and you are given $m = 0.2$ and $k = 13$, plug in the values and solve:

   $$0.2 = \frac{s}{13}$$
   $$s = 2.6$$

5. **The correct answer is C.** The best approach to this problem is to identify the relationships between the angles. Since a and b are vertical angles formed from the intersection of parallel lines and transversals, they are equal in measure. Since the same transversal (l_1) creates angle x, angle x is equal to angles a and b. Eliminate answer choices A and B. Angle c is a supplementary to angle x, which means that angle c + angle x = $180°$. There are no right angles in the figure, so angle c is NOT equal to angle x; answer choice C is correct.

6. **The correct answer is F.** The expression 4.2×10^{-5} is in scientific notation. The -5 exponent means that the decimal point has been moved five spaces

to the right of its original position. So, move the decimal five places to the LEFT back to its original position: 0.000042.

7. **The correct answer is E.** Multiplying by 0.01 is the same as dividing by 100, since $0.01 = \dfrac{1}{100}$. Move the decimal place two spaces to the left to get 0.03234.

8. **The correct answer is K.** To answer this question, you need to first expand the equation and then simplify it:

   $$\frac{x^2 - 2x + 1}{x - 1}$$
   $$\frac{(x - 1)(x - 1)}{x - 1}$$

   The $(x - 1)$ from the numerator cancels out the $(x - 1)$ in the denominator, so the equation is equal to $x - 1$.

9. **The correct answer is A.** This simple algebra problem asks you to solve for x. Combine like terms and isolate x on one side of the equation.

   $$9 - x^3 + 2 = 19$$
   $$-x^3 + 11 = 19$$
   $$-x^3 = 8$$
   $$x^3 = -8$$
   $$x = -2$$

10. **The correct answer is J.** With the information given, you can find that the measure of angle $WZY = 180° - (25° + 55°) = 100°$. Since WXY is opposite WZY in the same parallelogram, it also equals $100°$.

11. **The correct answer is D.** Since the circle at -1 is closed, that means that -1 should be included. Eliminate answer choices A, B, and E, which do not include -1. Since the graph goes to the right, the inequality must be greater than or equal to -1.

12. **The correct answer is G.** Solve for x, and keep track of the negative signs.

    $$93 - x = 342$$
    $$-x = 342 - 93$$
    $$-x = 249$$
    $$x = -249$$

13. **The correct answer is E.** You are given that $AB = 6$ and $BX = 10$. Use the Pythagorean Theorem to solve for AX:

    $$6^2 + (AX)^2 = 10^2$$
    $$(AX)^2 = 64$$
    $$AX = 8$$

If $AX = 8$ and $XC = 4$, then AC must equal 12. Given that $AB = 6$ and $AC = 12$, again use the Pythagorean Theorem to solve for BC:

$$6^2 + 12^2 = (BC)^2$$
$$180 = (BC)^2$$
$$BC = \sqrt{180} = \sqrt{(36)(5)} = 6\sqrt{5}$$

14. **The correct answer is F.** The formula for the area of a rectangle is $A = l \times w$, with l as the length and w as the width. The question states that the length of the parking lot is three times as long as the width. If w is the width, then the length is $3 \times w$, or $3w$. Therefore, the area of the parking lot is $3w \times w = 315$.

15. **The correct answer is C.** To solve this problem, set up a proportion: 3.5 miles is to x miles as 40 minutes is to 60 minutes. Cross-multiply and solve for x:

$$\frac{3.5}{x} = \frac{40}{60}$$
$$40x = 210$$
$$x = 5.25$$

16. **The correct answer is K.** First, divide the region into two rectangles, as shown:

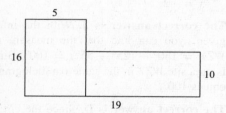

The first rectangle is 5 feet by 16 feet. The second rectangle is 10 feet by 14 feet (19 feet minus 5 feet). The area of a rectangle is calculated by multiplying the length by the width. Add the areas together:

Rectangle 1: $(5)(16)$ + Rectangle 2: $(10(14) =$ 220 square feet.

17. **The correct answer is A.** Given 32 ounces in a quart, you can calculate that there are 64 ounces in 2 quarts. 2 quarts, or 64 ounces, costs \$2.65. Divide \$2.65 by 64 ($2.65 \div 64$) to get \$0.04 per ounce.

18. **The correct answer is H.** Angles x and y are supplementary angles, so their sum is $180°$. Angle x is given as $125°$, so angle y is $180° - 125° = 55°$.

19. **The correct answer is B.** The first step in answering this question is to rearrange one of the given equations so that it is expressed in terms of y:

$$y + 3x = 9$$
$$y = -3x + 9$$

To solve for x, the next step is to plug $-3x + 9$ in for y in the second equation:

$$2x - \frac{1}{3}(9 - 3x) = 6$$
$$2x - 3 + x = 6$$
$$3x = 6 + 3$$
$$x = 3.$$

20. **The correct answer is K.** When multiplying fractions, multiply the numerators together and then multiply the denominators together and then reduce.

$$\left(\frac{5}{4}\right)\left(\frac{4}{3}\right) = \frac{20}{12} = \frac{5}{3}$$
$$\left(\frac{1}{3}\right)\left(\frac{2}{3}\right) = \frac{2}{9}$$

When dividing fractions, multiply the first fraction by the reciprocal of the second fraction and reduce.

$$\left(\frac{5}{3}\right) \div \left(\frac{2}{9}\right)$$
$$\left(\frac{5}{3}\right)\left(\frac{9}{2}\right)$$
$$\frac{45}{6} = \frac{15}{2}.$$

21. **The correct answer is C.** To solve this problem, combine like terms. Remember to keep track of the negative signs!

$$x^2 - (3x - 2) + 2x(4x - 1)$$
$$x^2 - 3x + 2 + 8x^2 - 2x$$
$$9x^2 - 5x + 2$$

22. **The correct answer is G.** First, factor the numerator and denominator:

$$\frac{x^2 - 6x + 9}{6x - 18} = \frac{(x - 3)(x - 3)}{6(x - 3)}$$

Next, cancel out an $(x - 3)$ from the numerator and denominator, which leaves you with $\frac{(x - 3)}{6}$.

23. **The correct answer is C.** You are given that $x = 3$ is one solution, which means that $(x - 3)$ is one of the factors of $2x^2 - 5x - a = 0$. Since the coefficient of the x^2-term is 2, you can set up the other factors

as follows:

$$(2x + \underline{\quad})(x - 3)$$

The x terms must equal -5, so apply the FOIL method to find the missing term:

$$-6x + \underline{\quad}x = -5x$$
$$-6x + x = -5x; \text{ the missing term must be } 1.$$

Use FOIL again to solve for a:

$$(2x + 1)(x - 3)$$
$$2x^2 - 6x + x - 3$$
$$2x^2 - 5x - 3$$

Thus, $a = 3$.

24. **The correct answer is F.** You are given that angle P is 55°. Since PQR is a right triangle, angle Q is 90°. So, angle R must be $180° - (55° + 90°)$ or 35°.

25. **The correct answer is E.** You are given that 1 gallon of paint can cover 36 square feet.

   The room is 8 feet by 12 feet, or 96 square feet. Set up a proportion:

$$\frac{1}{36} = \frac{x}{96}$$

Cross-multiply and solve for x:

$$36x = 96$$
$$x = \text{approximately } 2.666$$

The question asks you to round to the nearest whole gallon, so round up to 3 gallons.

26. **The correct answer is G.** You are given that $x \leq y$ and $y \leq z$. If $x = y$ and $y = z$, then $x = z$ could be true. Eliminate answer choices F, J, and K, which show that Roman Numeral I ($x = z$) is NOT true. If $x < y$ and $y < z$, then $x < z$ could be true. But $x > z$ could not be true in either case. So only II CANNOT be true, answer choice G.

27. **The correct answer is B.** The sine of an angle is the length of the opposite side divided by the length of the hypotenuse $\left(\dfrac{\text{opp}}{\text{hyp}}\right)$. You are given the measure of the opposite side, but you are not given the hypotenuse. So you must use the Pythagorean Theorem to find the measure of the hypotenuse:

$$(1)^2 + (5)^2 = (\text{hypotenuse})^2$$
$$1 + 25 = (\text{hypotenuse})^2$$
$$26 = (\text{hypotenuse})^2, \text{ so the hypotenuse} = \sqrt{26}.$$

Now, you can find sin C: $\left(\dfrac{\text{opp}}{\text{hyp}}\right) = \dfrac{1}{\sqrt{26}}$.

28. **The correct answer is F.** The easiest way to solve this problem is to cross-multiply and solve for x:

$$\frac{4x}{x - 1} = \frac{4x}{2x + 2}$$
$$4x(2x + 2) = 4x(x - 1)$$
$$8x^2 + 8x = 4x^2 - 4x; \text{ combine like terms}$$
$$4x^2 + 12x = 0; \text{ simplify by factoring out } 4x$$
$$4x(x + 3) = 0$$
$$4x = 0, \text{ so } x = 0$$
$$x + 3 = 0, \text{ so } x = -3$$

The two solutions are 0 and -3. The sums of these solutions is $0 + -3$, or -3.

29. **The correct answer is B.** This problem requires you to understand absolute value. Absolute value is the distance of the given value from zero on the number line, without regard to its sign. So, $|-2|^2 + |-5| - 3 = 2^2 + 5 - 3$, which is $4 + 5 - 3 = 6$.

30. **The correct answer is G.** Lines XY and ZW are parallel and are bisected by line AB. As you can see in the diagram from the question, these lines form two triangles. Because the lines XY, YZ, and ZW are equal, the sides of the triangles that are created are also equal. The triangle with $\angle s$ is a reflection of the triangle with $\angle t$, so $\angle s = \angle t$. If $\angle t = 45°$, then $\angle s = 45°$.

31. **The correct answer is C.** Here, you must first solve the inequality:

$$x^2 - 3 \leq 13$$
$$x^2 \leq 16$$

Because a negative number squared will yield a positive result, you must consider both the positive and negative values of x.

   $x \leq 4$ and $x \geq -4$. The greatest real value of x is if $x = 4$.

32. **The correct answer is F.** By definition, an isosceles triangle has a hypotenuse, c, and two legs, a and b, that are congruent. Use the measure of the hypotenuse given in the problem (12), and the Pythagorean theorem, $a^2 + b^2 = c^2$, to determine the length of one of the legs. Remember that $a = b$:

$$a^2 + a^2 = 12^2$$
$$2a^2 = 144$$
$$a^2 = 72$$
$$a = \sqrt{72}$$

The $\sqrt{72}$ can be reduced to $6\sqrt{2}$.

33. The correct answer is C. The formula for a circle is $(x - a)^2 + (y - b)^2 = r^2$, where (a, b) is the center of the circle and r is the radius of the circle. The question gives you the equation of the circle as $(x - 2)^2 + (y + 1)^2 = 4$. So, a is 2 and b is -1. The center of the circle, (a, b), is $(2, -1)$.

34. The correct answer is J. Find the slope by putting $2x - 3y = 6$ into the slope-intercept form ($y = mx + b$ where m is the slope):

$$-3y = -2x + 6$$

$y = \dfrac{2}{3}x - 2$. The slope is $\dfrac{2}{3}$.

35. The correct answer is D. This question is asking you to determine a weighted average. To answer the question, first calculate the total number of TVs:

$$(2 \times 5), (3 \times 20), (4 \times 15), \text{ and } (5 \times 10).$$

Next, add these values together and divide by the total number of houses (50):

$$\frac{(2 \times 5) + (3 \times 20) + (4 \times 15) + (5 \times 10)}{50}$$

$$\frac{10 + 60 + 60 + 50}{50} = \frac{180}{50} = 3.6.$$

36. The correct answer is H. Since you are given the radii of both circles, you can find the area of both circles. The radius of the smaller circle is 2, so the area is $\pi(2)^2$, or 4π. The radius of the larger circle is 6, so the area is $\pi(6)^2 = 36\pi$. Since the smaller circle is removed from the larger circle, simply subtract the area of the smaller circle from the area of the larger circle: $36\pi - 4\pi = 32\pi$.

37. The correct answer is B. By definition, the slope of any line is $\dfrac{\text{change in } y}{\text{change in } x}$. The question gives the slope of the line as $\dfrac{2}{3}$, which means that for every positive change of 2 in y, there is a positive change in x of 3. The question asks you to determine the x-intercept, or where $y = 0$. You are given a point on the line, $(-2, 2)$. Use the point-slope form of a line, $y = mx + b$, set y to 0, m to $\dfrac{2}{3}$, and solve for x:

$$(0 - 2) = \frac{2}{3}(x + 2)$$

$$-2 = \frac{2}{3}x + \frac{4}{3}$$

$$-\frac{6}{3} = \frac{2}{3}x + \frac{4}{3}$$

$-\dfrac{10}{3} = \dfrac{2}{3}x$, $x = -5$. The x-intercept is $(-5, 0)$.

38. The correct answer is J. From the graph, you can determine that the inequality is $x \geq -2$. However, that is not an answer given. So, you must solve the inequalities in the answer choices. Answer choices F and K do not contain a greater than or equal to sign, so they may be eliminated. Solve the remaining three inequalities:

Answer choice G $\begin{cases} 4x - 2 \geq 2x - 3 \\ 2x \geq -1 \\ x \geq -\dfrac{1}{2}. \\ \text{Eliminate answer choice G.} \end{cases}$

Answer choice H $\begin{cases} 5x + 5 \geq x \\ 4x \geq -5x \geq -\dfrac{5}{4}. \\ \text{Eliminate answer choice H.} \end{cases}$

Answer choice J $\begin{cases} 3x - 1 \leq 5x + 3 \\ -2x \leq 4 \\ x \geq -2 \end{cases}$

(remember to switch the sign when dividing by a negative number.) Answer choice J is correct.

39. The correct answer is D. By definition, the slope of any line is $\dfrac{\text{change in } y}{\text{change in } x}$. The question asks you to determine the slope from two points on the graph, so divide the change in y between the two points given by the change in x between the two points given:

$$\frac{y_1 - y_2}{x_1 - x_2} = \frac{5 - 3}{5 - 1} = \frac{2}{4}$$

$$\frac{2}{4} = \frac{1}{2}$$

40. The correct answer is K. You are given two of the three unknowns; plug $I = 2.25$ and $r = 0.03$ (the decimal equivalent of 3%) into the formula $I = Pr$:

$$2.25 = P(0.03)$$

Solve for P:

$$P = 75$$

41. The correct answer is E. Graph the rectangle on a coordinate graph.

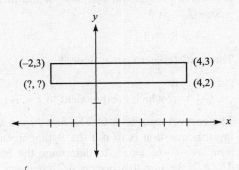

As you can see from the graph, the fourth vertex must be $(-2, 2)$.

42. The correct answer is F. Perpendicular lines have slopes that are the negative reciprocal of each other. Therefore, if one of the lines has a slope of $-\frac{5}{7}$, the slope of the other line must be $\frac{7}{5}$.

43. The correct answer is D. You are given that number of jars of jelly, j, is three less than twice the number of jars of applesauce, a. Put this into equation form: $j = 2a - 3$. Since none of the answers match this one, rearrange the equation: $j + 3 = 2a$.

44. The correct answer is G. The first step in answering this question is to factor the equation $3x^2 - 5x + 2 = 0$:

$$(3x - 2)(x - 1) = 0$$

To find the two solutions to this equation, solve for zero:

$$3x - 2 = 0$$
$$3x = 2$$
$$x = \frac{2}{3} \text{ (solution 1)}$$
$$x - 1 = 0$$
$$x = 1 \text{ (solution 2)}$$

The solutions to the equation given are $x = 1$ and $x = \frac{2}{3}$.

45. The correct answer is A. To solve this problem, you must first recall that the maximum value of the sine function is 1, and that the smallest value for a at this maximum value will be $\frac{\pi}{2}$. So, if $2a = \frac{\pi}{2}$, then $a = \frac{\pi}{4}$.

46. The correct answer is J. To solve this problem, replace y with $y - 2$, and z with $z + 1$:

$$x = 3(y - 2) - 4(z + 1) + 7$$
$$= 3y - 6 - 4z - 4 + 7$$
$$= 3y - 4z - 3$$

So, you went from $x = 3y - 4z + 7$ to $x = 3y - 4z - 3$. Subtract the two to see the difference:

$$(3y - 4z + 7) - (3y - 4z - 3)$$
$$3y - 3y = 0$$
$$-4z - (-4z) = 0$$
$$7 - (-3) = 10$$

Since the difference is a positive 10, that means that the original value of x was 10 greater than the new value of x. Thus, the value of x decreased by 10.

47. The correct answer is B. The first step in answering this question is to determine what we will call your critical numbers. Solve for x as if there were an equal sign instead of an inequality sign:

$$(x - 1)(4 - x) = 0$$
$$x - 1 = 0 \text{ and } 4 - x = 0$$

$x = 1$ and $x = 4$. Only answer choice B has both of these numbers, so answer choice B is correct. To make sure, choose a number that is greater than 4, like 5, and see if it is a solution to the inequality $(x - 1)(4 - x) < 0$:

$$(4)(-1) = -4 < 0; \; x > 4 \text{ is correct.}$$

Choose a number that is less than 1, like 0:

$$(-1)(4) = -4 < 0; \; x < 1 \text{ is also correct.}$$

48. The correct answer is H. You are given that the triangle is an isosceles right triangle, which means that it is a $45° - 45° - 90°$ triangle. One of the characteristics of this type of triangle is that the hypotenuse is $\sqrt{2}$ times the measure of each of the legs. So the ratio of the hypotenuse to PQ is $\sqrt{2} : 1$.

49. The correct answer is D. The tangent of any acute angle is the opposite side divided by the length of the adjacent side $\left(\frac{\text{opp}}{\text{adj}}\right)$. Cosine is equal to the length of adjacent side divided by the hypotenuse $\left(\frac{\text{adj}}{\text{hyp}}\right)$. Since $\tan x = \frac{3}{4}\left(\frac{\text{opp}}{\text{adj}}\right)$, then the adjacent side must be 4; eliminate answer choices B, C, and D. Now, figure out the measure of the hypotenuse by using the pythagorean theorem:

$$3^2 + 4^2 = (\text{hyp})^2$$

$$9 + 16 = (\text{hyp})^2$$
$$25 = (\text{hyp})^2$$
$$5 = \text{the hypotenuse.}$$

So, $\cos x = \dfrac{4}{5}$.

50. The correct answer is J. This question requires you to factor out the $(a+b)$ so that you end up with an equivalent, but simpler, equation. The equation $\dfrac{a+b}{b(a+b) - 2a(a+b)}$ can be simplified in the following way:

$$\frac{a+b}{a+b} \times \frac{1}{b-2a} = \frac{1}{b-2a}$$

By factoring out the $(a+b)$, the equation is reduced to $\dfrac{1}{b-2a}$.

51. The correct answer is D. You know that QRX is a right triangle, and $QR = 4$. Since X is the midpoint of SR, which is 8, RX must equal 4. $QX = 4\sqrt{2}$, since RX is an isosceles triangle where the hypotenuse is $\sqrt{2}$ times the measure of the legs of the triangle. Since $QX = 4\sqrt{2}$, PX must also equal $4\sqrt{2}$. So, the perimeter of triangle PXQ is $8 + 4\sqrt{2} + 4\sqrt{2}$, or $8\sqrt{2} + 8$.

52. The correct answer is K. The question states that the slope of the line is $\dfrac{2}{3}$. By definition, the slope of a line is the $\dfrac{\text{change in } y}{\text{change in } x}$, so set $\dfrac{2}{3}$ equal to $\dfrac{y_1 - y_2}{x_1 - x_2}$ and solve for t:

$$\frac{2}{3} = \frac{4 - (-2)}{3 - t}$$
$$\frac{2}{3} = \frac{6}{3 - t}$$
$$(3 - t) \times \frac{2}{3} = 6$$
$$2(3 - t) = 18$$
$$3 - t = 9$$
$$-t = 6, \text{ or } t = -6$$

53. The correct answer is A. To solve this problem, set up a proportion $\dfrac{\text{actual base}}{\text{actual height}} = \dfrac{\text{model base}}{\text{model height}}$

$$\frac{32}{56} = \frac{8}{x}$$

Cross-multiply and solve for x:

$$32x = 448$$
$$x = 14$$

54. The correct answer is H. The first step in answering this question is to rearrange the terms so that the x's are all on one side of the inequality, $-5x - 7 > 3x + 1$:

$$-7 > 8x + 1$$

The next step is to get x alone:

$$-8 > 8x$$
$$-1 > x, \text{ which is equivalent to } x < -1.$$

55. The correct answer is C. The first step in answering this question is to use the Pythagorean Theorem, $a^2 + b^2 = c^2$, to determine the length of AB. BD, the line that bisects AC, creates a second triangle, BAD. Use the length of lines BD and AD to determine the length of AD (let $AD = a$).

$$a^2 + 4^2 = 5^2$$
$$a^2 + 16 = 25$$
$$a^2 = 9$$
$$a = 3$$

Because you known that BD bisects AC, you know that the length of DC must also equal 3.

56. The correct answer is G. First, solve the equation for x:

$$x - 2 = \frac{2x + 5}{3}$$
$$3x - 6 = 2x + 5$$
$$x = 11$$

Only the interval $11 \leq x < 15$ contains 11, so answer choice G must be correct.

57. The correct answer is C. There are $360°$ in a circle. $\angle PRQ$ is $120°$, so the sector makes up $120° \div 360°$, or $\dfrac{1}{3}$, of the area of the circle. To answer this question, determine the area of the entire circle and take $\dfrac{1}{3}$ of the result to find the area of the sector. The formula for the area of a circle is $A = \pi r^2$. The radius, 9, is given in the problem, so plug 9 into the formula:

$$= \pi(9)^2$$
$$= 81\pi$$

You know that the sector is $\dfrac{1}{3}$ of the circle, so divide the area of the entire circle by 3:

$$81\pi \div 3 = 27\pi$$

58. The correct answer is F. Based on the figure, line a and line b are perpendicular lines, because they intersect to form right angles. Perpendicular lines have slopes that are negative reciprocals. In other words, if the slope of line a is m_a, the slope of line b is $\dfrac{-1}{m_a}$. You are given that the slope of line b is m_b, so $m_b = \dfrac{-1}{m_a}$. This is equivalent to $m_a = \dfrac{-1}{m_b}$.

59. **The correct answer is A.** The cosine of any acute angle is the length of the adjacent side divided by the hypotenuse $\left(\dfrac{\text{adj}}{\text{hyp}}\right)$. The tangent of any acute angle is the length of the opposite side divided by the length of the adjacent side $\left(\dfrac{\text{opp}}{\text{adj}}\right)$. The sine of any acute angle is the length of the opposite side divided by the hypotenuse. You are given that $\cos x = \dfrac{5}{7}\left(\dfrac{\text{adj}}{\text{hyp}}\right)$ and $\tan x = \dfrac{4}{5}\left(\dfrac{\text{opp}}{\text{adj}}\right)$. Sin x must equal $\dfrac{4}{7}\left(\dfrac{\text{opp}}{\text{hyp}}\right)$.

60. **The correct answer is G.** If each of the r boats that were used to carry the fishermen could accommodate a maximum number of m passengers, the total capacity of fisherman is rm. Since only one boat had 5 open spots and the remaining boats were filled to capacity, the number of fishermen was 5 less than the total capacity, or $rm - 5$. Thus $f = rm - 5$.

Reading Test Explanations

PASSAGE I

1. **The best answer is C.** The sentence before the quote states, "but, believe me, you cannot be too careful. Try and keep Mr. Rochester at a distance: distrust yourself as well as him." Mrs. Fairfax is suggesting that Mr. Rochester's feelings should not be trusted because they may not be genuine. This best supports answer choice C.

2. **The best answer is J.** Mrs. Fairfax states, "It is an old saying that 'all is not gold that glitters'; and in this case I do fear there will be something found to be different to what either you or I expect." This shows that Mrs. Fairfax believes Miss Eyre will discover that things may not turn out as she hoped or expected and may regret her decision. The other answer choices are not supported by the passage.

3. **The best answer is B.** Mrs. Fairfax says, "Gentlemen in his station are not accustomed to marry their governesses." She is pointing out a difference in Miss Eyre and Mr. Rochester's position and fortune and hinting that this difference is not a good thing. Mrs. Fairfax also clearly indicates that she is uncertain about Miss Eyre's future with Mr. Rochester. This information best supports answer choice B.

4. **The best answer is H.** Mrs. Fairfax is explaining that she would have cautioned Miss Eyre against forming a relationship with Mr. Rochester, but Miss Eyre had seemed mature and wise enough to conclude on her own that forming an intimate relationship with Mr. Rochester would be unwise. This best supports answer choice H.

5. **The best answer is D.** Mrs. Fairfax states, "Gentlemen in his station are not accustomed to marry their governesses." The words, "not accustomed to" imply that this is not a common occurrence, and that their relationship is not typical. The other answer choices are not supported by the passage.

6. **The best answer is G.** Mrs. Fairfax reminds Miss Eyre that, "all is not gold that glitters." Therefore, she is using the analogy of an object that appears to be gold, may not really be gold. In this way, Miss Eyre's relationship with Mr. Rochester may appear to be genuine and good, but it might not be. This best supports answer choice G.

7. **The best answer is D.** Mrs. Fairfax says, "Mr. Rochester, I dare say, is fond of you. I have always noticed that you were a sort of pet of his." Miss Eyre asks, "Why?—am I a monster? Is it impossible that Mr. Rochester should have a sincere affection for me?" Miss Eyre is indicating that she believes Mr. Rochester is truly fond of her and she is hurt that Mrs. Fairfax has not yet demonstrated that she believes or thinks this. The other answer choices are not supported by the details in the passage.

8. **The best answer is J.** Throughout the passage, Miss Eyre expresses her confidence that Mr. Rochester is not too old for her. She refutes Mrs. Fairfax's claim that people might mistake Mr. Rochester for Miss Eyre's father. Therefore, she is self-assured in her feelings. The other answer choices are not supported by the passage.

9. **The best answer is A.** Mrs. Fairfax implies that Mr. Rochester, in deciding to marry Miss Eyre, is not being his normally careful and proud self. Mrs. Fairfax is shocked and surprised by the marriage proposal.

10. **The best answer is H.** Mrs. Fairfax states, "I am sorry to grieve you . . . but you are so young, and so little acquainted with men, I wished to put you on your guard. It is an old saying that 'all is not gold that glitters'; and in this case I do fear there will be something found to be different to what either you or I expect." Mrs. Fairfax is expressing her fear that things may go wrong or not be as they appear and that Miss Eyre will end up getting hurt. The other answer choices are not supported by details in the passage.

PASSAGE II

11. **The best answer is C.** The first paragraph lists the main concerns of Abraham Lincoln that were addressed during the debates. The rest of the passage then provides details, definitions, and explanations about the concepts introduced in the first paragraph.

12. **The best answer is F.** In the second paragraph, Lincoln refers to the actions of the Founding Fathers. This provided historical evidence for his argument against the current state of slavery in America during the debates. The other answer choices are not supported by the passage.

13. **The best answer is D.** The passage states, "The Missouri Compromise and the Compromise of 1850 were at odds with the new Dred Scott decision, which denied that Congress had a right to exclude slavery in the states." This suggests that Congress may have initially had the right to exclude slavery. The other answer choices are not supported by the passage.

14. **The best answer is G.** The emphasis of these lines on the physical violence that was occurring over slavery in Kansas supports the idea that slavery was an issue that was dividing citizens and states.

15. **The best answer is A.** The passage states that, "the 'Spirit of '76'... was the hope of the Founding Fathers that slavery would be strangled within the original southern states over time." This best supports answer choice A.

16. **The best answer is H.** The passage states, "Lincoln's 'House Divided' speech and his arguments in the Lincoln-Douglas debates show that he believed that slavery was threatening to become a national institution. He saw the American public become increasingly indifferent to slavery." This best supports answer choice H.

17. **The best answer is A.** The passage states, "A key piece of evidence is that the Dred Scott decision was pushed back until after the election of 1856." The other answer choices are not supported by the passage.

18. **The best answer is J.** The Declaration of Independence is not specifically mentioned in this passage. The passage states, "He mentioned the unanimous abolition of the African slave trade as well as, the Northwest Ordinance and the lack of the word *slave* in the Constitution, to show that the Founding Fathers intended slavery to be strangled in the original Southern States."

19. **The best answer is D.** The passage states, "The Missouri Compromise and the Compromise of 1850 were at odds with the new Dred Scott decision, which denied that Congress had a right to exclude slavery in the states." The passage reports that the Missouri Compromise was used to regulate slavery in the territories. The passage also states that the supporters of slavery now favored the Dred Scott decision that effectively overruled the Missouri Compromise.

20. **The best answer is G.** The passage states, "In addition, the Democrats had drafted legislation in 1850 and 1854 that contained language which seemed to predict that Congress would not be able to exclude slavery in the territories because of Constitutional constraints." The other answer choices are not supported by the passage.

PASSAGE III

21. **The best answer is C.** The author recounts her first three performances, the roles she was most famous for, and her last performances. This best supports answer choice C.

22. **The best answer is J.** The author mentions that she appeared in *A Trip to Scarborough*, which was altered, from *Vanbrugh's Relapse*. The passage does not say that the author actually appeared in *Vanbrugh's Relapse*.

23. **The best answer is C.** According to the passage, the author was quite nervous and fearful about going on stage: "I then began to fear that my resolution would fail ..." This information best supports the selection of the word "courage."

24. **The best answer is F.** The author states that she played the character of Sir Henry Revel in *The Miniature Picture*. Therefore, she did not always play female characters. The other answer choices are not supported by the details in the passage.

25. **The best answer is D.** The author states, "The second character which I played was Amanda, in *A Trip to Scarborough*. The play was altered from *Vanbrugh's Relapse*." This suggests that the author acted in at least one, un-original play. The other answer choices are not supported by the passage.

26. **The best answer is G.** The passage states, "The second character which I played was Amanda, in *A Trip to Scarborough*." Then the author writes, "The third character I played was Statira, in *Alexander the Great*." Finally, the author writes, "The last character that I played was Sir Harry Revel, in Lady Craven's comedy of *The Miniature Picture*; and the epilogue song in *The Irish Widow* was my last farewell to the labor of my profession." Since you were able to determine that she first appeared in *A Trip to Scarborough*, Roman Numeral III, you would eliminate all of the answer choices that did not place Roman Numeral III in the first position.

27. **The best answer is B.** The narrator writes, "I stood mute and bending with alarm, which did not subside till I had feebly articulated the few sentences of the first short scene, during the whole of which I had never once ventured to look at the audience." Later in the night, the narrator says, "As I acquired courage, I found the applause augment; and the night was concluded with peals of loud approbation. I was complimented on all sides. I then experienced, for the first time in my life, a pleasure that language could not explain." This best supports answer choice B.

28. **The best answer is J.** Quotes from the passage include: "My dress was a pale pink satin,

trimmed with crêpe, and richly spangled with silver", "I leaned upon the Nurse's arm, almost fainting. Mr. Sheridan and several other friends encouraged me to proceed", and "The second scene being the masquerade, I had time to collect myself." Nothing in the passage suggests that the narrator received criticism for delivering her opening lines feebly.

29. The best answer is A. The crowd's applause stunned her and she momentarily lost her ability to think or reason the noise and crowd overwhelmed her hearing and other senses, answer choice A. The other answer choices do not make sense based on the context.

30. The best answer is F. Although a gentleman did comment on the narrator's performance, this was not the primary focus of these lines. The narrator speaks more about being filled with pleasure from hearing the applause and completing her first performance. These lines do not state that the narrator believed she was famous, nor do these lines tell the reader how the narrator believed she performed.

PASSAGE IV

31. The best answer is B. The passage states, "No single factor has been proven to cause ash decline. Ash yellows and environmental factors may work together to create ash decline." This best supports answer choice B.

32. The best answer is F. The passage states, "Verticillium wilt on ash can also result in cankers and dieback similar to ash yellows." The other answer choices are not supported by the passage.

33. The best answer is D. The passage gives the following reasons why it is hard to diagnose as ash tree: "Trying to diagnose a tree is difficult because symptoms could be caused by a variety of problems." "Ash yellows and environmental factors may work together to create ash decline." "A survey of several Midwestern states found that some ash decline was found to be independent of ash yellows." "Verticillium wilt on ash can

also result in cankers and dieback similar to ash yellows." The passage indicates that the trees may decline slowly, not rapidly.

34. The best answer is G. The passage states, "Ash yellows is caused by a *phytoplasma*: virus-like pathogens that are spread by insects."

35. The best answer is C. The passage states, "The decline of these trees may have a severe impact on the health of other plant and animal communities. Green ash provides nesting sites for several species of birds and other wild creatures. Insects and fish flourish in the cool waters made possible by the shade of ash trees." This best supports answer choice C.

36. The best answer is H. The passage states, "A survey of several Midwestern states found that some ash decline was found to be independent of ash yellows. The droughts in the 1980s may have caused the decline of ash trees in the Midwest." The other answer choices are not supported by the passage.

37. The best answer is B. The passage states that, "Insects and fish flourish in the cool waters made possible by the shade of ash trees." The paragraph discusses the importance of ash trees "in the ecology of North American forests." It makes the most sense, based on the context of the paragraph, that "flourish" means "prosper."

38. The best answer is F. Throughout the passage the author states that ash trees are important and necessary. It makes sense that the author would agree with a statement suggesting that a cure for a disease that kills ash trees be researched. The other answer choices are not supported by the passage.

39. The best answer is D. The passage states that ash yellows turns the leaves of ash trees "pale green or pale yellow," not bright yellow.

40. The best answer is J. According to the passage, there is no known cure for ash yellows. Eliminate answer choices F and H because they include Roman Numeral I. The remaining Roman Numerals, II, III, and IV, are supported by details in the passage, so answer choice J must be correct.

Science Reasoning Test Explanations

PASSAGE I

1. The best answer is B. Scientist 1 argues that technology "has played a huge role in helping humans to adapt to conditions on this planet." Scientist 1 goes on to explain some technological advances that might change the natural processes of the sun and says that there is "enough time and incentive to discover ways to thwart the natural progress of nature." This best supports answer choice B.

2. The best answer is H. According to Scientist 2, a significant drop in carbon dioxide levels could lead to the end of photosynthesis, which, in turn would result in dramatic temperature increases. Once the temperature reaches a certain point, the water on the surface and in the atmosphere will evaporate. This information best supports answer choice H.

3. The best answer is C. Scientist 1 states that humans could "develop technology that would stir the sun and bring new hydrogen to the sun's core. This would greatly extend the current phase that our sun is in." The passage clearly indicates that our sun is not yet in the Red Giant phase, so this technological advance could postpone the sun reaching that stage.

4. The best answer is F. Scientist 1 believes that in 7 billion years, humans will have more than enough time to "advance technology and find solutions to adapt to the atmospheric changes the Red Giant phase would bring." This suggests that Scientist 1 believes in human beings' ability to adapt and adjust to changes in Earth's atmosphere and environment. The other answer choices are not supported by Scientist 1's viewpoint.

5. The best answer is A. Scientist 1 believes that there is plenty of time for technology to evolve in time to change Earth's environment. Scientist 2, on the other hand, states that there is not enough time "for humans to evolve in order to meet large atmospheric and environmental changes, or to develop the technology needed to make Earth habitable." The other answer choices are not supported by the passage.

6. The best answer is H. According to the passage, the only thing that both scientists would agree on is the notion that the earth is going to undergo dramatic changes in the future. The other answer choices are not supported by the passage.

7. The best answer is B. According to Scientist 2, if "Earth's average temperature rises to above 70°C, the oceans will evaporate and Earth's water sources will be almost completely eliminated." If it was found that at one point in earth's history the temperature rose above 70°C and these things did not happen, Scientist 2's viewpoint would be weakened.

PASSAGE II

8. The best answer is G. The passage indicates that radon levels outdoors are rarely high enough to pose a threat, but radon is a concern indoors "because it can seep into the foundation of a home through the ground and accumulate in areas with little ventilation, where levels can then become threatening." This best supports answer choice G.

9. The best answer is D. The passage mentions the fact the radon is both colorless and odorless and produces no short-term symptoms, and that radon levels can vary from day to day, in order to emphasize the importance of regular monitoring. The fact that radon is a naturally occurring gas does not significantly contribute to the importance of continual in-home testing.

10. The best answer is J. The passage indicates that radon gas can enter a home "through many different pathways." This information is consistent with the findings. The other answer choices are not supported by information in the passage.

11. The best answer is A. Radon potential is defined as "an estimate of the radon level of a structure." According to the passage, Zone 1 includes areas with a high radon potential. Table 1 indicates that the pCi/L levels in Zone 1 are greater than 4. Therefore, a radon level of 5.2 pCi/L would be considered the most harmful.

PASSAGE III

12. The best answer is J. Table 1 lists characteristics of certain predators. Since "herbivore" is listed in the table, a herbivore is a predator. The passage also indicates that some scientists contend that herbivores are predators. According to Table 1, carnivores eat herbivores, which means that a herbivore is also a prey animal.

13. The best answer is D. The passage states that "the number of prey consumed depends on the number of prey present as well as the number of predators present." The other answer choices are not supported by the passage.

14. **The best answer is F.** According to Figure 1, predators are indicated by a series of x's. During the first year, the number of predators was higher than was the number of prey.

15. **The best answer is C.** According to Table 1, a deer is a herbivore, so eliminate answer choice B. Table 1 also indicates that herbivores can be selective eaters, which means that they may choose to eat a certain type of plant over other types of plants. This best supports answer choice C.

16. **The best answer is G.** To answer this question, find the location on Figure 1 where the line representing prey reaches its highest point. This occurs during the second year.

PASSAGE IV

17. **The best answer is B.** According to Table 1, animals and plants contribute to physical weathering. The passage states that plants also contribute to biological weathering.

18. **The best answer is J.** Table 1 shows that temperature variation can lead to physical weathering, specifically cracks and splits in rocks caused by mineral expansion and contraction.

19. **The best answer is C.** According to the passage, the "ultimate product of biological weathering agents on rock is soil." Plants and bacteria are organic, or living, and the passage indicates that they contribute to biological weathering. This information best supports answer choice C.

20. **The best answer is G.** Table 2 shows factors of chemical weathering. The presence of water contributes to almost all of the weathering mechanisms listed in Table 2. Therefore, you can safely assume that the presence of water is the greatest contributing factor to the alteration of minerals and rock.

21. **The best answer is D.** Table 3 indicates that lichens are rich in chelating agents and that chelating agents "trap elements of decomposing rock, resulting in etching and grooving." The other answer choices are not supported by the passage.

22. **The best answer is H.** According to Table 2, the result of hydrolysis is the disruption of "the chemical composition of the minerals, destabilizing the rock." Table 2 indicates that rainwater is the usual cause of this type of weathering, which best supports answer choice H.

PASSAGE V

23. **The best answer is B.** Figure 1 shows some of the internal anatomy of a sea anemone. According to this figure, the sea anemone's mouth is located at the center of its body. The other answer choices are not supported by Figure 1.

24. **The best answer is F.** The passage states that zooxanthellae "are a food source for the sea anemone." The passage also indicates that the clown fish "helps the sea anemone by actually cleaning the tentacles." This best supports answer choice F.

25. **The best answer is B.** The passage starts out by saying that sea anemones look like plants. Also, Figure 1 shows that a sea anemone looks more like a plant or a flower than an animal. Nothing in the passage suggests that a sea anemone looks like a clown fish, marine algae, or a rock.

26. **The best answer is H.** According to the passage, "when ocean currents are strong, the sea anemone will reduce its internal volume in order to decrease the surface area that is exposed to the current." This best supports answer choice H.

27. **The best answer is C.** Figure 1 clearly shows that the sea anemone's mouth is connected to its gastrovascular cavity by way of the pharynx. The other answer choices are different internal parts of the sea anemone, but they do not correctly answer the question.

PASSAGE VI

28. **The best answer is G.** According to Table 3, the average plant height of the plants grown in potting soil was 5.3 centimeters, and the average number of leaves on the plants grown in potting soil was 6. This best supports answer choice G.

29. **The best answer is D.** According to Table 2, after 14 days the soil/compost mixture that yielded the greatest average plant height was mixture 1, with an average plant height of 4.2 centimeters.

30. **The best answer is G.** The passage states that, in Experiment 2, "each pot contained a different soil type, and no compost was used." The other answer choices are not supported by the passage.

31. **The best answer is D.** Based on the data in Tables 2 and 3, soil from near the school was used in Pot 4 in Experiment 1 and in Pot 3 in Experiment 2. This would most likely account for the nearly identical results recorded. The other answer choices are not supported by the data.

32. The best answer is F. The passage indicates that 4 radish seeds were placed in each pot in Experiment 1. The only differences between Experiment 1 and Experiment 2 were the soil types used and the fact that no compost was used. Therefore, the same number of seeds (4) was planted in each pot in Experiment 2.

33. The best answer is B. Based on the data in Table 2, Pot 1 yielded the highest average number of leaves. Table 1 indicates that this pot contained 75 percent compost and 25 percent soil.

PASSAGE VII

34. The best answer is H. Figure 1 shows that the temperatures near the bottom of the lake are lower than the temperatures near the surface of the lake. The thermocline is shown as a layer separating the surface water from the deeper water. This best supports answer choice H.

35. The best answer is A. According to the passage, spring turnover "eliminates the temperature stratification that was established during the winter." This turnover "results in a relatively even distribution of O_2 throughout the lake." The graph shown in answer choice A indicates an even distribution of O_2 at every depth of the lake.

36. The best answer is J. The passage states that the thermocline is the "narrow zone of water undergoing rapid temperature changes," which separates the layers in the lake. This best supports answer choice J.

37. The best answer is A. According to the passage, each of the Great Lakes, including Lake Michigan, "tends to stratify, ... depending on the season." The passage goes on to say that this stratification occurs during the winter and the summer. Water in the Great Lakes is mixed during the spring and fall, which effectively eliminates the stratification.

38. The best answer is G. According to the passage, the stability of a lake's stratification depends on "both the inflow and outflow of lake water. Lakes with a lot of water flowing into and out of them do not develop consistent and lasting thermal stratification." This best supports answer choice G, since the question indicates that the river flows into the lake.

39. The best answer is D. Figure 1 shows that the temperatures near the bottom of the lake are lower than the temperatures near the surface of the lake. This best supports answer choice D.

40. The best answer is G. The passage states that the lake's depth, the amount of wind present, and the amount of water flowing into the lake affect the stability of the lake's thermal stratification. "Seasonal turnover" is the name given to the stratification of lakes, so it is the exception here.

Writing Test Explanation

Because grading the essay is subjective, we've chosen not to include any "graded" essays here. Your best bet is to have someone you trust, such as your personal tutor, read your essays and give you an honest critique. If you plan on grading your own essays, review the grading criteria and be as honest as possible regarding the structure, development, organization, technique, and appropriateness of your writing. Focus on your weak areas and continue to practice in order to improve your writing skills.